W9-ADK-600

THE IVP WOMEN'S BIBLE COMMENTARY

Edited by
CATHERINE CLARK KROEGER
& MARY J. EVANS

Administrative Assistant
ELIZABETH KROEGER ELLIOTT

InterVarsity Press
Downers Grove, Illinois

InterVarsity Press
P.O. Box 1400, Downers Grove, IL 60515-1426
World Wide Web: www.ivpress.com
E-mail: mail@ivpress.com

InterVarsity Press® is the book-publishing division of InterVarsity Christian Fellowship/USA®, a student movement active on campus at hundreds of universities, colleges and schools of nursing in the United States of America, and a member movement of the International Fellowship of Evangelical Students. For information about local and regional activities, write Public Relations Dept., InterVarsity Christian Fellowship/USA, 6400 Schroeder Rd., P.O. Box 7895, Madison, WI 53707-7895, or visit the IVCF website at <www.ivcf.org>.

See page 839 for interior photo credits.

Cover photograph: Erich Lessing/Art Resource, NY. Portrait of a young woman with writing materials. From Pompeii, 1st century A.D., Museo Nazionale, Naples, Italy.

ISBN 0-8308-1437-X

Printed in the United States of America ∞

Library of Congress Cataloging-in-Publication Data

The IVP women's Bible comentary/edited by Catherine Clark Kroeger and Mary J. Evans.
p. cm.
Includes bibliographical references and index.
ISBN 0-8308-1437-X (alk. paper)
1. Bible—Feminist criticism. I. Kroeger, Catherine Clark. II. Evans, Mary J.
BS521.4 .I97 2001
220.7'82—dc21

2001039360

P 20 19 18 17 16 15 14 13 12 11 10 9 8 7 6 5 4 3 2 1
Y 18 17 16 15 14 13 12 11 10 09 08 07 06 05 04 03 02

Project Staff

Senior Reference Book Editor/Project Editor
James Hoover

Associate Editor
Linda Doll

Assistant Editor
David Zimmerman

Copyeditor
Linda Triemstra

Design
Kathleen Lay Burrows

Design Assistant
Mark Eddy Smith

Typesetters
Gail Munroe
Marj Sire
Maureen Tobey

Proofreaders
Bill Kerschbaum
Allison Rieck

Editorial Assistants
Joice Gouw
Cindy Kerschbaum

Editorial Intern
Michelle Collins

Technical Support
Tricia Koning
Andy Shermer

InterVarsity Press

PUBLISHER
Robert A. Fryling

EDITORIAL DIRECTOR
Andrew T. Le Peau

PRODUCTION MANAGER
Anne Gerth

Contents

Supplementary Articles

Illustrations

Photographs

Tables

Figures

Diagram

PREFACE

Why a Women's Bible Commentary?

The majority of commentaries available to today's readers of Scripture are written from the perspective of white, Western, classically educated, middle-class males, and the questions asked and issues raised are almost always dealt with from that perspective. Usually the work is done with integrity, insight and good scholarship, and the usefulness of the commentaries is by no means limited to those who share the same background as the writers. The answers found in Scripture to questions asked by men often bear great relevance to women; their insights are likely to be genuine insights into what Scripture is saying. Nevertheless, inevitable limitations arise from their curtailed perspective. Many insights into the text are never revealed simply because the questions that might have revealed them have never been asked.

This commentary seeks to redress this imbalance. While it stands in its own right as a commentary on the biblical text, it serves as a complement rather than as an alternative to other commentaries. It unashamedly approaches the text from a particular and identified perspective, seeking to provide a resource for the whole church—both women and men—that will allow readers to notice and identify issues within Scripture that relate to women or reflect their unique perspective. It seeks deliberately to ask women's questions. It is not written simply "for" women as opposed to men; it is rather written "from" women. In other words, this commentary doesn't just look at passages about women, it looks at all of Scripture from a woman's perspective.

Women need the opportunity to have the Scriptures explained in ways that are relevant to their lives. The Old Testament bears witness to the importance of the Scriptures being read and interpreted to all God's people (Deut 31:12; Josh 8:34-35; cf. 2 Kings 23:2). Just as Ezra made sure the Word was not only read but also interpreted for both men and women (Neh 8:1-8), so today the Scriptures need to be read and interpreted for women. But all too often the interpretive voices of women have been lacking.

In the process of working on this commentary, we have found it exciting and encouraging to note how much there is in the Bible that has not been identified or expounded before—material that, once noted, can clearly be seen as coming from the text and not being read into it. Scripture attests to many women who received and interpreted God's Word within their own contexts—Miriam, Deborah, Hannah, Huldah, Elizabeth and Mary among them. This commentary seeks to follow in their footsteps, perhaps fulfilling the psalmist's words "The Lord gives the word: great is the host of women who proclaim it" (Ps 68:11 ERV, cf. NASB; the feminine plural "host of women" is obscured in many contemporary versions).

We hoped that we might give women freedom to write from the broadest possible range of their experience. Our contributors were encouraged to reflect both in their university offices and at their kitchen tables, from serious exegetical study to rumination on the real world in which women live. How does the Scripture speak to their sisters as they birth and breast-feed, bandage and console, earn their daily living, survive intolerable conditions, hold high office, and contemplate their own failures and shattered hopes? We want this commentary to address readers in the most common experiences of everyday life.

At the same time, we could not ignore recent challenges presented to women of faith. Much contemporary feminist criticism has viewed the Bible as hostile to women because it has been used for unjust oppression in contemporary societies. Some feminists have understandably viewed the Bible as inimical to the concerns of women and have employed what has been called a "hermeneutic of suspicion." Frequently efforts have been made to subvert the text in order to recover an underlying stratum that is supportive of women. This stratum is held to have been deliberately distorted by the biblical writers in order to yield a patriarchal message detrimental to women.

In contrast to such efforts, this commentary is written by women of faith who believe that all Scripture is inspired by God and given for the benefit of all humanity. The contributors have examined the difficult texts from a "hermeneutic of faith," a conviction that the Scriptures are meant for healing rather than hurt, for affirmation of all persons, especially those who are oppressed. Our contributors have examined the hard texts, the seeming contradictions and the paradoxes regarding women, and they have sought to move in new, faith-filled directions without minimizing the negative attitudes of individual biblical authors. (Jonah, for instance, had no sympathy for his audience, though he delivered a life-giving message; other figures in biblical history also learned that God had a far nobler and more gracious design than they had originally contemplated.) The Bible is God's Word, and we must deal with both its divine and human authorship—the God of truth communicating through frail and fallen human beings. Faithful believers may appropriately ask some very hard questions about text and context, original intention, and enduring significance.

Although much relevant material comes through the main commentary sections, certain areas of interest to women cannot be expounded thoroughly in the commentaries on individual books. For this reason a range of articles have been included, enabling major doctrinal issues (such as the Trinity and monotheism) and everyday concerns (such as parental influence, sibling rivalry and menstruation) to be looked at from a woman's point of view.

The chosen perspective is that of women, but the work of scholars from all around the world and from different denominational backgrounds have been included in recognition that we need to hear from those of different cultures and different backgrounds. Because we have been seeking to provide a voice for women and to ask new questions, the work of some younger and lesser known writers has been included alongside that of more recognized experts. There are a small number of male contributors, included not simply as a token but as a model, reflecting the conviction that, with effort, it is possible to set aside one's own perspective and to ask questions wearing, as it were, someone else's spectacles.

Because of the unique nature of this project, both a complement to other commentaries and an opportunity to ask different kinds of questions of the biblical text, each writer has been given a great deal of freedom. Some have chosen to discuss every paragraph of text within their assigned book; others have chosen to discuss major themes throughout their assignment; still others have focused on just a few significant passages, allowing other commentaries to fill in the gaps. For each book, however, the contributor has supplied an outline of its contents. There is considerable variety in points of view and style—not all agree, and not all reflect the views of the editors or the publisher. What all contributors do share is a conviction that the Scriptures can speak meaningfully to women's lives today. Difficult questions relating to text, context, content or significance have not been avoided; paradoxes and seeming contradictions have been honestly faced.

This commentary should be an invaluable asset for those who wish to gain an understanding of women's approach to Scripture as good news for themselves and others. Here is a commentary on the entire Bible that envelops the manifold experiences of and attitudes toward women. It argues for the full inspiration of the Bible and the full equality of women. Here is a resource that allows qualified evangelical women to interpret Scripture from their own stance. This will be an important contribution to feminist hermeneutics, albeit from a more conservative position than some other materials. Nevertheless it affirms the significance, power and essential dignity of women in all aspects of life. We offer this work in the conviction of the Puritan divine John Robinson, who proclaimed, "God has yet more things to break forth from his holy Word."

Catherine Clark Kroeger
Mary J. Evans

How to Use This Commentary

This commentary consists of individual articles on all sixty-six books of the Old and New Testaments (except that 1 & 2 Samuel and 1 & 2 Kings, respectively, have been treated together by one author). In addition, seventy-seven supplementary articles on a variety of theological and practical issues of interest to women have been spread throughout the commentary. A listing of these articles in the order in which they appear may be found in the "List of Supplementary Articles" on page ix. A complete alphabetical listing of both the main and supplementary articles may be found in the "Index of Articles" on pages 845-46. More than fifty illustrations, tables, figures and diagrams enhance the usefulness of the commentary, and a listing of where they are placed can be found on pages x-xii.

Abbreviations
A list of standard abbreviations used throughout this commentary may be found on pages xix-xx.

Authorship of Articles
The authors of the articles are indicated by their names at the end of each article. A full alphabetical list of the contributors, indicating their highest earned degrees and current position or location, can be found on pages xxiii-xxvii. The contribution of each author is listed alphabetically following their identification.

Bibliographies
Most articles carry a short bibliography with them at the conclusion of the article, though some do not. Contributors were asked to limit their bibliographic entries to five or six in most instances. When citing sources from their bibliographies, contributors list simply the author's last name and a page number within parentheses. All bibliographic references are listed in alphabetical order by their authors' last names, though the authors' initials are also included. Some bibliographies have been subdivided into categories (e.g., "Commentaries" and "Studies").

Cross-References
This commentary has been extensively cross-referenced in order to aid readers in making the most of the supplementary articles dispersed among the biblical books. All cross-references are found within parentheses and carry a note *"see."* Occasionally only shortened titles for articles may appear; thus "Violence" for "Violence, Abuse and Oppression" or "Purity Laws" for "Purity Laws Related to Women." Supplementary articles can most easily be located by checking "Index of Articles" on pages 845-46.

Indexes
Both a "Scripture Index" and an "Index of Articles" have been included in this volume to aid readers in finding relevant commentary for their purposes. Those who wish to see the

full range of articles contributed by any one author are encouraged to see the list of contributors on pages xxiii-xxvii.

Transliteration

Hebrew, Aramaic and Greek words have been transliterated according to the system set out on page xxi. Greek verbs generally appear in their lexical form (rather than the infinitive) in order to assist those with little or no knowledge of the language.

ABBREVIATIONS

General Abbreviations

2d ed. second edition
3d ed. third edition
c. circa, about (with dates)
cf. *confer* (compare)
e.g. *exempli gratia,* for example
Gk. Greek
Heb. Hebrew
i.e. *id est,* that is
lit. literally
LXX Septuagint (Greek translation of the Old Testament)
mg. margin
p. (pp.) page(s)
par. parallel passage(s) in another/other Gospel(s)
rev. revised

Bible Translations

AV Authorized Version (or KJV)
CEV Contemporary English Version
ERV English Revised Version (1881)
JB Jersusalem Bible
KJV King James Version (or AV)
NASB New American Standard Bible
NEB New English Bible
NIV New International Version
NJPS New Jewish Publication Society (Old Testament only)
NRSV New Revised Standard Version
RSV Revised Standard Version

Books of the Bible

Old Testament

Gen Genesis
Ex Exodus
Lev Leviticus
Num Numbers
Deut Deuteronomy
Josh Joshua
Judg Judges
Ruth Ruth
1 Sam 1 Samuel
2 Sam 2 Samuel
1 Kings 1 Kings
2 Kings 2 Kings
1 Chron 1 Chronicles
2 Chron 2 Chronicles
Ezra Ezra
Neh Nehemiah
Esther Esther
Job Job
Ps Psalm(s)
Prov Proverbs
Eccles Ecclesiastes
Song Song of Solomon
Is Isaiah
Jer Jeremiah
Lam Lamentations
Ezek Ezekeiel
Dan Daniel
Hos Hosea

Joel	Joel
Amos	Amos
Obad	Obadiah
Jon	Jonah
Mic	Micah
Nahum	Nahum
Hab	Habakkuk
Zeph	Zephaniah
Hag	Haggai
Zech	Zechariah
Mal	Malachi

New Testament

Mt	Matthew
Mk	Mark
Lk	Luke
Jn	John
Acts	Acts
Rom	Romans
1 Cor	1 Corinthians
2 Cor	2 Corinthians
Gal	Galatians
Eph	Ephesians
Phil	Philippians
Col	Colossians
1 Thess	1 Thessalonians
2 Thess	2 Thessalonians
1 Tim	1 Timothy
2 Tim	2 Timothy
Tit	Titus
Philem	Philemon
Heb	Hebrews
Jas	James
1 Pet	1 Peter
2 Pet	2 Peter
1 Jn	1 John
2 Jn	2 John
3 Jn	3 John
Jude	Jude
Rev	Revelation

Transliterations

Hebrew and Aramaic

Hebrew	Transliteration
א	' or nothing
ב	*b* or *v*
ג	*g*
ד	*d*
ה	*h*
ו	*w*
ז	*z*
ח	*h*
ט	*t*
י	*y*
כ	*k*
ל	*l*
מ	*m*
נ	*n*
ס	*s*
ע	' or nothing
פ	*p* or *f* or *ph*
צ	*ts*
ק	*q*
ר	*r*
שׂ	*s*
שׁ	*sh*
ת	*t* or *th*
◌ַ	*a*
◌ָ	*a* or *o*
◌ָה	*ah*
◌ְ	*e* or nothing
◌ֶ	*e*
◌ֵ	*e*
◌ֵי	*e*
◌ִ	*i*
◌ִי	*i*
◌ֹ	*o*
וֹ	*o*
◌ֻ	*u*
וּ	*u*
◌ֳ	*o*
◌ֲ	*a*
◌ֱ	*e*

Greek

Α, α	*A, a*
Β, β	*B, b*
Γ, γ	*G, g*
Δ, δ	*D, d*
Ε, ε	*E, e*
Ζ, ζ	*Z, z*
Η, η	*Ē, ē*
Θ, θ	*Th, th*
Ι, ι	*I, i*
Κ, κ	*K, k*
Λ, λ	*L, l*
Μ, μ	*M, m*
Ν, ν	*N, n*
Ξ, ξ	*X, x*
Ο, ο	*O, o*
Π, π	*P, p*
Ρ, ρ	*R, r*
Σ, σ/ς	*S, s*
Τ, τ	*T, t*
Υ, υ	*Y, y*
Φ, φ	*Ph, ph*
Χ, χ	*Ch, ch*
Ψ, ψ	*Ps, ps*
Ω, ω	*Ō, ō*
Ῥ, ῥ	*Rh, rh*
γξ	*nx*
γγ	*ng*
αυ	*au*
ευ	*eu*
ου	*ou*
υι	*yi*
῾	*h*

CONTRIBUTORS

ALSFORD, SALLY, PH.D. Senior Lecturer, University of Greenwich, London, England: **Atonement; Sin**

ANSLOW, CHRISTINE L., M.A., M.PHIL. Lecturer in Biblical Studies, Greenlane Christian Centre, Auckland, New Zealand: **1 Chronicles**

ATHYAL, SAKHI M., PH.D., D.MISS. Adjunct Professor, Asia Theological Seminary, Tiruvalla, Kerala, India: **Women in Mission**

BAKER, JILL L., PH.D. Candidate, Brown University, Providence, Rhode Island: **1 & 2 Kings**

BATTYE, LISA KATHERINE, M.A., B.S.N. Manchester, England: **Depression; Divorce**

BELLEVILLE, LINDA L., PH.D. Professor of New Testament, North Park Theological Seminary, Chicago, Illinois: **1 Timothy; Homosexuality**

BENHAM, PRISCILLA, PH.D. Former President, Patten College, Oakland, California. Deceased: (coauthor) **Intertestamental History and Literature**

BENTLEY, KRISTEN PLINKE, M.DIV. Minister of Christian Education, Second Presbyterian Church, Lexington, Kentucky: **Philemon;** (coauthor) **Galatians**

BLESSING, KAMILA A., PH.D. Vice President for Congregational Ministries and Director of the Incubation Center for Congregational Resources, Christian Board of Publications, St. Louis, Missouri: **John; Midwifery and Birthing Practices**

BOYLAND, PATRICIA B., PH.D. Instructor in Economics, Glendale Community College, Glendale, California: **Land Ownership and Economic Justice**

BRANCH, ROBIN GALLAHER, PH.D. Adjunct Faculty, Biblical Studies, School of Theology and Missions, Oral Roberts University, Tulsa, Oklahoma: **David's Wives; Deborah; Hannah; Sarah; Wicked Queens**

BROWN, CHERYL ANNE, PH.D. Lecturer in Old Testament and Acting Director of Biblical Studies, International Baptist Theological Seminary, Prague, Czech Republic: **Monotheism**

BUTLER, ANTHEA D., PH.D. Assistant Professor of Theological Studies, Loyola Marymount University, Los Angeles, California: **Zephaniah**

CARTER, PHILIPPA, PH.D. Assistant Professor of Religious Studies, McMaster University, Hamilton, Ontario, Canada: **Joshua; Women as Psalmists**

CHISHOLM-SMITH, LISA, M.PHIL.F. Coordinator, School of Lay Ministry, Anglican Diocese of Ontario, Kingston, Ontario, Canada: **Menstruation**

CHONG, LILY YUN CHU, M.A. Pastor, Anglican Sabah Diocese, Sabah, Malaysia: **Men and Women as Stewards of the Environment**

COHICK, LYNN H., PH.D. Assistant Professor of New Testament, Wheaton College, Wheaton, Illinois: **New Testament Use of Old Testament Quotations Referring to Women; Romans**

COLLINSON, SYLVIA WILKEY, PH.D. Lecturer, Baptist Theological College,

Perth, Australia: **Faith Development; Women Disciples**

CREEGAN, NICOLA HOGGARD, PH.D. Lecturer in Theology, Bible College of New Zealand, West Auckland, New Zealand: **Adultery; Use and Abuse of Language**

DEARBORN, KERRY L., PH.D. Assistant Professor of Theology, Seattle Pacific University, Seattle, Washington: **The Trinity**

DECKER-LUCKE, SHIRLEY A., S.T.M. Associate Editorial Director, Hendrickson Publishers, Peabody, Massachusetts: **Colossians**

DE GROOT, CHRISTIANA, PH.D. Professor of Old Testament, Calvin College, Grand Rapids, Michigan: **Genesis**

DOWD, SHARYN, PH.D. Associate Professor of Religion, Baylor University, Waco, Texas: (coauthor) **Galatians**

DOWSETT, ROSEMARY M., M.A. Training Minister at Large, Overseas Missionary Fellowship, Glasgow, Scotland: **Acts; Matthew**

EVANS, MARY J., M.PHIL. Lecturer in Old Testament, London Bible College, London, England: **Deuteronomy; James**

EVERY-CLAYTON, JOYCE E. WINIFRED, TH.D. Lecturer, Southern Baptist Seminary, Recife, Brazil: **Daniel**

EVES, AILISH FERGUSON, DIP.TH. Lecturer in Missiology and New Testament, London Bible College, London, England: **Judges**

FLESHER, LEANN SNOW. Associate Professor of Old Testament, American Baptist Seminary of the West, Berkeley, California: **Job; Lamentations**

GEMPF, CONRAD, PH.D. Lecturer in New Testament, London Bible College, London, England: **2 Timothy; Birth Pain Imagery**

GRENZ, STANLEY J., PH.D. Professor of Theology and Ethics, Carey/Regent College, Vancouver, British Columbia, Canada: **The Purpose and Value of Human Life**

GRIFFITHS, VALERIE, TH.M. Freelance Writer and Lecturer, Guildford, England: **Polygamy; Women as Leaders**

GRITZ, SHARON H., PH.D. Freelance Writer, Fort Worth, Texas: **1 Thessalonians; Hebrews**

HANCOCK, MAXINE, PH.D. Professor, Interdisciplinary Studies and Spiritual Theology, Regent College, Vancouver, British Columbia, Canada: **Menopause; The Wise Woman, the Foolish Woman and the Righteous Woman**

HARPER, ELIZABETH A., M.A. Director of Studies and Biblical Tutor, West of England Ministerial Training Course, Bristol, England: **Jonah; Micah**

HARRINGTON, HANNAH K., PH.D. Professor of Old Testament, Patten College, Oakland, California: **Ezra; Purity Laws Related to Women; Zechariah;** (coauthor) **Intertestamental History and Literature**

HILTON, JULIE ANN, M.TH. Teacher of Philosophy, Ethics and Religious Education, Langley Grammar School, Slough, England: **Isaiah**

HOPPIN, RUTH, B.A. Independent Researcher, Daly City, California: **Priscilla, the Author of Hebrews**

HOSTETTER, EDWIN C., PH.D. Professor of Biblical Studies, Ecumenical Institute of Theology, Baltimore, Maryland: **Habakkuk**

HOUTS, THE REV. MARGO G., PH.D. Interim Pastor, Head of Staff, Sturge Presbyterian Church, San Mateo, California; Adjunct Faculty, Fuller and San Francisco Theological Seminaries, San Francisco, California: **Images of God as Female; Paul's Use of Female Imagery**

HULL, GRETCHEN GAEBELEIN, LITT. D. Author and Editor, Cold Spring Harbor, New York: **God's Call to Social Justice**

IRVIN, DOROTHY, TH.D. Durham, N.C.: **Clothing and Textiles; Dwelling Places; Food and Water; Numbers**

JERVIS, L. ANN, TH.D. Professor of New Testament, Wycliffe College, Toronto School of Theology, Toronto, Ontario, Canada: **2 Peter**

JOHNSON-LEESE, J. J., S.T.M. Kirkwood, Missouri: **Infanticide;** (coauthor) **The Inspiration and Interpretation of Scripture**

KASSILLY, JANET NASAMBU, M.A. Teacher, Al-Madrasa Tus Saifiyatul Burhaniyah School, Nairobi, Kenya: **2 Thessalonians; Israel as the Wife of Yahweh and the Church as the Bride of Christ**

KEESMAAT, SYLVIA C., D.PHIL. Assistant Professor of Biblical Studies and Hermeneutics, Institute for Christian Studies, Toronto, Ontario, Canada: **Manipulation; Yahweh's Concern for the Disenfranchised**

KENT, DAN GENTRY, TH.D. Professor of Old Testament Emeritus, Southwestern Baptist Theological Seminary, Ft. Worth, Texas: **2 Chronicles**

KOPERSKI, VERONICA, PH.D., S.T.D. Associate Professor of Theology, Barry University, Miami Shores, Florida: **Nahum; Philippians**

KROEGER, CATHERINE CLARK, PH.D. Adjunct Associate Professor of Classical and Ministry Studies, Gordon-Conwell Theological Seminary, South Hamilton, Massachusetts: **1 Corinthians; Emotions of Women in Childbirth; Luke; The Relevance of Psalms for the Everyday Lives of Women; Titus;** (coauthor) **1 Peter;** (coauthor) **Ancient and Modern Slavery**

KROEGER, RICHARD CLARK, JR., D.MIN. Retired Presbyterian Minister (PCUSA), Brewster, Massachusetts: **Haggai**

LE CORNU, ALISON, PH.D. Director of Open Learning, London Bible College, London, England: **Proverbs; Singleness**

MACCINI, ROBERT GORDON, PH.D. Editor, Peacham, Vermont: **Women as Witnesses**

MAGDA, KSENIJA, TH.M. Director, Adult Education, Croatian Baptist Union, Osijek, Croatia: **2 John; 3 John**

MAGGAY, MELBA PADILLA, PH.D. President and CEO, Institute for Studies in Asian Church and Culture, Quezon City, Philippines: **Esther; The Power and Potential of Women**

MATHEWS, ALICE P., PH.D. Lois W. Bennett Distinguished Associate Professor of Educational Ministries and Women's Ministries, Gordon-Conwell Theological Seminary, South Hamilton, Massachusetts: **Hierarchicalism and Equality in the Home**

MAY, THE REV. GRACE YING, TH.D. Pastor, Chinese Christian Church of New England, Brookline, Massachusetts: (coauthor) **Wells**

MCCOY, JILL, B.TH. Lecturer in Liturgy and Theology, Ridley College, Melbourne, Australia: **Covenant and Community; Expectations of Women**

MCCRORY, JEFF H., JR., PH.D. Teaching Pastor, The National Presbyterian Church, Washington, D.C.: **Blessing and Cursing; Nehemiah**

MERCADANTE, THE REV. LINDA A., PH.D. B. Robert Straker Professor of Historical Theology, The Methodist Theological School in Ohio, Delaware, Ohio: **Violence, Abuse and Oppression**

MITCHELL, BEVERLY E., PH.D. Assistant Professor of Historical Theology, Wesley Theological Seminary, Washington, D.C.: (coauthor) **Ancient and Modern Slavery**

MORRELL, KEREN E., M.A. New Romney, England: **Hosea; Revelation**

MOTION, THE REV. MARGARET A., POST GRAD. DIP. ED., POST GRAD. DIP. TCHG. Dean of Studies, Wellington Centre, Bible College of New Zealand, Wellington, New Zealand: **1 John**

NASON-CLARK, NANCY, PH.D. Professor of Sociology, University of New Brunswick, New Brunswick, Nova Scotia, Canada: **Biblical Images of Women; Childbearing and Rearing**

NGAN, LAI LING ELIZABETH, PH.D. Associate Professor of Christian Scriptures, Truett Theological Seminary, Waco, Texas: **Amos**

OSGOOD, JOY, PH.D. Old Testament Lecturer and College Chaplain, Spurgeons College, London, England: **1 & 2 Samuel**

PEARSON, SHARON CLARK, PH.D. Adjunct Professor, Anderson University School of Theology, and Visiting Professor of Biblical Studies, Anderson University: **Holiness and Wholeness**

PETERSON, MARGARET KIM, PH.D. Assistant Professor of Theological Studies, Eastern College, St. Davids, Pennsylvania: **Marriage**

PHILLIPS, ELAINE A., PH.D. Professor of Biblical and Theological Studies, Gordon College, Wenham, Massachusetts: **Ecclesiastes; Exodus**

PIGOTT, SUSAN M., PH.D. Associate Professor of Old Testament, Logsdon School of Theology, Hardin-Simmons University, Abilene, Texas: **Leviticus**

POKRIFKA-JOE, HYUNHYE JUNIA, S.T.M., PH.D. CANDIDATE. Assistant Professor of Old Testament, Azusa Pacific University, Azusa, California: **Obadiah;** (coauthor) **Wells**

POLASKI, SANDRA HACK, PH.D. Associate Professor of New Testament, Baptist Theological Seminary at Richmond, Richmond, Virginia: **2 Corinthians**

POWELL, CLAIRE M., M.A. Former Lecturer in New Testament, All Nations Christian College, Ware, England: **Ephesians**

RAIKES, GWYNNETH MARIAN NAPIER, M.A. Dean of Women and Pastoral Studies, Chaplain and Lecturer in Spirituality, Oak Hill Theological College, London, England: **Joel; Psalms**

ROWELL, THE REV. GILLIAN M., B.A. International Project Director, Novi Most International, Chesham, England: **Ruth**

SANDERS, THE REV. CHERYL J., PH.D. Professor of Christian Ethics, Howard University School of Divinity, and Senior Pastor of the Third Street Church of God, Washington, D.C.: **Hagar**

SCALISE, PAMELA J., PH.D. Associate Professor of Old Testament, Fuller Theological Seminary, Seattle, Washington: **Jeremiah; Malachi**

SCHOLER, DAVID M., Professor of New Testament and Associate Dean for the Center for Advanced Theological Studies, Fuller Theological Seminary, Pasadena, California: (coauthor) **The Inspiration and Interpretation of Scripture**

SINTON, VERA M., M.TH. Tutor in Theology, Oxford Centre for Youth Ministry, Oxford, England: **Grief and Bereavement; Martha and Mary**

SKAGGS, REBECCA, PH.D. Academic Dean and Professor of New Testament and Greek, Patten College, Oakland, California: **Jude;** (coauthor) **Intertestamental History and Literature**

SMITH, MARSHA ELLIS, PH.D. Associate Vice President for Academic Administration, The Southern Baptist Theological Seminary, Louisville, Kentucky: **Feminine Adornment; The Manufacture and Use of Household Utensils; Occupation, Skills and Crafts of Women**

SPENCER, AÍDA BESANÇON, PH.D. Professor of New Testament, Gordon-Conwell Theological Seminary, South Hamilton, Massachusetts: (coauthor) **1 Peter**

STINTON, DIANE B., PH.D. Lecturer in Theology, Daystar University, Nairobi, Kenya: **Africans in Biblical History**

STUEBING, KATHLEEN W., ED.D. Lecturer, Theological College of Central Africa, Ndola, Zambia: **Parental Influence; Sibling Rivalry**

TAYLOR, MARION ANN, PH.D. Associate Professor of Old Testament, Wycliffe College, University of Toronto, Toronto, Ontario, Canada: **Ezekiel**

THURSTON, BONNIE BOWMAN, PH.D. William F. Orr Professor of New Testament, Pittsburgh Theological Seminary, Pittsburgh, Pennsylvania: **Mark; Paul's Greetings to Female Colleagues; Widows**

VOS, CLARENCE J., TH.D. Professor of Religion and Theology Emeritus, Calvin College, Grand Rapids, Michigan: **Women in Worship**

WAGNER, LILYA, ED.D., C.F.R.E. Associate Director, Public Service, Center on Philanthropy, Indiana University, Indianapolis, Indiana: **Changing Life Circumstances; Women and Philanthropy**

WEAVER, DOROTHY JEAN, PH.D. Professor of New Testament, Eastern Mennonite Seminary, Harrisonburg, Virginia: **Barrenness and Fertility**

WHITELEY, RAEWYNNE J., M.A. Doctoral Candidate, Princeton Theological Seminary, Princeton, New Jersey: **Song of Solomon**

WILLETT, ELIZABETH A. R., PH.D. Linguistics Consultant, Field Linguist and Bible Translator, Durango, Mexico: **Household Gods**

WU, JULIE LEE, PH.D. Vice President and Professor of New Testament, China Bible Seminary, Hong Kong, China: **Mary the Mother of Jesus**

The Inspiration & Interpretation of Scripture

How one reads the Bible is inextricably related to how one applies the biblical message. The primary goal in this article is to guide persons of faith toward a more meaningful and responsible reading and application of the Bible in their lives and for the Christian community.

The Inspiration and Revelation of Scripture

The Scriptures have played a central role in forming the identity of Judaism and the Christian church. From its inception, the early Christian community assumed responsibility to read, study and teach Scripture, which for them was the Old Testament (Acts 17:2-11; 18:24, 28; 1 Tim 4:13; 2 Tim 3:15-16). Gradually Christian communities began incorporating in worship and teaching other first-century writings (see 2 Pet 3:15-16) that became known as the New Testament. By the second century, these writings and the Jewish Scriptures were collected and paginated to form a more usable, comprehensive unit for distribution. Throughout the following generations these collections were circulated broadly, widely read in Christian communities and came to be recognized as the guiding norm for faith and practice. During the fourth and fifth century, the formal canonization of the Scriptures took place.

The Christian Scriptures are a remarkable collection of ancient religious documents resulting from the relationship between the Creator God and the created human race. Throughout most of the history of the church, the Scriptures have been recognized as possessing divine and human elements. The nature of Jesus as human and divine has been likened to the revelatory nature of Scripture as human and divine. Both reveal the redemptive nature and intentions of the divine for all time and for all people, yet both are expressed through their unique historical particularities. God's self-revelation in Scripture is truly mysterious and marvelous primarily because it is communicated through human and ordinary events in history.

Unlike sacred writings from other religious traditions, which often expound rules or instructions to be obeyed, God's mode of inspiration was not a divine, word-by-word declaration from a distant heaven recorded by an unreceptive hand. Rather, the Word of God came to individuals and faith communities in the midst of life and struggle. Through this faith conversation with God, ancient Israel and the early Christian community found identity, purpose and direction. Therefore Jewish and Christian Scriptures, while mysteriously inspired by God, remain imbedded in human history, dynamically addressing local particularities as well as universal concerns.

The essence of biblical inspiration should not be confined to single authors, times or the original inscriptions of Scripture. A more holistic approach toward understanding the inspiration of Scripture affirms the process guided by divine providence whereby God's word was revealed in community, was interpreted by the community and has been preserved by the community in its final canonical form.

Inspiration is the process by which the words of the biblical writers were constituted at the same time as God's written Word. Revelation refers to God's disclosures about God's nature, attributes and intentions for faithful living. While people can learn about God's attributes through creation (general revelation), Scripture functions as the special witness (special revelation). Dozens of human authors spanning a period of more than fifteen hundred years wrote, edited and collected documents. God's revelation came through prose, poetry, narrative history, genealogies, proverbs, drama, hymns, prayers, letters, sermons, apocalypses and other forms. Most of Scripture emerged as faith communities preserved stories orally, then in written form, and passed them from generation to generation. Some documents were letters written to specific congregations and individuals addressing particular human situations. Eventually they were woven into a collection of diverse yet unified documents. One central thread connecting this collection is God's redemptive interaction with human beings at real points of need. The drama for Christians culminates with God's unique self-revelation in the incarnation, the Word of God made flesh.

The revelation of God in Scripture becomes an ongoing, rich tradition for faith experience and expression. Gordon Fee understands God's self-revelation in history as a guarantee that God will continue to communicate to us in meaningful ways (36). This hope informs our understanding of biblical authority. The authority of Scripture is grounded in the conviction that God is the ultimate author and originator of the Word. Likewise the power of God's Word continues to convict, transform and empower the community of faith (e.g., 2 Tim 3:15-17). The central message of Christ crucified grasps the hearer, transforms the whole person and creates the body of Christ—the church. This "new creation" continues the work of Christ in each age (e.g., 2 Cor 5:17-21; Gal 6:15).

The Interpretation of Scripture

The appeal to Scripture's authority and how one interprets and applies Scripture are in some ways two sides of the same coin. This is to say that the authority of Scripture as the witness to the transforming and redeeming power of Jesus Christ can be jeopardized if one's reading of Scripture doesn't reflect this life-giving core. While the intrinsic authority of Scripture can never be annulled, distorted readings of Scripture can make its message meaningless and void. The history of biblical interpretation in the Christian church best illustrates this integral connection between biblical authority and interpretation. An appeal to Scripture's authority has been used by the Christian church in countless atrocities, not the least of which was to persecute and kill Jews, kill thousands in holy war, burn women suspected of witchcraft or of using pain relievers in childbirth, kill doctrinal heretics and torture and enslave Africans. The claim that "the Bible says so" has armed countless people with tools for oppression and enslavement, thereby subverting the life-giving good news of God's redeeming love in Jesus Christ.

How the church handles Scripture, how the church reads Scripture, how the church embodies Scripture becomes a reflection of God's transforming work in and through the body of Christ. A primary purpose of biblical interpretation must be to present a faithful reading of the text to shape and empower the church toward a life characterized by the central gospel message. The message is that Christ came to redeem all people through the cross, called them into a life of discipleship and created the community of faith as the physical presence of God's present work in the world.

Sources That Influence and Shape Biblical Interpretation

One challenge in biblical interpretation is the significant role of the reader. Feminist and liberation hermeneutics have done much to demonstrate that biblical texts cannot be read with pure objectivity. Nevertheless, many Christians believe that when they read the text, they automatically possess an accurate understanding of the text. Every reader of the Bible is also an interpreter of it, but all interpretations are invariably influenced by sources other than Scripture. Cultural, ethnic, social, gender and economic experiences factor into the interpreter's perspective and thus shape how a reader might understand a text.

Other external sources shape the interpretive process as well. Ecclesiastical traditions provide significant insight and direction as we seek to read the text faithfully, yet each church tradition also reads biblical texts through the experiences of its historical heritage. Different church traditions present diverse interpretations and applications of the Bible at many doctrinal points. Even the questions that individuals and church bodies take to the text are shaped by their ecclesiastical traditions. As with human experience and ecclesiastical tradition, one's capacity for reason and basis for knowledge change with times and cultures. Human reason can inform and bring clarity, or it can muffle and distort the message of Scripture.

Establishing that these external sources exist leads naturally to the discussion of what role they should play in biblical interpretation. Richard Hays establishes what he considers a "minimal guideline" for understanding the relationship between extrabiblical sources and the Bible. "Extra biblical sources stand in a hermeneutical relation to the New Testament; they are not independent, counter-balancing sources of authority. In other words, the Bible's perspective is privileged, not ours" (Hays, 296).

Until a few decades ago, biblical scholarship, interpretation and the teaching of Scripture was done primarily by men of European descent. Yet if the church can affirm in practice what it has always taught—that the Bible belongs to the whole church—then we must acknowledge that no longer should scholarly biblical interpretation be dominated by a homogeneous few. This shift is occurring as Asians, Africans, Hispanics, women and those in oppressed social situations write biblical interpretation. Readings that more easily identify the multiple contours of the text lead all to rethink theological and interpretive assumptions. Biblical interpretation involves listening to the whole people of God, each bringing a unique perspective to the interpretive process. As genuine dialogue occurs, increased sensitivities and respect for different readings of the text will result.

Nature of Biblical Texts and Their Message

How then do we allow the biblical text to speak out of its setting and through its inspired form? How can we be called into the text's service, instead of shaping the text to say what we want it to say? How do the divine intentions of Scripture become for us the privileged and authoritative perspective? And what guides our reading and contemporary application of the Bible? To address these important questions, an interpretive methodology that considers three circles of contexts as a guide toward a responsible reading of the Bible is suggested. These three circles of context are literary context, historical context and canonical context.

The literary and historical contexts focus on the original settings out of which the Scriptures were written. The literary context involves the literary forms and conditions of the message, literary devices, author's intent and the like. The historical context reveals what can be inferred about the setting of the original writing. To ignore the original literary and historical context of an ancient text may lead to a distorted reading of the text. Thus, before asking "What does this say to me?" one must first ask, "How did the text function authoritatively in its original setting?" Answering this question primarily comes through understanding the multifaceted issues of the literary and historical settings. The third circle of context, the canonical context, takes the interpretive process one step further. Its primary interpretive function is to ask, "How does the text function authoritatively for the church today?" The canonical approach seeks to allow each text to be heard and balanced against the entire canonical witness, acknowledging that although our times and place have changed, Scriptures continue with universal significance and authority. Diagram 1 presents visually the interconnection among these three contexts.

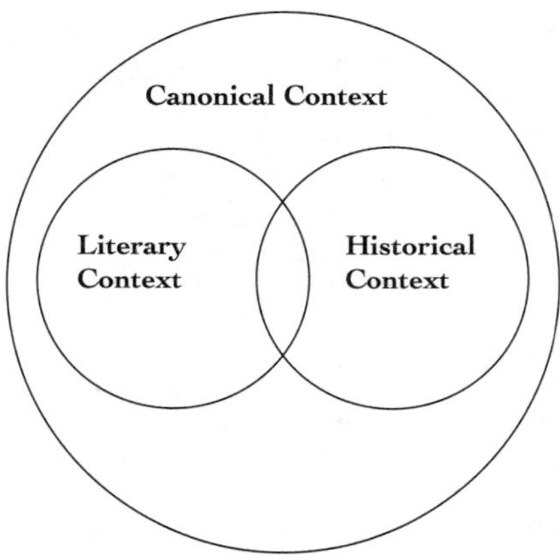

Diagram 1. Biblical Contexts

Literary Context. The first essential task in understanding the literary components of the Bible is to determine what words are included in a text. This task is not always so obvious. For most people, that means relying on linguistic experts in the field of textual criticism. These experts meticulously evaluate Hebrew and Greek manuscripts of biblical texts that were copied and recopied by ancient scribes to establish what they believe to be the most accurate Hebrew and Greek readings in existence. Because there are no original manuscripts in existence today, the textual experts work with thousands of copies of manuscripts, no two exactly alike. The vast majority of the differences are small or obvious copy errors, and no discrepancies detract from the overall message of the Bible or alter major doctrinal teachings. Among the better-known variant readings are the endings to the Gospel of Mark. Some ancient Greek texts end at Mark 16:8; some end at Mark 16:20; others have what is called "the shorter ending." Most study Bibles will refer to such variant readings of a text in the margins or notes.

Because most Christians are not trained in textual linguistics and do not have a working knowledge of Hebrew, Aramaic and Greek, they must rely on translations of the Bible. Translators attempt to bring an accurate reading of the text; however, changes in word meanings and cultural distance mean that differences of opinion are inevitable. Therefore certain biases exist in translations. Awareness of translation biases is important in selecting a translation from which to read and study. In general, it is best to select a translation that was completed by a committee with a variety of church traditions represented.

Closely related to the translation of the text is the meaning or range of meanings of words or phrases. Greek and Hebrew sometimes used words with nuances not understood or reflected in English translations. Thus to some extent the translator becomes interpreter as well. One example is what Paul meant by the Greek term *kephalē*, typically translated as "head" (e.g., Eph 5:23; 1 Cor 11:3-16). When we use the word *head* in English, it is commonly understood to mean an anatomical appendage or sometimes metaphorically one's brain. It is also a common metaphor for one who is a leader or director over someone. Occasionally it is used for the end or top of an object or the beginning or source of a river. We know which meaning to apply based on context. For example, the head (source) of a river is never viewed as a leader.

When Paul used the Greek term *kephalē,* it had twenty-five figurative uses alone. The most common figurative uses included "source of life," "beginning," "base," "origin" and "starting point." It was not assumed most commonly to mean "boss" or "leader." Therein lies a great challenge for translators and readers of Scripture. Should one assume a twenty-first-century meaning for a word that may not have meant the same in its ancient linguistic usage? Paul could have been using the term *kephalē* in a number of ways. One challenge of biblical interpretation is to attempt to determine a meaning or cluster of meanings based on context and Paul's use of the term elsewhere.

In conjunction with meanings of words are grammatical concerns that arise from the original languages. For example, one passage often quoted in isolation is Ephesians 5:22, "Wives, be subject to your husbands as you are to the Lord." Although this is not apparent from English translations, there is no verb in this sentence. Literally the Greek says, "wives to your husbands as to the Lord." Grammatically this sentence cannot stand alone and must draw its verbal sense from Ephesians 5:21, "Be subject to one another out of reverence for Christ." Translations that separate the two verses by a paragraph and the insertion of a subtitle mislead readers and distort the grammatical structure that ties these verses together. Another grammatical consideration is that the verb "be subject" (Eph 5:21) is a modifying verb to the main verb of Paul's discussion beginning in Ephesians 5:18, "be filled with the Spirit."

This example also illustrates one of the most basic yet often overlooked steps for responsible Bible reading. Each passage must be read in its larger literary context. Paul's directives to wives in Ephesians 5:22 can be understood only within Paul's larger discussion of the Spirit-filled and Spirit-guided marriage characterized by mutual submission, self-sacrificial love and respect (Eph 5:18-33). Paul's discussion of Christ's self-sacrificial giving up of self and rights out of love for his body, the church, becomes the guiding metaphor for how husbands should relate to their wives. There is no basis from this text to support the popular teaching that Paul is telling women to obey their husbands because the husbands as head of the house are the spiritual leaders and decision makers of the family. Careful reading of texts in their larger literary unit is the best remedy for such practices of proof texting, or reading into the text something that is not there.

Identifying the genre of biblical literature is another necessary step toward understanding how a text functioned and how it should be read today. Genre refers to the literary styles and motifs of literature. The Bible contains a wide variety of genres: poetry, prose, Gospel, letter, apocalyptic, historical narrative, proverb, drama, parable, hymns, prayers and more. This rich anthology of literature in the Bible is unlike any other ancient collection of writings. Such variety creates for the contemporary reader an additional interpretive challenge, however. The type or form of literature one reads will shape how one reads the text. In other words, sensitive readers understand that the content (what is said) of a passage is shaped and understood by the literary form (how it is said) of the passage. For example, apocalyptic literature (e.g., Daniel and Revelation), although common in the ancient world, is a genre relatively unknown to the average reader today. Therefore it is important to understand something about the unique function of such literary forms in the ancient world in order to understand how the content of the literature might have been read and understood in the early Christian church. Identifying the significant link between content and form will significantly shape how such apocalyptic literature is read as meaningful for us today.

Another literary genre common in the New Testament is the genre of letter. All the New Testament letters were written to people in the first-century Mediterranean world addressing specific concerns of those unique early church settings. Most of the New Testament letters were also occasional letters, which means that the letters were pastoral responses to specific written or verbal requests and questions of the recipients. Understanding the unique features and purposes of the letter literary form will shape how one reads what was said in the letter. This leads naturally to the second circle of context for biblical interpretation, the historical context.

Historical Context. Each document in the Christian canon reflects a general and specific historical setting as well as the particularities and life settings of each human author. One primary task in the interpretive process is to identify the historical circumstances that shaped the writings of Scripture. This process informs an understanding of the text and heightens awareness of the historical distance between the text and the contemporary reader. This realization should not diminish the authority of the text or be construed as a barrier to understanding it. Rather, acknowledging the historical particularities of the text should result in a more responsible reading of the text by enabling one to appreciate otherwise difficult discussions (e.g., head coverings in 1 Cor 11:2-16) and avoid anachronistic readings.

Any reading of the Bible should consider general and specific historical particularities of the text, the biblical author's stated concerns and the chronological placement in the author's life. For example, in 1 Timothy 5:3-16, Paul provides for the church at Ephesus guidance concerning widowed women under the age of sixty. They were not to be placed on the list of widows because their sensual desires would alienate them from Christ and bring them condemnation. Paul's requirement for such a widow was to remarry and be concerned with children and a household. In another New Testament letter (1 Cor 7:32-35, 39-40) Paul urges unmarried and virgin women in Corinth to stay single so that they may give all of their energy to the Lord's work rather than being anxious about the affairs of the household and a husband. Such biblical examples illustrate that Paul's varied audiences required different directives depending on the specific historical situations or spiritual crises that they faced. Third-party readers who have access only to one side of ancient conversations must take great care to hear and handle the text with integrity.

General historical information concerning the ancient Mediterranean world can also provide necessary insight for drawing out deeper meaning and significance of a text. The interaction between Jesus and the Samaritan woman (Jn 4) takes on deeper significance when we understand that in their world women did not have the prerogative of divorce, yet men could divorce their wives for virtually any reason. Reading the text from our perspective sees this woman as immoral at best. However, reading the text from her situation gives a different perspective: she is deeply wounded and vulnerable. General historical information about divorce laws helps us to make a more accurate evaluation of the interaction between Jesus and the woman. Although bridging the historical and cultural gap between the ancient world and our own is no easy task, sensitive readers can benefit greatly by careful and repeated readings of the text, along with a good study Bible and Bible dictionary.

Sensitivity to the Bible's literary and historical contexts along with a close, careful reading of a text will enable a clearer understanding of the author's intent and concerns. Such a method of study will respect the distinct life or voice of each biblical passage while showing how the text functioned authoritatively in its original setting.

Canonical Context. Informing one's reading of the Bible with sensitivity to the literary and historical contexts of individual texts is a vital and necessary component in biblical interpretation. Nevertheless, any study of the Bible that stops at this point remains incomplete, for the third circle of interpretation, the canonical context, bridges the gap between what the text meant and what the text means. The canonical circle of context insists that Scripture, as the authoritative written Word of God, continues to shape and inform the church's identity and life. This focus answers the theological questions of how we relate to God and understand ourselves in relationship to God and to the ethical questions of how we relate to one another in the Christian community and to the world. This level of biblical interpretation invites readers to go beyond the cognitive study of Scripture to the far more difficult task of embodying the Word and allowing its imperatives to come alive within. Biblical information becomes personal transformation.

Thus the crucial function of canonical context is to engage the ancient text with the contemporary reader and to allow the text to speak a meaningful, fresh word to each generation and social setting. To illustrate the point, let us consider how 1 Timothy 2:9-10 functioned authoritatively for the church at Ephesus and how it should function as God's authoritative word for the church today. If one considers the literary and historical issues, one can determine that Paul intended a specific change in behavior for the women in Ephesus: they were not to braid their hair or wear pearls, gold or expensive clothing. Therefore answering how the text functioned authoritatively in its original setting seems straightforward. Yet should this text function in the same way today even though our social setting is significantly different from ancient Ephesus? Should this passage become a dress code for women for all times and places? Is there something inherently evil about pearls, gold, braids and expensive clothing? Most of us never get to the point of asking such questions. We discount this passage as culturally conditioned with little personal trepidation over the moral and spiritual implications of not changing our behavior to fit the specifics of this text. The problem with this common approach to biblical interpretation is that every word of Scripture is culturally conditioned and culturally relevant. All of Scripture was shaped by its original historical settings, varied literary forms and the specific thought patterns and languages of the human authors who wrote and the communities they addressed. Therefore, on what basis (besides external sources such as intuition, experience or tradition) do we determine which texts are so conditioned by their original situation that they no longer speak to us in the same way and those ancient texts that transcend their historical particularities and should be understood as normative teachings for all times and all places? How can the inspired authoritative words of 1 Timothy 2:9-10 be meaningful and fresh for us today? Or can they be?

The canonical approach addresses these types of questions and assists the church in understanding how a text such as 1 Timothy 2:9-10 can be meaningful today. The canonical context of this passage goes beyond understanding the unique historical and literary concerns and attempts to place these biblical injunctions into a canonical perspective. One foundational premise to the canonical approach is the affirmation that all of Scripture is authoritative in its final canonical form. Therefore, within this interpretive model, it is not acceptable to determine as irrelevant specific texts because they are culturally conditioned. Nor is it acceptable to impose upon the contemporary church an ancient worldview or practice with relevance bound to a specific culture or time. This method seeks to allow the integral wholeness of the canon, not external sources, to shape the answer to how a text such as 1 Timothy 2:9-10 should be heard and become authoritative for the church today.

The canonical approach has several important methodological components to understand and practice in one's reading of a text. One basic principle is to study the entire canonical witness on any given theological or ethical question. This comprehensive approach usually identifies a consistent witness, a diverse witness or an isolated witness. If a consistent witness arises throughout the canon, then one can be fairly certain that the witness should be understood as a normative theological or ethical teaching for all times and places. For example, Genesis 1:1 states that God is the Creator of the universe. If one were to evaluate this proposition canonically, one would identify a thematic consistent witness throughout the Bible that affirms this basic theological teaching about God. Even though the canonical witness comes to us through diverse literary forms speaking to a variety of historical particularities over two thousand years, the message is the same: God is Creator. Therefore Genesis 1:1 should be understood as teaching a normative and universal theological and canonical teaching for all times and all places: the Jewish and Christian God is Creator of the universe. This universal application becomes the text's first and only meaning.

There are, however, many instances where a diverse witness results from a canonical inquiry. When this results, one must allow the diversity and ambiguity of the texts to stand. This guards against distortions that can occur when premature harmonization is attempted or when we read into the text something that is not present. Instead of trying to deny or harmonize the biblical witness, a responsible reader will understand that this canonical diversity is best explained when investigation of the historical particularities of each situation is understood. For example, Scripture's diverse witness to women's participation in Judaism and in early church leadership has received significant discussion in recent years. Although a few passages read in isolation seem to exclude women from church leadership (e.g., 1 Tim 2:11-12; 1 Cor 14:33-36), the larger canonical witness presents women's involvement differently (e.g., Deborah, Huldah, Anna, Priscilla, Syntyche and Euodia, Phoebe). Therefore, when we discover a diverse witness in Scripture, we should ask the literary and historical questions necessary to understand what circumstances prompted different directives.

There will also be instances when a text is an isolated witness. One such example is Acts 19:12, which as a narrative history describes how Paul's handkerchiefs and aprons were used to heal people. One can safely conclude in this instance that such an isolated text is not to be understood as a central, normative teaching of the canon that should guide and inform church practice, policy or faith expression.

The benefits of reading the entire canonical witness on any given theological or ethical question is to bring perspective and balance to each specific text and consistency in the treatment of various texts. This method of reading Scripture also functions as a corrective to those who develop a theological or ethical teaching by relying on a limited or isolated canonical witness. Such limited readings are in danger of distorting or misrepresenting the more prominent canonical witness.

Finally, a canonical reading of any given text encompasses, considers and integrates the literary and historical elements of a biblical passage to inform how a text should take shape in the life of the church today. This essential connection between these three contexts is necessary because of the inherent nature of Scripture as inspired literature embedded in history. This integrated approach to biblical interpretation acknowledges that a meaningful word for today cannot be understood apart from the original historical setting and inspired literary forms.

To disregard the literary form, historical setting and canonical voice of a text such as 1 Timothy 2:9-10 could easily turn this text into a proof text to support a normative, timeless dress code for all women. Thus a simplistic interpretive method prevails, and the church ends up with a biblical teaching claimed by interpreters as authoritative because the Bible says so. To apply this text in the same way that it was applied in first-century Ephesus takes the life out of the text. The text becomes distorted into law instead of gospel and results in Scripture and the church losing their transforming witness to our world.

Conclusion

How can twenty-first-century Christians read Scripture faithfully and with integrity? How can we allow the foreignness of its original historical setting and the ancient nature of the text to come alive as a fresh and convicting word for us today? These questions will be addressed throughout this commentary and answered from a variety of perspectives. We have presented one interpretive method that attempts to address the multifaceted nature of the inspired canon as well as honestly admitting the great challenge this presents for the contemporary reader. Our hope is that this model brings clarity and direction to our understanding and application of the Bible and that it becomes a framework for much creative and thoughtful work.

Bibliography

G. D. Fee, *Gospel and Spirit: Issues in New Testament Hermeneutics* (Peabody, MA: Hendrickson, 1991); G. D. Fee and D. Stuart, *How to Read the Bible for All Its Worth: A Guide to Understanding the Bible,* 2d ed.

(Grand Rapids, MI: Zondervan, 1993); J. Goldingay, *Models for Scripture* (Grand Rapids, MI: Eerdmans, 1994); J. B. Green, ed., *Hearing the New Testament: Strategies for Interpretation* (Grand Rapids, MI: Eerdmans, 1995); R. B. Hays, *The Moral Vision of the New Testament: A Contemporary Introduction to New Testament Ethics* (San Francisco: HarperSanFrancisco, 1996); D. M. Scholer, "Issues in Biblical Interpretation," *Evangelical Quarterly* 60 (1988) 5-22.

J. J. JOHNSON-LEESE AND DAVID M. SCHOLER

GENESIS

Introduction

Genesis is a book about beginnings. Genesis 1—11 describes how the cosmos came into being, how marriage arose, how it happened that men dominate women and that the ground unwillingly gives its produce, how culture and the many languages began. Against this primeval backdrop, the text continues in Genesis 12 by narrating the creation of God's people. Genesis moves from the universal to the particular and keeps a tension alive between depicting God as the Creator/Sustainer of the universe and of all humanity and God as the initiator of a special relationship with the chosen people. Genesis relates how and why the Israelites were set apart, what their particular calling was and how they lived out this vocation. Choosing the Israelites is not opposed to God's commitment to the whole world; rather, Israel's separateness is presented as a means to God's blessing the whole world.

Genesis, as a book about beginnings, shares features with the stories of beginnings told by other cultures. Human beings have explained the world in certain typical ways. For example, seeing the present reality as a fall from an ideal world is a persistent pattern in tales of beginnings. Understanding these typical patterns of thought allows us to perceive more clearly what Genesis shares with other stories and how it differs. Reading the text in comparison with other creation accounts, particularly with other creation accounts from the ancient Mesopotamian area, allows the specific content of Genesis to be highlighted. For example, when we understand that in the ancient Near East only monarchs were considered to be images of the divine, we can appreciate more fully the high status that is conferred on each one of us. According to Genesis, all human beings are created in the image of God (Gen 1:26-27).

In this single book, Genesis, we encounter many different literary genres. Each literary genre has its own goals and typical features, and each proclaims truth in its distinctive way. Recognizing the particular literary form that is being read allows readers to listen better to the text. However, identifying the literary genre is not always easy. Because this text was written in the distant past and arises from a different cultural context, we are involved in crosscultural communication when we read Genesis. The text does not always function as modern Westerners would expect, and for this reason also it is helpful to understand the text in its original cultural context.

One facet of the text that becomes apparent when Genesis is read in its original context is that its primary goal is not simply to convey accurate information about the past. Although it describes the past, its genre is not history, understood as recording the events of the past as they occurred. The family stories in Genesis tell of the lives of Israel's ancestors not only to inform but also to shape the present generation. By telling its story, the community instilled in generation after generation a sense of its identity, its calling as a people and its basis of hope for the future (*see* Covenant and Community).

Claiming that Genesis is not history as we think of a history book does not mean that the story it narrates is not rooted in events. The text reflects life in the ancient Near East. Customs that function in Genesis are present in other Mesopotamian texts. For example, the use of a surrogate mother in the narrative about Abraham, Sarah and Hagar was a typical way to deal with infertility. Especially significant for this commentary is the realization that the patriarchal culture reflected in Genesis is not unique to Israel. The privileging of male over female that we meet in this text occurs throughout the ancient world. The question arises whether the text is assuming patriarchy, endorsing patriarchy or calling it into question. In analyzing particular texts, I intend to demonstrate that on the whole the text challenges patriarchy and presents a vision of both women and men as full human beings.

The final text that we have before us in English translation is the result of a long process of formation. There is good internal as well as external evidence to support the hypothesis that much of what we now read was initially part of an oral tradition. The many stories of the matriarchs and patriarchs were passed on by word of mouth for many generations. Other texts probably originated in liturgies and perhaps were part of a covenant renewal ceremony or the various festival celebrations. Nowhere in the text are we told who the author is. Technically Genesis is an anonymous work, as are most ancient texts. Although the human author is not named, Christians believe that the final text is the Word of God.

Outline

1:1—11:32	Origins of Reality
12:1—50:26	Ancestral Narratives

Commentary

Not only Genesis 1—2 but also Genesis 3—11 are concerned with relating how the present reality came into being. We read of creation in the opening chapters, the transition from an ideal state to the real, then of the destruction of the world and a second beginning after the flood. The high status of human beings is reflected not only in the opening chapters but again in the genealogies in which humans are almost immortal and in Genesis 11 when God notices humanity building a tower and concludes that nothing will be impossible for them. Only when we begin the narratives of the ancestors in Genesis 12 do we recognize ourselves as limited, complicated beings and our present ambiguous reality.

Origins of Reality (Gen 1—11)

Creation (Gen 1—4)

In Genesis 1:1—2:4 we read of the creation of the world by decree. In an orderly, processional manner, the cosmos is created. In the first three days the stage setting is formed: the light and dark, the sky and seas, the land and vegetation. Then in the following three days the corresponding moving parts are introduced: the sun, moon and stars, the birds and the fish, animals and humanity. Finally, on the last day, God rests and establishes the sabbath. There is a pattern to the week as well as a pattern to each day.

In this account humanity is created last, the pinnacle of creation. Only before our creation does God reflect and specify what the task of humanity will be (Gen 1:26). This reflection is followed by a description of the act of creation: "So God created humankind in his image, in the image of God created he them, male and female created he them" (Gen 1:27). As we have noted, for human beings to be presented as the image of God is remarkable, given the ancient context. In that world, kings were understood to be the image of the deity, and this grounded their authority to rule. In other ancient Near Eastern creation accounts, when human beings are created, it was to relieve the lesser deities of their drudgery. Rather than being created as slaves, as in the Atrahasis Epic, according to Genesis all human beings share the status of royalty.

Genesis 1:27 lays the foundation for biblical anthropology. It tells us that to be human is to be related to God in a special way; only humanity is created in the image of God. Genesis 1:27 states that God created *adam* in his image. Some translations render this word "man" and some "humankind." Although translations may differ, there is no confusion concerning the intent of the text to include all human beings in the singular noun *adam*. This is a collective term for humankind; the pronoun *he* in the second line of the poem refers to this collective noun and does not indicate that only men are in God's image. All humanity, women and men, are God's image.

The preposition *in* in the phrase "in the image" merits some reflection. The Hebrew prepositional prefix *bet* is sometimes translated into English as "in," sometimes as "as." The context suggests which is the preferred rendering. Translation of the preposition *bet* with "in" has given rise to specu-lation about what particular quality of humans beings reflect the deity, and a long tradition in the history of interpretation of this text equates our ability to reason with our God-likeness. This interpretation has harmed women in that stereotypically men were considered rational and spiritual and women were considered emotional and physical. This translated into a hierarchy of being in which men more closely imaged God than did women.

More recently some scholars have suggested that "as" is a preferred translation. They claim that being God's image is a task, and they support their arguments with evidence from the ancient world in which the king ruled as the image of God. They point out that in the text of Genesis, being created as God's image is followed by a mandate giving humanity dominion over the earth. I suggest that the Hebrew language holds together what in English can be divided. By translating *bet* with either "in" or "as," English allows us to separate who we are from what we are called to do, and recently some Christians have made such claims about gender roles. For example, suggestions have been made that although both women and men are created in God's image and hence have the same status, yet God has called them to different roles. Men are called to leadership positions, and women are called to be followers. The biblical text, however, does not drive a wedge between our status and our calling. We are both "in the image" and "as the image."

Humanity's creation is followed by a blessing and command addressed to both the woman and the man. Hebrew verbs in the second person indicate whether the party addressed is masculine or feminine, singular or plural. The blessing and command are in the plural. Both male and female are to be fruitful and multiply, and both are to have dominion over the earth (Gen 1:28-30). There is no division of labor into the private or family realm for women and the public or work realm for men. Both are given the same blessing and called to the full range of responsibilities.

In the biblical text the polytheism of ancient Mesopotamian religions is absent. Rather than a pantheon of male and female deities, we have one deity. The cosmos is not inhabited by gods and goddesses who mirror and undergird the roles of men and women in society. Tikva Frymer-Kensky (1992) explores what happens when gods and goddesses are no more, when monotheism replaces polytheism (*see* Monotheism). She demonstrates first that the worship of goddesses is no guarantee that women are more highly valued. Her analysis of Sumerian religion and society leads her to conclude that this pantheon of male and female deities established and supported a patriarchal social system. Second, she claims that in biblical monotheism God is not male. Although God is addressed by the pronoun *he* and has predominantly masculine characteristics, nowhere in the biblical text is God presented as a sexual being. Because God is above and beyond sexuality, it is possible for both women and men to be in the image of God. Another implication of God's non-sexuality is that human beings are not defined first by their sexual identity. We are first members of the human race, and it is as human beings that we image the one God.

It has been argued that Genesis 1:26-27 supports not only monotheism but also plurality within the Godhead. In Genesis 1:26 God ruminates, "Let us make humankind in our image, according to our likeness," and in Genesis 1:27 we read, "So God created humankind in his image." The text fluctuates between singular and plural when referring to God. Although it is not possible to definitively interpret this plurality, in its original context it did not necessarily mean either the Trinity or a plurality of genders (*see* The Trinity). Rather, this text parallels Isaiah 6, a passage in which God is envisioned as a king on a throne. There also the text fluctuates between singular and plural, and there it fits with the image of God as a king who speaks both for himself and for his council. In a similar fashion, Genesis 1 depicts God as a monarch who creates by decree. In this context, the original understanding of the use of "we" in God's speaking is that it is the royal "we." God the king creates us in his image so that we can rule in his stead.

Genesis 2:4 begins a second creation account in which the picture of God and the process of creation differ from the picture of Genesis 1. This narrative presents creation as a project in which God takes a step and then decides on what the next step will be. First the *adam* is shaped from the earth *(adamah)*. God then breathes life into him and puts the *adam* into the garden he had planted. Then God notices that the *adam* is alone, concludes that this is not good and creates the animals. However, none of the animals meet the needs of the *adam* for companionship. Then God puts the *adam* to sleep, opens his side, builds a woman and

Men & Women as Stewards of the Environment

A bank in Sabah, Malaysia, published a poster calendar with a caption that reads "Together we care for the environment" against a backdrop of corals in our tropical coastal seas. The Chipko movement is an example of women and children adopting this attitude to protect trees and animals in India.

God created man and woman in his image (Gen 1:27-28) and entrusted them with tending the earth (Gunton, quoting Karl Barth; see Gen 1:26-28). The word *steward* in Hebrew carries the meaning of "guardian," and people of God are to tend and protect the earth as stewards. Stewardship is then a sacred duty.

In the New Testament God gave us this mandate through John 3:16, which says God loves the world and gave his only Son, Jesus Christ, that through him we might have redemption. Most of us use this verse to emphasize salvation. But the "world" here in Greek means "cosmos," not only the lives of men and women but also the created world. Because of the Fall, Satan's influence spoiled what initially was inherently good (Gen 1:31). However, God sent his Son to rescue humanity but also to save this world from destruction.

Therefore Jesus is not only our Redeemer but also the cosmic Christ. We are to bring back everything to him; "through him God was pleased to reconcile to himself all things, whether on earth or in heaven, by making peace through the blood of his cross" (Col 1:20). Paul says the creation waits for release from its bondage and decay and for restoration (Rom 8:18-21). We are God's agents, under the Great Commission sent to save souls and to see God's created world saved. Because we are citizens in the kingdom of God and children of God, we are to do what God has told us to do. When a father asks a child to do what is good, an obedient child will do so.

What then are the demands of our mission as children of God? In the light of kingdom values, we are accountable to live in ways that display concern for the world and its resources. We can work to lessen damage to the environment, being like salt and light (Mt 5:13-15) to preserve and stand up for what God has entrusted to us as guardians of creation. Wherever God puts us, we can bring about shalom and reconciliation.

Defilement of the environment is a grave concern, but as responsible children and citizens of God's kingdom we are to treat God's earth as God wants us to and not destroy it to satisfy our whims, greed and selfishness. It is therefore the responsibility of every man and woman of God to be the harbinger of this urgent mission. Jesus' coming can bring salvation not only to humanity but also to his cosmos.

As men and women of God, we are endowed with the gifts of the Holy Spirit to bring about reconciliation and restoration of this creation; we are to be faithful to our mission until Christ comes (Eph 4:11-13; Rom 12:6-8; 1 Cor 2:7-11; 1 Pet 4:9-11).

Bibliography

C. Seaton, *Whose Earth?* (Great Britain: Crossway Books, 1992) 113-19; C. E. Gunton, *Christ and Creation* (Grand Rapids, MI: Eerdmans, 1992); A. Gnanadason, "Towards a Feminist Eco-theology for India," in *Ecology and Development*, ed. D. D. Chetti (India: UELC/Gurukul Lutheran Theological College, 1991).

LILY YUN CHU CHONG

brings her to the man. Now the man has a partner who is fit for him. The narrative concludes by establishing the institution of marriage (Gen 2:24; *see* Marriage). The story has moved from the creation of a single human being who is then differentiated into male and female and concludes with a return to the original unity.

The structure of this narrative is circular. Rather than humanity being created last as the pinnacle of creation, the man is created first, and then the rest of creation is introduced to meet the needs of the man. First his physical needs are met by the creation of the garden, and then his social needs are met. The man names the animals, but among them is found no partner for the man. Only with the creation of woman is a suitable companion found.

In this narrative, the process of creation and the character of God are presented quite differently from Genesis 1. Rather than having the sequence of creation planned, God operates experimentally. Rather than creation by decree, he operates like a surgeon or plants like a farmer. This portrait of the deity is much more immanent than the transcendent portrait of God found in Genesis 1. There are tensions between these two pictures of God, but the text of Genesis makes no effort to harmonize them or emphasize one over the other. Both are presented as true; God is both transcendent and immanent, both omniscient and experimenting, both unlike and like us. The Western Christian tradition has typically been uncomfortable with such tensions in the text and has tended to elevate the majestic God of Genesis 1 at the expense of the craftsman God of Genesis 2. However, the text affirms both pictures. The two sides of God introduced here will appear again and again in Scripture. God is both the Lord before whom we bend the knee and our friend to whom we reveal our inmost thoughts.

Typically the first account of creation has never been used to malign and subordinate women. The second creation narrative, followed by the disobedience and expulsion of the man and woman from the garden (Gen 2:4—3:24), has been the classic text to ground claims about gender hierarchy. Phyllis Trible (73) documents the misogynous claims based on this text. In the past twenty-five years this passage has come under much scrutiny from a new generation of women. These biblical scholars have sought to recover the meaning of the text apart from the history of interpretation and to consider it anew within its ancient context. They have recovered much that is liberating for women, as well as much that remains problematic.

For example, Genesis 2:4-24 consistently reflects androcentric thinking, that is, men are the standard against which women are measured. The text is primarily about man and meeting man's needs. He is the center of the narrative. The man's needs for companionship have been met in the creation of woman, rather than the needs of both being met. We know only how he reacts to the creation of the woman; we hear nothing from her. We hear about marriage only from the man's point of view. We hear nothing about the woman leaving her father and mother and cleaving to her man.

What is the nature of the woman created in this second account? In the history of interpretation the woman has been described as derivative (created from the man's rib), as opposed to the autonomous male, and subordinate (created to be his helper). Both of these depictions are worth considering anew. It is correct that the woman is derived from the man, and this is indicated in the etymology of the Hebrew word for woman, *ishah*. "She shall be called *ishah*, for from *ish* was she taken" (Gen 2:23). Yet the text does not claim that woman is derivative and man is autonomous. The man is also derivative. He was taken from the ground, and in parallel fashion, we have seen that the text makes a word play on that: *adam* is taken from *adamah*. We are both derivative creatures.

Although the woman is derived from the man, it is not correct to assume that the woman created to be a helper is created to be man's subordinate. The Hebrew word *ezer*, in Genesis 2:20 is also used to describe God as our Helper or Deliverer (see Gen 49:25). The context of *ezer* indicates what sort of help is needed and if the helper should be considered an inferior or superior or equal. In the context of Genesis 2, the man needs help to alleviate his aloneness. He needs a friend, a partner, and he cannot find one in the animal kingdom. In this context, being a helper does not mean being man's subordinate but rather means being his partner and companion.

Tension in the text emerges from the words with which the man greets the woman and their context. Although she is created to meet his needs and is derived from him, when he greets her, he cries, "This at last is bone of my bones and flesh of my flesh" (Gen 2:23). He concludes that ontologically they are the same. It is significant that he does not notice difference but similarity. In this way the anthropology of Genesis 1 and Genesis 2 is identical. Both claim that we are first of all alike. We are human beings; we are in the image of God; we have the same bones and flesh. Only secondarily are we male and female. Our primary identity is not as women or men but as creatures in relation with God. According to these chapters there is no hierarchy of being in which man is elevated above woman.

The next episode in the second creation account describes the event that occasioned the transition from paradise to the real world (Gen 2:25—3:7): the disobedience of the man and woman. Since Augustine, the act of eating the forbidden fruit has been designated as the sin of pride. Woman and then man were reaching beyond what was theirs in an effort to be like God. They thought too highly of themselves and took something to which they were not entitled. Feminists, among them Valerie Saiving, have analyzed why and how this characterization is harmful to women. Women who have been socialized to think of others before themselves, to see themselves as caretakers and nurturers, do not need to hear that they are proud. This may be a message that men, often reared to be ambitious and achieving, need to hear. If it is correct to characterize the disobedience of Genesis 2 as that of pride, then a tendency that is typically male has been expanded to typify what is human. As a result, the particular weaknesses of women have gone unnoticed. Their tendency to passivity and lack of self-definition has gone unattended. However, pride may not be the best way to characterize the disobedience described in Genesis 2:25—3:7.

A close look at the text may suggest new insights. When the serpent engages the woman, he inquires concerning God's instructions. "Did God say, 'You shall not eat from any tree in the garden'?" (Gen 3:1). The woman replies, "We may eat of the fruit of the trees in the garden; but God said, 'You shall not eat of the fruit of the tree that is in the middle of the garden, nor shall you touch it, or you shall die' " (Gen 3:2-3). The woman is faithful in her reporting of the law as first being expansive and secondarily being limiting. Only after being told that they may eat from all the trees in the garden is a restriction placed on one tree. This prohibition, formulated in this way, accords with the character of God that we have encountered thus far. This is a deity who cares for humanity, who has created all to meet the needs of the man. This is a generous, benevolent deity who has constructed a world in which human beings will flourish.

God's character is contested by the serpent. He responds to her, "You will not die; for God knows that when you eat of it your eyes will be opened, and you will be like God, knowing good and evil" (Gen 3:4-5). God's truthfulness is attacked, and he is portrayed as a deceitful deity who does not want human beings to be like him. The woman's response is not to defend God and point to the generous treatment they have received. Rather, with the serpent's words in her mind, she considers the tree, notices its good qualities, eats and gives some to the man, who was with her. Her eating from the tree is the result of heeding the words of the serpent. She allowed God's character to be maligned, allowed herself to mistrust God's motives and, acting out of suspicion rather than trust, studied the tree. Perhaps the original disobedience is giving credence to slander.

This characterization of the woman's action fits with what follows. In the subsequent scenes, distrust and brokenness are rampant. The man and the woman distrust each other and hence clothe themselves. Then they fear God and hide. Finally they break faith with themselves as they pass on responsibility to another. All relationships are shattered, and we are left with oppression, disharmony, fear and subservience. This depiction of the disobedience also accords with our basic human nature as it is presented in Genesis 2. After meeting our physical needs, God notices that the man is alone and that this is not good. According to the text, man is not an autonomous being but needs companionship and connection. If our basic nature is to be in relationship with others, then it will follow that the most profound brokenness will involve the breaking of those relationships. This characterization of the woman's actions is appropriate to the text of Scripture and insightful in its description of who we are and how we are lost.

Interpreters have noted that the woman was approached by the serpent and the woman sinned, and many theories have arisen as to why it was the woman and not the man. Commentators have suggested that because women are morally weak and more gullible, the woman was the serpent's target. Anthropologists have suggested that the serpent approached the woman because in a hunting and gathering society, women are in charge of providing fruit and vegetables. Conversations about fruit of the tree would naturally be directed to her. Others have noticed the role that women play in ancient Mesopotamian literature, such as the Gilgamesh Epic, as the bearers of wisdom and knowledge; these interpreters understand this narrative to be influenced by that tradition. Whatever the reason the serpent had for approaching the woman, Genesis does not allow us to hold the woman more culpable of wrongdoing than the man. The text makes clear that the man was present during the exchange between the serpent and the woman. The woman speaks for both of them (Gen 3:2-3), and when the serpent addresses them, he uses the second person plural form of address (Gen 3:4-5). The episode ends by stating "she also gave some to her husband, who was with her" (Gen 3:6). Furthermore, God's response demonstrates that he holds the man, woman and serpent culpable. There is no basis in this text to hold the woman responsible for sin, suffering and death in a way different from that in which the man and serpent are held responsible.

In the next scene (Gen 3:8-24) God discovers the wrongdoing, passes judgment on it and exiles the man from the Garden of Eden. About this scene much has been written to lend support to patriarchy. Here too modern scholars have studied the text carefully and questioned the interpretation that grounds the subordination of women in Genesis 3:16. Theologically it is crucial to realize that this passage is not God's last word on gender relations. As Christians we confess that we are no longer under judgment; because of Christ's sacrifice, the judgment has been lifted. We are called to live as new creatures, empowered by the Holy Spirit, submitting to one another. Whatever the precise nature of God's judgment on the man and woman, this should not determine how we ought to live in relationship with each other. Furthermore, the words of God are better understood as descriptive rather than prescriptive. They do not indicate God's will. Rather, God describes what will result from the actions of the man and woman.

Carol Meyers's studies of ancient Israelite life and a close reading of the text have resulted in her unique translation of the woman's judgment. She translates Genesis 3:16: "To the woman he said, 'I will greatly increase your toil and your pregnancies. Along with travail you shall beget children. For to your man is your desire, and he shall predominate over you' " (95-121). According to Meyers, this judgment aptly describes the situation of women in ancient Israel. They toiled alongside their husband in the field, and in addition to field work, they had the burden of bearing and rearing children. For the survival of the community women needed to bear many children—between a high infant death rate and low average life span, the issue was not overpopulation but maintaining the population. Not having sexual relations and not bearing children would result in the death of the community. Hence the woman will be drawn to the man, and the man's desire will predominate over any reluctance of the woman. Again, whether or not we agree with this interpretation, the text makes it clear that these conditions are the result of human disobedience. The domination of women by men is not part of God's original good intentions for us.

Following the judgment, we read words that create hope. "The man named his wife Eve, because she was the mother of all living" (Gen 3:20). This act of naming is an act of authority over her at the same time that it recognizes the power that she has. Here too we have echoes from the ancient world. A title reserved for a female goddess in ancient Mesopotamia is here ascribed to a woman. Women have the power to bring life into the world, and because of this, life goes on. Second, God makes garments of skin for the man and the woman and clothes them (Gen 3:21). Here also we have an immanent picture of God. God is a tailor who dresses his creatures. Apparently the clothes they fashioned for themselves out of leaves were not good enough—they needed leather clothes. God's act has been interpreted as an act of grace; given that mistrust and brokenness have entered our relationships, we need to protect ourselves from one another. Clothing is needed, and God teaches us how to make clothing that will last. God is equipping the man and woman to survive in the new reality.

The second creation account began by noting the lack of a farmer and the subsequent creation of man. The narrative ends with God reflecting on the threat posed by the man and driving the man out of the garden (Gen 3:22-24). The woman is not mentioned. Somehow the woman created to meet the needs of the man has become invisible.

The role of Eve in the biblical narrative is not finished, however. Life in exile, out of Eden, begins with a birth announcement. In birthing Cain, Eve is fulfilling her role as the mother of all the living, and she names the child (Gen 4:1). Eve bears three sons, and the text mentions that she names two of them, Cain and Seth (Gen 4:25). Given the patriarchal cast of the text, the naming of the children by the mother is surprising. It puts Eve in a parallel role to the man. He bore the woman and named her; now Eve bears sons and names them.

The Sons of God and Daughters of Men (Gen 6:1-4)

The narrative in Genesis 6:1-4 is one of three accounts in Genesis 1—11 that describe features of our present life. In Genesis 2—3 we learned why we live here and not in Eden. In Genesis 6:1-4 we learn why our life span is 120 years, and in Genesis 11:1-9 we learn why there are many languages. In each case there has been a transgression of a boundary between the human and divine realm, and in each case God has punished humanity by imposing limits. In Genesis 6:1-4 the boundary is transgressed from the divine side. The sons of God see that the daughters of men are beautiful and take them. The language and sequence of events is parallel to the pharaoh's taking Sarah (Gen 12:10-20) and David's taking Bathsheba (2 Sam 11:1-5). In all three instances the action is initiated by the powerful males responding to the beauty of women, a motif that is widespread in the ancient as well as modern world.

The phrase "sons of God," which in context could mean lower-level deities, was translated in the Septuagint, the ancient Greek translation of the Bible, as "angels."

As a result, the traditional understanding of this strange phrase has been "angels." This passage is behind the enigmatic phrase of Paul in 1 Corinthians 11:10. In instructing women to have their head covered "because of the angels," he is protecting them from the amorous desires of the "sons of God" mentioned in Genesis 6:1-4.

Women in the Genealogies (Gen 4:17-26; 5; 10; 11:10-32)

In certain passages of Genesis and the rest of Scripture women are notable for their absence. The genealogies in Genesis are a case in point. Because the role of women is to bear children, we might expect that they would be listed regularly in the genealogies. With few exceptions, genealogies list fathers and sons, but mothers and daughters are invisible. Exceptions in Genesis 4:17-26 include that Lamech has two wives, Adah and Zillah. These wives bear sons, Jabel, Jubal and Tubal-cain, who are the founders of those who live in tents, those who play the lyre and pipe, and those who make bronze and iron tools. Lastly we learn that Tubal-cain has a sister, Naamach. This first genealogy perhaps preserves the memory of a higher status of women in ancient times as well as their role in the development of culture.

The last genealogy, Genesis 11:10-32, also includes the names of two women, Sarai and Milcah. The list gives us some background information about these women so that we will better understand the narrative that begins in Genesis 12. We learn that Sarai is barren and had no child and that Milcah is the daughter of Haran. Sarai's barrenness is significant because it creates tension when God promises progeny to Abraham. These few inclusions of women in the genealogies do not ameliorate the dilemma that the text poses regarding women. They are valued primarily as bearers of sons, and yet when the lists of ancestors are recorded, their contribution is not honored.

The Ancestral Narratives (Gen 12—50)

The rest of Genesis tells of God's chosen people through several generations. We learn how God's promises and covenant shaped the lives of Abraham and Sarah, Hagar and Ishmael, Isaac and Rebekah, Esau and Jacob, Rachel and Leah and their twelve sons and one daughter, Dinah. The collection of narratives relates the arranging of marriages, difficult births, infertility, surrogate mothers, sojourning, digging wells, dividing property, inheriting estates, sibling rivalry and surviving famine. In all these events God is at work creating a people to be a blessing to the nations. God's commitment to the whole world and the flourishing of all is continued.

Stylistically these chapters fall into two halves. Genesis 12—36 and 38 are narratives that have been loosely combined, while Genesis 37 and 39—50, the story of Joseph, is a coherent whole. The styles of the two halves as well as the status of the main characters are quite different. We move from stories about seminomads, living in extended families, vulnerable to drought, living on the margins of society, to a narrative in which a young man moves from rags to riches and becomes second in command in Egypt. This latter narrative builds so carefully that no scene is optional. From the dreams of the baker and butler to the hiding of the cup in Benjamin's sack, all the episodes are necessary to bring God's people safely to Egypt during a time of the famine.

These narratives have traditionally been named the patriarchal narratives, but more recently the significant role that women have played has been brought to the fore, and they are now typically called the ancestral narratives. Still, the role of women is quite limited and none of the women emerge as three-dimensional, complicated characters. We do not see women negotiating the same conflicts as Abraham does when he is confronted with God's command to sacrifice his son. The sibling rivalry between Jacob and Esau is more fleshed out in a way than the relationship between Rachel and Leah. The men have many roles in both the public and private domain. Abraham buys a field, negotiates well rights and divides property as well as being a husband and father. As such, when men look to the Bible for models, they find male characters whose lives contain ambiguities and are multifaceted. When women look to these texts, they tend to see flat female characters operating within narrowly circumscribed roles. The text does not provide women with as rich a legacy of complex women and their accomplishments and failings.

Sarah, Abraham and Hagar (Gen 12—23)
The narrative of God creating a chosen people begins with a promise made to an old man, Abram, that he will father a great nation (Gen 12:1-3). His wife, Sarai, is not present when the promise is given, and at this point no specifics are given. We do not know who the mother will be or if the child will be born or adopted into the family. However, as the narrative progresses we learn that Sarai (later Sarah) will be the mother and Abram (later Abraham) will be the father. The central conflict in the narrative involves the fulfillment of God's promise given the obstacles of Sarah's barrenness, Abraham's and Sarah's age, and both their characters (*see* Barrenness and Fertility; Sarah). When Isaac is born (Gen 21), we are convinced that he is the fulfillment of God's promise and that God gives life and hope.

The winding road leading to Isaac's birth reveals much about the respective roles of men and women in this ancient patriarchal culture and the way in which God

Hagar

Hagar, an Egyptian slave, is forced to submit sexually to the patriarch Abram in the role of surrogate mother. She twice encounters God in the form of an angel—first when she flees Sarai's abusive treatment while pregnant, and a second time after she and her son, Ishmael, have been sent away by their former slave masters to fend for themselves or die.

In the first instance, Hagar hears a divine mandate to return to her slave masters and to name her unborn son Ishmael, meaning "God hears." Hagar responds by giving God a name that means "God sees" (Gen 16:11-13). The second theophany occurs a few years later, when Hagar cries out to God in the wilderness after she and her son have been ousted by Abraham because of Sarah's jealous resentment. This time God opens her eyes, revealing a well of life-giving water and assuring her that the very thing needed for her family's survival is within her grasp. She is profoundly empowered by the promise that God will make of her offspring Ishmael a great nation (Gen 21:18-19).

Thus the same themes of divine promise and redemptive suffering commonly associated with the Hebrew patriarch Abraham and his wife Sarah also find fulfillment in the story of Hagar the Egyptian.

CHERYL J. SANDERS

works within this culture. Immediately after the promise is initially given to Abraham, we read that there is a great famine in the land, and Abraham and his household migrate to Egypt (Gen 12:10-20). On reaching Egypt, the narrative informs us, Abraham fears for his life. Because Sarah is beautiful, he surmises that the pharaoh will want her as a wife and will dispose of Abraham. He tells his wife to say that she is his sister so that the pharaoh will not kill him. The text does not tell us of Sarah's reaction to this plan. Only Abraham's emotional state and speech are recorded. Sarah's status in this transaction is as his property. She has no say in the arrangements, and we learn nothing of Sarah's response to becoming a wife of a man she does not know. He is a subject in the story; she is an object.

As the story continues, the pharaoh does indeed desire Sarah. He takes her into his house and showers Abraham with many gifts. The story would end here, and we would hear no more of Sarah, were it not for God's intervention. Abraham treats Sarah as disposable, but God does not. The pharaoh's house is afflicted with a plague. He correctly interprets the plague as a punishment, admonishes Abraham for lying to him, returns Sarah to Abraham and sends them off. Once again Sarah has no voice in the narrative. If we are interested in what Sarah thought of being returned to the man who was willing to sacrifice her for his safety, we will not find out from the text.

The plot of God's promise to Abraham and Abraham's response continues to thicken. In the next episode Abraham adopts his servant, Eliezer of Damascus, as his heir (Gen 15:2). Archaeological evidence indicates that this was a customary solution to the lack of an heir (Frymer-Kensky 1981). God responds to Abraham's solution by specifying that Abraham himself will father his heir (Gen 15:4).

Following this we read of Sarah's proposal that Abraham take Sarah's slave Hagar, have sexual relations with her and in this way obtain a child (Gen 16:1-2; *see* Hagar). Such a plan might seem preposterous to us, but archaeologists have discovered evidence that suggests it was a custom

Figurine of Egyptian slave woman grinding corn. (Genesis 16:1)

of the times. Documents from ancient Mesopotamia contain marriage agreements that state that if a wife was not able to bear children, then she was responsible for providing her husband with a surrogate (Frymer-Kensky 1981). Like Abraham, Sarah is behaving in a socially sanctioned manner to resolve the problem.

Abraham agrees to Sarah's plan. He has sexual relations with Hagar, who conceives and then looks with contempt on Sarah. Sarah in turn brings the matter to Abraham, and in a puzzling speech exclaims, "May the wrong done to me be on you! I gave my slave-girl to your embrace, and when she saw that she had conceived, she looked on me with contempt. May the LORD judge between you and me!" (Gen 16:5). Sarah's speech illustrates the complicated nature of polygamy and the role confusion it can create. Where previously there had been a clear hierarchy of Abraham, Sarah, Hagar, there now is ambiguity. As the second wife who has conceived, Hagar's position is not clear. Is she still subservient to Sarah, or has she become Abraham's favorite and surpassed Sarah? At this point Sarah must see how things stand with Abraham. Abraham's response shows that he relinquishes any power he might have over Hagar as well as his unborn child. He upholds the old order (Gen 16:6). This sequence of events is also reflected in ancient family laws that specify the status of a slave who becomes the mother of the master's children. Abraham stands within this tradition when he reinstates the status quo (Frymer-Kensky 1981).

Sarah then turns on Hagar, and Hagar flees. Sarah, herself a victim of a society that requires her to present children to her husband, has in turn victimized her slave. Class difference has proven stronger than sisterhood and has undermined solidarity between the two women.

As Abraham had dispensed with Sarah before, this time Abraham and Sarah together dispense with Hagar. However, God is not willing to abandon Hagar. The angel of the Lord finds her, inquires of her and gives her a task—she must return to her mistress and submit to her—and a blessing. God promises that she will be the mother of a great multitude and that she will bear a son, whom she will call Ishmael, because God has heard her affliction (Gen 16:10-11). In response to this revelation, Hagar names God (Gen 16:13). Hagar is the first woman to name God, an act that commemorates and honors her experience. The narrative contrasts her status according to the culture in which she lived and according to how Abraham and Sarah treated her and how God considers her. Her slave status relegates her to the level of disposable possessions, and even the child she bears does not change this. God, however, is not willing to dispense with her or her descendants. In God's revelation, he gives her a future, albeit a difficult future. She is to return and submit to her mistress, but she returns as a woman treated as a human being by God and equipped with inner strength.

The first episode in this narrative ends on a note of promise. Hagar returns and bears a son who is named Ishmael by Abraham (Gen 16:15-16). The promise of God to Hagar is in the process of being fulfilled.

The larger narrative of God's promise to Abraham continues with yet another reiteration and narrowing of the promise (Gen 18:1-5). For the first time we learn that Sarah is to be the mother of the son. Considering the patriarchal milieu of the story, this is interesting. The seed of Abraham is not enough to create the favored line; the mother must be Sarah. Abraham's response to hearing that Sarah will be the mother is to laugh and say, "Can a child be born to a man who is a hundred years old? Can Sarah, who is ninety years old, bear a child?" (Gen 17:17). Then Abraham suggests that Ishmael be considered the promised child (Gen 17:18). This is not to be, however. God repeats the promise, specifying the name Isaac, and that the child will be born within a year. However, Ishmael will not be forgotten. God instructs Abraham that Ishmael will also found a great nation, but the favored line will go through Isaac.

Up to this point in the narrative, we have not been told if Sarah is aware of the promise God made to Abraham. In the next episode Sarah finally learns that she is to bear a son. Her lower status is made painfully clear in that she is not directly addressed by God. Although God asks Abraham where she is and learns from Abraham that she is in the tent, the Lord continues to address Abraham. Because she is behind the door of the tent, she overhears the promise that she will bear a son (Gen 18:10). Like Abraham, she laughs upon hearing the news; however, unlike Abraham, she is reprimanded by God (Gen 18:13-14). The text then becomes enigmatic. We are told that Sarah is afraid and lies and says that she did not laugh. Then he tells her, "Yes, you did laugh" (Gen 18:15). Whom Sarah is addressing and who responds is not clearly indicated. In comparison with Abraham, Sarah is dealt with harshly, for Abraham was not reprimanded when he laughed.

In the final part of the narrative Abraham journeys south and resides in Gerar (Gen 20:1-18). Again Abraham declares that Sarah is his sister, and Abimelech, the king of Gerar takes Sarah. Abraham is more culpable on this occasion since the promise has specified that Sarah is the mother and that the child will be born within a year. Abraham is now disposing of the mother of the promised son. God again intervenes, and Sarah is returned to Abraham intact.

In Genesis 21 we read Isaac's birth announcement. God's promise has been kept. Abraham names him, and Sarah rejoices, creating a word play on the name Isaac, which sounds like laughter (Gen 21:6-7). Her joy makes abundantly clear that she has at last achieved the socially sanctified role for women, motherhood. To be barren at that time was to have no significant contribution to make, to have little status in the community, to have no security for old age. Sarah has finally moved from the margins to the center. Not only has she given birth to her son, but also her son has given new life to her.

We quickly learn that there is room for only one mother in Abraham's family. No sooner is Isaac weaned than Sarah sees the two brothers playing, becomes jealous of Ishmael as a rival for the inheritance and orders that Hagar and her son be cast out (Gen 21:8-10). This time Abraham does not so quickly defer to Sarah's wishes because of his tie to Ishmael. But God instructs Abraham to be compliant (Gen 21:12-13). Hagar and Ishmael once again are in the wilderness. Abraham has sent them out with some bread and a skin of water, provision for a day perhaps. In that place of death, Hagar lays down her son, goes off and weeps. God hears the voice of the boy and calls to Hagar. Interestingly, or troublingly, it is the voice of the child, the boy, that God responds to. At first sight the plight of Hagar has not moved either Abraham or God. However, it is to Hagar, not Ishmael—supposedly well into his teens at this time—that God speaks. He addresses her a second time. He encourages her to go and care for her son, for God will make him into a great nation. Her eyes are opened and she sees a well of water (*see* Wells). God provides her with a source of water that will endure—in contrast to Abraham's sending her off with a skin of water. Once again the weak and lowly that Abraham and Sarah dispense with are cared for by God.

Hagar's and Ishmael's story ends with the news that he lived in the wilderness and became an expert with a bow. His mother obtained a wife for him from Egypt (Gen 21:20-21). Hagar is looking after her son, providing a way into the future by obtaining a wife for him. The story has come full circle in that Hagar, from Egypt her-

Sarah

According to Jewish tradition, Sarah numbers with Esther, Vashti, Abigail, Michal, Jael and Rachel as among the world's most beautiful women. The biblical text introduces her as Sarai, the wife of Abram, and a woman with a problem: barrenness (Gen 11:29-30; *see* Barrenness and Fertility). The story of the patriarch and matriarch of the Hebrew nation in part tells how her problem is resolved. God makes a covenant with Abram to make him the father of a great nation (Gen 12:2-3). Does this covenant include Sarai?

Before the text clarifies this, it gives much insight into their marriage. Twice Abram passes off Sarai as his sister; he fears for his life because of her great beauty. During a famine, Abram and Sarai journey to Egypt. Abram's fortunes—livestock and slaves—increase largely because of Sarai. Then Pharaoh, upon learning of Sarai's true status, expels the couple and their possessions (Gen 12:10-20). Years later they repeat the ruse in Gerar (Gen 20).

Sarai dearly wants a child and gives Hagar, her Egyptian slave, to her husband (Gen 16; *see* Ancient and Modern Slavery). Custom allows a woman to claim a child by her husband and her serving maid as hers. Ishmael, the resultant child of the union, however, is not the child of the promise or the one who fulfills covenant, as Paul later points out (Rom 9:8-9).

The promise that the line of blessing will come through Sarai occurs in Genesis 17:15-16, and at this point she is renamed Sarah. Both prospective parents laugh at the news, for they are about one hundred and ninety years old respectively (Gen 17:17; 18:12).

Jewish tradition maintains that after Isaac's birth, the parents host a huge party; Sarah nurses all the infants, thereby proving her motherhood of Isaac.

Sarah dies at age 127 and is buried at Hebron in a cave near Mamre (Gen 23:19).

The prophet Isaiah encourages the Israelites to look to the rock—Abraham and Sarah—from which they came. Even as laughter erupted for Abraham and Sarah, so will Zion express joy and gladness (Is 51:1-3). Various New Testament writers number Sarah among God's faithful people, including Paul (Rom 4:19; 9:9), Peter (1 Pet 3:6) and the author of Hebrews (Heb 11:11).

ROBIN GALLAHER BRANCH

self has sought her future among her people. Her narrative is troubling in that she never becomes part of the chosen people. She was cast out and in the end stays out. She and Ishmael pay the price for Abraham's and Sarah's cruelty and negligence.

The preferred line is accomplished, but it comes with a price that the marginal bear disproportionately (*see* God's Call to Social Justice).

Although God's promise to Abraham and Sarah has been fulfilled, the narrative continues. In Genesis 22 God tests Abraham by requiring him to sacrifice Isaac. This chapter is troubling for many reasons, but the one that concerns us now is that Sarah is absent. God, according to the text, addresses only Abraham with this command and only Abraham and Isaac leave early the next morning. Where is the mother of Isaac? Why is the woman who was blessed with a son in her old age not part of the event? By ignoring Sarah this narrative tests the faith of women today. How are they to respond to a text that overlooks them?

Sarah's omission here is consistent with a larger pattern. When God enters a covenant relationship with Abraham, Sarah is also absent. From the beginning, God addressed his promises only to Abraham (Gen 12:1-3). Later, when God gives Abraham instructions concerning the sign of the covenant, it is clear that Sarah and all women are not directly in a covenant relationship with God. The sign of the covenant is circumcision of the foreskin (Gen 17:9-14). Women are part of the covenant people only indirectly, through the male to whom they are subordinate. In the New Testament women's status changes. Baptism becomes the sign of inclusion in the church, and all are baptized: Jew and Greek, slave and free, male and female (Gal 3:27-28).

Sarah's story ends with her obituary (Gen 23:1-2). She lived to 127, died in Hebron, was mourned by Abraham and was buried in a cave, the first piece of real estate that Abraham owned in the Promised Land. Buying this plot of land foreshadows that Abraham's descendants will eventually own the whole land. The narrative that began with God's promises that Abraham will be the father of a great nation has ended with Abraham having a son and owning a piece of property. The promise is being fulfilled.

The Daughters of Lot (Gen 18—19)

A subplot of the narrative about Abraham and Sarah concerns Abraham's nephew Lot. They have left Haran together (Gen 12:4-5) and settle in Canaan. At a certain point, their flocks became too large for them to live side by side, and there is strife between their herders. Abraham takes the initiative to resolve the conflict and proposes a generous solution to Lot. He suggests that they separate and offers Lot the first choice of land. Lot's selfishness contrasts starkly with Abraham's generosity. He chooses the best land for himself—the plain of Jordan (Gen 13:2-12). This episode ends with the narrator pointing out dark clouds on the horizon. "Now the people of Sodom were wicked, great sinners against the LORD" (Gen 13:13).

In the next episode concerning Abraham and Lot, the two are again contrasted. Angels of the Lord visit first Abraham and then Lot (Gen 18—19). The hospitality shown them by Abraham and Sarah functions as a foil to the inhospitable treatment they receive in Sodom. Lot compares favorably with his fellow citizens in Sodom but unfavorably with Abraham. When the angels come to Sodom, Lot, sitting in the gateway, rises to meet them and bows down to greet them. He invites them home with him to spend the night, wash and then continue their journey (Gen 19:1-2). He does not mention food or drink and is not as deferential in his speech. The angels turn down his offer of hospitality and decide to spend the night in the square. At this point Lot becomes insistent, and they agree to accompany him home. Although Lot prepares a meal and bakes unleavened bread for them, we do not have the impression of a whole household busy providing for guests as was the case in Abraham's hospitality.

While Lot is providing for his guests, the male population of Sodom surrounds the house and demands that he bring out his guests so that they may "know" them (Gen 19:5). Lot seeks to protect his guests and does so by offering the crowd his two virgin daughters (Gen 19:8). Lot's offer makes graphically clear the value of women relative to men. The practice of hospitality is a practice of men protecting men from men. Women are not protected, and women can be the means by which men are protected. They are the sacrificial lambs.

This offer astounds and horrifies modern readers. What are we to assume about Lot's offer? Are there clues in the text to indicate if it was condoned or condemned by God? Here an assessment of Lot's character is helpful. If Lot had throughout been portrayed as a righteous man, then his offer might be sanctioned by the narrator. However, Lot's actions both before and after this event show him to be self-centered. I suggest that the narrator wants us to conclude that Lot is not one of the ten righteous whom the angels have set out to find in Sodom and that his action is not condoned. As commentators note, his action is understandable, given the practice of hospitality in the context of patriarchy, but it is neither excused nor applauded. We are right to be horrified.

After the angels have rescued Lot from the mob, they instruct Lot to take his family out of the city, for the city will be destroyed. Lot begins by telling his two sons-in-law but does not communicate effectively. They think he is jesting (Gen 19:12-14). In the morning the angels again instruct Lot to take his family and leave, and again he lingers. Finally the angels take him, his wife and daughters by the hand and bring them outside the city. The angels tell them to run, flee for their lives and not look back (Gen 19:15-17). Lot asks that he may flee to Zoar, and the angels grant his request. Then destruction rains down on Sodom and Gomorrah. Lot's wife, we read, looked back and became a pillar of salt. This woman, who has remained unnamed, of whom we have heard nothing, who seemed to be absent when the guests came, who was not asked about offering her daughters to the mob, who is not informed directly about the impending disaster, is now turned into a pillar of salt for looking back. Humanly speaking, her punishment seems out of proportion to her crime; yet in Luke's Gospel Jesus puts her forth as a cautionary example for all who try to make their life secure: "Remember Lot's wife" (Lk 17:32-37).

The story is not over yet for Lot and his daughters, who remain unnamed. As the three of them move from the city to live in caves, the daughters fear that they will have no future because there are no men. The older daughter proposes that they make their father drunk, have sexual relations with him and in this way obtain children. The plan succeeds, and both daughters become pregnant by their father. Two sons are born, and both are named by their mothers. The first is Moab, who becomes the ancestor of the Moabites; the second is Ben-ammi, and he is the ancestor of the Ammonites. This narrative explains the origins of the people who will be troublesome neighbors to the Israelites throughout their history, and it presents them as the result of immoral behavior and as members of the extended family.

Rebekah and Isaac (Gen 24:1—28:9)

The family story of Abraham and Sarah continues into the next generation. Their son, Isaac, marries Rebekah, who bears Esau and Jacob. In this middle generation the relative importance of father and mother is reversed. Isaac is almost never the subject in these chapters (Gen 24:1—28:9). We read of Abraham arranging for a bride for Isaac, of Rebekah's difficult pregnancy and the oracle of God given to her about the twins she is carrying, and of Rebekah orchestrating that Jacob rather than Esau will get the blessing by deceiving Isaac (*see* Parental Influence). Isaac is the passive one, and God's promise is not made to him. Only when they move to Gerar and he fears for his life because the king might desire Rebekah is he the subject, but then he is no hero. Rebekah plays the more significant role and emerges as the more complicated figure. Given the milieu, her role is both surprising and encouraging.

Rebekah's story begins with Abraham's arranging for his oldest servant to acquire a bride for Isaac. The narrative has indicated that Sarah is dead and has foreshadowed the role of Rebekah by including her in a genealogy in Genesis 22:23. Rebekah is introduced as the daughter of Bethuel, who is the son of Nahor, a brother of Abraham. This is a culture in which cousin marriage is preferred, especially over marriage to local Canaanites or Hittites. Abraham's instructions to his servant are surprising in several ways. The servant is asked to swear an oath that he will not procure a wife for Isaac from among the local Canaanites but will travel to Abraham's homeland and there get a wife. Because of the seriousness of the oath, the servant clarifies the limits of his responsibility. He asks, "Perhaps the woman may not be willing to follow me to this land; must I then take your son back to the land from which you came?" (Gen 24:5). Although the marriage is an arrangement between the heads of the two families, the woman apparently has some say about where she will live. Abraham's response indicates that this is a plausible scenario. The servant's concern is not dismissed. Rather, the servant is told that he will be released from his oath if the woman is not willing to return with him (Gen 24:6-8).

The servant sets off and creates for himself a test that will allow him to select the right wife for Isaac. The scenario involves meeting the woman at a well, a variation of the type scene in which the hero meets his future wife (see Robert C. Culley, *Studies in the Structure of Hebrew Narrative* [Philadelphia: Fortress, 1976], 41-43, in which he compares three meetings at wells that lead to marriage). As Jacob met Rachel at a well (Gen 29:1-14), as Moses met Zipporah at a well (Ex 2:15-21), so the servant meets Rebekah at a well (*see* Wells). The test involves asking the woman for a drink. If the woman is the right one for Isaac, she will respond by giving the servant water as well as offering to give water to his camels (Gen 24:14). The servant's test will reveal her character. The servant wants a wife for Isaac who is generous and energetic. Interestingly, Abraham's instructions have specified only that she be from his country and his kindred. No character test was needed. Because the test of the servant does not indicate if she meets Abraham's criteria for a wife, we are left in suspense until the servant asks her who she is. When we learn that she is a member of Abraham's extended family, then we realize that God has providentially been orchestrating the meeting, as the servant had prayed (Gen 24:12-14).

The last hurdle is whether Rebekah's family will agree to the marriage. The servant makes his presentation to Laban, Rebekah's brother, and Bethuel. When they hear the whole story about Abraham, Sarah and Isaac, the servant's mission and God's providing, they respond affirmatively (Gen 24:50-51). Rebekah's consent or opinion in the matter is not explicitly sought. According to the practices of this culture, the male head of the household determines who will have sexual access to his daughter. Rebekah's future is his to decide. The only voice that Rebekah has, according to the text, is not about whether she will marry Isaac and go with the servant but about whether she will go with the servant right away. Although the text is not crystal clear, that seems to be the best reading of Genesis 24:54-59.

Rebekah is willing to leave at once, and the return journey begins. In the history of interpretation, much has been made of Abraham's leaving his home and traveling to an unknown land at God's command. Rebekah's departure has not been interpreted in the same way, and yet her story is similar. She may be the more courageous of the two, for she leaves her family, whereas Abraham takes his along. She too leaves her homeland to journey to the strange land, to become the wife of a man she has never met and become part of an extended family that is unknown to her. She places herself at great risk in all this because she is a woman and is dependent on the goodwill of the men in authority over her. Rebekah is one of the heroines that tradition has neglected.

The narrative of Rebekah's betrothal concludes with her marriage to Isaac. The text narrates that when she sees Isaac she covers herself with her veil, the servant relates to Isaac the success of his mission, Isaac takes Rebekah into his mother Sarah's tent, she becomes his wife, he loves her, and he is comforted after his mother's death (Gen 24:67). We learn of Isaac's feelings for Rebekah but nothing of her feelings toward him.

After love and marriage, children would normally follow quickly, but instead we again have a barren matriarch. This time the situation is quickly resolved after Isaac intercedes for Rebekah. The text tells us that the Lord granted Isaac's prayer, and his wife conceived (Gen 25:21). It is worth pointing out that Scripture understands God to be the giver of life. Conception is due to the grace of God, and children are gifts of God. In a most profound way, our lives are not our own, nor do they belong to our parents. They are given by God.

Rebekah's pregnancy is difficult, and she inquires of God. Her prayer reveals that she is at rock bottom, "If it is to be this way, why do I live?" (Gen 25:22). Her question captures the situation that many women experience. They are valued primarily as mothers, and yet pregnancy and childbirth can be very hard and can threaten their life.

God's answer reveals to Rebekah that she is to give birth to two sons (Gen

25:23). Rebekah has taken the initiative to inquire of God, and God has revealed to her the future destiny of her sons. In so doing, she is elevated in the text. Unlike Sarah, who heard God's will indirectly, Rebekah is the recipient of the oracle. The content of the oracle reveals that the younger will be preferred again. As Isaac was preferred over Ishmael, so too will Jacob be preferred over Esau. This revelation sets the stage for their actions (*see* Sibling Rivalry). When Esau sells his birthright for some lentil stew (Gen 25:29-34) and marries two Hittite women, making life bitter for Isaac and Rebekah (Gen 26:34-35), we understand that he is not fit to carry on the chosen line.

This oracle is also in the background when Rebekah acts to ensure that Jacob will receive the blessing, and not Esau. In this episode Rebekah listens when Isaac instructs Esau to bring him game, specially prepared, so that Isaac may bless Esau before he dies (Gen 27:1-5). She is not party to the conversation, yet she knows what is going on. She operates behind the scenes, but she controls the action. The text tells us that Isaac is old and sees dimly, and Rebekah arranges a plan that takes advantage of his blindness and results in Jacob receiving the blessing. Although such trickery makes us uncomfortable, the narrator does not condemn her actions. By placing the oracle about Jacob's preeminence with the birth narrative and by addressing this oracle to Rebekah, her actions accomplish the will of God. Rebekah's use of deception indicates her inability to steer events directly. Both men and women use deception when they are in the position of underdogs. Women who have to negotiate a patriarchal setting or men living as sojourners in a foreign land are relatively powerless. To level the playing field, they often resort to indirect means, to trickery, in order to survive and achieve their goals. A more recent parallel example of the use of deception is that of Christians in World War II who hid Jews and then lied to the Gestapo when they were questioned. Although lying is wrong, in these cases it was protecting innocent people. Lying is the lesser evil. In a sinful world, God works through morally ambiguous means.

Rebekah and Jacob's deception of Isaac succeeds, but then there are consequences. Esau learns that Jacob has stolen his blessing, hates Jacob and plans to kill him after his father, Isaac, dies (Gen 27:41). Rebekah, the listener, learns of Esau's plan. She tells Jacob to flee to her brother Laban for a time (Gen 27:42-44). Then we read of her addressing Isaac, complaining that if Jacob marries a local woman, her life will be of no use to her (Gen 27:46). Unlike her address to Jacob, she gives Isaac no instructions but only speaks about her worries. The differing rhetorical strategies reflect the dif-

Sibling Rivalry

Sibling rivalry arose spontaneously in Cain after sin entered human relationships and has been with us ever since. Cain and Abel were seeking God's favor, so God's response to Cain reveals God's answer to sibling rivalry (Gen 4:7). The lesson is that we are evaluated by what we do toward God and by how well we master sin. Scripture also illustrates God's prerogative to bestow favor as he wills, irrespective of human traditions. God chose Isaac over Ishmael, Jacob over Esau, Joseph over his brothers, Ephraim over Manasseh and David over his brothers—in each case reversing the traditional hierarchy based on age. While the overriding of gender hierarchy is less frequent in Scripture, God also challenged it by giving Miriam a prominent role with her brothers, Aaron and Moses, and by directing that Zelophehad's daughters should inherit his land in the absence of sons (Num 27).

Scripture decries situations in which human choices increased sibling rivalry. The favoritism of Isaac and Rebekah fueled the rivalry between Jacob and Esau, and rather than learning from his experience, Jacob obviously favored Joseph. Prolonged antagonism between siblings was the result in both generations. Ungodly traditions, another source of sibling rivalry, produced Ishmael and led to early rivalry with Isaac that resulted in Ishmael's banishment. Evaluation by physical appearance led Samuel to favor David's older brothers and earned Samuel the Lord's rebuke for an ungodly standard. But the most common source of increased sibling rivalry in Scripture is polygamous marriage. No polygamous family in Scripture is portrayed as happy, and the sibling rivalry leading to rape, murder and rebellion among David's children is one of the saddest examples of such rivalry. Current research indicates that sibling rivalry is still endemic in polygamous families, and it is also common in any family under marital stress due to adultery, divorce and remarriage.

A healthy pattern of sibling relationships emerges among Jesus' disciples, however, There is no indication of sibling rivalry even though two sets of brothers were among Jesus' twelve disciples. Andrew found Jesus first and brought his brother Peter to see Jesus. From that point we read much about Peter, including his being in the inner circle of three, but very little about Andrew. Although James and John were in Jesus' inner circle, John was closer to Jesus than was James.

Why, given these relationships, do we find no sibling rivalry among these brothers? Might it be that Jesus helped them to live by God's original instructions to Cain—to focus on pleasing God and mastering sin rather than on comparisons among themselves? When Peter compared himself with John after Jesus' resurrection, Jesus rebuked the comparison and called Peter to follow him (Jn 21:20-22). While acknowledging the inequities of our sinful world and endeavoring to alleviate them, Scripture calls us to deal with sibling rivalry by shunning comparisons and instead focusing on mastering sin and pleasing our Lord. KATHLEEN W. STUEBING

---

fering power relationships. Whereas Rebekah can instruct Jacob, her son, she cannot instruct Isaac, her husband. Isaac then takes the initiative and instructs Jacob not to marry one of the Canaanite women but to go to their homeland and find a wife there. Unlike Abraham, he does not send a servant to procure a wife but sends Jacob himself.

The final episode in Rebekah and Isaac's story is another narrative about a patriarch passing off his wife as his sister. Three times a similar story is told, and this too seems to be a type scene. Again the patriarch is sojourning in a foreign land, in Gerar. Although the Lord promises to bless Isaac in that place (Gen 26:1-5), when Isaac is asked about his wife, he claims that she is his sister. He, like Abraham, fears that the ruler will want her as a wife and will kill him for the sake of acquiring Rebekah (Gen 26:6-7). However, before the king has made any moves, he sees Isaac fondling his wife, calls him, upbraids him for lying and warns his people to leave the two of them alone (Gen 26:8-11). As in the previous episodes, the voice of the wife is missing.

The final words about Isaac and Rebekah record their burial in the cave of Machpelah (Gen 49:31). After Jacob has secured the inheritance, the spotlight shifts to his story. Rebekah has played a substantial role in ensuring that the line will continue according to God's plan. She has emerged as a competent, emotionally complicated, three-dimensional character. She was first of all a mother and chose to further Jacob's future even when it involved deceiving her husband. Her tactics are questionable, but she was not so much siding with her son against her husband as carrying out God's will for the family. In the end, it is not Rebekah who has undermined Isaac's authority but God. The patriarchal family structure has been challenged by how God has worked within it.

Rachel, Leah and Jacob (Gen 29:1—35:20)
Certain themes reappear in the stories of

the next generation: Jacob meets his future wife, Rachel, at a well; she is barren for a long time and uses her maid Bilhah as a surrogate mother; she pleads with God for children, and with God's intervention she conceives and bears the favored son; finally, deception is one of the means of accomplishing God's promises. However, certain new themes emerge as well: the relationship between the sisters Leah and Rachel, both wives of Jacob within a polygamous household; the relationship between Laban and his daughters; and the relationship between Jacob and his daughter Dinah. In this complex narrative, the women again play significant roles but roles that are largely sexually defined.

Jacob arrives at Haran, the land of his roots, and at a well inquires of shepherds about Laban (Gen 29:1-5). They assure him that all is well with Laban and point out that his daughter Rachel is approaching to water her sheep. (Here is one of the few places in which a woman and man have the same occupation and cooperate—an ancient equal-opportunity career perhaps.) Gallantly Jacob rolls away the stone from the well's mouth, waters her sheep, kisses her, weeps and then introduces himself as family (Gen 29:6-12). The sequence indicates his intense emotion. Rachel's response echoes his, for she runs to tell her father, Laban, who returns with haste, welcomes Jacob and brings him home (Gen 29:13-14).

After a month, Laban suggests that Jacob stay with him and work for some kind of payment. At that point we are introduced to the two sisters, daughters of Laban. Their appearance is described (Gen 29:17), but because the meaning of the Hebrew words is unclear, translations differ in how they render this verse. Leah is described as having "lovely" (NRSV), "weak" or "delicate" (NIV) eyes, or as being "tender eyed" (KJV). Rachel is described as "graceful and beautiful" (NRSV), "lovely in form, and beautiful" (NIV) or "beautiful and well favored" (KJV). Although it is not clear what the text is saying about the sisters' appearance, Rachel seems to be more beautiful and Jacob is drawn to her. He asks to be allowed to marry her, the younger sister, in exchange for seven years of service. Laban agrees, and Jacob works the seven years. Again we notice that the agreement is reached between the two men without any input from Rachel. Furthermore, the text makes clear that Jacob loved Rachel so much that the seven years seemed as nothing (Gen 29:18-20). However, we read nothing of Rachel's feelings toward him. In fact, nowhere in Genesis do we read of a woman loving a man. In all of the Old Testament historical narratives, only Michal, Saul's daughter, is reported as loving a man, David (1 Sam 18:20).

In a way parallel to Rebekah's manipulation of events to deceive Isaac, Laban manipulates events to deceive Jacob. He takes advantage of the darkness to substitute Leah for Rachel on the wedding night, and Jacob awakes in the morning to find he has been tricked. He confronts Laban, who makes a weak excuse. The matter is resolved by Jacob completing the seven days of the wedding feast with Leah and then immediately marrying Rachel and working another seven years in payment for her (Gen 29:21-30). After the treachery of Laban toward Jacob is exposed, the reader infers the anger of Jacob by his sharp, persistent questioning of Laban, but from Leah and Rachel we hear nothing. Their reaction to being manipulated by their father so that they end up being wives of the same husband is not recorded. Two other women whose voices are not heard in this narrative are those of the handmaids, Zilpah and Bilhah. They enter the household of Jacob as servants of their mistresses and are later given by their mistresses to Jacob.

The narrator does not explicitly comment on the creation of this complicated family, but divine retribution is at work in the plot. Jacob is pictured here reaping what he sowed. As he cooperated with his mother to take advantage of his father's blindness to trick him, so Laban takes advantage of the darkness to trick Jacob. Later in the story, Laban, who took Rachel's rightful place from her, will have his household gods stolen by Rachel.

The following episodes in the narrative detail the messiness of family life in a polygamous household (*see* Polygamy). Not only is there a favorite child, but also there is a favorite wife. In this household, Rachel is that wife. God, who has in the past protected the matriarch who was passed off as a sister, who sided with Hagar when she was cast out of Abraham's household, now has compassion on Leah (Gen 29:31). In succession Leah bears Reuben, Simeon, Levi and Judah, naming each of them. The names of the first three eloquently reflect her pain in being unloved, whereas the last name praises God. The movement in naming her sons suggests that her pain is diminished, and the text narrates that she ceased bearing children (Gen 29:32-35).

In seesaw fashion, now Rachel is desperate. Her request of Jacob, "Give me children, or I shall die!" (Gen 30:1), is especially poignant because we know that she will die giving birth to Benjamin (Gen 35:16-19). Her cry reflects the doubly precarious position of women valued primarily for childbearing. If they don't have children, they have no life; and if they have children, they risk losing their life. Jacob's response indicates his frustration. "Am I in the place of God, who has withheld from you the fruit of the womb?" (Gen 30:2). As pregnancies are understood to be caused by God, so also is barrenness understood to be from God (*see* Barrenness and Fertility). Rachel responds by giving her maid Bilhah to Jacob, so that she may become a surrogate mother. The plan succeeds, and Bilhah bears Jacob two sons, Dan and Naphtali, both named by Rachel (Gen 30:4-8). Unlike the narrative about Abraham, Sarah and Hagar, the text describes no tensions resulting from this arrangement.

However, the matter of offspring is not over yet. The focus shifts again to Leah, who counters Rachel's strategy by giving her maid Zilpah to Jacob. With her Jacob fathers two more sons, Gad and Asher, who are also named by Leah (Gen 30:9-11). The symmetry is now out of balance, so the scene shifts to Rachel. She obtains mandrakes, thought to enhance fertility, from Leah's son in exchange for allowing Jacob to lie with Leah that night. In a wry scene that reflects the relative powerlessness of a husband who is outnumbered by his wives, Jacob comes in from the fields to find that he has been hired by Leah (Gen 30:14-16). Then, in quick succession, Leah has not one but two more sons, Issachar and Zebulun, and then a daughter, Dinah (Gen 30:17-21). Again, these two sons, like all the other sons before them, are given theophoric names whose meaning is explained. Dinah, however, is named with no explanation. Finally God turns to Rachel, and she conceives and bears Jacob a son, Joseph (Gen 30:22-24).

At this point Jacob has completed his years of service for his wives, and he seeks to return to his home with his family. Laban makes him an offer that involves paying him with part of the flock, and Jacob agrees to continue working (Gen 30:25-34). Then the text describes that Laban tried to cheat Jacob and that Jacob used a counterstrategy that succeeded. Laban is no longer happy with Jacob, and rumors circulate that Jacob has stolen from Laban (Gen 30:35—31:1). Now God tells Jacob to return and promises to be with him. Jacob in turn confers with his wives (Gen 31:4-13). The silence of Rachel and Leah regarding their father's dealings with them is broken, and we learn that they also feel cheated by their father. They may have been competitors for Jacob's love, but they are united in their anger toward their father (Gen 31:14-15). In contrast to Jacob's speech, in which we are given the full particulars and understand clearly the basis for his claims, the narrative has not given enough information for the reader to know on what Rachel and Leah base their accusations. However, it is customary that the bride price paid by the suitor is echoed by the bride bringing a dowry into the marriage. Sons receive an inheritance, and daughters receive a dowry. Jacob paid a bride price of seven years service for each of his wives, but the text does not speak of a dowry, only that each took a maidservant into the marriage with her. It is probable that not receiving a dowry is the basis of the daughters' claim that they have been treated like strangers and cheated out of their money by their father.

Jacob and his household depart quickly, taking advantage of Laban's absence (Gen 31:17-35). The tension in the story escalates because we know that Rachel has stolen Laban's household gods (*see* Household Gods). Both Jacob and Rachel are tricksters here, but Jacob does not know of Rachel's theft. When Laban catches up with him, he demands to know why they departed without a proper farewell and why they have stolen his gods. Jacob defends his decision to leave and offers that anyone caught with Laban's gods will not live. Once again the patriarch puts the matriarch in danger by his words, only this time he does so unwittingly. Rachel hides the gods by sitting on them, and she asks to be excused from rising because she is menstruating (*see* Menstruation). Her deception succeeds, and Laban does not find his gods. The irony of the situation is clear—household gods are humiliated by being hidden under a menstruating woman. To Israelites who understood menstruating women to be unclean and as a result barred them from the temple, this is a comic situation.

In parallel fashion to the clarity of Jacob's reason for leaving and the ambiguity of the sisters' reasons, we again have clarity between Jacob and Laban concerning their actions, and their relationship is brought to resolution (Gen 31:49-50). However, we

Household Gods

Mesopotamian families had various household deities: deceased ancestors, personal deities and protective spirits. The ancestors of Laban and Jacob were Mesopotamian, so the teraphim (household gods) of Genesis 31 and other Old Testament references may parallel Mesopotamian "little gods" that fifteenth- to fourteenth-century B.C. Nuzi texts mention as figurines that represented deified ancestors. These deified ancestors functioned in divination in a family's house. Archaeologists have found many figurines in houses, but they have not identified any as ancestor figurines.

Personal gods assisted by protective spirits, both often feminine, were thought to protect the members and interests of the household. The biblical narrative in which Rachel steals her family teraphim seems to distinguish between the teraphim and the personal guardian deities of the family. Since Laban makes a treaty with Jacob that depends on Nahor's god as witness while the teraphim are missing, he must be referring to another deity. A letter from Canaanite Ugarit similarly supports distinction between personal deities and deified ancestors. It cites the gods of Tipat and the gods of Ugarit in parallel with the gods of the family, which implies that the family gods are gods rather than deified ancestors.

Household gods

Texts also distinguish between ancestors and personal deities with respect to their offerings. Whereas families executed prayer and offering ceremonies to personal deities each morning and evening, they made ritual offerings for deceased relatives only once a year. Burning incense or oil invoked the presence of protective deities, and lamps and incense burners are present frequently in excavated household shrines in the ancient Near East.

From the group of publicly known deities, patriarchs chose personal deities that related to their interests or to the neighborhoods in which they lived. Family members shared the same personal deity, and a woman's allegiance changed from her father's deity to her husband's when she married. Babylonian letters indicate that personal deities functioned as intercessors with national or city deities. The Canaanite goddess Asherah played this role when she interceded with the high god El in Ugaritic mythology. Israelite Asherah appears to have a similar function in inscriptions from Khirbet el-Qom and Kuntillet Ajrud that claim Yahweh's blessing and protection "through his Asherah."

Archaeologists have found female clay figurines throughout Israel and Judah, with a large number of them in Jerusalem; they probably exemplify the "carved image" and "idols, dung balls" that the Deuteronomists and prophets so vigorously opposed. The prevalence of such figurines throughout Israel and Judah is evidenced in that almost every domestic dwelling in tenth-century Tirzah (Tell el-Far'ah) and 45 percent of divided monarchy-era houses at Mizpah (Tell Beit Mirsim) had a female or an animal figurine. The jewelry, textile production tools and cooking equipment that surround the female figurines and other ritual artifacts at these and other sites like Beersheba and Tell Halif suggest that women petitioned images of the goddess for aid and protection, particularly while childrearing. The writing prophets consistently denounced syncretism just as they opposed the oppression of the poor. While the veneration of secondary deities, often imaged in concrete form, diminished after the exile, it continued in various branches of Judaism and thrives in some forms of Christianity today.

ELIZABETH A. R. WILLETT

---

are not given the same information about Rachel's action. We do not know why she took the household gods. Her deception of Laban is left unresolved, and we are not told if Jacob ever found out about her trickery.

The narrative about Leah and Rachel culminates with the family's arrival in Canaan. Jacob prepares to meet Esau, whom he fears is still his enemy. He divides his household with the hope that if Esau attacks one group that perhaps the other would escape (Gen 32:3-8). When he does meet Esau, he positions the maids and their children first, then Leah and her children and finally Rachel and Joseph (Gen 33:1-2). Who is most valued and who is disposable is painfully obvious. The encounter ends happily enough with a peaceful reunion between the two brothers. Jacob and his large household are now safely home, and the story of Jacob and Rachel and Leah is almost over. The last scene is devoted to Rachel's tragic death giving birth to Benjamin. The words of the midwife as she is delivering reinforce the assumptions of the culture: "Do not be afraid; for now you will have another son" (Gen 35:16-19; *see* Midwifery and Birthing Practices). Why Rachel should not fear is not obvious from the context. Her son does not and cannot deliver her from death. The story of Jacob and his sons continues, but we hear no more of his wives. Neither Leah's nor Bilhah's nor Zilpah's death is recorded, though the place of Leah's burial is recorded (Gen 49:31).

The narratives involving Rachel and Leah, Laban and Jacob, and Jacob and Esau are among the most colorful in Genesis. In their interactions with each other, we see both the pain wrought by broken relationships and the grace shown in reconciliation. The interactions are complex enough that we see the players in different lights. In this narrative the institution of arranged marriages and a polygamous household is drawn warts and all. The narrative assumes these customs, typical of a patriarchal culture, but also challenges them. As the story is told, the social conventions do not cohere with the nature of the female characters. Rachel and Leah are not property to be disposed of but are human beings who have feelings, who know when they are been taken advantage of, who can take initiative and who work to shape their lives. For example, at the one point in the narrative when we see a discussion on future plans between Jacob and his two wives, we see three adults who are united in their outrage against the injustice of Laban. When Rachel and Leah are treated as partners, they emerge as partners. They are not tricky or underhanded in this dialogue. Rather, something of value occurs when they are treated as partners—Jacob and his two wives come to be in solidarity concerning their move. This dialogue is a glimmer of how relationships between men and women could be if there was mutual respect and consideration.

The Rape of Dinah (Gen 34)
The narrative of the rape of Dinah is disturbing for several reasons. The chapter begins with Jacob and his family settling safely in Shechem, purchasing land from the sons of Hamor, the king of Shechem, erecting an altar and calling it El-Elohe-Israel, that is, "God, the God of Israel" (Gen 33:18-20). It seems that we are in the age of fulfillment. With Jacob's large family, God's promise of many descendents is being realized, and now the preferred line is securing a foothold in the Promised Land. In this context, Dinah, reintroduced as the daughter of Jacob and Leah, sets out to visit the women of the region (Gen 34:1). This constructive effort to secure good relations is the last time that Dinah will initiate action. From here on, the narrative tells what is done to her. She becomes a pawn, and we are not even told how she responds to the events swirling around her (*see* Violence, Abuse and Oppression).

When Dinah sets out, she is seen by Shechem, the son of Hamor. He seizes her and rapes her (Gen 34:2). Then the text narrates that he comes to love her, speaks tenderly to her and commands his father to get Dinah for him as his wife (Gen 34:3). Several things are problematic here. First, although the text clearly states that Hamor took Dinah by force, Dinah's brothers, when referring to this event, ask, "Should our sister be treated like a whore?" (Gen 34:31). A rape victim is not a whore (Heb. *zonah*). A whore or a prostitute acts independently of her father or husband; she claims the right to control access to her body and falls outside the socially sanctioned relationships of a patriarchal society. The brothers, in putting the question this way, could be drawing attention to the similarity between rape and consorting with a prostitute. Both involve a man having sexual relations that are not sanctioned. Dinah's rape is further complicated because the sexual union is not between members of the same tribe who both practice circumcision. Hence, in addition to the offense of rape, there is the offense of Dinah's being defiled.

The next episode in this sad story involves the negotiations between Shechem's family and Dinah's family to arrange their marriage. That rape is to be followed by marriage between the victim and the rapist is abhorrent to modern readers. In the laws of the Pentateuch that deal with raping an unmarried or unengaged woman the rationale for this practice is clarified. The laws are based on the principle that the woman is the property of a man. Hence the crime of rape is not against the woman. Rather, this violation is understood as an offense against her father. It is a property crime in which one man has damaged the property of another. The penalty for raping a single woman reflects this principle. In both Exodus 22:16-17 and Deuteronomy 22:28-29, the rapist is required to pay the father the bride price. The laws differ in whether or not the father can disallow the marriage. In Exodus 22:16-17, the marriage is at his discretion, whereas in Deuteronomy 22:28-29 the man automatically marries the woman. Although the laws in the Pentateuch are not a mirror image of what happened in society, in this case there is coherence between the narrative of Genesis 34 and the law in Exodus 22:16-17. As appalling as this situation is, in the ancient context it can be understood as a necessary evil. As a raped woman, she would no longer be eligible for marriage to another man, and hence marriage to her rapist gives her a socially sanctioned place in society.

In the negotiations between Hamor and Jacob, the reader knows that Jacob and the brothers already know of Dinah's rape. Yet, when the negotiating occurs, there is no mention of the illicit sexual relation that has occurred. Only in Shechem's generous offer to pay the bride price, no matter how high, might we infer an acknowledgment of wrongdoing and the need to make restitution (Gen 34:8-12).

As Hamor and Shechem have not been forthcoming, Jacob's sons return the favor. They claim that the obstacle between the union of Shechem and Dinah concerns circumcision. They agree to the marriage on the condition that Shechem and all the male inhabitants become circumcised. In this dialogue, Jacob's voice is not heard. The whole chapter is surprising because of the leadership role assumed by the sons on both sides. The sons of Jacob and Shechem are not deferential toward their fathers; and the sons, not the fathers, seem to be in charge.

Shechem returns to his people and convinces them of the benefits of mingling with the Israelites. All the males are circumcised (Gen 34:18-24). On the third day, when the men are still in pain, Simeon and Levi, full brothers of Dinah, enter the city, slaughter all the males and take Dinah from Shechem's house. The rest of the brothers come upon the slain and take all their possessions, including their wives and children, as booty (Gen 34:25-29). Then we learn of Jacob's disapproval: "You have brought trouble on me by making me odious to the inhabitants of the land, the Canaanites and the Perizzites; my numbers are few, and if they gather themselves and attack me, I shall be destroyed, both I and my household" (Gen 34:30). Jacob's statement is rebuffed by the brothers, who ask, "Should our sister be treated like a whore?" (Gen 34:31).

There are no heroes in this story apart from Dinah. From Jacob's closing remark and from the context of the chapter, we know that Jacob's securing a place for his household in the land is a crucial and precarious enterprise. Since they are few in number, brute force will not work. Dinah's effort to visit with the women of the place fits with their situation. Jacob's family needs to be in the business of building bridges and forging good relationships with the people in the area. However, the rest of the chapter graphically illustrates the dark side of patriarchy and its inability to promote abundant life for all. What begins as one man violating a woman is construed as an attack on male honor that must be avenged. The brothers take revenge, and the result graphically illustrates that revenge does not secure justice or promote peace. Their actions are out of proportion to the crime committed. The violence against one woman has led to the slaughter of all the males in Shechem and the taking of women and children as booty, with the result that Jacob and his household leave. This foothold in the land has been lost.

Rather than illustrating heroic behavior, this narrative documents human depravity. In this chapter light came into the world, and the darkness put it out. It paints a sobering picture of the sinfulness of the Canaanites as well as the chosen family. Opposition to God's promises comes not only from outsiders but also from insiders. The enemy is not only the other. The enemy can be Israel.

Tamar (Gen 38)

The narrative about Tamar is inserted into the longer narrative focusing on Joseph (Gen 37—50). Although the narrative style is distinct, key themes are central in both, such as the virtue of loyalty to family and the need to preserve life. In contrast to the narrative of Dinah, a woman who is a victim in a man's world, the narrative of Tamar shows a woman who succeeds at securing justice for herself (*see* Expectations of Women). Because of how it portrays both Tamar and Judah, it is one of the most hopeful narratives in Genesis.

The story begins by focusing on Judah, who chooses to settle away from his brothers, near a certain Adullamite, Hirah. He then sees a woman, the daughter of a Canaanite, Shua, and marries her. In short order Judah and his wife, who remains unnamed, have three sons, Er, Onan and Shelah, and Judah arranges that Er take Tamar as his wife. The narrative does not indicate whether she is Canaanite or Israelite, but because the milieu is Canaanite, Tamar is assumed to be Canaanite. Without going into detail, the text relates that Er was wicked, and the Lord put him to death. "Then Judah said to Onan, 'Go in to your brother's wife and perform the duty of a brother-in-law to her; raise up offspring for your brother' " (Gen 38:8). Although the focus of the custom is to preserve the line of the male, it also benefits the widow. She is given a place in a household, the chance to become a mother, and status and security. Onan, however, does not do his duty, spilling his semen on the ground, and the Lord puts him to death also. Judah sees a pattern emerging and fears that giving Tamar to Shelah will result in Shelah's death. He sends Tamar to her father's house until Shelah is grown (Gen 38:9-11).

Time passes, Shelah grows up but is not given to Tamar, Judah's wife dies, the period of mourning is over, Judah sets out to shear sheep at Timnah, and Tamar comes to hear of it. She puts off her widow's clothing, dons a veil, wraps herself and sits at the side of the road. Judah sees her, thinks she is a prostitute and goes over to her. They negotiate the payment (a kid) and the pledge: his signet, cord and staff. The deed is done, and Tamar reverts to her widow's role. Judah later sends his friend Hirah with the payment, but Hirah cannot find the prostitute, and no one seems to know of her when he asks. In the text there is variance in the way Tamar is described in the two scenes. Judah mistakes her for a common prostitute *(zonah),* whereas Hirah looks for a cultic prostitute *(qedeshah).* Perhaps this is the reason that Hirah cannot locate her. When Judah's initial attempt to pay the prostitute fails, he gives up, fearing that he would look foolish if he continued the search.

The next episode brings the plot to its climax. Judah hears that Tamar was with a man and as a result is pregnant. His response indicates how powerful the patriarch was at this time in Israel's history. Even though Tamar is not living in his household, he retains the right to determine who has sexual access to her. Her pregnancy indicates that she has been insubordinate. Without a hearing and from a distance, he finds her guilty and decides her punishment. "And Judah said, 'Bring her out, and let her be burned' "(Gen 38:24). Tamar, while being brought out like a lamb to the slaughter, sends word to her father-in-law. "It was the owner of these who made me pregnant." And she says, "Take note, please, whose these are, the signet and the cord and the staff" (Gen 38:25). Her statement and request are deferential in tone, as befits her subordinate status. She does not confront or accuse Judah, yet the evidence speaks loud and clear. Judah acknowledges the items and his own guilt and holds up Tamar for honor. "She is more in the right than I, since I did not give her to my son Shelah" (Gen 38:26).

In this resolution, patriarchy is both reflected and challenged. Judah's power is shown throughout; he has control over the lives of his wife, sons and daughter-in-law. Yet the narrative makes clear that Tamar is an independent agent who understands her situation can and does work to secure justice for herself. There is tremendous tension in the narrative between how Judah treats her and how she emerges in the narrative. She is treated as though she is his property to be disposed of at will, yet she is not his property. Her success calls into question the basic assumptions of the culture.

Judah also subverts patriarchy when he recognizes and honors Tamar as being more righteous than he. Insofar as he recognizes a higher standard to which they are both accountable, he undercuts his male privilege. The episode ends by noting that Judah did not lie with Tamar again. In doing so he is observing a widespread taboo that father and son do not have sexual relations with the same woman (Lev 18:15).

Tamar's successful deception results in her becoming the mother of twin sons, Perez and Zerah (Gen 38:26-30). She was duplicitous, and yet because God blessed her with children, we are encouraged to hold her in high esteem. She is one of the founding mothers of Israel, mentioned again in the genealogy of David (Ruth 4:12-20) and the genealogy of Jesus (Mt 1:3). Because of her courage, the line continued and life was preserved.

Potiphar's Wife and Asenath (Gen 39:1-20; 41:45, 50-52)

The narrative about Joseph (Gen 37, 39—50) is unlike the previous ancestral narratives. In those, women as well as men tended to be on the margins and often resorted to trickery in order to achieve their goals. Their status was insecure, and they quickly rose and fell. In this narrative, by contrast, we have a tale of an underdog who makes good by playing by the rules. His rise in status is due first to God's providential care, which is matched by Joseph's outstanding ability to interpret dreams, to administer a household, a prison and a land, and to remain virtuous in the face of temptation. He is the model hero for the establishment. Nowhere does he use trickery to advance his status or seek justice. Hard work, discipline and virtue pave the way out of servitude to prosperity.

The interesting women of the ancestral narratives are absent here. We have only two women, and both are undeveloped. The first, Potiphar's wife, is a stereotypical antagonist. She is both a foreign woman and a temptress. Although it is possible to be a positive foreign woman (Hagar) and a positive temptress (Tamar), Potiphar's wife is negative on both counts. She enters the plot of Joseph's rise to power when he

Preliminary sculpture of the head of an Egyptian noblewoman. (Genesis 39)

first comes to Egypt. His brothers have sold him to traders, either Midianites or Ishmaelites, who have taken him to Egypt and sold him to an Egyptian official, Potiphar. Potiphar sees that Joseph succeeds in all tasks assigned him, and Potiphar gives Joseph more and more responsibility, until he is managing Potiphar's entire estate.

This stable and prosperous situation is overturned by Potiphar's wife. In one of the few descriptions of appearance in Hebrew narrative, we are told that Joseph is handsome. This prepares for what follows: Potiphar's wife notices him and commands Joseph to lie with her (Gen 39:7). He refuses, giving as his reason that this would be an act of betrayal of his master's trust and a sin against God (Gen 39:8-9). Potiphar's wife persists in her entreaties, and one day, when no one else is in the house, she takes hold of Joseph's outer garment and again commands him to lie with her. Joseph is in a more dangerous situation now, and he flees from her, leaving his garment with her. She then uses this as evidence to back her claim that Joseph had attempted to lie with her (Gen 39:13-18). She convinces her husband, who becomes enraged and puts Joseph in prison (Gen 39:19-20). She has functioned as the stereotypical temptress, a duplicitous woman who is to be feared by all upstanding males. Like Dame Folly in the book of Proverbs, she is sexually aggressive, acts independently, is not loyal to her husband and brings men to ruin (*see* The Wise Woman, the Foolish Woman and the Righteous Woman). She is a woman who dissociates sexual relations and motherhood. She is a woman who has acted like a man motivated by lust.

Joseph meanwhile has persevered in his virtue, and in the end she does not ruin him. Rather, she is a catalyst to move the action along. Joseph ends up in prison, which will lead him to have an audience with the king, which will lead to his rise in position to second in command of Egypt. Because God is at work behind the scenes and because Joseph is virtuous, Potiphar's wife does not succeed in bringing him down.

This episode of the Joseph narrative is a cautionary tale teaching young men to avoid powerful foreign women. Although this message is helpful for young men to hear, there is no parallel story for young women. Even more than men, women need instruction on how to maintain their virtue when they are in a subordinate position. The situation of women experiencing sexual harassment from their male superiors is much more common than the reverse.

The negative portrayal of Potiphar's wife is softened by Joseph's marrying an Egyptian woman, Asenath, daughter of Potiphera, priest of On (Gen 41:45). We know nothing more about her, except that she bore Joseph two sons, whom he named Manasseh and Ephraim (Gen 41:50-52).

In the end, the chosen people are a mixed race. Semites and Egyptians will together form the people that will one day leave Egypt and settle in the Promised Land.

Bibliography. P. A. Bird, "Male and Female He Created Them: Genesis 1:27b in the Context of the Priestly Account of Creation," in *Missing Persons and Mistaken Identities: Women and Gender in Ancient Israel* (Minneapolis: Fortress, 1997) 123-55; T. Frymer-Kensky, *In the Wake of the Goddesses: Women, Culture and the Biblical Transformation of Pagan Myth* (New York: Fawcett Columbine, 1992); idem, "Near Eastern Law and the Patriarchal Family," *Biblical Archaeologist* 44 (1981) 209-14; S. P. Jeansonne, *The Women of Genesis: From Sarah to Potiphar's Wife* (Minneapolis: Fortress, 1990); C. L. Meyers, *Discovering Eve: Ancient Israelite*

Women in Context (New York: Oxford University Press, 1988); V. Saiving, "The Human Situation: A Feminine View," in *Woman Spirit Rising: A Feminist Reader in Religion* (San Francisco: Harper, 1979) 25-42; P. Trible, *God and the Rhetoric of Sexuality* (Philadelphia: Fortress, 1978); D. Williams, *Sisters in the Wilderness: The Challenge of Womanist God-Talk* (Maryknoll, NY: Orbis, 1993).

CHRISTIANA DE GROOT

EXODUS

Introduction

The book of Exodus reports unquestionably the most dramatic events in all of the Hebrew Bible. After 430 years of silence (Ex 12:40), God invaded the history of the covenant people in such a profound way that the deliverance from bondage in Egypt was paradigmatic for the future return from exile (Is 43:14-21) and, from the Christian perspective, for the deliverance from the bondage of sin as accomplished by the atoning death of Jesus Christ as the Passover Lamb (1 Cor 5:7; 1 Pet 1:18-19).

The Hebrew title of the book is *Shemoth* ("names"). As with the other books of the Pentateuch, the Hebrew title is based on the first key word of the text. In this case, it refers to the names of the children of Israel who went to Egypt. The text of Exodus deliberately establishes continuity, in spite of the centuries of intervening silence, with the events that closed Genesis. The English title, Exodus, is a transliteration of the Greek Septuagint title and addresses the theme of the first part of the book.

The historicity and date of the exodus from Egypt have prompted extensive and nuanced scholarly debate, which may be accessed in standard recent texts on the history of Israel. The following commentary is written from the perspective that the exodus was a historical event that involved the descendants of Israel as named in Exodus 1:1-5. Within that historical framework, there are two general positions regarding the date of the exodus, each one having significant supporting data as well as unanswered questions. The early date for the exodus, primarily determined on the basis of 1 Kings 6:1, is 1446 B.C., and the late date would locate the event in the middle of the thirteenth century B.C. Both fall into the Egyptian New Kingdom period, the former placing the exodus during the Eighteenth Dynasty and the latter putting it into the Nineteenth Dynasty, during which the name Rameses (cf. Ex 1:11) became prominent.

Although the issue of authorship is another hotly debated topic, it is not improbable that Moses, reared in the court of Pharaoh, was capable of recording the history of his people, the events that they experienced and the covenant words that God revealed to him (see the direct indications in Ex 17:14; 24:4, 7). This does not rule out the possibility of later editing, but there are reasonable bases for attributing the essence of these texts to Moses.

As the events of Exodus unfold, three fundamental themes emerge and are intertwined. They are revelation, redemption and relationship. God initially revealed himself to Moses at Horeb (Sinai), reasserting the covenant relationship established with Abraham, Isaac and Jacob and declaring the intention to rescue the people from bondage (Ex 3:6-10). God was revealed to the people of Israel by the sequence of mighty acts that led to their redemption and deliverance at the Sea of Reeds. Finally, God firmly established the intimate relationship with the people as he revealed the words of that covenant at Mount Sinai and gave instructions for the tabernacle and priesthood, both gracious provisions for the wayward people in their ongoing relationship with the holy God.

Undergirding these distinct themes is the truth of God's sovereignty. Sovereignty refers to God's all-encompassing control over every aspect of the universe. Thus God is able perfectly to accomplish good purposes, carry out the divine will and promises and work through the course of human history. His sovereignty is displayed through intervention in the creation that is his; it is also displayed in the choice of individuals to fulfill his purposes. God's justice and mercy, the covenant and the Torah, and the provision of salvation and redemption are all manifestations of God's indisputable and gracious rule of the universe. The choice and preparation of Moses is a stunning example of God's sovereignty. From a much more sobering perspective, so also is the case of Pharaoh.

The covenant is the instrument for restoring the relationship between God and humankind that had been broken in the fall. The covenant revealed at Sinai followed those made with Noah (Gen 9:8-17) and Abraham (Gen 15:10-21). The word *torah* means "instruction." The Torah given at Sinai contained instructions for the covenant people indicating how to conduct themselves so as to be pleasing to their sovereign.

While *redemption* is a term that is used frequently in conjunction with the deliverance and salvation that believers experience in Christ, initially the process of redeeming meant the payment of a price to buy back either persons or property. In the context of the exodus and the Israelites, it is linked closely with the firstborn. Israel was God's firstborn, and because Egypt would not allow God's firstborn to go free, the Egyptians would pay with their firstborn sons (Ex 4:21-23). In commemoration of this, Israel was to consecrate to the Lord every one of their firstborn males; the animals were sacrificed and firstborn sons were redeemed. God's deliverance of the people from Egypt is spoken of as redemption (Ex 6:6; 15:13) and was accompanied by a display of God's power. The Hebrew Bible refers to God as the Redeemer of Israel (e.g., Ps 78:35; repeatedly in Is 40—66). All of this provides the cultural and theological backdrop for the substitution of the blood of Christ (Eph 1:7), the firstborn over all creation (Col 1:15), for those who are his new creation. Jesus declared that he would give his life as a ransom for many (Mk 10:45), and 1 Peter 1:18-19 makes clear allusion to this truth.

Outline

1:1—13:16 Israel in Egypt
- 1:1-22 The Oppression of Israel
- 2:1-25 Birth, Preservation and Preparation of Moses
- 3:1—4:31 Call and Commissioning of Moses
- 5:1—11:10 The God of Israel Versus the Gods of Egypt
- 12:1—13:16 Instructions for Passover

13:17—15:21 The Exodus
- 13:17—14:31 Deliverance at the Sea of Reeds
- 15:1-21 Song of Victory

15:22—18:27 Tests in the Wilderness
- 15:22-27 Bitter Waters
- 16:1-36 Threat of Starvation
- 17:1-7 Thirst in the Desert
- 17:8-16 Attack from Enemies
- 18:1-27 Overwhelming Number of Disputes

Commentary

Israel in Egypt (Ex 1:1—13:16)

The Oppression of Israel (Ex 1)

It is important to read the events in Exodus 1 in conjunction with Joseph's words to his brothers in Genesis 45:7, "But God sent me ahead of you to preserve for you a remnant on earth and to save your lives by a great deliverance" (NIV). The ruthless oppression under which the Israelites suffered for at least part of the 430 years was preparatory for their understanding the depths of the meaning of deliverance.

During that time, the Israelites were fruitful, multiplied and filled the earth. The phrases in Exodus 1:7 are reminiscent of those in Genesis 1:28. These numbers caused the new king "who did not know Joseph" (Ex 1:8) to fear that the Israelites would join the enemies of Egypt in the event of war and leave the country. This suggests dynastic change, accompanied by significant perceived threat. It further suggests that the Israelite population was a necessary part of the Egyptian economy but had to be controlled.

The control tactics included oppressive slave labor, the harshness of which is stressed in the text. Subsequently, more direct means of extermination were attempted, first in Pharaoh's command to the Hebrew midwives to kill newborn boys and then to all his people to intervene in this manner. Most likely, Shiphrah and Puah are two representative names of a larger group of women who were engaged in midwifery (*see* Midwifery and Birthing Practices). It is significant that fear of God motivated them to disobey the king of Egypt, preserve the lives of the infants and present the matter to Pharaoh in a less than truthful fashion. In return God blessed them with families (lit. "houses"), an example of the measure-for-measure justice that is evident throughout the Scriptures.

Birth, Preservation and Preparation of Moses (Ex 2)

The parents of Moses, Amram and Jochabed, were both of the tribe of Levi. It is apparent that the extreme measures taken to deal with newborn Israelite males were relatively recent at the time of Moses' birth because Aaron was three years his elder. Miriam was old enough to have been appointed to watch the box into which Moses' mother put him after she could no longer hide him. When Moses was put into the Nile, it was technically in keeping with the edict, with the added protection of a carefully crafted ark. The Hebrew word *(tevah)* is used only here and of Noah's ark (Gen 6:14-16). Both crafts saved from the destructive force of water the life of an individual chosen by God.

These events are illustrative of God's sovereignty in overriding the designs of a fearful and brutal man. It is significant that the text concentrates on courageous women God was using to accomplish his purposes. Not only do we see the actions of the midwives, mother and sister; we find that Pharaoh's daughter happened to be at the river's edge as the basket went by. Even though the boy was immediately recognized as a Hebrew child, she was predisposed to respond positively to Miriam's bold offer to find a nurse for him. This meant acting directly contrary to Pharaoh's

Syrian synagogue fresco depicting the baby Moses rescued by Pharaoh's daughter from the Nile. (Exodus 2:5-6)

edict. Finally she sustained her interest, paying Moses' mother to nurse him and later adopting him as her son. In the context of the official policy toward the Israelites, these actions were extraordinary. The name that she gave to Moses is interesting from several perspectives. *Mosheh* is a Hebrew participle that, while it is related to his being drawn out of the water, also may have reference to his drawing the people out of Egypt. In Egyptian, it means "is born," and it may be related to several names of the Eighteenth Dynasty, Thutmose and Ahmose.

Not only was the sovereignty of God evident in the preservation of Moses' life, it was clear also in his preparation for his role as leader of the Israelites. The initial phase occurred as his mother nursed him, and it lasted long enough to give him a strong and profound sense of his identity as a Hebrew. The second part was in the court of Pharaoh. As Stephen put it in Acts 7:22, "Moses was educated in all the wisdom of the Egyptians and was powerful in speech and action" (NIV). This process continued until he was forty (Acts 7:23) and would mean acquiring the ability to write, likely access to literary works and the knowledge of court etiquette that would serve him well in the future confrontation on Pharaoh's turf. The third phase of his preparation surely seemed like the end of his career. As a result of his sin of murder, he fled into the wilderness. Following a mutually beneficial encounter when Moses defended the rights of Jethro's seven daughters and gained hospitality and a wife, Moses served as a shepherd of his father-in-law's sheep for another forty years. Contrary to all appearances, however, this aspect of Moses' education was indispensable as he learned the terrain and water sources of the Sinai Peninsula and gained skills necessary for leading difficult and recalcitrant groups.

Call and Commissioning of Moses (Ex 3:1—4:31)

Because God remembered and was faithful to his covenant promises, the angel of the Lord appeared to Moses at Horeb, the mountain of God. The fire that did not consume the bush attracted Moses; God's verbal identification of himself as the God of the covenant with Abraham, Isaac and Jacob caused him fear. Upon learning of his prospective role, Moses raised a series of objections. The first one was a question: Who am I? He compared himself with Pharaoh, an issue that God would later address. God's response at this point redirected Moses' focus from the intimidating prospect of Pharoah to things much more profound: God's presence and the ultimate goal of worshiping him.

Moses' second question followed logically on God's response. On behalf of the Israelites, he asked in effect, Who are *you*? In this context, God revealed not only the basis for his covenant name, Yahweh, but also his intention to fulfill the covenant promise. The literal meaning of *ehyeh asher ehyeh* (Ex 3:14) is "I will be who I will be." The imperfect tense of the verb form implies that God is the eternally self-existent One. The repetition of the verb suggests certainty. The root of this verb "to be" is the basis for the divine name Yahweh that is characteristically translated "Lord." In his response, God made it clear that he was God of the fathers, God of the people in bondage and God of the continuing covenant.

Moses' third objection posed the likely potential of disbelief on the part of the Israelites as they were asked to accept Moses' leadership in this adventure. In response, God demonstrated two signs as witnesses. The first utilized the rod that would become a regular feature in the drama; it became a serpent when Moses cast it to the ground and was restored to its natural state when he put out his hand to take it up again. In this Sinai context, the word for serpent is *nahash,* the appropriate term for that geographical region; when Moses replayed the sign in Pharaoh's court at the Nile, the rod became a crocodile *(tanin)*. The second sign was the immediate appearance of leprosy on his hand as Moses put it into his garment next to his heart and the subsequent removal of that uncleanness when God commanded him to repeat the action. In addition, the Lord told Moses that if the people did not believe the first two signs, Moses would have the capability to pour the waters of the Nile onto dry ground and see them become blood, a preview of the first plague.

Unconvinced, Moses claimed that he had not been a "man of words" for a long time, that he was "heavy of mouth and heavy of tongue" (Ex 4:10). While this appears to contradict the witness of Stephen (Acts 7:22) that Moses was "powerful in speech and action," it is important to recall that Moses was speaking from his immediate perspective of having been out of the Egyptian court for forty years while Stephen was representing the wider picture of Moses' activities throughout the process of leaving Egypt. After Moses' first attempt to address Pharaoh and the apparent failure of that effort, Moses raised the issue again, stating twice that he was "uncircumcised of lips" (Ex 6:12, 30). God reminded Moses that he is the Creator of all human abilities and impediments but promised his presence "with [Moses'] mouth" as well as instruction as to what he should say.

At that point, Moses said, "O my Lord, please send someone else" (Ex 4:13), a response that angered the Lord. Nevertheless, God continued with the intention to use Moses, indicating that Aaron would be his mouthpiece. Even Moses' recalcitrance under the vast reaches of God's sovereignty was effectively turned to good. Providentially, in the context where Pharaoh considered himself a deity, having Moses operating through a spokesperson for whom he would be "like a god" (Ex 4:16; 7:1) would likely raise his level of acceptance in the court.

As Moses was en route to Egypt, the Lord prepared him for the sobering events as they would unfold around the person of Pharaoh. Moses would see and participate in the painful process of the hardening of Pharaoh's heart. This is the tragic side of the doctrine of election, the process whereby God chooses in mercy to rescue individual persons from their utterly fallen and helpless state in sin and guilt and to make them holy and blameless as adopted children to the praise of his glory (Eph 1:1-6; Rom 8:29-30; 9:11-12; 10:14-17). This tragic side is called reprobation, teaching that God has eternally condemned the nonelect to eternal punishment for their sins. We see the complexity of this truth as God's hardening and Pharaoh's responsibility in hardening his heart are inextricably interwoven (Ex 4:21; 7:3, 13, 22; 8:15 [8:11 Heb.], 19 [8:15 in Heb.], 32 [8:28 in Heb.]; 9:7, 12, 34-35; 10:1, 20, 27). This horrifying and complex process was the subject of Paul's comments in Romans 9:16-18 as he wrestled with the implications of the truth of God's sovereignty.

As with all wicked individuals, the effects of Pharaoh's evil were not experienced by him alone. The slaughter of the Egyptian firstborn would be because of Pharaoh's refusal to free Israel, God's firstborn. The principle of measure-for-measure justice is apparent here: Pharaoh had exalted himself above humans in his assumption of deity and in his treatment of Israel as subhuman; thus God deprived him of his free will and bound him in rebellion, making him subhuman. The death of the firstborn would be the indication of this.

There is likely a thematic linkage between this mention of refusal to let the firstborn go and the resultant death and the next puzzling incident. The Lord met Moses on the way back to Egypt, threatening to kill "him" (either Moses or perhaps the firstborn son) because he had not circumcised this son. As the chosen deliverer of God's people, he had to be in obedience to the stipulations of God's covenant with them (cf. Gen 17:14). In some way that is not evident from the text, Zipporah, his Midianite wife, knew the proper action; she immediately circumcised her son with a flint. While her charge that Moses was a "bridegroom of blood" is cryptic, there are several possible symbolic connections to consider. First, the divine-human covenant relationship was often articulated in terms of marriage. The sign of the covenant with Abraham was circumcision. Moses' failure to live up to the stipulations of the covenant threatened her immediate family as well as the larger covenant family that it represented. To make that right involved the shedding of blood, as was characteristically the case.

The God of Israel Versus the Gods of Egypt (Ex 5:1—11:10)

The Initial Request (Ex 5:1—6:1). Moses and Aaron initially asked, in the name of the Lord, to celebrate a festival in the desert. Pharaoh's response was twofold. First, he rejected the request at the outset, demanding to know who the Lord was. As it turned out, the plagues were a definitive answer to his question. Second, he increased the workload of the enslaved people. It is instructive to note that Moses' obedience did not suddenly make everything easy. The situation got much worse, but there was a purpose: Instead of a temporary journey into the desert, Pharaoh would be responsible for driving the Israelites out and it would be the mighty hand of God that would undeniably accomplish the task.

The Covenant Lord and His People (6:2—7:5). While an initial translation of Exodus 6:3 might read, "I appeared to Abraham, to Isaac and to Jacob as El Shaddai; but [by] my name, the Lord *(Yahweh),* I did not make myself known to them," that does not do justice either to the immediate context or to the whole of the patriarchal account in Genesis. First, the next verse says, "I *also (gam)* established my covenant with them," indicating that the preceding statement is likely a positive one. Further, in Genesis the name of the Lord appears many times. The second part of this verse can be read as a question: "I appeared to Abraham, to Isaac and to Jacob as El Shaddai and [by] my name, did I not make myself known to them?" That fits better with the syntax that follows. While God did reveal himself by name to the patriarchs, the full implications of that name would now be manifested. The covenant Lord as identified in Exodus 3:14 was about to redeem them powerfully and then give the Sinai covenant.

The partial genealogy in Exodus 6:14-25 established the position of Moses and Aaron among the covenant people as descendants of Levi. It is of interest to note the number of women mentioned in this brief record and who they were. The mother of Moses and Aaron is named, as are the wives of Aaron and Eleazar. The latter carried on the line of Aaron after the deaths of Nadab and Abihu (Lev 10).

As the final preparation for the drama of the plagues, the expressed intentions of God are restated without ambiguity. Moses would be as God to Pharaoh, and Aaron would be his spokesperson. God would cause the heart of Pharaoh to be hard so that even in the face of tremendous miracles, he would reject the word of God through Moses and Aaron. God would deliver his people from Egypt with "great judgments," and Egypt would indeed know who the Lord was.

Unleashing the Plagues (Ex 7:6—11:10). It is possible that the ages of Moses and Aaron were indicated here because age was venerated in a tradition that valued wisdom, as Egyptian culture did. Egypt's wisdom circles included wise men and those who engaged in magic and sorcery. It is not surprising that the initial signs performed by Moses and Aaron could be imitated by the circles of those who dabbled in the arts of magic and deception and appealed to the darker supernatural powers that kept the people in blindness. Significantly, after Pharaoh's magicians manipulated their snakes and turned the waters to blood as Moses had done, Pharaoh's heart was hard, and he refused to listen.

Also evident in this narrative, however, are the limits beyond which those powers succumbed before the mighty hand of God. The magicians capitulated at the third plague when they failed to produce gnats and they acknowledged "the finger of God" (Ex 8:19). Furthermore, while the initial plagues affected all of the inhabitants, with the fourth plague of the flies, God announced and made a distinction between the Egyptians and the Israelites who lived in Goshen. As the onslaught intensified, the officials of Pharaoh were convinced, and many obeyed the instructions of Moses in order to preserve their property.

In the plagues God used timed and intensified aberrations in the natural phenomena of Egypt, some of which had been deified. They started and stopped at the expressed word of Moses. Most of them were announced ahead of time to Pharaoh, and it was often as a result of his pleading for relief that Moses called on the Lord to stop the plague. The plagues increased steadily in severity, and at each stage, there were clear moral purposes, articulated in the text, to be discerned.

First, the mighty acts of God gained freedom for Israel, demonstrated that they were God's people and showed them that he was their God. These events made an indelible mark on the corporate memory of Israel and were rehearsed as they sang the psalms (Ps 78:1-8, 44-51; 105:28-36). Second, in response to Pharaoh's challenge, the plagues demonstrated to him and to Egypt who God was and what his powers were. They were part of the hardening of Pharaoh's heart. As each of the plagues tore at the religion, social economy and persons of Egypt, Pharaoh appeared to repent, acknowledging his sin, requesting that Moses pray for relief and indicating that he would allow them to go and worship. Moses consistently intervened on his behalf despite his bad track record, and God extended him numerous opportunities to relinquish his self-worship. Nevertheless he rejected them all. Third, the Egyptians and Israelites were not the sole nations to hear of God's miraculous works; Pharaoh was raised up that God's name might be proclaimed in all the earth. Jethro heard and joined with the Israelites in worshiping God. As the Israelites were about to conquer the land, Rahab told the spies that the inhabitants of the land had heard of God's activities on their behalf (Josh 2:8-11). Centuries later, the Philistines expressed their fear of the God who struck the Egyptians with all kinds of plagues (1 Sam 4:8). Fourth, the plagues directly challenged the multiplicity of Egyptian deities and a stated purpose was to bring judgment on all the gods of Egypt. The last two plagues were especially sharp attacks because the sun was the primary deity and Pharaoh was its earthly representative. Finally, it is possible to see in the plagues a foreshadowing of cosmic eschatological plagues, including hail, fire, blood (Rev 8:6-8) and locusts (Rev 9:1-11). The two unnamed witnesses of Revelation 11:6 will have power to shut up the sky, turn waters into blood and strike the earth with every kind of plague.

As the first plague, Aaron struck the water of the Nile with the staff, and all of it became blood or turned blood red, bringing death to whatever was in it. The idiomatic use of "blood" *(dam)* to indicate color is evident in Joel 2:31 [3:4 in Heb.] and 2 Kings 3:22. Whether it was literally blood or undrinkable water, the significant factor was that the Nile was the heart of the nation's religion. Osiris was god of the underworld and the death and resurrection cycle. Ironically, the Nile was considered to be his lifeblood, and its annual flood in midsummer was a significant religious event. Not only was the Nile struck with death but also there was blood in every place where water collected and even on the "trees and stones" (Ex 7:19). These latter may have been idolatrous objects.

Seven days later, frogs came up and overwhelmed the land. The frog was a symbol of long life and an emblem of fertility. Frogs proliferating in uncontrollable numbers in the bedroom and bed of Pharaoh was the height of humiliation.

The next two plagues involved phenomena that would be the natural result of putrid water and dying frogs. Vermin and a dense swarm of flies descended. The vermin were a plague on humans and domestic animals, while the land was ruined because of the flies. Large golden flies were found among the jewels and military items buried with Queen Aahotep, who played a major role in the initial stages of expelling the foreign rulers, called Hyksos, from Egypt in the sixteenth century B.C.

With the plague directly on the livestock, several Egyptian deities were under attack. Apis was a bull god; Hathor, often represented as a cow, was the goddess of love and beauty. This was the first plague that involved the loss of property, and there were religious and economic implications as all the major domestic animals were smitten. The plague of boils brought physical suffering directly to humans as well as animals. In fact, Pharaoh's magicians were humbled and unable to stand in the presence of Moses.

The plague of hail occurred in February

when the barley and flax were ripe. Likely there had been some time in between during which the flocks and herds had been replenished, perhaps from those of the Israelites who had been protected in Goshen. Some time thereafter, Moses warned that the crops that had not been devastated by the hail would be destroyed by an invasion of locusts. At this point, the officials challenged Pharaoh's authority, in spite of the fact that he was a divine figure, appealing to the potential of utter ruin of Egypt.

The ninth plague was a direct assault on the sun god, Amun-Re. It was a darkness "that could be felt," possibly an intensification of the weather phenomenon in the Middle East called the *sharav,* in which winds from the desert raise huge quantities of fine dust in the air, even to the point of blocking out the sun. Amun was the god most closely linked with Pharaoh in his becoming a divine figure.

The culmination of the confrontation was the tenth plague. Prior to leaving the presence of Pharaoh, Moses tersely announced the conditions. At midnight, every firstborn son in Egypt would die. For the Israelites, however, there would be a distinction made if they followed the instructions for the Passover (see next section).

The question is often asked why there is no evidence of this dramatic series of events outside the biblical narrative. Characteristically, the Egyptians as well as other ancient peoples tended not to record those events that were defeats, and this was a stunning example of utter defeat.

Instructions for Passover (Ex 12:1—13:16)
While the word *pesah,* translated Passover, appears frequently with reference to the sacrificial animal for the festival, the related verb form as it appears in Exodus 12:13, 23 is not so common and merits some clarification. In Isaiah 31:5, the word is used in a classic illustration of poetic parallelism with the clear meaning of defending and protecting: "Like birds hovering overhead, the Lord Almighty will defend Jerusalem; He will defend it and deliver it; He will protect ('pass over') it and rescue it." Exodus 12:23 indicates that the Lord would see the blood on the door frames and protect the doorway, not permitting the destroyer to enter and strike down the people. This compelling image foreshadows the effective work of the blood of Christ, the Passover Lamb, as he bore the destructive wrath of God against sin.

These chapters give the instructions for the Passover in Egypt and the principles for its commemoration on an annual basis. These two focuses alternate as the Lord gave both sets of instructions to Moses, and he passed them along to the elders of Israel.

In preparation for the dramatic visitation against Egypt, the Israelites were instructed to take a lamb or kid on the tenth day of the month and keep it until the fourteenth day. It was to be a one-year-old male without defect, and the four days of guarding the animal would ensure its unblemished state. The importance of the family as part of the community is apparent in the instructions. While they were eating the flesh of the animal together in the house, the blood was put with hyssop on doorposts and lintels as a sign for the Lord to protect the house. The roasted sacrifice had to be consumed that night together with bitter herbs and bread made without yeast, and the people were to stay indoors. Finally, they were not to break any of the bones of the sacrificial animal (Ex 12:46; cf. Jn 19:36). The initial instructions did not attach symbolic significance to these elements of the meal. The unleavened bread was indicative of leaving in haste. In time, however, the bitter herbs would come to represent the bitterness of slavery and the unleavened bread purification from the leaven of sin. Yeast affects the entirety of a loaf of bread; so also the pollution of sin ranges much farther than its original starting point. In addition, fermentation leads ultimately to decay and death, a compelling representation of the results of sin being death. Paul used the figure to address the need to deal in a radical way with sin in the Corinthian congregation (1 Cor 5:6-8).

The Lord did pass through the land, striking down all the firstborn in Egypt, humans and animals. That the domesticated animals suffered as well might be another indication that they were being judged in their capacity as "gods" of the people. The firstborn of Pharaoh, the expected next ruler, would also have been considered one of those deities as the traditional origins of the pharaohs customarily involved the visitation of the god Amun to the mother of the pharaoh-to-be.

Pharaoh's final words to Moses and Aaron were a command to do just as they had requested with an added plea to bless him in the process. In keeping with the word of the Lord, the Israelites, men and particularly women, asked for silver, gold and clothing from Egyptians, who were eager to have them leave lest they all die. In so doing, they essentially received at least a partial payment for the years of slave labor. Further, these precious materials would be the voluntary offerings that were given toward the construction of the tabernacle.

Israel was to observe the annual celebration, keeping vigil for generations to come because the Lord had kept watch that night. Each aspect of their celebration was to remind them that God brought them out from Egypt with a mighty hand. Furthermore, to ensure corporate memory and continuity of the tradition, they were commanded to tell their children of God's intervention on their behalf.

The subsequent history of the celebration of the combined festivals of Passover and Unleavened Bread crossed the boundaries between home and family, on the one hand, and the corporate community as the central place of worship, on the other. Deuteronomy 16:2 indicates that the sacrifice was to take place at the location God would choose as a dwelling for his name. When major reforms occurred during the reigns of Hezekiah (2 Chron 30) and Josiah (2 Chron 35), a centerpiece of each was the corporate celebration of the Passover at the cleansed temple.

An additional element of the annual celebration was the consecration of firstborn males of humans and domestic animals, a reminder that the firstborn was the Lord's and that he had required of the Egyptians their firstborn. In the case of the livestock, this meant sacrifice. In regard to the firstborn sons, it meant redemption, the payment of a price as a substitute. Finally, to participate in the Passover celebration, one had to be or become a member of the covenant people which, for males, meant circumcision.

The Exodus (Ex 13:17—15:21)

Deliverance at the Sea of Reeds (Ex 13:17—14:31)

Although it is traditional to speak of the Israelites crossing the Red Sea, the phrase is *yam suf*, which means "sea of reeds." While the precise location is unknown, this possibly refers to the region north of the modern Gulf of Suez, which in antiquity was characterized by large, shallow lakes with extensive swampy areas. Whatever it was, it was not navigable without the miracle that dried it up and allowed the Israelites to walk across "on dry ground" (Ex 14:21-22, 29; 15:19). Furthermore, it was deep enough that the Egyptians were engulfed when the heaps of water returned.

As the Israelites exited Egypt, their path was determined by God and it was not the customary way toward Philistine country. That would have been the international trade and battle route that was too well-guarded for these newly-freed slaves who were not ready for major battle. In addition, God's design was to make them appear to be confused in the desert so that Pharaoh chose to pursue them, thus bringing destruction to Egypt.

The Philistines were one of five entities making up the Sea Peoples whose migration to the ancient Near East en masse occurred during the twelfth century B.C., evidenced by carved reliefs from the reign of Rameses III. This was well after the exodus, no matter which date is supposed for that event. Later editing of the text may have introduced the term, because it was well known as the designation of the coastal plain area in the land of Canaan, always controlled by the more powerful, cosmopolitan political forces who were characteristically enemies of Israel. It is also possible that while the major part of the Sea Peoples arrived in the twelfth century, there had been smaller groups of them already resident in the land.

Moses took the bones of Joseph to fulfill the oath taken by the sons of Israel (Gen 50:25). Hebrews 11:22 notes that this was indicative of the faith that Joseph had that God would bring the people out of Egypt.

When the army of Pharaoh overtook the Israelites, their fear made them cry out to the Lord and reproach the visible leader, Moses. His role as intermediary was paradigmatic as the drama unfolded. He encouraged the Israelites with the promise of God's deliverance but it seems that he also appealed to the Lord, who instructed him to raise the rod in order to dry up the sea. As with all tests in life, each step of the deliverance was accompanied by occasion for potential fear and the resultant need to trust God. It was not until the Israelites finally saw the Egyptians lying dead on the shore that they came to the point of fearing the Lord and putting their trust in him and in Moses.

While the entire army of Pharaoh died, Pharaoh is not mentioned as having perished, and there is no evidence of change of Pharaoh in either the early- or late-date scheme at the particular points when the exodus happened.

Song of Victory (Ex 15)

One of the ways of remembering God's mighty interventions on behalf of the people was through poetry. It appears that Moses and Miriam, called a prophet, taught the text of the song to the Israelites. In Miriam's case, the singing was enhanced by the rhythm of tambourines and dancing. It is important to note that her role in all of the events connected with the exodus and the period of wandering in the wilderness was a significant one. Centuries later, when God reminded the people of their deliverance from Egypt, he said through the prophet Micah, "I sent before you Moses, Aaron, and Miriam" (Mic 6:4).

The first part of the song (Ex 15:1-12) addresses the events that had already occurred, hailing God as the majestic and glorious warrior. Salvation had to do with victory over a real, powerful and threatening enemy. This song of victory celebrates the overthrow in graphic images. The right hand of God shattered the enemy, and his burning anger consumed enemies as fire would chaff. The boasting words of Pharaoh, each phrase added to the previous ones as if he had attempted to be convincing, are followed by the breath of God destroying them.

Exodus 15:13 serves as a transition to the promises regarding what the Lord would yet do for his people. While Hebrew verb tenses have some flexibility, especially in poetry, the verbs in this verse are all in the past (perfect) tense, representing what had already occurred and the surety of God's guidance to their ultimate goal. The major people groups whom they would encounter, Philistines, Edom, Moab and the Canaanites, all paradigmatic enemies, would be terrified and allow the people to pass by. As the final goal, God would bring them to the land and the place of his sanctuary, where he would rule as sovereign.

Tests in the Wilderness (Ex 15:22—18:27)

The route of the Israelites to the mountain of God and Mount Sinai cannot be identified with certainty, but the traditional location of the mountain in the southern part of the Sinai Peninsula is logical. It is a region that is isolated, rugged, far from the traveled routes of the northern part of the peninsula and separated from those routes by the central region that is extremely barren and desolate. What is evident is that the Israelites' journey was fraught with difficulties and their faith was tested. Likewise, they tested God. Because this path is so like that of the believer who has experienced the profound joy in redemption followed by the frustrations of life in a sinful world, there are timeless lessons to be gained from study of these incidents.

Bitter Waters (Ex 15:22-27)

The first test was severe. Three days without water was a crisis, and finding only bitter water added to the desperation. Because water is such an important element in that geographical context, many desert oases were named for wells, springs or pools. The name Marah would be a warning.

God's response was to show Moses a tree (or a piece of wood) that Moses cast into the water in order to restore it. The word translated "show" literally means "taught" and is related to the word *torah* ("instruction"). At that point, God stated an intention to test them to see if they would be obedient. Although the specific contents of the decree and the law were not articulated, the point was that they were to obey God. The reward would be freedom from the diseases that God had brought on the Egyptians. This may be a reference to far-reaching effects of the plagues, evidence of which they had seen. After the crisis, God brought them to a place with multiple springs.

Threat of Starvation (Ex 16)

A month after leaving, when the Israelites were in the desert of Sin, their circumstances seemed so bleak that they voiced their desire to return to Egypt, representing their previous estate in rather rosy colors complete with pots of meat and all the food they wanted. As Moses and Aaron addressed the people, they said that the Israelites would see manifested again the glory and power of God in a benevolent provision for them. They would have meat in the evening and bread in the morning. In this context, while both were promised, the manna was the focus of the narrative. A year later (Num 10:11), the quail were prominent. A recurrence of distress about food at the close of their sojourn at Sinai should come as no surprise, especially as they expressed disdain for manna that had gotten to be boring (Num 11:6). While God responded in mercy in the first instance, the complaining that resulted in their receiving meat in abundance and gorging themselves on it (Num 11:31-34) prompted a much more severe plague.

The descriptions of the manna in this account and in Numbers 11:7-8 indicate how extraordinary it was. Even the name expressed the Israelites' wonder at this substance: "They said to each other: *man hu?* because they did not know what it was *[mah hu]*" (Ex 16:15). It appeared as thin flakes like frost; it was white like coriander seed and tasted like wafers made with honey; and it looked like resin (Num 11:7-8). The miraculous nature of God's extensive, egalitarian and continuous provision is evident. It was sufficient to provide for all the people and to meet each individual's needs. God continued to provide it for the wilderness period, as the later editorial note in Exodus 16:34-35 states. Joshua 5:10-12 indicates that after celebrating the Passover in the land, the Israelites ceased to receive it.

When Moses recalled for the people the manna experience as they were about to enter the land, he reminded them that God caused them to hunger and then gave them the manna to teach them that "on bread alone humankind (*adam*) does not live but on everything that comes out of the mouth of God humankind lives" (Deut 8:3). Jesus identified himself as the "bread from heaven" (Jn 6) and as the incarnate Word of the Lord. After feeding the five thousand, the people asked Jesus for a sign, citing the fact that their ancestors had eaten manna in the wilderness. His responses rolled over them like multiple shock waves, each increasing in expectation and intensity. It was the Father who gave the bread from heaven; that bread would be a person who comes down from heaven and gives life to the world; Jesus is that bread of life, and those who partake of his flesh would live forever. In response, Peter said, "You have the words of eternal life" (Jn 6:68). Jesus was the Word coming from the Father; disciples of Jesus must feed on his words, thereby abiding in him.

The grumbling of the people against Moses and Aaron prompted a response from the Lord to the effect that this would be another occasion to test their obedience. It is significant that the Lord instituted the sabbath observance at this point prior to the giving of Torah at Sinai. The sabbath is regularly associated with sanctity. It is called a "a day of rest, a holy rest" (Ex 16:23). It was the culmination of the creation time cycle, and God sanctified it (Gen 2:2-3). It would be the sign of the Sinai covenant, and desecrating the sabbath was punishable by death (Ex 31:12-17). Observing the sabbath was an intrinsic part of the maintaining the relationship between the holy God and his people, and its importance transcends the stipulations of the Sinai covenant. That is one of the lessons evident in its position here. Setting that day apart in obedience to God was preparatory to receiving the full covenant.

Thirst in the Desert (Ex 17:1-7)

The Israelite community traveled at the command of the Lord, and it was his intention to lead them to Rephidim, a place with no water. It was to be another test of their ability to trust the Lord. In turn, their quarrelsome response was interpreted as their testing the Lord, especially as they were prepared to kill Moses. In that context, God required Moses to take a significant risk in walking ahead of them. He was commanded to strike the rock at Horeb with the rod so that water would come forth. Moses did as instructed, and although the text does not say so, it is assumed that the needs of the people were met by water coming out of the rock. In Paul's recital of the lessons to be learned from the wilderness events, he stated that the people drank "from the spiritual rock that followed them, and the rock was Christ" (1 Cor 10:4).

Even the place names given by Moses establish that this was yet another testing incident. Massah is related to the verb *nasah,* which means "to test," and Meribah comes from the verb *rib,* meaning "to strive or quarrel." A similar incident with the recurrence of the name Meribah occurred well into the years of wilderness wandering when the people arrived at Kadesh-barnea (Num 20:1-13). It is important to note briefly that these incidents were instructive for the psalmist (Ps 95:7-11) and the author of Hebrews 3—4, both of whom were concerned about basic unbelief and hardness of heart in the face of evidence of God's provision. The exhortation in Hebrews was to enter the "sabbath rest" (Heb 4:9-10), which meant leaving the life of disobedience and disbelief.

Attack from Enemies (Ex 17:8-16)
The Amalekites were nomadic descendants of Esau (Gen 36:12). The huge number of Israelites presented a threat to their use of the water sources. Deuteronomy 25:18 is more explicit on their vicious method of attack; they stayed on Israel's rear flank and cut off stragglers, having no fear of the Lord or compassion for human life. Thus, in the aftermath of the battle, the Lord declared his perpetual enmity toward the Amalekites, whose attacks continued against Israel into the period of the judges (Judg 6:3). A tragic turning point for the first king, Saul, was his disobedience in not putting to death Agag, the king of the Amalekites (1 Sam 15). In one of the compelling ironies of Scripture, centuries later it was Mordecai, of the tribe of Benjamin, a son of Kish (Esther 2:5), who saw the downfall of the wicked Haman the Agagite (Esther 3:1), who had plotted the destruction of the Jews.

The battle provided military training for Joshua, who would later command the army of Israel during the conquest. While it is clear that the upraised rod of God was a visible symbol indicating that the battle was the Lord's, there was significant human effort involved as well. When Moses tired and his hands sank, the Amalekites prevailed until Aaron and Hur, representing the tribes of Levi and Judah, sustained him.

As part of the subsequent ceremony, Moses built an altar, calling it "the Lord is my standard". The word is *nes* and refers to an upraised symbol and rallying point in battle. Moses was commanded to write about the event on a scroll *(sefer).* Writing is presented here in conjunction with and as the basis for oral recitation, two great sources for the traditions. The purpose was to record the sacred ban on Amalek.

Overwhelming Number of Disputes (Ex 18)
At some point after the incident en route back to Egypt from Midian, Moses had sent Zipporah back to her father. The text does not indicate why. Perhaps it had to do with his perception that the rigors of confronting Pharaoh would be overwhelming and they would be safer with Jethro. There may have also been issues related to their being foreigners in the Israelite context. Moses knew what it felt like to be an outsider, as the name of his first son, Gershom, testifies. The text emphasizes at this point the identities of Moses' wife and children.

A focus on the outsider status of these people sets the stage for the narrative to follow. This was a wonderful conversion story. Jethro heard of all that the Lord had done for Israel in bringing them out of Egypt and immediately gave testimony to the greatness of God above all other gods, echoing the line in the song of Moses "Who is like you, O LORD, among the gods?" (Ex 15:11). His allegiance to the God of Israel was expressed by his bringing a burnt offering as well as other sacrifices. The purpose of the burnt offering was to atone for sin in general (Lev 1:4). Together with Aaron, the priest of Israel, this priest of Midian ate in the presence of the God.

As perhaps a new convert, Jethro contributed to the community almost immediately. Seeing the congestion created by the large numbers of people coming to Moses with legal disputes, he gave Moses some practical advice on delegating responsibility. The qualifications of those chosen were important: They were to fear God, be people of truth and hate dishonest gain.

While this narrative ends with Jethro's return home, that seems to have been temporary as he appeared to help Israel again after their Sinai sojourn (Num 10:29-32).

At Mount Sinai (Ex 19:1—40:38)

Preparations to Receive the Covenant (Ex 19)
Once Moses and the Israelites arrived at the mountain of God, there were prepara-

tions that needed to take place prior to the encounter between God and the covenant people. Moses' role as intermediary is striking; he was up and down the mountain multiple times as he communicated God's promises as well as the procedures for purification to the Israelites and their expressed intention to be obedient to God. Paul noted that the law was put into effect by angels through a mediator (Gal 3:19; see also Acts 7:53 on the role of the angels), referring to the activities of Moses in this setting.

The promises of God followed a reiteration of God's strong care for them, having borne them on eagle's wings to their present safe haven. This image stems from the care a mother eagle gives to her young when teaching them to fly (Deut 32:11-12). These promises set Israel apart from all nations; if they were obedient to the covenant, they would be his treasured possession, kingdom of priests and a holy nation. These phrases identify members of the new covenant community in Christ (1 Pet 2:9; Rev 5:10).

Meeting with God was not to be dealt with casually. The people had to purify themselves, representative of their being holy and set apart. This involved washing their clothes and setting boundaries around the mountain to prevent them from going up until the sounding of the ram's horn. They were also told to abstain from sexual relations, which resulted in a temporary state of uncleanness (Lev 15:18).

The descent of God on the third day was preceded by thunder, lightning, a thick cloud and a loud trumpet blast. When God descended on the mountain, it was amid billowing smoke, in fire like that of a raging furnace and violent trembling of the mountain. These were phenomena to inspire the greatest dread and humility, recognizing the immensity of the God who controlled them. God chose to be manifested through these powerful expressions as the framework for articulating his word so that none should forget that, even as the word was graciously given to establish the relationship, God was unquestionably the Sovereign of the entire observable world. God did come down, an expression of condescension, but the people were called to meet him in humble fear.

Several times in this context, priests are distinguished as a separate entity from the people. While the descendants of Aaron were not officially designated as priests until Moses received instructions on the mountain, nevertheless the Israelites would have been familiar with the role inside and outside their cultural context. Jethro, for example, was a priest of Midian, and Egypt had a whole class of priests.

The author of Hebrews set the terror inspired by this drama in contrast to the joy of approaching Mount Zion, the heavenly Jerusalem, and the city of the living God through Jesus, the mediator of the new covenant (Heb 12:18-24). Nevertheless, that writer knew that the holy nature of God had not changed one iota and urged his audience to worship God with fear and awe because God is a consuming fire (Heb 12:28-29).

The Ten Words and the People's Response (Ex 20)

With Exodus 20, the genre changes from narrative about God's activities to primarily the instructive words (torah) of God. Torah reveals God's holiness by indicating that there are absolute standards of right and wrong and that punishment will be forthcoming when those moral absolutes are violated. It repeatedly calls for people to be holy as God is holy, and it articulates purity and cleanliness standards as symbolic of life lived in the presence of God. Torah reveals the depths of human sinfulness as it is painfully evident that those standards are repeatedly broken. Because torah demon-strates what sin is and how completely humans are captured by it, it serves to lead to Christ (Gal 3:24; see also Rom 7:7-13). In addition to these soteriological purposes, torah also sets the basic standards by which given social units function. Finally, Hebrews 10:1 suggests that what is evident of righteousness and goodness in the articulated torah is a shadow of the perfection that is to come. Redeemed humankind can see in torah an initial expression of the justice that will prevail when this world's injustices have finally been overcome.

These instructions relate to every area of life and may be generally addressed within the framework of three categories. The first is moral torah, which makes demands of the individual heart, mind and will. Summarized in the Ten Commandments and parts of Leviticus 19, the moral torah stands for all time and crosses cultural and temporal boundaries. Second, civil torah structures societal conduct and provides for proper administration of justice. The individual forms of some of these may change from the specific biblical articulation given the particular society, but the general principles remain the same because every social unit is made up of sinful humans. Actions that violate the moral torah may end up in courts, thus crossing into the civil sphere. The third category is ritual or ceremonial torah, which helps the covenant community understand what it means to approach a holy God in worship and makes community members aware that all of life is conducted in the presence of God.

When Jesus was asked which commandment was the most important, his response acknowledged that two fundamental principles summarize the Torah and the Prophets. He first said, "Love the Lord your God with all your heart, and with all your soul, and with all your mind, and with all your strength," following it with "Love your neighbor as yourself" (Mk 12:28-34; see also Mt 22:34-40; Lk 10:25-27). These distinctions can be seen in the Ten Commandments as well. The first four of the Ten Commandments address the relationship of humans to God, indicating God's sole right as Creator to the worship and undivided adoration of his people. The last six deal with horizontal relationships, compactly articulating the absolute justice and goodness that must attend all human interactions. In all of them, love is to be the dominating intention. While these commandments have prohibitions in them, they are designed primarily to direct love to the proper object by ruling out those things that quench or distort love.

All of the commandments were addressed to members of the community of Israel with singular forms of the verbs. Each individual was to hear and obey, and the community was to be of one heart and mind. The first and most important commandment was that there be no other gods before the Lord. They had been living for centuries in Egypt, where they were surrounded by elements of nature that were deified. They would be moving into the land of Canaan, where the same practices were evident. They were to be different in that their allegiance to and trust in the Lord was to be singular.

The second commandment against making idols was a specific application of the first. They were not to make images, bow down to them or serve them. This applied to any of the elements of nature that so easily became objects of worship, and the restriction is comprehensive. An idol reduced God to something that could be managed for the self-satisfaction of the one who exploited the idol. That this was continuously a sore temptation into which Israel fell was evident throughout their history. It would be their heinous idolatry that repeatedly brought judgment on them, culminating in the exile from the land. While other gods are nothing (1 Cor 8:5-6), worship directed to idols is nevertheless offered to demons (1 Cor 10:19-20; Deut 32:16, 17). The paradoxical tendency to rely on things that humans make and control transcends all cultures. Colossians 3:5 indicates that greed is idolatry.

God, who had bound his people to himself with covenant love, was jealous and would punish those who abused his covenant love and refused to be devoted exclusively to him. This sobering statement of punishment visited to the third and fourth generations of those who hate God is countered by the promise of unfailing covenant love *(hesed)* to thousands (of generations) of those who love God and keep his commandments. In this single verse the justice and the mercy of God are evident. Severe consequences often accompany choices to live in rebellion and rejection of God. These are sadly not limited to any given individual but affect a wide range of people. Often children are the tragic victims of these choices.

A literal translation of the third commandment reads "You shall not lift up the name of the Lord your God to emptiness because God will not hold guiltless the one who lifts up his name to emptiness." Just as an idol or an image trivialized the person of God, so frivolous use of his name was a terribly serious affront to the glory and majesty of God. God's name must be reverenced. Infractions of this commandment occur with sad frequency within the believing community that too often lightly and frivolously jokes about God.

In the parallel articulation of the Ten Commandments in Deuteronomy 5, several important differences occur in regard to the sabbath. In Exodus, the people were told to "remember" the sabbath; in Deuteronomy, the word is "keep." Remembering meant sustaining continuity with their past traditions; keeping implied protecting and guarding for the future. In conjunction with this, the reason given in Exodus for remembering the sabbath was that God had rested after creation. He had set the day apart and blessed it. They were to remember and do the same. In Deuteronomy 5:15 the sabbath was to be kept holy because it commemorated God's rescue of Israel from Egypt. Because the exodus event is the great paradigm for redemption that Christians experience in the risen Christ, it is not surprising that Jesus infused the sabbath with even greater meaning when he said, "The sabbath was made for humankind, and not humankind for the sabbath, so the Son of Man is lord even of the sabbath" (Mk 2:27-28). Jesus did not lessen the importance or value of sabbath, but as with many of the issues of law, he redirected the attention of the people to the necessary heart attitude of reverent worship to the Creator and Redeemer.

The fifth commandment is in a pivotal position between the first group that addresses humankind's relationship with God and the second that attends to interactions on the human level. Parents bring new life in the world, and they are to be accorded corresponding honor. This is a comment on the value of life and the order established by God, whom parents represent to their children. While this is a call to children to hold their parents in a special position, it likewise is a call to parents to be godlike and worthy of the honor. The responsibility of that position is addressed by Paul (Eph 6:2-4). After observing that this was the first commandment with a promise, he indicated that the nature of the parental obligation was essentially to follow the pattern established in Deuteronomy 6:5-9. It should be from parents that children learn how to love and serve God with their whole being. Clearly, human parents fail in this enterprise, some more drastically than others. Part of the honor accorded them is, in those cases, forgiveness and exerting every effort to live at peace (cf. Heb 12:14). Maligning parents who have been a severe detriment in one's life only leads to bitterness. It is significant that the punishment for cursing parents was death (Ex 21:17), and rebellion and disobedience received a like punishment (Deut 21:18-21).

The sixth commandment prohibits murder. Murder is the most drastic antihuman action, violating the image of God. Satan was a murderer, knowing that introducing sin meant introducing death. The term used is specific, referring to intentional and de-

---

Adultery

Adultery is forbidden by the Mosaic law (Ex 20:14) and Jesus' teachings (Mt 19) for men and for women. Along with murder, lying and idolatry—with which it is often linked—it is regarded as a heinous sin punishable by stoning. The grammar of the biblical narrative, however, suggests an underlying gender inequality. A woman's purity is more easily suspect than a man's, evidenced by the uncleanness of menstrual blood (e.g., Lev 22:10) and childbirth, and by the sense that a woman's purity belongs to the honor of the men related to her (*see also* Leviticus; Purity Laws Related to Women). Note, for example, the extreme vengeance of Dinah's brothers when she is raped at Shechem. Similarly the sin of adultery is most commonly considered a sin against a husband's honor (e.g., Lev 18:7). This same taint is suggested by laws that prevent a priest from marrying a woman sullied by marriage or prostitution (Lev 21:15).

Although the law refers always to men committing adultery with another's wife, adultery and prostitution are frequently mentioned together and thus associated with women (e.g., Jer 5:7). In the Prophets the symbol of Israel's unfaithfulness becomes the adulterous woman, and this symbol resonates its charges through Israel's travail and exile (e.g., Jer 3:8). Moreover, Old Testament men appear to be peculiarly insensitive to conviction of their sexual sin, unless confronted directly—witness David and Judah.

The double standard is further suggested by laws that require a virgin woman and her parents to bear the burden of proof of her purity (Deut 22:20-21) and by the ubiquity of male polygamy (*see* Polygamy). Moreover, the woman caught in adultery is brought to Jesus without her male partner (Jn 8:3).

Unless one believes that women were the primary adulterers in the ancient world, the close linking of adultery and women must be regarded as a part of a general cultural and religious patriarchy that defines women in terms of sexual status (*see* Numbers).

The larger trajectory of biblical history, however, suggests a profound reversal. The sons of Tamar and Rahab are a part of the genealogy of Christ (Gen 38; Josh 2; Mt 1:3, 5). Christ promises that the "last will be first" (Mt 19:30). And Christ not only loved and forgave the woman caught in adultery but also died outside the city in a place of horror and shame, sharing in the plight of shamed women throughout history.

Eschatologically the New Testament makes explicit what is hinted at the by the prophets—the restoration, in which the new Jerusalem is the bride of Christ (Rev 19:7) and becomes the vindication of Israel and simultaneously of all shamed women. In the new order the bride awaits the bridegroom, but no examination of virginity, no shame is in prospect—only the marriage supper of the Lamb (Rev 19:9). The images of women's adultery and idolatry, which resonated through the Old Testament, are overturned, to be replaced by those of love and honor in the beloved.

NICOLA HOGGARD CREEGAN

---

liberate taking of human life. It is not the same word as "to kill." Subsequent stipulations in the Torah deal with such issues as manslaughter, going to war and capital punishment. The punishment for murder was death (Ex 21:12).

With the seventh commandment, God forbade adultery (*see* Adultery), which is specifically violation of the marriage covenant. Violation of the love bond and that intimate union leads only to disaster, graphically illustrated on the human level in Proverbs 5:1-23; 6:20-29; 7:1-27. Marriage also represented in earthly symbols the intimate covenant love between God and his people, and broken marriages represented the spiritual adultery of the people of Israel (Hos 1—2; Mal 2:13-16). All manner of unacceptable sexual practices were rampant in the land that the Israelites were going to possess, and God warned them soberly against these perversions, stating unequivocally that they defiled the land (Lev 18). As with all of the commandments up to this point, adultery was punishable by death (Lev 20:10).

The eighth commandment prohibited stealing. Underlying this commandment is the intrinsic value of persons and property. While God is the ultimate Possessor of all creation, God has given to humans stewardship and ownership of specific aspects of the creation, and that ownership is not to be violated. The penalty for property theft was restitution (Ex 22:1-4). If, however, a person was stolen (kidnapping), the penalty was death (Ex 21:16).

The ninth commandment addressed giving false testimony against a fellow Israelite and had specific application to witnesses in court. The penalty for false witnesses was severe (Deut 19:16-21). That lying in general, however, is a heinous offense is evident throughout the rest of the Scriptures. Distortions of the truth lead to ruined reputations, lack of trust, irreconcilable pain and loss of life. The book of Proverbs repeatedly warns of the damage that false speech does. Jesus struck at the root of the problem of lying in calling the devil the father of lies and a murderer from the beginning (Jn 8:44). The end of liars, along with such offenders as murderers, sexually immoral and idolators, will be the lake of fire (Rev 21:8).

The final commandment against coveting completes the circle created by this comprehensive statement of ethics. Coveting means having an insatiable craving to possess that which does not rightfully belong to a given individual. It means desiring to serve oneself at all costs. This is clearly a violation of the first two commandments. It is the underlying attitude that can so easily surface in acts of murder, adultery, theft and false witness.

Having seen and heard the manifestation of God's presence and voice, the people were afraid and asked Moses to mediate from that point on. Moses attested to the great value of fear. It would protect them and keep them from sin. Then, while the people remained at a distance, Moses approached the thick darkness. Evidence of the paradox of God's presence and continuing mystery, here the thick cloud shrouded his manifestation, so often portrayed as blazing fire.

The Covenant Stipulations (Ex 20:22—23:33)

In these chapters, the categories of torah that are primarily represented are civil and ritual/ceremonial, with a heavier emphasis on the former. The primary social issues addressed are the treatment of Hebrew slaves, personal injuries, theft and property damage, sexual abuses, mistreatment of the disenfranchised (*see* Yahweh's Concern for the Disenfranchised) and fundamental practices of justice.

It is not surprising that the slavery issue would be a prominent one (*see* Ancient and Modern Slavery). First, the Israelites had just emerged from a context of slavery in which they had been harshly treated. Furthermore, the master/servant relationship was a part of the ancient socioeconomic structure, and there was the provision for selling oneself into bondage in order to deal with unmanageable debt. Therefore, principles for proper treatment of Hebrew slaves were essential. The Hebrew word is *ebed*, which may mean either "slave" or "servant." The point is that it is opposite of "free."

In a number of these social contexts, gender made a difference. This may be partly due to the cultural conditions, in which it was not possible for a woman to live independently. The protection of some household provided by the father, a husband or a master was necessary. The text deals with some of these combinations, one of which addresses the fact that a man might sell his daughter to be a servant. Although there are ambiguities in the passage, several principles are evident. First, she was not to be cast off, either by being sold to foreigners or by becoming marginalized and abused in the extended family context. Second, her lot was determined by the men who made up her social context.

In the broad category of personal injury and abuse, the matter of intentionality was prominent. If an individual died as the result of a premeditated attack, the killer was to be put to death. If "God lets it happen" (Ex 21:13), then there was a system to protect the slayer from those who would take revenge. This is briefly mentioned in the exodus context and developed significantly in conjunction with the criteria for the cities of refuge (Num 35:6-34; Deut 19:1-13).

Dishonoring parents by physical or verbal abuse was punishable by death, as was stealing persons. It is noteworthy that the same life value is put on women and men in every category of personal injury. Where there were differences was in regard to whether the victim was a slave or not. In cases of personal injury, balance in the administration of justice was essential. The measure-for-measure principle is stressed in this context as well as in Leviticus 24:17-22 and Deuteronomy 19:16-21. It did not imply that literal hands and eyes were to be removed but that the punishment must fit the crime. That was to avoid the all-too-human tendency to escalate the stakes in taking revenge when a wrong was committed. Even in this context, the text recognizes that compensatory payments were appropriate rather than strict measure for measure. These guidelines were established for court procedures. Jesus addressed the personal need to eschew any desire for retaliation by giving even more (Mt 5:38-42).

The injury case cited as foundational to the measure-for-measure principle was the woman who was struck in a fight. It is complicated by the possibilities that she was pregnant and that as a result of the blow, "her children" came out. If there was no serious injury, the punishment was a fine. Serious injury necessitated just retribution. While there is some potential ambiguity in the text, it seems likely that the injury addressed in this case is that which occurred to the woman. The fine applied to the prematurely born or miscarried children.

Because the society was an agriculturally based one, the cases regarding theft and property damage deal with ownership and responsibility for animals and land produce. While theft in general meant a twofold restitution, the relative value and necessity of certain animals meant that the payback when they were stolen was significantly more; five head of cattle for an ox and four sheep for one sheep. This principle of multiple restitution was to serve as a deterrent, and if the thief could not make the payment, being sold into slavery was his end. Additional cases of negligence and loss round out the material on property damage.

The instruction regarding sexual misconduct is limited in this context. In the first case, a man who deceived a virgin and slept with her was to take responsibility by paying the price and marrying her. The same stipulation is part of a much larger discussion of sexual improprieties in Deuteronomy 22:13-30. Likewise, the brief mention of the death penalty for one having sexual relations with an animal is only one of numerous abuses detailed in Leviticus 18.

On the basis of their bitter experiences as aliens in Egypt, the Israelites were enjoined to treat properly those in that marginalized condition. Further, just as God had heard the cry of the Israelites when they were in Egypt, he promised to hear and respond to the cry of disenfranchised persons who might in the future be oppressed by the Israelites. Justice is profoundly evident in God's response. If the Israelites treated widows or orphans unjustly, the number of widows and orphans in Israel would increase because God would kill the malefactors. Likewise, those who were financially disadvantaged were not to be abused, either in financial dealings or in matters of justice.

The justice principles that close this section on social and civil torah acknowledge the fundamental problems of effecting justice in a fallen world where lying, peer pressure, hatred and greed too often reign. The call for truthfulness as the basis of justice is compelling.

Indicative of the fact that the categories of torah overlap, presented among the instructions that deal with justice issues are important prohibitions of alien religious practices, including sorcery and sacrifice to and invocation of other gods. The command not to blaspheme may refer to God or to "judges," as the word *elohim* can mean both, and in this context it may have primary reference to the latter. The Israelites were also reminded to give to the Lord their firstborn and to demonstrate their separation by not eating improperly killed meat. The obligation to ensure that these regulations were kept most likely fell primarily on women, who were responsible for preparing food.

The sabbath guidelines, summarized at this point (Ex 23:10-12), also demonstrated the integration of ritual and social torah. Presented first in this context, the seventh year practices had social implications, including provision for the poor. These are expanded significantly in Deuteronomy 15, and Leviticus 25 addresses the seventh year and the Jubilee regulations. Likewise, even the command to observe one day in seven was for the refreshment of the members of extended household units that would most need it, the slaves, the aliens and even the working animals.

Moses then briefly summarized what came to be known as the three pilgrim festivals. Each of these is described at much greater length, and the alternative names appear in the parallel passages (Lev 23; Num 28:16—29:40; Deut 16:1-17). All of them were celebrations of the various ways in which God provided for them, and celebrants were to bring something back to God; they were not to appear before him empty-handed. Four ritual guidelines follow. First, they were not to offer sacrificial blood, the cleansing agent, with anything that contained yeast because the latter symbolized that which was old and evil. Second, the fat portion, always given over to the Lord (Lev 3:9-17), was not to be left until morning. That would represent a disdain for what belonged to the Lord. Third, the best of the first fruits belonged to God. Fourth, a young goat was not to be cooked in the milk of its mother. This last stipulation appears three times in the torah (see also Ex 34:26 and Deut 14:21). None of the references gives a reason as to why this was forbidden. It may have been a Canaanite religious practice or a magical rite. The Israelites were called to be separate from such practices.

In light of the preceding comment, it is interesting that the primary function of the accompanying angel was to bring them into the land inhabited by indigenous people groups who were idolatrous and to remove those peoples. This angel was intimately identified with the Lord. He was to be obeyed, and with him resided the power to forgive or not to forgive because the name of the Lord was "in the midst of him." The Israelites were called to worship the Lord God and, as a result, experience his blessings. This brief statement of blessings for covenant obedience is a microcosm of those articulated in Leviticus 26:1-13 and Deuteronomy 28:1-14.

Covenant Ratification (Ex 24)

The directive of the Lord to Moses made a distinction between him, the other ceremony participants and the people in general. Moses alone was allowed to approach the Lord; the others were to worship from a distance. Nevertheless, those who were invited to go up to the Lord were granted a vision of the God of Israel. Under his feet was something like a pavement of sapphire, clear as the sky. Although abbreviated, this corresponds to significant aspects of the visions of Ezekiel and John (Ezek 1; Rev 4).

In preparation for the ceremony, Moses repeated to the people what the Lord had said, they promised to be obedient, and he wrote down the contents of the covenant. He then built an altar, setting up the symbolic twelve stones and having young Israelite men sacrifice burnt offerings and fellowship offerings.

The purpose of the whole burnt offering was to atone for sin in general (Lev 1:4), while the fellowship offering was an expression of gratitude and, by virtue of its name (*zebahim shelamim*, "offerings of peace or wholeness"), a symbol of restored relationship. It was significant that the participants partook of the fellowship offering in God's presence following the burnt offering. The blood of these sacrifices was the central feature. It represented life given to make atonement (cf. Lev 17:11). Half of the blood was sprinkled on the people and half on the altar. Hebrews 9:19-22 re-presents this ceremony, expanding on the list of objects that were sprinkled with the blood and focusing on the blood as the means of cleansing and as necessary for forgiveness.

Following the communal meal, Moses ascended the mountain on the seventh day to receive the written torah on tablets of stone. He remained on the mountain for forty days and nights. The purpose of this time with the Lord was to receive the instructions for the construction of the tabernacle and the preparation of the priesthood (cf. Ex 25:40; 26:30; 27:8).

Instructions for the Tabernacle and Priesthood (Ex 25:1—31:11); Establishing the Tabernacle (Ex 35:4—40:38)

The great importance of the tabernacle and high priest's attire and functions is evident by the amount of space devoted to presenting the instructions and completion. The two sections about the sanctuary are separated by the devastating incident of the golden calf, in which Israel broke the fundamental bond of the covenant. Yet God determined to dwell in their presence, and the carrying out of the instructions emphasized that mercy. These two sections are treated together for the comprehensive picture of the tabernacle and its ministers.

The terms used to designate the place are instructive. First, it was called a sanctuary *(miqdash)*, a place set apart. The construction of the courtyard around the tabernacle created that defined space. At the same time, it was called a tabernacle *(mishkan)*, which means "dwelling place." God had chosen to dwell in their midst. In this sense, the tabernacle prefigured the incarnation of the Word of God. John 1:14 literally says that "the Word became flesh and tented among us." John continues with explicit reference to seeing the glory of God, clearly drawing his readers' attention back to the manifestations of divine glory in conjunction with the tabernacle. Finally, it was also called the "tent of meeting," indicative of God's intention to meet his people where they were. All three terms appear together in Exodus 39:40-41; see also Exodus 25:8-9.

The tabernacle was a tremendous visual lesson on the implications of approaching the holy covenant God. It was exquisitely beautiful and representative of the beauty and perfection of God, who had come to dwell in their midst. Planning and executing all of the beautiful components of the tabernacle were done with great care. The Holy Spirit filled Bezalel, the artist who oversaw the work. God appointed his assistant, Oholiab, and gave skill to all the artisans. At the same time, approach could not be casual or haphazard. The pathway was via blood sacrifice and subsequent symbolic cleansing. The process of taking the life of the animal, the mess, the bloodshed and the pain, were all grim reminders that sin is a horrifying and dreadful thing in the presence of God.

The chest or ark, described first, was the sole object in the Most Holy Place and held the tablets of the testimony inside. These tablets were the central feature because they contained the permanent statement of the covenant relationship. At certain points in Israel's history, this chest would also hold the pot of manna and Aaron's rod (Ex 16:34; Num 17:10; Heb 9:4; see 1 Kings 8:9; 2 Chron 5:10). The ark had a cover, above which extended the wings of two cherubim that faced each other. At this covering the Lord met with Moses, and when Moses entered the tent of meeting, he heard the voice of God speaking to him from between the two cherubim above the atonement cover (Ex 25:22; cf. Ex 33:11; Num 7:89). The cherubim figures were representative of the celestial beings who stood guard at the separating point between the throne of God and other spheres (cf. Gen 3:24; Ezek 1; 10).

Three additional objects were in the holy place of the tabernacle. The first was the table that held the bread of the Presence, twelve loaves of bread that were to be regularly set out before the Lord on behalf of the Israelites. Accompanying the table were plates, ladles, pitchers and bowls for the pouring out of offerings. The second was an elaborate lampstand that had six branches extending out from a central shaft, three on each side. All together there were seven lamps on the stand, which were to be tended and kept burning continually. There is possibly a symbolic connection between the lamps and the Spirit (see Zech 4:1-14; Rev 1). The third article was the altar for incense, which was positioned in front of curtain separating the Holy Place from the Most Holy Place. The incense was to be burned regularly every morning and evening. Burning the incense came to be symbolic of prayers of the saints (Ps 141:2; Rev 5:8).

Sacred articles that were placed in the courtyard of the tabernacle included the horned altar for the sacrifices and basin. The "horn" on each of the four corners was an extension upward beyond the top surface of the altar and likely served the practical purpose of containing the wood that was heaped up on the altar to keep the sacrificial offerings burning. It also came to be associated with a place of refuge from someone seeking to take a person's life (1 Kings 1:49-53). The basin and its stand were made of bronze, and specifically the material came from the mirrors of the host of women (*tsob'oth*) who served (*tsab'u*) at the entrance to the tent of meeting. That the gifts and skills of women played a significant part in the development of the tabernacle is clear (Ex 35:22, 25-26; 36:6). The word *tsaba'* often appears in a related plural form in conjunction with the "Lord of hosts" (*tseba'oth*) and has connection with war and cultic activities. The service of the Gershonites, descendants of Levi, was described by this term and was conducted at the tent of meeting (Num 4:23; cf. 8:24). A potentially ominous side of this activity is evident in 1 Samuel 2:22, where Eli's sons were sleeping with the women who were serving at the entrance of the tabernacle. The basin was for Aaron and his sons to wash their hands and feet before entering the tent of meeting. There was a "path" into the presence of God. First, sacrificial blood was shed at the altar. Then, the cleansing of the basin was necessary, and finally, the cloud of incense preceded the priest into the presence of God and protected him.

Anointing oil, incense and salt were important ingredients. Very likely the command to salt the incense is similar to the injunction in Leviticus 2:13 to season all the offerings with salt so that the salt of the covenant would not be lacking. Because salt preserves and enhances flavor, it was an appropriate additive to offerings that represented the relationship with the everlasting covenant God.

The maintenance of the elaborate cultic ritual would be accomplished by the half-shekel payment. It was to be collected in conjunction with the census but had a distinctly religious significance, because it was a ransom for the life of the one paying it and was called atonement money. While the original statement sounds like a one-time payment, it was collected at later points in history when the temple was being repaired (2 Kings 12:4; 2 Chron 24:9; 34:9).

Because the mediating role of the high priest was of central importance, the descriptive material in the text is primarily given over to the attire of the high priest, much of which was symbolic of his representing the people of Israel before God. On the ephod, Aaron bore the names of the children of Israel before the Lord as a memorial. The breastpiece was a square piece of material folded double and worn over the heart. It was made to be attached to the ephod and had twelve stones, one for each of the tribes. The Urim and the Thummim were put into the breastpiece, and they were to serve as a means for making decisions. It is not clear how they functioned or even what the words mean. The traditional suggestion is that the words meant "lights" (from *'or*) and "perfections" (from *tom*) and these objects worked in a way similar to the casting of lots. An indication of their use appears in Numbers 27:21 regarding Eleazar, who would obtain decisions from the Lord for Joshua by means of the Urim. It is also likely that the command to take judicial issues to the priests who would give decisions in the Lord's presence may also refer to their use of the Urim and Thummim (Deut 17:9-10). It was the ephod that enabled David to inquire of the Lord (1 Sam 23:4-6; 30:7-8). Not having any word from the Lord via prophets or the Urim is what drove Saul in desperation to the witch of Endor in his final hours (1 Sam 28:6). The Urim and Thummim were still expected to function after the return from exile (Ezra 2:63; Neh 7:65).

The high priest was also attired in a robe of blue with pomegranates and bells alternating around the hem. This was so that "his sound will be heard as he comes in to the sanctuary before the Lord, and as he goes out, that he will not die" (Ex 28:35). The text seems to indicate that God would be attentive to the sound of the high priest in his representative dress. The whole worship and ritual process was one of communication utilizing all of the senses, and that communication went both ways. Thus to speak of sounds and smells as being appealing to God recognizes something profoundly rich about sense in the expressed relationship between the Creator and his creatures.

Once dressed, the priests were consecrated for service. The process is described in detail in Exodus 29, and that material should be read in conjunction with Leviticus 8 for further definition and elaboration. The bull was offered first as a sin offering for the priest in order that, as intermediary for the people, his sins should be dealt with first. The first of the two rams was to serve as the burnt offering, consumed on the altar. The second ram was the ordination offering, and in addition to its blood being sprinkled on all sides of the altar, some of it was put on the right ear lobes, the right thumbs and the right big toes of Aaron and his sons. Traditionally this was to represent their need for care in how they listened, in what they did and in how they would conduct themselves. This procedure, however, applied not only to priests who were being ordained. When a person was cleansed from an infectious skin disease, he was to bring a guilt offering, and its blood was also put by the priest on the right ear, the right thumb and the right big toe of the individual whose cleansing was being celebrated (Lev 14:28). These actions symbolized the comprehensive efficacy of the blood of the sacrifice to make the person presentable before God.

The fat of the offerings was always the Lord's and was a pleasant aroma to the Lord. This expression is used more than forty times in the text, almost always in conjunction with God's acceptance of the offerings. Thanksgiving and propitiation are associated with the expression, with the former being more prominent. It is a profound acknowledgment of God's participation in accepting the offerings from his people. Idols were unable to smell (Ps 115:6); by way of contrast, God could, and God articulated acceptance of the worship of sincere hearts.

For generations to come, the burnt offering of two lambs was to be made twice daily, once in the morning and once at evening, at the entrance to the tent of meeting. This would indicate the continuing relationship between God and his people at that place where he determined to dwell and where he would meet with them. The tabernacle was set up on the first day of the first month of the second year. Thus it was ready for the celebration of Passover.

The Sign of the Covenant (Ex 31:12-18; 35:1-3)

Having stated the covenant stipulations, celebrated its confirmation and prepared for the ongoing rituals of approaching God, the importance of the sign of this covenant was again emphasized. First, keeping the sabbath was to be a distinctive sign, one that would remind the people that God was the Lord and that he set them apart, just as they were to set apart the sabbath. Furthermore, its eternal nature is stressed. They were to observe it as a lasting covenant and a sign forever, and the reason given for its observance was lodged in the act of creation. The sober side, articulated three times in these two passages, was that those who desecrated the sabbath were to die.

The Golden Calf and Its Aftermath (Ex 32:1—34:35)

It is a tragic irony that while Moses was on the mountain receiving the instructions regarding the tabernacle and the special position and function of Aaron as the high priest, Aaron was swept up into making and ministering before an idol, breaking the second commandment. He built an altar in conjunction with the calf and proclaimed a feast to the Lord, clearly an abuse of the name of the Lord. Even more insidious, his language about it made it sound like something good. Finally, he allowed the people to get wildly out of control.

God's words to Moses contained an ominous distancing. He called the Israelites "*your* people whom *you* brought up out of Egypt" (Ex 32:7). They had rejected his covenant and him by making the idol; he declared his intention to destroy them and make Moses into a great nation. In response, however, to the plea of Moses, God chose not to bring on the people the disaster he had promised. The Hebrew word *naham* means to change one's course of action. It can apply to humans and to God and with regard to the former is generally translated "repent." In regard to God's "repentance," it means that his intention, articulated at a given point in response to specific circumstances, has been altered best to address current developments (cf. Gen 6:6-7 ["was grieved" in NIV]; 1 Sam 15:11; Jon 4:2). In ways that are beyond human comprehension, this is part of the complexity of sovereignty.

When Moses descended from the mountain he carried the two tablets engraved with the writing of God. Seeing that the people had rebelled so blatantly against the covenant, he symbolically broke the tablets of the covenant. Then he burned the calf, ground it and made the people drink the powder mixed with the water. The possible parallels with the later legislation regarding the wife suspected of adultery (Num 5:5-31) are striking.

Aaron did not manifest great strength of character. When Moses asked what the people had done to make him succumb to the pressure, his response set the responsibility almost entirely on them and their fundamentally evil nature. Worse yet, he reduced what had been his active role in fashioning the calf to a passive one: "I cast it into the fire and this calf came out" (Ex 32:24).

The results of the people's rebellion and Aaron's capitulation were horrifying. The Lord called on those who were faithful to kill the idolaters. The Levites, Aaron's tribe, responded, and three thousand people died. In addition, the Lord inflicted a plague on the people. The choice made by the tribe of Levi was not an easy one. Because they chose what was right, they had to kill those who apparently were continuing in flagrant disobedience. This would be a horrifying task and was a severe punishment for failure to stand for righteousness in the first place.

The weight of responsibility felt by Aaron was undoubtedly crushing. Yet, in the sovereign workings of God, he would be the ideal high priest. He would know God's mercy and grace in a truly compelling way. Hebrews 5:2 is an acknowledgment of the reality of Aaron's situation. Because of his weakness, he would be able to deal gently with those who strayed. This constant reminder would spare him from any vestiges of temptation to pride. Moses continued in his office as intermediary, making a tremendous statement of willingness to sacrifice himself: "And now, if you will forgive their sin. . . . But if not, erase me, please, from your book which you have written" (Ex 32:32).

After the uncertainty created by this horrifying episode, Moses sought reassurance from God. He expressed his desire to know more of God's ways and reiterated his plea that God go with them, even though God had threatened not to do so. Because Moses found favor with God, the Lord promised to grant Moses' request. At that point, Moses, who already spoke face to face with God and who had entered into the cloud, requested to see the glory of God. *Glory* refers to the visible manifestation of the complete power, perfection and radiance of God's person.

Moses was allowed to experience what he was capable of seeing without being taken from this world by the overwhelming presence of God. Exercising abundant mercy, God compassionately hid Moses in the cleft of a rock and covered him "with his hand" while God's goodness passed in front of Moses. Moses' intimate interactions with God resulted in a brilliance so fearsome that Moses had to veil his face before the rest of the Israelites.

God's multiple responses to Moses are foundational to the knowledge of the divine character as it impacts the rest of the biblical text. He called Moses back to the mountain in order to give a second time the tablets of the covenant that had been broken. In an astounding demonstration of condescension, God came down in the cloud of glory and stood with Moses. God proclaimed the covenant name, Yahweh, signifying his intention to continue the relationship, which would be characterized by compassion, mercy, patience, unfailing covenant love and forgiveness. These elements of the Lord's name were repeated throughout the record of the history of Israel as they persisted in demonstrating their human failings and as God lavished on them mercy and forgiveness. At the same time, it was just as important to declare God's justice; he would punish those who were guilty. Only there could rest the true goodness and integrity of his name and character. The reward and punishment aspect as stated in verse 7 is a direct reflection of the covenant promise of Exodus 20:5-6.

Moses made a final statement of his plea that God personally accompany them, and the Lord stated a determination to do so. God promised to help them conquer the land and warned against making treaties with the inhabitants and succumbing to their idolatrous practices. God restated significant elements of the torah, with a distinct emphasis on ritual aspects that would take place in the context of the sanctuary. This too was a reassurance that God's presence would continue to be with them. Then the Lord told Moses to write the words of the covenant that were the declaration and assurance of the relationship.

In closing, it is important to ponder the condition of this people who had fallen so far and the unfailing grace of their God. It is no different from that experienced by believers, representatives of frail humanity, through the ages. Moses, as their leader, was painfully aware of the seriousness of their condition before the Lord. He persisted in his expressed desire for assurance because he knew the reality of the wrath of the Lord against sin. He did not take lightly or easily God's grace. He fasted again for forty days and forty nights (Deut 9:9, 18), recognizing his need to be prepared to be the covenant mediator, declaring the Word of God. This event of his life was a prototype of that of Jesus Christ, who, in preparation for his role as the perfect mediator of the new covenant, would fast in the Judean wilderness for forty days and nights. And so, just as the Ten Words were written again, graciously given to instruct and restore the Israelites to a right relationship with their covenant Lord, the Word Incarnate came to instruct and fully restore fallen humankind.

Bibliography. J. J. Davis, *Moses and the Gods of Egypt: Studies in the Book of Exodus* (Grand Rapids, MI: Baker, 1971); P. Jordan, *Egypt: The Black Land* (Oxford: Phaidon, 1976); B. J. Kemp, *Ancient Egypt: Anatomy of a Civilization* (London: Routledge, 1989); C. Rasmussen, *NIV Atlas of the Bible* (Grand Rapids, MI: Zondervan, 1989); W. A. VanGemeren, gen. ed., *The New International Dictionary of Old Testament Theology and Exegesis*, 5 vols. (Exeter: Paternoster, 1996); R. Youngblood, *Exodus* (Chicago: Moody Press, 1983).

ELAINE A. PHILLIPS

LEVITICUS

Introduction

What has Leviticus to do with women? On first glance it might seem little, if anything. The regulations are placed in the mouth of a man, Moses, and are directed primarily to men. No women play prominent roles in Leviticus as they do in Genesis, Exodus and even Numbers. The book focuses heavily on the role and responsibilities of the Aaronic priests, none of whom were women. Laws about women focus on childbirth and menstruation, the two most intimate and unique aspects of sexuality that set women apart from men, both of which resulted in the epithet *unclean.* And when women vowed themselves to Yahweh, they were valued less than men were.

The fact that Leviticus is perceived to some degree as a man's book is illustrated by the paucity of female commentators. Although several essays and journal articles have been written recently by women, men write more about levitical issues related to women than women do. Women seem to feel distanced from a book that ostensibly legislates their lower status and demeans their essential bodily functions. How can such a book be understood as canonical Scripture? Does it have a message for women today?

Each book of the Torah receives its Hebrew title from the first word or words in the book. The Hebrew title of Leviticus is *wayyiqra',* which means "and he called" (Lev 1:1; translations are the author's unless otherwise noted). When the Hebrew Bible was translated into Greek, the translators assigned titles to the books that reflected their content. Because Leviticus focused on priestly matters, it was given the title *leuitikos* ("priestly [book]"). The Latin Vulgate rendered this *Liber Leviticus,* from which the current English title is derived.

The date and authorship of Leviticus have been debated for some time and are still the subject of much discussion. The traditional view is that Moses wrote the entire book. The book itself designates Moses as the lawgiver through whom Yahweh communicated the decrees (e.g., Lev 1:1; 4:1; 5:14; 6:1, 8, 19; 8:1; 11:1; 12:1). However, when questions arose regarding Mosaic authorship of the entire Torah, Leviticus was questioned as well.

Critical scholarship of the nineteenth and twentieth centuries generally accepted the view popularized by Julius Wellhausen in *Prolegomena to the History of Ancient Israel* (1878). According to this view, the Torah was composed of four sources (J, E, D and P) that were gradually redacted together. Leviticus and other portions of the Torah were the product of a priestly writer (P) who wrote long after Moses. Wellhausen asserted that P was written sometime around 450 B.C. and reflected the priestly interests of the second temple period. References to the tent shrine were thinly veiled anachronisms of the second temple, and the sacrificial system reproduced the highly structured ritual system of the postexilic era. Because Wellhausen believed that religions developed from simple to complex, he assumed that P's complex religious system represented the latest strand of the Torah. This view of the Torah's composition was widely accepted, and even though Wellhausen's dates for the other three sources (J, E and D) were subsequently challenged, the postexilic date of P and therefore Leviticus remained virtually uncontested.

However, the study of comparative religion cast doubt on this scholarly consensus. The institutions once thought to be Israelite creations of a late period were discovered in other ancient Near Eastern societies antecedent to and after the Mosaic period. Highly developed ritual systems and priesthoods were common, and extensive law codes elucidated proper sexual relationships, outlined purification procedures for uncleanness and listed animals acceptable for food and sacrifice. While the existence of ancient Near Eastern parallels did not prove the antiquity of P, since such practices may have continued for some time and influenced P at a later date, the authenticity of Israel's institutions had to be reassessed.

As a result, commentaries on Leviticus increasingly affirm the antiquity of Israel's institutions as depicted in the book, even when a complex composition history is acknowledged (for instance, see Hartley, xxxv-xliii). In addition, recent terminological studies (see Milgrom, 3-35) comparing P with Deuteronomy and Ezekiel may demonstrate that P's composition date is preexilic, dating to the monarchy and the first temple.

The books of the Torah are notoriously difficult to date, and this is especially true of Leviticus, which contains no datable referents to the historical world surrounding it, such as wars, invasions or names of kings. Very little is known about the history of Israel's worship, and reconstructions of it remain speculative. Because interpreters' conclusions are principally determined by their methodological presuppositions, issues of authorship and date will continue to be debated.

The milieu of the ancient Near East provides fertile ground for comparing the institutions and practices prevalent in Leviticus, regardless of when one dates the book. Sacrifice was a common practice in these societies, and sacrifices akin to the ones in Leviticus are evident in other cultures. Priests were expected to maintain a higher degree of sanctity than were laypersons, and strict rules regarding ritual procedures were typical. Animals, particularly pigs and dogs, were regarded as unclean, and sexual discharges and childbirth were ritually regulated. Law codes similar to the ones found in Leviticus demonstrate that other ancient Near Eastern nations had highly developed standards of morality.

Was anything unique to Israel? In terms of practice and procedure Israel's institutions often mirror ancient Near Eastern ones. However, the motivation for Israel's laws is clearly grounded in relationship with Yahweh rather than superstition, demonology or magic, as in some of the other cultures.

Leviticus plays an integral role in the Torah narrative. Its place between Exodus and Numbers is no accident, for it contains information essential for Israel's survival as the people of God. In Exodus, God provided Moses instructions for building a tabernacle where God's presence could dwell in the midst of the people. However, while Moses received these instructions, the people attempted to provide themselves with a symbol of God's presence: the golden calf (Ex 32). In light of their stubborn sinfulness, God refused to abide among the people any longer "lest I destroy you on the way" (Ex 33:3). Moses interceded, focusing on God's merciful and just character (Ex 34:6-7), and God agreed to remain in the midst of the people. However, one question remained unanswered. The people's sinful character had not changed, so how could God possibly dwell in their midst? Leviticus provides the answer.

Although much of Leviticus deals with laws probably addressed to the whole congregation, certain sections focus on regulations about women: Leviticus 12 (the parturient woman), Leviticus 15 (the menstruant and the woman with an abnormal flow), and Leviticus 18 and Leviticus 20 (laws regulating sexual relations). In addition, Leviticus 21 specifies which women priests could marry, Leviticus 22:10-16 outlines rules regarding who may eat of the priestly sacrifices (specifically when a priest's daughter could partake), and Leviticus 27:2-8 details the valuations of women who offered vows. Interspersed throughout the Holiness Code (Lev 17—26) are individual laws about women. These laws and rituals raise interesting questions about the role of women in the Israelite cult and their status in Israelite society, questions that are fraught with difficulty.

The focus of this commentary will be on those sections of Leviticus that deal specifically with women. However, the book will also be considered as a whole, especially in light of its significance to women then and now.

Outline

1:1—7:38	Grace for People with God in Their Midst: The Sacrificial System
8:1—10:20	Mediators to a Holy God: The Inauguration of the Priesthood
11:1—15:33	Is Cleanliness Next to Godliness? The Laws of Purification
16:1-34	Pollution Control: The Day of Atonement
17:1—26:46	Family Values: The Holiness Code
27:1-34	Sanctuary Economics: The Value of Vows

Commentary

How can sinful people live with a holy God in their midst? By becoming pure and holy themselves. And how do they achieve purity and holiness? By observing proper ritual procedures that cleanse and sanctify them and by living according to God's moral standards. Although modern readers may find the ritual instructions tedious to read, the emphasis on order and detail indicates how seriously procedure, decorum and preparation in worship were taken. God's holiness is an awesome and formidable thing—it is not something to approach flippantly or without proper regard for one's own sinful state.

Grace for People with God in Their Midst: The Sacrificial System (Lev 1—7)

The first section of Leviticus is devoted to the most important ritual: sacrifice. Sacrifice served both to atone for sin and as a means of fellowship and devotion. As such, it was the language used to communicate between worshiper and deity.

Leviticus does not offer a rationale for sacrifice, nor does it explain in detail the purpose for each of the sacrifices. Instead it provides procedural instructions for the offerers and the priests, both of whom took part in the ritual. In animal sacrifices, the offerer brought the animal to the doorway of the tent of meeting (tabernacle) and laid his or her hand on the animal's head in an act of identification. Then the animal's throat was slit. The priest manipulated the blood of the animal, burned the appropriate portions on the altar and disposed of the remainder in accordance with the type of sacrifice offered.

The first three sacrifices—the burnt offering, the grain offering and the well-being offering—were voluntary sacrifices, which meant that they were brought at the offerer's initiative as an expression of gratitude, joy or dedication to God. This indicates that sacrifices were not solely for expiation. They were a means of fellowship with Yahweh whereby reverence could be expressed publicly through ritual actions. The purification offering and reparation offering were required sacrifices specifically prescribed for the expiation of sin. For an overview of each sacrifice and its purpose see table 1.

The sacrificial laws do not specifically mention women as participants, though the neutral terms *adam* (Lev 1:2; 5:4) and *nefesh* (Lev 2:1; 4:2, 27; 5:1, 2, 4, 15, 17, 21; 7:18, 20, 21, 25, 27; 23:29, 30) indicate that both men and women brought sacrifices. In ad-

Table 1. The Sacrifices of Leviticus 1—7

Leviticus	Sacrifice	Animal(s) offered	Blood manipulation	Method of sacrifice	Actions of worshiper	Actions of priest	Purpose
1:1-17; 6:8-13	Whole burnt offering	One of the following: bull, ram, male goat, turtledove or pigeon	Sprinkled around on the altar of burnt offering	Entire animal burned on altar; only the skin retained by the officiating priest	Chose animal, brought it to the door of the tabernacle, laid hand on its head, slaughtered the animal	Manipulated blood, skinned the animal, cut it into pieces, arranged the pieces on the altar, washed entrails and legs with water, burned entire animal on altar	General atonement; entreating Yahweh's favor
2:1-16; 6:14-23	Grain offering	None. Flour was mixed with oil, frankincense; could be uncooked, baked in an oven, cooked on a griddle or fried in a pan; was always unleavened. For first fruits, loose heads of roasted grain were offered.	None	A memorial portion of the grain offering was burned on altar; remainder was eaten by officiating priest	Brought grain (either in flour form, cooked or roasted grain); took a handful of it to give to the priest	Offered up memorial portion on altar	Similar to burnt offering; usually appears in conjunction with burnt offering as a daily sacrifice (Ex 29:39-41)
3:1-17; 7:11-36	Well-being offering (freewill offering, votive offering)	One male or female ox, lamb or goat	Sprinkled around on the altar of burnt offering	Fatty portions of animal (fat of tail and entrails, the kidneys and the lobe of the liver). Remainder eaten by worshiper	Chose animal, brought it to the door of the tabernacle, laid hands on its head, slaughtered the animal	Manipulated blood, burned fatty portions on altar	Expression of gratitude, joy; offered in fulfillment of a vow
4:1—5:13; 6:24-30	Purification offering	Priest offered a bull; leader offered a male goat; individual offered a female goat, lamb; if offerer was poor, two turtledoves, two young pigeons or a grain offering	For a priest and the congregation, blood was sprinkled seven times before the veil in the Holy Place, anointed on the altar of incense, and the rest was poured out at the base of the altar of burnt offering. For a layperson, blood was anointed on the horns of the altar of the burnt offering and the rest poured out at the base of the altar of burnt offering	Fatty portion of animal offered (fat of entrails, the two kidneys, the lobe of the liver). When offered for a priest or the congregation, the remainder was burned outside of the camp. When offered for a leader or an individual, the remainder was eaten by the officiating priest	Confessed sin; chose animal, brought it to the door of tabernacle, laid hand on its head, slaughtered the animal	Manipulated blood, removed fatty portions and burned them on the altar, took remainder of animal outside the camp and burned it there or retained it for food	Cleansed uncleanness and provided atonement for unintentional sin
5:14—6:7; 7:1-10	Reparation offering	Ram	Sprinkled around on the altar of burnt offering	Fatty portions of animal offered (fat of tail and entrails, the two kidneys, lobe of the liver); remainder eaten by the officiating priest	Chose animal and brought it to door of tabernacle; paid one-fifth of its value to the priest (if the sin was against God) or paid one-fifth to the person offended	Manipulated blood, burned fatty portions on altar	Atonement for sacrilege against God's holy things (sancta, God's name) and violations against fellow humans by deception, robbery or extortion

dition, Leviticus 12:6 and Leviticus 15:29 clearly state that women were required to offer burnt and purification offerings, and women with skin ailments would have offered the specified sacrifices for their cleansing (reparation, burnt, purification and grain; Lev 14:10-20). All sacrifices were presented on the altar of burnt offering at the doorway of the tent of meeting before Yahweh (Lev 1:3; 3:1-2, 7, 12-13; 4:4, 14, 23, 24, 28; 5:6; esp. Lev 17:1-7). Both laywomen and laymen had access to this sacred area.

The unadulterated bloodiness and violence of sacrifice evokes a visceral reaction from many modern readers. We live in a sanitized world in which our meat comes neatly dissected and packaged, and unless we grew up in an agricultural setting, most of us have never slaughtered an animal. The ritual of taking an animal to a public place, laying one's hand on its head in an act of identification and then slitting its throat seems horrifying and inhumane. But perhaps that is the point. Such ritual actions would have left an indelible impression on the participants, signifying that sacrifice was costly because blood (symbolizing life) was shed.

In many ways modern worship has also become sanitized. Sacrifices are conveniently packaged in offering envelopes or yearly donations to a charity. Some people consider the mere act of going to church a sacrifice, as if God should be grateful that an hour of precious time has been offered. There is no struggle to choose the best animal for the sacrifice, no long walk to a smoky, malodorous altar to stand before a holy God, no public confession of sin or testimony of God's grace and goodness, and no blood or mess. Of course, Christ's sacrifice eliminated the need for daily offerings of animals. But the New Testament indicates that Christians are to come before God with acceptable sacrifices of themselves (Rom 12:1), of praise (Phil 4:18; Heb 13:15) and of good works (Heb 13:16). Should our sacrifices be offered with any less concern for propriety, acceptability and costliness than those offered in the Hebrew Bible? Should not sacrifice require something of us, even to the extent that we get our hands dirty ministering to the homeless, the AIDS victims, the unloved? Should not the act of offering a sacrifice to a holy God leave an indelible impression on us?

Mediators to a Holy God: The Inauguration of the Priesthood (Lev 8—10)

A sacrificial system cannot be implemented without a consecrated priesthood. Thus these chapters depict the consecration of Aaron and his sons for their priestly duties (Lev 8), the inauguration of the sacrifices (Lev 9) and regulations concerning the priests (Lev 10:8-20). In the midst of these instructions appears a rare narrative, the story of Nadab and Abihu's offering of "strange fire" (Lev 10:1-7).

The priests were set apart from the rest of Israelite society as members of a holy institution. They alone had access to the most sacred areas of the tabernacle, and they alone consumed portions of all the sacrifices except the burnt offering. They were required to live according to different standards (Lev 21), were held responsible for maintaining the sanctity of the offerings made by the Israelites (Lev 22) and paid the ultimate price for abusing their position (Lev 10:1-3).

Women are not mentioned in these chapters. Their conspicuous absence leads to an obvious conclusion: women were not allowed to be priests. No reason for this is given in the biblical material, but one likely factor is that because women were unclean during parturition and menstruation (see Lev 12; 15), their ability to officiate would have been severely limited. The holy offerings were eaten by the priests who offered them, but unclean priests were not allowed to eat sacrifices until they were cleansed (Lev 22:2-9) and presumably did not officiate while unclean. Female priests, had they existed, would have been restricted from these activities during menstruation and for forty to eighty days after giving birth.

Although the absence of female priests has been viewed as discriminatory against women, it should be remembered that most men in Israel were also excluded from the priesthood since they were not from the family of Aaron (is this ethnic discrimination?). Even Aaronic men whose bodies were defective were not allowed to officiate as priests (is this prejudice against the physically challenged?). Although many ancient cultural practices were male-dominated or patriarchal, this does not mean that they were inherently sexist and misogynistic. Can such contemporary terms accurately characterize ancient practices that do not accord with modern standards of equality between the sexes? On the other hand, using the ancient practices of the Hebrew Bible as a basis to exclude women from participation in modern religious roles is also inappropriate.

Another matter that should be acknowledged is how many religious roles women could perform. Leviticus indicates that women entered the sanctuary (Lev 12:6; 15:29), offered sacrifices (Lev 1—7), made vows (Lev 27:1-8) and as laywomen had every access to the cult that laymen did. The Hebrew Bible elsewhere attests that women were prophets (Ex 15:20; Judg 4:4; 2 Kings 22:14), servers at the door of the tent of meeting (Ex 38:8; 1 Sam 2:22), judges (Judg 4—5; *see* Women as Leaders), singers (Ezra 2:65) and Nazirites (Num 6:2). The Nazirite vow is particularly interesting because it parallels in many ways the restrictions required of the high priest. Both were "holy" to Yahweh/God (Num 6:8; Lev 21:7). Their heads were dedicated or anointed to God (Num 6:7; Lev 21:12; cf. Ex 29:7; Lev 8:12). Both were forbidden to touch corpses, particularly of close family members (Num 6:6-7; Lev 21:12). Both were to abstain from wine, the Nazirite during the vow (Num 6:4), the priest while ministering (Lev 10:8; see Jenson, 50). Thus women or men who vowed themselves to Yahweh as Nazirites attained a level of consecration similar to that of the high priest.

The absence of women in the priesthood may be troublesome or disappointing to modern women. And it raises questions about whether this was God's intent, (although there is no overt command to keep women out of the priesthood), or accommodation to cultural practices, as in the cases of polygamy and slavery, which seem to have been accepted although never specifically approved (*see* Ancient and Modern Slavery; Polygamy). Nevertheless the focus of Leviticus is not on why persons were excluded from priesthood, as though it were a privileged life, but on the formidable responsibility of the priests to maintain the sanctity of the sacrificial system and the people. When this responsibility was not taken seriously, death was the consequence (Lev 10:2).

Is Cleanliness Next to Godliness? The Laws of Purification (Lev 11—15)

The laws of purification are perhaps the most puzzling section in Leviticus. These detailed regulations concerning proper food, the uncleanness of childbirth, skin diseases and bodily discharges are unfamiliar and strangely primitive. Such matters seem foreign to worship of God since they are physical conditions and, in the case of discharges and skin disease, out of the individual's control. Why would such persons be considered ritually unclean?

Some clarification of terminology is in order. The concepts of clean and unclean do not equate with our modern concepts of physical cleanliness or dirtiness. More importantly, they are not parallel to our concepts of sinless and sinful. Instead these are ritual states of existence, which might best be compared with the ideas of appropriate and inappropriate. Clean was a state of ritual appropriateness; unclean was a state of ritual inappropriateness.

Leviticus 10:10 illuminates the major terms associated with clean and unclean. The priests were to distinguish between the holy *(haqqodesh)* and the profane or common *(hahol);* between the unclean *(hattame')* and the clean *(hattahor)*. Obviously "holy" and "profane" are opposites, as are "unclean" and "clean." The chiasmus of the verse would seem to indicate that "unclean" and "profane" are synonymous, as are "holy" and "clean." However, this is not the case. To be unclean did not mean that one was profane or that one had necessarily committed some sort of sin. It meant that one was ritually impure. To be clean did not mean one was holy, since clean persons could still profane holy things (e.g., see Ex 20:25; Lev 18:21; 19:7-8, 12; 20:3; 21:4-6, 9, 12-15, 23; 22:2, 32) and defile the sanctuary by worshiping Molech (Lev 20:3; cf. Ezek 20:26; 23:38). Cleanliness was not the equivalent of godliness. It simply meant that one was ritually appropriate.

Most if not all interpreters assume that unclean persons were prohibited from entering the sanctuary because impurity threatened God's holiness, but nowhere in the priestly literature is an unclean person forbidden to enter the sanctuary (on the command to the parturient, see comments on Lev 12 below). Texts often cited in support of the idea that unclean persons could not enter the sanctuary include Leviticus 7:19-21, Leviticus 22:3-8 and Numbers 5:1-4. However, the texts in Leviticus do not refer to entering the sanctuary unclean but to ingesting holy sacrifices while unclean. Numbers 5:1-4 refers to the unique situation of the war camp, from which all unclean persons were excluded. But there is no prohibition against entering the tent shrine. Instead unclean persons were sent outside the camp to protect it from defilement in preparation for holy war (cf. Deut 23:9-14). This is not the situation in Leviticus, where only persons with skin ailments were sent outside the camp, not because they defiled it but so they would not defile other persons (Lev 13:45-46).

Thus what separated a clean person from an unclean person was the privilege of eating the sacred offerings. Being unclean meant that it was inappropriate for a layperson to eat of the well-being offering or for a priest to eat any of the sacrificial food.

Purity Laws Related to Women

The Pentateuch contains a system of purity and impurity that undergirds nearly every form of ancient Judaism. Impurities can be organized into three categories: death, leprosy and sexual discharges.

Although both men and women are equally susceptible to corpse contamination and leprosy, the sexual discharges of women are more contaminating than are those of men. For both men and women, sexual intercourse brings a one-day impurity, but women have the added impurity of a full week each month due to menstruation (*see* Menstruation). Anyone who touches the menstruant becomes impure (Lev 15:19). Other items susceptible to impurity (e.g., pots, clothes and food, Lev 11:32) are probably contaminated by contact with a menstruant as well. Any man who has sexual intercourse with a menstruant becomes impure for a week (Lev 15:24; cf. Ezek 18:6). At the end of her week of impurity, a woman probably bathes; less impure persons are required to do so (Lev 15:21-22).

A woman who has just given birth is impure for forty days if the child is a boy or eighty days if the child is a girl (Lev 12:2-5). For the first one to two weeks after childbirth the mother is regarded as a menstruant. After the initial, severe period of impurity, the mother remains impure at a lower level of intensity for the remaining thirty-three or sixty-six days. She is pure for the ordinary sphere of activity but still may not handle sancta until the end of this second stage, when she offers a concluding sacrifice (Lev 12:6).

The person with the most impure sexual discharge is a woman with an abnormal genital flow (i.e., she is menstruating outside of her normal period). She requires divine healing from her disease before she can undergo purification, an eight-day procedure, including ablutions and sacrifices (Lev 15:27-30).

Perhaps the best explanation for the biblical impurity laws is that impurity is a symbol for death. The most impure item in the biblical system is the corpse, and the second to it is the leper, a sort of living corpse (cf. Num 12:12; Job 18:13). Sexual discharges are probably impure because they are the fluids that give life but are wasting away from the body. The Israelite system lifts up purity as illustrative of the realm of life, the living God and his people, Israel, as opposed to impurity, representing death, lifeless gods and pagan nations.

Throughout the Old Testament women's impurities surface in various contexts. Women were forbidden contact with the Israelite military camp on account of purity concerns (Deut 23; 1 Sam 21:4-5). Rachel's declaration that she was menstruating kept her father, Laban, from looking underneath her for his stolen idols (Gen 31:35). The recoil caused by menstruation is often used symbolically in the Bible to describe the repulsion God has toward sin (Is 30:22).

In the New Testament, Mary offers a sacrifice after the impurity of childbirth (Lk 2:22-24). The woman who had been hemorrhaging for twelve years was undoubtedly a woman with abnormal menstruation (Mk 5:25-34). The woman reaches out fearfully to touch Jesus' garment. However, Jesus reverses the dynamics of impurity. Instead of the woman defiling Jesus' clothes, healing power flows from Jesus to the woman.

Bibliography

M. Douglas, *In the Wilderness: The Doctrine of Defilement in the Book of Numbers* (Sheffield: JSOT Press, 1993); J. Milgrom, *Leviticus 1—16,* Anchor Bible 3A (Garden City, NY: Doubleday, 1991); D. P. Wright, "Unclean and Clean—OT," *Anchor Bible Dictionary,* ed. D. N. Freedman et al (New York: Doubleday, 1992) 6:729-41. HANNAH K. HARRINGTON

If they did so, they profaned the sanctuary (Lev 7:19-21; 22:3-8). Unclean persons were also required to be cleansed. If they failed to do so they defiled the sanctuary (Num 19:13, 20; Lev 15:31).

The main threat uncleanness posed was to other persons, because uncleanness was communicable. Why it was communicable is not addressed in the laws, although it was viewed much like an invisible contagion that could be contracted through touch. The level of communicability varied depending on the type of uncleanness. Major uncleanness affected persons who had certain skin ailments, women after childbirth and persons with certain types of sexual discharges, such as menstruation and pathological genital discharges. This category is characterized by a lengthy period of uncleanness (seven days or more), a high level of communicability to other persons and objects, and typically a more extensive ritual purification. Minor uncleanness affected those who touched a person with a major uncleanness or a contaminated object or who had certain types of sexual discharges: involuntary seminal emissions and emissions during sexual intercourse. This category is characterized by its short duration (until evening) and minimal ritual purification procedures (bathing, washing clothes). See table 2 for an overview of human uncleanness.

The biblical material is unclear whether or not persons were expected to remain isolated within their homes for the duration of their uncleanness. Notably, the menstruant and the woman with an abnormal flow only contaminated objects like beds and chairs; no mention is made about persons or objects outside the home. Either they were expected to sequester themselves within the home or they could not communicate their uncleanness by touching others. The man with an abnormal flow communicated his uncleanness to persons by touch and to objects within and outside the home, which implies he was not restricted even while unclean. In any case, if proper precautions were not taken to limit the communication of uncleanness, persons potentially could contract uncleanness unknowingly and then eat of the well-being offerings or fail to cleanse themselves. This in turn would profane or defile the sanctuary and could result in the people's death (Lev 15:31).

The only rationale given by the biblical text for the purification laws is that Israel was to be holy (Lev 11:44-45). The concept of purity invaded every aspect of life, including the physical. What entered the body in the form of food, what was on the surface of the skin and what came forth from the sexual organs were all connected with purity. Although this sounds curious from a contemporary standpoint, which as-

Table 2. A Comparison of Human Sexual Uncleanness in Leviticus 12 and 15

Categories	**Parturient (Lev 12)**	**Unclean male, unnatural flow (*zub*, Lev 15:2-15)**	**Unclean male, involuntary flow of semen (Lev 15:16-17)**	**Unclean male/female, due to sexual relations (Lev 15:18)**	**Unclean female, menstruant (Lev 15:19-24)**	**Unclean female, unnatural flow (*zabab*, Lev 15:25-30)**
Type of uncleanness	Major/lengthy	Major/lengthy	Minor/brief	Minor/brief	Major/lengthy, no sacrifice required	Major/lengthy
Time of uncleanness	For a male child, seven days; for a female child, fourteen days	Until his unnatural flow ceases	Unclean until evening	Unclean until evening	Seven days	Until her unnatural flow ceases
Type of purification	"Bloods of purity" unique to parturient; male child, thirty-three days; female child, sixty-six days	Waiting period of seven days after flow ceases	N/A	N/A	N/A	Waiting period of seven days after flow ceases
Communicability	Not stated. But if "unclean as in her niddah" means she was unclean just as she was when she menstruated, then her communicability during the seven or fourteen days would be like the menstruant's.	Communicable to any objects on which he sits or lies (beds, chairs, saddles, anything underneath him). Communicable to persons who touch any of these contaminated objects. Communicable to any household vessels he touches. Communicable to persons who touch him, whom he touches without first washing his hands or on whom he spits.	Communicable to garments worn by the man at the time of his emission. Garments are unclean until evening and must be washed. Apparently not communicable to others.	Communicability is limited to female partner. Apparently not communicable to others or to inanimate objects.	Communicable to any bed or chair upon which she sits or lies. Communicable to anyone who touches any of these contaminated objects. Communicable to anyone who touches her. Especially communicable to a man who engages in sex with her.	Comunicable to any bed or chair upon which she sits or lies. Communicable to anyone who touches any of these contaminated objects.
Prohibitions regarding holy things and places	Cannot touch holy things during "bloods of purity." Cannot enter the sanctuary during "bloods of purity."	None	None	None	None	None
Method of cleansing	No bathing specified. Brings a year-old lamb for the burnt offering and a young pigeon or turtledove for the purification offering.	Washes garments, bathes his flesh (penis?) in fresh water and is purified. On eighth day, brings two turtledoves or two young pigeons for burnt and purification offerings.	Must bathe all of his flesh in water.	Must bathe in water	No bathing specified and no sacrifice required	No bathing specified. On eighth day, brings two turtledoves or two young pigeons for burnt and purification offerings.
Priestly actions	Priest offers sacrifice and makes atonement on her behalf. She is purified.	Priest uses one bird for the purification offering and the other for the burnt offering and makes atonement for the man. He is purified.	None	None	None	Priest uses one bird for the purification offering and the other bird for the burnt offering and makes atonement for the woman. She is purified.

sociates purity with morality, it is also strangely compelling. Every facet of a person—mind, personality and body—was integral to a life of purity.

Numerous attempts have been made to provide more functional rationales for the purity system. One rationale is the medical approach, which explains the laws as protecting the health of Israel by avoiding unclean animals that were disease carriers and practicing good hygiene. Another is the religious approach, which asserts that the laws protected Israel from the practices of neighboring nations. Third are various anthropological approaches, which associate uncleanness with lack of wholeness or abhorrence toward death. The first two approaches have largely been rejected by interpreters, the first because some of the clean animals were also disease transmitters, and good hygiene is not the point of the laws, although it may have been a byproduct. The second is rejected because the ritual practices of neighboring nations were more similar to Israel's than they were different. The third approach has been the explanation of choice for most recent interpreters, because it seems to provide a logical explanation for all the laws, especially those regulating sexual flows. However, associating uncleanness, particularly sexual uncleanness, with death or lack of wholeness because of the loss of blood or other bodily fluids also has its weaknesses.

Although death is associated with uncleanness (cf. Num 18), the concept is almost entirely absent from the laws of purification. The laws do not mention human corpse defilement and only briefly mention contamination from animal corpses. Perhaps most closely associated with death were persons with skin ailments. They were banished outside the camp, as were those who were corpse contaminated, and the appearance of their skin was comparable to death and decay (cf. Num 12:12). However, Leviticus never suggests that these skin ailments led to death but assumes that such persons would be restored to health.

The sexual defilements seem particularly unrelated to death. Loss of blood can potentially lead to death, but loss of blood during menstruation does not cause death, nor does normal loss of blood after childbirth. In addition, if loss of blood always represented loss of life, why were wounded persons or newly circumcised males not considered unclean? Even the pathological genital flows are not depicted as life threatening. Most importantly, emission of semen cannot be connected with loss of life since it so obviously produces life.

A simple contextual study of the word *blood* in Leviticus demonstrates that everywhere it is used it means "life," not "death" (see esp. Lev 17:11, 14). It seems odd then that parturient and menstrual blood would be exceptions to the rule. Perhaps the loss of these bodily fluids did not evince death, lack of wholeness or lack of fullness of life, all of which imply negativity. Rather, these fluids represented life, productivity and fertility. This would apply equally well to seminal fluid in intercourse. Life-producing fluids were unclean because of their association with the mysteries of life, not death.

The laws of purification are organized in four sections: laws of clean and unclean animals (Lev 11); laws concerning the parturient (Lev 12); laws of skin ailments (*tsara'ath;* Lev 13—14) and laws concerning natural and unnatural discharges (Lev 15). Only the purification laws in Leviticus 12 and Leviticus 15 will be discussed here, since they specifically concern women. (Women were subject to the food laws and the laws of skin ailments, even when not mentioned.)

Laws Concerning the Parturient (Lev 12)

The regulations in Leviticus 12 pertain to women's exclusive role in biblical Israel: childbearing. The flow of blood accompanying the birth of a child rendered the woman unclean for a certain period of time, depending on the sex of the child.

Birth of a Male (Lev 12:2-4). When a woman gave birth to a male, she was unclean for seven days "according to the days of the impurity *[niddah]* of her menstruation/infirmity *[dawah]."* Both *niddah* and *dawah* are used to refer to menstruation, although *niddah* is the more common term. Outside of Leviticus *niddah* is often used interchangeably with impurity (*tame';* Ezek 7:19-20; Lam 1:17; Ezra 9:11) and is sometimes even used in the opposite sense as purification (Zech 13:1; Num 8:7). *Dawah* means "to be ill" and is used three times to refer to the "illness" of parturition or menstruation (Lev 12:2; 15:33; 20:18).

After childbirth a woman was unclean for seven days like the menstruant (Lev 15:19). Whether or not the parturient was considered a menstruant during this time is unclear. In its first stages lochial flow closely resembles a heavy menstrual period. However, the text does not state that the parturient's uncleanness was communicable to persons or objects as menstrual impurity was (Lev 15:19-24), although the use of the term *niddah* may presuppose this. If, however, the parturient's uncleanness was communicable, she would have made her child unclean, a fact that seems too significant to be omitted. Unlike some other ancient Near Eastern countries, Israel had no cleansing ceremony for newborns and did not consider them unclean. Perhaps in the priestly system, uncleanness could not be transferred to children, or perhaps a parturient's *niddah* was not communicable.

On the eighth day the male baby was circumcised. This was followed by a thirty-three-day period during which the mother sat (or remained, dwelled) "in the bloods of purity." She was not unclean during this time (the word *tame'* is not used). Instead she was in a state of purification unique to the parturient, a purification associated with her blood. Lochia can last up to six weeks, but in its later stages it gradually slows and becomes lighter in color. The priestly writers recognized the uniqueness of this later lochial flow, since they did not relegate the new mother to the status of a *zabah,* a woman with an irregular flow of blood outside of menstruation. Instead the lochial flow was understood as purificatory blood. The woman was forbidden to touch holy objects or enter the sanctuary not because she was unclean but because she was in a unique process of blood purification. Notably, only the parturient of all the persons discussed in Leviticus 12—15 was specifically forbidden entrance to the sanctuary and access to holy things, and only the parturient underwent this special purification.

Birth of a Female (Lev 12:5). When a female child was born, the mother was unclean for fourteen days and in blood purification for sixty-six days. No reason is stated in the text for the doubling, resulting in extensive speculation. A few theories are summarized below.

1. A female child was considered less desirable or valued than a male child (based on Lev 27:2-7). Although the Hebrew Bible contains evidence of inequalities between the sexes, this view is weakened by the fact that the mother was unclean, not the child. If gender was the issue, it seems the child would be unclean rather than the mother, as was the case in the Hittite culture (see Milgrom, 763-64). Or if desirability or value was the issue, it seems there would be regulations for children, male or female, who were born with defects or illness, and this apparently was not the case.

2. A female child was viewed as more vulnerable to disease or demonic attack. Infant mortality was high in the ancient Near East, and childbirth was fraught with danger. However, why would the perceived vulnerability of the child create a state of uncleanness for the mother and not for the child?

3. A female child may produce a vaginal discharge (sometimes bloody) upon birth, and a woman's lochia sometimes lasts longer after the birth of a female child. Although these medical characteristics can occur, they do not account for the extensive time differences between males and females. In addition, it is unclear why a female child's flow would make her mother unclean if the mother's lochia did not render the child unclean.

4. The potential for the female child to menstruate or her potential motherhood made the mother unclean. However, it seems odd that a female's potential fertility would have any effect at birth, since she would not reach puberty for many years and at that point she would maintain her own uncleanness.

5. Because a male was circumcised on the eighth day (Gen 17:12; Lev 12:3), his mother's uncleanness was abbreviated to seven days. Heavy lochia can last ten days to two weeks, so in the case of the female child who had no circumcision ceremony, the mother's uncleanness extended a full two weeks, in accordance with the heaviest flow. Since the period of uncleanness was doubled, the period of purification was also. The statement of the male's circumcision interrupts the regulations (it is the only verse not focused on the mother), and the circumcision ceremony is the only distinction between male and female births cited in the text, suggesting it as the probable

reason for the difference.

The parturient was not commanded to bathe either after her initial uncleanness or at the end of her blood purification. Nevertheless, because bathing is an important part of other cleansing rituals, commentators often assume that the parturient was also required to bathe, suggesting that the priestly writers omitted this detail. However, bathing is not prescribed for *any* of the women who have flows of blood, which suggests that such a ritual was not required for them.

Sacrifice (Lev 12:6-8). After the period of purification was completed, the woman brought a year-old lamb for a burnt offering and a pigeon or turtledove for a purification offering to the door of the tent. The priest offered the sacrifices, and the woman's time of purification was complete.

Laws Concerning Persons with Discharges (Lev 15)

Five kinds of sexual discharges rendered persons unclean in varying degrees. The discussion of these impurities is arranged so that the two types of male uncleanness (unnatural [Lev 15:2-15] and natural [Lev 15:16-17]) and the two types of female uncleanness (natural [Lev 15:19-24] and unnatural [Lev 15:25-30]) are parallel, with the rule pertaining to both sexes in the middle (Lev 15:18). For an overview and comparison of sexual uncleanness, see table 2.

Laws Concerning a Male with an Unnatural Flow (the* zab*; Lev 15:2-15). A man who had an unnatural flow *(zab)* from his "flesh" (penis) was unclean. The type of flow is described in Leviticus 15:3: either a flow like slimy juice from his penis or some sort of stoppage of his penis. Gonorrhea is probably the disease being described.

The *zab*'s uncleanness was the most communicable of all the types of sexual uncleanness, implying that it was the most serious. A man could communicate uncleanness to inanimate objects, to humans who touched inanimate objects contaminated by him and to humans through direct contact with him. This high level of communicability may be due to the fact that an unclean man came into contact with more members of the community than an unclean woman would. However, this would not explain why his communicability within the home was greater. Only the *zab* could contaminate housewares (Lev 15:12), and in this respect he was comparable to the most reviled of unclean animals, rodents and reptiles (Lev 11:32-33).

When the *zab* was purified from his flow (i.e., healed), he counted seven days for his purification, after which he washed his garments and bathed his flesh (perhaps here a reference to just his penis or maybe his entire body) in fresh water. This rendered him purified. On the eighth day he took two turtledoves or pigeons to the door of the tent and gave them to the priest. The priest offered one for the purification offering and the other for a burnt offering and made atonement for the man on account of his flow.

Law Concerning a Male with a Natural Flow (emission of semen outside of intercourse; Lev 15:16-17). If a man had an emission of semen outside of intercourse, he was to bathe all of his flesh in water and be unclean until the evening. Apparently this uncleanness was communicable only to his garments and bedclothes, which were to be washed in water and were unclean until evening.

Law Concerning Emission of Semen During Sexual Intercourse (Lev 15:18). After a man and woman engaged in sexual intercourse, they were to bathe in water and be unclean until the evening. Uncleanness from sexual intercourse was apparently not communicable to other persons or to garments and bedclothes.

It should be stressed in this context that uncleanness from sexual intercourse was not sin. The Hebrew Bible does not view sex within marriage as sinful but as a God-given command and blessing (Gen 1:28). The reason the participants were unclean is because of semen's role in the production of life.

Laws Concerning a Female with a Natural Flow (menstruation; Lev 15:19-24). A woman who had a bloody flow from her flesh (vagina) was unclean for seven days, apparently regardless of whether her menstrual flow was shorter than that. The menstruant's uncleanness was communicable to others who touched her or who touched anything she had sat or lain upon. However, the text does not indicate that the woman could render other persons unclean if she touched them. Whether this was because a woman was expected to re-

Menstruation

In 2 Samuel 11:2-5, David observes Bathsheba bathing, and the reader is told that she "was purifying herself after her period." A ritual bath or *mikvah* following sexual abstinence during menstruation continues to be an important practice for some Jewish women, although such practices are criticized by others (*see* Purity Laws Related to Women). Scholars who view the regulations concerning menstrual impurity as oppressive, however, often neglect to mention that purification rites, including the washing of clothes and bathing in water, were also prescribed for seminal emissions and unusual penile discharge. What is striking about Leviticus 15 is how consistently the laws regarding bodily emissions are applied to both sexes. Not only are the discharges of males and females alike regarded as unclean, but chronic or unusual emissions for both males and females require precisely the same purification rites (cf. Lev 15:13-16, 28-30), and in both cases the uncleanness is transferable to other people and objects to a similar degree. Moreover, while a menstruating woman's period of uncleanness is longer than a man's following ejaculation—seven days as opposed to one—this disparity has a basis in physiological reality. The presence of a bodily discharge, not the bodily process itself, renders a person unclean. In the case of menstruation the discharge lasts for five days, and so the law allows for two extra days to be sure that all bleeding has ceased.

Other factors mitigate the apparent harshness of these regulations. First, in comparison with today's Western women, Israelite women menstruated much less frequently. They married young and had large families. Since menstruation does not occur during pregnancy and seldom occurs during breastfeeding, many women menstruated relatively rarely. Second, within a patriarchal context, in which women were treated more like property than persons, these laws arguably had positive impacts on women and placed some limits on male control of women's lives (see Greenberg). Third, there is evidence that women sometimes used these menstrual purity laws to their own advantage. In Genesis 31, for example, Rachel pretends to have her period in order to conceal Laban's stolen household gods and save her own life.

Despite such considerations and the consistency of these laws in theory, within interpretative traditions such laws have often been applied selectively and have functioned to legitimize more destructive notions that women are polluted per se. Typically menstrual regulations are retained, reintroduced or even amplified in faith communities, while regulations concerning male emissions are ignored or dropped. There is also textual evidence that in comparison with semen, menstrual blood is the focus of heightened concern in this purity code. Males who come in contact with menstrual blood during sexual intercourse are rendered unclean for seven days (Lev 15:24), whereas contact with semen during sex renders both the man and the woman unclean only until evening (Lev 15:18). In addition, several passages (Lev 18:19; 20:18; Ezek 22:10) specifically forbid sexual intercourse with a menstruating woman, suggesting that this act is a particularly serious violation. While problematic, this more intense ritual concern with menstrual blood likely reflects the Israelites' view of blood in general as symbolizing life, belonging to God and hence warranting special precaution (see Lev 17; 19). An explicit and metaphorical connection between menstruation and violent forms of bloodshed is made in Ezekiel 36:17-18. Similar blood imagery is used in Ezekiel 22 (especially Ezek 22:1-3). Although most readers would share Ezekiel's condemnation of violent and exploitive acts, some may object to his use of menstrual imagery.

An examination of biblical references to menstruation in their cultural context suggests that these texts do not oppress women in the manner or extent to which some critics have claimed (Delaney, 37). In addition, Jesus' public affirmation of the woman who sought healing for chronic bleeding (Mk 5:34) may imply that his redemptive purpose includes exposing the unjust application of such laws.

Bibliography

L. Chisholm-Smith, "Menstrual Impurity: An Examination of Leviticus 15 in Light of Feminist Concerns" (Toronto: Institute for Christian Studies, 1993); J. Delaney et al., *The Curse: A Cultural History of Menstruation* (Urbana: University of Illinois Press, 1976; rev. ed. 1988); B. Greenberg, *On Women and Judaism: A View from Tradition* (Philadelphia: Jewish Publication Society of America, 1981).

LISA CHISHOLM-SMITH

main within the home during her menstrual cycle or because she could not contaminate others merely by touching them is unclear.

The most significant communicability was if a man had sex with a woman during her period. If he did this "her impurity *(niddah)* [was] upon him and he [would] be unclean seven days and any bed which he [lay] upon [would] be unclean" (Lev 15:24). Thus a man who had sex with a menstruant became *niddah* himself and could communicate this uncleanness to inanimate objects. Leviticus 20:18 is much harsher, stating that a man and woman who engaged in intercourse during the woman's period would be cut off (see also Lev 18:19). Leviticus 20:18 may be a strengthening of the law in Leviticus 15:24, or Leviticus 15:24 may be a less stringent version of Leviticus 20:18. Possibly the context of the two laws is different. Leviticus 15:24 depicts a situation in which the woman's menstruation began as the partners engaged in sex; thus the couple did not knowingly have intercourse during menstruation. Leviticus 20:18 refers to a man and woman knowingly engaging in sex during menstruation (see Hartley, 212).

Leviticus 15 does not state that the menstruant was required to bathe and wash her garments or bedclothes. No sacrifices were required of her; at the end of seven days she was clean.

Laws Concerning a Woman with an Unnatural Flow of Blood (zabah; Lev 15:25-30). A woman who had a flow of blood that occurred at a time outside of her normal period or extended many days after her normal period was considered a zabah. She was impure as she was during her normal period, only the uncleanness extended for as long as the unnatural flow. Her uncleanness was communicable to objects (beds, chairs), as it was during her period. Anyone who touched these items was unclean until evening and had to wash his or her garments and bathe in water. However, no mention is made of what happened to a man who touched the woman or whom she touched.

Like the *zab,* when the *zabah* was purified (i.e., healed) she counted seven days and after that was purified. No mention is made of her having to bathe or cleanse her garments. On the eighth day she took two turtledoves or pigeons and brought them to the priest at the tent door. He used one for a purification offering and the other for the burnt offering and made atonement on her behalf because of her unnatural flow.

Motivation for the Laws for Sexual Discharges (Lev 15:31-33). The final verses of the chapter summarize the laws and indicate the motivation for them. Leviticus 15:31 states, "Thus you will separate (*nzr*) the people of Israel from their uncleanness so they will not die because of their uncleanness by their defiling my dwelling place which is in their midst." The use of the verb *nzr* in this context is unusual because it usually means consecration or dedication, as in the Nazirite vow. Nevertheless it accords well with Leviticus 10:10, where clean and unclean were to be kept separate or distinct *(bdl).* The Samaritan Pentateuch and Syriac versions replace the verb *nzr* with *zhr,* meaning "admonish" or "warn," which also suits the context. In either case, the only way the people could address their uncleanness was by being cleansed. This verse warns that failure to be purified would defile the sanctuary and the consequence was death (see also Num 19:13, 20).

Impact on Women. The purification laws are often regarded as particularly harsh toward women, since the two things unique to a woman's sexuality, menstruation and childbirth, were the very things that made her unclean. Because of the misconception that uncleanness restricted a person from the sanctuary, some interpreters have concluded that a woman's bodily functions in effect separated her from God for longer periods than did those of men.

However, the mere structure of Leviticus 15 indicates a balance between male and female sexual uncleanness. Both men and women became unclean due to the issue of semen or blood from the genital area regardless of whether it was a natural sexual function (semen; menstruation) or an abnormal, extended flow (flow from the penis; flow outside of menstruation). Both men and women with abnormal flows were unclean for the duration of the flow, were communicable and had to offer the same sacrifice at the conclusion. Neither sex was required to offer sacrifices at the end of a natural flow, and both of them were communicable to a certain degree. Differences between the sexes did exist. A menstruant's uncleanness lasted longer (seven days) than the ejaculant's (until evening), but the flow of menstruation lasted longer than ejaculation. At the same time, a man with an unnatural flow was more communicable than any other sexually unclean person, including the menstruant and the woman with an unnatural flow. Most importantly, uncleanness did not separate one from God. It merely meant one could not eat the well-being offerings.

A state of uncleanness did carry with it the danger of communicability and may have effectively resulted in isolation from the community for the duration. If so, this would have significantly impacted an unclean woman's ability to assist in agricultural and shepherding tasks or to participate in social events, since she was unclean monthly unless she was pregnant, nursing or in menopause. However, it should be noted that for many women, the times when they were pregnant or nursing far outnumbered the times when they were not.

Outside of the priestly literature, Deuteronomy and Ezekiel, the purification laws for sexual uncleanness are hardly mentioned. None of the birth narratives allude to the uncleanness of parturition or the required sacrifices at the end, although one New Testament reference occurs (Lk 2:22). Allusions to sexual flows in narratives are rare and occur in dubious circumstances. For instance, Rachel used her menstrual flow as an excuse to prevent her father from discovering the stolen teraphim she had hidden underneath her (Gen 31:35). David claimed his men were sexually clean in order to convince Ahimelech to give them the sacred bread (1 Sam 21:5). Bathsheba's purification from menstrual uncleanness is strategically placed in the narrative to implicate David (2 Sam 11:4). The paucity of references is surprising considering the emphasis uncleanness receives in the priestly literature. Perhaps this is an indication of the late date of the literature (thus the lack of influence on other portions of the Hebrew Bible). Or perhaps because ritual purity, especially sexual purity, was something maintained in private, its observance was not typically mentioned except under extraordinary circumstances. In either case, we are left without much of a context to judge how severely the laws impacted women's participation in Israelite society.

What can Christian women glean from the purity laws? Are these simply outmoded, culturally conditioned taboos from which Christ set us free? No modern Christian would suggest returning to the ritual systems described in Leviticus, but it is important to recognize how deeply ingrained the laws were even in the early church. The Gospels record Mary's observance of the parturient laws (Lk 2:21-24), and Jesus' command that a healed leper comply with the cleansing ritual as a testimony to others (Mt 8:4; Mk 1:44; Lk 5:14). Jewish Christians were reluctant to abandon the dietary laws (Rom 14:14, 20; Gal 2:11-13; cf. Acts 10—11), and although the New Testament never implies it, menstruants were sometimes denied communion and entrance into church services in early church history.

Nevertheless, Jesus was clearly unconcerned about his own ritual defilement (Mt 8:3; Mk 1:41; Lk 5:13; esp. Mt 9:20-22; Mk 5:25-34; Lk 8:43-48) and emphasized that true purity came from the heart and actions, not the physical state of the body (Mk 7:1-23). Elsewhere the New Testament focuses on having a pure heart (Mt 5:8), thinking pure thoughts (Phil 4:8), having pure bodies (1 Cor 6:18-20) and living lives acceptable to God (Rom 12:1). The command not to eat the Lord's Supper "in an unworthy manner" (1 Cor 11:27 NASB) may be analogous to Leviticus's prohibitions against partaking of the well-being offerings in an unclean state. So while the ritual laws of Leviticus were eventually abandoned, the principle of purity upon which they were founded continued to be stressed.

One other matter should be considered. Although we find it strange and perhaps awkward that Leviticus speaks so frankly of human bodily functions and their relationship to God, perhaps we have much to learn. Our physical bodies are of as much concern to God as our spiritual lives, and yet we tend to separate the two, especially in regard to sexual functions. Menstruation is ensconced in silence and hardly spoken of in polite company, much less in church. Even in modern society, menstruation tends to be viewed in a negative light as an inconvenience, a source of anxiety and embarrassment, and something to conceal. Our attitude toward this bodily function, which is necessary for fertility, is to try to ignore it and make it as unobtrusive in our lives as possible. Whether we like to admit it or not, we tend to consider menstruation unclean in a wholly physical sense and fail to recognize it for what it is: a cleansing of the uterus in preparation for the next egg and another opportunity to produce life.

Rather than a curse, menstruation is part of the unique, ingenious design of a woman's body. Its onset marks a young girl's entrance into sexual maturity, a rite of passage that ought to be commemorative rather than humiliating. This time is surrounded by legitimate anxieties and unanswered questions that should not be minimized or ignored but addressed with honesty and sensitivity. At the same time, it is important that women recognize the spiritual aspects of menstruation. Instead of being an inconvenience, the monthly cycle can remind a woman that God has created her uniquely female. Instead of being a shameful experience, menstruation signals a woman's miraculous ability to participate in the creation of life, regardless of whether or not she becomes a mother. And instead of being dreaded, menstruation can call a woman to a time of purging inner impurities of thought and mind even as her body cleanses her from within.

Pollution Control: The Day of Atonement (Lev 16)

Significantly, the purpose of the Day of Atonement was to cleanse the sanctuary from the contamination caused by Israel's uncleanness and sin (Lev 16:16, 33). This is why the ritual for the day comes immediately after the purification laws. As noted above, when properly cleansed and atoned for, uncleanness had no effect on the sanctuary. However, when unclean persons failed to cleanse themselves or when persons participated in certain sins, the sanctuary was defiled. Apparently these impurities accumulated on the sanctuary throughout the year like an invisible rain of pollution. Thus once a year a cleansing ceremony was performed that eradicated the accumulated filth and atoned for the people. As such, the Day of Atonement became the highest holy day of the sacred year.

The high priest performed the ritual for the Day of Atonement, and that ritual consisted of several rites. One rite cleansed the sanctuary (the Holy of Holies, the Holy Place and the altar of burnt offerings) from the impurities of the priests. Another cleansed the sanctuary from the impurities of the people. A scapegoat ritual removed the transgressions from the people, and burnt offerings atoned for the priests and the people.

Family Values: The Holiness Code (Lev 17—26)

Chapters 17-26 have long been viewed as a distinct section within Leviticus. Termed the Holiness Code (H), these chapters probably had a lengthy composition history, originating out of various social settings and reflecting the moral and ethical practices of Israel at various times. How and when the laws were compiled is still the subject of much speculation.

Characterized by the repeated refrain "Be holy, for I, the Lord your God, am holy," this portion of Leviticus contains a series of laws for maintaining the community's holiness through proper ritual and relational actions. That the people of Israel were to be separate and distinct from the other nations is a primary emphasis of these laws (especially Lev 18—20), yet similar laws are found in ancient Near Eastern law codes indicating common concerns.

Modern readers sometimes assume that

the Hebrew Bible law codes were ensconced in legalism with no regard for morality and relational integrity. This is an unfortunate misconception, because ritual was unequivocally connected with morality in the Hebrew Bible. One's relationship with God was affected by one's relationship with others. The following discussion will summarize only those laws within the Holiness Code that are directly related to women.

Laws Related to Sexual Sin (Lev 18)

The laws in Leviticus 18 concern two types of forbidden relationships: incest (Lev 18:6-18) and other forbidden sexual relations (Lev 18:19-20, 22-23). Each verse in Leviticus 18:6-17 begins with the statement "the nakedness of *x* do not uncover," which is a euphemism for engaging in intercourse. The family members prohibited are listed in table 3 and include relatives by blood and by marriage. The fact that sex with a daughter is not prohibited is puzzling. Judith Romney Wegner (41) asserts that since a father had a vested interest in maintaining his daughter's virginity to obtain her dowry, no prohibition was necessary. But this does not explain why other female relatives are also omitted (grandmothers, maternal aunts by marriage, cousins, nieces). Brothers arranged marriages for their sisters (Gen 24:29-59; 34:8-17), implying that they also had a vested interest in protecting their sisters' virginity, yet a prohibition against sex with sisters does appear in the chapter (Lev 18:9). Leviticus 18:6 states that a man is not to have intercourse with any flesh relative, so the omitted family members may be subsumed under that prohibition.

Leviticus 18:19-20, 22-23 addresses forbidden sexual relationships other than incest, including sex with a menstruant, adultery, homosexuality and bestiality. The

Table 3. Comparison of Prohibitions Against Sexual Relations with Family Members

Leviticus 18 **Prohibited sexual relationships, familial**	**Familial relationships not specifically prohibited (but see Lev 18:6)**	**Leviticus 20** **Prohibited sexual relationships, familial**	**Punishment**
Any flesh relative (v. 6)			
Mother (v. 7)			
Stepmother (v. 8)		Stepmother (v. 11)	Death
Full sister or half sister (v. 9)		Full sister or half sister (v. 17)	cut off
Granddaughter (v. 10)			
Stepsister (born to stepmother prior to marriage to one's father, v. 11)			
Paternal aunt (v. 12)		Paternal aunt (v. 19)	Bear guilt
Maternal aunt (v. 13)		Maternal aunt (v. 19)	Bear guilt
Paternal uncle's wife (v. 14)	*Maternal uncle's wife*	Paternal uncle's wife (v. 20)	Bear sin; die childless
Daughter-in-law (v. 15)		Daughter-in-law (v. 12)	Death
Sister-in-law (v. 16)		Sister-in-law (v. 21)	Will be childless
A woman and her daughter (the man's stepdaughter) at the same time; step-granddaughters (v. 17)	*Daughter*	A woman and her mother at the same time (v. 14)	All three burned with fire
Wife's sister while wife is alive (v. 18)			
	Female cousin *Niece* *Grandmother*		
Prohibited sexual relationships, nonfamilial		Prohibited sexual relationships, nonfamilial	Punishment
Sex with menstruant (v. 19)		Sex with menstruant (v. 18)	Both partners cut off
Adultery (v. 20)		Adultery (v. 10)	Both partners put to death
Offspring offered to Molech (v. 21)		Worship of Molech (vv. 1-5)	Death; God's face set against perpetrator; perpetrator cut off
Homosexuality (v. 22)		Homosexuality (v. 13)	Both partners put to death
Male/female bestiality (v. 23)		Male/female bestiality (vv. 15-16)	Death of animal and human partner

prohibition against worship of Molech (Lev 18:21) seems out of place in a series of forbidden sexual unions. However, it is connected to the preceding verse by the use of the word *seed.* Leviticus 18:20 states, "You will not give your lying of seed [intercourse] with your neighbor's wife." Leviticus 18:21 states, "You will not give from your seed [descendants] to pass over to Molech." Perhaps just as forbidden sexual unions were inappropriate uses of seed (semen), so was giving over the product of seed (children) to Molech. In addition, worship of Molech and other forms of false worship are often compared with playing the harlot (see Lev 17:7; 20:5-6), a figurative symbol of adultery against Yahweh (cf. Ezek 6:9; 16:1-63, esp. Ezek 16:15; 20:30-31 [Molech worship]; Hos 4:15; 9:1), again tying this prohibition to Leviticus 18:20.

Every law in this chapter except for one (Lev 18:21) mentions a woman and always in a prohibition regarding sexual intercourse. But the prohibitions are all directed at men (the verbs are second-person masculine singular, except one in Lev 18:23), probably because men were the sexual initiators. It seems unlikely that these laws were designed to protect women from the unruly impulses of men or to safeguard men's property rights (the sexuality of their women) or even to prevent genetic abnormalities caused by close intermarriage. Rather, the focus of these laws is like that of other levitical laws: ritual purity. Human sexuality was a ritual matter, as demonstrated already in Leviticus 12 and Leviticus 15. Here the concern is not with the sexual flows but their misappropriation in improper sexual unions. Both the introduction (Lev 18:3) and the conclusion (Lev 18:24, 26-27, 30) relate these restrictions to the practices of the nations whom Israel would drive out. Such sexual unions were abominations, making the entire land ritually unclean (*tame';* Lev 18:27) as well as the participants (Lev 18:30). Thus the people of Israel were to avoid these practices or face the possibility that they would be "cut off," or exiled (Lev 18:29) and ultimately "vomited up," or expelled, by the land itself (Lev 18:28).

Laws for Proper Relationships (Lev 19)

The laws in Leviticus 19 concern proper relationships, both divine-human and human-human. Many of the laws distinctly parallel or expand on the Ten Commandments (cf. Lev 19:2-4, 11-13, 15-18, 30 and the Decalogues in Ex and Deut). Laws relating to women include Leviticus 19:3, 20-22 and 29. Leviticus 19:3 states, "Every person will fear his mother and his father and keep my sabbaths, I am Yahweh." The term *fear,* or "show reverence," emphasizes the high degree of respect both parents were to receive. *Fear* is normally used with God as its object and only rarely with humans (Josh 4:14 is the only other example). Parallel to the commandment to honor one's father and mother in Ex 20:12 and Deut 5:16, the formulation here is striking in that *mother* appears before *father,* giving her the place of honor (*father* precedes *mother* in both versions of the Ten Commandments). In Leviticus this is the first command listed, receiving peiority over the sabbath command and the prohibition against idolatry. A child who cursed rather than honored his parents was subject to the death penalty (Lev 20:9).

Leviticus 19:20-22 specifies the penalty for a man who committed adultery with a slave woman betrothed to another. Because the woman was not a free person, neither she nor the man received the death penalty (cf. Lev 20:10). Instead the man was required to give a reparation offering because he had in essence stolen his companion's property (see Lev 6:2-7).

Leviticus 19:29 forbade a father from making his daughter a harlot. Fathers may have used their daughters as harlots in order to remove themselves from debt or to supplement income. However, this verse may refer to prostitution connected with foreign cults, since immediately preceding it is a stipulation against practices related to the cult of the dead (Lev 19:28). Prostituting one's daughter resulted in the prostitution of the land, just as false worship defiled the land (cf. Lev 18:24-30). Thus, making one's daughter a prostitute "profaned" her, and a father was forbidden to use his daughter for monetary or religious gain.

Leviticus 19 provides the best evidence that ethical and ritual demands were not separated in the priestly conception. Rather, the ethical was interwoven with ritual. Just as the structure of the Ten Commandments indicates, proper relationship with God expressed through ritual must be mirrored by proper relationship with fellow humans expressed through morality.

Penalties for Disobedience (Lev 20)
Every restriction in Leviticus 20 has a parallel in Leviticus 18 and/or Leviticus 19, but the emphasis here is on the penalties for breaking the laws. The death penalty is most often prescribed (Lev 20:2, 9-16), although the manner in which it was carried out is usually unspecified (but see Lev 20:16). Childlessness was the penalty in certain instances (Lev 20:20-21), indicating that some forbidden sexual unions would produce no fruit. Finally, some persons were "cut off" from their people (Lev 20:3, 5, 6, 17, 18). The meaning of this penalty is never spelled out in the biblical material, although usually it occurs in the context of ritual violations. Most likely, being cut off meant exile from the holy community and expulsion from God's presence (cf. Gen 4:14).

Laws Pertaining to the Priesthood (Lev 21—22)
The priests had been set apart by God to be representatives for the people. Therefore, because they themselves were consecrated as holy, the rules they followed were more stringent than those for the people.

The regular priests could not defile themselves by touching human corpses, except those of their closest family members: parents, children or siblings (cf. Num 19:11-22), and they could not disfigure themselves during mourning. They were forbidden to marry prostitutes or divorced women, probably to insure a pure lineage. If a priest's daughter became a prostitute, she profaned herself and her father because she was a member of a consecrated tribe. Her prostitution obviously would have compromised the purity of the tribe. In addition, if her prostitution was related to false worship, it would have threatened the sanctity of the priestly office. Consequently, a daughter who prostituted herself was burned to death. This presents an intriguing antithesis to Molech worship in which children were burned as sacrifices. In this case, a priest was required to burn his child, not as a sacrifice but as a punishment.

The high priest also could not demonstrate any visible signs of mourning, nor could he touch any corpses, not even those of his immediate family. He was required to stay in the sanctuary, lest by leaving he profaned it, and to marry a virgin from among his own people. He could not marry a widow, a divorced woman or a harlot "so he will not profane his seed among his people" (Lev 21:15). There was to be no question that the high priest's children were really his, so he had to marry a virgin.

Priests and their sons were allowed to eat portions of the sacred offerings (Lev 6:18, 26, 29; 7:6-10). Daughters, however, were allowed to partake of only the wave offerings, not the cereal, purification or reparation offerings (Lev 10:14; 22:12-13). If a priest's daughter married outside her tribe, she could no longer eat any sacred offering (Lev 22:12), but if she was widowed or divorced and without offspring, she could return to her father's house and resume eating them (Lev 22:13). These verses indicate that women within the priestly tribe had only limited access to the consecrated food.

Sanctuary Economics: The Value of Vows (Lev 27)

The final chapter of Leviticus is usually considered an appendix to the Holiness Code. It addresses vows paid to the sanctuary in the form of persons or animals (Lev 27:2-13), the dedication of houses or fields to Yahweh (Lev 27:14-25) and regulations for things dedicated to Yahweh (Lev 27:26-33).

The first eight verses are of most concern because of the value placed on human beings who made vows or who were vowed to Yahweh by another person. Because human sacrifice was not practiced in Israel and because the priests were the only ones allowed to serve in the sanctuary, if laypersons wished to dedicate themselves in a special way to God they could do so by paying their equivalent in silver to the sanctuary. The contribution was determined according to table 4.

The puzzling aspect of this passage is that in each age group males receive a higher valuation than females. Although this is often construed as evidence of the higher social value of males in Israelite society, it is more likely a reflection of each gender's physical strength (Hartley, 481) or the ability of each to contribute to Israel's subsistence (Meyers, 573-86). Notably, a five- to

Table 4. Valuation of Vows for Males and Females

Age	Male (in shekels)	Female (in shekels)
1 month to 5 years	5	3
5 to 20 years	20	10
20 to 60 years	50	30
60+ years	15	10

twenty-year-old female was valued higher than a male of one month to five years, and a woman aged twenty to sixty was valued higher than a male aged five to twenty or sixty and over. Thus age and gender determined the valuations, not gender alone.

In the modern world, where inequality between men and women, especially in wages, has been the source of much contention, Israel's valuation system may seem repugnant. But it was probably a means of standardization based on potential economic contribution, not a commentary on the intrinsic value of human beings. The greatest significance is that both men and women could be vowed or make such a vow as an extraordinary expression of dedication to God.

Conclusion

Although Leviticus may seem irrelevant since its ritual practices are no longer observed (at least by Christians), the principles it emphasizes are still pertinent. God is a holy God who commands reverence and worship in spirit and truth. This is a sober reminder for modern worshipers who may assume "fear of God" is obsolete and unnecessary in a theological construct of grace. While Christians can approach the throne room boldly (Heb 4:16; 10:19), they cannot do so flippantly or without proper regard for preparation of their hearts and minds (Heb 10:22). Instead, as living sacrifices, Christians must constantly assess whether or not they are acceptable, pure in mind, conscience and body.

Leviticus clearly has much to say about women. It indicates that, apart from the priesthood, women had equal access and accountability to the cult as men. It emphasizes that uncleanness was a male and female ritual responsibility and that sexual uncleanness was related to the production of life, not sinfulness, avoidance of foreign cults, hygiene or death. Leviticus portrays one's relationship with God holistically, as an integration of the mind, the conscience and the body. It demonstrates that moral issues and human sexuality directly affect relationship with God. Most importantly, it is a book about holiness and purity, characteristics requisite for all persons who have God in their midst.

Bibliography. ***Commentaries:*** J. E. Hartley, *Leviticus,* Word Biblical Commentary 4 (Dallas: Word, 1992); J. Milgrom, *Leviticus 1-16,* Anchor Bible 3A (Garden City, N.Y.: Doubleday, 1991). ***Other resources:*** P. P. Jenson, *Graded Holiness: A Key to the Priestly Conception of the World,* JSOT Supplement Series 106 (Sheffield: JSOT Press, 1992) 50; C. Meyers, "Procreation, Production, and Protection: Male-Female Balance in Early Israel," *Journal of the American Academy of Religion* 51 (December 1983) 569-93; P. Washbourn, "Becoming Woman: Menstruation as Spiritual Challenge," in *Womanspirit Rising: A Feminist Reader in Religion,* ed. C. P. Christ and J. Plaskow (San Francisco: Harper & Row, 1979) 246-58; J. R. Wegner, "Leviticus," in *The Women's Bible Commentary,* ed. C. A. Newsom and S. H. Ringe (Louisville, KY: Westminster John Knox, 1992) 36-44.

SUSAN M. PIGOTT

NUMBERS

Introduction

Scholars have noted the difficulty in following the book of Numbers. Although there is a narrative thread, readers may feel that a subnarrative or another literary form, such as a census list, interrupts. Refrains of songs, prophecy, proverbs, bibliographical footnotes and special legal provisions are also woven in. Numbers is said to have more literary forms than any other book of the Bible.

The overall theme is the transition from a desert life to life as a settled people, and the overarching event is the break between the generation that came from Egypt and the generation that was to enter the Promised Land. All of the earlier generation had to die because of their lack of trust in God and their unwillingness to accept the privations of the exodus when God had given them freedom and a chance to worship a God of their own. This last was important for peoplehood in a polytheistic world where their only available worship had been that of their overlords' gods. This made it impossible to sing the song of the Lord in a foreign land. If the ordinances about sacrifices seem long, they were necessary to people who had not been able to express their beliefs and convictions in worship.

In addition to demanding better food, the people disobeyed cultic precautions and refused to follow God's plan for entering Canaan from the south. After their refusal to move northward into Canaan and conquer it, the tribes continued in an easterly or southeasterly direction, crossing the Wadi Arabah below the south end of the Dead Sea. In addition, the tribes had to deal with the more powerful sedentary peoples in this area—Edom, Moab, the Amorites and Ammon, who blocked their way, especially King Sihon of the Amorites, at Heshbon. It seems that the way would have remained blocked had the king not summoned Balaam.

The final section of Numbers recounts the progress of the next generation toward the Promised Land, although not all of the earlier generation had yet died; Moses is still alive. A new census appears and new tribal lists.

Many Old Testament scholars are convinced that its books are best understood by noting repetitions, inconsistencies, differing points of view and differing language habits. Close study of these and other features has led them to conclude that the Pentateuch was not written by a single author, Moses, or at the time when Moses is placed in history. These scholars believe that the Pentateuch is composed of several separate documents, written at different periods between 900 B.C. and approximately 538 B.C. They represent different geographical areas, different views of history and differing theologies. These documents were edited into a whole that illuminates our understanding by preserving many of the differences. However, these writings were not arranged in the Old Testament in the chronological order in which they were written but usually in the order of the theological stages they deal with and sometimes by other criteria.

Those who accept Mosaic authorship of the Pentateuch see revelation as happening through the divine inspiration of a single author, Moses, in the composition and setting down on papyrus or parchment of a single document, with the possible exception of Deuteronomy 34, in which his death is recounted. Between the two extremes lie a number of mediating positions, including on the conservative side the view that the Pentateuch derives its essence but not its final form from Moses. Rather, it derives from successive efforts to update the text and adapt it to reflect changing circumstances. While there are those on the more liberal side who see the documents as a purely human product, others see divine inspiration acting on a multiplicity of human writers and human processes. Occasionally these earlier sources will be identified, such as proverbs, folk songs (Num 21:27) or written documents, such as The Book of the Wars of the Lord (Num 21:14).

The difference this makes in studying Numbers is that those who see significant editing of the book during the exile (586 B.C. to the edict of Cyrus, 538 B.C.) believe that the book reflects events of the exile and events leading up to it. Convinced that their exile had happened because of the sinfulness of the people and their rulers in Jerusalem, these authors/editors of the biblical text told the ancient story to make it clear that the Judeans' return from exile would be successful only if they carried it out in strict accordance with God's law. The people have been offered, through God's patience and longsuffering, a chance to learn from their history. The book's purpose would be to strengthen a different group of people, preparing in Babylon to reestablish land holding, self-government and national worship when the edict of Cyrus would allow them to return to the Promised Land.

In either case, what significance do women have in this book? The few references to women appear scattered and unrelated. However, if Numbers is understood to be preparation for a God-given opportunity to settle in as landholders and participants in a theocratic state and legal system, and as worshipers of their God and none other, then the passages concerning women fall into place. Women are mentioned precisely concerning their roles in land holding, land transmission and women's worship.

Outline

1:1-54	Census of Adult Men
2:1-34	Arrangement of Encampment by Tribes
3:1—4:49	Census and Duties of Levites
5:1-31	Laws for Exclusion from Camp
6:1-27	Nazirite Vows, Blessing of Aaron
7:1-89	Offerings in Completed Tabernacle
8:1-26	Purification of Levites
9:1-23	Instruction for Passover and Movement of Tabernacle
10:1-36	Order of March, Including Tabernacle
11:1-35	Complaint About No Meat
12:1-16	Aaron and Miriam Complain About Moses' Wife
13:1-33	Spies in Canaan
14:1-45	People Refuse to Attack Canaan
15:1-41	Instructions for Future Offerings
16:1-50	Rebellion of Korah
17:1-13	Aaron's Rod
18:1-32	Aaronite Priesthood, Levitical Tithe
19:1-22	Red Heifer, Uncleanness Related to Corpse
20:1-29	Death of Miriam, Waters of Meribah, Death of Aaron
21:1-35	King of Arad, Fiery Serpents, Bronze Serpent
22:1-41	Defeat of Sihon King of the Amorites and Destruction of Heshbon
23:1—24:25	Balak and Balaam's Blessings of the Israelites
25:1-18	Israelites' Idolatry
26:1-65	Second Census
27:1-23	Daughters of Zelophehad, Moses Commissions Joshua
28:1—29:40	Feasts and Offerings

30:1-16	Men's and Women's Vows
31:1-54	Destruction of the Midianite Men and Women
32:1-42	Territory of Reuben and Gad
33:1-56	Moses Writes Down the Stages of the People's Journey
34:1-29	Division of the Land
35:1-34	Territory of the Levites, Cities of Refuge
36:1-13	Addition to Law Concerning Women's Inheritance

Commentary

The Lay of the Land

It is helpful to have a map ready for constant reference when reading Numbers. Remote as they seem in time and space, the events in Numbers took place in the geographical areas that today are occupied by Egypt, Palestine, Jordan and Israel. In Numbers these areas are called Egypt, Sinai, Canaan, the hill country, the desert, Edom, Moab and Ammon. Often the people traveled from region to region, not town to town—a truly nomadic point of view.

One of the travelers' main complaints on the journey was the lack of food and water, as might be supposed in areas that for good reason are sparsely inhabited. However, they are not uninhabitable; survival there demands careful use of local agricultural and water harvesting capabilities.

Sinai, the Negeb and Other Deserts

Rainfall comes in the winter and is scanty. Water is available predominantly in the oases, where plants, animals and humans cluster around a well or spring augmented by rainfall. An oasis provides the opportunity to grow small gardens with date palms, fig trees, olive trees and other shade and fruit trees and bushes suited to the climate, such as oleanders. Grain is grown in the beds of nearby wadis.

A wadi, often called a river in the Old Testament, is a watercourse that flows with water after rains. Some of the water soaks through the sand or soil and is retained in the water table, while the rest rushes in torrents down the wadi, carrying good topsoil with it. Humans learned early to prevent the erosion of topsoil by building low dams of stone in the wadis. These dams served to catch the soil and to hold the water in the soil, forming beds of rich silt in which grains and legumes could be grown. The wadi banks and nearby hills could be terraced with loose stones; areas too small for a plow to turn were utilized for olive and other trees, vineyards and small gardens. The wadis, plus the many plants that spring up in the desert after the winter rains, suffice to feed limited flocks of sheep and goats.

Oases are occupied by tenacious communities, and water rights are carefully worked out and enforced. In light of what an oasis can support, the population figures of the tribes in the two census lists prove to be problematic. The first census list, 603,550 (Num 1:46), if we add the Levites, the males younger than twenty, the older males unable to go to war and an equal number of women, would give us a total of about two million people. Under normal circumstances these numbers would have overwhelmed the resources of a typical oasis inhabited by a few dozen to perhaps two hundred people.

Edom, Moab and Ammon

Tourists in Jordan who travel down the Desert Highway have a good view of the harsh terrain pictured in Numbers. Gravel-covered sand and rocky hills or mountains line both sides of the road, with only rare signs of water or greenery. The older King's Highway runs north and south also, but through much more mountainous terrain closer to the Dead Sea. Here too the small settlements are far apart, depending on soil and water. Water would be available only in springs and wadis.

However, even in antiquity, these areas were considered worth settling and defending; well-developed villages and significant industries are attested to from the Neolithic period (12,000 to 4,000 B.C.) onward, and settlements expanded as water-harvesting techniques developed.

Water harvesting means that winter rainfall can be caught, saved and kept as clean as possible until the rains begin again in the autumn. There are two ways of doing this: cisterns and reservoirs. As we know, water exposed to the sun produces green algae and then other organisms that feed on the plant life. This is what happens, although gradually, to water collected in open rock-cut reservoirs. Also, much water is lost to evaporation. However, since these processes happen over many months, it is worthwhile to cut such reservoirs, usually rectangular, into bedrock and plaster them inside with waterproof cement. Such cement was developed about 1000 B.C.

Channels are cut into the collection surface, usually the rock slope above the reservoir, to lead water into the reservoir. A typical ancient rock-cut reservoir might measure 50 by 100 feet and be perhaps 6 to 10 feet deep. Thus it would contain between 225,000 and 375,000 gallons, which would take care of the livestock of a community of several hundred people for much of the year.

A water-saving technique suitable for smaller amounts of water is the cistern, which is cut into rock and also cemented on the inside. It is cylindrical, narrowing toward the top. To stay free of algae, water must be kept dark, so the opening to the cistern is only about 20 inches across, and it is reclosed with a stone each time after drawing water (Gen 29:2-3). Rainwater collected in a cistern is (if the collection area is clean) of drinking quality and keeps well for a year or more. My recent measurements of household and field cisterns in Moab give volumes ranging from 15,000 to 25,000 gallons of water, although some are much larger.

Thus the barren appearance of Edom, Moab and Ammon is a little deceptive. The technology of rainwater saving, combined with inherited traditional knowledge of dry farming, enabled this area to produce far more food than would seem possible to a European or North American. Someone traveling in the Old Testament period from Edom northward on the east side of the Dead Sea, through Moab and Ammon, would have seen increasing flocks of sheep and goats. In broad wadis and other fields there would have been wheat, barley, buckwheat, peas, chickpeas, lentils and flax, and on the terraced wadi banks, vineyards and olive trees as well as figs and pomegranates. Home gardens would have yielded the vegetables and melons that the Israelites so missed in the desert (*see* Food and Water). In Moab and Ammon there would have been forests of pine, oak and pistachio.

The glowing report regarding Canaan brought back by the spies (Num 13—14) shows us a country similar to Moab, although usually even more prosperous in its fields, gardens, orchards and flocks. Not always, however. Remember that during the extended famine in Bethlehem, Elimelech and Naomi and their sons moved to Moab in order to survive.

Adultery (Num 5:11-31)

People have noticed that the Bible seems harder on women than on men in the matter of sexual morality. This observation culminates in the story of the woman taken in adultery (John 7:53—8:11), where we wonder how the scribes and Pharisees could not notice that adultery requires two people. Why then was the man not also hauled before Jesus? So the woman was guilty of a capital offense, for which the angry mob was ready to stone her, as prescribed by Deuteronomy 22:22. The mob did not bring its detective powers to bear on finding the man, for whom the same verse in Deuteronomy prescribed stoning. Nor are we told that the woman went into the act willingly. This may have been a rape (*see* Violence, Abuse and Oppression).

But for a married woman, according to Deuteronomy, the guilt of adultery does not require consent. The woman, even if she was raped, might have conceived a child who would inherit from a man who was not his biological father. That is what the laws intend to prevent. In such a case the woman was punished for something that the man did.

To understand this sin from an Old Testament point of view, we have to realize that nearly every woman was under the charge of a man. In a sense he owned her and owned some of her capabilities, mainly her ability to work and to bear children. In an age that had slaves and where free people never dreamed of having the rights we sometimes take for granted, that status of women did not seem as terrible as it does now.

To her father, since he married her off with a guarantee of virginity, a daughter's chastity was important. Society was organized to keep men and women apart, so she

---

Food & Water

In biblical times, people lived much closer to disaster than we do in the modern Western world. Diet varied greatly, with nomadic families having the most restricted diet: grains, legumes and milk products. The grains grown were wheat, millet and barley. Ezekiel 4:9 mentions spelt. The legumes were beans, lentils, peas and chickpeas (garbanzos). A grain eaten with a legume makes a complete protein, so they ate bread with cooked lentils (Esau, Gen 25:34) or pita bread with chickpeas (hummus, Ruth 2:14). Barley is less palatable than wheat or millet, and when times are good it is grown principally as animal feed. So the boy who donated five barley loaves (Jn 6:9) was very poor.

Sowing is timed to take advantage of the cold, heavy rains that fall only between November and April and to allow adequate time for the grain heads and legumes to fill out and ripen before the summer weather gets too dry. After the crops are harvested and gleaned, the grains and legumes are stored in burlap bags and carried around when the family moves. Wheat is threshed and stored but not ground until needed.

In biblical times, the sound of the upper grindstone rubbing against the lower as women did the daily grinding was a sound people were accustomed to hearing all day. Its cessation meant famine (Jer 25:10). The handling of the upper grindstone was a feminine skill, as illustrated by the story of Abimelech, whose skull was crushed by a well-aimed upper grindstone thrown from above by a woman (Judg 9:53; 2 Sam 11:21).

The other food source for nomads was milk from their sheep and goats. Without refrigeration, milk must be processed immediately. The milk, once soured in a goatskin churn, can be consumed within a few days as butter, drinking yogurt or spreadable yogurt (in Arabic *lebneh,* also known as yogurt cheese). For long-term storage, it is made into feta cheese or yogurt balls that keep for a year or more and are scraped and mixed with water for cooking in the winter. While sedentary families have olive oil, the only storable dietary fat for nomads is butterfat, which is used for cooking.

On special occasions a sheep or goat might be killed. In Old Testament times the most common occasion for meat eating was the sacrifice of an animal at the sanctuary or temple, when the family, after setting aside the priests' share, ate meat together (1 Sam 1).

Sedentary families had the same foods as the nomadic family but with the addition of products from gardens and orchards. Full nomads might not taste fruit from one year to the next, as food from trees and vines such as olives, olive oil, figs, pomegranates, fresh grapes, grape preserves and wine required year-round care from sedentary owners. These plants also required stone walls around them to prevent their being eaten by wild animals or the ever-present goats, as the prophet sings in Isaiah 5. The nomadic diet was bleak without vegetables (Num 11:4).

The earliest biblical reference to raising chickens is in the New Testament (Lk 22:34, 60), but doves were raised near every house for their eggs and flesh. They were among the cheapest of animal sacrifices and were particularly associated with women's worship (Lk 2:24).

Only small amounts of water for drinking, cooking, sponge baths and a little cleaning and laundry could reasonably be carried. It was not easy to water trees or gardens. Housing location had to take into consideration the availability of water, and tent dwellers had to carry their water unless they camped near it. If winter rain can be caught and kept, the remaining months are much more comfortable and horticulture can be extended. A big change took place (c. 1000 B.C.) with the invention of waterproof cement that could ensure retention of water in rock-cut pools or underground cisterns. Families who did not own a private cistern nearby had to carry their water. Ceramic jars of water would be fetched several times a day by women, from a perennial spring or a community well or cistern. Those who owned a donkey could carry several water skins in one trip.

Hosea 2 pictures a divorced woman who relies on prostitution to survive. She receives payment in kind: bread to eat, oil for food and for her lamp, and wool and flax for clothing. Water is also listed among her few needs; it could not be taken for granted.

DOROTHY IRVIN

---

would have no chance of becoming pregnant except after marriage.

To her husband, it was important that a woman's child was also his; only his heir must inherit his property. Everyone agreed that semen was the future child in liquid form, needing nothing more than the uterine environment to solidify and grow. Society and marriage customs were organized around this biological error.

If a married man had sex with another woman, it was not adultery and not sinful unless he had intercourse with a married woman or with a betrothed virgin (*see* Adultery). Interfering with another man's certainty about paternity was adultery for both parties and required stoning for both.

If a man raped a virgin who was not betrothed, the offense was against her father and could be compensated by paying fifty shekels of silver to him. This was the bride price, and they were married. The man could never divorce the woman. The rape was not considered sinful and required no remorse offering at the sanctuary. It was not adultery because it did not make another man's paternity uncertain, and it did not matter whether the perpetrator was married, since polygamy was allowed (*see* Polygamy). Thus the man did not offend against his wife or against another man. Society did not perceive that there was an offense against the virgin. It was a great task for Christianity to change such ideas, to protect women in their own right and not as they were related to a man's paternity.

If a man had sex with a woman who had no father—a slave, servant or day laborer—it was not adultery and must have been common when the woman worked for him (*see* Ancient and Modern Slavery). His only responsibility was to support the child. This is what made Abram hesitate to send Hagar away with Ishmael (Gen 16). He could not do this immoral thing merely at Sarah's behest. God had to approve the exception to the rule.

A man could relinquish his right to the paternity of a woman's son and dispose otherwise of the sexuality of a woman under his charge. Thus Lot could offer his daughters to save his visitors from sexual abuse (Gen 19:6-8). So could the man of Gibeah (Judg 19:24), who offers his virgin daughters and his visitor's concubine to the gang rapists. These count as stories about the principle of hospitality.

Abram could let the pharaoh take Sarai

as a concubine (Gen 12:10-20) and then triumph over what he gained in payment when the pharaoh discovered his error and returned Sarai without asking for his payment back. This counts as a success story, but one that draws a righteous rebuke (Gen 12:18-20; cf. Gen 20:9).

The Law and the Ordeal (Num 5:11-31)

Recorded law begins in ancient Mesopotamia with the cuneiform Code of Lipit-Ishtar, about 1850 B.C. The better-known Code of Hammurabi dates from about 1700 B.C. Egypt appears to have relied on oral tradition, so we do not know much about its legal system and values, but the surviving cuneiform law codes help us understand the Old Testament laws.

In the ancient Near East there are two main types of legal formulations. One type is casuistic law, or case law. Its formulation begins with phrases most simply translated "if." The description of the improper action is followed by a consequence. This tells the current judge how to handle the case. As cases and decisions accumulate, it becomes necessary to take into consideration how each case can vary, so subclauses are added.

A second type of law is apodictic law, in which a prohibition or a requirement is laid down. The Ten Commandments are in this form. Apodictic law specifies the end to which legal efforts should be directed; it expresses normative values rather than practical legal solutions.

Most scholars hold that only codes of casuistic law were intended for use in judicial situations. They would be applied to cases brought before a person trained in the legal tradition and specializing in juridical decisions. In Israel's early years, these would be the judges, described as having their origin when Moses' father-in-law, Jethro, realized that Moses could not handle all the cases brought before him. These judges continued in the tradition of Deborah and others, but the role was later largely taken over by priests. Such judges still exist in rural, traditional Arab communities of the Middle East.

The ordeal for the wife suspected of adultery seems to be a casuistic law. This type of case was brought to a priest, and its ancient purpose was to support the passing on of land to the biological son of the current owner. The important word is *biological*. As many ancient people saw it, the wife's obligation was to the principal man in her life, her husband. The woman's purity or impurity was not related to marital fidelity as a moral, emotional or spiritual commitment but to the genes of the heir. Where this attitude was predominant, the husband was not considered legally to owe marital fidelity, as we understand it, to his wife. His obligation was not to infringe on the rights of the principal man in his partner's life. If she had no principal man, he was not doing anything wrong. Taking Deuteronomy 22 into consideration, it seems that women had no rights apart from the rights of their fathers or husbands. However, the feeling that there was mutual obligation at some personal level was present at points in the Old Testament period (Prov 5:15-20; Mal 2:14-15).

The law discussed in Numbers 5:11-31 begins with "If any man's wife goes astray" and is clarified with other clauses: "if a man has had intercourse with her," and "[if] she is undetected" and "[if] there is no witness against her." Thus alternative situations are excluded. Intercourse must be suspected, and this ordeal is not for use when certainty can be reached by calling witnesses. It demonstrates reliance on God as the witness of hidden deeds, presupposes that the true answer will be made known without possibility of error and that the innocent will be protected.

Both possible outcomes are stated: "If . . . he is jealous of his wife who has defiled herself" or "if . . . he is jealous of his wife, though she has not defiled herself, . . . then the man shall bring his wife to the priest. And he shall bring the offering required for her, one-tenth of an ephah of barley flour. He shall pour no oil on it and put no frankincense on it, for it is a grain offering of jealousy."

The priest, in preparing to administer the ordeal, adds another condition that limits the use of this accusation, "while you were under your husband's authority." The possibility is acknowledged that there were times when the woman was not under her husband's authority. One such time might be when she had been betrothed but was not yet married. In that case, it appears that the prospective husband did not yet have the right to demand the ordeal. The alternative was for him to break off the marriage arrangements, as Joseph (Mt 1:19) planned to do, but he could not carry out an accusation of adultery, with its possible death penalty.

Or this might be a time when a husband had divorced his wife. This clause protected women from possessive vindictiveness, restricting men's authority to the times when they were married. It seems also to protect concubines, who otherwise might suffer the penalty applied to a married woman without having the married woman's claim to support or right to have her children considered legitimate and entitled to inherit.

The law still applies to women who are under their husband's authority but deprives the husband of the power of life and death. In the ancient world, men often held the power of life and death over their wives and children. But here his authority is restricted; he is not allowed to kill his wife on suspicion of adultery. Instead she must go through the process of the ordeal carried out by the priest.

Recourse to the ordeal is not optional. "This is the law" (Num 5:29). The man may not choose between this and taking the law into his own hands. He has the obligation to handle his jealousy by carrying his accusation to the priest. Only then shall the man be free from the serious iniquity of murder.

The woman was to drink a mixture of holy water, dust from the sanctuary floor and the ink (ink was made from lampblack or soot) with which the curse on her was written. If she became ill, her womb dropped and she suffered a discharge from it, she was guilty of adultery. Then she "shall bear her iniquity." This appears to mean that the death sentence (Deut 22:22) would be carried out. We do not know how dirty the sanctuary floor was, but the ingredients do not seem to be toxic. This ordeal seems to be slanted in favor of the woman. Any naturally occurring result would come from the psychological pressure stemming from awareness of guilt. Some authors have thought that the mixture would induce a miscarriage, at least in a guilty woman, but the law does not stipulate that it deals with a pregnant woman.

This law makes no distinction as to whether the woman initiated, consented to or resisted the deed. It would scarcely matter to the husband how it happened. For him, the important thing would be his certainty that he was the father of any child she had. Perhaps this helps us to understand how jolting the opening of the Gospel of Matthew must have been to its contemporaries. Joseph's acceptance of the angel's instruction not to be afraid to take Mary as his wife struck at the heart of patriarchal convictions about the value of women (*see* The Purpose and Value of Human Life).

Sometimes Old Testament laws seem peculiar and harsh, but this law must have been reassuring to women in those days. It limited the rights of husbands to entertain arbitrary and unfounded suspicions of their wives and to inflict capital punishment on them. It also set limits to the power of men who wished to control women without having given them the benefits and protection of marriage. It made betrothal, concubinage and the divorced state a little less one-sided. Thus, although it supported the values of patriarchy, it was a small step toward mutuality.

This ancient law, promulgated more than two thousand years ago, would not permit men to kill their wives, daughters or sisters on the suspicion of encouraging advances from another man. It would prohibit the murder of women family members in a moment of anger. It would require reporting to a public authority, as well as investigation of the circumstances of the allegation, and it would require turning the matter over to God's decision, as well as could be determined. A man who disobeyed the law and killed in sudden anger would be convicted as a murderer. For all of the strangeness of the ordeal prescribed, this law was intended, just as modern laws are, to keep women safe from angry, jealous, murderous men.

Inheritance and Marriage (Num 27:1-8; 36:1-5)

In an ancient agricultural society, people depended on land for sustenance. Together, marriage and inheritance formed an essential part of the system organized to feed the present and future family by determining land ownership into the next generations. People did not get married without knowing what they and their children would have to live on. As long as the family had land on which to set their tent or house, graze their animals and plant flax, wheat and other grains and legumes, and perhaps even a garden or orchard, they had the essentials of survival. Marriages were normally arranged by the parents of the groom and bride, as they still are among traditional families within large areas of the world (*see* Marriage).

Marriage was not usually an option for those who did not own land; they had to attach themselves to landowners for survival, either as slaves, indentured servants or day laborers. There were landless men and women in all three categories. Women, whether family members or employees, worked in the fields and with the flocks, as did men. Women also worked in every aspect of food production and preparation, spun, wove and made pottery. They produced and purchased raw materials and sold products (see below on Proverbs 31:31).

Work, especially farm work, was paid for in kind because coinage, throughout most of the Old Testament period, did not exist or was not readily available. Payment in kind meant that the worker received shelter, food and probably simple clothing.

Women who were slaves, indentured servants or day laborers often were required to have sexual intercourse with the landowner they worked for. If they were widows or orphans and had no principal man in their family, they may have had little choice. If no children resulted, it appears that the man had no legal obligation beyond the work agreement. If the woman had a child, the child belonged to the father but would not be an heir, because an heir was a male child of the legal wife or wives, in or-

---

Women's Rights in Biblical Times

Women's rights in biblical times were, by modern standards, sharply limited. Patriarchy placed all women, from the Hebrew slave in rural Palestine to the wealthy matron in Rome, under male authority. Yet the experience of an individual woman would have been affected by her situation: whether she was wealthy or poor, Jewish or Gentile, a Roman citizen or a slave, urban or rural, operating in a public or private sphere.

Old Testament Times

In many ways the Old Testament reflects the patriarchal world of its day. Wives and daughters were subject to their husbands and fathers and had little right to self-determination: fathers and husbands could overrule a woman's vows; an injury to a woman was viewed as an injury to her father or husband; and while a man could divorce his wife if she were "objectionable" (Deut 24:1), we read of no such rights for a woman. A raped woman was treated with suspicion and could be killed or married to her rapist. The stories of Lot offering his virginal daughters as sexual appeasements to violent strangers and of Abraham expelling Hagar from her home illustrate the vulnerability of women in this culture (see also the stories of the slave raped to death and of the sacrifice of Jephthah's daughter).

However, the Old Testament law does provide protections for women. Although a father could sell his daughters as a slave, he could not turn her into a prostitute. Widows were provided for, and women who were not overruled by their husbands or fathers could make and be held responsible for vows. When Zelophehad died without sons, his daughters were allowed to inherit his property. Although women were dependent upon men to protect their rights, those who were not so provided for could seek recourse: Tamar, for example, took steps to ensure that her right to bear a child was respected. When under the approval of her father or husband, a woman could act with great autonomy, as is the case with the industrious wife (Prov 31:10-31) who earns praise from her husband when she acts decisively and independently.

Arguably, the most important right in the Old Testament was that of membership among the people of God, and this right Israelite women had. Women received blessings, could benefit from the reading of the law, could participate in worshiping God and were not included among the uncircumcised. They could participate in sacrifices, consult a prophet independently and take the vow of the Nazirite. Deborah the judge, prophet and leader, Huldah the prophet, and Miriam the prophet, worshiper and leader played respected roles in the life of God's people.

New Testament Times

The women of the New Testament were also under a patriarchal system, but being part of the Roman Empire brought them some freedoms. Some women who had privilege, power or money obtained divorces; bought, sold and inherited property; and obtained freedom from slavery. Women such as Lydia, who sold purple cloth, and Chloe, who appears to be the head of a household, attained a degree of self-determination.

As was the case for Old Testament women, the most significant right for New Testament women was that of full membership in the community of God. In comparison with the surrounding first-century religions, in which women were often excluded and viewed as ritually unclean, Christian women were given considerable rights of participation. Jesus granted women the right to approach, learn from, be healed by, accompany and support him; he treated them with respect; and he entrusted them with the first preaching of gospel. To Paul, women were members of the body of Christ and potential co-laborers for Christ, and thus Paul was far more concerned with what women could do than with what they could not. Women prayed, prophesied and exhibited many gifts. Prisca and Nympha are examples of women with churches in their homes, in which they possibly were the patron or leader. Prisca taught Apollos, and Junia and Phoebe were called "apostle" and "minister." Many women are listed as workers in the Lord: Tryphaena, Tryphosa, Persis, Nereus's sister, Euodia and Syntyche, for example. For New Testament women, their encounter with Christianity was a liberating experience, granting them the right to approach God, to be a member of God's household and to exercise their gifts and energies for the work of the church of God.

Bibliography

M. J. Evans, *Woman in the Bible* (Downers Grove, IL: IVP, 1984); T. Ilan, *Jewish Women in Greco-Roman Palestine* (Peabody, MA: Hendrickson, 1996); C. S. Keener, *Paul, Women, and Wives* (Peabody, MA: Hendrickson, 1992); R. S. Kraemer, *Her Share of the Blessings* (New York: Oxford University Press, 1992); S. B. Pomeroy, *Goddesses, Whores, Wives and Slaves* (New York: Schocken, 1975); B. Witherington III, *Women in the Ministry of Jesus* (Cambridge: Cambridge University Press, 1984).

SHIRLEY A. DECKER-LUCKE

---

der of seniority. The slave's child could be kept on to work for the landowner and be supported by him, or the child could be hired out or sold. Heirs also could be hired out as laborers or sold, in case of necessity, but this was less likely, as they were more highly valued.

Females ordinarily did not inherit. If they were to take their father's land with them into marriage or to inherit their husband's lands as widows and then marry again outside the family, that would alienate land from the family that originally owned it. No family would accept a marriage plan by which their land holdings could be decreased.

Therefore the marriage and inheritance system called for women to be supported, but in a way that did not allow for family land falling into strange hands. A woman who married had a universally recognized claim to land to work on, but she ordinarily did not own that land. (Note that Job's sons all had houses, but his daughters did not.) A woman's welfare depended on the land-owning man to whom she was attached: her father, her husband, her son. If her father died before she was married, then her brother, like Laban, had the responsibility to see her suitably married. A son would maintain the family's claim to their land and his mother's claim to a livelihood from his father's land (*see* Widows). A daughter came into her importance when she married and, above all, when she had a son.

It cost a lot to marry a wife. Before the invention of coinage in the Persian period (approximately 625-330 B.C.) and probably even after, payment was in kind—flocks of sheep and goats and other goods. For those who had no possessions, indentured service was the means to pay for a wife. Thus Jacob worked seven years each for Leah and Rachel, building up Laban's fortune in flocks, as well as his own.

Although in principle (according to biblical, ancient extrabiblical and modern evidence) the bride price should be for the couple's use and for the bride, in practice the bride's share often was given to her father or brother and kept or spent by him. Leah and Rachel complain that Laban has used the money given for them (Gen 31:15), so they have no financial security apart from Jacob. Yet important comparative material from the ancient Near East shows that the bride often received and retained the bride price. One ancient text speaks of a woman sewing it into her garment, showing that her bride price is in small pieces but valuable, probably jewels or gold or silver. Until recently Arab women wore the bride price in the form of gold coins sewn to a headband or worn as a necklace. Although that custom is being replaced by bank accounts, the principle is still in use.

In some Middle Eastern societies today, when the groom's parents negotiate with the bride's parents, two sums of money are under discussion. The first, commonly called the bride price in translation, does not mean that the bride has been bought like a chattel. Rather, it means the amount of money necessary to give the new couple a start in life and includes their income and standard of living, housing and furniture, as well as gold wedding jewelry. This price must be paid at the time of the wedding. The jewelry and some of the bride price become bride's individual possession, and it is considered bad behavior if the groom tries to take it.

A second sum may be looked on as divorce insurance. Generally this money is not paid unless the husband divorces the wife; then she receives that sum for her support. This is intended by the bride's parents to make the groom think twice about divorce and to make sure that the wife, if divorced, will have something to live on. Until modern times, children remained with the father in the event of a divorce and were his financial responsibility. Today, however, there are different practices about child custody.

In low-income families, or if the bride's family is much poorer than the groom's family and therefore cannot be demanding, the divorce insurance may be low or nonexistent. Many women in the Arab world, like women in the United States, England and Europe, drop suddenly into poverty after divorce.

In biblical times women feared divorce because they could not initiate it, but men could divorce their wives apparently merely because they wanted to (*see* Divorce). Divorce was all the more cruel because it was unnecessary. Polygamy was an accepted practice; if a man was displeased with his wife, he had only to add another, especially if his first wife did not have children or did not have a son. It was not necessary to send away his first wife in order to take another, and concubines were allowed as well. It is easy to see why Jesus opposed divorce as it was practiced in his time (Mk 10:5). The woman's years of work as a wife did not entitle her to any share of the inheritance. It was always difficult for a divorced woman to marry again.

A well-negotiated wedding contract, especially if the bride came from a rich or powerful family, may have provided some insurance against the extreme poverty into which the wife fell when she was separated from land to work on and left without sheep or goats, flax or wool, fields or garden. Divorced or separated women could hire out as laborers, but if they were not well paid, they might still have to depend on friendly neighbors for gifts of essentials. Since men usually owned the means of production (land), divorced women had to look to men merely to live (Hos 2:5, 8).

Although a woman could claim support from the land of her principal man, it is not clear what she could own. Proverbs 31:19-31 tells us that some women had the power to invest, apparently on their own, in land and praises this as the activity of a competent woman. After describing the work of the valuable wife, the singer pleads, "Give her a share in the fruit of her hands." Men must often have claimed all the income when a wife's work was marketed.

For a balanced view, we must realize that few men in a tribal society had great individual power; their authority existed only in a chain of command in which male authority was determined by the interplay of birth order, age and wealth. The scope of their freedom to decide or choose in matters of employment, vocation, wife, political affiliation or life planning was extremely limited. In biblical society, all men but the most powerful rulers had far less self-determination than women today. But within that world, women for the most part had less than men (*see* Women's Rights in Biblical Times).

Nevertheless, women are people and even in ancient times had God-given rights within the system. Therefore, in unusual situations, unusual solutions were found to guarantee their rights without questioning the patriarchal structure. It is a little hard for us to find these rights spelled out in the Old Testament. Our best knowledge comes not from legal codes but from stories about the working out of women's claims: the story of Judah and Tamar (Gen 38), the book of Ruth, and the story of the daughters of Zelophehad (*see* Expectations of Women). An understanding of land ownership and how it operated in marriage is crucial to the question asked by the daughters of Zelophehad.

The Daughters of Zelophehad (Num 27:1-11; 36:5-12)

Zelophehad, when he died, left five daughters who appeared before Moses, Eleazar the priest, the leaders and the congregation to state what they thought would be a fair solution to their dilemma. There was no principal man in their family to own the land on which they might earn a living. If others inherited the land, their father's name would die out. They asked for equal rights to land ownership among their father's brothers (*see* Land Ownership and Economic Justice in Israel).

This was such a difficult question that Moses took it to the Lord, and thus the answer was divine and unquestionable. The Lord, always alert to the difficulties of widows and orphans, answered that in the absence of male direct descendants, women direct descendants would inherit in preference to male collateral descendants. This made sure the women had something to live on. This ordinance, together with the legal obligation of the next of kin as in Tamar's and Ruth's stories, provided for the support of women when the principal male died. Support does not mean that food, clothing and shelter were provided for women. Rather, they were allowed to support themselves and others by working on the land.

The ordinance (Num 27) does not talk about the possibility that the daughters might marry. But in Numbers 36 the other members of the tribe begin to worry that men outside the tribe might gain permanent control of their tribal lands by marrying women who inherited land. They receive reassurance from Moses; the daughters may marry within their father's tribe. Thus the tribal system of land ownership remains intact, while the daughters have freedom in choosing husbands within those limits. This seems to answer the concerns of each side. Female orphans will not be disinherited and impoverished. If they have brothers, the oldest brother has the obligations of the principal man.

Like all laws, this one can be disobeyed, but we see that ancient Israel had legal provisions to ensure that women, with their different status under the law, were fairly provided for, as fairness was envisioned at that time.

Miriam (Num 12; 20:1)

In Exodus 2 we are introduced to Miriam as a young girl of courage and initiative. In Numbers she is identified as the sister of

Moses and Aaron. The references to her as a person known to the hearer imply that she is to be identified with Miriam the prophet:

> Then the prophet Miriam, Aaron's sister, took a tambourine in her hand; and all the women went out after her with tambourines and with dancing. And Miriam sang to them:
> "Sing to the LORD, for he has triumphed gloriously;
> horse and rider he has thrown into the sea." (Ex 15:20-21)

When struck on its leather head with the hand, a tambourine provides a drumming noise together with the ringing of small metal disks. It is well suited to maintain rhythm and keep musicians together while singing or dancing.

Many Christian churches have no tradition of liturgical dance; the Catholic Holy Week liturgy in Spain is an exception. In many churches dancing is considered reprehensible. Yet liturgical dance was taken for granted in the Old Testament; it was done by men's groups (2 Sam 6:5) and also by women. Women's groups danced separately from men, with women leaders, as a traditional act of worship (*see* Women in Worship; Women as Leaders).

We have in the preceding verses a good description of what active prophecy could look like. We are accustomed to thinking of prophecy as the spoken word because we see it printed and then read it aloud while sitting or standing still. In reality prophecy was often sung and danced to the accompaniment of musical instruments. Prophets needed musical as well as religious training.

1 Chronicles 25:1-8 tells how David set up a system for training prophets to serve in the house of the Lord. These included men and women students. In Jerusalem the "sons and daughters" of Heman were trained to prophesy with lyre, harp and cymbals (1 Chron 25:5-8; 2 Chron 29:14). There is no indication that women's prophetic activity was different from men's or that support or compensation was different. The schedule for serving in the house of the Lord was determined not by rank, individual importance or gender but by drawing lots, which was understood as leaving the choice up to God.

Many of these prophecies were significant enough to be recorded in the Old Testament, although we cannot usually tell from the content whether they were composed by a man or a woman. An exception may be the Song of the Vineyard (Is 5:1-30); "let me sing for my beloved my love-song concerning his vineyard" (Is 5:1) is uttered from a woman's perspective if not by a woman. The songs of Hannah (1 Sam 2:1-10) and Mary (Lk 1:46-55) have in common with Miriam's song the prophetic concept of God as one who defends weak and insignificant people against the powerful (*see* Yahweh's Concern for the Disenfranchised). Many, if not most, of the weak were women.

The Pentateuch is concerned with origins, and Miriam, the originator and first leader of women's worship, is the sister of Aaron, the originator of male priests. We do not find lengthy descriptions of her job or specific rules for how it was to be carried out, as we do for the priests. This is because women's worship was carried out separately from men. Men knew that it existed but did not feel called to put down instructions and rules for how it was to be carried out. This fact preserved women's autonomy.

In the Old Testament, women sometimes led women's worship by receiving revelations from God, composing prophecies based on these revelations and handing on these prophecies by leading groups of women in worship. For example, the women of Shiloh had a liturgical dance to celebrate the annual feast of the Lord; it was common knowledge that the women danced without men present (Judg 21:19-24). This left them vulnerable to predatory men who were lacking in reverence for Yahweh.

Women were also prophets in the sense of foretellers of the future and advisers of public policy, like Huldah, and practiced other acts of worship, some approved and some disapproved (Jer 7:18).

In the Semitic tradition, women and men are separate in public. The custom of women celebrating and worshiping separately from men is attested to, and women had a separate area in Herod's temple, although there are no instructions for or evidence of such an area within the tabernacle summons or in Solomon's temple. It is not clear that they had a separate seating area in the village synagogues of Roman Palestine. These synagogues were often small, some less than fifteen feet square, with bleacherlike benches up the sides; it was scarcely possible to separate groups. Also, in a village, people went home at night, whereas those who came to Jerusalem to serve in the temple stayed for a longer time and were housed in the temple precincts, as was Anna (Lk 2:36-37). There separate areas for men and women would be expected.

In Numbers 12 we have a story about Aaron and Miriam that is difficult to understand. They did two things they should not have done, but it is hard to make a connection. They spoke disapprovingly of the Cushite woman whom Moses had married (*see* Africans in Biblical History), and they questioned his superiority as a prophet. The Lord calls them together with Moses and speaks from within a cloud at the door of the tent of meeting. Prophecies, the Lord says, are ordinarily revealed to prophets by the Lord in dreams. Not so, however, with Moses, to whom the Lord speaks directly. This astonishing mark of divine approval should have been enough, the Lord tells Aaron and Miriam, to make them see that Moses is superior to them as a prophet. His behavior is not to be questioned by them. For their arrogance, Miriam is stricken with a skin disease (sometimes questionably translated "leprosy"). Aaron admits their guilt and asks Moses for mercy for himself and for Miriam. Moses then asks God to heal her, so her punishment is lightened to a seven-day exclusion from the camp. The people waited for her to return, healed, before setting out again on their journey.

The lesson is clear that Moses had God's approval and was to be respected personally and as a prophet above all others. But Aaron, equally guilty in the text, received no punishment. We could conclude that this story teaches that it is much more offensive for women to question authority than for men. However, it could be that Miriam was the stronger character and took the punishment because she had been the prime mover. Yet in Numbers 12:11 Aaron speaks of having been punished like Miriam.

In Numbers 20, Miriam dies in Kadesh, in the desert of Zin, and is buried there. We do not know where Kadesh was, but the first audience of this text knew, and it is likely that Miriam's place of burial was mentioned because it was a shrine. The name of the city, Kadesh ("holy"), indicates that it was an important worship center and goal for pilgrimage. Perhaps it was a destination for women prophets and temple servants, who traveled to the tomb of this long-departed woman, famous for holiness and known to have been close to God.

So we know that Miriam was the first woman prophet and the first to lead women's worship, just as Aaron was the first to lead men's worship as prophet and as priest. It seems that they hold their positions by virtue of their being sister and brother to Moses, although it has been suggested that the religious and liturgical leadership of men and women could be expressed by describing them as brother and sister of Moses. The Aaronic priesthood had a divine mandate to be centrally important for men's religious activity, and the prophetic tradition of Miriam in leading women's worship was divinely maintained as being equally significant for women. We find few references to women's roles in prophecy or religious leadership in the Old or the New Testament, but those references never indicate any controversy about whether women should have these offices. The ancient writers take it for granted that women should and do. It must have been a great reassurance to women then to know that women's religious leadership was affirmed in the divinely instituted holiest of writings, acknowledged without hesitation in their social system, even by men, and maintained by temple training and jobs.

It is no accident that so many of the earliest Jewish followers of Jesus are named Miriam (Gk. Mariam, Lat. Maria): the mother of Jesus; her sister, the wife of Clopas (Jn 19:25); the mother of Mark; the mother of James and Joses and the children of Zebedee; the sister of Martha and Lazarus; and Miriam from Magdala.

Miriam, the mother of Jesus, was also a Miriam who was close to God (*see* Mary the Mother of Jesus). Perhaps she had learned to compose such songs at the Jerusalem temple, where this was taught. According to Luke, she prophesied in an inspiring hymn that she composed affirming God's preference and help for the poor and lowly (Lk 1:46-55). This hymn is in the ancient tradition of the Miriam for whom she was named and whose tradition she may have practiced (*see* Women as Psalmists).

Heshbon and Balaam (Num 21:21—24:25)

Earlier study of Numbers centered on trying to identify the route of Moses and his followers even though extrabiblical historical and archaeological evidence was lacking. No one thought of the prophet Balaam as someone likely to be verified by extrabiblical sources or archaeological finds when many more significant biblical men and women are not mentioned in historical sources outside the Bible. The relationship of archaeology to the text of Numbers 21:21—24:25 has turned out to be unexpected and strange.

It seemed reasonable that Tell Hisban, southwest of Amman and north of Madaba, was a natural place to start looking for Heshbon, city of Sihon, king of the Amorites. The continuity of name and of habitation promised well for biblical history. The city was destroyed by fire (Num 21:28), and the fire laid waste the territory all the way to Madaba. This probably refers to the villages surrounding Heshbon (Num 21:25). A team from Andrews University in Michigan, led by Siegfried Horn, began to excavate in the summer of 1968, having good reason to believe that they would come down on a burned level that would be datable by potsherds to about 1400 B.C., the presumed date of the exodus. Summer after summer they went down through successive layers, only to discover that habitation earlier than 1250 B.C. was not present at that site. The excavation did reveal, however, an immense open pool, cut into bedrock to catch and hold winter rainfall for summer use. They were delighted at this confirmation of Song of Solomon 7:4.

The lioness, as well as the lion, represented strength and ferocity. (Numbers 23:24)

The story of Balaam and the attempts of Balak son of Zippor, king of Moab, to hire him to prophesy against the Israelites is one of the most memorable in the Bible and has become a classic of world literature. It uses theology, mysticism and even folksy humor in teaching that God is the omnipotent planner and helper, in spite of working with poor material. In its emphasis on honest and inspired prophecy, regardless of payment and politics, it sets a standard against which the office of prophecy and the performance of individual prophets is to be judged. And it provides leadership principles for churches and church people in our day. It does all this while asserting the Old Testament's constant theme of the triumph of the underdog over the established powers, by the help of God.

However, the biblical view of Balaam is not simple. Although the story recounts that Balaam is consistent in his intention to obey God's instructions for his prophetic oracles, even though that was not what Balak wanted, and he tells Balak's messengers that is how it will be (a view echoed in Mic 6:5), other Bible passages do not understand his behavior that way. Deuteronomy 23:5 and Joshua 24:9-10 seem to imply that Balaam uttered a curse against the Israelites, which God would not listen to but turned into a blessing. He is described in 2 Peter 2:15 and Jude 11 as loving to receive gain from wrongdoing. Revelation 2:14 holds him responsible for teaching Balak to lead the Israelites into idolatry.

Numbers 25 begins with a story in which the women of Moab invite Israelite men to attend their religious feasts, at which worship of the Moabite gods was intertwined with eating the meat that had been offered to them. The implication that eating meat sacrificed to the gods meant worshiping them was an important issue in the early church. Worship of other gods was often described as harlotry in the Old Testament; here it is said to have been followed by sexual and religious misconduct.

God ordered Moses to hang all the chiefs of the people, a command that Moses passes on as a commandment to the judges to slay the men who have worshiped Baal. Phinehas slays Zimri, who had brought a Moabite woman, Cobzi, into his tent. It is hard to agree that Cobzi did anything deserving of death. She was worshiping her god; she did not know any other. The Lord also sent a plague on the people, but it killed fewer than it might have because of Phinehas's diligence in slaying a transgressor.

In the second story (Num 31) the Lord commanded Moses to execute the Lord's vengeance on Midian, so his troops slew the five kings of Midian and Balaam son of Beor, burned their cities and tent camps, and captured their wives, children and cattle for booty with which to reward the fighters. This was customary. Moses, however, is angry with the returning troops, asking, "Have you allowed the women to live?" He says that the women, at the instigation of Balaam, led the people of Israel, which seems to mean the men, to act treacherously against the Lord in the matter of Peor. We do not have the story about Balaam inciting Midianite women to lead Israelite men into idolatry. In Numbers 24:25 he seems to have gone home before the idea arose.

The men of Israel committed idolatry, and responsibility for their behavior is placed on Balaam and the Midianite women, although these women undoubtedly did not think they were doing anything wrong in inviting the Israelites to their worship feast. The Israelites are instructed to invite local foreigners to the Passover (Num 9:14), and this sort of invitation may have been a common form of hospitality in the ancient world, just as we invite visitors to our churches or Christmas dinner. All the Midianite women who had had sexual intercourse are slain, as well as their sons. The virgins were, so to speak, spared; the men can keep them. We can only imagine how the soldiers ascertained which group each woman was in.

The early church's view of Balaam was more favorable. His prophecy in Numbers 24:17, "a star shall come out of Jacob, and a scepter shall rise out of Israel," was understood as foretelling Jesus' birth. Thus Balaam is depicted, with the star, Mary and the baby Jesus, in Roman catacomb art.

While archaeological evidence for the exodus and the desert wanderings is lacking, one archaeological find verifies the historical existence of Balaam.

In the midst of the modern village of Deir Alla is Tell Deir Alla, a large habitation mound of mudbrick houses, dissolved into soil more than twenty-five hundred years ago. This site was chosen for excavation, beginning in 1959, by an archaeological team from the University of Leiden, the Netherlands. They excavated several trenches, coming upon a temple or shrine. Written on the white plastered wall of this building was an inscription in black and red ink dating from around 800 B.C. This is an unusual thing to find, and even though the inscription was damaged and some letters, even entire sections, were missing or illegible, the language was similar enough to biblical Hebrew to be read.

The inscription announces itself to be a book, or account, of Balaam son of Beor. He had visions at night and announced oracles on the basis of the revelations he received in his dreams. This is the same way that the biblical Balaam received his messages and exercised his prophecy. However, in this inscription, the revelation comes not from Yahweh my God (Num 22:18) but from the Shadday gods and the goddess Shagat. In the same form as the sections of Numbers concerning his prophecies, the Balaam inscription contains prose sections that introduce the blessings or curses; these are in poetry. The text is so broken that we do not know the reasons behind the oracles or to whom they were announced. However, the existence of this inscription attests to the continued fame of Balaam several centuries beyond the events described in Numbers.

Women's Vows (Num 30)

It was a common religious practice in the ancient Near East to make vows to give something to God or to do something for God. Worshipers might make such a vow after receiving a blessing from God. Or people might make a vow when in need or in danger, promising to make a certain offering to God if they were rescued or the wish was granted.

Because vows may involve significant amounts of wealth or time taken from other obligations, people may later not be so eager to fulfill them as when they made them. But vowing something to God and then not fulfilling the vow is reprehensible. Jephtha vowed (Judg 11) to offer to God the first thing that came out to meet him on his arrival home if God would give him victory over the Ammonites. God gave him victory, but Jephtha had to sacrifice his daughter.

So when the Old Testament takes up the question of under what circumstances a vow may be abrogated, it talks about an important aspect of religion. Numbers 30 is devoted to vows, but the men's section is short and simple. If men make vows, they must keep them.

A woman's vows are to an extent under the control of the principal man in her life. If her father or her husband objects to her vow when he first hears of it, the Lord excuses her from keeping it. However, she does not seem to be required to tell her father or her husband about her vow. If these men do not object to what she has vowed on first hearing of it, her vow stands. No one may object to a vow made by a woman who has no father or husband, such as a divorced woman or a widow,

What would a woman vow? The most likely vow would be to offer one of the standard sacrifices at the Jerusalem temple or at a local shrine. She might also vow to participate in traditional women's festivals, such as the four days in honor of Jephtha's daughter or the yearly feast of Yahweh at Shiloh (Judg 21:19). In many cases the vow would necessarily include the journey to Jerusalem or another sanctuary, perhaps a pilgrimage with other women.

The goods vowed, whether food offerings or precious metal, and the travel expenses would come out of the property of the woman or of her family. These expenses and the time away from work could be resented or prohibited at the whim of her husband or father if her right to keep her vow were not protected by law.

In the ancient world, not merely the biblical world, daughters and married women did not have much freedom. Their lives were, and in some places still are, under the control of the men in the family. So although this command that Yahweh delivered to Moses gives men control over the family assets and work schedule, it allows women some significant self-determination in their worship.

Conclusion

A look at the passages concerning women in Numbers reveals that many issues of importance to women are addressed. In every case, laws given to Moses by God protect women's rights in the family and inheritance system or in worship.

We see that these laws were carefully formulated to protect the male privileges on which social order and economic stability were thought to depend, particularly in the matter of the afterthought contained in Numbers 36:10-12. But we can also see that within that context they often secured women's rights in family and in religion.

Although the lives of women in the biblical period were different from ours and may seem restricted, Numbers assures us that rights, as they were seen at that time, for women were a concern of the legal system. Some of the most important rights of women were inalienable, and this is confirmed by their having been announced by God through Moses.

Bibliography. M. Douglas, *In the Wilderness: The Doctrine of Defilement in the Book of Numbers*, JSOT Supplement Series 158 (Sheffield: Sheffield Academic Press, 1993); O. Eissfeldt, *Hexateuchsynopse: die Erzählung der fünf Bücher Mose und des Buches Josua mit dem Anfange des Richterbuches* (Darmstadt: Wissenschaftliche Buchgesellschaft, 1922); C. H. Gordon, *Ugaritic Literature: A Comprehensive Translation of the Poetic and Prose Texts* (Rome: Pontifical Biblical Institute, 1949); J. T. Greene, *Balaam and His Interpreters: A Hermeneutical History of the Balaam Tradition,* Brown Judaic Studies 244 (Atlanta: Scholars Press, 1992); G. van der Kooij and M. M. Ibrahim, *Picking Up the Threads: A Continuing Review of Excavations at Deir Alla, Jordan* (Leiden: University of Leiden Archaeological Centre, 1989); M. Noth, *Numbers: A Commentary,* trans. J. D. Martin (Philadelphia: Westminster Press, 1968); D. T. Olson, *Numbers,* Interpretation (Louisville, KY: John Knox Press, 1996); H. Rouillard, *La Pericope de Balaam (Nombres 22—24): La Prose et les "Oracles"* (Paris: Gabalda, 1985); J. Sturdy, *Numbers* (Cambridge: Cambridge University Press, 1976); T. Thompson and D. Thompson (D. Irvin), "Some Legal Problems in the Book of Ruth," *Zeitschrift für die alttestamentliche Wissenschaft* 18 (1968): 79-99. The information on modern nomadic life comes not from publications but from my visits over twenty-five years with many women of the following Jordanian and Palestinian tribes: the Abu Riash, the Adwan, the Ajarmah, the Balqa, the Bani Hamida, the Bani Sakr and the Howeitat. To visit them is to enter a little-known corner of today's world, as well as the world of the Bible. To receive their hospitality is a great blessing.

DOROTHY IRVIN

DEUTERONOMY

Introduction

Although it is perhaps invidious to make such comparisons, Deuteronomy could be described as the most significant book in the Old Testament. It is indissolubly linked to the historical books; the common description of Joshua—2 Kings as the Deuteronomic history stems from the links, in vocabulary as well as theme and interest, between the two. There are also close connections between the interests and motivation of the Deuteronomist and the prophets. In the New Testament Deuteronomy is quoted directly thirty times, and there are a further eighty clear allusions. Deuteronomy brings together and reflects on the principles of covenant living. It provides a historical background for the nation of Israel, gives a sample selection of laws and rituals, and discusses the consequences, in terms of blessings and curses, if Israel does or does not keep the covenant.

However, the main purpose of Deuteronomy seems not to be just to provide information about what it means for Israel to live as God's covenant people. Most of the information is available elsewhere in the Pentateuch, often in more detail. Rather, Deuteronomy is a driving force, inspiring loyalty and action. It is in many ways the equivalent of a modern motivational video or seminar. It is the nearest thing that Israel had to a national constitution. It gives the people of each generation a sense of national identity and drives them to take seriously the implication of their identity as the people of Yahweh. One of the main links, with New Testament teaching and with the teaching of the prophets, is the stress that the essence of religion is not a set of beliefs and rules—although beliefs and rules may be important—but a personal relationship with the God who has chosen this people as his own. This relationship has to be lived in the context of everyday life. Deuteronomy provides data about what this means in practical terms and a stimulus and encouragement to live it. It stands as a refueling station for the people.

There is no doubt that Deuteronomy is in some sense to be seen as a covenant document, and it must be interpreted in the light of that, but in precisely what sense is not quite clear. It is structured in the form of a series of speeches given, apparently, by Moses just before the people entered into the Promised Land. It has sometimes been seen as a legal document, but that description does not do it justice. The laws mentioned are selective, illustrative rather than a comprehensive code. The selection is there to explain rather than to define the covenant and its requirements. As J. G. McConville puts it, "The point of Deuteronomy's legal section, as of the book in general, is to inculcate a spirit of law-keeping rather than to promulgate law as such" (1984: 154). We do not have here a textbook for lawyers or for leaders but a challenge for the whole people, children, women and men alike.

Although Deuteronomy is formulated as speeches rather than as direct treaty, strong links between Deuteronomy and other ancient Near Eastern treaty documents have been identified. However, there is debate as to whether it relates more closely to the Babylonian style of treaty that was more common in the first millennium B.C. or the Hittite style of treaty that was prevalent in the second millennium B.C. If the Hittite style is seen as a pattern that the writer was aware of, then Deuteronomy should be dated as basically Mosaic and the speeches could be seen as original, a copy (edited perhaps) of what Moses said to the people. If the later style is the background, then this supports the view that Deuteronomy was produced in the seventh century, around the reign of Josiah, and the speeches are a literary technique used to further the writer's purposes.

A key issue is exactly how Deuteronomy relates to the historical books that have come to be known as the Deuteronomic history. That there is some dependency between Deuteronomy and the historical books, which only came into their final form during the exile, is undoubted. The question is whether Deuteronomy is the foundation of the thinking of the historian—a kind of introduction to the whole spectrum of historical writing, constantly in the editor's mind as he organized the material—or whether the historical writings are the inspiration for Deuteronomy, which is formulated as a conclusion perhaps written during the time of Josiah and intended to draw the people back into a covenant relationship with God. Did Deuteronomy form the basis of Josiah's reformation, or did it arise out of it? A related question is whether the theology in Deuteronomy is formulated in the light of long-term reflection on the laws or whether the laws were formulated in the light of the theology. McConville argues that the "laws were framed expressly to encapsulate covenant principles," and thus he leans toward an early date (1984: 157).

The language of Deuteronomy is described as good seventh-century Hebrew, which means that if we are to accept the dating as essentially Mosaic then we must assume that the language was revised and updated around the time of Josiah, in the same way that modern translations re-present the biblical material so that it can be understood by contemporary readers. This would make good sense: Deuteronomy's prime aim of motivating people to own their identity as a covenant people and to actively live a covenant lifestyle would be harder to achieve if the language used no longer communicated. In some ways the disagreements over dating can be seen as stemming from the ongoing relevance of the book. It does have a timeless quality that speaks clearly to each generation. It has definite things to say to Josiah's kingdom and to the postexilic Israelites, but that does not take away from the dynamic relevance it would have had for the Israelites just entering into the Promised Land. So maybe it does not affect our appreciation and understanding of the message too much whether it was first presented to Israel during the covenant renewal ceremony at the time of Joshua or at the time of Josiah.

The overall theme of Deuteronomy is the call for Israel to be a covenant people and to be aware of itself as that, but it is worthwhile to note a number of subsidiary themes and motifs to look for as one reads through the book.

Grace and law. The Deuteronomist is concerned to show that God has been and continues to be gracious to Israel. Yahweh gives them the covenant and provides a stream of blessing for them. But there is also a concern to show the need for the law and for keeping the law—in obedience to their great God but also so that they can imitate and reflect him. As their God is holy, just and concerned for the poor, so must they be. Grace and law appear to be inextricably linked in the mind of the author. They are not in conflict; both of them must be seen in the context of covenant relationship with God.

The Deuteronomic principle. The idea that righteousness will bring blessing and unrighteousness disaster is often seen as at the heart of the Deuteronomist's thinking. It is clear that this principle is present. However, when the principle is developed to suggest that as God blesses the righteous, then those who are blessed, often interpreted as rich, must therefore be righteous, this becomes a travesty of Deuteronomy's teaching. The concept must again be seen in the context of relationship with God.

Humanitarian interests. The concentration on blessings coming from God does not override the responsibility for others. There is a particular responsibility to care for those who do not seem to be obviously blessed by God, those who if the Deuteronomic principle is applied unthinkingly could be seen as unrighteous.

Kinship. Related to the preceding is the sense that the whole community is viewed in family terms. Responsibilities of brotherhood and sisterhood carry through to all aspects of life. Business and government must be carried out in the light of this family relationship.

Opposition to alien religion. There is within Deuteronomy a consistent stress on the need for the eradication of Canaanite worship from within the Israelite community. Sometimes it has been thought that the Deuteronomist was against all religious ritual. There is little explicit interest in religious ritual and other cultic elements; that is left to other books like Leviticus. But this does not mean that Deuteronomy sees the cult as irrelevant. The condemnation of pagan practices includes the idea that there are religious rites that are not pagan and that must be protected from pagan influence.

The centralization of worship. Deuteronomy speaks often of "the place that Yahweh your God shall choose." In the light of Israelite history this is interpreted as a single, centralized sanctuary—namely, the temple. This is perhaps not quite as clear-cut as is sometimes assumed, but there does seem to be a strong assumption that corporate worship must take place in officially sanctioned situations.

Outline

1:1—4:49	Moses' First Speech: Historical Overview and Preliminary Challenge
5:1—26:19	Moses' Second Speech: Overview of the Law
27:1—28:68	Moses' Third Speech: Consequences—Blessings and Curses
29:1—32:52	Moses' Fourth Speech: The Ongoing Challenge
33:1-29	Moses' Fifth Speech: The Blessing on the Tribes
34:1-12	Conclusion: The Baton Is Handed On

Commentary

Moses' First Speech: Historical Overview and Preliminary Challenge (Deut 1—4)

If Israel was to have a clear sense of identity and an effective awareness of the meaning of its covenant partnership with Yahweh, then a historical perspective was vital (*see* Covenant and Community). If the nation was to move ahead along the path that God had called it to, then the people must know where they came from and how they got to the place where they stand now. To modern readers, immersed in individualistic thinking, this kind of historical overview is often seen as having only marginal relevance. However, even today, particularly among the older generations and perhaps especially women, interest in family background and genealogical information is growing fast. People do like to know where they come from. We need to grasp the significance of this first speech, get a feel for the community, for the sense of national pride and national shame that this speech inculcates. The response is meant to be "Where do we go from here?" and the final challenge spells that out. It is in the light of what has gone before that Israel is called to commit itself anew to following the great God who had entered into covenant relationship with the nation and set covenant demands before it. It may be that the writer has included the historical prologue in imitation of other Near Eastern treaties, but that would not lessen its impact for the Israelites.

For women, the awareness of history has always been important not so much in terms of dates and leaders but in terms of homes and relationships, the stories of the past. The only specific mentions of women in this first speech are when we hear of men, women and children destroyed by Israel in their progress to the Promised Land and in the mention of the wives left behind by the soldiers from the tribes who wished to settle on the eastern side of the Jordan. However, the history described was their history just as much as that of the men. It was the story of their lives and their experience, and it was to be passed on to their children that they might understand too. This speech was for "all Israel," men, women and children.

Introduction (Deut 1:1-5)

The precise site of the Israelite gathering is given, not so much because of any geographical significance but in order to give the impression that these were real people in a real situation. The two key points brought out are that it was forty years since they first set out for the new land and that the Lord Yahweh was behind the words that Moses spoke, just as Yahweh had been involved in the history of the long forty years that was about to be set out.

Land and Government (Deut 1:6-46)

The land is given; potential government structures are set up; the land is explored, feared, rejected and then unsuccessfully reclaimed. This chapter explains the reason for the forty-year period of wilderness wandering. Israel through disbelief and disobedience had lost the opportunity to claim the land forty years earlier. Two issues relating to leadership are raised. Deuteronomy 1:13 encourages Israel to "choose for each of your tribes individuals who are wise, discerning, and reputable to be your leaders." This implies a level of democracy that does not seem to be reflected in the practice of Israel elsewhere. Second, Moses states or perhaps complains that "even with me the LORD was angry on your account" (Deut 1:37) so that he was not able to enter the Promised Land. Deuteronomy 3:26 picks up the same point. Moses' great longing to enter into the land was not to be fulfilled because of the failures of the people that he led. The account in Numbers 20 is rather different. That passage puts the blame for the prohibition against Moses entering the land securely on his own shoulders. It perhaps seems a heavy punishment for a fairly trivial crime, striking the rock instead of speaking to it, but as a leader Moses had a strong responsibility to represent God rightly. Taking it upon himself to misrepresent God as being the source of his personal anger was a serious matter. It may be that the elderly Moses is seeking to shift or to share that blame, because he would not have been angry if it had not been for the people's attitude. However, it may be that the Deuteronomist wants to make the point that leadership has implications and consequences. The ultimate responsibility for the actions of the led will be the leader's and will be allowed to stand. There is perhaps some background here to the directive of James 3:1 that not many should presume to be teachers because they will be judged more strictly.

Desert Wanderings (Deut 2—3)

This is an abridged and foreshortened record of events of which Exodus and Numbers give us more detail. The intention here seems to be to provide the people with a sense of what had happened and to bring to mind the history that they would have known from the other sources. For the modern reader, this section raises uncomfortable issues relating to the conduct of holy war. Those who stood in Israel's way were destroyed. Whole communities of "men, women and children" (Deut 2:34; 3:6) were slaughtered. For ancient Israelites this would have been a great victory, a reason for pride. Although discussions of innocence and guilt occur elsewhere in the Old Testament and we know that even ten righteous Sodomites would have saved their city (Gen 18), that issue is not picked up by the writer of Deuteronomy. However, Deuteronomy 2:9, where Moses states, "The Lord said to me: 'Do not harass Moab . . . for I will not give you any of its land' " shows that we must beware of simplistic views of their triumphalistic nationalism. It is made clear that although the victories of Israel are the main concern, nevertheless the reader must be aware that the God who is leading Israel and who has instituted a covenant relationship with Israel does also have concerns for and dealings with other nations.

This bringing-you-up-to-date section concludes with a brief description of the land assigned to the two and a half tribes who decided to remain on the east side of the Jordan and with the explanation of why, in the next stage of Israel's progress into the land, Joshua and not Moses would lead them. One can hear the pathos in Moses' voice as he speaks of pleading to be allowed to see the task through to the end. It is easy to accept the reality of a speech like this. But whatever the basis of the prohibition of Moses entering the new land, the reality remains. Life moves on, new tasks call for new leaders, and it was important that Joshua was seen as fully supported and not just resentfully accepted by Moses. Maybe the editor was aware that Israel's leaders needed to accept the concept of graciously handing over to their successors, as some, such as Samuel, later did, and others, such as Saul, did not.

Linking the History and the Law (Deut 4)

Deuteronomy 4 forms a link between the historical prologue and the second speech giving an overview of the law. This kind of link is a clear indication that even if the main body of Deuteronomy consists of verbatim records of Mosaic speeches, at some stage an editorial process has blended all the different sections into a unified whole. This chapter focuses the mind of readers on their experience as individuals and as a nation. That experience leads them into relationship with God, and the motivational force of that experience challenges them to future obedience and service.

Deuteronomy 4:1-14 sets out the relationship between possession of the land and obedience to the laws and decrees that were about to be set out. The land and the laws were given to Israel by Yahweh, the God of their ancestors. The God who had cared for their ancestors and them in the past would continue to care for them and their descendants in the future. The land was the God-given place where the community could develop and flourish; the laws set out the pattern of God-ordained living that would enable the community to develop and flourish. Commitment to God and obedience to his laws were the key. The challenge that is put before the people at this crucial stage in the life of the community is to make it happen. The constant references to children, the importance of teaching children and providing for the future of their children, emphasize that this book is not just for the generation entering the land but for all those who will live in the land in the future.

It is made clear that the law is not to be kept just for its own sake but because it is God's law. The national identity was bound up with relationship with God, and if the people missed out on that fact, then everything else was irrelevant. Therefore the primary prohibition is of idolatry (Deut 4:15-31) and the primary reality is God (Deut 4:32-40). God is not to be represented as man or woman (Deut 4:16) or worshiped as being gender-specific. The task then is to "acknowledge today and take to heart that the LORD is God in heaven above and on the earth beneath; there is no other" and to "keep his statutes and his commandments . . . for your own well-being and that of your descendants . . . so that you may long remain in the land that the LORD your God is giving you" (Deut 4:39-40).

A brief note on the provision of cities of refuge for those in the tribes settling east of the Jordan leads in to the introduction to the law code (Deut 4:44-49).

Moses' Second Speech: Overview of the Law (Deut 5—26)

There are laws and instructions found elsewhere in the Pentateuch that are not contained here. This is not meant to be a comprehensive survey of everything that Israel was or would ever be required to do or not to do. It is a selection, a summary, meant perhaps to enable the Israelites to understand the kind of life that God wanted them to lead. It may be a summary, but it has comprehensive coverage. God was concerned about family life, social life, interaction with neighbors, religious practices, employment, warfare, food, religious beliefs and understanding, national government, the justice system, health and hygiene. In other words, there was no aspect of life that was not relevant to Israel's life as God's covenant people. There was no separation between the religious and nonreligious aspects of life.

There seems to be no particular prioritizing of laws. How you harvest your grapes, what feasts you attend, where you worship, whom you marry, how you treat your servants, how you plant, harvest and sell your grain—all of these are relevant to the overall question of how you live your life as the people of Yahweh, relating to him, obeying his commands and reflecting his character. There is also no priority of personnel. The law was for everyone. Particular ordinances may apply to particular subgroups within the community: employers, slaves, leaders, mothers, husbands, kings. But the law as a whole was for the community as a whole. It was a gift from God to the whole community to enable it to receive the blessing—that is, to enable Israel to live as God's covenant people, in constant relationship with him. In this context the law belongs equally to the men, the women and the children of Israel.

In a brief commentary like this there is not the space to give detailed comments on each of the requirements listed. So we too will make selections, based in a fairly arbitrary way on personal interest. We will try to get our own feel for the life that God wanted for his people and in doing so trying to gain that dynamic sense of the reality of God that was so much a part of the Deuteronomist's life and experience.

Overview of the Law (Deut 5)

The Ten Commandments form a preliminary summary, an overview, of all the other requirements of the law. These commandments, originally given years before at Sinai, were equally applicable, as the covenant was equally applicable, to the women and men about to enter the Promised Land and indeed to the women and men throughout the history of God's people. The rest of this main, central section of Deuteronomy can be seen as expanding on these commandments, as working out what it might mean in different situations or for different people. The covenant involves relating to God but also relationships with one another. The Ten Commandments deal with some of the implications of both. The list is not, and is not intended to be, comprehensive. However, it is extensive enough, especially when one looks at the expansions and developments in the following chapter, for the Israelite to work out what might have been said about their attitudes or behavior in other similar or even at that stage unforeseen situations. For Christian believers it is equally necessary to have both a broad sense of what it means to belong to Christ, an idea of the implications of that belonging within specific situations or circumstances, and the ability to apply general principles to new situations. In the New Testament era, it was considered possible to condense the law, or at least the Ten Commandments, still further to the twin commands of loving God wholeheartedly and loving one's neighbor as oneself (Mt 22:39-39; Mk 12:33; Lk 10:27). The New Testament makes it clear that keeping the law given to Israel is not an essential prerequisite for Christians of relationship with God; that comes, rather, through faith in Christ and through his work. Nevertheless this summary of the law is seen to have ongoing significance for Christians (Rom 13:9; Gal 5:14; Jas 2:8), and it could be argued that the Ten Commandments continue to form a good basis for Christian living.

Note that daughters and female servants are to be allowed to rest on the sabbath along with their brothers and male colleagues. This indicates that their need to rest is taken seriously and also that their participation in what might be called the religious requirements of the covenant are taken for granted. The requirement for the equal honoring of father and mother is paralleled later in Deuteronomy (Deut 21:13, 19; 22:15; 27:16; 33:9). In almost every case where parenting comes into question, mother and father are mentioned together.

The Heart of the Law (Deut 6)
It is possible to see this chapter as the hub around which the rest of Deuteronomy is centered, the heart of the Deuteronomist's message of covenant relationship. In it the writer conveys his conviction that the covenant was not just about ideas or status but about the whole of life. Lifestyle and belief are intimately linked. Blessing and obedience are two sides of the same coin. But what matters most of all is the love that links God and people together. It would be impossible for them to obey the law without loving God because the love of God was at the heart of the law. It would also be impossible for them to obey without the support stemming from the tremendous concern that God had for them. With New Testament insights we understand this concept in a different way from the ancient Israelites, but the heart of the gospel is found in incipient form within this chapter. Deuteronomy 6:4-5, "Hear, O Israel: The LORD is our God, the LORD alone. You shall love the LORD your God with all your heart and and with all your soul, and with all your might" is known as the Shema and became a key part of the ritual of later Judaism when the instruction to bind it on foreheads

Monotheism

Monotheism is essentially belief in one God (Gk. *mono,* "one," *theos,* "G/god"), although in biblical religion belief was never separated from action. Thus the Old Testament rejection of polytheistic idolatry is often formulated in terms of prohibitions against serving other gods ("serve" and "worship" derive from the same Hebrew verb) or following other gods.

There is widespread agreement that monotheistic belief within Israel developed over time, although scholars differ regarding the dating and exact nature of the process by which it developed. It is clear that one's perspective is shaped by hermeneutical presuppositions, specifically how one understands the formation of the Old Testament canon and the historical nature of the texts involved. Those who interpret the book of Genesis as literally historical according to present-day standards hold that monotheistic belief was present in earliest human history (Gen 4:26), while others trace it to the patriarchal/matriarchal period (Gen 12:8). Early Jewish interpreters identify Abraham as the first to believe that God is one (*Genesis Rabbah* 39.1; Josephus *Jewish Antiquities* 1.156). Still others trace the belief to Moses, to whom and through whom God revealed the Ten Commandments, the first of which is "I am the LORD your God, who brought you out of the land of Egypt. . . . You shall have no others gods before me" (Ex 20:1, 3). It must be noted, however, that this commandment does not explicitly deny the existence of other gods (cf. Ex 15:11). For this and other reasons, some interpreters attribute the explicit formulation of monotheism to Josiah's reform (621 B.C.), based upon the Book of the Law/Covenant, which many identify as at least the basic core of Deuteronomy (2 Kings 22—23).

It is often suggested that monotheism was the crowning achievement of exilic Judaism, when Israel finally rejected polytheistic idolatry—for which God had severely judged them—and affirmed allegiance to the one true and living God. Evidence for this is the fact that monotheistic belief is most clearly articulated in Deuteronomy (e.g.,

Deut 4:35, 39; 6:4), in Isaiah 40—66 and in postexilic prophets (e.g., Zech 14:9; Mal 2:10). The book of Judith (c. 130 B.C.) also gives expression to this view: "For never in our generation, nor in these present days, has there been any tribe or family or people or town of ours that worships gods made with hands, as was done in days gone by. . . . But we know no other god but him" (8:18, 20). However, although it is clear that only after the exile did polytheistic and syncretistic ideas largely disappear from the religion of the common people, this does not mean that monotheistic ideas were new at this time. There is still a strong opinion that sees Amos as the founder of ethical monotheism, and many would see even Amos as reinforcing old truths rather than introducing new ones.

Biblical monotheism is most fully expressed in the supreme creedal affirmation of God's self-revelation as one, the Shema: "Hear, O Israel, the LORD, our God, is one LORD" (Deut 6:4, author's translation). The Shema, recited twice daily by observant Jews, forms the most important core of Jewish prayer liturgy. We know that it was originally accompanied by a recitation of the Ten Commandments, as reflected in the Nash Papyrus (c. first century B.C.), the Mishnah (*Tamid* 5:1) and Mark's Gospel (Mk 12:29-30). Thus very early the Shema was associated explicitly with ethical conduct, particularly as embodied in the Ten Commandments, the quintessential expression of God's will for Israel and all humankind. To recite the Shema was to take upon oneself the yoke of the kingdom, that is, to place oneself in covenant relationship with Yahweh and thus under Yahweh's authority. The Shema, with its affirmation of Yahweh's oneness, is joined with the acclamation of Yahweh's rule in Zechariah 14:9: "And the LORD will become king over all the earth; on that day the LORD will be one and his name one." This combination of concepts has significant implications for biblical ethics, often designated as monoethics.

The existence of a variety of translations for the Shema's six Hebrew words reveals their inherent ambiguity. Some suggestions are "the LORD our God, the LORD is one"; "the LORD is our God, the LORD is one"; "the LORD our God is one LORD"; or "the LORD is our God, the LORD alone." Much of the debate centers on the word *ehad*, whether to render it as "one" or "alone." Those who opt for "alone" have to explain why the semantically difficult *ehad*, which in its plain meaning does not necessarily connote exclusivity, appears instead of the more precise word *levad* ("alone"). The term seems to have a special usage in this context and probably is intentionally ambiguous to inspire and allow for a multiplicity of interpretations. The most obvious meaning is "alone." Against the backdrop of pagan idolatry, Israel confessed that Yahweh alone is the only true and living God. But the word *ehad* carries additional connotations, all of which suggest that the biblical concept of monotheism, far from providing theological legitimation for that which is exploitive and alienating, can serve as a powerful redemptive model for all creation.

First, *ehad* means "unique." Thus the affirmation that "God is one" is not a quantitative designation, one vis-à-vis many, as in pagan monotheism or philosophical monotheism, but essentially qualitative. God is one in God's essence. God is not more than or better than but altogether different from—ontologically unique, "wholly other." God is distinct from, separate from, all creation, that is, God is holy (cf. Is 45:21-22).

Second, *ehad* connotes "unity," which implies wholeness (Heb. *shalom*). *Shalom* presupposes unity within diversity, that is, perfect relationship and functioning among constituent parts that form a perfect, harmonious whole. How is God a unity? We see two aspects. God exists in unity of relationship within the Godhead (cf. Gen 1:26). Traditional Christian trinitarian doctrine affirms that God is one in three Persons—Father, Son and Holy Spirit (*see* The Trinity). This relationship is expressed clearly in John 1:1: "In the beginning was the Word, and the Word was *with God* [emphasis added], and the Word was God." The word translated "with" *(pros)* is unusual in this context. It is related to the word *face* in Greek *(prosōpon)*, thus expressing personality.

The text signifies that "the Word was 'face to face' with God," that is, in eternal relationship with God.

Moreover, in God there is an inner unity, a perfect consistency of essence, though seemingly divergent to the finite human mind. This ontological paradox is articulated by Abraham Joshua Heschel: "He [God] is a being who is both beyond and here, both in nature and in history, both love and power, near and far, known and unknown, Father and Eternal . . . Creator and Redeemer" (118-19). Such a theological understanding—God as a unity who holds within Godself diverse elements—is foundational to the New Testament theology of the church as the body of Christ, which is a unity and at the same time diverse (1 Cor 12:4-27). In Ephesians 4:3-16, Paul explicitly connects monotheistic affirmation with teaching about diversity within the church and exhortation to unity.

The unity of God finds expression in the unity of the cosmos that God created, for God is one—as Creator. Already in the book of Isaiah these twin concepts are joined: "For thus says the LORD, who created the heavens (he is God!), who formed the earth and made it (he established it; he did not create it a chaos, he formed it inhabited!); I am the LORD, and there is no other" (Is 45:18). This is just one example of many such affirmations in Isaiah. The orderly structure and interworkings of creation are an expression of the oneness of God; without this unity, the cosmos would be nothing but chaos.

God's unity and the essential unity of creation gave rise to two ancient Jewish theological expressions that shed light on this important aspect of biblical monotheism. One was that early rabbis referred to God as "the Root" *(iqar),* which meant the elemental principle of the universe, the One from whom it came into being and the One by whom it continued to exist and hold together. The second is more explictly liturgical. The concepts of God as One and God as Creator were conjoined in the Jewish prayer formula for the Shema. The first of the two benedictions (blessings) immediately preceding the recitation of Deuteronomy 6:4 affirms that God is the Creator and Renewer of the world, expressing theologically that God is a unity in relationship with creation and that God imparts unity *(shalom)* to creation.

The unity of God in relationship to creation also has significant implications for ecological ethics, an area that has attracted feminists of many kinds to the extent that there now exists a distinct discipline called ecofeminism. Ecofeminism links women together with nature and holds patriarchalism responsible for oppressing both; ecofeminists maintain that women alone are uniquely suited to lead the way to restoration of planet Earth. In that many feminists also identify monotheism with patriarchalism (see below), they regard it as likewise unconcerned with or opposed to responsible behavior with regard to creation. This perspective, however, does not take into account the concept that God's essential unity finds expression in the relationship between the unity of God and the created cosmos. One who affirms the biblical truth of God's unity must act accordingly, devoting his or her energies to working for reconcilation between people and restoring and maintaining order, wholeness and harmony *(shalom)* in all of God's creation.

This leads to the third point: God is one, specifically in relationship with humankind, expressed in God's creation of persons in God's image and entering into relationship with those created. The fact that human beings are created in the image of God, who is one, has important implications for human relationships, as Stanley Grenz explains: "The image of God is primarily a relational concept. Ultimately, we reflect God's image in relationship" (169). "We should not be surprised that the image of God ultimately focuses on community. For the doctrine of the Trinity makes clear that throughout all eternity God is community, the fellowship of three Persons who constitute the triune God. . . . When God created humankind, God built into creatures . . . the unity-in-diversity and mutuality that characterize the eternal divine reality" (171).

The fact that all humankind is created in God's image has tremendous potential to effect unity and harmony in relationships within the diverse human community. It is no coincidence that Isaiah's emphasis upon God's oneness and sovereignty carries with it a new awareness of and commitment to the universality of God's salvation: "Turn to me and be saved, all the ends of the earth! For I am God, and there is no other" (Is 45:22). Far from causing alienation and exclusion, God's unity drives God to be concerned with the unity of the world and to strive to restore all people to *shalom* with God's self and with each other (Eph 2:11-22; cf. Is 57:15, 18-19). This compelling love (2 Cor 5:14) should also drive all who bear the divine image to engage in the same mission, to be instruments through whom God works to effect *shalom*.

Moreover, biblical monotheism, unlike philosophical monotheism, which posits that God is unmoved and apathetic, affirms that God is profoundly moved by and involved with humankind, especially in human brokenness and suffering. The book of Isaiah, which significantly advances the theology of monotheism, also highlights this truth. In Isaiah 57:15, God declares: "I dwell in the high and holy place, and also with those who are contrite and humble in spirit, to revive the spirit of the humble, and to revive the heart of the contrite"; likewise the prophet affirms that "in all . . . [Israel's] distress, he, too, was distressed" (Is 63:8-9; author's translation). According to New Testament theology, the ultimate Old Testament expression of this sympathy with humankind is found in Isaiah 53, which is understood as a prophetic pronouncement about Jesus, God incarnate, who suffered, died and rose from the dead in order to free humankind from the power and penalty of sin and to reconcile all people to God and to each other—indeed, to reconcile all things (cf. Col 1:15-22).

Monotheism is assumed in New Testament faith and practice, though some would question that it is possible to affirm at the same time monotheism and the deity of Jesus. Later generations of Christians would struggle with this issue and formulate complex theological dogmas, but the New Testament does not seem concerned to address the problem. Jesus affirms the oneness of God (e.g., Mk 12:29), as does the apostle Paul (e.g., 1 Cor 8:6; 12:6; Eph 4:6).

The connection between the oneness of God and the oneness of humanity has significant implications for ethics. We have already noted that the Shema was and is recited together with the Ten Commandments and that in Jewish practice to recite the Shema was and is to take upon oneself the yoke of the kingdom of God, that is, to submit to God's rule as revealed in the Torah. Likewise, an explicit connection between monotheistic belief and doing God's will is found in Zechariah 14:9. In this same way, the prophet Malachi bases his paranaesis on common belief in God's essential unity: "Have we not all one *(ehad)* Father? Has not one (*ehad*) God created us? Why then are we faithless to one another?" (Mal 2:10; cf. Mal 2:15). The answer to both questions is assumed to be yes; hence the implications are obvious. People must treat each other in ways that foster and/or maintain harmony *(shalom)* in relationships. A similar expression is found in Jesus' prayer for his disciples: "that they may be one. As you, Father, are in me and I am in you, may they also be in us, so that the world may believe that you have sent me. The glory that you have given me I have given them, so that they may be one, as we are one, I in them and you in me, that they may become completely one" (Jn 17:21-23).

The construct that monotheism emerged through a process of exclusion of all other deities, particularly feminine deities, has led many feminist scholars to view monotheism negatively. They conclude that monotheism represents the ultimate triumph of the "patriarchal God" and patriarchalism and thus provides ideological legitimacy for all that feminism opposes. Rosemary Radford Ruether summarizes the essence of this perspective:

> Emotional hostility [toward speaking of God in feminine terms] has deep roots in the Judeo-Christian formation of the normative image of transcendent ego in the male

> God image. The underside of this transcendent male ego is the conquest of nature, imaged as the conquest and transcendence of the Mother. To probe the roots of this formation of the male God image, it is useful to reach back behind *patriarchial monotheism* [emphasis added] to religions in which a Goddess was either the dominant divine image or was paired with the male image in a way that made both equivalent modes of apprehending the divine. (47)

This negative view of monotheism solely in terms of exclusion of all other gods derives more from Greek philosophical speculation than biblical religion. It corresponds to "philosophical monotheism" described by Aristotle in *Metaphysics* (book 12.1072b4-1073b14): God is "one, simple, unmoved, apathetic, immortal divine Being" (quoted in Lapide and Moltmann, 45-46). This interpretation of the background and essence of monotheism, however, mispresents the true meaning of the Hebrew words and concepts underlying biblical and early postbiblical beliefs. Biblical monotheism does not represent the triumph of one male God over all others (male or female) in some great, cosmic competition. Yahweh, the covenant name of Israel's God, often rendered in English as LORD, is neither exclusively masculine nor feminine, but both—and yet much more. Due to Hebrew grammar, texts often refer to Yahweh in masculine terms and with masculine pronouns, but Yahweh's essence and activity are articulated in feminine language and imagery as well. For example, God created humankind in God's image—"male and female" (Gen 1:27; emphasis through repetition); and masculine and feminine imagery is used to describe God's nature and ways (Is 49:15; *see* Images of God as Female). In truth monotheism is essentially a positive concept that, when embraced and put into practice, has potential to bring good to the lives of individuals and society, as well as the cosmos.

In summary, biblical monotheism is a positive concept, in that it affirms that God is unique and a unity. God's unity is a perfect consistency of essence that integrates diverse elements into a single whole, expressed most accurately in terms of the multivalent Hebrew word *shalom*. This *shalom* is also expressed in the unity of the cosmos that God created, as well as the human family created in God's image. Thus biblical monotheism has extremely important practical implications, as it provides all who affirm that "the LORD our God is One LORD" with the theological foundation for a right relationship with God, with fellow human beings and with God's creation.

Bibliography

S. Grenz with D. M. Kjesbo, *Women in the Church: A Biblical Theology of Women in Ministry* (Downers Grove, IL: IVP, 1995); A. J. Heschel, *Man Is Not Alone: A Philosophy of Judaism* (New York: Harper, 1951); P. Lapide and J. Moltmann, *Jewish Monotheism and Christian Trinitarian Doctrine*, trans. L. Swidler (Philadelphia: Fortress, 1981); R. R. Ruether, *Sexism and God-Talk: Toward a Feminist Theology* (Boston: Beacon, 1983).

CHERYL A. BROWN

---

and tie it to door frames was interpreted literally. What the passage is getting at is that Israel's relationship with God is to be such a key part of their lives that it would be normal for them to discuss it with their children around the breakfast table or while traveling or at bedtime. It was not something to be set aside for special occasions. It was a particular parental obligation to make sure that their children understood all of this. Because in the covenant blessings, obedience and relationship were all intimately related, turning away from God toward idols and following the gods of the peoples around would bring the edifice crashing down. Without wholehearted allegiance to God there was no relationship; without relationship there was no covenant; without covenant there was no blessing or land or community. For them to survive for more than one generation, the children must not only understand but also must grasp the concepts emotionally and spiritually and come into covenantal relationship with God on their own account.

Maintaining Allegiance (Deut 7)

Deuteronomy 7, with its emphasis on separation from and destruction of the surrounding nations, could come across as racist and encouraging the worst form of what today is called ethnic cleansing. However, we must guard against judging the events in the light of twenty-first-century values that would not have been understood by the writer or the participants in these events. As far as the Deuteronomist was concerned, the greatest danger to the survival of the covenant community was the absorption by the people of the beliefs, attitudes and practices of the other inhabitants of the area. This was to be avoided at all costs. God, their God ("the faithful God who maintains covenant loyalty with those who love him and keep his commandments, to a thousand generations. . . . He does not delay but repays . . . those who reject him," Deut 7:9-10) would enable them to overcome their enemies and those who prevented them from inhabiting the land as the covenant people. Such enemies, with God's help, were to be wiped out. In particular all the altars and sacred objects attached to pagan religions are to be destroyed in order to prevent them from polluting the land, which was to be holy to Yahweh. The language used within this chapter is extreme. The implication is that no thing and no person belonging to these peoples is to be allowed to survive.

However, as we shall see, elsewhere in Deuteronomy we have sections explaining how Israelites are to relate to the foreigners who live within their communities. Even here, the command not to intermarry implies that there must have been some left with whom they might have been tempted to intermarry. The drastic measures described here seem not to have been applied or even to have been intended to have been applied in such an extreme way as one might have thought. What was vital was that the Israelites realized how important it was for them to be separate and to maintain their identity and their wholehearted allegiance to Yahweh. Without this, there would be no Israel. There could be compromise on the detailed application of the rules, perhaps, but on this point the language had to be extreme. Any compromise here meant the annihilation of Israel.

Remembering God (Deut 8—11)

In Deuteronomy 8 we have an extended discussion, perhaps a sermon, on God's continuing care for Israel and the importance of remembering what he has done for them. This warning about the dangers of forgetting "Yahweh your God" can perhaps be seen as parallel to the warning to Christians in Hebrews 6:4-5 against leaving behind the faith that has once been known. There is a particular concern that the prosperity that God will give them will lead them to view themselves as rich and important people. As such, their pride will make them think that their wealth is the deserved result of their cleverness when it is "the LORD your God . . . who gives you power to get wealth" (Deut 8:18). It is apparent from Israel's later history that this warning was necessary and that it was not always heeded. Amos 4:1 is a well-known example of a rebuke to wealthy women who had set aside their responsibilities to God and to the covenant community.

The focus moves quite naturally from memory and forgetfulness on to a discussion of Israel's stubbornness. They must embrace endurance, the positive holding on to the things, beliefs and actions that are good, and avoid stubbornness, the determined holding on to things, beliefs and actions that God has forbidden and that would lead them away from him. In Deuteronomy 10:16 they are encouraged to "circumcise, then, the foreskin of your heart, and do not be stubborn any longer." It is clear that Paul's conviction that circumcision was significant only insofar as it worked as a symbol of a determined commitment to live in relationship with God is shared by and almost certainly stems from the Deuteronomist. This teaching would probably have been encouraging to Israelite women. They were only marginally involved in the symbol of circumcision, but if what really counted was circumcision of the heart, then they could be equally involved and their commitment as fully recognized.

Concern for All Parts of Life (Deut 12—19)

It is clear as we read through these chapters that the concept of different kinds of law was alien to the thought of the writer. There appears to be no distinction between civic, ritual (or ceremonial), and moral laws, although such distinctions have often been seen as significant within Christian thinking. Here the commandments appear to be arranged indiscriminately. Concerns for worship, for economics, for home economics or for the distribution of charity are mingled in what can only be seen as a haphazard way with laws about military systems, the legal processes or marriage. Presenting the laws in this way brings the details of the everyday life of ordinary women alongside the concerns of priests, rulers and military leaders. All of life mattered to God.

Deuteronomy 12:12 and Deuteronomy 14:26 illustrate that sacrifices and sacrificial feasts were meant to involve the whole household, including "your sons and your daughters, your male and female slaves." Sometimes Deuteronomy 16:16, which states that "three times a year [i.e., at the three major feasts] all your males shall appear before the LORD your God" is used to argue that women were irrelevant to or excluded from Israel's cultic life (*see* Women in Worship). However, the preceding verses in Deuteronomy 16 again make it clear that those involved in keeping the feasts were meant to include "your sons and daughters, your male and female slaves, . . . and the widows resident in your towns" (Deut 16:14-15). Thus the command for attendance by all the men is by no means to be interpreted as a restriction on the women. The reason women are excluded from the command is not made explicit. It is possible that a recognition of the fact that for pregnant women and those who are feeding young children travel would be difficult led to women being excused from compulsory attendance at the feast. In that context, where contraception was not available and weaning did not take place until the child was three years old or more, the proportion of women in those categories would be very high. Nevertheless, even without compulsion, it is apparent that many women are expected to be present at the feasts.

The danger of Israel being absorbed into the surrounding tribes was constantly in the mind of the Deuteronomist. He knew that intermarrying in particular but also making close friendships or even business relationships could entice the Israelites into involvement with the religious beliefs and practices of these tribes. For women, relationships tend to be especially significant, and they are also often key players in the transmission of religious beliefs. Deuteronomy 13:6-11, with its warning that any who respond to pressures from family or friends and get embroiled in the worship of other gods should be put to death, is perhaps particularly relevant to the women. This may seem harsh treatment, but the Deuteronomist was well aware that as the covenant relationship with God was the basis of the whole community, if that was threatened or compromised then the community was at risk.

Deuteronomy 15:12-17 is one of several regulations governing rules of employment. In this case the rule is that all Hebrews—that is, ethnic Israelites, but not necessarily foreigners now forming part of the community—who have become slaves are to be freed after six years of servitude and provided with a generous terminal bonus enabling them to start again (*see* Ancient and Modern Slavery). This is to be applied to female slaves in exactly the same way as male slaves. At first sight this appears to contradict the apparent restriction in Exodus 21:7, "When a man sells his daughter as a slave, she shall not go out as the male slaves do." However, it is likely that in Exodus the intention is to provide protection for a woman who has been taken as a slave wife, preventing her from being cast off after six years, rather than restricting the freedom of all bonded women.

Throughout Deuteronomy it is clear that all Israelites are seen as responsible for their actions. They will all be held accountable for their behavior. It is true that Deuteronomy 5:9 speaks of "punishing children for the iniquity of parents to the third and fourth generation of those who reject me," but this is apparently meant in general terms, implying that the behavior of one generation has long-lasting consequences. Deuteronomy 24:16 is very explicit that parents "shall not be put to death for their children, nor shall children be put to death for their parents." Israelite women did not always have full control over their destiny, but there is no lessening of this personal responsibility for them on those grounds. Women as much as men are members of the community and must take responsibility for their conduct. Deuteronomy 17 reinforces what has already been seen in Deuteronomy 13. As long as there are at least two or three witnesses to confirm the truth of any accusation, anyone—male or female—who is found guilty of idolatry is to be executed.

Further instructions about witnesses are given in Deuteronomy 19:15-20. There is no sign within Deuteronomy of the ideas that were incorporated into Israelite thinking at a later stage that the testimony of women is less valuable than that of men. Later readers may have taken it for granted, but there is no indication here or elsewhere that the witnesses whose testimony was required before anyone could be convicted or even put to death had to be male. (Judges 13 provides a somewhat humorous reflection on this topic. It is made plain that Samson's father, Manoah, felt that the testimony of his wife was not sufficient. He needed to hear the angel's message for himself. Their prayer for the angel's return was answered, but the angel came back to the woman, not the man. When the man eventually arrived and asked for clarification, he was told that his wife had to do what she had already been told. The angel did not have the problems regarding the testimony of a woman that Manoah seemed to have.) The implication of this is that the responsibility to be truthful and to ensure that injustice is avoided is given to each and every Israelite, men and women alike. The cooperation of all was needed if the community was to function properly, in this as in every other way.

Significance of Each Individual (Deut 20—26)

The instructions given for the treatment of female captives in Deuteronomy 21:10-14 take it for granted that a conquering army have the right to dispose of the conquered population in any way that it wishes. It is hard for those coming from a different cultural context to see this as anything other than appalling, but this approach would have been unquestioned within the ancient Near East, and we have to see these instructions within that setting. What is remarkable is that although the woman may have had no choice in the matter—the soldier who fancied her has every right to make her his wife—nevertheless her identity as a human being is at least to some extent recognized. She is not to be thrown into the new situation but must be allowed time to mourn for her parents and her past life. If the man has sexual relations with her, then even if he does not want to keep her, nevertheless he has made her his wife, and she is not to be treated as a slave but allowed to go free.

There are further indications within Deuteronomy 22 of the concept that women were to be viewed as the property of their father or their husband. It would be possible to note these indications and assume that women had no rights and were somehow slightly less than fully human. Any married woman who had sex with any man other than her husband was automatically deemed to be suspect. The integrity of

---

Polygamy

Polygamy describes the state of having more than one legal sexual partner, usually a woman. It is part of complex social structures controlling marriage, children, inheritance and barrenness. Polygamy is not just bound up with meeting male sexual desires.

Though some women use polygamy for their ends, those without choice or status are vulnerable to abuse and misery. Polygamy has usually been restricted to the wealthy and the childless. Polygamy has never been widely available, especially not in market and industrial economies.

In ancient Mesopotamia, monogamy was probably the norm, but childlessness could be solved by adopting an heir, using a concubine or the barren wife's slave (i.e., property) in her place or remarrying (Nuzi Archive, 1500 B.C.). The Old Testament reflects this background in patriarchal times and later, but polygamy was not as widespread as it is commonly thought. Jacob was originally tricked into it. The law accepted the possibility but protected the rights of the most vulnerable (Ex 21:10; Deut 21:10-17) and allowed a wife's divorce when human sin broke the relationship (Deut 24:1-4). The Bible provides evidence of the destructive influence of polygamy and warns that it leads to the downfall of kings (Deut 17:17; 1 Kings 11:1-6).

At the same time, the Old Testament laid down the ideal for marriage and the family: one man and one woman equal and identical in their humanity, different in their sexuality, complementing each other and together reflecting the image of God in a lifelong, exclusive and faithful relationship (Gen 2). The wisdom books never refer to polygamy, and Elkanah is the only ordinary man with two wives mentioned during the monarchy. The prophetic concept of marriage as a picture of God's faithful and exclusive relationship with his people assumes one wife (Hos 2).

Monogamy was also the norm in the New Testament, although divorce was easy for husbands. Jesus reaffirmed God's intention of lifelong commitment, adding stern words against trivial divorce (Mt 19:3-10). The early church saw monogamous marriage as a figure of Christ's relationship to the church (Eph 5:21-33). Polygamy apparently existed among new Christians, but leaders could have only one wife (1 Tim 3:2, 12). Polygamy remained legal for Jewish men until the time of the emperor Justinian.

Some missionaries have struggled with the place of polygamy in the church and have insisted on the divorce of polygamous wives and their children. The good news of the gospel had a hollow ring for women and children made destitute and outcast in this way. In the process of change, it is important to understand the function of polygamy in a culture and respond to that from a Christian standpoint. Today the newly converted remain in their situation at conversion, even though this may preclude them from leadership (1 Cor 7:20-24). Those unmarried at conversion are expected to embrace monogamy.

Helmut Thielicke, quoting Freytag, claimed that the Christian affirmation of the value and dignity of women in God's sight soon led new Christian communities to abandon polygamy for monogamy. Thus monogamy comes as the fruit of grace and *agape* love in marriage, but if it is imposed as a requirement for baptism, it marks a return to legalism and law. The increasing divorce rate in the West leads many into a form of serial polygamy. This may release some people from the misery of failed relationships but again exposes wives and children to abuse, devastation, poverty and deprivation. This is a major challenge for the church today.

Bibliography

H. Thielicke, *The Ethics of Sex* (New York: Harper & Row, 1964); E. Nida, *Custom, Culture and Christianity* (London: Tyndale Press, 1963); C. H. Kraft, *Christianity in Culture* (Maryknoll, N.Y.: Orbis, 1979).

VALERIE GRIFFITHS

---

the marriage relationship had been damaged; that affected the wronged husband, but it also affected the community. Therefore both parties to this crime must be executed. The possibility that the woman may have been an unwilling participant does not seem to have been considered relevant or even considered (Deut 22:22). The death sentence was in theory at least mandatory for all men and all women involved in adulterous situations. The concept of an innocent, raped woman is not part of the equation. The only time when rape seems to have become a possible factor is in situations where the woman was engaged rather than married and the sexual encounter had taken place in an isolated area. In this instance the possibility of the woman's innocence does come into play (Deut 22:25-27); it is accepted that she may have tried unsuccessfully to call for help and could thus be considered blameless. However, in general it was taken for granted that the best option for a virgin who has been raped was for her rapist to marry her. He had no choice in this matter, but apparently neither did she. She could be forced into a permanent relationship with the man who assaulted her (*see* Violence, Abuse and Oppression). Presumably the thinking is that if a girl has been raped, she is unmarriageable. Any marriage is better than no marriage, and therefore the man must be forced to take responsibility and ensure that the girl will be married—to him. Deuteronomy 22:28-29 makes it explicit that any compensation to be paid for the rape of a girl who was not yet betrothed is to be paid not to the girl but to her father. The implication of this seems clear; injury to a woman was viewed primarily as injury to her father or her husband. Surely this is proof of the fact that women were to be regarded as property.

These attitudes are alien and unacceptable as far as most modern readers of Deuteronomy are concerned. However, further investigation reveals that the attitude toward women that these verses seem to portray does not tell the whole story. It should be noted that statements like these are found almost entirely within what is known as casuistic or case law. The instructions deal with situations that existed. Where they did exist, then behavior needed regulating. The existence of the law does not necessarily mean that the Deuteronomist was commanding or even encouraging such situations to exist. In Deuteronomy 24:1, for example, the law states that if a man is divorcing his wife, then he must do it properly and not leave her in a state of unmarriageable limbo. In Matthew 19:8, Jesus explains clearly that these arrangements for divorce did not imply approval of the process of divorce (*see* Divorce). They were meant to be seen as a concession rather than an ideal. He does not present himself as changing Moses' instructions but as clarifying what was going on within the Deuteronomic text. Other regulations need to be viewed in the same way. Many of these laws include implicit recognition that the situations that they describe are oppressive. Within these oppressive situations the laws are geared to provide at least a level of protection for the women involved. For example, a daughter could be sold as a slave (Ex 21:7) but not as a prostitute (Lev 19:29). Women who were bought as wives or captured in war and taken as wives could not be sold as slaves or even neglected (Ex 21:11; Deut 21:14). A woman who displeased her husband could be sent away, but only with a paper that permits her to marry again without being declared an adulteress (*see* Adultery). The possibility that a man may bring an accusation against his wife on a jealous whim was recognized. However, if this were to happen, regulations were in place to ensure that proof of any charges must be provided before any action is taken (Deut 22:15-21).

The emphasis on the importance of each member of the community as a significant participant within the nation is found within the list of regulations as much as elsewhere in the book. There is no question of these rules being formulated for the benefit of the rich and powerful. At times it seems that the reverse is true. Deuteronomy 24 provides a number of instances of this. We have already noted that a divorced wife is to be protected by a legal paper. Deuteronomy 24:5 explains that newly married young couples, not a group with a vast amount of social influence, are to be given special consideration for the first year of their marriage. This prohibition on young bridegrooms going to war or being given heavy duties away from the home is an interesting one. The main reason stated for it is the happiness of the young bride. Stability of marriages was a crucial element in the stability of the community (*see* Marriage). The responsibilities of family life, in particular the maintaining of good relationships between husband and wife, are to be given a greater priority even than the defense of the country. This protected year allowed the young couple time to get to know each other, to form a new family unit. Perhaps today's churches could learn from this and make sure that gifted young couples are protected from heavy involvement in the front-line work of the church for the first year of their marriage. This regulation would also have given more opportunity for the wife to become pregnant. This means that if her husband did go to war in the future she was less likely be left as a childless widow without means of protection as she grew older (*see* Widows).

Special protection was likewise to be given to those who had fallen on hard times and therefore needed to borrow money. No lender was permitted to take as security for a debt anything, such as the millstone (Deut 24:6), that would mean that the borrower would be prevented from earning a living, paying back the money and regaining self-respect. The borrower was to be protected by the lender from being forced to end up in slavery. Similarly it was the lender's responsibility to make sure that the borrower's dignity—and need for a good night's sleep—was recognized and protected. It is interesting that the Deuteronomist considered the self-respect of the impoverished Israelite to be so significant that what seems peripheral instructions, not to go into their home to fetch a pledge (Deut 24:10-11) or leaving them with a blanket to sleep under at night (Deut 24:12-13), are included within the selection of laws, which inevitably had to be limited.

Just as those who had been successful enough so that they were able to lend money had responsibilities toward those who borrowed, so those who were successful enough to be employers had responsibility to those they employed (Deut 24:14-15). Workers, whether Israelite or alien, deserved their wages, and these were not to be kept back in order to aid the profit of the

Clothing & Textiles

In the Old and New Testament periods, clothing was simple. The main garment was formed by wrapping a single length of cloth around the body and fastening it. The few archaeological representations show men wearing a skirt, wrapped around the waist and held in place with a sash (sometimes translated "girdle"), usually woven. For additional warmth and dignity, an overgarment ("cloak" or "mantle") was worn. This garment could be taken in pledge for a debt but must be returned to the owner at nightfall, as the owner slept in it (Deut 24:11-13). This overgarment was probably fastened by a fibula, a bronze fastener similar to a safety pin. Sewn clothing, rather than wrapped and pinned, was not common until the late Roman period.

Women also wore a simple garment, a length of cloth that wrapped around, went under one arm and came forward from the back over the opposite shoulder. It was probably fastened with a bone or metal pin. A mantle, and perhaps a sash, formed part of a woman's wardrobe also.

Wardrobe may be too grand a word. Samuel received one new garment a year, woven by his mother, Hannah (1 Sam 2:19). Cuneiform labor contracts from Nuzi (near modern Mosul, Iraq) specify food, housing and one new garment a year as payment for employees, slaves or indentured servants. One new garment a year seems to have been the norm.

It does not appear that women in the Old or New Testament periods wore veils that covered the face. The only clear example is Tamar (Gen 38); veiling was something only prostitutes did. However, men and women probably wore a cloth head covering outdoors. This may be attested to as early as the Bronze Age tombs in Jericho, where a copper headband was found. The men's headband, as known from other periods, is woven.

Fabrics available were linen and wool, with some use of camel hair and hemp. Cotton was known to the Assyrians in the seventh century B.C. but was not cultivated in Palestine or Egypt until much later. Silk was probably not known. As a cooler alternative to wool, linen was the standard fabric for garments worn next to the skin or in warm weather. If well-washed and fine, it was comfortable and absorbent, but linen wrinkles badly and shows spots readily. Thus a smooth, clean linen garment became a simile for the purity of conscience to be expected of the church (Eph 5:27).

Flax was widely cultivated in the ancient world; its disadvantage was that it was labor intensive, requiring at least thirteen operations. No wonder cloth already woven ranked with gold and silver in value: "And the wealth of all the surrounding nations shall be collected—gold, silver, and garments in great abundance" (Zech 14:14).

Wool, by contrast, required less work. The sheep were shorn once a year, and for very coarse uses, wool could be spun straight from the fleece. Or it could be washed, carded to remove debris and line the fibers up, and arranged in rolags or wrapped around a distaff for faster spinning and finer thread.

If cloth was to be dyed or a pattern in contrasting colors was planned, the thread was dyed after spinning and before weaving. In the Old Testament period, thread was dyed in small stone pots with a hole in the top, through which the thread or yard could be dipped into the dye. A rill around the edge of the top surface caught the precious dye before it spilled and funneled it through a small hole back into the pot. Plant dyes were used, as was the purple coloring from the Mediterranean murex.

During most of the Old and New Testament periods weaving was done on the ground loom, made of sticks and large stones and stretching for 15 to 20 feet or more on the ground. The upright warp-weighted loom came into use in the Iron Age. The space-consuming ground loom could be used only outdoors and therefore only during the dry season; however, the warp-weighted loom, since it hung vertically from a beam, could be used indoors and in the winter, the rainy season. The vertical loom was also faster and easier to use than the ground loom. After the cloth was taken off the loom, it was fulled—an effective laundering and shrinking process (Mk 9:3) done by a specialist.

In the biblical world, clothing was considered important for privacy and sexual protection, so sexual intimacy was described in terms of clothing (Ruth 3:9), as were prohibitions (Lev 18:6-19).

The distinction between men's and women's clothing was significant and even seen as God-ordained (Deut 22:5). The gods and goddesses of Egypt, Syria and Mesopotamia were sometimes portrayed naked, but usually clothed. They often have distinctive clothing, especially headdresses, by which they can be identified. But in the Old Testament, God, although described with human characteristics and activities, is almost never spoken of as wearing clothing. Clothing for biblical people was gender-based, and their reluctance to ascribe clothing to God expresses an important theological insight. God is a spirit and therefore is neither male nor female. This conviction tends to get lost linguistically in Hebrew and in English, as grammar necessarily ascribes gender to God, and it is almost impossible to speak of God without attributing gender. If the people of the biblical world had attempted to picture God, they would have had to decide to picture God clothed or naked, and either way a choice for masculinity or femininity would have become evident. The people of the Bible not only refused to attempt the picture; they consistently prohibited the attempt to ascribe gender to God as idolatry and extremely sinful.

Usually we have understood the Old Testament prohibition against graven images to be intended to show that God is spirit, and we have missed its other intention—to show that God is not male or female. In the Bible, the lack of references to God's clothing and the lack of representations of God attest to God not only as spirit but also as gender-free.

DOROTHY IRVIN

boss. There are still areas of the world where to have to wait even one day for money that has been earned can cause real hardship. In many Western situations, to be paid daily would probably be inconvenient, but the point is still clear and still valid. Any employer must protect and not exploit employees. Not to do so means being answerable to God. Those who are successful enough to have fields that produce a harvest have responsibility not only to their employees but even to strangers who may want to find some food by scratching around in those harvested fields (Deut 24:19-20). The concept of community is real. Each one may be considered responsible for or may find themselves dependent on any other. Ensuring justice for those who had no one to defend them—the widow, the fatherless, the alien (Deut 24:17)—was the responsibility of all.

It is not clear whether or how often or in precisely what way the instructions about the responsibility for a man to marry his brother's widow were carried out. Even the illustration we have within Ruth 4 has its ambiguities. The possibility of the man not carrying out this responsibility is recognized. Whether the woman was given a choice is less clear. The rationale given for the regulation is that the memory of the dead man be preserved, a further indication of the importance of every individual. However, there is no parallel regulation relating to the inheritance of a childless man who died without having a wife. This regulation could have provided protection for women who otherwise may have been left with bleak prospects, and that idea may also have been part of the original motivation.

This extended selection of regulations and rules ends, as might have been expected, with a final summary or rather a final exhortation in Deuteronomy 26:16-19. Adherence to the rules is to be wholehearted. The spirit of every Israelite needs to be dedicated to keeping the spirit of the law. Their obedience should stem from their predetermined commitment to be in covenant relationship with God and should be based on their grasping of the fact that Yahweh their God has declared his commitment to Israel. They can then in reality be the holy people of a holy God.

Moses' Third Speech: Consequences—Blessings and Curses (Deut 27—28)

The first two speeches have set out the essence of what it means to be Israel: living in covenant relationship with this God, who has provided them with this land and given them these laws and decrees to live by. The third speech, through the medium of describing blessings and curses (*see* Blessing and Cursing), brings home to the Israelites the consequences of allegiance to God and obedience to the law or of turning from God and disobeying the law. Deuteronomy 27 describes the ceremony in which the people come together to proclaim the blessings and curses, concentrating on setting out the actions that will cause judgment to fall. Deuteronomy 28 provides a more general discussion of the consequences of keeping or failing to keep the law. Overall, sixty-five verses speak of curses and only fourteen of blessings. The reason for this apparent imbalance is not discussed within the text. It may be that the editor fears (or knows, if he is writing in the seventh century) that Israel will be much more inclined to disobedience than obedience and therefore spends more time in giving the warnings that might scare the people into avoiding disaster—perhaps parallel to the health warnings that are becoming more and more prominent on tobacco products throughout the world. Disobedience (like smoking) can seriously damage your health! Human nature being what it is, blessings are easily seen and understood; the negative consequences of attitudes and actions are harder to accept and understand and therefore need to be set out in more detail.

Ceremonial (Deut 27:1-13)

There is a great deal of symbolism in this chapter. Visual and even multimedia methods are set out to help the people to grasp the Deuteronomist's point, to feel his enthusiasm, to own their identity as God's covenant nation, that is, to be the people that God has called them to be. The words of the law are written on large stones, set up in a public place, on Mount Ebal. It would have been a massive task for all the laws, even the Deuteronomic summary, to be written in this way; perhaps it was the Ten Commandments, representing the whole law. But the symbolism is clear: the law was for all, to be seen by all, to be understood by all, to be obeyed by all. The nearby altar was to be built of ordinary stones picked up from the fields, not hewn to intricate shapes. The symbolism is again clear. God cannot be controlled or organized by human beings. The writing of the law is to be in the context of worship, whole burnt offerings recognizing God's sovereignty and fellowship offerings celebrating their relationship with this great God, in effect sharing a meal with him. The law, in spite of the curses that are about to be outlined, is presented in the context of relationship and celebration. It was important that everybody acknowledged personal ownership of the law and its provisions. The ceremony, in which the people divided into two—six tribes on Mount Gerizim for blessing and six on Mount Ebal for cursing—enabled this acknowledgment to take place. The two mountains may have been used because the whole people would not fit on one, but it is more likely that they are there to symbolize a choice between two ways forward, the way of blessing in relationship with God and the way of cursing separated from God. The fact that the altar was built on Mount Ebal, from where the curses were to be proclaimed, makes it clear that they were not to ascribe any superstitious significance to the mountains. Both Mount Gerizim and Mount Ebal were part of the land that God had given to them. Joshua 8:30-35 describes the carrying out of the instructions given here.

Ratifying the Law (Deut 27:14-26)

The dramatic recital of the curses must have been awesome. The whole nation is involved in accepting that those who take part in these activities, who commit these crimes, deserve to be cursed. No legal system can be effective if the people as a whole do not accept the validity of the laws within it. This ceremony is almost a national ratification of the law. The whole people, including women and men, concur that behavior including such things as dishonoring parents, depriving widows of justice, incest and violence against neighbors are unacceptable in their society. Anybody involved in these activities, including each one who takes part in this ceremony and makes this acknowledgment, deserves awful things to happen to them.

Relationship with God (Deut 28)

The pattern of curses and blessings found in Deuteronomy, relating as they do to breaking and keeping the covenant between God and Israel, are part of a known system of covenant validation in which legal codes are validated by a series of curses. However, in Deuteronomy, in spite of the amount of space given to the curses, it seems clear that they are primarily there to serve as a backdrop to the blessings. We have seen the way in which Deuteronomy as a whole forms a kind of national constitution explaining what it means for Israel, as a nation and as individuals, to live as the people of God. The primary focus of this life as God's people is their relationship, first with God and then with each other. Their lifestyle is to be holy; they are to keep the law not for the law's sake but because the law exhibits something of God's holy character, which they as his people are called upon to reflect. That is, the law pictures how their life in relationship with God could and should be worked out.

To be in relationship with God and to demonstrate that by a holy lifestyle means to be blessed. This blessing is not a reward for keeping the law. Rather, it is an automatic consequence of being in relationship with God, resting on his promises.

This blessing is clearly expressed in material terms. The obedient people can expect that material benefits, such as fertility, prosperity, peace and victory will be theirs because they remain in relationship with God. However, the real blessing is not those material benefits but the relationship. To belong to God's covenant people, that is, to belong to God, is to be blessed. In a similar way, to step outside of that relationship with God is to be cursed. Like the blessings, the curses too are seen in materialistic terms. If they turn away from God's path, then they will suffer famine, ill health, defeat and general ignominy. However, it does not appear that these curses were meant to be applied in a mechanistic way, implying that if they break this particular law they would suffer this particular consequence. The separation of the statement of the offenses in Deuteronomy 27 from the description of the consequences in Deuteronomy 28 is almost certainly a deliberate breaking of that link. Rather, the curses serve to persuade Israel that rejecting God or his plans for them will have awful, devastating consequences and that being out of relationship with Yahweh is a terrible state, to be avoided at all costs. In the light of this, the curse is presented more as an illustration of what it means to be outside the covenant, outside of relationship with God rather than as a direct punishment for those who do not keep the law. Deuteronomy 27:26, "Cursed be anyone who does not uphold the words of this law by observing them," can be seen as a summary of the more detailed curse statements, supporting the view of a unified curse that is faced by all who break the law and thus take themselves out of relationship with God.

If this is right, then we need to focus our interpretation of the blessings and curses within these covenant documents not on the individual elements of the blessing or curse narratives but rather on the single, significant blessing of being able to relate to God and the single curse of being outside of

Blessing & Cursing

The phenomena of blessing and cursing presumes an understanding of the universe in which divine powers affect living creatures, both humans and other organisms. This understanding predates biblical references and underlies any attempt to define these terms. Ancient people assumed that gods could intervene in life. Thus humans attempted to engage divine powers simultaneously to enhance their lives and diminish the lives of their enemies through blessing and cursing. Much of the literature on blessing and cursing in ancient cultures points to the mix of the religious and the magical. By religious is meant the relational connection between humans and gods, which underlies the attempt at blessing and cursing. By magical is meant the bypassing of the relational in which words themselves set in motion either blessing or cursing.

The Bible uses a number of different terms to connote blessing and cursing. The most common terms in the Old Testament are *barak* ("to bless"), *alah* ("to swear") and *kalal* ("to treat lightly"). In the New Testament the most common terms are *eulogeō* ("to bless"), *makarios* ("blessed"), *kataraomai* ("to curse") and *kakologeō* ("to speak against"). The root meaning for blessing is the bestowal of vitality, which can include fertility, prosperity and power. The root meaning of cursing is the opposite, that is, the removal of these vital powers. Blessing and cursing occur from God to humans, from God to organisms, from humans to humans and from humans to God. However, when humans bless God they are not transferring power to God but are responding to God's blessing on them (e.g., Ps 134:1, 3).

Biblical Meaning

The most important texts for understanding the root meaning for blessing and cursing occur in Genesis. When God creates the universe, he pauses twice to bless the creatures: first, all creatures (Gen 1:22), and second, the humans (Gen 1:28). God's blessing for vitality is the theme of Genesis, forming the structure of the narrative through genealogical lists.

The classic text for cursing is Genesis 3:14-17, the narrative following the disobedience of the human pair in the garden. God curses the snake and the ground; that is, God devitalizes both because of the actions of the snake and the humans. The snake no longer functions as it should but must crawl on its belly. The ground as well loses function, its fertility. The cursing theme, unlike the blessing theme, does not have a developed theology in the Bible, except for its use in Deuteronomy 27—28 and in the subsequent Deuteronomic history (Joshua—2 Kings).

Relevance for Women's Concerns

The investigation of blessing and cursing touches a large amount of biblical material. For the purposes of this commentary it is necessary to narrow concerns to focus on a major theme relevant to women, that is, God's involvement in ongoing life processes as opposed to God's intervention in history.

Blessing in the Old Testament is rooted in the ongoing process of family life: birth, rearing children, rites of passage, courtship and marriage, tending crops and animals, food, death, all activities of central concern to women. Women's activities in the Bible cluster around these processes, with some exceptions (e.g., Deborah in Judg 4—5). In Genesis, Abraham and Sarah await God's blessing for them, the birth of a son to Sarah. Laban blesses his daughter Rebekah before sending her to marry Isaac, hoping that she will fulfill this blessing by having children. Later, when aging Isaac desires to bless his eldest son, Rebekah intervenes to shift the blessing to the younger Jacob. The women in the book of Ruth bless the Lord because Ruth has given birth to a son. Eli the priest blesses Hannah and Elkanah after hearing Hannah's prayer for a son, Samuel (*see* Women as Psalmists). In the New Testament, Mary, after hearing of her pregnancy, reflecting Hannah's prayer in 1 Samuel, proclaims, "Surely, from now on all generations will call me blessed" (Lk 1:48).

This biblical trajectory of blessing associated with women raises the necessity of theologizing life processes, that is, of seeing God involved in the ongoing movement of life. Always there is the danger of confusing God with life, a danger that Bible readers must face and move beyond in order to comprehend the God of the Bible. If God is the Creator, then God is involved in life-giving events. It is here that the Bible speaks to women's roles as primary. Women give birth, nurture and rear children. The absence of men in these processes points to the need for reconsidering male nurturing as contributing to the blessing of God in creation. The current crisis in families points to the neglect of theological attention to family process, a theme that dominates Genesis and touches directly on the actions of women. Furthermore, there is a danger for men and women to lose vital contact with the God of creation by absenting themselves from family activities: preparing and blessing a meal, receiving guests in hospitality, providing for nurture of children and celebrating birthdays, weddings, anniversaries and rites of passage.

JEFF H. MCCRORY JR.

God's domain, no longer relating to him. These chapters present us with a joyful affirmation of covenant life and a solemn warning against any kind of rejection of God and his sovereignty. To see the curses and blessings in this way and to recognize that God's sovereignty allows him to show mercy when and where he decides, explains why, throughout the Old Testament, individual blessings and cursings did not automatically come into play. Not every good, law-keeping person lived a long and happy life; not every disobedient, law-breaking person suffered devastation and disaster. This was a real problem for Israel on occasions, something that psalmists and prophets alike found difficult, but it is interesting that they rarely, if ever, discuss the problem in the context of covenantal curses failing to come into play.

There is no doubt that at times in Israel's history the legalistic understanding of the curse as bringing disaster as a direct result of specific sin did arise in the understanding and practice of ordinary Israelites. This, however, does not seem to be the understanding that the writer of Deuteronomy intended, and it does not seem to be interpreted that way within the rest of Scripture. Everyone who breaks the covenant stands under the threat of the curse. That is a self-evident consequence of the fact that to break the law takes one outside of the covenant, and being outside of the covenant is what ultimately it means to be cursed. However, God's sovereign mercy also has to be taken into account. Everything depends on recognizing relationship with God as a living reality and not a mechanistic application of rewards and punishments.

Once we move away from the kind of formal covenant documentation that we have here, then it becomes much more apparent that the concept of cursing within the Old Testament is very different from the way that it was understood within the ancient Near East in general. There is no sign in Israel of the domination that the fear of curses had over life in ancient Mesopotamia. In spite of the preponderance of such rituals within contemporary literature, there is not a single example within the Bible of a curse-removing ritual being put into effect or even being known. It is significant that outside of stylized treaty chapters there is hardly any discussion of cursing. Blessings, not cursing, dominated Israel's religion. The Old Testament is full of instances of God's blessing showered on individuals, on families, on the nation. But nowhere do we read of God specifically cursing any human person or any object. God is first of all the one who brings blessings. Israel was convinced that because they had been chosen by God as his covenant people they were guaranteed his blessings whatever they did. It may be because of an awareness of that mistaken conviction that Deuteronomy spends so much more time on describing the curses, showing them that God's blessing cannot and must not be taken for granted.

Although the language of judgment and of punishment is often used by the prophets, the language of cursing is largely absent. Many of the curses outlined in Deuteronomy are identical with judgments proclaimed by the prophets. However, these judgments are never presented as simply the inevitable and unalterable fulfillments of previously issued curses. They are rather the prophets' method of indicating what it will mean for the people if they depart from the path that God has set out for them. Deuteronomy uses curses and the prophets use judgment oracles to make the same point: rejecting God's covenant by breaking the covenant laws means stepping out of relationship with God, and that can only be described as catastrophic.

Moses' Fourth Speech: The Ongoing Challenge (Deut 29—32)

Several speeches and some intervening comments apparently are contained within this section, but together these chapters form a kind of reprise, a review of all that has been covered so far. There is a further look back at Israel's history, an awareness of the importance of the law, a discussion of the consequences of keeping or failing to keep the covenant, a stress on the importance of handing on to their children a realization of their identity as Yahweh's people, and overall a sense of urgency and the crucial nature of the decision and the commitment that they as individuals and as a nation are being called on to make. This was a life-and-death situation for Israel, and the Deuteronomist was determined that all should be aware of it.

Covenant Partnership (Deut 29—30)

This section follows the treaty pattern quite closely. Deuteronomy 29:1-8 provides a historical prologue, a brief summary of the history detailed in Deuteronomy 1—3. Following the covenantal statement in Deuteronomy 29:9 we have in Deuteronomy 29:10-15 a setting out of the personnel involved in this covenant. On the one hand is Israel, making sure that it is understood that this included all the leaders; however, it was not just for the leaders but for the whole people. It included all the men, but it was not just for the men; the women were full participants within the covenant. It included all the adults, but it was not just for the adults; the children are involved. It included all full-blooded Israelites, but it was not even just for them; aliens who became part of their community were also involved. On the other hand we have Yahweh. The God who made promises to their ancestors wanted to commit to them in this solemn way.

The basic requirements of the covenant are described in Deuteronomy 29:16-19, stressing that this relationship with Yahweh was exclusive and that as covenant partners with him they were to behave differently from the surrounding nations. Women may not have had full recognition or rights within the society, but they are specifically mentioned. They, as much as the men, were considered fully responsible as far as the covenant requirements were concerned.

Deuteronomy 29:20-28 reemphasizes the disastrous consequences of turning away from God and rejecting his covenant. It was clear that sins could be forgiven. There were procedures within the system to enable the repentant sinner to be cleansed and restored. Nevertheless the deliberate and cynical rejection of God and his covenantal requirements would prove fatal. "The LORD will be unwilling to pardon them" and "will blot out their names from under heaven" (Deut 29:20). However, that was not how it was supposed to be, nor how it could be. Deuteronomy 30:1-10 emphasizes the benefits for those who do keep the covenant that will be freely available even for those who fail, if only they recommit themselves fully to God's service.

Deuteronomy is realistic. The strong stress on the importance of making the right decision at this point is because of the recognition that Israel might be tempted to make the wrong decision. There is also a recognition that they might fail; indeed almost an acceptance that they will fail. However, failure—seen as different from the kind of cynical turning away—is not necessarily the end of the story. Restoration is possible. In case this recognition that failure was likely made them think that it was indeed inevitable, Deuteronomy 30:11-20 stresses that the commitment they were being called on to make was not impossible. It was, with God's help, well within their grasp. The choice before them was clear: life or death. The Deuteronomist does not present the options in an objective or dispassionate way. He knew the consequences of each choice. He minded dreadfully that they did "choose life so that you and your descendants may live, loving the LORD your God, obeying him, and holding fast to him. For that means life to you" (Deut 30:19-20). Relating to God is the requirement of the covenant and its blessing and reward.

It is worth stressing that women and children are explicitly included as part of the covenant ceremony in Deuteronomy 29—30. The call to "choose life" is addressed to the women as much as to the men. The regular law reading, which they were commanded to undertake, was to be attended by all the women as well as all the men. It mattered that the women too "hear and learn to fear the LORD your God and to observe diligently all the words of this law" (Deut 31:12).

Preparing for a New Start (Deut 31—32)
Moses' part in the drama of Israel's life is almost over, but it is important that there is proper closure for him and a preparation for the new start for the people and for their new leader.

Deuteronomy 31:1-8 describes Moses' public retirement ceremony and his handing over to Joshua and prepares for the ordination ceremony to be described shortly. Joshua's leadership is affirmed by Moses, who makes it clear to Joshua and to the people that this is God's appointment. It is also made clear to Joshua and to the people that his task is to divide the land among the people, not to take it for himself. He is to "go with them," not to lord it over them, and the key to a successful individual ministry for him is exactly the same as the key to successful life for the people, that is, a trusting relationship with, obedience to and dependence on God. Moses presents Joshua with a personal mission statement.

Deuteronomy 31:9 gives instructions for the setting up of a ceremony in which every seven years the whole law is to be read to the whole people, men, women, children and aliens. It was perhaps the Deuteronomist's deepest concern that each generation should own the covenant and the law for themselves and that each generation should realize that the covenant was about life, and relationship was not just a list of rules. The importance of this concept to the writer is emphasized by this repetition of concepts that have been covered several times already. The law bears constant repetition, and so does the encouragement to constant reading for all people. Maybe we need to take a little more seriously that the encouragement includes children and fringe members in the corporate reading of Scripture.

Deuteronomy 31:14—32:4 is set in the context of Joshua's official ordination and recognition. Again the Deuteronomist's sense of reality comes across. Joshua needs to know the nature of his task and the difficulties that will arise. The people need to know again that the covenant needs to be worked at; that although failure is not inevitable they are likely to fail and therefore to hit disaster if they don't recognize the nature of the task ahead of them. There is no unthinking triumphalism. But for Joshua and the people there is the clear guarantee that if they walk with God, then God will walk with them. They are to remember the Rock who fathered them and the God who gave them birth (Deut 32:18). As a mother eagle God has overshadowed and upheld this pilgrim people (Deut 32:11). An understanding of a mother's love and care can deepen one's knowledge of God. It is always easier to remember songs than it is to remember speeches, and the people are therefore given a song to help them remember and take to heart all that has been told to them so far. The song is a tremendous proclamation of God, of his power and his goodness and yet a warning about the frailty of human beings and the dangers of turning away from God. Deuteronomy 32:44-47 comes as a final reminder of the importance of making sure that they and their children—maybe in spite of its somber sections the song was one that a mother could sing to her children as she worked and they played—should take everything to heart. "This is no trifling matter to you, but rather your very life" (Deut 32:47).

Deuteronomy 32:48-52 records the instruction to Moses to climb up to the mountain. This would be his chance to look out over the land that he would not enter and would also be his final resting place.

Moses' Fifth Speech: The Blessing on the Tribes (Deut 33)

It is not clear exactly when these blessings on the tribes were given. They are parallel to the blessings that a father might bestow on his children in the last days of his life, not necessarily spoken on his deathbed but counting as his last words; they remind us of Jacob's blessing on his sons (Gen 49). The blessings are set between two further statements reflecting on God's glory and care for Israel. The implication is that although Joshua was without any reservation on Moses' part proclaimed as leader of the people, it was into God's hands that Moses entrusted the tribes, his surrogate children. The blessings consist of a mixture of prophecy, encouragement and character assessment. There is no blessing recorded for Simeon. It is not clear whether there was a further verse, now lost, or whether Simeon had already been absorbed into the tribe of Judah. The dating issue comes to the fore again here. Was this a looking forward to the life that the tribes would have in the new land or a looking back on the life they did have put into the mouth of Moses?

Conclusion: The Baton Is Handed On (Deut 34)

There has been a lengthy preparation, but the end for Moses is recorded briefly and simply. He died and was buried, the Israelites grieved, life moved on. Moses was not forgotten. Joshua did not fully replace him. But nevertheless Joshua now had the main rule, and the new adventure was about to begin. God's covenant people were going to enter at last the land that God had set apart for them, and all Deuteronomy's hopes and fears, persuading, encouraging, convincing and challenging would be put to the test.

Bibliography. P. C. Craigie, *The Book of Deuteronomy* (Grand Rapids, MI: Eerdmans, 1976); T. E. McComiskey, *The Covenants of Promise* (Grand Rapids, MI: Baker, 1985); J. G. McConville, *Grace in the End* (Grand Rapids, MI: Zondervan, 1993); idem, *Law and Theology in Deuteronomy,* Journal for the Study of the Old Testament Supplement Series 33 (Sheffield: JSOT Press, 1984); C. J. H. Wright, *Deuteronomy* (Peabody, MA: Hendrickson, 1996). MARY J. EVANS

JOSHUA

Introduction

The book of Joshua is a book of transitions explaining the shift from the nomadic existence of Israel following the exodus to its settlement in the land God has provided, from bondage in Egypt to sovereignty in the Promised Land and most importantly from despair to hope. It is also a book in which these transitions are never achieved perfectly. Life can be a messy business even with God on one's side, and at the end of the book Israel has yet to possess the land completely. The book ends, however, and indeed begins with the relationship between God and his people firmly in place.

Joshua is as well a book of ambiguities. Despite the emphasis on God's sovereignty over history and care for Israel, his covenant partner, the book of Joshua can be disturbing for any reader. For women it can be especially disaffecting. From the superficial fact that few women appear in the narrative to the more important questions concerning whether or not the phrase "the people of Israel" includes women, the book poses special challenges for readers interested in the way the Bible speaks about and to women.

How should we read Joshua? How should we as women read Joshua? We should probably seek the women in the text. The most notable woman is Rahab, a prostitute in Jericho, whose memory lived on not only in Israel but also in the writings of early Jews and Christians. There are others, however, largely hidden; they include the women and girls who constitute part of Israel but whose voices are not heard: the daughters of Achan, who are punished along with their brothers for their father's sin, Achsah (Josh 15:13-19) and the daughters of Zelophehad (Josh 17:3-6). And we must not forget those women and men, girls and boys, who lived in Jericho and the other cities conquered by Joshua who were "devoted to destruction" under the covenantal policy of *herem* (Deut 20:16-18). Their inherent foreignness, exemplified primarily by their worship of other gods, poses a threat of corruption to the Israelites that must be wiped out. This policy not only emphasizes the loyalty God demands from his people but also acknowledges implicitly the tenuous nature of Israel's devotion to God.

The book of Joshua concentrates on the military conquest of the land. If war is a man's game, then Joshua would appear to be a man's book. But the military conquest of Canaan is contextualized within the larger framework of covenant loyalty. The notion of covenant provides the framework for the worldview of the Bible, and it is central in Joshua. Covenant provides the context for many of the most important biblical themes to emerge and solidify in this book, for in Joshua God's most extravagant promises to his people begin to come to pass. Joshua, like all the biblical books, is primarily about God and his relationship to his people and to his creation. God is portrayed as being interested and engaged with his people and their welfare. Sometimes, in the popular imagination, the God of the New Testament is loving, forgiving and merciful, while the God of the Old Testament is possessive, ruthless and harsh. Such a view oversimplifies God's self-revelation. Nevertheless, as readers of the book of Joshua we are challenged to come to terms with a God who destroys entire cities at the sound of a trumpet and who requires the death of the family of a man who disobeys God. In Joshua entire cities are placed under the ban *(herem),* so that their inhabitants are slaughtered as an offering to God. God, who so mercifully rescued his people from tyranny in Egypt, now installs them in a land by dispossessing the original inhabitants. While we, like many other exegetes, might struggle with the militaristic, inhumane tone of the book since Israel's victories over the inhabitants of Canaan seem barbarous and cruel, we also detect a view of God who is prepared to show mercy even when it violates the terms of his agreement with Israel. We encounter a God who relates to the marginalized and dispossessed in ways that subvert any attempts to advance a simplistic view of God as harsh, judgmental and punishing (*see* God's Call to Social Justice). The prostitute who declares the truth about God is saved with her whole household. In the words of Rahab, "the LORD has given you the land, and that dread of you has fallen on us, and that all the inhabitants of the land melt in fear before you" (Josh 2:9). And well they might.

Joshua, like all good stories and like human experience, is filled with conflict and opposition. There is little suspense, however. We, like Joshua's original audience, know that God's people will triumph and that the land will be taken. While for modern people the book of Joshua poses some special challenges concerning theodicy, it also assures its readers that no matter how dismal the odds, those who seek God and his will may hope for rescue.

Joshua is set in the period following the exodus, but it probably achieved its current form later. Scholars detect numerous sources in Joshua. The most basic evidence for its composite nature is the variety of genres we find in the book: from dry lists of Canaanite kings to lively narrative. The book serves as the fulfillment of God's promise to Abraham that he will bring the patriarch's descendants into the land (Gen 12:1-9). Throughout Joshua there are reminders both explicit and implicit of what God has achieved in the history of his people already as Israel prepares to consolidate its possession of the land. In many ways, moreover, Joshua's career recalls that of his predecessor, Moses: they both lead their people triumphantly across the water, they both affirm the importance of circumcision, and they both affirm the sanctity and significance of God's law.

Much of the narrative is concerned with how Israel is to prevent Canaanite religious practices from infiltrating its own cultic worship. Scholars are only now coming to reconstruct anywhere near a complete picture of the ancient Canaanite worship thanks to the discovery of the Ugaritic tablets at Ras Shamra in 1929. Scholarship on these ancient texts from northern Canaan shows how Israelite political and religious formulations were both similar to and different from those of the Canaanites. Pantheons of gods were acknowledged and worshiped by Israel's neighbors, and it is easy to see why much of the biblical record is intent on warning God's people to maintain their covenant loyalty to him.

The inhabitants of Canaan worshiped a variety of gods and goddesses, the most notable of which, given the number of references to them in the biblical record, are Baal and Asherah. Other Canaanite deities posed a threat to the monotheism of Israel, but it is Baal, the Canaanite storm god, with whom the biblical text is most often concerned. The God of Israel of course is depicted as more powerful. Unlike Baal and other ancient Near Eastern deities, he is not confined to a particular geographical area. He has been with and led his people from the dawn of time, in Ur, in Egypt and now in the land promised to Abraham. Nevertheless, that there are so many references to Baal and to other Canaanite gods suggests that not all of Israel maintained unwavering loyalty to the God of Abraham.

More intriguing for many scholars has been the possibility that at least some of the ancient Israelites worshiped a goddess as a consort to God. This view has garnered some credibility among scholars because of repeated references to cultic objects called *asheroth* at various Israelite sites and the fact that Asherah was the name of a Canaanite goddess. Although most scholars do not believe that the worship of a goddess, a consort of God, ever constituted part of the official cultic activity of the ancient Israelites, it is clear that Canaanite religious practices resonated with many of the people since they are warned so often against engaging in them. In the book of Joshua most of these warnings come near the end of the book, but the entire narrative demonstrates that in the God of Abraham and Sarah, the God of Israel who brought them out of Egypt, his people find their salvation. It is not only futile but also pernicious to seek it among the local deities of Canaan. The barren woman, the Canaanite prostitute, the sinful king all find their redemption in God. Whether one finds oneself in bondage in Egypt or in exile in Babylon, the God of Israel is not limited by the geographical location of those who would worship him.

If some or even many Israelites worshiped a goddess, there are no grounds for supposing that such idolatry emerged as a rebellion against the monotheistic worship of a male deity. Although the language used to talk about God in the biblical tradition is grammatically masculine, we need not suppose that the ancient Israelites were so unsophisticated that they could not imagine God as transcending sexuality (*see* Images of God as Female). The book of Joshua, with its overall depiction of God as warrior, however, offers few resources for thinking about God in less than robustly and traditionally masculine ways. Nevertheless the book of Joshua also challenges us to think of God as fiercely protective of his people and as loyal and steadfast despite their shortcomings. The covenant links God and Israel. The insistence on covenant loyalty, emphasized throughout the book of Deuteronomy, is illustrated with concrete examples of its significance in Joshua. The relationship of the events in Joshua to the presuppositions and theological position of Deuteronomy is important because of the widespread agreement among scholars that Joshua constitutes part of the Deuteronomic history. Joshua, along with Judges and the books of Kings and Samuel, constitutes a historical narrative that reflects the theological position and interests of Deuteronomy.

The structure of the narrative is illuminating. Although Joshua seems to be primarily about war, it is only in Joshua 6—11 that warfare is described. These battles, however, are horrific. They are undertaken by the men of Israel, who serve as the warriors for the nation. The men of Israel had a much greater degree of military obligation than do men in our own time. This aspect of a patriarchal structure is reflected in Joshua in other ways as well. Men wielded authority over the members of their households, whether they were wives, servants or children. At the same time, however, we should not equate authority with ownership. Although some parts of the Bible suggest that men owned their wives and children, this does not take into account all of the evidence (Wright, 220-21). On occasion—more often than not—the Bible records that the traditional, hierarchical social structures were subverted by God. Just as God is not bound by national boundaries, so God is not enslaved by social and political protocols. Repeatedly the oldest son does not inherit and the senior wife is not the most favored.

Similarly, in the case of the land of Canaan, possession may well be nine-tenths of the law, but God's will constitutes the remaining tenth and always prevails. The land belongs neither to the Canaanites nor the Israelites but to God: human beings have no claim on the land since technically they do not possess it. Having said that, God promises to give the Israelites the land for their own. As Christopher Wright has pointed out, there is some tension between the notion of Israel's possession of the Promised Land and the idea that God claims sovereignty over all creation (Wright, esp. 10-23). To complicate matters further, when Israel does come to possess the land it is not clear who is envisioned as constituting Israel. The phrases "the people" and "the people of Israel" would seem to be inclusive, yet often it is clear that only men are meant. In Joshua this tension is especially pronounced because of the militaristic theme of the book. Israel is a nation of warriors, of followers of God, the warrior par excellence. Ironically, however, God the warrior is, in

Joshua, most clearly understood by a woman, Rahab.

Most scholars agree that the book of Joshua reached its current form long after the events it relates. Critical scholarship classifies it as part of the Deuteronomic history, those books of the Old Testament (Joshua, Judges, 1 and 2 Kings and 1 and 2 Samuel) in which the theological themes of Deuteronomy are paramount. These themes include the necessity for Israel to maintain covenant loyalty, the centralization of cultic activity and the shunning of non-Israelites (Deut 10:11; 11:24-25; 31:6-8, 23; 5:32-33; 17:18-19; 30:10; Fretheim, Bailey and Furnish, 51).

Even the most skeptical scholars agree that Joshua includes ancient sources that have been used to put together a continuous narrative. Many scholars suggest that the book was put together in its present form during the exile in Babylon following the destruction of Jerusalem in 586 B.C. We can well imagine how the exilic community would have been both comforted and dismayed on hearing the message of the book of Joshua. Comforted because of the repeated assurances throughout the book that God is in solidarity with his people no matter how daunting the opponent, and dismayed by the realization that Israel had forsaken the covenant their ancestors had reaffirmed at Shechem (Josh 24).

The original audience appears to have much greater knowledge of those events than we do today. The author makes several allusions to things we can no longer know and refers to at least one source, the book of Jashar, no longer extant (Josh 10:13). Joshua helps explain why Israel's possession of the land had been so tenuous and why many indigenous inhabitants remained and continued to live, work and worship alongside their Israelite conquerors. This makes for an enormous degree of narrative tension in the book that is relaxed only because of the repeated assurances, both implied and explicit, that the God of Abraham and Sarah ultimately directs events.

Although Joshua reflects the theological concerns of Deuteronomy, it also looks forward to the practical social and political issues that will confront Israel in the future. Joshua ends on a note of optimism with the renewal of the covenant at Shechem, but the problems that the people of Israel face and indeed create in these early days foreshadow the danger that lies ahead. The covenant is a fragile possession subject to the frailty of the human partners. It depends on the cooperation of all living in the land to keep its requirements. It is also a robust and everlasting mark of God's grace. Although the people of Israel may forsake the covenant and their responsibilities, God is incapable of reneging on his commitment. His loyalty to his people, despite their apostasy, is a mark of grace. It also demands a response: those who reject that grace suffer the consequences, both in Joshua and throughout the biblical tradition.

Outline

1:1-18	God Commissions Joshua
2:1-24	Rahab and the Spies
3:1—5:15	Coming Home with God
6:1—8:35	Taking the Land
9:1—12:24	Consolidating Possession of God's Gift
13:1—21:45	Division of the Land
22:11—24:33	Affirmation and Commitment

Commentary

God Commissions Joshua (Josh 1)

Readers of Deuteronomy and Numbers have already learned that Joshua is to be Moses' successor. Joshua's name means "the Lord is salvation." It is changed, like the names of many biblical heroes, to reflect Joshua's special relationship to God (Num 13:16). Joshua begins his career as an attendant of Moses (Ex 32:17; 24:13; Num 11:28) and as one who guarded the tabernacle (Ex 33:11). There are several references to his commission to succeed Moses before it occurs in Joshua 1 (Deut 1:38; 3:21, 28; 31:3, 14-15, 23; Num 27:18-23; 34:17).

The opening verses of Joshua are emphatic that the outcome of Israel's military endeavors is to be credited to God. The bloody slaughter of Canaanites, which is recounted at various points in the book, is God's command to his people. The struggle requires strength and courage, fidelity to God's law; upon this success depends. In these opening verses Joshua is Moses' right-hand man. (Joseph is referred to in a similar way when his relationship to Potiphar is described [Gen 39:4; 40:4].) In Joshua 1:5 the Lord speaks directly to Joshua, assuring him and the reader that he is the legitimate heir to Moses' leadership and will enjoy the same divine protection as did his predecessor.

These opening verses, as well as confirming the steadfastness of God, attest to his extravagance. "From the wilderness and the Lebanon as far as the great river, the river Euphrates, all the land of the Hittites, to the Great Sea in the west shall be your territory" (Josh 1:4) There are conditions, however: Joshua is urged to be strong and courageous (three times), and God insists that the law be kept. This last condition helps explain the failure of Israel to possess the land completely. Although the people, presumably only the men, assure Joshua that "just as we obeyed Moses in all things, so we will obey you" (Josh 1:17), there has to be a degree of irony here since Israel did not obey Moses in all things. If these men speak not only for their contemporaries but also for their Israelite predecessors, they have short memories concerning the conduct of their forebears following the exodus. They are loyal both to God and to Joshua in this opening chapter, however, for they echo the divine exhortation to Joshua to be strong and courageous.

In this opening chapter we see the strategy of a military campaign with God rather than Joshua as the commander-in-chief. Alliances are solidified: the tribes of Reuben, Gad and the half-tribe of Manasseh, for example, agree to help with the campaign west of the Jordan even though their own possession will be to the east of the river. The book of Joshua opens and closes with reminders of the importance of God's law and the necessity of the people's fidelity. The Bible throughout insists that the God of Israel alone is worthy of worship. The gods of Israel's neighbors are described either as nonexistent or as powerless, which amounts to the same thing in practical if not theological terms.

Some scholars have argued that rather than a fairly rapid conquest, as it is portrayed in the first part of Joshua, we should think in terms of a slow settlement over many years or an uprising of economically exploited people, including, presumably, women (Mazar, 328-55). Whatever the case, the book of Joshua emphasizes military conquest. Despite the fact that it begins with fairly explicit militaristic overtones, however, scholars have emphasized the religious nature of the commissioning of Joshua and the preparation of Israel (e.g., Fretheim, Bailey and Furnish, 50).

Rahab and the Spies (Josh 2)

This chapter about Rahab deserves extended comment, not only because she is the most visible woman in the book of Joshua and maintained a fairly prominent place for herself in later Christian writings but also because her story both reflects and subverts some of the major themes in Joshua and the Hebrew Bible as a whole. In the course of her first appearance, Rahab is the central figure in the narrative (Josh 2:1-21). She directs the action and saves the spies. In her second and final appearance Rahab is far more passive (Josh 6:17, 22-25).

Although Rahab speaks in a Deuteronomic voice by declaring the sovereignty of Israel's God (Josh 2:9-11), the agreement the spies make with her violates the guidelines laid out in Deuteronomy 20:10-20 concerning holy war: "When you draw near to a town to fight against it, offer it terms of peace. If it accepts your terms of peace and surrenders to you, then all the people in it shall serve you at forced labor. . . . But as for the towns of these peoples that the LORD your God is giving you as an inheritance, you must not let anything that breathes remain alive . . . so that they may not teach you to do all the abhorrent things that they do for their gods, and you thus sin against the LORD your God" (Deut 20:10-11, 16, 18).

The ambiguity that arises over Rahab's (and the Gibeonites'—Josh 9—11) survival despite the policy of *herem* is noted by many commentators. The stories of Rahab and the Gibeonites, moreover, give a human face to the victims of Israel's conquest. Rather than being exceptional perhaps they are completely and wonderfully ordinary. The notion of Jewish and biblical exclusivism or separatism is too easy to exploit for anti-Semitic purposes. The story of Rahab represents a sympathetic portrayal of a marginalized Gentile, but more than that it demonstrates that yet again God's purposes are not dictated by social, political or even religious mores and norms. Rahab is the quintessential outsider: apparently marginalized even among her own people to the extent that she feels no compunction about betraying them, she too can be drawn into the warp and weft of God's design for his people.

As a person living on the limits, at the boundary of the city, Rahab's status is compromised within the social order by her profession. Rahab is a prostitute, or *zonah.* This word is the general term for harlot. Etymologically her name is connected with the sense of breadth or expansion, and this

---

Dwelling Places

Housing in the Old and New Testament periods was traditionally of three kinds: houses built of stone or mud brick and tents of goat hair. A less significant category is underground housing such as caves and disused cisterns.

Nearly everywhere in Israel, Judea, Ammon and Moab it is possible to quarry the limestone bedrock and build houses nearby. Stone usually would be used for temples, palaces and the houses of the rich. Amos prophesies against those whose dishonesty and greed have enabled them to disdain the common mud-brick houses: "You have built houses of hewn stone, but you shall not live in them" (Amos 5:11).

Far less expensive were houses of mud brick (adobe). Beginning in the Neolithic period (12,000 B.C.), topsoil was mixed with water, shaped into bricks and dried in the sun. The lower courses of mud brick, less sheltered by the overhanging roof than the upper, were more readily eaten away by the heavy rains of a Palestinian winter. Houses whose lower courses were of stone, with layers of mud brick continuing upward, withstood winter storms better (Mt 7:24-27). These lower rows of stone are often all that archaeologists find in place, the mud brick having dissolved into soil.

Roofs were of wooden beams that supported reeds covered with mud. These necessitated annual upkeep after the winter rains. Stone roofs were generally for public buildings and the dwellings of the rich, although they became more common, especially in towns, by the New Testament and early Christian periods.

In every period two-story houses were built. For them and for one-story houses the roof was used as part of the dwelling, as a food- or resource-processing area (Rahab dried flax on hers, Josh 2:6-8) and often for sleeping in the summer. An early building code required that a parapet be built around the edge of the roof (Deut 22:8). The simple mud-brick house had a doorway with a door of hanging cloth panel or wood. A door had projections top and bottom on the hinge side, which turned in sockets of stone. Windows were not common; single-room houses of stone or mud brick did not often have them, but large stone houses or palaces did. Cooking was usually done outside, on the ground in the courtyard. Rarely did a house have an indoor toilet (see Judg 3:24), but the concept and technology were in use elsewhere in the Near East before 1000 B.C. for royal dwellings. Lesser people used an uninhabited cave (1 Sam 24:3), a sheepfold strewn with chaff or a secluded area outdoors.

People whose livelihood came from flocks and fields continued to live in goat-hair tents in the summer and to retreat in winter to stone or mud-brick houses in town if they could afford to. The poorer, year-round tent dwellers moved with their tents and flocks into the warmth of the deep valley of the Jordan and Dead Sea, or in colder areas they shifted into caves or disused cisterns. Cave dwellings run the range from simple natural caves to elaborate ones enlarged by cutting into the rock or adding rooms on the outside. Simple, less comfortable caves are often used as seasonal herding stations or permanent animal stables. Today worshipers and pilgrims are shown to a cave under the Church of the Nativity in Bethlehem as the birthplace of Jesus (Lk 2:7-20).

Women may have been frequent or principal builders of mud-brick houses (Prov 9:1; Ezek 5:11) and were principally responsible for supplying the family with a house of spun and woven goat hair (Is 54:20). Goats' stiff, slippery, black hair is spun with a large drop spindle and plied double for strength. The plied yarn is woven on a simple loom that lies flat on the ground and is formed of sticks and rough stones. The woven lengths of heavy black fabric are sewn together to form a tent roof of the size needed for the family (Is 54:2), as well as side and interior panels. A tent weighs several hundred pounds and may be taken apart at some of the seams to be transported in pieces by camel. It is supported by tent poles held in place by long guy ropes woven of sheep's wool. Making and setting up the tent are the jobs of women, and they must be skilled at pounding in the pegs to withstand strong winds. This skill is praised in the story of Jael, who used her strength and abilities to defeat Sisera by pounding a tent peg through his skull as he slept (Judg 4:21).

Exterior wall panels are pinned to the roof, and inner panels divide the tent into rooms for different purposes. These woven panels provide visual privacy, but anyone can hear what is being said on the other side, as did Sarah (Gen 18:9-15). The long black tents are comfortable in a wide range of temperature and weather conditions, and their beauty became legendary: "I am black and beautiful, O daughters of Jerusalem, like the tents of Kedar" (Song 1:5).

The mobility of the tent enabled women to live near to and tend their grazing flocks or ripening grain or weave items for sale (Prov 31:24) without leaving their children. In polygamous systems, each wife was or is entitled to a room for herself and her children, whether in house, tent or cave.

God dwelt in a tent until the establishment of the united monarchy, when David, living in his house of cedar, raised the question of God's becoming sedentary and living in a more pretentious house. But God objected (1 Chron 17), preferring the traditional tent, and sent a message through Nathan, so no temple was built until the reign of Solomon.

DOROTHY IRVIN

may have negative connotations. The text makes no comment on Rahab's profession other than to imply that prostitutes apparently enjoyed a degree of autonomy in terms of covenant making and property not accorded to women whose sexuality met the sociolegal model or ideal.

Rahab is also a liar and a traitor—or more benignly, a part of the complex of biblical stories that relate how God's plan is forwarded by means of deception. The biblical view of deception is complex. It seems that God can use even deception to forward divine purposes. Although throughout the Bible many women and men engage in deception, it is not always explicitly condemned, especially when it advances the cause of the underdog and, more importantly, the unfolding of God's plan (e.g., Rebekah's deception of Isaac [Gen 27:1-40], Tamar's deception of Judah [Gen 38:1-26] or Jael's deception of Sisera [Judg 4:1-24; 5:24-31]). The Bible does not sanction duplicity capriciously: the Sinaitic covenant is clear that deception is sin (e.g., Ex 23:1, 7; Lev 19:11), and most narrative passages involving deception demonstrate that it is not to be emulated. Rahab's deception occurs in the interest of preserving God's people, which implicitly at least includes herself having recognized God's supremacy. The story of Rahab is less about how things happened than why. The narrative directs the reader to the triumph of God's will on behalf of his people. Rahab's confession, rather than her action, is the focal point.

We should note that the spies present a certain enigma to the reader. The amount of reconnaissance they engage in is exactly none, and their report to Joshua on their return is based entirely on the word of Rahab, who also devises their strategy for evading the king's men before their return to the Israelite camp (Josh 2:23-24). There are no reports that the spies went anywhere in Jericho save to Rahab's house. There is no suggestion that they spoke to anyone other than Rahab. Rahab has said all that needs to be said (Josh 2:9-11), but it is surprising that the spies take her at her word. This has led to the more negative appraisals of Rahab's character by writers who suggest that Rahab is portrayed as nothing more than a self-interested whore. Such claims are open to debate. Her confession does not read as a cynical ploy to seduce the spies with her supposed piety. It seems much more accurate to describe her as a righteous Gentile to whom Israel's God also directs his mercy. Her acknowledgment of God's power highlights the frequent inadequacy of Israel's commitment. Women like Ruth and Jael are women of non-Israelite ancestry who aid in the restoration of Israel's fortunes. It is Rahab whom we know by name in the narrative, not the spies commissioned by Joshua or the investigators commissioned by the king.

Rahab is not only a Canaanite but also a woman and a prostitute. In some ways Rahab is yet another example of the biblical theme of the vindication of the one least likely to succeed. Narratives related to this theme include those that describe the usurpation of birth order by the younger over the elder: Isaac over Ishmael (Gen. 17; 21), Jacob over Esau (Gen 25—27), Perez over Zerah (Gen 38:27-30), Joseph over his brothers (Gen 37; 44—45; 49), David over his brothers (1 Sam 16). Other stories are of righteous Gentiles: Tamar (Gen 38), Jethro (Ex 18), Jael (Judg 4:17-24; 5:24-27), Uriah (2 Sam 11). Yet other stories tell that even the barren are made fertile: Sarah (Gen 21), Rebekah (Gen 25:21), Rachel (Gen 30:1-24), Hannah (1 Sam 1), among others (*see* Barrenness and Fertility). This theme also embraces the essence of God's covenant-making activity with his chosen people: God constantly reminds Israel that they were not chosen because they were a great or mighty nation. God's liberation and redemption of Israel reveal more about the merciful compassion of God than the righteousness of Israel (Ex 20:2; Deut 9; 2 Sam 7). Like Israel, the figure of Rahab too is redeemed. She survives and becomes an exemplary figure for Christians in the New Testament, where she appears in lists of one kind or another, including the genealogy of Jesus (Mt 1:5) and as one of several examples of righteousness (Heb 11; Jas 2).

Rahab's appearance in the genealogy of Matthew's birth narrative bears witness to her tenacity within the tradition. Although it is not a genealogy proper, Hebrews 11 could be described as a genealogy of faith. Rahab is mentioned in a list of biblical heroes who demonstrated their faith through their actions. (Such lists are found throughout the roughly contemporaneous and antecedent literature. The most extensive is probably that of Sirach 44—47, although there are others: 1 Maccabees 2:51-60, for example.) Joshua is never mentioned as the one who brings Israel into the Promised Land, but Rahab is praised for giving friendly welcome to the spies. Thus Rahab becomes an exemplar like Moses (Heb 11:25) for those who would remain faithful to God. (Joshua is mentioned in Hebrews 4:8.) In James she is exemplary for her work of genuine hospitality as it should be practiced by all believers. Intriguingly, the epithet *harlot* persists with apparently no compulsion on the part of the author of either Hebrews or James to justify this or mention her repentance. The theological or ethical points these Christian writers make dictate to a large extent their use of Rahab: none of them, for instance, makes a virtue of Rahab's courage, and courageous she was. The reader's imagination, during any sensitive reading of Joshua 2, cannot help but dwell on the terrifying nature of the intrusion of the king's envoys and the fear of the consequences should Rahab's ruse not succeed. In addition, for the pious, prostitution was not an acceptable occupation for any woman in any era. Female sexuality is threatening if it is not channeled into socially acceptable or divinely ordained structures. At the turn of the era her story was used in theological discourse without apology for her harlotry. The preservation of this aspect of Rahab's character not only illustrates the sense these writers had of the grace and mercy of God but also their ability to assimilate the possibility that a prostitute, a woman, a pagan, could serve as a witness to the truth and as a moral exemplar.

Coming Home with God (Josh 3—5)

As we return to Joshua and Joshua 3, the text reminds its readers of the crossing of the Red Sea. There the Egyptian army acknowledges that the "LORD is fighting for them against Egypt" (Ex 14:25). In Joshua, it is men who constitute both the people of Israel and the army, since Joshua has told the members of the tribes of Reuben and Gad and Manasseh that "your wives, your little ones, and your livestock shall remain in the land that Moses gave you beyond the Jordan" (Josh 1:13-14). It appears, however, that the women of the other tribes who are to settle west of the river also cross over, since the children are circumcised at Gibeath-haaraloth or Gilgal (Josh 5:2-4). In these chapters the ambiguity in the term "people" or "people of Israel" is especially pronounced. The people who are circumcised are obviously men (Josh 5:4), and these chapters focus most clearly on the male priests and warriors who are crossing over, unlike the account in Exodus 14, where we imagine a somewhat rag-tag mass of refugees.

This section about the reinstitution of circumcision reminds us that so often within the biblical purview it is men on whom the focus rests. The rite of circumcision as a sign of the covenant (Gen 17:11) is one that is inscribed on the flesh of men. As the male priests were responsible for transporting the ark of the covenant into the Promised Land (Josh 3:14-17; 4:10-24) so now all the men of Israel reaffirm the covenant by undertaking circumcision (Josh 5:2-9). It is not so much that women are excluded as ignored. Although it is "all the people" (Josh 5:5) and "all the nation" (Josh 5:8) who are circumcised, obviously only men are meant. (Males are explicitly referred to earlier in the chapter [Josh 5:4].) We have to assume, however, that when Israel celebrated the Passover for the first time in the land the women also participated (Josh 5:10). We are told further that "the manna ceased on the day they ate the produce of the land, and the Israelites no longer had manna; they ate the crops of the land of Canaan that year" (Josh 5:12), which surely includes women among the Israelites.

Joshua 5 concludes with a somewhat obscure encounter between Joshua and the "commander of the army of the LORD" by the banks of the Jordan (Josh 5:13-15). This account of a theophany, an appearance of the divine, has obvious parallels with Moses' encounter with the burning bush (Ex 3). The passage is ambiguous, however. Joshua does not recognize the man for who he is but is interested in finding out if this warrior figure is on the side of Israel. The man's answer is ambiguous—he belongs to neither side (Josh 5:14). His response is startling; one would anticipate an unequivocal declaration that God is on Israel's side, but this is not the case. In a sense Joshua is asked whether he will be on God's side, that is, on the side of the holy. "It is the recognition of holiness, not one's nationality, suggests this story, that identifies one with God's people" (Fewell, 63).

Taking the Land (Josh 6—8)

As sensitivity to the voices of marginalized and colonized peoples has increased in public discourse, we cannot fail but imagine the terror of the citizens of Jericho and the other Canaanite cities destroyed by the Israelites as they are "devoted to destruction." From their point of view there is nothing to celebrate. Imprisoned in their homes, besieged within the city walls, the people of Jericho can do nothing but await death. They are not given the opportunity like their compatriot Rahab to declare or demonstrate their allegiance to God. Their city is devoted to destruction *(herem)* in order to avoid the possibility that their worship of idols and foreign gods might contaminate the Israelites and seduce them into forsaking God. The practice of *herem* is referred to several times in the Hebrew Scriptures (Lev 27:28-29; Num 21:1-3; Deut 20:10-20). It is a sacred act that is required by God, and consequences follow if it is not practiced, as Achan discovers in the book of Joshua and as Saul discovers later on (1 Sam 15). The divine requirement is tempered by the note that only those cities within Canaan are to be utterly destroyed in this way. In 2 Kings we learn that Israel disobeyed God in this regard by subjecting some Moabite cities to *herem* (2 Kings 3:19, 25).

The Israelites were not the only nation to practice *herem* during times of war. From the Stele of Mesha, the famous Moabite stone, we hear Mesha, a Moabite king, declare, "Now the men of the Israelite tribe of Gad had always dwelt in the land of Ataroth which borders our land, but I fought against that town and I captured it. I slew all of the people of the town as a satisfying offering to Chemosh." Here we learn that an eighth-century Moabite king places an Israelite city under the ban, subjecting it to *herem*, as an offering to his god Chemosh. So while we can conclude that *herem* was not solely a feature of Israelite warfare—it was practiced by other ethnic and national groups during this period—we should not shirk from the awful implications. Women did not go to war during this period, but they and their children were slaughtered as brutally as the warrior class due to their guilt by association—whichever side they belonged to.

While we can celebrate the redemption of Rahab's household out of all the people of Jericho because she alone recognized the truth of God, we should also remember that the other citizens of Jericho are never given the opportunity to declare their allegiance to the God of Israel. Their very existence poses a threat to Israel's ability to keep the covenant with God. *Herem* is a precaution to foster Israel's covenant loyalty. The destruction of others ideally leads to the preservation of Israel. Such terrible precautions, however, are still not enough to prevent apostasy in Israel later in its history.

While we can assume that Rahab is marginalized in Jericho as a prostitute who dwells at the limits of the city, we see that she and her household are not fully integrated into Israel. Although she and her relatives are saved, they are kept outside the camp. This is probably due to the restrictions imposed on Israel as they engage in warfare. God is present with his warriors in the camp, and it is therefore to be kept holy (Deut 23:14). The note about the preservation of Rahab is considered by many to be etiological or explanatory in that it accounts for how her family continued to remain in Israel despite the rigorous policy of *herem*. "But Rahab the prostitute, with her family and all who belonged to her, Joshua spared. Her family has lived in Israel ever since. For she hid the messengers whom Joshua sent to spy out Jericho" (Josh 6:25). Nevertheless this explanatory note is difficult to interpret. Is the verse meant to explain the continued existence in Israel of Rahab's descendants? Perhaps, but the text is silent as to whether or not she had children. Does it justify the continued existence of prostitutes? It is hard to believe that the writer or redactor of this text would place the responsibility for prostitution in Israel at Rahab's door. Perhaps the note seeks to explain the continued existence of Gentiles. Rahab, however, given her earlier confession (Josh 2:9-11), does not fit the usual portrayal of Gentiles as a category within Israel's national borders in the Deuteronomic history. Rahab herself, given her recognition of God, does not represent a threat to Israel.

For the most part Israelite women play no active role in the warfare; the women of the tribes of Reuben, Gad and the half-tribe of Manasseh remain east of the Jordan while their menfolk fight on behalf of the other tribes. One can only wonder how things would have turned out had women had the opportunity to consult with Joshua during these campaigns. As the daughters of Zelophehad persuaded Moses to petition God on their behalf (Num 27:1-11) perhaps the supplications of Israel's women could have persuaded Joshua and God to reconsider the protocol of war. Women were not consulted, however. They are largely invisible in this part of Israel's history. Nonetheless it should be noted that the apparently hard and fast policy of *herem* was pliable enough to respond favorably to the entreaties of Rahab. Her household is saved even as her city is reduced to ashes.

Rahab's acknowledgment of God's power and her consequent aid to the spies were enough to save her household but not enough to protect her city. This notion of collective guilt or—in Rahab's case—innocence is a persistent feature of the biblical understanding of responsibility and accountability. In Joshua 7, following the decisive victory at Jericho, Israel's fortunes suddenly shift, and they are almost routed in their next campaign against Ai. Although the reader learns that Achan has kept back some of Jericho's booty in disobedience to God (Josh 7:1), the rest of Israel cannot understand why their attempts to take the city of Ai fail so miserably (Josh 7:2-5). Joshua uncharacteristically berates God for bringing them into the land, since this failure to take Ai threatens the existence of Israel (Josh 7:7-9). It is interesting that Joshua suggests that Israel had a choice concerning where they would wind up: "Would that we had been content to settle beyond the Jordan!" (Josh 7:7). Settling east of the Jordan was not an option that most of Israel ever had. The reader has known the divine plan for Israel ever since God's conversation with Abraham (Gen 15). God is understandably impatient with Joshua and tells him that Israel has sinned and this accounts for the failed offensive against Ai. Joshua undertakes to discover who has violated the covenant through theft and deception following the battle at Jericho. The stakes are high, because God has threatened to subject Israel to *herem* unless the sin is discovered and punished (Josh 7:12-15). Achan, of the tribe of Judah, is discovered to be the perpetrator, and "all Israel stoned him to death; they burned them with fire, cast stones on them, and raised over him a great heap of stones that remains to this day" as God required (Josh 7:25-26).

Although Achan alone is responsible, "Achan son of Zerah, with the silver, the mantle, and the bar of gold, with his sons and daughters, with his oxen, donkeys, and sheep, and his tent and all that he had" (Josh 7:24) are destroyed in order to appease God and ensure the victory over Ai. Strikingly, Achan's wife is not explicitly mentioned as being subjected to the punishment that the rest of the household undergoes. It is inconceivable that Achan's wife would have escaped the fate of her husband and children unless we assume that Achan was a widower. Wright suggests that the failure to mention Achan's wife reflects his view that "the wife's legal status was essentially complementary to her husband's thus constituting a legal counterpart to the theological concept of 'one flesh' (Gen 2:24)" (Wright, 221).

The story of Achan and his family highlights the problem of individual versus corporate responsibility. One could argue that it is probable that Achan's family knew that he had disobeyed yet said nothing to their fellow Israelites. If so we are dealing with a case of a family sticking together despite the sin of the father. When interpreted in this way the story emphasizes the biblical theme that loyalty to God and his covenant must supersede family ties. The issue of the suffering of many (Israel's initial defeat at Ai) or several (the death of Achan's family) for the sin of one (Achan) is an issue that the biblical writers allude to on several occasions. For example, David's firstborn dies as a consequence of David's duplicity and sin (2 Sam 11). The Bible as a whole nevertheless is ambiguous on this topic. There are several assurances that subsequent generations suffer for the sins of their ancestors (Ex 20:5; 34:7; Ps 109:13-15; Is 65:6-7), but other passages reassure the reader that one is responsible only for one's own wrongdoing (Ezek 18; Jer 31:29-30). The Bible also speaks of those being preserved thanks to the righteousness of their forebears or relatives. For example, apart from Rahab's family here in Joshua, the life of Abijam is preserved, despite his evil ways, for the sake of his ancestor David (1 Kings 15:1-5). Overall the biblical literature insists that actions always have consequences. Those passages that speak of those consequences continuing in subsequent generations would be enormously powerful to those whose cultural background emphasizes kinship relationships across generations much more than our own does.

In Joshua 8 the destruction of Ai is recounted and then Israel's reaffirmation of the covenant. Ironically, immediately following the punishment of Achan, God concedes that in the case of Ai, Israel "shall do to Ai and its king as you did to Jericho and its king; only its spoil and its livestock you may take as booty for yourselves" (Josh 8:2). This surprising concession is all the more jarring following the destruction of Achan's household but highlights a clear distinction between booty and *herem* (Josh 8:26-27). In Joshua 6—8, therefore, the divine command is the controlling factor determining what Israel may or may not do.

Although the covenant stands as the foundation for God's relationship to Israel, it is not an inflexible rulebook. God's very presence abides with Israel—it does not merely exist in the law given to Moses. The law, however, is important, and Joshua 8 concludes with a reaffirmation of the covenant at an altar built by Joshua. Interestingly "all Israel" here includes "alien as well as citizen" (Josh 8:33), and all of Israel attend to Joshua as he copies and then recites the law. "There was not a word of all that Moses commanded that Joshua did not read before all the assembly of Israel, and the women, and the little ones, and the aliens who resided among them" (Josh 8:35). Although it is not a hard and fast rule, the words translated "people" or the "assembly" of Israel tend to refer to men in Joshua. That women, children and aliens are specifically mentioned here illustrates their membership in Israel and, more important, their responsibility and accountability under the terms of the covenant.

Consolidating Possession of God's Gift (Josh 9—12)

Following Israel's success in Jericho and Ai the indigenous inhabitants form an alliance to defend their land. The Gibeonites, however, do not join in but rather acted "with cunning" (Josh 9:4) and deceive Joshua and his fellow Israelites into promising them protection during the upcoming battles. Essentially they convince the Israelites that they do not come from a city nearby but from a land far away, which, according to Deuteronomy, should not be subject to the ban, to *herem*. Israel's encounter with the Gibeonites recalls Rahab's successful attempt to save her family. Her deception is directed at her own king, whereas the Gibeonites deceive the Israelites through an elaborate ruse. The agreement with the Gibeonites is interesting since, even when the trickery is discovered, the Israelites cannot go back on the treaty. The agreement with Gibeon stands over and above the objections of the Israelites (Josh 9:17-20). The Gibeonites' deception is tempered by their own Deuteronomic confession (Josh 9:9-10), which recalls the words of Rahab (Josh 2:9-11). The Gibeonite spokespersons have styled themselves as Israel's servants (Josh 9:8, 11), and Joshua determines that they shall be hewers of wood and drawers of water on behalf of Israel. The Israelites are true to their agreement with both Rahab and the Gibeonites—as members of the covenant community they do not bear false witness. Although Rahab was left outside the camp, the Gibeonites are drawn, albeit at a lowered status, into the very center of Israel—a decision that has surprising consequences.

The treaty with the Gibeonites is put to the test when Gibeon is attacked by the king of Jerusalem (Josh 10). Jerusalem is one of the last city-states in Canaan to be taken over by the Israelites much later under the leadership of King David. The attack is essentially a preemptive strike to avert a threat from the Israelites. It fails, however, despite the alliance that Canaanite Jerusalem makes with the kings of Hebron, Jarmuth, Lachish and Eglon, which are all cities in the south. The battle is swift and terrible between God and the Canaanites: "As they fled before Israel, while they were going down the slope of Beth-horon, the LORD threw down huge stones from heaven on them as far as Azekah, and they died; there were more who died because of the hailstones than the Israelites killed with the sword" (Josh 10:11).

It is God who triumphs, not the Israelites—he is the one in control. Although the Canaanite alliance is one made up of fearsome male warriors, the God of Israel is the greatest warrior whose decisive victory is measured in the greater number of soldiers he kills. The battle is a study in the superiority of divine as opposed to human power.

Notably, the kings themselves who represent the cities in the alliance initially manage to escape. They apparently do not lead the troops into battle. This seems to be a different pattern from that which obtains among the Israelites whether their leader is a king or a figure like Joshua. Joshua, Saul and David, for example, all play prominent roles not only in commanding their troops but also in being in the thick of things during battle. David is subtly excoriated for remaining in Jerusalem while his troops go out to fight (2 Sam 11:1), and at this time he falls into sin with Bathsheba. Joshua does not shirk the battle. The remainder of the chapter details Joshua's conquest of these and other cities in the south: "Joshua defeated the whole land, the hill country and the Negeb and the lowland and the slopes, and all their kings; he left no one remaining, but utterly destroyed all that breathed, as the LORD God of Israel commanded" (Josh 10:40).

Joshua 11 iterates much of Joshua 10, only this time the military campaign is in the north against a formidable alliance equipped with horse-drawn chariots. Again Israel prevails, and again the duty of *herem* is carried out, although the towns are not burned with the exception of Hazor. In addition, Israel takes booty, although all the people are struck down. Again we are to assume that *people* includes women and children. At the conclusion of the chapter we are told how successful Joshua's campaign was thanks to God.

In Joshua 10 and 11 two brief notes are interesting from the point of view of God's relationship to his people. First, concerning the famous episode in Joshua 10:13, when the sun "stopped in mid heaven," we learn that "there has been no day like it before or since, when the LORD heeded a human voice; for the LORD fought for Israel" (Josh 10:14). The assertion that on this one occasion God heeded a human voice is noteworthy; it suggests that God as a rule acts independently of human desires and aims, even as he acts on behalf of Israel. Second, we read later that "Joshua made war a long time with all those kings. There was not a town that made peace with the Israelites, except the Hivites, the inhabitants of Gibeon; all were taken in battle. For it was the LORD's doing to harden their hearts so that they would come against Israel in battle, in order that they might be utterly destroyed, and might receive no mercy, but be exterminated, just as the LORD had commanded Moses" (Josh 11:18-20).

We have suspected while reading Joshua that those people who concede the power of Israel's God, as Rahab and the Gibeonites have, will receive mercy. Here that suspicion is confirmed. Those whose hearts are hardened, who fail to acknowledge God's sovereignty must, for the sake of Israel's weakness, be destroyed. The idea that God hardened their hearts is a persistent dilemma throughout the biblical record. In the opening chapters of Exodus we repeatedly read that Pharaoh's heart was hardened (sometimes explicitly by God), and we have to read this in the context of God's utter sovereignty over his creation (Ex 9:12; 10:1, 20, 27; 11:10; 14:8). We should not forget, however, that God is merciful, sometimes forsaking even the conditions of his own covenant, toward those who acknowledge his sovereignty and power.

Division of the Land (Josh 13—21)

The chapters concerning the allotment of the land to the tribes and clans of Israel are essentially lists of geographical boundaries with some narrative sections interspersed. It is interesting perhaps that the land is divided according to tribe, so that the impression overall is given of a rigorous, organized apportioning, although several loose ends remain. Land that is still to be conquered is noted (Josh 13:1-7), giving the impression that although Joshua might not live to see it God will ultimately triumph and Israel will receive this land too.

The failure of the campaign to achieve total success is acknowledged throughout this section of the book (Josh 13:13; 15:63;

16:10; 17:12-13). Each of these verses notes the continued existence of certain peoples in the land side by side with the Israelites. Each time the failure is military in nature. The other two instances in which non-Israelites remain are the house of Rahab and the Gibeonites, who become servants to the Israelites, as do other Canaanites (Josh 17:13).

We are told that Joshua "took the whole land, according to all that the LORD had spoken to Moses" (Josh 11:23), thereby reminding the reader of the continuity between the promise to Moses and Joshua's vocation. But we hear the ominous note that Joshua was getting on in years and much of the land was still not consolidated under Israelite control (Josh 13:1). In fact, the conquest of the towns still to be taken in Phoenicia never took place (Josh 13:4-7). What this section of the book is most interested in is the distribution of the land to the twelve tribes. As God was the primary actor in the first part of the book, here the agency of human beings becomes more prominent; yet it is clear that God approves of the divisions that are made.

In Joshua 14 the purview of the text moves west of the Jordan and deals with the land's distribution there. It opens with an explanatory note as to why nine and a half tribes reside there despite the Levites not being allotted any territory. This is because Joseph's descendants were classed as two tribes: Manasseh, already allotted territory east of the Jordan, and Ephraim, who numbered among the western tribes.

In this lengthy exposition of the distribution of the land we must not forget Achsah, the daughter of Caleb, or the daughters of Zelophehad of the tribe of Manasseh. Othniel receives Achsah as his wife for successfully conquering Debir (Josh 15:16-17). Recalling Rahab, we again read of a woman petitioning a man or men as Achsah asks Caleb for springs (Josh 15:19-20; cf. Judg 1:12-15). Likewise the five daughters of Zelophehad—Mahlah, Noah, Hoglah, Milcah and Tirzah—are forced to petition the priest Eleazar and Joshua to grant them what is rightfully theirs according to the covenant (Josh 17:3-6). In Numbers we have the first part of this story where the women take their petition directly to Moses (Num 27:1-11). In that passage they base their claim for land on the need to keep their father's name alive in the absence of any male heirs. In Joshua, however, they simply recall Moses' verdict. Their claim to the land is endorsed by Moses and, of course, God.

What is interesting here is the apparent forgetfulness of the male authorities when it comes to acknowledging the legitimate claims of women. From Adam ("The woman whom you gave to be with me, she gave me fruit from the tree, and I ate" [Gen 3:12]) to Ahab ("Indeed, there was no one like Ahab, who sold himself to do what was evil in the sight of the LORD, urged on by his wife Jezebel" [1 Kings 21:25]) the disobedience of men is blamed on women. Yet too often the biblical heroes neglect to listen to women when they speak the just requirements of God. In Joshua we find both. Women are often forgotten, as in the case of the daughters of Zelophehad, but occasionally heeded: the spies in Jericho apparently judged the voice of Rahab authoritative enough to render any further surveillance of the city unnecessary.

Affirmation and Commitment (Josh 22—24)

Up to this point the reader has had to struggle to remember the tribes in the Transjordan, especially Reuben and Gad. Reuben, although the eldest of Jacob's sons by Leah, does not fare well among the tribes. He is recorded in Genesis as having slept with Bilhah, his father's concubine and the mother of his brothers Dan and Naphtali (Gen 35:22). There is therefore some irregularity concerning Reuben, since the tribe does not exactly prosper (Gen 49:3-4; Deut 33:6) and the Chronicler is explicit that his birthright was given to Joseph's sons, who also by being split into two (Ephraim and Manasseh) make the tribes' territories number twelve even though the Levites have no geographical area of their own. There is throughout the biblical tradition a bias against the eastern tribes of Reuben, Gad and Manasseh. Reuben and Gad are descended from Leah, the least favored of Jacob's wives, and Manasseh is the tribe from which arises the clan of Zelophehad, who managed to sire five daughters but no sons and elicits a crisis of inheritance (Num 27:1-11).

The allotment of the tribes reflects a degree of tension between inheritance norms and divine will. This motif occurs throughout the Bible primarily in the theme of the younger son usurping the older. Social norms are predicated, however, on the oldest son inheriting from his father. Incest also is universally condemned, and there are serious implications for it. Both the Ammonites and Moabites, two of Israel's most notorious enemies, trace their origin to the incestuous relationship between Lot and his daughters, for which Lot is held largely unaccountable (Gen 19:30-38). Concerning the tribe of Reuben the incest is not explicit, although is forbidden in the Mosaic law (Lev 18:8). Reuben's act of sex with Bilhah then has far-reaching consequences (cf. 1 Chron 5:1-2).

The tribes of Reuben, Gad and Manasseh trigger a crisis (Josh 22:10-20) when they build an altar west of the Jordan; this act is considered treachery by those tribes settled in Canaan. The threat of civil war looms as Israel decides to eradicate these members who appear to have forsaken God's command. Internecine war is avoided once the transjordanian tribes convince the rest of Israel that they are not disobeying after the manner of Achan (Josh 22:20) but are setting up a concrete witness to their loyalty to God. The rest of Israel relents once they are assured that the altar does not pose a threat to their existence by provoking God to punish the entire nation for disloyalty.

Although the dispute is settled, there is a clear division in Israel between those tribes living west of the Jordan and those who have helped conquer the land but have returned east. This marginalization of the eastern tribes reflects the episode in which Moses balks at promising the Transjordan to Reuben and Gad since he believes their request to settle there signals cowardice (Num 32). Although the transjordanian tribes are viewed negatively elsewhere in the Bible (Judg 11:29-40; 1 Chron 5:23-26), the author of Joshua does not comment negatively on Reuben until now (Josh 22:10-34). But the subtext is one of marginalization. The contribution of the tribes of Reuben and Gad to Israel's victory is undercut by the location of their settlement.

As the book draws to a close, a crisis is narrowly averted in a context that again draws attention to the corporate nature of Israel's responsibilities under the covenant. The construction of the second altar implicates all of Israel in the apparent rebellion

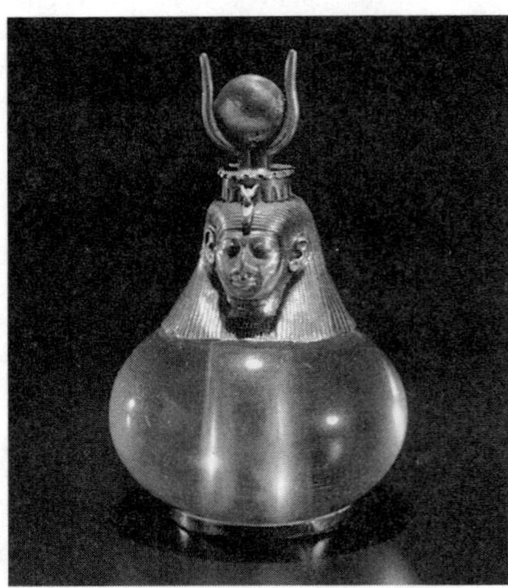

Crystalline and gold figurine of the Egyptian goddess Hathor. (Joshua 24:14)

of the tribes east of the Jordan. But this notion of corporate responsibility extends further than this. Throughout Joshua the family is represented by the oldest male and the nation by the king. This corporate identity becomes most critical for those most marginalized, and for the most part the biblical tradition insists on the responsibilities of Israel to those on the boundaries of the society. The stranger, the slave, the resident alien, while subject to Israel's law, should also benefit from it. Women, while acknowledged as having responsibilities to the covenant, often have difficulty in making their voices heard. In times of war, in times of misunderstanding, in times of forgetfulness, it is imperative that those with the least power speak out and that those in authority listen. The altar originally understood by the dominant western tribes as religious rebellion on the part of the tribes east of the Jordan was constructed by them to hold the western tribes accountable (Josh 22:21-29).

In Joshua 23, the crisis averted, we learn that Joshua is growing old and that although Israel has enjoyed some relief from its enemies there is still much to be done. Joshua assures the people that God will continue to work against Israel's enemies provided they remain separate from them. That Joshua has to warn them against intermarriage with Canaanite women and vice versa (Josh 23:12) suggests that Israel has not been entirely successful in fulfilling the requirements of Deuteronomy 7:1-3. It also shows that here the audience of Joshua's farewell address is assumed to be men, which may be the case if "all Israel" refers to "their elders and heads, their judges and officers" (Josh 23:2). As so many commentators point out, if the ban of Joshua 7:2 had been carried out completely, the warning against intermarriage would be redundant (Josh 23:11-13).

In the final chapter, as the covenant is reaffirmed at Shechem, the Israelites' promises to faithfully serve God and observe the law are tragically ironic given their subsequent failures in the succeeding books (Josh 24:16-18). Although we cannot be certain that women are present at this ceremony, it is likely that they were; all the people of Israel are responsible to keep the covenant requirements (Josh 8:35). Here the covenant requirements are essentially reduced to one: absolute loyalty to God, who has chosen Israel and guaranteed its survival. Joshua ends on a note of triumph with the covenant relationship between God and Israel reaffirmed. With the final notices concerning the death and burial of Joshua and Eleazar and the burial of Joseph's bones, the history of Israel from Genesis through to the conquest of Canaan is tidily concluded.

Conclusion

Reading Joshua shows that often things are not so simple as they appear. The voices of the disenfranchised or the marginalized make claims and counterclaims that God's leaders and agents need to hear. Caleb heeded his daughter; Joshua and Eleazar heeded the daughters of Zelophehad. But these women had to speak and make themselves heard. How many others have spoken but were not heard? Civil war is narrowly averted only because the elders hear out the eastern tribes when the tribes west of the Jordan zealously denounce the altar constructed as a witness. How often have the claims and practices of others been condemned by those not patient enough to take the time to listen and learn? Rahab at first seemed to be an enemy, but she spoke the truth about God. How often have people been ignored because they are not from the right class, or the right profession, or the right race or the right gender? Rahab not only rescues the spies but also teaches that not rules or social structures or traditions or even kings or generals or judges are sovereign but God.

As Rahab says, "God is indeed God in heaven above and on earth below" (Josh 2:11). This is probably the most important message we should draw from Joshua. God acts mercifully and graciously on behalf of those who acknowledge his sovereignty and enter into covenant relationship with him. Like the rest of the Bible, the book of Joshua lets us know that backing out of the obligations that are part of this privileged relationship has far-reaching consequences. Prior to their entry into the Promised Land the people of Israel had not demonstrated their willingness to maintain covenant relationship with God very consistently. Had they done so, those dimensions of Joshua that appear to be problematic, especially the divinely sanctioned policy of *herem,* might have been eased, since the problem is not so much the Canaanites' cultic practices but the susceptibility of Israel to adopt such false worship. The book of Joshua insists that our acknowledgment of and responsibility to God must come first. Only then can we be as confident as Rahab that no matter how appalling the situation God will act on our behalf. God, unlike his human partners, never fails to hear the voice of his people, no matter how marginalized, and he never, ever reneges on his promises.

Bibliography. D. N. Fewell, "Joshua," in *The Women's Bible Commentary,* ed. C. A. Newsom and S. H. Ringe (Louisville, KY: Westminster John Knox, 1998) 69-72; T. E. Fretheim, L. R. Bailey Sr. and V. P. Furnish, eds., *Deuteronomic History* (Nashville: Abingdon, 1983) esp.11-86; A. Mazar, *Archaeology in the Land of the Bible 10,000—586* B.C.E. (Garden City, NY: Doubleday, 1990); C. J. H. Wright, *God's People in God's Land: Family, Land and Property in the Old Testament* (Grand Rapids, MI: Eerdmans, 1990), esp. 3-23, 44-53, 227-28.

PHILIPPA CARTER

JUDGES

Introduction

Read as a connected narrative, Judges could be advertised as a modern blockbuster novel. Read as a disparate collection of heroic sagas from ancient Israel, it is often presented as exciting fodder for youngsters. But Judges is about adults in history, a story not of sanitized heroes in a saga but of assassins, of violent and sadistic women and men. Although they are real, they are at the same time caricatures, for in its pathos and humor as well as its horror this kind of storytelling is the generic ancestor of modern action or adventure films. The most pressing question is what led the Hebrew people to preserve among their holy books these accounts of their ancestors' immorality, oppression and violence.

Judges is an overview of the two hundred years between Joshua and Samuel, about 230 to 1050 B.C. The book of Judges has its own literary unity but is also a further episode in the Deuteronomic history from exodus to exile (Deuteronomy through 2 Kings) that was shaped by people sharing the same presuppositions about Yahweh's purposes for and demands on his people. Most scholars suggest that the original sources were collected and edited into the canonical book of Judges after the Assyrian captivity of the north in 722 B.C., around the time of the exile in Babylon in the sixth century B.C. Nuances in the stories may indicate the political and theological uses to which the stories were put during the long years of oral transmission before the book took its present shape (approval of the monarchy [Judg 21:25]; negative views of Ephraim [Judg 12:1-6] and Dan [Judg 17—18]).

This was the age in which Israel made the transition from being a pastoral, nomadic desert people to being settled in an agricultural lifestyle. The Canaanite peoples were more advanced civilizations, living in city-states while across the Jordan on Canaan's eastern flank were the peoples of the desert lands of Ammon and Moab. The early hint of the Iron Age is evident in references to the iron chariots and weapons of the Philistine coastal enclave.

These Yahwist people could initially hope only to colonize the less fertile uplands outside of the fortified cities. There was an obvious need for close cooperation and joint action among the twelve related tribes of the children of Israel, even more so as a nonjaundiced eye could see that they would be powerless against the superior equipment of their enemies.

In compiling these diverse accounts of the chaotic years between Israel's conquest of Canaan and the establishment of the monarchy the editors of the book of Judges discovered a recurring pattern that is explained in Judges 2:6-23. This pattern is the key to the main theological message of the book (see fig. 1).

The repetitive cycle of blessing, defeat and slavery, restoration and renewed conquest is presented as the result of rebellion against Yahweh's covenant and person. Life's pattern for Yahweh's people was not meant to be a repetitive mandala of failure but a straight path of obedience and order by living in covenant with him according to his revealed law. The text looks forward to the end of anarchy and the coming of true Yahweh-related kings (Judg 21:25).

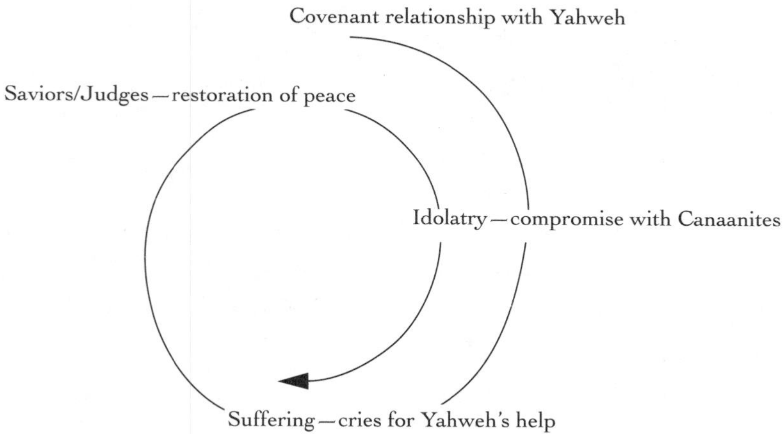

Figure 1. The cycle of rebellion, suffering and deliverance.

The double story of Gideon and Abimelech is the second key to the book. Here the vicious cycle of repeated failure turns into a downward spiral of accelerating decadence, corruption and defeat in which the judges themselves participate (see fig. 2).

The final chapters (Judg 17—21) are an ironic reversal of what was meant by the first entry into Canaan. Victory and displacement are turned against the Israelites; there are no judges and no accepted standards any longer.

Judges is a place for the destruction of an illusory hope in human heroes. The Israelites who had chosen "this day" to follow Yahweh in covenant (Josh 24:15, 21) failed to live happily ever after. Here are vivid descriptions of what happens when people fail to keep their part of the promises. Appalling things are done by those purporting to be saviors of God's people, whom we may have been wrongly taught to interpret as types of the Lord Jesus Christ. Yet God is not absent; he uses unexpected, meritless, even dissolute people to display grace in an age of decay. If you want a perfect hero, hear Jephthah: "the LORD . . . is judge" (Judg 11:27).

The excitement of battle stories does not mask the profound moral problem of God's allowing his people to be conquered precisely because they do not implement his genocidal program for the other peoples in Canaan. Yet Judges assumes that readers share the Deuteronomic view (Deut 9:5) of Canaanite societies: that they were deeply corrupt and that after long patience Yahweh intends to judge them through his people. The use of ironic humor to mock powerfully armed opponents beaten by the small, underestimated and marginalized Israelites signals that this is akin to the cowboy-and-Indian genre of modern storytelling. Narrator and reader stand at a safe distance from the horrors of the historical events. It is not now politically correct to view early United States history in such a way, yet in those lawless days when death and destruction were commonplace, people were much less squeamish than we are. The moral issues are sidelined as far as the worth of Canaanites is concerned (see, however, Judg 18:7, 28), but not for Israelites.

The values and culture of a patriarchal tribal society are abhorrent to many modern, Western people. Some modern commentators therefore interpret Judges as exploitative, seeing women as objects of male privilege and programs, used, abused, blamed and sacrificed. In Judges more than in any other book it is vital to hold to the principle that Scripture is God's Word in all that it affirms. In this light a study of some female characters shows Yahweh's empowerment, as in the case of Deborah (Judg 4—

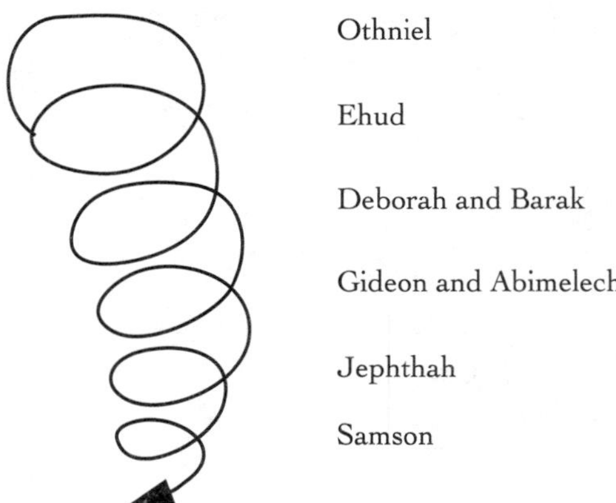

Figure 2. The downward spiral under the judges.

5), and heroism at the noticeable expense of men (Jael and the woman whose millstone killed Abimelech, Judg 4:11-24; 9:53). Women are comic, stereotypical manipulators in Samson's story (Judg 14; 16) and stereotypical victims in the last chapters (Judg 17; 19; 21). In the former, however, we are meant to laugh at Samson, but in the latter we are to shudder at the depths to which the Israelites sink. Even Jephthah's daughter (Judg 11:29-40) does not have to be interpreted as the helpless victim of parental egotism and abuse; she is an honored heroine here, as is her father in the view of the writer of Hebrews (Heb 11:32).

Far from being a learned legal figure meting out justice on the basis of God's law, the judge in this book has more affinities with the warlords of China: bandits who ruled and despoiled in times of decayed central government. Each biblical judge, major or minor, differs in function and in action. The judges may be seen as freedom fighters, terrorists to the opposition, or as charismatic leaders with unusual powers. They are in some sense saviors, and although attention to the geographical references indicates that each operated in a restricted area surrounding his or her tribal position in Canaan, the editors of the book of Judges see them as saving Israel as a whole. By the end of the period, fragmentation and intertribal warfare had replaced the initial attacks on the non-Israelites in the days of Joshua.

After a clear-headed view of the conquest of Canaan, the editors discern in the sagas they have received a recurring pattern of failure. Gideon's ambivalent refusal of kingship and naming of his son Abimelech ("my father, a king") turn the spinning cycle into a downward spiral. These later judges mirror the decay of Yahweh's people. In the final reversal the spin is out of control. The Israelites turn the energy and unity needed to face the Canaanites against themselves.

The geographical and historical background may be investigated through works in the bibliography. This commentary focuses on the narrative as theological history, the basis for a modern understanding and appropriation of the text.

Outline

1:1—2:5	Forward with Yahweh: An Alternative View of the Conquest
2:6—3:6	The Cycle of Judges

Commentary

Forward with Yahweh: An Alternative View of the Conquest (Judg 1:1—2:5)

Joshua, the previous episode of the book of Judges, leaves the impression of total victory and total commitment to Yahweh and his covenant. "Not one thing has failed of all the good things that the LORD promised"; "the LORD our God we will serve, and him we will obey" (Josh 23:14; 24:24). The realities of the situation were to be otherwise.

The first wave (Judg 1:1-26) into the south of Canaan, killing tyrants and razing cities, was in consciousness of God's inspiration. By his leading (Judg 1:1-2) Judah goes first. There is brotherly unity with Simeon and the exemplars of Caleb's family, including Othniel, later perhaps to function as a model judge (Judg 3:7-11). Caleb's daughter (Judg 1:14-15) is the first female character to be introduced, and she epitomizes the adventurous and committed spirit that was her father's legacy. She prefigures the positive leadership and examples of faith given by Deborah and Samson's mother.

The Israelites succeeded broadly in the south, but there are hints of trouble (Judg 1:19, 21). The northern wave of the conquest (Judg 1:27-33) is characterized by a refrain of failure: they "did not," they "could not." The phrases suggest a position of compromise with the local inhabitants that is ominous to readers conscious of Yahweh's command for the Israelites to be separate as the people of God (Deut 29).

The first appearance of an angel (Judg 2:1-5; cf. Judg. 6:11; 13:3) gives God's perspective. The people failed because they did not listen to God's voice, accepting his leading and obeying him. He is therefore no longer prepared to help them. They mourn but do not appear to repent.

The Cycle of Judges (Judg 2:6—3:6)

A dispiriting and unedifying series of tales about one's honored ancestors would not normally be preserved. At some point in the transmission and compilation of these sagas, however, a pattern seemed to emerge that ensured the book's preservation and gave it a permanent theological value.

The Failure of Joshua's Generation (Judg 2:6-10)

There is a sting in the text about the faithfulness of Joshua's generation (Judg 2:10). The Deuteronomic ideal of fathers teaching their children the things that the Lord had done for Israel was not fulfilled (Deut 6:4-9). The next generation did not know Yahweh in any meaningful sense. Was it willful failure of parents who settled in Canaan and forgot their experiences and God's promise, or was it willful children who found parental reminiscences about the desert boring, repetitive and irrelevant?

The Vicious Cycle (Judg 2:11-23)

The ways and gods of the Canaanites are found to be much more attractive than commitment to Yahweh, who had saved the Israelites and made them his people. Political as well as spiritual slavery to the pagans follows, sometimes for many years. Then his people's distress and sometimes their prayers (Judg 3:15) move Yahweh to send a judge to be a savior, a guide, a warrior for them. All is renewed; Israel is back at peace and in tenuous relationship with God. The cycle never stops. It is not an arabesque on the horizontal plane but a spiral spinning downward to disintegration.

The mandala of Tibetan Buddhism is one of many ancient religious beliefs in which the cycle of birth and rebirth in the seasons inspires a pattern of inescapable fate explaining all existence. In the revelation to Israel and then to the world in Christ, God offers and intends a new pattern. It is linear and upward, out of the spinning spiral, out of the pit. There is a future and a hope. There is a day of the Lord.

Testing and Training (Judg 3:1-6)

A number of reasons are given for the tribes' failure to take the land: inferior territory and weaponry (Judg 1:19), disobedience (cf. Josh 23:13-14), ignorance of the Lord and his power (Judg 2:10-11) and a rooted preference for Canaanite culture and religion (Judg 2:17-19; 3:6). It is clear in the traditions that this was not Yahweh's desire, but there are indications, perhaps conflicting ones, that suggest that he is still fulfilling a purpose: to punish (Judg 2:3), to test obedience (Judg 2:22-23) or to train them in warfare (Judg 3:2). These may reflect the explanations offered as the storytellers told and retold the sagas to following generations, reaching to find theological answers and applications appropriate to their diverse situations and audiences. Their mixed, pluriform interpretations in the final canonical book are helpful: facts and experience in human history may not be explicable in only one way. Yahweh has many ways of working out his ultimate purposes of discipline and of blessing (Rom 8:28).

Unexpected Heroes (Judg 3:7—5:31)

Othniel, a Paradigm (Judg 3:7-11)

Othniel, nephew and son-in-law to Caleb, is the first judge and has already been introduced (Judg 1:15). By conquering Kiriath-sepher he received from Yahweh's faithful hero, Caleb (Josh 14), his redoubtable and demanding daughter Achsah. Othniel wins freedom from Edom, which lasts for the ideal symbolic period of forty years. Othniel's character is unknown to us, but he functions as a paradigm judge in the sense that his experience follows exactly the cycle drawn out in the previous verses.

Ehud, an Assassin (Judg 3:12-30)

Ehud is a deceiver and an assassin, yet the text indicates that he is a hero. Distanced from the gruesome realities, told and retold in Israel through the passing years, Ehud's knifing becomes a basis for laughter at the enemy's expense. The most unlikely and inadequate of people, it tells us, can defeat the bloated oppressor.

Irony begins the tale. Left-handed Ehud is a man of Benjamin, which means "son of my right hand." Middle Eastern people always use the right hand; the left is the less honorable hand used for toilet purposes. A child with a tendency to left-handedness would be disciplined out of it then as now. The Hebrew reads "a disability in the right hand" (Judg 3:15), and this disability inspires Ehud and enables him to secrete an eighteen-inch blade under his garment on the right side, where anyone who frisks him will not suspect a weapon. He takes the tribute to Eglon of Moab, a single-handed, left-handed, one-man assassination squad.

Irony turns to bitter humor at the enemy's expense when Ehud announces to the king, "I have a message from God for you" (Josh 3:20). "The word of God is sharper than a two-edged sword," but Ehud was unaware of that forthcoming text and intent on doing more than allegorical damage to the oppressor of his people. Into the grossness of Eglon's overfed belly goes the short sword, and he collapses in a pile of his own excrement. The Hebrew is allusive, but this seems to be what is meant.

Ehud opens the door to freedom for his people while Eglon's servants overcome their embarrassment and open the door to find the tyrant messily dead. It is not necessary to presuppose that God approved of Ehud's strategy, but he makes use of it, turning it to a good purpose (Judg 3:15). This does not remove the moral problem but alerts us to the danger of wanting life's decisions to be wrapped in plastic, free of blood and guts and devoid of reality. If we were faced with another Adolf Hitler, would not assassination be devoutly wished?

Ehud is only the first of the unexpected, inadequate, undervalued and handicapped people out of whom heroes in Judges are made by Yahweh's grace (cf. 1 Cor 1:26-31).

Shamgar, an Unknown (Judg 3:31)
Shamgar is a judge whose name is known and who bears a resemblance to the Samson story to follow. Some scholars suggest that this verse may be a remnant of an incomplete editing process in the successive editing and selection process throughout the centuries. It may indicate, however, that even the outrageous Samson was not unique in those days.

Deborah and Barak (Judg 4:1—5:31)
In this stage of the spiral Israel is a terrorized and oppressed people living in the hills (Judg 5:6-8). This saga is full of incongruous contrasts. On one side is the overwhelming twenty-year-long military superiority of the Canaanites and their iron-furbished chariotry (Judg 4:1-2) based at Hazor, north of the Sea of Galilee. On the other side is Israel, whose "strengths" are a woman prophet, a spineless army commander and whole tribes that prefer not to get involved (Judg 5:15-18). Only God can bring victory in that situation, and his main agents are women.

Barak's Call (Judg 4:1-10). The text takes Deborah's status and responsibilities in Israel for granted. She is not introduced as an emergency substitute for the men who have failed to come forward (as some would interpret Judg 4:4; cf. Judg 5:6-7) Her standing in society is a secure and accepted one as a prophet through whom God speaks (*see* Women as Leaders). As such she, not her husband, is the accepted leader, a judge. She is unique in this book in combining roles of prophet and judge.

Within such a patriarchal society Deborah is enabled to act appropriately by being a married woman who can function as a matriarch, a mother figure (Judg 5:7). She is an initiator and a consultant prophet, and as such she passes on God's orders to Barak, who, whatever their relative ages, responds much like a son. Deborah is not the unexpected instrument but Barak, who triggers the emergency situation by his childlike overdependence on Deborah and implied lack of trust in God. His name, ironically, means "lightning."

The incongruity of God's working arises when Deborah has to step out of conventional societal roles, including that of prophetic instruction, to accompany the commander to the battlefield. Then the victor's glory, normally that of the soldier, always male, goes to a woman (Judg 4:9), whom we expect to be Deborah.

Sisera's Defeat, Jael's Triumph (Judg 4:11-24). In the main battle the Lord intervenes in some as yet unexplained way as Barak and Deborah take his troops down from Mount Tabor to the Kishon valley. The very ancient Song of Deborah (Judg 5:1-31; *see* Women as Psalmists) describes God's victory in language, implying an unexpected storm on the plain of Jezreel.

The culmination of victory, though, is through utterly unexpected people, in particular through a woman, Jael. The passage is constructed as a kind of sandwich in which the all-important bread on either side (Judg 4:11, 17-22) is the role of the other nonparticipants in the battle, the nomadic Kenites, who were Midianite in origin and whose political alliances are ambivalent at best (cf. Judg 1:16). It was in their best interest to maintain their role as the blacksmiths (Kenite means "smith") for the Jabinite cavalry.

The slaughter is complete except for the Canaanite supreme commander, Sisera, who makes his lone escape on foot. Jael acts as Sisera—and indeed any other Middle Eastern person—would expect from a female, a nomad and the wife of Heber the nonaligned Kenite. She is kind, hospitable, consoling and motherly, while even in his extremity he acts as the dominant male to a woman alone and defenseless. Then, in the helplessness of his exhausted sleep, Jael bangs a tent peg through his temple. (Tent-pitching was women's work, and she knew well how to use the stone tent peg and hammer.) "And he died!" (Laughter and cheers from the listening Israelites, male and female.) A defenseless, statusless, weaponless female becomes the victor over the erstwhile commander of "nine hundred chariots of iron." Commander Barak pants up, a late arrival who finds himself overtaken at the finish line by a mere female.

This sadistic murder of a defenseless man is heightened in effect by the incongruity of a woman, a mother figure, acting with such savagery. The implication of the text is that the failure of the male leader to accomplish his normal task has forced women to step across contemporary Israelite role boundaries and fulfill the divine purpose. It is not attempting to imply that women given power will always go over the top. The outcome is Israel's increasing dominance and eventual complete victory over Jabin (Judg 4:23-24).

Deborah's Victory Song (Judg 5:1-31). This ancient piece of poetry is in the genre of a triumph song, which emphasizes the triumph of the Lord through what appears to have been a sudden, overwhelming cloudburst that flooded the Kishon valley and bogged the chariots in mud (Judg 5:4-5). There is *Schadenfreude,* the bloodthirsty enjoyment of the oppressors getting their just deserts, a celebration of shattered bone, of smashed brain matter and spilled blood. "Perhaps many of us in the west cannot rejoice when God smashes oppressors because we have never been so oppressed or crushed by tyranny. . . . Deborah clearly votes for Jael, 'servant of the Lord.' Naturally you can disagree. If so, you can claim more refinement but less faith" (Davis, 88).

Three special matriarchs gain mention: Deborah (Judg 5:7), Jael (Judg 5:6, 24-27) and Sisera's waiting mother (Judg 5:28-30), a foil to triumphant Deborah and Jael. Deborah's leadership is celebrated alongside those who willingly responded to the battle call. There is sorrowful mention of the reluctance, neutrality or noninvolvement or appeasement policy of the northern

---

Deborah

Deborah, the Old Testament's only female judge, excelled also as a prophet, military leader and singer. This amazingly capable woman exercised legal functions in Israel first for twenty years during the oppressive Canaanite reign, then apparently for another forty years after the Israelites won a mighty victory (Judg 4:3; 5:31; *see* Women as Leaders).

Deborah, presumably an Ephraimite because she and her husband, Lappidoth, resided in Ephraim's hill country, adjudicated disputes under a palm tree. Jewish tradition maintains that this tree symbolized the fairness of her decisions.

The text shows Deborah as a woman who waits to hear from the Lord before acting. When the word of the Lord comes that it is time to fight, she summons Barak, a Naphtalite. Barak refuses to go into battle without Deborah. Scholars alternate between saying this represents cowardice to viewing it as further evidence of Deborah's high standing. Deborah agrees to accompany him but prophesies that the Lord will hand Sisera, the Canaanite commander, over to a woman (Judg 4:9).

The Canaanites come equipped with nine hundred iron chariots and weapons; the Israelites lack advanced weaponry. God sends a torrent of rain, making a muddy, impassable battlefield. The Canaanites perish in hand-to-hand combat. Sisera escapes on foot and seeks shelter in the home of Jael, a Kenite woman. While he sleeps, she drives a tent peg through his head. The battle changes the international power structure, for the Canaanites lose their arms.

The Song of Deborah (Judg 5), one of the Bible's oldest portions, recounts the battle and adds details absent in the prose text. Bright and fast moving, the song depicts the battle's preparations and the Israelites' deplorable living conditions: the Canaanites controlled the lucrative trade routes, forcing the Israelites to the hills. Deborah praises God's cosmic intervention and credits him with the victory.

Deborah's song mentions several women. Sisera's mother waits for her son in vain by a window, women are the conquerors' spoils of war, and Jael is the "most blessed of women" for her deed (Judg 5:24).

The prose text lists only the tribes of Naphtali and Zebulun as fighters. The song adds that Ephraim, Benjamin, Machir and Issachar contributed men but condemns Gilead, Dan, Asher and Meroz for declining to participate in the holy war.

Some Jewish traditions hold that Deborah wrote Psalm 68.

ROBIN GALLAHER BRANCH

---

tribes, including Naphtali (Judg 5:15-18), of whom Barak (Judg 4:6) was not the only fearful and reluctant warrior. He is here only by implication in the song. Tribes in the north were obviously in more danger and were perhaps less free and more endangered by a call emanating from Ephraim (Judg 4:5-6), but Israelite disunity is to be noted.

Monarchy: Yes or No? (Judg 6:1—9:57)

Gideon, the Doubtful Leader (Judg 6:1—8:32)

Gideon is a decidedly ambivalent figure, a doubtful and doubt-full role model. He is perhaps braver than Barak, but the incidents of his life—the call, the fleeces and the battle—need to be interpreted in the light of the outcome. He descends from the confession "the LORD is peace" (Judg 6:24) to syncretistic devotion to the ephod (Judg 8:27), which becomes a snare to him and his family (Judg 8:33). This is perhaps the idol of Baal-berith ("the Lord of the Covenant") worshiped by Israel after his death. His alternative name, Jerubbaal (Judg 6:32; 8:35), symbolizes his semidetached, compromised state of mind. He is a man struggling and overcoming his doubts, but in terms of the whole story we see a person who never gets to wholehearted commitment to Yahweh and who tends to self-aggrandizement after a battle that neither Gideon nor his three hundred troops has won. We see that the battle is the Lord's alone.

Following the era of Deborah the vicious cycle of repeated apostasy and conquest turns into a downward spiral of degradation and suffering. The devastation and famine created by the locustlike, periodic depredations of the nomadic, camel-equipped Bedouin Midianites and other peoples from beyond the Jordan is worse than any so far. The Israelites live in caves and holes in the ground, they suffer famine from the seasonal depredations by the people of the east, and as usual, they cry to Yahweh. This time, however, an unnamed prophet, not a judge, is God's first response to their desperation. Before more can be done, they and the reader need to be reminded of their disobedient apostasy (Judg 2:11-15), which is the cause of their predicament.

Gideon's call (Judg 6:11-24) follows the pattern of many others (cf. Moses, Ex 4), but there is a strong vein of irony here. A man hiding from the Midianites is addressed as "mighty warrior" (Judg 6:12) and is told to go "in this might of yours" (Judg 6:14) to deliver Israel when he not only pleads his personal and tribal insignificance but also has a mind full of doubts (Judg 6:13, 15). Obviously the prophet's message (Judg 6:7-9) has not found acceptance in him. But God has chosen this man and intends to empower him (Judg 6:12, 16), even though he still has questions and immediately requires a sign as proof (Judg 6:17-24).

It is a significant feature in the saga of Gideon that Yahweh is incredibly patient and willing to give sign after sign to stiffen the resolve and confirm the faith of this judge. Yet such a deep-rooted habit of doubt, worse than the fears of Barak, leads to a growing self-assurance and self-aggrandizement, the weak person's response to the gift of leadership.

Gideon's family are at best syncretists. His father sponsors the altar to Baal that Gideon is ordered to destroy. Through fear he obeys, but he does so under cover of night. Joash's reaction to the villagers' outrage indicates a level of noncommitment to either Baal or Yahweh that may have been typical of the time. Gideon's alternative name, Jerubbaal, derives from this incident. He is in opposition to Baal, but still he bears Baal's name.

Gideon, possessed by God's Spirit (Judg 6:34), declares war on the innumerable hosts of Midian encamped in the Valley of Jezreel. Then doubts set in again, and he tries God with his fleeces (Judg 6:36-40). This is very human, but we shall see in Gideon how a rooted propensity to doubt is not driven out by the Spirit or easily overcome by signs and wonders.

Yahweh is both gracious and patient in giving the signs, and yet he is not at the beck and call of Gideon. His plan is to reduce the army to a minimum, equip it with ludicrously inadequate weaponry and then send it out to fight the locust hordes of Midian. Yet again he uses the unexpected and inadequate. No human is meant to be able to claim glory in this victory.

Anticipating Gideon's need for proofs, Yahweh sends him down at night to overhear the Midianite's report of his dream and overcome his fears with the conviction

The Manufacture & Use of Household Utensils

Women were responsible for the daily activities of their households, and in wealthy families the matriarch at least oversaw the entire production.

In ancient times two types of hand mills were used. One consisted of a small stone being pushed and pulled across a much larger stone. The other type consisted of a bottom stone with a wooden peg in its center that pointed up through a hole in the center of the top stone. The top stone usually had a handle used to rotate it on the bottom stone. Grain dropped through the hole and ground between the two stones would sift out around the bottom stone as flour.

Pottery was probably used in the same ways that a modern household uses plastic containers for storage. Small utensils were made from stone, wood, bone and metal.

Animal skins were used to contain wine and other liquids. Baskets are mentioned often in Scripture, and basket sizes seem to vary greatly (see Judg 6:19; Jer 24:1-2; Mk 6:43; Acts 9:25).

A spindle, a narrow stick made of wood, ivory or bone, had a perforated round weight on one end to give it momentum as it spun. Spinning involved holding a distaff in one hand and operating the spindle with the other. The fiber from the distaff becomes spun thread as it twists onto the spindle (for looms, *see* Clothing and Textiles).

The earliest needles were made of sharp pieces of bone, but later needles were also made from ivory, bronze and iron.

Designs and sizes of lamps varied, but most were small enough to be carried easily. They contained oil and a wick and often had a small handle on one side.

Bibliography

A. Lucas, *Ancient Egyptian Materials and Industries,* 3d ed. (London: Edward Arnold, 1948); R. J. Forbes, *Studies in Ancient Technology,* 2d ed. (Leiden: E. J. Brill, 1965) 3:51-110, 138-63; R. J. Forbes, *Studies in Ancient Technology,* 2d rev. ed. (Leiden: E. J. Brill, 1964) 4.

MARSHA ELLIS SMITH

of victory. Gideon worships (Judg 7:15) and sets the attack in motion, again at night (Judg 7:19-25). The nomadic hosts are set to flight, and yet the battle cry is ambivalent: "For the LORD and for Gideon" (Judg 7:18).

In the aftermath of this famous and incongruous victory the saga shows Gideon the diplomat, a soother of the susceptibilities of the Ephraimites, who came late to the battle and wanted recognition and a share in the fruits of victory. Yet he is sadistic in his retribution toward those Israelites of Succoth and Penuel in Transjordan who refused him aid in the pursuit of the Midianite leaders.

Such a ruler fulfills the classic pattern of ancient Near Eastern despots. The Israelites recognize and approve these kingly qualities (which Samuel was later to describe, 1 Sam 8:10-22). Gideon's decision is for theocracy: the Lord as king (Judg 8:22-23). Monarchy has been offered and ostensibly rejected by Gideon, but his royal lifestyle and his naming of his son Abimelech ("my father, a king") show where his priorities lay.

The judge chosen and most closely fostered by God is the one who leads Israel into apostasy and the archetypal pseudomonarchy of Abimelech. Though the later chapters are promonarchy in their refrain, believing that Israel's chaos and degradation are caused by a kingless society (Judg 17:6; 18:1; 19:1; 21:25), here there are kings in all but name, Gideon and his son Abimelech, who makes himself king (Judg 8:22—9:57). In the text neither is approved.

In Ophrah, where he had a family altar to Baal at the beginning, Gideon's ephod is set up in a private shrine that was "a snare" to him and his family: "in my end is my beginning." From enslavement in Ophrah and doubt in a family that keeps an altar to Baal, he returns in the end to Ophrah and an ephod. Gideon/Jerubbaal seems to cause Baal to win in the end. This time we are left much lower down the spiral.

Abimelech, the Pseudo-King (Judg 8:29—9:57)

Abimelech breaks the expected next turn of the cycle. He is no judge or prophetic figure but a self-appointed half-Israelite who slaughters his way to three years of kingly power. Israel has no external enemy; he is the enemy within (Klein, 70). Jephthah's origins and early life might have predisposed him in the same ways (Judg 8:29-31; 9:4). But Jephthah is seen as a hero of faith (Heb 11:32), whereas Abimelech is an antihero, a negative embodiment of what monarchy can mean.

Shechem had a long history as a continuing Canaanite enclave with harmonious interrelationships with the Israelites. As son of his father's Shechemite mistress, denoted as a prostitute in the text ("concubine," 8:31), Abimelech is the least likely successor to his father's neodynasty when there are seventy legitimate half-brothers. At this stage, however, the unexpected and inadequate leader is not Yahweh's choice of deliverer—none is needed, for the land is at peace. Abimelech, ambitious to reign and supported by his pagan Shechemite relatives and his "worthless and reckless" followers (Judg 9:4), is the one from whom deliverance is needed. After the bloodbath, Abimelech's enthronement takes place under the oak at Shechem—financed by the shrine of Baal-berith or El-Berith ("the Lord/God of the Covenant"). Ironically this is the place where Joshua had affirmed loyalty to the covenant with Yahweh (Josh 24:1, 26).

The unexpected mouthpiece of God is Jotham, the surviving youngest son whose fable or parable of the trees (Judg 9:8-15) picks up on Abimelech's path to leadership. Jotham delivers his ironic story from Mount Gerizim, the mount of blessing (Deut 27:12-13). The bramble (brier or boxthorn) may make a brushfire blaze and threaten the majestic cedars of Lebanon, but how could such thorny, low bushes offer shade? Jotham is a youngest son with potential as one of Yahweh's unlikely instruments, yet he disappears. Yahweh is to repay Abimelech and bring him down. Only in this way can a man's curse be effectual (Judg 9:22-25).

The author or editor of Judges believes that nothing that occurs is outside Yahweh's overarching ultimate control, his sovereignty. The three years of conflicts between Abimelech and his erstwhile brethren are the result of "an evil spirit" sent by God (Judg 9:23). In contrast, his father was moved by "the spirit of the LORD" (Judg 6:34).

An unexpected opponent, Gaal, son of a

slave (*ebed; see* Ancient and Modern Slavery), speaks treason against Abimelech, whose father was king. But Gaal is not the deliverer. Fire is lit against the Tower of Shechem and Thebez. The bramble indeed starts a fire (Judg 9:15). Abimelech is not killed by Jotham or the boastful, drunken slave. He is killed by a woman without a name—but with a millstone. Again a woman uses a weapon with which she is familiar. Abimelech commands his armor-bearer to kill him to avoid this disgrace. Like the alien Sisera, that is how he is mockingly remembered: felled not by a sword but by an eighteen-inch stone, not by a warrior but a mere female. Death with ignominy comes for the self-styled king.

The Spiral of Decay (Judg 10:1—16:31)

Tola and Jair (Judg 10:1-5)

Two judges are mentioned with minimum detail but will act as contrasts to Abimelech. They have ministries over two decades and are buried in honor. They also contrast with Jephthah, whose saga is sandwiched between brief reports of prolific judges with large families (Judg 10:4; 12:8, 13), tragically unlike his own.

Jephthah: God Is Judge (Judg 10:6—12:7)

The Ammonites and Philistines are the next enemies to attack, and the brunt of the attack is felt by that vulnerable outlying enclave of Israelites, Manasseh, resident on the east of the Jordan. Again Yahweh speaks, perhaps through a prophet, and this time the response is bleak. His patience is at an end: "I will deliver you no more" (Judg 10:13). But the end is not yet. The community repents and returns to worship him, and "he could no longer bear to see Israel suffer" (Judg 10:16).

Faced with the enemy, the Gileadites turn to an outcast, illegitimate son of their clan, an outlaw and bandit chief, and choose him as their leader. Without a call narrative or a message from God it yet appears that this man is the one he approves, for God's spirit comes upon him (Judg 11:29).

The saga shows Jephthah guilty of child sacrifice as well as the genocidal slaughter of forty-two thousand defenseless Ephraimites. The focus of modern feminist rereadings is on the oppression and abuse of his unnamed, unmarried daughter. Some scholars have understood her to be treated as a tool, paying the price for her father's egotistic preoccupation with access to Yahweh's power, presence and victory. A few maintain that it was not her life that was sacrificed but her right to marry, hence the bewailing of her virginity.

Before the courts of heaven will Jephthah be condemned? The writer of Hebrews names him as a hero of faith, ignoring the unnamed, unmarried daughter sacrificed to fulfill an unnecessary vow. A careful rereading of the text within the pattern of Judges and in relationship to the whole Deuteronomic movement is needed to see what makes Jephthah a hero in spite of himself.

As illegitimate son of his father's prostitute, Jephthah is paralleled with Abimelech. Rejected by brothers and clan elders, he becomes an outlaw in Tob. Yet he is, or is to become, "a mighty warrior" chosen not by Yahweh, as Gideon was, but by those same elders responding to the crisis of the Ammonite attacks. Yahweh has talked of his sense of abandonment (Judg 10:13-14); now Jephthah experiences the same. Yet he is the savior that Yahweh intends to use: a person wounded by rejection, made hard by suffering.

The rejected one is now the preferred candidate of Gilead, whose elders are anxious for Jephthah's leadership. Although he points out the irony, Jephthah is prepared to be their head (not their king) and be brought "home"(Judg 11:9). This arrangement is made consciously in a ceremony before God (Judg 11:10). Perhaps the spiral is now on an upturn?

The sympathetic portrait of Jephthah continues with mention of diplomatic negotiations: a peace process! An outlaw bandit with every reason to have sadism in his psyche engages in diplomatic initiatives on the basis of historical background and careful, Yahweh-centered reasoning (Judg 11:23). Israelites had never taken Ammonite lands but had occupied those of the Amorites, who had opposed their passage to Canaan. For three hundred years these lands had been occupied without complaint, so any protest from Ammon is strangely late. Now, says his representative, "let the LORD, who is judge, decide" (Judg 11:27). This statement could be taken as the book's comment on the humans who are called by that name in Judges.

Diplomacy having failed, the battle is inevitable. So God's spirit falls on Jephthah as it did on Gideon before him. Yet as with Gideon, this enduement does not prevent Jephthah from making mistakes. Jephthah's vow to God, made out of insecurity and doubt and in order to guarantee victory, shows that he thinks and feels from the traumas of an undervalued child. His view of God is that of the Canaanite magic-centered religions, in which unmerited love is unknown and the spiritual bribery of vows may perhaps bring success at a price. The well-instructed Israelite remembers Deuteronomy 23:21-23 at this point, stressing that there is no compulsion to make vows but that vows made freely to God must be performed. Jephthah, not as well instructed, knew only the terror of breaking promises to the God of his fathers. His experience of fatherhood hardly prepared him to relate properly to the God of his father—or of his brothers.

Israelite tradition at no point approved human sacrifice, a fact that accounts for the embarrassed, elliptical style by which the writer indicates the fate of the daughter of Jephthah, "who did with her according to his vow" (Judg 11:39). The father's action is repellent to the faithful Israelite but is a tragically misplaced example of extraordinary determination to honor God by keeping his promise. Jephthah may have anticipated the need to sacrifice an expendable animal or a household slave (Judg 11:31 may read "whatever" or "whoever"). But his only child, his only daughter who comes out with music and dancing to greet his triumphant return . . . this is the end of all his joy, the end of his hopes for a future and a name, for descendants to carry on his memory. For his daughter must die, and she is a virgin. The pathos of the scene is increased by our knowledge that this man whose childhood experience had been so unhappy, having now achieved acceptance and even honor among his clan and people, is to lose his only child and destroy his future along with hers.

Yet Jephthah is committed to his vow, to his determination not to default against Yahweh. As he tells his daughter he treats her as a person in her own right, loved by him. She shares his understanding of the overriding nature of this vow. The narrative intent is to arouse pity in the hearer for such a misdirected but honorable father and admiration for such a loving and obedient daughter. She is allowed to go away to the hills for two months to "bewail her virginity" with her companions. This gave rise to a custom of yearly remembrance of her in Israel and may be in some way a recontextualized example of Israel taking over an existing Canaanite custom. To remain a virgin is to be bewailed, for the resultant childlessness means that this woman, named only by her relation to her father, will be without memorial and so forgotten in the future. Yet ironically she is remembered by the whole people. Because of her Jephthah also is remembered. He is a character with desperately tangled motives and beliefs but an example of faithfulness to his promises to God.

As is their habit, the tribe of Ephraim turn up after the battle is won to complain about their nonselection for this successful attack on Ammon. They threaten Jephthah, but he has had enough. In his state of grief and heroic sacrifice, how can he pander to such a self-serving clan? He is not prepared now for diplomacy and negotiation (cf. Gideon, Judg 8:1-3), so a pitiless internecine slaughter begins. Israelites have now sunk so low that interrelated clans turn against each other, clans recognizably different only by accent and pronunciation (Judg 12:6) but supposedly all one chosen people of God.

Ibzan, Elon and Abdon (Judg 12:8-15)

Three short accounts of judges from various regions follow. They too have short periods of leadership: seven, ten and eight years. But they contrast most noticeably with Jephthah in their productivity in terms of offspring: Ibzan with thirty sons and thirty daughters, Abdon with forty sons and thirty grandsons. Yet none of these people are named; their parents' contribution to Israelite history is all but forgotten. Without their advantages Jephthah is still the hero, though seriously flawed.

Samson: Grace and Disgrace (Judg 13:1—16:31)

Samson is a maverick fighter who failed to make much of an impact on the enemy, a person of childish tantrums and sadistic instincts harnessed to misused physical powers. He is a hulk of a man, yet a man to laugh at—a type familiar in ancient literature and modern films. The saga allows the reader to enjoy the discomfiture of the Philistine enemies yet to appreciate the irony of Samson's repeated capitulation to the wiles of women and his pitiful blindness at the end. With tragic irony we see that he, who was destined and equipped from conception to fight the enemy, finds all his closest relationships with Philistine women. It is ironic also that Samson's last recorded words are "let me die with the Philistines" (Judg 16:30).

Samson is not a type of Christ but a parable of Israelite history: chosen and destined for rule, greatly privileged and empowered by Yahweh yet consistently wasting his strength and cohabiting with the enemy. He has power without holiness. His failure of conscious commitment and intent to fulfill his destiny is overridden by God, who still "begins" (Judg 13:5) to save Israel from the Philistines. King David will later complete the task (2 Sam 8:1).

Most of the women in this saga are used by men, except for Samson's mother, Manoah's wife. She is entrusted with Yahweh's message, separated to God, mother of the deliverer. Here the laugh is on the husband. Samson uses women: "get her for me, because she pleases me" (e.g., Judg 14:3; 16:1). But these women are used by their people to defeat Samson and destroy his strength. The reader is expected to enjoy the stereotypical humor in the handling of intergender relationships and not take it too seriously.

An Annunciation Story: Samson's Birth (Judg 13:1-25). Israelites come under the domination of the Philistines for forty years. From their five towns of Gaza, Ashkelon, Ashdod, Ekron and Gath on the coastal plain this sophisticated and cultured people controlled the highlands. They were an Iron Age people dominating a Bronze Age Israelite community.

Like their nation, Manoah and his wife are in a barren state, but they too are visited by God's messenger (cf. Judg 6:7-10; 10:10-16), who announces that they will have a son. The story is determinedly focused on Manoah's wife. She is who gets the message, and she is perceptive and reticent in seeing who it is and not asking the person's name. Her husband bustles about determined to interview the man, to check for himself and take the dominant role in this encounter. But the angel comes at his own initiative, insists on turning the focus back onto Manoah's wife (Judg 13:12-13) and confirms the rightness of her sensitivity: "Why do you ask my name? It is too wonderful" (Judg 13:17-18). After the sacrificial fire is lit and the angel disappears, Manoah is all fear while his wife is the logical and reasonable one (Judg 13:22-23) who has to calm him. Samson's mother had the balance right!

The unique feature of this annunciation story is in the Nazirite restrictions imposed on the mother-to-be and on the child to be born. (For a woman who had had difficulty conceiving the ban on alcohol was good prenatal counseling.) But such a vow was usually a voluntary matter entered into by adults and not a matter of inheritance imposed on the unborn child from the womb. It symbolizes a state of separation or consecration to God that is acted out in the conditions mentioned (Judg 13:4-5): no drinking of wine, no breaking of the food laws, no cutting of hair or beard.

In many traditional spiritist religions, growing long hair and the cutting of hair have a quasi-religious or magical significance, and this seems to have been the way Samson came to interpret or misinterpret his state and his powers. The tale goes on to show how he breaks each of these conditions of his separation to God (Judg 14:6, 9; 13:4; 16:1-20) and how he fulfills his destiny only partially and always unintentionally. In spite of a miraculous conception to a wise and godly mother Samson's subsequent history is a disgrace: a misuse of grace.

Samson's saga from here on falls into two acts, Judges 14:1—15:20 and Judges 16. The recurring themes are of his dangerous encounters with unsuitable females, his secrets, his outbursts of rage and death-dealing power. Both end with his requests to God.

The Fateful Alliance (Judg 14—15). *Timnah and tantrums (Judg 14:1-20).* Samson, without respect to parents or reference to his destiny, breaks covenant by insisting on marrying a woman in Timnah. The Philistines are not the covenant people but are uncircumcised (Judg 14:3). Samson is driven by his hormones, breaking traditions and all the commitments of a Nazirite one by one. Yet he is also empowered by Yahweh (Judg 14:6), a wild spirit that comes and goes in his life but is "the spirit of the LORD." This seems far from the Holy Spirit and the ethics of the new covenant, but it is a wildfire force. It may be that after the passage of time the tellers of his saga looked back and saw that Samson's uncontrolled outbursts of tantrum and destruction fulfilled God's purposes in part without any conscious cooperation and intent on Samson's part. So they explain that this unruly physical strength was "the spirit of the LORD," as was his desire to marry a girl from Timnah (Judg 14:4; cf. Romans 8:28).

Samson goes on to break every Nazirite rule: killing a young lion, eating honey from a carcass and so involving his parents in unknowingly eating unclean food. Samson returns to his wedding feast, where it is presumed he will drink wine. Yet he does not lose God's presence; his strength remains as flourishing as his unshaved head. Only one part of the vow remains intact.

The text is full of secrets. The parents do not know about the lion and the honey, the people of Timnah do not know the answer to the riddle, Samson does not know that his wife is being pressured by her people. In all of this Samson remains his own man. He claims that his primary loyalty is to his parents rather than to his spouse, which is, ironically unknown to him, his wife's position also. The Torah has a strong covenant concept in marriage of leaving mother and father and cleaving to one's wife, involving a change of priorities and a mutual openness (Gen 2:24-25). This is hard enough when the parties are from a shared background, but Samson is marrying out of the covenant. He keeps his own secrets. He does not belong to anyone but himself.

When it turns out that the archetypal tears and nagging pleading of a sexual partner are at the instigation of his wife's Philistine relatives and friends, Samson is scathing. His new wife is but a "heifer" to be used by him or by others (Judg 14:18). He runs amok in Ashkelon in his frustrated rage and loss of face. But at least he is now attacking Philistines rather than sleeping and feasting with them. He returns to his Israelite parents' home. Is there now hope that he has learned his lesson and will work consciously to fulfill his destiny?

Loss of face, loss by fire (Judg 15:1-8). Some forms of marriage in the ancient Near East involved the wife continuing to live with her parents after marriage, being visited by her husband. His tantrum over and time having passed, Samson returns to claim his rights. His childish naiveté that all will be back to normal when he arrives with a ritual present is frustrated. He finds that his wife has been given to another (Judg 14:20). He is affronted. He has lost face yet again. Samson is not prepared to take the younger sister, who would be assumed to be the better deal, having more years of fertility before her. Instead he must get his own back.

In a clever but vicious plot the foxes are set alight to run and destroy the treasured harvest in the fields. The Philistines blame Samson's ex-wife's family and burn them too; in his revenge Samson attacks the community. At this stage the diagnosis moves up a notch: surely he is a sadistic, paranoid, manic-depressive? How did his parents let him get to this state? Was this child, whose name may be derived from the Hebrew for "sun," the overindulged light of their lives? In adulthood Samson always has to get what he wants when and how he wants it.

Contemporary Western susceptibilities about cruelty to animals may blind us to the reality that in most societies animals are regarded as pests for destruction or meat for consumption and as being at human disposal. The writers intend us to imagine the harvest destroyed and the prospect of empty stomachs for Timnah's people in the coming months. So they react with the vicious, illogical burning of Samson's ex-wife and her family. They are alike, these Philistines and Samson.

Samson at Lehi (Judg 15:9-17). The wild inroads on their people and property provoke the Philistines to move into the hills and raid the territory of Judah. In the conquest of Canaan this was the tribe first into battle, most faithful in its separation from and eradication of non-Israelite influences (Judg 1:1-8). Yet now they, the ancestors of the great king David, are appeasers. They want to keep the status quo and are prepared to surrender Samson. He is only a Danite, after all (Judg 13:2). Later generations would see Judah here representing

Israel in various points of its later history: a subdued, spiritless and weaponless people prepared to make the best of the foreign overlordship.

Samson seems to them to be willing to make the heroic sacrifice of his life, but his intent is kept secret from the people of Judah. He knows he can deal with the new ropes that bind him, although he is aware that he cannot hope to withstand three thousand of them if they attack (Judg 15:12-13). Samson, in contrast with Judah, cannot be bound and is empowered by God's spirit. Anything that comes to hand can become a weapon: his hands (Judg 14:6), the foxes on fire (Judg 15:5) and now the jawbone of a donkey. As God has used unexpected people throughout the book so far, so Samson uses unexpected weapons. He kills a thousand men. Perhaps it was not the numbers of Judah that he feared (Judg 15:12-13) but his unwillingness or powerlessness to attack his own, in admirable contrast to the succeeding chapters (Judg 19—21).

Samson: the new Moses? (Judg 15:18-20). Just as the miraculous story of his birth reminds the reader of the announcement of Isaac's birth to Abraham and Sarah, so this incident has echoes of Moses in the wilderness. Is there hope that Samson is to bring his people out of captivity in a like manner? The request he makes, though duly giving God the credit for his victory, concentrates on his personal safety, his physical needs and the gratification of the moment. Yet God graciously answers Samson's request. He does not throw away the weapon after use as Samson does. There is some resemblance between the instruments—Samson is much like the jawbone of a rebellious donkey.

The first act is over, and Samson seems set to rule in peace for twenty years to come.

The Same Old Cycle (Judg 16). Like Israel's people as a whole, Samson's life so far is one of commitment, misuse, slavery and deliverance. At the beginning of this second cycle our hope that he will become the new Moses is swiftly dashed. He ends up an abject, blinded slave. He is used as an animal and becomes a mockery to the Philistines. Yet God's purpose for his life is fulfilled in his dying.

First visit to Gaza (Judg 16:1-3). When it comes to sex, Samson always goes to Philistines. He risks his life in a foolhardy, vainglorious way, confident in his strength. He evades the secret plotters and humiliates the city by carrying off its gates on his shoulders. Against all expectation he gets away with it.

This incident is a prelude for the downfall to come. We shall yet see Samson brought down, literally back down to Gaza's coastal plain. All will see him then in daylight performing as a slave, shorn and subservient in the temple of Dagon, the god of the Philistines. But he will see nothing any more. In fact, he has never seen his life in the right perspective from the outset.

Delilah (Judg 16:4-20). The next, inevitable female is different, for Samson falls in love with her. Yet she, like the wife in Timnah, is loyal to her people and will use her wiles on this congenitally susceptible and gullible man. Delilah is a more despicable character, for she is motivated by money (Judg 16:5). There is again an interplay of secrets between Delilah and the Philistine plotters lying in wait (as they had done in Gaza, Judg 16:2) and the secret Samson is determined to keep lest he lose his powers (Judg 16:9).

Bound by bowstrings or ropes or even with his hair woven into the loom, Samson can break free. But he is enslaved to this woman, captured by her assertions of love, her desire to know his secret (Judg 16:15-17). By telling her his secret, he becomes helpless, his head in her lap, his hair shorn and unknowingly "weak . . . like anyone else" (Judg 16:17). His tragedy is to wake and try to shake off his bonds not knowing that "the LORD had left him" (Judg 16:20). His hair is symbolic—the important thing is that God has now declined to use him further.

So it was with Israelites throughout history: the desire to be like other peoples, the enslavement to their cajolings and gifts, and by this the loss of that separation to God for which they had been destined from birth. They are unaware that God had left them. In the days of Jeremiah and the exile, Samson's story would be particularly apt.

Death: revenge or martyrdom? (Judg 16:21-31). Samson's hair begins to grow, and the saga gives us a gleam of hope for him. He is the one who is destined to begin to release Israel from the Philistine yoke, yet he is yoked like an ox or a donkey turning the grinding millstones in the depths of Gaza. Here is Milton's Samson Agonistes, "eyeless in Gaza at the mill with slaves."

In the temple of their god the three thousand worshipers wait for the entertainment of the Israelite Hercules reduced to a circus event, his God humiliated before theirs. For the second time Samson calls on the Lord, but his heart is set on revenge for the loss of his eyes, not on his destined task. He is at best an unholy martyr, dying for his own cause rather than God's. Life for a sightless person in ancient times was desperate and purposeless.

The saga assumes that the Lord answers with the restored strength that Samson requires, for the Lord's own purposes. The pillars are pushed off their plinths, out of true, and the building collapses. In the rubble lie more dead Philistines than Samson had killed so far, and with them Samson. He died with the Philistines, but in death he is returned to the tomb of his father. Samson's story, as with most in Judges, shows God's patience with humans who make perverted use of the gifts he has given and who fail to cooperate with his divine purposes. Even in all its degraded motivations and misuse of strength, the story gives some hope for Israel's future (cf. Job 42:2).

The Grand Reversal (Judg 17:1—21:25)

On a superficial reading this last section of Judges, held together by the refrain "there was no king in Israel" (Judg 17:6; 18:1; 19:1; 21:25) and sharing two Levites among their characters, seems to be two appendices of undated earlier material cobbled together by someone reluctant to omit any research notes, regardless of their irrelevance. The first section, Judges 17—18, seems inconsequential or even boring: a man called Manoah loses his personal chaplain to a tribe of migrating Danites. In contrast, Judges 19—21 is the ultimate in horror, the unbearably sordid tale of a woman gang raped, the callous mutilation of her body, scenes of genocidal revenge that culminate in the abduction and rape of many more innocent girls. Why would such ghastly material be preserved in a Torah-loving, God-related society?

While Judges 2—16 rolls along secure in the pattern of cycle turning to spiral, the tale of increasing degradation of people and their leaders, the first chapter and the last five seem unrelated to this more coherent writing. Put these chapters in place, however, and it can be seen that there is a relationship between them. Judges 1 and Judges 17—21 are the envelope containing the message; they repeat motifs but subvert them. Now irony is bitter and deadly, and we feel the horror undistanced.

As at the beginning the Israelites consult the Lord, go out to conquer the people of Canaan and signally fail to fulfill their task, so now the degraded tribes of Israel consult the Lord and go up to fight Benjamin (Judg 20:18) and turn on Jabesh-gilead (Judg 21:8-12). Israel ends in anarchy, united in hypocritical ethical outrage yet viciously turning on each other. Now the text treats the Canaanites with sympathy as "quiet and unsuspecting" (Judg 18:7, 27-28), no threat to anyone, while a new Sodom, the most extreme symbol of Canaanite corruption, rises from destruction in Gibeah of Benjamin, in Israel (Judg 19:22-30). As the whirling spiral plummets down to disintegration, no one can persist in self-congratulatory assumptions about the stereotypical corruption of the other nations.

In this context there is no approval of the appalling suffering of the women depicted in these chapters. Life in those unstructured days was brutal, basic and sadistic for males as well as females. (Remember Jael.) Yet after the gang rape (Judg 19) even the most corrupted Israelites are appalled, as are the successive hearers of this tale. The most hardened criminals have their moral boundaries, as any rapist threatened in jail can attest.

As a musical coda echoes, repeats and brings to resolution the themes of a piece, so Judges 17—21 echoes past events within and beyond the text: Lot and Sodom, Gideon's ephod, Jephthah's vow, the ambivalent attempts toward monarchy. Then comes the resolution of all the themes: "In those days there was no king in Israel; all the people did what was right in their own eyes" (Judge 21:25).

With the echoes are resonances for the future. Whenever these stories were retold, they could be given an appropriate slant for the times. Hints of these appropriate retellings remain in the text as we have it. For

David and Solomon positive treatment of Judah and Bethlehem would be important. Later, as Jeroboam took the north into secession and set up his own priesthood and cult, the story of Manoah would be particularly apt.

Implicit in these chapters is the approval of the future peaceful days of Davidic monarchy, but the book as a whole shares the same ambivalence as 1 Samuel 8—10, either because it combines sources from different shades of opinion in the community or because it recognizes that kingship comes in various guises: Abimelech and Saul have something in common.

Micah and the First Levite (Judg 17:1—18:1)

Micah is not the judge, as expected, but an Ephraimite, the scapegoat tribe targeted throughout Judges. He is a negative person throughout: stealing from one's own mother is the ultimate in low behavior. Family life has reached the ultimate in corruption when his mother responds to the return of the silver with a blessing rather than a rebuke and uses some of it to make an idol for their private shrine. There are echoes of Gideon, then the refrain (Judg 17:5-6).

A Levite, symbol of the separation of the Israelites to the exclusive worship and service of God, leaves his post in Bethlehem of Judah, the idealized or model tribe, to search for a profitable place to be a private priest. All of this is against Deuteronomic principles for Jerusalem-centered worship (Deut 12; 18). But Micah says, "Now I know that the LORD will prosper me." Stolen silver has made an idol, and a disobedient Levite has become a family chaplain. The refrain (Judg 18:1) comments on Micah and leads in to the sequel.

Spying Again (Judg 18:2-10)

This incident resonates with and repeats with significant variations the old story of Israel's initial investigation and conquest of the land. It dates back to the days long before Samson, when the tribe of Dan is not yet settled in its region. Spies are sent out as before, but they are assured of God's approval from Micah's dubious priest, seeking land according to their own principles and methods. The area of Laish is occupied by innocuous, wealthy Sidonians, not by giants in fortified cities as described by faithful Caleb (reminding us that he features in Judges 1:12-15). These five spies, like Caleb and Joshua, are full of positive faith that God has ordained the land for them.

Stolen Shrine, Lost Security (Judg 18:11-26)

As the armed tribe of Dan set off, the erstwhile spies determine to steal the approving Levite priest, the shrine and its furnishings to set up their own center of worship in the far north, away from Judah and Jerusalem. The idol made from stolen silver is itself stolen, and the priest is willing to be seduced into a wider ministry (Judg 18:19-20). Micah's desolation is pathetic but self-induced, typical of the people of God in disobedience (Judg 18:24; cf. Is 46:1-7).

And the Levite Was . . . ? (Judg 18:27-31)

The unsuspecting people in Laish are overrun by these unprincipled Danites. They have no deliverer-judge, no near allies to help. The Danites set up their shrine with their coopted Levite. Then comes the revelation: this Levite's name was Jonathan, son of Gershom, the grandson of the great Moses. (The manuscripts' reading "son of Manasseh" rather than "Moses" probably originated in an attempt to avoid offense against the revered giver of the law.) Even that great family had been corrupted.

Though worship was centralized in Jerusalem about 150 years after this date, the separation of the northern kingdom (c. 922 B.C.) was followed by Jeroboam I's setting up separate shrines, one yet again in Dan (1 Kings 12:29), until the Assyrian captivity (722 B.C.).

An apparently inconsequential story has wider impact and resonances, a delayed change—unexpectedly exploding at the end. The desecration of true worship follows a society's failure of obedience in every aspect of its life before God.

The Rape of the Levite's Woman and Its Aftermath (Judg 19—21)

This Levite, like his woman, remains anonymous. Like Micah, the Levite is no hero but a man corrupt in the midst of a corrupted people. His relationship with his common-law wife, although stormy, is recognized and approved in her family. After an angry separation he goes to fetch the woman from her father's house in Bethlehem of

Judah, the place that Jonathan son of Gershom had left to go wandering (Judg 17:7). The repetitious account of the father-in-law's delaying tactics serves as a reason for the lateness of their journey and their need to stay overnight along the way. More than that, it serves to point out a deliberate contrast between Bethlehem, David's hometown in Judah, and inhospitable Gibeah, in the territory of Benjamin. We are led to assume that they would have been better off staying in non-Israelite Jerusalem than in Gibeah (Judg 19:12).

The text echoes with the memory of the angels' visit to Sodom (Gen 19). Yet these visitors are not angels, and there is no deliverance from the demands of the depraved local men planning to rape the Levite visitor. This is not a foreign stranger but a fellow Israelite and a Levite at that, yet they are intent on rape. Their host's offer to surrender his virgin daughter and the man's concubine to the mob comes as an affront beyond bearing, as it does in Genesis 19:8. These men thought of homosexual rape, the rape of the male, as being much the worse of two evils, involving a sexual connection abominated in Israelite culture and religion (*see* Homosexuality). The women are expendable. Their rape is wrong but not seen as so perverse (*see* Violence, Abuse and Oppression).

Repellent chauvinism lies behind the story, a tale told of a decadent people whose values are implicitly rejected by the book as a whole (Judg 19:1; 21:25). For this woman, however, there is no miraculous escape (cf. Gen 19:11). Her man throws her out to be gang raped throughout the night and to die on the doorstep with her hands stretched out (Judg 19:27). He is the crass, egotistic, pitiless male who uses females for his purpose and salvation. Yet the dismembering of her body, the gruesome call to arms, may be interpreted as the response of a guilty, traumatized and grief-filled person driven to the edge of insanity. Here at last is revulsion against corruption, a call to unity to reject such un-Israelite behavior, unworthy of a people brought out of Egypt. Yet it is also a call to civil war.

Before the assembled company the Levite gives a cleaned-up, self-serving version of what happened, this "vile outrage in Israel" (Judg 20:6). Appalled, they are united in judgment against Gibeah. Clan loyalty takes precedence over ethical principles. "Our own, right or wrong" seems to be Benjamin's philosophy, not loyalty to "their kinsfolk, the Israelites" (Judg 20:13). Like Ehud, the Benjaminites are left-handed sons of the right hand (Judg 3:15), but Ehud used his disability to profit Israel.

The Israelites replay the first scene in Judges, asking the Lord who shall go up first (Judg 1:1), and again Judah is indicated. Again they "go up" (Judg 20:18, 28), but this time they attack their own people. The resulting campaign is unsuccessful at first, echoing the past conquest of Bethel and Ai, when disobedience first lost and then won the battle (Josh 7—8). The comprehensive defeat eventually inflicted on Benjamin is attributed to the Lord at work, just as he had been against the Canaanites (Judg 20:35-48).

Two More Vows (Judg 21:1-24)

At Mizpah, a place associated with Jephthah's commitment to God, the Israelites also made two self-generated vows that are bound with a curse. The first vow is that no tribe would give its daughters in marriage with the Benjaminites (Judg 21:1). The second vow is that those who did not participate in the punitive war against Benjamin would be executed (Judg 21:5). Instead of avoiding marriage with the people of Canaan, they now ban their kindred. Afraid of the curse on those who do not fulfill vows, they find a loophole in their first vow by activating their second. Israel is yet reluctant that any of the tribes should disappear (Judg 21:6), so their solution is to provide wives for these Benjaminites while taking the promised retributive killing of the people of Jabesh-gilead, who had not participated in the war (Judg 21:8-11).

The fate of those women is tragic: they are given over to the people their male relatives had refused to fight. They are abducted during a religious festival to the Lord in Shiloh. They were in the right place but were living the wrong life. Yet those abducted, raped women were to be the mothers of the generations to follow.

Conclusion (Judg 21:25)

The people of God who refuse to obey God, make their own strategies and attempt their own deliverances end in degradation. It will be better with a king, hints the text, foreshadowing the Davidic dynasty appointed by God. All the rest is gloom and disintegration.

Yet here and there we have seen God graciously at work in patient, repetitive teaching of the same lessons and giving assurance and reassurance far beyond the boundaries of normal expectation. There are no unblemished heroes in Judges but God. He is the Judge.

Bibliography. A. Cundall, *Judges and Ruth* (Downers Grove, IL: IVP, 1968); A. Brenner, ed., *A Feminist Companion to Judges* (Sheffield: Sheffield Academic Press, 1993); D. R. Davis, *Such a Great Salvation* (Grand Rapids, MI: Baker, 1990); L. R. Klein, *The Triumph of Irony in the Book of Judges* (Sheffield: Almond Press, 1989); B. G. Webb, *The Book of Judges* (Sheffield: JSOT Press, 1987); M. Wilcock, *The Message of Judges* (Downers Grove, IL: IVP, 1992).

AILISH FERGUSON EVES

RUTH

Introduction

This beautifully constructed narrative concerns Ruth, a Moabite, member of a cursed race (Deut 23:3-6), who, through willful commitment to her impoverished mother-in-law Naomi, her people and her God (Ruth 1:16-17), becomes great grandmother to King David (Ruth 4:17). The redemption of Naomi through the birth of Obed, who continued the family line of Perez to David and ultimately to the Messiah (Mt 1:1-17), begs no special pleading. God chose an isolated, foreign woman to bring redemption to his chosen people Israel. Ruth is hailed as being worth more than seven, the number for perfection in biblical parlance, sons. Ruth had no status and no standing in the society she adopted, but God used the commitment and determination of this insignificant foreign woman to accomplish his purposes in salvation history. The book of Ruth is unequivocally a story about God's redemptive love.

Ruth is unusual in that it is a microtale concerning women and their struggles in a patriarchal society. For this reason, some scholars argue female authorship, and while this cannot be proven it is interesting to note that there is some consensus that it began as an oral story. The canonical book of Ruth may have originated in the women who were aware of Naomi's destitution on her return to Bethlehem and publicly rejoiced in the restoration of her family line. A written account of an oral tradition would embrace the classical style and language contained within the book and the various dialectical anachronisms while accounting for the editorial explanation of the sandal exchange (Ruth 4:7) and the genealogy (Ruth 4:18-22). Names in Ruth are important and reveal something of the characters who own them, in keeping with the Hebrew understanding that to know a person's name is to know his or her character. This adds to the speculation that the narrative is a parable but conflicts with the historicity of the account (Ruth 1:1; 4:7, 11-12, 18-22) and its geographical setting. One may conclude that through the passage of time characters have been given appropriate names in order to emphasize their personalities, while the story is historical.

The various arguments regarding date of composition are based on linguistic content, chronological evidence and the perceived purpose of the book. Evidence is inconclusive regarding pre- or postexilic dating. Assuming the genealogy is integral to the original copy, one may authoritatively claim that the book was compiled after David became king of Israel, but how long after remains unknown.

Ruth 1:1 sets the story "in the days when the judges ruled," roughly between 1220 and 1050 B.C., which Judges 21:25 tells us were days when "there was no king in Israel; all the people did what was right in their own eyes."

Women who feature prominently in Judges are Deborah, a prophet and leader of Israel (Judg 4—5); Samson's mother, who is told by an angel of the Lord that she will conceive and have a son (Judg 13); and Delilah, who betrays Samson to the Philistines (Judg 16:4-21). By contrast, Ruth's tale gives no account of political leadership, no mention of supernatural encounters and no account of treason.

Great social weight was accorded to clan loyalty during the time of the judges, as was continuance of the family line, always through the male. Israelites were divided into tribes, clans and families. A clan was united by blood relationship and common ancestry. Land belonged to a family rather than to an individual, and if a man died leaving no sons the inheritance went to his daughters; if no daughters, to his brothers; if no brothers, to his father's brothers; if no father's brothers, to the next of kin (Num 27:8-11). If a married man died, his brother was obliged to act as *levir* and marry the widow in order to secure his brother's family line (Deut 25:7-9). The firstborn son of this union would be regarded as the son of the dead man. While this law ultimately preserved patriarchal inheritance laws and protected family lineage, a byproduct was that the widow was provided for. Gleaning laws, too, protected the poor and the alien (Lev 19:9-10; 23:22). God was not reinforcing a patriarchal cultural framework through these stipulations; rather, through the provision of them, human integrity and dignity were to be given to those who were vulnerable because of the prevailing culture. In the telling of Ruth's tale we gain some insight into the vulnerability of women striving for survival in a male domain, where the reality of famine and the vagaries of war were harsh aspects of life, and procreation an essential element of it.

Judges gives no specific mention of famine, although localized famines in the region were not uncommon, due to lack of rain and also war. The Midianite strategy of ruining crops and livestock forced the Israelites into the mountains (Judg 6:3-5).

The Israelites were dominated by Moab for eighteen years (Judg 3:12-30). It may have been during this time that Elimelech took the drastic action of leaving Bethlehem with his wife and two sons, deserting his clan and abandoning its protection in search of food. The Moabites were descended from Lot, whose daughters plotted and committed incest with him in order to preserve the family line (Gen 19:30-38), a matter of crucial and fundamental importance in ancient times. The Moabites were not monotheists like the Israelites, and they worshiped other gods alongside their principal god, Chemosh (Ruth 1:15; Num 25:1-5; 2 Kings 3:27).

Outline

1:1-22	Death, Destitution and Covenant
2:1-23	Providence
3:1-18	Covenant
4:1-22	Redemption

Commentary

Death, Destitution and Covenant (Ruth 1)

The narrative opens in Bethlehem, which means "house of bread," but ironically there is no bread as the land is in famine. In search of food, Elimelech and his family go to Moab, another irony, for the Moabites failed to give food to the Israelites during the exodus, and they were cursed as a result (Deut 23:2-4). Circumstantial evidence suggests that an Ephrathite (Ruth 1:2; 4:11) had considerable social standing within the community; the context suggests Ephrathah was a location in Bethlehem. No longer under the influence of their father, Mahlon and Chilion marry Moabite women, possibly for reasons of self-preservation—in order to gain access to land, paid as a dowry, that they could farm. It is conceivable that there was a shortage of men due to war or famine and the Moabite women had little choice but to marry foreigners. The text gives no reason for the cause of deaths; this may be because God's anger caused by their intermarriage was assumed to be self-evident (cf. Num 25:1-5; Deut 23:3-6; Rom 6:23). However, the narrator seeks to focus on the dire predicament of the women. Elimelech had effectively deserted his clan in search of food; on his death and the death of his sons, Naomi's social standing is precarious, and the extinction of Elimelech's family line is conclusive. Ancient Israel placed a harsh social stigma on women with no children; to have been blessed with sons and then to have lost them was clear evidence of God's wrath. If her Moabite daughters-in-law remarry Moabite men they will not produce heirs for Elimelech or her sons.

With the prerequisite for social acceptability, stability and security—men—taken away from the women, Ruth 1:6 introduces an all-female cast, headed by Naomi, still in search of food. The women set out together for Judah, from whence Naomi came. But Naomi, possibly wishing to evade publicly facing up to her sons' intermarriage on arrival in Bethlehem, turns to her daughters-in-law and tells them to return to their mother's home until a husband is found for them (cf. Ruth 4:12; Gen 38:11). Naomi's worth is anchored in her status as wife and mother; she interprets her circumstances as being the result of God's judgment against her (Ruth 1:13, 21) and not against her menfolk (cf. Deut 23:2-4; Num 25:1). Naomi is past child bearing, unable to provide sons for Elimelech or husbands for her widowed daughters-in-law. Marriage will not, therefore, secure her future.

Naomi's blessing, "May the LORD deal kindly with you, as you have dealt with the dead and with me" (Ruth 1:8, which she repeats in Ruth 2:2 on discovering Boaz's identity), reveals a perspective that is almost alien in contemporary society: that of honoring and perpetuating the family of the dead. The women initially refuse to leave her, wishing to identify themselves with Naomi's people, who are also their husbands' people. There is kissing and loud weeping; the bereft women display their emotions and support one another in their desolation and grief. Orpah conforms to Naomi's wishes and leaves obediently with a kiss, but Ruth clings to Naomi in defiance. Naomi's observation that Orpah has returned "to her people and to her gods" (Ruth 1:15), and her appeal to Ruth to do the same suggests Naomi's disillusionment with Yahweh. She has no desire to convert Ruth and implores her to follow Orpah.

For Ruth, the prospect of returning to her mother's house was unappealing. As a widow she would be an added burden to her family or a servant for her brothers' wives until a husband was found for her. However, marriage is not on Ruth's agenda, for Ruth commits herself utterly to Naomi, Naomi's people and Naomi's God, specifically named as Yahweh. In doing this, Ruth unknowingly secures for herself the role of redeemer, for her covenantal confession reveals a loyalty and commitment that will be borne out in the rest of the text and that results in God's blessing. Justice is her prime motivating factor, for seeing Naomi's plight, she determines to stand by her mother-in-law until death separates them. Trapped within their cultural framework, both women face a bleak future. But Ruth proves through her actions that she perceives the God of the Israelites to favor the oppressed, and she is resolute in her determination to follow this through. The force of Ruth's pledge silences Naomi.

On arrival in Bethlehem the whole town is "stirred," and the women ask, "Is this Naomi?" (Ruth 1:19). The women of the town are shocked that this desolate woman is the one who left Bethlehem more than a decade previously (Ruth 1:4). Naomi finds return without her menfolk humiliating. Her circumstances have directly affected her outlook on life. She is consumed with self-pity and hopelessness; all her identity and worth were invested in her husband and her sons, and so sure is she that her grief will be permanent that she wishes her name, meaning "pleasant," to be exchanged for Mara, meaning "bitter" (Ruth 1:20). She left Bethlehem full, although in famine, because she had a husband and two Israelite sons. She returns to Bethlehem empty, because she is without husband or sons. The verbs (Ruth 1:20-21) are singular, indicating that Naomi perceives herself as alone, isolated in her affliction and despair, suggesting that her daughter-in-law, Ruth, counts for nothing. Naomi has only one perspective: as a woman she was the facilitator of Elimelech's family line in which was established her security and future.

Ruth 1:22 sets the stage for the rest of the narrative. In contrast to Naomi's analysis, the reality of the situation is that Naomi left Bethlehem with her family in a time of famine and she enters the town, accompanied by her daughter-in-law, in a time of plenty, "at the beginning of the barley harvest."

Providence (Ruth 2)

The narrator wastes no time in introducing Boaz as a wealthy relative of Elimelech's, a man of standing and worth, *ish gibbor hayil.* Matthew 1:5 identifies Boaz's mother as Rahab, the prostitute. Genealogies often jump generations, but it is interesting to note that Boaz has immoral ancestry, although Rahab, like Ruth, was an unlikely foreign female who, in her commitment to God's people, was used by God to secure his purposes for Israel (Josh 2; 6:25). Rabbinic commentators held that Boaz is the same Ibzan of Bethlehem attested to in Judges 12:8-11, but this is speculative, and the likelihood is that that text refers to a different Bethlehem.

Taking the initiative, Ruth, who is poor and alien, requests Naomi's permission to take advantage of the gleaning laws (Lev 19:9-10; 23:22). Naomi's emphatic reply, "Go, my daughter" (Ruth 2:2), suggests urgency; the women are desperate for food. Naomi's social standing, being an Ephrathite, may prevent her from joining Ruth, but it is more likely, in view of the women's comments, that she is too weak, physically and mentally, to assist with gleaning.

Having introduced the reader to Boaz, Ruth 2:3 reveals that Ruth is providentially working in Boaz's field. The repetition that Boaz was from Elimelech's family emphasizes his connection to Naomi and paves the way for what is to follow. Field boundaries were unmarked, often determined only with reference to surrounding ownership. Boaz notices the stranger in their midst on his arrival, and his question to the foreman (Ruth 2:5) indicates a desire to know who, among his male neighbors, is responsible for the unknown woman working in his field. Women usually belonged to men: fathers, husbands or brothers. The foreman discloses that Ruth belongs to no one but "came back with Naomi from the country of Moab" (Ruth 2:6).

Whether gleaning was common practice at that time is unclear, but it would indicate to Boaz the extent of Ruth's and Naomi's poverty. Ruth is unaware that Boaz belongs to Elimelech's clan and consequently has obligations to Naomi (cf. Deut 25:5-10; Lev 25:25). Boaz is benevolent toward Ruth, his welcome into his *familia* increasing by degrees as the day progresses. "I have ordered the young men not to bother you" (Ruth 2:9) could refer to Ruth's vulnerable situation in having no man to protect her, leaving her liable to sexual abuse. More probably gleaners were not welcome during harvest, for they were in effect reducing the quantity of crop gathered.

In lying prostrate before Boaz (Ruth 2:10), Ruth is paradoxically ensuring that Boaz does take notice of her, a foreigner. Boaz delivers a fine speech extolling Ruth in reply to her question, but he does not disclose that Naomi is a relative of his, and throughout the harvest period he takes no further initiative to secure the women's well-being. In keeping with his paternalistic role, he praises Ruth for leaving her homeland, her father and mother and coming to "a people you did not know before," conferring blessing upon her (Ruth 2:11-12). This pious blessing will be fulfilled through Boaz's actions (Ruth 3:13; 4:1-10) when Ruth goads Boaz into action on behalf of herself and Naomi.

Ruth responds to Boaz with grateful thanks (or is it intelligent manipulation?), pointing out that she has a lower status than Boaz's servant girls, thus emphasizing the calamity that has befallen upon her. Ruth is confident of her worth to Naomi (Ruth 1:17); working within her culture she gently lays claim to human dignity by emphasizing her precarious status to someone in power: Boaz. Ruth's tactic, conscious or not, has its effect, and Boaz offers the hungry Ruth sustenance, more than she

Reapers in Judah worked like these Egyptians harvesting grain. (Ruth 2)

can eat, welcoming Ruth into his household by inviting her to eat and drink with them and ordering his workers to look after her welfare.

On Ruth's return home with a large quantity of threshed barley (an ephah is approximately 15 to 20 liters or about 13 to 18 dry quarts) she arouses Naomi's curiosity and inspires her excitement. Ruth's disclosure of Boaz's name to Naomi emphasizes the key role that Boaz will play in their lives. Ruth 2:1 introduced Boaz; the narrator labors the point as his name is finally revealed to Naomi. Naomi uses a familiar phrase (Ruth 1:8) in praise of Boaz and reveals to Ruth that Boaz is a close relative and one of "our" kinsmen, that is, a family member with the right or obligation to redeem. Ruth's success in gathering food has been rewarded by Naomi's inclusion of Ruth in her clan.

Lest the reader begin to forget that Ruth is a foreigner, Ruth 2:21 immediately designates Ruth as the Moabite, a crucial element of the narrative, for in focusing on Ruth's foreign origins, the text simultaneously emphasizes God's inclusive love. Ruth retains her national identity even though Naomi has adopted her. Our distinctiveness as individuals is to be embraced, not dismissed or abused, when we join the community of God's people, enhancing its diversity and variety and adding to its richness.

The chapter concludes with Ruth gleaning in Boaz's field throughout the barley and wheat harvest and living with her mother-in-law, temporarily secure in work and food (Ruth 2:23; 3:1). The circumstances of the women have improved considerably; and this is not through their calculations but through the providence of God.

Covenant (Ruth 3)

Naomi takes the initiative as the chapter opens, and bearing in mind Ruth's commitment to her people (Ruth 1:16), she devises a scheme to motivate Boaz to fulfill his obligations as a next of kin (Ruth 3:1-4). Ruth is an activist and unafraid to claim God's provision for herself and Naomi through Boaz. Boaz, being a wealthy man of standing and a member of Elimelech's clan, is challenged by Ruth to act as *go'el* ("kinsman-redeemer"; Ruth 2:20) using similar imagery to that which Boaz used of Yahweh when he blessed her. Ruth, who has sought refuge under Yahweh's wings, now seeks refuge under Boaz's cloak. Typologically we may have a foretaste of the Holy Spirit overshadowing Mary (Lk 1:35) in Ruth 3:9.

The role of *go'el* was specifically concerned with buying back family land (Lev 25:25). While no specific mention is made of Naomi's land until Ruth 4:3, the ancient reader would understand that the redemption of land was a responsibility of the next of kin. But that was not the only responsibility (cf. Gen 38:8-9; Deut 25:5-10; Mt 22:23-25). Ruth, although free to marry whom she wished, was the widow of Elimelech's elder son, Mahlon (Ruth 4:10). Because levirate marriage is not possible for Naomi, should she find a male family member willing and able to comply, Ruth could claim a *levir* to continue the family line.

Boaz interprets Ruth's appeal as asking him to act as *go'el* and as *levir,* the latter being an invitation to marriage (Ruth 3:10). Ezekiel 16:8 uses similar phraseology, where the Lord rescues Jerusalem from destitution by spreading his garment over her nakedness.

Why Naomi instructs Ruth to approach Boaz in this way is something of an enigma. In Hebrew, "feet" (*regel,* Ruth 3:4, 7-8) is sometimes used as a euphemism for the sexual organs. Is Ruth making a sexual advance? This is possible, but unlike Ruth 4:12, the text is not explicit, so although we may want to know whether there was or was not a sexual encounter, the ambiguity suggests this is not an integral part of the story. The Hebrew word for "startle" or "tremble" (Ruth 3:8) reveals that Boaz, the strong man, was not merely surprised but frightened to find a woman lying near to him, suggesting no expectancy on his part to be visited in such a manner.

Boaz recognizes that Ruth's request is further evidence of her loyalty to God's people. Not only has she left her family and country; she is now prepared to further the line of her Israelite father-in-law in order to redeem the destitution of her mother-in-law. Self-sacrifice is sometimes perceived as a natural element of a woman's character and role. However, Boaz is right to commend Ruth, for her conduct is a model for both genders. Here on the threshing floor she reveals the extent of her commitment to Naomi, Naomi's people and Yahweh. Ruth is selfless and sensible; she has made an ethical choice, and now she is living by it. As female she initiates, as male Boaz responds.

But there is another *go'el* closer in line to Elimelech than Boaz. Boaz is content for this man to take on the role, thus indicating that the motivation for his actions is based more on family duty than on romantic love. If it is discovered that Ruth has visited the threshing floor, Boaz may be compromised when challenging the closer kinsman-redeemer to redeem the land and also to marry Ruth (Ruth 4:5). According to the Mishnah (*Yeb* 2:8), if a man was suspected of having intercourse with a Gentile woman he could not perform levirate marriage with her. The gift of barley is a sign for Naomi that Boaz is committed to both the women and a sign to the reader that the women are still in poverty and in need of food. Ruth 3 concludes with Naomi, Ruth and the reader wondering: Will the closer next of kin marry Ruth, or will it be Boaz? Naomi is confident that their future will be decided by the end of the day.

The theme of covenant pervades the narrative. Ruth has pledged her allegiance to Naomi, and in fulfillment of that pledge goes to the threshing floor to invite Boaz to take up his role as *go'el* and *levir.* Boaz in response to Ruth pledges that he will do for her all that she asks, and Naomi is confident this promise, his covenant, is to be relied upon. The shawl of barley is a sign of Boaz's covenant to the women.

Redemption (Ruth 4)

In calling the meeting of the town council at the town gate, where matters of legal and public concern were conducted, Boaz serves the purposes of Naomi and Ruth. Yet ultimately the men will determine the fate of the women. There is great similarity with the stipulations recorded in Deuteronomy 25:7-9 and the events described in Ruth 4:1-12, although the specifics differ.

Legally there were no provisions enabling a widow to inherit the property of her deceased husband (Num 27:8-11), but in practice it seems that Naomi is using Elimelech's land to galvanize the male members of her clan into action. Leviticus 25:25 indicates that selling the family land is clear confirmation of poverty and testifies to the practice of family members redeeming the land (buying it back) to keep it in the family. If the next near relative(s) will not redeem the land, Naomi will benefit from selling it, but the demise of Elimelech's line will be absolute.

The anonymous next of kin is initially willing to redeem the land and keep it from being sold out of the clan, until Boaz also imposes on him the responsibility of acting as *levir.* These are unusual circumstances, and it appears that Boaz has presented the next of kin with a predicament. If the man accepts his duty as next of kin and acts to redeem the land, it seems he will be obliged to act as *levir* and acquire "the widow of the dead man, to maintain the dead man's name on his inheritance" (Ruth 4:5). Levirate marriage is not an option concerning

Naomi and poses no threat to his estate, for she is past child bearing. But if he acquires or marries Ruth, he would forfeit the redeemed land on the birth of her firstborn son, for the son would be regarded as the firstborn of Mahlon, and all inheritance rights would go to that son. If Ruth were to have no more sons, the *levir* would have restored Elimelech's family line at the expense of his own.

Alternatively, if the next of kin redeems the land but refuses to act as *levir*, Boaz, who is also next of kin, could claim the role. If the union between Ruth and Boaz produced a son, the next of kin would forfeit the redeemed land. The kinsman-redeemer is not prepared to redeem the land if in so doing he is also obliged to marry Ruth or if there is any possibility that she marry someone else. Consequently the next of kin gives his "right of redemption" to Boaz. The editorial comment on the practice of sandal exchange indicates a passing of generations after the story is told (Ruth 4:7).

Boaz's public announcement is ironic, for Elimelech's and Mahlon's names are omitted from the genealogies. The line of descent is through Boaz in Ruth 4:21 and Matthew 1:5, fulfilling the blessing endowed on him by the elders (Ruth 4:12). It may be that Elimelech's line was also attributable to Salmon; if so, God's redemptive purposes in the restoration of his family have been superbly accomplished.

In keeping with the patriarchal framework of which he is a part, Boaz's proclamation is not couched in terms of compassion for the women but rather in terms of maintaining Elimelech's and subsequently Mahlon's name. Naomi embraced this framework wholeheartedly; her identity has been shattered through the loss of male lineage. From her perspective the task of women is to bear children for men. In contrast to this, while Ruth facilitates this agenda, her motivation is based on her commitment to Naomi and ensuring Naomi's survival. In adopting Yahweh as her God, Ruth becomes a liberator not only for the oppressed but also to the wealthy Boaz, for she has enabled him to fulfill his obligations. In the union of Boaz and Ruth, God has incorporated wealthy male Israelite and impoverished female Moabite in his redemptive purposes.

The elders confirm that they have witnessed the transaction, testifying to its legal status, and then confer blessing on Boaz by referring to Rachel and Leah, who with their maidservants Bilhah and Zilpah were the mothers of the twelve sons of Jacob (Gen 29), the ancestors of the twelve tribes of Israel. The blessing is fulfilled, for God uses Ruth to build the house of Israel, and the birth of Obed furthers the line of Judah (Leah's fourth son), which produces the great king David (Ruth 4:22) and also the Messiah (Mt 1:1-16). The elders pray that Boaz "may produce children in Ephrathah" (Ruth 4:11) and be famous in Bethlehem. Ephrath is where Rachel died in childbirth (Gen 35:16-20); it is also identified as "one of the little clans of Judah," from which "shall come forth for me one who is to rule in Israel, whose origin is from of old, from ancient days" (Mic 5:2; cf. Mt 2: 4-6).

The reference to "Perez, whom Tamar bore to Judah" (Ruth 4:12; Gen 38) incorporates Boaz's family heritage and also alludes to levirate marriage. Tamar, on the consecutive deaths of her husbands, waited for Judah's third son, Shelah, to grow up in order to marry him. But Judah failed to give him in marriage to Tamar. The plot that Tamar hatched to remedy the situation resulted in the birth of Perez (Ruth 4:18-22). Tamar and Ruth are both foreign widows; both are vital to God's purposes in establishing the line of descent for a family of major significance in Judah. The genealogy identifies Perez as Boaz's ancestor, and no mention is made of Elimelech or Mahlon or maintaining the name of the dead with his property.

Obed's conception is orchestrated by God (Ruth 4:13). The women praise God for Naomi's restoration and God's provision of a *go'el*, whose reward, in their eyes, should be fame in Israel. They recognize that Naomi's destitution has been overcome by the faithfulness of her daughter-in-law, who is better than seven sons. Ruth provided a grandchild for Naomi that her sons could not. Ruth has redeemed Naomi, Boaz has redeemed Ruth, and together they not only provided a forerunner for the messianic line but also became an essential part of it (Mt 1:5). God has used an isolated, foreign woman with no status in the society she adopts to bring redemption to his people through her obedience, which at every point in the narrative carried risk. She abandoned her roots more conclusively than Elimelech; she labored in a field where she was vulnerable to abuse, physical or verbal (*see* Violence, Abuse and Oppression); she went to Boaz at night, risking rejection. The women observe that Naomi's desolation has been reversed (cf. Ruth 1:19); in extolling Ruth they gently rebuke Naomi for perceiving the worthiness of her life only in terms of family lineage; in praising Yahweh they acknowledge God's providence in redemption. Unusually, it is the women who name the child and not Boaz, possibly because as the firstborn of a levirate marriage, the baby boy is reckoned by the women to be Mahlon's, although the genealogy attributes paternity to Boaz.

The genealogy concludes the narrative. The book began with the death of all the males in the family, but God's redemption is in clear view at its conclusion. Ruth, who sought refuge in the God of Israel (Ruth 1:16; 2:12), becomes great-grandmother to the shepherd boy David, the king of Israel and the seed of messianic hope.

Bibliography. A. Brenner, ed., *A Feminist Companion to Ruth* (Sheffield: Sheffield Academic Press, 1993); D. N. Fewell and D. M. Gunn, *Compromising Redemption: Relating Characters in the Book of Ruth* (Louisville, KY: Westminster John Knox, 1990); H. Fisch, "Ruth and the Structure of Covenant History," *Vetus Testamentum* 32 (1982) 425-37; R. M. Hals, *The Theology of Ruth* (Philadelphia: Fortress, 1969). GILLIAN M. ROWELL

1 & 2 SAMUEL

Introduction

"It was the best of times; it was the worst of times," writes Charles Dickens in his *Tale of Two Cities*—a world in transition where some things never change. In the Hebrew Bible the books of 1 and 2 Samuel directly follow from the verdict of the final editor of the book of Judges. The breakdown in moral and social order, described in Judges 19—21, was due to the fact that "there was no king in Israel; all the people did what was right in their own eyes" (Judg 21:25). Thus the stage is set for the social and political transition from a society organized on lineage lines to monarchical rule. Yet for the majority of people during this period, life proceeded much as before with its focus primarily on kinship ties and human relationships. Even for those directly caught up in the events surrounding the establishing of the monarchy, family concerns loom large, and much of the action in both 1 and 2 Samuel focuses on the developing and shifting relationships between the various characters. But what makes this story of supreme and lasting value is the divine dimension, for it is the genius of the Jewish-Christian tradition that God is never remote from human affairs but is active in them, working out his mysterious purposes in, through and sometimes despite the lives of frail and often failing human beings. The books of Samuel may recount Israel's transition to kingship, but the overarching message is that ultimately Yahweh, the Lord, rules over all. The only proper and safe response to his kingship is submissive dependence upon him.

Outline of 1 Samuel

1:1—2:11	A Mother's Prayer
2:12-36	A Father's Failure
3:1-21	A Young Man's Calling
4:1—7:2	The Glory and Power of Yahweh
7:3—8:22	Samuel as Judge
9:1—10:27	The Anointing and Commissioning of Saul
10:27—11:15	The Claims of Kinship
12:1-25	Samuel's Farewell
13:1—14:52	Saul Under Pressure
15:1-35	Saul's Failure
16:1-23	David as Court Musician
17:1-58	David as Champion of Israel
18:1—20:42	David and the Family of Saul
21:1—22:23	David, Saul and the Massacre at Nob
23:1—27:4	David on the Run from Saul
27:5—28:2	David in Philistine Territory
28:3-25	Saul's Descent into Despair
29:1-11	David and the King of Gath
30:1-31	David and the Amalekites
31:1-13	The Death of Saul

Commentary

A Mother's Prayer (1 Sam 1:1—2:11)

The importance of kinship ties in early Israelite society is well illustrated in the opening verse of 1 Samuel. Genealogies served as a charter of human rights, with membership in a kinship group bringing associated rights and duties, privileges and responsibilities. Within the patrilineal framework characteristic of Israelite society, women also ideally found their security and destiny. On one such woman attention is focused in this opening section, for the story of Hannah's faith and devotion to God was to mark a turning point in Israel's history.

Elkanah had two wives (1 Sam 1:2), of whom Hannah was almost certainly the first (*see* Hannah). But in a day when continuity of family line and name were of paramount importance, descendants were essential. Therefore, in the event of a first wife's being childless, taking a second wife was the norm if the husband's economic status permitted. Elkanah's other wife, Penninah, was fruitful, and she exploited every opportunity to celebrate her good fortune at the expense of her rival (1 Sam 1:6-7).

In ancient society barrenness was regarded as a curse from God (1 Sam 1:6), a personal disaster that condemned a woman to an uncertain future (*see* Barrenness and Fertility). Children, particularly sons, were an effective insurance policy for a mother in the event of her husband's death. It was all very well for Elkanah to protest, "Am I not more to you than ten sons?" (1 Sam 1:8). Maybe so, while he lived, but in the event of his demise, Hannah's future would be bitter (*see* Widows).

Hannah's prayer and subsequent dialogue with Eli (1 Sam 1:9-18) provide a number of insights into the state of contemporary religion in Israel and the place of women in it (*see* Women in Worship). In contrast to later restrictions on women's participation in the cult, Hannah takes the initiative and plays an active role. Her confidence in Yahweh, her conviction of his interest in her affairs and his ability to radically alter her situation, is expressed in a series of active verbs: "look . . . remember . . . not forget . . . give" (1 Sam 1:11). In a daring move of breathtaking faith she offers back to God that which she presently lacks, vowing to dedicate her as yet unborn son as a lifelong Nazirite.

In contrast to Hannah's simple faith, Eli's lack of spiritual perception as priest comes as a shock, and his question is a sad reflection on the common state of contemporary religious practice (1 Sam 1:14). But, convinced of the purity of Hannah's motives and character, he pronounces God's blessing on her petition (1 Sam 1:15-17), and in due course she gives birth to a son (1 Sam 1:20). For up to three years the child was hers, drawing his life from her breasts, on loan from God until he was weaned (1 Sam 1:21-24; cf. 2 Macc 7:27). For the rest of his life, she would lend him back to the Lord (1 Sam 1:25-28). Who but a mother can know the extent of Hannah's pain as she nursed her son for that precious period,

---

Hannah

Hannah, the favorite wife of Elkanah and the mother of Samuel, is known in Scripture for her perseverance, faith and joyous, prophetic song (1 Sam 1:1—2:11). Jewish tradition credits her with teaching David to pray.

Hannah, like many biblical women destined to bear exemplary sons, is barren (*see* Barrenness and Fertility). The taunts of Peninnah, Elkanah's other wife, and Hannah's own longings for a son make her life miserable (*see* Polygamy).

Finally, in great distress, Hannah goes to the Lord's temple at Shiloh and weeps. She vows that if the Lord would but give her a son, she will give him back to the Lord all the days of his life and a razor never will touch his head. The priest Eli, seeing her lips moving and judging her to be drunk, reprimands her. She replies graciously, as befits her name ("grace"). He blesses her and prays that the Lord will grant her request.

Hannah conceives and names the child Samuel, a play on words of the verb "to ask." She brings Samuel, once weaned, to Eli to live at Shiloh, thereby fulfilling her vow.

Hannah's song expresses her joy in God's deliverance. Calling God a rock, she praises him for his holiness. God knows hearts and weighs deeds. God upsets the status quo by routing the strong, letting the full go hungry and raising the poor from the dust. He gives the barren woman seven children and sets the needy next to princes. The Lord controls all aspects of life: poverty, wealth, death and life. She prophesies the coming of Israel's first king and the Messiah (1 Sam 2:10).

Each year when the family makes a pilgrimage to Shiloh, Hannah brings Samuel a new cloak. She had three more sons and two daughters (1 Sam 2:21).

Citing God's ability to raise the humble and fulfill his promises, the Magnificat of Mary borrows heavily from Hannah's song (*see* Mary the Mother of Jesus; Women as Psalmists).

ROBIN GALLAHER BRANCH

or the strength of spiritual resolve required as the time drew near to give him up? What heart-wrenching agony was involved in embracing her child and waving goodbye in the knowledge that from then on she would see him only once a year? The sacrifice Hannah brought that day in fulfillment of her vow (1 Sam 1:24) was far greater than any bulls or flour or wine offered in accordance with the law, for in giving up her son for the purposes of God, her action struck a chord in the heart of God.

There is a significant word play in 1 Samuel 1:27 that is hard to capture in English, for in Hebrew the same word *sha'al* means both "to ask" or "to request" and "to lend." God had granted Hannah her request, and a child had been born. Now she in turn, as though requested by God, was responding by lending that child to him. At the same time an implied contrast is set up between Samuel, the child asked for by Hannah in faith, who throughout his life was dedicated to God's service, and Saul *(sha'ul)*, the king asked for by the people in rebellion against God, a king whose dedication and service were to prove a much more complex affair.

Hannah's prayer in 1 Samuel 2:1-11 is effectively a song of praise to Yahweh in which she extends the sovereignty she has experienced in her life to the whole field of human relationships (*see* Women as Psalmists). It is a sovereignty that jars modern susceptibilities, for in practice we often prefer to domesticate the divine power to conform to our ideas of what is reasonable. Hannah will have none of that. Her conception of God's greatness soars to the heights of the absolute; there are no secondary causes in her portrayal of his majesty. It is the Lord who reverses fortunes, who elevates and relegates, who raises the humble and demotes the proud, apportions poverty and wealth, life and death as he sees fit (1 Sam 2:4-8). The language is poetic, the theological principle profound. This is forthright divine omnipotence, and only a fool would fail to bow down before such awesome majesty (1 Sam 2:3). With such a God on one's side victory is secure for his chosen and faithful ones, but to oppose his purposes is to be doomed to death and destruction (1 Sam 2:9). The only appropriate response therefore is to seek his favor as Hannah had done.

Doubt is sometimes expressed regarding the possibility of this song having been composed by a woman, but there is no inherent reason why Hannah could not have expressed in this way her joy at God's ability to transform human life, even if she may have adapted for her purposes existing phraseology (cf. Ex 15:1-18). As the story of 1 and 2 Samuel amply demonstrates, the

Barrenness & Fertility

The contrasting biblical motifs of barrenness and fertility have their theological roots in the Hebraic concept of God as lifegiver, a concept prominent throughout the Scriptures, from the creation of all living things in Genesis (Gen 1:1—2:25) to the "spring" or "river of the water of life" in Revelation (Rev 21:6; 22:1). Fundamental to the biblical worldview is the confession that God is Creator of all that exists and Lifegiver to all that has life.

At its most graphic level the concept of God as lifegiver appears in the depiction of God as a woman giving birth. For the Deuteronomist, God is "the Rock that bore you [the Israelites]" and "the God who gave you birth" (Deut 32:18), while for Isaiah God is the birthing woman: "Shall I open the womb and not deliver, says the LORD; shall I, the one who delivers, shut the womb? says your God" (Is 66:9). More frequently, however, God is depicted as the divine agent who bestows fertility upon humans by opening a woman's womb (Gen 29:31; 30:22), in this way enabling childbirth (*see* Birth Pain Imagery; Childbearing and Rearing). God creates fertility through "blessings of the breasts and of the womb" (Gen 49:25); and the promise for those who obey God's commandments is that "the LORD your God will make you abundantly prosperous in all your undertakings, in the fruit of your body, in the fruit of your livestock, and in the fruit of your soil" (Deut 30:9; cf. Deut 7:12-14; 28:1-14).

The biblical records highlight the significance of God's role in enabling childbirth by means of birth predictions delivered by personages divine and human: God (Gen 17:1-21; 18:1-15), the angel of the Lord (Gen 16:1-14; Judg 13:2-25; Mt 1:18-25; Lk 1:5-25, 26-38), a priest (1 Sam 1:17) and a prophet (1 Kings 13:1-2; 2 Kings 4:11-17; 2 Sam 7:1-17; 1 Chron 22:6-10; Is 7:14; 9:6-7). For their part the women respond to God's initiatives on their behalf by acknowledging God's essential role in the birth of their children (Gen 4:1, 25; 21:6; 29:32, 33, 35; 30:6, 18, 20, 23-24; 1 Sam 1:20, 27; Lk 1:25).

Alongside the Hebraic concept of God as lifegiver stands the correlated concept of barrenness as curse (*see* Blessing and Cursing). Barrenness, like fertility, is viewed in terms of divine action. If God opens the womb (Gen 29:31; 30:22), God also closes the womb (Gen 20:18; 1 Sam 1:5), prevents women from bearing children (Gen 16:2) and withholds "from [them] the fruit of the womb" (Gen 30:2). If fertility represents the blessing of God, barrenness represents not merely the absence of that blessing but at its most extreme a curse that God calls down on the disobedient: "But if you will not obey the LORD your God, . . . cursed shall be the fruit of your womb, the fruit of your ground, the increase of your cattle and the issue of your flock" (Deut 28:15, 18). By contrast, for those who obey God's commands, God will remove this curse: "No one shall miscarry or be barren in your land" (Ex 23:26); "you shall be the most blessed of peoples, with neither sterility nor barrenness among you or your livestock" (Deut 7:14).

For the biblical writers the barren woman is "desolate" (Is 54:1 par. Gal 4:27) and in "misery" (1 Sam 1:11), with a womb that is "never satisfied" (Prov 30:15-16). She suffers "reproach" (Gen 30:23) or "disgrace" (Lk 1:25), and she joins "the poor," "the needy" and "the widow" as a symbol for the disadvantaged and vulnerable within the Hebrew community (1 Sam 2:5, 8; Ps 113:7-9; Job 24:21). In corresponding fashion barrenness serves as a metaphor for the national tragedy of the Jewish people as they are exiled from their homeland (Is 49:21; cf. Hos 9:11-14, 16-17).

As biblical motifs, however, barrenness and fertility find their greatest prominence as they are juxtaposed in the accounts of women whose barrenness and desolation have been transformed by God into the joy of conception and childbirth. The biblical writers proclaim God's power to reverse the fortunes of the childless woman (Gen 18:13-14; Is 54:1-3; Lk 1:36-37; Rom 4:19-21), and they compare God's concern for the barren woman with God's corresponding concerns for the poor and the weak in society (1 Sam 2:2-8; Ps 113:5-9; *see* God's Call to Social Justice). These writers depict God as one who "sees" the distress of barren women (Gen 29:31), "hears" their cries for help (Gen 30:6), "remembers" them (Gen 30:22; 1 Sam 1:19), "grants their petitions" (1 Sam 1:17, 27), fulfills what has been "promised" (Gen 21:1) and "heals" their barrenness (Gen 20:17). The biblical texts are replete with the stories of women for whom God has turned barrenness into fertility: Sarah (Gen 11:30; 16:1; cf. Gen 21:1-7), the women of Abimelech's household (Gen 20:18; cf. Gen 20:17), Rebekah (Gen 25:21), Rachel (Gen 29:31; 30:1-2; cf. Gen 30:22-24), the wife of Manoah (Judg 13:2-3; cf. Judg 13:24), Hannah (1 Sam 1:1-2, 4-6; cf. 1 Sam 1:19-20), the Shunammite woman (2 Kings 4:14-16; cf. 2 Kings 4:17) and Elizabeth (Lk 1:5-7, 18, 36; cf. Lk 1:24, 36, 57). Most prominent among these stories of divinely enabled conceptions, however, is the account of Mary, the young woman "engaged" to Joseph (Mt 1:18; Lk 1:27), who as an unmarried "virgin" (Mt 1:23; Lk 1:26-27; cf. Mt 1:18, 24-25; Lk 1:34) gives birth to a child conceived by the Holy Spirit (Mt 1:20; cf. Lk 1:35).

Just as with the motif of barrenness, the imagery of fertility functions metaphorically with respect to the life of the nation. If the language of barrenness paints an image of dispersion and exile for the people of God (Is 49:21; Hos 9:11-14, 16-17), the unexpected fertility of the once barren woman stands as a symbol of God's ultimate reversal of their political fortunes (Is 54:1 par. Gal 4:27).

Bibliography

"Biblical Perspectives," in *Bioethics and the Beginning of Life: An Anabaptist Perspective,* ed. R. J. Miller and B. H. Brubaker (Scottdale, PA: Herald, 1990) 15-30.

DOROTHY JEAN WEAVER

---

danger for men, especially those in powerful positions, is the temptation to rely on their own resources. Women, lacking such positions of power in society, more easily recognized that their greatest resource was God. So Hannah's song, as a testimony to woman's spirituality, was preserved and ultimately found its echo in the song of another mother whose faith and submission to God also marked a turning point in the history not just of Israel but of the world (Lk 1:46-55; *see* Mary the Mother of Jesus).

A Father's Failure (1 Sam 2:12-36)

In line with the divine sovereignty so clearly pronounced by Hannah, the remainder of 1 Samuel 2 is an outworking of the principle that it is "the LORD . . . [who] brings low [and] also exalts" (1 Sam 2:7). A contrast is set up between Samuel, the son of Hannah, who ministers to the Lord in the presence of Eli the priest (1 Sam 2:11, 18, 21, 26), and Hophni and Phinehas, the sons of Eli. They demonstrate their lack of regard for the Lord (1 Sam 2:12) by abusing their privileges as priests (1 Sam 2:13-17), exploiting their position of power over the most vulnerable (1 Sam 2:22) and dishonoring their father by their refusal to heed his warning (1 Sam 2:23-25). It is worthy of note that at this period of Israel's history it was considered appropriate for women to serve at the tent of meeting (1 Sam 2:22; cf. Ex 38:8). It would be interesting to speculate to what extent the unbridled sexual passions of reprobate priests like Hophni and Phinehas contributed to women's subsequent exclusion from ministry, for it is often easier to remove a source of temptation and consider it blameworthy than to recognize the frailty of our human nature.

Woven into the explicit contrast between Samuel and the sons of Eli is also an implied contrast between Hannah, the mother who was willing to relinquish her son to God's service, and Eli, the father who was willing to see the service of God brought into disrepute by his overindulgence of his sons (1 Sam 2:17, 23-24).

1 Samuel 2:11 stated that "Elkanah went home to Ramah while the boy remained to minister to the LORD." The absence of any mention of Hannah highlights the emotional tension with which she had to live from then on. Physically she would have accompanied Elkanah back to Ramah, but it could no longer be fully home for her while her son remained at Shiloh. Yet she continued as best she could to lavish a mother's love upon him within the boundaries of his appointed destiny (1 Sam 2:19). Her sense of loss was at least partially alleviated by God's gift to her of further children in answer to the prayer of Eli, who recognized the depth of her ongoing sacrifice (1 Sam 2:20-21). However, Eli failed to put God's interests before family considerations. His weak remonstration against his sons' wickedness and failure to discipline their perversion of all that was holy (1 Sam 2:22-25) ultimately called forth God's judgment upon the entire family line (1 Sam 2:27-36; *see* Parental Influence).

A Young Man's Calling (1 Sam 3)

In the course of this well-known incident of Samuel's response to God's call in the night, there is a subtle shift in the relationship between Samuel and Eli. At the start Samuel was ministering to the Lord under Eli (1 Sam 3:1); by the end he was ministering to Eli and to Israel under the Lord (1 Sam

3:18-21). In the night he was still dependent for his spiritual training on Eli, his father in God and spiritual mentor. As yet he had had no personal experience by which to distinguish the Lord's voice (1 Sam 3:1-9). By the time morning comes, Eli recognized his dependence on Samuel for a revelation of God's will (1 Sam 3:10-17).

Being a prophet entrusted with God's message was never easy, but for a young man, little more than a child, Samuel's first test in faithfulness to God's word was an awesome trial of his spiritual resolve (1 Sam 3:15), even if his task was eased by Eli's mature acceptance of the Lord's sovereignty and essential goodness (1 Sam 3:18). The opening of the doors of the house of the Lord by Samuel (1 Sam 3:15) may be regarded as symbolic, for until now the word of God had been rare in Israel (1 Sam 3:1). With Samuel's appointment, access to God's mind and will was once again possible through God's promised prophet (1 Sam 3:19—4:1; cf. Deut 18:15-19).

The Glory and Power of Yahweh (1 Sam 4:1—7:2)

1 Samuel 4 serves as a bridge, recording the death of Eli's sons and of Eli, thus rounding off the opening unit of 1 Samuel. At the same time it introduces the theme of the awesome power of Yahweh, enthroned between the cherubim of the ark—a power that refused to be manipulated by a sinful people but that remained sufficient to strike terror into Israel's enemies.

The story opens with the defeat of the Israelite army by Philistine forces bent on extending their power from the coastal plain into the hill country inhabited by God's people (1 Sam 4:1-2). Acknowledging that their defeat was Yahweh's doing, the decision was taken to bring the ark of the Lord's covenant into battle as a visible material symbol of his presence, thus ensuring victory (1 Sam 4:3-4). Perhaps the Israelites would have done better to remember the events of Ai and the response of Joshua and the elders to Israel's defeat on that occasion (Josh 7:6). The Philistines meanwhile were sufficiently aware of aspects of Israel's history to quake at the prospect of facing Israel's "gods" (1 Sam 4:6-9), but victory was theirs and so also, by virtue of that victory, was the ark (1 Sam 4:10-11).

News of the ark's capture came as such a shock to Eli that it brought about his death (1 Sam 4:12-18), while his daughter-in-law, the wife of Phinehas, on hearing the same news went into premature labor and lived only long enough to name her child Ichabod (1 Sam 4:19-21). It was not her widowhood that caused her grief so much as the spiritual insight that "the glory has departed from Israel" (1 Sam 4:21-22). From the Philistine perspective the glory of Israel had been captured (1 Sam 4:11), but the wife of Phinehas was more astute. She acknowledged that the departure of the glory had been an active move on the part of God, whose continued presence with his people could not be guaranteed in the face of spiritual corruption at the heart of the nation's life. It was a corruption of which she must have been only too painfully and personally aware, for her husband had been seducing the female attendants at the sanctuary and had become the talk of the land (1 Sam 2:22-24).

Concluding that their defeat of the Israelites signified the triumph of their gods over Yahweh, the Philistines brought the ark of the covenant into the temple of Dagon to be placed as tribute at his feet. The error of their thinking, however, became obvious in the course of the succeeding days as the statue of Dagon was reduced to a crippled wreck (1 Sam 5:1-5), and the people succumbed to an outbreak of disease (1 Sam 5:6). Contemporary wisdom made the connection between the current plight of the inhabitants, the presence of the ark and the heaviness or glory of Yahweh (1 Sam 5:7; in Hebrew the same root, *kbd,* denotes both "glory" and "heaviness"). In the popular imagination the ark became an object of dread, the very approach of which was sufficient to cause panic and death (1 Sam 5:8-12).

The decision of the Philistines to return the ark "to its own place" (1 Sam 5:11; 6:2) was accompanied by a measure of spiritual perception lacking among the Israelites after their defeat at Aphek. The Philistine acknowledgment of the need for restitution for the wrong they had committed (1 Sam 6:3-5) and their eagerness to avoid repeating the error of the Egyptian pharaoh who had dared to challenge the authority of Israel's God were highly commendable (1 Sam 6:6). Yet there is an intriguing mixture of the spiritual and the pragmatic in the test they devised to discover whether the disasters that had struck them were divinely inspired or a chance occurrence (1 Sam 6:7-9). For cows to desert their young would be positive proof that a supernatural force was at work and, they hoped, indicate the divine acceptance of their guilt offering (1 Sam 6:10-12, 16-18).

This episode introduces the concept of the holy in ancient Israel. The Hebrew root *qdš* originally meant "separate" and could denote any object withdrawn from ordinary use and devoted to God. As such the object became imbued with his power. In its right place holiness was beneficial, for in some way it brought God's presence to bear on a situation. It was therefore a cause of rejoicing, blessing and reverent worship (1 Sam 6:13-15; cf. 2 Sam 6:11-19). But in the wrong place, handled in the wrong way or approached with a wrong attitude, holiness was potentially dangerous, as the descendants of Jeconiah and Uzzah found to their cost (1 Sam 6:19-20; cf. 2 Sam 6:2-10).

Samuel as Judge (1 Sam 7:3—8:22)

The ark had been returned to Israel, but it remained marginalized in the house of Abinadab at Kiriath-jearim until David restored it to its rightful place at the heart of the nation's life and worship (2 Sam 6:2-17). Yet God's gracious activity in the lives of his people was not confined to the ark. 1 Samuel 7:2 records a measure of spiritual awakening in the house of Israel that led to a renewed desire to return to the Lord. Seizing the moment, Samuel issued a prophetic call to repentance, a single-minded devotion to Yahweh and a steady dependence on his sovereign power to deliver "out of the hand of the Philistines" (1 Sam 7:3-4). Assembling the people, Samuel led them in a day of fasting and ritual cleansing (1 Sam 7:5-6) until proceedings were interrupted by the threat of Philistine reprisals. Confronted with such unexpected aggression, the people appealed to Samuel to intercede on their behalf that the Lord might rescue them "from the hand of the Philistines" (1 Sam 7:7-9). The divine intervention led to a dramatic victory (1 Sam 7:10-11; cf. Josh 10:11; Judg 5:4, 20-21) and a tenuous peace throughout the remainder of Samuel's days as judge (1 Sam 7:13-15).

The setting up of a memorial stone as testimony to the Lord's help "thus far" (1 Sam 7:12) casts an ironic shadow over the events of the next chapter, for if God could so easily save his people through a judge like Samuel, what need was there for a human king to fight Israel's battles (1 Sam 8:5, 19-20)? Small wonder that Samuel took the people's request as a personal slight, reflecting adversely on his office (1 Sam 8:6-7). From a human perspective he had little defense—he was old and, like Eli before him, had to accept the harsh reality that offspring will not necessarily share their parents' values (1 Sam 8:1-5). When Samuel took his concern to the Lord, however, he was told to comply with the people's request. It was not he who was being rejected but Yahweh himself as king (1 Sam 8:6-7). The sense of betrayal Samuel felt was but a faint echo of God's pain at his people's lack of covenant loyalty (1 Sam 8:8). Their desire for a human king, however misguided, could be accommodated in Yahweh's purposes (2 Sam 7:11-13), but the people needed to know the risks involved in substituting human rule for divine sovereignty (1 Sam 8:9-18). Human power almost inevitably leads to corruption and exploitation, and the monarchy in Israel would be no exception. There is an ominous reiteration of the clause "he will take" (1 Sam 8:11, 13-17); no family would remain untouched, no aspect of life unaffected. Samuel's warning fell on deaf ears; the lure of being like the other nations, instead of remaining significantly different, proved too strong (1 Sam 8:19-20). A new page in Israel's history had been turned. For good or ill, Israel was to have a king (1 Sam 8:21-22).

The Anointing and Commissioning of Saul (1 Sam 9:1—10:27)

The future king of Israel is introduced in the context of family life—a handsome young man, standing head and shoulders above his fellows, sent with one of the family servants to search for some of his father's donkeys (1 Sam 9:1-3). Unsuccessful in the task, the servant suggested calling on the insight of a local seer believed capable of informing them about the outcome of their journey (1 Sam 9:4-6, 8-9). The double significance of the servant's statement, "so that he will tell us our way" (1 Sam 9:8 Heb.), may have struck Saul in retrospect, but for the present his mind was taken up with more practical considerations such as his father's concern for their whereabouts and their lack of basic provisions (1 Sam 9:5, 7).

Enquiring of some local girls engaged in the daily task of drawing water, the two young men were drawn into the festivities accompanying the local sacrifice, at which the prophet Samuel was to officiate (1 Sam 9:11-14). To his surprise, Saul was accorded a place of honor among the invited guests with special provision made for him (1 Sam 9:19-20, 22-27). Unknown to Saul, Samuel had been informed of his coming and of his place in God's purposes (1 Sam 9:15-17). First Samuel 9:16 is important for its threefold emphasis on Israel as "my people," the use of the Hebrew word *nagid* ("leader") instead of the more usual word for "king" *(melek),* the clear echoes of Exodus 3:9-10 and the specific reference to deliverance from the hand of the Philistines, the significance of which becomes clear in ensuing chapters. Israel might be about to have its king, but it was a king who must operate within strict parameters under God.

One of the features of Hebrew narrative is the use of key words, phrases or formulae to evoke memories of different stories that are to be used as commentaries on the present text either by providing a thematic parallel or by suggesting a contrast in behavior. Saul's modest reply to Samuel's fulsome welcome of him as the one "on whom . . . all Israel's desire is fixed" awakens echoes of Gideon's response to his commission to deliver Israel from the hand of its oppressors (1 Sam 9:20-21; cf. Judg 6:15). Like Gideon, Saul is given three signs corresponding to his earlier expressed concerns (1 Sam 10:2; cf. 1 Sam 9:5; 1 Sam 10:3-4, cf. 1 Sam 9:7; 1 Sam 10:5-6, cf. 1 Sam 9:21). The signs were designed to confirm the authenticity of Saul's appointment and make good his perceived lack of resources and feeling of inadequacy. The implicit question, however, is whether Saul will rise to the occasion as Gideon did, and in particular how he will respond to the coming of the Spirit of the Lord upon him. Gideon's first task had been to rid his home locality of pagan foreign influences (Judg 6:25-32). Saul's anointing with the Spirit was to take place at Gibeath-elohim ("the hill of God"), where, provocatively, a Philistine garrison was located (1 Sam 10:5). Samuel does not spell out the connection, but supplied with the interpretive key of Gideon's story, of which Saul had already displayed knowledge, the instruction to do whatever "your hand finds to do, for God is with you" (1 Sam 10:7 RSV/Heb.; cf. Judg 6:16) was plain enough. Attacking a Philistine garrison would almost inevitably lead to an all-out Philistine assault. Hence Saul was instructed to go down to Gilgal to summon the people and to wait seven days for Samuel to come to offer sacrifices and reveal God's plan of campaign (1 Sam 10:8). The signs were fulfilled but not the commission. The Spirit of God came upon Saul at Gibeah, but at the end of the ecstatic experience Saul returned home, remaining silent regarding the momentous events of the last few days and leaving the Philistine garrison untouched (1 Sam 10:9-16).

If Saul had fulfilled his commission, the people's recognition of him as God's chosen deliverer would have been in little doubt. As it was, a public ceremony was necessary to discover the king (1 Sam 10:17-24), a ceremony that so closely paralleled the events of Joshua 7:10-18 as to evoke chilling memories of the dangers of failing to fully obey the will of God. No wonder Saul hid (1 Sam 10:22)! Being king in Israel brought many privileges (1 Sam 10:25-27), but the responsibility was awesome.

The Claims of Kinship (1 Sam 10:27—11:15)

The background to the events of 1 Samuel 11 is an incident that occurred in the time of the judges, when the men of Gibeah had violated the ancient laws of hospitality by first threatening to sexually assault a visiting Levite and then gang raping his concubine with such violence that she died (Judg 19:12-28). Knowing that he would not obtain justice locally, the Levite sent a bloody appeal to the rest of the Israelite tribes by the simple expedient of cutting up his concubine's corpse and dispatching the pieces throughout the land (Judg 19:29-30). In the ensuing conflict, in which the tribe of Benjamin fulfilled its kinship obligations to the men of Gibeah by rallying to their support (Judg 20:12-14), an oath was taken by the rest of the tribes that no one was to give his daughter in marriage to any man of Benjamin (Judg 21:1). Realizing subsequently that such an oath would ultimately condemn the tribe of Benjamin to extinction, a way was sought to circumvent it. Part of the solution was to permit the marriage of young women from Jabesh-gilead, a settlement that had not participated in the oath, to men from the tribe of Benjamin (Judg 21:2-14).

Contrary to common assumption, in a patrilineal society such as Israel, where descent was reckoned through the male line, kinship ties through the female line were still significant and could be called on when necessary, however tenuous the link. Examples are Jacob's fleeing to his mother's brother to escape Esau's wrath (Gen 27:42-44) or David's sending his parents to Moab when he was pursued by Saul (1 Sam 22:3-4). So when the inhabitants of Jabesh-gilead found themselves under threat from Nahash, their request for help from the people of Gibeah was as much a claim on kinship as an appeal to the power of the king (1 Sam 10:27—11:4).

Hearing a secondhand report of the threatened assault on the inhabitants of Jabesh-gilead, Saul reacted in the manner of the judges of former days (1 Sam 11:5-6; cf. Judg 14:19). Inspired by the Spirit of God, he evoked memories of the incident recorded in Judges 19, reenacting the bloody demand of the Levite for justice by cutting up his oxen rather than a human corpse and dispatching the pieces throughout the land. The accompanying threat of violent action on those who failed to comply with his command had the desired effect, and the people "came out as one" (1 Sam 11:6-7). United under Saul's leadership against a common enemy, the Israelites achieved victory, the inhabitants of Jabesh-gilead were rescued, and Saul's suitability for the role of king was confirmed in action (1 Sam 11:8-15).

Samuel's Farewell (1 Sam 12)

In the aftermath of the celebrations, Samuel made his farewell speech to the people, declaring his faithfulness as a leader from his youth until old age (1 Sam 12:1-5). Then, like Moses on the edge of the Promised Land (Deut 29:2—30:20), Samuel reminded the people of God's faithfulness to his covenant and of Israel's history of disobedience and faithlessness, a disloyalty that had found contemporary expression in the request for a human king (1 Sam 12:6-12). The Lord had complied with their request (1 Sam 12:13), but they and the king had to choose between good and evil, blessing and curse, between faithful and obedient service of God (1 Sam 12:14) or the path of rebellion that would lead to the Lord's "hand" being against them (1 Sam 12:15, 25). They had seen his might at Mizpah, expressed against the Philistines (1 Sam 7:10); now let them see a token of that same power against themselves when it might be least expected (1 Sam 12:16-17).

The visible effect of Samuel calling on the Lord (1 Sam 12:18) served to confirm his status as God's appointed mediator (1 Sam 12:19, 23). Israel might have an established king, but real power remained with Yahweh, whose word through his prophet was to be obeyed (1 Sam 12:20-21, 23-24), if only to avoid the chilling consequences of disobedience (1 Sam 12:25).

Saul Under Pressure (1 Sam 13—14)

How much time passed between Saul's anointing and the action of these chapters is uncertain, as are all figures relating to Saul's reign, as the confusion of 1 Samuel 13:1 testifies. By this stage Saul had a son of military age; when he was anointed king, Saul had been a young man whose military prowess had not yet been proven (1 Sam 9:2; 10:27). As many as fifteen to twenty years may have passed since Saul's original commission to deal with the Philistine presence in the land (1 Sam 10:5-7). In the end Jonathan took the initiative and not Saul, even though the victory gained was attributed to his father (1 Sam 13:2-4). The king's commission having at last been carried out, the command of 1 Samuel 10:8 came into effect, and Saul went down to Gilgal to call out the Israelite forces and await the coming of Samuel to communicate God's battle plan.

The Philistines predictably responded to what they regarded as the rebellion of a subject people (1 Sam 13:19-22) and amassed their troops like "the sand on the seashore" for number (1 Sam 13:5). This description of the forces ranged against Israel recalls again the story of Gideon, who, like Saul, had been confronted with an innumerable enemy (Judg 7:12). Gideon's triumph with a mere three hundred men had demonstrated his trust in God and obedience to God's command (Judg 7:2-8). How would Saul fare in the present situation? Watching his fearful forces drift away, Saul's resolve to wait for Samuel broke (1 Sam 13:6-8), and he attempted to secure his men's loyalty and commitment by performing the ritual sacrifice preliminary to battle (1 Sam 13:9-12). There is a certain irony in the fact that Samuel had waited years for Saul to begin to fulfill the purpose for which Yahweh had appointed him king, and yet Saul could not wait a week for God's prophet. And it was for his disobedience, fear and ultimate lack of trust in God's sovereign control of the situation that Saul was judged unworthy of the role of *nagid* over God's people and was told that his kingdom would not survive his death (1 Sam 13:13-15).

The implied contrast between Saul and Jonathan is continued in the ensuing events of the war against the Philistines. Jonathan's decisive action (1 Sam 14:1-15), taken in dependence upon God (1 Sam 14:6) but without the knowledge of his father (1 Sam 14:1), successfully turned the tide of battle and instilled such a divine dread in the Philistine army that they fled from the uplands in terror (1 Sam 14:15-16). Saul turned to God for counsel and advice, but then, in response to the developing chaos in the Philistine camp, did not wait for an answer and set off in pursuit of the enemy (1 Sam 14:18-23). In a misguided attempt to ensure the continuation of the divine favor, Saul imposed a fast on his men, threatening the curse of death on anyone who failed to comply (1 Sam 14:24). The rashness of this decision, however, deprived his army of greater success against the Philistines (1 Sam 14:29-30), led to a violation of Israel's food laws (1 Sam 14:31-35) and inadvertently put his son's life at risk (1 Sam 14:25-28). Having cleared the Philistines from the hill country, Saul again turned to enquire of God, although this time it was only on the suggestion of Ahijah the priest (1 Sam 14:36-37). Recognizing that the divine silence signified sin in the camp (*see* Sin), lots were cast, yet when Jonathan was isolated, Saul was swayed not by love of his son (cf. 2 Sam 18:5, 33) but by the strong feelings of his troops that the one to whom so much of the victory was owed could not merit death (1 Sam 14:38-45). Thus Saul's oath was set aside and Jonathan was spared, to come to terms with the realization that in the dogged pursuit of his own ends his father would be willing for him to die.

The closing verses of the chapter summarize the extent of Saul's military victories (1 Sam 14:47-48) and introduce other members of his family destined to play their part in future events (1 Sam 14:49-51).

Saul's Failure (1 Sam 15)

The chapter begins with a reminder to Saul that despite being king, he is still subject to God's word communicated through his prophet (1 Sam 15:1). Appointed as God's agent of judgment upon the Amalekites because of their ruthless assault upon the Israelites during their journey to the Promised Land (1 Sam 15:2-3; cf. Ex 17:6-14), Saul was sent to engage in a holy war. However, in conjunction with his troops, he allowed material considerations to determine what was preserved and what was destroyed (1 Sam 15:4-9). Forewarned by God of Saul's disobedience, Samuel proved to be unimpressed by Saul's claims to have fulfilled his commission and brushed aside all his excuses and attempts to shift the blame to his men (1 Sam 15:10-21). Would Saul never understand that greater privilege brings greater responsibility, and in relation to God partial obedience is no obedience (1 Sam 15:17-19, 22-23)? By his refusal to listen to and obey God's word, Saul had effectively disqualified himself as God's appointed ruler.

Faced with such a decree absolute, Saul pleaded with Samuel to accompany him back to the assembled troops and, when the old man refused, attempted to physically restrain him (1 Sam 15:24-27). The tearing of the prophet's robe became a symbolic act, with Saul's attempt to grasp power that was not his to command matched by God's removal of the kingdom and its power from him in favor of one better qualified (1 Sam 15:28-29). All that was left to Saul was a saving of his face before his troops and an execution of the divine will by Samuel, who killed the Amalekite king who in his time had brought much unnecessary suffering to many women by cutting down their sons in their prime (1 Sam 15:30-33). It was the final parting of the ways for the two men, who were never to meet again during Samuel's lifetime (1 Sam 15:34-35).

David as Court Musician (1 Sam 16)

In the aftermath of Saul's rejection, Samuel was sent to anoint a new king, the one of God's choosing, from among the sons of Jesse (1 Sam 16:1). Samuel's immediate response to the command gives an early hint of the darker side of Saul's character that would stop at nothing to protect his throne (1 Sam 16:2-4).

The scene depicted in 1 Samuel 16:5-13 is marked by its similarities with and contrasts to that of 1 Samuel 9. On both occasions the setting is a community feast. In 1 Samuel 9 the honored guest was the young man Saul; here it is the family of Jesse, among whose sons will be the Lord's anointed. In 1 Samuel 9 attention was drawn to Saul's physique (1 Sam 9:1; cf. 1 Sam 10:23-24), but when Samuel is impressed by the appearance and stature of Jesse's eldest son, he is gently rebuked by the Lord (1 Sam 16:6-7). In 1 Samuel 9:21 Saul drew attention to the insignificance of his family and tribal connections. Here David is regarded as so insignificant, even by his family, that he is not included in the reckoning of those eligible to meet the prophet (1 Sam 16:8-11).

Unlike Saul, David was given no signs and no initial commission to fulfill, yet the divine ordering of circumstances was as apparent in his case as in Saul's; ironically, his first task as the Lord's anointed was to serve the existing king (1 Sam 16:14-23). Saul's rebellion against the word of the Lord had led to the removal of the divine protection from him, and his susceptibility to spiritual forces (1 Sam 10:10-11) now became his undoing. Popular belief in the calming properties of music (1 Sam 16:15-17) culminated in the bringing of David to Saul's notice and the entering of one more young man into his service (1 Sam 16:18-22; cf. 1 Sam 14:52), ostensibly as one of his armor-bearers but in reality because of his ability to bring relief to Saul in his trouble (1 Sam 16:23). The contrast between the two is summed up in the key statement that "the Spirit of the LORD departed from Saul," whereas of David it is said that "the LORD is with him" (1 Sam 16:14, 18).

David as Champion of Israel (1 Sam 17)

The story of David and Goliath is probably the best known of all the incidents in 1 Samuel, although no summary of that victory can do justice to the subtleties of the narrative as the chapter unfolds. Many scholars choose to focus on whether the account constitutes an alternative tradition of how David entered Saul's court, since the court musician (1 Sam 16) is apparently unknown to the king in this incident (1 Sam 17:55-58). But anyone who has had a teenage son will know that even a few months' absence, coinciding with a growth spurt, can effect such change as to make him unrecognizable even to close friends. As 1 Samuel 17:15 reports, David was still fulfilling his familial responsibilities by traveling back and forth from Saul's court to his father's home.

During one of these absences the Philistines invaded the territory of Judah, and in the ensuing confrontation Goliath issued his challenge for any man to engage him in personal combat, the outcome to determine the course of the battle (1 Sam 17:1-10). The effect on the Israelite army was one of dread. Even the king, who stood a head taller than any of the others and had his own armor (1 Sam 17:38-39), had no stomach for the fight, preferring instead to offer rich rewards to any man who overcame the giant (1 Sam 17:25). The arrival of David brought a new dimension to the scene (1 Sam 17:20-32), even while it awakens echoes of another young man sent on an errand by his father (1 Sam 17:12-19; cf. 1 Sam 9:3-5). Saul's journey had led to his secret anointing and commission to deal with the Philistine menace; David, already secretly anointed, regarded that same Philistine menace as an affront to the living God (1 Sam 17:26).

David's outspoken reaction and willingness to fight Goliath brought him to the king's notice (1 Sam 17:31-32). Convinced by David's testimony of God's ability to deliver, Saul expressed his desire that the Lord may be with David in the ensuing conflict, unaware that that was precisely the difference between David and himself (1 Sam 17:33-37; cf. 1 Sam 16:13-14). So David triumphed over his enemy, and victory that day went to the Israelites (1 Sam 17:40-54).

Saul's question of Abner (1 Sam 17:55-56) is understandable in the context of his promise to give his daughter in marriage to whoever killed Goliath, for the relative wealth and status of the family involved in such an alliance was an important issue, as David was only too well aware (cf. 1 Sam 18:18, 23).

There is much confusion regarding the status of married women in ancient Israel, and it is often too easily assumed that they were their husband's property by virtue of his payment of the *mohar,* a term that is often translated "bride price," thus confirming the notion that women were bought and sold (*see* Marriage). But marriage was a form of gift exchange, still common today in some traditional societies. The gift of the woman, it was hoped, would enable her husband's name and lineage to be preserved. Such generosity on the part of the bride's father required reciprocation in order to maintain the balance and due order in the relationship of the two families involved in the marriage alliance. The nature and size of the *mohar* were determined by the status and relative need of the girl's family. Thus Saul, who needed Goliath killed, could regard that exploit as sufficient *mohar* for his daughter Merab, while the privileges and benefits of becoming the king's son-in-law were considered sufficient to justify the risk involved in killing the giant.

David and the Family of Saul (1 Sam 18—20)

While David was establishing his claim to one member of Saul's family, he had already won the respect and affection of another. Jonathan's spirit had been captivated by David's manner of speaking. Here was a young man who, like himself, believed that "nothing can hinder the LORD from saving" (1 Sam 14:6; cf. 1 Sam 17:37). The covenant formed between them effectively made them brothers, with all the privileges and responsibilities such kinship brought in terms of provision in time of need, protection from harm and preservation of name and honor. The covenant was sealed by the superior party, in this case Jonathan, sharing with David all that marked him off as being the king's son and potential heir to the kingdom (1 Sam 18:1-4).

Jonathan's generosity throws into sharp contrast his father's attitude. Saul also perceived David's potential in relation to the kingdom (1 Sam 18:5, 13-17) but, responding out of his own rejection by Yahweh, expressed his jealousy and fear of David (1 Sam 18:6-9, 12) by attempting to take his life either directly (1 Sam 18:10-11) or by the hand of the Philistines (1 Sam 18:17-25). David discovered there were further conditions attached to his marrying Merab, which he declined (1 Sam 18:17-19), while the *mohar* requested for Michal was little more than an invitation to sign his own death warrant (1 Sam 18:25). The NRSV loses the plot and the point in mistranslating 1 Samuel 18:27. In meeting the king's demand for evidence of the death of one hundred Philistines and doubling it (1 Sam 18:25-27), David not only cast doubt on the king's estimation of his daughter's worth but in accordance with the law of reciprocity placed the king in his debt to the tune of one hundred Philistines. (The humor of such a turning of the tables on a king who sought his death would not have been lost on the original audience.) The killing of David became Saul's great obsession (1 Sam 18:29), gradually taking over his life and adversely affecting his relationships with his son and daughter, whose loyalties were torn in the face of their father's unreasonable hostility toward David.

Aware of his father's intentions, Jonathan first warned David of the danger and then successfully interceded for him, reminding Saul of David's faithful and fearless service on Israel's behalf (1 Sam 19:1-6). The resulting reconciliation was short-lived, however, as once again Saul's murderous intentions against David surfaced (1 Sam 19:7-10). This time Saul's daughter Michal rescued David. Her perceptive insight into her father's intentions (1 Sam 19:11), daring initiative (1 Sam 19:12-13), and plausible and persuasive arguments, made to both servants and Saul (1 Sam 19:14-17), gained David time to escape. It was a remarkable performance by a woman whose heart at this juncture was all David's own (1 Sam 18:20).

David fled for spiritual sanctuary to Samuel (1 Sam 19:18). Saul's pursuit was ultimately defeated by spiritual forces that overwhelmed the soldiers sent to capture David (1 Sam 19:19-21). Despairing of his men's ability to accomplish their task, Saul finally went himself. But even in his state of rebellion, he too was still susceptible to God's Spirit and thus distracted from his original intention (1 Sam 19:22-24).

David used the respite to return to Jonathan, bewildered as to the reason for Saul's implacable hatred. A scheme was devised to expose where Saul's heart lay (1 Sam 20:1-3). In ancient Israel, family ties and responsibilities were paramount, and David's desire to be present at an annual sacrifice for his clan at Bethlehem would, in normal circumstances, have been sufficient excuse for his absence from the king's table. If, however, the king were to react violently to the news, that would be indication of his evil design on David's life (1 Sam 20:4-7). David's fears of betrayal were allayed by Jonathan's renewal of the covenant between them, although on this occasion there is a shift in the balance of the two parties. Jonathan acknowledges his dependence on the covenant love of David and the future dependence of his descendants (1 Sam 20:8-17; cf. 2 Sam 9:7; 21:7). His prayer, that the Lord will be "with [David] as he has been with my father" (1 Sam 20:13), recognizes that the future belongs to David, not Saul.

Tragically for all concerned, David's suspicions of Saul's intentions were confirmed. Although his absence was at first unremarked, by the second day his nonappearance was questioned (1 Sam 20:24-27), and the king's description of him as the "son of Jesse" (1 Sam 20:27) introduces a chilling note of distance to the relationship between them. Jonathan elaborated on the preplanned excuse—David had been ordered by his brother to be present at the family gathering. How could he refuse such an injunction (1 Sam 20:28-29)?

In the absence of David, Saul directed his anger against his son, accusing him of perversely and shamefully putting his own future at stake because of his misplaced loyalty to David (1 Sam 20:30-31). The reference to Jonathan's mother as "perverse" and "rebellious" is ironic in that the description more aptly fits the father. But it was true that while David lived, none of Jonathan's mother's hopes and dreams for her son's future as king would be fulfilled.

Saul's solution was simple: David must be put to death. When Jonathan questioned his father's logic, he only narrowly escaped death at his father's hand (1 Sam 20:32-33; cf. 1 Sam 14:39, 44).

The prearranged signal having been given to David (1 Sam 20:19-23, 35-40), he and Jonathan met to say farewell, pledging loyalty to one another again before they parted (1 Sam 20:41-42). They only ever met once more (1 Sam 23:15-18).

David, Saul and the Massacre at Nob (1 Sam 21—22)

On the run for his life, David once again headed for spiritual sanctuary, this time to Ahimelech, the priest at Nob. Ahimelech's reaction to his coming is surprising, for why should a priest be afraid of David, alone and unarmed? Or was he perhaps afraid for David, because he was aware of Saul's previous attempts to capture David at Ramah? If that is the case, then his opening question (1 Sam 21:1) may be intended as a warning that while David might be alone, Ahimelech was not alone. One of Saul's servants, and a fairly responsible one at that, was present at the sanctuary (1 Sam 21:7). Quick on the uptake, David spun Ahimelech (and the listening Doeg) a story plausible enough to account for his presence but false enough to provide Ahimelech with a future defense should he need one. If Ahimelech were questioned by Saul, he could state that he had helped David but he had been told that David was on a secret mission for Saul (1 Sam 21:2-9).

Armed with provisions and the sword of Goliath, David fled to Gath but found that his reputation as military champion had gone before him (1 Sam 21:10-11). The question of the servants of Achish, "Is this not David the king of the land?" is heavily ironic in the circumstances, as once again David was forced to live by his wits, this time by pretending to be witless (1 Sam 21:12-15).

Turning his back on human settlement, David made for the hills, gathering about him a band of four hundred men who, like himself, found themselves forced to make a livelihood outside the bounds of normal society. His first concern, however, was for his parents, whose protection he sought by calling on kinship ties extending back three generations to Ruth, his great-grandmother (1 Sam 22:1-4; cf. Ruth 4:17).

If David's parents were now beyond Saul's reach, the same was not true for Ahimelech and his extended family. Saul's obsession with David had become all-consuming, leading him to accuse even his closest officials of conspiring against him (1 Sam 22:6-8). In his tortured imagination it is "the son of Jesse" who is lying in wait for him, incited to rebellion by his own son. Why should his servants behave in this fashion? Who was the "son of Jesse" anyway, and what possible benefit could they receive from his hand? Did they not know that fields and vineyards and positions of power lay in the king's gift (1 Sam 22:7; cf. 1 Sam 8:14)? The bait was cast and was seized by Doeg, who gave his account of events at Nob (1 Sam 22:9-10).

Ahimelech and his kinsmen were summoned and accused of encouraging David in his rebellion. Rather than defending his actions by using the alibi David had provided for him, Ahimelech boldly seized the opportunity to challenge Saul's interpretation of events, proclaiming David's loyalty and denying any conspiracy against the king, either on David's part or his own (1 Sam 22:11-15). Ahimelech's speech marks yet another turning point in the life of Saul: the voice of God, through his priest, coming to Saul for the last time. It was an appeal to reason, but it fell on deaf ears. The king, who on a previous occasion had disobeyed God's command to destroy the Amalekites, now counteracted God's word by commanding the destruction of the settlement of the priests (1 Sam 22:16-17). Saul's Israelite officials refused to be party to such sacrilege, so it was left to Doeg, the Edomite shepherd turned butcher, to fulfill the king's command (1 Sam 22:18-19; cf. 1 Sam 15:3). In the ensuing carnage, only Abiathar escaped and made his way to David, leaving him to regret his earlier failure to kill Doeg and thus save the lives of a community. All that remained for him now was to offer sanctuary to Abiathar, whose life, like David's, was now in permanent danger from Saul's murderous intent (1 Sam 22:20-23).

David on the Run from Saul (1 Sam 23:1—27:4)

Characteristic of the period covered by these chapters is the contrast in the attitudes and actions of Saul and David and the manner in which each is guided. Having given shelter to Abiathar, the lone survivor of the massacre at Nob, David had access to and made use of the divine oracle, submitting plans and proposals to God's will in order to determine God's way for him (1 Sam 23:2, 4, 9-12; cf. 1 Sam 30:7-8). Saul, in his single-minded intent to destroy David, was dependent on information received from human sources as to David's whereabouts; this information, though accurate, failed to keep pace with David's movements (1 Sam 23:7-8, 13-15, 19-21; 24:1-2; 26:1-4). David's determination to wait for God's judgment on the situation (1 Sam 24:5-7; 26:9-11) was rewarded by divine protection and provision for his needs. Sometimes that provision was physical (1 Sam 23:5; 25:18; 27:8-9) and sometimes spiritual, in the form of Jonathan's encouragement (1 Sam 24:15-18), Abigail's prophetic words (1 Sam 25:28-31) or even Saul's reluctant admissions that the future did indeed lie with David (1 Sam 24:16-21). Saul became the victim of his erratic emotions, driven by his desire to defeat David, even as the Philistine menace pressed in upon his kingdom, demanding his attention (1 Sam 23:27-28) and ultimately his life.

Embedded in the heart of these events is the lengthy account of David's dealings with Nabal and Abigail. Described by his wife as one whose name is "fool" "and folly is with him" (1 Sam 25:25), the story of Nabal serves as an oblique commentary on the foolishness of a king who was also guilty of treating David in an unworthy manner.

Whatever his reasons for initially helping Nabal's shepherds, David's assistance constituted an act of unsolicited generosity for which some reciprocal action of goodwill on Nabal's part was only to be expected in a traditional culture (1 Sam 25:4-16). David had provided security for those who, in terms of their ability to defend themselves, were less well off than himself (1 Sam 25:7, 15-16). When shearing time came and the positions of relative need and supply were reversed, David's humble request for some share in the festive provisions was unremarkable (1 Sam 25:4-9) and bears no resemblance to a protection racket assumed by some modern, Western commentators.

Nabal, however, responding according to character (1 Sam 25:14, 17), gave a surly display of negative reciprocity, returning "evil for good" (1 Sam 25:21). He had no intention of sharing his well-deserved wealth with any upstart who happened to come along (1 Sam 25:10-11). To such a reply, designed to shame and dishonor David among his men, there seemed only one response. Let Nabal discover what his shepherds had been protected from—a marauding band of cutthroats bent on destruction and pillage (1 Sam 25:12-13). The reference to killing all the men (1 Sam 25:22) leaves unanswered the question of what would happen to the women.

One of Nabal's servants had the presence of mind at this juncture to report to Abigail the current state of affairs and the impending disaster threatening them all because of Nabal's refusal to listen to reason (1 Sam 25:14-17). The parallel with Saul in this respect is striking (cf. 1 Sam 20:32-33; 22:14-16), making the servant's statement about the disaster hanging over his master and his household all the more somber in its implications for the royal family.

If Nabal was Saul's alter ego, then Abigail is Jonathan's, acting decisively to redeem the situation by doing what Nabal should have done (1 Sam 25:18; cf. 1 Sam 13:3; 14:1). Like Jonathan, she chose not to tell her nearest kin of her actions (1 Sam 25:19 is almost an exact parallel to 1 Sam 14:1) but set out for a personal encounter with David in the desert (1 Sam 25:19-20).

Abigail's command of household supplies (1 Sam 25:18), which reflected the general authority of women in the domestic sphere (*see* Occupations, Skills and Crafts of Women), was surpassed in her case by her command of language in the public arena. Uttering one of the longest recorded speeches given by a woman in the Old Testament, she prophetically expressed Yahweh's ultimate design for David as leader over Israel with a lasting dynasty and urged him to avoid the guilt that would come from a needless shedding of blood (1 Sam 25:26-28, 30-31). Her husband was a fool, everybody knew that; her regret was that she had not seen David's men before they encountered Nabal. Then this unfortunate incident would never have arisen (1 Sam 25:23-25). She encouraged David with the knowledge that he was secure in God's keeping, while the life of his enemies would depart as swiftly as a stone from a shepherd's slingshot (1 Sam 25:29).

Abigail's tact and diplomacy, eloquence and persuasive speech dramatically turned the course of action and had the effect of restoring David to an attitude of dependence on God rather than relying on his own schemes of revenge. By her perceptiveness and wisdom she ably demonstrated that although women seldom held center stage for long in Israel's history, their intervention at strategic moments was often pivotal (1 Sam 25:32-35).

Returning to her drunken husband, Abigail wisely bided her time before conveying to him how near an escape he had had. Nabal's subsequent death from heart failure served to confirm to David the truth of Abigail's prophecy that his future could safely be left in God's hands (1 Sam 25:36-39). It was a future that David desired Abigail to share, along with Ahinoam of Jezreel. Abigail's freedom to determine her destiny contrasts sharply with that of Michal, who in David's absence had been given by her father to another man in a political move designed to dishonor David and sever any possible future claim to Saul's throne on the grounds of marriage to the king's daughter (1 Sam 25:39-44).

In his encounters with Saul during this period, David repeatedly pleaded his innocence of any intent to harm the king, even though on two occasions the king's life had been at his mercy (1 Sam 24:2-15 26:13-20, 22-24). His appeal to the king's more rational nature was seemingly rewarded by the king's recognition of his own folly and wrongdoing (1 Sam 24:16-19; 26:21). But the reprieve on the first occasion had been short-lived (1 Sam 24:22; cf. 1 Sam 26:1-4), and David suspected that the king's promise not to harm him would prove useless in practice (1 Sam 26:21). He eventually removed himself from all possibility of death at Saul's hands by taking refuge as an armed mercenary in the service of Achish, king of Gath (1 Sam 27:1-4). Saul and David would never meet again.

David in Philistine Territory (1 Sam 27:5—28:2)

Even among the Philistines, David's life was preserved and blessed by God. Fooling Achish about his intentions and actions, David set about destroying Israel's enemies in the Negeb region (1 Sam 27:1-12). Only when the Philistines planned a major invasion of Israel did David's position become untenable, for as the bodyguard of Achish, who trusted him implicitly, his place at his master's side seemed guaranteed to involve him in fighting against God's people (1 Sam 28:1-2).

Saul's Descent into Despair (1 Sam 28:3-25)

The narrative concerning David breaks off at 1 Samuel 28:2 and reverts to Saul's predicament. Confronted with an invading Philistine army, the mere sight of which was sufficient to inspire terror, Saul was at a loss to know what to do. Not for him, however, was the solace of a revelatory dream, divine oracle or prophetic word. Instead there was only the despair of a grand, divine silence (1 Sam 28:4-6) and a descent into the darkest depths of necromancy as in his desperation he sought one final encounter with Samuel, calling him up from the dead so that once more the prophet might "tell me what I should do" (1 Sam 28:7-16). The echo of Samuel's words at Saul's anointing (1 Sam 10:8) is deeply ironic, for Saul's failure to do what the prophet had told him had led to his downfall (1 Sam 28:17-19). Now his only reward was a chilling message of doom and the final naming of what he had feared all along, that the "neighbor" to whom the Lord had given the kingdom was indeed David (1 Sam 28:17). Overwhelmed with fear of a known future, nothing remained for Saul but the shame of having his most basic needs provided for by an acknowledged medium, a member of a group that he had earlier endeavored to legislate into oblivion (1 Sam 28:3, 9). It was the last recorded act of kindness to Saul in his lifetime, a shared meal between a doomed king and a despised practitioner of magical arts, the bonds of a common humanity overriding the prejudice of the one and the fear of the other (1 Sam 28:20-23).

David and the King of Gath (1 Sam 29)

The narrative focus returns to David to resolve his dilemma as the supposedly loyal subject of a Philistine king. Fortunately for him and for the future of Israel, the other Philistine rulers were not so convinced as Achish of David's loyalty (1 Sam 29:1-4). Ironically, the very verse that had sparked off Saul's suspicion of David's aspirations to the kingdom now at last came to David's defense and saved him from involvement in an assault on that kingdom (1 Sam 29:5; cf. 1 Sam 18:7-9). Parting from Achish on the best of terms, David returned to his home in Ziklag (1 Sam 29:6-11).

David and the Amalekites (1 Sam 30)

Arriving at Ziklag, David discovered that in his absence the settlement has been attacked by Amalekites, the inhabitants carried off and the place set alight (1 Sam 30:1-3). Despite his personal grief and the danger from his troops, who doubtless blamed his involvement with the Philistines as the cause of all their woes, "David strengthened himself in the LORD his God" (1 Sam 30:4-6). The contrast with Saul's weakness in the face of forthcoming battle could not be more marked. The king's enquiry of Samuel, through the medium at Endor, brought only knowledge of certain death in battle the following day. David's enquiry of the Lord through Abiathar, the priest from Nob, brought confidence of success in the battle awaiting him (1 Sam 30:7-8). Saul's death was to encompass his three sons and inevitably many of his troops, who had accompanied him to war (cf. 1 Sam 28:19). David's victory ensured recovery of all the people and property that had been captured, restoration of his honor and prestige among his men as their families were restored to them and gaining of sufficient plunder to satisfy all his troops and enable him to make gifts to the elders of numerous settlements in the south of Judah (1 Sam 30:9-30). This generous gesture the men of Judah were to reciprocate later, when they crowned him king in Hebron (2 Sam 2:4).

The Death of Saul (1 Sam 31)

When Saul was appointed *nagid* of God's people, it was for the purpose of delivering them from the hand of the Philistines. When he met his death, it was at his own hand to avoid capture and abuse by those same enemies (1 Sam 31:1-6). Yet they still cut off his head, exposed his body to the birds by pinning it to the wall of Beth-shan and celebrated his defeat by placing his armor in the temple of their goddess of war (1 Sam 31:8-10). In Israelite thought, for a man to remain unburied was a fate almost worse than death itself (cf. Is 14:3-20; 2 Sam 21:10). That Saul and his sons were spared this final ignominy was due to the kindness and bravery of the men of Jabesh-gilead, who reciprocated Saul's earlier action on their behalf when he had intervened to save them from shame and disgrace at the hands of Nahash and by so doing had established himself as the first king of Israel (1 Sam 31:11-13; cf. 1 Sam 11:1-15).

Outline of 2 Samuel

1:1-27	David's Lament
2:1—4:12	Rival Kings in Israel
5:1-25	The Defeat of the Philistines
6:1-23	David, Michal and the Ark of God
7:1-29	Building a House
8:1-18	David's Military Triumphs
9:1-13	David and Mephibosheth
10:1-19	War with the Ammonites
11:1-27	How Are the Mighty Fallen
12:1-31	God's Judgment and Mercy
13:1-39	The Rape of Tamar
14:1-33	The Return of Absalom
15:1—16:23	Absalom's Rebellion and Ahithophel's Revenge
17:1-29	Hushai's Advice and David's Escape
18:1-33	The Death of Absalom
19:1-43	David's Return
20:1-26	Sheba's Rebellion
21:1—24:25	Appendix

Commentary

David's Lament (2 Sam 1)

News of Saul's death and the loss of many men reached David at Ziklag. The opportunist messenger claimed to have been the last person to have seen the king alive and, in obedience to the king's final command, had administered the deathblow that Saul was too weak to accomplish (2 Sam 1:1-10). The messenger no doubt hoped to be rewarded, but David applied to him the standard by which he had operated, for "who can lay a hand on the LORD's anointed, and be guiltless?" (cf. 1 Sam 26:9). So the Amalekite died (2 Sam 1:13-16), and David mourned the death of Saul and Jonathan, described here as the glory of Israel (2 Sam 1:19; cf. 2 Sam 1:25). In a lament designed for posterity (2 Sam 1:17-18), David called down a curse on the fields of Gilboa, which had seen the final exploits of the two men, loved in life and undivided in death (2 Sam 1:21-23).

Women played a special role in the early musical life of Israel and the surrounding nations (*see* Women as Psalmists; Women in Worship). They were the performers and sometimes the composers of songs of triumph in time of victory (Ex 15:20-21; 1 Sam 18:6-7) or laments in the face of death and defeat, as here. David cannot bear to think of the Philistine women celebrating the defeat of Saul and Jonathan (2 Sam 1:20), so he calls on the daughters of Israel to lament the passing of their king whose previous victories had provided them with rich materials for their dresses and ornaments of gold (2 Sam 1:24; cf. Judg 5:28-30).

The mention of fine apparel turns David's thoughts back to Jonathan, whose covenant love for David had first been indicated by his lavish gift of robe and tunic, sword, bow and belt (1 Sam 18:4), the marks of royalty he had been prepared to relinquish to his friend and covenant brother. His was a love that had stood the test of time, adverse circumstances and his father's murderous intentions (2 Sam 1:25-27). Faithful to the end, Jonathan had fallen with his father on the heights of Gilboa, but his heart had always been David's, and the loss of the steadfastness of that covenant love David grieved most of all. Would there ever again be anyone he could trust so implicitly?

Rival Kings in Israel (2 Sam 2—4)

Relying on the divine oracle about the way ahead, David moved with his wives and men from Ziklag to Hebron, where he was anointed king by the men of Judah (2 Sam 2:1-4). From there he began his path to the throne of all Israel by sending a message of thanks to the people of Jabesh-gilead for their kindness to Saul. He also hinted broadly that their best interests in the future lay not with their dead master (the point is emphasized) but with himself, the newly anointed king of the house of Judah (2 Sam 2:4-7). But there was another newly anointed king—Saul's surviving son Ishbaal, ruling from Mahanaim, across the Jordan. The real power behind the throne, however, was Abner, the cousin of the late king and commander of Ishbaal's army (2 Sam 2:8-11).

Civil war between the opposing forces began when a physical contest, designed to while away the time and provide some sport for two groups of young men sitting in the shade beside a pool of water, escalated into full-scale hostilities in which Abner and his men came off worse and were forced to flee (2 Sam 2:12-17). In the ensuing chase Abner was singled out by Asahel. Asahel and his brothers Joab and Abishai were kin to David, the three being sons of his sister Zeruiah (1 Chron 2:16) and employed in his service. Recognizing who was pursuing him, Abner attempted to persuade the young man to turn aside and chase someone else, but Asahel was determined to go for the glory of taking on the opposing commander and refused to listen (2 Sam 2:18-21). Unwilling to run Asahel through with his spear, Abner turned the butt end toward him with the intention of winding him and effectively bringing his pursuit to an end, but the speed of the young man was such that the force of impact was enough to kill him (2 Sam 2:22-23). On such events the course of history turns, for although the pursuit of Abner and his men ended as the sun went down, the death of Asahel at the hand of Abner was to be long remembered and ultimately avenged in a society in which kinship considerations were still paramount (2 Sam 2:24-32; cf. 2 Sam 3:22-30).

The Death of Abner (2 Sam 3)

While the civil war dragged on, David's influence, political power and substance were increasing all the time, as is indicated in the

---

David's Wives

The Bible records that David had eight named wives and numerous concubines; Jewish tradition accords him more but does not name them. The Bible gives this tradition weight because of Nathan's scathing prophecy in which the Lord says, "I gave . . . your master's wives into your bosom" (2 Sam 12:8). Perhaps Saul's wife Ahinoam and his concubine Rizpah became David's wives as well.

David's choice in wives reflects his physical attractiveness, good fortune and political astuteness.

David won his first wife, Michal, by bringing her father, Saul, two hundred Philistine foreskins (1 Sam 18:27). Michal loved David and saved his life from Saul, but she expressed contempt when he worshiped publicly. She died childless (1 Sam 18:20, 28; 19:9-17; 2 Sam 6:16, 20-23).

David's second wife, Ahinoam of Jezreel, bore him Amnon (1 Sam 25:43). The biblical text lists only two Ahinoams. If David's wife and Saul's wife were the same, perhaps David took her because Saul had given Michal to Palti (1 Sam 25:44).

Abigail, David's third wife, came to him after her husband Nabal died. Both beautiful and intelligent (the only person in Scripture described by these two adjectives), Abigail brought him wealth and standing in Judah (1 Sam 25:2-3). Abigail bore him Kileab.

Maacah, daughter of Talmai, king of Geshur, bore David Absalom and Tamar. Haggith bore him Adonijah, Abital bore him Shephatiah, and Eglah bore him Ithream (2 Sam 3:2-5). Bathsheba bore him the child of their adulterous union who died (2 Sam 12:20) and four other sons: Shime, Shobab, Nathan and Solomon, his heir (1 Chron 3:5). Jesus' genealogy splits at Nathan and Solomon, showing Bathsheba's preeminence (Mt 1:7; Lk 3:31).

The text depicts David's family as unhappy, perhaps because David did not participate adequately in his children's upbringing (1 Kings 1:6; *see* Parental Influence). Amnon seduced his half-sister Tamar; her brother Absalom killed Amnon. Both Absalom and Adonijah rebelled against David, and David grieved mightily at Absalom's death (2 Sam 18:33; *see* Grief and Bereavement).

ROBIN GALLAHER BRANCH

---

number of wives he was able to support at Hebron. Of the sons born to him there, three were to figure large in his reign. Amnon, Absalom and Adonijah each had a different mother, a point of no small significance in the years ahead (2 Sam 3:1-5).

Polygamy was a matter of fact in ancient Israel, the number of wives a man had being limited only by his desire and his ability to support them and their offspring. One of the difficulties and dangers of the practice, however, was that although the children shared a common father, they tended to separate into distinct groupings on the basis of maternal bonds. Just as resentment and jealousies might arise among the wives, so it might arise among their progeny (consider the tensions and rivalry within Jacob's family [Gen 29; 30; 37]; *see* Polygamy).

If David succumbed to the temptation to have too many women in his life (cf. 2 Sam 11), Abner and Ishbaal fell out over one—Rizpah, the daughter of Aiah, who had been Saul's concubine, although she played no visible part in the events of 1 Samuel. Unlike wives, concubines were regarded as property and as such were inherited. For Abner to have slept with Rizpah was no slight affair but a direct challenge to Ishbaal's position as king. How justified was Ishbaal's accusation is a moot point. It may have been nothing more than his father's inherited neurosis reasserting itself in a jealous suspicion of Abner's real aspirations (2 Sam 3:6-7). But Abner was not prepared to submit to such vindictive outbursts as David had experienced at Saul's hand. He knew of the divine promise to ultimately give Saul's kingdom to David and considered that the time had come to put that promise into effect (2 Sam 3:8-10). Ishbaal could do nothing to resist the proposed alliance and meekly complied with David's demand for the return of Michal, Ishbaal's sister and David's first wife (2 Sam 3:11-16). Since David had never divorced his wife, his demand for her return was not illegal, but the contrast between David's inclusion of her in a political deal with Abner and Ishbaal and the palpable grief of her present husband, Paltiel, as his wife is taken away from him is marked (2 Sam 3:15-16).

As for Michal, who can guess her emotions? She had loved David dearly during the short time she had been his wife in the rustic simplicity of her father's court. But to discover, on her arrival at Hebron, that she was only one of a number of wives in the royal harem would have been a bitter pill to swallow and cause her to wonder whether

her return was an affair of the heart or a matter of politics. To have the daughter of Saul as wife would undoubtedly be a point in David's favor when he appealed to the men of Israel to change their allegiance.

Having won over the elders of Israel, Abner met with David; the deal was sealed over a festive meal, and David sent Abner on his way "in peace" (2 Sam 3:17-21). The repetition of the words "in peace" in the following verses (2 Sam 3:22-23) serves to heighten the enormity of Joab's crime as he put personal and family vengeance above political considerations and the king's honor (2 Sam 3:24-27). On hearing the news of Abner's murder, David was appalled, calling down judgment on Joab's house for such a betrayal of Abner's trust (2 Sam 3:28-29) and personally lamenting his death, just as earlier he had lamented the death of Saul and Jonathan (2 Sam 3:31-39).

The Death of Ishbaal (2 Sam 4)

Without Abner, Ishbaal lost courage and was no longer sufficiently in command of himself to lead anyone else. Nor was Jonathan's only surviving son a suitable candidate on whom the Israelites might pin their hopes, for he was lame and unable to walk without aid, let alone fight (2 Sam 4:1-4). Some decision was called for, and Baanah and Rechab, the sons of Rimmon, took it, killing Ishbaal during his siesta. Traveling day and night to David's headquarters at Hebron, they brought him the head of their victim as gory proof of his demise (2 Sam 4:5-8). The brothers' miscalculation of David's character and ignorance of the fate of a previous messenger of death were their undoing. Significantly David does not refer to Ishbaal as "the LORD's anointed" but as "a righteous man"; yet the fate of the sons of Rimmon was the same as that of the Amalekite who earlier had dared to claim that he had been responsible for the death of the king of Israel (2 Sam 4:9-12; cf. 2 Sam 1:13-16).

The Defeat of the Philistines (2 Sam 5)

With the death of Ishbaal the way was clear for David to become king over all Israel (2 Sam 5:3-4). David's choice of Jerusalem as capital was politically astute, for its capture from the Jebusites had made it crown property and thus set apart from tribal territory and local allegiances (2 Sam 5:5-10).

There is some dispute among historians about whether the capture of Jerusalem occurred before, during or after the Philistine incursions (2 Sam 5:17-18, 22). But in two decisive battles, in both of which David's dependence on God is stressed (2 Sam 5:19-21, 23-25), the Philistines were defeated. So at last the original purpose in granting Israel a king was accomplished, as God's people were rescued from the hand of the Philistines (cf. 1 Sam 9:16).

Secure in the knowledge that "the LORD, the God of hosts, was with him" (2 Sam 5:10), David set about building a house for himself commensurate with his increasing power. For the material palace he formed an economic and political alliance with Hiram, king of Tyre (2 Sam 5:11), while to achieve a more extensive physical house or lineage, he entered into a series of marriages and sexual relationships (2 Sam 5:13-14). None of the women are named, although their sons are. If Saul had been haunted by the knowledge that he would establish no dynasty, David's problem was more likely to be which one of his many sons would succeed to his throne and what would happen to the rest.

David, Michal and the Ark of God (2 Sam 6)

One thing was certain: the next king would not be a grandson of Saul, for Michal remained barren throughout her marriage (2 Sam 6:23). Some would say it was a result of God's judgment on her for failing to participate in the general celebration surrounding the bringing of the ark of God to Jerusalem (2 Sam 6:12-19). Others would attribute her failure to conceive to David's refusal to have anything more to do with her after the argument they had on that occasion. Michal had been deeply offended at David's display of enthusiasm as he danced before the ark on its journey (2 Sam 6:14-16). It was one thing for a king to spread his sexual favors around in the privacy of his harem, but to make a public exhibition of himself before every servant girl who chose to ogle at his energetic cavorting was something else (2 Sam 6:20). The bitterness of Michal's reproach may well have expressed her sense of frustration and disappointment at being no longer the sole object of David's conjugal bliss. But her remarks must have struck David as a bit extreme, coming from the daughter of a man who had stripped naked in the company of prophets and whose behavior on that occasion had become proverbial (1 Sam 19:24). It was the first and last time that any dialogue between the two was recorded, and Michal was left to ponder whether keeping up appearances before fellow human beings (1 Sam 15:30) was as important as enjoying a relationship with God, as David so manifestly did.

Building a House (2 Sam 7)

The ark had been placed in a tent as an interim measure (2 Sam 6:17). David planned to build a more substantial house for it, but he was forbidden to do so by God. God had no need for a fixed house, choosing rather to move from place to place with a tent as his dwelling (2 Sam 7:1-7); the statement suggests that the temple, like kingship, was ultimately a divine concession to human desire (cf. Acts 7:47-50). Yet David's longing to honor God would be recompensed (2 Sam 7:8-11). He had desired to build God a house, but instead God would build "a house" for him, a lasting dynasty, an established kingdom. (In Hebrew, the same word for house, *bayit,* can refer to either a material building or a human lineage.) Successive kings of David's lineage could look to God's promise to be their father and experience in their lifetime the divine love and discipline accorded to them as sons (2 Sam 7:11-16).

The prophecy was always greater than any individual human descendant of David. Even when the kingdom of Judah fell and the line of Davidic kings came to an end, the prophecy was still preserved as a signpost of hope, pointing to *the* son of David, yet to be raised up by God, who would build a lasting house for God's name and whose throne and kingdom would be established forever.

Nathan's faithful communication of God's revelation to David overwhelmed him (2 Sam 7:18-20). Once before he had declared "Who am I and who are my kinsfolk?" (1 Sam 18:18). Then he had been addressing Saul and expressing his reluctance to become the king's son-in-law. Now he was addressing the sovereign Lord of all, and there was no reluctance in being his servant forever (the word *servant* is mentioned ten times in David's prayer), only a sense of awe that both he and his people should be singled out for such blessing (2 Sam 7:19-29).

David's Military Triumphs (2 Sam 8)

Because the focus of 2 Samuel is primarily on David and his personal relationships with other human beings and with God, little space is given to the record of his military triumphs, which effectively extended his control from the river Euphrates to the brook of Egypt, as the Lord had promised to Abraham (2 Sam 8:1-14; see Gen 15:18). In Israel the beginnings of an administrative system, which included David's sons, were set up to assist the king in his just ordering of the country (2 Sam 8:15-18).

David and Mephibosheth (2 Sam 9)

As part of his covenant with Jonathan, David had promised to care for his descendants (1 Sam 20:14-15), so Mephibosheth, the sole surviving son of Jonathan, was summoned from Lo-debar (2 Sam 9:1-6). To him David restored all the land that had belonged personally to his grandfather but that had devolved to David by right of accession to Saul's throne. Because of Mephibosheth's incapacity, administration of the property was committed to Ziba, a former servant of Saul and a man of some personal wealth and stature in his own right (2 Sam 9:9-11). Mephibosheth was to live in the royal palace and always dine at the king's table (the point is noted three times in 2 Sam 9:7, 11, 13), as befitted the grandson of a king.

It has often been observed that David's act of kindness had the undoubted political benefit of enabling the king to observe any inclination on Mephibosheth's part to aspire to his grandfather's throne. Against the likelihood of such a move, however, was the reality of Mephibosheth's disability—he was crippled in both feet (2 Sam 9:3, 13)—and in his own estimation, and doubtless in the estimation of others, of no more worth than "a dead dog" (2 Sam 9:8). It was an expression David had once used when seeking to assure Saul that he need fear no harm from David's hand (1 Sam 24:14). David had meant it. Did Mephibosheth?

Would he keep covenant loyalty with David as his father, Jonathan, had done, or prove to be as unpredictable as his grandfather (cf. 2 Sam 16:1-4; 2 Sam 19:24-30 for David's uncertainty in this matter)?

War with the Ammonites (2 Sam 10)

The extensive treatment of Israel's campaign against the Ammonites, rather than mere inclusion in the summary of 2 Samuel 8, is in no small measure due to the fact that it provides the backdrop against which the tragedy of David's affair with Bathsheba is played out (2 Sam 10:7-19; 12:26-31).

No attempt is made by the narrator to explain why the Ammonite king Nahash had shown kindness to David, in contrast to his treatment of the inhabitants of Jabesh-gilead (1 Sam 11). The fact that he had was sufficient reason for David to send a delegation to express his sympathy to Nahash's son, Hanum, on the death of his father (2 Sam 10:1-2). The misinterpretation of David's motives by the Ammonite nobles led to an unprovoked act of negative reciprocity (cf. 1 Sam 25:21) designed to humiliate the messengers and thus the one who sent them (2 Sam 10:2-5). Fearing reprisal measures for such an assault on David's honor, the Ammonites hired an extensive force of foreign mercenaries and thus precipitated war with Israel.

Early battles led by Joab and David so effectively dealt with all the Ammonites' allies that any future help from them could no longer be expected, leaving the Ammonites exposed and vulnerable to attack the following spring, the time when kings habitually went to war.

How Are the Mighty Fallen (2 Sam 11)

Spring came, and so did the Israelite army under its commander, Joab. Of David there was no sight or sound. It could only be assumed that he was otherwise engaged with his affairs in Jerusalem. He was, but the affair in question was to have repercussions David never could have envisaged as he strolled one evening on the roof of the palace. As befitted the king's status, the palace would have been built above the other houses clinging to the slopes of the hill on which Jerusalem was located, and from his vantage point the king could look out over the houses below and, if he so chose, look in on activities normally hidden from public view. He saw a woman, a beautiful woman, bathing after her monthly period, unaware of her exposure to the view and fantasies of a king with a string of sexual conquests behind him. It was easy for David to discover whose house it was and who was the woman in residence. According to contemporary convention she was identified as the daughter of Eliam and the wife of Uriah, one of David's mighty men (cf. 2 Sam 23:39), even now in the field, fighting the king's battles (2 Sam 11:1-3).

The invitation to the palace would have caused Bathsheba no suspicion; she was a married woman, and was not her grandfather Ahithophel one of the king's most trusted advisers (2 Sam 16:23; 23:34)? Her encounter with the king is passed over in a single verse, which effectively communicates how insignificant the whole affair was in the mind and intentions of the king. He sent, she came, he slept with her, she returned home (2 Sam 11:4). For her it would have been impossible to resist the advances of a man in such a powerful position, a man who was capable of taking whatever or whomever he wanted. Had he not obtained back Michal, even though she was married to another man? What would happen to Uriah if she refused the king on this occasion? What would happen to her if she acceded to the king's proposal? She knew the law (Lev 20:10; Deut 22:22-24), but what would be the use of crying out for help in the king's private chamber? Who would believe her word against that of the king? And to what law was the king subject? Perhaps their sin would not be discovered, and the king, having indulged his idle fancy, would forget about her and turn his mind to other conquests of a military variety. Uriah had been gone for some time on the king's business. Perhaps he would come home soon, and then her honor would be safe once more.

The confusion in the mind of Bathsheba can only be imagined, but the turmoil of her thoughts eventually settled on a single harsh reality—her worst nightmare come true. A month later (or was it two months, just to be sure?), David received a terse little note: *harah anoki* ("I am pregnant"). Only two words, yet they formed the hinge on which the reign of David turned (2 Sam 11:5).

Harah anoki: the only words spoken by Bathsheba in the whole episode encapsulated the tragedy of her position. Not for her the excitement of new life stirring within and the prospect of forthcoming celebration but a sense of impending shame and doom, for now the whole question of her honor was at stake in the public domain, as was David's, for adultery was adultery, however exalted the position of one of the participants (*see* Adultery).

Harah anoki: David saw the situation as a problem to be solved, and the solution, at least in his mind, was simple. Summon Uriah home on some trumped-up military concern, give him a couple of days' leave to spend some time with his wife and then, when the child was born, pass it off as premature and pray that the community gossips wouldn't notice the child was full-term. No problem (2 Sam 11:6-13)!

The deviousness of the king's plan was undone by the high principles of his loyal soldier who, although a foreigner, had accepted the conditions of holy war to which David had once subscribed (1 Sam 21:4-5). The irony of Uriah's reply to the king in 2 Samuel 11:11 has often been remarked, as the faithful soldier refused to enjoy any privilege denied to the rest of the king's troops. They were camping in the open field, devoid of female company; how could he choose to go home and lie with his wife? The irony was double, for not only had David chosen to stay at home with his own wives, but also he had been lying with the wife of Uriah, and the very thing Uriah was refusing to do, David had already done. So vehement is Uriah in his refusal to do "such a thing" that he even swears by David's life, unaware that for that strength of principle he was about to lose his life, as he carried back to Joab the king's instructions for his own death (2 Sam 11:14-15). It was to be a well-planned accident, a military decision that in hindsight might be regarded as foolhardy, leading as it did to the death of a number of others besides Uriah. But the whole matter was airily dismissed by the king: "Do not let this matter trouble you, for the sword devours now one and now another" (2 Sam 11:25), a somewhat cynical expression destined to return to haunt the king to the end of his life (2 Sam 11:16-25; cf. 2 Sam 12:10).

The death of Uriah was duly mourned by his widow, who then became David's wife and bore him an even more premature son (2 Sam 11:26).

God's Judgment and Mercy (2 Sam 12)

It is sometimes maintained that so great is the patriarchal bias of the Old Testament, Bathsheba is virtually invisible for the greater part of 2 Samuel 11—12. Two observations counter such a position. Second Samuel 11:27 reads, "The thing that David had done displeased the LORD," and "the thing" in question is lying with Uriah's wife. Other kings in the ancient Near East might assume that they were entitled to take any woman they desired and by so doing dishonor their husbands, but kingship in Israel was different, for ultimately it was Yahweh who ruled, and to him all men, including the king, were accountable. Moreover, however much Bathsheba might seem to be relegated to the background in 2 Samuel 11, it is only necessary to ask "Who is the lamb in the parable told by Nathan?" to realize that she was not invisible to Yahweh but was rather the focus of his concern.

The story Nathan told was masterly, perfectly designed to appeal to a king who had once been a poor shepherd (2 Sam 12:1-4). In passing judgment on the rich man who did "this thing" without pity, David unwittingly passed judgment on himself. The prophet's statement "You are the man!" brought home to David the stark truth that all his plans and scheming had been exposed to the view of Yahweh all along (2 Sam 12:5-7).

The divine judgment perfectly matched the dimensions of David's sin. The "sword" that had so conveniently removed Uriah in a foreign land would turn back on David's house, bringing death to those he loved (2 Sam 12:7-10). He had dishonored Uriah in taking his wife for himself, so Israel would see him dishonored as his wives were taken by another man. David's action had been shrouded in secrecy, but his public recompense would take place in daylight (2 Sam 12:11-12). He had brought shame to Bathsheba, for which he deserved to die. His confession of guilt before God secured his forgiveness, but as events stood, Bathsheba still would have nowhere to hide her shame. As long as their ill-conceived child lived, the palace gossips would have a field day, for any woman with eyes in her head would know that the child was full-term when it was born, despite claims of it being early. A little arithmetic would make them realize why David had been in such a hurry to marry Uriah's widow after her husband's unfortunate but possibly convenient death.

The death of the child was a severe mercy, but it was nonetheless a mercy, a token of the divine compassion for Bathsheba in the longer term. It served to substantiate the claim that the child had been premature and therefore more likely to become another infant mortality statistic, and it removed the possibility of any future gossip occasioned by an innocent query as to the child's identity. ("Oh, that's David and Bathsheba's first child, you know, the one that was born early." And the women would smile knowingly at one another and in their hearts despise the royal couple for presuming they could be deceived.)

David prayed that the life of the child might be preserved, but he did not mourn the child's passing (2 Sam 12:15-23). Instead he comforted Bathsheba, now acknowledged as "his wife," a person loved and honored for her own sake. A child was born, and they named him Solomon, meaning "peace and wholeness," because in him Bathsheba's life was complete once more (2 Sam 12:24-25).

The Rape of Tamar (2 Sam 13)

The tragedy of Tamar's rape is introduced in such a way as to establish links with and draw parallels to the story of Bathsheba. Like Bathsheba, Tamar was beautiful; like Bathsheba, she became the object of a man's seeing (2 Sam 13:5-6, 8), a seeing that aroused such unbridled passion and desire as to lead to illicit sexual union and subsequent disaster.

With the help of Jonadab, a shrewd character, a plan was devised by Amnon, Tamar's half-brother, to bring her into his presence that he might look upon her (2 Sam 13:3-6). The king, responding to what seemed like an innocent request for Tamar to minister to the need of her brother (the relationship is emphasized in 2 Sam 13:6-8) and stimulate his jaded appetite, sent her to her doom (2 Sam 13:7-8). At what point were Tamar's suspicions aroused that there was more to this encounter than she had been led to expect? Was it when she discovered that Amnon wanted to watch her prepare the food and she could feel his eyes on her, running all over her in a way that made her feel embarrassed and uncomfortable? Was it when he refused to eat and sent all the servants out, leaving the two of them alone? She had not anticipated this; the king had said nothing about her having to feed Amnon (2 Sam 13:9-10; cf. 2 Sam 13:7). She brought the cakes to the bedside and held out to him her token of sisterly affection. His response was alarming, his grip on her viselike: "Come, lie with me, my sister" (2 Sam 13:11). The brutal proposition jarred her sensibilities; this was not how things should be. Ignoring the rising panic in her heart and the fear that gnawed inside, she tried to reason with him, to appeal to his better judgment. If he so desired her, let him ask the king. They might share the same father, but with different mothers marriage was permissible (Gen 20:12); what he was suggesting was not. The house rules of Leviticus 18 had been drawn up precisely to protect someone like her from the illicit sexual advances of members of her family (Lev 18:11). What he was suggesting was foolishness *(nebalah)*. They would be scorned and ridiculed by all. She could not agree to his proposal to lie with him. He "forced her and lay with her" anyway, forcing an entrance and ravaging the inner sanctum of her personal identity so that the child in her died (2 Sam 13:11-14; *see* Violence, Abuse and Oppression).

His lust satisfied, Amnon's desire turned to revulsion. Once more he spoke to her: "Get out" (2 Sam 13:15). No longer was she his sister but a spurned woman. Bravely she stood her ground. To send her away was even worse than rape, for there was nowhere for her to go (2 Sam 13:16). At least marriage to Amnon would in some measure restore her honor and secure her future. The law on this matter was clear (Deut 22:28-29), and however harsh it might seem there was no viable alternative, for no other man would ever want to marry a violated woman, and a woman on her own had no future worth contemplating.

But Amnon was a law to himself. Summoning his servant back, he commanded him to throw Tamar out and bolt the door (2 Sam 13:17). There was no way back for her now. Even the words of his command deny her personhood, for there is no personal name, no female noun; she is *zo't* ("this female thing"), and by this term his true opinion of her is expressed. He may have used the word *sister* to achieve his ends, but in reality she was always only an object in his eyes, and as an object she is now discarded (2 Sam 13:18).

For Tamar there remained one last appeal for justice, a visible demonstration of her loss of personhood. No longer a virgin, she tore (the sleeves of?) the robe that signified her status and symbolized her own death with the characteristic actions of the bereaved (2 Sam 13:18-19). It was thus that Absalom found her, and the perceptiveness of his initial question shows an awareness of the workings of his brother's mind and the tendency of his thoughts (2 Sam 13:20). Too late to protect Tamar from Amnon's clutches, now only retribution and revenge were possible.

The responsibility of defending Tamar's honor lay primarily with David, as Tamar's nearest male kin. His inaction and silence are open to various interpretations, of which the Septuagint addition to the Hebrew text is but one possibility (see NRSV text), and even that is ambiguous. Did David maintain silence lest the suitability of Amnon as his successor might be called into question? Or did he see in his firstborn a reflection of his own moral indiscretion that effectively rendered him impotent in his exercise of family discipline (*see* Parental Influence)?

Absalom's silence was more ominous. His response to Tamar's silent admission of events might suggest an attitude of indifference to her plight and a desire to keep the scandal within the family. However, as events were to prove, Absalom's refusal to say anything, whether good or bad, was a deliberate ploy designed to deceive his brother and lull him into a false sense of security (2 Sam 13:20-22). The revenge was well-planned (2 Sam 13:23-27), its final execution swift (2 Sam 13:28-29).

The report that reached the king was wildly exaggerated: all the king's sons were dead apart from Absalom. The sword had indeed fallen with a vengeance (2 Sam 13:30). But Jonadab restored a measure of reality. Absalom had no quarrel with the king's sons en masse; only Amnon had died (the point is made twice), his fate sealed from the day he had so casually raped his sister (2 Sam 13:32-33). The return of the rest of the king's sons confirmed Jonadab's appraisal of the situation, but of Absalom there was no sign. He had fled, seeking refuge with his maternal grandfather, the king of Geshur. So David was bereft of two sons in one day (2 Sam 13:34-39).

The Return of Absalom (2 Sam 14)

Absalom's return was brought about by Joab, who perceived the king's desire to be reconciled. To achieve his end he called on the services of a woman from Tekoa, in the hill country of Judah, whose divinely inspired wisdom had earned her respect and renown in her village and beyond (2 Sam 14:1-3; *see* The Wise Woman). Relying on Nathan's example, she approached the king with a story that was sufficiently true to life to be a plausible appeal to the king's justice and mercy (2 Sam 14:4-7).

The extensive legislation on behalf of widows in Israel is some indication of their precarious position in society, although much depended on whether the widow had children or not and whether those children were male or female, minors or old enough to take their place in the adult community (*see* Widows). To have adult male sons was to be relatively blessed, for they could look to her interests and protect her rights. But her two sons had fought, and as a result one had died. Contemporary justice demanded revenge, but in this case such justice would leave her vulnerable and lead to the extinction of her husband's lineage and the family's association with the land, "the heritage of God" (2 Sam 14:7, 15-16; cf. Ps 16:6).

The king's immediate response showed his willingness to temper justice with mercy in the case of the woman's son, but in a masterly exchange, she pressed her point until David swore that not one hair of her son's head would fall to the ground (2 Sam 14:8-11). Once again, in passing judgment on another, the king was passing judgment on himself, as the woman bravely pointed out (2 Sam 14:13-14). To leave his own son banished and estranged was to act in a way contrary to the mercy of God, who does not punish us as we deserve. To a king only too aware of the blood of another man on his own hands it was a powerful message, delivered by a woman whose attitude throughout was one of humble deference to the king's person (the phrase "my lord the king" is used nine times), wisdom, discernment and essential goodness (2 Sam 14:9, 17-20).

The king's compassion and forgiveness did not quite match that of the woman in the story. "The young man Absalom" (2 Sam 14:21) was recalled to Jerusalem, but it was another two years before he was admitted to the king's presence, and even that audience was obtained only by Absalom taking forthright action against Joab to achieve his purpose (2 Sam 14:21-33). He should have remembered that Joab always took reciprocal action against any offense.

Absalom's Rebellion and Ahithophel's Revenge (2 Sam 15—16)

Convinced by his father's coolness toward him that he had no chance of inheriting his father's throne legally, Absalom began to make plans to obtain it by alternative means. He was already a popular figure with the masses, a man of striking good looks, crowned with a mass of luxuriant hair that was cut once a year and, somewhat ostentatiously, weighed (2 Sam 14:25-26). To improve his image further Absalom obtained a chariot and horses and fifty men to run before him. He set about winning the hearts of the people by establishing himself as an appeal judge for those who, like the wise woman from Tekoa, considered local judgment inadequate or unjust (2 Sam 15:1-6).

Having patiently laid his plans, Absalom obtained the king's permission to travel to Hebron, ostensibly to pay a vow made to the Lord during his self-imposed exile in Geshur. Without asking why it had taken Absalom four years to fulfill this vow, David gave his permission. "Go in peace" were his final words to a son bent on civil war and his own destruction (2 Sam 15:7-9). Accompanied by a party of two hundred men who were unaware of the real purpose of proceedings, Absalom made his way to Hebron. A more ominous addition to the party, who did know precisely what was planned, was Ahithophel, David's trusted counselor and Bathsheba's grandfather (2 Sam 15:10-12).

At last David learned of the treachery planned by his son. Unprepared for a full-scale battle and anxious to avoid the sacking of Jerusalem, he chose to flee accompanied by his officials and personal bodyguard (2 Sam 15:13-18). But he left behind ten concubines to look after the house.

After his passivity (2 Sam 13-14), David became a man of action again. He left the city as a penitent, walking barefoot with his head covered and weeping as he went, acknowledging once again his dependence on God for the future ordering of events (2 Sam 15:30). But his political brain was in gear once more, accepting Ittai's determination to remain with him wherever his path might lead (2 Sam 15:19-23). He persuaded Abiathar and Zadok to return to the city with the ark of the covenant, so that through their sons, Jonathan and Ahimaaz, a line of communication might be set up to keep him abreast of events in Jerusalem (2 Sam 15:24-29). And he encouraged Hushai to swear loyalty to Absalom in order to act as foil and counter to the advice Absalom would receive from Ahithophel (2 Sam 15:32-37). It was Ahithophel's counsel to Absalom that David feared the most. In matters of war and state Absalom on his own would be no match for his father. With Ahithophel at his side, God alone knew of what he might be capable.

As David continued on his way, he was met by Ziba, the steward of Mephibosheth. Bearing provisions for the king's party, Ziba maintained that Mephibosheth had remained in Jerusalem in the hope that present events would prosper his aspirations to the throne. The unlikelihood of Absalom rebelling and then meekly handing over the kingdom to someone else suggests that Ziba was an opportunist who exploited the present situation to further his interests as the expense of his master (2 Sam 16:1-4). The temporary success of Ziba's plan may reflect David's desperate need of the provisions he had brought or a deeper underlying suspicion of any of Saul's descendants, a suspicion that proved well founded in the next character he met. The manner in which Shimei cursed the king (2 Sam 16:5-8) suggests that the events of 2 Samuel 21 had already occurred. As usual, a son of Zeruiah was only too ready to shed blood (cf. 1 Sam 26:8-9; 2 Sam 3:27; 20:10), but the king, as befitted a humble penitent, took it all submissively. Time would prove the validity of Shimei's judgment and whether it was of God (2 Sam 16:9-14).

Meanwhile, in Jerusalem Hushai was gaining an entrance to the court of Absalom, allaying the latter's natural suspicions with a speech that is heavy in its ironic affirmation of Hushai's loyalty to "the king" as the one chosen by the Lord and his people (2 Sam 16:15-19).

Having seized his father's throne, Absalom proceeded to occupy his father's bed. Ahithophel's advice that Absalom should engage in sexual relations with the concubines of the former king was governed by both political and personal considerations. By taking his father's concubines, Absalom would publicly establish his claim to all his father's estate, since concubines, being property, were inherited (cf. 2 Sam 3:7; 12:8). The fact that David was not dead, however, made Absalom's action a calculated insult, guaranteed to seriously affect his relationship with his father (cf. Gen 35:22; 49:3-4). At the same time, whether Absalom realized it or not, he was being used to satisfy Ahithophel's personal desire for revenge against David for the dishonoring of his granddaughter more than ten years before. In normal circumstances such a dishonoring of a family would have been avenged long since, but when the guilty party was the king, it was necessary to wait for an appropriate opportunity. The presence of the royal concubines left in Jerusalem was a chance too good to be missed. And so the final element of Nathan's prophecy was fulfilled in the place where all David's troubles had begun—on the roof of his palace (2 Sam 16:20-23).

Hushai's Advice and David's Escape (2 Sam 17)

Knowing that Absalom would be immediately occupied, Ahithophel offered to set out at once in pursuit of David, in order to exploit the advantage already gained by the unexpectedness of the rebellion. Ahithophel's speech is all haste and action, appropriate to the needs of the situation (2 Sam 17:1-4), but fatally for Absalom, he decided to consult Hushai also. In a speech that conveyed the impression of wisdom by its great length and use of vivid imagery (2 Sam 17:8, 10, 12-13), Hushai deliberately slowed the pace of proceedings, advising caution and proposing the gathering of a huge army out of all Israel, which Absalom would lead in person (2 Sam 17:1-14).

The acceptance of Hushai's advice, rather than Ahithophel's, earned sufficient time to enable word to be sent to David via Zadok and Abiathar (2 Sam 17:15-16). An important link in the communications chain between the priests and their sons was an unnamed servant girl whose movement between Jerusalem and the neighboring village of En-rogel would have aroused no suspicion (2 Sam 17:15-17). Jonathan and Ahimaaz, by contrast, were regarded as a security risk, and once spotted, they were pursued by some of Absalom's servants. Their safety and ultimately that of the king was dependent on the quick thinking of a woman at Bahurim who first covered the well in the courtyard of her house, where the two men had hidden, and then sent their pursuers off in the wrong direction (2 Sam 17:17-22).

Knowing that in a prolonged campaign the cause of Absalom was doomed, Ahithophel went home to Giloh, set his affairs in order and hanged himself (2 Sam 17:23). Did he suspect that when David returned to Jerusalem, he would know who had suggested to Absalom the sexual exploitation of the king's concubines, and knowing, would also deduce why such a calculated insult had been designed? Ahithophel preferred to order his own destiny, choosing a death that was short and self-inflicted to the rage of "a bear robbed of her cubs" (2 Sam 17:8).

Meanwhile David came to Mahanaim, where Ishbaal had been crowned (2 Sam 2:8-10); there he was encouraged and strengthened by support, both moral and material (2 Sam 17:27-29), and there he organized his troops for the battle ahead.

The Death of Absalom (2 Sam 18)

Slipping easily back into his role as army commander, David divided his men into three companies under the leadership of Joab, Abishai and Ittai. His proposal to accompany the army was vetoed, however, on the grounds that his death would be worth more to the forces of Absalom than the loss of even half his army. To what extent Joab in particular preferred the king not to be present so that Absalom could be dealt with once and for all is debatable. All the men knew that the king's heart was not in this battle, and David gave strict instructions that for his own sake Absalom was to be treated gently (2 Sam 18:1-5). In the end he wasn't. Absalom's hair, which for so long had been his crowning glory, became entangled in tree branches, and he was left suspended and helpless. His plight was reported to Joab by a soldier who, having heard the king's command for his son to be spared, was unwilling to harm him (2 Sam 18:6-13). Joab had no such scruples and proceeded to use Absalom as target practice. Absalom died as an object of sport, unable to defend himself, and his body was thrown in a pit rather than restored to his father for a proper burial (2 Sam 18:14-18). When news of Absalom's death reached the king, David was overwhelmed with grief (*see* Grief and Bereavement), and the day of victory became a day of mourning as the king's anguish for his son spread out to engulf his returning troops (2 Sam 18:19-33; cf. 2 Sam 19:1-4). Estranged in their lifetime and ineffectively reconciled, it was only with his son's death that David's true feelings for Absalom found expression in the reiterated use of his name (five times in two verses), the repeated phrase "my son, my son" (three times) and the heart-broken statement "Would I had died instead of you."

David's Return (2 Sam 19)

Ever one to have an eye for political reality, Joab took the king to task for his excessive grief. Absalom had actively rebelled against his father, seized his throne and taken up arms against the king. Yet the message David was communicating to his troops was that he would rather Absalom had lived and they had all died. Unless a more appropriate response was made to the victory the men had won for him, he would lose their support, and the last state of affairs would be worse than the first. So the king suppressed his tattered emotions and went out for the march past his troops to ensure their continuing support (2 Sam 19:5-8).

Bereft of Absalom, David temporarily lost his political judgment. The memory of his exploits against the Philistines was sufficient to earn him renewed support throughout all the tribes of Israel (2 Sam 19:8-10). Yet strangely, and in the long term foolishly, David chose to appeal to his own tribe of Judah to escort him back to his capital (2 Sam 19:11-15). Whatever the reason for this decision, it was in effect a rebuff of the friendly overtures of the northern tribes. This rebuff was to bring a sour note to his homecoming (2 Sam 19:41-43), contribute to the ensuing rebellion of Sheba (2 Sam 20:1-2) and bear even more bitter fruit at the outset of the reign of his grandson Rehoboam (1 Kings 12:16).

Just as his departure had been marked by a series of encounters with various people, so also was David's return. Shimei, who had cursed him on his way previously, now hastened to make peace (2 Sam 19:16-23). Ziba, who on the former occasion had profited from his tale of his master's duplicity, came too (2 Sam 19:17-18), but this time so also did Mephibosheth, countering Ziba's claim that he had entertained hopes of the throne returning to the house of Saul (2 Sam 19:24-30).

The coming of Barzillai was less problematic, for the old man's sincerity and transparent regard for David shine among the mixed motives governing the actions of many of the others close to the king. By contemporary standards Barzillai was a very old man, having survived to the age of eighty, and on the grounds of his age he graciously refused the king's offer to accompany him to Jerusalem, preferring rather to live the rest of his days on his ancestral land (2 Sam 19:31-40).

Sheba's Rebellion (2 Sam 20)

Returning to his home in Jerusalem, David's first action was to ensure future protection and provision for the ten concubines he had left to look after the house. Ironically Absalom's abuse of them for his own ends condemned them to a fate similar to that which his sister Tamar had experienced because of Amnon—an unnecessary and unnatural widowhood for the rest of their life. In Tamar's case it had been because no other man would want to marry her; in the case of the royal concubines it was because David was unwilling to dishonor them further by acting as though his son's violation of them was of no account (2 Sam 20:3).

In the aftermath of Absalom's death David had promised command of his forces to Amasa (2 Sam 19:13), either to win back the loyalty of those who had rebelled against him or perhaps because of a personal desire to remove from office one whose propensity to kill had been expressed too often for David's comfort (2 Sam 19:22). Joab, however, did not take kindly to his loss of position, and at the earliest opportunity he removed Amasa from the reckoning for the post of commander-in-chief (2 Sam 20:4-13).

Joab's pursuit of the rebellious Sheba took him to the far north of the country to the walled settlement of Abel, where Sheba had taken refuge. Calmly and methodically Joab prepared for a major assault on the city, but he was forestalled by the intervention of a wise woman who offered an alternative way of proceeding, the way of words rather than warfare, of peaceful negotiations rather than unnecessary violence. Her intervention demonstrated that although in ancient Israel women lived mainly outside the public arena of power and politics, that fact often enabled them to approach problems with a fresh perspective and bring divinely inspired wisdom to bear on seemingly intractable situations. The woman was listened to by Joab and by the men of her city. Sheba alone died, the town of Abel was preserved, David's kingdom was restored and his kingship secured (2 Sam 20:14-22).

The closing verses of the chapter provide another list of David's officials similar to that in 2 Samuel 8:15, with one significant addition, that of Adoram, who was in charge of the forced labor. Even in the reign of David, the prophetic warning given by Samuel regarding "the ways of a king" was finding ominous fulfillment and providing a foretaste of worse to come (2 Sam 20:23-25; cf. 1 Sam 8:11-17; 1 Kings 5:13-16; 12:12-16).

Appendix (2 Sam 21—24)

The final chapters of the books of 1 and 2 Samuel form an appendix composed of various sections deriving from or relating to different periods in David's life.

The Devotion of Rizpah (2 Sam 21:1-14)

Just as a whole family was regarded as a unit, so that whatever happened to one member affected all (2 Sam 3:30; 14:7), so also in the religious sphere the notion of corporateness applied. Here the whole people (of God) were regarded as one, with the offense of any individual affecting the spiritual well being of all. This principle had determined the defeat of Israel at Ai, after the sin of Achan (Josh 7:1), and it is the same principle that underlies the events of 2 Samuel 20, which probably occurred early in the reign of David over all Israel.

A persistent famine, regarded as a sign of divine displeasure, led to an enquiry of God as to its cause. It transpired that Saul had broken the covenant made with the Gibeonites in the days of Joshua (Josh 9:3-27). Whatever the rights and wrongs behind the original event, the covenant itself was inviolable, and Saul's misguided zeal on behalf of his people constituted an offense for which the Gibeonites required retribution. If retribution did not come from Saul, then it was required from contemporary representatives of his family who, together with him, were regarded as a single person in law (2 Sam 21:1-6; cf. Josh 7:24-25).

Faithful to his covenant with Jonathan and his descendants, David handed over instead the offspring of Merab and the two children born to Saul through his concubine Rizpah. We are not told the feelings of Merab, the wife of Adriel, concerning the sacrifice required of her. But Rizpah, bereft of Saul and now also her sons, faced a bleak future, and her single desire was to honor what remained to her, even if it was only the dead bodies of her children and Saul's grandchildren (2 Sam 21:7-9). In line with contemporary practice, known from other sources, the Gibeonites denied the corpses a decent burial and exposed the bodies to the ravages of the "the birds of the air . . . [and] the wild animals" (2 Sam 21:10; cf. 1 Sam 17:44, 46). Rizpah's devotion throughout a long, hot summer ensured that the dead were at least spared that ignominy. By her lonely, gruesome vigil she brought about a shift in popular opinion and the behavior of the king, for as a result of her action David, by returning their bones to their ancestral land (2 Sam 21:11-14), honored the remains of Saul, Jonathan and the seven who had been impaled.

Other Battles Against the Philistines (2 Sam 21:15-22)

The remaining section of this chapter, a record of a series of local skirmishes with Philistines, honors the prowess of David and his men in battle and provides an insight into the formation of David's reputation as the one who had saved Israel from the hand of the Philistines (cf. 2 Sam 19:9). That reputation rested on more events than those recorded in 1 Samuel 17:50—18:30 and 2 Samuel 5:17-25.

A Song of Deliverance (2 Sam 22)

This psalm, which is included also in the wider Psalter (Ps 18), expresses David's thanks to God for rescuing him from all his enemies and the dangers to which he had been exposed in the desert. (The language of 2 Samuel 22:5-6, 17 should not be taken as simply metaphorical; it may well reflect the experience of being swept away by flash floods in the desert wadis in the winter months.) So David praises God as his rock, his refuge, his deliverer, his shield and savior (2 Sam 22:2-3), intervening on his behalf (2 Sam 22:7-16), protecting and preserving him from harm, guiding his path and strengthening him in battle against all his enemies (2 Sam 22:18-49). To God alone and his covenant love David ultimately attributes all his success, and to God alone honor and glory are due (2 Sam 22:50-51).

David as Charismatic Leader (2 Sam 23)

The same attitude of humble dependence on God is reflected in the oracle with which this chapter opens. David may be king, but God alone has exalted him, and David acknowledges that his exercise of kingship will be of benefit to his people only when it is exercised in "the fear of God" (2 Sam 23:1-7). If David was most great when he was most dependent on God, the remainder of this chapter illustrates something of that greatness in the list of those whose loyalty he inspired (2 Sam 23:8-39), the "mighty men," whose devotion to him extended even to their willingness to risk their lives to meet his every wish (2 Sam 23:13-17). Conscious on that occasion of the power of his personal charisma for good or evil, David was careful to honor their commitment by offering to God as holy the water they had obtained for him at such potential cost to themselves. Yet at the end of the list of warriors is the name of Uriah the Hittite, a sober reminder of charisma and power misused that had sent a good man to his death to cover up the sin of his king.

David as Shepherd of Israel (2 Sam 24)

A similar misuse of power is reflected in the opening section of the final chapter of 2 Samuel, when David fails the test of his determination to rely wholly and solely on the Lord. In the ancient world a census was usually for one of two purposes: to determine a king's military might and human resources or the people's potential to pay taxes to further the king's glory (2 Sam 24:1-9). Neither was appropriate in Israel, for both constituted a fulfillment of the worst of the excesses of kingship predicted by Samuel (1 Sam 8:10-18). Once again David had to learn the hard way that ultimately Yahweh ruled in Israel, and by his mercy alone his people were preserved (2 Sam 24:10-16). Thus David was brought back to his roots and the realization that the people he ruled were as vulnerable to his misuse of power as his sheep had ever been in Bethlehem. His role as king was to care for the people as a good shepherd (2 Sam 24:17), under the sovereign hand of God upon whom all life depended and who alone was to be worshiped (2 Sam 24:18-25).

Bibliography. R. Alter, *The Art of Biblical Narrative* (New York: Basic Books, 1981); S. Bar-Efrat, *Narrative Art in the Bible,* Journal for the Study of the Old Testament Supplement Series 70 (Sheffield: Almond Press, 1989); V. P. Long, *The Reign and Rejection of King Saul: A Case for Literary and Theological Coherence,* Society of Biblical Literature Dissertation Series 118 (Atlanta: Scholars Press, 1989); C. L. Meyers, *Discovering Eve: Ancient Israelite Women in Context* (New York: Oxford University Press, 1988); S. J. Osgood, "Early Israelite Society and the Place of the Poor and Needy: Background to the Message of the Israelite Prophets" (Ph.D. diss., Manchester, 1992).

JOY OSGOOD

1 & 2 KINGS

Introduction

It is generally accepted that 1 and 2 Kings were originally one volume, since there is no break in the continuous narrative. In the Septuagint and the Vulgate, 1 and 2 Kings are known as 3 and 4 Kingdoms. This is because 1 and 2 Kings are considered to be the sequel to 1 and 2 Samuel, entitled 1 and 2 Kingdoms in the Septuagint and Vulgate. Kings was divided into two books when it was translated from Hebrew into Greek, perhaps because more space was required for the Greek, since it writes vowels while Hebrew does not. Much of the material from 1 and 2 Kings is paralleled in 1 and 2 Chronicles. Chronicles was compiled later than Kings, some time around 400 B.C.; it presents a history of the Hebrews from Adam (Genesis) to Kings, concluding with Ezra and Nehemiah.

The author of 1 and 2 Kings is not known. Early Jewish tradition attributes authorship to Jeremiah, who was a contemporary of Josiah and the last kings of Judah (639-586 B.C.). Jeremiah was exiled and sent to Egypt (Jer 43:6-7). He may have written Kings while in exile, since Jeremiah 52 essentially repeats 2 Kings 24:18—25:31, which refers to exile. However, the end of 2 Kings seems to indicate familiarity with events of the Babylonian captivity rather than Egypt. In this case, one may speculate that 1 and 2 Kings were written by an unidentified author in Babylon around 550 B.C. It is more likely that several different authors utilized primary sources that no longer exist. The link with Deuteronomy is undisputed, although scholars differ as to whether they see Deuteronomy as the foundation on which the historical writings were based or a conclusion written in the light of the history.

There are several themes in 1 and 2 Kings. These include proper and improper cultic activities, righteous kingship, loyalty to Yahweh, consequences of improper and disloyal behavior toward Yahweh, the Jerusalem temple, prophecy and fulfillment and united and divided monarchy. There are four major prophecies. Nathan the prophet predicted that a Davidic descendant would rule over his kingdom and build a temple to Yahweh (cf. 2 Sam 7:11-16). Ahijah predicted the division of the united kingdom due to Solomon's apostasy (1 Kings 11:29-39); he also predicted the Fall and exile of Israel due to the sins of Jeroboam (1 Kings 14:15-16). Isaiah predicted the Fall and exile of Judah (2 Kings 20:17-18; 22:16-17).

The united kingdom was ruled by three kings: Saul (1046-1011 B.C.), David (1011-971 B.C.) and Solomon (971-931 B.C.). After Solomon's rule there were twenty kings in Judah and twenty kings in Israel prior to the fall of each kingdom. Israel fell to the Assyrians in 724 B.C., and Judah to Nebuchadnezzar in 586 B.C. The house of David ceased to rule over Israel, the northern kingdom, at the death of Solomon; the golden age of the united kingdom lasted only about eighty years.

Outline of 1 & 2 Kings

United Kingdom

1 Kings 1:1—2:12	David's Final Days
2:13—11:43	Solomon's Rule

Divided Kingdom

12:1—14:31	Division of the Kingdom

Israel and Judah

15:1-8	Abijam of Judah
15:9-24	Asa of Judah
15:25-32	Nadab of Israel
15:33—16:7	Baasha of Israel
16:8-14	Elah of Israel
16:15-20	Zimri of Israel
16:21-28	Omri of Israel
16:29-34	Ahab of Israel
17:1—19:21	Elijah and Elisha
20:1—22:40	Ahab of Israel
22:41-50	Jehoshaphat of Judah
22:51—2 Kings 1:18	Ahaziah of Israel
2:1—8:15	Elisha Stories
8:16-24	Jehoram of Judah
8:25-29	Ahaziah of Judah
9:1—10:36	Jehu's Reform
11:1-20	Athaliah of Judah
11:21—12:21	Jehoash (Joash) of Judah
13:1-9	Jehoahaz of Israel
13:10-13	Jehoash of Israel
13:14-25	Elisha's Final Acts
14:1-22	Amaziah of Judah
14:23-29	Jeroboam II of Israel
15:1-7	Azariah (Uzziah) of Judah
15:8-12	Zechariah of Israel
15:13-16	Shallum of Israel
15:17-22	Menahem of Israel
15:23-31	Pekahiah of Israel
15:32-38	Jotham of Judah
16:1-20	Ahaz of Judah
17:1-6	Hoshea of Israel
17:7-14	Fall of the Northern Kingdom to Assyria

Judah and Assyria

18:1-16	Hezekiah of Judah
18:17—19:37	Sennacherib Attacks Jerusalem
20:1-21	Hezekiah's Decline
21:1-18	Manasseh of Judah
21:19-26	Amon of Judah
22:1—23:30	Josiah's Reforms

The Fall of Judah

23:31-35	Jehoahaz of Judah
23:36—24:7	Jehoiakim of Judah
24:8-17	Jehoiachin of Judah
24:18-20	Zedekiah of Judah
25:1-30	Fall of Jerusalem and Exile

Commentary

United Kingdom (1 Kings 1—11)

David's Final Days (1 Kings 1:1—2:12)

1 Kings opens with an elderly David who was no longer able to rule; he was feeble and could not keep warm. David's servants decided to find a young woman to care for him. The Hebrew word *betula* ("virgin" or "maid") may refer to someone who has not experienced sexual intercourse (Gen 24:16; Num 31:18) or it may mean "young (unmarried) girl," as found in the Akkadian *batultu*. In the case of David, a young unmarried woman, one worthy of functioning as a nursemaid for the king, is meant. Abishag was retained to comfort the aged king in his last days but not to function as a sexual partner. As is seen later in the story, Abishag presumably retains her virginity, since Adonijah attempts to persuade Bathsheba to ask Solomon to give Abishag to Adonijah in marriage (1 Kings 2:13-25).

In the ancient world, women could occupy positions of authority and have professions. Women, especially foreign women, could function as queen, prophet, poet, author, magician, witch and sorceress. In Egypt, women had numerous personal freedoms and enjoyed many of the same legal rights and obligations as men. Women could contract business deals, run businesses or farms, take oaths and act as witnesses in court. They could divorce and remarry; they could inherit and bequeath property such as land, houses, furniture and jewelry. Some of the professions open to women included temple dancer, singer, musician, priestess, professional mourner, gardener, nanny and servant; some women were taught to read and write, and some even became doctors. Apparently the only positions not normally open to women were government jobs.

It was a natural assumption that upon David's death Adonijah would become king, since he was the eldest son. He quickly set about gaining supporters, winning over Joab and Abiathar the priest, both officers in David's court. In addition, Adonijah was able to demonstrate military strength, with chariots, horses and "fifty men to run before of him" (1 Kings 1:5). Their support of Adonijah was crucial if he was to become king. Adonijah's jubilant group of supporters proceeded to the stone Zoheleth near Enrogel in order to perform a coronation ceremony that would establish him as legitimate king.

Nathan and Bathsheba reminded David that he had named Solomon as successor, or *nagid* ("crown prince"). They also informed him of the coup d'etat that was in progress. It was imperative for David to act quickly and publicly proclaim Solomon his heir. Otherwise, upon David's death there would have been chaos in the kingdom and a divided monarchy would have resulted. These actions seem to represent the culmination of Nathan's and Bathsheba's political aspirations. One may question the accuracy of Bathsheba's and Nathan's assertion that Solomon was already heir to the throne. Was this a legitimate promise that David made, or were Bathsheba and Nathan using David's weakened and confused state for their political gain? Upon Solomon's accession to the throne, Bathsheba would become queen mother, an important political office (*see* 2 Chronicles).

Solomon's accession is sometimes said to mark a departure from charismatic to hereditary kingship in Israel. Charismatic kingship describes the reign of a leader anointed by God regardless of heredity or merit to whom is given special power, such as Solomon's wisdom; the status of such a ruler is further made manifest in his or her gaining support and control of the army. Israelite kingship was established because of the people's desire to be like other nations, and their kings were fashioned accordingly. When the people of Israel first requested a king (1 Sam 8), they were warned of the evil that kings can do (1 Sam 8:10-18). Originally God was to be the King of Israel, while the judges (charismatic leaders appointed by prophets) were to be military leaders; creating the office of king would change that balance. Now the king was political, military and religious leader of the people, with God ultimately in control. With the appointments of Saul and David, that control is evident. The accession of Solomon, however, marks a transition;

Solomon becomes king not only because he was "chosen by God" but also because of his heredity. From this point, kings will ascend to the throne based on heredity or military might.

Solomon's appointment and anointment were different from Adonijah's self-coronation in that they were conducted with the full support of David and his court. This was made evident in the public announcement of Solomon's kingship and the ensuing symbolic rituals. Solomon's service was held at Gihon, an established sacred spring in Jerusalem and the site where the ark of the covenant was sheltered. Purification by water has an important significance in the ancient world. Solomon rode David's mule to Gihon; his legitimate succession was confirmed through blowing trumpets and shouting "Long live King Solomon!" (1 Kings 1:34). Zadok the priest "took the horn of oil from the sacred tent [i.e., the tabernacle] and anointed Solomon" (1 Kings 1:39). The act of anointing was an ancient religious rite common among the people of Israel, Canaan and Egypt. It was considered to confer grace and symbolized that the Spirit of God had taken hold of the recipient (cf. 1 Sam 10:10). Solomon was considered the anointed of Yahweh (cf. 1 Sam 24:7, 11; 26:9, 11, 16), having been officially installed as the divinely appointed king of Israel, and Adonijah was regarded as an enemy of Solomon's court. The role of prophet in the appointment of a king seems to have changed as the role of kingship evolved from charismatic selection into hereditary succession. As the focus changed with David and Solomon away from charismatic leadership, the prophets' message became one of the ruler's obedience to Yahweh.

When David's death was close, he wanted to entrust the kingdom to Solomon. David's instructions included blessings and curses: follow in the ways of God and you will be blessed; stray from them and you will be cursed. This applied not only to Solomon but also to the nation as a whole. However, Solomon represented the people and was responsible for the nation's moral character.

Solomon's Rule (1 Kings 2:13—11:43)

Purging Enemies (1 Kings 1:13-46). Adonijah, who had promised to support Solomon, spoke to Bathsheba, requesting that she convince the king to give him Abishag in marriage. Now that Solomon was king, Bathsheba enjoyed a great deal of power. Adonijah knew this and appealed to the strongest source next to Solomon. This, however, was no minor petition, as Adonijah insists. It represents a significant political move on his part, as he again attempts to acquire power in the kingdom. Even though Abishag was not David's wife or concubine, she had been connected to him in a significant way. This association was quite strong, as seen in Solomon's response to Bathsheba: "Ask for him the kingdom as well! For he is my elder brother" (1 Kings 2:22). If Adonijah had married Abishag, it would have been equivalent to marrying a newly widowed queen mother or wife of the king. Moreover, if the couple were to have children, the oldest male would pose a threat to Solomon and any heirs or appointed successors of his. Bathsheba's request gave Solomon the excuse he needed to put Adonijah to death and permanently remove him as a threat to the throne.

Solomon's Government (1 Kings 3:1—4:34). Solomon made an alliance with Pharaoh and married his daughter. We are never given the name of the pharaoh or the name of his daughter. It was unusual for a pharaoh to allow a daughter to marry outside Egypt. According to the ordinances put forth in Deuteronomy (Deut 7:1-5), it was also forbidden for Israelites to marry foreigners. Politically, however, Solomon was behaving astutely. In this way, Israel would not be attacked by Egypt, since the pharaoh would not want to risk his daughter's safety. Nor would Solomon want to anger his new father-in-law by attacking Egypt. Solomon and his new wife lived in the city of David until the palace, temple of the Lord and Jerusalem's city wall were constructed.

Jerusalem was originally the Jebusite "stronghold of Zion." Early in his reign David captured and occupied this fortification, renaming it the city of David (cf. 2 Sam 5:7, 9; 1 Chron 11:4-7; 8:11). Seven years after conquering this site, David moved his capital there from Hebron. His palace was constructed just above the destroyed Jebusite citadel and just south of the later temple mount. Excavations have revealed not only a possible site for David's palace but also public buildings, residential areas, a defense system including the so-called stepped-wall structure, subterranean water system, terraces and evidence of city planning. Water was abundant in this strategic location, which offered excellent defense against intruders. It was through tunnels that brought water into the city that David was able to enter the city, undetected, and capture it. It has long been assumed that David entered via a tunnel known as Warren's Shaft; however, recent excavation has determined that Warren's Shaft is a dead end. Newly discovered channels reveal a maze of tunnels, any number of which could have been used in David's sacking of the Jebusite city.

During David's reign this city became the seat of the royal house. David brought the ark of the covenant here from the house of Abinadab (cf. 2 Sam 6:1-12); the ark symbolized the unity of the tribes and the covenant between God and his people. In addition, kings from the Davidic dynasty were buried in the city. The city of David grew, and David eventually built an altar in the area that would later become the temple mount, thus establishing a thriving metropolis and cult center in Israel. David had visions of building a temple in Jerusalem; although plans for the complex were begun by David, Solomon and Nathan the prophet prior to David's death, it would not become reality until the time of Solomon. David did, however, build a palace next to the tent of meeting that housed the ark of the covenant; this palace was called the "house of cedar" (2 Sam 7:2), the "house of the warriors" (Neh 3:16) and the "tower of David" (Song 4:4). Until the cult center was finished, people worshiped Yahweh and offered sacrifices at established sacred high places (1 Kings 3:2). Once the temple was completed, however, high places that once had been acceptable for worship and sacrifices to Yahweh were now forbidden. The temple became the only official site for veneration of Yahweh. This became a major point of contention between Judah and Israel in their relationships with God.

Solomon offered sacrifices at Gibeon, since it was the most important high place. At Gibeon, the Lord appeared to Solomon in a dream, offering to grant whatever he requested. Solomon requested wisdom and a discerning heart, in order to administer justice and rule fairly among the people of God. After the Lord had blessed Solomon with wisdom and discernment, these gifts had to be demonstrated. The story of the two prostitutes was not meant to test the wisdom and judgment of Solomon but rather to establish his abilities. The two women were able to represent themselves in the highest court of law, before the king. This means they did not need male representation in the legal system, and they enjoyed rights similar to those of men under the law. A high opinion of a mother's care for a child is shown here.

When a king first comes to power, it is expected that new officials will be named. The offices to be filled included high priest, secretary, recorder, commander-in-chief, priests, a master of district officers, priest and personal advisor to the king, master of the palace, master of conscripted labor and twelve district governors. Some of these employees were sons of people from David's administration. This suggests continuity in administration and an expectation of loyalty on the part of Solomon and employee alike. Several of the officials' names seem to be of foreign origin. It is not surprising to find that David and Solomon employed non-Israelites at their court. These people came from nations that had long-established and well-organized court administrations. It would be of advantage to employ experienced people, in order to make the Israelite royal household and kingdom run smoothly.

Each of the twelve districts was responsible for supplying rations for one month a year to Solomon and his administration. In addition, neighboring nations, such as the Philistines and Egypt, brought tribute (i.e., gifts), as did people who came to visit the king. In this way the king and governmental employees could exist and receive reimbursement for their services. Spreading the responsibility of provision among the twelve districts meant that no single district would be unduly burdened with the task of financing the government. Solomon's consolidation and organization marked a departure from theocracy to monarchy.

Building the Temple (1 Kings 5:1—7:51). David could never build a temple because he was constantly at war. But Solomon was ruling in peace, and he was ready to undertake this daunting task. He negotiated with Hiram of Tyre for cedar from the trees in Lebanon; in return he would provide food for Hiram's royal household, which included the required labor forces. Solomon conscripted thirty thousand men from all over Israel who were sent to Lebanon to work with Hiram's men in shifts. There were as well seventy thousand carriers, eighty thousand stonecutters in the hills and thirty-three hundred foremen as supervisors. The extent of the disruption caused by this massive program perhaps explains Solomon's unpopularity by the end of his reign.

Solomon also built a seaport at Ezion-geber and manned the ships with Phoenicians (professional sailors) who taught his men to sail. According to 1 Kings 9:26, Ezion-geber was located at the northern tip of the Gulf of Aqaba, near modern Elat. It is possible this naval port was created to control trade to the south with people such as the Egyptians and the Queen of Sheba. Ezion-geber was Solomon's first and only seaport. He was, however, allowed access to Phoenician ports on the Mediterranean because of his alliance with them.

The use of conscripted labor was common practice in the ancient Near East. The Hebrew word for "slave" is *ebed,* which comes from the root *abad* ("to work"). The word *slave* (sometimes also translated "servant") was used in numerous contexts. For example, in the ancient texts a subordinate was slave to a higher-ranking individual; all subjects in Israel and Judah were slaves to the king (1 Sam 17:8; 19:5; 29:3); even royal officials and courtiers were slaves to the king; the Israelites were slaves in Egypt (Ex 13:13-14; Deut 5:15; 24:18); and they were slaves (or servants) to God. Freemen of any ethnic background who were in debt could legally sell a child into slavery or sell himself or herself into slavery to a creditor for six years. At the end of the six years, the debt was considered paid and the slave was again a freeman. Slaves of foreign descent, however, made up the majority of state workers. These slaves, or forced laborers, were obliged to perform tasks prescribed by the needs of the state. Those who composed this class were usually war captives from foreign lands and conquered native inhabitants (such as the Canaanites). This was the work force that Solomon used to build the temple and royal palace in Jerusalem. Solomon had a heavy hand that took its toll on this labor force, physically and spiritually; ultimately his heavy-handedness became a major factor leading to the division of the kingdom (1 Kings 12:4).

Construction on the temple commenced in Solomon's fourth year as king. His construction of the temple, royal palace and the city plan imitated those of Neo-Hittite and Aramean royal cities. Solomon's intention was to create the temple under the Davidic dynasty, establish a strong bond between the temple and royal line and centralize the state religion (Shiloh). The interior layout of the sacred areas had a tripartite division that was typical of numerous ancient temples. The three areas the interior was divided into are the *ulam* ("front," "porch," "portico" or "entrance hall"), the *hekal* ("sanctuary" or "nave" [RSV]) and the *debir* (the Holy of Holies or Most Holy Place; Meyers, 357). It seems that this pattern was meant to direct the worshiper from the outer world into spaces that became smaller, more holy and more restricted; only the high priest could enter the holiest space. The *ulam* served as the entrance hall; admission into the portico was through an open entrance. The portico was a transitional area, where one's thoughts turned from the daily activities of the mundane world to sacred meditation. The main room, or *hekal,* was separated from the portico by two double-hung doors made of cypress and olive wood. The *hekal* hosted many of the cultic activities and rituals, and the temple furnishings were housed here as well. The Most Holy Place was located at the innermost end of the complex. It was separated by two double-hung olive wood doors. The floor of this room was elevated and accessed by several steps. The Holy of Holies measured 30 x 30 x 30 feet (or 9.0 x 9.0 x 9.0 meters), a perfect cube; there were no windows and no light wells in the ceiling: light could not penetrate, and nobody could look in.

The ark of the covenant was housed in the Holy of Holies. Two cherubim of gilded olive wood were placed in this inner chamber, along with the ark. The cherubim stood side by side, with their wings touching the side walls. The interior of the shrine was dressed with cedar paneling from floor to ceiling, and the floor was covered with pine planks. The interior, including the altar, was overlaid with pure gold. The second and third floors were most likely used as priests' residences, offices and classrooms.

Solomon included a great deal of artwork in the temple. It has generally been assumed that the Israelites did not create artwork for fear of violating the second commandment (Ex 20:4). However, Solomon's designs, with cherubim, twelve oxen to hold up the molten sea, festoons, palm trees and open flowers, illustrate his understanding of this commandment: artwork in itself is not bad. The problem arises when artistic representation is venerated. In other words, the commandment warns against making representations of spiritual things and then worshiping them as idols. It is not forbidden to create artistic renderings of that which exists in God's realm.

Solomon's palace was constructed adjacent to the temple on the temple mount. However, it took longer to complete the palace than the temple, about thirteen years. It seems that Solomon's concern for his glory had become greater than his concern for the glory of God. His palace was longer and wider than the temple and very ornate, bespeaking a marked extravagance.

The temple furnishings were as elaborate as the temple, and Solomon engaged a certain bronzeworker from Tyre, Hiram, to fashion all of the bronzework in the temple. He commissioned a golden altar, a golden table for the bread of the Presence, lamp stands, golden floral work, lamps, tongs, pure gold dishes, wick trimmers, libation bowls, ladles and censers and golden door sockets. He installed all these, plus those that David had made, in the temple. Most of these fittings and utensils were used by the priests while performing ceremonies in the temple; the basins were used for ritual washing, lamps for light, shovels for sacrificial food, small golden altars for incense offerings. The hybrid cherub (Akkadian *kuribu*) seems to have originated in the winged lion or bull with the head of a bird, ram or human, types that are well known from the iconography of Mesopotamia and Egypt. Biblical cherubim combined all these features. The cherubim were guardians representing the strength and protection of God.

Dedicating the Temple (1 Kings 8). The most important item to be set up in the temple was the ark of the covenant, representing God's permanent presence among his people. It was placed in the Holy of Holies with the cherubim spreading their protective wings over it. It was not until the priests had left the holy place that the glory of Yahweh filled the temple.

David had identified Mount Zion as the site for the temple. In the ancient world it had long been established that gods lived on mountaintops, because such places were beautiful, grandiose, mysterious and close to heaven—the perfect place for a god to dwell. Therefore ancient worshipers constructed altars and temples on hilltops and mountain summits to better communicate with their deity. To be sure, Moses met Yahweh atop Mount Sinai. But Yahweh had certain characteristics that distinguished him from other gods; he was mobile. Most other gods found their dwellings in specific locations and rarely left them. Yahweh not only moved with his people but also led them into a new land and dwelled there with them; he would later follow them into exile. Another attribute of Yahweh was that he came down from his lofty dwelling place to meet humankind.

In general, ancient Near Eastern people traveled to the place where the gods were and built altars on high places to be sure their prayer would be heard. Yahweh, conversely, sought after the Israelites and ultimately humankind, manifesting himself in various mystical physical phenomena, such as a pillar of cloud and fire. This sort of divine self-revelation was unique to the relationship between Yahweh and the people of Israel. Even more amazing was the fact that Yahweh promised to interact daily with his chosen people. He made himself available to their religious leaders in a sort of traveling residence, the tent of meeting (tabernacle; cf. Ex 29:42, 30:18), while his contract with humankind was symbolized in the ark of the covenant, which was moved among the people (cf. Egyptian portable divine barques). He was perceived as a sort of nomadic God, with a mobile home.

The tabernacle had previously sufficed as the house of God. When the Israelites, especially their kings, were becoming more sedentary, only the temple was a suitable and grand enough residence for Yahweh. The Solomonic temple in Jerusalem represented the permanent dwelling place of Yahweh. There was a clear understanding that the temple in no way contained or restricted Yahweh, but it was assumed that he could always be found in the temple. This sort of permanence not only symbolized God's presence among his people but also reflected the fact that the Israelites were no longer nomadic. Their days of wandering were over, for they too had found a permanent dwelling place in the land of Israel. The temple was thus an important cultural feature that served to unify the nation.

In the ancient world, cult and state were not separate entities; religion and state were so intimately connected that it is difficult to determine where one ended and the other began. The king was considered to be God's viceroy or regent on earth, managing not only matters of state but the cult as well.

The temple/palace economies of the ancient world were essential to the socioeconomic nature of the community. In Egypt and Mesopotamia the temple collected surplus food and raw materials from all over the country, stored it in repositories, then distributed it to all governmental employees who could not engage in food production because of their work. These groups include the king, his family, the king's officials, priests and temple personnel, scribes and royal laborers. The temple not only collected foods and raw materials; it also made clothing, owned herds, had orchards and farmland producing its foodstuffs, and sheltered widows, orphans and war captives. It standardized weights and measures, stabilized interest rates and at times participated in judicial matters. With the construction of the temple, all of those materials could be collected in a central location and distributed as necessary.

The temple functioned as a school. The precinct priests educated other priests and officers of the court. The temple had an extensive library on subjects such as medicine, science, religion, politics, historical writings, annals and economic and legal matters. People who wanted to study came to the temple for their education. When they worshiped at the temple, people offered valuable gifts of precious metals, minerals or cash as their sacrifice. These contributions would be collected and considered part of the temple treasury. The king also collected a national treasury from taxes and war booty and stored it in the palace. Both treasuries, however, were under the control of the king, who could do whatever he saw fit with the wealth.

Once the temple was finished, Solomon spoke a prayer of dedication to Yahweh before the entire assembly of Israel. In essence, this dedication was a joyful ceremony of singing, dancing, ritual, prayer, banquet and other festivities. Yahweh was believed to be living in the temple when the ark of the covenant was placed in the *debir*, since it is the most important symbol of the divine Presence. At this point the spirit of Yahweh filled the temple. However, Yahweh's presence is not limited to this place. Rather, as 1 Kings 8:27 states, God's Spirit may be found everywhere in highest heaven and on earth and the depths of the sea. The *debir* served to remind the people of God's constant presence among them on earth and served as a meeting place between heavenly God and earthly human.

Solomon dedicated not only the temple but also the people of Israel to Yahweh. Solomon vividly and passionately confirmed his and Israel's position and responsibilities before God, as well as God's responsibilities to his people. Solomon reaffirmed the Davidic covenant, which established God's omnipresence, attentiveness to his faithful people and punishment for disobedience. In this passage Yahweh is described as a caring, attentive, patient and forgiving deity. Through God's eyes, ears and presence, the prayers of the people shall be heard and acted upon. Disobedience will be punished, but forgiveness is available upon confession and repentance.

God Appears to Solomon (1 Kings 9). The temple is consecrated by God, and this is where his name, eyes and heart will dwell forever. The name, eyes and heart of God are the essential parts of his being (in anthropomorphic terms). Yahweh's name separates him from and elevates him above all other gods; the eyes represent God's continuous presence, opinion and judgment; the heart represents God's mind, character, innermost self, loyalty and conscience.

Solomon mounted a great building campaign and fortified Jerusalem, Hazor, Megiddo, Gezer, Beth-horon, Baalath and Tamar. Cities were designed and used for various administrative purposes. For example, some cities were established for storage of armament, for chariots and horsemen or as military supply centers for food and clothing. Archaeological evidence for this activity may be found at Hazor (stratum X), Megiddo (strata VA-IVB) and Gezer (stratum VIII). These settlements were placed at militarily strategic points. In contrast, Jerusalem served as Solomon's political and religious center. Since he was ruling during a time of relative peace, his building projects were not interrupted by war. As for conscripted laborers, only non-Israelites were forced to work on these building projects. The Israelites served as Solomon's construction supervisors, army, government officials, military officials, commanders, captains and charioteers.

Queen of Sheba (1 Kings 10). Solomon's reputation as a wise leader, great imparter of wisdom and follower of Yahweh was known far and wide. The queen of Sheba was so intrigued by his fame that she journeyed to meet him in order to test him by asking difficult questions. She traveled with a large caravan and brought valuable commodities with her, including copious quantities of spices, gold and precious stones. She was immediately impressed and ultimately overwhelmed with Solomon's wisdom, his court, temple, palace, the temple and palace furnishings, food and administrative order. She was amazed that all the reports she had heard about him were true, so she gave the cargo in her caravan to him as tribute. Solomon, equally dazzled by Sheba, gave her riches from his royal bounty, far outweighing what she had given him.

The reason for the queen's visit to Solomon may have been to strengthen or initiate trade relations. Solomon was beginning to expand his sphere of influence, controlling numerous overland trade routes. If the relationship between Sheba and Solomon were to become unfriendly, this could potentially block trade with East Africa, so it was in the queen's best interest to remain on friendly terms with Solomon. She was a powerful leader who was accepted into Solomon's court just as any other head of state would be. Her entourage was large, and there was no question about her ability or legitimacy as a ruler because of her gender.

The queen of Sheba conducted herself with the dignity and stature of a head of state. She did not seem to abuse her power or to underestimate it. In order for a woman to achieve her stature and position, she would have had to obtain and retain the respect of the people, the military and religious leaders and the palace court, all of them primarily male-dominated groups.

Solomon and the queen of Sheba were immediately friends, and she remained with Solomon, as his guest, for an unknown period of time. According to Ethiopian legend they had a love affair that resulted in the queen's pregnancy, although she was not aware of this upon her departure from Israel. The child, a boy, was born after she had returned to Sheba.

Legend has it that when Solomon's and Sheba's son, Menelik (whose name is known from extrabiblical sources), grew up, he visited his father in Israel and traveled to Ethiopia as well. In the Ethiopian story, Menelik carried the ark of the covenant to Ethiopia, thus transferring the seat of Yahweh's presence from Israel to Ethiopia and establishing the powerful Abyssinian Dynasty. To this day, the Ethiopians claim, according to the *Kebra Nagast* (the book of The Glory of the Kings), that the ark of the covenant is housed in the church of Mary Zion in Axum.

Solomon possessed land from the Euphrates River in the east to the land of the Philistines in the west and down to the "Wadi of Egypt" (Wadi el-Arish; 1 Kings 8:65; 2 Kings 24:7) in the south. This meant he was in control of two important trade routes: the Via Maris and the King's Highway. He imported chariots and horses from Egypt and Que and exported them to the Neo-Hittites and Arameans. Solomon's kingdom controlled most of the trade that passed through Israel, thus accumulating a great deal of wealth from import/export taxes and transit duties. For example, Solomon received in one year 666 talents of gold (1 Kings 10:14), which is equal to 50,349.60 pounds or more than 25 tons. People from near and far came to hear his judgments over specific problems. It was unusual for a king to deal directly with people in this way. Kings of other nations usually delegated legal matters to judges or priests, hearing only the most important cases themselves. Solomon dealt directly with his subjects. As a result, gifts and payments made Solomon a very rich man.

Solomon's Downfall and Death (1 Kings 11). It was common for a ruler to have numerous wives. In the ancient world, death during childbirth was common; the survival rate for children and their chances of reaching adulthood were very low. The inability of a couple to bear children was also a common problem. Therefore numerous wives would ensure a male heir to the throne. Moreover, upon conclusion of a treaty, in order to ensure good relations, a princess or prince would be offered in royal marriage. Solomon had seven hundred foreign wives of royal birth and three hundred concubines. God had instructed the Israelites not to marry foreign women because they would begin to follow foreign gods (1 Kings 11:2). This is what happened to Solomon; he began to worship Ashtoreth, Molech and Chemosh, and he built cult places for the idols of all of his wives. Because of this violation, not only Solomon's reign but also the spiritual well-being of Israel would never be as peaceful, strong and prosperous as it once was.

It would seem that polygamy was common among kings, leaders and the wealthy (*see* Polygamy). It was expensive for a man to have many wives, and only the wealthy could afford such a luxury. Much later, the Talmud established that a common man could have as many as four wives, and kings, eighteen. In the book of Kings, common men had only one wife, while kings had many.

From this point on, Israel (soon to be the kingdoms of Israel/Samaria and Judah) will struggle with its relationship with Yahweh. When Solomon decided it was acceptable to worship foreign gods, he made a public statement. A king is inevitably influential, and thus Solomon led the nation down a path to destruction.

Divided Kingdom

Division of the Kingdom (1 Kings 12:1—14:31)

Jeroboam the son of Nebat, an Ephraimite who was one of Solomon's officials, was chosen to become ruler of Israel, the northern kingdom. Ahijah, a prophet from Shiloh, vividly described to Jeroboam what would happen. The prophet tore his new cloak into twelve pieces, telling Jeroboam to choose ten. Ten of the tribes of Israel would be taken from Solomon and his heir, Rehoboam, and would be given instead to Jeroboam. This was Solomon's punishment for worshiping other gods. Two tribes, Judah and Benjamin (together with the Levites), would remain in the hand of Solomon's son and successor, since this tribal land included Jerusalem, the city where the temple was. Only because of Yahweh's promise to David and David's faithfulness to Yahweh would the southern tribes continue to belong to Solomon's heir. Solomon, upon learning of this divine plan, attempted to kill Jeroboam, who fled to the court of Shishak, king of Egypt, until Solomon died.

Rehoboam as Successor (1 Kings 12:1-24). Upon the death of Solomon, his son Rehoboam attempted to control the northern kingdom of Israel and the southern kingdom of Judah, but without success. The rupture occurred over the "heavy yoke" that Rehoboam was going to impose, reinforcing his father's forced labor schemes. The northern tribes united behind Jeroboam and broke away from the united monarchy. This was God's punishment. From this point on, Israel and Judah were two separate nations with two different fates; they were so treated by Yahweh and by the Assyrians.

Jeroboam Organizes the Northern Tribes (1 Kings 12:25-33). Even though the kingdom was divided, everyone's responsibilities to Yahweh at the temple in Jerusalem remained the same. The people were still required to go there to perform cultic duties. With his people traveling regularly to Jerusalem, now located in Judah, Jeroboam feared one day they might transfer their allegiance to Rehoboam; the kingdom of Israel would revert to the house of David, and Jeroboam would be killed. Jeroboam resolved to create two new high places in his kingdom so that his people would not have to go to Jerusalem to satisfy religious obligations. These high places would be much more convenient, and the journey much less strenuous, for people who lived so far away from Jerusalem. Jeroboam built shrines at Bethel in the south and Dan in the north, furnishing them with altars and golden calves. It is possible that these altars were intended to encourage Yahweh worship and the calves were symbols, not intended to be seen as idols.

Jeroboam Consecrates Priests (1 Kings 13:1-32). Jeroboam succeeded in driving the people of Israel even further from God. The golden calf was extremely close in appearance to the bull image found in the Canaanite worship of Baal. Baal, the leading Canaanite god, was the deity of storm and fertility; his rain fell on the fields and made them fertile. This cult posed the greatest challenge to the Israelites. Since the bull is a symbol of strength and virility, its imagery was also applied to Yahweh in several biblical passages (cf. Gen 49:24; Ps 132:2, 5; Is 49:26; 60:16). Biblical passages instruct Israel to divorce itself from the adverse influences of calf/bull worship, since it was the leading cause of the Israelites' unfaithfulness to Yahweh (Ex 32:2-6, 19-20; 1 Kings 12:28-31; Hos 13:1-3). Numerous calf and bull statues have been discovered during archaeological excavations in Israel at sites such as Ashkelon, the "bull site" in Samaria, Hazor and Ugarit. This worship violates the second commandment forbidding the making an image of anything and venerating it (Ex 20:4).

Jeroboam's Decline (1 Kings 13:33—14:20). The story of the visit of the Judean prophet is enigmatic, but the point is clear. Jeroboam's failure to keep God's law was the source of his, his family's and his people's downfall.

Jeroboam's son became ill, and the king sent his wife to Ahijah the prophet in Shiloh to ascertain the reason. It should be noted that he sent a woman as representative of the king and the kingdom. She clearly had freedom to travel and freedom to consult the prophet. Upon her arrival, Jeroboam's wife discovered that Ahijah had been expecting her, because he had received a message from Yahweh. Once again Jeroboam's conduct was the focus of God's judgment. Despite numerous warnings from God, Jeroboam and Israel continued to worship other gods; they even made Asherah poles. When Jeroboam's wife returned to Tirzah, the boy died. His death is presented positively: as a reward for his faith he was to be buried decently, the only one of Jeroboam's descendants to be properly mourned. Jeroboam reigned for another twenty years, and the events of his reign are detailed in the annals of the kings of Israel.

Rehoboam's Decline (1 Kings 14:21-31). Rehoboam, Solomon's son, was not faithful to Yahweh and continued to lead Judah astray by establishing high places, setting up sacred stones, making Asherah poles and allowing male cultic prostitution. As a result, in Rehoboam's fifth year as king, Pharaoh Shishak of Egypt invaded Judah, raided Jerusalem and carried away the temple treasures, including the gold shields that Solomon had made. Shishak is generally taken to be Sheshonq I (945-924 B.C.) of Dynasty 22, thus providing a nice synchronism with Egyptian chronology.

Israel and Judah

1 Kings 15—16 summarize the character and some of the events of the reigns of the kings of Judah and Israel. 1 Kings 17—19 depart from this summary to discuss the work of Elijah the prophet. 1 Kings 20—25 return to the synopsis of the kings and their actions. The writer(s) of 1 and 2 Kings were mainly concerned with the details of events as they related to Yahweh. Only those events and deeds that pertained to the worship of and obedience to Yahweh were recorded. The reader is invited to learn about all the other events of the kings' reigns in the annals of the kings of Judah or the annals of the kings of Israel. According to these passages (1 Kings 15—16; 20—25), the kings of Israel and Judah were seen as good or bad. This determination rested solely on the religious behavior of a king; either he was faithful and worshiped only Yahweh, or he was unfaithful and worshiped other gods. Table 5 includes the names of the kings of the northern and southern kingdoms, the approximate dates of their reigns, their status as king and their prophets (LaSor). Because of confusion over overlapping reigns (coregencies) and sometimes politicized dating when a king began to seek power rather then when he took over, it is extremely difficult to be precise about dating. We can be broadly accurate, but all dates are to some extent approximations. This explains differences between lists in different commentaries. The dates that are included in the table represent approximations and do not attempt to harmonize all discrepancies.

Difficulties in dating should not detract from the message that Kings delivers. The author(s) and editors were looking back at the history of the Jewish people, trying to interpret what had happened to them and why. They saw the hand of God at work in the miracles that occurred according to the annals. They found God in history and concluded history is a revelation of God, the story of Israel being a sort of (auto)biography of God.

Table 5. Kings of Judah and Israel and Their Prophets

Judah (southern kingdom)			*Israel (northern kingdom)*		
Rehoboam	931-913	bad	Jeroboam I	931-910	bad
Shemaiah			Ahijah the Shilonite		
Abijam	913-910	bad	Nadab	910-909	bad
Asa	910-870	good	Baasha	909-886	bad
Azariah; Hanani			Jehu, son of Hanani		
Jehoshaphat[1]	873-848	good	Elah	886-885	bad
Jehu, son of Hanani; Jahaziel; Eliezer, son of Dodavahu					
Jehoram (A)[1]	853-841	bad	Zimri	885	bad
Elijah					
Ahaziah (A)	841	bad	Tibni	885-880	bad
Athaliah	841-835	bad	Omri	885-874	bad
Joash	835-796	good	Ahab	874-853	bad
Zechariah, son of Jehoiadah; Joel (?)			Elijah, Micaiah		
Amaziah	796-767	good	Ahaziah (B)	853-852	bad
Uzziah			Elijah, Elisha		
(Azariah)[1]	790-740	good	Jehoram (B)	852-841	bad
Isaiah, Micah			Elisha		
Jotham[1]	751-732	good	Jehu	841-814	good
Isaiah, Micah			Elisha		
Ahaz[1]	735-716	bad	Jehoahaz (A)	814-796	bad
Isaiah, Micah			(Elisha)		
Hezekiah[1]	728-687	good (reformer)	Jehoash[1]	798-782	bad
Isaiah, Micah			Elisha		
Manasseh[1]	696-642	bad	Jeroboam II[1]	793-753	bad
			Hosea, Amos, Jonah		
Amon	642-640	bad	Zechariah	753	bad
Josiah	639-609	good (reformer)	Shallum	752	bad
Habakkuk, Huldah, Zephaniah, Jeremiah					
Jehoahaz (B)	609	bad	Menahem	752-742	bad
Jeremiah					
Jehoiakim	608-597	bad	Pekahiah	741-740	bad
Jeremiah; Uriah					
Jehoiachin	597	bad	Pekah[2]	752-732	bad
Jeremiah			Oded		
Zedekiah	596-586	bad	Hoshea	731-722	bad
Jeremiah					
597 B.C., fall of Jerusalem; 586 B.C., destruction of temple in Jerusalem			724/722 B.C., fall of Samaria		

[1]Coregent [2]Rival kingship

Israel had only one king, Jehu, who is given approval by the Judean authors. He reigned for 27 years; nineteen bad kings ruled for a total of 182 years. Seven of these kings (and Jezebel) were assassinated; one committed suicide; one died of battle wounds. Judah had eight good kings and twelve bad kings; the good kings ruled for a total of 224 years, and the bad kings for 121 years. Four of these kings were assassinated; two died of battle wounds; three died in exile. Israel existed 209 years after the death of Solomon; Judah survived 345 years after the death of Solomon. A bad king was one who worshiped Baal, Asherah and other deities, built high places, allowed male cultic prostitution and practiced magic, divination, witchcraft and astrology. Good kings were those who expelled the male prostitutes, removed idols, cut down and burned Asherah poles and eliminated illegitimate high places. Some kings were tepidly good; for example, Jehoshaphat followed in the ways of Yahweh but allowed the people to worship other gods as they pleased. God promised David there would always be an heir from the Davidic dynasty on the throne in Jerusalem. For 1 Kings 15—25, only select kings and their deeds will be considered.

Asa of Judah (1 Kings 15:9-15). Asa is one of the few kings who is described as good (cf. 2 Chron 13:23—16:14). He initiated a large-scale and widespread reform by expelling all male prostitutes and removing all previously built idols; he also removed his (grand)mother Maacah as queen mother, because this position was cultic, and she had made an Asherah image; Asa cut down the Asherah image and burned it. It did not matter that Asa did not remove all of the high places from the land; he had successfully reestablished the worship of Yahweh in Judah. But all was not well in Asa's kingdom, for he was constantly at odds with Baasha of Israel over the border that they shared. Asa enticed Ben-hadad of Damascus to break his alliance with Baasha and realign with him by offering the temple treasury, which he had just replenished. With Ben-hadad's agreement, he attacked Israel, giving Judah the upper hand temporarily.

Omri of Israel (1 Kings 16:21-28). Zimri (885 B.C.) lasted as king only seven days. After another usurper, Tibni, attempted to take the throne, Omri became king in the thirty-first year of Asa's reign and reigned for twelve years (882-871 B.C.), six at Tirza and six at Samaria. Omri was the first ruler to bring stability to the northern kingdom, both domestically and on an international level. Because of this solid structure, the Omrid dynasty would last longer than any other in Israel, a total of thirty-three years. It is assumed Omri was a worshiper of Yahweh because his name could be a shortened form of Omriyahu, which means "Yahweh is my protection." Omri is the first Israelite king to be mentioned on the Moabite stone (the Mesha stele), an inscription of King Mesha of Moab (lines 4-8). He is also mentioned in several Assyrian inscriptions. Omri's origin is mysterious, for neither his parents nor his tribe are mentioned; he suddenly appears as "commander of the army" (1 Kings 16:16). Nevertheless, scholars postulate his origins probably lay in a family who served as foreign mercenaries during David's time and who came to embrace Yahweh. This may be seen in Omri's name and that given to his (grand)daughter Athaliah.

Omri's foreign policy consisted of treaties and diplomacy with Israel's neighbors. He made numerous treaties and sealed them with royal marriages. For example, Omri's son Ahab was married to the Phoenician princess Jezebel. Omri also reduced the longstanding animosity between Israel and Judah by relinquishing some land and sealing the treaty with the marriage of his (grand)daughter Athaliah to prince Joram. Thus Israel was at peace with its neighbors. Omri cultivated and maintained Canaanite religion on the part of the state, making Canaanite religion equal to that of the Israelites. While this achieved stability within certain sectors of society, it created problems in others, for the conservative Yahwists were outraged. This provoked the work of prophets such as Elijah, Elisha and others from this time.

Partway through his reign, Omri decided to move his capital from Tirza to Samaria. Omri purchased the hill of Samaria from Shemer (1 Kings 16:24) for two talents of silver, and he built his new capital there. Archaeological excavations at Samaria have uncovered an upper city or acropolis, the royal quarter and a lower city along the slopes and base of the hill. Around the royal quarter there are two large fortification walls. The inner and earlier wall measures about 587.5 feet or 178 meters east to west and about 293.5 feet or 89 meters north to south. It was about 5.25 feet or 1.6 meters thick and made of fine ashlar masonry fashioned in the header-stretcher style.

Inside the wall, one building is particularly noteworthy. It was located along the southwest wall; consisting of a central courtyard surrounded by rooms, these remains are considered to be part of the palace. A second, outer wall was constructed later. It was considerably larger and stronger than the first, though little of it remains. It was a casemate wall, with rock-cut foundations; only the foundation survives. The casemate wall was 33 feet or 10 meters thick; it consisted of two parallel walls with perpendicular partitions between them. The walls and partitions were made of ashlar blocks and stone, while the hollow spaces were filed with rubble. This made for an extremely strong wall. The contemporary buildings were constructed similarly. Their foundation stones were set into rock-cut trenches, with header-stretcher walls. Built on top of that, the upper courses of the foundations were made of smooth, well-dressed ashlar blocks set without mortar. The superstructures were made of mud brick. This is a building technique that the Israelites learned from the Phoenicians. Finally, numerous ostraca have been discovered at Samaria in the Ostraca House. Sixty-three pottery sherds, written in Hebrew, mostly inscribed with black ink, recorded shipments from surrounding towns as tax payments to the royal house.

Ahab of Israel and Elijah (1 Kings 16:29—2 Kings 1:18)

Ahab of Israel (1 Kings 16:29-34). Ahab (874-853 B.C.), the son of Omri, became king during the thirty-eighth year of Asa's reign as king of Judah. Ahab diligently continued the domestic and foreign policies of Omri. He maintained good relations with his neighbors and continued to balance Canaanite, Israelite and conservative Yahwistic elements of society. Ahab ruled in Samaria for twenty-two years and is described as being even wickeder and more evil than Omri. His wife was Jezebel, the daughter of Ethbaal, king of Sidon; they converted Ahab to Baal worship. He built an altar and temple to Baal in Samaria and made an Asherah pole and worshiped it.

It is important to understand how much power Jezebel had. As a Phoenician princess she would have been high priestess of the chief cult, in this case Baal Melqart, and her father would have been high priest of the cult of Ashtoreth (Astarte). This made an extremely powerful bond between religion and state, as the father and daughter could control the economy, politics and religion. Once she arrived in Israel, Jezebel assumed an equally powerful role in its religion and government. She was an essential pillar of Ahab's reign, an important supporter of the Baal and Asherah cults, and she gained the temporary support of the people of Israel. The relationship between Ahab and Jezebel seems to have been one of mutual respect. Jezebel enjoyed a great deal of flexibility, independence and responsibility in the day-to-day running of the kingdom. She was an active member of the government, functioning as queen and high priestess. She supported 450 prophets of Baal and 400 prophets of Asherah. She had routine access to the king's seal and used it at will. She was seen as the legitimate heir to Ahab's throne. It has been suggested that Ahab was happy to have Jezebel involved in religion and politics in this way, because it strengthened his reign (Yee, 849; Brenner). It would have been to Ahab's advantage to give Jezebel such authority, in order to keep the Canaanite population happy.

Thus the marriage between Ahab and Jezebel was one of equal partners in life, religion, politics and governing. Ahab was supposed to be devoted to Yahweh; instead he allowed his foreign wife to lead him, and ultimately Israel, astray. Jezebel knew she had ultimate power and authority as queen. She manipulated the law in order to acquire Naboth's land. Tempting as it might be, one should never allow the power of one's position to override good sense (cf. 2 Kings 9:14-29).

Elijah (1 Kings 17:1—19:21). Chapters 17—19 are a welcome relief from the narrative of the actions of the kings of Israel and Judah. They provide a foundation for the ministry of Elijah the Tishbite, the great prophet who is introduced in 1 Kings 17. The village of Tishbeh was located in the area of Gilead. Elijah's work as prophet began with Ahab, toward the end of his reign. Elijah is instructed to inform Ahab about a coming drought. After delivering this message Elijah was commanded to go to the brook of Cherith, east of the Jordan River, where his daily nutritional needs would be met by Yahweh. When that brook dried up, Elijah was to go to a village called Zarephath, which was part of Sidon and out of Ahab's jurisdiction; there he was to reside with a widow who would provide for his daily needs.

When Elijah met the widow, she was gathering sticks for a fire upon which to make a meal. The widow expected this to be the last meal she and her son would eat, as her supply of flour and oil had run out; she was convinced starvation and death would soon follow. Elijah commanded her to make the cake anyway, because Yahweh would continue to provide flour, oil, water and everything necessary to survive the drought, until Yahweh sent rain again. Elijah lived with the widow and her son for many days; while he was living with the widow, her son became ill and died. The widow petitioned Elijah, in order to ascertain the reason for God's great anger toward her, such that he would take away her only son. Elijah immediately held the boy and prayed that God would restore his life, which he did. Zarephath was in Sidonian territory, a Phoenician area where Baal was worshiped. Though Baal was seen as responsible for fertility and agricultural prosperity, rain, life and death, for three years Yahweh had caused drought and famine, demonstrating that Yahweh, not Baal, is ultimately in control.

The widow was to learn from her first encounter with Elijah that Yahweh provides these life-giving forces. Yahweh miraculously sustained the widow, her son and Elijah during a drought. The widow should have renounced Baal immediately and pledged loyalty to Yahweh, but she did not. When the widow's son died, he was brought back to life by Yahweh through Elijah. Only after such a dramatic episode could the widow be convinced Yahweh truly is the sovereign God of the universe. Yahweh is the sustainer of life. Just when the widow had lost all hope, Yahweh stepped in and provided for her every need. She had only to trust Yahweh to provide for her and the boy, by faithfully reaching into the jar of flour and the jug of oil to make the bread-cake. Every time she reached for the supplies, she was demonstrating her faith in Yahweh as her provider. God continued to reach out to this woman until she learned that Yahweh was greater than Baal. In Luke 4:26 Jesus affirmed the significance of the widow who, though a foreigner, was considered worthy to serve God through helping Elijah.

Elijah was deemed a criminal and enemy of the state because he prophesied against the royal cult of Baal. He prophesied that death and destruction would come to Ahab, his kingdom and household, should he continue to worship Baal instead of Yahweh. This was perceived as a threat, and Elijah's death was ordered.

1 Kings 18:16-46 narrates the contest between Baal and Yahweh (cf. Ex 7, Moses and Aaron in Pharaoh's court). Elijah challenged the prophets of Baal to a test, to see whose god was more powerful and ultimately in control of the universe. The contest took place on Mount Carmel, where Elijah proclaimed himself to be the last prophet of Yahweh; as such, he alone would compete with and be victorious over the prophets of Baal and Asherah. Elijah spelled out the rules: they would take two oxen, one for Baal and the other for Yahweh, cut them into pieces, and place the pieces on wood, arranged as a hearth; but they were not to set it on fire. Whichever deity could set fire to the wood and animal pieces first was the supreme God.

Elijah encouraged the prophets of Baal to go first. Once the ox had been prepared, they began to call on Baal to send fire, but

Syrian synagogue fresco depicting Elijah on Mount Carmel. (1 Kings 18:19)

there was no answer. Elijah taunted them, encouraging them to yell louder, since perhaps their god did not hear them, or possibly he was sleeping or not there. After an appropriate time had passed, Elijah called all the people of Israel over to his hearth, around which he dug a trench; he prepared the ox and wood and poured four large storage jars of water over the offering and the wood, soaking them three times. The water drenched the offering and the wood and filled the trench. Then Elijah prayed to Yahweh for fire to demonstrate that Yahweh is the God of the universe. Suddenly fire consumed the offering, wood, water, stones and ground. Israel was immediately reminded of Yahweh's greatness. The prophets of Baal were all killed by the astounded people. Even Ahab was convinced.

Upon learning of the fate of her prophets, Jezebel raged against Elijah and threatened his life. Elijah fled to escape her wrath. Arriving in Beersheba, Elijah embarked on a journey into the desert. He was so distraught that he prayed for death. Instead an angel appeared to him, giving him food and drink. Thus strengthened, he traveled for forty days and nights to Horeb, where he found a cave in which to rest.

In spite of Elijah's feelings of despair and aloneness, God still had work for Elijah. Yahweh instructed him to go to Damascus in order to anoint Hazael king of Aram, Jehu king of Israel, and Elisha as prophet. God promised Elijah those who rejected Yahweh and have harassed Elijah would be put to death either by Hazael or Jehu, but the seven thousand people who had been loyal to Yahweh and did not worship Baal would be protected.

When Elijah found Elisha, he was plowing with twelve yoked oxen. Elijah signaled to Elisha that it was time to go; so, after bidding farewell to his parents, he joined Elijah. A prophet's job was not in general a prestigious position. Rather, it was a dangerous and humble assignment. A prophet was a spokesperson for God, an interpreter of God's will, an intermediary between God and the people. Although prophets did speak of the future, their predictions were usually made with respect to a promise of God's reward or punishment for good or bad behavior. When a prophet was commissioned by Yahweh to deliver a message to the people or a king, the communiqué was generally not filled with good news. Prophets frequently conveyed a warning of God's wrath unless the contents of the announcement were obeyed. People did not want to hear this, nor did they want to be told they were worshiping the wrong deity,

Jezebel sealed letters with Ahab's seal not unlike this Hittite king's. (1 Kings 21:8)

especially when their ancestors had been venerating this god for generations. Thus a prophet's message consisted of warnings of destruction and chaos if abhorrent ways were not abandoned. This is the sort of situation in which a king would not hesitate to kill the messenger. Yet, within a message seemingly consisting only of bad news, the way to redemption was always signaled.

Wicked Queens

Among the Bible's most notorious persons are two queens, Jezebel and Athaliah, members of the house of Omri.

Jezebel, daughter of Ethbaal, king of Sidon, wed Ahab, king of Israel, and brought the worship of Baal Melqart to Israel. She persecuted the prophets of God (1 Kings 16:31; 18:4, 13, 19; 2 Kings 3:2, 13; 9:7, 22), swearing that she would kill Elijah. Elijah took her threat seriously and fled (1 Kings 19:1-3).

Upon hearing of her husband's despondency because Naboth refused to sell the king his vineyard, Jezebel conspired to kill Naboth (1 Kings 21:5-16). Elijah rebuked both Ahab and Jezebel for Naboth's murder; he prophesied that dogs would devour Jezebel (1 Kings 21:23). At the order of the new king, Jehu, she was thrown from a window, and horses trampled her body (2 Kings 9:30-37). In the New Testament she becomes the symbol of apostasy and harlotry (Rev 2:20).

Athaliah is alternately called the daughter of Ahab and his granddaughter (2 Kings 8:18; 2 Chron 22:2). If she was the former, then perhaps Jezebel was her mother; certainly she took Jezebel as a model in terms of behavior and religious beliefs. Parallel accounts in 2 Kings 11 and 2 Chronicles 22 tell Athaliah's story. Athaliah married Jehoram, king of Judah. When he died, to "no one's regret," quips the text (2 Chron 21:20), their son Ahaziah assumed the throne. He too fell victim to Jehu's purge of the house of Omri. His death created a political vacuum.

Athaliah assumed the throne by murdering all her relatives. But one escaped, the baby Joash, saved along with his nurse by his aunt, Jehosheba (2 Kings 11:2). Athaliah ruled six years, until Jehoiada, a priest and Jehosheba's husband, organized an elaborate coup complete with military and priestly sympathizers. Jehoiada ordered Athaliah taken from the temple, and she was killed at the Horse Gate (2 Kings 11:16).

ROBIN GALLAHER BRANCH

The prophets' messages were thus paradoxical, including doom and gloom as well as promise and guidance. Elijah had been delivering unpleasant messages and fighting to stay alive for a long time; in essence, he was burned out and needed a break. God provided a colleague who would become areplacement, Elisha. However, before Elisha could take over, he needed some training.

Ahab (1 Kings 22:1—22:28). Ahab hoped to acquire a parcel of land, near his palace in Samaria, from Naboth, a Jezreelite. This land was already in use as a vineyard and had been in Naboth's family for generations. When Ahab offered to purchase it or trade for land of equal fertility, Naboth rejected the offer, stating this land had belonged to his forefathers and could not be given up so easily (1 Kings 21:3). This was Naboth's ancestral property; it was the inheritance of his forefathers. Thus Naboth's refusal was based on his legal rights, as well as religious principles. The phrase "inheritance of my forefathers" may suggest several things. The word *inheritance* (Heb. *nahalah*) can refer to property, portion or inheritance, suggesting God gives or assigns land to Israel, the tribes or individuals. God alone has the authority to bestow or transfer land, because it is an integral part of the covenant bond made with Israel, the tribes and individuals. According to Leviticus 25:23, all land belongs to God, and inhabitants are merely long-term tenants; Yahweh determines who holds the land. This plot had been in Naboth's family for a long time, perhaps since the time of the Israelite occupation. When a family settled and developed a portion of land, their entire life was spent maintaining and cultivating it. But, more importantly, the family burial plot would also have been located there. Therefore it was well within Naboth's rights to refuse to sell this land to anyone, even the king. Behavior such as Naboth's was unacceptable to Jezebel, as a Phoenician; in Phoenicia a subject could not refuse the request of a king in this manner (Brenner, 20-27).

Jezebel intervened, attempting to make things right for Ahab by scheming to kill Naboth. She forged letters from Ahab to the elders, instructing them to set a trap for Naboth. Convinced this was Ahab's wish, they stoned Naboth to death; and Ahab took possession of the vineyard. Jezebel must have received an extensive education as a child, since she was able to write letters, presumably in Phoenician. She apparently knew how to write Hebrew as well, although she may have ordered a scribe to write or translate what she dictated. Nevertheless, she was acutely aware of judicial matters, since she was careful to obtain Naboth's land legally, even if by treachery.

Although these were Jezebel's actions, God intended to punish Ahab and Jezebel equally for their actions by making Ahab's house just like those of Jeroboam and Baasha: there would be no more male heirs, for Ahab was just as guilty of Naboth's death as Jezebel. Moreover, Jezebel would be eaten by dogs in the district of Jezreel (cf. 1 Kings 14:11). This was the prophecy that Elijah delivered to Ahab, as a result not only of his and Jezebel's sins but also for leading Israel astray. In 1 Kings 21:27, Ahab reacts by tearing his clothes, putting on sackcloth, fasting and acting despondently. Yahweh sees Ahab's remorse and explains to Elijah that because Ahab humbled himself, evil will not afflict Ahab while he is alive; rather, it will fall on his son's house. However, since Jezebel seems to have remained as intransigent as ever, a special punishment is reserved for her (cf. 2 Kings 9:30).

Micaiah is an excellent example of facing a difficult situation with strength, dignity and courage. He knew the message he was to deliver would not be to the king's liking. Yet he delivered it anyway. Jehoshaphat had an open mind with respect to the information that he set about gathering; Ahab had already made up his mind to go to war. Jehoshaphat's open mind allowed him to make the right decision and listen to the warning that Micaiah delivered.

Ahaziah of Israel (2 Kings 1:1-18)

Moab rebelled against Israel and Ahaziah (853-852 B.C.). The injured king, Ahaziah, instructed his prophets to seek a prediction of recovery from Baal-zebub, the god of Ekron. Tell Miqne-Ekron is an important site, as it was one of the five cities of the Philistine confederation. This site was excavated from 1981 to 1996 (Dothan and Gitin; Gitin). An inscribed limestone slab, found in the final season, positively identified Tel Miqne as Ekron. Yahweh sent Elijah to intercept Ahaziah's prophets in Samaria and ascertain the reason for consulting a false god and to inform them that the king would die. The fire that consumed Ahaziah's subsequent messages is a potent symbol, used throughout the Elijah/Elisha cycles to indicate the power of the Spirit of God. Since Ahaziah did not have a male heir to replace him, Jehoram (852-841 B.C.) became king of Israel in the second year of Jehoram's (853-841 B.C.) coregency with his father, Jehoshaphat, king of Judah (two different men, both named Jehoram).

Elisha (2 Kings 2:1—10:36)

Elijah Goes to Heaven; Elisha Installed (2 Kings 2:1-25)

It was no secret to Elijah, Elisha and all the prophets of Yahweh that Elijah would be miraculously taken up into heaven. Elijah asked Elisha what gift he could bequeath to him. Elisha's answer was unexpected; he asked for a double portion of Elijah's spirit. This was unusual because Elisha was not Elijah's son but rather his attendant. Usually the rightful heir (generally the eldest son) would receive a double portion of the estate. The other siblings would inherit a single portion. But Elisha had been a loyal underling and perhaps as close to Elijah as an eldest son would be. Normally an heir would ask for property, goods or cash. However, in this case Elisha requested a portion of Elijah's spirit, either because Elijah did not have any material goods or more likely because Elisha was to be Elijah's spiritual heir, having been appointed to succeed Elijah as prophet. When Elijah was eventually taken up to heaven, Elisha received a double portion of Elijah's spirit.

Yahweh's and Elijah's spirits settled on Elisha, making him a particularly powerful prophet. Elisha was empowered and transformed into a state of being that was similar to Elijah's. Elijah therefore had one portion of divinity (Yahweh's Spirit), while Elisha had two, Yahweh's and Elijah's spirits: double the power, twice the intensity. This was demonstrated symbolically when Elisha removed and tore his garment, not only to mourn the passing of his mentor but also to show that he had shed his old being. He had inherited the prophetic spirit of Elijah, symbolized by donning his master's mantle.

Because of his prophetic work and assumption, Elijah is a significant figure in Jewish and Christian traditions, in present and eschatological contexts alike. According to Jewish tradition, Elijah is the protector of every Jew, adult and child. Traditionally he protects the boy from harm during circumcision, where a chair is set aside to symbolize Elijah's presence. Even though Elijah resides in heaven, he is seen as a frequent visitor to earth, performing miracles and spreading good will among humankind. He is also viewed as intimately involved in the fate of Israel. Elijah is perhaps best known for his role in the Passover. During the ceremonial meal, four cups of wine are poured and drunk. The fourth and final cup, drunk at the close of the banquet, is called the cup of Elijah, symbolizing hope and expectation. It is thought that Elijah will return in order to restore the people of Israel and deliver them to God. At this time the family will be restored, the hearts of sons will turn to their fathers as the fathers turn to their sons (Mal 3:24); neighbors will be at peace, wars will end, arguments and disagreements between individuals will cease, and there will be a time of great peace. Elijah will also act as a bridge between God and humankind, a sort of messenger from God. Furthermore, Elijah will be a herald for the Messiah.

Elijah's responsibilities concerning the coming of the Messiah and the day of the Lord are vast. His special status is due to the way in which he was raised into heaven. He has been elevated and exalted, almost to the point of messiahship, because he was taken up into heaven without having died. He is assumed to have a special body and being, which allows him to travel between heaven and earth, endowing him with the highest powers of angelhood.

Elijah's main task as herald is seen as twofold: to announce or introduce the Messiah to the world and to be involved in the plan of salvation. Just as the Messiah is about to arrive, Elijah will cause Israel to repent, solve all legal battles from time immemorial and settle all cultic questions and differences of opinion. Jewish belief in an end time is important, for it is during this time that the Jews will be restored as a nation and will enjoy political ascendancy as they had prior to the diaspora.

In Christian tradition, Elijah's role raises more questions than it answers. For example, some equate Elijah with John the Baptist, since he was the forerunner of Jesus the Christ (i.e., the Messiah). John 1:21 denies that John the Baptist is Elijah, but it suggests that John the Baptist could have come in the spirit and power of Elijah, in much the same way that Elisha was empowered by Elijah (Lk 3:2). Prior to John the Baptist, there had been no prophetic activity for two to four hundred years. When John the Baptist emerged from the wilderness dressed in clothing much like that of the prophets of old (especially like Elijah's, 2 Kings 1:8), it is easy to imagine how he might be mistaken for Elijah. Elijah and John went to the wilderness to hear a still small voice, both announced the arrival of the Messiah, both preached repentance; and both were persecuted. There were, however, more differences than similarities. For example, John the Baptist came primarily as a preacher; he was an "inspired rebuker of a country's sins and he bade them prepare for the reception of that country's Lord" (Seiss, 247). John did not restore anything, nor did he fulfill the prophecy found in Malachi 4:4-6. John the Baptist did, however, proclaim the message of Jesus Christ, who came to initiate the first part of redemption. He also came in the spirit and power of Elijah, which means he was like Elijah, though not the same person.

Similarly Elijah and Moses share many characteristics. For example, each had prophetic power and delivered messages that produced harsh outcomes, each spoke the authoritative word of God, both took flight eastward to escape a king's wrath, both parted water (2 Kings 2:13), and both complained of mistreatment as a servant of Yahweh. Furthermore, some interpreters have identified as Moses and Elijah the two witnesses to whom God has given great power (Rev 11:3).

Once Elisha returned and proved he had replaced Elijah, his first task was to purify the water and land that had been made impure. A series of anecdotes about the acts of Elisha is inserted into the document at this point (2 Kings 2:22—9:13).

As Elisha made his way back to Samaria, he experienced humiliation and mocking from the young men of Bethel. He cursed them in the name of God, and two shebears were sent to eat them up. The shebear, who ferociously defends her cubs, is a symbol of the way God protects his children (see also Hos 13:8). This incident is hard for modern readers to comprehend or accept. It seems a gross overreaction on Elisha's part. However, it may be that the mocking of Yahweh's prophet is to be seen as a deliberate rejection of Yahweh's power and authority, a crime that was seen as worthy of the death penalty within Israel.

Moab Revolt (2 Kings 3). Jehoram (852-841 B.C.), the son of Ahab, became king of Israel during the eighteenth year of Jehoshaphat's reign as king of Judah. This passage contains a variant account of the ascendancy of Jehoram to the throne of Israel (1 Kings 1:17-18). Jehoram tore down the sacred stone of Baal that his father had made. But he made his own mistakes, clinging to the ways of Jeroboam and causing Israel to sin with him.

Mesha, king of Moab, raised sheep and paid a substantial tribute to the king of Israel annually: one hundred thousand lambs and ram's wool (cf. 1 Kings 16:21-28). After Ahab died, however, the king of Moab rebelled and stopped sending this payment to Israel. Jehoram contacted Jehoshaphat, king of Judah, told him of the situation and secured his aid in attacking Moab. The Edomite king joined them in the fight as well. They traveled by way of the desert of Edom, and after seven days' march they ran out of water. Jehoshaphat requested a prophet of Yahweh who might help them understand the situation.

Elisha was present and asked Jehoram why he did not contact his own prophets. Jehoram replied that Yahweh brought them to this place, and it should be Yahweh who is petitioned. Through Elisha, God instructed them to dig ditches, which would miraculously fill with water; then Moab would be conquered by the three kings. The water, blood-colored in the light of the morning sun, symbolized death to the Moabites and God-given life to the Israelites. Ultimately Moab was conquered. Mesha's rebellion is celebrated in an inscription of his on a stele (the Moabite Stone) discovered in 1868 in Dhiban and now in the Louvre Museum in Paris.

Human sacrifice (2 Kings 3:27) did sometimes happen in Israel, although it was strongly condemned. There is no mention here of the anguish of the boy's mother or the rest of his family as he is killed in an attempt to influence the course of the battle.

Elisha Stories (2 Kings 4:1—8:15). 2 Kings 4 opens with a miracle. A widow and her two sons were in financial trouble. Her husband had died and left a significant debt, for which ultimately the family was responsible. In the ancient world, when people could not pay their debts, they could sell themselves or their children into slavery for a limited period of time or until the debt was paid. The deceased man's creditors were threatening to take the widow's two sons and indenture them in this way. So the widow sought help from God through Elisha. The prophet instructed the widow and her sons to collect empty storage jars. Then, using the partial jar of oil that she had, they were to fill the empty storage jars. The miracle was that there was only a little oil to begin with, and yet the partial jar of oil filled all the empty jars. They were able to sell the jars of oil and live off the profit. This woman was able to save her sons from slavery by negotiating a business deal that satisfied her dead husband's creditors. This glimpse into the difficulties faced by the poor speaks volumes. Economic and social injustice is not ignored by a just and merciful God who makes special provision for the poor (cf. the story of Elijah and the widow, 1 Kings 17:8-16; *see* Yahweh's Concern for the Disenfranchised; Land Ownership and Economic Justice in Israel).

Elisha befriended a couple living in Shunem. They liked him and recognized he was a holy man; they made a room for him in their house, so he could stay there whenever he was in town. The wife and husband cooperate in hospitality; she envisages, he supplies. Elisha was grateful and wanted to do something nice for them. Since the woman was content with her life, Elisha resolved that because they had no children and her husband was old, she should have a son. He announced she would have a son by the same time next year; the Shunammite woman became pregnant and had a son.

But one day the boy became ill and died. The woman was distraught; she laid the boy on the bed in Elisha's room and sought out the prophet. Her expectation was that only Yahweh, through his prophet, could help. Just as Elijah had done (1 Kings 17:17-24), Elisha was able to bring the boy back to life. Life in the ancient world was hard and sometimes dangerous. It was important that men and woman were not left alone in the world. Domestic life required a great deal of hard work, between household chores and the field. One person could not do it alone; therefore tasks were divided among family members.

It is likely there was an age difference between the woman and her husband, so his death would most likely occur before hers. Should the Shunammite woman have become widowed, without a son, she would have had to bear all these responsibilities (assuming there were no *go'el* ["redeemer"] or *levir* ["husband's brother"]). A brother-in-law is not mentioned; if there had been a brother-in-law, he would have been required by levirite law to marry his brother's widow. If there were a son, the boy would inherit all his father's possessions and be responsible for the well-being of his mother. This is why Elisha felt it was so important for this woman to have a son.

Throughout this passage, the focus is on the woman rather than her husband. She is the initiator. This may be an indication that he is elderly—although still fit enough to work in the fields—or it may imply that a greater faith was found in her.

In one of two catering incidents, an outbreak of food poisoning is contained. Whether Elisha's ability to combat the effects of the poisonous stew is a sign of miraculous power or a greater knowledge of the property of foods is not clear. In the second incident, a man from Baal-shalishah brought Elisha twenty loaves of barley bread baked from the first ripe grain and some new grain. Elisha instructed the man to give it to the people to eat. The man was perplexed because there were one hundred people, and twenty loaves would not feed that many. Elisha replied by saying that God would provide enough for all, with some leftovers. The multiplication and provision of food is a favorite biblical theme (cf. Mk 8:1-21; Jn 2:1-11). Normally catering is seen as the province of women, and concern for the provision of food affirms the significance of that role.

Naaman was a powerful commander in the army of the king of Aram, who was greatly respected because, through him, the Lord gave victory to Aram over Israel. He was a brave soldier, but he had leprosy. The army of Aram had taken an Israelite girl captive, and she became a servant to Naaman's wife. With a remarkable display of initiative for a slave girl, she suggested that Naaman go to see Elisha in Samaria. Naaman discussed it with the king, who supported this idea and wrote a letter introducing him to Elisha. Naaman also took silver, gold and clothes as offerings. This letter was meant to be a document explaining why a foreign high commander was traveling in Israel, so that the king of Israel would not feel threatened.

Elisha gave instructions to Naaman that would lead to curing the leprosy. However, Naaman hesitated, expecting more than merely to be sent to the Jordan River for cleansing. Fortunately his servants convinced him to follow these instructions, and he was healed, recognizing that God had restored him. It was important for Naaman to follow God's instructions, through Elisha, in order to show faith and obedience. In addition, this celebrated military commander was healed in a humble manner, without pomp and circumstance, which was important not only for his physical recovery but his spiritual healing as well.

Naaman expected the prophet to stand, call loudly on the name of the Lord and wave his arms around to effect a miraculous recovery. Instead Naaman was sent to the river, where he was to dip seven times. In this way neither Naaman's nor Elisha's actions could be seen as greater than God's. Naaman could conclude without a doubt it was God who cured him, not Elisha. Naaman attempted to pay Elisha for what he had done, but the prophet would not accept the gifts. This is because, as a true prophet, he was not in the business to become rich, as many false prophets were. Rather, his daily and long-term needs were provided by God, not through riches that were brought to him in return for a prophetic word. Naaman vowed never again to worship deities other than Yahweh. Coming from Aram, he assumed that the power of the Israelite God was local—hence the request to take soil back home with him. Jesus uses the story of Naaman to indicate that salvation was not to be restricted to the Jews (Lk 4:27).

Gehazi, Elisha's servant, thought Elisha should have accepted Naaman's treasures. Gehazi ran after Naaman and his entourage with a false message. Naaman was only too happy to give these things to Gehazi; he doubled the amount of money and clothes, even sending two servants along to carry all these items. Gehazi hid everything in his house and returned to Elisha. When confronted, Gehazi lied, but his evasion was fruitless. Having lived with Elisha, Gehazi should have known better, but he was consumed by greed. For this, Gehazi and all his descendants would be cursed with leprosy forever. The misrepresentation of Yahweh has always been seen as serious offense, particularly for those involved in his service.

The incident with the ax head is a further example of Elisha apparently being given miraculous powers to meet the needs of the people.

Once again Aram and Israel were at war with one another. Through Elisha, God had been advising the king of Israel about the military plans of the Arameans, so that Israel could be prepared. When the king of Aram heard this, he became angry and ordered the capture of Elisha, assuming it would be to the Arameans' advantage to eliminate the king's advisor.

Ben-Hadad, king of Aram, besieged Samaria. The siege lasted so long there was great famine in the city; people turned to cannibalism. The king of Israel thought Elisha had caused the problem, somehow influencing God; he did not understand that Elisha was God's messenger.

The Aramean army had abandoned camp because, miraculously, they heard a huge army of Hittites and Egyptians coming toward them. The phrase "the kings of the Hittites and the kings of Egypt" (2 Kings 7:6) is a puzzling one. Most scholars speculate that the word *Miṣrayim,* which usually means Egypt, in this case refers to an area called Musri in northern Syria near Cilicia (Que) and is an anachronism in the text (Cogan & Tadmor 1988, 82-83). In addition, these are not the Bronze Age Hittites of central Anatolia; rather, they represent the Iron Age Neo-Hittite kingdoms of Syria. The city of Samaria was restored, as predicted, with commodities and resources from the plundered Aramean camp. The battle, famine, cannibalism and high prices for food were past. Such deliverance appeared impossible, but God works in unexpected ways. This passage brings to mind the angel's challenge that remains a challenge to believers today: "Is anything too wonderful for the LORD?" (Gen 18:14).

2 Kings 8:1-6 is the sequel to the earlier story of the Shunammite woman (2 Kings 4:8-37). Based on Elisha's warning of famine, the Shunammite woman took her family and moved into the land of the Philistines; once the famine had ended, she returned to Israel and attempted to reclaim her house and land. When she had abandoned her house and land, it was taken over by new occupants, which was legal in the ancient world. But since Elisha the prophet had instructed her to do this, the situation was a bit different; the land and house should be returned to the Shunammite family. This is another case in which a woman, showing a great deal of initiative, represented herself, her husband and son before the king (cf. 1 Kings 3:16-28). The king recognized her legal right to the land, house and possessions and dispatched a guard to ensure its rightful return. The family returned after seven years, so it may have been that this was a Jubilee year, when all debt was forgiven and loaned property was returned to its rightful owner. However, the image of the seven lean years is another biblical motif.

2 Kings 8:7-29 recounts the fate of Ben-Hadad, king of Aram, and Hazael his son, and the future of Aram's relationship with Israel and Judah; the reigns of Jehoram (853-841 B.C.), son of Jehoshaphat, king of Judah; Ahaziah (841 B.C.), king of Judah; and Jehoram (852-841 B.C.), son of Ahab, king of Israel.

Jehu's Reform (2 Kings 9:1—10:36)

When Elisha heard that Jehoram of Israel had been injured, he sent a junior prophet to Ramoth-gilead with a flask of oil, in order to find Jehu (841-814 B.C.), son of Jehoshaphat (not the king of Judah), son of Nimshi, in order to anoint him and proclaim him king of Israel. This was done in private, but when the officers learned of this they immediately blew trumpets and proclaimed Jehu king of Israel. Harking back to the time when kingship was a divinely chosen office, rather than being based on hereditary succession, Yahweh reached outside the royal family of Israel and chose Jehu as leader, in order to cleanse the nation of the idolatry that had been practiced there for so long. Elisha combined a prophetic role, fulfilling the command given to Elijah in 1 Kings 19:16, with a political role, inaugurating Jehu's rebellion.

Jehu Kills Ahaziah (2 Kings 9:14-29)

While Joram (Jehoram of Israel) was recovering in Jezreel from wounds suffered in the battle against Aram, Ahaziah visited him. Jehu's company approached the gate of Jezreel, and the gatekeeper asked whether they came in peace; Jehu questioned how peace could exist as long as idolatry and witchcraft, brought by Jezebel, were still flourishing. Jehu killed Jehoram of Israel and Ahaziah of Judah. If Israel was in any sense to be God's people, then justice was vital. Crimes like the confiscation of Naboth's vineyard had to be stopped.

Jehu Kills Jezebel (2 Kings 9:30-37)

Then Jehu proceeded to his encounter with Jezebel. When he arrived, she was looking out a window, perhaps hoping to seduce Jehu with her painted face. Although Jezebel's husband, Ahab, had long since died, she continued to be a commanding presence in the land. As mentioned earlier (1 Kings 16:29-34), Jezebel was well-educated, a powerful leader politically and religiously, and she was well supported by the people, at least in the beginning. However, as with many of the kings, her actions were intolerable; and it was clear the tide was turning in favor of Jehu's rule over Israel. Thus, when Jehu ordered three eunuchs to throw her down to the ground, they complied. She died under the trampling of horses' feet. Jehu ordered her body to be buried, since she was a king's daughter and had been ruling almost like a king. But when they went to fetch her body, only the head was left; it had been prophesied that when Jezebel died, the dogs of the city would eat her body, save for the head, which would be unrecognizable (1 Kings 21:22). Jezebel suffered a death that was commensurate with her great disobedience to Yahweh. Although Jezebel had effectively ruled a part of Israel for a short time, she is not recognized as such in the king lists. Her official standing would have been that of queen mother, upon the accession of her son, Ahaziah. Her omission from the king lists may well be due to the fact that she was regarded as a foreign usurper on the throne.

Though often secluded at home, women might observe much through a window. (2 Kings 9:30)

Jezebel serves as an excellent example of a woman serving in the highest position possible. She was educated and cunning and demanded and obtained the respect of the military, religious leaders and most of the people. She was, for the most part, a great leader. Her shortcoming was her unwillingness to worship only God, maintaining the Baal and Asherah cults. Because of these unacceptable traits she was condemned to death, denied a traditional burial and her memory defiled. Jezebel serves as a positive and negative example to women in leadership positions.

Ahab's Family Killed (2 Kings 10:1-7)

Jehu killed the surviving male members of Ahab's family, as Yahweh had instructed. It was standard practice to rid the land of all surviving members of a rival royal family, so that they did not conspire against the new king. 2 Kings makes no comment and raises no criticism about the extent of the violence used by Jehu, but Hosea 1:4 gives a strong indication that Jehu exceeded his brief.

Priests and Prophets of Baal Killed (2 Kings 10:18-36)

Jehu, through deception, gathered the prophets of Baal from all over the land. He lured them into the great temple of Baal and killed them. He destroyed the sacred pillar of Baal with fire and tore down the temple, thus effectively destroying Baal worship in Israel. He did not, however, stop the worship of golden calves at Dan and Bethel. Jehu's reward for carrying out God's orders would be to have a descendant on the throne of Judah for four generations. From this time the population and territory of Israel began to decline.

Hazael of Aram took the territory east

of the Jordan and retained it. Jehu ruled for twenty-eight years; when he died, he was buried in Samaria.

Athaliah of Judah (2 Kings 11:1-20)

When Athaliah (841-835 B.C.), widow of Jehoram, king of Judah, saw that her son, Ahaziah, was dead, she tried to destroy the rest of the royal family of Judah. However, Jehosheba, a daughter of king Jehoram and sister of Ahaziah, removed and hid Joash, son of Ahaziah, so he would not be killed along with the other royal princes. As elsewhere, women are seen as acting in evil and good, destructive and creative ways. Joash remained hidden in the temple of Yahweh for six years while Athaliah ruled. Jehosheba may well have saved the Davidic line from extinction. The name Athaliah means "Yahweh has manifested his glory" or "Yahweh is just." In 2 Kings 8:26 she is called the granddaughter of Omri king of Israel (cf. 2 Chron 22:2), and in 2 Kings 8:18 she is called the daughter of Ahab (cf. 2 Chron 21:6).

Athaliah was educated by Jezebel and thus exposed to the Sidonian princess's influence, political and religious. She appears to have inherited her mother's cruelty and desire for power. It is clear she was a member of the royal houses of Israel by birth and Judah by marriage. Her marriage had evidently been arranged to improve diplomatic ties between the two kingdoms. Athaliah was given in marriage to the Judean crown prince Jehoram as part of a peace settlement. This put an end to hostilities that had existed between Israel and Judah since the death of Solomon, although this new treaty did not remain in effect very long.

Nevertheless, Athaliah gained an extremely high rank, that of wife of the king, with the related responsibilities. Once her son, Ahaziah, became king of Judah, Athaliah apparently obtained another powerful position, queen mother and confidant to the new king (cf. 2 Chron 22:3). When Ahaziah died, Athaliah took on the duties of ruler and nearly wiped out the house of David, save for Joash, in order to secure her position. She ruled as an absolute monarch, attempting to apply Omridic political principles (cf. 1 Kings 16:21-28), building a great temple to Baal and extending certain rights and privileges to the cult as an accommodation to the Canaanite population. Much of the population supported her, but the priests of Yahweh, some of the military and Judeans of full citizenship did not. They conspired to have her removed. As ruler of Judah, Athaliah would have had to perform certain ceremonial rites at the temple in Jerusalem.

The king played an important role in the state religion, especially at the temple. So Athaliah almost certainly participated in sacrifices, rituals and ceremonies in her capacity as the representative of God on earth, the basis for her divine right to rule. In fact, Athaliah was comfortable in the temples of Yahweh and of Baal. She wielded considerable power religiously and militarily. Despite efforts to have her removed, Athaliah's cunning, political organization and strength allowed her to rule for seven years. She was the only female king mentioned in Judah or in Israel. It is disappointing, however, that she could not have been a better religious leader, for which she was to suffer the consequences.

In Athaliah's seventh year, Jehoiada the priest, husband of Jehosheba, summoned the commanders of the Carites (a special detachment of foreigners) and the guards. He brought them to the temple, revealed Joash and commissioned them to protect him at all costs. The boy was recognized as chosen by Yahweh to be king, and they gave him the swords and shields that once belonged to David. When the guards were in place, Jehoiada conducted the coronation ceremony, giving Joash the crown and a copy of the covenant; then the guards and the people proclaimed him king. When Athaliah heard the noise, she shouted "Treason! Treason!" a somewhat ironic statement, since Athaliah was a usurper. Fittingly, she was put to death outside the area of the temple of Yahweh.

Thereupon, indicating a new start for the people as well as a new king, Jehoiada the priest, Joash the king and the people all promised loyalty to Yahweh and to worship only him. They went to the temple of Baal that Athaliah had built and tore it down, smashing the altars and idols and killing Mattan, the priest of Baal. Then the Carites, the guards, Jehoiada and the people marched from the temple of

Yahweh to the palace where Joash had taken the throne; he was only seven years old. Everyone rejoiced: Athaliah had been slain, Baal had been abolished, and all was peaceful.

Jehoash (Joash) of Judah (2 Kings 11:21—12:21)

2 Kings 12—15 describes eight of the remaining kings of Israel except for the last one, Hoshea (731-722 B.C.), as well as the kings of Judah who ruled to the beginning of Hoshea's reign. Like a number of his predecessors, Joash began well, instituting repairs to the temple. Care for God's house was often seen as a significant sign of recommitment to Yahweh.

In 2 Kings 14, Jeroboam II comes to power in Israel, and in 2 Kings 15 Azariah (also known as Uzziah) begins his equally long reign in Judah. These reigns, coming at a time when world powers like Assyria and Egypt were less interested in this region, brought a great deal of prosperity to both nations. Amos and Hosea in the north and Micah and Isaiah in the south describe the prosperity and the corruption, oppression and injustice that were brought in with the prosperity. Women were involved as oppressed (Amos 1:13; 2:7) and as oppressors (Amos 4).

Ahaz of Judah (2 Kings 16)

With 2 Kings 16, the sins of Judah intensify. Ahaz (735-716 B.C.) became king (overlapping Jotham's reign) when he was twenty years old; he reigned for sixteen years in Jerusalem. He worshiped pagan deities similar to those that had been worshiped by Israel and the peoples who occu-

---

Infanticide

Infanticide is a parent's intentional decision to kill a child or to place an infant in a circumstance that will culminate in death. A related practice is abandonment, or leaving an infant to die or to be found and sustained by a stranger.

Extant primary sources from Greco-Roman, Jewish and early Christian authors refer to both practices. Hundred of sources, ranging from legal documents to personal letters, show that infanticide existed in many ancient cultures. Egyptians were generally known for rejecting infanticide (Diodorus Siculus 1.80.3; Strabo *Geography* 17.2.5) and for rescuing exposed infants.

Of note is the select infanticide of females (see, e.g., Apuleius *Metamorphoses* 10.23; Ovid *Metamorphoses* 9.666-84, 704-13). Demographic statistics often reflect a proportionately larger number of males than females (e.g., Dio *Roman History* 54.16.2). Studies pertaining to negative attitudes toward women in the ancient world suggest that selective female infanticide was not only possible but also probable. Primary evidence does not, however, speak unequivocally, and care should be taken when evaluating extant evidence.

Biblical data provide little insight into the extent of these practices in ancient Israel and the early church. The Old Testament disparagingly refers to the sacrifice of children to gods (e.g., Deut 12:31; Lev 20:2-5; 2 Kings 16:3; 17:31; 23:10; 2 Chron 28:3: 33:6; Jer 19:5; Wis 12:5-6). Two incidents recorded in Israelite history—Jephthah's killing of his only daughter as fulfillment of a vow made to God (Judg 11:30-40) and Abraham's willingness to sacrifice Isaac in response to God's demand (Gen 22)—stand as unique incidents. Their significance is more closely linked with Israelite faith history than with any conclusions that might be drawn concerning abandonment and infanticide. The New Testament documents provide even less explicit material, although the

Gospel tradition consistently affirms the value of children (e.g., Mk 10:15-16; Lk 18:17).

Contemporary with the New Testament are the works of a first-century Jewish historian, Josephus, who speaks against infanticide (Josephus *Against Apion* 2.24). A Hellenistic Jewish philosopher, Philo, also appeals to the law, concluding that infanticide is murder (Philo *On the Special Laws* 3.110-19). These texts undoubtedly reflect the broader Jewish attitude (Philo *On the Virtues* 131-33; also see Diodorus Siculus 40.3.8; Tacitus *Historiae* 5.5).

From the writings of Clement of Alexandria and Justin Martyr (see Boswell, 138-79) it can be inferred that some people within the church abandoned infants, even though official church teachings consistently rejected the practice and spoke harshly about infanticide (e.g., Basil *Letter* 199.33; Lactantius *Divine Institutes* 6.20.18ff; Tertullian *Ad Nationes* 1.5, 16; *Apologeticus* 9.1-8). In the fourth century the Christian church denounced infanticide (Gardner, 6).

Bibliography

J. Boswell, *The Kindness of Strangers* (New York: Pantheon, 1988); P. A. Brunt, *Italian Manpower 225 B.C.-A.D. 14* (Oxford: Clarendon, 1971); J. F. Gardner, *Women in Roman Law and Society* (Bloomington: Indiana University Press, 1986); M. Golden, "Demography and the Exposure of Girls at Athens," *Phoenix* 35/4 (1981) 316-31; B. Rawson, ed., *The Family in Ancient Rome* (Ithaca, NY: Cornell University Press, 1986).

J. J. JOHNSON-LEESE

pied the land before the coming of the Israelites. When Israel and Aram waged war against Judah in the reign of Pekah (752-732 B.C.), Ahaz sent a message to Tiglath-pileser III (745-727 B.C.), king of Assyria, asking for his help against these combined forces. This was a grave error on Ahaz's part, for he should have put his trust in Yahweh for the safety of his realm. Moreover, Ahaz built an altar, similar to the one he had seen when he met Tiglath-pileser in Damascus; he placed it inside the temple and instructed Uriah the high priest to use it. He also dismantled and removed many of the temple furnishings. He did these things to make the king of Assyria feel more at home. Ahaz was venerating the king of Assyria the way he should have been revering Yahweh. When Ahaz died, his son Hezekiah succeeded him.

In 2 Kings 16, Judah becomes a vassal state, and Israel continues its inevitable slide toward destruction and exile. The prosperity under Jeroboam and Azariah was shown to be no more than a mirage.

Hoshea of Israel (2 Kings 17:1-6)

Since the time of Pekah (752-732 B.C.), the northern half of the kingdom of Israel had been annexed by Tiglath-pileser III and Hoshea was made puppet king of Israel in the twelfth year of Ahaz, king of Judah. The servant of Assyria, Hoshea reigned for nine years; he was to be the last king of Israel. Shalmaneser V (727-722 B.C.), Tiglath-pileser's son and successor, discovered that Hoshea had contacted So, king of Egypt, and began paying tribute to the Egyptians instead of to Shalmaneser. There is at this stage no way of identifying So.

Hoshea was thus arrested and put in jail. Shalmaneser invaded Samaria. In the ninth year of Hoshea (c. 724/722 B.C.), after a three-year siege, Samaria fell, and its population was deported. The Israelites were relocated to Assyria; they were settled in Halah in Gozan on the Khabur River and in the territory of the Medes. Deportation was a common practice among the Assyrians.

Fall of the Northern Kingdom to Assyria (2 Kings 17:7-41)

The deportation was due to Israel's having worshiped gods other than Yahweh and following the abhorrent practices that their kings had introduced. They had established sacred stones, set up Asherah poles, worshiped other gods at high places and generally provoked the Lord to anger. Time and time again they were warned not to follow these evil ways, but they would not listen. They rejected God, his commandments and the covenant he had made with them. Even after the fall of Israel, the kings of Judah generally persisted in their evil practices.

Possession of Israel was given to peoples from other parts of the Assyrian Empire who were resettled in Samaria. It was thought that a number of disasters happened because they did not worship the local god. So a priest from Israel was sent back to Samaria to teach the immigrants the ways of Yahweh. They did learn to worship Yahweh, but they also worshiped their native gods, and their descendants were never seen as part of God's covenant people.

Elamite prisoners led into exile by an Assyrian soldier. (2 Kings 17:6)

Judah and Assyria (2 Kings 18:1—21-26)

Hezekiah of Judah (2 Kings 18:1-16)

Hezekiah (728-687 B.C.) became king of Judah and reigned in Jerusalem for twenty-nine years. He was considered a great king because he genuinely sought to serve Yahweh, and he rid the land of Baal and Asherah. He defeated the Philistines and defended Judah against the Assyrians. The writer, wanting to emphasize Hezekiah's righteousness, tells us that God blessed him in all that he did—perhaps an exaggeration given the extensive defeats that are also described. In Hezekiah's sixth year Samaria was captured. In Hezekiah's fourteenth year, Sennacherib (705-681 B.C.) of Assyria attacked the fortified cities of Judah and captured them. Hezekiah offered to pay tribute to Assyria and become the king's vassal. All the remaining gold and silver from the temple were removed and given to Assyria.

Sennacherib Attacks Jerusalem (2 Kings 18:17—19:37)

Sennacherib sent his officers to deliver a message to Hezekiah: since nobody could save Jerusalem from the Assyrians, not even their God, it would be better to surrender and lead a good life in submission rather than suffering the consequences of futile resistance. They even claimed that God had sent them—the use of religious language to try to manipulate events is nothing new. Discernment was needed then as much as it is today.

Hezekiah was distraught and sent Eliakim to consult with Isaiah. Yahweh promised to deliver Jerusalem from Sennacherib, and Judah was saved yet again.

Hezekiah's Decline (2 Kings 20)

Hezekiah became ill and was at the point of death. But because of his loyalty and his prayer, Yahweh added fifteen years to Hezekiah's life. More important, Judah was saved from Assyria for that length of time.

Hezekiah received a messenger from Merodach-Baladan II, king of Babylon (721-710 B.C.). The Babylonian king had heard of Hezekiah's illness and probably used this as an excuse to discuss an alliance against Assyria. Hezekiah showed the messenger all the riches and other valuable things in his palace. Isaiah's anger with Hezekiah almost certainly stems from the possible alliance. Far from supporting Judah, Babylon eventually destroyed it. Finally, Hezekiah constructed a tunnel to bring water into the city. That tunnel still exists, and people can walk through it.

Manassah of Judah (2 Kings 21:1-18)

Manasseh (696-642 B.C.) reigned for a total of fifty-five years, including twelve years of coregency with Hezekiah. His was the longest reign of any king of Judah or Israel. He rebuilt the high places and worshiped Baal, Asherah and the starry hosts. He practiced child sacrifice, even offering his son; he practiced sorcery and divination and consulted mediums and spirits. He even put an Asherah pole in the temple of the Lord in Jerusalem. From this point on, God condemns Judah to destruction.

Amon of Judah (2 Kings 21:19-26)

Amon (642-640 B.C.) became king at twenty-two and reigned in Jerusalem for two years. He copied Manasseh's style and was assassinated by his officials. Josiah (639-609 B.C.), Amon's son, became king as a result of a popular revolt. He was eight years old when his thirty-one-year reign began. He went back to Hezekiah's method of kingship, setting in place reforms and repairing the temple.

Josiah's Reforms (2 Kings 22:1—23:30)

When, during the temple work, the Book of the Law was found, Josiah was notified. He realized that God must be angry with the people of Judah, since they had not followed these laws for a long time. Josiah sent his senior officials to Huldah the prophet to inquire about the book.

Huldah is a prophet of whom we know very little, yet tradition gives her a position of great importance. She was a the wife of Shallum, the keeper of the wardrobe, and a court or temple prophet. The two southern gates of the temple mount, the Huldah Gates, were named after her. Many think it was odd for Josiah to consult Huldah instead of Jeremiah or Zephaniah. Numerous apologies have been made for this choice, but Jewish tradition has given it importance. Perhaps Huldah possessed greater authority and prominence than originally thought. Huldah delivered the message of God with confidence and obedience. Her message was one of destruction for Jerusalem and a peaceful death for Josiah (2 Kings 23:29-30; 2 Chron 34:38). The prediction of destruction came to pass; however, Josiah died in the battle of Megiddo (2 Kings 23:20-30; 2 Chron 35:20-24), not peacefully, as foreseen by Huldah. To some, this suggests that the report of her predictions was authentic, that her predictions were made prior to these events rather than being attributed to her anachronistically.

Josiah rid Judah of all cult shrines, idols, Asherah poles and prostitutes. He celebrated the Passover (cf. Deut 16:1-8), which had apparently not been celebrated since the days of the judges. He removed the mediums, spiritualists, household gods, idols and everything detestable to Yahweh. He cleansed the temple, clearing out all the illegitimate priests and replacing them with legitimate ones; he also took away all the vessels and idols of Baal, Asherah and other deities. The possibility is raised that with this full covenant renewal, judgment could be averted. But it becomes clear that the people were not as repentant or as committed as Josiah. Never before or after was there a king like Josiah, who turned so fully to Yahweh.

Josiah was killed at Megiddo in a battle between Pharaoh Necho II of Egypt (610-595 B.C.) and Assyria. Josiah had unwisely sought to prevent Egypt from allying itself with Assyria but succeeded only in bringing Judah under Egyptian control.

The Fall of Judah (2 Kings 23:31—25:30)

The last ruling kings of Judah were Jehoahaz (609 B.C.) and Jehoiakim (608-597 B.C., both sons of Josiah), Jehoiachin (597 B.C., Jehoiakim's son) and Zedekiah (596-586 B.C., Jehoiachin's uncle). None of them followed Yahweh as they should have; they were harassed and interfered with by the Egyptians and Babylonians, who were vying for control in this territory. Jehoiachin surrendered to Nebuchadnezzar (605-562 B.C.; or Nebuchadrezzar, Babylonian Nabu-kudurri-usur), king of Babylon, and was taken prisoner. Nebuchadnezzar finally took Jerusalem in 597 B.C., deporting Jehoiachin and his court to Babylon. Nebuchadnezzar installed Zedekiah as the puppet king of Judah. Anti-Babylonian feeling was strong, and at the instigation of Egypt (2 Kings 25:1-26) Zedekiah rebelled against Nebuchadnezzar. In the ninth year of his reign (588 B.C.), Babylon again marched against Jerusalem and besieged it. The city remained under siege for two years before Nebuchadnezzar finally entered the city, destroying the imperial guard, palace, temple and all the houses in Jerusalem. The captured officials were carried off to Babylon, and some were executed there. Those who had been left behind were governed directly by a Babylonian official named Gedaliah. He attempted to convince the remaining Judahites that Babylonian rule would not be so bad, if only they would settle down and respect him. The Judahites responded by assassinating the governor and fleeing to Egypt.

This may be when Jeremiah entered into exile in Egypt. Jehoiachin, who had been taken prisoner and removed to Babylon, was finally released in his thirty-seventh year of exile. Nebuchadnezzar's son, Evil-Merodach (562-560 B.C.; in Babylon his name was Awel-Marduk, "Man of Marduk," Sack) freed him from custody and gave him a position of honor and a seat at his table for the rest of his life. The account of 1 and 2 Kings ends at this point.

The destruction wrought by Nebuchadnezzar II is attested vividly by archaeological excavations at Ashkelon. Ashkelon would have been included in the area described as "all that belonged to the king of Egypt from the Wadi of Egypt to the River Euphrates" (2 Kings 24:7). Ashkelon was located in Philistia, which, along with Judah, was dominated by Egypt during the reigns of Pharaoh Psamtik I (664-610 B.C.) and his son Necho II (610-595 B.C.). Egypt's control reached as far north as Megiddo. Nebuchadnezzar's encounter with the Egyptians began at Carchemish on the Euphrates River. Nebuchadnezzar was victorious; encouraged by this victory, he continued his campaign southward. Nebuchadnezzar was able to take the cities of Syria by surprise, as he attacked during the winter months, the rainy season, when the amount of rainfall is substantial.

In the month of Kislev (November/December) 604 B.C., Ashkelon fell to the Babylonians (Stager; cf. Babylonian Chronicle). This destruction was prophesied by Jeremiah (Jer 25:8-11; 46:2-6). The port city of Ashkelon had been a thriving metropolis, having attested relationships with numerous foreign countries. The archaeological record has preserved the exact moment of that day when Nebuchadnezzar razed the city: smashed pottery, charcoal, vitrified brick, charred wheat and collapsed roofs were evident throughout the city. In one of the shops in the bazaar, a woman, approximately thirty-five years of age, was found sprawled on her back, having attempted unsuccessfully to prevent a large storage jar from hitting her head (Stager 69). No doubt exists as to the nature of this attack: it was swift, brutal and complete.

Conclusions

What does 1 and 2 Kings, a sixth-century B.C. document, have to do with modern people? Several important themes run throughout 1 and 2 Kings: proper and improper cultic activities, righteous kingship, loyalty to Yahweh and consequences of improper, disloyal behavior. Several prophecies specify the ramifications of Israel's and Judah's misbehavior: a divided kingdom due to Solomon's apostasy, the fall and exile of Israel and Judah. In addition, God promised there would always be a descendant of the Davidic dynasty on the throne in Jerusalem. God also spelled out the terms of his contract with David and, ultimately, Israel: follow in the ways of God and you will be blessed; stray from them and you will be cursed. Although these terms sound relatively simple, they proved to be extremely difficult for Israel and Judah to execute; this ultimately destroyed them.

It is necessary to note that the material that the author(s) of Kings included in this narrative is extremely selective. The author(s) cited several extrabiblical annals, now lost, that chronicled the events of each ruler's reign. From this assumed, vast database, only information that pertained to the relationships among the kings of Judah and Israel, the people and God was extracted. In other words, the primary concern of the writer(s) of Kings was to show the loyalty or disloyalty of the kings and the people to God. The book of Kings has a direct point to make, and it makes it against the background of the warning of the evil that kings do (1 Sam 8) made at the time of the establishment of the kingship at the people's request.

Perhaps the most important theme of Kings is loyalty to Yahweh. This meant that Israel and Judah were to worship only Yahweh. Neighboring peoples, such as the Egyptians, Philistines, Phoenicians and Mesopotamians, worshiped numerous deities. When they conquered new territories, they incorporated the local gods into their pantheons as well, so as not to anger the host deity. The most influential pagan gods were the ones that controlled fertility. Since Israel was primarily an agrarian society, fruitful fields and abundant children were of primary concern. One bad year of crops could send a family into debt for a long time. To ensure productive crops, it was customary to worship these popular fertility deities just in case. The priests and prophets of Yahweh attempted to convince people that Yahweh was in control of not only the fertility of crops and families but of the fertility deities as well.

But it was difficult to turn the ancient polytheistic mind to monotheism. Israel and Judah were warned on numerous occasions that their behavior had to change, or they would face the consequences. For them the punishment would be destruction and exile. While this seems to be extremely harsh, it was not until these events occurred that the Jews began to understand what God had been saying to them all along.

The exile was God's punishment for the disobedient Judah and Israel. The land of milk and honey was taken away; this was the price they had to pay for disobedience. God promised David there would always be an heir to the Davidic dynasty on the throne in Jerusalem; and so there was, until the fall of Jerusalem in 597/586 B.C., when the throne of Judah was abolished.

This is why it is so important to link Christ with the house of David: God keeps his promises. It is also important to note that God works with imperfect people; he is forgiving, but his tolerance has limits. Even David, who was considered to be the consummate king, had numerous faults. He sinned, made mistakes and used bad judgment on occasion, but God forgave him and continued to use him for his work. This does not mean that people may go forth and sin boldly (as Luther once said); rather, they may rest in the knowledge that nobody is perfect, and God will work through humankind's imperfections. Even though God held Judah and Israel responsible for their actions by exiling them to Mesopotamia, he was able to use this situation to the advantage of the Jews, as they were brought into a new and better relationship with God by it. Sometimes one has to be banished to the wilderness before hearing that still small voice.

If the exiles learned nothing else, it was that God would go to great lengths to get their attention. While they were in Babylon, they learned God was not restricted to the temple in Jerusalem; he was with them wherever they went and in whatever circumstances they found themselves. Now the Jewish people could have direct contact with God. They could find him anywhere, and the high priest was no longer needed for them to be able to communicate with God. They could approach Yahweh themselves. The lessons the Jews learned while in exile have proven to be valuable lessons and great news for Jews, Christians and Muslims.

The book of Kings also carries good news for women and sheds some light on the significant role of women in the ancient world. Several women played a prominent role in the development of this narrative. Women probably enjoyed a much greater, freer role in ancient Israelite society than many scholars have been willing to admit. It is not surprising to find women of position and influence in the Old Testament. It must be remembered that there is a wealth of ancient literature from Egypt, Mesopotamia, Anatolia and Greece, while there is a dearth from Israel. Either the ancient Israelites did not feel the need to write down all their goings on, or they used perishable materials, or archaeologists have yet to discover that hypothetical but much anticipated extensive archive.

Mainly we have the Bible, which is a selective compilation of information from more ancient primary sources and should not be considered as comprehensively representative of ancient Israelite society. Yet the Bible is careful to include powerful, well-respected, well-educated and intelligent women who helped to shape religious and political history. In the book of Kings, women are shown occupying the same positions as men; this message is conveyed by the writer(s) without shock or disdain, nor is there anticipation of such a reaction from readers. For example, the book of Kings portrays the queen of Sheba and Athaliah as possessing great powers as rulers of their respective lands.

Kings also suggests women and men had equal access to the law. For example, the two prostitutes, one of whose child had died, represented themselves in the high court before Solomon; there were no male intermediaries. Some scholars have suggested that only women who were widowed, divorced or prostitutes had their own legal status. However, that view seems to be negated by the actions of the Shunammite woman, who represented not only herself before the king, but her husband and son as well. It may also be assumed that men and women were subject to equal judgment in decisions, with punishments and rewards commensurate with their deeds and petitions. The two prostitutes and the Shunammite woman had to abide by the king's decision. Jezebel and Athaliah are rulers who commit unforgivable acts in God's estimation: they brought pagan deities into Israel and Judah and encouraged the people to worship them. As is seen over and over again, this is the downfall of numerous male rulers who accordingly were also reprimanded by God. Thus God does not distinguish between male and female when it comes to obedience or disobedience; both receive equal treatment.

Bibliography. A. Brenner, *The Israelite Woman: Social Role and Literary Type in Biblical Narrative* (Sheffield, England: JSOT Press, 1994); T. Dothan and S. Gitin, "Ekron of the Philistines," *Biblical Archaeology Review* 16/1 (1990) 20-25; S. Gitin, "Park 2: Olive Oil Suppliers to the World," *Biblical Archaeology Review* 16/2 (1990) 33-42, 59; M. Haran, "The Disappearance of the Ark," *Israel Exploration Journal* 13 (1963) 46-58; W. S. LaSor, "1 and 2 Kings," in *New Bible Commentary,* ed. D. Guthrie et al. (Grand Rapids, MI: Eerdmans, 1970), 320-68; C. Meyers, "Temple, Jerusalem," *Anchor Bible Dictionary,* ed. D. N. Freedman (New York: Doubleday, 1992) 6:350-69; R. H. Sack, "Evil-Merodach," *Anchor Bible Dictionary* 2:75-76; Y. Shiloh, "Jerusalem," in *The New Encyclopedia of Archaeological Excavations in the Holy Land,* ed. E. Stern (Jerusalem: The Israel Exploration Society, 1993) 2:698-712; L. E. Stager, "The Fury of Babylon: Ashkelon and the Archaeology of Destruction," *Biblical Archaeology Review* 22 (1996) 56-61; P. A. Viviano, "Hulda," *Anchor Bible Dictionary* 3:321.

JILL L. BAKER

1 CHRONICLES

Introduction

The two books of Chronicles (one book in the Hebrew canon) were written after the return from exile in Babylon of the people of Judah, probably about the same time as the books of Ezra and Nehemiah and perhaps by the same writer. This writer is unknown, though traditionally he was thought to have been Ezra, and this may be so. It is possible that these books were written about 400 B.C., though some scholars place them at a later date.

When the exiles returned to Judah from Babylon, they expected great things. The prophecies of Isaiah, Micah and others foretold a glorious future for God's people. However, the reality for the exiles was quite different. Enemies surrounded them, once again they battled with the temptation to intermarry and integrate with other nations, the rebuilding of the temple was forbidden for a long period, and their identity as the people of God was in danger of being lost. Ezra, Nehemiah, Haggai and Zechariah tell the story of their struggles and the way their difficulties were overcome.

It was clear that the exile had created a huge gap between the history of Israel and Judah as recorded in the books of Kings and the present reality. Yet they were the same nation, with the same God; their genealogies went back to the same ancestors.

The Chronicler wrote his history to bridge the gap, to show the continuity of God's plan for his people, and to rekindle their hope and expectation and assurance that God was still among them, still working out his purpose for them. He did this by taking the genealogies they knew so well from the Pentateuch and carrying them forward to his day. His genealogies are selective; he includes, adds or omits names according to what he sees as being important.

He also demonstrates that the kingdom God established under David is ongoing in the nation of Judah after the exile. Israel, the northern kingdom, had rebelled against God and its chosen king (2 Chron 10:19), and its kings are barely mentioned in the Chronicler's writings. However, representatives of the northern tribes still lived among the people of Judah (see 2 Chron 11:16) and were a part of the remnant God had preserved. Their genealogies are also included briefly, and the unity of all Israel under David and Solomon is emphasized.

Since the time of David, the center of the worship of Yahweh had been Jerusalem. And so an important emphasis is the preparation for and building of the temple in Jerusalem and the regulations laid down for the worship of Yahweh.

Another theme of the Chronicler is that God hears and answers prayers when the people of God trust in and obey him. This is illustrated in the lives of the kings but also in the lives of simple people such as Jabez (1 Chron 4:9-10).

The Chronicler's purpose was to restore and build up God's people in a time of uncertainty and disillusionment, and to do this he focused on continuity and commitment: the continuity of God's plan and purpose for the people and the people's commitment to faithful worship of and service to their God, Yahweh.

The Chronicler used genealogical records from Genesis to Joshua and historical records from Samuel to Kings, along with material such as prophecies or official archives and writings (1 Chron 29:29).

Outline

1:1—9:44 Genealogies
10:1—29:30 Israel United Under David
- 10:1-14 Summary of Saul's Reign
- 11:1—12:40 Establishing David's Reign
- 13:1—16:43 The Ark Brought to Jerusalem
- 17:1-27 The Lord Builds a House for David
- 18:1—20:8 Battles
- 21:1-30 The Census
- 22:1-19 Preparations for the Temple
- 23:1—26:32 Preparations for Temple Worship
- 27:1-34 Army and Administration
- 28:1—29:9 Plans and Gifts for the Temple
- 29:10-30 Solomon's Anointing & David's Death

Commentary

Genealogies (1 Chron 1—9)

Adam to Noah's sons (1 Chron 1:1-4) is a selective list of names that establishes the beginning of Judah's history. Japheth and Ham and their descendants are listed in 1 Chronicles 1:5-16, but these are side shoots. Shem's descendants as far as Abraham (1 Chron 1:17-27) are the direct ancestors.

Abraham's sons Ishmael and Isaac are mentioned in 1 Chronicles 1:28, but the descendants of Keturah are another side shoot (1 Chron 1:32-33). In 1 Chronicles 1:32 Keturah is called Abraham's concubine, although in Genesis 25:1 she is said to be his wife. These verses emphasize the importance of the main line of descent over the side shoots. Abraham's son through Sarah, Isaac, carries on the main line. Sarah was as important as Abraham to the plans of God. Even when Abraham was careless of her safety, God protected her (see Gen 12:10-20; 20:1-18; 17:15-16).

Esau (1 Chron 1:35-54) and his descendants are a further side shoot explored before Jacob's sons are named in 1 Chronicles 2:1-2. In 1 Chronicles 2:3-4 the story of Judah's two wives and their children is briefly told (see Gen 38). Judah had three sons by a Canaanite woman, whose name is not given, though her father's is, and two by his daughter-in-law, Tamar.

Tamar, married first to Er and then to Onan, who both died, was not given Shelah as husband as was her right under law. Because of Judah's betrayal, she tricked Judah into intercourse with her, and from this union came Perez and Zerah. Judah's assessment of her was that she had been more in the right than he (Gen 38:26); she had taken her rights under law that he had withheld from her. God expects his people to fulfill their obligations to others. Even though her actions might not fit in with our ideas of right and wrong, God vindicated her, and she became an ancestor of Jesus (Mt 1:3).

Through Perez the line is carried on down to Jesse and his sons (1 Chron 2:5-17). Zeruiah and Abigail, David's sisters, were, it seems from 2 Samuel 17:25, stepsisters, daughters of his mother and a man named Nahash, presumably before her marriage to Jesse. Zeruiah's and Abigail's sons became great warriors and leaders in David's army and rather a handful for him at times (2 Sam 3:39; 19:22-23). Zeruiah, mentioned twenty-six times, must have been a prominent woman. Her husband is never mentioned. David is established in this genealogy as of pure descent through the chosen line.

Other descendants of Perez through Hezron appear in 1 Chronicles 2:18-55. The names of several wives and concubines appear in this list, perhaps for the purpose of identifying different branches of a family or because the women were notable in some way. The daughter of Caleb, Achsah (1 Chron 2:49) is important because her role in the story is told twice (Josh 15:16-19; Judg 1:12-15). The Caleb spoken of here is the son of Hezron, and the Caleb of Joshua/Judges is the son of Jephunneh, mentioned in 1 Chronicles 4:15 with three sons. Perhaps this verse is misplaced from 1 Chronicles 4:15.

Achsah had no hesitation in asking her father for the water that was needed to make her inheritance of land fruitful. We often get the idea that women were subservient and limited to home duties, but throughout the Bible we see women acting with decision and with God's blessing in many other roles besides wife and mother (see, e.g., Sheerah, 1 Chron 7:24). God doesn't push people into molds; humans do.

David's wives and descendants are listed in 1 Chronicles 3:1-24. First we read about his sons and then the line of kings from Solomon to Jehoiachin, who was taken captive into Babylon. Next are seven generations of Jehoiachin's descendants, from the exile and afterwards, presumably up to the time of the writer—the sons of Elioenai. This is the central part of the genealogical record in 1 Chronicles.

One sister, Shelomith, is mentioned. 1 Chronicles 4 goes back to Judah and his descendants. Again, one daughter, Hazzelelponi, is included. These girls were notable for some reason not recorded.

1 Chronicles 4:9-10 is a picture of the Chronicler's belief that God hears and answers the prayers of his people. The name Jabez, given by his mother, sounds like the word for pain, but instead of changing his name in order to change his circumstances, Jabez called out to God for blessing, and his request was granted. Trust in God is better than human strategies.

Notice how various family clans specialized in linen work and pottery (1 Chron 4:21-23; *see* Occupations, Skills and Crafts of Women). This would no doubt include men and women using their God-given skills (see Ex 35:30-35). Uri and Bezalel are mentioned in 1 Chronicles 2:20.

The other sons of Jacob and their descendants are now followed up, including the mention of several women (1 Chron 4:17-19, 27). In 1 Chronicles 4:24-43, Simeon's descendants are given. Their cities were among Judah's, and during the time of Hezekiah they pushed south and east to find places to settle, destroying the previous inhabitants.

Reuben was Jacob's firstborn but lost his birthright when he had intercourse with his father's concubine. In doing this he was laying claim to his inheritance as firstborn, but his father was dishonored by this action, seen as rebellion, and Reuben lost his inheritance. Concubines were often used as pawns in power plays (see 2 Sam 16:21-22).

Settling across the river Jordan, the Reubenites were in a vulnerable position and were among the first to be taken into exile along with Gad and the half-tribe of Manasseh (1 Chron 5:26). Because of this the genealogical record is fragmentary, although full records had once been kept (1 Chron 5:17).

Gad, living in Bashan next to Reuben, had joined them and the men of Manasseh in warfare against Arab tribes. Notice again that God heard and answered their prayers because they trusted in him (1 Chron 5:20) and because they acknowledged that the battle was God's. However, 1 Chronicles 5:23-26 gives the reason for the capture of the half-tribe of Manasseh by Tiglath-pileser (or Tilgath-pilneser) of Assyria: they were unfaithful to God and worshiped idols. The Chronicler always points out that disobedience and unfaithfulness to God results in disaster.

1 Chronicles 6:1-81 deals with the descendants of Levi. Levites were appointed to serve in the temple to assist the priests. Some Levites were musicians, some had other duties, but only Aaron's descendants were priests, presenting offerings on the altar and making atonement for the sins of the people. Their towns and pasturelands are listed.

The descendants of Issachar, Benjamin, Naphtali, Manasseh, Ephraim and Asher are given briefly in 1 Chronicles 7 to round off the genealogies, although Dan and Zebulun are omitted. Wives and sisters are again noted, particularly Sheerah (1 Chron 7:24), who had a talent for city building. Also mentioned are Zelophehad's daughters (1 Chron 7:15), who spoke up for women as inheritors of property (Num 27:1-11; 36:1-12: Josh 17:3-4). Serah from the tribe of Asher is also mentioned in Numbers 26:46. She is obviously a woman of importance, but details are not given.

Throughout the genealogies other women are mentioned. Some of them are from other nations and married into Israel. One of the problems that Ezra and Nehemiah faced was intermarriage of the men of Judah with women from surrounding nations. They dealt with this strongly, sending the women and children away (Ezra 9—10; Neh 13:23-28). The difference was that these women did not worship God, nor did they bring up their children in God's ways. Rather, they led their husbands astray. The Chronicler shows that men and women who turn to God are accepted by God and become his people, whatever their background.

1 Chronicles 9:1 notes that the genealogies of all Israel have been recorded, though not all are included in Chronicles.

In 1 Chronicles 9:2-34, after a brief mention of the cause of the exile—Judah's unfaithfulness—the writer comes back to the situation of his time. The exiles had returned to Judah; some had resettled their properties and towns, while others lived in Jerusalem. Among these were representatives from Judah, Benjamin, Ephraim and Manasseh. Priests, descendants of Aaron, continued the work of the temple worship with the help of the Levites, including the Levite gatekeepers who traced their lineage back to the earliest gatekeepers of the tabernacle (1 Chron 9:20), and to those appointed by David and Samuel (1 Chron 9:22). Various priests and Levites were given special tasks (1 Chron 9:28-32), while musicians were responsible to keep worship of God going day and night. The continuity of the performance of these tasks by men descended from those appointed by God or his representative, the king, was important, demonstrating the continuity of God's presence and the validity of the appointments.

While, generally speaking, only men are mentioned in the genealogies, the work of their wives is implicit, for they care for the children who become the next generation, and without them there would be no next generation. Their work is vital in every age, whether society recognizes it or not, for proper nurture and care of children is central to the well-being of any nation and is highly valued by God, which is why women were excused from compulsory attendance at festivals.

In 1 Chronicles 9:35-44 part of the genealogy of Benjamin from 1 Chronicles 8:29-38 is repeated. This gives the immediate ancestors and descendants of Saul. The writer is about to begin his selective history of Israel, which will encourage his readers to put their trust in God and worship God alone. They already knew the stories, but through the Chronicler they would see them from a different viewpoint as he showed them God at work, dealing with nations and individuals according to their trust in God.

The lessons to be learned are that God will always respond to an obedient, trusting human being. God will always be faithful to his promises; he will always forgive those who repent and turn from their sins (*see* Sin). But sin will bring judgment on those who will not acknowledge or repent of their sins. Because this is his message, the Chronicler deals with his subjects accordingly. Saul did not repent, so judgment fell. David did repent, so his sins need not be dwelt on. Rather, the true desire of his heart, which was to love, serve and obey God, is emphasized. Other kings and individuals either obeyed or disobeyed God, either trusted God or turned to other gods and nations for help, and each reaped the consequences of the choice—reward or judgment.

Israel United Under David (1 Chron 10—29)

Summary of Saul's Reign (1 Chron 10)

The genealogies have emphasized the tribes of Levi, Judah and Benjamin. From Levi come the priests and temple workers, those who are set aside for God's service. From Benjamin comes King Saul, and from Judah comes the enduring kingly line of David. These tribes also form the kingdom of Judah, with the tribe of Simeon and many Levites who moved to Judah after the division of the kingdom (2 Chron 11:14.)

Kings and priests together are representatives of God to the people and of the people to God. The king is God's representative as ruler and shepherd to care for and protect them, to be an example of godly living to them. The priest brings the people to God for forgiveness of sin through the sacrifices and also teaches them the way to worship God and live as God's people. The tribe of Levi was scattered throughout Israel in order to represent the whole nation.

In 1 Chronicles 10 the Chronicler does not dwell on Saul's life but rather begins with the defeat that led to his death. Here the results of disobedience and unfaithfulness are spelled out (1 Chron 10:13-14). Despite Saul's disobedience, he was nevertheless king, and the actions of the citizens of Jabesh-gilead (1 Chron 10:11-12) are included to emphasize their loyalty to him as king and their gratitude to him for rescuing them from the Ammonites (1 Sam 11:1-11).

The Chronicler shows the promises of God flourishing in the ground of obedience and faithfulness, repentance, love, and trust. When Saul failed, God had ready David, son of Jesse, to take over the kingship (1 Chron 10:14).

Establishing David's Kingdom (1 Chron 11—12)

At the time Chronicles was written, David's kingdom was long gone. The glorious days of victory over enemies and supremacy among the nations were only a memory. But other things flourished in David's reign that could and must still flourish in every age, and these things the Chronicler wanted to present to his contemporaries.

David's Anointing (1 Chron 11:1-3). The writer skips over the long years of hiding from Saul and the seven years of David's rule over Judah in Hebron. The account begins as "all Israel" (NIV) joined to make David king as Samuel had promised so long ago (1 Sam 16:1). God's word does come to pass. Samuel and Kings show us that there had been a long training period, but this is not one of Chronicles' themes. The people recognized that David was one of them, that he had led them to victory in the past and that he was God's choice. They accepted the covenant he made with them, and he was anointed as king.

True leadership is not just authority but involves care, commitment, compassion and humility. David had once been the least in his father's family, concerned with the care and protection, nourishment and well-being of his father's sheep. He was raised up by God to a place of power and authority, but his task was still to shepherd God's people (1 Chron 11:2), to see that they were nourished by his word, to care for their spiritual and physical well-being. For this he must humbly rely on God, just as he had done as a shepherd of sheep.

The City of David (1 Chron 11:4-9). The city of Jerusalem is important. It is Zion, the chosen city; there God promised to live among his people and be their God (e.g., Ps 132:13-18). After the exile God had brought the people back to this city, where his worship had again been established. To go back to the city's beginnings was to reiterate its importance. It lay in the midst of the united kingdom of Israel, a central focus. It was also David's city, the historical emblem of a strong center of government and worship. What it once had been it could become again, if the lessons of faithfulness and obedience to God were learned.

Why did David become powerful? Because Yahweh Sabaoth (Yahweh of Hosts) was with him (1 Chron 11:9). In Chronicles we see that true power is always found in God's presence, in living in God's will. Men and women who rely on and are confident in God are truly powerful, even though they may seem weak and insignificant in the world's eyes.

David's Mighty Men (1 Chron 11:10-47). The chief characteristic of these men is their loyalty to King David. They gave him support as his kingdom began to extend (1 Chron 11:10). God had promised this extension of territory, but it was brought into being through faithful, brave, devoted men. David had the vision that God had given him, but these men were God's provision to bring it to fruition. In the New Testament we see how the apostle Paul was encouraged by faithful men and women who prayed for him and worked with him in spreading the gospel of God's kingdom (see, e.g., Rom 16; Phil 2:19-30; 4:2-3).

1 Chronicles 11:15-19 illustrates the lengths to which loyalty would go. To David the water of Bethlehem symbolized freedom to return to his own land as king. To the three mighty men it was a chance to express their loyalty and to show their courage and daring, their willingness to risk their lives for their leader. The water they brought back was poured out as an offering to God because such devotion was a worthy offering. The men had risked their lives to obtain it, making it almost a blood sacrifice; it appears that David felt unworthy of such devotion, which belonged to God alone.

There were degrees of brilliance and greatness of exploits among these men, but each was a "mighty" man. Notice too that not all were Israelites (1 Chron 11:39, 41, 46). People like this were needed in the years after the exile, men and women whose loyalty was to God, who worked for the good of the nation, who were willing to give their lives for God's sake and through whom God could work out his purposes. These were the people the Chronicler was encouraging.

Peace and Success (1 Chron 12). This chapter looks back to David's time in exile. Warriors came to David from Benjamin, Gad, Judah and Manasseh (1 Chron 12:1-23). Some had probably served under him when he was a leader of Saul's army. Perhaps some knew God's promise that he would be king and wanted to be on the winning side. Perhaps they saw in David a quality lacking in Saul. But their coming meant David's success in battle.

Saul's tribe was Benjamin, and the Benjaminites were especially skilled. Saul needed them, but they chose to follow David. David seems to have been wary of them (1 Chron 12:17), but the Spirit clothed Amasai to give a prophetic message of encouragement. They were with him because God was with him. God would give peace ("success") to David and to those who helped him.

So while David was in hiding from Saul, a fact that the writer and readers knew well and that did not need to be reiterated, God was building him up by sending strong supporters. Saul's opposition was powerless against God's provision, which was also an ongoing sign to David that God would fulfill his promises. Likewise, whatever opposition the Chronicler's readers were facing, however strong and invincible it seemed, victory would be theirs if they would trust in God and live in obedience; God's support of them would be powerful and unfailing. God is always working to bring about his purposes. Like these warriors (1 Chron 12:23, 38), God's people need to know his will and be united in determination to see it come to pass, rather than, as is often the case, arguing about unimportant things and hindering God's plans. Unity in every thought is not possible, but unity in purpose and action is.

Feasting and joy followed the recognition of David's kingship by representatives of all Israel at Hebron (1 Chron 12:38-40; see 1 Chron 11:1).

The Ark Brought to Jerusalem (1 Chron 13—16)

The First Attempt (1 Chron 13). In order to bind the tribes of Israel into a united kingdom, there had to be a central focus beyond David. This was the worship of Yahweh, the God who had brought Israel out of Egypt. Loyalty to this God would ensure unity. The ark of the covenant was the place where God had promised to meet with his people (Ex 25:22), and yet it had languished in Kiriath-jearim for many years after being sent back from the Philistines, who had captured it in battle (1 Sam 7:2).

The Philistines had learned that the ark could not be treated lightly, as God's judgment fell on them (1 Sam 5). The Israelites had learned that it was not a magic talisman with which to manipulate God (1 Sam 4) and that its presence could bring both judgment and blessing (1 Sam 6:19—7:1; cf. Mt 10:34-35). They were to learn these lessons again.

Saul had not used the ark to enquire of God during his reign (1 Chron 13:3), but David wanted God to be the true ruler of the people. If God was to be the center of the nation, the ark must be brought to Jerusalem. David's plan met with the approval of military leaders and of all the Israelites (1 Chron 13:6).

The picture in Chronicles is of a celebration in which all Israel, from as far south as the borders of Egypt to the far northern boundary, could participate with joy and excitement. The ark is called by the Name (cf. Deut 12:5), and it must be brought to Jerusalem in a worthy manner. It was placed in a new cart with king and people accompanying it, worshiping with music and singing. The celebration abruptly ended as the oxen stumbled and Uzzah, reaching out to steady the ark, was struck dead. His concern apparently was for the safety of the ark. Perhaps it was his family that had faithfully cared for the ark for many years, so why did God respond so devastatingly (cf. Ex 19:10-23)?

The holiness of God means that his commands cannot be ignored. Numbers 4:5-6, 15, 17-20 clearly states how the ark must be carried and that no one must see or touch it other than those appointed by God to do so. Uzzah was an innocent victim of the carelessness of the leaders of Israel, king and priests, who had not obeyed God's command. We may not understand the stipulations God makes, but we dare not disobey them. Jesus differentiated between what God says and the way human beings interpret or add to what he says (e.g., Mt 12:1-14). God is the one who appoints servants, men and women, and gives them gifts to use in the service he chooses for them.

David's reactions ranged from anger (1 Chron 13:11) to fear (1 Chron 13:12). His anger was because God had arbitrarily upset all his plans and so made him look foolish. There may have been an element of pride in his own faithfulness that caused him to be angry when God apparently rejected his efforts. Perhaps the name Perez-uzzah ("outbreak against Uzzah") hints that he felt God was at fault in this. Then came fear as he realized the obedience and reverence needed before this awesomely holy God and perhaps became aware of his own arrogance and presumption.

The ark was left in the house of Obed-edom. If he is the same man as mentioned in 1 Chronicles 15:18, 21, 24, he was a Levite, although 1 Chronicles 13:14 calls him a Gittite, a man from Gath. Obed-edom and his household experienced God's blessing upon them in every way as they reverently cared for the ark. The lesson is that God's requirements must be obeyed and God's holiness honored. If this is not done, the results of disobedience will follow.

David's Blessings (1 Chron 14; cf. 2 Sam 5). Between the two parts to the story about the return of the ark, the writer shows God blessing David in his family life, in his battles and among the nations, as if to say that God did not abandon him because he made a mistake, for David was truly seeking him, and God sees what is in a person's heart.

In 1 Chronicles 14 we see Hiram, king of Tyre, acknowledging David as king of Israel and as one with whom he wanted to establish good relations. More importantly (1 Chron 14:2), we see that David acknowledged that God had established him as king, not because of who David was but because of God's love for and promises to his people.

The Chronicler has nothing to say against David's taking many wives. This was a sign of power and prestige and a way to seal alliances with other nations. The birth of sons was considered a sign of God's blessing (see comments at the end of this section).

In contrast to Saul (1 Chron 14:8-12, 13-16), David enquired of God when the Philistines attacked, and he received and followed instructions for the battle. This time God broke out against David's enemies as he had "broken out" against Uzzah (1 Chron 13:11). In Uzzah's case the breaking out was due to disobedience on the part of those who should have known better, including David. The victory over the Philistines followed David's doing things God's way.

Because of God's blessings, David's fame and a healthy fear and respect because of his obvious power spread to the nations around him. This summary of what God did for David because he sought God contrasts with the summary in 1 Chronicles 10:13 of what happened to Saul because of his underlying disobedience.

We know that the multiplication of wives despite the warnings of Deuteronomy 17:17 brought great tragedy to David later. God's plan for man and woman as presented in Genesis 2:24 is that they be one flesh, working together, helping each other. It is impossible to be one flesh with more than one wife. Also it creates competition, jealousy and rivalry among wives and children (*see* Polygamy).

It is easy to father many children, but it is not easy to be a good father to many children. So David failed his many wives and children (*see* Parental Influence). But the Chronicler describes only the apparent blessing. He is concerned to present the underlying desire of David's heart, which was to honor and obey God. That David does not always succeed in this is proof of his humanity, but God responds to his desire and to his repentance. Nevertheless, as we know, the results of sin, mistakes and failures must follow, and they did so for David (see 2 Sam 12—1 Kings 1).

The Ark Comes to Jerusalem (1 Chron 15—16). This time (1 Chron 15:1-3) David made careful preparation for the ark's journey to Jerusalem. First he prepared a place and a tent for the ark, presumably a new tent, for the tabernacle was left at Gibeon (1 Chron 16:39; 21:29) and was brought to Jerusalem by Solomon (2 Chron 5:2-10). Then David acknowledged God's decree that the Levites should carry the ark (see Num 3:5-10, 25-26, 31; 4:15; Deut 10:8), and finally he again summoned all Israel to bring the ark up to Jerusalem. God is the God of every Israelite; every one of them belongs to God and owes devotion and service. All must be represented as the ark is brought to its place, which would be consecrated for its sacred purpose.

Levites were summoned and ordered to consecrate themselves for the task ahead (1 Chron 15:4-15; 2 Sam 6:12 omits this careful preparation). This time the ark would be carried on poles on the shoulders of the Levites, in the way God had stipulated through Moses. The Philistines had once sent the ark back to Israel on a new cart, but they did not have access to God's instructions. As always, God expects his people to know and fulfill his commands.

In 1 Chronicles 15:16-24 there is still celebration, but this time the Levites who were skilled in music were put in charge so that everything would be detailed and ordered. Each musician knew what his responsibility was. Doorkeepers were appointed; the priests were to blow the trumpets (see Num 10). Much careful study and preparation had been done so that God would be honored. The musicians and singers were skilled, and the songs were joyful (1 Chron 15:16), not only because God is worthy of the best but also because their hearts were overflowing with joy and thanksgiving. This was not a celebration demanded by an autocratic God but an outpouring of genuine love for God. Such an outpouring of love is evidence of true worship.

God responded by protecting ("helped," NIV, NRSV) the Levites so that none would die (1 Chron 15:26). Clothed in fine linen, symbolizing holiness and purity, David and the Levites brought the ark to Jerusalem along with all Israel. Their rejoicing was exuberant, wholehearted, sincere. Yet as

Michal, Saul's daughter, watched, she despised David for his lack of dignity. Perhaps the Chronicler is again noting the lack of true love for Yahweh of Saul's house as compared with David's (see also 2 Sam 6:20). Michal saw David's actions as demeaning to himself and to her. She did not realize that to exalt God by true love and worship does not bring humiliation to the worshiper but rather lifts him or her into closer fellowship with God.

Michal had been a pawn in Saul's dealings with David, first given to him as wife, then given to another man when David was Saul's enemy (1 Sam 25:44). David had demanded her back when he was asked to become king over Israel as well as Judah (2 Sam 3:14). With Michal as his wife, David's claim to the throne of Saul had more credibility with Saul's followers. The fact that her husband loved her and that presumably she was happy with him was of no concern to David (2 Sam 3:15-16). No wonder then, humanly speaking, that Michal was scornful of David's devotion to Yahweh when her well-being was not important to him.

Many wives have been suspicious of a devotion to God that is not expressed in devotion to wife and family, and rightly so, for true love for God is expressed by love for one another. But Michal, as a princess of her time, was expected to put the welfare of her country and people before her own interests. How did God expect her to react in the face of this unfair treatment? She was censured by David for not recognizing the rightness of his motives and actions, in this case to honor God, and for allowing her personal bitterness to take hold of her. Sacrifice is required of all God's people, men and women, a willingness to put God first. Michal put herself before God and held on to bitterness and an unforgiving attitude. Her whole life was blighted (see 2 Sam 6:23). Despite the unfairness of her situation, she could have put her life into God's hands and trusted him, but she did not. Michal despised David's way of worshiping God. God is more interested in wholehearted, sincere worship than in the way it is expressed.

Worship and Thanksgiving (1 Chron 16). The ark was brought and placed in the prepared tent. Offerings and sacrifices were made before it, with the king very much involved. The king also blessed the people, and each Israelite man and woman received a share of the sacrificial meal in Yahweh's name, a symbol of their share in the blessings God promises for his people when they love and seek him.

What was the relevance of the ark to the people of the Chronicler's day, when it was no longer in their possession? Why does he place such an emphasis on it if it can have no place in postexilic worship? The ark was the place where God met with his people, and even though it was no longer there, God was still among his people. David's bringing the ark to Israel's capital symbolizes the need to have God at the center of the nation, though David may also have thought that it would add legitimacy to his regime.

Levites ministered before the ark in prayer, in music, in praise, in thanksgiving—not to the ark but to Yahweh, the God of Israel. This had not been their task previously, but now that the Israelites were settled in their land, their former tasks were to a great extent gone. Notice that God gifted them to take up this new role.

1 Chronicles 16:8-22 is the same as Psalm 105:1-15. These verses call for thanks and praise for all that God had done in the past, for God's faithfulness to his covenant promise to Abraham, Isaac and Jacob to give them the land of Canaan, and for God's protection of his people. These promises were made to a people few in number, just as those who returned from exile were few in number, and God would be faithful to those promises.

The reference here to the covenant God made with Israel picks up the references to the "ark of the covenant" in 1 Chronicles 15:25-26, 28-29. The ark was symbolic of that covenant, and the covenant remained although the ark had gone. Remembering and telling what God has done in the past is necessary, and so is continual looking to God in the present and into the future (1 Chron 16:11).

1 Chronicles 16:23-33 (see Ps 96:1-13) is a song of praise for Yahweh's greatness, glory and sovereignty over all things. The recognition of who God is—his splendor, majesty, holiness, beauty, strength, glory—brings forth spontaneous praise from all creation. The next verses (1 Chron 16:34-36; see Ps 106:1, 47-48) first sum up the absolute goodness of God's character.

The foundation of all God is and does is goodness and love. A cry for deliverance brings assurance of that deliverance and a response of thanks and praise. Deliverance came to Israel many times over the centuries, but the exiles who returned from Babylon had experienced it in a particularly miraculous way, and how could they not respond with deep thankfulness, praise and worship?

The ongoing worship of God before the ark in Jerusalem and in the tabernacle at Gibeon was established by David (1 Chron 16:37-43) so that everything would be done in accordance with God's requirements (1 Chron 16:40). There is no other record of the tabernacle being at Gibeon apart from these references in Chronicles, but that the sacrifices continued in the way God had appointed is important to the writer and his readers. Notice, though, that the writer throughout places more emphasis on the ark and the accompanying worship of Yahweh than on the sacrifices on the altar at Gibeon, though sacrifices were offered (see 1 Chron 15:26; 16:1-2, 39-40). Although sacrifice is necessary, the presence of God and relationship with him are vital. Many times in Israel's history the people concentrated on ritual performances and sacrifices, not realizing that their hearts were far from God; in the end, only a remnant survived because of this fact (see Amos 5:22-27).

The Lord Builds a House for David (1 Chron 17)

David's plan to build a permanent place for the ark of the covenant was an expression of his devotion for God. Why should he have a beautiful palace to live in, while the ark remained in a tent? The idea was good, his motive was good, and when David expressed his idea to Nathan the prophet, he too thought it was right, advising David to go ahead because God was with him.

The idea was good, but it was not God's purpose (1 Chron 17:3-6; see Is 55:8-9). God does not require a settled place to live, for he lives everywhere. The ark had moved through the desert, to Gilgal, to Bethel, to Shiloh, to the Philistine cities, to Beth-shemesh, to Kiriath-jearim. Wherever it went the presence of God had been seen, in judgment or blessing. Its mobility had helped to make clear the fact that God is not limited to any one place. Later experience showed that a temple could hinder worship of God, giving a false sense of security (see, e.g., Jer 7:4). However, 1 Chronicles 17:4 indicates that a house would be built, but not by David.

God reminded David that he had been involved powerfully in all of David's life (1 Chron 17:7-10) as he was raised from being a shepherd boy to being king of Israel. What David needed to focus on was not his power to do something for God but God's power to do something for him and for Israel. And God assured him that he would provide for Israel, protect them from their enemies, plant them firmly in their homeland.

Rather than David building a house for God (1 Chron 17:10-15), God would build a house for David. God would raise up David's son; God would establish his kingdom and throne forever. (2 Samuel 7:14 states the judgments that would fall if that son disobeyed God, but this is omitted here.) This son would be the one to build a house for God. 1 Chronicles 22:8 and 28:3 tell us that David could not build the house because he had been a man of war, shedding much blood, whereas Solomon continued the building of the kingdom by more peaceful means such as alliances. The name Solomon comes from the Hebrew word for peace, *shalom*. The emphasis in Chronicles on David's son is stronger than in 2 Samuel 7, where David's kingdom and throne, rather than his son's, would be established forever. The point is that David's kingdom and his power were dependent upon God, and what God would build far exceeds anything David or his son could build. David's attention was drawn away from himself and placed where it should remain, on God.

David's Prayer (1 Chron 17:16-27). When David did focus on God, he realized how small he was and how great God is, and this is expressed in his prayer. He was overwhelmed as he considered the incredible grace of God shown to him, treating him as if he were someone important instead of, as he now realized, someone of little consequence. Why had God made this promise? It was his will to do so. David acknowledged God's sovereignty over his servants. God can do as he wishes with them.

Who is God? What is his nature? God is unique, the only God, the redeemer of his people. God makes his name known by his great and awesome acts, and is faithful to his promises to his people. David took God at his word. The establishment of David's kingdom would increase the recognition of God's greatness. God's promise gave David courage to pray, because it affirmed their relationship and God's continuing involvement in his life. David acknowledged God's faithfulness with the words "Do as you promised" (1 Chron 17:23).

The Chronicler's readers, knowing that David's descendants no longer ruled, must have been puzzled by the declaration that David's kingdom would be established forever. The stipulation in 2 Samuel 7 that disobedience would cause God to judge the king had been demonstrated, but why was there no king once the exile was over? If this promise did not hold, what about the other promises God made to his people?

With every promise God makes there must be a response from his people. David responded in belief. Later generations counted on the promise to keep them from destruction (e.g., Amos 6:1-7; Jer 7:1-15) but felt no obligation to obey God's commands. Nor did they believe the words of God spoken through his prophets. The remnant who returned from exile had to learn to listen to God's word through his prophets and to obey him. Though it seemed God's promise had failed, they must trust him.

God's promise to David did not fail. He kept his word, even though his people did not. When disobedience brought about the apparent end of David's dynasty, God continued to work out his plan, and from David's descendants came the king who rules forever, Jesus. God does not change. Faith, obedience and trust still ensure that his people receive his promises.

Battles (1 Chron 18—20)

Although David as a man of war could not build the temple, his battles were crowned with success by God, who gave him victory everywhere he went (1 Chron 18:6, 13). And from the booty won from these battles, much was put aside for the future temple (1 Chron 18:8).

In 2 Samuel 8—21 these battles are recorded along with the details of David's adultery and the murder of Uriah, and the rebellion, rape and murders among David's family (*see* Adultery; Violence, Abuse and Oppression). In 1 Chronicles the emphasis is on David's expansion of the kingdom and God's blessing on him. It is clear in 2 Samuel 12:13 and in Psalm 51 that David repented of his sins and that God continued to use him.

This is the same grace that is available to all God's people and that will encourage the Chronicler's generation and future generations to acknowledge sin, repent and press on with confidence in God. The central lesson is that the sovereign God will bless those who trust in him. He will encourage them and give them success when they walk with him in humility and obedience. David's God was still sovereign in the Chronicler's day, still working, and his power had been displayed in the incredible return of his people to their land. God is the basis of true faith. Success can be found not only in victory and wealth such as David knew but also in trusting God in every circumstance, even those of the returned exiles who had expected much but seemed to have little (see Hag 1:6).

Moabites, Arameans, Edomites (1 Chron 18; cf. 2 Sam 8). 1 Chronicles 18:2 omits the judgment David passed on the defeated Moabites (2 Sam 8:2). The Philistines to the west (also 1 Chron 14:8-16), the Moabites to the east and the Arameans to the north were all defeated, and the territory of Israel expanded as God had promised (see Gen 15:18-21; Deut 1:7; 11:24; Josh 1:4). The king of Hamath sent gifts and congratulations, allying himself with David. The Edomites, to the southeast of Israel, were also brought under submission by Abishai, Zeruiah's son and David's nephew.

David as king ruled with justice and righteousness. These characteristics of God are what he expects from his people (see, e.g., Amos 5:24), especially those in leadership. David put into place the necessary structure to organize the kingdom as it enlarged. His nephew Joab, Zeruiah's son, was commander of the army (1 Chron 11:4-6). The recorder kept the official records and probably oversaw the protocol and ceremonial details of the kingdom. Zadok the priest was in charge of the tabernacle at Gibeon (1 Chron 16:39), and Ahimelech led the worship in Jerusalem. (Zadok came into greater prominence under Solomon; see, e.g., 1 Chron 29:22.) David's bodyguard included non-Israelites, such as the

Cherethites and Pelethites. Some of David's most loyal warriors were non-Israelite (1 Chron 11:26-47). David's sons were also chief officials (2 Sam 8:18, "priests," NIV "royal advisors").

Ammonites and Arameans (1 Chron 19:1—20:3). In 1 Samuel 11:1-11 Nahash the Ammonite was Saul's enemy, defeated by him as his reign began. Perhaps the Nahash mentioned here is his son. At some time it seems Nahash and David had made a treaty, because the word for loyalty (NIV "kindness") is *hesed,* the word used for God's covenant love and faithfulness. David wanted this feeling of mutual obligation to be extended between himself and Nahash's son.

To reject David's overtures of friendship, and especially in such a humiliating fashion, was to declare war. David did not immediately react, but the Ammonites enlisted the help of the Arameans, and this made the intention of war clear. Joab and his brother Abishai routed the first army, and then a second, larger one formed with the addition of more distant Arameans was defeated by David and "all Israel," with their commander Shophach killed. The numbers given in Chronicles vary from those in 2 Samuel 10, with those in Chronicles generally being larger (e.g., 1 Chron 19:18; cf. 2 Sam 10:18). The groups previously controlled by the Arameans then became David's vassals, bringing a further expansion of territory up to the Euphrates River in the north.

1 Chronicles 20:1-3 gives an abbreviated presentation of the capture of Rabbah, the Ammonite capital. This final blow to the Ammonites had been left until spring, and Joab led the army while David remained in Jerusalem. It is at this point that 2 Samuel 11 tells the story of David and Bathsheba, and Uriah's murder. After the capture of the city (according to Chronicles), David took the king's crown and plundered the Ammonite cities, probably making their citizens assist in the destruction (1 Chron 20:3).

Philistines (1 Chron 20:4-8; cf. 2 Sam 21:15-22). 2 Samuel 12:1—21:14 deals with the rebellions, rape and murders in David's family. 1 Chronicles continues with the theme of victories in battles against the Philistines, taking up three of the four occasions of battle mentioned in Samuel. Each battle involves giants. In Chronicles Elhanan is said to have killed the brother of Goliath, whereas 2 Samuel 21:19 says he killed Goliath (cf. 1 Sam 17, the story of David and Goliath). It has been suggested that Elhanan was David's family name, but Chronicles could be clarifying the account in 1 Samuel. These three victories over giants show once again the power of Israel's God as the weak overcome the strong.

The Census (1 Chron 21; cf. 2 Sam 24)

The main purpose of this narrative is to show how the temple site was chosen and purchased. This is not made clear in 2 Samuel 24. Following David's acknowledgment of sin and repentance, although judgment falls, it is followed by God's mercy and forgiveness and the provision of the site for the temple.

1 Chronicles 21:1 tells us that Satan incited David to take a census as a means of attacking Israel. 2 Samuel 24:1 says that God incited David to take the census because he was angry with Israel. As in Job 2:10, all things ultimately were seen to come from God's hand, for Satan could not go beyond what God allowed. In Job 1—2 and Zechariah 3:1, "the Satan" or the adversary is shown working within God's council or court. However, later Judaism preferred to attribute evil to Satan rather than to God. It has been suggested that Persian dualism, in which good and evil are equal opponents, influenced this shift of emphasis after the exile. But it is probable that the Chronicler prefers to present evil as coming from Satan, while still accepting that God is the ultimate authority. In that case, God allowed Satan to incite Israel in order to bring about God's purpose—David's repentance. If God permits it to be done (Chronicles), then in a sense he has done it (Samuel), because everything is subject to him, including Satan and his followers.

Why should taking a census be a sin? Twice in Numbers (Num 1; 26), God told Moses to take a census of the people for a specific purpose. In Exodus 30:11-16 God told Moses that whenever a census was taken, each person numbered must pay a ransom for his life. Obviously David was not taking this census at God's command but for his own purposes. Perhaps pride caused him to want to know the numbers of fighting men. Perhaps he was beginning to attribute his success in battle not to God but to himself because of the size and skill of his army. The Chronicler emphasizes that battles are won because of trust in God (2 Chron 13:18; 14:11; 16:8). The census may have been for the purpose of increasing taxation or forced labor, an unjust motive. Israel had sinned against God (how is not stated in Chronicles); David was not seeking God and was determined for his own purposes to take a census. Satan took advantage of his wrong motives, and God did not intervene to stop the process.

In the end, David recognized that the blame lay with him (1 Chron 21:17). If he had been walking close to God, listening to and obeying his voice, his people would have been spared the calamity that fell on them. As soon as David recognized his sin (1 Chron 21:8), he confessed it, taking responsibility for his actions. Our human tendency is to blame someone or something else, as Adam and Eve did in the garden. Nevertheless, 2 Samuel 24:1 shows that the sin was not David's alone. Israel too had incurred God's anger. The people were not just innocent victims of David's sin.

David's Choice (1 Chron 21:2-6). David gave Joab the order to count the Israelites. Joab knew that David's action was wrong (1 Chron 21:3, 6) and protested. He said that it would bring guilt on Israel. 2 Samuel 24:5-8 tells us that the census took nine months and twenty days. Presumably in all this time David did not seek God. The number of men is smaller in Chronicles than in Samuel, perhaps because the tribes of Levi and Benjamin are not included.

Results (1 Chron 21:7-14). David at last realized his sin (1 Chron 21:8) and turned to God to ask forgiveness. God forgave, but the results of sin must come. Gad the seer offered David three options: famine for three years, enemy attack for three months, or a plague for three days. Leviticus 26:25-26 says that these three calamities are the natural results of turning away from God.

David placed himself and his people in God's hands, for there mercy may be found. God sent the destroying angel (as in Ex 12:23) to carry out his command, and seventy thousand men died. (If the word *elep* is translated "unit" instead of "thousand," this would give the lesser number of seventy units, but it is not certain how many men would be in a unit; see note on 1 Chron 23:3).

David watched his people suffering, his men dying, his military strength being depleted. He recognized once more that God is the source of all power; God brings victory or defeat. In all the success, prosperity and victories that God had given him, David had lost his focus on God, had ceased to trust God and begun to trust himself.

Mercy, Repentance, Sacrifice (1 Chron 21:15-30). God stopped the destroying angel as he stood over the threshing floor of Araunah (Ornan). In Chronicles he is shown with his sword drawn (1 Chron 21:12, 16), until he is told to sheath it (1 Chron 21:27). Previously the sword of the destroying angel had been drawn against Israel's enemies (Num 22:22-35; Josh 5:13-15), but now it was extended over Israel. As soon as David saw the angel, he and the elders, clothed in the sackcloth of mourning and repentance, fell face down. They were representing, interceding for, the whole people. David acknowledged his fault. As king, he had the responsibility to shepherd and teach his people, leading them by example, and he had failed them (1 Chron 21:17).

The purchase of the threshing floor has echoes of Abraham's purchase of the field with the cave of Machpelah (Gen 23). The full price was paid for land and sacrifice. As he had done for Gideon (Judg 6:26), God sent fire from heaven to consume the sacrifice, signifying his acceptance of the offering, and the plague was stopped. According to Chronicles, David paid six hundred shekels of gold, whereas Samuel mentions sixty shekels of silver. Perhaps sixty silver shekels was the price for the site of the altar, and the six hundred gold shekels the price of the entire site later used for the temple. The Chronicler is emphasizing the importance of this whole area as the place where the temple would be built (1 Chron 22:1).

Once David saw that God had answered him, he offered sacrifices. Notice that David had been afraid to go to Gibeon to inquire of God, because of the sword of the angel of the Lord, the judgment of God (1 Chron 21:30). Presumably he and the elders had been on their way to Gibeon when they saw the angel standing over the threshing floor. 2 Chronicles 3:1 tells us that this is Mount Moriah, perhaps providing a link to the place where many years before Abraham had been stopped from killing his son Isaac and a substitute sacrifice provided. Once more judgment had been averted by God's mercy at this place.

Preparations for the Temple (1 Chron 22)
The theme of this chapter is the building of the "house of God" (1 Chron 22:2, 5-8, 10-11, 19). If David could not build it, he could prepare and provide for it (1 Chron 22:3, 5, 14).

The Declaration (1 Chron 22:1). The place where judgment had been stopped and David's prayer answered was the place where the temple would be built and sacrifices for sin would continue to be offered. Until now the altar had been in Gibeon (1 Chron 21:29). Both it and the tabernacle would be united in the temple, sacrifice and worship together again. Jerusalem would be the nation's religious center.

The Materials (1 Chron 22:2-5). A great quantity of materials had been gathered together. As God had given abundantly to David and to his people, so David gave generously in return. Then David provided skilled workers and the best of materials, for God is worthy of the best. God is the one who gives skills (Ex 35:30-31), and those who use them to the full for God bring him honor.

David was also concerned that the house be magnificent, known throughout the world as a reflection of God's magnificence, splendor and fame. David honored God and expressed that in what he provided for the temple. All these preparations cost a great deal in money, time and effort (see 1 Chron 22:14). Some of these materials had been taken as booty from defeated nations (see, e.g., 1 Chron 18:8).

We see in 1 Chronicles 22:2 that non-Israelites in the land were used in these preparations. Although the NIV says David "appointed" them as stonecutters, they were more likely to have been forced labor gangs, as the "set" of the NRSV might suggest (see 2 Sam 20:24, "Adoniram was in charge of forced labor"). The beginnings of the use of foreigners for forced labor is seen in Joshua 9:21, 27, and 1 Kings 9:21-22; 2 Chronicles 2:17-18 and 2 Chronicles 8:7-8 show Solomon's increased use of non-Israelites in this way. 1 Kings 5:13 says that Solomon also conscripted Israelites to help build the temple in shifts of one month in Lebanon and two months at home. This was not a popular move (see 2 Chron 10:4).

The Builder (1 Chron 22:6-16). Solomon is said to have been "young and inexperienced" at the time of David's preparations (1 Chron 22:5; 1 Kings 3:7). If he was to build this great house for God he needed to be prepared for the task. God had brought peace to Israel by giving David success in war (see 1 Kings 5:3). But Solomon would be a man of peace and rest (1 Chron 22:9). He was God's choice (1 Chron 22:9-10) and would reign in peace by God's grace (see also 1 Chron 17:10-14; 2 Sam 7:11-16; Deut 12:10-11). The Scripture speaks of the rest that God will give his people in the land and of the place he will choose for his name where sacrifices will be made.

David charged Solomon to build the house. See also the charge in 1 Kings 2:1-9, where some of David's enemies are to be dealt with after his death. These are not included here, because the Chronicler's focus is on the temple. David was unable to build it because of the blood he had shed and the wars he had fought (1 Kings 5:3).

Just as Moses had done for Joshua long before, David pointed out Solomon's need for discretion, understanding, obedience and absolute confidence in God, shown by strength and courage (1 Chron 22:11-13; cf. Deut 12:10-11; Josh 1:6-9). Moses had prepared the people to enter the land; Joshua led them in. David had made preparations for the temple; Solomon would build it. The parallels show the importance of this temple.

The vast quantities of gold, silver, bronze and iron were ready, provided at "great pains." This was not inherited wealth but hard-won in battle. The workmen, skilled in every facet of the work, from stonecutters to the finest detailed workmanship, were also ready. David therefore commanded Solomon to begin work. 2 Chronicles 3:2 tells us that the building began in the second month of the fourth year of Solomon's reign. This may mean there was a delay in beginning the work, or it may mean that Solomon, who was made king before David's death (1 Chron 23:1; 1 Kings 1:32-40), had been coregent with David for four years.

The reminder of David's zeal for God's house and Solomon's faithful action in building it and establishing worship of God in it was a further encouragement to the Chronicler's contemporaries to rebuild the temple and establish the worship of God in it. Following David's example, after the exile Ezra, Nehemiah, Haggai and Zechariah urged the people not to neglect the rebuilding of the temple and its service. Ezra (Ezra 8:24-34) brought gold, silver and articles for temple use. The people too gave freewill offerings (Ezra 2:68-69; Neh 7:70-72). The prophets exhorted the people to put God first and begin the building (Hag 1:8) and promised God's presence and help (Hag 1:13; 2:4; Zech 4:9).

The Helpers (1 Chron 22:17-19). The leaders in Israel were ordered to help Solomon in his task, for this was vital to the well-being of the whole nation. All needed to devote themselves to seeking God and to joining in the building of the temple. See 1 Chronicles 29:6-9, where leaders and officials willingly gave gifts for the temple, and the people rejoiced in their wholehearted response.

Preparations for Temple Worship (1 Chron 23—26)

1 Chronicles 23—27 seem to break up the narrative, as 1 Chronicles 28:1 follows on from 1 Chronicles 23:2 very well (unless they refer to two separate assemblies of leaders). These chapters may have been added at this point at a later date, but they continue the temple theme of 1 Chronicles 22 by detailing David's organization of the Levites in its service. They also show the importance of the worship of God in the life of his people. His holy things must be handled by those who are set apart to do so. Even mundane tasks such as cleaning, which are always present, are holy tasks when undertaken for God.

Worship of God is to be orderly, not haphazard. As we read Genesis 1 we see God's orderliness, as well as his power and authority. Orderliness in worship honors him (1 Cor 14:40), as does giving the best of time, skill, willingness and obedience. Whether priest, gatekeeper, musician or temple worker, each must honor God in ministry, for God had come to dwell in Jerusalem (1 Chron 23:25).

This chapter begins with David making Solomon his heir. If the two ruled jointly until David's death, it would have helped a smooth transition of kingship—a lesson David learned after the attempts made by his sons Absalom and Adonijah to take the throne.

The Levites (1 Chron 23). David called an assembly of leaders, priests and Levites in order to put in place the system of worship for the new temple. The Levites thirty years old and over were counted in order to regulate their duties: supervisors, officials and judges (Deut 17:8-13; cf. 2 Chron 19:4-11; 34:13), gatekeepers (1 Chron 26:12-18) and musicians (1 Chron 25).

Note that the age of those who could serve in the temple is twenty years in 1 Chronicles 23:24 (see also Num 4:3, 23 [thirty years of age]; Num 8:23-26 [twenty-five years]; 2 Chron 31:17; Ezra 3:8 [twenty years]). The age may have varied according to numbers available or required. The census was legitimate this time, to enable the temple worship to be established.

As noted on 1 Chronicles 21:5, some commentators feel that the number of thirty-eight thousand is unnaturally large and prefer to translate the word for "thousand" as "unit," "group" or "clan." This would mean there were thirty-eight units or groups.

The Levites were grouped by their descent from the sons of Levi: Gershon, Kohath and Merari (1 Chron 23:7-23). This established the continuity of Levites in the time of David and Solomon with the first Levites and their work in the tabernacle under Moses and Aaron. And the Levites of the Chronicler's day could claim the same ancestry, so the continuity remains. The writer reminds his readers that Aaron and his descendants were set apart to be priests (see also 1 Chron 6:49), while the descendants of Moses are simply Levites (1 Chron 23:13-14). Eleazar's line was carried on through his daughters, who married their cousins (1 Chron 23:22; cf. Num 27:4; 36:6). In the Levitical and priestly lines mothers were particularly significant because of their role of educating the young.

The original Levites had carried the tabernacle and its furnishings from place to place in the desert. The twenty-four thousand or twenty-four units involved in the temple service (1 Chron 23:4) were to help the priests, their duties varied and prescribed by David (1 Chron 23:28-32).

Praise and worship, service in the outer temple area and involvement in preparation of offerings were all part of their responsibilities (cf. Num 3:5-9, 31; 18:1-7).

The Priests and Other Levites (1 Chron 24). The Chronicler breaks into the account of the Levites to deal with Aaron's descendants, the priests, as in 1 Chronicles 23:13. Nadab and Abihu lost their lives (Lev 10:1-2). Aaron's two other sons, Eleazar and Ithamar, became the ancestors of the priestly line. Two of their descendants, Zadok and Ahimelech, joined with David in dividing the priests into groups for service under heads of families, the "officer of the sanctuary [or holy officials] and officer of God" (1 Chron 24:5).

Impartiality and fairness in the choice is emphasized. The casting of lots also indicates that God was being consulted, while the king, the officials and the heads of priestly families were also involved (1 Chron 24:5-6).

The list of Kohathites and Merarites from 1 Chronicles 23:16-23 is repeated with the addition of one more generation. The Gershonites are not mentioned. Lots were cast for the Levites as for the priests; everything was handled with fairness, with no preference given to those descended from oldest sons. Jaaziah and his sons are not mentioned elsewhere in connection with Merari but could be descendants of his (1 Chron 24:26-27).

Musicians (1 Chron 25; cf. 1 Chron 6:31-47). The musicians are grouped under three family heads: Asaph, Heman and Jeduthun (or Ethan, 1 Chron 6:44). These family heads were descended from Levi (see 1 Chron 6:33-47), and their ministry included prophesying with musical instruments (1 Chron 25:1-3). Heman is named as the king's seer (1 Chron 25:5). Asaph and Jeduthun are also called seers (2 Chron 29:30; 35:15).

The musicians also were to thank and praise God (1 Chron 25:3) and minister at the house of God (1 Chron 25:6; see also 1 Chron 16:4-6). Their role was vital in the worship of God. They were trained and skilled in music (1 Chron 25:7). They were supervised (1 Chron 25:2-3, 6) by the heads of their families and also by the king (1 Chron 25:6), because of the huge responsibility involved. They too were divided into twenty-four groups and given their duties by lots, with no difference made between teacher and student.

1 Chronicles 25:4 lists the names of Heman's fourteen sons, given by God to exalt him. The names from Hananiah to Mahazioth can be read as poetry, or psalm headings, as follows (see major commentaries for additional comments):

> Be gracious to me, Yahweh, be gracious to me;
> You are my God.
> I exalt, I praise [my] helper,
> Sitting in adversity I said,
> Clear signs give plentifully.

The fact that Heman's daughters are mentioned is sometimes thought to indicate that they too were involved as temple musicians, as 1 Chronicles 25:6 ("they were all under the direction of their father") might imply, although the larger context seems to militate against this interpretation. However, in Psalm 68:25-26 girls did take part in the music at the "processions of my God, my King, into the sanctuary," while Nehemiah 7:67 mentions men and women singers (*see* Women in Worship).

The Gatekeepers and Other Officials (1 Chron 26). The gatekeepers (1 Chron 26:1-19; cf. 1 Chron 9:17-27) came from the descendants of Korah and Merari, the sons of Levi. An Obed-edom is said to be the son of Jeduthun in 1 Chronicles 16:38. In 1 Chronicles 13:13-14 Obed-edom is called a Gittite (a Levite from Gath? or a Philistine who joined the tribe of Levi?). Whatever his origin, his role as a gatekeeper is affirmed in 1 Chronicles 15:18, 24. Obed-edom was also a musician (1 Chron 15:21; 16:5). His family was capable and strong.

The gatekeepers could assist in other ways, ministering in the temple (1 Chron 26:12), or as 1 Chronicles 9:28-29 indicates, taking care of articles and furnishings used in the temple service and flour, wine, oil, incense and spices used in the offerings. Shelemiah's son Zechariah is called a "wise counselor" (NIV; see also 2 Chron 23:4-6, 9-13; 31:14-19). Gatekeepers guarded the holy place, kept out those who should not enter. Theirs was a place of responsibility and privilege (see Ps 84:10).

Other officials (1 Chron 26:20-32) included Levites in charge of two treasuries: treasures of the temple under descendants of Gershon, and treasures of dedicated things, spoils taken in war by David (1 Chron 18:10-11; 2 Chron 5:1), and others (1 Chron 26:28), under descendants of Amram (1 Chron 26:23), specifically the family of Shubael, who was descended from Moses' son Gershom. Some of these dedicated things were set aside for repair of the temple either at this time or after the temple was built.

From the Izharites (1 Chron 26:23, 29) came officials and judges who moved throughout Israel (see also 2 Chron 19:8-11). The Hebronites (1 Chron 26:23, 30-32) were given responsibility in the king's service and in the Lord's work (1 Chron 26:30) over the tribes west of the Jordan (seventeen hundred men) and those east of the Jordan (twenty-seven hundred men). Why more men were required to the east of the Jordan, where there were fewer tribes, is not clarified.

Army and Administration (1 Chron 27)

This chapter seems to depart from the temple theme of 1 Chronicles 23—26, but it expands the description of organization of the temple to organization of Israel. The leaders of the groups in this chapter are included in those whom David summoned to give instructions regarding the temple in 1 Chronicles 28:1 and 1 Chronicles 29:1. These groups, along with all Israel, were involved in the temple preparations (see 1 Chron 29:6). Unity in Israel, as in all nations, was difficult to attain. The Chronicler shows that love and worship of Yahweh is what had bound and held Israel together in David's day, and the same would apply after the exile.

The chapter is made up of four lists: commanders (1 Chron 27:1-15), tribal leaders (1 Chron 27:16-24), stewards or administrators (1 Chron 27:25-31) and advisers (1 Chron 27:32-24).

Each division (1 Chron 27:1-15) served for one month of the year under their commander. Either twenty-four units or twenty-four thousand men were in each division. The commanders did not come from every tribe. Judah, Levi, Benjamin, Ephraim and two other tribes were represented. Presumably the leaders were chosen for their capability. They "served the king," but whether the divisions were an on-call army or used all the time for other purposes is not stated. Many of the same names occur in the list of David's mighty men in (1 Chron 11:10-31). Asahel (1 Chron 27:7), who died before David became king over all Israel (2 Sam 2:18-23), was succeeded by his son.

In the lists of tribal leaders or officers (1 Chron 27:16-24) twelve tribes are mentioned, but Gad and Asher are omitted, while Ephraim and the two halves of Manasseh make up the twelve. These leaders are called officers rather than tribal elders, so they may have been appointed by the king, perhaps to take part in the census.

1 Chronicles 27:23-24 give a slightly different slant to the account in 1 Chronicles 21:2, 5-6. Here David is said not to have numbered those twenty and under (cf. Num 1:3) because of God's promise to Abraham (Gen 15:5), whereas 1 Chronicles 21 seems to indicate a lack of trust. Joab was stopped from counting the men because of God's wrath, rather than his distaste for the task as in the earlier account.

Twelve administrators (1 Chron 27:25-31) were placed in charge of David's property in Jerusalem and in outlying villages: his storehouses, fields and workers, wine and oil, and livestock. Some of this would have been accumulated while he was hiding from Saul in Philistia and attacking Israel's enemies (1 Sam 27:8-9), and some would have been booty from his wars during his reign.

Among the advisers (1 Chron 27:32-34) Jonathan and Jehiel are not known from elsewhere. Ahithophel later supported Absalom against David, while Hushai remained loyal (2 Sam 15). "The king's friend" may be an official title. Abiathar and Joab were with David before he became king. They remained loyal during Absalom's rebellion but supported Adonijah (1 Kings 1:7). Jehoiada son of Benaiah is not mentioned elsewhere, though Benaiah, son of Jehoiada, is (1 Chron 27:5; 11:22-24; 18:17), and a Jehoiada is mentioned in 1 Chronicles 12:27.

Plans and Gifts for the Temple (1 Chron 28:1—29:9)

The Assembly (1 Chron 28:1). 1 Chronicles 28 continues the account broken off after 1 Chronicles 23:2 of the choosing of Solomon to be David's successor. David summoned all those involved in leadership, as detailed in the previous chapters. The Chronicler's account simply records the transition of power from David to Solomon, leaving out the intrigues of 1 Kings 1 as irrelevant to God's plan.

God's Choices (1 Chron 28:2-7). David had wanted to build God a house, but God chose someone else to do it. David, as a warrior, was not the one to build the "house of rest" (1 Chron 28:2). See 1 Chronicles 22:9, where Solomon as a man of peace and rest would build it, and Psalm 132:7-8, 14 for the temple as God's footstool and resting place.

Yet God had chosen David from among Jesse's sons to be king, and God had chosen Judah out of all the tribes of Israel. God had chosen in the past, and again he chose for the future. Solomon should be king after David and should build the temple. God gave him the promise of an established kingdom, just as he had to David. He chose Solomon to be his son (see Ps 2:7).

Solomon was given tremendous privilege, and his responsibility was to be unswerving in obedience. This would involve his choice; it was not forced upon him. God's choices were an assurance to Solomon and to the people that his involvement with them was ongoing, his commitment to them was for all time. The concept of the king as God's son also emphasized the king's responsibility to rule as God's representative, with God's justice and love. For the Chronicler's readers, the lessons were clear: God's choice of them as his people remained, but as in the past, their choice must be to remain obedient and faithful. In order to see the promises fulfilled, God's people must trust him and obey him.

The Charge (1 Chron 28:8-10). David charged Solomon to be careful to follow all God's commands. The king's obedience was vital, because the people would follow his example, and so the land would remain in their possession and could be passed on as an inheritance. The requirements for Solomon and the people were wholehearted devotion, willingness of mind, purity of motive, determined seeking after God and completion of the work God had given.

Yahweh searches (Heb. *darash*), knowing hearts and understanding motives (1 Chron 28:9), and Solomon must search for God in the same way, seeking to understand and know God, so that he could walk in his ways. If, rather than search to know God, Solomon rejected him, God in turn would reject Solomon.

The Plans (1 Chron 28:11-12). Part of the work given to Solomon was the building of the temple. David had spent much time in prayer and planning for the temple because it was to be the outward sign of God's presence with his people. As he prayed and thought, he drew up the plans for it, the Spirit of God directing him (1 Chron 28:12, 19; cf. Ex 25:9, 40; 31:1-11; 40:16).

The Preparations (1 Chron 28:13-19). There were instructions for the priests and Levites, as given in the previous chapters, along with the details of articles to be used in the temple service. These were to be of the finest gold and silver. Again David had felt God's hand directing him in all these details. He was concerned that everything be well-organized but at the same time God-directed. The "chariot" on which the ark was to rest (1 Chron 28:18) perhaps hints at the Chronicler's recollection of the magnificence of the vision that Ezekiel saw long after David's day and that he describes in Ezekiel 1.

The Promise (1 Chron 28:20-21). The preparations being completed, Solomon could go ahead and build, confident of God's powerful presence with him. The promise is like that of Moses to Joshua (Deut 31:6, 8; Josh 1:5). David also ensured that Solomon had the support of everyone in the work; the officials and all the people were ready to help.

Prayer, preparation and planning are prerequisites for all service for God. Knowing his will and doing things as he directs are central, and counting on his promise day by day is an ongoing necessity.

The people of the Chronicler's day needed to take heart in their difficult situation and know that as they put God first and obeyed him faithfully, they would find him faithful. Times for them had changed; David and Solomon and the glories of their kingdoms were long gone, but God was still the same, his word as true and powerful as ever, and they were still his people. Their temple was insignificant in comparison with the magnificence of Solomon's temple, but God was not limited by a temple building; his glory filled the whole earth.

The Joy of Giving (1 Chron 29:1-9). To build a temple suitable for almighty God to live in is impossible. Who could do it well enough? Perhaps Solomon felt his inadequacy (cf. 1 Kings 3:7).

David's devotion for God led him to give huge quantities of the best of his kingdom's and his own resources (see also 1 Chron 22:2-5). The word used for David's personal or special treasures *(segullah)* is the same as is used of Israel as God's treasure (Ex 19:5). David would not offer to God what cost him nothing (cf. 1 Chron 21:24) but gave what was personal, valuable, for he knew that he owed everything he had to God's generosity.

Having given his best, David challenged the leaders, officers, commanders, officials. They were challenged to consecrate themselves. Priests were consecrated to serve God (see Ex 28:41), which meant a lifetime of devoted obedience to God. Their work and words and actions were to honor God. In the same way, these leaders were challenged to give their whole selves to God, their gifts being an outward expression of their devotion to him. True consecration is always expressed in giving, because true consecration comes out of true love, and true love always involves sacrifice and giving, as God showed by his example (cf. Mk 12:41-44; Lk 7:47).

The leaders gave willingly, just as many years before the Israelites had given willingly and generously for the tabernacle (Ex 35:20-29). A "daric" (1 Chron 29:7) is a Persian coin, the Chronicler helping his readers to understand the huge amount offered by using a term they understood. In David's time there were probably no coins.

The willing response by the leaders brought great rejoicing to both people and king, because of the wholehearted devotion that brought it about. Joy always follows selfless, unconditional giving.

Solomon's Anointing and David's Death (1 Chron 29:10-30)

Before summarizing Solomon's anointing and David's death, this section focuses on several aspects of praise (1 Chron 29:10-20). As David thought of God's majesty, power and splendor (1 Chron 29:10-13), he exulted in God's exaltation over all things. God's sovereignty and incomparable greatness are incredible and bring forth praise, thanks and worship from his people, who owe him everything.

Recognition of God's greatness brings realization of David's and Israel's insignificance (1 Chron 29:14-16) and also the source not only of all they have given but the source of the generous spirit of their giving as well. Everything comes from God. His people lived in the land as aliens and strangers in the sense that their days there were transient; just as their ancestors had come and gone, so would they all. Like a shadow they would not "abide" or have security in themselves (1 Chron 29:15; NRSV "hope," Heb. *miqweh*). They were there by God's grace alone, not by right. God, however, is a God of abundance. He does not stint in his giving, which is why the people had been able to give so generously (1 Chron 29:14). If God's people will not give generously, they are implying that their God does not give generously.

God is the one who searches out the heart (1 Chron 28:9; see also Ps 26:2; 139:23). David was confident that God would find integrity, willingness and honesty in his heart (1 Chron 29:17-20). David could see these things also in the hearts of the people who had given so willingly, and his prayer was that God would keep these attributes there along with loyalty. For Solomon, he requested wholehearted devotion that would enable him to obey God, so ensuring that his kingdom would be established, and to complete the temple. All the people then joined with David in praising God.

The second acknowledgment of Solomon as king (1 Chron 29:21-25) is then recorded. Following on from the hasty anointing of Solomon as king, as detailed in 1 Kings 1, the Chronicler shows him being accepted by the whole assembly (1 Chron 29:20), in the context of sacrifices and burnt offerings, feasting and celebration. (This is perhaps an expansion of the statement in 1 Chronicles 23:1, or else 1 Chronicles 23:1 may be a reference to the first anointing of 1 Kings 1.) The words "a second time" do not appear in the Septuagint and may not be in the original, but this acknowledgment of Solomon was a separate occasion from that given in 1 Kings 1, which was characterized by factions and divided loyalties (see especially 1 Kings 1:9, 19, 25). This acceptance is shown in connection with the officers and mighty men, and Solomon's brothers, the king's sons.

These were the ones whose loyalty was divided in 1 Kings 1, but the Chronicler shows these divisions overcome.

Zadok the priest replaced Abiathar, who had supported Adonijah's claim to kingship (see 1 Chron 16:39; 1 Kings 2:35; 1 Kings 1:39, where Zadok anointed Solomon). Perhaps this occasion was a public acknowledgment of Zadok's priesthood as well, a reappointment or promotion. After all the difficulties of succession, Solomon was clearly shown as God's choice, as he was rewarded with exaltation and splendor.

In a summary of David's life and death (1 Chron 29:26-30), David's reign over all Israel is reiterated. The first seven years over Judah only is incorporated into the total rule over Israel (see 2 Sam 5:5; 1 Kings 2:11). God had kept his promise to David (1 Chron 17:11-14), giving him long life, wealth and honor, and a son to succeed him as king.

The writer gives the sources (see, e.g., 1 Chron 10:13; 11:3; 17:1-15; 21:9-13, 18-19) from which he has chosen the details he wishes to emphasize to enable his readers to be trusting and obedient and to see God's blessing in their time. David's influence reached not only to Israel but also to many other kingdoms (1 Chron 14:17; 18:6, 13), as did the lives of those kings who followed God after him (2 Chron 17:10; 20:29).

It is God's purpose to reach out to other nations, to display his glory to them, through his people, but first his people must become strong in their faith, loyalty and obedience to God. David's life is an example of how God can use such people.

Bibliography. R. Braun, *1 Chronicles*, Word Biblical Commentary 14 (Waco, TX: Word, 1986); R. B. Dillard, *2 Chronicles*, Word Biblical Commentary 15 (Waco, TX: Word, 1987); M. Wilcock, *The Message of Chronicles*, Bible Speaks Today (Downers Grove, IL: IVP, 1987); H. G. M. Williamson, *1 and 2 Chronicles*, New Century Bible (Grand Rapids, MI: Eerdmans, 1982).

CHRISTINE L. ANSLOW

2 CHRONICLES

Introduction

The church father Jerome is supposed to have said that "the book of Chronicles . . . is of such importance that without it anyone who claims to have a knowledge of the Scriptures makes himself a fool" (Dillard, ix), and yet this is a neglected book among Christians. As the *Mercer Dictionary of the Bible* warns us, "the study of Chronicles is for the careful student rather than the casual reader" (Bain, 146). A close friend has called Chronicles a cure for insomnia.

One scholar has said that Chronicles tells us about four things: David (in 1 Chronicles), the temple, the festivals, and the Levites and their suborders (DeVries, 636). The last three of these four major themes are most prominent in 2 Chronicles.

The author of Chronicles emphasized ritual and musical matters. He believed in serving Yahweh through Jerusalem, the temple and the official and formal worship system, emphasizing the central place of Jerusalem and the temple. It sounds as if he had been reading Ezekiel and Malachi. The only hope for the returning refugees was in becoming a worshiping congregation centered upon the temple. And no joyful ceremony could be complete without music. In 2 Chronicles there are intricate, detailed descriptions of the festivals.

In the Chronicler's opinion, the Levites had yet to achieve the honor and influence that were rightfully theirs (DeVries, 636). Julia O'Brien has written, "Chronicles' high estimation of the Levites is perhaps its outstanding characteristic" (O'Brien, 21). 2 Chronicles was written from the priestly point of view. Of course, there is emphasis on the prophets too. But there are more references to the Levites in the Chronicler's work than in all the rest of the Old Testament (Clines, 29).

We might add a fifth theme for Chronicles: the Chronicler pointed out the principle of retribution (Gottwald, 515). People who sin are punished. This is especially true of those who abuse the priests and the prophets. The wonderful stories of this book illustrate this truth over and over again.

We may also be surprised and gratified by how many references are significant for women. Two women are particularly important, one negatively and the other positively: Athaliah and Huldah.

Outline

1:1—9:31	The Reign of Solomon
10:1—16:14	The Reigns of Rehoboam, Abijah and Asa
17:1—21:1	The Reign of Jehoshaphat
21:1—23:21	The Reigns of Jehoram, Ahaziah and Athaliah
24:1—25:28	The Reigns of Joash and Amaziah
26:1—28:27	The Reigns of Uzziah, Jotham and Ahaz
29:1—32:33	The Reign of Hezekiah
33:1-25	The Reigns of Manasseh and Amon
34:1—35:27	The Reign of Josiah
36:1-23	The Reigns of Jehoahaz, Jehoiakim, Jehoiachin and Zedekiah

Commentary

The Reign of Solomon (2 Chron 1—9)

First Kings tells all of the good things about Solomon (961-922; references to dates are from Bright), and then 1 Kings 11 tells us how badly he turned out. (There are several broad hints along the way about how badly things were going, if we have the perception to pick up on them.) Second Chronicles is different. It concentrates on the good part, leaving the negative aspects of the story to other authors whose purpose in writing is different. "Solomon son of David established himself in his kingdom; the LORD his God was with him and made him exceedingly great" (2 Chron 1:1).

Solomon's Good Beginning (2 Chron 1)

According to Chronicles, Solomon was devout without exception. He was selected by the Lord to succeed his father without any of the political manipulations reported in 1 Kings, and—again unlike Kings—he had the full support of his people. The story is so unfailingly positive that one who reads only Chronicles might wonder why the kingdom was divided after his death. Early in his reign Solomon was humble, and when he was given his choice of whatever he wanted the Lord to give him, he asked for the wisdom and knowledge necessary for leadership. He was granted those gifts, with many material blessings in addition.

Solomon as Worship Leader (2 Chron 2—7)

We know that the Chronicler emphasized ritual and musical matters. This is one reason Solomon was so important and why most of the information about him in 2 Chronicles relates to the temple. In this context we find 2 Chronicles 7:14, surely the verse from 2 Chronicles that more Christians know about than any other: "If my people who are called by my name humble themselves, pray, seek my face, and turn from their wicked ways, then I will hear from heaven, and will forgive their sin and heal their land."

Solomon was the one who built the temple, relying on the plans and preparations David had made (2 Chron 2—4). He made crucial use of skilled craftsmen and building supplies from their northern allies in Phoenicia, again following David's pattern (2 Chron 2:7-10, 13-16; 4:11-17). The Chronicler provides us with all of the details of the construction. One is touched by the elaborate decorations, which must have been breathtaking in their beauty.

When the shrine was completed, Solomon held an elaborate ceremony of dedication (2 Chron 5:1—7:11), which included processions, numerous sacrifices, musical praise and extended public prayer. According to Solomon's understanding, the building of the temple in Jerusalem and the Lord's blessings on it constituted the Lord's choice of a place where he would permanently place his name, in fulfillment of the long-given promises such as those in Deuteronomy 12. The Lord responded to Solomon's elaborate prayer with fire from heaven that consumed the burnt offering and sacrifices, "and the glory of the LORD filled the temple" (2 Chron 7:1). It has been said, "Old Testament history reached a high-water mark on the day Solomon dedicated the temple to God" (Yancey, 79).

Where are women in this complicated and important story? Apparently hidden in the crowds. They do feature more prominently later in the book.

Solomon's Other Activities (2 Chron 8—9)

Solomon's building projects may have been the most important aspect of his administration. After the temple he constructed a palace and built or rebuilt several cities, fortresses and storage towns (2 Chron 8:1-10).

Eventually he married, or rather began to marry. He married the daughter of the pharaoh of Egypt. This marriage is important for several reasons. The daughter of the pharaoh was not a believer in the Lord (2 Chron 8:11; 1 Kings 11:1-8). Also vitally important is the fact that in the ancient Near East a marriage between royal houses was for diplomatic and economic reasons. Marriages like this were a part of Solomon's foreign policy. One scholar calls this Solomon's state department. This is how Solomon kept the peace. This is how he established trade relations. Apparently spiritual considerations played little or no part in the proceedings. The frequent biblical prohibition against marriage with foreigners was always religious, never racial, but here there is no question of Solomon's wife wishing to become a follower of Yahweh.

Solomon was evidently highly regarded, because previously pharaohs had refused to give their daughters in marriage to foreign kings. In fact, this is the only Old Testament reference to an Egyptian princess marrying a non-Egyptian. So Solomon must have built quite a reputation (Clements, 28).

Second Chronicles is greatly concerned with the status of the Levites and their suborders and with the prescribed feasts and festivals. The Chronicler's Solomon starred at this point (2 Chron 8:12-15), as he had in temple construction. He was also active in land and sea trade, which enriched him and his kingdom. These riches are detailed in 2 Chronicles 9:10-11, 13-28.

Solomon and the Queen of Sheba (2 Chron 9)

The queen of Sheba was the undisputed ruler of an ancient realm. Her story is told to accent Solomon's wisdom and wealth, but the story also indicates her importance and influence. She had "a very great retinue and camels bearing spices and very much gold and precious stones." She was also a woman of considerable intelligence and insight: "She discussed with him all that was on her mind" (2 Chron 9:1).

This queen learned of Solomon's reputation and made a fifteen-hundred-mile journey to see for herself. When she became aware of his accomplishments, his lifestyle and his wealth, she was gracious and voluble in her praise. She provided him with elaborate presents, another indication of her status. It is clear that the approval of this woman is seen as adding to Solomon's significance or status.

The Reigns of Rehoboam, Abijah and Asa (2 Chron 10—16)

The Chronicler may have been able to overlook Solomon's many shortcomings, but he had a harder time maintaining that pattern with the kings who followed. His motto was apparently Be Positive—Always Be Positive, and it helped that he omitted the story of the northern kingdom of Israel and concentrated only on the southern kingdom of Judah.

The Division of the Kingdom (2 Chron 10)

But the Chronicler did have to mention that the original kingdom was divided after Solomon died. The seeds of the catastrophe must have been sown throughout Solomon's years, but the matter came to a head when the young king-to-be, Rehoboam (922-915), went to the ancient shrine center of Shechem so that the nation as a whole could recognize his accession to the throne.

The leader of the northern tribes was Jeroboam the son of Nebat, Solomon's former labor leader (2 Chron 10:2), who eventually would in time be Jeroboam I, the first king of what became the northern kingdom of Israel. Jeroboam expressed his people's desire for relief from the heavy burdens of labor and taxation that Solomon had placed on them.

Rehoboam followed the wrong instincts and listened to the wrong advisers. He decided on a harsh, threatening approach, and the people of the northern tribes rejected it. In consequence, the one unified nation of considerable international influence was instantly turned into two modest kingdoms doomed to generations of struggle against their neighbors and against each other (see 2 Chron 12:15). The division of the kingdom in 922 B.C. has been called the greatest catastrophe in national history. It certainly had some of the longest-reaching effects. Rehoboam retained the two tribes of Judah and Benjamin in the south (with Simeon apparently also included), while Jeroboam ruled over the ten tribes in the north. We can only imagine what continued effects this national tragedy had on the wives and mothers of Judah and Israel and their families.

Rehoboam's Inept Leadership (2 Chron 11—12)

Did the adjective *inept* ever apply to anyone so well as to Rehoboam of Judah? His pride, naiveté and attempted tyranny had split the kingdom, so the first thing he did was try to force it back together. The Lord, through his prophet, stopped him. However, Rehoboam had to fortify the border cities and fortresses on his side of the new boundary and had to cope with the economic loss and political confusion that he had caused.

2 Chronicles 11:18 seems like an insignificant verse, but it is not. It is representative of numerous similar references throughout the rest of the book. It is the first reference to the queen, one of the wives of the king of Judah. She became the mother of the crown prince and, after her husband's death, the queen mother. It reminds us that it has long been customary to consider someone to be an authentic Jew if the mother was Jewish. It is extremely significant that the divine record would be so careful to include these influential women. "During the entire period of the monarchy the *King's mother* (not his *wife*) has a special position in the state, beginning with Solomon, who bows down to his mother (1 Kings 2:19), up through the mother of King Jeconiah who was exiled together with him to Babylon (2 Kings 24:15). Note Jeremiah 22:26 (Goitein, 12). This recognition of the queen mother is an exceptional emphasis in the ancient Near East (Durham, 291; Hackett, 97). There are other indications, for instance from archaeology, that women were prominent in the royal administrative system of Judah (Mazar, 41-42).

Rehoboam's mother's name is listed: Naamah the Ammonite (2 Chron 12:13). Unfortunately Rehoboam, like many royals and nobles of those times, followed the example of David and Solomon in taking many wives and concubines.

2 Chronicles seems to talk as if Reho-

boam was close to the Lord in the beginning but strayed away from him later. 1 Kings seems to consider him unfaithful from the start. At any rate, "he abandoned the law of the LORD, he and all Israel with him" (2 Chron 12:1). As punishment, the Lord sent the Egyptian pharaoh Shishak against him in 918 B.C. This first Egyptian ruler named in the Bible captured Rehoboam's fortifications and threatened Jerusalem. One is not surprised that Shishak would favor the northern Hebrew kingdom over the southern, since Jeroboam I of Israel had spent his exile in Egypt. Rehoboam and his officials heeded the warnings of the prophet Shemaiah, so the Lord relented and spared Judah from destruction. This familiar pattern of judgment and grace is found throughout the book of Judges and also in the story of the kingdom.

Nevertheless the Lord's judgment on Jerusalem through Shishak was severe: the enemy ruler took away the treasures of the temple and the palace. 2 Chronicles 12:9 says, "He took everything." Rehoboam maintained a show of continued dignity by replacing Solomon's famous shields of gold with similar implements of bronze. It is a fitting metaphor for a ruler who "did evil, for he did not set his heart to seek the LORD" (2 Chron 12:14). Through his inept leadership, he was able to turn gold into bronze.

Abijah (2 Chron 13)

Rehoboam's son Abijah (915-913) was next. His mother's name was Micaiah, listed in the introduction to the information about the king, as is the custom throughout most of 2 Chronicles. We do not have enough information to say that Abijah was like his mother, but he was like his father: "He committed all the sins that his father did before him" (1 Kings 15:3). He too fought against Jeroboam I of Israel all of his life (1 Chron 13:2). Unlike Rehoboam, Abijah was at least partially successful, probably because of the Lord's faithfulness to his promises to David and Solomon and his favor for Jerusalem, and because Jeroboam I's sins were always pictured as even worse than those of his counterparts in Judah.

Asa (2 Chron 14—16)

It is not always true that the good die young. Abijah ruled only three years, while his son, Asa (913-873), reigned for forty. And Asa "did what was good and right in the sight of the LORD his God" (2 Chron 14:2). He was exactly what Judah needed at that time, a reforming king. He destroyed the foreign altars and the high places of pagan worship that had begun to creep into the land during the time of Solomon and that flourished during the next two reigns. He broke down the symbols of Canaanite fertility religion, sacred pillars and poles. He encouraged his people to seek the Lord by word and by example. Accordingly the land had rest during his time.

Asa saw to the defenses of the kingdom, as all of the kings of those times had to. Thus, when an immense Ethiopian army came against Judah, he was ready. He asked the Lord for help, he received it, and he was victorious. He followed the military victory with spiritual victory. Inspired by prophetic support, he led the people in a far-reaching spiritual renewal. This pattern of covenant renewal was followed by subsequent kings, such as Hezekiah and Josiah.

One curious incident involving King Asa's mother sheds more light on the influence of women in the royal court of Judah. His mother was Maacah, King Abijah's widow. Asa found it necessary to remove her from her position as queen mother because she had made an image for Asherah, the Canaanite goddess. This may be seen as a negative for women, but it indicates that their actions were taken seriously and seen as significant, even when they were worthy of judgment.

Asa spent his final years in continual warfare and in estrangement from the Lord. In order to hire as an ally Ben-hadad of Syria (Aram), he stripped the temple and palace of their treasures, which evidently had been replaced after Shishak's invasion and would be removed and replaced again. The king of Syria attacked Asa's enemy, Baasha, the king of Israel, and forced him to break his siege of Ramah. The problem, according to the Lord's messenger, was that Asa had relied on a foreign alliance rather than on the Lord. Asa's response was the opposite of what one would want. It is the first biblical record of royal persecution of a prophet and a sad end to a promising reign.

The Reign of Jehoshaphat (2 Chron 17:1—21:1)

If kings like Asa were seen as average and ones like Rehoboam as poor, there were those like Jehoshaphat (873-849) who were viewed more positively. He was a good king. He was somewhat naive, but he was godly and sincere.

Jehoshaphat's Reforms (2 Chron 17; 19)

Jehoshaphat, the son of his mother, Azubah, was another reformer. He did several positive things that turned Judah in a better direction. He "sought the God of his father and walked in his commandments, and not according to the ways of Israel. . . . His heart was courageous in the ways of the LORD" (2 Chron 17:4, 6). As a result, he removed the high places and sacred poles, or Asherim, from Judah.

Jehoshaphat was not merely satisfied with following the Lord himself; he sent official and levitical teachers throughout the land to instruct the people in the Lord's law. He reformed Judah's judiciary, ensuring justice for his people, as ancient kings—especially the kings of the Lord's people—were supposed to. He enjoyed national prosperity and international security.

Jehoshaphat's Mistakes (2 Chron 18)

Jehoshaphat's naiveté is most evidenced by his cooperation with King Ahab of Israel, the wickedest person ever to sit on a Hebrew throne. How else can one explain his close alliance with Ahab (some say Jehoshaphat was his vassal, or perhaps the two of them feared the threat of their near northern enemy, Syria/Aram, against whom Israel fought for almost a century), formed through the marriage of the daughter of Ahab and Jezebel, Athaliah, to Jehoram, the son of Jehoshaphat. This marriage had later, unfortunate consequences for Judah.

This alliance led to Jehoshaphat's going into battle alongside Ahab to retake the Transjordanian city of Ramoth-gilead. It was inappropriate for Jehoshaphat to get into that fight, and the Lord tried to warn him. He used the message and example of the absolutely fearless prophet, Micaiah, who dared to stand alone against Ahab and his sycophantic court prophets.

Further evidence of Jehoshaphat's naiveté is apparent in his letting Ahab talk him into dressing in his royal robes and taking Ahab's place in the front of the battle, while Ahab disguised himself as an ordinary soldier and stayed back in the ranks. Jehoshaphat's naiveté almost got him killed.

Jehoshaphat's Military and Commercial Campaigns (2 Chron 20)

The Moabites, Ammonites and Edomites in Transjordan were long-time bitter enemies of the Hebrew people, partly because they were related to them (Gen 19:30-38; 25:30). The king and all of the people of Judah, including the women (2 Chron 20:13), sought the Lord in humility, and he gave them a notable victory over these traditional enemies. Jehoshaphat was less successful in his commercial endeavors.

The Reigns of Jehoram, Ahaziah and Athaliah (2 Chron 21:1—23:21)

Jehoram, Husband of Athaliah (2 Chron 21)

Jehoram (849-843) was the one of Jehoshaphat's several sons who succeeded to the throne. One is not long left in doubt about what sort of king he would be. He showed his appreciation for this customary privilege of the firstborn by having his brothers killed. He was more like the kings of Israel than the kings of Judah.

As he describes this wicked king, the Chronicler reminds readers that Jehoram had married Athaliah, the daughter of Ahab and Jezebel.

A part of the Lord's punishment of Jehoram was for all vassal territories like Edom and Libnah to revolt against him, but this did not change his life pattern. He not only built high places—apparently regional pagan shrines—but also "led the inhabitants of Jerusalem into unfaithfulness, and made Judah go astray" (2 Chron 21:11). His consequent punishment was even more personal and severe. When he died, no one was sorry.

Ahaziah, Son of Jehoram and Athaliah (2 Chron 22:1-9)

The good news about Ahaziah (843-842), Jehoram's youngest son, is that he ruled for only one year. The bad news is that his mother was Athaliah, granddaughter of Omri, king of Israel, and daughter of Ahab and Jezebel. She has been called as evil as both of her parents—but one hopes not! Significantly, Ahaziah's mother "was his counselor in doing wickedly" (2 Chron 22:3). Both mothers and fathers bear responsibility for the influence and effect they have on their children (*see* Parental Influence).

During the brief time that Ahaziah was king in Judah, his uncle Jehoram or Joram was the ruler of Israel. They cooperated in a military expedition against Syria (Aram), during which Jehoram of Israel was wounded. During his incapacitation, a general named Jehu rebelled against the king and the house of Ahab, and Ahaziah, who was visiting his uncle, was also killed.

Athaliah (2 Chron 22:10—23:21)

With her son suddenly dead, the queen mother, Athaliah (842-837), seized power in Judah. She was the only woman ever to sit on a Hebrew throne. She set out to have all of the members of the royal family killed—these included her grandchildren—and would have succeeded but for the heroic efforts of Jehoshabeath, Ahaziah's sister and the wife of the priest Jehoiada, who hid Ahaziah's son Joash from harm.

Jehoshabeath kept the young prince Joash hidden for six years in the temple area while Athaliah reigned. Finally Jehoiada felt that the time was ripe to act. He enlisted military and spiritual leaders who pledged to support the rightful king of David's line. Plans were carefully laid to catch Athaliah off guard and present her with a fait accompli. Thus the existence of Joash, alive and well, was revealed to the citizenry, and he was officially proclaimed king.

When Athaliah learned what was going on, it was too late. She charged everyone with treason—it is a common practice to defend oneself and one's actions by charging everyone else with crimes. Besides, treason is an ironic charge brought by the woman who had almost all of the royal family of Judah destroyed. Athaliah and all of her followers were executed, though she was executed outside of the sacred temple precincts.

Jehoiada's next step was to lead the people in spiritual renewal, specifically a renewal of the ancient covenant. It should be noted that the Old Testament covenant was not automatic. It had to be renewed by each new generation. Each individual had to choose to be a part of the covenant community (*see* Covenant and Community). Under the leadership of the priest, the citizens of Judah would return to being the Lord's people again. They tore down the temple of Baal, with its altars and images, and killed the priests of Baal. True worship was purified and reorganized. Everyone looked forward to a new day under a young, new king.

The Reigns of Joash and Amaziah (2 Chron 24—25)

Joash (2 Chron 24)

Joash (837-800), the son of his mother, Zibiah, was only seven when he became king. Under the influence of the priest Jehoiada he made an admirable start. The end of the story is not so uplifting. Joash's first significant act was to properly refurbish the long-abused temple. The people throughout the country were generous in their financial support of the project, which enabled it to be carried to an appropriate conclusion.

In his latter days, however, with his uncle Jehoiada dead, Joash had a change of heart. He and his people abandoned the Lord for sacred poles and idols and suffered the consequent judgment. They ignored the prophets whom the Lord sent to them.

Jehoiada had been such an outstanding leader that he had been buried "among the kings" (2 Chron 24:16). His son, Zechariah, was apparently the same type of person. The Lord inspired him to assume a prophetic role, but "by command of the king they stoned him to death in the court of the house of the LORD" (2 Chron 24:21). The Lord sent Syria (Aram) against Judah as punishment. The destruction was great, and Joash was severely wounded in the fighting. His servants conspired against him and "killed him on his bed" (2 Chron 24:25). Unlike the priest Jehoiada, King Joash was not buried "in the tombs of the kings" (2 Chron 24:25).

Amaziah, Joash's Mirror Image (2 Chron 25)

Amaziah (800-783), the son of Joash and Jehoaddan, succeeded his father. Unfortunately Amaziah was like both the early Joash and the later Joash. "He did what was right in the sight of the LORD, yet not with a true heart" (2 Chron 25:2). After serious missteps in enlisting a sufficiently strong army, Amaziah successfully attacked Edom (Seir) to the southeast. For some reason he began to worship the gods of the defeated Edomites that he took back to Jerusalem. To this sin he added the transgression of silencing the Lord's prophetic messenger.

Amaziah experienced unpleasant relations with his contemptuous contemporary, Joash of Israel. When he tried to force the issue, the Lord used the occasion as an avenue of judgment on his idolatry. When the battle between the two nations was joined, Judah was soundly defeated and Amaziah and other hostages were captured. Joash of Israel added to Judah's sorry plight by breaking down a considerable section of the defensive wall of Jerusalem. He also stripped the temple and palace of their accumulated treasures. Amaziah suffered a death similar to that of his father.

The Reigns of Uzziah, Jotham and Ahaz (2 Chron 26—28)

Uzziah, the Best So Far (2 Chron 26)

Uzziah (Azariah, 783-742), the son of his mother, Jecoliah, was only sixteen when he became king, but he was a good one, better than average, and served for an unusually long time. "He did what was right in the sight of the LORD" (2 Chron 26:4). He was effective in his commercial ventures (2 Chron 26:2 refers to the southern seaport of Eloth or Eliat) and in his military endeavors. With his enemies subdued, he strengthened the defenses and organized and strengthened the army in Jerusalem and throughout the country. He supported agriculture, which contributed to the prosperity of individual citizens and of the nation.

That is the good news, but as was so often the case, there was also bad news. Uzziah suffered a lapse toward the end of his life. When he became strong and famous, he also became proud. He violated the sanctity of the temple by entering the sanctuary to make offerings on the altar of incense, which only the priests were supposed to do. The priests withstood him and condemned his rash action. He became furious, but he also became leprous. He spent the rest of his life in quarantine, and his son Jotham became co-regent and king in all but name. Uzziah was even buried separately from his predecessors and successors.

Jotham (2 Chron 27)

Jotham's (742-735) mother was Jerushah. He was like his noble father, with the exception that he did not violate the temple. Though he was faithful personally, he failed at leading the people in a closer walk with the Lord. He continued his father's pattern of upbuilding Jerusalem and defeating enemies.

Ahaz, the Worst So Far (2 Chron 28:1-15)

How could good men like Uzziah and Jotham have a grandson and son like Ahaz (735-715)? (Could it have something to do with Ahaz's mother?) Some people consider him to be the worst king in Judah. He was more like the kings of Israel than like his ancestor David or his father and grandfather. The list of his misdeeds makes for discouraging reading: he cast images of the Baals, he sacrificed his sons as burnt offerings, and he worshiped at the pagan high places. The Lord allowed him to be dominated by Syria (Aram).

Syria defeated Judah, killed many and took many captive. One of Ahaz's sons and at least two important officials were also killed. The people of Israel took advantage of Judah's weakness to engage in excesses of looting and enslavement, which were checked only by the courageous opposition of a northern prophet and several prominent leaders. The Lord did choose Syria and Israel as his instruments of judgment on Ahaz and Judah, but this did not excuse excessive cruelty or inhumanity on their part.

Ahaz's Most Serious Blunder (2 Chron 28:16-27)

Ahaz made many mistakes during his lamentable sixteen-year reign, but the mistake with the longest-lasting consequences was his appeal to Tilgath-pilneser of Assyria for help against Syria and Israel. It was like a mouse asking the cat for help to get rid of other mice. Assyria attacked Judah's northern neighbors and within ten years subjugated them. However, Assyria did not stop there but extended control into Judah. Judah became little more than an Assyrian province.

At this time, during this Syro-Ephraimite war (Syria and Israel—also called by the name of its most prominent tribe, Ephraim) against Judah, the prophet Isaiah urged Ahaz to trust in the Lord. He even gave him the famous Immanuel sign to reassure him (Is 7:14). However, Ahaz refused to listen or to trust. He was determined to go his own way. As a result, the Lord's people suffered for generations. It was the beginning of Gentile domination. Judah suffered defeats at the hands of other enemies, but none compared with the trouble Ahaz brought on himself. Alas for the temple! Ahaz plundered the temple and the palace in order to give tribute to Assyria.

Did Ahaz learn his lesson? Hardly. In fact, when trouble came he became more faithless to the Lord than ever. He sacrificed to the gods of Damascus—they had defeated him, so they obviously had to be stronger. He closed the temple and built altars in every corner of Jerusalem. In every city of Judah he built high places where he could make offerings to other gods. It was a relief to everyone when he was gone. He too was buried outside the royal cemetery.

The Reign of Hezekiah (2 Chron 29—32)

How could a perverse father like Ahaz have a good and godly son like Hezekiah (715-687/6)? At any rate, Hezekiah, the son of his mother, Abijah, along with his great-grandson, Josiah, was among the best of Judah's kings. The Bible gives him high praise (2 Kings 18:5). He was like David (2 Chron 29:2; 31:20-21). His importance can be seen in the Chronicler's giving him about 70 percent more space than did the author(s) of Kings (Japhet, 912).

Hezekiah's Reforms (2 Chron 29—31)

Hezekiah was a reforming king. All the perverse things that Ahaz had done, he undid. Most important, as far as the Chronicler was concerned, he again centralized worship in Jerusalem. He reopened the temple and repaired it. He reconsecrated the priests and Levites. He admitted that the people of previous generations had been unfaithful and had suffered because of it. Hezekiah led his people in covenant renewal, a return to the sacred agreement with the Lord that had guided the nation for centuries, and did so with impressive fanfare and ceremony.

The kingdom had split under the inept Rehoboam, but Hezekiah and later Josiah did what little they could to provide links with the northern tribes. Hezekiah encouraged people in Ephraim and Manasseh to return to Jerusalem for an observance of Passover, which had not been properly observed for generations. It was a time of outstanding spiritual opportunity for the people of both areas and for the young king of Judah. It was like the days of David and Solomon. Unfortunately most of the people who remained in what had been the northern kingdom of Israel, which had fallen to Assyria in 722 B.C., were contemptuous of Hezekiah's overtures.

The king's reforming zeal was shared by his people and by the priests and Levites who supported him. There is an intriguing note as a part of the detailed descriptions of the activities of these temple functionaries. As a part of what was apparently a census of them and their families, the Chronicler specifically mentions that the daughters of the priests were enrolled on the census lists (2 Chron 31:18), another practice that stood out from the common custom of the world of that day.

The Invasion of Sennacherib of Assyria (2 Chron 32:1-23)

Hezekiah's greatest military challenge came with the invasion of Judah by the mighty Sennacherib of Assyria in 701 B.C. In a sense Hezekiah was responsible for this invasion, because of his increasing spirit of independence from his Assyrian overlords. His spiritual reforms were paralleled by political reforms. In those days to be dominated by a power such as Assyria involved at least the implicit recognition of the overlord's gods. By leading his people back to the Lord, Hezekiah distanced himself from the common practice. Sennacherib arrived to bring him back into line.

Hezekiah prepared for the onslaught as best he could. Jerusalem, on its hills, has always been weak at the point of adequate water. The only water supply that the people had was to catch rain in reservoirs. And during certain times of the year, they did not catch much. Hezekiah's workmen cut a water tunnel a third of a mile long through solid rock underneath Jerusalem. They dug from both sides, wound around and met in the middle, only a few inches off. This diverted water from the springs outside the walls and was the first time that Jerusalem had ever had water flowing within its walls. Thus the necessary water would be available to those defending the city instead of to those attacking it. He strengthened the defenses of the city and organized and encouraged the defensive forces. He particularly urged the people to trust the Lord to help them against their human foes.

Despite Hezekiah's optimistic words, the situation did not look good for Judah. Sennacherib had already conquered almost all of Judah. According to his records, he had captured forty-six of Judah's cities and towns and had shut up Hezekiah in Jerusalem like a bird in a cage. Lachish was the last outpost to fall. During the siege of Lachish, Sennacherib sent messengers to Hezekiah to ridicule him and his God and to demoralize Jerusalem's defenders. The words of the Assyrian messengers indicate that they considerably misunderstood the nature of Hezekiah's spiritual reforms; they thought that instead of leading the people back to the Lord the Judean king was displeasing the Lord. They boasted that none of the gods of any other nation had been able to protect their people from Assyrian attack.

Characteristically, Hezekiah's response was spiritual. He prayed to the Lord and turned to the prophet Isaiah for guidance. The Lord's response was more dramatic than any of them could have dared hope. He sent an angel to strike down the Assyrian army, so that Sennacherib was forced to return home in disgrace. In the supposed safety of his royal city of Nineveh, his sons killed him with the sword.

Hezekiah's Illness and Its Aftermath (2 Chron 32:24-33)

At about the same time, Hezekiah became critically ill and lay at the point of death. He prayed again, this time for physical deliverance, and once again the Lord heard him. Like Uzziah before him, in his time of victory and strength he became proud. Hezekiah, however, learned his lesson—he was like David and acknowledged his shortcomings. He and his people were spared, and he lived to enjoy great riches and prestige.

The Reigns of Manasseh and Amon (2 Chron 33)

How could a good and godly king like Hezekiah have a son like Manasseh? They are as different as Mount Everest and the Dead Sea. What role did Manasseh's mother, Hephzibah, play? Manasseh was the worst king ever in the south, so bad that 2 Kings blames him for the ultimate fall of Judah, despite the fine efforts of his grandson Josiah, who came after him.

Manasseh's Ungodliness and Repentance (2 Chron 33:1-20)

Manasseh (687/6-642) was only twelve years old when he began to reign, apparently as co-regent with his father. He ruled for a record fifty-five years. He was not merely as bad as the Israelites, like some of his predecessors; he was as bad as the Canaanites. "He did what was evil in the sight of the LORD, according to the abominable practices of the nations whom the LORD drove out before the people of Israel" (2 Chron 33:2; see also 2 Chron 33:9). Not only was Manasseh submissive to his foreign overlords; he was enthusiastic about it. He seemed glad to serve Assyria. What did this mean religiously? The Lord was considered to be merely one of many gods. Canaanite fertility cults revived. Local sanctuaries were rebuilt.

The pattern is monotonous as well as tragic. Manasseh undid all of Hezekiah's careful reforms, instead engaging in the apostasies of his grandfather Ahaz. Yet some of his apostasies stand out. He built pagan altars and idols in the temple area, shed much innocent blood (2 Kings 21:16) and practiced child sacrifice (2 Chron 33:6). Worst, he led the people of Judah after him, so that the summary says that "they did more evil than the nations whom the LORD had destroyed before the people of Israel" (2 Chron 33:9).

The Lord warned Manasseh and his people, but to no effect. Therefore punishment was inevitable. Once again God used Assyria as his instrument of judgment. The invaders took Manasseh bound to Babylon. Second Kings does not tell this part of the story, but the severe judgment had its desired effect (the purpose of the Lord's judgment is always redemptive, to bring us back): Manasseh had a change of heart. He prayed, and the Lord—always gracious—

heard his prayer and restored him to his throne in Jerusalem. Manasseh's later years were spent in fortifying his capital city, removing the emblems of pagan worship to which he had been so devoted and restoring the true worship of the Lord. Although behavior can be changed, the effects of behavior cannot easily be obliterated. The people who had so fully shared his apostasy did not fully share in his repentance. They continued to worship in ways that were at least questionable, led by their new king.

Amon's Brief Ungodliness (2 Chron 33:21-24)

Amon (642-640) was as bad as Manasseh, but he did not reign as long. He was like his father in his unfaithfulness but unlike him in his repentance: he never acknowledged his need for God's forgiveness. His servants conspired against him and assassinated him in his palace. He left the throne to his eight-year-old son, Josiah.

The Reign of Josiah (2 Chron 34—35)

How could a person like Amon (640-609) have a son like Josiah? (Again, could it have something to do with his mother?) He was perhaps the brightest star of the Judean monarchy and is one of true heroes of 2 Chronicles (see also 2 Kings 23:25). Someone influenced the boy and later the young man to do what was right in the sight of the Lord and walk in the ways of his ancestor David without turning aside to the right or to the left (2 Chron 34:2). One person who did was the strong and influential prophet Huldah.

Josiah Seeks the Lord (2 Chron 34:1-7)

One key to Josiah's life and character is that he began to seek the Lord early, when he was sixteen, during his eighth year on the throne. He gave practical expression to this impulse four years later when he began reforms to undo the negative influence of his father and grandfather. He purged Judah of its high places, fertility cult symbols, images and altars to Baal.

Huldah and Her Work (2 Chron 34:8-28)

Perhaps the most important act of Josiah's administration came in his eighteenth year as king, when he began to refurbish the temple that for so long had been either neglected or abused. The most effective political and spiritual leaders of the nation were enlisted in the project, along with the Levites and the public, who contributed the necessary funds.

During this significant remodeling the workmen uncovered a dusty old scroll. Hilkiah the priest and Shaphan the secretary examined it and eventually read it to the king. To their consternation, the book turned out to be a law scroll, containing all or part of our book of Deuteronomy and thus filled with the Lord's commandments, which neither king nor people had been observing, in part because they were unaware of them. The king tore his clothes as a sign of grieving and anguish.

It is significant that Josiah instructed his advisors, "Go, inquire of the LORD for me" (2 Chron 34:21), and they took the law scroll to a woman. She was a prophet, evidently prominent in Jerusalem, named Huldah. She is the most significant female figure in 2 Chronicles. The committee, made up of five of the most highly placed men of the kingdom, went to her to "inquire of the LORD . . . concerning the words of the book," and apparently nobody objected to taking the scroll to a woman for authentication. Her authority was undisputed, even unquestioned. Nobody asked for a second opinion. This fact raises doubts about the common assumption that women of the time were all uneducated and downtrodden (*see* Expectations of Women). Huldah at least was a clear example of a learned and influential woman.

Huldah was married to Shallum, the keeper of the wardrobe. Tradition makes her a relative of Jeremiah. Her husband's family obviously had court connections. They lived in an affluent part of the city (Sampson, 19). This was the day of Zephaniah, Habakkuk and Jeremiah, but the delegation did not go to one of them. Perhaps they were less well known, or perhaps Jeremiah was still considered too young. But Huldah was obviously the most important spiritual leader in the Judean capital.

Huldah was a true prophet of the Lord. She used the traditional prophetic formula when she spoke: "Thus says the LORD, the God of Israel" (she used it twice, 2 Chron

34:23-24). Her message of judgment was also in the pattern of the messages of the prophets before the exile. She was even direct with Josiah: "Tell the man who sent you to me" (2 Chron 34:23).

Disaster is coming, Huldah said, speaking for the Lord in true prophetic fashion, because the people have forsaken me for false gods. "My wrath will be poured out on this place and will not be quenched" (2 Chron 34:25). It was not a pleasant message, but she did not hesitate to proclaim it boldly. She did have a somewhat positive word for Josiah personally: Because he was penitent and humble, he would not have to live to see the trouble come.

Josiah's Response to Huldah's Message (2 Chron 34:29—35:19)

In an appropriate response to Huldah's prophetic proclamation, the king began to lead the people in a dramatic ceremony of covenant renewal. They recommitted themselves to the Lord and to their covenant obligations. Though it may have been somewhat shallow, the resulting revival experience was perhaps the most widespread of the Old Testament.

Josiah read to the assembled people the words of the law scroll and "made a covenant before the LORD, to follow the LORD, keeping his commandments, his decrees, and his statutes, with all his heart and all his soul, to perform the words of the covenant that were written in this book" (2 Chron 34:31). The people made a similar pledge. All the days of Josiah, the people "did not turn away from following the LORD the God of their ancestors" (2 Chron 34:33).

As a symbol of the renewed covenant relationship, Josiah also led the people in observing the Passover, which had been so infrequently or inappropriately observed throughout the generations (2 Chron 35:1-19, especially 2 Chron 35:18). 2 Chronicles 35 is the final example in the book of the considerable emphasis on the feasts and festivals and the Levites who were so important in their observance.

Josiah's Untimely End (2 Chron 35:20-27)

The old saying may not always be true that only the good die young, but it was true of Josiah. In the latter years of the seventh century B.C. the power struggle in that part of the world was approaching its climax. Cruel Assyria, overextended and weakened, was about to reap what it had sown for more than a century. Babylon had revolted under the father of Nebuchadnezzar and would soon be part of bringing Assyria down. Egypt wanted to maintain the balance of power, so Pharaoh Neco (also Necho) marched eastward through Judah to try to bolster Assyrian resistance. He probably also wanted to carve out a section of Syria-Palestine for himself.

Josiah opposed him for both reasons. In 609 B.C. he resisted the Egyptian incursion. The two forces met at the ancient fortress of Megiddo, where Josiah was mortally wounded. His attendants took him back to Jerusalem to die. He had been thirty-one years on the throne, and dead at thirty-nine. His friend Jeremiah and everyone else grieved. We do not know whether it was because of Josiah's courageous but perhaps naive resistance, but Neco was too late to help Assyria. Its last outpost had already fallen in 610 B.C.

The Reigns of Jehoahaz, Jehoiakim, Jehoiachin and Zedekiah (2 Chron 36)

Josiah's sons—Jehoahaz, Jehoiakim and Zedekiah—were not like him, and the short rest of the story of Judah is not a happy one. Forgettable kings came and went quickly, like the slots of a revolving door. The final twenty years were years of political chaos and even further spiritual decline.

Jehoahaz (2 Chron 36:1-4)

Jehoahaz (609) was the second son of Josiah, but the people justifiably did not like his older brother, so they made him king instead. He reigned for three months. Then the pharaoh deposed him, exacted heavy tribute on the land and carried him off into Egypt, the first Jewish exile and the first Jewish leader to die in exile. In a sense, national history begins and ends in Egypt.

Jehoiakim, Strong in His Wickedness (2 Chron 36:5-8)

Josiah's oldest son was named Eliakim, but pharaoh changed his name to Jehoiakim (609-598). This indicates that he was little more than an Egyptian puppet. Remember also that he was not the people's choice. He was so selfish, materialistic and ruthless that no one grieved when he died. Jeremiah had to oppose him every year he ruled.

Jehoiakim did reign for eleven years, during which time Nebuchadnezzar of Babylon took full control over that part of the world. But Jehoiakim could not read the signs of the times. He foolishly rebelled against his Babylonian overlord, looking instead to weak Egypt for help. In 598 Nebuchadnezzar arrived to punish the rebel. Chronicles talks as if he were taken into exile in Babylon, though Kings seems to say that he died (perhaps he was assassinated) in Jerusalem during the siege. We can only imagine what was happening in the lives of the women of the land.

Jehoiachin (2 Chron 36:9-10)

Jehoiachin (598/7) was a young man when he was suddenly thrust upon the throne (2 Chron 36:9 says "eight," 2 Kings 24:8 says "eighteen"). He too reigned for three months. He hardly had time to do "what was evil in the sight of the LORD" (2 Chron 36:9) before Nebuchadnezzar carted him and his family off to Babylon, along with the treasures of the palace and temple. In all Jehoiachin spent thirty-six years in exile. We call it the first deportation, in 597. It began the exile and undid the exodus. It was a blow from which Judah never recovered.

Despite all this, Nebuchadnezzar was surprisingly lenient. He looted Jerusalem but did not destroy the city. He took many captives to Babylon, the cream of the leadership of the country. Perhaps there were ten thousand exiles in all. The prophet Ezekiel went to Babylon during this time.

Zedekiah and the End (2 Chron 36:11-21)

Nebuchadnezzar made Josiah's third son, Zedekiah (597-587), king in the place of his young nephew. He was the last of the Hebrew kings, ruling for ten years, but his fate hung in the balance every day of that time.

The Chronicler's assessment of Zedekiah is negative and familiar, but perhaps Zedekiah was more weak than wicked. He was dominated by inferior officials, generally pro-Egypt in sentiment, whom Nebuchadnezzar had thought not important enough to transport to Babylon. He was susceptible to whatever pressure was put on him. He followed the advice of whomever he spoke with most recently. He did often call on Jeremiah for advice, but neither he nor his people would ever do what the Lord told him through the faithful, longsuffering prophets.

Eventually Zedekiah rebelled. Nebuchadnezzar returned, and by this time he had run out of patience. He was determined to put an end to the rebel center. After a lengthy and excruciating siege, he captured Jerusalem. Not in haste but later, deliberately, he sent his troops back into the city to dismantle the defensive walls and burn to the ground every building of significance, including the famed temple. Many people had starved during the siege, and many died in the battle; Nebuchadnezzar deported many of the rest. Since that day up until the present, there have always been more Jewish people outside of Palestine than in it.

Even in Despair, Hope (2 Chron 36:22-23)

In his short, final paragraph the Chronicler reminds us that fifty years later (538 B.C.), during the first year of Cyrus the Great, the founder of the mighty Persian Empire that followed Babylon, the Lord began the long and involved process of returning his people home. As Jeremiah had promised, the enlightened Cyrus allowed any captive peoples who wanted to return to their homelands and rebuild their lives, including their worship centers.

And so Chronicles, the last book in the Hebrew Bible, concludes with an upbeat reference to the rebuilding of the temple. The Hebrew people felt that to be a suitable conclusion to the Hebrew Bible in its entirety (Gottwald, 108, 514). "The very last words of the Hebrew Bible are: 'Let them go up' to the Jerusalem temple" (Stuhlmueller, 15).

Bibliography. D. C. Bain Jr., "Chronicles, First and Second," in *Mercer Dictionary of the Bible,* ed. W. E. Mills (Macon, GA: Mercer University Press, 1991); J. Bright, *A History of Israel,* 4th ed. (Philadelphia: Westminster John Knox, 2000); R. E. Clements, "Solomon and Origins of Wisdom in Israel," *Perspectives in Religious Studies* 15/4 (fall 1988); D. J. A. Clines, *Ezra, Nehemiah, Esther,* New Century Bible Commentary (Grand Rapids, MI: Eerdmans, 1984); S. J. DeVries, "Moses and David as Cult Founders in Chronicles," *Journal of Biblical Literature* 107/4 (December 1988); R. B. Dillard, *2 Chronicles,* Word Biblical Commentary 15 (Waco, TX: Word, 1987); J. I. Durham, *Exodus*, Word Biblical Commentary 3 (Waco, TX: Word, 1987); S. D. Goitein, "Women as Creators of Biblical Genres," *Prooftexts: A Journal of Jewish Literary History* 8/1 (January 1988); N. K. Gottwald, *The Hebrew Bible: A Socio-Literary Introduction* (Philadelphia: Fortress, 1985); J. A. Hackett, "1 and 2 Samuel," in *The Women's Bible Commentary*, ed. C. A. Newsom and S. E. Ringe, rev. ed. (Louisville, KY: Westminster John Knox, 1998); S. Japhet, *1 and 2 Chronicles: A Commentary*, Old Testament Library (Louisville, KY: Westminster John Knox, 1993); E. Mazar, "Royal Gateway to Ancient Jerusalem Uncovered," *Biblical Archaeology Review* 15/3 (May/June 1989); J. M. O'Brien, *Priest and Levite in Malachi*, Society of Biblical Literature Dissertation Series 121 (Atlanta: Scholars Press, 1990); E. Sampson, "Who Is Huldah? What Is She? (That All Clergy Ignore Her?)," *Daughters of Sarah* (July-August 1985); C. Stuhlmueller, *New Paths Through the Old Testament* (New York: Paulist, 1989); H. G. M. Williamson, *1 and 2 Chronicles*, New Century Bible Commentary (Grand Rapids, MI: Eerdmans, 1982); P. Yancey, *Disappointment with God: Three Questions That No One Asks Aloud* (Grand Rapids, MI: Zondervan, 1988).

DAN GENTRY KENT

EZRA

Introduction

The church father Origen and the Jewish rabbis maintain that Ezra and Nehemiah were originally one book in the Hebrew canon. The thought was that an ancient editor compiled the memoirs of Ezra and those of Nehemiah, along with other sources, into one book. It has often been suggested that this editor also wrote Chronicles and may have been Ezra. The Talmud claims that Ezra wrote the majority of Chronicles and that Nehemiah completed the task. All three books use lists frequently, emphasize Jewish religious festivals and the temple and use a similar vocabulary of late Hebrew.

Recently the view that the Chronicler wrote Chronicles, Ezra and Nehemiah has been challenged. Chronicles refers to some of the same individuals as Ezra/Nehemiah but often prefers a different form of their names. Also, the perspective of the Chronicler can be seen as more international than the separatist attitude found in Ezra/Nehemiah. Different themes are pursued in the two sets of literature; for example, the issue of mixed marriages is not addressed in Chronicles, although the account of Solomon's life would have been a natural place to make at least an implicit protest against intermarriage.

There are many sources in the book of Ezra. Some of the most obvious are Ezra's memoirs (most of Ezra 7—10, both first person and third person sections); official memoranda, including the edict of Cyrus in both versions (Ezra 1:2-4; Ezra 6:2-5); letters of Rehum and Shimshai to Artaxerxes and his reply; the letter of Tattenai and Shethar-bozenai to Darius I (Ezra 5:7-17) and his reply and Artaxerxes' commission of Ezra (Ezra 7:12-26); lists of personnel, including those who had returned with Zerubbabel (Ezra 2:1-70), those returning with Ezra (Ezra 8:1-14) and those who had married foreign wives (Ezra 10:18-44); and inventories of important items (vessels and bowls, Ezra 1:9-11; Ezra 9:26-27). Many of these sources no doubt came from archives in the Jewish community, most likely at the temple, but some may have come from official Persian archives.

The issue of the date of Ezra is complex. Scripture is clear that Ezra worked under Artaxerxes, but we are not told if this was Artaxerxes I or Artaxerxes II. If the former is correct, then Ezra's journey to Judah was in 458 B.C., and if the second is correct, then his journey was in 398 B.C. However, no fourth-century B.C. persons or events are mentioned; therefore it is unlikely that the material was collected much later than 400 B.C. If the Chronicler is responsible for the final editing of Ezra, this again places it in about 400 B.C., the approximate date of the youngest person in the genealogy lists of 1 Chronicles 3 and Nehemiah 12.

Ezra is an account of two returns of the Jewish people from exile in Babylonia to Judah. The first takes place in 538 B.C., when Cyrus, the Persian emperor, took over the Babylonian Empire and allowed foreign captives to go back to their native lands. The Cyrus Cylinder extols the emperor's generosity in not only allowing conquered people to return to their homelands but also rendering financial assistance to them. He financed temple building projects and allowed captives to reclaim their sacred images and vessels. Ezra tells how the spirit of God moved not only upon Cyrus but also upon fifty thousand Jews of Babylon who took advantage of Cyrus's policy and returned to Judah (Yehud; Ezra 1:5). Sheshbazzar and Zerubbabel are the key Jewish leaders of this return. The local population in Palestine did not react favorably to the separatist attitude of the returning Jews or to their claims to property in Judah. The locals fiercely opposed the Jews, who soon became discouraged and stopped their work on the temple. However, in 520 B.C., with the encouragement of God's prophets Haggai and Zechariah, the task was begun anew. The temple in Jerusalem was completed in 516 B.C., seventy years after its destruction by the Babylonians.

The second return took place in 458 B.C. (in my view) under Artaxerxes I, another Persian king. Artaxerxes authorized Ezra to go to Judah and establish governance there, including the teaching of the laws of the Jewish God. Close to eighteen hundred Jews accompanied Ezra to Judah. Ezra was noted for his expertise as a scribe and teacher of the law. His interest was not simply academic but also practical: "to study the law of the LORD, and to do it, and to teach" (Ezra 7:10).

The homeland to which the Jews returned was the Persian province of Judah. It was situated in the lower half of the land of Israel just west of the Dead Sea area. It extended about twenty-five miles from north to south and thirty-two miles from east to west. Approximately one-third of this land was desert. Before the Babylonian conquest of Judah, the Davidic kings had ruled the area from Jerusalem for about four hundred years.

One significant issue in the book that involves women is the matter of divorcing pagan women with their children. The implication is that a mother will most likely rear her children according to her religion, even if it conflicts with that of the father. The power of the one who rocks the baby to sleep is considered more influential than that of the father. To be sure, in ancient times, nurture was more exclusively the mother's responsibility than it is in many cases today.

Although God hates divorce in principle (Mal 2:16; Mk 10:9), it was sanctioned in the Old Testament in certain cases, particularly where there had been adultery (Deut 24:1; see also Mt 19:9). Ezra could have argued that the Jews had committed spiritual adultery with God by choosing pagan wives. In any case, for Ezra's small, struggling community, surgery was necessary to secure the continuation of the people of God. Although proselytization was possible within the law, the situation here seems to be intermarriage with pagans. Thus in Ezra's community the next generation of Jews was threatened by marriage with foreigners. Ezra's decision to impose divorce on the offenders, however, should not be taken as prescriptive for all marriages in which one partner is a believer and the other one is not. Indeed, Paul counseled that if the unbelieving spouse is content to remain with the believing partner, the two should stay together (1 Cor 7:13). Ezra instituted a radical measure for an extreme situation.

Outline

1:1—6:22 The First Return of the Jews
7:1—10:44 The Second Return of the Jews

Commentary

The First Return of the Jews (Ezra 1—6)

Ezra begins with "the word of the LORD," and one of the main themes of the book is the power of the divine word. The writer notes that the prophetic word that the Jews would return from exile after several decades of captivity has been fulfilled (Jer 25:1-12; 29:10). The implication is that God's word can be trusted; his covenant to Israel continued throughout times of chastisement and trouble. Ezra's ministry illustrates the power of God's word. As Ezra teaches the sacred word to the people, they are convicted and make positive changes affecting the course of their lives.

When Cyrus took the throne of Babylon he allowed foreign captives to go home. The Cyrus Cylinder tells of the emperor's wish that all captive people in Babylon would return to their homes with their gods and pray to these gods on his behalf. After a time of preparation approximately fifty thousand Jews, "everyone whose spirit God had stirred" (Ezra 1:5), made the trek from Babylon to Judah, a walking distance of about nine hundred miles, or five hundred miles as the crow flies. They were laden with freewill offerings from their neighbors and the authority and financial support of the Persian government. Their task was to rebuild the temple of Yahweh in Jerusalem.

The sacred vessels that Nebuchadnezzar had stolen from the Jerusalem temple in 586 B.C. were, with the blessing of Persian authorities, being restored to the site by these Jewish returnees. The unveiling of more than five thousand pots, pans and other utensils of gold and silver and the responsibility of conveying them almost a thousand miles to Jerusalem was an awesome task. The expedition probably took about four months (see Ezra 7:8-9). The caravan would have proceeded from Babylonia north following the Euphrates River and then turned south through the Orontes Valley of Syria to Judah. For women and children the journey would have been particularly arduous. Resettlement in a new environment would have brought inevitable challenges. Transplanting families is never easy.

Credentials were important to every Israelite, and Ezra 2 lists the returnees by families. The list of ordinary, lay families makes up over half of the cited names. The family line was the most common way of personal identification and represents more than 50 percent of these names (Ezra 2:3-19). To have no roots was unthinkable. In addition, from a practical point of view, the maintenance of one's genealogy and its official registry provided credentials for property reclamations in the land.

Family registers were maintained by local officials (cf. Neh 7:5) and individual families (1 Chron 5:7-8; 9:22). Without proof people could still remain Israelites, but priests would be disqualified. These family lists give evidence of God's preservation of his people from generation to generation, for these returning Jews could trace their lineage back to the preexilic Israelites who witnessed and participated in God's miraculous exploits on their behalf. The genealogies of the returning exiles were proof that they were linked to the glorious past of Moses, Joshua, Gideon, Samuel, David and Solomon. Zerubbabel, the leader, has the most significant credentials. He is a grandson of Jehoiachin, one of the last kings of Judah. The returnees were the chosen people. This matter was especially important since the returnees would confront local peoples who would either challenge their claim to be the only, true Israel (Ezra 4:2) or seek to assimilate with them and thereby contaminate their pure lineage with pagan ways (Ezra 9:2).

Several women are mentioned in the list of returning exiles. An interesting inclusion is Hassophereth (Ezra 2:55). While some scholars read this term as a name, the word literally means "the female scribe." Female scribes are rare throughout Jewish history. S. D. Goitein tells of Ibn an-Nasikha, "son of the female copyist," in Iraq during the Middle Ages. Also, Miriam of Yemen, the daughter of a renowned scribe, wrote a beautiful and accurate codex of the Pentateuch. She writes, "Please be indulgent of the shortcomings of this volume; I copied it while nursing a baby" (Yamauchi, 614).

Another woman, the daughter of Barzillai, is listed as the individual through whom the bloodline continued (Ezra 2:61). Her husband is identified with his wife's family. Mesopotamian records reveal that when a father had only daughters, the children of these daughters could belong to the mother's family (cf. 1 Chron 2:34-36).

Finally, the list of cult personnel includes women. They are singers in the worship service. Thus, at this stage of Israel's history, women participated in cultic functions (*see* Women in Worship).

The first order of business for the returning exiles when they reached Jerusalem was to rebuild the altar of God at the ruined temple site. Regular daily offerings were begun as soon as possible, and the foundation of the house was laid. With the restoration of their cult and community in their native land, the Jews experienced a renewal, a sense of getting back on track. The second temple building program was begun in the same month as the work on Solomon's temple, in the second month of the year (Ezra 3:8; cf. 1 Kings 6:1).

The description given of the worship service records that the priests and Levites were in charge of the service. The latter provided both vocal and instrumental music. Trumpets were made of beaten silver (Num. 10:2) and blown by the priests. Cymbals were played by both priests and Levites. *Anah* ("to respond," Ezra 3:11) is understood by the RSV and other versions to indicate antiphonal singing. That is, the choir was divided into two sections with one group singing a response to the other. The Jews sang the same song that was sung at the dedication of the first temple (Ezra 3:11; 2 Chron 5:13). The congregation of worshipers was ecstatic; they gave "a great shout." Some of them were weeping, however, as they recalled the glorious Solomonic temple and compared it with the present, humbler edifice (Ezra 3:12).

Ezra 4 focuses on the opposition that the Jews faced in the sixth to fifth centuries B.C. It records several occasions of persecution: during the reigns of Cyrus (539-530 B.C., Ezra 4:1-5), Xerxes (485-465 B.C., Ezra 4:6) and Artaxerxes I (464-424 B.C., Ezra 4:7-23). The author ends the chapter with the current problem: the order of Darius I (522-486 B.C.) to stop work on the temple.

Opposition came from the people who had remained in the land and intermarried with foreigners. They resented the newcomers from Babylon claiming rights to property in Judah and rebuilding their homes and temple. Initially, under Cyrus's reign, the local people had offered to help with the rebuilding effort but had been rebuffed by the returning Jews. The writer of 2 Kings explains that the people of Samaria were syncretistic; they "worshiped the LORD but also served their own gods" (2 Kings 17:24-33). Even though they claimed to worship as the returning Jews did, they mixed pagan gods, rituals and beliefs into the religion of Israel.

After the Jews refused to include the people of the land, the latter began to oppose them. At first, they used simple discouragement tactics, but later they hired counselors against the Jews in an attempt to scare and frustrate them (Ezra 4:5). Under Xerxes' rule the local officials wrote a letter of complaint against the Jews to the emperor. Still later, Rehum, Shimshai and their associates wrote to Artaxerxes I complaining that the Jewish returnees were rebuilding a notoriously rebellious city, Jerusalem, and that when they had finished they would not pay their taxes.

This apparent digression into later accounts of opposition shows that the passage of time did not cool the enemy's antagonism, and even an emperor who had sanctioned the return could not be counted on to intervene. People who attempt to do something for God will invariably encounter opposition. Human benefactors and human antagonists come and go, but the message is that those who are truly doing God's will can be assured of divine blessing.

Ezra 5 introduces two new characters into the drama of the return and rebuilding of the Jewish community. The prophets Haggai and Zechariah began to encourage the Jews in about 520 B.C. (Hag 1:1). They were needed at this moment when the Jews were opposed from without and discouraged from within. Not only persecution but also economic hardship had taken their toll and stopped the building effort. Haggai admonished the community that they had not

Darius I giving audience. (Ezra 6)

put God first but had attended only to their own needs and therefore God had been against their efforts (Hag 1:9). The community responded promptly with repentance and an eagerness to redouble their efforts on the temple. Zechariah encouraged the community and its leader Zerubbabel that God's Spirit would enable them to finish the building operation even though their resources and energy had dwindled (Zech 4:6-7).

Tattenai, the governor of the province *Abar Nahara* (Across the River), is probably the same individual as Ta-attanni, governor of *Ebernari,* mentioned in a Babylonian record dated 502 B.C. Judah as well as all of Syria-Palestine would have been under his control, and he would have been subject to a higher official, Ushtani, over the combined satrapy of Babylon and Ebernari. Shethar-boznai was probably Tattenai's assist-ant.

Tattenai visited Jerusalem and reported to Darius I, the Persian emperor in 520 B.C. Tattenai requested from Darius that a search be made in Babylon for the original decree of Cyrus authorizing work on the new temple. A search was made and the decree of Cyrus authorizing the building of the temple at Jerusalem was found in the "fortress of the archives" at Ecbatana, one of the three capitals of the Persian Empire.

Darius was adamant when he discovered the decree of Cyrus authorizing the Jews to complete their temple. "Keep away," he ordered Tattenai and his cohorts (Ezra 6:6). Zerubbabel was given whatever money and protection he needed as well as animals and food for the daily offerings. Darius had rebuilt other temples throughout the empire, including the temple of Amon in Egypt and the temple of Eanna at Uruk. At the time he was dealing with the Jewish temple project he was probably also directing the restoration of the Egyptian temple at Sais. The order of Darius ends with a serious threat: those who would interfere with the Jewish building project would have their homes reduced to rubble and would be impaled on a beam of their own house. Derek Kidner notes a certain amount of poetic justice: the one who tampers with God's house is punished by the destruction of his own house. The inclusion of a threat of this nature is typical of royal decrees in Assyrian and Aramaic documents. According to the Behistun Inscription, Darius I impaled three thousand leading citizens of Babylonia when he conquered Babylon.

There were mixed emotions at the dedication of the temple. Some elderly Jews remembered the magnificence of Solomon's temple and wept at the lesser grandeur of the present temple. Others, having grown up in Babylon and seen the more than one thousand temples there dedicated to pagan gods but not a Jewish temple among them, were thrilled that Yahweh too now had a house of worship. The dedication of the first temple was much more elaborate (cf. 1 Kings 8:63), but God's presence was within the new temple, and that was the important point.

Joy is the dominant emotion in the temple dedication, and the word is repeated throughout the chapter (Ezra 6:16, 22). The Jews rejoiced as they celebrated the Passover, the feast that was originally instituted after the Israelite exodus from Egyptian bondage. Indeed a sort of second exodus had taken place among these people. Just as God had miraculously delivered the early Israelites under Moses from the bondage of slavery in Egypt, so also these Jews of the late sixth century B.C. had been unbelievably released from captivity in Babylon and allowed to journey to the Promised Land.

The first part of Ezra ends with victory. The Jews had miraculously obtained victory over great opposition. God had moved upon the Persian authorities and given the Jews imperial support. There was no need to work undercover or apologetically. There was no compromise regarding the temple's location or the materials needed to build it. There were no constraints put on the Jewish community, and the local opposition was quenched. The Jews were given imperial authority to do a first-class project for God.

The Second Return of the Jews (Ezra 7—10)

The narrative moves ahead several decades at the beginning of Ezra 7. The text changes style from historical narrative to biography and even autobiography as it presents Ezra's memoirs.

Ezra (lit. "help") was both priest and scribe. He was a descendant of Seraiah, who was the high priest killed by the Babylonians at the fall of Jerusalem (2 Kings 25:18-21). As a scribe, Ezra was probably a sort of secretary for Jewish affairs in the Persian government. He had an official position, since he represented the king on his mission. He had religious as well as political responsibilities. Scripture says he was skilled in the law of Moses. *Mahir* ("skilled") literally means "quick." Ezra was determined not only to study the law but also to do it and teach it to the Jews. For him, Bible study was not just an intellectual exercise but also relevant to daily life.

Artaxerxes I fully supported Ezra's mission. The king authorizes any who wish to accompany Ezra to the province of Judah to do so and provides a monetary grant from the king and his counselors. Artaxerxes orders Ezra to maintain the temple and its cult with this money and to do "according to the law of your God, which is in your hand" (Ezra 7:14). All temple personnel would be exempt from taxes. Artaxerxes' concern is that the God of the Jews be pleased with him and his family. Of course, he is also concerned about the contentment of the people of his realm. Ezra is commanded to teach Yahweh's laws to the Jews and establish a system of justice in accordance with it. Even capital punishment is put under Ezra's authority (Ezra 7:26).

The Persian kings were known for their interest in codifying law. Darius I was concerned that Egyptian law be codified. He ordered his satrap in Egypt to collect the wise men of Egypt and put them to work on it. So also Artaxerxes commanded that Ezra teach the laws of Yahweh to the Jews. Later, Darius II ordered the Jews of Elephantine to keep the Feast of Unleavened Bread and insisted that sacrifices be offered at the reconstructed temple to the "God Yahu." These emperors wanted to ensure the stability of the various societies they governed.

Artaxerxes issued a formal order to all the treasurers of Beyond the River that whatever Ezra needed (up to a certain limit) he was to receive (Ezra 7:21). According to Jacob Myers's calculations, the amounts offered by Artaxerxes total 3-3/4 tons of silver, about 650 bushels of wheat, 607 gallons each of oil and wine, and unlimited salt. With a typical Jewish blessing, "Blessed be the LORD, the God of our ancestors," Ezra gives glory to God for putting it into the heart of the king to support the temple building program (Ezra 7:27).

Ezra 8 relates the journey of Ezra's company from Babylon to Judah about eighty years after Zerubbabel's initial caravan. This generation of Babylonian Jews was linking up with those among their ancestors who had volunteered to return to the land of Judah under Cyrus's original decree. All but one of the individuals listed in Ezra 8:1-14 are from families that had been involved with Zerubbabel's return. Thus the faith of these ancestors had made a distinct impression on their children's children—so much so that several decades later another generation of the same families stepped out with an active faith in God. The inspiration for this journey was not just from Ezra, although he was the inspired leader. The faith of grandmothers, grandfathers and even great-grandparents was motivating their descendants generations later. This does not mean that every Jew who was from the same clan as those who had returned under Zerubbabel was inspired to make the trek with Ezra. Families remained incomplete in Babylonia and in Judah. However, the faith of the first returnees was a catalyst awakening the desire of many individuals to return with Ezra.

Few Levites volunteered to join the expedition, and thus Ezra sent for some of the leading men among the community to urge some of the Levites to come with the caravan (Ezra 8:16-17). Two families of Levites were all that was needed to fill out the number of Levites. These two clans contributed thirty-eight Levites to the journey. From the beginning of Ezra's leadership among the Jews one is impressed that he appeals to heads of families rather than commanding the people with the authority granted him by the Persian emperor.

Ezra's faith in God is admirable even if at times it seems naive. Ezra gathered his group to fast to plead for God's protection on the journey since he had told the king he did not need an escort. One wonders about the wisdom of refusing royal protection for a group laden with such valuables. Perhaps Ezra did not want to arrive in Judah with an ostentatious royal delegation that might immediately put the local population on the defensive and create unnecessary friction (cf. Neh 2:7-9).

Ezra links the responsibility of the priests to safeguard the sacred vessels to the fact of their holy status. Ezra reminds the priests that they are holy, the vessels are holy and the valuables too are dedicated to God. As chief cultic personnel, the priests have an obligation to deliver the holy vessels to the temple personnel at Jerusalem. These particular contributions were not just from Babylonian Jews but also from the king and various royal officials.

The journey from Babylon to Jerusalem took four months. Persian custom agreed with Jewish religious custom of dating from spring to spring. Although some scholars argue that the Jews resumed a fall-to-fall calendar after the exile, Ezra would probably have left on Nisan 1 (April 8, 458 B.C.) and arrived on Ab 1 (August 4, 458 B.C.).

Upon arrival in Jerusalem, Ezra delivered the valuables to the priests and Levites there, and sacrifices were offered in worship to God. Ezra gave God the glory for protecting the group from ambushes along the way (Ezra 8:31). The worship service included sin offerings and burnt offerings. Burnt offerings were offered every morning and evening in the temple cult to ensure the maintenance of Israel's relationship with God as commanded by the law. Sin offerings were sacrificed for purification and atonement.

The last two chapters of Ezra focus on the problem of intermarriage between the Jewish community and the people of the land. Malachi too complains of Jewish men divorcing their Jewish wives and marrying wives "of a foreign god" (Mal 2:10-12). Suggestions have been offered for why the Jews intermarried with pagan women. The latter may reflect wealthy families among the people of Judah and Samaria, an attractive alternative for Jews suffering economic hardship. Maybe there was a general lack of available Jewish women, since most of the Jews who had made the arduous journey from Babylon with Ezra were probably men. In any case, Jewish law prohibited marriage with any of the local population of the land of Canaan (Deut 7:1-6).

What is surprising about this episode is that Ezra did not bring up the problem. Leaders of the community came to him and told him what many had done. Ezra then meets with the community. This event does not occur until the twentieth day of the ninth month after the group's arrival in Jerusalem (Ezra 10:9). Intermarriage must have been going on for some time, because children had been born (Ezra 10:44). What was the impetus for bringing this matter to Ezra's attention at this point?

As noted above, a central focus of Ezra's mission was to teach the law to the Jews. It may very well be that learning the law from

Ezra was the catalyst for the concern about intermarriage and conviction came about because the people were studying the word of God. Deuteronomy 7, for example, is clear that Israel was not supposed to intermarry with the Canaanites (some of the very ones mentioned in Ezra 9:1) because they were a holy people and this mixture would compromise their relationship with God. The Jewish community of Ezra's time could easily identify with the Israelites of the Torah who were delivered from Pharaoh's bondage, for they too had been rescued, protected and empowered. However, parts of the Torah would probably have disturbed them and pricked their consciences. They could not have failed to notice the emphasis on Israel as a holy people, separated from pagans and their evil practices (cf. Lev 20:23-26; Deut 7:1-6). Some scholars insert Nehemiah 8 immediately before Ezra 9, thus making the reading of the law the even more obvious catalyst for the events of Ezra 9.

Ezra's influence lay in the fact that he was genuinely morally scandalized (Ezra 9:3). He was overwhelmed with disappointment in his community, especially with the leaders who had intermarried. He fasted, fell on his knees, prayed, and tore his clothes, hair and beard in great distress. According to Edwin Yamauchi's translation of *mesomem,* Ezra was "reduced to shuddering." Ezra must have been in this condition for hours; he was still in the same place at 3 p.m., the time of the evening sacrifice (Ezra 9:5).

Ezra's prayer reveals his complete identification with his community. Although he is innocent, he intercedes for the offenders in the first person plural. He approaches God with great humility admitting that God had been more than merciful to Israel and had treated them better than they had deserved. He does not offer excuses for what happened but gives God glory for bringing them again to the Promised Land and for a brief time brightening their eyes (Ezra 9:8). He humbly considers his community a remnant that escaped (Ezra 9:15). Nevertheless the fact that Ezra intercedes with such eloquent fervor and genuine appeal indicates that he was not only convinced of the magnitude of the Jews' sins but also confident that God could be merciful to them if they truly repented.

Ezra's concern and fervent intercession brought results. The offenders decided to divorce their wives and send away their children. Initially Ezra did not order these divorces (*see* Divorce). Rather, he waited for the initiative to come from the people. He recognized the pain the divorces would cause to many families in his community, and he waited for the offenders to realize that this was the best plan of action. Although he had the Persian authority to impose any punishment he wished on those who violated the Jewish law, Ezra wanted the community's willing agreement.

Shecaniah, a member of the congregation, spoke up and suggested that the offenders divorce their foreign wives (Ezra 10:2-4). Jehiel, his father, might be the same Jehiel as mentioned in Ezra 10:21, 26, a man of the family of Elam who had married a pagan woman. Shecaniah may have been grieved about his father's error. In fact, six members of Elam were involved in intermarriages.

Why were the children of these mixed unions put away as well as their mothers? According to Babylonian custom, divorced women took their children with them and could not remarry until the children were grown. In many ancient cultures the woman had the responsibility to give birth to and rear her children (*see* Childbearing and Rearing). Fathers were far less significant in these early stages. In addition, men sometimes had multiple wives and many children (*see* Polygamy). The mother, who nurtured the child daily, would often be the child's greatest influence and advocate (*see* Parental Influence). A good example of this is Bathsheba, who insisted that David honor his promises to her son, Solomon, over his half-brothers (1 Kings 1:17). A mother could be expected to rear her children according to her native religion and customs. Simply put, pagan mothers produce pagan children. When Nehemiah later confronts the same problem, he is appalled that the children are not even speaking Hebrew, the Jewish language. Rather, the children are hearing and learning their mothers' native, foreign languages.

Ezra put the congregation under oath to do as Shecaniah proposed (Ezra 10:5). Ezra continued to fast as he mourned the plight of the people. He then called for an assembly of the people in Jerusalem on pain of confiscation of property and excommunication. Within three days, the people came and sat in the street of the temple, trembling because of the seriousness of the matter and also because they were standing under a torrential rainstorm. It seemed that even heaven was weeping.

It appears from Ezra 10:15 that there were some dissidents. Perhaps they were sheltering relatives or friends or felt that the decree was too harsh. To be sure, God hates divorce (Mal 2:16). Breaking up a family is contrary to God's perfect plan for humanity from the time of the Garden of Eden, where the man and woman were considered one flesh (Gen 2:24). Jesus quoted this passage from Genesis and added, "Therefore what God has joined together, let no one separate" (Mk 10:9).

Nevertheless Ezra was faced with a dilemma. If he allowed intermarriage to continue, he would lose the next generation of Jews who, having been brought up by pagan mothers, would not adhere to the law of Moses and would influence their peers to act the same. Thus Ezra chose the lesser of two evils: divorce, although it would be painful for many families, would preserve the people of Israel into the next generation. He chose a radical cure for an extreme situation.

The divorces were handled with care. The elders and judges investigated each case individually. They did not try to rush the matter or make hasty decisions. Altogether the hearings took three months (Ezra 10:16-17).

The list of offenders is shocking. In all, 111 persons, 27 of whom came from priestly families, had intermarried with foreign women. Myers estimates that the whole congregation numbered about 30,000. The offenders even included the descendents of Joshua, the high priest of Zerubbabel's time. In addition to clergy, the list includes mostly upper-class men. None of the temple servants, whose origin was questionable at best, were offenders. They had clearly forsaken their pagan backgrounds and adopted the pure religion of Israel. They were trusted even with assisting Levites at the temple courts. The lowest socially acceptable classes appear to be the least involved (cf. Ezra 9:2). The matter was serious indeed: the leadership had spiritual cancer. The holy people had been violated.

A word about the children is in order. The children of these mixed marriages were born in the Promised Land. Since Ezra had returned to Judah only nine months prior, the children involved were either the fruit of mixed marriages begun in Babylon or the children of Jews already in the land when Ezra came. If the former is the case, one would question how Ezra could have been unaware of the problem. More than likely the problem was not with Babylonian women but with local pagan women. Foreign women, if they had accompanied their husbands and Ezra on the journey from Babylon, would have probably accepted the religion and culture of the returning Jews. Like Ruth, they had cast their lots with the people of God knowing full well that the future lay ahead of them like an uncharted path. Prior loyalties of homeland, gods and foreign customs would have probably been put aside early on. It is more probable that those Jews who had been living in the land of Judah alongside syncretistic families for decades would have slowly compromised their original standards and begun to assimilate with the local population. This trend would then have influenced some of the men who had returned with Ezra.

Ezra's community with its radical emphasis on pure lineage can be compared with other ancient Jewish communities who did not emphasize marriage with Jews only. For example, the Elephantine Jewish community of approximately the same time period as Ezra, who lived in Egypt, was syncretistic. These people worshiped Yahweh as well as Anath. They are part of history only; today they do not exist. Ezra's radical measures were timely and vital for the continuation of pure religion.

Bibliography. D. Kidner, *Ezra and Nehemiah: An Introduction and Commentary,* Tyndale Old Testament Commentaries (Downers Grove, IL: IVP, 1979); J. Myers, *Ezra and Nehemiah,* Anchor Bible 14 (Garden City, NY: Doubleday, 1965); H. G. M. Williamson, *Ezra and Nehemiah,* Word Biblical Commentary 16 (Waco, TX: Word, 1985); E. Yamauchi, *The Expositor's Bible Commentary: 1 Kings-Job,* vol. 4, ed. F. E. Gaebelein (Grand Rapids, MI: Zondervan, 1988).

HANNAH K. HARRINGTON

NEHEMIAH

Introduction

The book of Nehemiah is the second portion of a two-part work, Ezra-Nehemiah, which renders theological evaluation on the early history of the postexilic Israelite community, beginning with the edict of the Persian king Cyrus in 538 B.C. and extending to the final work of Nehemiah, around 424 B.C. The two-part work, as a theological evaluation, presents in narrative not a strict chronological account but a constitution or plan for how the exiles are to live after the debacle of the failed Zionist and monarchical experiment. Of particular interest to this commentary is the question of the emerging community identity in the context of political subjugation by Babylonian, then Persian and possibly Greek superpowers. How are we to live and constitute ourselves as the people of God in such an environment? is the operative question that drives the theological analysis. Such a question is relevant given the postmodern search for identity in the context of competing powers, either in the larger mix of sociopolitical power moves or in the narrower relational matrix of gender issues.

Gradually, through usage in the Christian church, Ezra-Nehemiah evolved into two separate books. The Hebrew Bible, both the Palestinian Aleppo Codex and the Babylonian tradition represented in the Leningrad Codex, knows the two books as one work. In the Hebrew manuscripts, the lack of Masoretic notes at the end of Ezra and the tally for verses at the end of Nehemiah prove this point. Also, thematic and common material unite the two works. Beginning with Origen in the third century, Christian reading practice finally produced a change even in Jewish usage, which resulted in the two separate books of the English Bible. For the purposes of this commentary, however, we will consider only the book of Nehemiah, bringing in passages from Ezra as they touch on theological topics.

Ezra-Nehemiah portrays a history that begins with the edict of Cyrus in 538 B.C. (Ezra 1:1). According to the text, the edict declares that the Israelite captives may return to Jerusalem and build a temple for their God. Ezra 1—6 narrates the immediate return and subsequent construction of the temple (515 B.C.) prior to the arrival of Ezra and Nehemiah. The activity of Ezra and Nehemiah, after the construction of the temple, coincides with the reign of a later Persian king, Artaxerxes I (465-424 B.C.). The text tells us that Ezra arrives on the scene in the seventh year of Artaxerxes, or 458 B.C., and that Nehemiah subsequently arrives in the twentieth year, or 445 B.C. Nehemiah travels back to Persia and later returns to Jerusalem for additional reform prior to 424 B.C. The timeline of dates and events is important for the theological analysis of the book of Nehemiah due to the questions raised in such a period of destruction and rebuilding. People were looking for an answer to the question regarding what sent them into exile. Why had God judged them? What could they learn from their reliance on temporal power such as the monarchy? During the exilic period, the books of Samuel and Kings took their final shape, both probing for an answer to the question of community identity in relation to temporal power. Furthermore, these people were wondering what they had learned of God's identity and how what they had absorbed affected their self-understanding. Was God resident in the monarchy and in the Zion tradition? And thus were they as well determined by the kings and the inviolability of Zion, "the city of the great King" (Ps 48:2)? Or was their identity fixed to a deeper understanding of God's presence in their midst, that of the desert sanctuary or "among the exiles by the river Chebar" (Ezek 1:1)? These questions and more come to light only if we grasp the significance of the dates and events of Ezra and Nehemiah.

Scholars have debated to no consensus the date and author for Ezra-Nehemiah. The reader may consult the many commentaries and dictionaries for detailed discussion of possibilities. Various people have suggested two different dates for the work, 400 B.C. or 300 B.C. The first option, just after the final events narrated by the text, relates the community identity questions more to early postexilic issues. The latter date locates identity questions to the context of subsequent challenges for Israelite self-understanding in light of the rising Samaritan community and its claim for God's presence on Mount Gerazim. Since the work, as with most biblical texts, does not name its author, we do not know for sure who wrote Ezra-Nehemiah. Scholars have suggested the Chronicler, Ezra with help from Nehemiah or some unnamed redactor/author, either in the early or late postexile. Regardless of the author's identity, the two-part work consists of prior existing documents: the memoirs of Ezra (e.g., Ezra 7—10) and Nehemiah (e.g., Neh 1—7), Aramaic letters and documents (e.g., Ezra 6:3-5), lists of exiles and other items (e.g., Ezra 2:1-70 = Neh 7:7-73), and third-person accounts (e.g., Ezra 1—6). Thus whoever constructed the final work used previously existing materials in the process. In doing so, this redactor/author shaped the raw materials into a theological paradigm, which helped the Ezra-Nehemiah generation understand its identity in the presence of God and prompts us to examine our struggle for identity in the presence of competing powers.

The analysis of this commentary follows the English Bible. The Hebrew Bible verses are at times out of sequence with the English text. For the purposes of this commentary it is necessary to include a brief portion of the book of Ezra as well as a detailed outline of the book of Nehemiah. Ezra-Nehemiah is a theological report on the exilic community and could be entitled "A Narrative Plan for the Postexilic Community." Together they might be outlined:

Ezra

1:1—6:11 Return and Temple Building Prior to Ezra
7:1—10:44 Ezra: Return and Reform

Nehemiah

1:1—7:73 Nehemiah: Return and Rebuilding the Wall
8:1—12:26 Celebration of the Restored Community: Ezra and Nehemiah
12:27—13:30 Nehemiah: Further Reforms After Ezra (?)

Outline

1:1-11 The Law of Moses and Work
2:1-20 Cooperation with Powers
3:1-32 Shared Tasks and Work
4:1—6:14 Work and Opposition
7:1-73 Reform and Cooperation
8:1-12 The Law of Moses and Celebration
8:13-18 Law and Obedience
9:1-38 Appropriating Tradition
10:1-27 Shared Tasks and Covenant
10:28-39 The Law of Moses and Covenant
11:1—12:26 Shared Tasks and Community
12:27—13:30 Reform and Regulation

Commentary

The Law of Moses and Work (Neh 1)

The first unit in the book contains a report to Nehemiah in Susa (Persia), supposedly in 445 B.C., the twentieth year of Artaxerxes I, regarding conditions in Jerusalem and a prayer of Nehemiah prompted by the report. Hanani, a kinsman of Nehemiah, brings word regarding the wall and the conditions of the people. This raises immediately the issue of community restoration, which has begun in the prior book of Ezra. The people are ashamed and discouraged, and the walls are in ruins. The condition of the community elicits from Nehemiah a prayer that sets the foundation for community renewal and rebuilding. Twice in the prayer Nehemiah refers to Moses. In content as well Nehemiah grounds community renewal in the "commandments, the statutes, and the ordinances" (Neh 1:7) of the law. Thus the book of Nehemiah begins as does the work of Ezra (Ezra 7:14, "law of your God") with the law of Moses. The reform of the exilic community starts with recognition of God's presence neither in the monarchy nor in the Zion tradition but in the Torah or instruction of Moses, which arose before there was a king or a particular place associated with God's presence.

By casting back into the foundational experience of early Israel, in the exodus from Egypt and resultant law giving, the book of Nehemiah sets a theological course different from that of preexilic Israel. Israel had moved into the land from the plains of Moab and before long desired a king, even though they had a king in the Lord (1 Sam 8:7). As well they desired a fixed location for their God, even though the tabernacle and the later temple were at best only conditional meeting places (Jer 7:4). The new community plan bypasses the compromised path to a new way in the wilderness, that of gathering around the Lord and his presence expressed in the law of Moses. The new work to take place begins from this new yet ancient starting point.

There is no reliance on temporal power for the renewal of the community. Nehemiah in his prayer does not ensnare the community in a proven false thicket, that of the monarchy and Zion, but references the authentic expression of God's presence, the law of Moses. Feminist theological analysis, whether by females or males, has critiqued the power structures of society, modern and ancient, exposing the coercive moves of societal structures. It is instructive that Nehemiah does not begin with power structures but with theological description of what it means to be the people of the Lord. It is from the law of Moses, not temporal power, that work will proceed.

Cooperation with Powers (Neh 2)

The next section of Nehemiah reports a conversation between Nehemiah and Artaxerxes, a report on the return to Jerusalem and a report on Nehemiah's initial inspection and the hint of opposition, which becomes a central theme later in the book (Neh 4:1—6:14). The text tells us that Nehemiah, as cupbearer of the king, has intimate access to Artaxerxes, such that Artaxerxes notices his moods and feels free to address him with questions. Nehemiah as well does not hesitate to speak frankly with the king. Such intimacy is peculiar in ancient royal courts. But it is not peculiar to Ezra-Nehemiah, nor is it out of character in the evaluation of foreign kings as carrying out the will of the Lord (e.g., Ezra 1:1, the edict of Cyrus, and Ezra 7:11-36, the letter of Artaxerxes).

The judgment of Ezra-Nehemiah, and in particular Nehemiah 2:1-8, on foreign powers is important in two respects. First, by elevating foreign powers to the status of doing the will of the Lord, the text sends the ancient as well as the modern reader in search of God in each person and situation. Because God can accomplish things through secular powers the reader must look to cooperate with whatever powers may be in charge. This theological thrust does not condone the misuse of power by secular authority or by regnant rule, yet it does assign any subjugated group or person the task of finding positive pathways in the midst of what may be a seemingly compromised power matrix. A person or group can move forward with what is just and right even though not in complete charge of her, his or their destiny. And it may be that help will come from unlikely quarters. Second, in spite of elevating foreign powers, the text empowers subjugated individuals to act. Ezra and Nehemiah are not helpless victims of an oppressive regime. They are leaders within their community with limited but important power to direct community restoration. Nehemiah can and does do something for the refugees in Jerusalem. He and his people are not without authority and responsibility. They can and do take action, albeit within the power of the Persian state, to make a difference.

The return to Jerusalem, the inspection and opposition emphasize the preceding points, that Nehemiah and the community begin to work within the restricted powers that overshadow them. The work they begin, however, does not proceed without conflict and hardship. Sanballit the Horonite, Tobiah the Ammonite and Geshem the Arab serve as foils for the protagonist Nehemiah, as do Rehum the royal deputy and Shimshai the scribe serve for those who would build the temple (Ezra 4:9, 23).

Shared Tasks and Work (Neh 3)

Ezra-Nehemiah is replete with lists (e.g., Ezra 2:2-63; Neh 12:1-26). The modern reader is at times frustrated with reading such lists, as is the case with reading the genealogical reports in the book of Genesis. But such lists have a distinct theological purpose: to emphasize the detailed as well as the shared nature of the Lord's work. The list in Nehemiah 3 is no exception. The list purports to bring to the reader those who worked on the wall. It sounds to the modern reader like a list of volunteer helpers at a community event. The list names each family grouping, where they worked and what they accomplished on the wall. Of particular notice is the inclusion of women, "Shallum . . . and his daughters" (Neh 3:12).

The shared nature of community restoration is one of the major themes of Ezra-Nehemiah, evident in the many lists. In an era of foreign subjugation, the community cannot afford to engage in hierarchical leadership paradigms. Initially, such a top-down power move would draw the attention of the Persian rulers. Also, such a style of leadership would not galvanize the community with the importance of their cooperation. Each person needs to know that her or his work is important and that they are valued, one next to the other. The phrase "next to them" (Neh 3:4, 5 and so on) shouts this point by its redundant appearance. The people under the leadership of Nehemiah and others work together. The book of Nehemiah has much to say to the continuing discussion of how people exercise leadership. The text tells through these lists that everyone helps; thus that each has a task, has dignity and contributes to the work instigated by Nehemiah under the authority of the law of Moses. If one wants to find examples of egalitarian leadership, the book of Nehemiah provides them.

Work and Opposition (Neh 4:1—6:14)

One of the elements that unites the books of Ezra and Nehemiah is the theme of work and opposition. Both parts of the single narrative employ this theme to structure the community project (Ezra 1—6; Neh 2:9—7:73). The flow of the text of Nehemiah in 4:1—6:14 moves from outside opposition to inside opposition and then returns to outside opposition. Opposition begins upon commencement of the building task, as is foreshadowed in Nehemiah 2. When work begins, Sanballat and others first taunt and then plan an attack on the wall builders. The text then reports that Nehemiah and others set guards over the wall building, such that some would work and others would guard. The writer of Nehemiah uses this literary mechanism of opposition and response (cf. Ezra 1—6) in the three units that touch on work and opposition. Someone threatens and the community responds, someone threatens and the community responds. The mechanism emphasizes the shared community response as well as the meeting and overcoming of opposition. Those reading such a story would understand first, that in any endeavor there will be opposition, and second, that in order to succeed people must work together.

The initial opposition comes from outside the community, from Sanballat and his associates. It is easy for a community in learning self-definition to perceive that all its enemies are without. It is difficult to understand that enemies can also come from within. The second unit in the cycle reports internal opposition. Evidently there was in the postexilic community infighting between those who had remained in the land and the new immigrants freshly returned from exile. The text tells us "there was a great outcry of the people and of their wives against their Jewish kin" (Neh 5:1). Interesting is not only the situation that gave rise to the outcry but also the source of the complaint, "people and their wives." As in the case of wall building, women are part of the solution to community building. In this instance, women are at the forefront of justice issues. The problem at hand is differing taxation on the two Jewish groups. Nehemiah responds by calling an assembly to remedy the malpractice and then in addition serves as a model by limiting his use of tax funds. Again, the report of the internal opposition uses the same literary mechanism as the report of the external opposition.

The import of internal opposition next to external opposition underlines the need for self-critique in any restoration process. There is always the temptation for oppressed groups or persons to assume an irreproachable hermeneutic stance. People can deceive themselves into thinking that because they are oppressed they are beyond critique and that their interpretive stance is correct. By including a unit on internal opposition, the book of Nehemiah draws even the oppressed under the eyes of God's presence. The law of Moses does not differentiate between injustice of oppressors or the oppressed. All are capable and culpable.

The third unit of oppression and work returns to the outside theme. Sanballat, Tobiah and Geshem now plot to draw Nehemiah away from his work for a conference, and when this does not work, they threaten him in order to strike fear into the project. In both cases, Nehemiah responds (again the literary mechanism) and the threat is aborted. This last section emphasizes the fear that is involved in undertaking a task as a subjugated people. Even though the enemies are in the wrong according to Persian instruction (Neh 2:9, "king's letters"), they possess power to intimidate. This is the case in many situations of power abuse. Whether in a community project, in a marriage or in the workplace, regardless of the law or the accepted norms, people can intimidate others. The book of Nehemiah sends a signal to victims of intimidation that they can and should persist with proper behavior despite threats from those who want to disrupt and discourage. Those who do persist will succeed—the wall is completed.

Reform and Cooperation (Neh 7)

This unit completes the first half of what is known as the Nehemiah memoir (Neh 1:1—7:73; 11:1—13:31). The unit consists of two parts, the reports of the gate closing and the genealogy of returning exiles. Appropriately, this section of Nehemiah closes the section on building the wall, which is the symbol of community boundary and identity, with a list of those within who returned. The list is identical to the list found in Ezra 2:2-70 (= Neh 7:6-73).

The closing of the gates and the taking of the genealogy draw together two continuous threads that run through Ezra-Nehemiah: reform and cooperation. The gates are literally and figuratively the outer limit for the community. The city of Jerusalem is yet to be populated, a task that Nehemiah will undertake in Nehemiah 11. Nonetheless it is the location for community identity. Guards must stand watch during the night because "the people within it were few and no houses had been built" (Neh 7:4). The major task of Nehemiah's reform is not just to build a wall but also to establish boundaries for the emerging postexilic community. The wall is the physical symbol of community identity.

Boundary issues are not limited to women's concerns but have emerged in the context of feminist critique of patriarchy. In the biblical text as well as in contemporary society, males have excluded females from full identity through the lack of access to property. The book of Ruth illustrates this point well. Ruth must glean in the fields of Boaz in order to find her identity through marriage and the resultant heir produced for Naomi. She by herself cannot establish her identity, being a foreigner and landless. The gate report in Nehemiah 7:1-4, although not specifically aimed at women, does point to the necessity of place in establishing identity. When people have a home, they can find themselves. This is true for the homeless on our streets as well as the homeless living in suburbia, who find through either divorce or financial disaster that they no longer have an identity because they no longer can claim a place. With the guarding of Jerusalem, Nehemiah secures a place so that the people can find their identity.

The second thread running through this text comes to us from Nehemiah 7:6-73. Already we have emphasized the shared tasks of the community (Neh 3), the cooperation needed in rebuilding identity. The presence of lists in Ezra-Nehemiah sends signals of identity formation as well as egalitarian cooperation. The list appearing here separates those who could prove their ancestry (Neh 7:6-60) from those who could not (Neh 7:61-65). Such a division points to the need to establish community boundaries. As well, the list tells who contributed to the reform effort, underlining the shared task theme. This is not a top-down reform effort or a five-year plan sent down from above. The building of the wall and the concurrent reform are the result of many hands. These many hands give the community ownership and pride of accomplishment.

The Law of Moses and Celebration (Neh 8:1-12)

Nehemiah 8 begins what many think is the center of Ezra-Nehemiah, the reading of the law and the resultant actions (Neh 8:1—12:26). Some interpreters have cited the resumption of the Ezra memoir here, begun in Ezra 7—10. Regardless of literary evaluation, this section does bring together the yet separate reforms of the two postexilic leaders. First, Ezra the priest/scribe and Nehemiah the governor appear together for the first time, signaling the cooperation of the sacred and secular realms in renewal. Second, Ezra reads the law of Moses establishing the basis upon which the new community will build itself, picking up the uncompromised themes of law and covenant and letting fall the tarnished Zion and monarchic traditions. Finally, the law of Moses elicits response from the people, who celebrate the Feast of Booths (Neh 8:13-18) and enter into a new covenant (Neh 9).

The text tells us that on the first day of the seventh month Ezra appeared before the Water Gate to read the law (Neh 8:1). The resultant action on the second day in celebrating the feast of booths links the reading section (Neh 8:1-12) to the obedience section (Neh 8:13-18). Significant is what is read, the manner in which Ezra reads the law and the way the people respond to the reading,. Ezra stands on a platform and reads the law of Moses. This is significant in a society that had for years been a society of kings and privilege. The book of Kings reports that the kings were responsible for the destruction of Jerusalem and the resultant exile. The kings are no longer in charge. The law is now the center of community identity. People look not to power structures but to a law book, which all hear and obey. This is important because in principle it places issues of justice and righteousness above temporal rule (i.e., right now makes might). For the women in the crowd and for future generations, rule by law opens the possibility for better treatment. In practice it may take time for women to be treated as equal partners with men, but at least this move from a rule of persons to a rule of law, effected in the reforms of Ezra and Nehemiah, pushes in the direction of equal treatment under the law.

When Ezra reads from the law he is surrounded by community leaders, who with him address the entire community, which contains women and men. All get a chance to hear the words and respond. The presence of leaders standing alongside and the mixed audience underlines a consistent communal theme running through Ezra-Nehemiah. All read, all hear, all are responsible for their lives under the rule of law. The pronoun *we* represents the view of these texts as they understand community formation. It is we who stand and we who hear. It is no longer the king's problem. We must take responsibility for ourselves.

Finally, the people respond by standing up when Ezra opens the book. They then shout "Amen!" and worship the Lord. While Ezra is reading, teachers, the Levites, help the people to understand what is being read and the impact it has on their lives. This sounds like a Reformation church service, where the priests no longer read in Latin but put the Bibles in the pews and preach to the congregation, who all the while read along. Significantly, the people and their teachers, the Levites, now locate reverence for the Lord in the book. Again, the emphasis on a religion of law raises issues of justice and righteousness, which set a course for equal treatment of genders that we in the biblical community have yet to fulfill.

Law and Obedience (Neh 8:13-18)

When Ezra stands to read the law, the people do not listen and leave. They become not only hearers of the word but also doers of the word. The evidence for this is their response to the law of Moses in keeping the Feast of Booths (cf. Ezra 3:4). The heads of the families come together to study, and upon finding the command of the Lord, they act.

The theme of law and obedience is not particular to women's issues, but it does relate to the rights of oppressed groups. When a dominant group rules in a society the tendency is for them to abuse the rights of those out of power. The establishment of the rule of law does mitigate abuse because it raises the criterion for judgment above the coercive force of the rulers. However, the laws may embody the power imbalance that rule of law is meant to redress. In Israel for the first time since Moses' time, the people reinstitute and cooperate with the rule of the Lord and bypass the power structures of the monarchy. And even if the law of Moses contains laws that in the judgment of some may hinder righteous treatment, it nonetheless moves Israel away from the dead end of the abusive monarchy. The fact that Ezra and Nehemiah publish and enact this new system is significant for the postexilic community and for us who seek patterns of rule for our day.

Appropriating Tradition (Neh 9)

A significant question for any renewal movement is how much of the past to keep and how much to reject. The people's confession and Ezra's prayer provide an analysis of how the postexilic community envisioned its relationship with the past. After the people confess not only their sins but also those of their ancestors, Ezra rehearses covenantal history beginning with Abraham. The prayer is in two parts, the narrative of what the Lord did with Abraham and the post-Egypt community, and what Ezra wants the Lord to do with the postexilic community. Notice that the trouble, in the assessment of text, begins not with Abraham but with those who left Egypt.

The significance of the prayer is its analysis of Israel's history under the rubric of covenant. Ezra does not reject the history but sees within it what is good, the covenant relationship with the Lord, and wants now to take what is good and reconstitute it for the new community. In doing so Ezra finds within the tradition Abraham, covenant and Yahweh's identity worth keeping. Many people today view tradition as the enemy of establishing a new and better community. Those who hold such a view at times reject the past as the oppressive structures of patriarchy, seeing nothing there to build on for a better future. Conversely, some would lay aside the present for a return to an idyllic past where all was ordered according to goodness and light. Ezra's prayer rejects both these tendencies, the first, idealistic arrogance, and the second, romantic nostalgia, for a measured sifting of the tradition. There is nothing about tradition that makes it of itself good. Nor is there anything about postmodern thinking, or its predecessor modern thinking, that makes it better just because it is current. Neither tradition nor postmodernism is the criterion for their validation. Ezra's prayer helps us understand that it is the presence of the Lord in justice and righteousness acted out in the covenant relationship with people that is the criterion for whether a movement is good. This judgment refuses to hail either novelty or nostalgia as king, looking for the identifying marks of the Lord in its midst as central. Thus, in assessing any liberation or reform movement, we must not hail it as valid without the prior sifting according to established criteria, here and for biblical people, what it means to proclaim the Lord's identity in our midst.

Shared Tasks and Covenant (Neh 10:1-27)

On the signed covenant we find again another list of names, here the leaders of the people. We have treated the theme of lists and shared responsibility before in this commentary (see Neh 3). The repeated list theme underscores the judgment of the preexilic community that this is not the monarchy but the shared responsibility of the group. This is again the shared *we* versus the blaming *you* or *them*. In an age of victimization and deflection, it is refreshing to hear a direct claim for responsibility. It is not the problem of our mothers and fathers, it is not the kings, it is we who stand before God and acknowledge first that the Lord, not we, is righteous and that we are responsible.

The Law of Moses and Covenant (Neh 10:28-39)

The narrative in Nehemiah 10:28-39 is a continuation of the covenant making begun with Ezra in Nehemiah 9:38. The leaders' names appear on the document, and now the rest of the people pledge to follow the covenant stipulations, particularly those of intermarriage, sabbath keeping and temple tax, tithe and first fruits. As is the case in the Sinai legislation, the law follows the Lord's actions in establishing the community. At Sinai God gave the people the law as a way of living out the covenant relationship begun in the gracious action at the exodus. Here God has again acted for the people in bringing them out of exile (note the exodus themes throughout Ezra-Nehemiah) and consequently gives them the law as a way for establishing good relations.

There has been within the Jewish and the Christian traditions the tendency to elevate the law above or place it before God's gracious actions, which establish the relationship within which the law makes sense. God first acts in grace and then in continuing grace gives the law. This is the flow of the book of Exodus as well as Ezra-Nehemiah. The implication of this biblical flow for women's concerns in particular, and for any liberation movement in general, is that the grace and freedom of God contain the restraints of the law. God in grace sets people free, in Egypt and now in the postexilic community, so that they can live within the boundaries of the Lord's reign. God does not set people free to do as they please or to establish their ethos and morality. This is not freedom but license. The Bible, and in particular Ezra-Nehemiah, knows nothing of unrestricted freedom. It knows only the freedom to do the right thing, to worship the Lord. This biblical move from grace to law, or better, law within the confines of grace, illustrates the Bible's understanding of freedom. We are set free to serve the Lord (Ex 8:1).

Shared Tasks and Community (Neh 11:1—12:26)

Here we return to the theme of lists. The first list (Neh 11) reports the population resettlement of Jerusalem and the surrounding region. The second list (Neh 12) reports the priests and Levites who returned to the land from the exile with Zerubabbel and Jeshua. The latter list seems out of place in the book of Nehemiah, relating more to the narrative of Ezra in Ezra 1—2. Both lists highlight the shared task theme.

Reform and Regulation (Neh 12:27—13:30)

Nehemiah 12:27 resumes the Nehemiah memoir, which broke off in Nehemiah 7:73. From Nehemiah 12:27 to the end of the book, Nehemiah narrates in first person the continuing reform according to the law of Moses. Prior to the reforms, though, Nehemiah reports a celebration at the dedication of the wall. All these activities may have once been part of the report that Nehemiah wrote to the Persian king in order to justify his employment. It is logical that Artaxerxes may have requested such a report and obtained it from Nehemiah when he returned to Susa (Neh 13:6).

The first section of the memoir (Neh 12:27-43) reports the celebration at the wall dedication. Nehemiah requests that the people divide into two companies and march around on top of the wall, one group going left and the other going right. As in the case of the law reading, Nehemiah and Ezra are present, though here, in contrast to the Ezra memoir, Nehemiah takes center stage. The celebration is once again a symbol of egalitarian cooperation and community identity. By including the names of various groups, Nehemiah points to the joint effort and now joint celebration. Shared joy characterizes the report: "They offered great sacrifices that day and rejoiced, for God had made them rejoice with great joy; the women and children also rejoiced. The joy of Jerusalem was heard far away" (Neh 12:43).

Celebration and thanksgiving bring the project of Ezra and Nehemiah to a close. The report of celebration endorses the reform efforts of the postexilic community. Biblically this is important, for it puts a stamp of approval on the type of community that emerges out of the Ezra-Nehemiah project. By ending on a note of celebration, the book validates the community as a model for future communities. This type of organization becomes the model not only for their time but also for contemporary reflection on community building. The theological validation that "God had made them rejoice" (Neh 12:43) sends a signal to biblical readers that this program is not a false start, as was the monarchy, but is the kind of rule that God intends. This does not mean that we in our reform efforts must duplicate the Ezra-Nehemiah community. But it does mean that the foundation for a biblically valid organization should incorporate the elements of God's law, the Scriptures and shared work and rule. These are the valid components of what it means to live with the Lord in our midst.

The latter sections of the Nehemiah memoir (Neh 13:1-30) cohere in the repeated phrase, "Remember me, O my God" (Neh 13:14, 22, 29, 30). After reading again the law of Moses, the people and Nehemiah launch further actions to bring their community into order with God's commands. The reforms touch the issues of separating from foreigners, removing improper people from the temple building, enforcing the tithe, policing sabbath observance and removing foreign spouses. The book closes with a summary statement of Nehemiah's accomplished reforms (Neh 13:30-31).

The reforms of Nehemiah may seem petty to us, but to postexilic people the reforms established identity in relationship to the Lord and within the surrounding culture. Two themes run through these closing verses. The first is the theme of grace and law. The community in response to the grace of God begins to order its life within the boundaries of the freedom it has received. The second theme is the identity theme. Nehemiah and the people make distinctions between themselves and their culture through their reforms. By separating themselves from foreigners, they declare who they are. By observing the sabbath, they exhibit distinctive behavior. In our culture, we might characterize these moves as intolerant or prejudicial. Yet in order for a person or a community to establish identity there must be separation from the surrounding environment. Without separation of some sort, people have no distinct identity. Beyond the separation and beyond the concern of Ezra-Nehemiah lies the issue of how those who have separated themselves then treat others outside the community. This is not the issue in Nehemiah 13:1-30. What is at the forefront is the need for separation in order to establish identity.

JEFF H. MCCRORY JR.

ESTHER

Introduction

Esther has been compared with such similar pictures of Jewish life in exile as Daniel, where the usual structures that ordered and supported Israel's existence were no longer operative. As in the time of the judges, when Israel's social and political organization was yet primitive, crisis brings to the fore men and women like Esther and Mordecai as instruments of deliverance, and they must act in an environment in which open profession of their faith and ethnicity can be dangerous.

Set within the reign of Ahasuerus, the Persian king known to the Greeks as Xerxes I, who ruled roughly between 486 to 465 B.C., the book in its present form was likely written within a century of the events it describes, probably from Susa or in Palestine. The author is unknown, though Augustine believed it was written by Ezra, while Clement of Alexandria and others thought Mordecai was the author, based on the writer's familiarity with Persian words and customs and access to official documents (Esther 9:32). Mordecai's narrative seemed to be one of the sources for whoever organized the final Hebrew material (see Esther 9:20). Scholars posit at least five Esther stories, the most prominent of which are those of the Masoretic and Septuagint texts, the latter a Greek translation with six deuterocanonical chapters added from Semitic and Greek sources. These more devotional sections, written in a later period, seem to have been added to balance the perceived secular nature of the book, making up for a puzzling lack of reference to God or the religion of Israel. This commentary opts for a reading based on the shorter Hebrew or Masoretic version.

Esther as a literary form has been regarded as myth or a historical romance or, on the other extreme, as strictly history. Most likely the book is based on a nucleus of historical material, reworked in such a way that it acquires the quality of fine literature. The work has a symmetry that to others suggest fiction—Gentiles against Jews as personified by "Haman the Agagite" and "Mordecai the Jew"; the contrast between the straightforward intransigence of Vashti and the artful vacillations of Esther; the fall of Haman and the rise of Mordecai as vizier; the prospect of an anti-Semitic pogrom and the eventual slaying of the "enemies of the Jews." Such symmetry, however, seems a function not only of the author's sense of poetic justice but also the sense that the world is providentially ruled. It shows a fine literary hand as well as a confident faith in happy outcomes as arranged by uncanny forces at work in the seemingly ordinary coincidences of everyday life.

The book is primarily a story of deliverance and only secondarily a festal legend, a narrative that recounts the historical grounds for the celebration of the feast of Purim. The casting of *pur,* or the lot, functions as a central metaphor in the story but is incidental to the main plot, which is the threatened extinction of the Jews and their relief and deliverance through human acts of courage and sagacity combined with what look like accidents of history.

A Jewish woman is queen in a pagan court when Jews were subjects in an alien empire and vulnerable to plots and resentments. This is the central coincidence in the story and explains why our attention is focused on Esther and not on Mordecai even if he seems more like the main hero. Mordecai does appear as a more consistent character, and his greatness is such that it is recorded in Persian annals, his deep and abiding identification with and service to his people extolled in the final chapter (Esther 10:2-3). But the work is rightly the book of Esther, for on her the story turns and moves from anxious despair to certain hope. This reversal has been wrought through the inner transformations of this woman who seemed docile and timid but emerged valiant and strong.

There is some substance to the notion that the book is the only one in the Bible "with a conscious and sustained interest in sexual politics" (Fox). Here is a society of men who, when thwarted, resort to political power to reinforce a dominant position. The figure of Vashti sets off the patriarchal context of the time without much comment. Her fall represents the discomfort of king and nobles before women of independent will and prefigures the dangers and risks taken by Esther when she crosses the line to oppose Haman and appeal to an erratic, irascible husband with no apparent principle for governance other than the whim of impulse and the thoughtless carelessness of arbitrary power.

Known simply as the Scroll, being among the five Megilloth or Rolls, Esther is read through in the presence of women as well as men during Purim, observed by Jews in commemoration of their deliverance and the spontaneous rejoicing, feasting and community sharing that followed (Esther 9:18-19.).

Outline

1:1—2:23	The Fall of Vashti and the Rise of Esther
3:1-15	Haman Plots to Destroy the Jews
4:1-17	Esther Chooses to Intervene on Behalf of the Jews
5:1—7:10	A Curious Reversal
8:1—9:19	The Deliverance of the Jews
9:20-32	The Feast of Purim Instituted
10:1-3	Conclusion

Commentary

The Fall of Vashti and the Rise of Esther (Esther 1—2)

The Social Backdrop (Esther 1:1-9)

The story begins in Susa, one of three capitals of the Medo-Persian Empire where most of its kings resided in winter. The scene opens with Ahasuerus displaying the pomp and circumstance of his court. Persian society is depicted as amusing and potentially dangerous, decadently opulent but also overregulated, where even drinking was according to the law, a reference perhaps to the relaxation of the strict decorum usually required in royal banquets, where guests drank only whenever the king did or were forced to drink continuously by a king whose wishes cannot be balked at. The word *dat* ("law") is used for all kinds of royal decisions, from simple instructions to servants to rules for a court audience to imperial edicts announcing the extermination of a people (Esther 4:11; 3:12). The law rules over almost every detail of life, yet such prescriptive rigidity has at its base the fragile ego and volatile temper of a despot (Esther 1:12).

Vashti's Refusal Turned to Sexual Politics (Esther 1:10-22)

Lightheaded from seven days of drunken merrymaking, Xerxes ceremoniously sends seven eunuchs to bring Queen Vashti before him in full regalia, to parade her beauty to the crowd of possibly intoxicated men. Why did Vashti refuse? The author treats the reasons behind this with reticence. We surmise it may be out of a sense of rank (the Persian queen by tradition had to come from one of the seven noble families) or dignity—she didn't want to be displayed as one more of Xerxes' prized possessions. Note that the royal parties were segregated according to gender; elsewhere, in Belshazzar's feast, his harem women were present, but the queen came in only on account of the writing on the wall (Dan 5:3, 10). Josephus believes Persian law prohibited wives from being viewed by strangers, so Vashti may have refused out of respect for this custom that the king was so flagrantly violating. Tradition has it that Persian wives could be present at banquets but usually left before the drinking. Whatever was the reason, such was the power of Vashti's refusal that it threw the king into a dark rage and made the princes nervous, perceiving a threat to their hegemony: "this deed of the queen will be made known to all women, causing them to look with contempt on their husbands" (Esther 1:17).

Vashti's fall has been read as a repudiation of strong-willed women. Not really; note how in this chapter the courtiers are depicted as somewhat ridiculous. Memucan, fearing that the queen's behavior will contaminate the ladies of the empire, unwittingly broadcasts the deed by his counsel. A private act of domestic insurrection gets widely publicized by an official edict, and the intractable realm of male-female relations becomes a matter for yet another state regulation: "every man should be master in his own house" (Esther 1:18-22). This prelude to Esther's story licenses a questioning approach to the text; while satire is perhaps too strong a word for it, there is the hint that we are dealing with characters that are not to be taken too seriously.

That every man should "speak according to the language of his people" (RSV) may refer to the tendency within a bicultural marriage for the household to follow the mother's linguistic and cultural heritage, seen here as a form of capitulation on the part of the husbands in this polyglot empire (cf. Nehemiah's finding that half of the children of the Jews who had married foreign women spoke their mothers' tongues and did not know Hebrew, Neh 13:23-24).

Esther Is Made Queen (Esther 2:1-23)

The main characters in this story, Esther and Mordecai, do not appear until now, where they are introduced as representatives of a colonized people, subject to the wishes of a changeable king who is manipulable, susceptible to the self-serving suggestions of those around him (*see* Manipulation).

Esther initially appears pliant and passive, a foil to Vashti's intransigence. Adopted by Mordecai, she obeys him as a father even after she ascends to her position as queen (Esther 2:7, 10, 20). The narrative makes no mention of her inner state as she is "taken" into the palace and the king's bed; she submits to the beauty contest and the regimen required for it without comment. Artlessly self-effacing, she does not ask for supplemental beauty aids when it is time to present herself before the king (Esther 13; 15).

The contest seems to have neither familial nor political significance; the women had no need of childbearing potential or the right pedigree that makes for sound alliances, but only beauty and the capacity to please the king sexually (Esther 2:4, 14). Nevertheless, while she is treated as a sex object, Esther stands out not only for her physical but also personality gifts; naturally winsome, she finds favor in the eyes of all who see her (Esther 2:9, 15).

Haman Plots to Destroy the Jews (Esther 3)

Mordecai Defies Haman (Esther 3:1-6)

It is not clear why Mordecai refuses to bow before Haman; like Vashti's, his reasons are unstated, save for a vague reference to his being a Jew. The text is silent about the connection between his show of unrewarded loyalty (Esther 2:21-23) and the rise of Haman as vizier, and there is no suggestion that obeisance to him has cultic significance as in the book of Daniel. "To see whether Mordecai's words would avail" (Esther 3:4) might mean that the court officers, before whose remonstrances Mordecai was impervious, finally brought the matter to Haman to see whether Mordecai's ethnicity exempts him from the king's order. Besides injured pride (the Hebrew word used for Haman's anger against Mordecai is the same as that of the king's for Vashti), Haman's fury might have to do with an undercurrent of racial animosity, as shown by his resolve to destroy not only Mordecai but also his people. Whatever was its original motive, the conflict now seems more than a personal battle between a recalcitrant subordinate and an overweening court favorite. It has been enlarged into a primal blood feud between "Mordecai the Jew" and "Haman the Agagite," who is four times described as "enemy of the Jews" (Esther 3:10; 8:1; 9:10, 24).

The Jews Sold to Destruction (Esther 3:7-15)

The plight of the Jews is left to chance, the propitious time of their annihilation determined by the casting of *pur*. Their continued existence as an unassimilated people in the empire is put to question before a mercurial, suggestible monarch too thoughtless and lazy to execute his own decisions. Described in the abstract as a "certain people," subtly denigrated as "scattered" and "dispersed" and therefore powerless and insignificant, the Jews are downgraded to the level of goods: to destroy them is to profit the king with ten thousand talents of silver, presumably the amount likely to be gained when the spoils are taken. This fabulous sum is about 68 percent of the total revenue of the Persian Empire, which ran to around 14,560 Euboeic talents, according to Herodotus. Posturing as a munificent king dispensing largesse, Xerxes hands over the Jews and their possessions to the scheming Haman.

The imperial machinery is then set into motion, the awful genocide couched in the passive voice: letters are "written" and "sent" throughout the empire, the fate of the Jews inexorably worked out with the impersonal precision and swiftness of the Persian pony express system. The letters were sent to "every province in its own script and every people in its own language," a respect for ethnic diversity that ironically is put to the service of destroying a people whose alleged crime is their distinctiveness.

This chapter is the midpoint of the story's movement; it marks the shift from Mordecai to Esther as main actor in the story. From now on the story is told from Esther's point of view, and it is she who, aided by fortuitous circumstances, shall move the plot and bring the crisis to a resolution.

Esther Chooses to Intervene on Behalf of the Jews (Esther 4:1-17)

Mordecai Mourns and Sends a Message (Esther 4:1-9)

News of the Jews' threatened extinction brings dismay and bewilderment to Susa and great lamentation among the Jews. Nowhere is the vast carelessness and callousness of power so telling as in the scene of Haman and the king sitting down to drink after consigning a whole people to their death (Esther 3:15). Mordecai reacts with howling grief, puts on sackcloth and ashes and goes to the king's gate to attract Esther's attention. Esther's maids and eunuchs predictably tell her, and clueless, she sends him clothes. Upon Mordecai's refusal, she orders Hathach, one of her eunuchs, to find out what the dramatic gesture was all about. Hathach goes out to Mordecai in the "open square of the city," a fact that underscores Esther's cloistered existence and some difficulty in communicating. The exchange of messages through Hathach indicates knowledge of her Jewishness and friendliness on the part of the court servants.

Esther's Choice (Esther 4:10-17)

Esther is tested and then transformed. She initially meets Mordecai's urging for her to intervene on behalf of her people with fear and a timidity born out of a sense of the limits set by law and her own doubtful power over the king.

Mordecai's famous reply is a pointed warning and an encouragement. "Do not think that in the king's palace you will escape" (Esther 4:13) puts squarely before Esther the fact of her solidarity with her people, a sense of common peril that in her isolation she might have found less compelling than the more immediate danger of death and disfavor from a lover who for a month has been disinterested.

At the same time, Mordecai expands Esther's horizon by putting forward a historical opportunity that she could lose if she chooses to keep silence: "relief and deliverance will rise for the Jews from another quarter, but you and your father's family will perish. Who knows? Perhaps you have come to royal dignity for just such a time as this" (Esther 4:14). Esther is brought to a sense of what is possible beyond the danger posed by a precipitate presence before an impetuous monarch of unsteady passions. It is likely that she has come to royal position for a time such as this; to fail to act is to miss her historical cues and fade from racial memory as her ancestral line sinks to oblivion. There is no mention of God, but there is at least enough confidence that providence so guides history that the possibility of rescue is already in place. And in case Esther fouls up, some alternative instrument will rise for the Jews' relief and deliverance.

The effect of this speech is immediately palpable as we see Esther suddenly transformed into her own person, ordering her former guardian to assemble all the Jews in Susa and hold a fast on her behalf. She moves from being a docile ward to a decisive, active partner in saving her people, from fear to resolute dauntlessness, and from a diffident faith in her powers to a daring attempt to test the limits of her constraints: "I will go . . . though it is against the law; and if I perish, I perish" (Esther 4:16).

A Curious Reversal (Esther 5—7)

These three chapters detail the swift turnaround of events for the Jews. Within two days, radical reversals happen through a series of coincidences that compel the sense of a force other than human sagacity in the doing of history.

Esther Makes Her Move (Esther 5:1-14)

Esther puts on her royal robes, the formal grandeur of her office as queen and her attractions as a woman in full force as she stands before the king for a chance audience. She finds the king in a magnanimous mood but responds to his offer of "even to the half of my kingdom" by inviting him and Haman to a dinner she had prepared. Contrary to comments that Esther's sitting down to dinner with Haman is "psychologically improbable," on the premise that one normally wishes one's enemy to be at a distance, Haman's deliberate inclusion suggests that Esther had coolly designed a plan that requires the presence of both principals. A number of speculations have been advanced as to her reasons for doing so, the most straightforward being that she did not wish to give him opportunity for a conspiracy behind her back.

Still, it is a puzzle why she delays and passes up another opportunity to state her request. Some account this to a female quality in Esther, an indecisiveness that delays at the critical moment. Others attribute it to the need to pique the king's curiosity and get him in a momentum for reflex action. But all this risks spoiling the king's generous mood, which experience shows is fairly short-term. And in any case, the idea of a second banquet does not seem premeditated, since, unlike the first one, it is yet to be prepared and hangs on the king's willingness to grant in advance her as yet unstated request.

It seems that Esther was feeling out the king's disposition; she sensed perhaps that the king was merely on his ritual grand gesture and she must cast about for telltale signs that her petition, if known, would likely turn his expansive impulses into swift and irreversible action. She seizes upon a second invitation as an index of whether truly "I have won the king's favor" and if he is disposed to grant what she wishes. The elaborately deferential preamble of her speech indicates she is aware she might be testing the king's patience, and so she subtly represents her project as something the king wants: "tomorrow . . . I will do as the king has said" (Esther 5:7-8).

The effect was to lull Haman into thinking that the banquet was a mere social visit (Clines). Haman went out "happy" and boasted to his wife and friends of the singu-

---

The Power & Potential of Women

The book of Esther has been interpreted as a classic stereotyping of how women shoulder their way to power. Straightforward women like Vashti lose their position, while Esther gets her way through recourse to feminine charm and cunning artifice. She is like Mary and Hannah and other women in the Bible who become national heroines only as they fulfill their assigned roles as wives. She is faulted for lacking an interior life, being uninspired by religious faith, seen as conforming to a seemingly general biblical policy of allowing women to talk to God only in a procreative context.

The first part of this critique glosses over the fact that the author of Esther treats

Vashti and Esther with respect. Esther, it is said, has Vashti's looks but not her willfulness; while this may be true, the contrast mostly ends there. Vashti refuses to come when bidden before the king, while Esther dares to come unbidden; both deeds take courage.

Far from being treated as an object lesson to self-assertive women, Vashti is held up as a victim of Xerxes' egotistic instability and the princes' insecurity; she is punished for an act of defiance in a patriarchal society nervous of female power. As with Mordecai, her recalcitrance is treated with great reserve; both are proudly intransigent, but there is no hint in the text that the reasons behind this are reprehensible. We are merely given the sense that her plight foreshadows the dangers and risks that Esther, already vulnerable as a member of a subject people, faces when set to the task of reversing the erratic decisions of an intractable monarch.

Esther needed to deploy all the physical, intellectual and psychological resources at her disposal. Shrewd strategy and subtlety rather than open confrontation are her only options in a society that requires careful submission to decorum. Her pliability, her lack of protest over her treatment as a sex object, her voicelessness are signs of learned helplessness in a context of severe restraints. Like all the Jews, who must adjust to powerlessness in an alien land, Esther had to tread softly through the landmines of power.

From the perspective of a colonized people, her way to power is understandably oblique and roundabout, something that perhaps looks like feminine wiles to those who come from aggressively straightforward cultures and are raised in a political tradition with a highly developed language for rights.

The notion that Esther comes to power largely through a traditional role ignores the fairly marginal influence of a wife in a setting where the king can put her away at will and has a thousand other women to take her place in bed. Like most women who start out with a limited sense of their potential, Esther comes to her own because she grows, moving from fear and timidity to resolute courage.

Mordecai, like most men, is himself constant because he is always certain of his position. Esther has had to grow and gather enough ego strength to become what she was meant to be in God's plan. She develops from a woman with a restricted view of the possibilities of her personal attractions and royal position to a woman testing the limits of what she can do. Mordecai has opened to her a window, enlarging her understanding of the possible meaning of what to her might have looked like a decorative and ceremonial life. Once aware of her place and its potential significance within the larger canvas of Jewish history, she sets out on her errand of deliverance with grit and decisiveness.

Contrary to the perception that the Bible exalts women mainly for their procreative functions, we have here a heroine whose importance to the Jewish people does not lie in child bearing. Like Deborah, she rises at a critical moment and rallies her people for a war of resistance. Unlike Deborah, however, she was not, before this, in a position of authority within the Jewish community. She grew into it by an evident transformation in her inner life.

The fact that women sometimes never get the chance to fulfill their potential in the same way is deeply lamented in the haunting story of Jephthah's daughter (Judg 11). In a moving gesture of loyalty to Yahweh, before whom her father had made a rash vow, she offers herself for sacrifice. All she asks is that she be left alone to wander on the mountains for two months to "bewail [her] virginity." To bewail her virginity involves not merely that "she had never slept with a man" but that at a time when what women can become is tied up with being wives and mothers, it is a thing of grief that she dies before she sees the full flowering of her womanhood.

It is perhaps an anachronism to criticize the Bible for stories on women whose main significance is in their traditional roles as wives and mothers. God's Word is progressively revealed in history and as such mirrors the status of women as it finds it in a particular time and society. Yet even so, there are subtle shades to each picture, hints toward a future significance defined no longer within the confining terms of gender but by the capacity to respond to God's initiatives. Mary, for instance, is blessed not only because of the fruit of her womb but because she "believed that there would be a fulfillment of what was spoken to her by the Lord" (Lk 1:45). Characterized as thoughtful, the mother of Jesus is also author of the Magnificat, the first theological reflection in the New Testament of what the coming of the kingdom means.

The same literary subtlety is evident in the portrayal of Esther. While she rises to importance in Jewish history through her connection as wife to the king, she becomes truly queen mainly by the exercise of her wits. Mordecai's star also rises, it is worth noting, because of his connection to her. The shared leadership of the two cousins is a refreshing contrast to the assumption of male supremacy in the Persian court.

The fact that we do not see Esther in dialogue with God or aided by the charisma of the Spirit falling down upon her as with the judges seems mainly due to the author's literary decision to keep the story at ground level. Though the call to a fast is indication of an intense spirituality, we do not see her wearing piety on her sleeve. Her supposed irreligiousness is characteristic of the book; we are being told a story of what it means for a people of God to survive in pagan society without benefit of supernatural intervention, preferring instead to see his presence in the ordinary details of our lives.

There are many and varied ways by which women come to power. Some, like Vashti, get to be there by birth or pedigree and so are naturally self-possessed and conscious of what is due them. Some, like Esther, need to rise from a sense of limitation to a sense of what is possible under the sovereign hand of God.

Whatever place we are coming from, whether as timid wives of potentates or modern career women aware of what they can do, this story tells us that we can all grow, find within ourselves unsuspected resources and win strength out of weakness.

MELBA PADILLA MAGGAY

---

lar honor to which he has been elevated. Still he could not bear that Mordecai would neither rise nor tremble; the solution was to clear Mordecai out of the scene by having him hang on the gallows.

A Tragicomedy of Errors (Esther 6—7)
Haman's fall begins with a series of coincidences. The king gets insomnia that same night and happens to read of Mordecai's forgotten deed; Haman, eager to hang Mordecai, comes early to court and arrives at the moment the king wants advice on how to honor Mordecai. The next day the king's reaction to Esther's request, momentarily on hold, turns decisively in her favor when the king chances upon Haman falling on her couch, begging for his life. These incidents, together with the central fact that a Jewish woman sits as queen of Persia at a time when the Jews are threatened, mark the many turnings toward a reversal of their fortunes.

Moreover, the story is fraught with ironies, turning things upside down for Haman. The night Haman has Mordecai's gallows made, the latter's loyal deed is brought to the king's remembrance. The next day Haman is forced to perform for Mordecai the honors he intended for himself. Humiliated, he mourns with his head covered and hurries to his house, only to find not comfort but premonitions of impending doom from his wife and friends. From a master plotter who holds all the cards, Haman is now led away in haste by the king's eunuchs, helplessly overtaken by the whirlwind force of circumstances. Finally, by a timely suggestion from a sympathetic servant who quickly saw fit to direct the king's outrage to Esther's advantage, he ends up hanging on the gallows he had made.

Both principles—synchronicity and peripeteia—operate in the story as a counterforce to *pur,* a metaphor for the reckless chance by which the Jews have been fated to perish. By an overwhelming series of coincidences, events are overturned, and we sense an overruling power that orders human life.

It has been suggested that these coincidences function as a kind of deus ex machina without the deus; there is a glaring absence of any reference to God. Unlike Daniel, who is rescued from the den of lions by supernatural intervention, the Jews in Esther get delivered not by miracles but by a chain of events triggered by growth in the inner resources, intellectual and spiritual, of people like Esther who at the outset do not seem to be natural leaders. Unlike Deborah and others in the time of the judges, Esther grows and rises to power without benefit of the Spirit coming upon her. This most secular of the Bible's books gives us instead an organic sense of God's sovereign strength as it works itself out in history. Even while unnamed, the sense of a Providence disguised as chance compels the recognition that while evil seems strong and life can be fragile, there is at ground level a force that can be trusted to thwart badness and turn things for good.

The Deliverance of the Jews (Esther 8:1—9:19)

At this juncture of the story the Jews begin their ascendancy. It has been suggested that the narrative is properly read as ending in Esther 8, the next two chapters being appendices to an older, proto-Masoretic text. Nevertheless it seems best that the Hebrew text is read in its entirety as it now stands.

Persian Law Circumvented (Esther 8:1-17)

The chapter opens with Esther rising to power and her cousin Mordecai along with her. Haman's decree, however, still stands. Esther this time falls at the king's feet and pleads with him in tears, her speech prefaced by four conditional clauses subtly playing on the king's suggestibility and his evident regard for her. The first two clauses are formulaic, characteristic of her earlier court speeches: "If it pleases the king, and if I have won his favor." Piled on these are new rhetorical inventions: "if the thing seems right before the king, and I have his approval" (Esther 8:5), which perhaps rose out of her consciousness that she was asking something unprecedented and needed to fall back on the power of her attractions.

The motif of Persian law as both rigidly fixed and randomly fixable takes center stage. The king is unable to revoke his previous edict but gives wholesale authority to the two cousins to find a way of circumventing it. Again the machinery of the empire's legal system is put into motion. The writing of the new edict in every people's script and language is especially extended to the Jews. The king's swift horses were used by the couriers, and wherever the news spread there was joy and feasting among the Jews.

From a subject people in fear of their lives, the Jews find gladness and light and honor among the general population, augured by the resplendent rise of Mordecai. While neither priest nor prophet nor king—leadership roles in the old Jewish society—Mordecai appears in full glory as a new type of leader in an alien empire. With his ascendancy, fear of the Jews falls upon the peoples, a mixture perhaps of the superstitious awe and obsequious deference accorded those whom the gods seem to regard with peculiar favor. This is what Haman's wife had sensed, in a rather primitive but prophetic way, about the Jews.

Jews Gain Ascendancy (Esther 9:1-19)

The thirteenth day of Adar and the outcome of its battles are summarized as "the very day when the enemies of the Jews hoped to gain power over them, but which had been changed to a day when the Jews would gain power over their foes" (Esther 9:1). The plight of the Jews reversed from defenseless powerlessness to powerful resistance: "no one could withstand them," for the fear of them and of Mordecai had turned the tide of official support and had apparently weakened those who wished to inflict them hurt.

The theme of control, of gaining power and mastery, is reinforced by accounts of military victory, of doing "as they pleased to those who hated them," and the completion of Haman's fall with the slaying of his sons. It is possible that it is within this larger thematic framework of gaining complete mastery over their foes that Esther asks for another day of slaughter, finishing off remaining anti-Semites in Susa. Comments have been made that Esther has become bloodthirsty and vindictive, her request for an extension an unnecessary overkill. An alternative reading could be that in the context of intrigue and power play in the capital, she who previously had been shown to be a cool and brilliant strategist saw the need to stamp out remnants of the forces allied with Haman and his sons.

This is not, as David J. A. Clines puts it, a story of bloodletting but of power, a perception that finds support in the scrupulous refusal to take the usual spoils of victory. The movement from helplessness to mastery, from a sense of threat to relief and of grief to joy, appropriately finds expression in the spontaneous celebrations of the fourteenth and fifteenth days of Adar.

The Feast of Purim Instituted (Esther 9:20-32)

In contrast to the dominant legal system whose legitimacy depends on the wayward whims of a potentate, Mordecai and Esther institutionalize a practice that the Jews had already taken the initiative to do: the feast of Purim. In a social context where a decree can be legal yet lethal, set into motion by fatuous royal fiat, the Jews create an ordinance that originates from popular impulse and finds enduring force in a community's grateful memory of deliverance.

Mordecai's Letter and the People's Response (Esther 9:20-28)

To preserve the memory of this part of their history, Mordecai puts it into writing and enjoins the Jews to turn the reflex of merrymaking into a permanent feast kept through the generations, with the added feature of sending gifts to the poor. Note the downplaying of Esther's and Mordecai's role and the pronounced exaggeration of the king's in the process of deliverance. What seems to matter historically is that the chance lot fixed by *pur* for the Jews had been overturned, and so, conscious of "what they had faced in this matter, and of what had happened to them" (Esther 9:26), the people give sanction to the perpetual celebration of the feast, an ordinance arising from popular consensus and quite unlike the divinely instituted festivals found in the Torah.

Esther's Letter Confirming the Feast (Esther 9:29-32)

The shared leadership and "full written authority" of Esther and Mordecai stand behind another letter confirming the institution of the feast. Esther's command "fixed" the practices of Purim by recording it in writing, a detail that shows the importance put on written records by this book, perhaps because memory fails and a time comes when a whole generation forgets God and his doings in history (cf. the dramatic impact on Josiah by the recovery of the book of the law in 2 Kings 22).

Conclusion (Esther 10)

The book concludes with a reference to Xerxes' levying of a tribute, not only on the immediate territories but also on far-flung "coastlands" (RSV), which may refer to the Ionian lands on the western extremity of the empire. *Mas* in biblical Hebrew means corvee or forced labor, but in rabbinic Hebrew means tax; mention of it suggests the heavy hand of imperialism on subject peoples. At the same time, we are told that in this vast and powerful empire Mordecai had risen to the heights of honor and power, second only to the king. His achievements had enough historical significance to be recorded in the empire's royal annals. His concern for the welfare of the Jews lingers in the memory of his grateful people.

Mordecai's rise and the story of Esther show that one can lead a significant, rewarding life in a foreign court and use it in the service of one's people, maintaining solidarity and an ethnoreligious identity in an alien culture. Human history, it seems, is both free and guided. While we may be subject to thoughtless injustice as exiles in alien lands, there is always the possibility of rescue through the chance provisions of an unseen power and our inner resourcefulness. We are not captive to random fate or to the apparent hopelessness of a history dominated by the vast carelessness of unprincipled power.

Bibliography. D. J. A. Clines, *The Esther Scroll, the Story of the Story,* Journal for the Study of the Old Testament Supplement Series 30 (Sheffield: JSOT Press, 1984); M. V. Fox, *Character and Ideology in the Book of Esther* (Columbia: University of South Carolina Press, 1991).

MELBA PADILLA MAGGAY

JOB

Introduction

The book of Job is a theodicy, an attempt to defend the justice and goodness of God in spite of the existence of evil in the world. This fact makes the work significant for women in every time and place, because much violence and evil have been wielded specifically against women. As a result, women have frequently found themselves left alone, in suffering and pain, asking "Why?" and "How long?"

The book of Job seeks to answer the question, Why do the righteous suffer? This question is raised in the light of a traditional emphasis within Old Testament wisdom literature on divine retributive justice, that God will reward the righteous but punish the wicked. This emphasis is exemplified in passages like the following:

For the perverse are an abomination to the LORD,
  but the upright are in his confidence.
The LORD's curse is on the house of the wicked,
  but he blesses the abode of the righteous.
Toward the scorners he is scornful,
  but to the humble he shows favor. (Prov 3:32-34)

Similar passages can be found throughout Proverbs and other Old Testament books. The book of Job challenges such an emphasis, exploring experiences that seemingly contradict it and daring to ask difficult, even uncomfortable, questions. In doing so the author or authors challenge the established religious institutions and forge forward to institute a more satisfactory answer to the problem of evil.

Reticence about the authorship of Job is well advised, for the book makes no reference to its author. In general commentators have remained silent on the topic and instead have focused on questions related to composition. The book as it appears in the canon is complex, which strengthens the probability of more than one author and leads one to suggest that several sources have been combined. It is commonly concluded that the book is built from four major sources.

This introduction begins with questions related to genre. Two major genres are represented in the book, the introductory and concluding prose narratives (Job 1—2; 42) and the poetic texts found in between (Job 3—41). The prose passages are simple and frequently compared with folk tales. In contrast, the poetic pieces are difficult and complex, filled with unusual words and thoughts. This has led many commentators to conclude that the two genres represent the work of more than one author and that the poetic pieces have been inserted into what was originally one simple prose narrative. Also, Elihu does not appear until Job 32 or after Job 37, which leads most scholars to suggest these chapters are a later insertion. Finally, some suggest that God's speeches (Job 38—41) were added or modified later.

Several complications lead some interpreters to suggest additional sources or corruptions in the text. Job 28 suddenly breaks into a discussion of mining, metallurgy and wisdom, which leads to the argument that it is a later insertion. In the third cycle Bildad's speech is unusually short (Job 25), Zophar's speech does not exist and a couple of Job's speeches seem contradictory. Consequently some scholars want to add part of Job's speech to Bildad's (i.e., Job 26:5-14) as well as create a speech for Zophar from Job 24:18-20, 22-25 and Job 27:8-23.

Thus scholars tend to suggest several stages in the compilation of the book. However, all such conclusions are speculative, because we have no concrete manuscript evidence to support the stages suggested. It seems reasonable to accept the supposition that an astute poet used an existing prose tale as opportunity to stage the debate found in Job 3—41. Simultaneously, the argument for the later insertion of Elihu's speeches and perhaps the later insertion of Job 28 is logical. However, it does not seem necessary to doubt the authenticity of the third cycle or God's speeches. In any event, the book in its current form is what we have to read and has been created for that purpose. Theories about sources may give us some understanding about differing genres and styles but do not assist our comprehension of the final product. For the purposes of this commentary the book will be read as a unified whole and each piece as a distinct part of an overarching rhetorical conversation.

Also difficult are questions related to date and location. For the latter, there are few clues in the book. The story is situated in Edom, but this does not necessitate Edom as the location for composition. The story provides no clues beyond the initial locating of the characters, and the geographical location plays no significant role for meaning.

The dates proposed for the book range from the tenth to the third century B.C. The story is placed in the patriarchal period, but this does not necessitate that date for its authorship or composition. Ezekiel referred to Job as an important person alongside Noah and Daniel (Ezek 14:14-20), and traditionally Job has been understood as one of the oldest books in the canon. But modern scholars are skeptical of this claim to antiquity. The book makes no references to historical events. However, some internal evidences suggest affinities with other canonical books and could lead one to conclude the work in its final form is post-Babylonian exile. Alleged are affinities between Job 3 and Jeremiah 20:7-18 and stylistic similarities between Job and Isaiah 40—55. These connections suggest a time either before the early sixth century B.C. (if Job is prior) or in the late sixth or early fifth century B.C. (if Job is later). However, there is no way of determining which text(s) came first. Job 7:17-18 is related to Psalm 8, but it is impossible to date this psalm. Finally, Job 3:4 seems to reflect on Genesis 1:3, a text often dated around the sixth century B.C.

Although Job is an ancient text, the popularity for reading it in contemporary culture is overwhelming. It seems this is due to the age-old struggle to comprehend the juxtaposition of a loving God and the problem of evil. From the time of the ancients to today, we have all struggled with why the righteous suffer. While this commentary will present a few examples of interpretive responses to particular passages of Job from feminist or womanist perspectives, its ultimate goal is to suggest a universal reading of critical concerns raised in and from the book.

Outline

1:1—2:13	Opening Narrative
3:1-26	Job's Lament
4:1—14:22	First Discourse Cycle
15:1—21:34	Second Discourse Cycle
22:1—31:40	Third Discourse Cycle
32:1—37:24	Discourses of Elihu
38:1—42:6	Discourse Cycle of the Lord
42:7-17	Closing Narrative

Commentary

Opening Narrative (Job 1–2)

Critical to reading Job is a clear comprehension of the opening narrative. Contemporary readers often find Job too complicated and consequently seldom read it in its entirety. Much of this has to do with the fact that readers have not paid close enough attention to or have not accepted the clues for reading that the narrator provides in the first two chapters. The first set of critical clues is given the opening verse: "There was once a man in the land of Uz whose name was Job" (Job 1:1). What does this sound like but the beginning of a fairy tale, which consistently begins with a similar phrase, "Once upon a time . . ."? Having read this many will be concerned about the question of historicity. Although some contemporary scholars assess these opening chapters of Job as historical narrative, many categorize the opening as folk narrative.

Perhaps this conclusion is best understood, or at least more easily accepted, by a discussion of what comes next: "That man was blameless and upright, one who feared God and turned away from evil" (Job 1:1). This is a key statement for understanding the book. The Hebrew words here, *tam* and *yashar*, will be found many times throughout the book to emphasize and thereby remind the reader that Job is indeed an upright (righteous) and blameless man. Often it is suggested that by making such a claim the individual, namely Job, has fallen into the sin of conceit and is being punished for his sin. However, the narrator, not Job, declares Job's righteousness. If the ensuing discussion is to have any relevance, readers must be aware from the beginning that Job's integrity has been established.

Significant for understanding Job 1:1 is to first become aware of who is speaking. The narrator opens the narrative with a stock phrase that may be intended to tell readers that we are entering the world of make believe. This is not to suggest that there never has been a Job-like character, and in many ways the point of the book is not lessened whether or not Job is a single historical figure. If Job is not an actual historical figure, then the ensuing description of his character, family and wealth are to be understood in this context. This allows the depiction of Job's life as perfect to be understood as exaggerated to make a point.

A second reading hint flows out of Hebrew narrative conventions with regard to the narrator. The narrator is omniscient, is committed to providing clues for reading and always tells the truth; consequently, information provided by this source is critical for ascertaining meaning in the story. With this in mind, the astute reader will accept as fact the narrator's assertion that Job is blameless and upright. When we wade through the poetic discourse cycles we may be persuaded to doubt this statement. Don't do it!

The opening statements are essential and in line with the tale's purpose. They prepare us for the theodicy that is to come, for by establishing a character who is prosperous, upright and blameless, the author has prepared us to struggle with why the righteous suffer. If Job is truly without blemish or blame, then he is the perfect foil for the ensuing doctrinal debate.

In Job 1:2-5 Job's wealth and character are delineated. Note that Job has the perfect number of sons and daughters. Seven is the number of perfection and completion in the Old Testament, thus the perfect number of sons. In addition, a man does not want to have too many daughters because when they marry, each will require a dowry. Note also that three pairs of items are numbered: seven sons and three daughters, seven thousand sheep and three thousand camels, and five hundred yoke of oxen and five hundred donkeys. The pairs each add up to some multiple of ten and thus create an extremely orderly account of Job's wealth. In Job 1:4 we get a description of the festivities of Job's children immediately followed by a lengthy description of Job's burnt offerings for each in case they may have sinned or cursed God in their hearts. Job is a man of wealth, sound piety and faithfulness. In five short verses we are given a picture of perfection, the ideal worshiper of Yahweh. But this is all about to change.

The next seven verses (Job 1:6-12) may

be the most difficult verses in the book. Critical to understanding this section is the distinction between the New Testament Satan and the figure represented here. In the New Testament Satan is the supremely evil being who acts on his own volition exhibiting powers by which humans are frequently overcome. They must therefore look to God for deliverance. In Job, Satan has a different function. In these verses Satan is the accuser, the one who goes "to and fro on the earth" and brings back a report to God.

In this section we encounter the first dialogue of the story, and it takes place between God and Satan. In response to the initial exchange that concerns Satan's recent activities, God asks, "Have you considered my servant Job?" This question is followed by God's describing Job as blameless and upright, *tam* and *yashar*, the same Hebrew words found in Job 1:1. The repetition is key to the story. Twice within eight verses we have been told that Job is upright and blameless, first by the narrator, who can be trusted, and now by God.

Satan answers God's question with a question: "Does Job fear God for nothing?" (Job 1:9). It seems, according to Satan, that God has been protecting Job from harm as well as assuring the increase of his wealth. This accusation evidences the dogma of divine retributive justice. Next Satan throws down the challenge: "But stretch out your hand now, and touch all that he has, and he will curse you to your face" (Job 1:11). God accepts the challenge and gives Satan the "power" to touch anything Job has, except Job's physical being (Job 1:12).

This dialogue creates the need for theodicy and consequently is the place where interpreters, as well as interpretations, go their separate ways. Where one goes from this point affects where one ends up in an analysis of the book and therefore in an understanding of God's presence in the midst of evil.

Always affecting our reading of the biblical text are our preunderstandings and presuppositions, which come from many places. An extensive conversation on preunderstandings and presuppositions is far too complex for this presentation, yet raising the point is critical for understanding diverse responses to Job 1:6-12. It is impossible to provide a comprehensive analysis of responses in such a brief work, but a few examples may prove helpful.

Excursus: Three Female Perspectives

Perspective 1. Many contemporary, white, educated, middle-class, American women have experienced God as Santa Claus, the one to whom we bring our wish list of things to be done with full expectation that they will be taken care of. And that has frequently been our experience, so when some sort of crisis enters our life we are astounded and immediately respond with phrases such as "Why me, Lord?" "What did I do wrong?" Our theology reflects our privileged status. We expect God to deliver us from evil, and when that does not happen we cannot imagine why. When we read of God's competition with Satan in Job 1:6-12 we are enraged, for we believe that God ought not to do such a thing; we question the justice of God.

Perspective 2. Naomi Southard, in an article about spiritual resources for Asian American women, notes that many Asian American women speak about particular theological themes as they struggle against exploitive power (see Southard, 379). The foundation for community for Asian American women is the ability and opportunity to embrace one another's suffering; similarly the Asian American experiences oneness with God, as God in Christ is a cosufferer. This relatedness or connectedness to one another's suffering results in self-empowerment.

Southard suggests that Asian American women must not allow themselves to suffer because they have accepted a dictum that suffering is their lot or that it is the antidote for being unworthy or the goal of faithful living. Rather, she coins the phrase "wise suffering," which means one consciously seeks a difficult path in hopes for radical transformation.

To support these fundamental ideals Southard looks for images of God that Asian American women will find to be empowering and transformational. The implications for Job 1:6-12 are readily apparent. Many Asian American women struggle with a God who imposes suffering upon humans for no apparent reason and consequently question the justice of God. They will look outside the biblical text to find transforming, liberating images of God.

Perspective 3. Clarice Martin finds the autobiographical work of Maria W. Stewart (1835) to be representative of the African American religious perspective on suffering and evil. According to Martin, Stewart did not attempt to "absolve the deity of responsibility for injustice," that is, the work of theodicy, but worked under the assumption that "God is near to and works on behalf of the powerless and disenfranchised in the interests of divine justice" (Martin, 23).

The combination of God's mighty acts (as evidenced in the exodus) and human response reverses the suffering and evil of oppression, although oppression thwarts the God-intended ordering of society. Divine fiat alone does not bring freedom and liberation, but the work of the divine in combination with conflict, struggle and overt human choice (Martin, 24). The implications for Job 1:6-12 are that Job's distress is viewed as an unfair oppression caused by Satan and that God is understood as working with Job to bring deliverance and resolution.

These three perspectives represent three different responses to Job 1:6-12. White American women and Asian American women question the justice of God when they encounter Job 1:6-12. However, their reasons for this judgment vary greatly, as do their ultimate responses to the text. Many white American women harbor anger against God or turn away from God when they encounter this pericope. Many Asian American women ask the same questions about God's justice, but rather than harboring anger against God, they look to alternative sources for images of transformation and liberation. Finally, many African American women attribute the evils of Job's distress to Satan and focus on God as the one who will deliver, but not without some work and effort on Job's part. When, as the book goes on, resolution does not come, they may accuse Job of not doing his part, which can focus on the need for repentance or a lack of humility.

Each response embraces in some way the traditional wisdom teaching of retributive justice. Representative white American women are prepared to question, be angry at and even reject a God who does not reward good behavior with blessings. Representative Asian American women question and turn away from a God who disciplines in search of a cosufferer or another, more liberating image. Representative African American women have not accepted the doctrine of divine retribution in the same way. It is understood that they will often suffer at the hand of another for no logical reason: what I am describing is racism. However, if an African American woman concludes that Job has not been delivered because he has not done his part, then she has accepted the concept that punishment is the result of sin.

In *On Job,* Gustavo Gutiérrez remains faithful to the basic premise of Job by challenging the doctrine of divine retribution. Gutiérrez, a priest and a theologian, struggles to make sense of Job within the context of a slum, Rimac, in Lima, Peru, where some of his parishioners literally do not know where their next meal is coming from. Thus in approaching the book of Job Gutiérrez asks, "Are suffering human beings able to enter into an authentic relationship with God and find a correct way of speaking about God?" (15). The implications of this question become clear when Gutiérrez reads Satan's question in Job 1:9 much differently from the examples we have discussed so far. Instead of focusing on God and God's justice, he looks at humanity's role and suggests that Satan's question is asking whether humans are capable of having a disinterested faith. In other words, are humans capable of worshiping God if they have no hope or expectation of receiving anything in return? For Gutiérrez, Satan's question is about the human capacity for faith, and this is what is being tested. Satan's claim is that no human, not even Job, is capable of remaining faithful (i.e., full of faith) in the midst of suffering and will curse God.

Calamaties (Job 1:13-19). Satan dismantles Job's fortune and family. Within one day Job loses his herds to thievery and fire, his servants to the sword and fire, and his children to a great wind. This is cataclysmic and heightens the narrative. Within a few short hours Job moves from being the wealthiest man in the land to abject poverty. His immediate response is found in Job 1:20-21: "the LORD gave, and the LORD has taken away; blessed be the name of the LORD." The narrator interprets

Job's acts and words of lamentation for us: "In all this Job did not sin or charge God with wrongdoing" (Job 1:22). It would seem Satan was wrong and God was right. Humans are capable of disinterested faith. But Satan is not so easily convinced.

Job 2 opens with a parallel, almost verbatim account of Job 1:6-8. However, this time God seemingly gloats over Job's response to Satan's test. But instead of conceding, Satan raises the stakes by suggesting that Job will curse God if he is physically afflicted. God gives Satan permission to act with the condition that he must spare Job's life. In our next view of Job we find him covered with sores and scraping himself with a potsherd. This final blow has forced him to leave his community and sit outside its walls as one who is unclean. This is the lowest point one can reach in life; the next level down would be death, something that Job will ask for in the near future.

In the meantime we encounter Job's wife (Job 2:9). These are the only words spoken by a female in the story, and they do not bode well for women as she berates Job for his integrity and exhorts him to curse God and die. Job's wife does not have the capacity for disinterested faith. But let us be aware of her literary function in the text. Her words serve as a foil for the words that Job speaks next: "Shall we receive the good at the hand of God, and not receive the bad?" Then the narrator tells us again that Job did not sin with his lips (Job 2:10); Job remained blameless and upright (cf. Job 2:3).

The infamous three friends make their entrance at the end of the chapter. The narrator tells us that Job's appearance was so altered that the friends were not able to recognize him from a distance. This fact distressed them and caused them to lament. When they reached Job, they sat with him for seven days and nights without speaking because his suffering was so great. These introductory comments from the narrator are significant, for they tell us that the friends had tremendous compassion for Job. It is important that we hear their ensuing words within this framework.

Job's Lament (Job 3)

Although Job does not curse God, he does curse the day he was born. Job 3 is a lengthy lament that begins with ten verses of imprecations against "that day," as though it were an enemy. Two additional sections, each introduced by the interrogative complaint "Why?" follow these initial verses. This complaint is a common form, often found in the lament psalms, that suggests the current distress is incomprehensible to the speaker. After cursing the day of his birth, Job picks up a second theme (Job 3:11-19) summarized by his opening statement, "Why did I not die at birth?"

In Job 3:20-26 Job completes his lament with a third and final theme:

> Why is light given to one in misery,
> and life to the bitter in soul,
> who long for death, but it does not come (Job 3:20-21)

His suffering has so overcome Job that he longs for relief by means of death.

Since lament is an acceptable form of expression in the Old Testament, Job still has not sinned with his lips. Although Job has used many words to explicate his pain and suffering, he has not cursed God.

First Discourse Cycle (Job 4—14)

The first of three lengthy discourse cycles between Job and his three friends begins in Job 4. Throughout these cycles the friends present varying arguments based on their commitments to the doctrine of divine retributive justice. Job responds to every discourse, sometimes addressing the friends' statements and at other times attending to something different. Frequently Job's conversation confronts the dogma of retributive justice.

Traditional Doctrine (Job 4—5)

Eliphaz speaks first. His opening phrase is courteous and gentle: "If one ventures a word with you, will you be offended?" (Job 4:2). He affirms Job's former virtuous acts. Eliphaz's initial exhortation is that Job has become impatient and dismayed now that the tables are turned. His ensuing argument is built on the simple precept that humans are not righteous but are imperfect. From this fundamental truth Eliphaz moves to an accusatory statement: God frustrates the crafty and helps the wise, but if the wise act in crafty ways then they too shall be frustrated. He concludes that those who are disciplined by God are in the end happy because God's discipline is good and leads to healing. Implicit is the assumption that Job has sinned and is being punished accordingly. Eliphaz's challenge to Job is to turn to God, acknowledge his sin, plead for deliverance and consequently preserve the idea of divine justice and traditional doctrine.

An Opposite Scenario (Job 6—7)

Job's response must be read in light of the narrator's statement about him in Job 1:1. Bear in mind throughout his discourse that he is blameless and upright. We may find such a premise difficult to hold throughout our reading of the book. Readers often fall into the trap of debating whether any human can be blameless and upright (Eliphaz's argument in Job 4). This brings us back to the stated premise of the book and its genre. The opening narrative is intended to establish a man of such integrity and righteousness that, given the dogma of divine retributive justice, he should encounter only blessings in his life. The fact that an opposite scenario has been created is to establish that sometimes bad things happen to good people (and vice versa) and to consequently seek to understand God's justice in the midst of this reality.

Job begins with an enigmatic discussion on the weight of his calamity, which he suggests exceeds all ordinary misfortunes and therefore surpasses what would or should be required. Job requests death so that he will not curse God. He proclaims that the three friends are "treacherous like a torrent-bed" (Job 6:15) and further challenges them to show him his error; so he establishes his integrity. In Job 7 he complains of the difficulty and brevity of life, a motif frequently found in the lament psalms, and suggests this truth justifies his complaint (Job 7:7-11; note the parody on Psalm 8 in Job 7:17-18). He ends with a tongue-in-cheek response directed to God: "If I sin, what do I do to you, you watcher of humanity? . . . Why do you not pardon my transgression and take away my iniquity? For now I shall lie in the earth; you will seek me, but I shall not be" (Job 7:20-21). Job is not making a confession of sin; rather he is provoking God to act on his behalf.

Repentance Urged (Job 8)

Bildad, speaking for the first time, also intends to show Job the error of his ways and therefore stimulate him to turn to God in repentance. Bildad's opener, "How long will . . . the words of your mouth be a great wind?" (Job 8:2), is less courteous than Eliphaz's opening comment. Bildad suggests Job is accusing God of perverting justice and says that Job is perhaps suffering for his children's sin. He concludes that if Job will be upright, he will be restored, and if blameless, accepted by God. The irony of these final verses is considerable. As the friends shake their heads in wonderment over who has sinned and where, Bildad proclaims that all Job needs to do is to be upright and blameless, the exact language used to describe Job in the opening chapters.

Complaints About Injustice (Job 9—10)

It seems that Job responds to Eliphaz rather than Bildad in this section (cf. Job 9:2 with Job 4:17). Job struggles with the idea of a hearing before God (Job 9). This is the first of three instances where Job will raise such an idea, but he quickly states, "Who has resisted him, and succeeded?" (Job 9:4). Job fears that God will not listen and concludes the idea is futile, because the Creator has the advantage of strength and there is no one to act as judge over God. These realizations are followed by complaints of injustice in which Job accuses God of mocking the calamity of the innocent and prospering the wicked. In effect Job struggles with the doctrine of divine retributive justice.

Finally Job lists three alternative means for bringing resolution to his situation, but each proves to be insufficient (Job 9:27-34). He pleads for God to take the rod of suffering away from him so that he can speak without fear, for he states, "I know I am not what I am thought to be" (Job 9:35). Ultimately Job begs God to leave him alone so that he might find some comfort (Job 10:20).

A Multitude of Words (Job 11)

With Zophar's opening words comes the end to courteous conversation. Zophar begins with biting remarks concerning Job's language, calling it a multitude of words, babble and mockery. He attacks Job's statements of innocence while praying that God will speak the secrets of wisdom to Job. His final words are the most crushing: "Know then that God exacts of you less than your guilt deserves" (Job 11:6). Zophar concludes by exhorting Job to repent of the sin that has led him to this point of suffering so that he may be restored.

Desiring Greater Wisdom (Job 12—14)
Job begins the final dialogue of this cycle with some biting remarks of his own: "No doubt you are the people, and wisdom will die with you" (Job 12:2). For Job also knows the traditional wisdom (Job 12:3; 13:1-2). He judges his friends harshly as he exclaims, "Those at ease have contempt for misfortune" (Job 12:5). Job desires a greater wisdom and accuses his friends of speaking falsely. The three friends are worthless physicians, their "maxims are proverbs of ashes" (Job 13:12), and if they would only keep silent, that would be wisdom. The doctrine of divine retributive justice is worthless.

Again Job requests a trial. Job has prepared his case and, despite the risk of coming before God, will speak confident of his innocence and pending vindication. Yet his fear of God is evident: "Only grant two things to me . . . withdraw your hand . . . and do not let dread of you terrify me" (Job 13:20-21; cf. Job 9).

Finally Job toys with an idea for escaping the present distress: "Oh that you would hide me in Sheol" (Job 14:13). Job is not thinking about death and resurrection but suggesting that he might be concealed in Sheol until God's wrath dissipates.

Conclusions. Eliphaz, Bildad, Zophar and Job struggle with the doctrine of retributive justice throughout this discourse. Not until his final speech (Job 12—14) does Job begin to challenge the dogma in any significant way. By the close of his third response, Job has concluded that the wisdom of the three friends is old, traditional and not helpful for his current experience and circumstance. Job makes it clear he is striving to understand the rules of life in a new way.

We, members of the contemporary Christian church, also struggle with the doctrine of retributive justice. We, like Job, have encountered situations where this dogma does not fit our experience and consequently makes no sense. We, like Job, need to think about suffering in new ways.

Gutiérrez's work helps for developing a new model. He suggests two types of language are applicable: the language of piety and the language of lament. Of the first, the contemporary human sufferer must come to terms with the God of gratuitous love. The inference is that God's love exhibited toward us is born out of grace and does not come as the result of our goodness. The concept is reminiscent of the parable of the laborers in the vineyard (Mt 20:1-16), in which the owner of the vineyard recruits workers several times throughout the day but pays each the same wage. In response to complaints the owner states, "Am I not allowed to do as I choose with what belongs to me? Or are you envious because I am generous?" In other words, the owner has the freedom to be gracious. How much more the Creator of the universe? Critical to creating a new model for thinking and talking about the justice of God is the profound truth that our God is a God of gratuitous love and that the blessings of God come to each of us as an act of grace.

The second means for speaking about God is the lament. Gutiérrez states that this genre is not only accepted by God but is God-ordained due to its prophetic nature. Implicit within this language is a fundamental challenge to the human contribution to suffering. Frequently one person's suffering is the product of another's behavior or a consequence of the outworking of institutional and societal agendas. Under these circumstances the lament prophetically challenges the ills of social structures and calls humanity to reform. For those who know they are not what they are thought to be (cf. Job 9:35), the lament is a God-ordained, prophetic tool that challenges those at ease who have contempt for misfortune (cf. Job 12:5).

Second Discourse Cycle (Job 15—21)

The battle lines have been drawn, and Job and his friends become even more confrontational as each one is increasingly more convinced of his stance.

Tradition Threatened (Job 15)
Eliphaz begins with rhetorical questions intended to ridicule Job: "Should the wise answer with windy knowledge?" (Job 15:2). These caustic questions build to an accusatory statement that summarizes Eli-

phaz's primary concern: "But you are doing away with the fear of God" (Job 15:4).

In Job 15:7-16 the questions continue. Eliphaz's emphasis is upon tradition. Job's responses move away from traditional wisdom, and this is quite threatening for Eliphaz. He accuses Job of choosing "the tongue of the crafty" (Job 15:5) and states, "Your own mouth condemns you, and not I" (Job 15:6).

The discourse closes with a lengthy diatribe about the retribution visited upon the wicked as has been observed by Eliphaz (Job 15:17; cf. Job's experience, Job 19) and passed on by the sages. The assumption is that Job will receive the same retribution if he does not turn from his current mode of thought.

Miserable Comforters (Job 16—17)

Job's second response to Eliphaz is one long lament. Claus Westermann distinguished three categories for the lament: the lament of one's current distress, the lament against the enemies and the lament against God. All three types are found in this response. Job begins, as has become the norm, with stinging remarks: "miserable comforters are you all" (Job 16:2). Next he launches into an accusatory complaint against God, for Job understands God to be the one attacking him. The imagery created is of an enemy chopping his body to bits with a sword (Job 16:13-14). The section culminates with Job's attestation of innocence (Job 16:17).

Assuming that death is imminent Job insists that his murder must be avenged. The language used creates a powerful allusion to the blood of Abel crying from the ground against Cain (Gen 4:10-11). Similarly Job calls to personified earth to avenge his death. There is no one to pledge a surety for Job; all have turned away from him and are appalled by him. All hope is gone. The imagery is typical for the laments and reflects the manifestation of the doctrine of retributive justice. Anyone who has fallen from blessing, as Job has, was thought to have committed some heinous sin against God. Consequently the community would have ostracized him.

The Extent of Retribution (Job 18)

Bildad's second speech picks up where Eliphaz left off. The wicked shall be torn from their tent, no memory of them will remain, and they will have no descendants because they do not know God. Retribution is understood to be extensive.

Plea for Vindication (Job 19)

The intensity of Job's speech toward his friends is heightened, and he speaks with a new confidence. He first confronts the friends' behavior: "These ten times you have cast reproach upon me; are you not ashamed to wrong me?" (Job 19:3). He goes on to say, "Even if it is true that I have erred, my error remains with me" (Job 19:4). This is not a confession of sin (cf. Job 9:21; 10:7; 16:17) but a statement to suggest that the friends' judgment is inappropriate. If Job has sinned that is between him and God.

In Job 19:7-20 Job blames God for his physical infirmities as well as his estrangement from friends, family and servants. The lament culminates in a plea for the three friends to take pity on him because God has touched him for ill.

Job's discourse culminates with wishes that his words could be written down and inscribed forever. He states, "I know that my Redeemer lives" (Job 19:25). All that is certain is that Job expresses trust in some sort of redeemer (a better translation would be "vindicator"). The Hebrew word is *go'el* and refers to a member of one's family who will vindicate one's honor or take care of one's debts (e.g., Lev 25:25; Deut 25:5-10; Ruth 2:20). It is not clear whom the *go'el* is associated with in this text. But Job is convinced he will be vindicated before God. When this will happen is unknown. Job 19:26 could be read in such a way as to suggest the idea of resurrection. But the doctrine of resurrection appears quite late in Hebrew thought (cf. Dan 12:1-3) and is not mentioned anywhere else in Job. What is clear is that Job expects to be vindicated in the presence of God, a foreshadowing of the coming theophany (Job 38—42). Job threatens his friends by suggesting that they will pay at the edge of the sword if they persist in their accusations against him.

Fate of the Wicked (Job 20)

Zophar gives yet another dogmatic rendition of the fate of the wicked. The only thing new is the concession that the wicked may have prosperity for a time, but it will not endure. This is probably another jab at Job.

Complaints About the Wicked (Job 21)
Job responds by stating conclusions that depart so radically from traditional teachings that they probably should be classified as complaints. Job concludes that the wicked remain unpunished by God even though they renounce God; the traditional belief that the sins of the fathers are visited on the children is untrue; and the righteous and wicked alike die and are covered by worms. Job calls the friends' traditional doctrines on the fate of the wicked "empty nothings" and "falsehoods" (Job 21:34). In the third discourse cycle we will find Job's extreme views on the fate of the wicked somewhat tempered (cf. Job 27:1-23).

Conclusions. In the second discourse, Eliphaz counters Job's experiential claims by emphasizing that he has seen the wicked cursed as traditional wisdom teaches. Zophar adds that the wicked may be prosperous for a time, but such prosperity will not endure. To these discourses Job gives three very different responses.

In this discourse cycle Job has made considerable movement theologically. In Job 16—17 he lamented his current hopeless situation and, convinced of his impending death, compelled the earth to avenge it. At that point he did not request a hearing but insisted that God be held accountable. This context reflects Job's struggle with the doctrine of retributive justice, for he viewed his impending death as unjust.

In Job 19 Job shamed his three friends for continually reproaching him instead of showing compassion. This points to a major theological shift. Job no longer holds to the pretense of respectful, cordial theological debate but ironically shames the behavior of his three friends instead of proclaiming his own shame. His laments have become prophetic as they confront the behavior of the three friends.

Job has recast the image of the fate of the wicked as he insists that they remain unpunished by God though they renounce God (Job 21). His complaints against God's neglect in this area are a prophetic reminder to all humanity of injustices served and experienced.

Third Discourse Cycle (Job 22—31)

In this discourse cycle Job and his friends have become rigid in their stances. As a result, their speech is extremely candid and confident. The friends, with the exception of Zophar, attribute the characteristics of the wicked to Job. In response Job proclaims his innocence all the more and accuses God of neglecting the poor.

A List of Accusations (Job 22)
Eliphaz brings his strongest accusations against Job. He begins by noting that no humans, not even the wisest, are of use to God. Of Job he says, "Is not your wickedness great?" (Job 22:5). The ensuing inventory of iniquities that Eliphaz attributes to Job includes exacting pledges from family members; withholding clothing, water and food from those in need; and not lending assistance to widows and harming orphans. This list reflects the Israelite ethic. One who is righteous and in good standing in the community would respond in a positive manner when confronted with each of the needs listed.

In Job 22:12-20 Eliphaz launches into a discourse about the transcendence of God and accuses Job of thinking that God is far away and unable to see or know his iniquities. All of these accusations are made in an effort to persuade Job to remove his unrighteousness and return to God. Eliphaz concludes with assurances that God will be faithful to forgive and restore if Job will only humble himself.

A Turning Point (Job 23—24)
Job's initial response to Eliphaz's third attack is to plead for a hearing with God. This is the third time Job has requested a hearing (cf. Job 9:32-34; 13:20-22), and unlike the others, this time Job is convinced that he would be acquitted. But, he concludes, God is nowhere to be found.

As Job contemplates an encounter with God his focus turns to his continual commitment and devotion to the law, which stands in sharp contrast to God's plans for harm. Job restates his fear of entering God's presence (Job 23:15; cf. Job 13). However, this time Job's confidence in his innocence seemingly overcomes his fear of God.

In Job 24, Job accuses God of ignoring

the prayers of the poor who have been victimized by the wicked. He emphasizes the heinous acts of the wicked against the widow, the orphan and the needy. While this catalogue of sins stands in parallel to that cited by Eliphaz against Job, this time Job brings the accusation against God. Job suggests the wicked go unpunished for their crimes, while the prayers of the poor for deliverance are ignored. Job is no longer focused solely on his plight and no longer views poverty as a punishment from God for sins committed. Instead he accuses God of ignoring the atrocities that the poor suffer at the hands of the wicked. Although Job has noted several times (e.g., Job 21) that the wicked go unpunished, this is Job's first acknowledgment that the poor suffer unjustly. It is therefore a significant turning point in the dialogue.

Job 24:18-25 is difficult. These verses reflect dialogue we are accustomed to hearing from the friends rather than Job. Some scholars suggest the verses are out of place and attribute them to Bildad or Zophar, who never speaks in this cycle. Others suggest the verses should be understood as if Job were quoting the three friends. Each of these solutions is hypothetical, yet if we attribute these words against the wicked to Job his discourse appears to be schizophrenic. However, they could be read as Job's resistance to the severe accusations he has just made. If the prayers of the poor are never heard and the wicked are never punished, then what hope is left? If these are Job's words, then he continues to struggle with the doctrine of divine retributive justice in that he cannot give up the hope that one day the balances will be evened out. Even if this is the case, the traditional dogma has still been significantly altered in that the present-day poor are viewed in a new way, as are the prosperous.

No One Righteous (Job 25)

Bildad's final speech is unusually short and biting. He begins by establishing God's power and might in contrast to a mere mortal. He no longer focuses his attention solely on Job but states that no one can be righteous before God, for human beings are weak (cf. the transition from Job 25:2-3 to Job 25:4) and nothing more than worms. Although a similar theme has been established elsewhere by Eliphaz (cf. Job 4:17-21; 15:14-26), Zophar (cf. Job 11:5-12) and Job (cf. Job 9:2-12; 12:9-25; 14:4), this is the first time it has been stated as a self-accusation.

The Omnipotence of God (Job 26—27)

Building off Bildad's power motif, Job's sarcastic response is filled with the same. Job accuses Bildad of speaking from a spirit he does not recognize, presumably an evil one. Job proclaims the omnipotence of God in a hymn. Many interpreters have suggested these final verses of Job 26 are out of place and should be attached to the end of Bildad's speech. However, they fit with Job's discourse as a transition from his caustic remarks against Bildad's lack of power and wisdom to his commitment to hold fast to his righteousness (i.e., innocence; Job 27:6). The hymn reveals Job's agreement with the doctrine of an all-powerful God, and its juxtaposition to Job 27:1-6 shows his disagreement with Bildad's worm theology. If Job is innocent, then humans have the capacity to be more than worms. Job's disagreement with Bildad's doctrine is so intense that he introduces his restatements of innocence with an oath: "As God lives" (Job 27:2) or "Far be it from me" (Job 27:5).

In Job 27:7-23 Job makes statements of ill will against his friends, whom he now calls his enemies, for the first time since the dialogues began. Many scholars have suggested these verses are the lost speech of Zophar, since the view of the wicked found in this discourse conflicts with Job's earlier comment that the wicked are not punished (cf. Job 21:7-34; 24:2-17). However, such a view does not take into account the possibility of fluctuating human emotions. Job's statements in Job 21 and Job 24 are extreme and might best be understood as reactionary complaints. We have seen the extremity of Job's statements against the wicked tempered in Job 24:18-25 in connection with Job's shift to solidarity with the poor. It has been noted that total rejection of the doctrine of retributive justice would not allow Job to have any hope for the poor. Consequently it does not seem out of place for Job to swing back to a more moderate position on retributive justice.

In Job 24 Job's tempered view allows the poor to hope for justice. If our current text is read as an imprecation against Job's enemies, it reveals Job's hope that he will eventually be vindicated and his friends proven to be enemies who will experience the consequences they suppose for Job. Job uses their words against them, which is ironic, and by so doing he condemns them to the fate of the wicked they so confidently proclaim.

Wisdom Inaccessible (Job 28)
The emphasis of this lengthy hymn is the inaccessibility of wisdom. While humans have the capacity to find precious metals and gems, they are not able to find wisdom because God alone knows the way to wisdom. God sees everything and seems to have placed wisdom somewhere. The hymn ends with a traditional idea: the fear of the Lord is wisdom.

Request for a Hearing (Job 29—31)
These chapters contain Job's final words. He will not speak again until commanded to do so by God in the closing chapters. Job 29—31 is one long speech that builds rhetorically, incorporating elements typically found in the lament, to Job's final request for a hearing.

Job contrasts his happy past with his present distress and delivers his final plea for a hearing heightened by the language of lament throughout. Most significant to these chapters are Job's claims of benevolence to the poor, the widow and the orphan. These claims counter the accusations made against him by Eliphaz (Job 22) and stand in sharp contrast to the accusations Job makes against God (Job 24).

Also significant are the numerous oath statements (Job 31). By the close of this discourse cycle Job's confidence in his vindication before God overshadows any fears he may have had (cf. Job 13; 23). He pledges his past life and deeds as surety of his innocence and integrity (Job 31).

Conclusions. In this final discourse, the arguments of Job's friends reach their height of condemnation as Eliphaz articulates Job's wickedness in detail (Job 22) and Zophar concludes all humans are worms (Job 25). In response Job for the first time brings harsh words of condemnation against the three (Job 27).

Job has made dramatic shifts away from the dogma of divine retribution. In Job 27 he tempers his complaint against God's lackadaisical attitude toward the wicked (cf. Job 21) after having brought severe accusations that God ignores the prayers of the poor (Job 24). Job is guilty of raising severe complaints against God, but he does not curse God. As Gutiérrez suggests, these laments are the prophetic proclamation that all is not well and things are not as they ought to be.

In Job 24, Job exhibits considerable solidarity with the poor as he has become fully aware that the wicked frequently prosper at their expense. Still, hope is present in the view that ultimately the wicked will be punished and the faithful rewarded. While this new stance on the wicked and the poor represents a shift in Job's thinking, it does not eliminate the traditional doctrine. Gutiérrez's language of piety with emphasis on the God of gratuitous love fills the gap. The only constant in which we may have hope is God's grace.

Discourses of Elihu (Job 32—37)

Because of the style and language (there are many Aramaic words) and the seemingly interruptive nature of Elihu's discourses, many scholars suggest that they were written by another author. However, there is no textual evidence to suggest that Job ever existed without these chapters. Thus we will read them as a critical part of the whole and determine their contribution.

Job 32 consists of a narrative introduction to Elihu's four discourses (Job 33—37). In the first five verses the narrator gives us critical information for understanding this discourse. According to the narrator the three friends cease to speak because they have deemed Job "righteous in his own eyes" (i.e., self-righteous). The narrator makes much of the fact that Elihu has become angry because Job has sought to justify himself rather than God and because the three friends have found no answer. Also highlighted is the fact that Elihu has waited to speak because the friends are older and supposedly wiser.

According to Elihu, nothing has been accomplished thus far. Thus Elihu can no longer keep his silence and proclaims that "the breath of the Almighty . . . makes for understanding" and it is "not the old that are wise" (Job 32:8-9). Elihu says to Job and the old men, "Listen to me" (Job 32:10).

The introductory discussion on theodicy is relevant here. The fact that Job does not work at justifying God in the face of evil is to say that he is not doing the work of theodicy; instead he persists in claiming his innocence and consequently that the traditional doctrine of retributive justice does not fit his experience. In Job 24 he goes so far as to suggest that many who are righteous suffer unjustly. In other instances he exclaims that the wicked go unpunished (Job 21). At one point he accuses God of ignoring the prayers of the poor (Job 24:12); at another point he claims God has caused the righteous to suffer (Job 24). He cries for vindication on numerous occasions (Job 9; 13; 23), yet he never curses God or calls God unjust. Job also struggles with the doctrine of divine retributive justice. Though he holds on to his integrity and continually proclaims his innocence, he still struggles to make sense of his predicament as well as that of many others. In the end he is certain of two things: if he is allowed a hearing he will be vindicated; and his experience does not fit with the doctrine that his friends preach to him.

Elihu's wisdom is also grounded in the doctrine of divine retributive justice. In Job 33 he makes the simple argument that God is greater than any mortal and therefore challenges Job's right to contend against God. He suggests that God warns humans to turn aside from their evil deeds through dreams and by chastening them with pain. He even suggests that an angelic mediator may offer a ransom so healing can occur, but this will happen only after a confession of sin. In Elihu's mind, Job finds himself in his current state due to his sin. In fact, Elihu is appalled that Job contends with God (cf. Job 34:18). The doctrine is so solidified in Elihu's mind that one ought not even question it but assume that one's pain is directly related to one's sin, since God cannot do wickedness and will not pervert justice. And so he concludes that Job speaks without knowledge and wishes for him to be tried to the limit. Job speaks as a wicked one and adds rebellion to his sin.

In Job 35 Elihu does provide a bit of sound wisdom when he argues, "If you are wicked or righteous, what do you do to God? Your wickedness and righteousness affect other humans" (paraphrasing Job 35:7-8). This is the point Gutiérrez tries to emphasize when he affirms the language of lament (see *Conclusions*, first discourse cycle). Elihu's attack on Job is misplaced, but the truth of the statement stands.

Elihu particularizes his argument (Job 36) by suggesting the afflictions of the wise are intended as motivation for them to turn from their evil ways in order that they might live in prosperity once more. This is the only gracious statement Elihu makes. While a similar argument was made by the three friends early in the discourse cycles, by the end the friends were speaking as if Job had been wicked all along and his punishment deferred. Elihu does not discuss the state and plight of the wicked. Instead he emphasizes the revelatory function of suffering (cf. Job 33:19-33; 36:5-15).

Elihu closes his discourses with a hymn that proclaims the power of God. As he proceeds through the hymn he raises questions for Job: "Do you know" the workings of God? While these questions foreshadow those that will come in the next chapter, when God speaks for the first time, in Elihu's mouth they serve to justify God and condemn Job. But Job will not be condemned when God speaks.

Discourse Cycle of the Lord (Job 38:1—42:6)

After thirty-four chapters of human debate over the dogma of divine retributive justice, God finally enters the conversation. God speaks out of the whirlwind, which is a frequent setting for theophany (i.e., God appearing to humanity) in the Old Testament. However, it would seem that God is little concerned with Job's petty questions. God has a much larger agenda and begins by asking numerous questions of Job. The questions are somewhat playful, at times sarcastic (e.g., Job 38:21) and seemingly intended to refocus the conversation on the mysteries of the cosmos, of which Job is a small part. Job is commanded to "gird up your loins like a man" (Job 38:3) and to declare his answers to God. After the first round of questions (Job 38:4—39:30) God demands a response from "faultfinder" (Job 40:2) Job, who declares himself speechless for the first time since the inception of the book (Job 40:3-5).

God begins a second set of questions, which focus on God's ability to create and control the chaotic forces of nature as depicted by Behemoth and Leviathan, primeval monsters frequently used in ancient literature as symbols of chaos and evil. The rhetorical effect is to suggest that although humans often experience aspects of creation as overwhelmingly powerful and chaotic, God is in control.

Job begins his second and final response to God with two significant summarizing statements: God can do all things, and God's purposes will never be thwarted (Job 42:2). These are the only answers Job receives for his question about why the righteous suffer. His question has not been answered, and yet Job seems satisfied, so much so that he retracts his utterances (Job 42:3). It is unclear whether this retraction refers to Job's initial question or some aspect of his dialogue. In any event, it seems the clouds have lifted and he now understands the world as well as his situation in a new way. Job, once so confident in his vindication before the Lord (Job 23), upon seeing God despises himself and repents in dust and ashes (Job 42:6).

Frequently this final statement of repentance creates difficulty for reading the book in its entirety. Job does not deny his precatastrophic righteousness and consequently legitimate the adversities recently experienced. Rather, Job repents of his speech before God throughout the last thirty-four chapters. Perhaps the best summary for this is found in God's challenge to Job: "Will you even put me in the wrong? Will you condemn me that you may be justified?" (Job 40:8). This is the only challenge Job receives from God; the remainder of his speech is affirmed (cf. Job 42:7).

Although Job has not cursed God, he also has not exhibited a disinterested faith. His frequent petitions for vindication before God (cf. Job 9; 13; 23) flow out of accusations that God has repeatedly brought severe and unjust attacks against him.

Closing Narrative (Job 42:7-17)

Job 42:7-9 pronounces a negative verdict on the doctrine of divine retributive justice. God's wrath is kindled against Eliphaz the Temanite (inclusive of the friends) for, as God states, "you have not spoken of me what is right, as my servant Job has." Rigid

Midwifery & Birthing Practices

Biblical midwifery incorporated delivery of newborns, precoital counseling of couples, caring for pregnant mothers, assisting during crises such as miscarriage or the death of the mother, and massaging the child in the womb to position the baby for head-first delivery. If the birth was delayed, the child might be given a temporary name and called forth with the formula "[Name], come out!" Many of these functions are combined in Genesis 35:16-20, wherein a midwife assists at Benjamin's difficult birth. Benjamin's temporary name *ben-oni* ("Child of My Labor"), given by Rachel just before her death in childbirth, is a calling-forth name. After the birth, the midwife cleaned and clothed the baby. She also presented the newborn to the parents for adoption—a necessity because relationship was determined by contract rather than kinship. Adoption was accompanied by a formula such as "This is my beloved son" or by naming the child, as when Jacob confers the permanent name Benjamin. If there was no adoption, the child was regarded as stillborn. If this cultural background is assumed in Romans 8:23, Paul's metaphor of groaning while awaiting adoption becomes clear: without God's adoption, we never become spiritually viable.

Most of the biblical references to midwifery describe the work of God or the angel of the Lord. This image is important in the biblical themes of creation (e.g., Job 38:8-11) and salvation. In Isaiah 66:7-11, a prophecy of the new creation, God is presented as midwife to mother Zion. In Psalm 22:9, the speaker acknowledges God as midwife. In Luke 1:26-38, the angel Gabriel acts as midwife to Mary, giving her precoital counseling. In the Synoptic Gospels, Jesus is given two sets of adoption formulas, proclaiming his origins to be divine and human. God implicitly acts as midwife in being the ultimate originator of these adoptions. In the baptism narrative (Mt 3:17 and par.; cf. Mt 17:5 and par.), the formula "This is my Son, the beloved" acknowledges that God is Jesus' legal parent. (God is mother and/or father, since either may adopt.) The human legal adoption occurs when Joseph names Jesus. The angel who instructs Joseph to name Jesus is acting as midwife at God's behest (Mt 1:20-23).

Jesus is presented as midwife when he commands, "Lazarus, come out!" (Jn 11:43). The flow of blood and water from Jesus' side on the cross (Jn 19:33-37) is widely held to be one of John's anti-Docetic reminders of Jesus' natural birth. However, if this is a birthing image, it is also the new birth of creation, incipient in Jesus' death on the cross. Jesus takes the role of mother as he gives his blood for the life of the world. Since John makes it clear that God brings this event to finality, again God is the midwife. God as midwife also appears in Paul where the Holy Spirit "helps us in our weakness" as "the whole creation has been groaning in labor pains" awaiting new birth in Christ (Rom 8:22, 26).

Bibliography

D. C. Benjamin, "Israel's God: Mother and Midwife," *Biblical Theology Bulletin* 19 (1989) 115-20; V. R. Mollenkott, "God as Midwife," in *The Divine Feminine* (New York: Crossroad, 1983) 32-35.

KAMILA A. BLESSING

adherence to the dogma that the righteous are blessed and the wicked punished is condemned. The three friends are required to bring sacrifices of repentance, and Job is to officiate, which affirms Job as righteous. Job is in the precarious position of having to pray for the three, Eliphaz, Bildad and Zophar, whom he has so recently condemned (cf. Job 27); his prayers for them are accepted. All four have been reconciled to God.

The concluding verses of the book parallel the opening as Job's fortunes are restored by God twofold and Job regains his stature in the community. Many readers struggle with these concluding verses, as they seem to reestablish the doctrine of divine retributive justice. Again Gutiérrez helps us make sense of the text. We, like the characters in the story (cf. Job 42:11), are so culturally immersed in the dogma of blessings for the righteous and punishment for the wicked that we miss God's grace. Job's fortunes are not restored as a result of some righteous act. Job is no more righteous now than he was at the start of the story. The restoration of Job's fortunes and status is an example of God's gracious activity and in no way nullifies the main point of the book, that is, the doctrine of divine retributive justice is an inadequate depiction of God's presence in our world.

While the three female perspectives depicted in the excursus above offer slightly different interpretations of God's agreement with Satan, each evidences an expectation of blessing for the righteous and punishment for the wicked. Much contemporary biblical scholarship has embraced multiculturalism and diverse interpretations of the text. While this movement in the field is to be affirmed, it leads to new levels of confusion and complexity that scholars have yet to work through. Although varied interpretations are deemed meaningful and legitimate for particular cultural groups, scholars continue to search for a hermeneutic that is universally meaningful. It seems that Gutiérrez has come near to achieving this goal by providing a common language that speaks to the core of our humanity. This language recognizes our common state: immersion in the doctrine of retributive justice; our common call: disinterested faith and the prophetic language of lamentation; and our common hope: God's grace.

Bibliography. D. J. A. Clines, *Job 1—20*, Word Biblical Commentary 17 (Waco, TX: Word, 1989); G. Gutiérrez, *On Job: God-talk and the Suffering of the Innocent*, trans. C. Martin, "Biblical Theology and Black Women's Spiritual Autobiography," in *A Troubling in My Soul: Womanist Perspectives on Evil and Suffering*, ed. E. M. Townes (Maryknoll, NY: Orbis, 1993); C. A. Newsom, "Job," in *The New Interpreter's Bible*, vol. 4, ed. L. E. Keck et al. (Nashville: Abingdon, 1996); N. P. F. Southard, "Recovery and Rediscovered Images: Spiritual Resources for Asian American Women," in *Feminist Theology from the Third World: A Reader*, ed. U. King (Maryknoll, NY: Orbis, 1994) 378-91.

LEANN SNOW FLESHER

PSALMS

Introduction

The Psalms are personal poems and Israel's hymns. Many have titles indicating authorship and, sometimes, circumstance of writing. I have chosen to take these titles at face value, though it is possible that "of David," for example, could on occasion mean "for" or "after" David. The titles may classify the psalm as a *maskil* or teaching psalm (e.g., Ps 32), although the meaning of some descriptions is now lost in the mists of history (e.g., *miktam*, Ps 56—60). Modern theologians tend to classify the Psalms by form, theme or supposed situation. Hence we can recognize wisdom psalms (e.g. Ps 37; 73; Ps 78), penitential psalms (e.g., Ps 51; 130), pilgrim psalms (e.g., Ps 120—134), nature psalms (e.g., Ps 29; 104), praise psalms (e.g., Ps 145—150) and so on. The royal psalms (e.g., Ps 2; 45; 110) are worthy of special note. These portray Israel's king as one appointed by the Lord to lead the people in a true fear of the Lord. They look beyond the current king to an ideal king yet to come, a king whom the New Testament identifies as Jesus Christ the Messiah.

The Psalms reflect that ancient Israel was a strongly patriarchal society. Men headed each family "house" (Ps 112; 128), and men served in the temple (Ps 133). A number of individual men are mentioned, especially in book 4: Abraham, Jacob, Joseph, Moses, Aaron, Phinehas, Samuel, David and others (see especially Ps 77; 78; 99; 105; 106; 132). The worldview reflected in the Psalms is one in which the male is normative and the self is assumed to be male. So, for example, Psalm 1 begins, literally, "Blessed is the man who" (NIV). The literal term "man" *(ish)* may refer to males and females, just as the plural "men" may at times incorporate all God's people (Ps 78:25), male and female. In a similar way, "son of man" *(bene adam)* may mean "human being," either male or female (Ps 12:8; 89:47).

By contrast, references to women are relatively few and mostly symbolic. "Woman"/"wife" *(ishah)* occurs three times (Ps 58:8; 109:9; 128:3), and these references reflect something of the normative role and function of women in Israelite society. All women were viewed in terms of their role in relationship to a man. They were wives, mothers, daughters, sisters, potential wives or servants, valued for their beauty, moral strength and ability to bear children (Ps 45:11-16; Ps 68:12-13, lit. "beauty of the house"; 127:3-5; 144:12). The classic example is the princess of Psalm 45, who is rich, beautiful, desirable and blessed, especially with the promise of children.

Specific literal women are rarely mentioned. For example, except for the title, Psalm 51 makes no mention of Bathsheba, nor does Psalm 113 explicitly mention Hannah. Recent studies have revealed how women played a crucial role in Israel's story, especially in the exodus. Yet when Psalm 105 recalls this story, Moses and Aaron are remembered by name as "sent" by the Lord, but no mention is made of Miriam or her singing (Ps 105:26, 43; cf Ex 15:20-21; Mic 6:4).

The most commonly encountered group of women in the Psalms are mothers. This reflects the fact that the normative role for women in Israel was a domestic one. They were to marry, bear children and look after them and the household of which their responsible male was the head. In a family-orientated society, mothers were the link that bonded family members together (Ps 50:20; 69:8). But childbearing and rearing in ancient Israel was a difficult and risky business (reflected in Ps 58:8). Hence motherhood was by far the most highly valued and desirable role to which a woman could aspire (Ps 113:9). To any Israelite, one's mother mattered (Ps 35:14; 116:16). This understanding of motherhood gives added significance to Psalm 87's picture of Zion as a mother city, in whom are the springs of life (Ps 87:5-7).

Because kinship to some responsible male determined a woman's social identity, it also inevitably determined her personal and social security. Apart from this relationship, Israelite women had few rights and little power. They were, for example, given in marriage, and marriage determined their legal status. Economically they were almost totally dependent on their responsible male relation. Consequently women in the Psalms are often portrayed as vulnerable.

This is particularly true of another commonly encountered group, the widows. The Hebrew for "widow" is closely related to the words for "silent" and "desolate" (*see* Widows). In a society in which husbands assumed full economic responsibility for their wives and children, any woman with no male to support her would indeed be desolate. Without a voice to speak for her, maybe even her survival would be at stake. Four of the five references group widows with orphans (Ps 68:5; 94:6; 109:9; 146:9). Together (sometimes with "strangers" added), they represent the poor, vulnerable and underprivileged in Israelite society: those without family able to bear the responsibility for supporting them. Such an unenviable position would understandably find its expression in lamentation (Ps 109). The prayer that a man's wife will become a widow (Ps 109:9) seeks not only his death but also lasting shame on his name, as people see his widow and children publicly reduced to a life of poverty, isolation and destitution.

In a similar way, the barren woman (Ps 113:9) represents those who would normally be considered not blessed, or even cursed (*see* Blessing and Cursing). As the place where human life began and was formed, a woman's womb was particularly precious. It was regarded as being under the direct control of the Lord, who opened or closed it at will (Ps 139:13; *see* Barrenness and Fertility). Since, under the old covenant, children and wealth were promised to those who obeyed the Lord (Deut 7:12-14; Ps 127:3), barrenness was commonly viewed as a sign of his disfavor. Furthermore, children, and sons in particular, were meant to provide for their parents' old age; hence barrenness was a failure of role that could lead to divorce (*see* Divorce). A woman without children would be vulnerable; at risk of being classed with the poor and needy of Israelite society.

The psalmists never explicitly examine, let alone challenge, these patriarchal assumptions. Yet there are hints that the Lord is not content with the status quo. When compared with the Israelite norm, for example, the Lord gives an unusually high priority to caring for widows, orphans and barren women (Ps 68:5; 113:9). Knowing their particular need for protection from the "wicked" (Ps 94:4-7), the Lord has pity on them and takes on the role of responsible male for them, becoming their protector, upholder, provider, father and judge (Ps 68:5-6; 113:9; 146:5-9).

Thus it appears that by being forced to accept a subordinate position in society, the women of Israel were perversely privileged. Though their position was often, in earthly terms, unenviable, yet it also uniquely qualified them to be objects of the Lord's compassion and recipients of the Lord's help.

The fact that in the Psalms' worldview, the male is normative gives added significance to the several occurrences of feminine imagery and metaphor. Psalm 73, for example, by using a participle of the verb *zanah* ("to prostitute oneself," "play the whore"), pictures the wicked as unfaithful wives, wronging the Lord their husband (Ps 73:27). Motivated by greed for wealth, their infidelity reveals itself primarily in arrogance. Similarly, Psalm 106 portrays Israel on entry to the Promised Land as a woman prostituting herself by mingling with the nations (Ps 106:34-39). This metaphor is developed further in the book of Hosea, especially Hosea 2:2-13.

The Psalms sometimes personify countries and cities as female. This is not too surprising, as the Hebrew words for "city" and "land" are feminine. Thus "Rahab," for example, almost certainly stands for Egypt (Ps 87:4; 89:10). Psalm 9:14 personifies the holy city, Zion, as a woman, and Psalm 48:11 speaks of the towns of Judah (and by implication, their inhabitants) as her "daughters" (cf. Ps 97:8; 137:8).

Whether or not feminine imagery is used of God in the Psalms, to any significant extent, is a matter for debate. Some interpreters claim that two psalms picture God as midwife (Ps 22:9; 71:6), but in both cases the emphasis seems to be more on protection from the time of birth than assistance with the birth. Some point to the large number of feminine nouns used in relation to God, often in association with steadfast love. I have highlighted some of these as they occur: nouns like faithfulness and righteousness (*emunath* and *tsedaqah,* Ps 36:5-6). However, one must be wary about drawing conclusions from this observation because, with Hebrew abstract nouns, there is no necessary correlation between grammatical gender and meaning. The most one can surely say is that the psalmists are evidently not hesitant to use such feminine terms when describing the attributes of the Lord God. On occasion they seem deliberately designed to contribute to the poetry of a psalm (e.g., Ps 57:10).

Women reaching out to God in the midst of crisis situations may find great support and consolation in the Psalms. Hence we find forthright condemnations of violence (Ps 5:9; 7:1-2; 10:2, 7-10; 17:11; 27:12; 31:4, 10-13; 37:32; 38:11-12; 52:2-3; 54:3; 35:12-14, 20-21; 56:5-6; 59:3; 64:1-6; 69:4, 19-20; 86:14; 140:1-5), passionate appeals to God for deliverance (Ps 59:2; 139:19; 140:1, 4) and deep assurances of God's power to give safety and support (Ps 10:17-18; 12:5; 28:8-9; 34:6; 35:10; 103:6).

As Hebrew poems, the Psalms are deeply rhythmic and steeped in many kinds of parallelism. Most are written in couplets or triplets of two or three units per line, with each unit arranged around a tone syllable. Like most poems, the Psalms deal with a wide range of human experiences and emotions, from deep sorrow to exultant joy, from anxious distress to confident trust, from agonized longing to grateful satisfaction. "Trouble" in particular is a common experience, to which the psalmists' consistent response is "pray and trust," on the grounds that the Lord God is consistently loving and trustworthy (e.g., Ps 20; 46; 77). All the Psalms are written from such a faith perspective, which is the primary key to understanding them.

As Israel's hymns, the Psalms may incorporate musical directions. In Psalm 9, for example, "Selah" means "pause," probably for a musical interlude, and "Muthlabben" (see title) is probably a tune. Such directions indicate the Psalms were either deliberately written or adapted for public worship. As with many of today's worship songs, the fact that they are often written in the first person singular does not render them any less suitable for this purpose. After all, individual faith is a prerequisite for genuine and lively worship. The main themes are adoration, remembrance, confession, thanksgiving, instruction, testimony, petition and praise. Thus the Psalms reveal that worship is essentially a response to God's revelation in creation and salvation, and they still provide a pattern for worship. Organized into five books, each ending with a doxology, the collection emphasizes from beginning to end the truth that to worship the Lord is the greatest possible privilege and brings lasting blessing.

Outline

1–41	Book 1
42–72	Book 2
73–89	Book 3
90–106	Book 4
107–150	Book 5

Commentary

Book 1 (Ps 1–41)

Psalm 1 affirms that the only sure and lasting happiness for people is found in friendship with the Lord. This involves deliberately rejecting the "advice" of all wrongdoers and daily delighting instead in "the law of the LORD" (Ps 1:1-2). The result is true eternal prosperity, often pictured in the Old Testament in terms of natural fruitfulness (Ps 1:3; cf. Ps 128). The contrast with "the wicked" reassures the people of God that though sinners may seem prosperous, appearances are deceptive. Eternity will prove it, for the awesome truth is that "the LORD watches" (lit. "is knowing," Ps 1:6).

Psalm 2 explores people's natural rebelliousness to God's rule, which provokes God to derision, wrath and judgment. The psalm pictures the Lord emphatically introducing "my king," to whom he has committed the powers of judgment, originally referring to David (cf. 2 Sam 7:8-11). The New Testament treats this psalm as a prophecy of Christ (e.g., Acts 4:25-26; 13:33). The nations' rebelliousness contrasts with the response of the wise. Aware of the Lord's wrath, they will worship him rightly, demonstrate their allegiance ("kiss" him) and consequently find in him security and happiness.

Psalm 3 is the first of many psalms written by David when he was in trouble (see title; cf. 2 Sam 15:14). His characteristic response is to turn to the Lord in prayer in spite of discouragement from those around. His personal knowledge of the Lord (Ps 3:3, "a shield around me, my glory") assures him that prayer works. This assurance overcomes fear and prompts specific prayer and witness. David's witness focuses on how, night and day, the Lord supplies all his needs, especially his present need for "deliverance" (*yeshu'a,* fem., Ps 3:7-8).

Psalm 4 is constructed around a tenet of wisdom (Ps 4:4; cf. Job 31:30; Prov 13:3) and its present application. Leading up to it is David's experience: when disturbed by slander against himself, instead of responding in kind, he turned to prayer. His confidence of an answer is based not on his faithfulness but on God's setting him apart "for himself" (Ps 4:3). Psalm 4:6 adds a reminder that he is not alone in his suffering and prayer. Therefore, despite the situation, he knows gladness and peace, for both are the Lord's blessings to his faithful people.

Psalm 5 finds David troubled by the violent duplicity of his enemies. He lays his concerns before the Lord "in the morning," then watches for an answer (Ps 5:1-3). His priorities are to seek first God's guidance "in . . . righteousness" for himself, then God's justice for the wicked, and finally God's protective blessing for all his people (Ps 5:8-12). His confidence that God will answer is rooted in an understanding of wickedness as transgressive rebellion against God and in the knowledge that the Lord is righteous and steadfastly loving. "But" (Ps 5:7, 11) contrasts the behavior and fate of the wicked and the righteous.

Psalm 6 graphically describes David when suffering from some serious illness. He faces the real prospect of death, filled to the soul with "terror" at the thought that God must be angry with him (Ps 6:1-3; cf. Ps 88). His appeal to the Lord's steadfast love (*hesed,* Ps 6:4) implies that a consideration of his desire to worship and his deep distress will move the Lord to saving action. Such sincere prayer is quickly answered, and those who have been taking advantage of his weakness in turn experience terror and depart in shame.

Psalm 7 finds David pursued because of an alleged injustice toward an "ally" (Ps 7:1-4). Cush (see title) is possibly an unknown relation of Abner (see 2 Sam 3). David's prayer is for personal salvation and judgment, on the grounds that he is innocent while unnamed others are guilty and that God is "my shield" and the just judge of all peoples (Ps 7:8-11). A metaphor of conception, pregnancy and birthing (Ps 7:14) focuses on the progress of evil rather than good. David's vivid picture of judgment taking place leaves him so sure of the Lord's righteous power that, instead of dwelling further on his plight, he looks forward in praise.

Psalm 8 is a God-centered celebration of his glory. In delighted wonder, David praises his royal greatness and grace. The former, evident in creation's vastness and variety, leaves David feeling small and weak. Yet, paradoxically, this great God commits his defense to humble "babes and infants," which metaphorically includes spiritual children (cf. Mt 18:3). David asks but already knows the answer: humans are privileged creatures because Israel's covenant Lord is the Creator-King of "all the earth" (Ps 8:1, 9). The verbs (Ps 8:5ff.) reflect his grace in creation and redemption, for Psalm 8 is messianic (cf. Heb 2:5-18).

Psalm 9 gives praise for a recent victory in battle that prompts David to affirm that the Lord is "enthroned" (Ps 9:7) as the "Most High," just judge of the whole world (Ps 9:2-8). Those who know him trust him to be their "stronghold" in trouble (Ps 9:9-10); they praise, witness and pray, for though they have already experienced saving grace, there is still much to pray for. By contrast, those who "forget" God find he makes himself known to them in judgment (Ps 9:15-17), forcing them to recognize their mortality and by implication his immortal greatness. Note the city's description as a "daughter" of the land (Ps 9:14; cf. Ps 97:8), a term also used by Jeremiah and Zechariah.

Psalm 10 tackles the classic wisdom question: Why do the wicked prosper? They like to think God doesn't exist, doesn't care, doesn't know or will not judge. Their blasphemous pride contrasts with the meek innocence of their victims. The psalmist prays for justice and, beginning with "But you do see!" (Ps 10:14), refutes their arguments. A true knowledge of God's observant and caring character leads to the affirmation of Psalm 10:16; as "king forever," the Lord does know, does care, will hear the prayers of the helpless and will "do justice" for them (Ps 10:17-18).

Psalm 11 logically follows Psalm 10. Tempted to abandon trust in God, David replies that because the Lord is enthroned in heaven and their personal "refuge" (Ps 11:1), the righteous do not need to flee from the wicked in fear. Again this psalm affirms that the Lord does see their plight, does care, and though he will "test" all people, he will ultimately punish the wicked and bless the righteous because he is righteous (Ps 11:5-7). The blessing will be to meet God personally ("behold his face," Ps 11:7).

Psalm 12 observes that evil pervades society. David sees people suffering and recognizes the cause as sin. Lies especially are prevalent; they are the manifestation of selfish pride. David's response is not despair but prayer for help (Ps 12:1, root *yash'a,* "save"), which the Lord answers with a promise to act on behalf of the poor and needy. This evokes renewed confidence in the Lord and his Word. Note the contrast between the purity of the Word of God and the duplicity of the lies of the wicked.

Psalm 13 finds David, shaken by pain and sorrow, feeling forsaken by God because his enemy has gained the upper hand. However, instead of turning from God, he turns to God in a prayer that seeks understanding as much as salvation. For a brief moment he entertains the thought that his enemy may triumph but quickly corrects himself with a reminder of the Lord's "steadfast love" and past goodness (Ps 13:5-6). So he can praise the Lord even in the midst of sorrow, confident that the joy of salvation will return.

Psalm 14, which is virtually identical to Psalm 53, introduces a character familiar in wisdom literature. The "fool" (*nabal,* Ps 14:1) is one who chooses to ignore God and is morally responsible for the consequences. Living without regard to the Lord leads to sinful behavior (Ps 14:1-3; cf. Rom 3:10-18), oppression of God's people and their longing for salvation. Hope (Ps 14:7) is certain because the God who sees everything is already working with and for the righteous. Even their present suffering is only his discipline; he will deliver his people and thereby thwart the fools.

Psalm 15 begins with a question. The Lord's home is intended to be the believer's home too, but on what conditions may believers enjoy their privilege? Psalm 15:2-5 provides the answer: the Lord's home is holy; therefore they too must be holy (cf. Ps 24:3-5). They will express this in four ways: integrity of character (Ps 15:2, "walks" and "works" must match), a disciplined tongue, just dealings with other people and a right attitude to money. Fulfilling these requirements results in eternal stability.

Psalm 16 is David's personal thanksgiving for preservation from death and a messianic prophecy that finds its deepest fulfilment in Jesus Christ. It reveals the depth and breadth of David's faith as he expresses total trust in God. His attitude is humble, prayerful, devoted, outward looking and uncompromising. His assurance encompasses contentment, gratitude, confidence and constancy. His hope is of eternal joy, for he trusts the Lord not only to conquer death but also to give life. The New Testament maintains that David's experience foreshadows a far greater deliverance from death: Christ's resurrection (Ps 16:10, cf. Acts 2:25-28; 13:35-37).

Psalm 17 finds David being unjustly persecuted, probably by Saul. Knowing his cause is just and his motivation open to God's eyes, he turns to God in urgent, sincere and confident prayer. He knows that God, like a doting parent (Ps 17:8), will hear, save, guard and hide him. He testifies to the character of God, who is greater than all his enemies. Their lives are centered on "this world"—their bellies and their children (Ps 17:14)—David's is centered on the prospect of seeing God's face, which gives him the confidence to expect victory.

Psalm 18 is David's thanksgiving to God for rescuing him (see title; cf. 2 Sam 22). With vivid imagery he describes how, motivated by delight in righteousness, the Lord used the forces of nature as instruments of salvation. This prompts a meditation: the Lord is so perfect that he must be the only true God. David attributes every success to the multifaceted humble "help" (Ps 18:35, *anawah,* fem., "humility"), which stems from his "steadfast love" (Ps 18:50). Observing that his enemies had no such "living rock" to save them, he resolves, as "head of the nations," to witness among them (Ps 18:41-49; cf. Rom 15:9).

Psalm 19 speaks of God's self-revelation in creation and in the Word. The former leads observers to the limited knowledge that God is gloriously real. The latter, by teaching righteousness and warning of sin, leads to inner revival, wisdom and joy. Therefore it is precious. The right response to God's revelation, modeled by David, is to seek cleansing and preservation from sin, that one might be "acceptable" to God (Ps 19:12-14). For God is Israel's holy covenant Lord. His way of salvation may not yet be fully revealed, but clearly David knows him personally. The joyful notion of marriage is noted (Ps 19:5).

Psalm 20 was probably a prayer before King David went into battle. God's people seek his sevenfold blessing for "the day of trouble" (Ps 20:1-4), on the grounds of confidence in his name (i.e., character) and presence with them (signified by Zion). Individually and corporately they affirm their faith, contrasting their "pride" and prospects with those of the surrounding nations (Ps 20:5-8). Their confidence in the Lord's holy might assures them that he will hear and help "his anointed" king (cf. Acts 10:38). Finally they address the Lord directly, summing up all their requests in one word, "victory" (Ps 20:5, 9, root *yash'a,* "save").

Psalm 21 fulfills Psalm 20:5. Recognizing that all victory comes from the Lord, God's people gladly give him the glory and praise for King David's victory in battle. In the process they reveal the closeness of David's personal friendship with the Lord and the depth of his trust, which gives them confidence to assure him of continuing victory in the future. Here again David foreshadows the Messiah. Psalm 21:10 seems cruel but reflects the fact that, as their only hope for the future, children were taking the rightful place of God in these enemies' lives (cf. Ps 17:14-15).

Psalm 22 finds David in the midst of some tragedy, feeling "forsaken" (Ps 22:1), "yet" still believing that God is holy, "enthroned" and trustworthy (Ps 22:3). The Scriptures and experience confirm it. Therefore he turns not from but to the Lord

Violence, Abuse & Oppression

Women, especially Christian women, can have difficulty determining what counts as violence, abuse and oppression. It may be easier for us to recognize the victimization of others than to identify such problems within our circle and family. Our difficulties in recognizing abuse come honestly. The Christian belief system and Scriptures are often understood to teach unrestricted self-sacrifice, endless forgiveness, humility as a chief virtue and sin as pride and self-will. While these can represent valid components of a Christian theology, an uncritical appropriation of them often blinds women to the violence in their lives and in the lives of those close to them. It can also stop women from following Christ in opposing such injustice.

Traditional Christian writing, preaching and advice historically have come from people who possess some societal power. They are thus more familiar with power's temptations and benefits. Those with power are often less clear, however, about the effects of violence, abuse and oppression on the unwilling recipients of it. Thus much Christian exhortation is often presented with the sinner, rather than the victim, in mind.

To make matters more complex, few have taken into account that not just gender but class, race and economics are interwoven. However, the voices of the formerly voiceless, including women, have begun to speak. And many of them have heard a clear, strong message in Scripture against taking advantage of the vulnerable or creating situations of oppression. From their experience and a renewed reading of the Bible, many abused persons have been able to identify oppression, share their knowledge and learn what heals and frees.

Identifying Violence, Abuse and Oppression

Violence, abuse and oppression are about coercion. A person or group uses methods of control, normally considered illegitimate, to further their goals. This control can be interpersonal or institutionalized, overt or covert. All forms further the unequal distribution of power, whether between individuals or within society. Racism, sexism and ageism are institutionalized forms of violence, abuse and oppression. Often the methods of control remain covert. When religion is used to justify coercion, it can be especially hard to detect and oppose. But religion can also bring reconciliation and peace, and that is the undergirding message of the gospel.

Making distinctions among these three forms of control can alert women to the subtle harm that exists here. Violence, when involving bodily harm, is an overt form of coercion, but threats, intimidation or reminders of past harmful acts can count as violence. Abuse can be a more elusive form of coercion, including withdrawal, neglect or deceit. Abuse can be slow-acting and cumulative. Our age did not invent the concept of emotional abuse, for Scripture makes clear that abuse can include scorn, mockery and insult (Job 30:9; Ps 22:5-7; Lk 6:22).

Oppression, although it can be interpersonal, is often on the social level. It is about setting up a hierarchy in which one person or group is privileged and others dispossessed. Scripture uses a number of different words to describe oppression, but all involve harming and gaining control over others. Passages often pair oppression with affliction, misery and poverty and show that it can come in the form of overwork, fraud, deceit, pressure or injury. Social oppression from within Israel is the kind most often referred to in the Old Testament. In spite of this witness, we are often blindsided by this injustice, since we expect oppression to come from outside our community, to be obvious or to happen to others.

All of these behaviors can function interpersonally or institutionally, inside the church or out, within families and in society. As women we experience these three forms of harm more often than we realize. Because this is so deeply rooted in history and society, we cannot expect intelligence, education, class, wealth or status to provide protection. Yet there are deep resources of help in our faith and Scripture, if we are able to see them and receive God's grace in new ways. First, however, we need to understand that violence, abuse and oppression cloud the mind and paralyze the will of victims.

The Effect: Bondage to Anguish

Scripture identifies what it feels like to receive violence, abuse and oppression. One feels abandoned, overpowered, reduced, enslaved, foolish and even insane. The victim becomes "broken-spirited" and experiences affliction, suffering and loss. One may often feel angry at God, be unable to keep God's precepts and despair of life. There are good reasons for these feelings—we have been abandoned, let down or used by others, often by the people closest to us.

But we do not have a theological term for this experience. Victims often feel guilty about what has happened to them. This common occurrence is why we need a category to describe the results of violence, abuse and oppression. Therefore I propose that the victim feels anguish: the pain of being sinned against to the point of powerlessness. Anguish needs to be marked out as different from personal wrongdoing or sin. Anguish happens when our healthy expectation for interpersonal interdependency is subverted. Someone has used us for his or her ends. The distinguishing experience from the victim's perspective is that she has been rendered helpless, whether chronically or only for a moment.

While everyone is gifted by God with personal will, it is not a pristine thing unaffected by conditions and experiences. All of us have trouble motivating our wills to turn toward God, but victims have an additional problem. The trauma of being victimized can paralyze or reduce the ability of the will to break free. It is especially dangerous when there are few resources with which to avoid it. The more powerful the abuse or the fewer the resources, the more deeply one is put in bondage to one's anguish. Once trapped, the will is weakened or paralyzed, and outside intervention is necessary to break the grip (e.g., Ex 6:6).

Theological Pitfalls and Helps

Given that powerlessness is the distinguishing mark, it is tragic that frequent questions for the victim are "How much of this did I bring upon myself?" "Is this the result of my sin?" "Christian theology, with its focus on personal sin, does not often help victims. While it is true that "all have sinned and fall short of the glory of God" (Rom 3:23), it is also true that we are all sinned against, some more and some less.

Victims often wonder if God condones what has happened to them, especially since in the Bible God gets angry and even acts violently on occasion. There is a subtle distinction here, for Scripture indicates that God hates violence, abuse and oppression, especially when done to the most vulnerable, such as aliens, orphans and widows. When God exhibits anger it is not the uncontrolled passion that humans exert. Instead, God allows perpetrators to have their sins turn back upon them. This serves a higher goal than retributive justice, that is, good being rewarded and evil being punished. God's fury is against sin in order to restrain it (Ex 22:21-27).

Thus God's relationship to chaos and order is not one-sided. God restrains evil and preserves order to keep chaos at bay, but sometimes disruption is necessary. Then God is free to disturb the status quo, especially when that system has perpetuated such evils as oppression and alienation. Not all human order has divine mandate, especially when it has become the purveyor of violence, abuse and oppression. This wisdom can help victims who feel guilty about disrupting human structures, even a marriage that has become abusive. Alternatively it counsels caution to those who feel they must take revenge. The Bible promises that evils such as violence, abuse and oppression will ultimately be done away with by God. In the meantime, God disrupts or protects human order.

This does not mean, however, that victims must practice immediate, unlimited forgiveness or that they should not exercise legal means to have their abuse addressed. Both assumptions can come from an unbalanced use of Christian teaching on personal sin, humility and Jesus' work on the cross. While forgiveness is a worthy goal and can free the victim from spiritual bondage, true reconciliation is not achieved without the repentance of the sinner. Ideally the most complete healing comes when the perpetrator helps in the victim's restoration. As for appropriate legal redress, it can be part of healing and reempowerment for the victim, while also serving to warn against or restrain evil. Finally, the witness of Jesus does not teach us to welcome or endure victimization but to work against it. We see the deep human propensity to scapegoat and victimize when we see the misunderstanding and mistreatment of this righteous, innocent God-man. Jesus' life, words and actions condemn and undercut, rather than condone, this human sin.

Bibliography

L. Mercadante, "Anguish: Unraveling Sin and Victimization," *Anglican Theological Review* 82/2 (spring 2000); idem, *Victims and Sinners* (Louisville, KY: Westminster/John Knox, 1996); A. S. Park, *The Wounded Heart of God* (Nashville: Abingdon, 1993); C. E. Gudorf, *Victimization* (Philadelphia: Trinity Press International, 1992); J. G. Williams, ed., *The Girard Reader* (New York: Crossroad, 1996).

LINDA A. MERCADANTE

---

in prayer. God's answer comes suddenly, prompting David to public witness and praise. Convinced that God has been good to him, David knows he will prove equally good to all nations and generations. The New Testament sees the hope of Psalm 22 fulfilled in Christ's death, resurrection and exaltation (see Mt 27:39-46; Jn 19:23-28; Heb 2:9-12).

Psalm 23 reflects David's experience (cf. 1 Sam 17:34-37). The shepherd image implies that God accepts the responsibility to care for those who know him. His priorities are to keep them spiritually healthy and growing (food, water, rest, restoration and guidance, Ps 23:1-3). Though they are not protected from "the darkest valley," the shepherd is always there to protect them through it (Ps 23:4). Rooted in "goodness and mercy" (Ps 23:6), the preplanned richness of God's care gives David confidence to face whatever the future may bring. All that matters is to be with him.

Psalm 24 may perhaps celebrate the return of the ark, the symbol of God's presence, to Jerusalem (cf. 2 Sam 6:12-15). David identifies the Lord as sovereign Creator, then focuses on his relationship with "those who seek him" (Ps 24:3-6). His holiness necessitates their salvation, so he grants them "vindication" (*tsedaqah,* fem., "righteousness") as a blessing. The picture of the Lord's greatness gradually builds up, from transcendent Creator, via personal Savior and covenant Lord to "King of glory" and "Lord of Hosts" (Ps 24:7-10). And as the picture builds, so does the praise.

Psalm 25 is a prayer for guidance and a meditation on the God who guides. In a time of trouble for all Israel, David prays for protection, instruction, pardon and deliverance. Knowing he does not deserve an answer, he appeals to the Lord's steadfast love and goodness, then "waits" for God (Ps 25:5, 21). He meditates on the God who longs to befriend and guide people but requires first their humility, obedience and reverence. Finally, aware that obedience means loneliness and suffering, he prays for saving grace for himself and all God's people.

Psalm 26 finds David falsely accused but maintaining his innocent integrity. Aware of the Lord's faithfulness to him, he has been, is now and always intends to be faithful in return. His fidelity is expressed in right inward attitudes (unwavering trust,

---

The Relevance of Psalms for the Everyday Lives of Women

The Psalms from earliest times have been a source of inspiration and strength. They are used as prayers, sung as hymns and repeated from memory in times of special need or celebration. The convents of Macrina and Olympias were said to resound constantly with a chorus of women chanting the Psalms. These hymns of Israel give expression to the praise in the hearts of believers and reflect at times their deepest despair.

Psalm 68, often considered the most celebratory of the Psalms, places women in the midst of the worshiping community. As singing had accompanied the ark during its long journey from Sinai to Zion (Num 10:35-36), so now women musicians celebrated the arrival of the ark of the covenant in Jerusalem (Ps 68:24-27; cf. 2 Sam 6:12-15). Their song exalted the victorious march of Yahweh through the wilderness and ultimately to the heights of Mount Zion.

At times of deepest significance the voices of women were essential. After a victory, women led the expressions of praise and thanksgiving. *Kosharoth* (Ps 68:6 [68:7 Heb.]), rendered in the NRSV as "prosperity," might better be translated "jubilations," perhaps an allusion to the jubilation of Near Eastern women over a victory (cf. Ex 15:20; Judg 11:34; 1 Sam 18:6-7; 2 Sam 1:20; Ps 48:11; 97:8; Jer 31:4). They too were foremost in expressions of lament (cf. Judg 11:38, 40; 2 Sam 1:24).

Women took a vital part in the proclamation of God's good news. The NASB version of Psalm 68:11 reads "The Lord gives the command; / The women who proclaim the good tidings are a great host." Calvin, in his *Commentary on the Psalms,* says, "Notice is taken of the women who announce the army, for it was the custom anciently for women to sing the song of triumph, as Miriam, the sister of Moses, with her companions, sounded the praises of God upon the timbrel, and the women celebrated David's victory upon the harp, when he slew Goliath, and routed the Philistines."

Here, as in Isaiah 40:9, it is women who are called to herald the saving acts of God. While some modern translations obscure the gender, the proclaimers here and the individual proclaimer in Isaiah 40:9 are clearly feminine. Women are unequivocally called on to bring good tidings to Zion and to lift their voices in witness to God.

The faith and influence of mothers are stressed, so that the psalmist in Psalms 86 and 116 refers to himself as "the child of your serving girl" (Ps 86:16; 116:16), while the loss of a mother is mentioned with grief (Ps 35:14). Psalm 128:3 depicts the joy and blessing of fruitfulness for women. God's presence during childbirth is an important concept for women. Psalm 22:9-10 pictures God as a midwife who delivers an infant, places it on her lap in order to clean it off and then starts it on the process of breast-feeding. Thus the process of maternal bonding is divinely initiated. The Jerusalem Bible renders these verses as "Yet you drew me out of the womb, you entrusted me to my mother's breasts; placed on your lap from my birth, from my mother's womb you have been my God." God is intimately concerned with both the physical and spiritual dynamics of birth.

A similar image occurs at Psalm 71:6, with a representation of God as midwife, bringing to birth and supporting the new child. In antiquity it was the skilled hands of the midwife who first drew forth the infant into the world and aided it to take its first breath. The task of the midwife was not only to deliver the child but also to provide for its needs in the first few critical hours of life. Competent care of the newborn is essential for the survival of the individual child and more broadly of the human race. Thus we have here a picture of God as both giver and sustainer of life, present at the time of crisis, the One in whom all humanity must ultimately trust. God is also pictured as a household mistress who gives both instruction and nourishment to her maidservants (Ps 123:2)

The psalmist prays that sons may be as flourishing young plants (or high towers), and daughters as sculptured pillars in the palace (Ps 144:12). The image bespeaks strength, stability and beauty. A corner pillar is critical in bearing the weight of the roof, but its form is an important architectural feature. The Jerusalem Bible suggests that perhaps the psalmist has in mind carved female figures to decorate the exterior of the building, beautiful yet capable of tremendous strength. The most famous example would be the caryatids adorning the Porch of the Maidens in the Erechtheum on the Acropolis in Athens. The key position of the daughters in the palace emphasizes their importance as prime supports in the household of faith.

Expressions of God's love of all persons and the universality of the eschatological response strike a special chord in female readers (Ps 68:31; 72:10; 87:4-6). A particular problem with which women struggle is that of the hostile emotions, which David in particular so vehemently expresses. The so-called imprecatory psalms are in point of fact remarkable for the honesty of their emotion. More often than we might like to admit, we too have entertained less than charitable thoughts toward others. The psalmists lay these emotions before God and find their way through to a dependence on divine mercy and faithfulness. The appalling sentiments can guide us to attitudes of faith and serenity.

This attitude of spiritual expectancy has many ramifications. In Psalm 37:7 the Hebrew command to "be still" or "to be silent unto" is translated in the Septuagint version by the Greek verb *hypotassō*.The same Septuagintal rendering of the command to "be still" is found in Psalm 62:1, 5 (NRSV "waits in silence" with the included concept of readiness to hear and to respond). *Hypotassō* is usually translated "submit" in its New Testament occurrences as they apply to women. The term has a far broader range of meanings than is often supposed, and these might greatly enrich our understanding of marriage and of interpersonal relationships. CATHERINE CLARK KROEGER

Ps 26:1), and right outward behavior (shunning the wicked [Ps 26:4-5], witnessing "aloud" [Ps 26:6-7] and delighting in worship [Ps 26:8]). On this basis he asks the Lord to "test" him thoroughly (Ps 26:2) and trusts that his prayer for vindication, preservation and redemption will be answered favorably, with grace to continue faithful.

Psalm 27 was written in a "day of trouble" (Ps 27:5), probably when David was hiding from Saul (cf. 1 Sam 22-24). The strength of David's faith reveals itself in his courageous confidence and his single-minded longing for the Lord's company, beauty and wisdom. Recalling past help, he trusts the Lord again to lead him through trouble, hide him in trouble and deliver him from trouble. Even though parental love (Ps 27:10), viewed here as the most steadfast of human relationships, should fail, God will still be faithful. So David prays for favor and guidance and receives sufficient grace to look forward with faith, convinced that the Lord is worth waiting for.

Psalm 28 begins with David's humble prayer for help, preservation and justice. The first two, personal pleas are quickly answered, prompting him to praise. Note how inner trust in the Lord leads first to receiving his help, then to inner joy and outward thanksgiving. How God answers the third plea is not revealed, but clearly David knows God not only as his "rock," "strength and shield" (Ps 28:1, 7) but also as the builder or breaker of all human lives and the shepherd of his people. As such he can always be trusted.

Psalm 29 focuses on God's transcendent, majestic glory as revealed in a thunderstorm. On earth, "the voice of the LORD" is conveyed in seven strikes of thunder and lightning (Ps 29:3-9). The devastating destruction they cause signifies especially his sovereign power to judge (e.g., Ps 29:10, the flood). Recognizing only one appropriate response, David calls all heaven to worship. In doing so he reveals the motivation for worship (giving the Lord his due glory [Ps 29:1-2]), the essence of worship (discerning and responding rightly to his voice [Ps 29:3-9]) and the consequences of worship (the blessings of strength and peace [Ps 29:11]).

Psalm 30, though a deeply personal thanksgiving, has an undeniably cultic setting (see title; David never built the temple but probably dedicated the site; cf. 2 Sam 6—7). The opening and closing personal praise, an example to be imitated by all God's people, is rooted in experiences of God's "favor" (Ps 30:7), especially in answered prayer and in dealing effectively with human pride. Such experiences confirm the truth that though "favor" and "anger" are aspects of God's nature (his responses to faith and sin respectively, Ps 30:4-7), "favor" is by far the greater (Ps 30:5).

Psalm 31 finds David beset by enemies seeking to trap him. He has succumbed to depression, physical illness and near paranoia. But instead of complaining or arguing, he trusts in the Lord his "refuge" (*ma'on,* Ps 31:2, 4), whom he knows to be righteous, faithful, good and steadfastly loving. In the face of growing opposition, this trusting knowledge of God leads him to keep praying and praising and to encourage all God's people to do likewise. Note how the protective "hand" of God is contrasted with the violent "hand" of his enemies (Ps 31:5, 8, 15).

Psalm 32 records David's experience following his adultery with Bathsheba and murder of Uriah (2 Sam 11). This psalm reveals the devastating effects of sexual sin. It may involve manipulation and exploitative treatment of others, as was the case with David, but it can create an equally deep wound in the soul of the perpetrator (cf. 1 Cor 6:18-19). Four different words reveal sin to be the unhappy, frustrating, weakening burden that drives David to seek forgiveness via sincere confession and petition. The Lord responds in generous, "steadfast love" (Ps 32:10), adding to the desired forgiveness protection, deliverance, a promise to guide the forgiven sinner and a warning against future stubbornness. Hardly surprising then that in this penitential psalm David's prevailing emotion is joy! Note how the psalm divides people into only two groups.

Psalm 33 expounds Psalm 32:11. The righteous may rejoice for two reasons. Both the "word of the LORD" and the "eye of the LORD" are indications of his "steadfast love" to all the earth, creating "all" (Ps 33:6) and observing "all" (Ps 33:13). But only those who "fear the LORD" will benefit from the counsel (Ps 33:11) and salvation they respectively provide (contrast Ps 33:10, 16). So the psalm hinges around the truth of Psalm 33:12, which is applied in the prayers of Psalm 33:8, 22. The conclusion explains why believers may rejoice even in times of distress (cf. Ps 32:6).

Psalm 34 (cf. 1 Sam 21:10-15). Thrilled by the experience of answered prayer, David invites all God's people to discover such happiness by looking to the Lord in reverence. To his followers (Ps 34:11, "children"), he reveals the secret of "fear," insisting that life without spiritual discipline leads only to death (Ps 34:11-14, 21; cf. 1 Pet 3:9-12) and implying that the pursuit of righteousness requires prayer and entails suffering. Assuring them that the Lord will hear and answer their prayers, he contrasts their experience of redemption with the "condemnation" faced by the "wicked" (Ps 34:15-22).

Psalm 35 is David's prayer for salvation and vindication on the grounds of his innocence. His unidentified enemies are guilty of conspiracy to murder, false accusation, ingratitude, mockery and public deceit. Nevertheless, recalling the truth prompts David to hope rather than despair. By contrasting their behavior with his, their vociferousness with other people's silence, their false observation with the Lord's true observation and their evil with his righteousness, he encourages himself and his supporters; they will joyfully praise and witness again. Psalm 35:14 recognizes the acute grief occasioned by the loss of one's mother. The deep attachment formed between mother and child was understood as lifelong and powerful.

Psalm 36 begins with David meditating on the deceitful sinfulness of his "wicked" oppressors (Ps 36:11). He then compares that with the Lord's powerful and precious steadfast love (*hesed,* masc., Ps 36:5-9), likened to the protection of a parent bird (Ps 36:7). Along with faithfulness (*emunath,* fem.) and righteousness (*tsedaqah,* fem.), *hesed* operates in judgment and salvation. It welcomes "all people" (Ps 36:7) yet is sought and fully experienced only by the "upright" who "know" the Lord (Ps 36:10). To them it gives security and the blessings of spiritual food, drink, life and light. By contrast, "evildoers" face defeat. Therefore David prays that *hesed* may continue.

Psalm 37 is full of the elderly David's spiritual wisdom. He recognizes only two kinds of people: the righteous and the wicked. On the basis of the stark contrast between their behavior and their prospects he advises those troubled by the wicked not to succumb to "fretting," anger or evil but to trust, pray and wait for the Lord to act (Ps 37:1-9). Personal experience confirms that God will judge the wicked and vindicate the righteous because he "loves justice" (Ps 37:28). The proverb holds true (Ps 37:16; cf. Prov 16:8); it is worth waiting and living for the Lord.

Psalm 38 is a penitential psalm in which David's heavy conscience leads him to identify the cause of his present suffering as the Lord's anger. His sin has rendered him vulnerable to illness, depression, isolation and violent opposition. Against all these he admits he is powerless. Yet still he believes God is "my God" and "my salvation"; still he sees himself as essentially a follower "after good" (Ps 38:20-22). Therefore he finds comfort in remembering that the Lord knows, and in sure hope of a favorable answer eventually, David devotes himself to waiting, repentance and prayer. Psalm 38:11-12 parallels the fear and despair of many an abused woman.

Psalm 39 finds David hot with emotion but resolved to suffer in silence before "the wicked" because he believes the Lord is disciplining him (Ps 39:1-3, 9-11). He does, however, voice his concerns in a prayer that reveals the depths of his depressive self-pity. Via a philosophy akin to that of Ecclesiastes (life is "fleeting," Ps 39:4-6, 11-13; cf. Eccles 6:12) he eventually decides to focus on the Lord rather than dwell on life's troubles (Ps 39:6-7; cf. Ps 77). Thus prayer gradually revives faith, which in turn produces (slightly!) more positive prayer—for deliverance from sin, relief from discipline and renewed happiness.

Psalm 40 prefaces an urgent prayer for deliverance (Ps 40:11-17; cf. Ps 70) with a description of David's salvation, praise for this and innumerable other blessings and testimony to the resulting effects. Worship is transformed by a new awareness that the Lord requires inner righteousness, and witness becomes more open and unrestrained. Prayer is directed first to his spiritual need, because he knows that only steadfast love and truth can deal with the evil and sin that threaten to overwhelm him. The New Testament relates Psalm 40:6-8 to the substitutionary work of Christ (see Heb 10:5-9).

Psalm 41 pictures David suffering from some serious illness. His "trouble" (Ps 41:1) is that his enemies, including one supposed "friend" (probably Ahitophel; cf. 2 Sam 15-18; Ps 55), are taking advantage of his weakness to plot and rebel (Ps 41:5-9; cf. Jn 13:18). His response is first to remind himself of spiritual truth concerning the Lord's care, then to bring his need to the Lord in prayer, seeking spiritual and physical healing. Answered prayer (whether already experienced or still anticipated) leads to reassurance, strengthened faith and praise, a fitting end to the first book of Psalms.

Book 2 (Ps 42—72)

Psalms 42 and 43 are a pair, written by a temple gatekeeper (cf. 1 Chron 26) while away from Jerusalem (Ps 42:6). They portray the same distressing inability to worship at the temple and the same taunting by onlookers, which leaves the psalmist feeling distant from God (Ps 42:1-3, 9, par. Ps 43:2). The solution to this spiritual dryness is sought in a question-and-answer refrain, which runs through both psalms (Ps 42:5,11; 43:5). Psalm 42 traces the writer's gradually increasing discernment. Spiritual hunger leads to joyful memories of past worship (Ps 42:1-4), which lead in turn to remembrance of the Lord (Ps 42:6). The psalmist realizes that God is still in control (Ps 42:7, "your cataracts . . . waves"), still present in steadfast love (Ps 42:8) and still trustworthy (Ps 42:9, "my rock"). The inner tensions, however, remain unresolved until, implicitly recognizing the limitations of human reason, the psalmist turns the questions into prayers, seeking God's vindication and guidance (Ps 43:1, 3). Only then do God's light and truth begin to replace darkness and fear, and once again God becomes "God my exceeding joy" (Ps 43:4). The deeply personal style emphasizes the necessity of individual faith as an essential prerequisite for true corporate worship.

Psalm 44 recognizes from Israel's history the truth that victory in battle is not the result of military might but the gift of God, then applies it to some present situation. "Yet" introduces a problem: what are God's people to make of the reality of present defeat (Ps 44:9-16)? They lay the problem before the Lord, insisting that they have remained faithful to him. Three times they ask "Why?" (Ps 44:23-24) but can only persevere in prayer on the basis of the Lord's steadfast love. The New Testament's answer is that nothing can separate believers from God's love (Rom 8:18-39).

Psalm 45 depicts a wedding (possibly Solomon's; cf. 1 Kings 3:1) against a backdrop of war. The focus is on the king, whose grace and majesty derive from God. Because he fights for truth and righteousness, he enjoys God's approval; his rule is blessed. The bride too is a person of dignity and worth, to be respected near and far. His bride's function is to forget her past and worship the king. Obedience makes her desirable; she produces children for him and attracts pagans ("Tyre") to his court (Ps 45:10-16). Psalm 45 acknowledges the difficulty that a woman may have in adjusting to new surroundings (Ps 45:10). She must view not only the splendor of marriage but also the inherent worth of the bridegroom (Ps 45:7). The psalm clearly looks beyond Solomon to Israel's perfect king, identified by the New Testament as Jesus Christ (Ps 45:6; cf. Heb 1:8-9), whose bride is the church (e.g., Rev 19:7-8). Psalm 45:16-17 ultimately applies to him.

Psalm 46 probably celebrates the victory of 2 Kings 19:35. The refrain reflects Hezekiah's words (Ps 46:7, 11; cf. 2 Chron 32:7-8). Sennacherib of Assyria claimed the title "great king" (2 Kings 18:28), but the psalmist insists the Lord is greater. He is his people's strong "refuge" from trouble (Ps 46:1-3), "a river" ensuring their survival (Ps 46:4-7) and the ruler of the whole world. Note the power of his presence and his word, which keeps his city (*ir*, fem.) secure. Hence the closing challenge: "behold . . . be still" (Ps 46:8-10), for God's "exaltation" cannot be thwarted. The psalm unknowingly looks forward to realities associated with Jesus Christ's return (Ps 46:4-5, 8-9).

Psalm 47 is an enthusiastic song in praise of who the Lord is and what he has done for his people. It implies that the latter testifies to the former; his loving support of one chosen people reveals him to be the "awesome," "Most High," "great king over all the earth" (Ps 47:2, 7; cf. comment on Ps 46). Therefore "all you peoples" are encouraged to join in worshiping him (Ps 47:1, 6). The loud exuberance of their worship reflects their appreciation of God's great victories and their unashamed desire to witness publicly to him.

Psalm 48 (cf. Rev 21) proclaims that Zion is holy, beautiful, mighty and enduring, but only because the Lord dwells in her. The city (*ir*, fem.) of God is a witness in "all the earth" to the truth that he is indeed "the great king" (Ps 48:1-8; see comment on Ps 46). Psalm 48:6 uses the simile of a woman in labor as describing the extremity of human distress (*see* Emotions of Women in Childbirth). Hence believers gathered in Zion (Ps 48:1, 9-11) praise and meditate upon his nature ("steadfast love . . . name") and his achievements ("victory . . . judgments"). But appreciation of the city has a further purpose: to motivate God's people to witness, especially to "the next generation," that "this [emphatic] is God . . . our guide forever" (Ps 48:12-14). For "towns" (Ps 48:11) see comment on Psalm 97:8.

Psalm 49, a wisdom psalm, presents "all . . . peoples" with a "riddle" (Ps 49:1, 4). Recognizing death as a universal concern, the psalmist shows how no one has an answer to its finality. The refrain focuses on the futility of human successes in a life without God. Wisdom recognizes only two ultimate destinies: either people will go "like sheep" to death or they will be received by God (Ps 49:14-15). The psalmist's certainty is an implicit challenge to the listening "peoples" to learn wisdom and "fear" God alone (Ps 49:15; cf. Ps 49:5-6). The promise of ransom is fulfilled in Christ (Mk 10:45).

Psalm 50 An awesome picture of God the judge leads Asaph (cf. 1 Chron 16:4-6) to affirm that judgment begins with God's people, called to be "faithful" (Ps 50:1-6). "Hear" is a covenant reminder that ritual sacrifices are worthless unless they symbolize a genuine, thankful, inner love for the Lord (Ps 50:7-15; cf. Deut 6:3-4). To the wicked who deceive themselves about this, God issues a warning. God requires his people to obey his word and live his way. The wicked slander even their brother, the son of the same mother. The kinship of those who occupied the same womb was considered especially deep. But God's purpose goes beyond conviction. So after encouraging reform and prayer, finally he assures his people that obedience will be met with salvation.

Psalm 51, a penitential psalm, clarifies the nature and consequences of all sin by describing David's sin (Ps 51:1-14; cf. 2 Sam 11—12). Genuine penitence has led David to recognize the immense damage it has done, especially to his "inward being" (Ps 51:6). His idea of having been conceived in sin applies less to the event than to his awareness of the depth of sin's hold on him. Fortunately he knows God well enough to know his priorities. Hence his confessional prayer for deliverance is thorough, covering every aspect of his need for salvation, from mercy, via cleansing and renewal, to joyful restoration. A restored appreciation of the preciousness of salvation rekindles his concern for others and prompts promises of evangelism, praise and genuine worship.

Psalm 52 denounces Doeg for a deliberate betrayal and massacre of priests (1 Sam 22). Behind his specific sins, David discerns a love of evil rather than good and a trust in riches rather than God. He prophesies that judgment will be meted out on the principle of Deuteronomy 19:19-21. Violent destruction will be met with violent destruction, thereby vindicating the righteous. By contrast, David's confident trust in God's steadfast love meets with blessing; flourishing like a tree in God's presence, he promises eternal trust, gratitude and testimony to the God whose name is "good" (Ps 52:8-9).

Psalm 53 almost repeats Psalm 14, except that "God" replaces "the Lord" (Ps 53:2, 4, 7), and Psalm 14:6 is replaced by Psalm 53:5. These changes shift the psalm's emphasis from salvation of the righteous to God's rejection and judgment of foolish "evildoers."

Psalm 54 Twice betrayed by the "insolent . . . ruthless" Ziphites (1 Sam 23:19-24; 26:1-4), David looks to God's might (*geburah,* fem.) to save him. "But" (Ps 54:4, lit. "behold") marks the turning point in his mood; as prayer brings reassurance so he reaffirms faith in "God . . . my helper." Now he knows that God will uphold his life and "put an end" to the Ziphites (Ps 54:4-5). Underlying his judgment he perceives the age-old battle between their "evil" and God's "good" (Ps 54:5-6). So confident is he that already he looks forward to giving thanks for answered prayer.

Psalm 55 When a friend, possibly Ahithophel, suddenly betrayed him (Ps 55:2-14, 20-21; cf. 2 Sam 15—18), David found himself haunted by unwelcome emotions. His first impulse was to run away, but instead he sought relief in prayer. The confused structure and language reflects the "burden" (Ps 55:22) of his hurt feelings. Recognizing the "evil" of the situation, he pleads for a drastic solution (Ps 55:9-15; cf. Gen 11:5-9). In the midst of the storm of emotion, he reminds himself that the Lord is his sure hope for salvation and justice and finds comfort in continuing to trust God. Psalm 55 has been particularly effective in helping abused women. It describes the feelings of betrayal by an intimate who was trusted (Ps 55:12-14, 20-21), the mockery of shared spiritual fellowship (Ps 55:14), the terror that the victim knows (Ps 55:3-5, 9-11), the breach of covenant (Ps 55:20), the deceptive mien (Ps 55:21) and the need for shelter and safety (Ps 55:6-8). In all of these crises, one's hope can be in God, who will hear the prayers of desperation and uphold the oppressed.

Psalm 56 again reflects 1 Samuel 21:10-15 (cf. Ps 34). Outwardly oppressed by enemies who plot his downfall, inwardly David experiences immense conflict between fear and faith, sadness and joy. However, as he prays, he recognizes the essential difference between the enemies arrayed "against" him (Ps 56:4, 11, "flesh," "mere mortal") and God the "Most High," who is "for" him (Ps 56:2, 9; cf. Rom 8:31-39). This prompts a double affirmation of trust in God and his Word. Thus, with the conflict resolved, a grateful David looks forward to living "in the light of life" (Ps 56:12-13).

Psalm 57 Trapped in a cave with his pursuers (Ps 57:4, 6; cf. 1 Sam 24), David prays for God's merciful protection on the grounds that God acts "for me" (Ps 57:2). He pictures "God Most High" as a parent bird sheltering chicks (Ps 57:1-2). Salvation is rooted in his "steadfast love and faithfulness" (Ps 57:3, 10; *hesed,* masc.; *emeth,* fem.), in the light of which David determines to continue "steadfast" (Ps 57:7, lit. "established"). Finally, although his faith is deeply personal, his praise will be public, because his overriding concern, expressed in the refrain (Ps 57:5, 11), is to see God glorified "over all the earth."

Psalm 58 begins with David castigating not literal "gods" (Ps 58:1) but wicked people who have evidently been abusing their positions of power. Their guilt encompasses injustice, wrong thinking, violence, error, lies and stubborn self-will. Sin has pervaded their lives from birth. The graphically venomous language of the sevenfold (cf. Ps 79:12) imprecatory prayer that follows is not merely gratuitous; it poetically matches the evildoers' "venom" (Ps 58:4). David is not interested in personal vengeance; rather, by destroying the powers of injustice, he wants to see God relieving the righteous of their sufferings and vindicating himself as "the Lord," a just judge "on earth" (Ps 58:10-11).

Psalm 59 David's unnerving experience while living under surveillance and constant threat (cf. 1 Sam 19:1-11) drives him to pray first for his immediate need, then for an outworking of justice that will benefit the Lord and his people. Each prayer is followed by a consideration of the situation, first from a human perspective, then from the perspective of faith. David's clear conscience contrasts with his enemies' evil deeds, plans and words. Eventually a new assurance of security in God "my fortress" (Ps 59:9-10, 16-17) results in a resolve to watch and sing for him.

Psalm 60 is one of David's prayers before battle (see 1 Chron 18—19). Whether literal or metaphorical, an earthquake has left God's people "reeling" (Ps 60:2-4). Diagnosing the cause as God's anger, David prays first for restoration and only then for victory. The latter prayer is grounded in God's promise that only he has the right to "divide" his people (Ps 60:5-11). It not only confronts him directly but also highlights the "instruction" this psalm aims to convey (see title), namely, the truth that God's people need his help in battle rather than human help because victory is his work.

Psalm 61 finds David praying at "the end of the earth" (Ps 61:1-2), accompanied by some loyal supporters. A faint heart suggests the king is running away from trouble (Ps 61:2; cf. Ps 55:6-7); Psalm 61:6-7 suggests threats to his life and his throne. Using familiar imagery (cf. Ps 31:2-3; 57:1) he humbly seeks God's protection and lasting presence (Ps 61:4, "tent"). As one who has sworn to fear God's name (which represents his character), David considers such blessings part of his God-given "heritage" (Ps 61:5) and promises to match God's steadfastness with a daily steadfastness in his worship.

Psalm 62 is distinguished by the repeated "alone" (*ak,* Ps 62:1, 2, 4, 5, 6, 9). Though the prolonged lies of his enemies have weakened him, David will neither complain nor "be shaken." "Alone" highlights the contrast between their sole purpose (Ps 62:4) and his, which is to "wait" in faith for God his rock, salvation and fortress (Ps 62:1-2, 5-6). So sure is his faith that he urges all people to trust in God always, arguing that worldly status, power and desires are nothing when compared with the power and steadfast love of God, which will be revealed in just judgment.

Psalm 63 follows the progress of David's soul at a time when he was being pursued into the desert by either Saul (1 Sam 23—24) or Absalom (2 Sam 15—18). Regarding insomnia as a welcome opportunity to pray, David discovers that meditating on God's power, glory and steadfast love satisfies his thirsty soul, prompts a desire to worship God, and renews joy and strength. Like a young bird, the satisfied soul then "clings" to God for protection (Ps 63:7-8), which produces in turn a renewed confidence that God will act in judgment against David's enemies.

Psalm 64 pictures David complaining to God about the steadfastly cunning character of the unidentified enemies pursuing him (probably Absalom; cf. 2 Sam 15—18). Their "evil" is expressed in "bitter words like arrows" (Ps 64:3), but they forget that God has arrows too. He will shoot them just as "suddenly" (Ps 64:7-8; cf. Ps 64:4) against those who speak evil, causing "everyone" to "fear" (Ps 64:9; cf. Ps 64:4), witness and "ponder." So, knowing his prayer for preservation will be answered by the God of justice, David confidently encourages the "righteous," including himself, to "take refuge in him" and exchange their complaining for rejoicing.

Psalm 65 probably originally sung at harvest time, is a thanksgiving for God's goodness. First for the goodness of God's holy presence (Ps 65:4, "house . . . temple") demonstrated especially in answered prayer, forgiven sin, elective privilege, satisfied desire, "awesome deeds" of salvation for his people and the hope (lit. "confidence") of salvation for "all" (Ps 65:1-5). Then for goodness of God's sustaining provision shown in creation, especially his sovereign control of nature, nature's worldwide testimony to him and its carefully nurtured rich fruitfulness, which more than supplies human need (Ps 65:6-13). Praise is indeed due to him!

Psalm 66 first exhorts "all the earth" to worship God (Ps 66:1-2), then invites them to "come and see what God has done" for his people, especially through the testing experience of the exodus and journey to the Promised Land (Ps 66:5-12). Recognizing that God's purpose was to refine his people, the anonymous psalmist then applies the lesson in a personal commitment to grateful worship followed by an invitation to "come and hear" a personal testimony to answered prayer. Knowing that words and works must match, the psalm closes with a personal example of acceptable worship (Ps 66:20; cf. Ps 50:13-14).

Psalm 67 takes an ancient blessing (Ps 67:1; cf. Num 6:24-25) and relates it to the truth that through the blessing he pours out on his people, God intends all nations to be blessed (Gen 12:2-3; cf. Gal 3:8-9). After a good harvest, the psalmist encourages God's people to seek future blessing in accordance with this principle, to pray that the nations might share their privilege of knowing God's "way" and his "saving power" (Ps 67:2), to share God's concern to care justly for all peoples and to recognize blessing when it comes.

Psalm 68 may celebrate the arrival of the ark of the covenant in Jerusalem (Ps

68:24-27; cf. 2 Sam 6). It exhorts individuals, congregations and nations to praise God. David gives many reasons for praise. They include God's care for the needy, his provision of rain in the wilderness and the Promised Land, victory over enemies (by means of his Word, Ps 68:11-14; cf. Ps 68:33), his choice of Mount Zion as a home and his daily saving power. Psalm 68:12-13 probably reflects the housekeeping role of women. They apportion the spoil (Ps 68:12) as they had previously despoiled the

Women as Psalmists

When the exiles returned from Babylon, both Ezra and Nehemiah note that their numbers included female singers (Ezra 2:65; Neh 7:67). It is unclear whether these women were employed as performers in the temple. Although the priesthood was hereditary and male, women were not excluded from worshiping in the temple, and so it is conceivable that women might have served as liturgical musicians and singers. Like men, they would have been expected to observe the divine laws of ritual purity to honor the sanctity of God's holy place.

Whether or not women acted as cultic musicians in the temple, the Bible is clear that women sang at public events, either in celebration or lament. The book of Ecclesiastes, for example, refers to women, "the daughters of song," who presumably performed funereal dirges (Eccles 12:4; cf. Jer 9:20).

Often the songs that women sing in the Bible are related to Israel's victory in struggles against an enemy. One such example is the Song of Miriam (Ex 15:20-21). In this passage Miriam leads the women in dancing and singing to celebrate God's triumph over Pharaoh's army and the safe passage of the Israelites across the Red (Reed) Sea. Deborah, another female prophet, also praises God in song (Judg 5), calling on kings and princes to listen as "I [Deborah] will make melody to the LORD, the God of Israel" (Judg 5:3; *see* Deborah). David's defeat of the Philistines finds women singing and celebrating (1 Sam 18:6-9), and here their song incites Saul to a jealous rage. He worried that such extravagant and public praise of David undermined his own authority as king. Notably, since it is uncharacteristic of the songs that women sing in the Bible, the praise is not of God but of the human warriors.

A final, more private example of this type of victory psalm is found in Judges. Jephthah's daughter emerges from the house following Jephthah's victory in battle "with timbrels and with dancing" (Judg 11:34). Although this has implications for the vow Jephthah made before going out to fight (Judg 11:30-31), it is difficult to believe he did not anticipate that his daughter would emerge first, dancing and singing in a typical celebration of her father's military victory.

The most compelling accounts of women as psalmists perhaps are those songs from the lips of women addressing God's response to their individual situations and dilemmas. Hannah, barren for so long and subject to the taunts of her cowife, Peninnah, praises God when she finally conceives Samuel (1 Sam 2:1-10; *see* Hannah). In the New Testament, Mary sings a psalm of praise, traditionally known by many Christians as the Magnificat, when Elizabeth blesses her pregnancy (Lk 1:41-55; *see* Mary the Mother of Jesus). In both cases the women are not only recipients of God's grace but also proclaimers of it. Both Hannah and Mary look beyond the limits of their particular situations to remind all of us that God looks with grace and mercy on the marginalized. Conversely they warn us of his judgment on the proud and the arrogant. In this, like those of Miriam and Deborah, their songs are prophetic in nature.

Whether it is the defeat of an enemy or the birth of a baby, all these women, in their capacity as psalmists, prompt us to remember that nothing falls outside the purview of God.

PHILIPPA CARTER

wealth of Egypt (Ex 3:21-22; 11:2-3; 12:35-36). The prayer for God to act (Ps 68:1-3, 28-31; cf. Num 10:35) seeks further honor for his "awesome" majesty (Ps 68:32-35).

Psalm 68 identifies the participation of women in praise and proclamation. It appears to have been composed for a procession in which maidens accompany musicians and singers as they march in celebration (Ps 68:25). The young women play on the timbrel, an instrument used almost exclusively by women. It was a terracotta vessel with the hide of an animal stretched across the top; its use was associated with prophesying and dance (Ex 15:20-21; Judg 11:34; 1 Sam 18:6-7; Jer 31:4, 13); for women singers in Israel, see 2 Sam 19:35; 1 Chron 25:5-8; 2 Chron 35:25; Ezra 2:65; Eccles 2:8).

The language and sentiments of this psalm are reminiscent of the song of victory sung by Deborah (Judg 5). Indeed, Psalm 68:8 echoes Judges 5:5. In this case, the primary victory is that of God, who led a slave people out of bondage, through the wilderness into freedom. Now the central shrine will be at Jerusalem, and there a temple will be erected on Mount Zion. Ultimately believers from many nations will join the throng of worshipers marching to the holy temple.

Egyptian women dancing and playing the tambourine. (Psalm 68:25)

God is mentioned as the protector of widows and orphans who provides a home for the desolate (Ps 68:5-6), or as Martin Luther translates it, "gives the lonely woman a house full of children." The benefits of God's triumph, however, were more spiritual than material.

Psalm 69 finds David in deep distress, suffering from false accusation, insult and gossip. He seeks salvation on the basis that though he was not always blameless, his present situation is an undeserved result of spiritual zeal (Ps 69:1-12; cf. Jn 2:17). Remembering that God knows his plight, he prays according to the Lord's "abundant" steadfast love and mercy (Ps 69:13-21). For his oppressors he requests just discipline, on the principle of Deuteronomy 19:19-21. "But as for me . . . But I . . ." (Ps 69:13, 29) contrasts their behavior, which displeases the Lord, with David's desire to please him and thereby encourage others who are similarly oppressed.

Psalm 70 is the same prayer for deliverance that ends Psalm 40 (Ps 40:13-17). On the basis of his urgent need and his previous experience of God's saving help, David makes five specific requests. For his enemies, he seeks confusion, dishonor and defeat; for his supporters he seeks joy and the grace to witness to God's greatness. All five are summed up in one word: "help" (Ps 70:1, 5).

Psalm 71 Again in trouble, the elderly David refuses to escape into despair or fantasy. Instead, again he prays, remembers the past and focuses single-mindedly on his friendship with the Lord (Ps 71:1-6; cf. Ps 27). His spiritual maturity shows in the way remembrance, prayer and focus are turned to exuberant praise. God is his rock of refuge, the basis of his hope, the motivation for his witness and the ground of his confidence. So the praise builds up to a final great crescendo and a personal promise.

Psalm 72 is Solomon's prayer, soon after he ascended the throne, that he would be a good king. He prays for righteous compassion, a reflection of the Lord's righteous compassion and an everlasting, worldwide kingdom. Solomon never did fulfill his own vision of God's ideal king, but the psalm is clearly looking toward a greater king than Solomon (cf. Mt 12:28). It foresees Christ's kingdom of peace, prosperity and justice reigning "from sea to sea" (Ps 72:8) and ends the second book of Psalms with praise to the God who alone can answer the prayer.

Book 3 (Ps 73—89)

Psalm 73 Asaph (see 1 Chron 16:4-5) gives poetic testimony to God's goodness (Ps 73:1). When life became difficult for him, he observed others who mocked God yet lived at ease (Ps 73:3-12). The contrast tempted Asaph to self-pity, complaint and the verge of unbelief (Ps 73:13-14), until he sought the Lord's company (Ps 73:17), gained the eternal perspective of true wisdom and recovered his spiritual balance (Ps 73:18-28; cf. Ps 73:2): this life, though it is unfair, is not everything. The wicked are heading for destruction; therefore "it is good to be near God" (Ps 73:28). Asaph remembered (Ps 73:28) and reaffirmed (Ps 73:25) his commitment. As assurance flooded in (Ps 73:26), he resolved that his experience would result in witness (Ps 73:28).

Psalm 74 conveys the stunned incomprehension of bereavement as Asaph, following Babylon's invasion (587 B.C.), observes a devastated Israel with neither temple nor prophet (Ps 74:1-11; cf. 2 Kings 25:9-17). However, faith ("God my King," Ps 74:12) means his questions (Ps 74:1, 10-11) lead to prayer rather than despair. He urges God (Ps 74:2, 18-23) to "remember" his covenant and act now, for his name's sake and for his "dove" (a love term implying helpless innocence, Ps 74:19). "Yet God" (Ps 74:12) is the turning point; looking back via the exodus to creation, Asaph realizes that Babylon's transient destructive power is nothing compared with God's eternal saving power (Ps 74:12-17).

Psalm 75 answers the questions of Psalm 74:10-11. A word from God reminds Asaph that the Lord keeps the earth stable and rules all its peoples, including the proud, insolent "wicked" (Ps 75:3-5). Therefore, though God will act in judgment (Ps 75:10), he will decide when (Ps 75:2). In response Asaph gives thanks that the Lord's name is near (Ps 75:1; God's "name" represents his powerful person, capable of "wondrous deeds") and rejoices in the truth that present status and future destiny are in God's hands (Ps 75:6-9). The cup in God's hand (Ps 75:8) is a picture of God's will (cf. Jer 25:15).

Psalm 76 praises God for a victory, probably over Assyria (Ps 76:5-6; cf. 2 Kings 19:32-36), which has vindicated God's mighty presence among his people and revealed his glory (Ps 76:1-4). On this basis Asaph foresees a far greater, worldwide victory (Ps 76:7-12), when God's judgment will surely (note the prophetic perfect tenses, Ps 76:8-9) be revealed in the simultaneous salvation of the "oppressed" and defeat of human "wrath" (*hemoth,* "heats," Ps 76:10). The Lord is "awesome" (*nora',* "to be feared"), ruling even the lives and deaths of princes. Therefore Asaph urges everyone to worship God while there is still opportunity (Ps 76:11-12).

Psalm 77 reveals Asaph struggling because, despite constant prayer, his life is still pervaded by misery (Ps 77:1-4). Recalling his experience of the Lord's steadfast love, he asks whether the covenant promises are forever forgotten and wallows in grief that God has changed (Ps 77:5-10). But by choosing to redirect his thoughts from self to the Lord (Ps 77:11-12), Asaph gains a new perspective. He realizes that God is the same "holy . . . great" covenant redeemer and caring shepherd of his people as he was in the exodus (Ps 77:13-20). The psalm ends abruptly as this truth suddenly lifts Asaph's depression.

Psalm 78 tells Israel's history, focusing on the exodus (cf. Ps 105, 106, 136). The prologue, typical of wisdom literature, explains the purpose: to teach future generations an obedient, trusting faith (Ps 78:1-8). The role of parents in passing God's law to future generations is stressed (Ps 78:5-7). An important aspect of motherhood is the perpetuation of her faith in her children. The story is one of persistent care in the face of persistent rebellion. An abundant experience of God's generous compassion and power left Israel without excuse for turning to him only in crisis (Ps 78:23-34). Asaph identifies the heart of the problem: faithlessness (Ps 78:22) and forgetfulness (Ps 78:42). The Lord's discipline (Ps 78:31,

33, 60-64) reveals his priorities: spiritual care comes before physical. Though the men are apparently held directly responsible for the sin, their dependent women inevitably suffer too (Ps 78:63-64). "Ephraim" may reflect some northern threat against David's throne (Ps 78:9-11; cf. Ps 78:67-71).

Psalm 79 observes Israel's humiliation following the Babylonian invasion (Ps 79:1-4; cf. Ps 74). The dead lie unburied while the neighbors mock. Yet Asaph's chief concern is for God's "name" (Ps 79:9-10). He recognizes the invasion as just punishment for Israel's sins (Ps 79:5, 8) but reminds the Lord that these are the covenant people (Ps 79:1-2, 13). His agonized questions and prayers seek forgiveness and salvation (Ps 79:9), that they might praise him again (Ps 79:13). And for the nations, punishment, that they might know the Lord is true and just (Ps 79:6, 10, 12). For God's answer, see Psalm 75 and Ezra 1 (cf. Lk 18:7).

Psalm 80 sees Asaph deeply concerned by Israel's suffering, traditionally associated with God's anger (Ps 80:4-6). Using the familiar analogy of a vine, he recalls how it was God, their Shepherd-King (Ps 80:1), who made them great (Ps 80:8-11). So why does God apparently no longer care (Ps 80:12)? Turning distress to a prayer refrain (Ps 80:3), Asaph remembers first God's power ("God of hosts," Ps 80:7), then the covenant ("Lord," Ps 80:19). The specific request to make strong one favored by God (Ps 80:17) refers originally to the Davidic king but prophetically to the Messiah. It is answered in Jesus Christ; will we therefore keep Asaph's vow (Ps 80:18)?

Psalm 81 urges Israel to celebrate a festival, traditionally that of tabernacles, in obedience to God's decree (Ps 81:3-5; cf. Lev 23:34). To this end Asaph encourages loud praise (Ps 81:1-3) and attentive listening to God's Word (Ps 81:6-16), which reminds the people of God's blessings during the exodus. These include relief, rescue, answered prayer and even testing, admonishment and punishment for disobedience. Assuring them of his desire to continue blessing (Ps 81:10, 14-16), the Lord warns that it nonetheless depends upon their choice. Will they listen and live in God's way or go their own way (Ps 81:13; cf. Deut 30:15-20)? Only the former truly satisfies (Ps 81:16).

Psalm 82 pictures God the judge, looking down from heaven on human injustices, questioning the perpetrators and demanding justice (Ps 82:2-4). God's words reflect his nature (cf. Deut 10:17-18). Psalm 82:5 is probably the explanation preceding God's sentencing of the guilty (Ps 82:6-7): they do not understand the destabilizing effects of their wickedness. Jesus understood the guilty to be human rather than spiritual beings (Jn 10:34-35). Asaph's introduction (Ps 82:1) and prayer (Ps 82:8) make clear that God's right to judge applies to "all the nations."

Psalm 83 describes an unknown conspiracy to "wipe . . . out" Israel (Ps 83:4) involving the nations of Psalm 83:6-8. On the basis that Israel's enemies are God's enemies (Ps 83:2-5) and that he has proved victorious in similar situations in the past, Asaph prays for their defeat (Ps 83:1, 9-18). In particular, he recalls the victory of Deborah and Jael over Sisera and Jabin (Ps 83:9019; cf. Judges 4—5). Whether by coercion or conversion, he longs to see these pagan nations shamed into seeking the Lord and acknowledging that God alone is "the Most High over all the earth" (Ps 83:6-18; cf. Phil 2:10-11).

Psalm 84 reflects the Korahites' (gatekeepers; see 1 Chron 26) seasonal pilgrimage to serve in the temple, revealing their love and longing for Zion, symbol of God's presence (Ps 84:1-7; cf. Ps 120—134). Zion meant a safe and happy home, even for small nesting birds (Ps 84:1-4), a refreshing, growing strength for pilgrims in dry places (Ps 84:5-8) and unlimited protective blessing for all who "walk uprightly" (Ps 84:10-12). Therefore the psalmist recognizes the truth and adopts the attitude of Psalm 84:10 and prays especially for the king (Ps 84:8-9), the representative and protector of all God's people.

Psalm 85 combines thanksgiving for one undeserved restoration (Ps 85:1-3, probably from exile) with prayer for another (Ps 85:4-7, possibly a rebuilt Jerusalem). Recognizing that Israel's sin had provoked God's wrath, the psalm implies that repentance and pardon have already happened. But though the sin is forgiven, spiritual joy is still lacking, and they pray for revival (Ps 85:6-7). In response (Ps 85:8-13) God promises peace, his presence among them and good gifts, presumably including revival, if they renounce their folly (Ps 85:8 footnote) and "fear" God, that is, worship properly (Ps 85:9). The simultaneous display of divine characteristics (Ps 85:10-11) was fulfilled in the Messiah.

Psalm 86 is composed of fragments of Davidic psalms and other Scriptures. The result is a prayer for help in trouble based on the psalmist's covenant-servant relationship with the "LORD" (Ps 86:2-3). It includes petition (Ps 86:1, 6), without failing to praise (Ps 86:5). Psalm 86:8-13 pictures the Lord as uniquely great yet steadfastly loving "toward me" (Ps 86:13). In response come not only wholehearted thanks but also the unique request for an undivided heart and the resolve to live accordingly (Ps 86:11-12). Having settled the priorities, Psalm 86:14-17 then details the petition, rooting it firmly in Scripture (Ps 86:15 is Ex 34:6). For Psalm 86:16, see Psalm 116:16.

Psalm 87 considers God's city (Ps 87:1-4) and foresees the heavenly city (Ps 87:5-6; cf. Rev 21). Zion is a community of individuals (Ps 87:4-6) from every nation, including Israel's enemies Egypt (Rahab), Philistia and Babylon. Also noteworthy is the inclusion of Ethiopia or Cush (cf. Ps 68:31; Is 18). In common, they all "know" the Lord and are registered as belonging to Zion (cf. Rev 21:27). In their change of citizenship, conversion is implicit. "This one . . . [was] born there" emphasizes God's loving initiative in the process (cf. Ps 87:1), picturing Zion as the mother city in which are the springs of life (Ps 87:7; cf. Gal 4:26). The spontaneous response to this is exuberant praise (Ps 87:7).

Psalm 88 Heman (see 1 Chron 25:5-6) is deeply depressed by some longstanding illness (Ps 88:15). Even friends have shunned him (Ps 88:8, 18). He graphically imagines death: a distant, cheerless, hopeless future of decay (Abaddon) and oblivion (Ps 88:3-12). Worst of all (Ps 88:10-12) would be the total separation from God. His only comfort has been prayer, but after death, it would be pointless. Heman associates suffering with God's wrath (Ps 88:7, 16) but knows the Lord also as God of steadfast love (Ps 88:11) and "my salvation" (Ps 88:1). Therefore he continues in desperate prayer (Ps 88:13-18). If only he could have read Romans 8:35-39.

Psalm 89 Ethan (see 1 Chron 15:16-19) praises the Lord's steadfast love, as seen in the Davidic covenant (Ps 89:3-4), and God's mighty rule, as seen in salvation (Ps 89:10; "Rahab" = Egypt) and creation (Ps 89:5-18). Israel's king is the Lord's anointed servant (Ps 89:18-20). The Lord promises to remain with him in intimate Father-son relationship and to grant absolute victory and an everlasting dynasty (Ps 89:21-37), a messianic promise (Acts 13:22-23). However, some disaster prompts Ethan to accuse God of renouncing his covenant in implicitly justified wrath (Ps 89:38-45). He deeply feels the shame and prays for mercy (Ps 89:46-52). The third book closes with customary praise (Ps 89:52).

Book 4 (Ps 90—106)

Psalm 90 is a reflective prayer on the eternal greatness of God as compared with human mortality and sinfulness (Ps 90:2-11). God's wrath against sin means he is rightly to be feared (Ps 90:11); yet he is also the "LORD" of steadfast covenant love (Ps 90:13-14). So Moses confidently approaches God in prayer on behalf of his people (Ps 90:12-17), who find in him a secure and stable home (Ps 90:1; *ma'on,* "dwelling" or "refuge"). This and the six requests of Psalm 90:12-17 suggest a context of the wilderness wanderings, when Israel was living in tents and grumbling against the Lord.

Psalm 91 vividly testifies that, although believers may face every kind of danger (Ps 91:3-7), they will survive by abiding and trusting in God, whose four names emphasize his power and covenant love (Ps 91:1-2). Their experience of absolute security is contrasted with that of the wicked, who face God's punishment (Ps 91:8). Those who make the Lord their home (Ps 91:9; *ma'on,* cf. Ps 90:1) may confidently rely on God's protection (Ps 91:10-13). God promises it (Ps 91:14-16), plus answered prayer, his personal presence, blessing and salvation *(yeshu'a)*. Satan later used Psalm 91:11-12 out of context (Ps 91:1-2) to tempt Jesus (Mt 4:5-6).

Psalm 92 is a sabbath poem with wisdom features. The sabbath (root *shabat,* "to cease") should be filled with meditation on the Lord's works (Ps 92:5), especially on the contrast between God's destruction of "the wicked" (Ps 92:7-9) and exaltation of "the righteous" (Ps 92:10-14). The "dullard" cannot understand this (Ps 92:6), but the psalmist has experienced it (Ps 92:11) and understands that it demonstrates the Lord's eternal greatness (Ps 92:8) and righteousness (Ps 92:15). Such understanding results in joyful praise and witness (Ps 92:1-4), spiritual growth (Ps 92:12-13) and fruitfulness, even in old age (Ps 92:14).

Psalm 93 is a poem (note the repetition) that may have been prompted by a recent flood. "The LORD is King" (Ps 93:1; lit. "reigns") sets the theme: God's throne is established from eternity (Ps 93:2) to eternity (Ps 93:5). The psalmist draws four conclusions: the world shall never be moved (Ps 93:1); the Lord is greater than any flood that may threaten Israel (Ps 93:3-4); God's word is eternally sure (Ps 93:5; cf. especially Gen 9:11); God must be worshiped in holiness (Ps 93:5).

Psalm 94 is a prayer for "vengeance" (*neqamoth,* Ps 94:1) upon "the wicked" who are brazenly abusing God's people, especially the vulnerable whom God had promised to protect (Ps 94:3-6; cf. Deut 10:18). Far from being vengeful, the psalm requests God's just discipline, and soon (Ps 94:1-3). The plight of widows, orphans and strangers is called to God's attention; the wicked are fools for claiming their Maker and Ruler is blind to their sin (Ps 94:6-11). Reassured by this truth and by personal experience of covenant love, the psalmist concludes that God's apparent inactivity means discipline, not desertion; God will yet execute justice for his people (Ps 94:12-23).

Psalm 95 calls God's people to wholehearted, corporate, exuberant worship of their "great God" (Ps 95:1-3), because he is King and Creator of land, sea and people (Ps 95:3-6) and the Shepherd to whom they belong (Ps 95:7). Worship, however, involves far more than joyful singing; beginning with humble listening, it is ultimately expressed in obedient living (Ps 95:6-11). The illustration (Ps 95:8-11; cf. Ex 17:1-7) warns believers against maintaining the outer rituals of worship with a hardened heart. Hebrews 3:7—4:13 equates God's "rest" (*menuhah,* Ps 95:11) with salvation and explains how God's anger against sin means it cannot be regarded with complacency.

Psalm 96 (cf. 1 Chron 16:23-33) tells all who know the Lord to praise him and to witness daily to his salvation and his glory (Ps 96:1-3). The aim is that all people might worship God rightly before it is too late (Ps 96:4-9), because God is "coming to . . . judge the world with righteousness and the peoples with his truth" (Ps 96:13). Worship makes sense because God is the whole world's mighty Creator, compared to whom "idols" (*elilim,* Ps 96:5) are literally nothings. God rules the whole world, maintaining stability and justice (Ps 96:10). Hence all creation is called to join in God's praise (Ps 96:11-12).

Psalm 97 looks toward the day when "all the peoples" will see the Lord's awesome glory (i.e., righteousness made visible, Ps 97:2-6; cf. Sinai, Ex 19:16-18; 24:17). Unbelievers will know shame as they realize the futility of their proud idol worship (Ps 97:7). But the Lord's "faithful" will rejoice in his salvation (Ps 97:8-12). Indeed, if they obey (Ps 97:10, lit. "you who love the Lord, hate evil!"), salvation is certain, and they may begin rejoicing now. "Towns" (Ps 97:8) is literally "daughters," reflecting the family relationship and allegiance of all God's people (cf. Ps 87:5; 1 Pet 2:17).

Psalm 98 gives praise for an earthly victory (Ps 98:1-3), attributing it solely to the Lord. The psalmist sees it as God's "vindication in the sight of the nations" (Ps 98:2; their previous wrong impression of God is put right), as a sign of covenant fidelity to his people (Ps 98:3) and as a foretaste of his final victory (Ps 98:9; cf. Ps 96:13). The Lord is supreme king (Ps 98:6) and righteous judge (Ps 98:9), not only of Israel but also of the world. Therefore "all the earth" (Ps 98:4-8), the people and the natural world, is encouraged to join the praise.

Psalm 99 What is God like? "Holy" (Ps 99:3, 5, 9), which means uniquely perfect in greatness (Ps 99:1-3), justice (Ps 99:4-5) and mercy (Ps 99:6-9). God's holiness is seen in heaven (Ps 99:1-3), where he is the great King whose kingdom reaches out from "Zion" to "all the peoples." God's holiness is seen on earth (Ps 99:4-5), where he is the judge in whom perfect power meets perfect justice. So Psalm 99:6-9 speaks of God's holiness as encountered by sinners, recalling three who, in answer to prayer, discovered that God is the Savior in whom perfect justice meets perfect mercy (Ps 99:8). This clearly points toward the cross of Christ.

Psalm 100 is a call to "all the earth" to worship the Lord gladly together (Ps 100:1-2). Why? God is God (Ps 100:3), the one true God of all peoples. God is their Maker and Shepherd; they belong to him. God is good (Ps 100:5), especially to those in covenant relationship with him. He is steadfastly loving and faithful to his promises. The emphasis on joy implies that true worship must be freely offered from a heart full of gratitude and love. Only then will it please God (Ps 100:4, "bless his name").

Psalm 101 shows David far more aware of the responsibilities of kingship than the perquisites. First he aimed to be a good servant and witness to the Lord (Ps 101:1, 8). David's burning personal ambition was to attain "the way that is blameless" (Ps 101:2); therefore he set himself high standards. In his private life he aimed for purity and integrity (Ps 101:2-4). In public he would steadily oppose all evil but support "the faithful," who shared his love for the "way that is blameless" (Ps 101:5-8). David failed and had to repent, leaving his greater Son to fulfill the vision.

Psalm 102 is the prayer of "one afflicted" personally (Ps 102:1-11) and because Zion is suffering (Ps 102:12-22). The experience is one of extreme weakness (Ps 102:4-5), sleeplessness, loneliness, derision and depression (Ps 102:6-9). Attributing this to God's wrath (Ps 102:10), the sufferer turns from pitying self to reaffirming faith (Ps 102:12). God is eternally all-powerful (Ps 102:12, 26-27) and compassionate (Ps 102:13, 17-20). The psalmist trusts the time for action has come (Ps 102:13), prays again (Ps 102:23-24) and hears the answer (Ps 102:25-28): the Lord does not change, and therefore his people are secure. Psalm 102:25-27 points to Jesus Christ, who through suffering obtained victory over suffering (cf. Heb 1:10-12).

Psalm 103 sees David recalling his richly satisfying experience of salvation and telling himself to "bless the Lord" wholeheartedly for it (Ps 103:1-6). He remembers how the Lord's nature (Ps 103:8) has remained the same since Moses' day (Ps 103:6-18; cf. Ex 34:6-7). God is the eternal Ruler of all creation (Ps 103:19) yet understands our transient human nature and cares for his people as a father cares for his children (Ps 103:13-18). Therefore all creation should bless God (Ps 103:19-22). Psalm 103:17-18 implies that only the obedient can truly bless God, that is, produce worship that pleases him, and so continue to experience his steadfast love *(hesed)*.

Psalm 104 considers creation and sees in it God's glory; that is, God's great and holy nature made visible (Ps 104:1, 35). The One who "causes" creation (Ps 104:14) is its master, using and controlling it for God's own purposes (Ps 104:2-9). People are part of creation, yet special. God provides abundantly for the physical needs of all living things (Ps 104:10-23), but provision for people also meets their inner needs (Ps 104:15). All life depends on God (Ps 104:24-30), but his goodness is a moral goodness (Ps 104:35). So the psalm ends with prayer that all creation, including the psalmist (Ps 104:31-35), would continue to please God.

Psalm 105 calls God's people to "remember" what he has done, then to rejoice, praise and witness (Ps 105:1-6; cf. 1 Chron 16:8-13). God's "wonderful works" arise out of fidelity to his "everlasting covenant" with Abraham (Ps 105:7-11). They are evident in God's historical provision for Israel (Ps 105:12-45), especially in God's special protective relationship with the patriarchs (Ps 105:12-15) during famine (Ps 105:16-25) and throughout the events of the exodus (Ps 105:26-42), culminating in possession of the Promised Land and the law (Ps 105:44-45). These works reveal God's purpose (Ps 105:45): to produce a people as faithful to him as he is to them.

Psalm 106, the first of four psalms based on a popular song (Ps 106:1; cf. 2 Chron 7:3; Ezra 3:11), encourages God's people to give thanks for his faithfulness despite their persistent sin from the exodus onwards (Ps 106:6-39). They were forgetful, rebellious, lustful, jealous, idolatrous, faithless, grumbling and disobedient, which provoked the Lord to anger and punishment. Psalm 106:28-31 recalls the seduction of Israelite men by Moabite cult prostitutes. Phinehas intervened when a sexually transmitted disease rages through the camp (Num 25). "Nevertheless," for their sake and his own, many times God saved them (Ps 106:8, 44-45). On this basis the psalmist again prays for salvation (Ps 106:4-5, 47) and leads in praise (Ps 106:48). Acculturation and intermarriage brought pagan worship, including the sacrifice of sons and daughters to Canaanite gods (Ps 106:34-39). In its infidelity, Israel is likened to a prostitute.

Book 5 (Ps 107—150)

Psalm 107 expounds the same song as Psalm 106:1, telling how God has "redeemed" four groups of people (Ps 107:2-3). The lost (Ps 107:4-9) wandered in the desert and became weak. The rebels (Ps 107:10-16) disobeyed God's word and brought imprisonment upon themselves. The fools (Ps 107:17-22, "sick" = foolish) allowed sin in their lives and brought sickness upon themselves. The complacent (Ps 107:23-32) relied on themselves until the Lord's storm humbled them. In each case, when they cried to God, he saved them, providing (respectively) guidance, liberation, healing and peace. Note the power of the Lord's word (Ps 107:20, 25). The refrain (Ps 107:8, 15, 21, 31) exhorts them all to thanksgiving and praise; Psalm 107:33-42 sets the example. The point, worth heeding (Ps 107:43), is that God's steadfast love is shown to the undeserving, and God's concern for their spiritual health takes priority.

Psalm 108 combines the second halves of Psalm 57 and Psalm 60, both of which are attributed to specific incidents in David's life (Ps 108:1-5 are Ps 57:7-11; Ps 108:6-13 are Ps 60:5-12). Psalm 108 may have been produced for more general use, whenever believers are threatened by aggressive enemies. It emphasizes the singer's resolve to remain steadfast (Ps 108:1) and trust in the Lord for victory and salvation (Ps 108:6, 13).

Psalm 109 sees David facing verbal vitriol from people he loves (Ps 109:2-5), possibly colleagues at Saul's court. Psalm 109:6-7 may record their words, but Psalm 109:8-31 records David's (cf. Acts 1:16-20). He charges his "accusers" (*soten,* Ps 109:20, 29) with unkindness and cursing (Ps 109:16-18), curses them (Ps 109:8-15) and prays (Ps 109:18-29) for salvation, justice and appropriate punishment, according to Deuteronomy19:19-21. Though hot with anger, David preferred prayer to personal revenge (see Rom 12:19). Psalm 109:9-15 reflects the dependence of wives and children on the man who headed their household. David seeks to vindicate himself and the Lord (Ps 109:21, 27), whom he continues to trust and praise (Ps 109:30-31; cf. Ps 109:1).

Psalm 110, possibly used for David's enthronement (2 Sam 5:6-12), begins with two promises from the Lord. Psalm 110:1-3 pictures the king exalted by God and ruling alongside him (Ps 110:1). The New Testament applies this messianically to the ascended Jesus Christ fifteen times (e.g., Mk 16:19; Heb 10:12-13). Psalm 110:3, which is obscure, probably pictures David strong and young, leading his willing people in battle. Psalm 110:4 promises he will also be "a priest forever." For the significance of this see Hebrews 5—7 (cf. Melchizedek, Gen 14:18-20). Following Psalm 110:3, Psalm 110:5-6 foresees a last day of judgment, after which comes peace and final victory (Ps 110:7).

Psalm 111 and Psalm 112 are acrostics, probably meant to be learned together.

Psalm 111 reflects God's character as seen in his "works" (Ps 111:2-9), especially those done for the covenant people (Ps 111:5, 9). These include the provision of food (Ps 111:5), the Promised Land (Ps 111:6), the law (Ps 111:7-8) and redemption (Ps 111:9). They reveal God to be righteous, gracious, merciful, generous, faithful, just, holy and awesome (Ps 111:3-9). They are matched by God's words (Ps 111:7). "Forever" (Ps 111:3, 8-10) means God's character will never change. God's people should respond with praise, thanks, study and delight (Ps 111:1-2). The conclusion (Ps 111:10) is a classic wisdom saying.

Psalm 112 explains that God's people are like him: righteous, gracious, merciful, generous and just (Ps 112:3-5; cf. Ps 111:3-5). They delight in God's will (Ps 112:1) and live by it (Ps 112:3-9). When "evil tidings" come, they remain unafraid (Ps 112:7-8), knowing that in the Lord they have security now (Ps 112:2-3) and forever (Ps 112:6). Children and riches were generally understood as blessings (Ps 112:1, "happy" = blessed) promised by the Lord to those who kept the covenant (*see* Blessing and Cursing). By contrast the "wicked," who chose not to fear God, experience anger as they watch the righteous honored (Ps 112:9-10; the horn symbolized power).

Psalm 113 is a meditation on the Lord's greatness (Ps 113:4-9) designed to promote continual praise (Ps 113:1-3). God's name represents his nature; uniquely great (Ps

113:4-6). From his heavenly throne, God sees and rules everything, not only in Israel but also throughout heaven and earth. God is distinct from ("above") creation but far from distant. God's glory is his nature made visible. He reveals it in his personal care for poor and needy individuals (Ps 113:7-9) The psalmist's example is Hannah, whose words are quoted (1 Sam 2:8; *see* Women as Psalmists). A "barren woman" could be rejected by her husband and consequently be homeless (*see* Barrenness and Fertility). A women enthroned among her children could indeed be joyful.

Psalm 114 is a poem praising the way the Lord brought Israel out of Egypt to the Promised Land. God's purpose (Ps 114:2) was to make a holy dwelling place ("sanctuary") over which to rule ("dominion"). Psalm 114:3-6 vividly pictures creation on three occasions during the exodus (Red Sea, Mount Sinai, River Jordan) responding supernaturally to the commanding presence of its mighty Creator (Ps 114:7). Psalm 114:7-8 implies God has not changed; as he brought water from rock (Ex 17:6; Num 20:10-11; cf. 1 Cor 10:4), so he still works miracles for his chosen people ("Jacob" emphasizes their weakness).

Psalm 115 prays for help, not simply because God's people need it but also for God's sake (Ps 115:1-2), because the watching world denounces him (Ps 115:2). This prompts a comparison between the Lord and the world's "idols" (Ps 115:3-7). God "does whatever he pleases"; the idols can do nothing. The logical conclusion is that it is better to trust the Lord (Ps 115:8-11). If priests and people do so, they can confidently look and pray toward future blessing (Ps 115:12-15). However, throughout this life God allows people to choose whom they will trust and praise (Ps 115:16-18). This temple song makes every worshiper's choice clear.

Psalm 116 testifies to answered prayer. The psalmist was facing death (Ps 116:3) and prayed for help (Ps 116:4). The Lord heard (Ps 116:1-2) and saved (Ps 116:6-8). Psalm 116:3 recalls the emotions; Psalm 116:6 implies foolishness ("simple"); Psalm 116:10 suggests personal victory over temptation. But the experience of salvation is not confined to the past; it affects life now and in the future (Ps 116:12-19). Life now is full of confidence and gratitude (Ps 116:9, 12). The future will be one of lifelong willing service (Ps 116:15-16), especially prayer (Ps 116:13, 17) and witness (Ps 116:14, 18-19). "Child of your serving girl" (Ps 116:16) indicates the faith of the psalmist's mother. In Jewish tradition, a true Jew is one whose mother is Jewish.

Psalm 117 is a call to "all . . . nations" to praise the Lord for his steadfast love *(hesed)* and fidelity or truth *(emeth)* to Israel (cf. Ps 100). God never intended that those who knew his covenant love should keep it to themselves; they were meant to witness to all peoples that his love is great and his truth eternal. The Lord is the God of all peoples and therefore worthy of praise by all peoples (cf. Ps 145:10-12; Rom 15:11).

Psalm 118 (cf. Ps 106, 107, 136) was probably sung in festival procession. It calls God's people (Ps 118:2-4) to praise and witness to his steadfast love *(hesed)*. The king leads, with personal testimony (Ps 118:5-9), to *hesed* in salvation (Ps 118:10-18) and acceptance (Ps 118:19-28). When Israel's enemies threatened (Ps 118:10-14), victory from the Lord (Ps 118:13) brought assurance (Ps 118:6-7), wisdom (Ps 118:8-9), joy (Ps 118:14-16; cf. Ex 15:2, 6) and hope (Ps 118:17-18). At the temple gates, the king seeks admission (Ps 118:19). The gatekeeper implies that sinners are unacceptable in the Lord's presence (Ps 118:20; cf. Ps 24:3-4), but the king is welcomed (Ps 118:22-27). Here the psalm also speaks of a righteous king yet to come, who will become the cornerstone, a messianic prophecy fulfilled in Jesus Christ (Mt 21:9, 42; Eph 2:20; 1 Pet 2:4-8). Although Psalm 118:27 is obscure, the psalm evidently ends with thankful worship.

Psalm 119, an alphabetic acrostic, pictures the believer as a pilgrim (Ps 119:19, 54) encountering various difficulties, among them temptation (Ps 119:36-37), mockery (Ps 119:42), despair (Ps 119:81-82) and persecution (Ps 119:150). Mindful of past errors (Ps 119:67) and personal weakness (Ps 119:141), the pilgrim's wholehearted response is to look to Scripture and pray to its author in a telling mix of praise and supplication (e.g., Ps 119:10, 145, 171). Almost every verse is a prayer incorporating a different synonym for God's Word. In that Word the pilgrim finds moral protection (Ps 119:9-16), delight (Ps 119:14), direction (Ps 119:33-40), freedom (Ps 119:45), comfort (Ps 119:49-56), wisdom (Ps 119:98-104), peace (Ps 119:165), hope (Ps 119:166), even life (Ps 119:93). It permeates body (e.g., Ps 119:6, 59, 171-72), soul (Ps 119:20, 167), memory (Ps 119:55), heart (Ps 119:80), mind (Ps 119:97-100) and will (Ps 119:106, 173). Yet this is not bibliolatry. God's Word is kept because it is *God's* Word, a lighted path (Ps 119:35, 105) through the dark wilderness of this world for all who seek God (Ps 119:2). Knowing its power and stability, (Ps 119:89-91), the pilgrim promises, with God's help, to keep it (Ps 119:57-64) and to share it (Ps 119:13). Here is one who, by treasuring God's Word (Ps 119:11, 127), can testify to happiness (Ps 119:1; cf. Ps 1:1-2) even in the midst of tears (Ps 119:136).

Psalms 120 through 134, the Songs of Ascents, were sung by pilgrims heading for the temple.

Psalm 120 is the cry of the believer in the world facing hostility (Ps 120:2) and a basic incompatibility (Ps 120:5-7): "I am for peace; . . . they are for war" (Ps 120:7). Lying and deceitful words are especially hurtful (Ps 120:2). Revenge is considered (Ps 120:3-4). Arrows (Ps 120:4) are instruments of retribution, and coals represent God's wrath. But personal vengeance has no place in a believer's life. So revenge is finally rejected in favor of prayer (Ps 120:1), humble acceptance of the situation (Ps 120:3) and peace (Ps 120:7), especially in the believer's words.

Psalm 121 Traveling through hills, the home of outlaws, would frighten any Israelite pilgrim (Ps 121:1). The believer's reaction is to look to the almighty, all-knowing Creator of the hills (Ps 121:2), who is the perfect helper. Bound by covenant to "Israel," "the LORD" watches over his people untiringly (Ps 121:3-4). God promises them threefold protection: their vulnerability to natural dangers (sun and moon) is offset by his constant companionship (Ps 121:5-6; cf. 2 Cor 12:9). Their vulnerability to evil is offset by God's power to save (Ps 121:7). Their waywardness is offset by God's power to guide (Ps 121:8). These promises become ours in Christ.

Psalm 122 The believer finds the security sought in Psalm 121 in Jerusalem (cf. Heb 12:22-23, which equates Jerusalem with the invisible church). The hostility and alienation one experiences in the world (Ps 120) is replaced by joy and fellowship in "the house of the LORD" (Ps 122:1). In Psalm 122:3-5 the unity of God's people is a testimony (Ps 112:4; "as was decreed" is lit. "a testimony"). The city, "bound firmly together" under the rule of one king (cf. Eph 4:3-6), is the center of "judgment," that is, just decisions. David prays for its peace (Ps 122:6-9). He is selflessly committed to seeking its good (Ps 122:8-9).

Psalm 123 The pilgrim has had "more than enough of contempt" from the proud (Ps 123:3) and seeks the Lord in prayer. Prayer involves personal contact with God (Ps 123:1), who sits enthroned in heaven. The psalm implies that God is ready and able to answer with "mercy," which can transform the situation. For every believer, whether male or female (Ps 123:2), access to God in prayer is constant; the believer adopts the attitude of a servant and looks to God. The Lord is pictured both as master and as mistress of a large household who assign tasks to servants both male and female (cf. Prov 31:15). Servants do not dictate; they submit to their Lord's will (Mt 6:10).

Egyptian wall painting of a slave girl dressing her mistress. (Psalm 123:2)

Psalm 124 David illustrates his experience of deliverance by means of a giant beast (Ps 124:3), a flood (Ps 124:4-5), a wild beast (Ps 124:6) and a bird trapper (Ps 124:7). Whether these imply one deliverance or more, Psalm 124:8 is common to all (cf. Ps 121). The Lord made and rules everything. Constantly protective of his people ("on our side," Ps 124:1-2), God has the authority and power to control their lives (Ps 124:6). God's salvation is full salvation (Ps 124:7, "the snare is broken," escape is complete). So David looks beyond personal experience to the eternal truth of what the Lord is like (Ps 124:8, "the name of the LORD").

Psalm 125 God's people are threatened by a "scepter of wickedness" (Ps 125:3), maybe Assyria. How should they respond? By trusting in the Lord (Ps 125:1). They will then know lasting stability, like Zion (Ps 125:1); security for the Lord surrounds them (Ps 125:2); and assurance, for God is in control (Ps 125:3). The psalmist prays also for blessing (Ps 125:4) and peace (Ps 125:5), highlighting the need for righteousness outside ("those who are good") and inside ("in their hearts"). The contrast with "those who turn aside" (Ps 125:5) provides a further motivation to trust in the Lord.

Psalm 126 looks back to a restoration beyond Israel's wildest dreams (Ps 126:1), possibly the return from exile. Recognizing it as solely an act of God, the people had responded with exuberant praise, a witness to the watching world (Ps 126:2-3). But in Psalm 126:4 the psalmist turns from past to present, and the mood changes. Exuberance is replaced with dryness (Ps 126:4) and joy with tears (Ps 126:5). Perhaps the hardships of life in a war-torn land are taking their toll. They pray for further restoration (Ps 126:4-5), in confident trust that the Lord will give what they seek (Ps 126:6; cf. Ps 30:5). Compare Psalm 85.

Psalm 127 Solomon has big plans but realizes he cannot fulfill them alone (Ps 127:1). "Unless" implies the Lord is willing to join him in the work, but only if allowed to do so. He promises to take on all the anxiety involved and give his cworker sleep (Ps 127:2). "Beloved" *(yadid)* implies the promise is prompted and guaranteed by their intimate relationship (cf. 2 Sam 12:25). So the psalm contrasts two sorts of working: restless, "anxious toil" and restful cooperation with the Lord. Psalm 127:3-5 illustrates the fact that only the latter leads to happiness and success. Children are a joyful gift from God, and generations of offspring can fill God's house with enduring purpose and praise.

Psalm 128 promises happiness (Ps 128:1-2, happiness = blessing, Ps 128:4) in the present (Ps 128:2-4) and in the future (Ps 128:5-6). Psalm 128:2-4 pictures a secure and healthy family; the wife's fruitfulness refers to every part of her life, not only to her many children. Psalm 128:5-6 is a prayer for happiness that lasts. Psalm 128:1, 4 explain that this happiness depends not on circumstances but on each individual's attitude to God. As a general Old Testament rule, happiness comes to "everyone who fears the LORD," though there are exceptions (e.g., Job). Psalm 128:1 recognizes that genuine fear of the Lord always expresses itself in outward conformity to "his ways" (Ps 128:1).

Psalm 129 portrays the believer suffering in a hostile world (Ps 129:1-3). However, those who attack God's people provoke his righteous wrath, and God punishes them (Ps 129:4; the "cords" probably relate to the plowing image of Ps 129:3). So they attack, "yet they have not prevailed" (Ps 129:2). The expressions in Psalm 129:5-8 could be statements of faith or prayers. Either way, the believer is confidently looking forward to what God wills and has already promised (e.g., Deut 32:39-43). Such uncomfortable verses belong to the uncomfortable truth of God's righteous wrath.

Psalm 130 The believer realizes that the sins of God's people are also serious and have serious consequences. This results in depression (Ps 130:1). God's righteous wrath, before which none can stand (Ps 130:3), could prove their greatest danger (cf. Ps 129:4). But alongside beliefs about sin are beliefs about God (Ps 130:4, 7) that lead simultaneously to urgent prayer (Ps 130:1-2), trusting (Ps 130:4) and confident waiting (Ps 130:5-6); the morning always comes. Thus grows an awareness of redemptive grace that covers "all . . . iniquities" (Ps 130:7-8). The hope in God's Word (Ps 130:5) is so sure a fact (Ps 130:8) that all God's people are called to share it (Ps 130:7).

Psalm 131 Aware of the dangers of pride, believers reject it and cultivate humility (Ps 131:1). Aware of the dangers of a restless spirit, believers cultivate a calm, childlike dependence on God (Ps 131:2) summed up in the word *hope* (Ps 131:3). The "weaned child" is one who no longer fractiously demands its mother's milk (cf. Heb 5:12-14). On the basis of experience, the psalmist finally urges all God's people to "hope in the LORD . . . forevermore" (Ps 131:3; cf. Ps 130:7).

Psalms 132 through 134 see the pilgrims arriving at Zion (Jerusalem) and finding blessing.

Psalm 132 recalls David's promise to find a "dwelling place" for the Lord, the hardship involved and the people's eager support (Ps 132:1-10; cf. 2 Sam 6). His prayer seeks a home for the ark, the symbol of the Lord's powerful presence; a right-eous priesthood; joyful worshipers and a favorable answer (Ps 132:8-10). This prayer is met by the Lord's promise to make Zion his home, to bless Zion and David (Ps 132:11-18). Psalm 132:16 answers Psalm 132:9. David's dynasty depends on his descendants' obedience (Ps 132:12), but Psalm 132:17-18 is unconditional; among them would be one all-victorious king (Acts 2:30-36).

Psalm 133 God's people are "kindred" because they all belong to his family, but they are also meant to live as kindred, that is, "together in unity." This is objectively "good" and subjectively "pleasant" (Ps 133:1). The unity of believers is like "precious oil . . . running down" (Ps 133:2), which speaks of abundant richness and consecration (Lev 8:12). It is like "dew . . . on the mountains" (Ps 133:3), which speaks of life-giving refreshment. It is essential to the blessing called "life forevermore," which the Lord ordains for his people (Ps 133:3).

Psalm 134 pictures the pilgrim entering the temple on Mount Zion. Zion is God's home, open day and night, from which he blesses his people (Ps 134:3) as they worship him (Ps 134:1-2). So pilgrims are first reminded of their calling (Ps 134:1, "servants") and of God's holiness (Ps 134:2); then they are urged to "bless the LORD," that is, to please him. Only then may they expect blessing from the Lord (Ps 134:3), who alone, as "maker of heaven and earth," has the knowledge and the power to bless people.

Psalm 135 is a compilation of other Scriptures (e.g., Ps 115:3-8; 136:18-22). The result is a psalm of praise grounded in the Lord's choosing of Jacob/Israel as "his own possession" (Ps 135:4). God's choice reveals his good (Ps 135:3), unique (Ps 135:5) and enduring (Ps 135:13) greatness, summed up in his "name." This greatness is seen in creation (Ps 135:6-7) and the exodus (Ps 135:8-12) and in contrast to the impotent idols (Ps 135:15-18). God never fails his people (Ps 135:14). This is the psalmist's personal testimony (Ps 135:5), on which basis everyone is urged to "bless the LORD," to please him (Ps 135:19-21).

Psalm 136 is the fourth psalm to expound the theme of the first verse (cf. Ps 106, 107, 118). Designed for antiphonal singing, it testifies to God's "steadfast love" *(hesed)*, as seen in creation (Ps 136:4-9) and redemption (Ps 136:10-22, amplifying Ps 135:8-12). Psalm 136:10-22 highlights three elements of redemption: deliverance from Egypt via the miracle at the Red Sea, guidance through the wilderness to the Promised Land and victory over the "great kings" who chose to oppose God's people. Psalm 136:23-26 concludes that *hesed* is shown in rescuing Israel and in providing for "all flesh." Hence "give thanks" is a call to all people everywhere.

Psalm 137 is a lament dating from the exile. The Babylonians treated captives well (Jer 29:4-7) and preferred to see them happy (Ps 137:3), but the faithful tearfully continued to remember their home and the Lord's (cf. Ps 132:13-14). Their agony prompts a question (Ps 137:4), a vow (Ps 137:5-6) and a prayer against Edom and Babylon (Ps 137:7-9; cf. Obad 10-14; 2 Kings 25:9). "Remember . . . against" (Ps 137:7) is a plea for divine justice according to Deuteronomy 19:19-21. Psalm 137:8-9 is prophetic (cf. Is 13:16; Jer 51:56), with "happy" reflecting contentment at justice done rather than emotional pleasure. Infanticide (Ps 137:9) was a cruel but common sequel to heathen victories (2 Kings 8:12; Is 13:16; Lk 19:44; *see* Infanticide).

Psalm 138 is a thanksgiving for answered prayer (Ps 138:3) "in the midst of trouble" (Ps 138:7). The answer did not change the situation; it strengthened the one who prayed (Ps 138:3) and led to worship, witness and trust in the Lord. The worship is grounded in God's "name" (character) and word (Ps 138:2). The witness envisages "all the kings of the earth" praising the Lord, who values humility even in kings (Ps 138:4-5; cf. Phil 2:5-11). The trust is now (Ps 138:7) and for the future (Ps 138:8). The attribution may mean "of the Davidic school," as there was no temple (Ps 138:2) in David's lifetime.

Psalm 139 An elderly David recognizes God's omniscience (Ps 139:1-6) and omnipresence (Ps 139:7-12) not as dry doctrine but in the context of personal relationship. God knows and cares for David (Ps 139:1-5) because God made David (Ps 139:13-

16). All human lives belong to God, who has the power of life and death (Ps 139:13, 19). No one can escape God's presence (Ps 139:7-12), and nothing is hidden from him (Ps 139:13-16). Yet, far from intimidating David, this truth leads him to wonder (Ps 139:6), praise (Ps 139:14) and prayer (Ps 139:19-24). Longing to see all people fully submissive to their Creator, David seeks justice for the wicked (Ps 139:19-22) and sanctification leading to eternal life for himself (Ps 139:23-24). The understanding of a fetus as an individual person known by God (Ps 139:13-16) and the continuity of identity from embryo to adult militate against abortion (*see* The Purpose and Value of Human Life). Prenatal influence is profound both mentally and spiritually. The pregnant woman is a vehicle within whom God is at work on a human soul.

Psalm 140 probably reflects Saul's pursuit of David (1 Sam 22—26). David is suffering from the malicious plans (Ps 140:2), words (Ps 140:3) and deeds (Ps 140:4) of "evildoers" (Ps 140:1) who seek to trap him (Ps 140:5). His response is prayer (Ps 140:6-11). On the grounds of covenant commitment (Ps 140:6), experience (Ps 140:7) and justice, David asks the Lord to bring their evil down upon them (Ps 140:9). The violent (Ps 140:1, 4) must suffer violence; the trappers (Ps 140:5) must be trapped (Ps 140:10; cf. Deut 19:21). Psalm 140:12-13 affirms David's faith: God always "executes justice" for the poor and needy (*see* God's Call to Social Justice); therefore he is worthy of worship. With its condemnation of violence and appeal to God for deliverance, this psalm is helpful for the meditations of battered women.

Psalm 141 Still oppressed by "evildoers" who want to trap him (Ps 141:9-10; cf. Ps 140), David's response is again prayer (Ps 141:1-4). He seeks an audience (Ps 141:1-2), then requests help: guarded speech (Ps 141:3) and a guarded heart (Ps 141:4). Psalm 141:5-7 reveals his thinking about the situation. He would accept even rebuke from "the righteous" but wants nothing to do with the "wicked" except to pray against them. Knowing they are heading for judgment, he turns from evil (Ps 141:4) and toward God and remembers his double security, "in" the Lord and "from" the trap (Ps 141:8-10). The final plea follows the same principle as Psalm 140:10.

Psalm 142 is specifically attributed to the period when David was hiding from Saul (1 Sam 22—26). Feeling imprisoned and alone (Ps 142:4, 7), he takes his "trouble" to God in prayer (Ps 142:1-2). Prayer makes sense because God knows (Ps 142:3) and sees (Ps 142:4) all that happens to his people. The "right hand" (Ps 142:4) is where one might expect to find help. Prayer makes sense because God is his people's refuge (Ps 142:5), and God is able to "deal bountifully" with them (Ps 142:7). So David makes a specific request, "Save me" (Ps 142:6), and looks forward to restored freedom and friendship (Ps 142:7). This psalm is particularly helpful to women hiding from abusers.

Psalm 143 Still pursued by enemies (Ps 143:3), David can endure no more (Ps 143:4, 7). He needs God's help urgently but fears he might be under judgment for some sin (Ps 143:2, 7). Nevertheless he knows the way to face trouble is by trusting prayer to God, who controls everything. So, after requesting a favorable audience (Ps 143:1-2), David presents eleven distinct needs, including assurance of God's covenant love (Ps 143:8), instruction and guidance (Ps 143:8, 10), deliverance and preservation (Ps 143:9, 11) and the destruction of his enemies (Ps 143:12). The ground on which he asks all this is that of covenant commitment, "for I am your servant" (Ps 143:12).

Psalms 144 through 150 close the Psalter with effervescent praise.

Psalm 144 was probably written when the Lord delivered David from Saul (cf. Ps 18). First he offers praise for past victories (Ps 144:1-4), picturing the Lord as his defensive military base. Note the repeated "my": this strong God is *my* God, a truth on which David meditates in Psalm 144:3-4. Then, in a context of continuing praise, he prays for continuing victory (Ps 144:5-11). Finally he adds a prayer for the future prosperity of his people (Ps 144:12-14) and God's (Ps 144:15). Psalm 144:15 recognizes the constant need to focus more on the One who blesses than the blessings.

Psalm 145 is an acrostic. For David, praise is a deliberate, daily (Ps 145:1-2) response to God's character and work. God's "name" (Ps 145:2, 21) sums up his character: great (Ps 145:3), good (Ps 145:7, 9), gracious and merciful (Ps 145:8), faithful (Ps 145:13), and just and kind (Ps 145:17).

"Merciful" (from Heb. *raham,* "to love") conveys a motherly compassion. God's work (Ps 145:4-20) is seen in redemption ("wondrous works," Ps 145:5, are usually redemptive), in revelation and in ruling creation justly and kindly. Notice "all" (Ps 145:9-21): God rules over all, caring for all who sincerely love him but destroying all the wicked (Ps 145:20). Therefore God is worthy of worship from "all flesh," forever (Ps 145:21).

Psalm 146 focuses praise on the happiness (Ps 146:5) of having the Lord to trust. Mortality renders people unreliable (Ps 146:3-4), but experience of God proves him always trustworthy (Ps 146:5-10). "Jacob" emphasizes the weakness and need of God's people, but their Creator is also "the LORD their God," committed to them in covenant love (Ps 146:5-6). Psalm 146:7-9 recalls God's special care for the needy and how God meets their various needs. God's concern for righteousness (Ps 146:8-9) and absolute rule ensure their eternal security (Ps 146:10). Hence the call to all God's people (Zion) to "praise the LORD."

Psalm 147 is corporate praise from all God's people. The imperatives "praise . . . sing . . . praise" (Ps 147:1, 7, 12) begin three sections that each juxtapose themes of redemption and creation. God's "understanding . . . beyond measure" of creation guarantees his care for the needy among his people (Ps 147:1-6). God's general care for all created life forms the backdrop for his special delight in people of genuine faith (Ps 147:7-11). And God's many blessings form the backdrop for the greatest blessing of all, the agent of all other blessings: God's Word (Ps 147:12-20). This is the distinctive and powerful possession of God's people, for which they are most to praise him (Ps 147:19-20).

Psalm 148 calls for universal praise in the heavens (Ps 148:1-6) and on earth (Ps 148:7-14). The downward order of praise (Ps 148:6-11, from greater to lesser) poetically balances the upward order (Ps 148:7-14, lesser to greater), culminating in the specifically equal call to people of both sexes and all ages (Ps 148:12). In each case a reason follows the call to praise: because the Lord is their Creator (Ps 148:5) and because he raises up strength for his people, who are "close to him" (Ps 148:14); "the horn," a symbol of strength, may refer either postexilically or prophetically to "a strong leader."

Psalm 149 begins and ends with God's "faithful" people singing his praise (Ps 149:1) and sharing his glory (Ps 149:9). Psalm 149:2-4 encourages them to rejoice in God's favors. Psalm 149:5-9 encourages them to rejoice because God rules the whole world justly. Justice means that, although God longs to bless all peoples, some will receive punishment instead (Ps 149:7-8). The task of God's people is to cooperate in accomplishing God's will; hence the picture of them happily relaxed yet with swords in their hands (Ps 149:5-6). The tension between resting in victory accomplished and fighting for victory still to come is one with which every believer continually lives.

Psalm 150 turns the final words of book 4 (Ps 106:48) into a tenfold doxology, an imperative to unceasing and all-encompassing praise. Praise to God who is mighty and does mighty deeds (Ps 150:1-2). Praise from every living thing (Ps 150:6), including human praise, by every available musical means (Ps 150:3-5).

Bibliography. L. C. Allen, *Psalms* (Waco, TX: Word, 1987); R. Davidson, *The Vitality of Worship* (Grand Rapids, MI: Eerdmans, 1998); T. Longman, *How to Read the Psalms* (Downers Grove, IL: IVP, 1988); M. Wilcock, *The Message of Psalms 1-72* (Downers Grove, IL: IVP, 2001); idem, *The Message of Psalms 73-150* (Downers Grove, IL: IVP, 2001).

GWYNNETH MARIAN NAPIER RAIKES

PROVERBS

Introduction

The book of Proverbs belongs to the corpus of biblical and extrabiblical literature known as wisdom literature. This corpus is characterized principally by its focus on life on earth, giving the collective wise words probably passed down and modified through the decades and centuries about the joys and pitfalls to be encountered and handled. Wisdom literature of this kind is also to be found emanating from ancient Egypt in particular, in addition to other ancient Near Eastern countries and Africa (Golka). Proverbs 22:17—24:22 is closely allied to the Egyptian wisdom book *Instruction of Amenemope,* for example, but these Hebrew texts presuppose and affirm a belief in and relationship with YHWH, the one God, to whom wisdom is ultimately attributed and without whom sense becomes nonsense (e.g., Prov 15:33). Similar theological, literary and social perspectives are found in Job and Ecclesiastes.

There is thus evidence to indicate multiple sources in Proverbs, incorporated by various authors and coupled with an overall editorial working that may have taken place at different stages. The book attributes certain sections to various individuals: Solomon (Prov 1:1; 10:1; 25:1), Agur (Prov 30:1) and Lemuel (Prov 31:1), as well as indicating the involvement of scribes (Prov 25:1) and hinting at a wider, more generally public origin in the "words of the wise" (Prov 22:17; 24:23). Efforts at dating the various sections allow for Solomonic authorship at least of Proverbs 10:1—22:16 and probably of Proverbs 25—29. In addition, *Amenemope* is thought to date to at least 1000 B.C., thus coinciding with the Solomonic era. Solomon's marriage to Pharaoh's daughter could have provided access to Egyptian wisdom material. The mention of Hezekiah (c. 716-687 B.C.) in Proverbs 25:1 indicates some type of editorial work, however, and for many years the opinion that Proverbs 1—9 was a later addition (basing this on literary or theological grounds) held sway, with a postexilic date being generally but not universally agreed on. Some recent scholarship challenges this, however, with one or two scholars stating that there is "no compelling evidence for placing those chapters, or any part of the book, substantially later than the rest" (Weeks, 5). Proverbs 1:1-7 also seems to form a self-contained unit that was a later addition designed to serve as a general introduction to the collection. Nothing is known of Agur and Lemuel other than their names and the possibility that they were not Israelites (Massa is thought to have been in northern Arabia, although the Hebrew text also permits translation of this word as "the oracle").

In the opinion of certain scholars, the proverbial form originally grew among ordinary (illiterate?) people and was passed down orally (Golka, 13) as folk sayings, often in the home. Other scholars have long talked of wisdom schools based in the royal court; in these schools, wisdom sayings were compiled from various sources, including that of surrounding nations and folk sayings, and used to train young male bureaucrats in response to the need for stable state administration. Certain similarities with literature serving this purpose from other nations lent weight to the idea. However, this view necessarily downplays the surprisingly wide range of interests and topics treated. Further examination of both purpose and nature of wisdom literature as found in Proverbs and elsewhere increasingly suggests that the existence of such schools is at best hypothetical, and some scholars now favor a setting of the home rather than the royal court.

At the same time, there is evidence to suggest that sages, at least of the early period, pronounced their wisdom at the city gates (see Job 29:7-25), and certain sections seem to have a royal flavor (e.g., Prov 16:12-24; 31:2-9). Whatever the case, the text indicates explicitly and implicitly that the wisdom of the book was directed at men and that these men were still of an age when such instruction was necessary or appropriate to the circumstances. The tone is exhortatory rather than educative in an informative sense and assumes a reasonable degree of prior knowledge and experience in life. The original, overall setting is thus somewhat obscure, if it can truly be identified.

The various indications of authorship in the text also largely correspond with significant distinctions in literary style. There is general agreement that the book subdivides into eight readily identifiable sections (Prov 1:1—9:18; 10:1—22:16; 22:17—24:22; 24:23-34; 25:1—29:27; 30; 31:1-9; 31:10-31, albeit with minor modifications among scholars) that correspond generally to movement between sources and authors. Three primary literary styles also permit grouping as instruction literature (Prov 1—9; 22:17—24:22; 31:1-9), sentence literature (Prov 10:1—22:16; 24:23-34; 25—29) and poems and numerical sayings (Prov 30; 31:10-31; McKane).

Characteristics that account for such labeling are easy to find: references to hearing run as a refrain throughout Proverbs 1—9 in particular but are also found in Proverbs 22:17—24:22 as well as once in the address to Lemuel given by his mother (Prov 31:2). Each time the purpose is to instruct and advise, with the instruction carrying a particularly personal emphasis as opposed to the general, observational wisdom offered to all and sundry in the sentence literature. This latter takes a stylized form: two lines written in such a way that the second line backs up, sheds light on or contrasts the first. Thus mothers feature alongside fathers in these couplets in such a way as to make primarily a literary point, although references to mothers teaching (Prov 1:8; 6:20) may indicate a more prominent instructive role in Hebrew society than the notion of wisdom schools might allow for. Numerical sayings are found in the words of Agur, while the last verses of Proverbs 31 form the only alphabetic acrostic in the book.

Outline

1:1—9:18	Acquiring Wisdom
10:1—29:27	Acting Wisely
30:1-33	The Truth of God's Words
31:1-31	A Final Portrait of Wisdom

Commentary

The comments that follow divide the book into three major sections: Proverbs 1—9; Proverbs 10—29, with a subsection focusing on Proverbs 22:17—24:22; and Proverbs 30 and Proverbs 31.

Acquiring Wisdom (Prov 1—9)

As has been indicated previously, Proverbs 1—9 forms a self-contained unit within the greater whole. A number of clear characteristics within these chapters bind them together. In these sections a father addresses his son(s) with an instruction to "hear"; a woman speaks as a personalized characterization of Wisdom, referred to henceforth as Lady Wisdom; and a strange (Heb.: "strange," "foreign," "loose") woman appears with the express intent of pulling the unwitting away from the paths of righteousness, in this commentary referred to as the Femme Fatale.

However, odd proverbs more characteristic of the style of the rest of the book also find their way in, as do passages speaking of wisdom in a less personalized form. In general the tone is instructional, although this incorporates the use of a number of short anecdotes. The unit is presented as a finely crafted literary entity in which the principal characters and themes are introduced, developed and brought to a climax through a series of interwoven and closely related threads that require readers to look both back and forward, up and down, and to develop a capacity for themselves similar to that which the son is urged to acquire. Here the universal message of the book is to be found, and despite the obvious male thrust of these opening chapters, it is equally appropriate to contemporary women and men.

Women feature prominently in these chapters. Many, however, have felt their portrayal to be demeaning, indicating a serious disrespect on the part of the writer(s) and of their society. Attempts to sweeten the pill have focused on the fact that wisdom is personalized in female form, but this takes little account of Femme Fatale, sometimes referred to as Dame Folly. Nor does it take account of the other instances, all brief, in which women's role in society is portrayed in fairly realistic terms: capable teachers in the home, appreciated wives, but with their weaknesses and foibles just as throughout all generations. The fact that these portraits are presented generally with a view to the effect and influence, positive and mostly negative, that diverse types of women have on men (never the reverse) is disconcerting only until one realizes that this section depends on the contrast of gender in order to communicate its message. Standing back from the text enables one to see that the section and probably the book was written by men for men and that the major portrayals of women are much larger than life and verging on the incredible. This indicates that something more than a literal opinion on womanhood is being offered. The key is possibly found in the fact that the female is principally used to portray a source of influence and occasionally example. More will be said of this later. Suffice it for now to suggest therefore that inclusive translations of the Bible may well do this section, if not the book, a disservice.

These observations lead to a number of guidelines regarding interpretation of the passage that the comments to follow will respect. Given its holistic nature, and with the exception of Proverbs 1:1-7, these chapters have all been taken as instruction emanating from a father to his son(s). Proverbs 1:1-7 is generally agreed to have been an editorial appendage. If this is understood in terms of an afterthought, then there would be grounds to consider the subsections as unrelated one to another. If, however, these verses introduce the whole that is to come, then it is reasonable to assume that the intention of the final editors was that the section should be understood in this way.

Linking to this is the question of the setting: Is the father a sage of a proposed wisdom school and the son(s) his pupil(s) receiving instruction? Or is the argument of those who prefer a home environment more persuasive? It is inappropriate here to enter these arguments. However, such considerations focus on the question of who and discount the why. Those who propound the existence of wisdom schools tie this in with training for positions within the civil service or the royal court, an argument supported by Proverbs 16:1—22:16.

Given the aforementioned questions raised by this view, however, a reasonable alternative might be to endow the whole book with a greater sense of urgency than is usually the case and hence to see it as preparation for a specific event. Entry into public service might be a possibility, but the overall tenor would lend itself equally to specific preparation for entry into adulthood, or even more precisely, marriage. This latter could well help to explain the frequent references to women, who at the time of speaking would be in many ways an unknown in terms of relationships other than the maternal and sororital (sisterly). Marriage would involve leaving the parental home, accepting new responsibilities and getting to know a new wife with whom the young man would rear a family. Avoiding marriage to a difficult wife would be important. Future life would demand calculated decisions and choices in the face of moral and social dilemmas and challenges, which would require not only an act of the will and an acceptance of personal responsibility but also wisdom.

A final observation to be made is the fact that this section puts more emphasis on the ontology of wisdom rather than the functioning. The son is urged to get wisdom and is offered plenty of opportunity to acquire the skill of being wise. Hence this section contrasts significantly with Proverbs 10—29, even allowing for Proverbs 22:17—24:34, which shows certain similarity with Proverbs 1—9. This point has been made somewhat dryly by the categorization of the former as instructional and the latter as observational literature. However, such categorizations reduce the vitality of these chapters, whose clear intention is not simply to convey wisdom but to teach and demonstrate how wisdom is to be acquired. The proverbs—the wisdom examples as found in Proverbs 10—29—function more in the capacity of tools, the handling and use of which the son is to perfect in order to acquire a skill, than they do ends in themselves, as specific examples of wisdom that the son should memorize and put into literal practice. Therefore the proverbs are important, but the major focus is on what the son will do with them.

Despite the fact that the purpose of the section is stated at the beginning (Prov 1:2-6), the overall message of these chapters is summarized at the end: "Lay aside immaturity, and live; / and walk in the way of insight" (Prov 9:6). The intervening chapters show how this is to be done.

A Call to Understanding (Prov 1:1-7)

These verses provide the key to all that follows. Highlighting the weaknesses of youth (simplicity; lack of prudence, reflecting youth's characteristic impetuosity) and maturity of age (a tendency to rest on laurels; thinking themselves already wise through lifelong experience), all are encouraged to acquire and to go on acquiring wisdom. While warning that it is possible to be discerning without understanding, wise and yet not hear, wise and continue to learn, true wisdom is presented as the acquisition of understanding. The purpose of the book is thus to impart wisdom and instruction in such a way that they can be known and received. The call to understand incorporates basic observational skills: look and learn, then reflect—bringing to mind Mary's pondering of Jesus' revelation to her (Lk 2:51). Common sense is also called for: observation and reflection should reveal that certain courses of action have beneficial results while others have negative repercussions. This is where the need for YHWH's revealed wisdom becomes apparent, since there are occasions when either the expected or the logically deserved doesn't come to pass.

The fear of the Lord is the prerequisite for this to happen (Prov 1:7). The phrase is repeated five more times in Proverbs 1—9 and reoccurs throughout the rest of the book. The fear of the Lord is cited as the beginning of wisdom (Prov 9:10), which results in the ability to avoid evil (Prov 16:6) and which is a fountain of life through which one may avoid death (Prov 14:27). It is allied to humility (Prov 22:4) and hence indicates an attitude of heart and a way of life rather than a literal fear felt by the weak and vulnerable in front of strength and power. Terms such as *awe, reverence, respect* and *devotion* might illuminate the concept further. In this verse, however, it is in juxtaposition to fools, who despise wisdom and instruction. It is perhaps appropriate to see a parallel between the fear of the Lord and Proverbs' concept of understanding, since this latter involves the humility of incomplete knowledge and recognition that wisdom and instruction are imparted by others rather than found in oneself. This contrasts significantly with the arrogance displayed by fools, who despise instruction through pride and self-sufficiency. The human tendency to analyze, structure, dissect, reconstruct and hence dominate, control and master must find its correct locus in YHWH, the giver of these skills and the origin of knowledge.

Learning the Lesson (Prov 1:8—2:22)

Functioning as a type of subsection, this passage presents an instance in which wisdom needs to be exercised and walks the son through its outworking. The son is to understand that situations will arise that will potentially pull him down. He is vulnerable to the pull of the crowd (Prov 1:14) and to the appeal of forbidden fruit (Prov 1:13). Thus he should learn not only that one reaps the fruit of one's ways (Prov 1:18-19) but also that illicit gain rots life to the core, choking to death the freedom of honesty and integrity (Prov 1:19). However, he should also learn, perhaps more important, that there is a different world, one that will openly tempt and entice him with its ease of living and easy gain but has different values that he would do well to understand. These are the values of putting oneself first, of disregard for others, of get, get, get, . . . with death and destruction as a result.

Lady Wisdom confirms this. Presenting the material almost as a videotape that the son is to watch attentively and understand, the father begs the son not to succumb, giving a minicommentary on the previous scene and reprimanding those who scoffed and neglected to equip themselves so that they could avoid the final, inevitable result of their action. Proverbs 1:29-33 gathers the observations and pleas under the overall umbrella of the fear of the Lord. Those who reject this, choosing another authority, as did the sinners (Prov 1:8-19), must reap the benefit of their actions. The way of avoiding this inevitable, however, is to listen to Lady Wisdom by hearing and understanding previous instruction and by paying attention to her voice on every occasion when there is opportunity to ignore her teachings.

Yet as before, the son seems to be called to understand in greater depth. Lady Wisdom is also communicating a message about herself. Found in the most public places (Prov 1:20-21), she is evident and available to all. At the same time she is often found precisely where she is not expected—these public places would not have been commonly frequented by women. This same message may even be the point of the female personification of Wisdom: a patriarchal society would not necessarily look to its women for public guidance and advice, and this being the case, her message not to disregard her is all the more potent.

Many scholars see in Lady Wisdom elements of a goddess figure imported from surrounding nations. However, other than the power of her words, her power is limited. She speaks as one with authority but no desire or perhaps ability to coerce; she employs no wiles, in direct contrast to the alluring but open enticement of the sinners (Prov 1:10), yet she is equally forthright in her desire to influence the young man's course of action. Herein lies a further thrust of her message: responsibility for listening and taking action is the hearer's, not hers. However, the sobering fact is that there comes a time when it is too late to seek her, even though this is done diligently (Prov 1:28). To seek Wisdom diligently after calamity is to mock her, a hypocritical act; therefore she goes into hiding. A complacent attitude is particularly dangerous (Prov 1:32): as opposed to fools, who despise wisdom and instruction (Prov 1:7), and the simple, who turn away from following wisdom, refusing to evaluate, consider, listen, understand, and hence thoughtlessly following all their inappropriate impulses (Prov 1:32), the complacent can't be bothered to listen.

So Lady Wisdom declares her hand. Will the son understand?

The father aims to ensure he does. "Accept my words," he urges. "Treasure up my commandments" (Prov 2:1). Just as Lady Wisdom cried out to passersby, so the son must cry out with equal urgency (Prov 2:3) for insight and understanding. His task is to seek, bringing to mind the woman searching for her lost coin (Lk 15:3-10). Wisdom belongs to the Lord, however, who communicates knowledge and understanding (Prov 2:6). Neither can be understood as a gift suddenly bestowed, therefore, but rather both demand perpetual listening. Through this communicative dialogue, therefore, the wisdom seeker can be sure that his understanding (evaluation) is appropriate. While thus emphasizing the ongoing process of the acquisition of wisdom, the son should also gain encouragement from the fact that the Lord "stores up sound wisdom for the upright" (Prov 2:7), an indication that the more experience in walking wisely that one has, the more upright one is and the more one can have confidence. As a result—note, not as a reward—the son will experience the protection of YHWH (Prov 2:7-8). This process will enable the seeker to understand righteousness, justice and equity (Prov

2:9), the primary goals of the instruction as expressed in Proverbs 1:3. Wisdom will thus come into his heart, which is not possible for fools (Prov 14:33), with the corresponding blessing of well-being (Prov 2:10).

The odd switch to the first warning about Femme Fatale seems to be provoked by the reference to perverted speech (Prov 2:12, referring to Prov 1:11-14?), although with the subtler link of forbidden fruit. At one level the father does appear to be warning the son against an adulterous woman—a natural warning should the son be preparing for marriage or adulthood. But at another level, perhaps lying closer to the intention of the text, the son is being asked to understand once again: understand this woman's role alongside the original sinners of Proverbs 1:8-19 and Lady Wisdom of Proverbs 1:20-33; understand the nature of the various appeals being made on his life; understand, therefore, that here is a new type, one that will creep up on him imperceptibly, that he won't instantly recognize it for what it is, one that will strike where he is most vulnerable, taking him by surprise, flattering him and appealing to his vanity and manhood. The vocabulary of Proverbs 1:18-19 emphasizes how gradual the descent to death is. As opposed to a quick death of violence that comes almost as rightful dues from easily identifiable foolish actions, this path to death can start without the son realizing. It is doubly dangerous since the fact that death is the inevitable consequence is not immediately evident. The serpent of Genesis 3 comes quickly to mind.

The father concludes (Prov 1:20-22) by encouraging the son to learn the lesson just presented. In so doing, he will join the ranks of the upright, with the corresponding expectation of living a life of security and blessing.

Commending Wisdom (Prov 3:1—4:27)

Having laid the foundations, the father goes on to flesh out his teachings. Indicating that simply to recognize that wisdom is a vital requisite of life is already to be wise (Prov 4:7), he introduces new aspects of wisdom. These include loyalty and faithfulness (Prov 3:3-4), with the urge to make them part of one's being: the heart is the place of understanding and the neck, a particularly vulnerable part of the body, is a place of beauty. The message is clear. Once the skill of understanding is acquired, then it must be kept in the forefront of life (Prov 3:21-22). This is security—head up, no need to look down (Prov 4:25-26), analogous today perhaps with touch typing or piano playing. When the unexpected arrives and takes one by surprise, one's previous experiences and the father's teaching will guide one through (Prov 3:25-26; cf. Prov 4:1-5, where the warning not to forget and turn away brings to mind James's mirror, Jas 1:23-24). Yet a real danger of living wisely lies in the temptation to trust in these attributes per se and in the corresponding blessings of favor and good repute, which also potentially lead to self-sufficiency and complacency. The son(s) must trust in God, not these things (Prov 3:5-8). So wisdom also involves recognizing the dangers of wisdom. Disregard may invoke YHWH's loving discipline (Prov 3:11-12), a much more comforting concept than inevitable negative consequences.

As if intoxicated by the blessings of the wise life (Prov 3:13-18), the father commends wisdom to the son(s), citing yet new reasons: wisdom is part of the created order, and humanity's task is to work in conjunction with this, acknowledging YHWH's far superior knowledge and understanding (Prov 3:19-20).

Peppered throughout these chapters is the notion of blessing resulting from wisdom: life (Prov 3:22); long life, often associated with the land (Prov 2:21; 4:10); healing (Prov 4:22) and security (Prov 1:33). Commentators observe dryly that experience must have proved otherwise, hence the more refined or realistic picture grappled with in Job and Ecclesiastes. Yet this belittles the wisdom, particularly its origins of experience, that the book seeks to portray, and we do better to view these benefits as generally but not guaranteeably true in a fallen world. They are principles rather than promises.

Warnings Against Foolishness (Prov 5)

Once again the appearance of Femme Fatale seems to be provoked by reference to speech (cf. Prov 1:12, 16). One has the impression that the father means to go in another direction but is always drawn back—perhaps himself a prisoner of the influences he warns against? Yet here Femme Fatale's dangers are more explicitly outlined, and she has a significantly higher profile than previously. Of particular note are the penalties for listening to her, many of which are negative parallels to the blessings received through being wise. As before, therefore, it is appropriate to take the text on two levels: a genuine warning against an adulterous relationship with its draining, life-sucking, debilitating effects; and a lived example of how external, tempting influences, once given room, will imperceptibly invade and take on ever greater dimensions.

The contrasts between Femme Fatale (Prov 5:3-14) and the "wife of your youth" (Prov 5:15-19) are also marked, with the latter embodying beauty, love and affection, and one again has the impression of the father showing a videotape in which the son (or sons; note the change from Prov 5:1 to Prov 5:7) is presented with a futuristic choice.

Living Wisely (Prov 6:1-19)

Picking up and developing themes and styles from previous chapters (especially Prov 3:9-10, 27-35) that give a foretaste of Proverbs 10—22, Proverbs 6 prepares the son(s) for living in society. Proverbs 3:27-35 had already emphasized the fact that one's neighbor has no place in which to be kept. One is not to exercise any manipulative or controlling power over others; here the son is to learn that neither should he give others the same sort of power over him (Prov 6:1-5). The crooked speech of Proverbs 6:12 recalls the same in Proverbs 4:24 and contrasts with looking straight ahead as well as bringing the renegades of Proverbs 1:8-19 to mind. Those who look sideways, who allow themselves to be deflected from the path of righteousness will create havoc for themselves and others and spend time on worthless pursuits. Even the ant knows better than that!

Influences and Temptations (Prov 6:20—8:36)

And so begins the lead up to the climax of the section: My son, by now you should know where your greatest dangers are, and you should know what you have to do. Influences and temptations will vie for your attention, each of which has been portrayed for you here in female form, representing the emotional and moral pulls and desires exerted on your life.

Femme Fatale flits on stage one final time (Prov 6:24-25) before making her grand finale in order to make sure there is no uncertainty regarding her identity. She is clearly not a run-of-the-mill prostitute (Prov 6:26), and the verses that follow raise questions about which of the two is being referred to. Again these are verses that seem to blur the edges between Femme Fatale as a somewhat surreal representation of evil temptation, a readily available prostitute and an adulterous woman. As previously, it seems reasonable to allow those three distinctions to stand, noting that the emphasis is of concern for the son's well-being and right action. While these women are not presented as honorable, neither is the focus on condemning them for their roles. They are rather presented as analogies of danger to beware of, not because of their gender but because through use of gender in this way the son is better equipped to learn the required lessons.

Etruscan gravestone with married couple still together in death. (Proverbs 5:15-19)

Proverbs 7—8 then bring the two principal women into high relief: the long build-up in the previous chapters is over, both can now be seen for who they truly are, and the relationship between them is highlighted. Lady Wisdom can preserve the son from Femme Fatale, in particular from her words (Prov 7:4-5).

Yet Proverbs 7 in particular provokes a good number of questions, as it is not easy to understand who this personage is, or more precisely, what motivates her. She is readily identifiable through her dress (Prov 7:10), already suggesting that any wise son should distance himself if he saw fit. The fact that he doesn't could in many ways be seen as the ultimate purpose of the anecdote. Femme Fatale is thus free to make her approach. Yet what does she want? Her actions are not typical of normal behavior of her gender, leaving women readers perplexed. She has a husband and security (Prov 7:19-20); she speaks of love (Prov 7:18) yet is not in a position to have a long-term relationship; and she is willing to risk all she has for an apparent one-night stand. She is portrayed as taking the initiative. She lies in wait and speaks, yet the return for her is obscure. Did she already know the son? One presumes not, yet her action is remarkably forward were he a stranger. In addition, she habitually walks the streets and must therefore be well known. Yet no hint is given as to why she acts in this way. Such an explanation might make her more

The Wise Woman, the Foolish Woman & the Righteous Woman

The book of Proverbs offers a kaleidoscope of womanly images. A "mother's teaching" is offered in counterpoint to a "father's instruction" (Prov 1:8; cf. Prov 6:20; 31). Wisdom, allegorized in the majestic feminine, prophetically confronts society. Wisdom is to be attended to as the source of understanding "the fear of the LORD and . . . the knowledge of God" (Prov 2:5), as well as the way to long life, riches and honor.

Wisdom continues to dominate the early chapters of Proverbs, her sound advice contrasting sharply in Proverbs 5—7 with the seductions of folly, personified as the adulterous woman (most memorably characterized in Prov 7:11-23). The language and style of the seductress, depicted as an unfaithful wife engaging in prostitution, is specifically sexual, and the warnings to the young man are given in sexual terms. Yet in the larger frame, opened in Proverbs 1 and closed in Proverbs 8, sexual seduction also functions as a metaphor for whatever takes the heart away from hearing and obeying God's truth—the picture of the unfaithful wife a parallel to such prophetic passages as Isaiah 50 and 54 and the book of Hosea.

The parallel between Wisdom as characterized in Proverbs 8 and New Testament passages concerning the pre-incarnate Christ (Prov 8:23-32; cf. Jn 1:1-4; Col 1:15-18)

has long been a source of devotional contemplation. However, the context makes it clear that the writer does not see Wisdom as one with Yahweh but rather as an attribute of God and, metaphorically, as the agency of divine action in creation. Wisdom is a metaphoric or allegorized figure akin to allegorized attributes of God in Psalm 85:10, which medieval thinkers rendered as the Four Daughters of God—love, faithfulness, righteousness and peace.

The contrasting parallel passages in Proverbs 1—8 reach a climax in the rival festal invitations of Wisdom, characterized as a great lady, and "the woman Folly" (see Kidner, 77-84). But Proverbs continues to pick up themes of wisdom and foolishness. One collection of sayings that reflect feminine concerns occurs in Proverbs 11:12-23, where matters of conversation, wise political counsel and business are included with two proverbs regarding womanliness. The "good wife" is compared with one "who brings shame" (Prov 12:4). The "wise woman [who] builds her house" is contrasted with "the foolish one" who "tears it down with her own hands" (Prov 14:1). Various figures of this foolish woman occur from Proverbs 14 on: the quarrelsome or contentious or nagging wife; the prostitute or unfaithful woman. The young person is warned to love wisdom rather than to dissipate energy on any substitute, and by this romancing of wisdom, Wisdom becomes identified with the lyrically idealized faithful marriage partner of Proverbs 5:15-23.

The collection closes with a set of summations that constitute the "oracle" taught to King Lemuel by his mother (Prov 31:1-9), giving a mother's instructions prophetic or oracular status, the mother becoming the embodiment of wisdom. In the character sketch of the capable wife, the enactments of the allegorical figure of Wisdom, from prophetic wise woman to instructing mother and faithful and beloved wife, coalesce in the idealized but human and womanly form, the "woman who fears the LORD" and therefore "is to be praised," exalted above the "many women" who have "done excellently" (Prov 31:29-30).

Like a prism, Proverbs catches the swirl of Old Testament ideas about and stories of women and distills them into the three strands of wise woman, foolish woman and righteous woman. Examples of each and discussions about them are to be found throughout the Bible. Allegorized or personified Wisdom also occurs in Job 28, suggesting it to be a very ancient concept, one elaborated by later Jewish writers (Murphy, 133-50). A number of wise women are described in the Old Testament: Tamar, who catches Judah in his hypocrisy, is one (Gen 38). Her story is particularly complex, since she acts the part of the prostitute or foolish woman in order to be the wise woman who takes her place within the genealogy of the kings of Israel and of the Messiah (Mt 1:3, 16). Rahab is the harlot who wisely gives assistance to the Hebrew spies and so becomes a faithful wife, mother in Israel and heroine among the faithful (Josh 2; Mt 1:5; Heb 11:31). Ruth becomes a part of the maternal chain leading up to the birth of the Messiah through her wisdom in embracing her mother-in-law, Naomi, and her mother-in-law's people, land and God. In Ruth's story, mother-in-law and daughter-in-law are shown to be wise women as they plan to gain the protection of Boaz in an action grounded in knowledge of Israel's ancient laws and of the even more ancient "way of a man with a girl" (Prov 30:19). Abigail, intelligent and beautiful, brokers peace between her churlish husband, Nabal, and the angry king-in-waiting, David (1 Sam 25). The aged Bathsheba demonstrates dignity and wisdom as she secures the succession for her son Solomon; the difficulty of meeting with David in the presence of the young woman who had become his attending concubine is not overlooked in the story (1 Kings 1:11-35). During the exile, Esther acts wisely and decisively to divert a pogrom, her brilliant action and personal courage celebrated in the feast of Purim.

Women who functioned as wise women or whose wisdom earned them this title play significant historical roles in key incidents. The wise woman of Tekoa, summoned by Joab, convinces David to bring Absalom back from punitive exile (2 Sam 14:1-21), and a wise woman acts on behalf of the city of Maacah to convince Joab to withdraw (2 Sam 20:14-22). Claudia V. Camp argues for a tradition of women sages on which the feminine allegorical form of Wisdom in Proverbs could be based.

A number of wise women emerge from within the New Testament as well. Priscilla, with her husband, Aquila, teaches and disciples new converts at Ephesus and Rome (Acts 18:18-26; 1 Cor 16:19; Rom 16:3). Eunice and Lois, who teach Timothy the Scriptures (2 Tim 1:5; cf. 3:15), carry on the tradition of the wise mothers of Israel. Phoebe is commended as "a deacon of the church" who is to be welcomed by the church as an apostolic emissary (Rom 16:1), continuing the tradition of wise women within the larger community.

But as there are examples of wise and righteous women, so also are there examples of unsound, faithless and dangerous women—or of the dangers of unsoundness and faithlessness characterized or allegorized in feminine form. The preacher of Ecclesiastes complains of "the woman who is a trap, whose heart is snares and nets" (Eccles 7:26). He claims to have found one faithful man among a thousand, "but a woman among all these I have not found" (Eccles 7:28). Delilah, who betrays Samson to the Philistines (Judg 16), is not only a person but also a paradigm. When Israel walks in the path of obedience and wisdom, the nation is described as a beloved and fruitful wife (Is 56). When Israel turns away from God's wisdom, the nation becomes the faithless wife portrayed in Proverbs, and God becomes the betrayed husband. The most poignant portrait of this betrayed relationship is in the story of Hosea and Gomer. Christ's love for the church is also depicted as husbandly, the righteousness of the church depicted in feminine terms as a bridelike "splendor" (Eph 5:25-32).

Biblical allegorical images of the wise, foolish and righteous woman are glimpsed again in Revelation. The church or perhaps the nation of Israel becomes the childbearing mother who is under supernatural protection (Rev 12). The world system of commerce is portrayed as Babylon, the "great whore" who defies God and his rule (Rev 17; cf. Is 13—21). The new Jerusalem is seen as a bride wearing "fine linen, bright and pure," with the explanation added, "Fine linen is the righteous deeds of the saints" (Rev 19:8).

Bibliography

C. V. Camp, "The Female Sage in Ancient Israel and in the Biblical Wisdom Literature," in *The Sage in Israel and the Ancient Near East*, ed. J. G. Gammie and L. G. Perdue (Winona Lake, IN: Eisenbrauns, 1990) 185-203; idem, "The Wise Women of 2 Samuel: A Role Model for Women in Early Israel?" *Catholic Biblical Quarterly* 43 (1981) 14-29; D. Kidner, *The Proverbs: An Introduction and Commentary*, Tyndale Old Testament Commentaries (Chicago: IVP, 1964); R. E. Murphy, *The Tree of Life: An Exploration of Biblical Wisdom Literature*, 2d ed. (Grand Rapids, MI: Eerdmans, 1996).

MAXINE HANCOCK

---

credible as a nonallegorical figure, but its absence inclines one to interpreting her as symbolic.

This is backed up by aspects of her conduct that bring to mind other scriptural passages. 1 Peter 5:8 speaks of "your adversary the devil," who "prowls around, looking for someone to devour," with the corresponding warning to be sober and watchful. There are links too with Genesis 3, in which words play such a vital role. In a similar way to the serpent, here Femme Fatale leads the son to believe that he can play with fire and not be burned, or more precisely, that the experience is pleasurable and the repercussions insignificant.

There is much to reinforce the idea, therefore, that Femme Fatale, rather than being a human being, is the personification of evil and temptation, just as Lady Wisdom personifies wisdom. The vignette depends on the son's simplicity (Prov 7:7) and aims to equip him in the skills of sobriety and watchfulness by alerting him to the existence and the way of working of a form of evil temptation able to destroy him.

In stark contrast, Lady Wisdom takes the stage in Proverbs 8, vying with Femme Fatale for the son's attention. Wisdom's message is still to the simple (cf. Prov 7:7), and her appeal begins by her emphasizing the wisdom and benefits of accepting her. Little has changed from her previous messages, and again one is struck by the emphasis on words (Prov 8:6-9). Lady Wisdom speaks what is noble and right, but she still depends on the listener to understand and to seek knowledge in order for the truth of her words to become apparent (Prov 8:9). This fact reiterates a facet of her personality already previously noted and one to surface later also: only by taking her at her word and experiencing it is her message proved true. Almost as if to add weight to her message, she emphasizes her role in just government (Prov 8:14-16), her presence therefore aiding in issues of authority and responsibility. She is unabashed at proclaiming her inestimable worth (Prov 8:11), which constitutes truth (Prov 8:7), counsel, sound wisdom, insight and strength (Prov 8:14)—indispensable properties for ruling, since they ensure peace, justice and stability.

Then, as if overcome by her glory, as a bud finally breaks open to allow the full flower to reflect the sun's glory, she presents her credentials—and what a curriculum vitae. Present at the creation of the world, used by YHWH in that creation and now rejoicing in that created world, she enjoys an intimate relationship with YHWH, is his own, and is the principle by which he ordered the world. Not only is she the means by which humanity fears the Lord, but she is also the means by which the universe is structured. By implication, those who find her and live by her align themselves to that same order, finding peace and tranquility.

Once again scholars are tempted to see parallels between Lady Wisdom and Greek and Egyptian goddesses (Isis, Ma'at) on account of language and function, particularly that of fertility and creation, with much corresponding discussion revolving around Proverbs 8:22 and the verb translated "created," "possessed" or "begot" (Fontaine also suggests "conceived," 148). Since the New Testament links this passage to Jesus (Jn 1:1-14; 1 Cor 1:24; Col 1:15-17), questions are raised not only about Lady Wisdom's identity and relationship to YHWH but also about Jesus' relationship to the Father. Is he a created being, an Arian argument still held by Jehovah's Witnesses, or a preexistent being (*see* The Trinity)? Arguments can be made for each possibility, but "possessed" seems to accord most readily with the interpretation of wisdom being here a personification rather than a hypostasis, thus conforming the most consistently to the presentation of Lady Wisdom throughout these chapters.

Application (Prov 9:1-18)

Proverbs 9 summarizes all that has gone before. Lady Wisdom offers the simple her feast—a potent invitation, given the need for the simple to so practice the art of understanding that it becomes akin to eating and inwardly digesting, then becoming a source of nourishment and well-being (note the analogy of eating honey in Prov 24:13-14). Proverbs 9:7-12 might seem to be an odd collection of unrelated sayings, yet these sayings have their place as a practical application of what has gone before as well as preparation for that to come. Femme Fatale's final sortie gives the impression of a damp firecracker, her message vain, empty and unappealing, her voice petering into insignificance when set against that of Lady Wisdom.

Understanding the two women as representations of wisdom and evil has its dangers, particularly if one follows the line that they are portrayed as women in order to present an often adverse source of influence, to emphasize their otherness from the son(s) and to highlight the need for an acceptance of choice and responsibility. Does any doctrine of original sin fit into this, for example (*see* Sin)? Yet closer scrutiny reveals that this doctrine may be reinforced rather than challenged by this approach. The texts in which Lady Wisdom appears present little difficulty for interpretation in that she is never taken to be a truly earthly figure. She is apart, symbolic, and her role is never confused with that of human women in any respect. No homely, wifely or even feminine role model is portrayed through her. In contrast, however, it can be difficult to distinguish whether the Femme Fatale is a literal earthly personage or a symbolic antithesis to Lady Wisdom. This confusion of locus permits an understanding of evil that truly resides outside humanity yet has pervaded life to such an extent that it is now part and parcel of human nature.

This interpretation could also lead to a presumption that human beings have the capacity within themselves to resist evil. Yet the whole purpose of these chapters is to sensitize the son(s) to the character and use of wisdom, without which no resistance is possible. The son(s) must acquire skill in its use, which will involve accepting not only Lady Wisdom's words but also her helping hand (Prov 1:24).

Acting Wisely (Prov 10—29)

These nineteen chapters can be subdivided into various subsections. Proverbs 10:1—15:33 is sometimes termed proverbs of Solomon. Proverbs 16:1—22:16 is sometimes thought of as a royal section on account of more frequent reference to kings and kingship than is found in the rest of the book; this fact perhaps contributes to the view that the setting for the book was originally the royal court. The proverbs in this section are less antithetic than are those in the previous sections. Proverbs 22:17—24:34 bears strong resemblance to the Egyptian *Instruction of Amenemope.* It attributes the contents to "the wise" (Prov 22:17) and contains a small allusion to the first chapters' Femme Fatale (Prov 23:26-28) as well as various references to "my child" (e.g., Prov 23:15, 19, 26). The author of Proverbs 25:1—29:27 is said to be Solomon, but the imparted wisdom is recopied by the men of Hezekiah (Prov 25:1). However, all these subsections share much both in terms of content and of style. For this reason they will be considered as a whole, with a brief specific comment on Proverbs 22:17—24:34 following.

These chapters are also far less personally direct and directed, and reference in the comment to follow is therefore made to sages (plural) rather than continue with the singular characteristic of Proverbs 1—9. The two-line couplet briefly introduced in Proverbs 1—9 (e.g., Prov 9:7-12) is now the exclusive medium of communication. There are occasional instances of close or exact repetition (e.g., Prov 19:12 and Prov 20:2; Prov 19:5 and Prov 19:9) and occasions when two or three couplets combine thematically to form a longer section. Analogies with nature are common, and while the sages show themselves principally concerned with people, animal welfare does not escape their attention (Prov 12:10). Wry snippets of humor also poke through (Prov 27:14). However, the couplets do not lend themselves to ready analysis either in the order or in the way in which they are presented. Themes, observations, examples and criticisms tumble in haphazard fashion, presenting an impression of only partial coherence and yet a visual, dynamic picture of life in all its diversity. It is almost as if the sages take their pupil(s) on a walk around the city and comment on features of life as they occur. This diversity encourages the reader to draw the various threads together and begin to sense an overriding message that quickly relates to Proverbs 1—9: there are two alternatives in life, and while overt exhortation to choose one rather than the other is rare, the implied message is clear. Once again, to take heed is wisdom, and these chapters reinforce and reiterate the teaching about wisdom of the first nine chapters.

However, while Proverbs 1—9 focused on the skill of recognizing evil, understanding its principal forms and outworkings, and understanding one's relationship with it (and hence being set primarily in a spiritual context), these chapters broaden the concept of wisdom by placing it in a largely although by no means exclusively social context. Of note, nevertheless, is the somewhat insular flavor that at times emerges. Mention of the law (e.g., Prov 28:7, 9) reminds one of the specific nation to whom this wisdom is directed, yet a nation consisting of all the sectors of society found throughout the world and concerned with its treatment of foreigners, who are not necessarily to be trusted (Prov 27:13).

These social relations occupy much of the sages' attention throughout, and it is clear that one of the purposes of wisdom is to promote and maintain social stability as well as corporate and individual well-being. These chapters portray a largely dualistic worldview, with people and actions falling into one of two groups: those commended by the sages, and those condemned, or at least warned against; those with an advantage in life as opposed to those disadvantaged. Polarization of extremes is hence characteristic of the proverbs, as is the direct cause-effect viewpoint frequently propounded with little allowance made for middle ground. Thus actions and attitudes are often seen as having their inevitable consequences, whether good or bad. Accompanying this view is the underlying tendency to suggest that righteousness will ultimately triumph over wickedness (Prov 11:31), despite the fact that hard evidence may indicate otherwise.

The sages communicate their message by commenting on a myriad of matters they deem important. The most major of these are as follows.

Character Attributes

Of major concern is the type of person one is. The fool is roundly condemned, accredited with numerous failings: hasty, unconsidered or slanderous speech (Prov 10:8, 14, 18), lack of common sense (Prov 10:21), enjoyment of wrongdoing (Prov 10:23), confidence in his wisdom (Prov 12:15), unashamed of his behavior and action (Prov 13:16), unable or unwilling to learn from mistakes (Prov 26:11) and to turn away from evil (Prov 13:19) even if pressed hard to do so (Prov 26:22). Generally contrasted with the wise, whose virtues are the positive counterparts to the fool's misdemeanors, the fool is characterized by an overall lack of self-control and respect (even of parents, Prov 15:20) that the sages compare with a city broken and left without walls (Prov 25:28). Unchanneled or inappropriately directed energy is unproductive and senseless and can be harmful.

The sluggard is no better off. He is lethargic, even when his personal safety and well-being are concerned (Prov 26:13-16), always wanting but never getting (Prov 13:4) and therefore endangering his life (Prov 21:25). His inactivity contrasts with the out-of-control action of the fool. The sluggard too earns the sages' condemnation.

The wicked feature most prominently in the sages' teaching, however, although their punishment and the fact that their actions are an abomination to the Lord are often pinpointed more than is the precise nature of their wickedness, and sin as a general concept is rarely spoken of. Nevertheless, wickedness is found in the mind (Prov 10:20) as well as in shameful and disgraceful acts (Prov 13:5). It manifests itself in deception (Prov 11:18), is treacherous (Prov 12:5) and speaks evil (Prov 15:28). Punishment is certain (Prov 16:4) and takes various forms: expulsion from the land (Prov 10:30), contempt (Prov 18:3) and distancing from the Lord (Prov 15:29), to name but a few.

In contrast to these attitudes and actions (cf. Prov 29:27), the sages extol the righteous, whose virtues are multiple. Portrayed as being those whose thoughts are just (Prov 12:5; "just" here is juxtaposed to deceitful) and who rejoice in seeing justice done (Prov 21:15), these people stand firmly rooted and secure (Prov 12:3, 7) and are able to look to YHWH for protection on account of their righteousness (Prov 10:3; 18:10). They are a blessing to the society in which they live (Prov 11:11); they are generous (Prov 21:25-26) and considerate, even to animals (Prov 12:10). They have every hope that their desires and hopes will be fulfilled (Prov 10:24; 11:23). They are rewarded by joy and satisfaction (Prov 10:6; 11:28) and are able to live secure in the knowledge that their wisdom delights the living (Prov 23:24) and that their name will continue to be cited favorably after their death (Prov 10:7). Their righteous lives have long-term influence morally (Prov 20:7) and practically (Prov 13:22). They are people of prayer to whom YHWH listens (Prov 15:8, 29), and their righteousness is linked with delivery from death (Prov 10:2; 11:4), of their being saved (Prov 11:6) and of walking in a straight way (Prov 11:5). Of particular note is their speech, through which they advise and guide wisely (Prov 10:22, 31), having carefully considered what to say (Prov 15:28). Hence they are able to speak words of value (Prov 10:21) that impart life to the hearer (Prov 10:11).

Righteousness is therefore seen holistically, as a way of life that incorporates every diverse aspect involved in living. The way of becoming righteous, nevertheless, is through the acquisition of wisdom. Real wisdom is the ability to transfer understanding into action, accepting the corresponding responsibility. Hence the responsibility each has for his or her actions is emphasized and is the means by which one's reputation is established (Prov 20:11). So the wise leave the presence of a fool (Prov 14:7; think of the young man who did not shun the advances of Femme Fatale in Prov 7), heed admonition (Prov 15:31-32) and acquire wisdom (Prov 19:8).

Proverbs does seem to suggest that one's well-being is directly related to the common sense exercised in the making of choices (Prov 12:8), and these chapters often have a pragmatic flavor: do what is right, not just because of its intrinsic rightness but because the results are to one's benefit (Prov 11:17). Hence general well-being, encompassing even prosperity (Prov 19:8), health (Prov 3:8; 16:24) and honor (Prov 12:8), to a degree is one's own to determine. Yet this cannot be done independently. Counsel and advice from others is part of the process (Prov 15:22). In part it seems that this is because one's own view is limited (cf. Prov 14:12); wisdom is consistently portrayed throughout the book as being something shared and cumulative (Prov 12:15). It is personally and individually acquired (e.g., becoming prudent, Prov 15:5), yet it grows and develops through living, observing and reflecting in society, not only on a daily basis but from one generation to the next.

As was seen in Proverbs 1—9, wisdom is dynamic, ever-changing: a person (Lady Wisdom) rather than a text, a skill rather than a dogma. One of the potent aspects of the book as we now have it is therefore its hand-me-down nature, from father to son(s), from those times to these. This wisdom needs the mind and cannot be bought (Prov 17:16), and it demands a wholehearted commitment (Prov 17:24). This in itself requires humility, another virtue extolled by the sages, sometimes once again for pragmatic reasons (Prov 29:23), but just as often cited as an inherent component of the overall concept of the fear of the Lord.

Fear of the Lord

As an umbrella extending over all the wisdom offered throughout the book lies an awareness that YHWH is omnipresent, the source and reference point of all life. Nothing is hidden from God, ranging from good and bad actions to the contents of people's hearts (Prov 15:3, 11), and since humanity is created by the Lord (Prov 14:31), we are intimately known by him. People are examined by the Lord through his spirit (Prov 20:27), whose word is final (Prov 21:30). It is clear that despite one's individual responsibility to acquire wisdom, in reality even this comes from the Lord (Prov 20:12). Hand in hand with wisdom are the dual notions of the word and commandment (Prov 13:13), which demand respect, and the way (Prov 15:10), which must not be forsaken. Yet one's relationship with YHWH is paramount, and this involves humility and commitment (Prov 22:4). Interestingly, the first eleven verses of Proverbs 16 focus on contrasting human ways, plans, thoughts and intentions with YHWH's, while the following few verses speak of earthly kingship almost as if to emphasize the need for those who are the most exalted in earthly terms to judge themselves according to YHWH's person and ordinances. The wry observation that in response to the common need to blame someone else for one's mistakes, one often blames the Lord (Prov 19:3) must strike a chord in each reader and encourage reflection about one's attitude and understanding of YHWH. The Lord made everything for a purpose (Prov 16:4) and serves a self-ordained purpose in the life of humankind (Prov 17:3). God orders and hence understands creation's steps better than men and women themselves (Prov 20:24).

A number of verses seem to promise rich blessing, preservation from calamity, long life and honor as a "reward" for fearing YHWH (Prov 22:4; 28:14). Experience may challenge such a chain and force reflection about the interpretation of these and other similar proverbs and the message imparted. It is perhaps useful in such instances to distinguish between principles, promises, hopes and truths and acknowledge that the book in general portrays a picture of an overall created order in which principles and structures exist yet are often violated in the fallen world. While Wisdom adheres to these principles, acquisition of it, to which the book calls students, involves recognizing and reflecting on the ideal, comparing it with evidence and experience, and then to understand.

Values

The values that one holds are linked to the type of person one is. Proverbs doesn't challenge those aspirations to wealth, status, honor, stability, security and longevity common to all humanity; on the contrary, much of the wisdom offered uses these rewards as motivational elements to achieve its aims. Nevertheless, they are portrayed as fragile concepts, vulnerable to misuse, lending themselves to gross over- or underestimation, easily rocked or destroyed. Many of the couplets focus on highlighting their relativity. Money and wealth are highly influential and can lead to questionable attitudes (e.g., Prov 14:20; 19:6). Attitudes of heart, generally linked to one's relationship with the Lord, are of far greater importance and relevance to life (Prov 16:8, 19). While on occasion wealth is clearly linked with righteousness (Prov 15:6), it is more common to find suggestions that the two are uneasy companions that vie for precedence (Prov 16:16). Their power to influence unjustly is acknowledged (Prov 17:8), but bribes are not universally condemned if their purpose is conciliatory (Prov 21:14).

Similarly, while status, honor and reputation are accepted features of life, they too must be judged according to pragmatic reality (Prov 12:9) and higher values (Prov 19:22; 22:1). The converse positions of shame and loss of reputation are nevertheless generally indications of misdemeanor (Prov 10:5, 9).

While not setting out to undermine those structures and values in society around which it revolves, Proverbs submits them to a higher series of moral values, indicating that only when the former find their place in relation to the latter will they have any chance of fulfillment. Thus if the riches, honor and life cited as the reward for humility and fear of the Lord (Prov 22:4) are not forthcoming, then humility coupled with poverty is still to be preferred over pride with injustice (Prov 16:19).

Social Relations

A heavy emphasis is put on the establishment and maintenance of social stability and harmony. Specific topics include treatment of neighbors, who must be respected (Prov 14:21), whose good nature must not be abused (Prov 25:17; 27:14) and whose friendship is often more worthwhile than that of a close relative (Prov 27:10). But their presence can all too easily tempt one to envy, anger and wrath (Prov 27:4). Other issues are social interaction (Prov 26:17); morale (Prov 25:20); issues of trust in terms of who can and can't be trusted and why (Prov 25:19); revenge, which serves no purpose and ultimately belongs to YHWH (Prov 24:28-29; 20:22); general friendship (Prov 22:24); respect for authority (Prov 24:21-22); and the influence one exerts on others (Prov 23:13-14). This last is often linked to the more general theme of how the strong in society treat the vulnerable, identifying the vulnerable as the poor, widows, children and slaves (*see* The Purpose and Value of Human Life; God's Call to Social Justice; Ancient and Modern Slavery).

Discipline, even corporal punishment (Prov 23:13), is recommended as having positive benefit, presumably basing this on the belief that if the recipient understands it is for his or her good, then the end justifies the means. Elsewhere self-interested violence is roundly and consistently condemned (Prov 16:29; 21:7), and thus the use of the rod should not be used to justify child abuse. Nevertheless, the observation that mere words are not enough to discipline a servant (Prov 29:19) reveals a questionable assumption that those of inferior status may not have the interior wherewithal to take heed.

Issues of justice also arise when considering the vulnerable, and the need to exercise justice is another theme omnipresent throughout the book—justice not only in action (Prov 17:26) but also in attitude (Prov 14:21) and word (Prov 17:4), with an emphasis on proactive justice as well as reactive and revolving around notions of equity (Prov 29:14), partiality (Prov 28:21) and manipulating a situation for one's ends (Prov 17:8, 23). The Lord is also seen to take an active part in its establishment and outworking (Prov 16:11; 22:22-23), with the same expectation being made of the wise. Rulers are often singled out as a result of their particular responsibilities in this area. Justice often seems linked to the cause-effect mentality, so that one gets one's just desserts in life, good and bad (Prov 14:14); nevertheless this, as already mentioned, is not necessarily borne out by experience and should therefore perhaps be taken as a principle rather than a promise.

At the same time, Proverbs warns that in many areas of life, all may not be as it seems and that appearances can be deceptive. Kisses are not necessarily an indication of friendship (Prov 27:6); flattery may have an ulterior motive (Prov 29:5); wine, which appears attractive on the outside, has an untoward side (Prov 23:29-35); those who appear wealthy may not be (Prov 13:7), and even wisdom can be feigned (Prov 17:28). Hence, while issues of principle still stand, they must be tempered with a discernment that pierces to the heart of the matter.

Family

The stability of society is something seen as essentially maintained through the family. Time and again the need for parental respect is emphasized (Prov 10:1; 13:1; 15:20; 20:20), generally for the well-being of the child but also stated as an nonnegotiable principle: "If you curse father or mother, / your lamp will go out in utter darkness" (Prov 20:20). The household is a respected entity (Prov 15:27), and providing for one's ancestors is seen as a mark of a good man (Prov 13:22). Unlike goods and chattels, however, a prudent wife is not inherited (Prov 19:14) but is rather a gift from the Lord. Despite the fact that "he who finds a wife finds a good thing, and obtains favor from the LORD" (Prov 18:22), most of the wives mentioned are sources of irritation (Prov 19:13; 21:9, 19) and even a means of the Lord's punishment (Prov 22:14, "The mouth of a loose woman is a deep pit; / he with whom the LORD is angry falls into it."). This last recalls the Femme Fatale of Proverbs 1—9, especially given the allusion to her speech, while the former references serve as reminders of the male focus of the book, rendered more palatable (possibly) if the wisdom offered is in preparation for the young man's marriage. Mothers would no doubt have corresponding comments to daughters regarding husbands, had the opportunity to express them been offered, and modern women might well interpret the contentious behavior of these Old Testament wives as having a potentially direct correlation with their husbands' treatment of them.

Words and Speech

Social harmony is not only a matter of external structures; it is potentially destroyed by something as simple as speech, and the use of speech is another favorite theme of the sages and of the book. Words are portrayed as a primary means by which matters even as great as life and death are governed (Prov 13:3; 18:21). Although at times it is difficult to determine which aspect of life is being referred to (eternal, physical, quality), words have power to build up or destroy the overall constructive order necessary for the well-being of society and of the individual. Hence words are a means of perpetuating or desecrating justice (Prov 12:17, 19, 22; 14:5, 25) and of initiating, maintaining or disabling constructive and peaceful relationships (Prov 12:18; 15:1; 21:23). The "whisperer" (Prov 26:20-22) is identified as the cause of much mischief. Discretion in speech is therefore applauded, as is the ability to hold one's tongue (Prov 25:2-7), and one's ability to ignore damaging words is highlighted (Prov 12:16). Proverbs also observes realistically that it is not only the content of one's speech that can be destructive; too much speech, whatever its nature, prevents necessary work from taking place (Prov 14:23).

While these chapters touch on a multitude of aspects presented by life, their overall purpose seems to be twofold: encouraging the acquisition of wisdom in order to promote the well-being and stability of society and the individual and in order to cultivate those character attributes pleasing to God—perhaps a form of Old Testament sanctification? Proverbs 24:30-34 functions as a vignette exemplifying some of the components of acting wisely: observing what happens around and about, focusing on an element that attracts attention for some reason, considering and understanding. Proverbs 22:17-19 amplifies this by establishing the ultimate purpose of such understanding as being that of trust in the Lord.

Today's reader might find many individual proverbs oddly enigmatic, provoking a number of questions. Does a gracious woman always get honor, as Proverbs 11:16 seems to suggest? Are there no other factors? Is the saying therefore encouraging women to be gracious in order to receive honor? If so, should men be violent in order to get riches? How should the twofold coupling of men and women, honor and riches be understood? Similarly, to interpret many proverbs too literally leads to the possibility of improbable conclusions. For example, Proverbs 12:21 might seem to suggest that any ill that befalls an apparently righteous person indicates lack of righteousness. This idea is explored in Job (Job 4:7) yet repudiated by the end of that book. These proverbs cannot be taken as literal truths but rather an expounding of thought-provoking observations and principles. So the overall and continuing dynamic message of the book to look around, observe, reflect and understand is reinforced.

Themes and Sources (Prov 22:17—24:22)
Similarities between this section and Proverbs 1—9 are found in the return to an overall instructional tone rather than observational, together with the sense of a one-to-one personal address (Prov 22:20; 23:15). Familiar themes also surface: the need to build and maintain personal righteousness, in part by keeping a distance from people, actions and attitudes that adversely taint and influence (Prov 22:24-25), in part by ensuring growth in wisdom through rooting all learning in the fear of the Lord (Prov 23:17; 24:21) and self-control of emotions and attitudes (Prov 23:17; 24:1). The nature of wisdom is briefly explored (Prov 24:3-7, 13-14) as well as the recurrent emphasis on the need for parental respect and the pleasure parents experience when their children exhibit wisdom (Prov 23:22-25). Warnings are given against the harlot (Femme Fatale? Prov 23:26-28) and intoxication with wine (Prov 23:20-21, 29-35). Instruction is given on reacting to or dealing with evildoers and enemies (Prov 24:17-20).

The link of this section with *Amenemope* has been so long taken for granted that few have questioned it. Nevertheless, some are beginning to do so: J. Ruffle, for example challenges many of the similarities ostensibly found between the two texts in areas such as parallelism and order, as well as particularly emphasis and content. Ruffle proposes as a result the hypothesis that the passage "was contributed by an Egyptian scribe working at the court of Solomon [and was] based on his memories of a text that he had heard and maybe used in his scribal training" (in Zuck, 329). Once again, to enter the debate here is inappropriate, but its presence highlights the continuing degree of uncertainty regarding the identity of authorship and source that characterizes parts of the book.

The Truth of God's Words (Prov 30)

This chapter contains various subsections and somewhat discrete elements: reflections on a relationship with YHWH (Prov 30:1-9) and numerical sayings in which the speaker marvels about and comments on some of life's profundities, interspersed with occasional cautionary reflections focusing, as in Proverbs 10—29, on aspects of social tension and evil or foolish behavior.

The change of authorship (Prov 30:1) not only signals a further change of style but also introduces the only occasion in the book in which self-confessed lack of wisdom is bemoaned. Ironically the questioner displays the qualities that previously the book has cited as integral to wisdom: humility and awareness of his need (Prov 30:2; cf. Prov 15:33) and the acknowledgment of YHWH as the source of all wisdom (Prov 30:3; cf. Prov 2:6). These verses can be taken as examples of wisdom in action with the assurance that the sought-after wisdom will be given (Prov 2:3-9). Already the seeker recognizes God's existence, which is seen in creation, and emphasizes the importance of the name—that which not only identifies but also reveals identity (Ex 3:14).

The truth of the words of God is proved through taking refuge in them (Prov 30:5), taking God at his word, without which his protection cannot be experienced. God's word is thus corroborated only once one puts it into practice; one must beware the temptation, all too human and often linked with the psychological need to be right, to make God's word a shield and use it to justify oneself and one's position. In reality God justifies himself. Adding to God's words (Prov 30:6) therefore might refer to adding one's use, and rebuke comes when they don't work as one thinks they should. One's emphasis proves one a liar, putting oneself in the place of God. Proverbs 30:7-9 expresses a realistically pure spirituality. Both excessive abundance and lack distract from true discipleship, encouraging self-sufficiency on the one hand and on the other action known to contravene YHWH's law (Ex 20:15). Both, as do falsehood and lying (30:8), result in a distancing from YHWH, removing one's integrity, which is so integral to seeing him.

One's place vis-à-vis those around one provides the content of Proverbs 30:11-14, recalling once again the notion of cumulative wisdom and the need for parental respect (Prov 30:11), as well as a willingness to recognize one's faults (Prov 30:12). Parental respect is taken up again in Proverbs 30:17, where the eye is made culpable and punishable. Wisdom is gained through respectful, not scoffing, observation of those more experienced, leading to reflection, not rejection. This latter renders one vulnerable to attack of the sort that makes it impossible to regain the right path. Correct use of a gift is constructive; abuse results in loss of that attribute. Those with "lofty" eyes (Prov 30:13) bring to mind the self-righteous Pharisee (Lk 18:9-14), while those with a survival-of-the-fittest mentality, exhibiting a violent, destructive nature, always willing to persecute the vulnerable, are included among this list of those whose attitudes and lives are clearly not governed by genuine fear of the Lord.

The numerical sayings generally follow a pattern in which the last of the cited examples provides the climax and often its real raison d'être. Examples of unfulfilled need and longing speak of lack of satisfaction tinged with grief and highlight a distinction between need, desire and demand (Prov 30:15-16). Complete fulfillment of the need on which each depends for its existence can never take place. To long for such a fulfillment is acceptable, yet to demand is to abuse the relationship between Creator and created. The leech's two daughters are thought to be the two suckers found at the head and tail of the leech. The relative unattractiveness of these scenarios is contrasted by instances of fulfillment and satisfaction (Prov 30:18-19) in which each plays its ordained role. In so doing, a mysterious yet beautiful liberty is exercised that defies comprehension and provokes wonder and awe.

The adulterous woman is then presented (Prov 30:20) as one who demonstrates an illegitimate fulfillment, satisfying her hunger yet becoming prisoner of a need to defend herself, of her conscience, and thus unable to fly free. She has usurped the position of another, providing a link with the following three verses (Prov 30:21-23) in which other roles are inappropriately assumed or exercised. Here, however, the theme becomes one of dignity and worthiness, coupled with an implicit questioning regarding competency. The earth's shuddering may reflect fear of the consequences at the hand of ineptitude or revenge but equally affirms the dignity of each person regardless of status—a dignity lost should the bearer find himself or herself out of one's depth or making use of an inappropriate resource.

One doesn't need to have high status to be wise (Prov 30:24-28): wisdom at its most basic means ensuring practical provision of food and secure dwelling places and community and communal cooperation coupled with humility and accessibility. Nevertheless, leaders, typically those with status, are expected to behave with the dignity inherent to their role as well as to fearlessly exercise the duties implicit to that role: protection, example and guidance (Prov 30:29-31, although note certain difficulties of translation). The advice on what to do after having blown one's trumpet or plotted in an underhand manner (Prov 30:32) draws many of the previous threads together, reiterating the need for individuals neither to esteem themselves too highly nor plan to undermine someone else. The inevitable consequences of such action, analogies of which are expressed so vividly in Proverbs 30:33, are bitterness, injury and conflict.

A Final Portrait of Wisdom (Prov 31)

This last chapter of the book raises a number of enigmas. It is divided into two separate sections (Prov 31:1-9, 10-31), with the final twenty-one verses in the form of an acrostic poem in which each line begins with a letter in the order of the Hebrew alphabet. Of immediate note is the heavy female emphasis throughout. Lemuel's mother (possibly the queen or a queen mother; see Prov 31:4) addresses her son in Proverbs 31:1-9, the first occasion that a woman instructs. Proverbs 31:10-31 focuses on the qualities of a good wife (Prov 31:10). Scholars debate over whether Lemuel's mother was also the author of Proverbs 31:10-31, with no convincing conclusions being drawn.

Lemuel, apparently a young or potential king, is urged by his mother to use and channel his strength in ways that benefit the weak and vulnerable rather than serve

Occupations, Skills & Crafts of Women

The daily activity of a woman in biblical times was governed by her occupational role and was partially determined by her socioeconomic level, culture, geographical area, marital status and age. While the occupational roles of women in the Old Testament continued into New Testament times, the freedom that Jesus Christ brought to women touched their hearts and must have permeated every aspect of their lives.

Common Occupations

The primary job of women was to make certain that the home operations ran smoothly. Food preparation required grinding grain for bread, baking bread, hauling water from a well or spring, harvesting or buying vegetables or meat, cooking, serving meals and cleaning up. Apart from daily food preparation, women were responsible for clothing the family, cleaning the home and probably in many cases helping in the fields. Usually the mother or other older female family members taught young children in the home. As the children grew older, sons went to school outside the home, but daughters continued their domestic education with their mothers.

Women living in rural areas and poor women in rural or urban areas would do most of the work themselves or perhaps engage the help of other female relatives or children. Urban and wealthier women could pay for help inside the home or could buy more items outside the home.

The importance of children caused a woman's role as mother to be crucial to a family's survival. The significance of a large number of children was a religious and symbolic one in many cultures, but the economic factor was also important. Particularly in an agricultural society, the workload of a family may make it essential to bring more children into the home. This was sometimes accomplished by incorporating extended family into a household but also depended on the birth of children. The birthing of children created two other occupations for women: midwifery (Gen 35:17; Ex 1:15-21) and wet nursing the babies (Ex 2:7; 2 Kings 11:2).

Women who had fewer responsibilities in the home had more opportunity to work outside the home. The woman described in Proverbs 31:10-31 is gifted in the business world and in the skills and crafts of the home. Lydia (Acts 16:14-15) sold purple fabric. Both women lived in urban areas and seem to have been of the middle or upper socioeconomic stratum.

Unique Occupations

Some women served as political leaders. Two examples are not necessarily to be emulated: Jezebel, wife and queen of Ahab (1 Kings 16:29-32), and Athaliah, wife of Jehoram and mother of Ahaziah, who ruled Judah after her son's death (2 Kings 11; 2 Chron 22:1—23:21). Esther, as queen to Ahasuerus, had an opportunity to show concern only for herself but chose to take a courageous stand that saved the lives of many people. The Queen of Sheba (1 Kings 10:1-13), Cleopatra of Egypt and Hatshepsut of Egypt are also examples of women in politically significant positions.

In the Old Testament, men and women who were said to be wise were sought as advisers and counselors. Joab brought one such woman from Tekoa to advise David (2 Sam 14:1-20). In a battle situation Joab was advised and aided by a wise woman (2 Sam 20:13-22).

Women were not allowed to be priests, nor were they allowed into the inner courts of the temple. However, they did have roles in religious life. Deborah ruled as a judge (Judg 4—5); the work of Priscilla and her husband, Aquila, helped to spread the gospel (Acts 18; Rom 16:3; 2 Tim 4:19). Female deacons, or deaconesses, seem to be addressed in 1 Timothy 3:11, although some scholars say that passage refers to the wives of deacons. Paul uses the word *deacon* to refer to Phoebe (Rom 16:1). And the presence of women prophets is undeniable: Miriam (Ex 15:20), Huldah (2 Kings 22:14-20; 2 Chron 34:22-28), Noadiah (Neh 6:14) and Anna (Lk 2:36-38). A woman named Jezebel in Thyatira who calls herself a prophetess is condemned (Rev 2:20).

Dishonorable Occupations

Women and men engaged in some occupations that were questionable or dishonorable. Seers and oracles were found in many ancient cultures, as were witches and sorcerers. Prostitution existed in brothels, in the worship of certain gods and goddesses, and in the courts of kings as concubinage. One prostitute, Rahab (Josh 2), is listed in the genealogy of Jesus Christ (Mt 1:5).

Some women were sold or captured into slavery or servanthood (*see* Ancient and Modern Slavery). Some were house servants; others learned various crafts and trades. In the Greco-Roman world, a female child was often unwanted and after birth was left to die from exposure (*see* Infanticide). Sometimes these girls were found and sold into slavery or prostitution.

Skills and Crafts

Women were almost exclusively responsible for spinning fiber into thread, a task that necessitated detailed knowledge of one of several looms. Women were also involved in weaving that thread into cloth, thereby gaining experience with one of three types of weaving looms. They then took that fabric and sewed it into clothing for their families.

Basketry involved harvesting plants, preparing the plant fibers and plaiting the strips into baskets. Food handling, preserving and processing vegetables and fruits, and baking were other skills in the ancient woman's repertoire. Acquiring these skills enabled women to move outside the home into business when the opportunities presented themselves.

Scripture contains evidence of women engaged in singing, playing instruments and dancing (1 Sam 18:6-7; 2 Sam 19:35; Ps 68:25; Eccles 2:8). Poetry is heard in the Song of Miriam, the Song of Deborah and the Magnificat of Mary (Ex 15:20-21; Judg 5; Lk 1:46-55; *see* Women as Psalmists).

Bibliography

J. M. Arlandson, *Women, Class and Society in Early Christianity: Models from Luke-Acts* (Peabody, MA: Hendrickson, 1997); A. Brenner, *The Israelite Woman: Social Role and Literary Type in Biblical Narrative* (Sheffield: JSOT Press, 1985) 15-83; C. Osiek and D. L. Balch, *Families in the New Testament World: Households and House Churches* (Louisville, KY: Westminster John Knox, 1997).

MARSHA ELLIS SMITH

---

his own ends. The "women" able to destroy him (Prov 31:3) hark back to Proverbs 5:8-10 and Femme Fatale, liaison with whom was equally destructive. No detail is given here about how or why women might be viewed in this way or perform this role, all the greater a conundrum given the fact that this advice comes from a woman. One can only assume the warning is seated either in the notion that the sexual act weakens men or that perhaps the danger of Femme Fatale is that she approaches, demands and usurps. By controlling, manipulating, possessing she weakens the king physically, in reputation and hence in prowess and ability to exercise his duties. His strength is rather to be used proactively, speaking for those without a voice, defending those in need of defense. Alcoholic beverages too can overcome one's powers of self-control, becoming master rather than servant, and although the queen mother acknowledges times and situations when they can be of benefit despite their potential danger, her concern is that her son should not compromise his ability to perform his duties efficiently, responsibly and with justice. She is called a valiant and virtuous woman.

Proverbs 31:10-31 has attracted much attention over the years, discussion focusing primarily on the identity of the wife (or woman; Hebrew permits both translations). Is she what she appears to be, the epitome of every man's conjugal dreams, or is she fulfilling some other role? Women's hearts quail at the prospect of the former, despite the fact that many twenty-first-century women seem to lead this type of life, juggling demands of work, family, house, church, society's poor. This omnicompetent woman has no blemish other than her perceived perfection.

No doubt men too look askance—their habitual raison d'être disappears, swallowed up in a whirlwind of feminine activity that means she provides food and clothing for the family, she oversees the servants, she buys and sells and conducts business, she rolls up her sleeves and works. She even has time and energy to look to the needs of the poor, offer charity and teach. She makes independent decisions (Prov 31:16), evaluates her own performance (Prov 31:18) and exercises sound judgment (Prov 31:26). She is active in both the public and the private spheres. The husband, meanwhile, confident in his wife's abilities and in her desire to do him good (Prov 31:11-12) and primarily on account of the reputation of his wife, devotes himself to civic causes (Prov 31:23), taking his place as judge at the city gate among those who administer justice (cf. Gen 19:1; 23:10; Ruth 4:1-12).

The passage reflects a remarkable perception of the value and dignity in women's occupations. The housewifely skills—not the most recent technology—sustains and nurtures human life. Women's abilities in the marketplace and in real estate are no less admired. The woman herself takes pride and pleasure in her excellent work (Prov 31:13). Both husband and wife exhibit qualities of wisdom and contribute to the good order of society. Their children grow to mature adulthood, standing on their own two feet and expressing their own opinions. The passage clearly indicates that the husband appreciates his good fortune, in no way sees himself diminished and is able to give all credit to his wife (Prov 31:28-29).

It seems likely therefore that this chapter is not intended to be exemplary or exhortatory. Scholars now recognize the ways in which this female paradigm of virtue mirrors aspects of Lady Wisdom's person and message. Lady Wisdom's parting invitation (Prov 9:4-6) was to enter her house and eat and drink with her; this final chapter can be seen as a phenomenological portrayal of her overall message set in the now-established household of wisdom. This idea is further backed up by the preceding chapters' suggestion that the life of

Spinning woman with work basket. (Proverbs 31)

a wise person is prosperous (Prov 8:18), where wisdom is valued (Prov 3:15) and bestows favor in return (Prov 4:6). Confident, even in face of an uncertain future (Prov 1:33), Wisdom is a public figure (Prov 1:20-33), industrious (Prov 8:22-31), strong (Prov 8:14) and female. All these aspects are found in the Femme Idéale of this chapter.

Nor is it probably coincidental that the man is seated at the city gate, where Lady Wisdom originally spoke (Prov 1:21). There is again something of reversal or combining of gender roles, the Femme

Idéale of Proverbs 31 portraying a number of aspects of typically male pursuits. As was the case for Proverbs 1—9, one wonders whether the allocation of a female personage is subtly to reinforce the message that wisdom is often found where it is least expected. Or perhaps the writer intends somehow to fuse Lady Wisdom's words with her young male attendant, originally observer rather than practitioner, bringing them together in such a way that this (the young man's future?) life of wisdom now has flesh and bones, soul and spirit, is practiced rather than preached. The son has eaten the sweet honey of wisdom (Prov 24:13-14), digested it and made it his own. In this way also, gender issues so important to the modern reader are sidestepped: the actor is male and female.

This chapter then might be seen to address a vital question that the message of the rest of the book has raised implicitly and explicitly throughout: If wisdom is essentially the personal acquisition of understanding and learning, what is one to do as a result of it? Put it into practice. Do not simply allow it to influence one almost surreptitiously, but actively seek and seize opportunities where righteousness can take root, grow and become an integral and unconscious part of life, not simply left at the level of the cerebral, of self-development. The necessary self-centeredness of the acquisition of understanding and wisdom is challenged and balanced by an outward, exterior focus and application that feeds back to the learner as he or she reflects and evaluates. Twentieth-century educational scholarship calls this an experiential learning cycle, the major additional component in Proverbs being the insistence on setting all reflection and evaluation within a worldview that has YHWH at its center: the fear of the Lord.

So the Femme Idéale of Proverbs 31 provides a fitting conclusion and summary to the book, bringing together theory and practice, learning and application, male and female, as well as issues of choice and rejection. The life portrayed is not one of passive, easy self-indulgence but rather an example of conscious decisions and choices that demand and impart strength (Prov 31:17, 25) of willpower and conviction. As the young man of Proverbs 1—9 needed to understand and be equipped for the task, so Proverbs 31 equally personifies a message found not only here but implicit throughout Scripture: "I have set before you life and death, blessings and curses. Choose life" (Deut 30:19). To do so is wise, and wisdom is life (Prov 8:35).

Bibliography. D. Atkinson, *The Message of Proverbs* (Downers Grove, IL: IVP, 1996); C. R. Fontaine, "Proverbs," in *The Women's Bible Commentary,* ed. C. A. Newsom and S. H. Ringe (Louisville, KY: Westminster John Knox, 1992); F. W. Golka, *The Leopard's Spots: Biblical and African Wisdom in Proverbs* (Edinburgh: T & T Clark, 1993); D. Kidner, *The Proverbs* (Chicago: IVP, 1964); W. McKane, *Proverbs: A New Approach,* Old Testament Library (London: SCM, 1970); J. Ruffle, "The Teaching of Amenemope and Its Connection with the Book of Proverbs, in *Learning from the Sages,* ed. R. B. Zuck (Grand Rapids, MI: Baker, 1995) 293-331; S. Weeks, *Early Israelite Wisdom* (New York: Oxford University Press, 1994); R. N. Whybray, *The Book of Proverbs* (Cambridge: Cambridge University Press, Cambridge, 1972); R. B. Zuck, ed., *Learning from the Sages* (Grand Rapids, MI: Baker, 1995).

ALISON LE CORNU

ECCLESIASTES

Introduction

Women who investigate the biblical text eventually encounter the alternately disturbing and reassuring realities expressed in Ecclesiastes. While scholars differ as to whether these views are a comfortable fit with orthodoxy and debate how to label and understand the various attitudes expressed, Ecclesiastes unquestionably speaks to the frustrating and tedious nature of much of life, the anguish over the brevity of life and finality of death, and the pain of incessant injustice.

Recurring expressions and the structure of the book contribute to its profound message to women. Foremost among the expressions is the phrase that frames the message (Eccles 1:2 and 12:8) and is the hallmark of Ecclesiastes: "Vanity of vanities! All is vanity" or "Meaningless! Meaningless! . . . Utterly meaningless! Everything is meaningless" (NIV). It is significant to note that the Hebrew word *hebel,* which is translated "vanity" or "meaningless," means literally "vapor" or "breath." In other words, it refers to the transitory nature of all of existence and is an appropriate metaphor for life. This is a sobering thought, but it does not necessarily follow that everything is meaningless. Instead, the expression is frequently used in the superlative form, indicating ultimate pain and frustration at the temporary and elusive nature of all aspects of life that are so profoundly important.

Several additional phrases maintain a high profile. The first is "I saw"; what follows is a sensitive perception of the way things are. Second, most of the book speaks from the perspective of "under the sun." The writer observed the complex and often perverse functioning of the universe as a result of the Fall (Rom 8:20-21). Thus the text speaks frankly in terms that sound pessimistic, wounded and even fatalistic. A third phrase is "chasing after the wind," an apt metaphor that is used in conjunction with *hebel* to describe an enterprise that yields no tangible results. Finally, the author repeatedly returned to the refrain "eat, drink, and be satisfied," urging the immediate appreciation and enjoyment of what is present and known, wholesome advice in light of the uncertainty of all that is yet to come.

From the standpoint of structure, there is a constant counterpoint in Ecclesiastes between the presentation of a transitory and pain-ridden life and life that acknowledges the divine presence. The former is more prominent because that is the majority of each person's experience. Nevertheless there are those fleeting moments when the presence and participation of God in the world is profoundly evident. This literary structure helps to convey the message that is also clearly articulated in words.

Additionally there is a slow evolution of thought throughout the book from overwhelmingly negative attitudes at the outset to a more balanced outlook, even to the point of including two sets of tart, down-to-earth proverbs (Eccles 7:1-14; 10:1—11:6). After the midpoint of Eccelesiastes 5:1-7, which addresses intentional approach to God, there is a noticeable increase in the expressed perception that life is not only transitory; aspects of it are fundamentally evil (Eccles 5:13, 16; 6:1-2; 8:8-13; 9:3; 10:5). The observations take on a moral character, neutral objectivity is distinctly out of the question, and the end of the matter is the basic need to fear the judgment of God (Eccles 8:12; 11:9; 12:13-14).

The Hebrew title of the text is Qohelet and is related to *qahal,* which means "assembly" or "congregation." Perhaps Qohelet was one who addressed a congregation; in other words, a preacher. In light of what is said in the text, this is a rather interesting sermon. It becomes even more intriguing when the issue of authorship is raised. While there is a wide range of suggestions, all based on differing analyses of linguistic considerations as well as references within the text, as to the actual date of composition, it is evident that the reader is supposed to think of Solomon, the paradigmatic wisdom figure, recording his observations about the multifaceted life he had lived (Eccles 1:1, 12, 16; 2:1-9; 4:13; 12:9). The ambiguous identity of this personage is heightened by the fact that *qohelet,* used only in this book, is a feminine noun form. There are possible parallels with the public and challenging preaching of the woman Wisdom in Proverbs 1:20-33. Even though the descriptions of this author uniformly depict a man, *qohelet* once is accompanied by the corresponding feminine form of the verb (Eccles 7:27).

No human enterprise, no matter how earnest and valuable, is sufficient to meet life's ultimate needs. "Under the sun," the following are true: The more knowledge one has, the more grief (Eccles 1: 3, 18; 8:16-17); even after expending a life's effort, the very things striven for are empty and must be left upon death (Eccles 2:11, 18-23; 4:7-8; 5:10-12, 14-15); pleasure provides no lasting satisfaction and yet the desire for pleasure is insatiable (Eccles 1:17; 2:1-3, 10-11; 6:7); the injustices of life are inescapable (Eccles 4:1-2; 5:8-9); in the face of inevitable death, there is a lack of lasting personal importance (Eccles 2:15-16; 3:18-20; 9:11-12).

Nevertheless a new perspective is gained in God's presence. Because Qohelet painted the world with all its intolerable darkness, the faint glimmers of light at the recurring mentions of God are all the more tantalizing and thought provoking. What humankind needs is supplied by God, beginning with time and stability (Eccles 3:1-14), work and pleasure, relationships and knowledge (Eccles 2:24-26; 4:9-12; 5:18-20; 9:9). In the midst of this counterpoint comes the ultimate paradox that hope and meaning are found in the prospect of judgment (Eccles 3:17; 11:9). Nothing is trivial, no injustice will be overlooked forever, and fear of the Judge will be the best security (Eccles 12:13-14).

Ecclesiastes does not easily fall into an outline form, but it may be addressed in successive units, the scheme of which is presented below and will serve to direct the commentary. The division points are arbitrary, as will be evident in the obvious flow from one section to the next.

Outline

1:1-11	Prologue: Statement of Primary Themes
1:12—2:16	Initial Program of Investigation: Research, Exploration and Reporting
2:17-26	The Emotional Side: Despair Followed by Acknowledgment of the Hand of God
3:1-17	God and Time
3:18—4:16	Investigating Social and Psychological Stresses 1
5:1-7	In the Presence of God Perspectives Change
5:8—6:12	Investigating Social and Psychological Stresses 2
7:1-14	A Collection of Proverbs
7:15—8:6	Observations of a Pragmatist
8:7—9:12	How to Think About the Future: Death, Justice, Enjoyment
9:13—11:6	Making the Case for Wisdom Literature
11:7—12:7	At the Threshold of Darkness: Thinking Now About Old Age
12:8-14	Epilogue

Commentary

Prologue: Statement of Primary Themes (Eccles 1:1-11)

The varied sources of personal anguish are introduced at the outset of the sermon and resonate in each woman's heart. Weariness and endless toil are foremost among them, perhaps as a reflection of the curse pronounced on the ground and human effort (Gen 3:17-19). The intrinsic lack of satisfaction and constant desire for something more are pitted against monotony from every perceivable direction. Finally the ultimate insult to the rigor of laboring through life is the anonymity that death brings. Nevertheless there is another side to the picture even at this point. While the repetitive nature of existence does lead to ennui and frustration, it also bespeaks stability. That the natural world is predictable has a degree of assurance in the face of uncertainty, especially the uncertainty associated with death.

Initial Program of Investigation: Research, Exploration and Reporting (Eccles 1:12—2:16)

The descriptions of Qohelet that are suggestive of Solomon appear primarily in this section. Qohelet held a royal position in Jerusalem. His wisdom was the defining factor pressing him to investigate "all that is done under heaven" (Eccles 1:13) and guiding him through the potential pitfalls of his chosen course. His wealth and status enabled him to engage in the varied projects described in Ecclesiastes 2:1-11. These statements are reminiscent of the wealth that Solomon amassed as a result of commerce and tribute (2 Chron 9). Three times (Eccles 1:17; 2:3, 12) Qohelet indicated that his research program ranged into areas of folly as well as wisdom, and his attitude toward women appears to have been part of that folly (Eccles 2:8; cf. 1 Kings 11:1-8). His preliminary conclusion was a capsule of what follows in the book. Objectively something about wisdom seemed to be better than folly, but the prospect of personal mortality dampened the moral compulsion to act wisely (Eccles 2:15-16). Furthermore, even in the early stages of investigation, the pain of knowledge is evident. God has laid an "evil matter" on humankind (Eccles 1:13 lit.); some things are irreparably twisted (Eccles 1:15); and with wisdom is bound to come anger or distress and pain (Eccles 1:18).

The Emotional Side: Despair Followed by Acknowledgment of the Hand of God (Eccles 2:17-26)

Qohelet's response to the inevitability of death and the apparent futility of hard work intensified. He expressed hatred for life and its inevitable stresses. All were pronounced evil and a vapor because that for which everyone labors passes out of one's control, a crisis of significant proportions. Each of the book's characteristic phrases appears in this context, and the emotional anguish associated with the enterprise is palpable. It is evil and accompanied by anger and pain. Nevertheless the heart that perceives the giving hand of God in all things will enjoy God's provision, even in the midst of distress.

God and Time (Eccles 3:1-17)

Implicit in the preceding conclusion is a call to rein in the anxious imagination about the unknowns in the future. This poem about time imparts confidence that there is appropriate and planned order to all circumstances. In the ancient world, where the individual was bound into the community, women were integral to each passing phase of life. The poem commences with the extreme points, giving birth and accepting death. Events that are parallel to starting and stopping life come next—planting and uprooting, killing and healing. Work in the fields and the home, relationships and emotional responses are all represented. As even the structure of the poetry indicates, life's experiences are balanced, and both good and evil are to be expected. Nevertheless these good and evil counterpoints are not presented with uncompromising rigidity. On the contrary, the aspects that are good switch positions with those that are evil as the poetry develops. That is reflective of the experienced uncertainty as humankind progresses from milestone to milestone in the time-bound sphere. The closure to the list has the significant pairing of love and hate, followed by war and peace.

Then comes another paradox. While there is a profound sense of eternity planted deep in the hearts of humankind, it is impossible to know anything beyond the present. Nevertheless there is a call to trust God and to act in accordance with belief in God's providential ordering of events. The premise that what God does will endure forever introduces a forceful moral component into the way humankind chooses to deal with the vicissitudes of life; people are to fear God because the injustices of all time, past, present and future, will be brought to judgment.

Investigating Social and Psychological Stresses 1 (Eccles 3:18—4:16)

Qohelet returned to the painful reality of mortality, coming to grips with the humiliating aspects of it. In the disintegration of the physical body and the return to dust, humans are no different from animals. That, in conjunction with the call to enjoy work, is again reminiscent of Genesis 3:17-19. After the honor of being given the mandate to care for the earth (Gen 2:15), being reduced to dust was a searing reminder of the corruption of sin and death.

Qohelet remarked on the tainted motives, envy and lack of contentment, that prompt all human achievement and drive a person to endless striving. And yet the fools who do not work but fold their hands "consume their own flesh" (Eccles 4:5). Qohelet recognized the nurturing power of mutually interdependent relationships, especially in contexts where human frailty is particularly evident. Lack of contentment on the individual level is paralleled in the sociopolitical arena; loyalty fades fast with each successive ruler.

In the Presence of God Perspectives Change (Eccles 5:1-7)

Even when God is the primary objective of the quest, there are cautions for the one who seeks that encounter. It is a fool who approaches God with no sense of remorse over evil and with an excess of words. Qohelet twice used the figure of dreams, which come and go haphazardly and are beyond conscious control, to illustrate the dangerous potential toward sin that lies in multiple words. The text is particularly emphatic about vows, words uttered with moral intent in the presence of God, and the necessity of carrying through on them. Recognizing that God is actively and personally responsive to words, Qohelet's advice is simple and profound: Listen, and fear God.

Investigating Social and Psychological Stresses 2 (Eccles 5:8—6:12)

In light of the divine Presence, the previously articulated sources of personal anguish are now recognized as a grievous evil (Eccles 5:13, 16; 6:1-2). In passing Qohelet cast a somewhat jaded and resigned glance at oppression, injustice and lack of contentment. What continued to bring distress, however, was that personal effort seemed to be thwarted no matter what the context, and death nullified all endeavors. The weight of wealth and honor and labor contrasted sharply with *hebel* and chasing after wind. What Qohelet continued to see with frightening clarity was that a death-ridden world is an unmitigated evil; "under the sun" is darkness. Nevertheless the toil that enables a person to eat and drink is a gift of God. All can and must be enjoyed, fleeting as the experiences might be.

A Collection of Proverbs (Eccles 7:1-14)

Contemplating death and mourning continues as a persistent theme, and it is better than the frivolity in which the author had also engaged. Many of the proverbs are evaluative; recognition of something that is better implies the ability to discern between good and evil. Qohelet explored wisdom and folly and concluded that wisdom and knowledge have a protective function that wealth does not have.

Another glance at the matter from "above the sun" followed. God ordained good and evil, and it is an exercise in futility and hubris to think that humans can change these things.

Observations of a Pragmatist (Eccles 7:15—8:6)

Qohelet's statement in Ecclesiastes 7:15 sets the stage for the forthcoming observations: "I have seen everything in the days of my breath *[hebel]*." Life was exceedingly transient, yet it had been sufficient for him to experience all the perversities "under the sun," and he was left without idealistic expectations or a false sense of personal righteousness or wisdom.

Nevertheless Qohelet was driven again to determine as much as possible about the depths of wisdom, all the while recognizing that it was impossibly far off (Eccles 7:24). The irony is that Qohelet more systematically than ever pursued the quest: "I turned my mind to know and to search out and to seek wisdom and the sum of things" (Eccles 7:25). Again this intention included a foray into the dark side of folly and madness, but now Qohelet linked them with wickedness. The mention of folly, joined in Proverbs with the figure of an adulterous woman and the known experiences of Solomon, may have prompted the next rueful observations about the woman whose heart and hands are snares. This is not the statement of a misogynist. Instead it acknowledges from the perspective of the Solomon figure the horrifying bondage of relationships with evil partners and is reminiscent of the good advice King Lemuel received from his mother (Prov 31:1-3). Avoiding this trap is dependent on one's relationship with God.

Qohelet's next utterance, introduced here with the feminine verb form (Eccles 7:27), posed again the incomprehensible riddle of being human. Driven to seek order, Qohelet meticulously went through the data one by one, this time in terms of persons, but still the results were impossible to categorize: "One man *[adam]* among a thousand I found, but a woman among all these I did not find. See, this alone I found, that God made human beings [*ha'adam*] straightforward [or upright], but they have devised many schemes" (Eccles 7:28-29). In other words, the perversity of the human heart and mind complicates existence exceedingly; the ambiguity of the poetry reinforces that conclusion.

How to Think About the Future: Death, Justice, Enjoyment (Eccles 8:7—9:12)

Qohelet again confronted present and future unknowns and the power of death and wickedness, and more firmly lodged the discussion in the context of God's inscrutable but ever-present control (Eccles 8:12-13, 15, 17; 9:1, 7, 9). There is a blending and merging of opposites; the righteous and the wicked all face the same encounter with death (Eccles 9:2-3), and no one knows when the divide will be crossed and how (Eccles 9:11-12). In that framework, life is then opposed to death and life is deemed better because, cruel as it might be, life still has memory, deep emotions, companionship and the prospect of personal engagement.

Making the Case for Wisdom Literature (Eccles 9:13—11:6)

The second collection of proverbs is introduced by a narrative with a predictable twist; the wisdom of a poor man saved a city, and yet he was neither remembered nor honored for his wisdom. Nevertheless the value of wisdom is recognized, and there follows a series of memorable word pictures and tidbits of advice that encapsulate keen observations about nature and human nature. The fool is prominent, illustrating characteristics to avoid. Reversals and ironies abound, chance is acknowledged, and yet there is also some degree of predictability in cause-and-effect sequences. There comes a point, however, beyond which advice and observation cannot penetrate. The mystery of God's creation is lik-

Pyxis (a round decorated box used by women to store small possessions) depicting women holding distaff and hand-held loom. Seated figure glances toward the door of the marriage chamber. (Ecclesiastes 11:6)

ened to the miracle of life ("bones") developing in the mother's womb. Humankind is given the mandate to be active stewards of creation in spite of the fundamental inability to predict or control the outcomes of those endeavors.

At the Threshold of Darkness: Thinking Now About Old Age (Eccles 11:7—12:7)

From the vantage point of light and vigorous youth, the audience of Qohelet is urged to think ahead to the vast time chasm of darkness and to the test that is old age. While everything is pronounced *hebel,* nothing is inconsequential because God will bring each person into judgment, a good reason to fear God and remember the One who created humankind. Only that mindset will provide sufficient preparation for the grim task of navigating through physical disintegration until death and assisting others on that journey. The poignant metaphors of old age and death are heartrending. These are the days in which no pleasure is found, when vision dims into darkness, limbs once strong give way, teeth fall out and hearing fades, sleep escapes, all desire is gone, and terrors invade because of frailty. The vessel bearing life is shattered and returns to dust (Gen 3:19). At this extremity, Qohelet extended a profound source of hope; the spirit goes into the care of God who gave it. This is the closing answer to all the expressed despair at the prospect of death.

Epilogue (Eccles 12:8-14)

Having acknowledged the spirit's return to God, it is difficult to construe Ecclesiastes 12:8 as a final frustrated outcry against lack of meaning. Rather, it reiterates the brevity, from beginning to end, of the human endeavor. The epilogue then presents the qualifications of Qohelet and the value of carefully articulated words of wisdom. Finally, lest the message have gotten lost, the best chosen lifestyle is one that is founded on the fear of God and obedience. In the prospect of judgment lies ultimate hope.

Bibliography. J. L. Crenshaw, *Old Testament Wisdom: An Introduction,* rev. ed. (Atlanta: John Knox, 1998); D. C. Fredericks, *Coping with Transience: Ecclesiastes on Brevity in Life* (Sheffield: Sheffield Academic Press, 1993); D. Kidner, *The Wisdom of Proverbs, Job, and Ecclesiastes: An Introduction to Wisdom Literature* (Downers Grove, IL: IVP, 1985); T. Longman III, *The Book of Eccelesiastes,* New International Commentary on the Old Testament, ed. R. K. Harrison and R. L. Hubbard Jr. (Grand Rapids, MI: Eerdmans, 1998).

ELAINE A. PHILLIPS

SONG OF SOLOMON

Introduction

The Song of Solomon, or more accurately the Song of Songs, is one of the most beautifully written books in the Bible, full of evocative imagery and superb use of language. Yet it is one of the most difficult books to interpret. In essence it is love poetry, and as such it is unashamedly erotic, so much so that early Christian commentators quote a Jewish saying that the book should not be studied until the reader has reached the age of thirty. Issues of authorship, date, form, canonicity and interpretation are controversial and interwoven; key themes include the voice of the woman, the community of women, eroticism and the Bible, the place of God, links with the Garden of Eden and notions of beauty and richness of imagery.

The title "Song of Songs" is the literal translation of the Hebrew *shir hashirim* (Song 1:1) and refers to the superlative nature of this song or poem. The superscription "which is Solomon's" has been taken to mean either that he was the author (in 1 Kings 4:32 Solomon is said to have written 1,005 songs) or that it was written about him. There is little internal evidence for its authorship. It cannot be determined whether the reference to a king in Song 1:4, like the shepherd references, is intended to be taken literally or figuratively. It has been argued that the man's reference to sixty queens and eighty concubines (Song 6:8) places the book on his lips early in his reign; alternatively this is a comparison meaning that the bride is more beautiful than the famed beauties of Solomon's courts. Similarly references to Solomon in Song 3:7-11 and Song 8:11-12 may be for poetic effect rather than being of historical significance. Suggestions of a postexilic date for the book would rule out Solomon as author.

The Song of Songs has a predominantly ahistorical character, which makes the task of establishing a date difficult. If the author is Solomon, then it must have been written in the mid-tenth century B.C. The reference to Tirzah in Song 6:4, if it is contemporary with the writing of the book, would date it to the period when Tirzah was the capital of the northern kingdom and thus before the early ninth century, when Samaria was built. However, there is no definitive way of telling if this is a contemporary or historical reference. The Song has a large number of words that are unique to it in the Bible; attempts to establish the date from parallels between these and other languages had resulted in a preexilic dating by some scholars and a postexilic dating by others. The bulk of modern scholarship tends toward a later date, possibly the fifth century B.C., a date supported by the placement of the book at the end of the Writings in the Hebrew Bible.

The ahistorical nature of the Song together with its poetic genre makes it difficult to identify any specific setting. It has been posited that the sophisticated language and references to the king belong to a royal court, and thus it is an elitist artistic composition, or alternatively that the subject matter belongs to folk poetry in popular culture, perhaps as used in betrothal or marriage ceremonies (*see* Marriage). The references to Jerusalem and surrounding areas may be evidence that it was written there or may reflect the central place of Jerusalem in Judaism, which could therefore be expected to be used as a literary motif.

The earliest evidence for the canonical inclusion of the Song of Songs comes in first-century debates, where the majority of rabbinical opinion deemed that the Song of Songs "defiles the hands," that is, was canonical; Rabbi Aqiba (d. A.D. 135) argued that "all the Writings are holy, but the Song of Songs is the 'Holy of Holies.' " By A.D. 100 its position was secure in the Jewish canon, being placed in the third section, the *ketubim,* or Writings, in the Jewish division of the Bible. It was later classified as the first of five *megilloth,* the scrolls read during the great feasts of the Jewish liturgical year, and was particularly associated with Passover. Its acceptance within the canon was based on its interpretation as expressing the relationship between God and the people of God. Similarly within the early Christian church, the Song of Songs was present in lists of canonical books in the late first and second centuries, attributed to Solomon.

Another area of controversy is the literary form of the book. There is consensus among scholars that it takes the form of poetry rather than prose; however, questions remain. Is it a disparate collection of poetry unified only by the theme of love poetry? a compendium, heavily edited? a single unified literary work? a collection of poems by the one author? There is no consensus on which of these is true; however, whichever of these viewpoints is supported seems to make little difference in the final interpretation.

There is within the Song of Songs a coherence of style and structure, albeit possibly the product of later editing, within which a series of discrete units can be identified. Scholars have reached no agreement as to the number of units, ranging in their analysis from six to thirty-one; this is complicated by the difficulties in assigning textual units to each of the speakers whom scholars have distinguished.

There are two main strands of interpretive tradition for the Song of Songs. The first is the natural, literal meaning, whereby the Song is a poetic composition that explores the dimensions of human love. This interpretation is exhibited in the Septuagint, wherein the translator tends to use extremely literal language, to the extent of being more bluntly erotic than the Hebrew text. This literal interpretation was common in the first century but was largely displaced by the allegorical interpretation in the second and third centuries and did not return with any frequency until the eighteenth century. Such an interpretation is consistent with a reading of the Song of Songs as wisdom literature, testifying by implication to a God who is concerned with every detail of human life.

The allegorical strand of interpretation, in which the Song is understood as expressing the relationship between God and Israel (in Jewish exegesis) and Christ and the church (in Christian exegesis), dominated from the third to the eighteenth centuries and provided a rich resource for sermons and commentaries. It is exemplified by Bernard of Clairvaux, whose *Sermones in Canticum* make up an eighty-six-sermon series on selected verses and themes from the Song, exploring the spiritual dimensions of human experience. The Song was a relatively popular sermon text for the sixteenth-century Reformers and their followers, notably Martin Luther, John Calvin and the Puritan divines, again interpreted allegorically. Such an allegorical reading emphasizes links between the Song and prophetic literature, in which the marriage relationship is used as a model of the relationship between God and Israel (see Hos 1—3; Jer 2—3; Ezek 16; 23; Is 50; 54; 62); in Christian thought it also reflects the language of Ephesians 5.

In contemporary interpretation there is a move to draw together allegorical and literal readings of the text in order to more fully experience its richness. In this view the Song is understood as more than just a celebration of human love; it is intended by its authors to be read symbolically, describing the intense love between God and God's people, using the language of human love as the least inadequate way of describing that love. There is a renewed interest also in the garden setting in relation to theology of the land and to the Garden of Eden.

Perhaps the most conspicuous characteristic of the Song of Songs is that well over half the book is spoken by a woman. Women are largely silent in the Bible, whether by deliberate choice or simple omission; female authorship is rarely seriously posited of biblical texts. The lovers, male and female, are equal in the way they give voice to their relationship; the volume of the woman's speech outweighs the man's speech. Nor, in contrast with other writings of the period, is any inferiority implied in the woman's appearance, intelligence, will or emotions. The man and the woman each have freedom in word and act, although there are hints of the limit of the woman's freedom in the actions of the night watchmen (Song 3:3; 5:7). Desire is reciprocal: man and woman meet in full mutuality in the Song, each enriching the other's life.

Throughout the Song the woman appeals to the daughters of Jerusalem. This chorus functions as her peers, those to whom she gives advice as one who has learned from experience. They allow the woman to give voice to her love and represent the role of the hearer—the community—in validating love. Communities of women have traditionally provided support, encouragement and advice. In the Song of Songs they are similarly called on to be tradition bearers in the wisdom of love, that between a woman and a man and that between humanity and God.

The Song of Songs, like the book of Esther, does not specifically mention God. However, its place in the canon among the Writings presupposes the presence of God, as Creator of all things, which forms such an important basis for imagery in this book. It is common among the Writings to assume rather than explicitly invoke the presence of God amid ordinary life. Furthermore, the Song contains a vast number of quotes from and allusions to other Old Testament texts, thus placing it firmly within the tradition of the covenant relationship of God with Israel. Thus the allegorical interpretation of the Song of Songs finds God in the person of the male lover.

The language of the Song of Songs is dominated by garden imagery. This evokes recollections of the Garden of Eden (Gen 2—3), the place where man and woman live in harmony and walk with God. In the Song of Songs we see suggestions of the restoration of that harmony, which had been destroyed in the fall.

The Song of Songs, as a poetic work, is rich in its use of language. It has a lyrical quality and is full of the language of the senses: seeing, touching, tasting, hearing and smelling. One of the difficulties in understanding such rich metaphorical language is in determining whether images are literal or figurative. In some cases the absurdity of the images points to their being figurative, such as the man's lips as lilies distilling liquid myrrh (Song 5:13). In others it is less clear, such as the reference to the man as shepherd (Song 1:7-8) and king (Song 1:12), which when taken literally have given rise to speculation about the book's authorship.

Images, similes and metaphors are drawn from nature, art and architecture, particularly in the lovers' praise of each other's bodies. These descriptions are not intended to be literal but rather to evoke the beauty they find in one another. A sense of playfulness pervades the Song.

Outline

1:1	A Frame of Reference
1:2-6	Inviting Love
1:7—2:7	Finding Complementarity
2:8-17	Yearning Fulfilled
3:1—6:3	Searching for the Lover
6:4—8:4	Exploring Dimensions of Love
8:5-14	Universalizing Love

Commentary

A Frame of Reference (Song 1:1)

The opening verse provides a frame of reference for the book. The title "Song of Songs," a superlative form, denotes this as the highest of all songs; the relative clause, "which is Solomon's," may be understood as denoting Solomon as author, probably alluding to 1 Kings 4:29-34, or as subject of the song (see discussion of authorship above). Perhaps more importantly it establishes the Song's significance within the Writings and points to wisdom as a possible premise for interpretation.

Inviting Love (Song 1:2-6)

The woman, with an invitation to love and a brief self-description, introduces the Song of Songs. The love invited, *dodim,* encompasses all aspects of lovemaking (cf. Prov 7:18; Ezek 16:8; 23:17; Song 1:4; 4:10; 5:1;

7:13). The woman is the initiator in the Song's presentation of the relationship, as she proclaims the superlative nature of her lover and of their love. The self-description of the woman, speaking to the chorus, the daughters of Jerusalem, challenges stereotypes of beauty within some traditions. No longer is beauty akin to fairness of skin; here, darkness of skin, accentuated by time in the vineyards, is celebrated.

Finding Complementarity (Song 1:7—2:7)

What follows is a dialogue between the lovers, each extolling the beauty of the other using imagery drawn from the world around them. It begins with the woman's question to her lover, using language that he then adopts and develops in his response, a pattern that is often repeated in the Song. Where one pauses, the other picks up the conversation, creating a sense of the complementarity of the lovers. The woman's opening question is of particular interest, as she demands that her lover tell her the whereabouts of his flocks. Whether she means this literally or figuratively, as an allusion to his dwelling, this is no submissive or passive stereotype of a woman.

The woman's reference to her lover as shepherd (Song 1:7) and king (Song 1:12) has precipitated a great deal of speculation about the identity of her lover. The shepherd analogy is consistent with the lover's drawing upon pastoral imagery in his description of the woman (Song 4:1-2; 6:5-6); however, some interpreters have questioned this on the grounds of incompatibility with the description of him as king. This assumes that the language of love in the Song is uncharacteristically literal. Furthermore, the Bible provides a precedent for a shepherd king in the person of David. And if the Song is interpreted allegorically, it coheres with the wider biblical witness of God as shepherd and king.

The mutual extolling of beauty, which assumes the presence of both lovers from Song 1:7—2:2, shifts to remembrances of the past and a sense of yearning on the part of the woman for her now apparently absent lover. She concludes with a formal caution to the "daughters of Jerusalem": "do not stir up or awaken love until it is ready!" This formula reappears twice more (Song 3:5; 8:4) and speaks of the pain experienced when love comes at the wrong time, when one is unable, unwilling or not yet ready to consummate it. This caution anticipates two late scenes (Song 3:1-5; 5:2-7) in which the mistiming of love is dramatically portrayed.

Yearning Fulfilled (Song 2:8-17)

Here the yearning is fulfilled—the desired lover appears. This section is dominated by the image of the beloved as a young stag or gazelle and the incredible bounty of creation, reminiscent of the Garden of Eden (Gen 1—2). There is a sense that creation looks on love and smiles, giving its blessing. We know that spring will inevitably follow winter, yet it is a source of surprise and joy; so too the arrival of the lover is heralded as inevitable, also bringing joyous surprise. Song 2:16-17 reminds us of the mutuality of the lovers, each belonging to the other, a principle taken up in 1 Corinthians 7:4.

Searching for the Lover (3:1—6:3)

The third chapter of the Song begins with the woman's search for her missing lover. This and the similar account in Song 5:2-8 speak of the dangers inherent in love that is ill timed. They have been particularly rich grounds for allegorical interpretation, with images of the soul's search for God and God's search for the soul (particularly Song 5:2) and the need to respond to God's love. The depth of human passion becomes an expression for the passionate love of God.

Although the woman searches for her lover, the compromised position of women is seen in the actions of the watchmen, who are said not only to find her (Song 3:3) but also to beat her (Song 5:7). Those who are supposed to be the protectors become the aggressors.

The description of Solomon (Song 3:6-11) has little connection with what precedes or follows it; it intrudes into the flow of the Song. It contrasts strongly with the monologues and dialogues of the lovers, and while some commentators have seen this section as evidence that the Song is by or about Solomon, it is perhaps more helpful to understand it, with its references to a royal wedding, as an idealizing of the love of the woman and her lover.

However, in Song 4:1 we return to the lovers. This is the first extended description of the physical beauty of the woman, using evocative similes from the world around the lovers. The language is figurative: there are dangers in trying to find parallels for every

Glimpse inside window reveals intimate scene. (Song of Solomon 2:9)

element. There is a rich use of garden imagery, which harks back to the Garden of Eden, when all creation was good. Unlike many stereotypes of woman as temptress, here her physical beauty is something to be celebrated and enjoyed, the very gift of God. If we follow the allegorical interpretation, this section suggests that humanity is a source of great joy for God; it speaks of the great love and tenderness felt by God for God's people.

A similar pattern can be found in Song 5:1—6:3. The search for the lover is again followed by a vivid description of the beloved. However, this time the search, the mistiming of love, is tragic. The lover comes to the woman; she is too slow, and he leaves. Her search for him ends not in the joy of reunion but in the sorrow of assault. The extended description of the beloved is, unlike Song 4:1-15, of the lover, the one who is absent. Yet again the language used is that of the land, that of the garden, which becomes the language of love.

Exploring Dimensions of Love (Song 6:4—8:4)

This section further explores the dimensions of love. The descriptions become more explicit; there is a sense of growing passion. The language of the Song of Songs is unashamedly erotic. A number of commentators have in recognition of this opted for an allegorical reading of the Song of Songs as less offensive. However, the offense of such language lies in a view of human embodiment and sexuality as fundamentally evil, part of creation marred by the fall. An alternative view, grounded in creation, is that the human body and sexuality are part of the rich blessing of God and therefore are to be celebrated. Like so many of God's gifts in creation, sexuality has the potential for great good but can be misused for evil. The pleasure of heterosexual love exhibited in the Song of Songs coincides with the general tenor of wisdom literature, which identifies the place of God in everyday life.

Song of Songs is lavish in its descriptions of beauty. Beauty is perceived through the eyes of love and is of a superlative nature. It is to be recognized and celebrated. The language used to depict the beauty of man and woman is concrete and visual. One would not be wise to use these images to try to create a portrait of either the man or the woman; taken literally the images appear ludicrous. This highlights the way in which culture shapes our notions of beauty. A description of a woman as black and beautiful (Song 1:5) or more sustained descriptions (e.g., Song 4:1-15) affirm notions of beauty other than traditional white Western stereotypes and challenge assumptions associating light with good and pure, and dark or black with bad and sin. The Song of Songs presents a world in which such simplistic assumptions cannot be made.

Universalizing Love (Song 8:5-14)

This section contains a number of apparently disparate fragments that echo other parts of the Song. Most significant among them is the climax provided by Song 8:6-7, which universalizes the love exhibited elsewhere in the book. As such, these verses bear the greatest resemblance to traditional wisdom literature. Love is portrayed as a primeval force of intimacy, stronger than the chaos of a creation marred by sin and death.

Song 8:5 appears to have no connection with the other material in this section; however, taken with Song 8:8-12 it forms a fitting conclusion to the song. Again prompted by the questioning of the daughters of Jerusalem, it surrounds the lofty pronouncement about love (Song 8:6-7) with the story of the awakening of that love—from birth, past the protective custody of the brothers (Song 8:8-9), to the woman's affirmation of her beauty, maturity, independence and love (Song 8:10-12)—returning to the imagery of the vineyard (Song 1:6). The structure of the beginning of the song is repeated in inversion, first a section of self-description and then in conclusion, the woman's call to her lover. However, this story of love is not completed. There is no ending, only an unresolved invitation to love.

Song of Songs could be understood as a superb love poem, evocative and rich in imagery. As such, it sets forth a high standard for mutual love and encourages the celebration of love and beauty. However, as we understand the further dimension of God's love, it becomes an intimate invitation into relationship with God, celebrating the goodness of love, the beauty of passion and the tenderness of God.

Bibliography. A. Bloch and C. Bloch, *The Song of Songs* (New York: Random House, 1995); A. Brenner, *The Song of Songs* (Sheffield: Sheffield Academic Press, 1989); E. Davis, *Song of Songs* (Louisville, KY: Westminster John Knox, 2000); R. E. Murphy, *The Song of Songs* (Minneapolis: Fortress, 1990); M. Pope, *Song of Songs,* Anchor Bible 7C (Garden City, NY: Doubleday, 1977).

RAEWYNNE J. WHITELEY

ISAIAH

Introduction

The longest composition in the corpus from the Hebrew prophets, the sixty-six chapters of the biblical book of Isaiah are held together by common themes and phrases, such as "the Holy One of Israel," "Zion," "justice," "salvation" and "righteousness." Sections from earlier passages are quoted or alluded to in later passages, and other areas of continuity exist such as details about the prophet (e.g., Is 6—9; 36—39; 40:1-8) and the collapse of Babylon (Is 13—14; 46—47). However, modern scholars have claimed to detect the work of at least two, possibly three, prophets within the book. The historical context of the literature spans more than two centuries, and literary studies point to the style of more than one author. For the purposes of this commentary I shall explore both perspectives, for and against unity, and leave readers to decide for themselves.

Arguments Concerning the Unity of Authorship

At the outset of this discussion it is important to state that the inspiration of the book of Isaiah is not in question. Whether a human author or authors penned the sixty-six chapters of Isaiah in its entirety or in its various parts, the book remains the enduring Word of God.

The unity of the composition of Isaiah was not questioned until the scientific inquiries of the eighteenth century. External evidence from various sources favors unity. These sources include the Dead Sea Scrolls, which reveal no break in the writing between the critical thirty-ninth and fortieth chapters of Isaiah, and the apocryphal book of Ecclesiasticus, a writing not forming part of the accepted canon but found in the Septuagint, an ancient Greek version of the Old Testament.

Furthermore, in the New Testament, the prophet Isaiah is uniformly considered to be the author of the entire corpus. In addition, even Jesus quoted the prophet from the later disputed chapters. It is perhaps strange therefore that knowledge of another great author or school of authors is not categorically recorded, remembered or even thought about until the eighteenth century. It could even be argued that the geographical background throughout the sixty-six chapters is localized in Judah. Jerusalem and Zion are continuously addressed, whereas Babylonian territory is never definitively described.

However, although most biblical scholars can agree that Isaiah wrote the first thirty-nine chapters of the book, beyond that there is little agreement among critics. Chapters 1—39 deal clearly with the period of Isaiah's lifetime in the eighth century, chapters 40—55 look ahead to the return from exile, and chapters 56—66 look even further ahead. Those who argue for three distinct sections must accept and explain the common themes and terminology throughout the whole. Those who argue for unity must accept and explain these divisions. For the rest of the introduction, therefore, I shall discuss background information and textual commentary in line with these divisions, referring to them as First, Second and Third Isaiah without prejudice as to whether they represent distinct authors or not.

The Prophecies Concerning Jerusalem

Isaiah, the son of Amoz (2 Kings 19:2), lived in the second half of the eighth century B.C. during the reigns of four kings of Judah (Uzziah, Jotham, Ahaz and Hezekiah). He is broadly associated with Isaiah 1—39, although Isaiah 34—35 are thought to reflect the message, tone and style of what is sometimes called Second Isaiah. The prophet, whose name means "the Lord is salvation," lived all of his recorded life in Jerusalem. He married a so-called prophetess who bore him two sons, Shear-jashub, meaning "a remnant shall return" (Is 7:3), and Maher-shalal-hash-baz, meaning "the spoil speeds" or "the prey hastens" (Is 8:1-4; cf. Is 5:26-29), which are obviously symbolic names indicative of the contemporary political scene and the prophet's message. However, his wife is not reported as having an independent prophetic ministry. Her only action in the narrative is one of childbearing. Thus, although Israel did admit female prophets, possibly her title is honorary by virtue of her marriage to Isaiah. She may have been specifically mentioned because of her influence on him, contributing to his insightful use of maternal imagery.

Isaiah's ministry begins at the age of twenty-five at the death of King Uzziah (c. 742 B.C.), when Isaiah has a vision and prophecies (Is 6:1-13). Often using the rhythmic appeal of poetry, he speaks to God's people amid political, spiritual and military upheaval. Uzziah's reign had been one of peace and prosperity, but disputes between the southern and northern kingdoms would eventually lead to the downfall of both nations. The kingdoms had divided into the house of David, or Judah, and the house of Jeroboam, or Israel, in 930 B.C.

During the reign of Jotham (742-735), Judah and Israel were under assault from Assyrian and Egyptian armies, and Isaiah warned against making alliances with powerful neighbors, advising trust in God. Nevertheless, Ahaz and Hezekiah eventually ignored the prophet, and although Judah survived the Assyrian onslaught, it was swallowed up by the nations in whom the people put their trust (Is 30:1-5). Meanwhile, Israel had fallen completely to the Assyrians in 722, when Samaria was lost. In terms of the northern kingdom, Hoshea was Israel's last king. This meant that from that moment the Assyrians were twenty miles from the border of Jerusalem.

Isaiah's language at this time is lyrical and picturesque as he declares that the people of Jerusalem have "refused the waters of Shiloah that flow gently" in place of "the mighty flood waters of the River [Euphrates]" (Is 8:5-8). As if the poetry were not enough, Isaiah resorts to the dramatic act of walking around the streets of Jerusalem naked during the reign of Hezekiah, a sign of the way in which the king of Assyria would lead away his captives (Is 20:1-6). Although Hezekiah began to reform Jerusalem as a result of Isaiah's warnings, eventually his impatience got the better of his faith, and he revolted against Assyria (Is 36—37). Sennacherib swiftly crushed the rebellion and overran much of Judah (701 B.C.). Yet, despite the inevitable disintegration of Judah's nationhood, the prophet of Jerusalem predicted a coming savior to deliver God's people (Is 9:3-7; 19:16-25).

The Prophecies Concerning Babylon

Soon after 590 B.C. Jerusalem fell again, this time to the Babylonians, and all leading citizens were exiled to Babylon in 586. Isaiah 40—55 (or Second Isaiah as we may label these chapters) do not reveal an individual author by his life and personal identity but by the nature and content of his message. Even so, Isaiah of Jerusalem was known to have gathered a group of disciples around him to safeguard his messages for future generations (Is 8:16), and the messages from Second Isaiah may have come from this circle of disciples. Although some scholars see this as predictive prophecy by Isaiah of Jerusalem, others argue that it was written around the mid-sixth century (c. 540 B.C.).

The message of these chapters is directed to a group of exiles in Babylon. They are defined as upper- and middle-class members of Judean society (2 Kings 24:12-16). The prophet preached that God would save, restore and revive the people. He encouraged what must have been a demoralized and doubting audience. Although the fall of Jerusalem is stated to be a past event (Is 51:17-23), the prophet also speaks of the imminent fall of Babylon (Is 43:14-15; 47:1-15). This is a new exodus, the work of God. Cyrus, a little-known king of southern Persia, is named as the instrument through which God will set the Jewish people free (Is 44:28—45:4). In typical Hebrew fashion then, these chapters wrestle with the spiritual significance of the political and social events of the time.

The chapters of Second Isaiah hold the gods of Babylon in contempt. The prophecies attack idolatry and urge a return to God's law (e.g., Is 44:10-11; 57:13). But they speak of God's love not only for Israel but also for the whole world. Second Isaiah includes the poems of the suffering servant, one of which refers to "the servant" as "a light to the nations, that my [God's] salvation may reach to the end of the earth" (Is 49:6). Whatever the identity or possible multiple identities of the servant in Isaiah 40—55, the way of God to the salvation of the world was to be the way of suffering and service.

Exiled Jews slowly began to return home in 539, when Babylonia fell to the Persians.

The Final Chapters

Some scholars contend that yet another prophet completes the final section of the book of Isaiah (Is 56—66). It reflects the outlook of Second Isaiah, if indeed not the predictive prophecy of First Isaiah, for the messages these chapters contain are similar to the idealism of Isaiah 40—55. However, amid the optimism there are notes of despair.

Under the original edict from Cyrus, the temple in Jerusalem had finally been rebuilt in about 515 B.C. under the authority of Darius I (Ezra 6:1-5). The book of Malachi gives information concerning this time. It appears that despite the temple's existence, the true covenant religion of Yahweh was still being syncretized with folk religion and magical practices. Lack of holiness is blamed for the social evils that were occurring, including injustice and sexual immorality.

Thus, although the final section of Isaiah, sometimes called Third Isaiah, is concerned with the return of the Jewish exiles to Jerusalem and the building of a new community there—especially the temple—the positive advances are overshadowed by the prophet's frustration with those who would thwart God's plan of salvation. The final verse (Is 66:24) is a graphic and gruesome description of the fires of hell for those who rebel against God, righteousness and justice. To end the reading of this passage on a more hopeful note, Jewish custom dictates that the verses about "the new heavens and the new earth" (Is 66:22-23) be repeated after the reading of this verse, thus reiterating the optimism and encouragement offered by the earlier chapters of Isaiah.

Outline

1:1—12:6	Oracles About Judah and Jerusalem
13:1—27:13	Oracles About the Nations and About Judah's Restoration
28:1—39:8	Justice, Judgment and Deliverance
40:1—55:13	Restoration and Blessing
56:1—66:24	Obedience and Vindication

Commentary

We will look within the writings of Isaiah for themes that are of interest to women and men who care to look beyond the usual biblical interpretation. In exploring a number of thematic headings, we will reconsider what was envisioned and spoken of by the prophet in light of the particular position of women today.

Traditional God Language and the Book of Isaiah

The biblical God is the "unnamable" YHWH, Spirit and Holy Mystery. Moreover, Isaiah's preferred terminology for God is "the Holy One of Israel" (Is 12:6). It can be argued that exclusively masculine naming and imagery of God—Father, King, Warrior, Lord—distorts this biblical image of mystery that is complex, hidden from human reason and beyond gender. Nevertheless, the history of power struggle and gender dominance in the church provides a comparable pattern or paradigm into the arena of language that represents God. The church has a history of male, hierarchical dominance. The ensuing struggle for women to be recognized, heard and included is evident. The same can be said of God-language. There was a reason in ancient times for the exclusion of feminine symbols in preference for masculine, but in our time feminine symbols are not exclusively suggestive of the world, the flesh, pantheism and immanence. Thus, contrary to the ancient Near Eastern context, feminine language for God does not destroy the biblical and philosophical notion of divine transcendence. Confining the masculine to the realm of the mind, the spirit and the divine, while confining the feminine to the realm of the body, matter and the sinful is, when we consider the terminology of the Bible as a whole, unbiblical and ungodly. One contemporary proposal is to complement masculine imagery for God with feminine imagery making use of biblical materials. The book of Isaiah is a rich and remarkable resource for such a project as it contains numerous maternal images for God.

God is compared with "a woman in labor" (Is 42:14) and described as a mother carrying a child, giving birth and nurturing her offspring (Is 46:3-4). God is associated with a woman who cannot forget the child she has nursed and who, by definition, must have compassion for the child of her womb (Is 49:15).

Images of God as Female

The consistent witness of the church is that biblical references to divine gender must be understood relationally and analogically, for the God of the Bible is neither male nor female (sex), neither feminine nor masculine (gender). If understood univocally, gendered terms would contradict the affirmation that God is Spirit (Jn 4:24), lacking physicality (Deut 4:15-16) and the Holy One who is qualitatively other (Is 6:2-3; Hos 11:9; Rev 4:8).

With its masculine analogies dominating church life, the Bible's witness to the divine feminine—including feminine analogies that Jesus used (Lk 13:20-21; 13:34 par. Mt 23:37; Lk 15:8-10; Jn 3:5)—lay dormant until awakened by feminist scholars. Their gender consciousness activated, faith communities debate how to regard the Bible's privileging of the divine masculine and whether feminine and masculine analogies may be used in an equivalent way.

Those who view the Bible's privileging of the divine masculine as normative oppose any equivalent use of feminine and masculine analogies. For them, the inspired authors intentionally limited the divine feminine—through restricted grammatical forms and relative infrequency—in order to preserve God's character. Remove these restrictions, they argue, and the God of the Bible will be compromised. For example, extrabiblical forms such as Our Mother God and She inevitably distort perceptions of God by introducing sexuality and blurring transcendence. This approach sanctions patriarchal constructions of gender.

Those who view the Bible's privileging of the divine masculine as nonnormative advocate using feminine and masculine in equivalent ways. For them, the biblical pattern reflects God's accommodation to ancient patriarchal culture, in which the masculine was used to dignify and elevate. The litmus test for orthodoxy is not reproduction of biblical forms and frequencies but conformity to the biblical meaning of God's character. Accordingly, the orthodoxy of Pévé Christians in Africa who call God "she" is measured not by the gender of the pronoun but by the meaning assigned to it. *She* introduces sexuality and blurs transcendence only if users have those meanings in mind; the Pévé do not. This approach transcends patriarchal constructions of gender.

The female or feminine analogies that follow both reflect and transcend their social location. At times their meanings parallel those found in patriarchal constructions, such as nurture (Num 11:12) and immanence (Ps 131:2). At other times patriarchal constructions are transcended, as when the feminine denotes divine power (Is 42:14; 46:3-4; Hos 13:8) and transcendence (Gen 1:26-28).

Imagery Drawn from Women's Biological Activity

1. A mother suckling her children and responsible for their care (Num 11:12).

2. A mother who gave birth to the Israelites (Deut 32:18). Translations sometimes conceal female analogies, as in "unmindful now of the God who fathered you" (JB); the Hebrew verb for "fathered" refers exclusively to birthing by females.

3. A woman in labor whose forceful breaths are an image of divine power (Is 42:14). God threatens to come in power, a force likened to the air expelled from the lungs of a woman in transition.

4. A mother who births and protects Israel (Is 46:3-4; *see* Birth Pain Imagery). In contrast to idol worshipers, who carry their gods on cattle (Is 46:1), God carries Israel in the womb. God's promise to redeem Israel is secured by maternal compassion and protective power.

5. A mother who does not forget the child she nurses (Is 49:14-15).

6. A mother who comforts her children (Is 66:12-13).

7. A mother who calls, teaches, holds, heals and feeds her young (Hos 11:1-4). While first person syntax permits either parent to be speaking, the series of activities are those that a mother would likely do. Hosea may be presenting YHWH as Israel's mother over against the Canaanite mother/goddess figure.

8. Other maternal images (Job 38:8, 29; Ps 90:2; 131:2; Prov 8:22-25; Is 45:9-11; Acts 17:28; 1 Pet 2:2-3). Links between El Shaddai and breasts *(shaddayim)* and between divine compassion and womb *(rehem)* have been theorized.

Imagery from Women's Cultural Activity

1. A woman who exercises dominion; bearing the image of the transcendent God, she rules the earth as God's representative (Gen 1:26-28).

2. A seamstress making clothes for Israel to wear (Neh 9:21; cf. Gen 3:21; *see* Occupations).

3. A midwife attending a birth (Ps 22:9-10, 71:6; Is 66:9); midwife was a role only for women in ancient Israel.

4. A woman in authority, to whom her servant looks for mercy (Ps 123:2).

5. A woman working leaven into bread (Mt 13:33; Lk 13:20-21), equivalent to the masculine image of God in the preceding parable of the mustard seed.

6. A woman seeking a lost coin (Lk 15:8-10), equivalent to the masculine image of God in the preceding parable of the shepherd seeking a lost sheep.

Additional Images

Divine protection is analogous to the action of a bird sheltering her young (Ruth 2:12; Ps 17:8; 36:7; 57:1; 91:1, 4) or hovering overhead (Is 31:5). Divine guidance is likened to an eagle (Deut 32:11-13; Ex 19:4)—male and female eagles share the parental role of education and protection. Jesus' desire to protect Jerusalem is expressed through imagery of a hen (Mt 23:37 par. Lk 13:34).

The fierce image of God as a mother bear is associated with maternal attachment to one's offspring (Hos 13:8). God's rage against those who withhold gratitude is that of a bear "robbed of her cubs."

The Holy Spirit (Heb. *ru'ah,* feminine; Gk. *pneuma,* neuter) is associated with the birthing process (Jn 3:4-5; cf. Jn 1:13; 1 Jn 4:7; 5:1, 4, 18; Rom 8:20-23). Some ancient church traditions referred to the Holy Spirit in feminine terms, the Syriac church retaining a feminine pronoun until about A.D. 400.

Wisdom (Heb. *hokmah,* feminine; Gk. *sophia,* feminine), identified with God and personified as a woman (Prov 1:20-33; 8:1—9:6; 31:10-31), develops into wisdom Christology. Jesus Christ does the work that *sophia* does (Mt 11:16-30; Lk 7:35; Col 1:15-17) and is designated "the *sophia* of God" (1 Cor 1:24; cf. 1 Cor 1:30; 2:6-8; Eph 3:9-11).

Despite disagreement over form and frequency, those who seek to include the divine feminine in the church's discourse acknowledge one or more of three benefits. Feminine analogies clarify who God is by enriching the church's vocabulary, as well as clarifying who God is not by countering idolatry that results from literalizing masculine analogies. These analogies help equalize gender relationships and validate the public ministry of women by challenging patriarchal gender constructions; created in God's image, women and men alike can represent divine transcendence, immanence, power and nurture. And these analogies enhance spirituality; by seeing their work as work that God also does, women and girls gain a greater sense of their inestimable value.

Bibliography

E. A. Johnson, *She Who Is* (New York: Crossroad, 1992); V. R. Mollenkott, *The Divine*

Feminine (New York: Crossroad, 1987); G. Ramshaw, *God Beyond Gender* (Minneapolis: Fortress, 1995); L. J. Swidler, *Biblical Affirmations of Woman* (Philadelphia: Westminster Press, 1979); P. Trible, *God and the Rhetoric of Sexuality* (Philadelphia: Fortress, 1978); J. W. H. Van Wijk-Bos, *Reimagining God* (Louisville, Ky: Westminster John Knox, 1995).

MARGO G. HOUTS

However, we must be aware that all the pictorial language used in relation to God—whether it involves male or female imagery—is indeed pictorial. To push the imagery too far leads to idolatry. The range of imagery used by Isaiah prevents us from using any single image too literally.

The revelations of prophets are a paradigm for the intertextuality of biblical literature, that is, the investigation of the connection of literary texts with each other and with society. Such investigation gives rise to a dynamic dialogue between different biblical texts, culture and reality. We can also look toward the signs and symbols in language that produce layers of meaning in a single text. Subsequently, biblical revelation is concerned necessarily with the past, the present and the future, and features the divine message and human concern. This is especially true of the book of Isaiah. The messages it contains go beyond the truth and significance of their original context and reach out above, below, behind and beyond to encapsulate glimpses of God's world out of reach to the minds of the original authors. Just such a function of sacred texts makes the Bible still relevant, authoritative and inspirational in the lives of women and men today.

Appropriately, then, from a woman's perspective, theological reflection from Isaiah invites the audience to face difficulties and dream dreams. Avenues of hope are offered to a demoralized people. I say "appropriately" because women have been so often subject to oppression in the world and the church because of their biological sex and gender. All such women need support and encouragement to face hardships with courage, to never give up the vision of a just world, to step out in confidence when detractors would undermine their opinions and autonomy. Significantly, the words of the prophets are written in poetic language. Prophetic speech is an appeal, and appeals, as such, have a rhythmic form. Perhaps we should learn from the prophet's method as well as his message and make more use of poetry and rhythm in modern proclamations of the message.

Isaiah presents the reader with a strong image of God as "friend" (Is 41:8). This friendship of the Lord is a model developed by contemporary theologians, female and male (e.g., Sallie McFague and Derych Sheriffs). The same text is alluded to by James in his New Testament letter (Jas 2:23). And in a passage that begins with a reference to the vineyard (Jn 15:1-8; cf. Is 5:1-7), John the Gospel writer reveals to us how Jesus developed the language of friendship (Jn 15:12-15). Furthermore, in language redolent of Lamentations, Isaiah 49:14-26 "engages dialogically the voice of the Judahite community" (Newsom, 75). There is talk of reintegration, preparation and survival as the prophet speaks directly to the exiles. Tod Linafelt develops his analysis of the passage in Isaiah by commenting on the striking similarity between the opening line of Isaiah 49:14 and Lamentations 5:20, which is followed by a response from Yahweh in the persona of a mother (Is 49:15). Linafelt remarks that Yahweh's extended response answers the desolation of Lamentations: the return of the children that Zion had lost (Linafelt, 354-57). Linafelt shares Carol A. Newsom's conviction that Isaiah "utilizes the language and symbols of Lamentations as a means of imagining the return of the Babylonian exiles to Judah" (Linafelt, 356; cf. Newsom, 75). Thus the image of Yahweh as mother provides an especially strong rhetoric of survival.

When we survey the feminine images in the book of Isaiah, we find a collection of different messages, positive and negative. The language of Isaiah 1—4, especially Isaiah 3:16—4:1, denounces the women of Jerusalem for governing their men. While today's readers might accept that Isaiah was addressing a social injustice, they also have to question the conventional social hierarchy of the prophet's times. Similarly, Isaiah 50 places a female figure central to the text, but she is shamed and turned into an economic slave. She is subject to a male-initiated divorce by means of a document and sold because of debt, thus losing all personal freedom (*see* Ancient and Modern Slavery; Divorce). Sin is blamed for this situation, but the woman's suffering is not self-induced (*see* Sin). Athalya Brenner finds much of the prophet's propaganda judgmental, authoritarian, undemocratic, monologic, imperial, self-righteous or chauvinistic (Brenner, 136-50). I sympathize with this assessment, but we must be careful to take into account the historical particularity of the human author. The metaphors, imagery and symbolism are relevant to the times and cannot be judged easily by twenty-first-century ideology.

Brenner's criticisms, nonetheless, may suggest a first step in recontextualizing the biblical message of the prophet. We should not perpetuate the ignorance of an earlier time any more than we would want our own shortsightedness to be perpetuated. Thus, in a hermeneutic of faith toward the text, believing that God speaks through the Hebrew prophets, we can investigate the significance of the historical word for today. Obviously all biblical interpretation needs the rest of Scripture: the covenant, God's judgment and blessing. In First Isaiah the context is God's message to Judah in the eighth century, when the people were in fear of the Assyrians. Similarly, in Second Isaiah we find God's message to the exiles when the end of their captivity is imminent. Prophecy is used to confront people in their particular situation and time, and it rarely translates literally or word-for-word to a new age and circumstance.

Because some voices are overtly manifest in the prophetic texts while others are submerged, we do well to pay close attention to those that are often overlooked. Isaiah 40:1-11, for example, uses feminine imagery for both God and Zion as it offers guidance for life. In Isaiah 62:1-6, Jerusalem and the land are personified as female in the language of fulfillment, blessing and salvation for all the people. The feminine imagery is complemented by familiar images of God addressed as father (Is 63:16; 64:8) and God as warrior (Is 63:1-6), but the masculine images are often weighted more than the feminine ones. Nevertheless, we should not give exclusive attention to one and not the other.

An unusual scenario is depicted in Isaiah 54:1-10. God is portrayed as a husband who is sorry for abandoning his wife, and Jerusalem/Zion (the grieved and forsaken wife) is taken back in an act of love and reconciliation. However extraordinary this image might be in the context of a sixth-century oracle, it obviously should not be literalized. Perhaps the image says more about how bereft the nation of Israel is when separated from Yahweh and conversely how much the Lord yearns for an everlasting relationship between them to exist. This extraordinary "compassion" of the Lord has been the focus of some of Phyllis Trible's theology as she has explicated feminine and maternal imagery for God. The Hebrew word for compassion is *rahamim,* which is closely related to the Hebrew for womb *(rehem).* In the book of Isaiah these two concepts are often closely aligned

Wooden statue of a non-Egyptian woman with child. (Isaiah 46:3-4)

in God-language that depicts God's relationship with Israel (e.g., Is 46:3-4; 49:14-15). Furthermore, it is possibly significant that the feminine-gendered *Shaddai,* translated "LORD Almighty" (NIV), is the one who hovers over Jerusalem, protects, delivers, spares and rescues (Is 31:5).

In the chapters of Third Isaiah we find an expansion and elaboration of the feminine imagery for God first introduced in chapters 40—55. Significantly, the feminine voice (God), for the sake of justice and righteousness—for the sake of Zion—"will not keep silent" (Is 62:1). The concept of God as mother is reintroduced in Isaiah 66:7-14. There is an interchange of ideas here as the feminine is represented in the place of perfection (Zion) and in God. Ultimately, God is described as comforting Jerusalem "as a mother comforts her child" (Is 66:13).

Feminine images are not guarantors of egalitarianism in a patriarchal social construct. The politicization of gendered images has to be considered. Consider the image of the daughters of Zion in Isaiah, which refers sometimes to the whole of Jerusalem and sometimes to a specific group of women, a rhetorical device singling out women as particularly responsible for behavior the prophet of Yahweh decrees unacceptable (Is 3:16-26; 32:9-14). Sometimes the motif personifies Jerusalem or Zion as a "whore," a religious apostate engaging in fertility rituals, rites of child sacrifice and necromancy (Is 1:21-23; 57:3, 6-13). It is the "filth of the daughters of Zion" that causes judgment to hang over Jerusalem (Is 4:4). "She" then requires "comfort" when "her penalty is paid . . . double for all her sins" (Is 40:1-2).

While some scholars have uncovered women's active roles in the music of the religious cult (Is 32:9-14; *see* Women in Worship) and in mourning rituals (Is 3:16—4:1; *see* Grief and Bereavement), many readers will still be troubled by the apparent misogyny of the language and imagery. We must remember that readers are drawn into the text by the speaker and cooperate with the prophet in order to understand the text. In the natural way of things, readers side emotionally with the speaker (Brenner). It takes a concerted exegetical effort to read against the grain of an author's predispositions. The opponents of the prophet's propaganda do not have a voice. Brenner calls for a balanced reading of the text that takes into account the distasteful elements of the text as well as the glorious and inspirational passages. It is not sufficient to ignore passages that do not suit our contemporary views any more than it is right to infuse social, moral and theological authority into them in an unquestioning way. Essentially, however, the Hebrew prophets chose powerful life metaphors and symbols that carried the dynamic reality of their messages. Our job as interpreters may be to *recontextualize*—to enable symbols from the past of ancient archetypal significance to find expression anew in our context. In today's world, for example, the language of corruption, hypocrisy and deceit might replace that of harlotry and religious apostasy as a more effective indictment of society.

Perhaps another reaction is to view such texts with equanimity; the Bible by virtue of its historical particularity does contain sexism and patriarchal concepts. The conventional social hierarchy of God/ adult males/adult women, children, slaves and other chattel is seldom disputed. Nevertheless, we can look beyond the human fallibilities reflected in the text in interpreting biblical literature. Such interpretation discovers the Word of God as revealed by the Spirit and in keeping with the person and message of Jesus Christ.

Beauty and the Suffering Servant

Women have long been made aware of the aphorism that one must suffer in order to be beautiful. This concept carries a double irony in light of the ideas of beauty and the suffering servant in the book of Isaiah and in light of the Christian interpretation of this servant in the lives of women and men today.

When a contemporary Western woman opts out of the beauty and fashion industry, she refuses to be defined by patriarchal concepts of acceptable appearance. She can attract ridicule, for fashion and beauty (at least societal concepts of beauty) are instruments of power. This was especially true in biblical times as the culture made womanhood dependent on attractiveness to males. Today the beautiful and fashionable woman is an object of men's desire and an appendage to the successful man. She may have a degree of success and power, but it is frequently on men's terms: she has played by the rules and looks the part. Some women may object to this analysis, and there surely are social restrictions on men's appearance as well, but imagine the wife of a successful politician who is an accomplished lawyer not conforming to societal expectations of beauty and fashion. Imagine that she should dye her hair purple, wear clothes from Oxfam International and forswear makeup. This would obviously be unacceptable, especially in light of her husband's position. (If she were an unattached maverick academic, she might get away with it!)

The point, in reference to the book of Isaiah, is that beauty is of no significance to the final Redeemer. Isaiah's suffering servant is not a glorious king of beauty but an inconspicuous servant: "he had no form or majesty that we should look at him, / nothing in his appearance that we should desire him" (Is 53:2). However, the Hebrew Bible draws a sharp distinction between beauty existing as being and beauty existing as an event. Beauty is spoken about in terms of blessing. Salvation occurs when the blessing is returned to the people. In the beginning of Israel's history the promise of salvation is connected with the beauty of the land, the beauty of creation and the people of God's inheritance. This gift of blessing is the gift of life. As Claus Westermann (585) says, "Here, the selective tastes of the elite play no part." From a large variety of words, beauty is a descriptive quality of salvation because salvation is a blessing expressing satisfaction, even paradise: "The unspoilt effect of God's blessing is accompanied by beauty and by life that is considered and experienced as beautiful" (591; cf. Is 58:10-11; 62:2-3, 5).

There are four so-called servant songs in the book of Isaiah (Is 42:1-4; 49:1-6; 50:4-9; 52:13—53:12). They can be identified as separate and self-contained poems, although they are also comprehended as an integral part of the prophet's message. At times this message is of a specific individual, "the servant," whom God will raise to deliver the people of Israel. Yet this servant is identified in various ways, including, in the context of the Babylonian exile, Cyrus of Persia (Is 41:2-3; 45:1-7) and the nation of Israel (Is 49:3). Often, however, the servant is an enigmatic and unknown figure. He is an unlikely messianic figure to a Jewish reader because this servant suffers rather than demonstrates his power as an all-conquering king. Nevertheless, the last servant song (Is 52:13—53:12) has exerted a powerful influence on the Christian understanding of Jesus as the Messiah of the Old Testament speculation because of its correspondence with the passion of Jesus.

The savior figure is a defender of justice and righteousness. A king from the royal lineage of David (Is 9:2-7; 11:1-5), the figure is also a prophet, anointed to "bring good news to the oppressed" (Is 61:1). Jesus echoes these words in Nazareth (Lk 4:18-19). Christianity has focused considerable significance on the last of the four servant songs because it describes an individual who heals and redeems others through vicarious suffering (Is 52:13—53:12). Nevertheless, there are other interpretations of this passage. It has been interpreted as expressing Israel's confidence in the power of God to intervene on their behalf, to heal their wounds, to forgive their sins; it is as such a hymn of thanksgiving. Ultimately the question of who the servant is and how deliverance of the people can be achieved is subject to multiple interpretations. The emphasis of the passage, however, is repeated throughout Isaiah's tradition of transformation from defeat to victory, from humiliation to exaltation.

Some interpreters, such as Susanne Heine, have remarked on the special significance of this kind of Messiah in the lives of women. Initially, the significance of Jesus Christ the man is vital to humanity because it is considered especially necessary for a man in a patriarchal society to oppose the seduction of gendered power. Beyond this insight, however, a pattern of serving, renouncing, suffering and dying would not be interpreted as unusual for a woman either in ancient societies or in contemporary ones. The incarnation is where the Other draws near: near to the feminine in representing her otherness in male form yet near to the masculine also by representing her servanthood as a man. Part of the scandal of the particularity of God's incarnation in human history is that by living out the life of a man he is conceived in a way that society can perceive him; simultaneously, by his adopting the life pattern of a woman in terms of status and reception, he becomes an affront to the world. As Heine says, "A woman could not represent the humiliated because she herself is already where the people are. . . . Jesus the man turns things upside down. Jesa the woman would always have been at the bottom." In the same vein, theologian James Cone has articulated that "God is black" as a metaphor to identify the particular way the salvific work of God identifies with the oppressed. "God's identity is found in the faces of those who are exploited and humiliated because of their color. But I also believe that 'God is mother,' 'rice,' 'red,' and a host of other things that give life to those whom society condemns to death" (Cone, 83).

The Old Testament provides many images, concepts and words with which to understand Jesus, none more so than these servant songs of Second Isaiah, even though in their original context they referred to the prophet or a contemporary deliverer of the people or Israel. This is another instance of intertextuality, this time across the two Testaments of the Christian Bible. Isaiah 42:1 refers to the "chosen" whom God upholds (redolent of Mt 3:17), and Isaiah 42:1-9 describes the role that Yahweh's servant is expected to fulfill. This role resembles the calling of a king, but the whole of Isaiah 40—55 makes it clear that this role will be fulfilled not with the usual exercise of power but by a calling of great personal cost and adversity that nevertheless restores the relationship of God and humanity. This calling is what God asks of Jesus and is reflected in Jesus' life and death. Furthermore, "his law"—not the law of Yahweh but the law of the servant—establishes justice and hope for the nations. Isaiah 49:1-6 contains the aforementioned "light to the nations" that the servant represents. In a symbolic way this is as true for Jesus as it is for Israel and the church. Isaiah 50:4-9 and 52:13—53:12 contain an increased emphasis on suffering and in Christian theology are part of the powerful thrust of the Old Testament toward the New Testament.

Zion and Justice

The book of Isaiah opens with the prophet's vision concerning Zion—Judah and Jerusalem (Is 1:1; cf. Is 2:1). When Jerusalem and Judah neglect the cult and law of Yahweh, Zion suffers (Is 3:1, 8). In biblical literature Zion, while being another name for Jerusalem, is also the place Yahweh desires to inhabit (Ps 132:13), probably an association with the ark placed in the newly constructed temple of Solomon in Jerusalem, the city of David. Thus Zion is more than a geographic location. Yahweh is king, and indestructible Zion is a place of refuge (Is 8:9-10, 16; 14:32; 17:12-14). As Zion is a sign of the kingdom that exists at the point where heaven and earth meet, Isaiah recognizes that Zion will endure even beyond the destruction of Jerusalem (Is 1:21-26; 29:1-8). Zion is an inclusive community that does not exclude any of God's people. In Isaiah 66:7-11 Zion is even portrayed as a mother. She labors and strives for the birth of her nation. Zion feeds and nurtures her people. Furthermore, she is characterized by justice and righteousness.

Zion is given symbolic and physical references. Zion is, symbolically, "the mountain of the LORD" (Is 2:3; 27:13; 40:9), a place of victory (Is 28:16) and a place of pilgrimage (Is 33:20; 51:11; 52:8). Zion is the palace of a great king; the place of victory and cosmic rule; the presence of and access to Yahweh. Encoded in these descriptions is reference to an actual building—the temple (Is 44:26, 28; 45:13; 49:16-18; 52:9). However, the temple is a culture-specific symbol, and we are far removed—both historically and culturally—from the experience that prompted this symbol. Nevertheless, the temple works first as a symbol of the presence of Yahweh among the people and the access to atonement in the kingdom of God, and much later in biblical history as a description of the relation of the body to the Holy Spirit (1 Cor 6:19). Clearly the concept of Zion in Isaiah 40—55 is set in the context of another exile and a new exodus of God's people (beyond that of Genesis and Exodus). Furthermore, in Isaiah 40—55 the rebuilding of Jerusalem/Zion is in direct contrast to the destruction of Babylon. Counterpoint to the redeemed "daughter Zion" is the ill-fated "daughter Chaldea" and "virgin daughter Babylon" (Is 47:1, 5; 52:2). The people of God exit from Babylon and enter into Zion; they leave slavery and receive salvation (Is 46:13; 48:20; 51:3, 11; 52:8). Jerusalem is the "holy city" (Is 48:2; 52:1), and outside its walls are people who are outside of the covenant. "We are dealing with a Zion-centred form of nationalism deliberately composed as a polemic against the competing Babylon-centred nationalism enveloping the Judaean exiles" (Sheriffs, 54).

Zion is partnered with the recurring divine epithet of "the Holy One of Israel"; however, this image of God—transcendent, majestic Creator of everything (Is 6:3; 40:12-23) and Lord of history (Is 10:5-7; 45:1-7)—also has an ethical dimension in Israel. In the presence of the Holy One the prophet sees his moral depravity and is forgiven (Is 6:5-7); the Holy One declares the holy city, Zion, a place of justice and peace (Is 11:6-9; 56:1-8). Furthermore, social justice can never be replaced by religiosity and ritual (Is 1:11-16; 58:1-14). Even in the temple of the new Jerusalem the emphasis is not on its splendor but its openness to strangers (Is 56:3-8) and all the world's nations (Is 2:2-4; 66:18-21).

Justice in Zion, then, is the exercising of righteousness (Is 28:16-17; 33:5-6). There is no salvation for Zion if justice is not executed there (Is 1:27; 51:1-3; 56:1). And what is justice? Isaiah 1:10-17 gives warnings to return to the ways of God and the law, and to help the oppressed, give rights to orphans and defend widows (cf. Is 10:2). Isaiah 5:23 describes the corrupt who let the guilty go "for a bribe," thereby depriving "the innocent of their rights." Isaiah 29:21 describes "those who cause a person to lose a lawsuit, / who set a trap for the arbiter in the gate, / and without grounds deny justice to the one in the right" as unacceptable in the ethic of "the Holy One of Israel." Further admonitions occur in Isaiah 59:4, 8-9, 11, 14-15.

If the book of Isaiah were to be divided into five sections of roughly equal length (Is 1—12; 13—27; 28—39; 40—55; 56—66), all except one would begin with an attack on arrogance and an appeal for justice, culminating in a hymn or prophecy for salvation. All except one would be addressed to the people of Jerusalem. The one exception is Isaiah 40—55, which begins "Comfort, O comfort my people" and is addressed to the exiled community of Israel in Babylon during the sixth century B.C. The polemic of Israel as the "vineyard" (sour "wild" grapes instead of those suitable for good wine, Is 5:1-6) reveals the reasons for the exile. Isaiah 5:7 acknowledges that Yahweh's expectation of justice was disappointed. Justice is integral to the character of God (Is 5:16; 30:18).

Justice is likewise essential to the nature of the promised deliverer of God's people prophesied in First Isaiah.

> For a child has been born for us,
>   a son given to us;
> authority rests upon his shoulders;
>   and he is named
> Wonderful Counselor, Mighty God,
>   Everlasting Father, Prince of Peace.
> His authority shall grow continually,
>   and there shall be endless peace
> for the throne of David and his kingdom.
>   He will establish and uphold it
> with justice and with righteousness
>   from this time onward and forevermore.
> The zeal of the LORD of hosts will do this.
> (Is 9:6-7; cf. Is 16:5; 42:1, 3-4)

The deliverer from the house of David speaks with justice and even wears it (Is 11:1-5). Such an ethic brings a kingdom of remarkable peace, the lion lying down with the lamb (Is 11:6-9). Not only "a king" reigns "in righteousness" in Zion but "princes . . . rule with justice" (Is 32:1). Thus at the Second Vatican Council (1962-1965) the book of Isaiah was quoted as an important statement on peace and social justice: "He shall judge between the nations, / and shall arbitrate for many peoples; / they shall beat their swords into plowshares, / and their spears into pruning hooks; / nation shall not lift up sword against nation, / neither shall they learn war any more" (Is 2:4). Similarly, "the effect of righteousness will be peace, / and the result of righteousness, quietness and trust forever" (Is 32:17; *Gaudium et Spes*, paragraph 70).

What is more, the justice of Yahweh is "a light to the peoples" (Is 51:4-5) extending salvation beyond the exiled group in Babylon to the known world. There is a moral obligation to "maintain justice" (Is 56:1) in Zion. The salvation of the Lord and deliverance of the people is then unhindered, for justice and righteousness work hand in hand in Zion in an everlasting covenant (Is 59; 61:8).

But what does justice mean for women? For many, the recognition, affirmation and understanding of difference is the beginning of justice. However, this is not mere toleration but dialogue. Feminism had to come to grips with its own monologic, imperial voice when it began as a movement of privileged white women. But this situation has changed in the last twenty years. Most women have rejected the abstract idea of a woman and engaged with the distinctive particularities of the Other. There is celebration and conflict. Perhaps the most important outcome of justice within feminism is the diffusion of power in making decisions, shaping procedures, influencing culture and distributing resources equitably. The quest is not for a homogenous community with a shared set of principles and values but a union of diversity. All people are invited to contribute to the formation and continuance of this community. Those at the margins are being brought into the central arena of debate.

This arena of communicative justice probably goes far beyond the type of distributive justice the prophet Isaiah had in mind. Certainly some biblical interpretations have led to clinging to hierarchical power structures in the church and have hindered a real dispersal of power. But such a distribution brings true justice as people at the margins of society are no longer dominated by the dictates and discourse of those at the center or top of society. However, it can be seen as threatening by those who already hold power, hence not all of the Christian church has embraced communicative justice (*see* God's Call to Social Justice). Some grassroots movements have prospered; nevertheless, a real change will occur when these groups are not separated from or overwhelmed by but integrated with the dominant groups. Only then, under the model of communicative justice, will believers be operating fully in the kingdom of God (Gal 3:28-29).

Garlands for Ashes (Is 61—62)

Some years ago I was involved with a group of women who were survivors of childhood sexual abuse. Designed as an opportunity for group therapy and run by a trained Christian counselor, the group met over a period of ten weeks. The course was titled "Garlands for Ashes," an image taken from Isaiah 61:3 (cf. Is 28:1-6).

On the first day of the course we were given these words from Isaiah to carry close to our hearts during the ten weeks of meetings. Isaiah 46:3-4 states:

> Listen to me, O house of Jacob,
> all the remnant of the house of Israel,
> who have been borne by me from your birth,
> carried from the womb;
> even to your old age I am he,
> even when you turn gray I will carry you.
> I have made, and I will bear;
> I will carry and will save.

These inspirational words of great consolation were given by the prophet to comfort the exiled Jews in Babylon, but identification with their plight appeared obvious to us. Were we not exiled, taken from our rightful homes, the innocent and natural state of childhood? Were we not the people of God? These words of Isaiah cut straight into our hearts. We had survived, and God had brought us that far. God was promising to take us further—out of bondage, out of misery, out of exile.

The Commission of the Lord's Anointed (Is 61:1-4)

A continuation of the songs from the servant of the Lord (Is 61:1-4) indicates that the same speaker addresses the same audience. The setting was still one of captivity viewed from the perspective of Babylon and, in turn, the desolated city of Jerusalem. For the original hearers it would have been a promise of literal manifestation. The city of Jerusalem and the temple would be rebuilt, and the exiles would be repatriated and restored. Jesus quoted this same passage at the outset of his ministry (Lk 4:16-21), claiming that the Scripture was fulfilled in the presence of his audience. The form and content of the blessings from the Sermon on the Mount are derived from this passage. Jesus did not create these ideas; he relied on the inspiration of Scripture and the eternal Word of God to develop his ministry and message. Jesus' interpretation is notably spiritual, however, for even John the Baptist had to learn that "the release to the prisoners" was not necessarily a literal rendition of the promise. It is also notable that Jesus omits the words "the day of vengeance" in his rendering of the passage from Isaiah. It appears that this was a final stage yet to be fulfilled (cf. Mt 25:31-46).

Thus, as one commentator has put it, "the prophecy is seen in the bud, the flower and, by implication, the full fruit" (Kidner, 622). For the women in the "Garlands for Ashes" course it was a promise of literal and spiritual fulfillment. It is not difficult for victims of abuse to identify with the "oppressed" and "brokenhearted" or even with "captives," "prisoners" and those who "mourn." The memories of abuse and its effects are overwhelming, often imprisoning victims in a world of solitude and distrust; they grieve for a lost childhood and a damaged process of maturation. This commission of the Lord's anointed thus gave the group hope; hope of repairing the damage but also of complete restoration: "to give them a garland instead of ashes, / the oil of gladness instead of mourning, / the mantle of praise instead of a faint spirit. / They will be called oaks of righteousness, / the planting of the LORD, to display his glory" (Is 61:3). We were being offered and promised beauty instead of ugliness (self-image); joy instead of despair (emotional healing); praise instead of heaviness (spiritual healing). Furthermore, we were not going to be weak and vulnerable anymore; we were no longer going to be victims. We were promised instead strength and grace and blessing ("oaks of righteousness"). This would come, we were warned, over time. Oaks do not mature overnight, but the promise and the seed were there. Isaiah 61:4 was applied to our broken relationships, our damaged sense of self, our histories of neglect and further abuse.

The Abundant Recompense (Is 61:5-7)

What, then, did these next few verses of Isaiah have to say to us? The text spoke of the people of God being served by foreigners, of enjoying the wealth of those who had taken it from them (Is 61:5-6). Even more strangely, the people of God were promised a "double portion" of joy for their suffering (Is 61:7). The prophet may have had the context of the priestly figure of Israel in mind. Therefore, no longer subject to servitude and slavery, Israel's full inheritance of kingship and priesthood was at last going to be enjoyed. Jesus' words "Blessed are the meek, for they will inherit the earth" (Mt 5:5) recall the language of Isaiah 61:7 and Psalm 37:11.

Similarly Jesus said, "Blessed are those who hunger and thirst for righteousness, for they will be filled" (Mt 5:6), which recalls "the heritage of the servants of Yahweh and . . . their righteousness from me [Yahweh]. . . . Everyone who thirsts, come to the waters. . . . Why do you spend . . . your labor for that which does not satisfy? . . . Eat what is good, and delight yourselves in rich food" (Is 54:17—55:2 RV). To our ears this was the language of great blessing. Moreover, it was set in the context of an "abundant recompense" for the experience of undeserved suffering. It is not suggested that Zion did not sin. From the prophet Isaiah's perspective, sin against Yahweh from the king down to the ordinary citizen of Jerusalem was responsible for the downfall of the nation. Survivors of childhood sexual abuse were not, however, accused of sin for their misfortune. Therefore the "double portion" of joy and prosperity appeared to compensate for great loss.

The Song of the Justified (Is 61:8-11)

This latter idea was endorsed in the song that followed. God is a lover of justice who hates theft and wrongdoing. God is faithful and will "make an everlasting covenant with them" who have suffered (Is 61:8). Poignantly, the words "Their descendants shall be known among the nations, / and their offspring among the peoples" (Is 61:9) were hard to bear for those whose childbearing potential had been robbed in their abuse. Yet others who feared sex and intimacy were challenged to consider and ponder these words. Ultimately, we were told by the prophet that "all who see them will acknowledge in them a race whom the LORD has blessed" (Is 61:9 NEB). At the time we did not understand the implications of these words, but over time testimonies of this realization were to come from others to members of the group.

The song of the justified continued into further realms of happiness, celebration and growth for the individual (Is 61:10-11). In its original context this eulogy is gender-inclusive; the bridegroom and the bride are blessed and exalted. The "robe" was an external garment conferred from outside, but the "shoots" in the "garden" came from within (cf. Rom 3:22; 8:10). This act of grace from God sprang from justice, and to those who felt scourged by a sense of terrible injustice such a prophecy appeared right and satisfying.

The Beauty of Zion Renamed (Is 62:1-5)

Isaiah again presents us with the figurative image of Zion as a woman. This was a helpful symbol for the women in the group to identify with, as the passage included phrases like "her vindication" and "her salvation" (Is 62:1). *Vindication* (some commentators prefer the translation "righteousness") suggested a clearing of any blame or suspicion and a further justification. *Salvation* suggested a sense of being preserved against loss and adversity rather than being delivered from sin and its consequences. Then some important information was given to us in the next verse: "you shall be called by a new name / that the mouth of the LORD will give" (Is 62:2). Feminists have long discussed the significance of naming in our society. Typically a daughter takes the name of her father and a wife the name of her husband. In both cases, the woman is identified with reference to a man; her autonomy is subsumed in the status of the male. In its original context the suggestion of "a new name" is tied up with the imagery of Zion as the bride and Yahweh as the husband. There is also the sense of a new start, a new beginning, when the people of God encounter the Lord in a covenant relationship.

I took this word from God seriously indeed. I had long hated carrying the name of the abuser in my life, so approximately nine months after the course I chose and legally adopted a new name for myself. More than one friend has commented on the value and significance of my new name; I managed to include a reference to my mother and my father in my newly devised surname. Usually the mother is not mentioned in the name of her child. I went on to graduate with three academic qualifications in this name.

Isaiah 62:3 was interpreted as the special relationship between God and Zion—between Yahweh and the women in the group. The imagery of a husband was offensive to some in the group, but the language was mediated by replacing the idea of a human male being with God. It never occurred to the group at the time that this imagery somehow reflected masculinity back to God, although undoubtedly it did.

Four names are mentioned in the verse that follows: Azubah, Shemamah, Hephzibah and Beulah—"Forsaken," "Desolate," "Delight" and "Married" respectively (Is 62:4). One commentator has suggested that Yahweh understood as husband is to be associated with the idea of fidelity ("Married"), whereas in the surrounding Canaanite cults, Baal as husband is merely a symbol of pleasure and fertility ("Delight"; Kidner, 622). The point for us in the group was another type of symbolism: not being termed *forsaken* meant not being isolated and alone in our experiences anymore.

Our "land" no longer being termed *desolate* was more comparable to Isaiah's original context. The land of Zion was part of the original covenantal promise and blessing from God to the people, and included crops, livestock, rain and children. Through the exile Zion was left barren and empty. Women in the group believed they were somehow removed from these blessings from God because in their bodies ("land") they felt bereft, empty and neglected. Therefore, to be delighted in and to be "married" suggested a concept of trust and intimacy in relationship that few of us had ever experienced, even though some members of the group actually were married.

A City Not Forsaken (Is 62:6-12)

Just as Yahweh promised never to rest until Jerusalem was reestablished, we understood that God had promised not to abandon us in our journey of healing and restoration (Is 62:6-7). At the time I do not believe we considered whether the mentioned "sentinels" were of any relevance to us, but further down the road I can see that Yahweh ensured that there were others standing watch over me just as others stood guard over the safety of Jerusalem. Others have prayed for me, supported me, comforted me, counseled me and even protected me from danger. The course leader may well have intended this in asking us to seek out three friends to support us with prayers and encouragement throughout the course.

More promises to Zion follow in Isaiah 62:8-9. Historically these promises were realized and then suspended; prophets continually reminded the Jews that failure to keep the covenant of Yahweh would result in a cessation of blessing. In the now-and-not-yet dimension of prophetic revelation the Christian gospel preaches an eschatological new age of final fulfillment, but the oracle of Isaiah continues with an imperative for those in bondage to claim their freedom, which in turn liberates others who are captive (Is 62:10-11). The pattern and example for the group meant that our courage

Depression

God strengthen me to bear myself; that heaviest weight of all," wrote Christina Rossetti (1830-1894) before medicalization of the human condition made the word *depression* popular. Few people reading this will not have felt like her at some time in their lives. It should not surprise us, therefore, to find that many great people in the Bible experienced depression. People like Hagar, with nothing left (Gen 21:15-16); Naomi, returning "empty" (Ruth 1:21); Hannah, anorexic and sad for years (1 Sam 1:8); Tamar, grieving the loss of something she would never have (2 Sam 13:19).

Scripture never shrinks from pointing to a God "who consoles the downcast" (2 Cor 7:6). Nonetheless, depression tends to deaden the sense of God's presence for even the most committed Christian. This could be why we are often told the sadder details of many lives in Scripture, which contains an extraordinary mass of evidence that God notices and cares about even the most private, complicated pain. For example, we read how Rebekah's daughters-in-law "made life bitter" (Gen 26:35); Michal, though first lady, was spurned (2 Sam 6:23); Leah felt fruitful but unloved, while Rachel felt loved but unfruitful (Gen 29:31); Sarah, "sensible, brave and very beautiful," was suicidal (Tob 6:12; 8:10, 20); a woman Jesus healed had been bent over for eighteen years (Lk 13:11). We find ourselves learning from women who overcame depressive situations from positions of powerlessness. Esther refused political oppression; Zipporah angrily protected her livelihood (Ex 4:25); Judith employed her intelligence to prevent war (Jdt 16:25).

Jesus' words in Luke 6:21 invite us to accept that for some people depression will be part of life, so no one has the right to teach or to believe that depression is in some way inconsistent with faith. This does not, however, mean there is nothing a depressed woman can do about it. She can talk about her feelings with friends and ask them to help her remain rooted in reality. She can expect "trials" (1 Pet 1:6) and become alert to depression-prone situations. She can learn coping techniques, like assertiveness, and how to handle anger and guilt, and read psalms (Ps 22, 31, 42, 56, 69). She can make changes in her life situation. She can practice trust in God and challenge negative thinking (Phil 4:8). She can tackle depression arising from poor diet and poor physical fitness. She can seek and accept professional help when necessary and reach out to offer support to others.

She can anticipate "a future with hope" (Jer 29:11; Rom 5:3-5) and take heart from Jesus' attitude. He did not condemn Mary of Bethany when grief and resentment and disbelief hindered her from coming to meet him (Jn 11:20, 33). He did not refuse the silent prayer of the woman who touched him for her healing after twelve years of suffering (Lk 8:43-48).

LISA KATHERINE BATTYE

---

to go forward and heal was an avenue that others could follow to their own liberation and healing.

The new name promised to the community of Israel (Is 62:2) is revealed in Isaiah 62:12: "They shall be called, 'The Holy People, / The Redeemed of the LORD'; / and you shall be called, 'Sought Out, / A City Not Forsaken.'" In the context of our community as adult female survivors of childhood sexual abuse it was a promise that God had not abandoned us. Rather, we had been sought and found; and we would not be left desolate.

Thus the counselor for "Garlands for Ashes" took us through a program of sessions that echoed these themes. First we learned of God's intent and promises for us. Then we surveyed our ground, which included our family background and the incumbent shame and guilt we carried. We thought about the ashes of destruction (the abuse and its ingredients: powerlessness and betrayal, ambivalence and confusion). We had to confront the way in which we had survived: the resulting ways of relating to others, the roles we played and the construction of our self-image. The counselor developed the symbol of the garden (Is 51:3)—our lives—and together we identified weeds and work to do. We began to perceive the possibility of order restored through choice, free will and ultimately forgiveness.

We recited a group prayer during the course: "Our Lord Jesus, you were wounded for each one of us. May the blood from your wounds be poured like healing ointment into our wounds. May we experience cleansing, release, freedom from bondage, great new life—and finally joy! We have great faith that you will answer this prayer because we know that it is your deepest desire. We love you, wounded Healer. Be health now for each one of us. In Christ's name, Amen." Again, the images from the writings of Isaiah, the portrayal of the suffering servant identified by Christianity as the Messiah Jesus Christ, were vividly portrayed (Is 52:13—53:12).

Conclusion

The book of Isaiah has played a central role in Christian liturgy and theology. Isaiah is more often quoted in the New Testament than is any other book of the Old Testament apart from Psalms. The church has adopted much of its language and imagery, including the suffering Messiah (Is 52:13—53:12), the Sanctus (Is 6:3), the winepress (Is 63:3) and the new Jerusalem (Is 65:18). Excerpts of Isaiah inspired Handel's *Messiah* (Is 7; 9; 34; 40; 52; 53; 60). Yet the Zion-centered visions of justice and peace are a distinctive aspect of Jewish literary and religious tradition too. And the scriptural texts on these issues of hope, justice and peace have played a major part in the discussions of postmodern, liberation and feminist theologians.

For many people the significance of language is paramount, as it constructs the individual and collective understanding of power, consciousness and the social. Thus such analysis has had a profound effect on the work of many theologians over the last thirty years. The assertion is that who we are as humans is not merely innate or given but produced in history.

Furthermore, meanings get produced and reproduced through the ordinary power relations of everyday life. Politics is potentially more dominant than theology in a secularized society. However, spirituality is a dominant discourse in a postmodern world because postmodernism is attracted to the hearing of difference, to many existential stories rather than an overarching metanarrative. This has been the opportunity for theologians to re-present biblical narratives such as the oracles of Isaiah in light of many different experiences, including the experiences of the oppressed and previously unheard.

Some readers unfamiliar with these new interpretive methods may be wary of their legitimacy, and to be fair, the methods are not guarantors of eternal truth. However, as I hope I have demonstrated in this exploration of pastoral and theological implications for a reading of Isaiah that gives close attention to the Other, prophetic language concerning the eighth and sixth century B.C. can still enliven the faith of people today. It does so by an appeal to contemporary concerns and a close examination of the texts in their original context. All conceivable voices are considered, and the imagery and language used is assessed in terms of the limitations imposed by the context of the author's society. Then it is assumed that the eternal Word of God might still challenge and comfort today's generation of believers and unbelievers.

I have attempted to highlight only certain issues: the need for bigendered and nongendered language for God in theology and liturgy that the prophecies of Isaiah support; the concept of servanthood that gives honor to the individual and not subjection to a chosen few; the relationship between the city of God and justice; and the pastoral words that can reinvest self-esteem and dignity into the lives of the victims of abuse.

Placing those who are apparently far removed from grace and blessing in the arena of interpreting the Bible can produce extraordinary results that enlarge the concept of Christian community and humanity. The process can promote compassion and increase understanding of others, often others whose lives are very different. It is an opportunity for empathy, for learning and for change. It is a practical theology. This commentary is by no means comprehensive, and I do not envisage these hermeneutical methods as a singular model for interpretation. The whole Bible requires a multitude of approaches. The theology of the Old Testament, including the oracles of Isaiah, comes to us in the form of an enculturated story. Some elements of the story are temporary in their significance, but others are permanent with a trajectory through the whole of Judeo-Christian Scripture. Exegetes are required to recontextualize these eternal elements so that the Word of God continues to be heard.

However, this commentary is not a complete solution to the intricacies of all sixty-six chapters of the book of Isaiah. It is an approach to reality, part of a bigger picture still hidden from view but promised.

> For as the new heavens and the new
> earth,
> which I will make,
> shall remain before me, says the LORD;
> so shall your descendants and your
> name remain.
> From new moon to new moon,
> and from sabbath to sabbath,
> all flesh shall come to worship before me,
> says the LORD. (Is 66:22-23)

Bibliography. A. Brenner and C. Fontaine, eds. *A Feminist Companion to Reading the Bible* (Sheffield: Sheffield Academic Press, 1997); A. Brenner, "Identifying the Speaker-in-the-Text and the Reader's Location in Prophetic Texts: The Case of Isaiah 50," in *Feminist Companion* 136-50; J. Cone, "God Is Black," in *Lift Every Voice: Constructing Christian Theologies from the Underside,* ed. S. B. Thistlethwaite and M. P. Engel (San Francisco: Harper & Row, 1990); S. Heine, *Matriarchs, Goddesses and Images of God* (Minneapolis: Augsburg, 1989); D. Kidner, "Isaiah," in *New Bible Commentary,* ed. D. Guthrie, J. A. Motyer, A. M. Stibbs and D. J. Wiseman, 3d ed. (Leicester: Inter-Varsity Press, 1970); C. L. Hess, "Becoming Midwives to Justice: A Feminist Approach to Practical Theology," in *Liberating Faith Practices: Feminist Practical Theologies in Context,* ed. D. M. Ackermann and Riet Bons-Storm (Louven, Belgium: Peeters, 1998); T. Linafelt, "Surviving Lamentations," in *Feminist Companion* 344-59; C. A. Newsom, "Response to Norman K. Gottwald, 'Social Class and Ideology in Isaiah 40—55,'" *Semeia* 59 (1992) 73-78; D. C. T. Sheriffs, " 'A Tale of Two Cities'—Nationalism in Zion and Babylon," *Tyndale Bulletin* 39 (1988) 19-57; P. Trible, "Journey of a Metaphor," in *God and the Rhetoric of Sexuality* (Philadelphia: Fortress, 1978) 31-59; C. Westermann, "Beauty in the Hebrew Bible," in *Feminist Companion* 584-602.

JULIE ANN HILTON

JEREMIAH

Introduction

The book of Jeremiah reveals God's presence in a world falling apart and God's gift of hope for life beyond the catastrophe. God's word through the prophet Jeremiah showed a theological basis for comprehending this chaos and believing in the future. The materials collected in Jeremiah continue the ministry of his preaching for generations afterward.

The book's order and arrangement are not chronological or logical. Readers must recall earlier passages, discover words or ideas that hold together a collection of disparate parts and reflect on the way juxtaposed passages interpret one another. Jeremiah and the skilled scribes who composed the book constantly use contrast and analogy to guide readers.

The theology of Jeremiah's message also resists systematizing. Two paradigms for God's dealings with the people remain in tension. God upholds the covenant requirement of judgment and simultaneously reaches out to help. The two cannot be separated in the book of Jeremiah.

Jeremiah's ministry began in the thirteenth year of Josiah (627/6 B.C.) and continued past the conquest of Jerusalem (587/6 B.C.) During these decades Jeremiah's prophecies provided God-given analysis of conditions within the former northern kingdom, Judah and Jerusalem, as well as the momentous events that shaped the region. When he began, the Assyrian Empire was in decline. Judah enjoyed increasing security and independence. Under Josiah's leadership, Judah briefly renewed its covenant commitment to God's law and became something like the kingdom God had called it to be. By the end of Jeremiah's ministry, however, the king was in prison and the people had been deported to Babylon or had fled to Egypt. Every institution that had defined the identity of God's people had been overthrown.

The remaining pillar of national existence was God's word. Earlier collections of prophecies, prayers and narratives were slowly assembled into the book we know today. A scroll could traverse space and time to go where the prophet could not. The latest date in the book is 561 B.C. (Jer 52:31-34), and the narrative continues for an unspecified number of years afterward. The earliest possible date for the book as we have it is several years after 561 B.C. At that time Jews were living in Babylon, Egypt, the territory of Judah and other places in the Babylonian Empire.

Little is known about the lives of Jews during the exilic period, but it is not hard to imagine some of the questions that troubled their minds. Among these questions might be, Why was Judah overthrown? How was God involved? Had Judah and Jerusalem been warned and given a chance to repent? Is God finished with Judah? What will the Jews' future be without a king and a kingdom? Can Jeremiah be trusted as a true prophet? The book has been arranged and composed to address this later audience and the generations of readers after them. One purpose of the book is that they "may turn from their evil ways, so that I may forgive their iniquity and their sin" (Jer 36:3).

Readers of Jeremiah need a basic knowledge of the order of events and the identity of significant individuals and groups.

In 721 B.C., Israel, the northern kingdom, was conquered and made part of the Assyrian Empire. A large part of the population was deported. Idolatry was the major cause of the northern kingdom's destruction (Hos; 2 Kings 17). Jeremiah points to the similarities between the northern kingdom and Judah. The name Israel, and its alternates, Jacob and Ephraim, is used for the northern kingdom, the covenant people of God from Sinai to the present and the descendants of former northern kingdom citizens.

In 605 B.C., in the fourth year of Jehoiakim, the Babylonians, or Chaldeans, defeated Egypt and Assyria at Carchemish and took over Assyria's former sphere of influence. Nebuchadnezzar became king of Babylon, and Jehoiakim became his vassal.

In 598-597 B.C., after Jehoiakim rebelled, the Babylonians besieged Jerusalem. During the siege Jehoiakim died and Jehoiachin succeeded him. When the Babylonians conquered the city they took Jehoiachin and other exiles to Babylon, looted the temple and put Zedekiah on the throne as their vassal. Jeremiah gave special attention to the exiles who had been forced to accept Babylonian rule while the rest of Judah continued to resist.

In 588-587 B.C. Zedekiah rebelled, and Babylon besieged Jerusalem.

In 587-586 B.C. the Babylonians conquered and burned Jerusalem and the temple, exiled Zedekiah and many others and appointed Gedaliah governor over the remainder of Judah.

In 539 B.C. Cyrus conquered Babylon sixty-seven years after Nebuchadnezzar became king.

Outline

1:1-3	Superscription
1:4-19	Jeremiah's Call
2:1—4:4	Israel Breaks Faith with God
4:5—6:30	The Enemy from the North
7:1—10:25	False Worship
11:1—17:27	The Broken Covenant and Prayers for Help
18:1—20:18	The Last Chance Refused
21:1—24:10	Failed Monarchy and False Prophecy
25:1-38	The Lord's People Among the Nations
26:1-24	Jeremiah Among the Prophets
27:1—29:32	The Lord Reigns
30:1—33:26	The Book of Comfort and Hope
34:1—36:32	Examples of Faithlessness and Faith
37:1—44:30	Siege, Conquest and Aftermath
45:1-5	A Promise for Baruch
46:1—49:39	Prophecies Against the Nations
50:1—51:64	Judgment on Babylon
52:1-34	The End of Judah and Jerusalem

Superscription (Jer 1:1-3)

Jeremiah was born into a priestly family living in Anathoth. This town was part of the tribal territory of Benjamin, although it was located two miles north of Jerusalem, in Judah. Centuries earlier Solomon had banished the priest Abiathar to Anathoth as punishment for supporting Adonijah, his rival for the throne of their father, David. Jeremiah's family may have been Abiathar's descendants.

Jeremiah's prophetic ministry, when "the word of the LORD came" to him (Jer 1:2), began in Josiah's thirteenth year as king and continued until Jerusalem fell to the Babylonians in Zedekiah's eleventh year. In Jeremiah 40—44, however, Jeremiah's prophesying continues for some time after that date.

Jeremiah's Call (Jer 1:4-19)

Before Jeremiah's birth God had chosen him and set him apart to serve as a prophet to the nations. Jacob and Samson also were chosen before birth, but there is no evidence that Jeremiah's mother was told, as Rebekah and the wife of Manoah had been. Hannah dedicated Samuel to the Lord's service before he was conceived, and Samuel was also called to be a prophet while he was a youth. All three women had been childless before giving birth to their chosen, dedicated sons. The only hint that Jeremiah's mother had anything in common with these other mothers is a possible meaning of Jeremiah's name, "Yahweh loosened," which could be a testimony by a previously childless woman (i.e., "the Lord has loosened my womb, enabling me to conceive and give birth").

Jeremiah objects that he is only a youth. For Levites the age of majority was variously twenty (1 Chron 23:24), twenty-five (Num 8:24) or thirty (Num 4:3), but Jeremiah could have been much younger. He will become a responsible adult when he takes up the divine commission and begins to speak the words that God puts in his mouth.

The second half of the account introduces the main themes of the next two sections of the book and relates them to

Jeremiah's prophetic role. Jerusalem and Judah are guilty of idolatry and deserving of judgment, which the Lord will bring in the form of conquerors from the north. The fortified cities of Judah on which the people rely will fall, but God's presence to save and protect will be found in the divine word spoken by Jeremiah. To fulfill his call Jeremiah will have to suffer like a city under attack but not surrender (cf. Jeremiah's "prayers for help").

Israel Breaks Faith with God (Jer 2:1—4:4)

An implied narrative underlies this collection of short, mostly poetic prophetic sayings. It is the story of God's relationship with Israel and the kingdoms that became Israel and Judah. The Lord had brought Israel out of Egypt, preserved them in the wilderness and given them the land. But Israel was unfaithful, worshiping other gods. The two kingdoms rebelled and made alliances with other countries. As a result, Assyria has conquered the northern kingdom. Judah now stands under threat of judgment. Judah is worse than Israel because it has not taken warning from the northern kingdom's example. God urges survivors and descendants of the northern kingdom to acknowledge their rebellion, apostasy and disobedience, and to return. If they do, they will come back to the land and live under godly rulers. Israel and Judah will be reunited, and the nations will come peacefully to Jerusalem. God also urges Judah to cease its evil doings and make a radical recommitment to the Lord in order to escape divine judgment. The purpose of this implied narrative is to persuade the audience to accept the comparison of Judah and Israel, to acknowledge their guilt and the justice of divine judgment, and to return. The promises offered to repentant Israel apply to the audience also.

Jeremiah 2:2 and Jeremiah 3:6-11 provide the key to interpreting this collection of sayings. The story of Yahweh and Israel is told as a metaphor of a husband and his unfaithful wives. The social and legal aspects of marriage in ancient Israel made it a suitable image in several ways. A husband might have more than one wife, but a wife could have only one husband at a time and was required to remain loyal to him. A wife could not divorce her husband for any reason. If she left him for another man or men, she committed adultery (*see* Adultery; Divorce). The husband, however, could divorce his wife if he found something objectionable about her or disliked her. A married woman's livelihood normally depended on the land owned by her husband or the male head of his household (*see* Numbers). The intimacy of marriage adds a dimension of compassion and anguish to the metaphor, which could simultaneously convey God's freedom and authority, Israel's dependence and their love for each other.

The marriage began happily, but Israel behaved like a harlot. Yahweh waited, hoping that she would return. The prophetic words of accusation against Israel (Jer 2:2—3:5) fit this part of the story. Accusation was necessary because Israel refused to acknowledge her sin. Israel did not return to Yahweh, so he divorced her, sending her into exile. Judah observed Israel's harlotry and its consequences yet committed adultery. She seemed to return but did not admit her sin. God judges Israel, who has suffered for faithlessness, to be less guilty than Judah. Judah should have learned from Israel's mistakes. Therefore God in mercy invites Israel to return. Jeremiah 3:6 dates this invitation in the reign of Josiah, a hundred years after the end of the northern kingdom. Some descendants of northern-kingdom Israelites still lived in the land of Israel. Josiah had removed the illicit altars from Bethel and all the towns of their territory. Because of God's mercy, they have another opportunity to confess the extent of their rebellion, acknowledging the truth of all the prophetic accusations and the justice of God's judgment (see Jer 3:22-25).

Because Judah sinned in the same way as Israel, the prophetic accusations also apply to Judah during Jeremiah's ministry. Jeremiah 4:4 implies that Judah and Jerusalem had an opportunity to repent and thus avoid at least some of the judgment brought upon them by the Babylonians. In the context of the book, addressed to an audience who had experienced that judgment and still suffers its effects, the call to repentance includes the promise of an end to divine wrath. The analogy with Israel holds out hope for Judah and Jerusalem and their survivors after 586 B.C. Like Israel, they must acknowledge past and present sin and God's justice before they can receive the promised blessings of return and restoration. Thus the extended metaphor of Yahweh's two adulterous wives shows postexilic readers of Jeremiah how to understand the earlier prophecies as being addressed to them.

Using the metaphor of the unfaithful wife, Jeremiah shows that it would be impossible for the people to initiate reconciliation with God. The law forbids remarriage of a woman to the husband who divorced her if she had been married to another man in the interim. Since this kind of remarriage would bring guilt on the land, how much more would the metaphorical remarriage of promiscuous Israel to God defile the land? Only God can initiate this reconciliation by inviting Israel to return and repent.

The wording of God's invitation in Jeremiah 3:12-14 goes beyond the marriage metaphor. *Rebel* is a political term, used often of the people's transgressions against God but never of a wife's behavior against her husband. *Guilt* has a broad range of meanings not limited to sexual sin. The last charge, "[You] have not obeyed," is masculine plural, as is Jeremiah 3:14 and the rest of this section (except Jer 3:19).

God's relationship to Israel originated with deliverance and blessing. God was a fountain of living, life-giving water to them. The divine farmer had protected Israel as the first fruits of the harvest or had planted them as a vine from the best cultivated stock. As a father, God had given the people a pleasant land for their inheritance.

Accusations against Israel for betraying this relationship and rebelling against God fill most of this section. These prophetic speeches use varied imagery, vivid similes and extended metaphor to accuse and convince the audience. They employ negative, offensive rhetoric to break down the nations' resistance to confession. Judgment came to Israel because they said, "I have not sinned" (Jer 2:35). Throughout this section the accused parties are always the nations of Israel or Judah or their leaders rather than individuals. Nations and their leaders are seldom amenable to gentle persuasion. Even bitter denunciations may not provoke repentance.

They broke faith by worshiping other gods and by forming illicit political alliances with other nations. The leaders forgot what the Lord had done for them. They chose to depend on cracked cisterns instead of a flowing spring. They gave up their freedom to become slaves. The vine from choice stock became wild. Who has heard of a nation changing its gods as they had? Apostasy made less sense for Israel than for anyone else because deities other than Yahweh are worthless and powerless. Yet they worshiped those deities ignorantly, saying "my father" to the tree that represented Asherah, a goddess, and addressing the stone that stood for the male deity Baal as the one who "gave me birth" (Jer 2:27). The poetry likens Israel to a female donkey or camel in heat, reduced to acting on instinct while searching for another deity with which to mate. The audience was expected to feel revulsion for this foolish behavior. If they acknowledged this picture of themselves they would have to admit their guilt.

Israel as the Lord's bride at the exodus and Israel and Judah as unfaithful wives are the most prominent image in these chapters of the people's relationship with God. Israel tried to hide and deny its promiscuous activity, yet even the strongest lye and soap could not remove the guilty stain visible to God's eyes. God charges Israel with teaching other "wicked women" how to find lovers (Jer 2:33).

God experiences the loss in several ways. Israel's early devotion and dependence in the wilderness is a precious memory that they have betrayed by forgetting the Lord. A woman's work and expertise made a major contribution to the support of the typical household in Israel and Judah (*see* Occupations, Skills and Crafts of Women). In Jeremiah 2:20 God addresses the feminine personification of Israel under the metaphor of a draught animal that refuses to serve. God is husbandman, not husband, in this metaphor. In the Old Testament a wife is never said to serve her husband, but Israel was called to serve God from the beginning.

Personified Israel is also guilty of violating the ethical standards of the Lord's household. God accuses Israel of violating the law by murdering the innocent poor. There were no mitigating circumstances for these killings, such as nocturnal burglary.

The people by their whorings have polluted the land given to them as a heritage. Jeremiah 2:7 expresses the same idea without the metaphor: "you [masc. pl.] defiled my land" by idolatry. As a result, rain has not fallen.

The implied audiences for Jeremiah's prophecy and for the book would have been appalled at the idea of a wife deserting her husband and proudly choosing a life of prostitution. Why would a woman give up the economic and social security of her husband's household and risk her livelihood on a succession of lovers? This is presented as yet another image of the senseless, inexplicable choice Israel made in turning away from the Lord.

Contemporary readers who live in societies where women enjoy legal and economic independence read the same image and do not find it inexplicable. A woman leaves her husband because she has been abused. We have rightly learned to reject the justifications given by men and women for abusing their children or spouses and to conclude that the abuser is at fault (*see* Violence, Abuse and Oppression). From this perspective, the image does not work. What was meant to demonstrate God's justice and lead hearers to recognize their sin now prompts some readers to take sides against God. Since nothing can justify abusing one's spouse or children, they reason, then nothing that Israel or Judah did can justify God's judgment. This reasoning becomes another way of saying that a God who judges in wrath is incompatible with a God who saves and nurtures in love.

The ethical implications of this image are also serious. If God as husband must punish Israel and Judah as wives, then aren't human husbands who desire to be like God obligated to punish their wives in analogous ways? One can understand the powerful temptation of this reasoning. Human beings aspire to lord it over others (Lk 22:25), to exercise divine rights over the lives of people with whom they live and work. Careful attention to the details of Jeremiah 2:1—4:4 shows that it is not intended to teach human husbands how to treat their wives. The marriage image is scattered. The passage regularly uses other images or nonpictorial expressions that depict God's relationship to Israel and Judah. God is not merely a husband, bound by law and custom. God is their sovereign Lord and Creator. Israel and Judah are not individual women but nation-states possessing territory granted to them by God and responsible to conduct their national affairs in accordance with God's will. The marriage image is a powerful rhetorical tool in individual oracles and also in the construction of the collection, but it must not divert attention from the full scope of the message.

The Enemy from the North (Jer 4:5—6:30)

Many of the short, poetic sayings in Jeremiah 4:5—6:30 describe the enemy who will come from the north to execute God's judgment. Judah lay in the fertile strip between the Mediterranean Sea and the Arabian desert. Invaders from Mesopotamia passed around the desert and approached from the north (see Jer 4:13-17; 6:1).

This enemy is typical of ancient Near Eastern conquerors. They will be mounted on horses and chariots, and equipped with the most effective armaments, including the bow, javelin and sword. The army will be so vast that it will sound like the sea. Its warriors will attack cruelly, show no mercy and kill efficiently, like predatory beasts. Their power will be so awesome that the description approaches mythic proportions (Jer 4:13). The enemy will appear as clouds or like a whirlwind, traveling faster than eagles.

The Neo-Babylonian Empire had established itself only a few years before with victory over Egypt at Carchemish, so Jeremiah's audience was not familiar with their language. Yet Babylon was also an ancient kingdom. A thousand years earlier the old Babylonian Empire had held sway in the region. Neither Babylon nor Nebuchadnezzar is mentioned by name in these chapters, but the rest of the book makes this identification obvious. The Babylonians besieged and conquered Jerusalem twice during Jeremiah's ministry, in 597 and 587/6 B.C. The devastation and desolation envisioned in these chapters matches other Old Testament depictions of the result of Babylonian conquest (e.g., Jer 33:10; Lam 2:15-16).

The oracles in this section are not arranged according to chronology or linear logic. Their purpose, like the purpose of Jeremiah 2:1—4:4, is to convince God's people of the justice of divine judgment and to provoke repentance. Individual sayings invite Jerusalem to "wash your heart clean of wickedness so that you may be saved" (Jer 4:14) and "take warning [accept discipline] . . . or I shall turn from you" (Jer 6:8). Other oracles cite invitations that the people had rejected, prophetic warnings that they had ignored and suffering as discipline or refining to which they had refused to respond. Jeremiah had been assigned to search Jerusalem for "one person who acts justly and seeks truth" (Jer 5:1) so that God might pardon the city, but none were found. He had been appointed assayer and refiner, but the refining proved to be in vain. The fire of the divine word in the prophet's mouth finally could bring only judgment.

This collection addresses an audience for whom the Babylonian conquest was certain. The audience is instructed to accept the prophet's explanation of Babylon's success as divine judgment on Judah and Jerusalem. The oracles and brief prose comments address several concerns that such an audience might have.

Jeremiah is the implied speaker (Jer 4:10) who charges God with deceiving the people with false assurances. Hadn't the prophets and priests who spoke in Yahweh's name said, "It shall be well with you" (Jer 4:10)? Three passages, however, make it clear that their words had not been from the Lord. Jeremiah 6:14 uses a medical metaphor to expose the damage done by the prophets who preach "Peace" when there is none. Such prophets persuaded the people to reject the Lord's warnings of judgment and to conclude that "no evil will come upon us" (Jer 5:12). This was an attractive word, and the prophets and priests may have benefited materially for giving the people the message they wanted to hear.

Jeremiah 5:19 articulates the question of audiences after the judgment: "Why has the LORD our God done all these things to us?" The short answer is that they worshiped other gods in the land that their God had given them. Forsaking the Lord and making oaths in the names of other, false deities begins a list of sins (Jer 5:7). The key verb from Jeremiah 3:4-14, "break faith," reappears in Jeremiah 5:11 but without the marriage metaphor. Only Jeremiah 4:30 accuses Jerusalem of harlotry, warning her that her lovers desire to kill her rather than help her. These "lovers" may have been other nations sought as allies.

Only the reference to "lovers" identifies the metaphor in Jeremiah 4:30 as describing a prostitute. Dyed clothing, gold jewelry and makeup were marks of wealth and position; David praises Saul for having enriched the nation so that Israelite women could possess these luxury items (2 Sam 1:24). The name of Job's daughter Keren-happuch (Job 42:14) means "vial of eyeliner"; eyeliner was a black mineral powder that made the eye look larger, and the name reflects Job's restored wealth. Jezebel painted her eyes and adorned her head to communicate her wealth and status when she confronted Jehu about his assassination of Ahab (2 Kings 9:30-33). If her purpose had been seduction she probably would not have addressed Jehu as "murderer of your master." Rahab is well known for the red thread taken from her robe (Josh 2:18, 21), but red is not the uniform color of prostitutes. The curtains of the tabernacle included red thread, and red yarn was part of some rituals of purification. The worthy wise woman is so diligent and skillful that she can clothe her household in red dyed apparel (Prov 31:21). Such a woman would not dress her family in garments of harlotry. Gold jewelry was worn by brides (Is 61:10; Ezek 16:11, 13) but also by anyone who could afford it, including men (Is 3:16, 18-23; Ex 33:4-6). A woman's jewelry could include anklets, bracelets, necklaces, rings for ears, nose or fingers and toggle pins to fasten outer garments. Israel and Judah minted no coins, and women did not own land, so jewelry was a woman's portable asset. A prostitute would dress to display her wealth to potential clients because her success and therefore her expertise would be evident (cf. Ezek 23:40). A city seeking allies would show off the strength of its defenses, the skill and armaments of its soldiers, the abundance of its provisions and the popularity of its leaders. Jerusalem's efforts, however, will fail.

To depict this failure Jeremiah 4:31 employs another feminine metaphor for Jerusalem, the image of a woman in labor. "I am fainting before killers," she says. The picture is one of pain and vulnerability, and it serves as an image of military conquest. The pregnant woman cannot avoid labor, nor can she control when it will begin or how long it will last. A woman in her first labor wonders how bad the pain will become, how long her strength will last and if she will survive. People listening outside the birth room hear her cries of pain and her gasps and pants in the extremity of her efforts. The woman in labor is not able to escape or fight back. This is a picture of a city without defense and without hope of avoiding the judgment.

Twice in these chapters God asks the rhetorical question: "Shall I not punish them for these things?" (Jer 5:9, 29). This collection of oracles makes the case for judgment on Judah and Jerusalem. The charges of idolatry and seeking illicit alliances are only two of many indictments. God charges them with wickedness, rebellion, foolishness, transgression, apostasy, sin and corruption. Prophets and priests speak falsehood. Everyone cheats and takes unfair advantage of others (*see* God's Call to Social Justice; Yahweh's Concern for the Disenfranchised). Individuals covet their neighbors' wives and commit adultery (Jer 5:8, not a metaphor). They swear to a lie, steal property and people and fail to make just legal decisions in the cause of orphans and the needy. They are guilty of slander, oppression and violence. These violations can be traced to their refusal to heed the Lord's law, or instruction. Judah's and Jerusalem's suffering at the hands of Babylon will be God's punishment, not just the natural result of Babylon's imperial ambitions. They had refused to heed warnings, repent and walk in God's way. Therefore "your ways and your doings have brought this upon you" (Jer 4:18).

Neither the Lord nor the prophet rejoices in the judgment. God's efforts to find a reason to pardon and the terms of endearment, Daughter Zion, and *bat ami*, "Daughter, my people," are consistent with the images of tender care in Jeremiah 2:1—4:4 (husband, parent) and the references to the good that God had done for them. The cry of anguish (Jer 4:19-22) expresses the prophet's participation in the people's anguish amid judgment. He hears the trumpet announcing the attack and sees the desolation of the land, the city and its temple. He feels his heart beating and can't help but cry out. His internal organs writhe like the womb of a woman in labor. He wants the enemy army to disappear. In Jeremiah 4:22 God's voice emerges. In the Old Testament, only God calls Israel or Judah "my people."

God's wrath for the people's suffering under the violence and oppression of their neighbors was expressed in the judgment brought by the enemy from the north. But the people's suffering under that judgment and the devastation of the country also caused God grief. Divine compassion helps to explain why God promises three times in these chapters, "I will not make a full end of you" (Jer 4:27; 5:10, 18).

False Worship (Jer 7—10)

A loose collection of prophetic sayings accuses and condemns Judah and Jerusalem for various forms of false worship. In the first unit God commissions a sermon at the temple, which should have been the site of exclusive, pure worship of the Lord. Jeremiah is told to urge the people to reform their way of life by obeying God. They had a false understanding of what the temple meant, thinking that its existence guaranteed their security because the Lord would always defend it. God reminds them that their relationship had begun with the command to walk in God's way and that their well-being depended on their obedience to the divine law. Expiatory sacrifices were pointless when the people were violating the Ten Commandments. The temple would be destroyed, as the earlier sanctuary at Shiloh had been, and the people would be exiled.

A long poem (Jer 10:1-16) contrasts Yahweh, the Creator, with manufactured idols. The poem's humor is sarcastic. There is no need to fear the gods of other nations because one can see them being made. Someone cuts down a tree, carves it, plates it with precious metals, attaches it with nails to its base and dresses it in clothing. The Lord, the living God, made the earth and the heavens and continues to produce the rain, lightning and wind. The God of Israel claims authority over the nations because their deities are a delusion, incapable of speech or moral action.

The queen of heaven was one of the other gods worshiped in Jerusalem and Judah. Jeremiah does not give her a name, but she seems to combine characteristics of Astarte and Ishtar. In Babylonian mythology

Ishtar was the consort of Tammuz, whose rites were observed at the Jerusalem temple in the preexilic period (Ezek 8:14). As her title indicates, she was a high god with a wide range of powers. (Yahweh is called "the God of heaven" several times in the Old Testament, but never the king of heaven.) Her devotees believed she granted fertility as well as success in battle. Nor was she a deity for women only. Whole families honored her by baking cakes for her (Jer 7:18). Apparently no priests were needed for this activity, which took place all over Judah and in Jerusalem.

Worship of the queen of heaven persisted in Israel from the time of the united monarchy at least into the exilic period. Solomon constructed a high place for her outside Jerusalem (1 Kings 11:5, 33). Hers may have been one of the altars Manasseh erected in the temple to the hosts of heaven (2 Kings 21:3-5) that Josiah subsequently destroyed (2 Kings 23:13). The refugees who forcibly removed Jeremiah and Baruch with them to Egypt determined to resume worshiping her there (see below, Siege, Conquest and Aftermath, Jer 37—44).

In the valley of the son of Hinnom, at Topheth (the "fireplace"), the people of Judah sacrificed their daughters and sons to Baal by burning them in the fire. Ancient depictions of a comparable practice at Carthage and the burials excavated there show that the victims included infants and toddlers. "I did not command," God says, "nor did it come into my mind" (Jer 7:31). The people could not excuse themselves by claiming to emulate Abraham or to fulfill the command to dedicate firstborn sons to the Lord. The law regarding the firstborn called for an animal substitute.

Voluntary child sacrifice in the Old Testament is related to prayers for help. Ahaz of Judah had passed his son through the fire as a sacrifice. Second Kings 16:3 does not specify the occasion for Ahaz's offering, but the Syro-Ephraimite war and the beginning of the Assyrian crisis in Judah occurred during his reign. The king of Moab once sacrificed his son on the city wall in the hope of bringing a siege to an end. Hiel, the man who rebuilt Jericho, offered two sons as foundation sacrifices. Jephthah sacrificed his daughter in fulfillment of a vow because the Lord had given him success in battle (*see* Judges). If the people sacrificing their children at Topheth were the same ones who believed the other prophets' false message of peace and security, then some of their sacrifices were made when they did not think they were in imminent danger. Such corruption of the people's spirit and of the land will bring a terrible judgment. This valley, just outside of Jerusalem to the west and south, will be filled with corpses, buried and unburied, that will become food for carrion-eating beasts and birds.

The audience is called to lament and wail in anticipation of the devastating judgment to come. Wailing for the dead was done publicly, in the streets and squares of towns and cities, by relatives and colleagues (*see* Grief and Bereavement). Women or men skilled in composing and performing dirges led the public mourning. David (2 Sam 1:17; 3:33) and Jeremiah (2 Chron 35:25) are the only named authors of dirges for the dead in the Old Testament. David's brief lament for Abner protests the manner of his death. The dirge for Saul and Jonathan describes how they fought, where they died, the people's loss and David's grief. David ordered that the song be taught to the people (2 Sam 1:18; cf. Jer 9:20).

The lament or dirge is also a form of judgment prophecy (e.g., Ezek 2:10; 19:1, 4; Amos 5:1). It describes the manner of death before the nation or leader is gone. The dirge to be sung and taught by these women (Jer 9:20) is also a word from the Lord. The ministry of women skilled in mourning will enable the people to weep. Music may touch the heart and inspire tears, but more is at stake in this ministry than emotional release. Jeremiah's audience will mourn under the leadership of these skilled women only when they acknowledge the truth of God's word of judgment. The dirge will have to be sung over and over to reach the rebellious listeners, so the women are commanded to teach it to their colleagues and to the generation who will succeed them. It is a song describing the victory of death.

The prophet also mourns for the people, and his voice speaks God's grief over their suffering and despair. The people whose words are quoted (Jer 9:19-20) have lost their false confidence. They are called "daughter, my people" four times in Jeremiah 8:18—9:1. This term of endearment is God's special name for the Israelites, but the rest of the poem is filled with stunning anthropomorphisms (e.g., sick, hurt, dismayed). The reasons for the people's suffering are present within the passage and in the following two closely related verses. Their suffering is the result of judgment for unfaithfulness (i.e., idolatry and falsehood). In this poem, however, God, through the prophet, mourns their hurt more than God's own.

Salvation and restoration are offered to God's people when their just measure of correction is complete, but they still suffer because their conquerors extend oppression beyond their warrant from God. Objects of just judgment become recipients of divine mercy, as the prayer in Jeremiah 10:23-25 asks. The poem in Jeremiah 8:18—9:1 demonstrates that wrath did not destroy or replace the Lord's love for Israel. The prose comment in Jeremiah 9:24 summarizes the paradoxical divine character, recognized by all who truly know the Lord: "I act with steadfast love, justice, and righteousness in the earth, for in these things I delight."

The Broken Covenant and Prayers for Help (Jer 11—17)

The Lord's covenant with Israel will no longer protect them. Their distant ancestors had accepted God's terms at Sinai—obedience and exclusive worship—but while they had lived in the land they had persistently refused to keep those terms. Therefore the Lord declares through the prophet as covenant mediator that they had broken the covenant. Only the overlord who had initiated the covenant had the right to declare it broken, and Yahweh did so only after watching the people refuse to heed repeated warnings. Therefore God will not listen to the people's prayers for help or to intercession by Jeremiah. Most of the material in this section relates in some way to this initial unit. The covenant theology in Jeremiah 11:1-17 offers a rationale for the dissolution of order and hope expressed in the prayers and prophecies constituting these chapters.

Varied metaphors show how the people's persistent disobedience has hardened into habitual evil. They are as unable to change themselves as Cushites, from the area of Ethiopia and the Sudan, are unable to change the color of their skin and as leopards are unable to remove their spots. Judah's sin is engraved on their hearts, the organ of thought, decision and commitment. Their commitment to idolatry is cut deeply, as by a sharp point on a stone tablet.

Exile, loss of the land and dissolution of institutions of national life will be consequences of covenant violation. The sufferings of individual women and of personified

Sarcophagus of mourning women. (Jeremiah 9:20)

Jerusalem are highlighted. For example, instead of picturing soldiers dead on the battlefield, Jeremiah 15:8-9 lists uncountable widows and bereaved mothers. God had promised Abraham descendants as numerous as the grains of sand on the shore, and the number of widows will exceed that count (*see* Widows). A mother who had been especially blessed with seven sons will be all the more bereaved.

The verses that say the queen mother and the king will lose their royal power may have been addressed to Jehoiachin and his mother, Nehushta, who were exiled together. In 1 and 2 Kings all but two of the mothers of the kings of Judah appear in the formulas introducing each king's reign. This formula usually includes the name of the woman's father and her hometown. Perhaps the office of queen mother gave political power and influence to families outside the Davidic royal line. Bathsheba arranged Solomon's succession and served as an adviser after he became king. Other queen mothers probably used their political skills and the power of their fathers' families to put their sons on the throne and to secure an influential position for themselves. Athaliah, the mother of Ahaziah, ordered the assassination of the royal family and assumed the throne. Her grandson Joash was rescued by his aunt Jehosheba, however, and eventually deposed Athaliah. In the course of his religious reform Asa removed Maacah as queen mother because she had set up an Asherah image (*see* 2 Chronicles for more about Athaliah and Maacah). Jehoiachin, the last king to take the throne as a result of political processes internal to Judah, reigned for only a few months before he surrendered to Babylon. Perhaps Nehushta had influenced the choice of her son. Nothing is known about how she exercised her office as queen mother. Her status at court is implied by the lists of exiles taken in 597 B.C.; she is listed after the king and before the other court officials.

Personified Jerusalem will also be humbled by conquest because she is guilty of worshiping other gods. Jeremiah 13:20-27 emphasizes the humiliation of nakedness (see also 2 Sam 10:1-5; Is 20:1-4). Having the freedom and means to maintain the privacy of one's body is a basic human need. By exposing the private parts of the conquered enemy the victors deprived them of dignity and revealed that they were powerless to defend themselves or others in their care. Being stripped and exposed was sometimes the experience of slaves (e.g., personified Babylon in Is 47:1-4; *see* Ancient and Modern Slavery). In Old Testament law stripping does not precede execution by stoning, even in the case of adultery.

In the feminine personification of Jerusalem a conqueror's abuse of prisoners of war intersects with a husband's punishment of his adulterous wife. Within the metaphor of a marriage, God threatened to strip and expose personified Israel (Hos 2:3, 10) and Jerusalem (Ezek 16:35-43) for their religious and political adultery. Since this punishment is never specified in cases of adultery elsewhere in the Old Testament, there are at least two ways to understand its relationship to the metaphor in Hosea, Ezekiel and Jeremiah. Exposure and humiliation may have been a lesser punishment that a husband could choose instead of stoning. Ezekiel 16:36-37 presents stripping as a logical punishment for adultery, doing to Jerusalem what she had already done to herself. Stripping is not a substitute penalty in Ezekiel 16:40 and Hosea 2:3; in both contexts death will follow immediately.

The punishment of exposure may have been imported into the metaphor of Yahweh and his wife from the realm of warfare. It may have had no place within the bounds of known or accepted behavior by an Israelite husband, but because it was a common practice of conquerors, it was included in the story of what Israel and Jerusalem would experience. When applied to a personified nation or city the threat of exposing nakedness is metaphorical, but it is the conqueror's act, not the husband's. Fortifications constituted a city's clothes. A naked city has had its walls breached or its gate broken down so the city can no longer control who enters to plunder, destroy and kill. A naked country has been stripped of the crops that feed and clothe its people. Israel and Jerusalem experienced breached walls and stripped fields, but there is no narrative account of individuals stripped and exposed by the Babylonians in 597 or 587/6 B.C.

Does the abuse pictured in Jeremiah 13:22, 26 go as far as rape? Knowledge of human nature and the violence done by conquering armies makes it impossible to exclude the possibility. In the expression "your skirts are lifted up," the word *skirts* may be a euphemism for the private parts (cf. Is 47:3; Nahum 3:5). This clause would function as a euphemism for rape by naming the step before the act. A related expression, "uncover the skirts of," with an active form of the same verb and a different noun, serves as a euphemism for marital relations (Deut 22:30). However, having one's nakedness "uncovered" may refer to no more than being seen (Ex 20:26).

In the next clause, "your heels suffer violence" (Jer 13:22; NRSV "you are violated"), "heels" may stand for the sexual organs or the buttocks. The verb is a unique passive form of a rare verb with a wide range of meaning but never specifically rape.

The final expression, "I will lift up your skirts over your face," may indicate exposure only, or it may point to rape. In Nahum 3:5 the same judgment is spoken against Nineveh personified as a woman. The nations will see her nakedness and shame and will respond by throwing filth at her. The sight of her exposed body will incite contempt.

In the poetry of Jeremiah, Jerusalem almost always functions as the personification of its population, the king and other leaders, and the political, religious and social power held by its people and institutions. When Zion's walls are torn down, the nation-state's way of life will also be overthrown. The personification of the city as a woman fits the social patterns of the ancient Near East. Like the women in the typical Israelite household, the city stays home while the men go out to work, trade, establish political relationships and fight. The men's success is displayed in the richness of the city's ornaments and the strength of its defenses. The female figure appears as the passive party, the one for whom men work and do battle. Conversely, the failure of male leaders, diplomats and armies is evident in what happens to the city and the land (another feminine noun). The descriptions of the judgment on the nation therefore often depict the ruin of women. This rhetoric was supposed to appeal to the male leaders of Judah on a visceral level. In their desire to protect a vulnerable woman they might listen to the Lord's word through the prophet and obey. The judgment came in part to put an end to violence against real, individual women. Readers of Jeremiah should resist the tendency to think of women in general as passive, vulnerable and defenseless and guard against the temptation to take perverse pleasure in portrayals of women's suffering.

The juxtaposition of Jeremiah 13:22 and Jeremiah 13:26 illustrates a frequent phenomenon in Jeremiah: God and the Babylonians do the same things. Compare, for example, Jeremiah 13:14 (God) and Jeremiah 21:7 (Nebuchadnezzar). God has chosen to bring the kingdom of Judah and Jerusalem to an end "by his [Nebuchadnezzar's] hand" (Jer 27:8). As a result, a large part of the portrayal of God in Jeremiah corresponds to the portrayal of Nebuchadnezzar and the Babylonians. One might even say that God takes responsibility for the horrors of warfare and subjugation as practiced by the Babylonians. For the first audiences of Jeremiah the prophet and Jeremiah the book the only alternative to this theological explanation would have been to acknowledge the victory of Marduk, the god of Babylon. The Lord also took a risk by choosing to depend on the worldly power of Nebuchadnezzar and the Babylonians to carry out the divine plan, for they retained freedom to act according to their values and ambitions. They exceeded their mandate from God and suffered judgment. In the interim, God used the available means to overthrow the stubbornly rebellious kingdom of Judah and bring to an end the oppression and violence being done within it.

In Jeremiah the theme of God's anguish and grief over the suffering of the people under just judgment and excessive Babylonian violence distinguishes the Lord's plan from Nebuchadnezzar's imperial goals. These chapters also include brief summaries of God's plan for Judah, including restoration to the land.

Most of Jeremiah 11—17 deals with a particular consequence of the broken covenant. The point has been reached when God will not enter into negotiations for covenant renewal. The covenant curses must come into effect. Moses had interceded effectively on behalf of Israel on two occasions when the Lord was ready to break all ties with them. But after declaring the covenant broken, God forbids Jeremiah to pray for the people. A series of prayers by the people alternating with words from God illustrate this decision (Jer 14:7—15:9). Although the people express repentance, asking God to "remember and do not break your covenant with us" (Jer 14:20-21), the Lord does not relent.

These chapters also include three of Jeremiah's prayers for help, or "Confessions" (Jer 11:18—12:6; 15:10-21; 17:14-18). In each prayer Jeremiah contends with God over the pain and distress he suffers as a prophet. His relatives had plotted to kill him if he did not stop prophesying. Jeremiah had received the Lord's words with joy, but his audience cursed and persecuted him for bringing a message of doom and ridiculed him when those prophecies were not immediately fulfilled. Jeremiah's complaints serve as evidence against the people of his audience. His enemies are the very people who stand under divine judgment, and persecuting Jeremiah compounds their guilt. Jeremiah follows the conventions of some Old Testament lamenting prayers and asks for vindication from his enemies. When judgment falls on Judah and Jerusalem those prayers will be fulfilled. Jeremiah's survival depends solely on God, who had promised to be with him and defend him.

Jeremiah's social isolation was part of his ministry in another way. The Lord commanded him to remain unmarried, childless and uninvolved in community rituals surrounding marriage and death. This unique way of life would be a demonstration of the judgment to come. Jeremiah was deprived of children and therefore a future for his name, as the people will be. Jeremiah did not participate in mourning rites as a sign that no one will be left to bury the dead or comfort the bereaved. Jeremiah did not attend wedding feasts because God will banish the people from the land and leave no one to laugh or sing.

Readers of these chapters are not left to despair, however. Jeremiah 16:10-15 summarizes God's plan for Israel, including restoration after exile. There will even be hope for nations who reject their false gods and know the Lord.

The Last Chance Refused (Jer 18—20)

The material assembled in these chapters shows how the people to whom Jeremiah ministered refused their last chance to repent and be spared. Two examples from pottery making illustrate this development. Jeremiah watched a potter change his plan for a lump of clay. It could be remade into another shape while it was still moist and malleable. Once a pot had been fired, however, the only way to change its shape was to break it and render it useless. God had planned good things for Israel, but they had disobeyed. Through Jeremiah the Lord had declared the plan to break and destroy them, but they could still choose to turn from their wicked ways and let God shape their future for good. They refused God's offer, however, and chose to be shaped by their own plans. Their national life and institutions would maintain their way rather than the Lord's. The city and people shattered by divine judgment will be like a shattered pot that cannot be mended. After their decision there will be no turning back from disaster.

Once again the central indictment of idolatry is presented as the reason for judgment. The city gate near the pottery shop led to the valley of the son of Hinnom, where people burned their children as offerings to Baal. The theory behind the practice of child sacrifice is never explained in the Old Testament. It may have been thought of as a way to acknowledge dependence upon the deity. By offering up the children through whom their lives would be continued, parents entrusted their existence to the god. Jeremiah 19:4 labels this practice murder.

A particularly horrible picture of judgment follows this indictment. Jerusalem will be besieged, and the starving people will resort to cannibalism (Jer 19:9; cf. Ezek 5:10). Thus one of the covenant curses will come into effect (see Lam 2:20; 4:10, which lament this horror during the conquest of the city). Second Kings 6:24-30 is the only narrative account in the Old Testament of this measure of desperation.

Rejection of the divine word takes the form of persecuting the Lord's prophet. His enemies plotted against Jeremiah, beat him, put him in stocks and planned to kill him. Jeremiah's prayer for vindication coincides with God's announced judgment.

Jeremiah's prayer (Jer 20:7-13) follows one of the conventions of an Old Testament lament when he blames God directly for his suffering. In Jeremiah 20:7 he accuses God of enticing or deceiving him and prevailing over him, using the same verbs as his traitorous friends speak (Jer 20:10). God had succeeded at what they had only planned. Both verbs can have a sexual connotation ("seduce," e.g., Ex 22:16; Judg 16:5; and "force [sexually]," e.g., Deut 22:25; 2 Sam 13:11, 14). Nevertheless, this prayer also includes a statement of confidence in God's help. Jeremiah believes the truth of the judgment oracles he has had to deliver.

The sixth and final prayer for help is uniformly negative. This poem does not say anything directly about the message Jeremiah has preached or the persecution he has suffered, although they are the reason for his misery. Instead Jeremiah curses the day he was born. The Lord had consecrated Jeremiah a prophet before birth, so he could have avoided the burden of God's call only by never being born. His father had received with joy the announcement "A child is born to you, a son" (Jer 20:15).

Jeremiah curses this messenger just as he has been cursed for bringing unwelcome news. If he had died in the womb, he could have avoided the sorrow and shame that have filled his life. If the anonymous messenger is the subject, Jeremiah 20:17 is hyperbole. The only way a man could have killed him in the womb would have been to kill his mother before he was born. Jeremiah stops short of saying this, just as he does not directly curse his mother. Alternatively, God may have been the one who could have killed him instead of consecrating him.

Jeremiah's question about the meaning of his life suggests a parallel question about the meaning of Israel's life. In these chapters the Israelites in Judah have turned down their final opportunity to repent. They have voluntarily forfeited their special role among the nations as the Lord's chosen people. What will prove to be the meaning of their national life if it ends like this? Jeremiah's survival provides a hint that there will be a future for God's people too. Although Jeremiah's hearers decided against God's word, they were not able to kill God's prophet.

Failed Monarchy and False Prophecy (Jer 21—24)

The monarchy was the heart of pride, security and hope for the people of Judah and Jerusalem. The collective message of the prophecies in these chapters is that the Lord would bring to an end the monarchy and the nation-state ruled by it. Individually and collectively the last four kings of Judah had failed God's basic requirement for royal rule: They had not executed justice and righteousness. Kings were responsible for delivering the oppressed from the ones who exploited them and protecting the weak from violence and murder. Jehoiakim, however, had been one of the oppressors. In order to build his grand new palace he had pressed people into forced labor, and in order to achieve his greedy goals he had killed innocent people.

There is a word from the Lord for each of Judah's last four kings. Zedekiah will be handed over to Nebuchadnezzar, whose victory is certain. Shallum (Jehoahaz) will never see Judah again and will die in Egypt. No one will mourn Jehoiakim. His corpse will be treated no better than a donkey's. Coniah (Jehoiachin) will die childless in exile. These kings failed to care for the nation entrusted to them, so they and their people will be scattered from their land.

In spite of this, the Lord's plan for Israel and Judah will include return from exile and a new king. The new king from David's line will reign in accordance with God's will, so that he will be named "the LORD is our righteousness" (Jer 23:6).

People claiming to be prophets were also responsible for Judah's stubborn commitment to sin. False prophets claimed to speak the Lord's word although the Lord had never spoken to them. A true prophet had stood in the privileged circle of the Lord's council and heard and seen the word in person (Jer 23:18). Prophets who turn the people to worshiping other gods were to be killed (Deut 13:1-5). Such prophets worked in Jeremiah's time also, undermining the people by encouraging disobedience to God. The ministry of true prophets should have the opposite effect, turning the people away from evil and back to God.

The preaching of judgment was a way of causing the people to recognize the sin in their lives so that they could repent. The false prophets preached peace and well-being, so the people saw no need to change. In the political situation their message of peace meant that Babylon would not conquer and destroy Judah as Jeremiah prophesied. Even after the first conquest of Jerusalem and the exile of Jehoiachin the false prophets preached peace, supporting the belief that the guilty parties had been exiled and the worst was over. God shows Jeremiah two baskets of figs to illustrate the opposite message. The figs that were too rotten to eat represented Zedekiah and the new leaders of Judah, who would not escape disgrace and destruction. The exiles of 597, however, were represented by the good figs. Only those people who accept divine judgment will be able to receive the future God will offer. They will return and be built up in the land. The Lord will change their hearts so that they will choose only the Lord as God and live according to the divine will. They will once again become the Lord's covenant people.

The Lord's People Among the Nations (Jer 25)

This chapter serves as a hub within the

book, linking the judgment on Israel and Judah with the violent expansion of the Neo-Babylonian Empire under Nebuchadnezzar. It claims for the God of Israel a scope of authority as wide as the known world and a direct responsibility for the military and political affairs of the other nations. (In the Septuagint the oracles against foreign nations [Jer 46—51] are all found in the middle of Jeremiah 25.) The world of the ancient Near East was falling apart, but the Lord had not lost control. The Babylonians' hegemony would last seventy years; then they will be repaid in accordance with the way they exercise their rule.

Jeremiah Among the Prophets (Jer 26)

The account of Jeremiah's trial establishes him as a true prophet. The people who heard the oracle threatening the destruction of the temple charged him with a capital crime. They did not believe that such a word could have come from God (cf. Deut 18:20). Yet the court ruled that he had spoken the Lord's word in the Lord's name. Readers of the book know that the prophecy came true.

Jeremiah was a member of the long line of prophets whom the Lord had sent to call Israel to repentance. In every generation the purpose of their prophesying had been that the people would listen and turn, so that God would withhold the threatened disaster. After the verdict the elders recalled Hezekiah's repentance when Micah preached the destruction of Jerusalem. Jeremiah's first audience did not follow Hezekiah's example. The appeal, however, continues to address hearers and readers.

A true prophet ministered at the cost of great danger and pain. This narrative illustrates the complaints in Jeremiah's "Confessions" that the people made plans to kill him. Uriah, who prophesied in words like Jeremiah's, was killed by Jehoiakim.

The Lord Reigns (Jer 27—29)

Early in the reign of Zedekiah emissaries from Edom, Moab, Ammon, Tyre and Sidon came to Jerusalem, apparently to plot rebellion against Nebuchadnezzar. Jeremiah met them with a word from the Lord for the kings they represented. Every kingdom in the region must submit to the rule of Nebuchadnezzar. The Lord, as Creator, had the authority to make this demand. To illustrate his message, Jeremiah wore a yoke, a familiar image of political servitude. If the other nations accepted Nebuchadnezzar's yoke peacefully they would avoid exile or ruin at his hand. Judah had already experienced one deportation, in 597 B.C., but Jerusalem might be spared destruction.

The Lord had granted the Babylonians three generations of rule before they would be enslaved by other nations (Jer 27:7; cf. seventy years in Jer 25:12; 29:10). Their hegemony had a time limit, but it was long enough that adults in Jeremiah's audience could not hope to see the end. The kingdom of Judah as they had known it could never be the same after a seventy-year hiatus.

Other prophets offered a different message, which they said was from the Lord. Hananiah, in Jerusalem, and Ahab and Zedekiah, among the exiles in Babylon, said that God had already broken the power of Nebuchadnezzar. The exiles and the booty taken from the temple will return within two years. The worst was over. There was no need to repent. Hananiah illustrated his message by breaking Jeremiah's yoke. Prophets and diviners in the neighboring countries also said that their kings and people would not have to serve Nebuchadnezzar.

Jeremiah sent a collection of prophecies in writing to the Jewish exiles already in Babylon. Little is known about the conditions in which they lived except that they were kept together as one or more communities. God told them to build houses and plant gardens, arrange marriages and have children. It is unlikely that intermarriage with non-Jews was allowed by this command. The three generations of Jews (Jer 29:6) corresponds to the three generations of kings (Jer 27:7). For Babylon's seventy years the exiles' well-being will coincide with Babylon's. Therefore they should pray for the good of Babylon, their conquerors' capital, as they had once prayed for Jerusalem. The exiles could submit to Nebuchadnezzar by living peacefully. Their mandate was to survive and flourish until Babylon's time was over. The adults who received Jeremiah's letter would not be alive to see the restoration. But if they believed and obeyed, then their grandchildren would be part of the hopeful future the Lord had promised. Exiles who taught lies and flouted divine law cut themselves off from that future (e.g., Ahab, Zedekiah and Shemaiah; Jer 29:23, 31-32). Meanwhile God will hear their prayers and be with them in exile.

After the terrifying upheaval of conquest and deportation it must have been tempting to preach and to believe that everything would soon be back to normal. This belief was another way of denying the need for change and the radical reconstruction that had already begun. God's people will emerge from Babylon's seventy years transformed and made new.

The Book of Comfort and Hope (Jer 30—33)

The Lord's promises of restoration for Israel and Judah receive their fullest description in these chapters. Poems, prose sayings, narrative and prayer set forth the new future planned by God in the context of present judgment. Much of the book is devoted to explaining the necessity of this judgment, but these chapters indicate why God's people will be saved.

Salvation and restoration will be possible because of God's everlasting love and faithfulness. Family relationships are the metaphors for this enduring commitment. The Lord is the close relative who redeems or ransoms. Israel is God's firstborn son and virgin daughter. Rachel weeping for her missing children is a picture of God's grief. Motherly mercy, felt in the womb, welcomes Ephraim's repentance.

The principle of measured judgment is also present. Punishment will continue until God's plan is accomplished. But when Israel's conquerors exceed that just measure of punishment, God will intervene to deliver them.

The Lord promises a new covenant that will be different from the first. Their sins will be forgiven; not even the memory of them will cloud the new relationship (Jer 31:34; cf. Num 14:20-23; Mt 26:28). God will transform every person's will and desire to be consistent with God's will. Hearts once inscribed with sin will be a tablet for God's law. Then no one will have to teach them to choose the Lord's way.

The collection of poems in Jeremiah 30:5—31:22 moves forward and then backward in its chronology of the promised future. God is present and will save Israel, who is living in terror and distress (Jer 30:5-11). Their pain seems incurable because it is a consequence of their sin, but God will heal them (Jer 30:12-17). Jerusalem will be rebuilt and populated and ruled by a prince who is one of God's people, but not until the time of judgment is complete (Jer 30:18—31:1). The people who survive the wrath will be built up in the land. Crops will grow and festivals will be celebrated in gratitude to God (Jer 31:2-6). The people are addressed as "virgin Israel" (Jer 31:4). Although they were guilty of unfaithfulness in the past, they will be wholly true to God.

Moving backward, Jeremiah 31:7-14 describes how the people will come back to the land and settle in it. The Lord will gather them out of all the nations where they have been scattered and provide them with comfort, water and a smooth path. Even the weakest and most unlikely travelers will be able to come, including women who are pregnant or in labor. A people who once needed the services of women skilled in mourning will be led by women dancing with joy. What will happen before this to enable them to return? The final poem (Jer 31:15-22) begins by evoking the image of Rachel, who died in childbirth. She weeps for the children of Israel who have been taken in to exile. Her weeping is answered like a prayer. There is hope for a future because the lost children will come back. Those lost ones are personified as Ephraim, who acknowledges his sin, asks God to bring him back and repents. God, as Ephraim's father, has mercy on him. The answer to Ephraim's prayer is addressed to Virgin Israel, God's daughter. She has repeatedly turned to and from God, but God will forget her unfaithfulness and welcome her home.

The enigmatic new creation, literally, "female encircles he-man" (Jer 31:22), has many possible interpretations. Unusual words appear in a unique combination to express the unprecedented nature of God's creation. The nation that was dead will live again, so that Rachel will embrace a strong son. The status of women will be enhanced so that a woman can protect a male warrior as well as he can protect her. God will transform the people spiritually so that Israel, as fickle daughter, will firmly embrace faith in the Lord, the valiant One.

During the final siege of Jerusalem, Jeremiah fulfilled the obligation of redeemer for his cousin, Hanamel, by buying his field. The purpose of this custom was to keep ancestral land in the possession of the family. In the tenth year of Zedekiah, however, Hanamel's field in Anathoth may have already been occupied by the Babylonians. Jeremiah was being held in the court of the guard. In spite of these things, Jeremiah obeyed God's command by redeeming the field and using the transaction as a sign act. He had the deed prepared by a professional scribe, Baruch. It was witnessed, sealed and stored in a jar to demonstrate God's promise. Jeremiah was doing what the people will be able to do when they return. "Houses and fields and vineyards shall again be bought in this land" (Jer 32:15).

Jeremiah's prayer and God's answers set this apparently foolish act in the context of Israel's past and the Lord's plan. God's people were about to lose the land because of their persistent disobedience. How could they hope to hold it again? The answer is found in God's character: for God "nothing is too hard" (Jer 32:17, 27; cf. Gen 18:12-15). The Lord will give the new covenant people a single-minded capacity to honor and obey.

Examples of Faithlessness and Faith (Jer 34—36)

These three chapters are arranged in reverse chronological order. Their purpose is to present contrasting examples of faith and faithlessness. Looking backward, these incidents justify the judgment on Judah. Looking ahead, they advocate continuing adherence to God's law and the prophetic word.

During the siege of Jerusalem Zedekiah made "a proclamation of liberty" for male and female debt slaves (Jer 34:8). Like Josiah, he led the people to make a covenant to keep the terms of the Sinai covenant. One may speculate that the slaveholders benefited by having fewer mouths to feed. Documents from Nippur show parents who sold their children into slavery during a siege of the city to ensure that they would be fed. The slaveholders, they believed, would take care of their investment. The only reason given in Jeremiah 34, however, was the public explanation that a Judean should not hold another Judean as a slave. The covenant law allowed a poor person to sell himself or his child into servitude to raise funds to pay debts. Their service was limited to six years. The fact that female slaves were also released at that time probably indicates that they had not become secondary wives. The people in Jerusalem who could afford to hold slaves had not been releasing them at the end of their term of service. Zedekiah's proclamation of release resembles the ancient Near Eastern practice of *mesharum* acts in which a king could alleviate some of the burden on the poor, redistribute wealth and gain personal support.

Soon, however, the Babylonian forces withdrew from Jerusalem in response to the advance of the Egyptian army. People in Jerusalem hoped or believed that the Babylonians would not return. The slaveholders reneged on their promise and took back the slaves they had just released. In so doing they not only violated again the provisions of the law but also took the Lord's name in vain by breaking the covenant oath they had sworn by that name. They would suffer under the curses of the covenants they had violated.

Jeremiah 35, dated during the reign of Jehoiakim, stands alongside Jeremiah 34 to invite comparison. The Rechabites were a mysterious, isolated group that had originated in the ninth century B.C. (2 Kings 10:15-28). Through almost three centuries they had lived by the standards of their founder. Women, men and children did not live in houses, engage in agriculture or drink wine. At God's command Jeremiah used them in a sign act to call his audience to account. When the Rechabites refused to drink the wine Jeremiah offered them, saying that they had to obey their ancestor's command, Jeremiah's word from the Lord invited his audience to examine themselves. The Rechabites had remained obedient to stringent commands from their ancestor and over many generations had maintained their way of life despite constant pressure to conform to the majority lifestyle. The people of Israel and Judah, however, had not been obedient to the word of the Lord for even one generation, even though God had spoken directly to them and sent prophets to call them to repent.

The events of Jeremiah 36 begin in the

fourth year of Jehoiakim, the year that Nebuchadnezzar defeated the Egyptians at Carchemish and became king of Babylon and overlord of the king of Judah. In the context of Jeremiah 34—35 the incidents of Jeremiah 36 serve as another example of unfaithfulness and disobedience to the Lord's word. The collection of prophecies written in the scroll described the disasters threatened against Judah. Jehoiakim's response epitomizes contempt and rejection of the divine word. His actions were the opposite of Josiah's upon hearing the scroll of the law. Instead of tearing his clothes in contrition, Jehoiakim cut the scroll into strips. Instead of sending the scroll to a prophet to be authenticated, he sent men to arrest Jeremiah and Baruch. Instead of instituting concrete changes in national life in accordance with God's word, Jehoiakim burned the scroll so that no one else could hear it.

The account of the two scrolls serves another function for readers of Jeremiah and other prophetic books. It is impossible to know what parts of the book were included in the first scroll or in the second, to which many similar words were added. Written words, read from a scroll, can still be the living word of God. Prophetic words addressed to earlier times and different circumstances remain relevant. Prophecies threatening judgment should be heard as invitations to repent and be forgiven.

Siege, Conquest and Aftermath (Jer 37—44)

Eight chapters recount the end of Jeremiah's ministry from the time of the final Babylonian siege of Jerusalem to some months or years later in Egypt. The section is bracketed by the people's false hope in Egypt as help and refuge. During the final siege Pharaoh Hophra approached Jerusalem with an army. When the Babylonians withdrew to face the Egyptians, people in Jerusalem believed they had been saved. The Lord's word through Jeremiah, however, denied that hope. Pharaoh would return home, and the Babylonians would defeat and burn Jerusalem. After the conquest some Jews tried to escape Babylonian rule by emigrating to Egypt, although Jeremiah warned them against it and prophesied the conquest of Egypt also.

The lifting of the siege became the occasion of Jeremiah's imprisonment in Jerusalem on a charge of deserting to the enemy. He had tried to go to Anathoth on family business, possibly relating to his cousin's field. He was arrested at the gate of the city, beaten and incarcerated in the house of Jonathan. These chapters highlight the political aspect of Jeremiah's message. Again and again the word from the Lord calls for submission to the king of Babylon. Before Jerusalem fell, individuals could save their lives by giving themselves up to the besieging forces. The king could save the city from burning and have his life spared if he would surrender to the Babylonian officials. Jeremiah's last word for Zedekiah included a report of a vision. Jeremiah saw the women of the king's household being led out of the conquered city to the Babylonian leaders and heard them taunting the king for listening to unreliable advisors. The courtiers who opposed the Lord's word thought Jeremiah should die for undermining the courage of the defenders and the populace with his announcements of Babylon's certain victory. Zedekiah preserved Jeremiah's life by ameliorating the conditions of his imprisonment, but he never submitted to God's word.

Jeremiah had one courageous ally while he was being held in the court of the guard. Ebed-melech, from Ethiopia, or Nubia, was an official in the palace (*see* Africans in Biblical History). He gained permission from the king to remove Jeremiah from the muddy cistern where the anti-Babylonian advisors had left him to die. God gave Ebed-melech a special promise that his life would be preserved when the city was taken because he trusted in the Lord.

In the eleventh year of Zedekiah, after almost two years of siege, the Babylonian forces breached the wall and took the city. Even then Zedekiah did not surrender. He fled but was captured near Jericho and brought before Nebuchadnezzar at Riblah, in Syria. There he suffered an agonizing judgment. The last thing he saw before being blinded was the slaughter of his sons and the rest of the captured Judean nobles. In chains, Zedekiah was exiled to Babylon along with the Judeans who had surrendered and the survivors remaining in the city.

The Babylonians treated Jeremiah differently. They took him from the court of the guard to Ramah, a few miles north of Jerusalem, with the other captive survivors. With Nebuchadnezzar's permission, Nebuzaradan released Jeremiah and let him choose to go to Babylon or to remain in Judah. Jeremiah chose to join Gedaliah, son of Ahikam, whom the Babylonians had appointed governor. Gedaliah came from a family of courtiers who had supported Jeremiah's ministry in various ways; the king's daughters were also with him at Mizpah.

Gedaliah's leadership offered hope to the people who remained in the land. The Babylonians left behind the poor people who owned nothing but gave them farmland and vineyards once owned by the exiles. Judeans who had fled during the Babylonian crisis returned from the neighboring countries and received a share in the harvest. Somehow, part of Judah's army had survived in the open country. Gedaliah persuaded some of them to accept Babylonian rule and submit to his authority. He assured them that they would suffer no reprisals and granted them the towns that they held as well as their portion of the harvest. Not everyone agreed with his optimistic view of conditions in Judah, however.

One of the commanders did not accept Gedaliah's terms. Ishmael, a member of the royal family, plotted with Baalis, king of the Ammonites, to assassinate Gedaliah. They wanted to overthrow Babylonian rule. In the theology of Jeremiah this plot represented continued resistance to the Lord's will, not admirable patriotism. Another of the commanders, Johanan, son of Kareah, warned Gedaliah, but he refused to believe it. So Ishmael and his accomplices killed Gedaliah at his table, along with other Judeans and some Babylonian soldiers.

Ishmael's rebellion prevented a first step toward return and reunion for northern kingdom Israelites. Eighty men from the former northern kingdom cities of Shiloh, Shechem and Samaria stopped in Mizpah the next day on their way to Jerusalem. They were dressed in mourning and carried incense and offerings for the temple. Ten of them bought their lives with bribes of food, but Ishmael killed the rest and disposed of their corpses along with the rest of his victims in a large cistern. Johanan and his forces caught up with Ishmael and freed his captives. Each man had reason to fear Babylon. Ishmael escaped to the Ammonites, and Johanan set out for Egypt with the mixed group under his leadership.

Johanan and his people inquired of the Lord through Jeremiah. The divine word was unequivocal: Do not go to Egypt. God promised to plant them in Judah and build them up. God would be with them and save them from Nebuchadnezzar, who would give them back their land. The people did not believe this word, and they refused to obey it. Johanan and other leading men accused Jeremiah of colluding with Baruch in order to hand them over to the Babylonians for death or exile. The group emigrated to Egypt, taking Jeremiah and Baruch with them.

The last phase of Jeremiah's ministry returns to the core issue of false worship. The Jewish refugees had disobeyed God and had gone to Egypt. Although they had experienced disaster and had the divine word readily available to them, they chose to return to the worship of the queen of heaven. They made vows to her and fulfilled them by offering libations and cakes in her image—perhaps a star, the moon or a female form.

The worshipers of the queen of heaven had worked out an alternate theological explanation for what had happened to Judah during the preceding half century, one that contradicted the Lord's word through Jeremiah. When the queen of heaven had been worshiped in Judah in earlier times the people had prospered, enjoying peace and plenty of food. Josiah's religious reformation, beginning in 621 B.C., had put a stop to the veneration of the queen of heaven. Neglect of her offerings caused the suffering Judah experienced in the years that followed. They reasoned that renewed offerings might bring about a restoration of peace and prosperity.

The final word of prophecy reported from Jeremiah in Egypt is another announcement of judgment. People who had experienced the consequences of idolatry in Judah will experience it again. The truth of God's judgment against them had been confirmed by the Babylonian conquest. Disbelieving, they had disobeyed again. So proof will be offered once more when God gives Pharaoh into the hands of Nebuchadnezzar.

This commitment to apostasy and to an alternative theology among the refugees in

Egypt demonstrates the need for the book of Jeremiah. No one knows what happened to Jeremiah, but the book that bears his name continues to bring the living word of God to the nations.

A Promise for Baruch (Jer 45)

The unit that concludes this portion of the book is dated to the fourth year of Jehoiakim, the year in which Baruch wrote the scroll at Jeremiah's dictation. The Lord promised Baruch his life as a prize of war during the chaotic, dangerous years to follow because of Baruch's response to the message of the scroll. Jehoiakim had closed his mind to the Lord's word, but Baruch had responded in sorrow because he believed it. This brief chapter contrasts Baruch the believer to the idolatrous Jews in Egypt. It also gives another example of the fulfillment of God's word. Baruch had survived through all these disasters because God had promised he would.

Prophecies Against the Nations (Jer 46—49)

Babylonian expansion through Syria-Palestine and into Egypt appeared to be the result of their ambition and military prowess, but Jeremiah revealed another cause. The Lord as Creator claims sovereignty over all nations and exercises the authority to appoint their ruler by naming the king of Babylon. Nebuchadnezzar will be God's instrument for bringing judgment upon Judah and its neighbors. More than a score of cities, nations or regions are listed as recipients of divine wrath (Jer 25:19-26). The upheaval and suffering that accompanied Babylon's rise were not proof of the victory of Marduk, patron deity of Babylon, over the gods of the conquered nations, including Yahweh. On the contrary, the king of Babylon was Yahweh's servant.

Superscriptions within Jeremiah 46 relate prophecies against Egypt to Babylon's victories. An oracle in Jeremiah 46:3-12 describes the failure of Egypt's ambitions ("Let me rise, let me cover the earth," Jer 46:8). Egyptian forces had defeated the Babylonians and made Judah Egypt's vassal, but at Carchemish, Nebuchadnezzar was victorious. This oracle claimed that victory for the Lord and warned the king and the people of Judah to accept Babylon's authority.

Some people in Judah continued to put their hopes in Egypt. God used prophecies such as Jeremiah 46:14-26 to warn them against this misplaced trust. Egypt looked and sounded strong, but Pharaoh, their gods and their armies will fall before the Lord and the enemy that will invade from the north. The Babylonians broke off the final siege of Jerusalem when the Egyptian army approached, and the population hoped that they had been delivered. The Egyptians could not save Judah from the judgment, and they could not save themselves. Since Nebuchadnezzar did not invade Egypt until 568 B.C., this oracle had continuing relevance after the fall of Jerusalem. Egypt would not be a safe place for refugees.

The final two verses in Jeremiah 46 repeat Jeremiah 30:10-11. Like Jeremiah 46:26, they balance the announcements of Nebuchadnezzar's victories in the rest of the chapter with the promise of a limit to Babylonian rule. When Israel's just measure of punishment is complete, the Lord will make an end of Babylon and bring them back from captivity.

The Philistine cities along the Mediterranean coastal plain lay in the path of imperial armies. Babylon defeated Ashkelon in 604 B.C. and Egypt conquered Gaza in 601. This oracle about the first occasion could have been reused in preparation for the second. Prophecies about Babylonian victories supported Jeremiah's unwelcome message that Judah and Jerusalem must submit to their rule. Ashkelon's conqueror from the north was a sword in the Lord's hand. If the Philistines had allied with Tyre and Sidon to resist Babylon, then they may be an example of what will happen to nations who oppose the Lord's plan.

Envoys from Moab, Ammon, Edom, Tyre and Sidon met with Zedekiah in 594 B.C. to plan a revolt against Nebuchadnezzar. The account of God's word through Jeremiah for these messengers and their kings (Jer 27) provides a context for reading the collections of prophecies concerning Moab (Jer 48), the Ammonites (Jer 49:1-6) and Edom (Jer 49:7-22). The Lord, the Creator, had given all these lands into the power of Nebuchadnezzar. Any nation that refused to submit to his rule would be punished by sword, famine and pestilence. The judgment prophecies in Jeremiah 48—49 assert the Lord's authority over these nations and give vivid descriptions of their terror and loss.

The main reason for judgment in each case is misplaced trust. Moab was arrogant and relied on its fortified cities and wealth. The Moabites magnified themselves against the Lord and trusted their national deity, Chemosh. The Ammonites also believed that their treasures made them secure. Edom trusted in its capacity to terrorize other nations. The coming conquest will destroy every false object of trust. Shame and mourning will replace pride.

In Genesis these three nations were closely related to Israel. Edom came from Esau, Jacob's twin. Moab and Ammon were sons of Lot, Abraham's nephew. Their territories bordered Israel and Judah on the east. Their sins included offenses against Israel. Moab had ridiculed Israel, and Ammon had taken land and towns from the tribe of Gad. Yet each nation also receives a tender word from God. The Lord's heart moans and mourns for the people of Moab. The Ammonites are called "faithless daughter" (Jer 49:4), the same title by which God addressed Israel in Jeremiah 31:22. The Lord offers shelter in the midst of judgment to Edom's widows and orphans. After the judgment is complete, God promises to restore Moab and the Ammonites to their lands.

The remaining three oracles are about peoples increasingly distant from the land of Israel. The Lord's sovereignty extends northeast to Damascus, across the Arabian desert and as far as Elam, on the far side of Babylon. Their destruction has nothing to do with Judah or Israel, although Damascus had been an ally and an enemy. These prophecies have been included in Jeremiah because they support the Lord's authority to rule all nations.

Judgment on Babylon (Jer 50—51)

This collection of judgment prophecies against Babylon seems to contradict the commands to serve the king of Babylon (Jer 27:7, 12) and to pray for and seek the peace of Babylon (Jer 29:7). Jeremiah's announcement that Babylon will be "desolate forever" (Jer 51:62) dates to the fourth year of Zedekiah, only shortly after the message of Jeremiah 27—28. The book explains this difference by the promise of a limited period of power, seventy years, for Babylon. The promised return of the exiles and their descendants will be linked to the end of their captors' power. God will summon the exiles to flee before Babylon is destroyed. The prophecies of Babylon's destruction refer, according to this chronology, to the end of the seventy years. The time of restoration for Egypt, Moab, the Ammonites and Elam must also follow Babylon's fall.

The expansion of the Babylonian Empire had been the Lord's tool for bringing the kingdom of Judah and the city of Jerusalem to an end. Yet these chapters announce judgment on Babylon for cruel oppression and for sinning against God. This transformation mirrors the change seen in Jeremiah 30—31, and especially in Jeremiah 30:12-17. In a gracious non sequitur, God's word transforms the exiles and survivors from objects of a just punishment to the recipients of mercy and vindication. The concept of a "just measure" of punishment helps to explain this change (Jer 30:11, cf. Jer 10:24). When the Babylonians and their supporters, acting according to their ambitions and character, exceed the "just measure," then they are liable to judgment.

God did not change sides arbitrarily. The Creator who had granted power to Nebuchadnezzar is free to take it away (Jer 51:15-19, a duplicate of Jer 10:12-16). Like Judah, the Babylonians will be judged because they had sinned against, challenged and arrogantly defied the Lord. Theirs was a land that had gone "mad over idols" (Jer 50:38), so they will be punished. In answer to lament prayers like that of personified Jerusalem (Jer 51:34-35), the Lord will redeem Judah from its captors and take revenge for Jerusalem and for the temple. Babylon will "fall for the slain of Israel" (Jer 51:49).

Babylon's punishment will also be measured. The oracles against Babylon repeat several of the themes and specific expressions from the judgment sayings against Judah earlier in the book. Babylon's enemy will also come from the north. Jeremiah 50:41-43 duplicates the description of the invaders from Jeremiah 6:22-24 but substitutes "Babylon" for "Zion." Babylon's warriors will become weak like women, and its king will suffer anguish like a woman in labor. They will be powerless to defend and save the city. The city of Babylon personified as a woman appears frequently in these chapters, intensifying the picture of the city as a victim.

"Do to her as she has done" (Jer 50:15, 29) summarizes the principle exemplified in

Emotions of Women in Childbirth

An analysis of biblical texts reveals sympathy with women in childbirth and a familiarity with their vicissitudes throughout the event. Though contemporary mothers are often reticent to disclose their emotions, Hebrew society acknowledged their suffering, with little effort to conceal or ignore a familiar aspect of life.

Jeremiah twice speaks of Moab and Edom, whose "hearts . . . shall be like the heart of a woman in labor" (Jer 48:41; 49:22; cf. 50:43). Prevailing emotions may be terror and shock at the suddenness with which a woman is gripped by a force beyond her control (Jer 13:21; Mt 24:8). Isaiah's composition reflects an observation of birth (Is 26:17-18). There follows a description of a false pregnancy in which the woman undergoes labor pains but "[gives] birth only to wind" (Is 26:18; cf. 33:11). This is a bitter conclusion for a woman who has wanted a child and must accept the disappointing reality.

In the biblical texts we find described intense fear, panic (Ps 48:5-6), agony (Is 13:8), anguish (Jer 6:24; 49:24; 50:43) anger, bewilderment, despair (Is 21:3-4), a sense of isolation and of being overwhelmed by forces within a woman's own body that cannot be controlled. Ancient observers noted writhing (Mic 4:9-10), trembling (Ps 48:66) and groaning (Jer 4:31; 22:23) as indicators of the distress that women experience during delivery. Even God is portrayed as a woman in labor, gasping and panting (Is 42:14).

Modern research reveals that many women fear that they will not have sufficient strength to deliver their children (see Is 37:3; 2 Kings 19:36). Hosea writes of an obstetrical crisis (Hos 13:13-14): the time has come for the birth, but the child is not in a proper position. In this dire strait, delivery is impossible. Mother and child will be lost unless there can be an appropriate intervention.

God is the one who brings relief (Hos 13:14). The NRSV and the JB use the first lines as questions, whereas the NIV construes them as assurances. Few readers recognize that these words that Paul quotes (1 Cor 15:55) were first spoken to a symbolic crisis of pregnancy. They speak directly to deliverance from a desperately dangerous situation known only to women. The emphasis is not on the danger and desperation of childbirth gone wrong but on Yahweh, who can and does deliver.

Many of the biblical texts end with the assurance that Yahweh, sometimes portrayed as a midwife, will bring the child safely to birth (Mic 4:9-10). Labor will be concluded in joy (Is 66:7-12; Jn 16:21). In seeking to suppress the fear that these passages might inspire, we have often failed to recognize the positive support that they offer to parturient women. We have forgotten too the descriptions of immense joy at the arrival of the child. Some recent studies indicate that women are better served by preparation for the pain that they may well expect to experience. These studies indicate that mothers more often desire to gain control over panic rather than pain. In this respect, selected texts have been effectively used to enable expectant mothers to anticipate birthing with confidence and calm. CATHERINE CLARK KROEGER

Jeremiah 30:16. God had threatened Jerusalem, "I will kindle a fire . . . it shall devour" (Jer 17:27; 21:14), and also said "the Chaldeans shall . . . set [Jerusalem] on fire" (Jer 32:29). Jeremiah 52:13 reports that the Babylonian commander burned the temple and other large buildings. The same threat is spoken against Babylon in 50:32: "I will kindle a fire . . . it will devour." Like Jerusalem, Babylon will become "a heap of ruins, a den of jackals, an object of horror and of hissing, without inhabitant" (Jer 51:37).

The principle of corresponding judgments breaks down in the end, however. The Lord will pardon the remnant of Jews who are spared and will not abandon them. Israel and Judah will join in an everlasting covenant with the Lord while Babylon will remain desolate forever.

The End of Judah and Jerusalem (Jer 52)

The book concludes with a chapter borrowed from 2 Kings 24:18—25:30. It reports the final siege and fall of Jerusalem and the immediate aftermath. Then the account jumps forward to the latest date in the book, the thirty-seventh year of Jehoiachin (560 B.C.). Since Jehoiachin had reigned in Jerusalem for only a matter of weeks during the Babylonian conquest in 597 B.C., the use of his regnal year in the date formula is a small act of defiance. Jews were subject to the king of Babylon, Evil-merodach, but the former, rightful king of Judah still lived. In that year, roughly halfway through the seventy years of Babylonian hegemony promised by Jeremiah, Evil-merodach released Jehoiachin from prison, acknowledged his royal status and gave him the dubious honors accorded to other captured kings. Fragments of documents detailing the allowance of grain, wine and oil for Jehoiachin and his sons have been discovered in the excavations of ancient Babylon. It is impossible to determine whether the provisions were generous or meager. Jehoiachin's favored status continued until his death, an unspecified number of years later.

By the addition of Jeremiah 52, the completed form of the book communicates important assurances to an audience late in the exilic period and beyond. The treatment of Jehoiachin illustrates the truth of God's promise to the exiles, "in [Babylon's] welfare you will find your welfare" (Jer 29:7). Jehoiachin would have been fifty-five years old in his thirty-seventh year. His long life serves as a reminder that the royal Davidic line was not extinct (but cf. Jer 23:5-6).

Bibliography. R. E. Clements, *Jeremiah,* Interpretation (Atlanta: John Knox Press, 1988); P. C. Craigie, P. H. Kelley and J. F. Drinkard Jr., *Jeremiah 1—25,* Word Biblical Commentary 26 (Dallas: Word, 1991); A. R. P. Diamond, K. M. O'Connor and L. Stulman, eds., *Troubling Jeremiah,* Journal for the Study of the Old Testament Supplement 260 (Sheffield: Sheffield Academic Press, 1999); G. L. Keown, P. J. Scalise and T. G. Smothers, *Jeremiah 26—52,* Word Biblical Commentary 27 (Dallas: Word, 1995); P. J. King, *Jeremiah, An Archaeological Companion* (Louisville, KY: Westminster John Knox, 1993); J. A. Thompson, *The Book of Jeremiah,* New International Commentary on the Old Testament (Grand Rapids, MI: Eerdmans, 1980).

PAMELA J. SCALISE

LAMENTATIONS

Introduction

Lamentation is a genre common to the ancient Near East and, consequently, to early Israel. There are numerous examples of lament in the Old Testament, many of which appear in the psalms. The book of Lamentations is a compilation of corporate laments written in response to the destruction of Jerusalem by the Neo-Babylonians in 587/6 B.C. Many interpreters have suggested these laments were recited annually during the days of fasting held at the ruined temple site throughout the time of exile (cf. Jer 41:5; Zech 7:1-7; 8:19).

The book of Lamentations consists of five individual pieces most likely composed independently and artfully redacted into one rhetorical piece. Lamentations 1—4 share common vocabulary, stylistic devices and an acrostic structure. Such consistency suggests a group, or school, of lament traditionalists as composer(s). For many years the authorship of the book was attributed to Jeremiah due to an erroneous interpretation of 2 Chronicles 35:25; however, the laments described in Chronicles were for the death of Josiah, not the destruction of Jerusalem.

Scholars have noted that the imagery and language of Lamentations are common to the prophetic literature, as well as the wisdom, deuteronomistic and kingship traditions. Although this statement is true, it ignores the distinct rhetorical emphasis of Lamentations. The most notable similarities between the laments and the prophetic tradition are found in the use of female imagery and personification. In Lamentations Jerusalem is personified as female, sometimes as a woman scorned, sometimes as a young girl, but most often as Yahweh's daughter (often virgin daughter; e.g., Lam 1:3; 2:2, 4, 5, 8, 10, 13). In contrast in the prophetic literature, Israel is most often personified as an adulterous wife who must be punished.

Rhetorically the female imagery is used in prophetic literature to shame Israel into repentance. In Lamentations the imagery is used in an attempt to persuade God to deliver Jerusalem from her distress (i.e., exile). While the result is the same—reconciliation between Israel and God—the object of persuasion differs in each genre. Both genres rise out of a shame-based culture and therefore utilize tactics that play on this cultural norm for the purposes of motivation.

Outline

1:1-22	Jerusalem Personified as Female
2:1-22	The Day of the Lord's Anger
3:1-66	Traditional Responses to Suffering
4:1-22	Jerusalem's Punishment Too Severe
5:1-22	The Cry for Restoration

Commentary

Jerusalem Personified as Female (Lam 1)

From the start Jerusalem is personified as female. Several female images are used to describe her former and current state.

In Lamentations 1:1 Jerusalem is compared with a lonely widow who was formerly a princess among the provinces. None of her lovers (i.e., allies) have comforted her; she is now a slave in exile. Daughter Zion has lost her majesty, and all have seen her nakedness, a shameful state as well as an allusion to her wantonness. Her downfall is directly related to her sin, described as uncleanness in her skirts, which is an allusion to the prophetic imagery of Israel as harlot.

However, the imagery *emphasized* in Lamentations 1:1-11 is that of the helpless, victimized female, as evidenced by references to Jerusalem as lonely widow and slave, the inhabitants as young girls and children, and the epithet daughter Zion. Juxtaposed to these images are numerous references to enemy victory and mockery.

The images of helpless females in distress intertwined with laments over enemy victory as well as confessions of sin work together to create a scenario that plays into the cultural expectation of a parent's responsibility to discipline and protect a child (Weems, 15-22). To ignore the second responsibility, protection, is to bring shame onto oneself as well as one's family; similarly, the widow is taken care of by the family, or at least by the community. In other words, God is being called into account for not sufficiently protecting his children. Although God's discipline for sins committed is understandable and acceptable, destruction by the hand of those forbidden to enter the sanctuary is not. Note that the only petition found in these opening lines is a request that God see the enemy triumph and the consequent affliction of Jerusalem.

In Lamentations 1:11 the speaker changes as Jerusalem laments on behalf of herself. The lament begins with petition for God to attend to Jerusalem's pitiful state followed by accusations of God's attacks against Jerusalem. Although Jerusalem has fallen at the hands of the Neo-Babylonians, she holds God accountable. The images become increasingly more severe: a fire sent from heaven that penetrates deep into the bones, the binding of transgressions into a yoke to be hung around Jerusalem's neck, rejecting all warriors and crushing the young men, treading on the virgin daughter as if in a wine press.

These accusations stand in sharp contrast to the image of Jerusalem as virgin daughter stretching out her arms in search of a comforter where there is none to be found. Juxtaposed is the image of mother Jerusalem concerned for her helpless children in the absence of any earthly assistance. Jerusalem is an exiled orphan. Her final appeal is for God to discipline her enemies as she has been disciplined for her transgressions.

God is held accountable to his severe parental discipline brought to bear on a weak virgin daughter while her evil dominating enemies rejoice. Implicit within the contrasting metaphors is a petition for God to redeem and restore.

The Day of the Lord's Anger (Lam 2)

Much is made of the day of the Lord's anger as proclaimed by the prophets and the ensuing destruction of Jerusalem (Lam 2:1-10). The poet again depicts God as the destroyer of Jerusalem, its temple, festivals and traditions. God's discipline is portrayed as severe as Jerusalem is humiliated and destroyed in fierce anger, without mercy. The destruction moves from general to specific, climaxing with the ironical description(s) of God destroying God's sanctuary. The fierce anger of the Lord juxtaposed to the destruction of daughter Zion surfaces God's obligation to discipline and protect, thus preparing for and legitimating the lament that is to follow.

A compassionate poet depicts the inhabitants of Jerusalem as infants and babes without sustenance (Lam 2:11-19). In an attempt to console, the poet emphasizes

Jerusalem's innocence through the use of feminine epithets as well as claims that her prophets were deceptive. Simultaneously the enemies are pictured as continually mocking her destruction. Ultimately the poet exhorts Jerusalem to cry to the Lord for deliverance because her punishment has been fulfilled.

Seemingly inspired by the poet, daughter Zion laments over the destruction of her children (Lam 2:20-22). Her lament begins with a pointed question: "To whom have you done this?" set in contrast to the festivities of the enemies. The concluding focus on the day of the anger of the Lord that no one survived mirrors the emphasis of the opening verses (Lam 1:1-10) creating an inclusio.

In the end, the poet's language obligates God to redeem and restore Jerusalem as her punishment has been sufficient and as God is also responsible to protect his daughter from the mockery of enemies.

Traditional Responses to Suffering (Lam 3)

The third chapter of Lamentations is made up of allusions to three distinct Old Testament genres: Joblike expressions of despair and trust (Lam 3:1-24), traditional wisdom teachings on suffering (Lam 3:25-39) and a traditional individual lament psalm (Lam 3:40-66). This chapter is distinct from the remainder of the book as its language is capable of fitting a multitude of settings.

If Lamentations 3:1-24 is an intentional allusion to Job (e.g., cf. Lam 3:1 and Job 9:34; Lam 3:2 and Job 19:8; Lam 3:4 and Job 30:30), then its function is to proclaim Jerusalem's current distress incomprehensible while striving to justify the acts of God (i.e., theodicy). Theodicy was a common means of coping with suffering in the ancient Near East, as it is today.

Lamentations 3:25-39 focuses on several traditional responses to suffering as found in the book of Proverbs. Lamentations 3:25-30 emphasizes teachings on patience and taking the long view of things (cf. Eccles 7:8). One's patience will be rewarded; the Lord will not reject forever (Lam 3:31; Ps 30:5) because of the abundance of God's steadfast love (Lam 3:32; Ps 36:5, 7, 10). The Lord sees all the works of iniquity (Lam 3:34-36; Ps 10:14; 35:22), and both blessing and calamity come from the Most High (Lam 3:38; Job 2:10; Is 45:7).

The chapter closes with a fairly typical individual psalm of lament (Lam 3:40-66) that emphasizes God's shunning, resulting in enemy victory, and the poet's complaint. From the midst of the distress the poet cries for the Lord to hear and deliver. In Lamentations 3:57 the Lord responds to the cry for a hearing, after which the poet reviews the crimes of the enemies and petitions for their destruction. Unique to this lament is the reference to the fate of the young women in the city (Lam 3:51, an allusion to the feminine imagery of Lam 1—2) as well as the substitution of a petition for deliverance with imprecations against the enemy. The latter substitution is not unprecedented, but does reflect a malicious, backward approach to deliverance.

Jerusalem's Punishment Too Severe (Lam 4)

Jerusalem, formerly the precious child of God, is depicted as an impoverished mother unable to feed her children. In addition, her royalty, once pure and vital, now sits on ash heaps in a sickly state. This further allusion to Job is combined with accusation (Jerusalem's punishment is greater than that of Sodom, Lam 4:6) to proclaim the current chastisement too severe. The desolation of Sodom was quick and complete, but for Jerusalem the life drains away bit by bit. The final imagery drives home the point—Israel's devastation is so severe that mothers boil their children for food (Lam 4:10).

The anger of the Lord may be likened unto the day of the Lord proclaimed by the prophets (e.g., Amos 5:18-20). Originally the day referred to a time when God would come in judgment to destroy the Israel's enemies; however, the prophets turned the expression back onto Israel. Lamentations 4:11 depicts the Lord coming in hot anger against Jerusalem (cf. Lam 2:1-10). The blame for the devastation is put on the prophets, priests and elders but not the royalty.

Curiously, the lament does not end with an overt petition for deliverance or a petition of any type. Instead, personified Jerusalem directs God's attention to the inabilities of Jerusalem's allies (probably referring to Egypt, Lam 4:17-19; cf. Jer 37:5-10) as well as the proclamation that Jerusalem's punishment is completed and Edom's about to come (Lam 4:21-22; cf. conclusion). This reference, along with the book of Obadiah, would suggest that Edom (the descendants of Esau), who should have been an ally, may have taken some kind of active role in Jerusalem's destruction by the Neo-Babylonians (see Ezek 25:12; 35:3, 15; Ps 137:7; Jer 40:11; Is 34; Mal 1:2-5; Joel 3:19). Jerusalem has been shamed before the nations, and consequently so has God.

The Cry for Restoration (Lam 5)

Personified Jerusalem initiates her closing lament (Lam 5:1-18) with a petition for God to remember the shame that has befallen her. The imagery is of the vulnerable orphan enslaved under a foreign master and scraping for daily sustenance. The labor is difficult and demanding, the treatment cruel and abusive, causing the community to mourn. The Davidic monarchy is no more, and Mount Zion is desolate, because she has sinned. God is reminded that the current generation pays for the sins of their ancestors. The description of Jerusalem's current deplorable state coupled with this noteworthy reminder prepares the hearer for Jerusalem's final plea.

That which has been implicit finally becomes overt as personified Jerusalem petitions for restoration (Lam 5:19-22). A masterful redaction of independent sources has built to this moment.

Throughout the book God has been reminded of his parental responsibility to discipline and protect (Lam 1—2); of the many ways Jerusalem has been shamed before the nations (cf. Lam 3:58-66; 4:12, 21-22; 5:1-14); of God's participation in the destruction of the city, its temple, its palace and its sacraments (cf. Lam 1—2); of the enemies' impending discipline (cf. Lam 3:64-66; 4:16-22); of God's obligatory patience and steadfast love (Lam 3:25-39); of Jerusalem's continued deplorable state; of God's anger and consequent severe punishment (cf. Lam 2, 4); of the incomprehensibility of God's chastisement (cf. Lam 3:1-24; 4:1-10) and the duration of the discipline (cf. Lam 2:17-18; 5:7). After 260 verses of rhetorical lament the poet comes to the main petition.

In the preamble the poet contrasts Jerusalem's loss of king with God's unending reign. Juxtaposed to the eternal nature of God's reign are two interrogative complaints: Why have you forgotten us completely? Why have you forsaken us these many days (Lam 5:20)? The first addresses the severity of the discipline; the second, its duration. Given the preceding arguments, the only comprehensible reason for God not to restore would be an utter rejection of Jerusalem, which, according to the covenant, is inconceivable. The book ends with the poet's ultimate argument: Jerusalem must be restored because she belongs to God.

Bibliography. F. B. Huey Jr., *Jeremiah, Lamentations*, New American Commentary 16 (Nashville: Broadman, 1993); L. E. Keck et. al., eds., *The New Interpreter's Bible* 6 (Nashville: Abingdon, 2001); T. Linafelt, *Surviving Lamentations: Catastrophe, Lament and Protest in the Afterlife of a Biblical Book* (Chicago: University of Chicago Press, 2000); R. J. Weems, *Battered Love: Marriage, Sex, and Violence in the Hebrew Prophets* (Minneapolis: Fortress, 1995); C. Westermann, *The Psalms: Structure, Content and Message* (Minneapolis: Augsburg, 1980).

LEANN SNOW FLESHER

EZEKIEL

Introduction

The book of Ezekiel, a carefully structured collection of writings addressed primarily to the exiles in Babylon, contains insights into life in Jerusalem and wrestles with the deep questions surrounding the exile. Until the modern period, when critical scholars posited that Ezekiel's materials had been reworked by later disciples, Ezekiel was assumed to be the author of the book. However, many scholars have returned to the earlier consensus about the book's essential unity and Ezekiel's role as author.

Although little of Ezekiel's personal life is revealed in the book, his experiences of God and his dramatic sign presentations have made him the subject of psychological studies. D. J. Halperin, for example, attributes the exceptional features of Ezekiel's prophecy to a pathological fear and hatred of female sexuality arising from sexual abuse he supposes Ezekiel suffered as a child. This approach, which is problematic and has not been affirmed by most commentators and psychologists, nonetheless highlights an important interpretive issue, namely, the predominantly violent and negative images of women. A more fruitful approach involves consideration of the book's purpose, setting and circumstances, the rhetorical function of prophecy, knowledge of the written traditions that Ezekiel inherited, separation of women as literary figures or metaphors from real women and appreciation of the differences between life in the ancient and modern world.

A series of dates within the book places Ezekiel's prophetic activity between 593 B.C., the fifth year of the exile in Babylon when Ezekiel received his call (Ezek 1:2), and 571 B.C., the twenty-seventh year of exile (Ezek 29:17). The primary setting of the book is Babylon, though Ezekiel's visions transport him back to Jerusalem and many of his oracles provide insights into life in Jerusalem. King Jehoiachin, his wives, mother, servants, princes, palace officials, warriors, skilled craftsmen and smiths, and a number of other leaders and upper-class Judeans, including Ezekiel, were taken to Babylon in 598 B.C. as prisoners of war (2 Kings 24:11-16). The number of captives is debated, and it is not clear whether women and children were included in the numbers. However, there is little doubt that whole families were taken into captivity by Nebuchadnezzar.

Like the Assyrians before them, the Neo-Babylonians used exile as a way of controlling and punishing conquered peoples. Some indication of the treatment of women in captivity and exile is afforded by stone reliefs that show women and children walking or riding in carts driven by mules or oxen separated from men and older boys who were sometimes in chains. Touching scenes of women and children weeping with their hands raised in prayer, of mothers nursing babies and bending over to give a small child a drink from an animal skin call attention to the difficulties faced by families on the journey into captivity (Albenda, 17-19).

The journey into exile ended with settlement in small communities in Nippur. The conditions under which the Judean exiles were settled are not known, but an extant letter listing the rations for Jehoiachin suggests that the exiled king and his family were well provided for. Also positive is Jeremiah's letter (Jer 29:5-7). Further, the presence of elders in the Judean settlement of which Ezekiel was a part points to some form of self-government; the text suggests that Ezekiel exercised considerable independence in terms of his lifestyle and his prophetic role.

Still, exile disrupted the most basic patterns of private and public life. The challenges the exiles faced in terms of confronting their losses, making sense out of their situation, keeping their families together and facing their future were immense. Moreover, many of the women sent into exile were women of status, power, ability and prominence. The discovery of Hebrew seals belonging to women suggests that some women during the eighth to the sixth centuries may have been accustomed to having legal rights in matters of signing contracts and other such documents. Some women may have been literate (aniconic seals, which consist of words only and not pictures, may indicate literate owners in a predominantly illiterate society; Avigad, 22-24, 30, 45).

The book of Ezekiel provides only limited glimpses into women's lives, but from comparable biblical and extrabiblical sources, archaeology and sociological studies of ancient and modern societies, we may draw a fuller picture of the lives of women in exile.

The primary focus of women would have continued to be the family. Hence, marriage, birth rituals and the nurture and education of children would have been central to a woman's life. In addition, women would have been involved in the production as well as preparation of food and clothing and in providing a healthy, safe and ritually pure home environment. Moreover, women's responsibilities extended to the care of the sick, the dying and the dead. However, the financial, physical, spiritual and psychosocial resources available to women in exile had changed (i.e., the availability of food and perhaps domestic help, the loss of the temple). Women would have learned new skills because of economic constraints, their changed status and differences in climate, geography and environment.

Faced with socioeconomic conditions that have been likened to the conditions in premonarchic Israel, women and men may have experienced shifts in gender roles resulting in greater power and perhaps even more equality with men in the family (Eskenazi, 33). Ezekiel's message about individual responsibility would accord with this, though issues related to women's impurity and the exclusion of women from the new temple remind readers that the term *equality* must be carefully nuanced. Little is known about women's roles outside of the family, though some women were professional mourners and others prophets. Judean women were also surrounded by a new culture, which presented different religious, social and moral values and rights. Babylonian women, for example, could own and freely dispose of their property, initiate divorce proceedings and inherit a part of their husband's estate. Still, they rarely held official positions and could not act as a witness of a contract (Dandamaev, 48-49). Female slaves and prostitutes were also an important part of Babylonian society.

The task of surviving captivity with spiritual, moral, ethical, community and family values intact undoubtedly rested on the shoulders of women and men. While the book of Ezekiel portrays the male leaders of the community deliberating about the theological issues related to the captivity, women undoubtedly discussed these issues among themselves and with their husbands and were expected to respond to the challenges of Ezekiel's message. Women played a role in keeping their families centered in their faith through sabbath keeping, circumcision, festivals and purity laws. To them would have fallen the vital task of teaching their children day-to-day lessons, including how to resist syncretism. In so doing they were helping to establish the boundaries against the outside world that studies of comparative minority groups in exile suggest are critical to survival (Smith, 64-65).

The book of Ezekiel provides few glimpses into the lives of individual women. Ezekiel's wife is the only real woman in the book, and what is known about her is limited. Women are mentioned as weeping for Tammuz and as prophets. They are also cited as potential defilers of righteous men, victims of war and perhaps the intended audience of the story of Samaria and Jerusalem. Moreover, images of women feature prominently in Ezekiel's oracles and extended narratives in the first half of the book.

The most important and problematic female image is the city as the wife of the Lord. Cities in the ancient Near East often had a patron deity, and the city was frequently envisaged as the wife of that deity. Hosea, Isaiah and Jeremiah used this commonplace notion and developed the idea of Jerusalem as the Lord's unfaithful wife. However, Ezekiel graphically depicts Jerusalem and Samaria as unfaithful women who are punished by their lovers at the request of their husband. Other texts make reference to Jerusalem as the unfaithful wife and pollutant (menstruant; see Galambush, 130-41).

The language and images that Ezekiel uses to depict God's relationship with Jerusalem and Samaria presents challenges for women because the prophet depicts women's bodies, their bodily functions and their sexuality explicitly and negatively. Most contemporary readers find Ezekiel's negative images of women to be problematic and offensive. Some recent interpreters have even described his language and imagery as pornographic.

A critical issue in this discussion is the nature of metaphorical language. Some interpreters focus on what was meant or signified by Ezekiel's metaphoric language in its historical and canonical context. Others suggest that metaphorical language is problematic when it is not heard or read as a finger pointing beyond itself but rather becomes the finger (Weems, 110-13). An example of metaphorical language becoming the finger would be when a reader concludes that Ezekiel's image of God as the shamed husband violently retaliating against his wife models or justifies spousal abuse.

Ezekiel's purpose was to offend and shock his readers. His mission was to confront God's people with their sin that had severed the covenant bond, to correct their faulty ideas (about God, God's promises and the nature of the covenant relationship), to warn them of the imminent fall of Jerusalem and to inform them of God's plans for restoration. However, modern readers experience even more shock and offense because they do not share the ancients' assumptions. Questions loom about the continuing influence of Ezekiel's negative and objectified portrayal of women's bodies and sexuality and the model of using violence to control wives.

Still, the focus on woman's uncleanness and infidelity is largely restricted to texts that feature the unfaithful female city. Other references to real and imaged women are much more positive (e.g., Ezekiel's wife, the lioness, the women prophets who are judged for their actions alongside their male counterparts and not for anything linked to their nature as women and the feminine images linked to the new temple).

Finally, there is danger in letting the offense of Ezekiel's depiction of unfaithful wives block the message of the text. Although the marriage metaphor raises interpretive issues, its richness as a metaphor should be acknowledged. From first love to strained relationships, divorce and reconciliation, the complexities of love and of covenanted relationships can be explored (see Weems, 64-67, 72-78). Even though the book of Ezekiel presents numerous interpretive challenges, it continues to draw women and men into a deeper understanding of God, of sin and of grace and the demands of a covenanted life with God. It also holds a message of hope of restoration and new life for those who, like the suffering exiles of the sixth century, need to be filled with God's life-giving Spirit and given hope for the future.

Outline

1:1—3:27	Ezekiel's Initial Vision and Call
4:1—5:17	Messages of Judgment
6:1—7:27	Oracles of Judgment and the Knowledge of the Lord

8:1—11:25	The Temple Vision
12:1-20	Exile Reenacted
12:21—14:11	True and False Prophecy
14:12—15:8	A Righteous Few Cannot Save
16:1-63	A Love Story Gone Wrong
17:1—18:32	A Riddle and a Proverb
19:1-14	The Lioness and the Vine
20:1-44	Israel's History Revisited
20:45—21:32	The Sword
22:1-31	Jerusalem, the Guilty City
23:1-49	The Story of Two Sisters
24:1-14	The Cooking Pot
24:15-27	The Death of Ezekiel's Wife
25:1—32:32	Oracles Against the Nations
33:1-33	Ezekiel, the Sentinel
34:1-31	The Divine Shepherd
35:1—36:38	Judgment and Restoration
37:1-28	Restoration of the House of Israel
38:1—39:29	Prophecies Against Gog
40:1—48:35	The New Jerusalem

Commentary

Ezekiel's Initial Vision and Call (Ezek 1:1—3:27)

Ezekiel, identified as the son of Buzi and as a priest, was one of the exiles who had been taken from Jerusalem and relocated by the Chebar Canal, an area in Babylon that Nebuchadnezzar wanted to rebuild. Cut off from Jerusalem and the temple, Ezekiel was not able to exercise his priestly duties. However, in the fifth year of his exile, Ezekiel received the call to his new vocation as prophet.

Ezekiel's Vision (Ezek 1:4-28)

Ezekiel's initial vision was of four astoundingly brilliant creatures reminiscent of the cherubim that supported the ark of the covenant of the Lord (1 Sam 4:4; Ezek 10:14-19). The creatures seemed to carry a four-wheeled, chariotlike vehicle that could move everywhere (the ark was called a chariot, 1 Chron 28:18). Enthroned on this vehicle was the appearance of the likeness of the glory of the Lord. Ezekiel's response is suggestive of the vision's theological significance: God was not confined to the temple in Jerusalem. Instead, God's throne could easily move and God was therefore present among the exiles. Moreover, as God's message would clarify, the sovereign and holy God demands covenant loyalty.

In his description Ezekiel likens the sound of the wings of the living creatures to "the thunder of the Almighty" (Shaddai). The etymology of "Shaddai" is obscure, but one option is "the God of the two breasts" or "the double breasted One."

Ezekiel 1 has inspired the imaginations of artists and songwriters and the hearts of the faithful who, like Ezekiel and his fellow exiles, need a renewed vision of God. When circumstances make communal and private worship impossible or difficult (e.g., caring for newborns or the sick), an assurance of God's presence, power, holiness and accessibility brings hope and comfort. It offers a new perspective on circumstances that seem impossible to change or perhaps unjust (cf. Rom 8:38-39 and the circumstances faced by African American slaves). A renewed vision of God's holiness also prepared the way for the message of judgment that Ezekiel was to bring.

Ezekiel's Call and Commission (Ezek 2:1—3:27)

The vision of God's glory is followed by Ezekiel's call to speak God's words to a rebellious people. Although Ezekiel is addressed by God as "mortal" or "human," the Spirit enters him and sets him on his feet so that he hears his assignment. Ezekiel is sent to "the sons of Israel," and the brief rehearsal of Israel's past focuses on the sins of the fathers and their sons. Although women are not named explicitly, they are assumed to be included in the designation "the sons of Israel," which is often translated "descendants of Israel."

Ezekiel obediently eats a scroll that contains words of lamentation, mourning and woe; ironically, it tastes as sweet as honey. Ezekiel is again told to speak God's words to Israel. Taken back to the Chebar Canal, Ezekiel sits in a state of shock for seven days. He is then charged to be a sentinel or watchman for Israel. Ezekiel is to warn the people of the sentence of death that God will bring if repentance does not follow the warning. The messenger is held responsible for delivering God's warning, though he is not responsible for the people's response.

The final scene of Ezekiel's call takes place in the valley, where the glory of the Lord appears to Ezekiel again. Ezekiel is to be shut up in his house, bound with cords and unable to speak until God speaks through him to offer the people the opportunity to hear or refuse to hear God's word. The meaning of this section is difficult (see Block, 151-62); however, most commentators understand this text to point to the fact that some of Ezekiel's ministry would involve periods of silence. As God's chosen, Spirit-filled prophet, Ezekiel is bound to carry out God's orders explicitly. God fixes the limits of the prophetic task, and Ezekiel's words will be God's words.

What follows in the book is to be read in light of these opening chapters, which establish God's character as holy, transcendent, relational and omnipresent; the nation's character as rebellious and stubborn; and the prophet's character as obedient messenger and his task as sentinel.

Messages of Judgment (Ezek 4—5)

The Siege of Jerusalem (Ezek 4)

Through a series of sign acts, Ezekiel conveys God's message. The first sign involved a map of Jerusalem drawn on a mud brick surrounded by models of siege instruments and an iron plate or griddle that blocked the view of the prophet. In this sign act, Ezekiel represented God, whose separation from the besieged city was symbolized by the impenetrable griddle. God was allowing his wrath to be enacted on his beloved Jerusalem. The message would have unnerved and bewildered the exiles, whose hope for the future still rested in Jerusalem and the promises contained in God's eternal covenant with David.

The second and third sign acts continued the theme of siege. Ezekiel's action of lying on his left side for 390 days may symbolize the duration of the iniquity of Israel (counting back 390 years from the fall of Jerusalem in 586 B.C. to the time of Solomon). The action of lying on his right side for forty days may represent one generation and symbolize the exile. The significance of the numbers, however, is debated.

In the third sign act, Ezekiel takes on what was traditionally a woman's task. The prophet is commanded to take six different grains and vegetables and make bread for himself in the presence of an audience. The recipe highlights the shortage of food, especially ritually clean food, that would accompany the siege and the fact that bread would be made with whatever particles of grain and vegetables could be found. This bread was to be of a certain weight, eaten at a fixed time each day and cooked on human dung, which would render it unclean. When Ezekiel protests, the Lord empathizes with his feelings of revulsion and allows him to cook the bread on cow dung, which, when mixed with straw, was commonly used as fuel for a cooking fire.

Unless Ezekiel was working with ingredients that were ready for baking, he may have had to consult his wife about how to prepare the grains and vegetables. Alternatively, she may have been involved in soaking, milling and grinding the grains (*see* Food and Water). The sight of a male preparing an unusual loaf of bread in an unusual fashion would have caused a stir among the captives, particularly among the women. The message conveyed was one that women especially might have taken to heart: it would have been their responsibility to provide food for their families, even in treacherous times.

The Shearing of Ezekiel and Jerusalem (Ezek 5)
In yet another sign act, Ezekiel is commanded to shave his head and beard. This act was a sign of shame, mourning or both. The hair is then weighed and divided into three piles, which symbolize the fate of Jerusalem's inhabitants.

The interpretation of the sign act contains a rehearsal of Jerusalem's failures. The city has rebelled against God's ordinances and statutes and defiled God's sanctuary by becoming more wicked than the nations. God's response to Jerusalem is one of jealous anger. Men, women and children will be judged by God and punished through famine, pestilence, wild animals, bloodshed and the sword. It is difficult to imagine the desperation that would lead parents to eat their children and children to eat parents. The motif of cannibalism, however, is found in a number of ancient treaty curses (Lev 26:29; Deut 28:53-57; see also Block, 204). Moreover, the story of the mother who shared the flesh of her son with another mother during the siege of Samaria (2 Kings 6:24-31) puts a human face on this harsh message.

Jerusalem is personified as a female in Ezekiel 5, but the figure of the woman is not elaborated on, nor is God figured explicitly as a husband.

Oracles of Judgment and the Knowledge of the Lord (Ezek 6:1—7:27)

The focus of Ezekiel's message shifts from a condemnation of Jerusalem to an address to the whole land. A further oracle, however, promises that God would spare some who, through the experience of exile, would remember God, repent and return to a true knowledge of God.

Another threat of judgment follows the word of hope. Ezekiel is told to clap his hands, stamp his feet and utter, "Alas!" The message is that God's judgment on those who carried out "vile abominations" is death by sword, famine and pestilence and desolation to the land. Death and desolation also bring the knowledge of God's lordship, a theme throughout the book.

Ezekiel develops the theme of judgment further by emphasizing the imminence of "the end" to the land of Israel. To those exiled from the land, whose hopes for release and return to the homeland centered on the presence of God in the land, this series of oracles would be disturbing. God is portrayed as an angry covenant God whose longstanding patience and compassion are spent. The time of reckoning has come. The cry of Ezekiel, the sentinel, is again that God must punish the inhabitants of the land. But God's actions as judge are not seen as impetuous, capricious or even unexpected. The inhabitants would be judged according to their ways.

The description of the time of war (Ezek 7:14-22) contains images that are appropriately male. However, Ezekiel also uses a female image in his description of men's response to the day of wrath. In despair, the men flung their silver into the streets and treated their gold, which had been their most valued asset, as unclean. The term *unclean* most often describes menstrual impurity, though it can be used as an expression or image of extreme uncleanness. Ezekiel's training as a priest sensitized him to issues of purity and impurity, and most likely he had the image of menstrual impurity in mind as he attempted to shake his hearers out of their lethargy and bring them to an awareness of the imminence of God's judgment and of their personal accountability for what had happened and would happen.

The Temple Vision (Ezek 8:1—11:25)

Nearly fourteen months after his initial vision, Ezekiel experiences another encounter with God in which he is shown why the Lord is abandoning his temple and Jerusalem. Ezekiel 8 opens with a description of Ezekiel at home with the elders of Judah, a group of men who exercised leadership among the exiles, sitting before him. Although the reason for the elders' visit to Ezekiel is not given, the elders seem to have recognized Ezekiel as God's prophet among them and came to hear a word from God.

Their "sitting before" the prophet suggests deference to Ezekiel's words. The elders then spread God's message to others. Presumably this would have been how women heard God's words of judgment and hope.

The first scene of cultic sin involved an image of an idol set up as guardian at the entrance to the inner court. The details about the idolatrous image, the worshipers and their activities are not given. The message, however, is that the covenant God demands exclusive worship. The presence of rivals in God's sanctuary evokes not only the Lord's jealousy but also his pain as those whom he loves bring other lovers into his presence.

Though the identity of the image is not certain, it was most likely the Canaanite goddess Asherah. According to Ugaritic mythological texts, Asherah was the consort of the chief god, El, and the mother of the gods, perhaps even Baal. At various times in Israel's history, Asherah was incorporated into Israelite religion. Recent scholarship suggests that syncretism was alive in the late sixth century in Judah and that in the minds of some indiscriminate worshipers of the Lord, Asherah was the Lord's female consort or at least a hypostasis of his female side. Some scholars identify the queen of heaven, for whom cakes were made in Jerusalem (Jer 7:18; 44:19), with Asherah.

The second scene of cultic sin is fleshed out in greater detail, though it is still somewhat obscure. Seventy men recognized as elders of the house of Israel were involved in clandestine worship of cult images engraved on walls. They claimed that God could not see them and had left the land, but ironically, the all-seeing God had not left, though he was about to leave because of such idolatrous acts.

The third scene moves to the entrance of the north gate of the temple, where women sat weeping for (the) Tammuz. In this oracle the presence of women in God's holy place is not challenged (but see Ezek 43). This third abomination centers on the women's activity of sitting and weeping for (the) Tammuz. That women played an important role in mourning rituals throughout the ancient world is well attested in written and iconographic sources. The question is for whom are the women mourning in this sacred space?

Most often commentators suggest that the reference is to Tammuz, a Mesopotamian god well attested from the third to the first millennium B.C. Tammuz (Dumuzi) is often mentioned in poems and laments uttered by his wife, his sister and his mother. According to one tradition, Dumuzi courted and married the goddess Ishtar (the Sumerian goddess Inanna), who then banished him to the underworld to take the place of her sister. The women then wept for the dead god. In another text, Dumuzi's death is linked to his life as a shepherd. Dumuzi's association with death and his affinity with women form the basis for the cult that involved women mourning for his death. Moreover, many scholars see a connection between the myths about Dumuzi/Tammuz and Inanna/Ishtar and cultic fertility rites that are related to the seasons. The sexual union of these gods was thought to be associated with the fertile growing season and the god's death with the dry season. The dry season (June/July), named after Tammuz, was when the ritual of weeping was generally undertaken. Accordingly it is thought that the third abomination was the worshiping of a Babylonian fertility deity by Judean women in the temple. How Tammuz came to be present in the temple is a further question, though Israel's flirtation with Baal, who was revered as a dying and rising fertility deity, and with Asherah was longstanding.

However, if the women were weeping "the Tammuz," it is possible that the reference is to a special kind of mourning lament or ritual and not Tammuz (Block, 294-96). Perhaps the women were using a Tammuz-like liturgy of mourning to grieve the departure or death of the Lord, which the elders had just announced. If this was their offense, their mistake was that the Lord was not dead. His absence was not to be equated with his death. Alternatively, the women may have incorporated features of the Tammuz cult into their faith and equated the Lord with Tammuz. The thought of associating or assimilating the God of Israel and the youthful and charming lover Dumuzi, "the wild bull, who has lain down [and] lives no more," seems incredible (Jacobsen, 102). The fact that the women were carrying out their ritual in the sixth month instead of the fourth month supports an interpretation that associates the women's worship with syncretistic practice that incorporated Babylonian rituals into the worship of the Lord.

The final scene of cultic sin involved twenty-five men with their backs to the temple and their faces toward the east, worshiping the rising sun. Whether the men understood themselves to be self-consciously committing apostasy or whether they were in their minds legitimately incorporating solar symbolism into worship of the Lord is unclear. Their worship, however, is deemed spurious. In addition to carrying out such cultic sins, the Judean worshipers are judged for their social sins. God's response to such spiritual and moral degeneration is anger that will lead to judgment. The time for pity and mercy has passed; God will no longer listen to their cries.

These four scenes of cultic sin suggest that God is equally the covenant God of women and men. God demands covenant faithfulness, which expresses itself in purity of worship and life of all who have entered into a covenant relationship with God.

Punishment by Slaughter (Ezek 9)

The punishment announced in Ezekiel 8:18 is enacted from the temple outwards. In Ezekiel 9, the man in white linen is sent through the city to place a mark on the foreheads of the faithful. The ones without the mark are struck down. Perhaps Ezekiel's reference to foreheads is intended to evoke memories of unleavened bread. Six executioners are directed to kill all who are not marked on their foreheads. A seventh man marks the foreheads of those who are remorseful over the city's apostasy. Concerned that God will destroy all who remain, Ezekiel passionately appeals to God for mercy, but God's response gives little hope.

Focus on God's Glory (Ezek 10)

The theme of judgment continues as the agent of deliverance becomes the agent of judgment. God directs the man to take burning coals from the chariot throne and scatter them over the city. The chariot throne is described again in great detail, reminding readers of the glory, holiness, transcendence, separateness and omnipresence of the God who is bringing judgment on his rebellious people. This long section also builds tension for readers who anticipate the departure of God's glory from the temple.

Further Judgment (Ezek 11:1-13)

Ezekiel is shown twenty-five public officials who were involved in wicked schemes and evil counsel. Their ambiguous saying, "the time is not near to build houses; this city is the pot, and we are the meat" (Ezek 11:3), likely means that the leaders felt that attention should be given to defenses and not to building for peace. This attitude ignored Jeremiah's counsel about the foolishness of resistance to Babylon and reflected the smug self-confidence of those left in Jerusalem. The prophetic condemnation of this group reveals that they had butchered many people; the dead were the meat in the city, which was the pot. The city would provide no protection for the wicked leaders, who would meet their end at Israel's borders. God's judgment of this group would ultimately lead them to recognize his lordship. This section concludes with the notice of the death of Pelatiah. The ominous nature of the death of the man whose name means "the Lord delivers" prompted Ezekiel to cry out in despair, "You are wiping out the remnant of Israel!" (note that the NRSV translates this as a question; cf. Ezek 9:8). Ezekiel's statement/question shows that he does not yet understand God's thinking. Ezekiel's reaction to Pelatiah's death makes it clear that he considers the remnant to be those in Jerusalem. The Lord corrects this misconception; the true remnant is to be found in exile, where the Lord has been their sanctuary. The true remnant is defined by proximity not to the land but to God.

A Message of Hope and the End of the Vision (Ezek 11:14-25)

The scene of despair is followed with a message of hope to the exiles, who had been written off by those remaining in Jerusalem. Though they had been scattered, God assures them that he has been a sanctuary to them. Moreover, God promises to gather them and give them the land of Israel and the necessary inner resources that will enable them to become God's faithful and obedient covenant people. God's glory then leaves the city, and Ezekiel is returned to the exiles. Although the elders of Judah were undoubtedly the first exiles to hear about Ezekiel's vision, the exiles are designated as those to whom Ezekiel tells "all the things that the Lord had shown me" (Ezek 11:25).

Exile Reenacted (Ezek 12:1-20)

Ezekiel is commanded to perform an action that will be seen by and later interpreted to his fellow captives, who are described as blind, deaf and rebellious. Still, the fact that God gives Ezekiel a further prophetic word implies that there is hope for the exiles, who may yet understand and repent. Ezekiel was to mimic an exile. He was to bring out his baggage, dig through the wall, carry it out in the dark and cover his face so that he could not see the land. The wall was most likely the mud brick wall of his home, though it is possible that it was a low retaining wall that surrounded the captives' compound. Ezekiel's bemused neighbors might have wondered if this latest sign action meant that they would soon return to their homes, but they found out that the oracle concerned the capture, blinding and exile of Zedekiah and the annihilation of all his forces.

The short sign act of a weak and trembling prophet reiterates the message of a violent end and a desolate land for God's people who have practiced violence. God's justice is not arbitrary.

True and False Prophecy (Ezek 12:21—14:11)

A new twist on an old proverb (Ezek 12:21-28) begins a section that focuses on issues related to true and false prophecy. It begins with the citation of two familiar proverbs that reflect cynicism and unbelief regarding the words uttered by prophets about the future. The proverbs are cleverly turned to remind the exiles of the truth of God's prophetic word. God's judgment was coming, and it was to come soon.

Prophesying Out of Their Own Minds (Ezek 13)

Ezekiel 13 contains two sections that concern prophets "who prophesy out of their own minds." The first group of prophets is judged for uttering delusions and lies to God's people by assuring them of peace when there is no peace (Ezek 13:1-16).

The oracle against the daughters of Ezekiel's people (Ezek 13:17-23) is one of the few Old Testament oracles addressed specifically to women (cf. Amos 4:1-3; Is 3:16—4:1; 32:9-12). Moreover, it is the only oracle directed to women who are involved specifically in prophecy. In Old Testament times, a relatively small number of women are designated as prophets, though the nature of their prophetic ministries is varied and not always clearly defined: Miriam (Ex 15:20), Deborah (Judg 4:4; 5:7, 12), Huldah (2 Kings 22:14-20; 2 Chron 34:22-28), Nodiah (Neh 6:14) and Isaiah's wife (Is 8:3). Later rabbinic tradition recognized seven women as prophets to Israel: Sarah, Miriam, Deborah, Hannah, Abigail, Huldah and Esther (*b. Meg.* 14a). Female prophets were well known in Mesopotamia, and their influence on Judean women in Babylon was most likely considerable. However, although the women who received Ezekiel's oracle are described as prophesying, Ezekiel does not flatter them with the designation prophet, since the methods and intentions of their prophetic work are deemed fraudulent. Indeed, commentators often appropriately identify these women as sorcerers, witches, charlatans or practitioners of black magic.

The mantic and magic acts of these women are difficult to determine with precision because the Hebrew text is not clear. The bands attached to the inquirers' wrists and the veils of varying sizes that covered their heads were part of the magic art that seems to reflect a Mesopotamian influence. Perhaps these items placed on the wrists and head reflect a non-Israelite equivalent of rabbinic phylacteries. Ezekiel describes the intention of the magical acts as an aggressive "hunt for souls." It is unclear as to what was involved in pursuit of "souls," a key word in this passage. Had these women adopted a Babylonian conception of the soul as being independent of and external to the body, or did they understand the term in its more usual sense as designating the human person (Block, 413-16)? In either case, they followed the Babylonian practice of appealing to their deities and demons in their magical acts. But the Lord's name was not to be called on in acts of divination. By so invoking the name and power of the Lord, they profaned his name. Furthermore, the magical deeds effectively directed evil power against others to the end that some died who should not have died and others lived who should not have lived. Moreover, the women's nefarious activities affected the moral and spiritual order, as the righteous were disheartened and the wicked encouraged. The women's actions became a source of power and income. They may have received the barley and bread as payment for services rendered (cf. 1 Sam 9:7). Alternatively, they may have used them in their divinations by casting them on water or by offering them as food for the gods (Block, 416). In any case, their practices were unauthorized and their so-called prophetic ministry deemed to be false.

God's response to these women was judgment. God would tear their bands from their arms and remove their veils, which would free the souls they were hunting. Moreover, the women would no longer prophesy, for they would see no more visions and practice no more divinations. The incompatibility of magic and divination and true prophecy is set out in Deuteronomy 18, where improper and unauthorized methods of mediating the powers of life and death are delineated before the qualities of true prophesy are described. God's response to the victims, though, was deliverance. In contrast to the designation of the so-called prophets as "your people," God calls the "hunted" or "haunted" souls "my people" five times, suggesting God's great compassion for those who are victims of deception, exploitation and the occult. Block also calls attention to the cluster of references to "my people" (Block, 415).

That many of the exiles were drawn to women who seemed to have divine knowledge and power over death and life is not surprising, because they lived with such uncertainty, instability and fear. However, then as now, such practices are not value-neutral but rather exceedingly harmful. God has and continues to provide resources for the community of faith when it experiences times of confusion, pain, judgment, illness, death, prosperity or blessing. This passage warns those in crisis to avoid the lure of the occult and to hold on to their relationship with the God who cares for his people. Moreover, although this unique passage on women affirms the right of women to be prophets, it also warns that women are also capable of practicing illegitimate ministries that are rooted not in God but in human ideas and pagan divination practices. Along with the capacity for good comes the capacity for evil.

Idolatrous Elders (Ezek 14:1-11)

In this scene, a group of elders came to Ezekiel for a message from God. But the word they received was not one they expected. Rather, the issue of their worship of idols alongside of their worship of Lord was raised. Whether they had adapted idolatrous Babylonian practices or whether they were continuing idolatrous observances from Jerusalem is not known. In any case, they seemed to be blind to the fact that God demanded an exclusive allegiance from his covenant people. Repentance from the evil of idolatry was required. Prophets who falsely spoke God's word to those who indulged in pagan practices are condemned alongside of the idolatrous inquirers.

A Righteous Few Cannot Save (Ezek 14:12—15:8)

The exiles' conviction that a righteous remnant would save Jerusalem from final destruction is shown to be out of line with a basic principle of justice. According to this principle, if and when God judges a land, not even the presence of righteous persons would save the land or their children. Instead of being saved by the righteous, each person is responsible for his or her position before a righteous and just God. This principle of individual responsibility (cf. Ezek 18) is important for women, who would now be judged on their merits and not on those of the men who are the heads of the household. However, the sons and daughters who would escape the coming devastation of Jerusalem were not to be regarded as being saved by their righteousness. Rather, their unrighteous deeds and ways would demonstrate that God was fully justified in punishing Jerusalem.

The short parable of the vine (Ezek 15:1-8) declares the message of the destruction of Jerusalem again and attacks the exiles' optimism and false sense of security as the royal vine of God's planting (cf. Ps 80:9-12). God originally intended that the vine he had planted should produce fruit (cf. Is 5:1-7). Ezekiel does not even mention the fruit of the vine; it is as though its days of production are long gone. Instead, the uselessness of its wood is observed and its end declared (cf. Jn 15:1-6).

A Love Story Gone Wrong (Ezek 16)

God's word of judgment is communicated by means of a love story between God and

Jerusalem that quickly goes awry. This oracle is renowned for its length, its distinctive rehearsal of Jerusalem's ancestry and history and its poignant portrait of Jerusalem as the Lord's unfaithful wife. Ezekiel transforms the metaphor of the city as the wife of its patron god: the wife is not the benevolent goddess/wife but the unfaithful human wife of a shamed and dishonored God. At the same time, Ezekiel builds on the metaphor of apostasy as adultery, which assumes an exclusive covenant relationship between God and Israel that included obligations and consequences. In his attempt to shock his audience into a recognition of their situation in relation to God, Ezekiel explodes the metaphor of Jerusalem as wife to include graphic and offensive references to the female body and a portrayal of God that, when taken out of its metaphorical context, proves highly problematic. When these pictures of women are read out of their literary and cultural contexts, serious interpretive and theological problems occur. Ezekiel, however, intends that men and women identify themselves as the unfaithful lover of the God who throughout is assumed to be just and holy. God's rage is to be distinguished from human rage, which would be affected by pride, ego and other aspects of fallenness.

Jerusalem's Early Years (Ezek 16:1-14)

The description of Jerusalem as an abandoned newborn points to significant cultural differences between the world of the text and the world of readers. Postnatal care for a newborn child involved cutting the umbilical cord, bathing in clean water, rubbing in salt and wrapping in cloth. Newborns may have been salted to clean and strengthen the skin, to ward off evil spirits and demons or perhaps to prevent bacteria from developing in the swaddling clothes. The details regarding the neglectful state in which the baby was tossed out to die also point to ancient customs regarding legal rights and responsibilities for infants (*see* Infanticide). But the newborn Jerusalem was rescued from sure death by the Lord, who in declaring, "In your blood, . . . live!" formally adopted her (Ezek 16:6; Block, 481). The child became the Lord's possession.

The young woman grew sexually mature but remained naked. Signs of physical maturation were generally viewed positively in the ancient Near East. However, because menstruation was linked not only to fertility and blessing but also to impurity, its onset was viewed with ambivalence. Ezekiel's emphasis on the woman's body, her nakedness and fertility foreshadows the depiction of the woman's subsequent prostitution, nakedness and punishment. Her vulnerability is noticed by her rescuer, who then performs the ancient Near Eastern custom that symbolized declaration of betrothal, that is, spreading a garment over a woman (Ezek 16:8; cf. Ruth 3:9).

The marriage is formalized by a solemn oath and covenant and the declaration "you became mine." The emphasis is on the husband's role as initiator, magnanimous provider and enabler of his beloved "possession" (Ezek 16:8-14). Although many brides in ancient times brought dowry items like silver, gold, jewelry, linens, textile, furniture and household utensils into a marriage, this foundling bride came naked. The hierarchical nature of this marriage reflects the broader patriarchal culture of the ancient world. It also functions to build readers' expectation that the spouse on whom such commitment and gifts of love are lavished would respond in gratitude if not in kind, since mutuality in marriage was known in the Old Testament world (cf. the relationship between the lover and the beloved in Song of Songs and the expression "my man," used by a wife of her husband [Block, 483-84]). The fine adornment and diet of the bride mark her as royalty. Although the primary referent of the bride metaphor is Jerusalem, the language also suggests an allusion to the temple as bride (cf. references to female images for the temple as "the beauty of his adornment" [Ezek 7:20] and "the delight of [his] eyes" [Ezek 24:21]; Block, 486).

Religious and Political Harlotries (Ezek 16:15-34)

However, placing her confidence in beauty and forgetting her benevolent spouse, Jerusalem became a prostitute. Many of her acts of promiscuity involved a perversion of the gifts bestowed on her as the new bride by her loving husband. Perhaps the most perverse act of Jerusalem's religious promiscuity was sacrificing the children she had borne to the Lord. Here the figure of the mother, who is most often depicted positively as nurturer and caregiver in the Old Testament, slaughters her children as food for her lovers. Child sacrifice was practiced though never sanctioned in Israel and Judah. There is intense irony in the image of the once rescued infant growing up to slaughter the children she bore to her rescuer.

The force of the language of Jerusalem's growing promiscuity with her political enemies is often masked in translation (e.g., "offering your body" [Ezek 16:25 NIV] for lit. "spreading or parting your legs"; the Egyptians, "your lustful neighbors" [Ezek 16:26 NIV] for lit. "big of phallus"). The offense of the language is intentional. The momentum of the narrative builds, and the harlot's behavior is deemed to be shocking even to the Philistine "women," Jerusalem's neighboring cities. But Jerusalem is no ordinary prostitute. She solicits her clients instead of being solicited, and she offers them gifts given to her by her husband.

Punishment (Ezek 16:35-42)

In the honor-shame culture of the ancient world, an unfaithful wife brought dishonor to her husband. She was considered to be a social reprobate deserving punishment. According to Middle Assyrian laws, a husband had the legal right to whip his unfaithful wife, to pull out her hair, to mutilate her ears or genitals, to tie her up and throw her into a river or from a tower or to make her a slave. The punishment of the wife's lover, who was considered to be a thief, could be either comparable or inconsequential, but it was never more serious than the woman's (Roth, 183).

Ezekiel's metaphor assumes that the husband, who in this case is a righteous God and holy covenant partner, had the right to punish his wife. But neither the law nor the narratives attest to the kind of marital violence that is found in Ezekiel's extended metaphors (cf. Ezek 23). Anger and vengeance were the more expected responses to sexual violations in the Old Testament world. Moreover, adultery, like murder and child sacrifice, was considered a capital offense deserving of death. In ancient Israel, punishment was based on compensation and penalty. Under such a system, capital punishment was reserved for crimes for which compensation was impossible (e.g., bringing someone back to life, restoring virginity, restoring the brokenness of adultery). The fact that adultery was a crime for which compensation was impossible makes Israel's eventual restoration all the more a miraculous and gracious act of God.

Furthermore, the custom of stripping a woman as part of divorce proceedings is also attested (Ezek 16:37; Hos 2:2-3). Thus the depiction of God's "bloody and impassioned fury" (Ezek 16:38 Jewish Publication Society) toward his wife is not unexpected in its context. Readers are expected to sympathize with the wronged divine husband. Jerusalem's lovers carry out the punishment. The unfaithful wife is exposed, stripped, stoned and pierced with swords. Ezekiel 16:38 suggests that these penalties are for murder as well as adultery, a fact that may lessen in a small way the misogynist tone of the passage. The metaphor of the Jerusalem as unfaithful wife may break down in Ezekiel 16:41, for details regarding the city's demise "in the sight of many women" are included. This notice of the female audience may continue the metaphor of the city as female or may warn women against imitating Jerusalem's wantonness. In the end, God's fury and rage are satisfied. He is no longer shamed and promises to be angry no more.

Like Mother, Like Daughter (Ezek 16:44-63)

Ezekiel moves from a graphic depiction of Jerusalem's sin to a comparison built on the proverb "like mother, like daughter." Only a mother and sisters who bring dishonor to their roles as wives and mothers are named here. A more positive and literal casting of this proverb might include a consideration of such honorable matriarchs as Sarah, Rebekah, Rachel or even Deborah, who is named "a mother in Israel" (Judg 5:7). But Ezekiel uses the proverb to cast a negative light on Jerusalem as a daughter and mother. Although news of restoration is usually positive, the news of Jerusalem's restoration continues the critique in that she will have to share her good fortune with Sodom and Samaria and their daughters. This shameful situation is regarded as further punishment for Jerusalem. Still, God promises to remember his covenant and establish an everlasting covenant with Jerusalem. Her sisters are not included in this covenant directly, though they will benefit from it in that they will be given to Jerusalem as daughters. In the end Jerusalem will remember and feel shame for all that she did.

This long chapter overflowing with troubling images of marriage and sexuality was intended to offend and has succeeded in doing so for many readers. Without denying the dangers inherent in Ezekiel's extended metaphor, it is important to hear its message within its historical, cultural and literary context. By using the figure of the unfaithful wife, Ezekiel intended to shock his predominantly male audience into listening to God's message about their infidelity to the covenant and their imminent punishment. The message is about fidelity in relation to the covenant bond between God and God's people. The love story gone wrong explains the reasons for God's judgment on Jerusalem. It holds forth hope for restoration of deeply severed divine-human relationships. It seeks to bring its readers to a place of awareness, a deeper understanding of God's ways, God's expectations, God's desires and promises and a deeper knowledge of the history of God's people. To be sure, it raises important questions about God's character as God is imaged as a compassionate rescuer, a deeply passionate and generous lover who responds to the wantonness of his wife with jealousy, anger and vengeance and ultimately with promises of restoration. But these questions need to be studied with an appreciation for the text's genre and in light of the rest of Scripture.

A Riddle and a Proverb (Ezek 17—18)

In Ezekiel 17, the eagles represent Babylon and Egypt, and the vine is Zedekiah, who sought to be liberated from Babylon and looked to Egypt for help. His act of rebellion against Babylon invites God's retribution. What seemed to Zedekiah to be a shrewd political solution to Judah's troubles did not address the underlying moral and spiritual issues that were at the heart of Judah's problems. The message to the exiles, who were looking for a political solution to their troubles, was clear. In the epilogue, God becomes the great eagle, and he promises the continued existence of the Davidic line through a special shoot. This tender twig planted on towering Mount Zion flourishes, bears fruit and provides shelter for all species of birds. Other trees (nations) will recognize God's lordship over history. God's final promise that what he has spoken, he will perform, is a word of hope for the community of faith who later recognized a messianic promise in this epilogue.

A popular proverb that encapsulated an attitude of fatalism that was causing moral, social and spiritual degeneration among the exiles is challenged (Ezek 18). Instead of placing the responsibility for God's present judgment on the shoulders of previous generations, Ezekiel declares that each person is responsible for his or her life. Ezekiel explores the issue of individual responsibility from a number of different angles. The various subjects of Ezekiel's cases are male, and the crimes are typically male (especially defiling another man's wife or approaching a menstruous woman; Block, 562 n. 39). However, the principles that are fleshed out are universal and inclusive. They are ultimately liberating for women, who must take responsibility for their spiritual and moral lives before God. Male and female members of the house of Israel are expected to live a righteous life, and both are offered life on condition of repentance. Finally, although this passage repudiates the old proverb that allowed adult children to blame others for their circumstances, the proverb seen in its best light reminds parents of their responsibilities for teaching their children and their children's children the ways of God so that they will know how to live a righteous life before God.

The Lioness and the Vine (Ezek 19)

Following a chapter that focuses on fathers and children, Ezekiel 19 features the figure of a mother imaged initially as a lioness and then as a vine. The image of mother raises issues relating to the vocation of motherhood. Moreover, although the chapter allows for positive reflection on the importance of mothers, it is a lament and ultimately leads readers to thoughtful reflection on pride, ambition, disappointment, sin and judgment.

The chapter begins and ends with a reference to a "lament," which is a technical term for a dirge that was composed and sung at the death of an individual. Characteristically, a lament was a short composition written in a 3+2 meter that addressed the dead person, celebrated his or her life, lamented the death and called listeners to join in the mourning ritual. Many prophets effectively adapted this ritual form to address the living (individuals, communities and cities), to celebrate their past and to declare their imminent disaster, judgment and death. In this the first of Ezekiel's laments, there is considerable debate about the identity of the individual or entity mourned.

The first part of the lament features the lioness, which is extolled as a mother in her role as caregiver and educator of her cubs. The lioness succeeded in raising a strong lion that learned (presumably from her) to tear the prey and devour people. Her hopes and ambitions for her son were dashed when he was trapped and led away captive by the Egyptians. Her losses, however, did not defeat her. She took another of her cubs and made him a strong lion. Again her role as an ambitious, perhaps controlling, yet effective trainer and teacher is underlined. As his mother's pride, his prowess and strength and violence are celebrated. Like his brother he devoured people. In his ravages against the land and its inhabitants, he raped widows or perhaps the women who were made widows by him. It is similar to a reference to princes making widows and calls attention to the fact that women of all times have been victims of war. This second lion was also trapped, taken into exile and imprisoned. The first section of the dirge ends with the acknowledgment of the virtual death of the second cub. Although the figure of the lioness has disappeared, his removal has once again dashed her expectations and ambitions.

The second part of the lament features the mother again, though this time she is likened to a vine. Planted by water, the vine bears fruit, produces strong and proud branches and luxuriant leaves and grows tall. The double references to the height of the vine ominously suggest the sin of pride. The association of women and pride is also made in Isaiah 3:16, where the women of Zion are called haughty, and in Ezekiel's description of Sodom and her daughters (Ezek 16:49-58). But the once fruitful, vinelike mother is uprooted and destroyed by wind, fire and drought. The luxuriant vine that produced branches fit for a ruler's scepter is left without a mighty branch, no scepter for a ruler. The lamentation ends with images of death. The mother vine is left without life and hope. The final notice suggests that the death of the mother that is lamented in the funeral dirge has taken place.

The interpretive question remains as to the identities of the mother(s) and her (their) progeny. One approach is to look for close correspondence between symbol and reality and to identify the lioness, her cubs and the vine with historical figures. Hamutal, the wife of Josiah and mother of Jehoahaz and Zedekiah, is undoubtedly the strongest candidate for the mother figure (2 Kings 24:18). When this identification is made, this lament provides considerable insight into Hamutal's life as a maternally ambitious, powerful and at least initially successful mother and queen as she prepared and put forward first one son and then a second as king of Judah. The suggestion has been made that the funeral lament may have been for Hamutal, whose great plans came to naught with her exile and death in Babylon (Clements, 84).

However, for a number of reasons, including the fact that no textual evidence corroborates the detailed picture of Hamutal that emerges from this text, many interpreters prefer to identify the mother as a collective entity such as Israel, Judah, its royal house or Jerusalem. The view that the mother represents Judah collectively is supported by Genesis 49, which may be the text that inspired this lament. In that passage, which includes several verbal links with Ezekiel 16, Judah is figured as lion, lioness and vine. However, the positive images of the lioness and the vine in Genesis 49:8-12 are transformed into negative images in Ezekiel 19 as the death knell is sounded for the once blessed royal house of Judah. If the feminine figure refers to the city, nation or royal house of Judah, the lament suggests to its hearers that the rulers that the lioness produced or that sprouted from the vine have come under judgment and have fallen. Furthermore, when a collective interpretation of the feminine figures is made, the identity of the cubs is opened up for discussion. Most commentators concur that the first cub is Jehoahaz. Difference of opinion exists, however, when it comes to identifying the second cub as Jehoiachin, in which case the vine may be identified as Nehushta, who was exiled with her son to Babylon (2 Kings 24:12).

Positively, this chapter calls attention to the importance of a mother's role in the producing, nurturing, socializing, education and vocational formation of children. Moreover, the story of the lioness and her cubs paints a portrait of the intimate bond between mother and child as the mother's ambitious hopes, pride and disappointments are revealed. But the greatest hopes and dreams of the lioness and the vine for their progeny came to naught. The story of the vine points to the ultimate destruction of the progeny and the mother. This lament then underscores a common theme in Scripture relating to the impact of the failures and successes of children on their parents. Moreover, the images of life, water and fruitfulness that are transformed into images of death and the desert call to mind the contrasts between the righteous and the wicked in Psalm 1. The lioness and the vine may have neglected teaching their children the ways of the righteous to the peril of their children and ultimately themselves. Human sin brings death. The appropriate response to the losses that sin breeds is lament. Though this chapter gives no hope, elsewhere Ezekiel teaches that God in his mercy can bring new life to the dead (Ezek 37:1-14). Moreover, the positive image of the lion of Judah is redeemed when the Messiah is designated as the Lion of the tribe of Judah (Rev 5:5). Finally, that the career that his ambitious mother viewed as successful led to the ravishing of women and the death of men reminds readers that women as well as men can be involved in processes that lead to the abuse and death of others.

Israel's History Revisited (Ezek 20:1-44)

The elders who came to Ezekiel with a question for him to ask of God were undoubtedly shocked by the long and grim rehearsal of Israel's history that they were given. Ezekiel's description of Israel's past as one of constant rebellion and disobedience was not the history they had idealized. It was history recast by a prophet, preacher and visionary whose task it was to warn his contemporaries of coming judgment, and the elders undoubtedly recognized the message as one they had heard from Ezekiel before. The story begins in Egypt, where God chose Israel and made himself known by name. God promised liberation from Egypt and the gift of a new land on the condition of the rejection of the idols of Egypt. God's chosen people defied him, but God held back his anger for the sake of his name.

The story continues with an account of life in the wilderness, where God tried to teach his people to live by giving them laws. There, however, they rebelled, and God held back his anger for the sake of his name and relented of his decision not to bring them into the Promised Land. The pattern of grace, rebellion and restrained anger continues even with the new generation in the wilderness. What follows is a problematic statement that God gave them bad laws and rules that could not lead to life—most notably the sacrifice of firstborn. Many solutions to the theological problems raised by this text have been offered. One possibility is that Ezekiel is referring to a perverse twisting of the law that the firstborn belonged to the Lord, which was being used by God's covenant people to justify the practice of sacrificing children to the Canannite god Molech. From the perspective of divine providence, Ezekiel could understand this "misunderstanding" or bad law as being part of God's larger plan to punish his rebellious people. Alternatively, it has been proposed that the so-called bad laws are not to be identified with the laws given in Egypt or at Sinai but rather were laws given specifically to the second generation in the wilderness that are not preserved (see Block, 636-41, for a full discussion). Ezekiel's account of the sins of past generations continues with a description of the idolatry that took place upon entry into Canaan.

Finally, Ezekiel's grim history reaches the present, and the elders are told that God will not respond to their inquiries because they are no better than their forebears and are accountable for following their pattern of rebellion. Their desire to be like the nations is met with censure and an affirmation of God's kingship. In the end they are promised a new exodus, another wilderness experience and a purging of the rebels that ultimately would create a people who would acknowledge the Lord and worship on his holy mountain. God's restored people would respond to his gracious acts on their behalf by humbly acknowledging their past and by recognizing that the Lord's actions are rooted in his covenant faithfulness and integrity.

The Sword (Ezek 20:45—21:32)

This section contains four oracles that make reference to a sword. In the first oracle (Ezek 20:45—21:7), Ezekiel speaks of a forest fire that will sweep through the land and that will be recognized as an act of God's judgment. Then to his audience, who mocks him as a spinner of riddles, Ezekiel explains that the south stands for Jerusalem and the forest fire for the avenging sword of the Lord that will slay the right-eous and the wicked to the end that all will recognize the destruction as the Lord's. Ezekiel is to respond to the report with grief and dismay to impress upon his audience the grim nature of the news.

The second oracle (Ezek 21:8-17) begins with a song that describes a sword that is sharpened, polished and ready for slaughter. It will be used as an instrument of God's judgment against his people. Clapping and perhaps even a sword dance accompanied the words of this dramatic and forceful oracle.

The third oracle concerns the sword of Babylon's king (Ezek 21:18-27). Ezekiel uses a military map marking two alternative assault routes to point out the king of Babylon's choices. In order to make the right military decision, the king uses three different methods of divination. Jerusalem's fate and that of its prince, Zedekiah, is sealed. The Babylonian king will be the Lord's agent of destruction.

In the final oracle (Ezek 21:28-32), the sword is brandished against the Ammonites, who had earlier been spared. The sword is then to return to its sheath and receives judgment. The sword probably refers to Babylon, though some commentators interpret the sword as Ammon.

Jerusalem, the Guilty City (Ezek 22)

This chapter consists of three oracles that center on Jerusalem. In the first, Ezekiel is asked to judge Jerusalem, "the bloody city." The ascription to Jerusalem of a phrase that had earlier been used to describe Nineveh (Nahum 3:1) would have been shocking for the exiles. However, the catalogue of Jerusalem's sins left no doubt that punishment was inevitable. Women are noted among the crime victims: mothers (and fathers) are treated with contempt, strangers (possibly women) are cheated, widows and orphans are wronged. Moreover, women are victims of sexual violence. Menstruating women are ravished. A verb that suggests abuse is used instead of the expected euphemism for intercourse. Further, neighbors' wives, daughters-in-law and sisters are violated. These and other heinous sins lead to God's judgment. The attention that Ezekiel gives to women as the victims of crimes starkly contrasts with the extremely negative representations of women in other chapters. Moreover, it is intensely ironic that Jerusalem, which is implicitly personified as a woman in this chapter, allows other women to be victimized.

In the second oracle against Jerusalem (Ezek 22:17-22), God's people are declared to be dross. They are to be thrown into a furnace, where they will experience God's wrath and come to know that their suffering comes from God.

In the third oracle (Ezek 22:23-31), Jerusalem's princes, priests and prophets are shown to be spiritually and morally bankrupt. Moreover, those whom they lead are also corrupt. God can find no one to "stand in the breach," so judgment is inevitable. The blame for ruination is laid on the spiritually and morally corrupt individuals of Jerusalem.

The Story of Two Sisters (Ezek 23)

Ezekiel 23, like Ezekiel 16, is a long oracle that is based on the figure of the city as promiscuous female figure married to the Lord. Like Ezekiel 16, it is replete with marital and sexual images that are intentionally graphic, lewd and offensive.

The story of the sisters, Oholah and Oholibah, begins with an account of their youthful harlotry in Egypt. The text explicitly notes that "their breasts were squeezed and their virgin nipples were handled" (Ezek 23:3 New Jewish Publication Society). This early period is referred to again in Ezekiel 23:8, where Oholah's early sexual history is described in terms of the experience of the Egyptian men who had poured their lust on her. When these verses are read through the eyes of those who are sensitized to contemporary issues relating to the abuse and victimization of women, they are read as a male perspective on child abuse or rape (note the passive voice and absence of the female perspective). Though such a reading raises the question of the effect of language on readers, it does not interpret the text in light of its narrative purpose, which is to shock readers into an awareness of the longstanding unfaithfulness of Samaria and Jerusalem to their covenant Lord.

Oholah's sexual history continues with a lurid account of her blatant unfaithfulness to her husband, who had taken both sisters as wives. Her abandoned husband handed her over to her lovers, who exposed her nakedness, seized her children and violently killed her. In death, she became proverbial among women for the ruinous effects of marital unfaithfulness. Oholah's story is the story of Samaria, whose relationship with Assyria led to her demise in 722 B.C. and marked the end of the northern kingdom.

One of the women who observed the demise of Oholah was her sister, Oholibah. But the lessons of history were lost to her. Like her sister, she lusted after handsome Assyrians. Her feelings soon turned to Babylonian men, whose pictures sculptured on walls had incited her lust, but even their love did not satisfy her. Her lust turned back to the Egyptians and the wantonness of her youth. The male genitals, which are usually referred to euphemistically in the Old Testament, are crudely likened to those of asses. Some commentators suggest that the focus on the size of the male member reflects a particularly male perspective on sexual experience. Oholibah's passion, however, also extended to the "semen" or "emissions" of stallions. This coarse language is intended to disturb the audience or reader whose response of aversion may not be unlike that of her divine lover, who observes Oholibah's wanton lifestyle and turns from her in disgust. Her story told the tale of Jerusalem's political and religious history. It recounts her fickle relationship with God and her various political allies and enemies.

The message of divine judgment on Jerusalem is delivered four times and comes as no surprise to readers. The divine judgment is administered by former lovers, who now hate her. The story moves from describing the horrible demise of the city and its inhabitants to the punishment of the whore, who is left disfigured and exposed without the desire to continue her profligate lifestyle. The third divine judgment is a poetic lament that may have been a popular song adapted to convey again the message that Oholibah would experience the same demise as her sister. The image of drinking from a cup of desolation and woe is used figuratively to convey the reception of God's judgment and wrath. The image of a woman drinking from a cup that brings horror and desolation also recalls the ordeal of the suspected adulteress in Numbers 5:11-31. However, unlike the case in Numbers, witnesses and evidence of infidelity are plentiful. The poem concludes with the grotesque picture of Oholibah drinking deeply from the deep, wide and overflowing cup of intoxicating wine. She drains the cup and then, desiring more wine, gnaws on the cup's broken pieces. In her final moment, she tears out her breasts. This act starkly contrasts her early experience of having her breasts caressed and her later longing for those experiences. It is a particularly violent image of self-hatred and grief. The cup of judgment was given because Jerusalem had forgotten the Lord and cast him behind her back. Jerusalem, to her peril, had failed to heed God's many warnings about the importance of remembering the God of the covenant.

Views of women bathing excited both literary and artistic notice. (Ezekiel 23:40)

The chapter closes with a general accusation of adultery and bloodshed against the sisters. They are accused of engaging in idolatry, sacrificing children, defiling the sanctuary, profaning the sabbath and engaging in drunken orgies. The description of the sisters' allurement of their lovers is detailed. But beneath the actions of the literal adulteresses, lie the cultic meaning of their actions, for the incense and oil that they sets before their lovers belong to the Lord. The righteous men who will punish them are not identified. Their identification as righteous may be because their cause is regarded as just or because they are right-eous in comparison with the sisters (Block, 762). After the case against the sisters is made, punishment is announced. The punishment is particularly violent; an army is summoned and the sisters are handed over to be terrorized, plundered, stoned and hacked with swords. Children are also killed and houses burned. At this point, the extended metaphor breaks down as the punishment is leveled not only against the two sisters but also against the inhabitants of the cities they represent.

Ezekiel 23:48 introduces an unexpected admonition to women that they take warning and not imitate the sisters' wantonness. This warning seems to shift the burden of the prophetic message from the house of Israel to individual women and their sexual mores. Whether the concluding verses narrow the focus of the application to real women or not, the message of the chapter is not to be limited to women. All readers are to learn from the hard lessons of Israel's persistent unfaithfulness, which led to disaster and death.

The Cooking Pot (Ezek 24:1-14)

This strong word of judgment is dated to the day Nebuchadnezzar began his long siege of Jerusalem. It marks the climax of the judgment oracles against the rebellious house and the "bloody city." The oracle begins with what was likely a cooking song that has been likened to "Polly, put the kettle on."

The interpretation of the allegory or parable is fairly complex, although its basic message is unclouded. The cooking pot is Jerusalem. The use of cities and pots as symbols for women and the association of this city and pot with blood may suggest the image of Jerusalem as a menstruant (Galambush, 137). The contents of the pot is most often rendered as "rusty," though the noun literally means "diseased," which suggests that what is inside the pot is diseased or corrupt (Block, 776-77). This rendering corresponds well with the later emphasis on the impurity of the meat and may also correspond to the notion of the uncleanness of uterine blood (Galambush, 137-38). Further references to blood assume knowledge of the levitical laws about bleeding an animal killed for food and disposing of its blood by pouring it out and covering it. Not only did Jerusalemites not follow God's prescriptions, but also they sacrilegiously poured blood out on the bare rock, which may allude to the sacrifice of children at high places or to crimes involving bloodshed. God's response is to take vengeance on the city. The focus then shifts to God, who as the chef takes over the job of cooking. God repeatedly attempts to purify the meat (the citizens of Jerusalem), but the city's diseases and lewd filthiness are such that it cannot be cleansed. God then addresses the city using second person feminine forms and declares that opportunity for cleansing has passed and that the city will be judged in accordance with her wanton behavior. She will get what she deserves until God's fury is spent.

A reader cannot help but read the present text in light of the extended metaphors in which Jerusalem is personified as a whore (Ezek 16; 23). The proximity of Ezekiel 23 has the effect of heightening the female images in this text. Jerusalem is a bloody city, unclean, diseased and sexually defiled. Ezekiel declares that her punishment is not only imminent but also deserved. Jerusalem offers no hope for the exiles. Neither can her citizens remain complacent about their future in God's city.

The Death of Ezekiel's Wife (Ezek 24:15-27)

God's most difficult word to Ezekiel was the announcement of his wife's imminent death. Ezekiel's wife is described as "the delight [or desire] of your eyes," an expression used of persons or objects that one loves to gaze on and that implies that Ezekiel and his wife had an intimate relationship (1 Kings 20:3-6; Lam 2:4; Song 5:16). Nothing else is known about Ezekiel's wife, but she would have been involved in his prophetic ministry. She not only witnessed his sign acts but also supplied the materials used from her household goods (pots, an iron plate, a knife, baking supplies and gear for exile) and perhaps even instructed Ezekiel about baking bread and taught him the cooking song. She supported her husband in his ministry, which would have invited the laughter, mocking and anger of their community. She may have been involved in entertaining the elders and others who came to their house.

Ezekiel was instructed to refrain from showing outward signs of mourning. In response to the inquiries of those who knew that there must be a reason that he was not displaying the customary signs of mourning for the woman they knew he loved, Ezekiel explained that they too were about to lose the delight of their eyes, the Lord's temple and sons and daughters left behind in Jerusalem. They were also to follow Ezekiel's lead in not showing outward signs of mourning. When the destruction came, the exiles would acknowledge the Lord God and Ezekiel would be recognized as a true prophet. His tongue would also be loosed, an action that signified a change in Ezekiel's prophetic role: judgment was over. Ezekiel could begin the work of reconstruction. Although the text does not comment on Ezekiel's personal response to the ultimate sign of his wife's death, he obediently carried on his ministry alone and in pain, perhaps comforted only by the fact that God became known through these terrible acts. The deaths of Ezekiel's wife and of the Lord's symbolic wife, Jerusalem, mark the virtual end of the use of feminine personification of Jerusalem in the book. Indeed, Jerusalem is never mentioned again by name.

Oracles Against the Nations (Ezek 25:1—32:32)

This collection of oracles marks a dramatic shift in the focus of Ezekiel's message. Oracles of judgment against the enemies of God's people effectively delay the news of the fall of Jerusalem and provide a transition to the more positive news that follows.

Grief & Bereavement

Grief is a process with characteristic stages and tasks. The initial reaction to bereavement is likely to be shock or disbelief, and feelings may be numb. Then grief becomes sharper, with outbursts of sadness and anger. There may be feelings of guilt or intense loneliness. The Bible gives us many examples of mourning in its narratives, and in its poems people pour out sorrow, rage or tenderness to God (Job 30:16; 2 Sam 1:23-27; 18:33). The terrible pain is not minimized, yet it gives hope beyond the horizon of suffering.

Societies develop traditions for grieving that bring people together for support. Hebrew mourning was not as elaborate as in the surrounding cultures. Customs implying superstitious veneration of tombs or attempts to contact the dead through mediums were forbidden. Yet Abraham's burial place in Hebron is remembered. People who desecrate tombs are condemned.

Two texts (Ezek 24:16-18; Jer 16:5-7) describe grief expressed by audible sobs and laments and visible signs such as shaving the head and rubbing it with ashes. Others offer the mourners food to acknowledge the death. Both Ezekiel and Jeremiah were asked to forego the customs, but this is not a model for a godly (or manly) approach to bereavement. It is meant to be shockingly inhuman behavior conveying a symbolic message to the observers.

Jesus silenced the perhaps artificial wailing at Jairus's house (Mk 5:38-39), but he weeps and feels indignation at Lazarus's tomb (Jn 11:35, 38). In both cases Jesus says the victim is not dead but sleeping, and Paul develops this metaphor (1 Thess 4:14; 1 Cor 15:20). Such language, used glibly, has encouraged some Christians to remain in denial, feeling guilty about their desperate grief. It needs to be clear "sleep" implies there is something beyond death to wake up to. When God raised Jesus to new life, the disciples were glad but soon had to face sadness that they could no longer see and touch him.

More women than men are widowed, and they have been more likely to suffer loss of money and status at the same time. Justice and care for widows is an Old Testament principle, underlined in the New. It was embraced by the Jerusalem church, which ran into administrative difficulties putting it into practice (Acts 6:1).

Infertility can be like bereavement for men and women, but a woman's self-image has often been linked with childbearing. Her biological clock runs down more quickly. When Paul speaks of Abraham with Sarah "hoping against hope" for a promised child, he describes a chain where suffering produces perseverance, then character, then hope (Rom 4:18; 5:3-4). This is not an inevitable or easy road. It involves pouring out anguish to God and accepting our need for support from other people while we gradually let go of one set of hopes for the future. The hope that emerges is increasingly grounded in the trust that God loves us now (Rom 5:5) and will one day defeat death and wipe every tear from our eyes (Rev 21:4). VERA M. SINTON

Oracles against Israel's most geographically immediate neighbors—Ammon, Moab, Edom, Philistia, Tyre and Sidon—are followed by a lengthy collection of oracles against Egypt. Set exactly between the oracles against the six nations and the oracles against Egypt are words of promise for Israel. It was comforting for the exiles to be assured that God would judge their enemies, that God was sovereign over the nations and that through judgment, the nations would know the Lord. The theme of God's self-disclosure through judgment is central to this collection. In addition, the oracles serve to warn readers of the consequences of pride, conceit, arrogance, selfishness and vengeance. They also demonstrate the breadth of Ezekiel's prophetic ministry.

The oracles against the nations contain little that pertains specifically to women. Cities, towns and nations that are gendered as feminine are then referred to as feminine entities. In the descriptions of the impending devastations of the nations, women are possibly mentioned as victims only in Ezekiel 30. If the pronoun "they" is taken as "women," following the Septuagint, or if a textual error is assumed, then the women are designated as those who go into captivity. Similarly, it is possible to interpret the reference to "her daughters" (Ezek 30:18) as the women of Tehaphnehes or all Egyptian women instead of the outlying towns.

A further reference is made to women in the laments over Egypt. In Ezekiel 32:16 mention is made of "the daughters of the nations" who shall mourn the death of Egypt by chanting this lament. The picture of women from all nations cooperating to perform this universal mourning is truly remarkable. A similar picture is painted in Ezekiel 32:18, where the daughters of majestic nations are summoned to wail with Ezekiel over Egypt, which is about to descend to the lowest part of the netherworld. This is probably another reference to women's involvement with death rituals as professional mourners.

Ezekiel, the Sentinel (Ezek 33)

This new phase in Ezekiel's ministry of hope begins not with the expected news of Jerusalem's fall but with his recommissioning as a sentinel to warn Israel of potential judgment. This text is similar to part of Ezekiel's initial commissioning as a prophet, though his initial call to be a sentinel was private and this second one is public. What follows provides an illustration of Ezekiel's work as sentinel. Ezekiel cites a comment that was circulating among the exiles that implied that Ezekiel's preaching had been taken to heart by some. But the exiles were left with a feeling of despair, and they did not understand how God's justice worked. The divine response offers great hope. God calls the wicked to life by offering them forgiveness if they turn from their wicked ways. The hypothetical cases that are presented are similar to those in Ezekiel 18:21-30. In the end the notions of individual responsibility and divine justice tempered with mercy are affirmed.

The fall of Jerusalem is announced by one who had escaped from the captured city. Ezekiel was freed to speak. His first address is to those who remained in Jerusalem who were justifying their expropriation of land by inferring from the gift of land to one man, Abraham, that they deserved the land that was left by those who had died or who had been taken into exile. However, their sins are exposed, including the defiling of one another's wives, and they are judged. Here Ezekiel alludes to Leviticus 26 to show that there will be no quick return to the land. The punishment is a clear and exact reversal of the blessings of Leviticus 26:6-10. By leaving the last curse—exile (Lev 26:27-53)—unspoken, Ezekiel allows his audience to come to the sobering conclusions that the people of Jerusalem will join the exiles, not vice versa. Through the final judgment of the desolation of the land, unlike the one that has just happened, God's people will recognize the Lord. This reference to "I am the Lord" also alludes to Leviticus 26:1-2 and shows that the purposes of the curses are not solely punitive but also didactic. If the people learn to acknowledge who God is, then there is the possibility of future redemption.

Ezekiel's second address also raises the issue of the people's hardened hearts. The exiles finally recognized him as a prophet, and he became quite popular as an entertainer. Even so, they did not take Ezekiel's message seriously. Ezekiel is assured that those who hear the message without acting on it would eventually recognize him as a true prophet whose words should have been heeded.

The Divine Shepherd (Ezek 34)

Although this chapter contains little that is specifically related to women, it declares the good news of a loving Shepherd, the promise of new life and future hope that lies beyond the pain, trouble and suffering experienced in this life. These texts, which brought hope to African American slaves, continue to speak to women and men in the community of faith who need to hear of God's words of hope and love.

The chapter begins by condemning the shepherds of Israel who looked after themselves and terribly neglected God's flock. Included in God's abused flock are the weak, the sick, the injured, the lost and the neglected: they are all prey to wild beasts. God promises to deal with the shepherds and rescue his flock from the shepherds. This loving and caring portrait of God, the Shepherd, continues with God's promises to take thought of his flock and seek them out, rescue them, find the lost, bandage the injured, sustain the weak, bring them back into their land, pasture them on the mountains of Israel, feed them and let them lie down. However, even among the flock, there are those who abuse and greedily exploit other sheep. They will be judged, and God promises again to rescue the weak. God then appoints his servant prince David as shepherd of his sheep. He promises to establish a covenant of peace that will bring peace and security to the flock who will then know God's presence with them and their identity as God's people, the sheep of his pasture. The idea of restoration in this chapter comes through even more clearly by comparing its imagery with that of Jeremiah 23, on which it seems to draw.

To the exiles who were sheep without a shepherd, this message would have brought hope and comfort. It assured them that their future would be under the care of a loving, shepherd God who would reestablish his covenant that promised peace, land and a relationship with God. To Christian readers, Ezekiel's vision takes on more particularity as Jesus is identified as the Davidic Messiah, the good Shepherd who came to seek, find, heal and save the lost sheep and establish a new covenant and the new kingdom.

Judgment and Restoration (Ezek 35—36)

Ezekiel 35:1-15 begins with an oracle of judgment against Mount Seir (Edom), which at first sight seems misplaced in the midst of oracles of hope. However, when it is read with the prophecy to the mountains of Israel that follows (Ezek 36:1-15), it provides a message of hope for the exiles. It confirms God's sovereignty over all nations and lands and announces the judgment and removal of a long-standing enemy who stood in the way of God's plans to restore the land to Israel. The message to the mountains of Israel begins with words of judgment against Edom and other foreign nations who insulted and slandered God's people. A magnificent description of the restoration of the mountains follows: its land would be cultivated, its population would increase, its towns and waste places rebuilt and the Lord acknowledged. This prophecy provides a dramatic contrast to Ezekiel's earlier words about the coming desolation of the mountains of Israel. Now that the devastation has taken place, restoration is possible. This message would have undoubtedly encouraged the captives living far from the land of promise. It also encourages all readers that new life, new hope and new promises are possible following times of painful judgment, devastation or separation from God and the house of faith. Ultimately it points to the eternal city of God.

Before the exiles are given exultant words of restoration, the Lord explains the problem of how the exile had the effect of profaning his name before the nations. As a means of vindicating his name before the nations, God proposes to cleanse his people, give then a new heart and spirit, return them back to an ancestral land abounding in fruitfulness and to rebuild and repopulate the waste places. The people's response to God's merciful acts would be recognition of their evil ways, personal remorse, and recognition of his lordship. The clear emphasis of this text is on God's doing. The planned renewal and restoration had nothing to do with human worth, human initiative or action, since God's chosen people had continuously proved unfaithful to the covenant. God would act for the sake of his name so that Israel and indeed all the nations would recognize him as Lord.

Within the initial rehearsal of Israel's past sins, the Lord says that Israel polluted the land by their ways and actions and that their conduct (the capital crimes of bloodshed and idolatry) was like the uncleanness of a woman in her menstrual period. For their defilement of the land, Israel was scattered among the nations. According to Levitical law, menstrual blood rendered a woman (and anything or anyone whom she touched) ritually impure for seven days. This comparison of Israel's crimes with the uncleanness of a woman is problematic since the involuntary pollution caused by menstrual blood is of a different order than the pollution caused by the voluntary acts of murder and idolatry. Several explanations have been offered for Ezekiel's use of this unusual simile. Medieval Jewish expositors associated the image of an unclean woman with Ezekiel's consequential metaphor of Jerusalem as God's wife. Accordingly, the exegete Kimchi explained that God in his punishment of Israel is like a husband who puts his unclean wife away while she is impure but then draws her near once she becomes pure (Greenberg, 2:728). More recent commentators have associated this female image of uncleanness with other images of feminine uncleanness and blood in the book, especially with Ezekiel's depiction of Jerusalem as a woman (Ezek 16; 23). Implicit then in this association of the sins of bloodshed and idolatry with menstrual uncleanness is the prevalent metaphor of Jerusalem, the unclean wife of God, condemned as the city of bloodshed and idolatry.

Restoration of the House of Israel (Ezek 37)

The chapter begins with an account of Ezekiel's extraordinary vision in which God showed him a valley filled with dry bones. Ezekiel preached to the bones, and the bodies of the dead were reconstituted. Then when God's Spirit entered the bodies, they lived.

Is this most famous of Ezekiel's visions to be interpreted literally as pointing to the idea of individual resurrection and life after death, as many Jewish and Christian readers have thought? Or is it a metaphor for the return of the seemingly dead exiles to Israel, an interpretation that would accord well with many other promises of return in Ezekiel? To be sure this text points to God as the giver of life, even life to bones that are dead and dry. The fact that the bones are in the open shows that they belong to people who had been cursed/desecrated, as scattering an enemy's bones or leaving them unburied was common in the ancient Near East. This further points to the miraculous and merciful work of God in restoring Israel. The text is also given to restore hope to those who like the exiles experience life to be more like death. African American slaves found great encouragement in Ezekiel's message of hope and new life beyond their present pilgrimage on earth. The more literal interpretation is also supported by the identification of the bones as "the whole house of Israel" (Ezek 37:11), which suggests that the promise of life and restoration is being offered to the long dead remnants of the northern and southern kingdoms. This understanding fits with the oracle that follows, which envisions a reunification of the two former kingdoms into one. Whether one adheres to a literal or metaphoric interpretation of the vision, its message of hope continues to bring great comfort and promise to women and men whose experiences have left them hopeless and despairing of life. New life is to be found through the life-giving spirit of God.

In the symbolic action of the two sticks (Ezek 37:15-28), the message is given that the former northern kingdom (Joseph/ Ephraim) and the southern kingdom (Judah) will be united. Ezekiel 37:24-28 refers again to Leviticus 26 to show that Israel will get a fresh start with the Lord. God promises to gather the dispersed Israel to the land of promise under the leadership of God's servant David; there they and their descendants will live in obedience, cleansed from sin forever. Further, God promises to establish an everlasting covenant of peace with them and dwell in their midst. Finally, God's restoration of his people, and his presence in their midst, will bring the nations to acknowledge that God sanctifies Israel.

This text also is hard to interpret. The northern kingdom had fallen in 722 B.C., and it is difficult to understand how it might be or might have been restored, though there have been a number of attempts to find the missing kingdom. This prophecy seems to point to a fulfillment that goes beyond a promise of the return of the exiles to the land. Indeed, it seems to point to restored nationhood in its fullest sense in the more distant future. Many Christians regard Jesus' coming as the inauguration of the messianic kingdom alluded to here but suggest that the fulfillment is not completed. The concluding reference to God's sanctuary in the midst of his restored people looks ahead to the final vision of the temple in Ezekiel 40—48.

Prophecies Against Gog (Ezek 38:1—39:29)

These chapters have long been regarded as the most enigmatic and difficult in the book. Questions about placement, authorship, genre, meaning and application abound. Gog is presented as an enemy who assembled an enormous army and planned to launch a military attack on the unfortified and peaceful land of Israel. At stake in the battle are the greatness, holiness and sovereignty of God. The battle takes on cosmic dimensions as God wages a great war against the forces of evil with pestilence, bloodshed, torrential rain, hailstones, fire and brimstone. In the end the nations will know that God is the Lord. God triumphs over the forces of evil. The battle and its morbid aftermath are described vividly and symbolically in Ezekiel 39. Dead bodies become food for birds and beasts. Indeed the scene is later described as a gory sacrificial feast for creatures that assist in God's triumph over evil. The weapons of Gog's defeated army provide fuel for Israel for seven years. Gog's dead take seven months to bury in the Valley of Hamon-gog. Earlier, the bones of Israel and Jacob had gone unburied. In the new land where God will dwell with Israel, however, purity demands the burial of Gog's dead. When the great battle ends, God will be vindicated and Israel will dwell in peace. His glory will be known among the nations, who together with Israel will understand that Israel's defeat and exile were caused by their iniquity and not because of any weakness on God's part.

The theological message of these chapters is clear in spite of all the other questions it raises. The holy and sovereign God reigns over all history and will ultimately triumph over evil. Readers of all periods can rejoice that God is in control over human history and that God will ultimately triumph over evil. Such knowledge brings comfort and security. Those who seek particular meaning in the language of the text risk having history overtake their interpretation.

The New Jerusalem (Ezek 40:1—48:35)

The book of Ezekiel concludes as it began, with a new vision of God. Initially God revealed that he was present with the exiles in Babylon and was withdrawing his presence from the temple in Jerusalem. To conclude, God returns to dwell in the midst of a new temple among his restored people, who are now reestablished in the land. The final vision comes after twenty-five years of waiting, of suffering, of disappointment and of separation from the temple and Jerusalem. Unlike so much of the book, which looks to Israel's sinful past and present to explain existing and imminent disasters, the final vision points to a happy future that is spent in God's presence. As many scholars have observed, this final section portrays Ezekiel as a type of Moses who leads his people in a new exodus to the new Promised Land, receives new laws directly from God on a Sinai-like mountain and exercises a priestly role in the consecration of the new altar.

In his vision, Ezekiel is brought to a new city that was set on a high mountain in Israel. There an unnamed heavenly being guided him through the new temple complex. The tour began at the wall outside the temple area and gradually approached the temple. The guide carefully measured the dimensions of the various structures, and Ezekiel noted many of the fine architectural details. Ezekiel, who had been trained as a priest and separated from the temple for twenty-five years, was obviously captivated by the functional and symbolic significance of the various structures. When they reached the gate that faced east, Ezekiel witnessed the return of the glory of the Lord to the temple. God spoke to Ezekiel and announced that he would dwell in the midst of his people forever on the condition that they did not defile God's name by their "abominations" (Ezek 43:6). This reference to prostitution is the only explicitly feminine image in this final section of the book. It calls to mind Israel's former life, which was so dramatically imaged as an unfaithful wife in the first half of the book. Feminine images and references to women in general are noticeably absent from Ezekiel's vision of the future.

At this point Ezekiel receives his final commission to speak and write about the temple and all its laws so that God's people might follow its plan and its laws. An example of what Ezekiel was to write about follows with the elaborate description of the altar and the regulations for sanctifying it before its use. Ezekiel 44 sets out further regulations that prescribe admission to the sanctuary. These regulations apply only to men, since women, because of their potential uncleanness, were not able to minister in or enter the holy space. Foreigners also (perhaps foreign slaves) were denied entry into the temple lest they profane God's holy place. In the past, those who were "uncircumcised in heart and flesh" had worked in the temple (cf. 1 Kings 11:4). But in the new temple, they were excluded since they were not part of the community of faith. The work that foreigners had previously done was now assigned to Levites who because of their involvement with idolatry could no longer serve as priests but still could serve in the temple. The priestly duties were assigned to the male descendants of Zadok, and regulations about their clothing, appearance, behavior and inheritance are given. The Zadokites who were to perform the most holy ministries were set apart and were to be kept clean, literally and ritually. It is within this context that the restrictions about the kind of woman that a priest might marry must been seen. A priest could marry only a virgin Israelite or a widow of a priest who by virtue of her marriage to a priest would have been in a special category of holiness. Women are also mentioned in a list of family members whose death provided the only exception to the rule that priests could not enter a house where there was a dead person whose body would defile him.

The final chapters of the book contain a collection of further laws about the use of the temple, various celebrations (Passover, sabbath and New Moon), the responsibilities of the prince and the boundaries and tribal divisions in the restored land. Of special interest are the inheritance laws for the prince, which mandate that inheritance must pass on to the prince's sons. Even gifts made to servants eventually would revert to the prince and his rightful male heirs. This system of inheritance was a continuation of what was normative in the ancient world (cf. the challenge of the daughters of Zelophehad, Num 27:1-11). Also of note is the description of the sacred kitchen where the priests were to boil the guilt and sin offerings and bake the meal offerings. This area was separate lest the holiness of the offerings consecrated the worshipers. Other kitchens were located in the four corners of the outer courtyard, where the levitical servers were to prepare the portions of the sacrifices and offerings that were going to be eaten by the worshipers. Cooking and baking were normally done by women, but special meals, especially sacrificial ones, were prepared by men—in this case, by Zadokite priests and Levites.

When Ezekiel was brought from the kitchen area of the inner court to the entrance of the temple, he saw water flowing down from the altar (Ezek 47:1-12). The volume of water increased dramatically as it moved out of the temple area. The river brought life to everything in and around it, even to the lifeless waters of the Dead Sea. Though the swamps and marshes along the coast continued to provide salt, the rest of the areas touched by the river produced trees that bore fruit for food and leaves that brought healing. This is a measure of the perfection of this new era. Everything that was bad about the Dead Sea would be gone as the good things about it were retained (e.g., the sea's production of salt is inconsistent with its support of freshwater marine life). Although some commentators have interpreted this vision literally and tried to locate the source of this water on Mount Zion, its meaning more correctly lies in its rich symbolism. The water, which symbolized God's presence, brings life, fruitfulness, health and healing not simply to the temple but to the entire area, which included the wilderness. To the exiles, this vision brought hope. It promised that when God's presence was reestablished in the temple the blessings of new life, healing and fruitfulness would flow and transform the lives of those near his presence and also others (cf. Rev 22:2, where the leaves bring healing to the nations, and Jn 7:38, where the living waters flow from a believer's heart). God desires to bless and renew his people, not because they deserve it or earn it but rather because of his gracious love.

Female images are noticeably absent from Ezekiel's vision of the new temple and city. This may be because Ezekiel 40—48 emphasizes issues not related to gender, such as architecture, ritual and territorial divisions, and describe the sanctuary from which women were now excluded. The absence of female images may also be because of the strong symbolic association of Jerusalem and the temple with women and defilement in Ezekiel 1—24 (Galambush, 148-51). The new temple, which was marked by holiness, was not to be associated with any type of defilement, and women posed such a threat. Still, some interpreters have seen implicit feminine images in the new temple, which unlike the old temple is fertile. Thus Julie Galambush writes, "This life-giving stream . . . is reminiscent of the flow of blood that earlier characterized the woman Jerusalem. This stream, however, like the blood contained within this temple, is both clean and cleansing, the inverse of menstrual or other uterine blood. The flow from the interior of the new temple is a sort of symbolic amniotic fluid, a provider and sustainer of life" (154). That water is used as an image of fertility elsewhere in the Old Testament suggests that feminine imagery is at least implicit in the image of the waters of life (Ezek 47; cf. Song 4:12-15; Ps 46:4; Ps 87; Jer 31:12). The new city is not called Jerusalem or even the new Jerusalem, lest old associations with the unfaithful and unclean wife be made. Rather the new city is named "The LORD is There" (Ezek 48:35). Though the city is described as being perfectly symmetrical and accessible to all, God's presence makes it a holy city.

Bibliography. P. Albenda, "Woman, Child and Family: Their Imagery in Assyrian Art," in *La femme dans le Proche-Orient Antique, XXXIIe Rencontre Assyriologique Internationale Paris 7-10 Juillet 1986,* ed. J.-M. Durand (Paris: Editions Recherche sur les Civilisations, 1987) 17-21; N. Avigad, *Corpus of West Semitic Seals,* revised and completed by B. Sass (Jerusalem: Hebrew University, 1997); D. I. Block, *The Book of Ezekiel Chapters 1—24* (Grand Rapids, MI: Eerdmans, 1997); R. E. Clements, *Ezekiel* (Louisville, KY: Westminster John Knox, 1996); M. A. Dandamaev, *Slavery in Babylonia: From Nabopolassar to Alexander the Great (626-331 B.C.),* ed. M. A. Powell and D. B. Weisberg (rev. ed.; DeKalb, IL.: Northern Illinois University Press, 1984); T. C. Eskenazi, "Out From the Shadows: Biblical Women in the

Postexilic Era (Sixth to Fourth Century B.C.E.)," *Journal for the Study of the Old Testament* 54 (1992) 25-43; J. Galambush, *Jerusalem in the Book of Ezekiel: The City as Yahweh's Wife,* Society for Biblical Literature Dissertation Series 130 (Atlanta: Scholars Press, 1992); M. Greenberg, *Ezekiel 21—37: A New Translation With Introduction and Commentary,* Anchor Bible (Garden City, NY: Doubleday, 1997); D. J. Halperin, *Seeking Ezekiel: Text and Psychology* (University Park: Pennsylvania State University Press, 1993); T. Jacobsen, "Toward the Image of Tammuz," in *Toward the Image of Tammuz,* ed. W. L. Moran, Harvard Semitic Series 21 (Cambridge: Harvard University Press, 1970) 77-101; M. T. Roth, "Gender and Law: A Case Study from Ancient Mesopotamia," in *Gender and Law in the Hebrew Bible and the Ancient Near East,* ed. V. H. Matthews, B. M. Levinson and T. Frymer-Kensky (Sheffield: Sheffield Academic Press, 1998) 173-84; D. L. Smith, *The Religion of the Landless: The Social Context of the Babylonian Exile* (Bloomington, IN: Meyer-Stone Books, 1989); R. J. Weems, *Battered Love, Marriage, Sex and Violence in the Hebrew Prophets* (Minneapolis: Augsburg Fortress, 1995).

MARION ANN TAYLOR

DANIEL

Introduction

Daniel was not a typical prophet called to admonish God's people but a bureaucrat serving God in the hostile environment of pagan Babylon (modern Iraq). Thus in the Hebrew Bible, Daniel is grouped with the Writings rather than with the Prophets. The book's emphasis is apocalyptic, with strange dreams and visions of the future.

Two closely related languages are used: Hebrew (Dan 1:1—2:4; 8:1—12:13) and Aramaic (Dan 2:4—7:28). The latter was more widely spoken internationally, even as early as the eighth century B.C. (2 Kings 18:26), and was the official language of the Persian Empire.

The book divides naturally into two: Daniel's youth and suffering in Babylon (Dan 1—6) and Daniel's visions as an old man—visions about world history and the suffering of God's people (Dan 7—12). Although the halves seem unrelated, there are definite signs of literary unity. The basics of Daniel 2 reappear in Daniel 7; the destruction "not by human hands" (Dan 2:34) parallels that "not by human hands" (Dan 8:25); "God . . . will set up a kingdom that shall never be destroyed" (Dan 2:44) parallels "the holy ones of Most High; their kingdom shall be an everlasting kingdom" (Dan 7:27).

Although Daniel speaks in the third person in Daniel 1—6 and in the first person in Daniel 7—12, many interpreters deny that Daniel wrote the book. Rather, the author is said to be a pious scribe who lived during a severe persecution of Jews by Antiochus Epiphanes (175-163 B.C.) but took the name of an ancient hero and set his tale in sixth-century Babylon. Intricate arguments meant to explain this complicated process do not convince, and it is best to read the book as a revelation from God to the exiled Daniel during the Babylon and Persian empires. The exile was punishment for centuries of apostasy, a "period of wrath" (Dan 8:19) but also of repentance and learning for God's people and of anticipation of the Messiah.

Outline

1:1-21	Daniel, a Young Israelite in Babylon
2:1—6:28	Pagan Rulers Dream and Scheme in Babylon
7:1—12:3	Daniel Also Dreams in Babylon
12:4-13	Daniel, Receive Your Inheritance

Commentary

Daniel, a Young Israelite in Babylon (Dan 1)

Details of the final turbulent years of Judah and of the collapse of Jerusalem appear in 2 Kings 24—25. The summary of Daniel 1:1 may be dated in 605 B.C., the year in which Nebuchadnezzar invaded Syria, Palestine and Egypt. The phrase "The LORD let King Jehoiakim of Judah fall into his power" (Dan 1:2) introduces a theme of the book: God's rule over all, even powerful earthly rulers.

It was common for a conqueror to take hostages and valuable items back to "the treasury of his god" as a thank offering. So Daniel found himself carried off to Babylon about eight years before the main group (Is 39:7; Jer 25:11) and stayed there until 538 B.C., "the first year of King Cyrus" (Dan 1:21). Undoubtedly the propaganda effect of the kidnapping of four handsome, intelligent youths wore off during their three years of study and preparation in the royal court. Finally came graduation, with top grades in "the literature and language of the Chaldeans" (Dan 1:4), in "literature and wisdom" (Dan 1:17) and "in every matter of wisdom and understanding concerning which the king inquired of them" (Dan 1:20), including a typically Babylonian subject, "visions and dreams" (Dan 1:17). The top grades of the Jews, their adaptation to a new culture and their personal faith and integrity bear eloquent testimony to the dedication of unnamed parents and Israelite teachers. However, the main reason for their success was that "God gave knowledge and skill" (Dan 1:17)—the same God who gave the king of Judah over to the enemy.

Ashpenaz was responsible for the selection of the four Jews just as the eunuch Hegai was responsible for the selection of Esther, another victim of the Babylonian invasion. The phrase "God allowed Daniel to receive favor and compassion from the palace master" (Dan 1:9) is similar to Esther 2:9 and Genesis 39:21. *Favor* is a key word in Esther, the secret of her survival and success in the pagan court. Joseph survived and succeeded for the same reason. Will it work for Daniel?

Daniel's request for permission not to "defile himself" (Dan 1:8) and his choice of vegetarian food were motivated by the fact that the king's food would have been consecrated to idols, and to eat it would have constituted idol worship. Also, sharing the king's food implied loyalty to him (Dan 11:26). The Jews' refusal for these ritual (Lev 11) and moral reasons, their superior physical appearance and high grades in the tests undoubtedly called everyone's attention to them. These Jews will not compromise with pagan culture where this is opposed to God's law. Nor will they be fanatics, unwilling to benefit from secular education for fear of losing their faith.

The change from Hebrew names, all of which contain the name of God, to new, pagan names that do not and that may even use the names of pagan gods was common (2 Kings 23:34; Gen 41:45; 43:32). So

Daniel, meaning "God has judged," became Belteshazzar, meaning "protect the life of the king." Possibly the main reason for the change was to obliterate ethnic identity and speed up acculturation.

Pagan Rulers Dream and Scheme in Babylon (Dan 2—6)

Daniel Interprets Nebuchadnezzar's Dream (Dan 2)

Dreams, worry, insomnia, every possible type of astrologer, a cruel demagogue in crisis but making absurd demands are common today. And in South America, where I live, Daniel's reaction is not uncommon either. He accepted the challenge, asked for prayer and afterward expressed gratitude to God.

The frustration of waking up and realizing he had forgotten an important dream was a dangerous portent, and the king's subsequent threats and promises increased the astrologers' tension and panic. Daniel's rational behavior—discreet questions and explanations—contrasts with the king's screaming petulance; Daniel prefers a courageous interview to speculation.

Prayer (Dan 2:20-23; cf. Job 12:13, 15, 18, 22) is another theme of the book, and Daniel's dependence on God contrasts with the astrologers' complacent self-sufficiency. After prayer, action; and just as Joseph's God-given administrative ability saved Egyptians from death (Gen 41:55-56), so Daniel's God-given courage saved Babylonian seers from execution. This is an example of the fulfillment of God's promise to Abraham: "In you all the families of the earth shall be blessed" (Gen 12:3).

Daniel 2:25-49 forms a unit framed by these phrases:

> "among the exiles from Judah a man" (Dan 2:25)
> "Are you able . . . ?" (Dan 2:26)
> "There is a God in heaven who reveals mysteries" (Dan 2:28)
>
> "Nebuchadnezzar fell on his face" before Daniel (Dan 2:46)
> "[Nebuchadnezzar] worshiped Daniel" (Dan 2:46)
> "Your God is . . . a revealer of mysteries" (Dan 2:47)

Thus a nameless exile whose ability was doubted became "ruler over . . . Babylon . . . and over all the wise men" (Dan 2:48).

The dream is about "what will happen at the end of days" (Dan 2:28), a phrase used of the messianic age (Is 2:2; Jer 48:47). The statue, when struck by a rock "cut out, not by human hands" (Dan 2:34), crashed to the ground, its splinters scattered to the four winds, while the rock "became a great mountain and filled the whole earth" (Dan 2:35). The sharp contrast between carefully crafted but ultimately fragile manufactured objects and the raw simplicity, power and solidity of that which comes from God is striking.

Daniel's interpretation is that Nebuchadnezzar's glorious, worldwide reign will be succeeded by inferior ones until a strong but "brittle" (Dan 2:42) kingdom appears. This "divided" group will also fall before the flying rock, which many understand to refer to Christ.

After Babylon came the Median kingdom, then the Persian and the Greek. Perhaps the list should read Medo-Persian, Greek and Roman. Daniel 2:44 suggests that the order is not necessarily chronological, for the rock destroyed all the kingdoms simultaneously and then grew in size and importance. Evidently a destructive but indestructible kingdom will succeed the kingdoms of this world. These kingdoms and their history are in the hands of the one true God, and only God's people can interpret that history.

Daniel accepted Nebuchadnezzar's "worship" (Dan 2:46), in accordance with classic prophetic teaching (Is 49:23; cf. Phil 2:10-11; Rev 21:24-26).

Daniel's Friends Survive the Fiery Furnace (Dan 3)

His ego boosted by the dream, "Nebuchadnezzar made a golden statue" (Dan 3:1). The phrase pulsates through the first half of the chapter. The statue was huge, strategically located and to be worshiped by all.

Names of the guest list appear in order of importance: provincial governors were called satraps in the Persian period. The pomp of the dedication ceremony, complete with herald and an orchestra of instruments with Greek names, was marred by the threat of dreadful punishment for any who refused to be cowed, unthinking worshipers; by the undercover work of the astrologers; and by the rage of the king.

"There are certain Jews whom you have appointed over the affairs of . . . Babylon" (Dan 3:12), as well as insinuating that the king is to blame, introduces the theme of anti-Semitism and reminds readers of Haman's accusation (Esther 3:8-9). Just when it seemed that Jews could survive in a pagan culture and even be a blessing there (cf. Esther 2:19-23), we discover that the astrologers are jealous of the Jews' promotion and able to convince a power-hungry Nebuchadnezzar.

The irrational fury of the dictator who cannot cope with dissidents and even kills those who are on his side contrasts with the Jews' calm behavior, faith and courage. No true Jew could "fall down and worship the golden statue" (Dan 3:5) and so break the first two commandments (Ex 20:3-4). Daniel 3:16-18 replies to Daniel 3:15: "If you do not worship, . . . you shall be thrown" / "If our God . . . is able . . . let him deliver us. . . . But if not, . . . we will not worship." No doubting of God; no claiming immunity from suffering; no fanaticism. Just total faith in God's sovereign power to save, or not, as he wills. Nothing that God can do will make these men love him less.

A long prayer and hymn appear in some Bible versions between Daniel 3:23-24 and come from Greek versions of the Old Testament. Most likely they are not part of the original text.

The king's new decree (Dan 3:29) is another example of dramatic inversion (cf. Dan 2:5), as is "Three men . . . fell . . . into the furnace. . . . King Nebuchadnezzar . . . rose up quickly" (Dan 3:23-24). Once again the demeanor of the king contrasts with that of God's people, quietly "walking in the middle of the fire," accompanied by a fourth person, perhaps an angel (Heb 1:14).

The verb *deliver* pulsates through the second half of this chapter and reappears in Daniel 6:14 ("save"); 6:16, 20; 12:1.

Daniel Interprets Nebuchadnezzar's Dream (Dan 4)

God's sovereignty and the phrase "grew great and strong, its top reached to heaven" (Dan 4:11, 20, 22, 30) are key themes in a chapter that highlights the struggle between divine and human greatness, with the pagan king reading out the final score.

The chapter is well-structured: the king praises the Most High God, the king dreams, the dream is interpreted and fulfilled, and the king praises the Most High God.

The descriptions in Daniel 4:4, 29-30 are in harmony with archaeological discoveries, and references to the strange illness, lycanthropy, occur in several later texts. The conversion of the king does not appear in Babylonian court records. But the language used is general, merely a grandiose salutation with little religious significance. Similarly, the phrase "a spirit of the holy gods" (Dan 4:8, 9, 18; 5:11-12; Gen 41:38) appears to be nothing more than a popular way of describing someone interested in spiritual things.

The enormous tree is a frequent theme in ancient literature (cf. Ezek 17; 31). The treetop touching the sky is reminiscent of Babel (Gen 11:1-9).

The "messenger" or "watchman," as the Portuguese Bible and other translations say, is "a holy watcher, coming down from heaven" (Dan 4:13, 17, 23), a phrase used of angels (Job 5:1; 15:15). "Seven times" (Dan 4:16, 25) is often interpreted as seven years, though it is perhaps better to see it as referring to an indefinite period of time (as in Dan 4:26), where the duration of the period, when "you learn that Heaven is sovereign," cannot be measured (cf. Dan 7:25; 12:7).

Nebuchadnezzar was terrified because he did not understand his dream; Daniel was terrified because he understood it only too well—it spoke of the end of an era. Nebuchadnezzar is "driven away from human society" and eating "grass like oxen" (Dan 4: 33), a huge contrast with the dignified Jewish vegetarians (Dan 1).

Daniel Interprets Belshazzar's Dream (Dan 5)

In a book that touches on the grandeur of the Babylonian court—a large, if not always competent, staff, good food, gold images, orchestras, palaces, roof gardens—the reception room for one thousand guests is no surprise. Excavations have uncovered the palace throne room, which is one quarter the size of a football field. Three of its walls were covered in white plaster, and the fourth had a design of blue enameled bricks. A magnificent setting for a magnificent party, comparable to that of Esther—but with women present (cf. Esther 1:9-12).

The host, Belshazzar, dominates Daniel 5—7; he was the oldest son of Nabonidus, the last Babylonian king. It would seem that, due to his father's many military exploits abroad, Belshazzar was de facto ruler and therefore able to promise to make another "third in the kingdom" (Dan 5:7, 16), after himself and Nabonidus. But why the reference to "his father Nebuchadnezzar"? Since the word *father* is used loosely elsewhere (2 Kings 2:12), we may suppose that Belshazzar was a descendent or protégé of Nebuchadnezzar.

The party took place on the eve of the destruction of Babylon by the Medo-Persian army in 539 B.C. Once again a historical detail confuses, for the leader of the invading army was Cyrus, not "Darius the Mede" (Dan 5:31). Possibly this is a reference to Darius I, the second successor to Cyrus as head of the Persian Empire.

The party, a *festa* in classic playing-the-fiddle-while-Rome-burned style, is characterized by the repetition of key words: *kings, nobles, wives, concubines, wine, drink*. The drinking from the "vessels of gold and silver . . . taken out of the temple in Jerusalem" (Dan 5:2-3) accentuates the idolatry of Daniel 5:4.

A spotlight focused on the plain white wall and "the palm of the hand which wrote" (Dan 5:5 lit.). The king was terrified and his advisors confused yet again. The almost photographic descriptions of royal emotions are a high point in the book.

The "queen," because she is mentioned separately from the "wives" (Dan 5:2-3), reminds Belshazzar of his father's times and orders him around, is normally understood to be the queen mother. Her intervention recalls Pilate's wife's (Mt 27:19).

The question "You are Daniel?" (Dan 5:13) and the promise of purple robes and a gold chain are small historical details; Daniel's refusal of gifts is similar to his refusal of luxury food. Faithful Jews did not need help from Gentiles (Esther 2:15).

Just as in Daniel 2, only God and his people can discern patterns of human history. Daniel's interpretation begins and ends with God: "God gave . . . Nebuchadnezzar kingship [and] greatness" (Dan 5:18); "the God in whose power is your very breath" sent the hand, "and this writing was inscribed" (Dan 5:23-24). The details of dictators' methods and their tragic end have a contemporary ring.

"MENE, MENE, TEKEL, and PARSIN" (Dan 5:25) is literally "counted, counted, weighed and divided." The concept of God weighing human actions is not uncommon (Job 31:6; 1 Sam 2:3). The scales show that, for all its apparent weight of glory, the Babylonian kingdom is weightless, a nothing in comparison with the truly weighty item, God's omnipotence (cf. 2 Cor 4:17).

There are different accounts of the fall of Babylon, and most agree about the basics. The ancient historian Xenophon, for example, reports that Cyrus and his troops diverted a stream to facilitate access to the city and that they entered it when the inhabitants were at an all-night drinking party. Belshazzar's end recalls Luke 12:16-21—fools are fools because they forget God (Ps 14:1), despise him (Dan 5:2) and do not repent as did Nebuchadnezzar (Dan 4:34-37).

Daniel Survives the Den of Lions (Dan 6)

Even under Darius (Dan 5:31), governor of the Medo-Persians, Daniel, now about eighty years old, remains at the top, as the frame to the chapter shows: "Daniel distinguished himself" (Dan 6:3); "Daniel prospered" (Dan 6:28). Several pairs of phrases give a rhythm to the chapter: God's rescue (Dan 6:16, 20); the king's distress and subsequent joy (Dan 6:14, 23); the decree of death for those who will not worship the king and then for those who will not worship Daniel's God—the dramatic inversions seem unending.

The Medo-Persian Empire stretched from Libya, Egypt and Turkey to the River Indus. It was ably administered, mainly by satraps, local governors whose duty was to ensure "that the king might suffer no loss" (Dan 6:2) of territory and tax revenue. Esther 8:9 mentions 127 satraps in the period approximately fifty years after the fall of Babylon. As in Daniel 3, however (and in Esther 1:19; 8:8), the Persian bureaucracy ironically traps itself in its efficiency: the weak king is caught in the net of his unchangeable laws and lying lawyers. Their claim that they had "all . . . agreed" (Dan 6:7) did not include Daniel, officially one of them. The contrast between a corrupt bureaucracy that kills even its own people and Daniel's "excellent spirit" (Dan 6:3), his lack of "corruption" or "negligence" (Dan 6:4-5), is marked.

Daniel's "windows . . . open toward Jerusalem" (Dan 6:10) recall the prayerful hope of Solomon (1 Kings 8:41-43) and the tearful lament of exiles (Ps 137:4-6). Daniel remembers the holy city, even after sixty years abroad. His praying "three times a day" (Dan 6:10) recalls Psalm 55:17. The lying malice of the conspirators is evident in their description of the distinguished national figure as merely "one of the exiles from Judah" (Dan 6:13). Similar disrespect for religious freedom, private and public, is common today, and the resulting conflicts of loyalty (Acts 5:29) bring intense suffering.

The lions' den was not a cage as in modern zoos. Some envisage a deep pit, an open cistern (Gen 37:24; Jer 38:6) or perhaps a long tunnel. The king's sleepless night recalls Xerxes' sleepless night before another miraculous intervention by God (Esther 6:1; cf. Ps 121:4).

The episode suggests parallels between Daniel and Jesus Christ, an "innocent" (Mt 27:24) who also was trapped, interrogated, arrested (after prayer), condemned to a cruel death, buried in a sealed tomb—and miraculously delivered.

Several reasons combined to guarantee Daniel's deliverance: God sent his angel and shut the lions' mouths (Dan 6:22; cf. Heb 11:33), and Daniel "was found blameless before [God]; and also before you, O king, I have done no wrong"; "he had trusted in his God" (Dan 6:22-23). This interweaving of God's sovereignty and human responsibility is a recurring biblical theme.

So is the theme of the ultimate victory of the righteous over enemies and over death. This eschatological dimension is heightened by a possible interpretation of the deliverance from the lions as a foretaste of the radical changes in the animal world that will mark the age yet to come, when all creation will be renewed (Is 11:6; 65:25; Hos 2:18; Rom 8:21-22).

The apparently excessive cruelty (Dan 6:24) has caused concern. Possibly not all of Daniel's accusers were killed, but only the conspiracy's leaders. The Greek translation of the Old Testament, the Septuagint, insists that only two died. It was Persian custom to kill criminals' families.

Darius's doxology reminds us that throughout the Old Testament the chief function of "signs and wonders" (Dan 6:27) is to call the attention of unbelievers to the God of Israel, with a view to their worshiping him (Ex 7:5; 8:10; 9:20; Josh 4:24; 1 Kings 18:37; cf. Jn 9:1-4; 11:14-15).

Daniel Also Dreams in Babylon (Dan 7:1—12:3)

Nations Stripped of Authority (Dan 7)

Now Daniel "lay in bed" (Dan 7:1), dreaming disturbing dreams—but while Nebuchadnezzar had broadcast his, Daniel affirmed, "I kept the matter in my mind" (Dan 7:28). Nebuchadnezzar needed to find an interpreter; Daniel's interpreter was on site. Aramaic (an international language to deal with international questions) is used until Daniel 7:28, and there are clear parallels with Daniel 2.

Daniel 7:1 (and Dan 8:1) is dated before Daniel 5:1, and as in the first half of the book, the chapter order in the second half is chronological. The mysterious animals "like a lion" (Dan 7:4), "like a bear" (Dan 7:5), "like a leopard" (Dan 7:6) and the horn with eyes "like human eyes" (Dan 7:8) recall the four-faced man, lion, ox and eagle of Ezekiel 1:4-21. Both men lived in Babylon, and archaeological excavations reveal that Babylonians used such creatures as part of their decor (Millard, 137). Because Daniel graduated in Babylonian sciences and culture and then spent about sixty years of his life in Babylon, it is not surprising that God spoke to him through familiar things, in a cultural form that he understood. The rational element is further emphasized by "wrote down" (Dan 7:1; cf. Dan 10:21; 12:4, 9), "considering" (Dan 7:8), "the truth" (Dan 7:16, 19, 20) and an explanation (Dan 7:23).

It is tempting to try to ascertain the precise relationship between different animals and different kingdoms but not always possible or even helpful to do so. And it is easy to miss seeing the whole picture while wading through piles of wings, ribs, teeth, horns and numbers. The key idea is that each animal is powerful, distinct, unique. Maybe it is not so important that the first one is a lion (or whatever) representing Babylon, but it is important that it is stripped of its wings, unable to fly, powerless. The second animal is insatiable; the third, a leopard (or something) with four heads and four wings suggests many leaders, speed of movement. The fourth is terrifying in its cruelty. Different kingdoms mean different styles.

The content and symmetry of the chapter may be summarized:

human history judged—only some survive (Dan 7:2-12)
the goal of human history—"one like a human being" rules (Dan 7:13-14)
human history judged—only the saints survive (Dan 7:15-25)
the end of human history—"the Most High" rules (Dan 7:26-27)

The "four winds of heaven" (Dan 7:2) and "one like a human being, coming with the clouds of heaven" (Dan 7:13) contrast with the manufactured statue (Dan 2). The winds symbolize God's worldwide power; one Hebrew word serves for "wind" and "spirit." The great sea symbolizes God's created world (Gen 1:6-7). As winds, sent by God, whip up the sea, so God stirs up human kingdoms (Dan 7:17; Is 27:1; 51:9).

The continuous rise and fall of empires that constitutes human history stops only when the last and most terrifying of all appears with iron teeth and the destructive possibilities implicit in ten horns. Then the "little horn," probably a reference to Antichrist (Rev 13:5-6), with human eyes and boastful lips, will contend against God's people and even defeat them for a while. As in Revelation 5:1-5, the frightening clarity of his vision caused Daniel great sadness.

After the cruel chaos of human history comes a vision of final judgment. The "Ancient One" is variously understood: King David? the elders of Israel? angels? the Trinity? It is best to see here a reference to the eternal God (1 Kings 22:19), whose wheeled throne in a flame of fire (Dan 7:9) recalls Ezekiel 1:15-28. Daniel 7:10 recalls Deuteronomy 33:2 and Psalm 68:17.

Exodus 32:33, Isaiah 65:6 and Revelation 20:12 also refer to the "books," God's file on human behavior. A scene of majesty, purity, judgment—and power, for even the last, terrifying beast is consumed by fire, while others survive only "for . . . a time" (Dan 7:12; 2:21). So human kingdoms end—and God's begins.

High points of the chapter and book are Daniel 7:13-14 and Daniel 7:26-27. "Son of man" often means an ordinary human being (Ps 8:4) or even a special one, a prophet (Ezek 39:1). But Jesus used this name of himself (Mt 25:31-32; 26:63-65); therefore the phrase may refer to Jesus' humanity. So God the Father, the "Ancient One," grants to the One who comes "with the clouds of heaven" (Dan 7:13; Rev 1:7), all "dominion and glory and kingship" (Dan 7:14; 2:44; 3:33; 4:31; 6:22; cf. Mt 28:18-20). It is possible to see a fulfillment of Genesis 1:26, the perfect Son of Man exercising perfect dominion over all creation.

"The holy ones" (Dan 7:18) are God's people of all ages and places, and their suffering is more than persecution. This great tribulation is a satanic attack from the Antichrist, a blasphemous tyrant whose goal is "to change the sacred seasons," or calendar of Jewish holy days, and the moral teaching of the law of Moses (Rev 13:6-7). As for the "time, two times and half a time" (Dan 7:25), while some interpret "time" as "year" or even as "decade" (Dan 4:16, 23), it is probably best to understand it as a chronologically indefinite period (for three and a half, cf. Lk 4:25; Jas 5:17)—but it will end. Antichrist will be destroyed!

In spite of what some contemporary thinkers say, we have not yet seen the end of history. Nor will history crawl to its end in a meaningless whimper. God has planned its end and the end of that suffering of his people that will increasingly be a mark of the future. In his pastoral encouragement of suffering believers, Daniel emphasizes that final victory is certain (Dan 7:18, 21-22, 27; 8:25; 12:1-4; cf. 2 Tim 2:12).

Kings of Media, Persia, Greece (Dan 8)

The date (Dan 8:1) is approximately 544 B.C., two years after Daniel 7:1 and about seven years after the fall of Babylon. This chapter, written in Hebrew (Jewish language to deal with Jewish interests), differs from preceding ones in its precision about geographic location, the angel's name and the names of the kingdoms.

The vision has three elements—war between the ram and goat, an all-powerful small horn in action and a question of how long this will last—and ends with a terrified prophet (Dan 8:1-18). Its interpretation includes an explanation of the ram and goat and the small horn plus a time ("many days from now"; Dan 8:19-26)—and ends with a terrified prophet.

"I . . . saw myself in Susa . . . by the river" (Dan 8:2) may suggest that Daniel did not live and work in Susa, capital city of Babylon. Josephus registered how Daniel built himself "a tower at Ecbatana, in Media. . . . It was a most elegant building. . . . Now they bury the kings of Media, of Persia, and Parthia in this tower." Commenting on Daniel 8, the same writer concluded: "Indeed it so came to pass, that our nation suffered these things under Antiochus Epiphanes, according to Daniel's vision. . . . In the same manner Daniel also wrote concerning the Roman government, and that our country should be made desolate by them. All these things did this man leave in writing, as God had showed them to him" (Josephus *Antiquities of the Jews* 10.11.7).

Historical detail is spelled out clearly: after the rapid advance of the ram (Persia, a kingdom whose mascot was a ram) comes the goat (Greece in general, Dan 8:21), then the "large horn" of Alexander the Great, on whose sudden death the empire was divided among four generals (Dan 8:22).

The "little [horn]" (Dan 8:9), the "king of bold countenance" (Dan 8:23), dominates, conquering all and extending his tentacles to the "beautiful land" (Dan 8:9), Israel (Jer 3:19), even reaching "the host of heaven" (Dan 8:10), the stars (or the saints? cf. Dan 7:25; 12:3; Mt 13:43), some of which are thrown from the sky. The picture is of great arrogance (compare Babel; Dan 3; Is 14:12-15), of contempt even for "the prince of the host"—and of short-lived glory.

In Daniel 8:10-12 the emphasis falls on what the small horn did: desecrating the temple, taking away the burnt offering, throwing "truth to the ground" and "prospering in what it did." The temple was desecrated and destroyed on December 25, 167 B.C.

In the parallel verses, Daniel 8:24-25, the emphasis falls on what happened to the small horn eventually: he became strong, caused devastation and succeeded in what he did; he destroyed the powerful and the holy people. "He shall make deceit prosper," consider himself superior, "even ris[ing] up against the Prince of princes." He will be destroyed, but not by human power.

The time span for these dramatic events is indicated:

> twenty-three hundred "evenings and mornings" (Dan 8:14; the two daily sacrifices?)
> "the appointed time of the end" (Dan 8:19)
> "the evenings and the mornings . . . many days from now" (Dan 8:26)

Not a few interpreters date this starting from Antiochus's campaign against Judah, which began in 171 B.C., and ending with Judas Maccabeus's reconsecration of the temple on December 25, 165 B.C. This is a period of six years, three months and twenty days, that is, twenty-three hundred days. Others understand mornings and evenings as years.

So has the appointed time been and gone? Sometimes understanding prophecy is like peeling onions: layer after layer, and tears of frustration. This prophecy has been fulfilled. The temple was desecrated; later, temple worship was restored; and we can date those events. Deceit does prosper, and many of God's people have already been destroyed. However, take off another level of the historical onion, look at the future through (still misty) New Testament eyes, and it is clear that this prophecy will be fulfilled again. One day, that "small horn" will seem a toy in comparison with the final arrogant, blasphemous beast, the Antichrist (Rev 13:1-8).

The angel Gabriel, whose name means "man of God," interpreted the vision (Dan 9:21; cf. Lk 1:19, 26) about "the appointed time of the end" (Dan 8:19; Is 2:2; Jer 3:24; a phrase used of dramatic, divine intervention in human history), warned about a delay in its fulfillment and ordered Daniel to seal it (Dan 8:26; contrast Dan 12:4). All of this reappears in Revelation 10, but in Revelation 22:10 the sealed scroll is opened because "the time is near."

Daniel's fear at the sight of the heavenly messenger was followed by a loss of consciousness (Dan 10:9; Rev 1:17) and by emotional exhaustion (Dan 8: 27; "exhausted" is used of Nebuchadnezzar in Dan 2:1). The stress came from Daniel's vision of the wrath of God, a wrath visible when proud nations rise meteorically and then crash, when God's sinful people bring disaster on themselves. To reflect seriously on such topics is to react as Daniel did. Our world too is often beyond understanding, and contemplation of coming, deserved wrath is a sure recipe for stress—unless, like Daniel, we are able to see beyond to the final, certain victory of God's people, for the enemy "will be broken, and not by human hands" (Dan 8:25; 2:44).

God Worshiped as Lord of All (Dan 9)

The date (Dan 9:1; 5:31; 6:1; 11:1) is approximately 539 B.C., and this chapter provides a counterpoint to the preceding one. In Daniel 8 a vision and an angel disclose the truth about the future. In Daniel 9 the inspired Scriptures have already disclosed the truth about the future. And there is no incompatibility between the two. Gabriel is still around, as are the "abomination that desolates" (Dan 9:27), mathematical puzzles, wars and the destruction of the sanctuary. In our generation, fascinated by dreams, visions and futurology, it is necessary to give due importance to the written truth of God.

So Daniel unearthed the Jeremiah scrolls—one wonders who smuggled them to Babylon—and began to research the Scriptures (Dan 9:2), the first time this word is used of prophetic books and an indication of their authority and status, even granted the relatively short time elapsed since their composition. Daniel found the reference to seventy years, calculated the sums and, realizing that the period was ending, turned to prayer, fasting and reflection on the meaning of even earlier Scriptures for his generation (cf. Ezra 9:6-15; Neh 1:5-11; 9:6-37). Some commentators suggest that long prayers of national confession were an integral part of Jewish life.

The chapter structure carries a message, with the arithmetical references (seventy years, seventy sevens, seven sevens, sixty-two sevens) framing the long prayer and confession (Dan 9:4-23). It tells us that it is possible to devote too much time and effort to counting up numbers and not enough to understanding the principles of divine judgment. These principles are that the God of Israel—glorious, righteous, merciful and powerful—and the sin of Israel—blatant rebellion against God's law—cannot enjoy peaceful coexistence. Though the covenant-keeping God is a God of mercy in spite of sin, the holy God is a God of repeated warnings about judgment, a God of judgment. Daniel concludes: "He has confirmed his words, which he spoke against us. . . . Just as it has been written in the law of Moses, all this calamity has come upon us" (Dan 9:12-13).

The magnificent, courageous words "Now, O Lord our God" (Dan 9:15-16) invite God to repeat that unparalleled intervention in his people's history that was the exodus from Egypt. However, instead of approaching God with a shopping list of requests, Daniel approaches him with another list:

> "your people . . . your name
> your righteous acts . . . your anger and wrath
> your city . . . your holy mountain
> your people . . . your servant
> your desolated sanctuary . . . your eyes . . . your name
> your great mercies . . . for your own sake
> your city
> your people . . . your name"

It is almost as though Daniel is putting God into a very tight corner! But God did not complain. Rather, "at the beginning of your supplications a word went out" (Dan 9:23). The words that describe Gabriel's task—"give wisdom and understanding . . . declare . . . consider . . . understand" (Dan 9:22-23)—stress that religious experience, even the ministry of angels, has an objective content that enables us to discern between truth and error.

So to Jeremiah and the number puzzle. Following from a moment similar to Daniel 9:4-19, Jeremiah 25:8-10 gives precise details of the invasion to be headed up by Nebuchadnezzar and promises that the resulting servitude and exile will last seventy years. Then Babylon will be enslaved, and so the exile will end. But Daniel complicates this simple piece of mathematics. By my calculator, (*7* x *7*) + (*62* x *7*) = 483 (Dan 9:25). Then I must add another *7* (Dan 9:27), making a grand total of 490. And Jeremiah's *70* has become *70* x *7* = 490. Why? What does it mean?

One commentator has named this seventy weeks/years/units of seven "the dismal swamp of Old Testament criticism" (Montgomery, in loc.), and it is difficult not to get bogged down. The decree to "rebuild Jerusalem" (Dan 9:25) was issued . . . in 539 B.C. (2 Chron 36:22-23)? in 458 B.C., when Ezra began his journey to Jerusalem? in 444 B.C. (Neh 2:1-8)? After the decree comes the 483-year interval, which takes us up to . . . ? Many say to about the first coming of Christ in the flesh, then to his death: "an anointed one shall be cut off" (Dan 9:26). This was followed, not long after, by the destruction of Jerusalem by invading Roman armies. Others note the change of tone in Daniel 9:26, where the anointed One gives way to a different ruler, and suggest an accompanying time interval. After the sixty-two sevens, which followed the seven sevens, comes a complete change. After someone who will "destroy the city and the sanctuary[,] its end shall come. . . . To the end there shall be war. . . . He shall make a strong covenant . . . [there] shall be an abomination that desolates" (Dan 9:26-28).

In his teaching about the end of all things, Jesus recalled "the desolating sacrilege, . . . as was spoken of by the prophet Daniel" (Mt 24:15) and taught that it will immediately precede his second coming (Mt 24:3-35). On that basis, "the decreed end is poured out on the desolater" (Dan 9:27) refers to the final, inglorious end of the enemy of God and of his people.

A Man Promises to Fight Princes (Dan 10:1—11:1)

The date is 537 B.C., and some exiles had returned to Jerusalem with Zerubbabel (Ezra 1—2). Daniel was officially an exile until "the first year of King Cyrus" (Dan 1:21; 539 B.C.), but thereafter he continued to live in Babylon, his adopted home. Daniel's vision about a war dominates the beginning and end of this section, but as in Daniel 9, the main thrust of the chapter is something else. Not prayer because of the war/desolation to come, but a glorious Man who strengthens Daniel for the war to come.

At the beginning of his exile, Daniel fasted; now, at its end, he does the same. Passover was celebrated on the fourteenth day of the first month, and the Feast of Unleavened Bread from the fifteenth through the twenty-first, so the vision of the great Deliverer was particularly appropriate for the time of year. And Daniel's sadness may be related to his dismay that more Jews did not return to Jerusalem to rebuild the temple and receive the blessings God had for them there.

Table 6. Comparison of Daniel 10:5-11 with Daniel 10:16-19

Daniel 10:5-11	Daniel 10:16-19
I saw a man (Dan 10:5)	one in human form touched my lips (Dan 10:16)
I was left alone . . . I heard the sound of his words (Dan 10:8-9)	I opened my mouth to speak (Dan 10:16-17)
I fell . . . to the ground (Dan 10:9)	I retain no strength . . . no breath is left in me (Dan 10:16-17)
a hand touched me (Dan 10:10)	one in human form touched me (Dan 10:18)
pay attention to the words I am going to speak to you (Dan 10:11)	let my lord speak (Dan 10:19)
stand up . . . I stood up (Dan 10:11)	be strong and courageous (Dan 10:19)

The "great war" (Dan 10:1) is the war of Daniel 10:12-14. The location and content of the vision recall Ezekiel 1:1-28, and the description (Dan 10:5-6; 7:13) recurs in Revelation 1:12-16. Both texts record prostration before the glorious Son of Man (Dan 10:7-9; Rev 1:17). As with Daniel, Saul fell to the ground, speechless (Acts 9:7), though his companions saw nothing. Daniel's companions fled anyway.

The repetition of a simple structure stresses the emphases of Daniel 10:5-11 and Daniel 10:16-19, as shown in table 6.

The human touch, accompanied by the tender words "greatly beloved" (Dan 10:19), was just the encouragement Daniel needed to cope with the message about a trip delayed for twenty-one days, about answers to prayer delayed for twenty-one days. And all because of a spiritual battle (Eph 6:12; Rev 12:7) between spiritual beings: "the prince of Persia" (Dan 10:13, 20), that is, Persia's demonic representative; "the prince of Greece," Greece's demonic representative; and God's representative, Michael. God will not stand on the sidelines forever. When his people are threatened he will enter the fray and engage in battle, as the Septuagint says, at "the end of days." Although much contemporary teaching on territorial spirits focuses on Daniel 10:13, it is impossible to infer the existence of hierarchies of demons ruling over distinct geographical areas from this text.

Unlike Daniel 7 and Daniel 9, this

chapter ends before we are told the final score but not before we are reminded again of the relation between visions (Dan 10:1) and truth (Dan 10:21; Ex 32:32).

Kings Go to War (Dan 11:2—12:3)
The "three more kings," those who succeeded Cyrus on the Persian throne, were Cambyses, Smerdis and Darius Hystaspis. The "fourth . . . far richer than all" was Xerxes, followed by the all-conquering Alexander the Great (336-323 B.C.), his sudden death and the subsequent carving up of the empire into four in 301 B.C. Details of the post-Persian period follow.

Historical records describe how, during that period, two dynasties fought to control Palestine: the Ptolemaic, or southern group, and the Seleucid, or northern group. At times they did try to live at peace, but mostly it was war and more war. The Ptolemaic army was eventually defeated, and from 198 B.C. Seleucids ruled Palestine. But trouble began again when the Seleucid ruler, Antiochus (196-187 B.C.), greedy for more victories, tried once too often and was routed by "a [Roman] commander" (Dan 11:18). His son, Seleucus IV, ruled from 187-175 B.C., but no one has much to say about him. The big problem was the other son, a "contemptible person on whom royal majesty had not been conferred" (Dan 11:21), Antiochus Epiphanes (175-163 B.C.). He ignored all claims to the throne by Seleucus's son and "through intrigue" (Dan 11:21) "obtain[ed] the kingdom."

Antiochus Epiphanes' reign of terror began when he rolled into Jerusalem; killed the "prince of the covenant" (Dan 11:22), possibly the high priest, Onias III; bribed followers generously; invaded Egypt once and then decided to do it again. But he was turned back and spent his rage "against the holy covenant" (Dan 11:30), against Jerusalem (169 B.C.). The apocryphal book of 1 Maccabees also describes how many Jews fell "by sword and flame, and suffer[ed] captivity and plunder" (Dan 11:33). The temple was desecrated by an altar to the god Zeus (Dan 11:31; 8:13; 9:27; 12:11). Some Jews capitulated before the invader's flattery, but some resisted, sparking the Maccabean revolt (168 B.C.). The "little help" (Dan 11:34) may refer to the Maccabees.

So it is real history, with even an arranged marriage and a Cleopatra, and there for all to read in the history books. And Daniel foresaw everything, about 370 years before it happened. As noted in the introduction, today many believe that the book of Daniel was written by a scribe who lived during Antiochus Epiphanes' reign and that claims about the prophet Daniel foretelling history are unfounded. However, their argument stands or falls on the assumption that predictive prophecy of this nature is impossible. If that assumption is rejected, then the argument is unconvincing.

In a less specific way, Daniel 11:36-39 continues to describe Antiochus's reign, clarifying the reason for the name *Epiphanes*, a Greek word meaning "God manifest" (cf. Dan 11:36-37) and promising that the disrespectful, self-exalting ruler "shall come to his end, with no one to help him" (Dan 11:45). In fact, he died insane.

Many, however, understand Daniel 11:40-45 to apply to Antichrist, the ultimate arrogant, blasphemous small horn before whom many countries will fall (Dan 11:40-41), though Edom, Moab and Ammon, traditional enemies of God's people, will be spared. Consumed by "great fury to bring ruin and complete destruction to many" (Dan 11:44), Antichrist will set up camp by "the beautiful holy mountain," Jerusalem (Dan 11:45), only to find that the much-promised "end" or "appointed time" (Dan 11:27, 29, 35, 36), his end, has finally arrived. However, rather than capitulate quietly, Antichrist will inaugurate one last reign of terror, a "time of anguish" (Dan 12:1; Mt 24:21).

How to survive the dangerous times before God intervenes in history to bring about final victory for his people is an important theme of Daniel 7—12. The secret? Keep the covenant, know God, resist the enemy, be wise, trust in God's protection (Dan 12:1), make sure your name is "written in the book" (Dan 12:1; Rev 20:12, 15), "lead many to righteousness" (Dan 12:3), refuse to "be running back and forth" to increase knowledge (Dan 12:4) outside the words of the scroll. The final victory is nothing less than everlasting life after death (Dan 12:2; Is 26:19), the final tragedy nothing less than everlasting shame and contempt (Is 66:24; Mt 3:12).

Daniel, Receive Your Inheritance (Dan 12:4-13)

The order to "keep the words secret and the book sealed" (Dan 12:4) indicates that no more prophecies will be given and that what has been revealed is of great value and must be preserved for posterity, "until the time of the end" (Dan 12:4, 9; contrast Rev 22:10).

The closing vision incorporates several of the key elements of the whole book but with significant differences. Two angels question the glorious Man who stands "upstream" (Dan 12:6); more powerful is he than the roaring waters and those nations who depend on them. Questioned, the Man swears "by the one who lives forever" (Dan 12:6-7); that is, God swore by himself, and not by raising only one hand, as was usual (Deut 32:40), for this is a more than solemn oath.

However, neither the angels with their "How long?" (Dan 12:6) nor Daniel with his "I heard but could not understand" (Dan 12:8) could calculate the "time, two times, and half a time" (Dan 12:7; 7:25).

Some commentators translate the words that follow as "When the power of the shatterer of the holy people has been finally broken." A reference to Antichrist? Daniel too wanted more details about "the outcome of these things," but the Man's lips were sealed. "Go your way, Daniel." It is enough to know that "the time of the end" (Dan 12:9) will come; enough to know about the only options—"purified, cleansed, and refined" or "wicked" who "continue to act wickedly" (Dan 12:10; cf. Ps 1:6).

Daniel 12:11, however, seems to open up the subject of mathematical puzzles again, and for that reason many understand it to be a postscript. By the calculator, 1,290 days are about 3.5 years (Dan 7:25), but 1,335 days are 3.7 years, and commentators struggle to fit parts of history (past, present or future) into these 3.5 years. Nevertheless, the overall message is clear, having been repeated several times throughout the book. It is well worth persevering, even during intense suffering; there is blessing for "those who persevere"; the end will surely come.

The threefold, closing message to Daniel is almost another blessing: he will "rest," that is, die (Is 57:2); he will "rise" from the dead; he will receive his "reward." The message is a magnificent promise for the lifelong exile about whose family and descendants we know nothing. The God who has looked after Daniel right from Daniel 1 will not forget him "at the end of the days."

Bibliography. A. Millard, *Treasures from Bible Times* (Belleville, MI: Lion, 1985); J. A. Montgomery, *A Critical and Exegetical Commentary on the Book of Daniel,* ICC (Edinburgh: T & T Clark, 1927).

JOYCE E. WINIFRED EVERY-CLAYTON

HOSEA

Introduction

In the book of Hosea, we find an astonishing blend of sexual and spiritual history, of intense emotional pain and of psychological insight turned into prophetic proclamation. The experiences of Gomer and Hosea are far from comfortable. Gomer, in her sexual wanderings, becomes a metaphor of errant Israel. Beyond the turmoil in her soul, she must be aware, however dimly, that her condition is being made to portray the wider confusion and moral deterioration of Israel. In her anomalous position as prostitute and her repudiation by her husband, she does not stand alone. Perhaps even for her there is a way to make meaning of the bewilderment that has swept over her soul. Many a woman in such straits cannot understand herself, her actions or how to extricate herself from a downward spiral toward disaster. Despite the stern measures taken by her husband, Gomer might find the hope of restoration and reconciliation.

The situation is not less distressing for Hosea. He is asked to bare the anguish of his soul, to share his sense of rejection, jealousy and humiliation. In this crucible of torment he comes to see a wider message of the heavenly Husband whom Israel has rejected, betrayed and scorned. He comes to understand that even the ruin of his marriage might find its significance in the oracles of God. Beyond that he comes to experience the outlook of God in perhaps a more intensely personal way than the other prophets.

The prophecies of Hosea pulsate with the love of God for his people. His love is contrasted with the lustful desires his people have for Baal. Yahweh proves to be the better lover, allowing his people freedom to choose their way in life. Generously he warns them of the consequences of their actions. He cautions them time and again through the prophets, who act as sentinels of the soul of Israel. They are given many opportunities to repent but prefer to allow themselves to be seduced. For this they will be judged and punished as the covenant dictates. God, the holy One, will not remain angry with them forever; he exercises his divine grace and mercy and promises a renewed, permanent relationship with him.

Hosea uses poignant metaphors to convey his message. The most noticeable metaphor is that of marriage. The marriage of Yahweh and Israel has reached a crisis point, and divorce is imminent. Hosea speaks of a future eschatological hope in which this relationship will be restored, not in Hosea's generation, not until the end of time. This familiar theme is taken up and used throughout the New Testament, where the church is referred to as the bride of Christ. In the book of Revelation the faithful people of God become part of the intimate, exclusive marriage with him that he yearned to have with them from the beginning.

Hosea's message has four major interconnecting components. The first expresses Yahweh's constant love rejected by his people at every turn. The second examines Israel's unfaithfulness demonstrated by a threefold rejection of Yahweh: turning to other gods, placing their livelihood in the hands of their self-appointed monarchy rather than trusting in Yahweh's leadership, and making foolish alliances with foreign nations. The third theme covers the consequences of Israel's sinful actions demonstrated by their judgment and subsequent punishment at the hands of foreigners. The final theme is one of hope as Yahweh's people are renewed in his love, restored to him, forgiven, no longer to be punished but reunited in an unending relationship.

Little biographical material is available about Hosea's early life. He was the son of Beeri and, most probably, a professional prophet who had been ministering to Israel before the prophecies recorded were pronounced. No mention is made of his call: it is simply stated that the "word of the Lord came to him." The kings mentioned in Hosea 1:1 give the range of his ministry (about 780-692 B.C.). Most of his ministry took place during the latter years of Jeroboam's reign and around the time of the fall of Samaria (755-722 B.C.).

Hosea's writing is filled with sexual allusions. No other biblical author, save that of Song of Solomon, exhibits so strong a degree of sexual awareness. He married a woman named Gomer with whom he had three children. This marriage would be used to reflect the turbulent relationship of Yahweh and his people, climaxing in the marriage's restoration.

The prophecies are mostly aimed at the northern kingdom of Israel, also referred to as Ephraim, but some warnings are directed at Judah in the south. Under Jeroboam, Israel enjoyed stability, wealth, peace and prosperity. However, after his death there followed economic and political decline that caused the nation to seek alliances with

Egypt and Assyria. They played one off against the other until they were finally defeated by Assyria and carried into exile (722 B.C.).

During Jeroboam's reign, the strict religious regulations of the covenant that formed the basis of Israel's relationship with Yahweh were relaxed. Baal worship was not only tolerated but also encouraged until it was thoroughly mixed with the practices and ceremonies of Yahweh worship. The religious and secular authorities neglected Yahweh, depending instead on their own wisdom and faulty insight. Hosea warned that their failure to depend on Yahweh and their unfaithfulness in all areas of life would bring devastating consequences. Indeed they lost everything: their monarchy, religion, wealth, land, homes and, ultimately, many of them their lives.

Hosea's generation paid a high price for their unfaithfulness, but future generations still had the hope of a renewed relationship with Yahweh if they heeded the warnings.

Outline

1:1—2:1	The Prophet and the Prostitute
2:2-23	Israel the Unfaithful Wife
3:1-5	Hosea Buys Back His Wife
4:1—5:7	The Case Against Israel
5:8—6:11	Advancing Judgment
7:1-16	Corrupt and Half-Baked
8:1-14	Trumpets and Whirlwinds
9:1-17	Festivals and Punishment
10:1-15	Punishment for False Hearts
11:1-12	A Parent's Love
12:1-14	Israel's Past
13:1-16	Yahweh Alone Can Save
14:1-9	At Last Israel Returns

The Prophet and the Prostitute (Hos 1:1—2:1)

Hosea's prophetic ministry begins with an unusual instruction that dramatically affects his personal life. He is to endure the shame of marriage to a woman who sold her sexual favors. His marriage would be under the scrutiny of a nation as it reenacted the failing relationship of Yahweh and his people. For this woman, marriage may have been an escape from the life she had been living. Or perhaps she married reluctantly knowing that her behavior would be severely restricted.

Hosea is the first to use the marriage metaphor to describe the relationship between Israel and God and to portray spiritual unfaithfulness in terms of broken marriage vows. Within the constraints of this metaphor it is logical to see Yahweh in the role of husband. A husband provided for all of his wife's needs, and she was dependent on him. In a similar fashion Israel should have been dependent on Yahweh, but like Hosea's wife, Israel seemed unable or unwilling to remain faithful.

The covenant of Exodus formed the basis of Yahweh's relationship with Israel. Marriage, too, is viewed as a type of covenant, a binding agreement between two parties (cf. Ezek 16:8, 59; Mal 2:14). As the natural order of marriage is one husband, one wife, so the covenant relationship is one God, one people. No one else is involved, just the two committed and faithful to each other.

In Hosea's day the community worshiped other gods in direct contravention of the covenant (*see* Covenant and Community). This worship was akin to marital infidelities. Israel had been warned before concerning her unacceptable behavior but throughout her marriage was never constant. Marriage was too mundane, too restrictive for Gomer and Israel. They took their husbands for granted, no longer appreciating the patterns of life that they provided.

Yahweh had rescued Israel from slavery, given them his protection, called them his people and made a covenant with them (*see* Ancient and Modern Slavery). In return he required that they keep the terms of the covenant. Hosea had rescued Gomer from a life fraught with danger. There would be no one to protect her from clients and no provision when her looks faded. Hosea had given her respectability and a secure life. She threw it all away, as had Israel. The picture is one that everyone would understand: a wayward wife, a loving husband; an idolatrous nation, a compassionate God. Hosea's message was conveyed in a manner that its recipients should have understood, but waywardness and self-indulgence had blinded them to the spiritual realities being played out in the marriage of Hosea and Gomer. Yahweh, the God of their ancestors, was not relevant to their situation, in which life was good, prosperous and peaceful. They paid homage to Baal in the same way that their Canaanite hosts had done long before Yahweh appeared in Canaan with his people. The fertility rites produced wonderful results, so lip service was all that was deemed necessary for Yahweh.

Some commentators regard this metaphor with disgust because they perceive it as casting a female character in a role that personifies all that was evil in Israel and implying that women are rebellious, unfaithful and liable to turn against their husbands. Later, however, these attributes are ascribed to a male Israel. Neither, as some assume, does the text give a husband permission to mistreat his wife under the guise of justifiably punishing her for misdemeanors (*see* Violence). It is an illustration from life to explain the deterioration in the relationship between Yahweh and his people. Israel is depicted as a woman who sells herself for material gain, and the imagery works. No other relationship is as intimate and exclusive as marriage (*see* Marriage), and that is how Yahweh felt about his people. Within marriage certain behavior is unacceptable. If such behavior continues, the relationship will break down and ultimately end in divorce (*see* Divorce).

Hosea's Family (Hos 1:3-9)

No biographical material is included other than that Gomer was the daughter of Diblaim and a prostitute. Perhaps her beauty attracted men who sought only to exploit her. Would she now conform to the role of wife? Or would the pull of her former life be too strong and enticing?

We have no means of knowing what Gomer thought about the marriage or whether she had any feeling for Hosea. Like most marriages it would have been arranged. Gomer could be viewed as a pawn to illustrate a point as she played her part in this living metaphor.

God's instruction that Hosea should marry the woman has puzzled many commentators. The text indicates that the marriage provided a metaphor. It may be, however, that Hosea was attracted to Gomer and married her willingly, though he might not have done so without divine permission. As with the marriages of Gilead and Samson (Judg 11:1; 14:4), God had a purpose even for this anomalous union.

Often the biblical attitude toward prostitutes was more positive than that exhibited today. Jesus declared that harlots and tax gatherers walked into the kingdom of heaven before the chief priests and elders (Mt 21:31). A repeated theme is that of the penitent prostitute who embarks on a new path of life (Mt 21:32; Lk 7:36-50; Heb 11:31). As Jesus, the descendant of a prostitute (Josh 2:8-11; 6:22-25; Mt 1:5), affirmed the sinful woman, so the early church cherished the ministry of transformed courtesans who exerted a powerful influence in Christ's kingdom. While Gomer's sexual conduct was deplorable, she may have possessed other redeeming features, including potential for a productive and fulfilling life for herself and her family.

Gomer conceived and had a son. The text says this first child was Hosea's—presumably Gomer had curtailed her promiscuity for a while. The other two children may have been the product of her affairs. The names given to Gomer's offspring reinforce Yahweh's message to his people. Jezreel ("God scatters") carries the warning of judgment, although the name also includes the idea of sowing and reaping. The people are to be judged and incur a heavy punishment. Jezreel is a valley between the mountains of Samaria and Galilee made famous by the massacre of his rivals that brought Jehu to power (2 Kings 9:21-28, 30-37; 10:10).

Gomer's second child, a daughter, was named "not pitied" or "no compassion." Neighbors and associates would be curious about the shocking name given to the baby, for it amounted to a curse of divine rejection, giving Hosea the opportunity to explain its significance to the inquirers. The root of the word means "womb" and carries with it the meaning of a mother's tender love and compassion. One wonders, with such a mother as Gomer, whether the girl was denied the motherly love usually given to a growing daughter (*see* Parental Influence).

It was a shocking name to give to a child but also a shocking warning. Yahweh had consistently shown compassion to people who repeatedly proved themselves to be unfaithful, but he would tolerate no more. They had failed to keep their part of the covenant, so he was under no obligation to keep to his side. For the time being Judah would retain its position, with deliverance coming from the Lord rather than military might. But Judah finally fell to Babylon in 587 B.C.

Children were breastfed by their mother or a wet nurse until about the age of three. There would therefore be approximately a three-year age difference between each of Gomer's children. The message of Hosea was protracted by the birth of each child. With the naming of the third child Yahweh no longer acknowledges Israel as his people. The "I AM" who had rescued them from Egypt (Ex 3:14) is now "I am not."

Yahweh's People (Hos 1:10—2:1)

The tone changes from one of judgment to one of eschatological hope and restoration. The ancient promises to the patriarchs still stand (see Gen 32:12). After a period of harsh punishment in exile, those who had been scattered in judgment will be gathered in restoration. The two kingdoms will once again be united under one leader. The population shall again flourish as a result of a renewed relationship with God. The names of the children will be reversed in an act of leniency in which Israel shall again be the people of a compassionate God.

Israel the Unfaithful Wife (Hos 2:2-23)

In this section, Israel takes the place of Gomer as the unfaithful wife (*see* Israel as Wife of Yahweh). Yahweh brings a case against his people. The images of Israel alternate among those of unfaithful wife/mother, children and the land, while Yahweh appears in the roles of plaintiff, prosecutor, judge and enforcer of punishment.

Bringing the Accusation (Hos 2:2-13)

Yahweh calls the children as witnesses against their mother. The NRSV translates the Hebrew word as "plead," but the meaning is closer to "make an accusation against." Israel is simultaneously mother and children, corporate and individual. A distinction is made between Israel as a whole, the unfaithful wife, and the children, a segment of Israel's population. Identifying their roles within the court case is not straightforward, so viewing them as separate entities may simplify matters. The purpose of this trial is to prove Israel's adultery (*see* Adultery); it is not a divorce case even though the wording of Hosea 2:2 suggests a Middle Eastern divorce formula and echoes the meaning of the third child's name ("not my people"), here not my wife, not her husband.

The hope is that individual elements within Israel can persuade her to give up her prostituting ways. If she will not listen and remove the paraphernalia of prostitution, Yahweh will strip her naked. She had flaunted herself in her harlot's garb; now she is forced to experience the shame of going naked for all to see. Israel, the nation, will be stripped of its glory, prosperity, military might, religious cult and monarchy, and exposed as sinful, disloyal and vulnerable.

God is pictured as stopping the support of his adulterous wife. He does not enable flagrant promiscuity. The food, clothing, water, material comforts and wealth—which were his contractual obligations in the marriage covenant (Ex 21:10; Ezek 16:10)—were abrogated when the covenant was broken. The stripping bare was the lesser of two punishments for an adulterous wife (Ezek 16:39), the other being stoning. Yahweh distances himself from the behavior, but he waits for his repentant wife to return to him. Most of Hosea 2 clearly

Israel as the Wife of Yahweh & the Church as the Bride of Christ

The name Yahweh clearly distinguished the God of Israel from other gods, or Elohim. Yahweh alone is the Creator, Revealer and Governor of history and humankind, Judge and Savior, Possessor of the kingdom that is as wide as creation, a living God and the Lifegiver.

Israel is portrayed as the "wife of Yahweh" in God's saving Israel, through Moses, from the hands of the Egyptians (e.g., Ex 3:13-15; 14; 21:1-17; 34:28). Israel understood itself as the people of God, by God's call linked with the new covenant: "I will take you as my people, and I will be your God" (Ex 6:7; 19:5; 23:22; 7:6; 14:21; 26:18; Lev 26:9-12; Jer 32:38-41).

The early church appropriated this image (1 Pet 2:9-10; Is 43:20-21; Ex 19:6), and hence the church is the new eschatological community of God (2 Cor 6:16; Ezek 37:27; Heb 8:10; Jer 31:31-34; Rev 21:3). This new people of God, formed out of the remnant of Israel and from many Gentiles, arises out of the love and grace of God (1 Pet 2:10). It is a purchased people, acquired at the price of Jesus' blood (Acts 20:28). The church is the new people of God through the new covenant by faith in Jesus Christ and the circumcision of Christ, baptism (Tit 2:14; Ezek 37:23; Lk 22:20; 1 Cor 11:25; 2 Cor 3:6; Gal 2:11; Heb 8:8-12; Jer 31:31-34).

The church is the whole body, or congregation, of persons who are called by God the Father to acknowledge the lordship of Jesus, the Son, in word, in sacrament, in witness and in service, and through the power of the Holy Spirit to collaborate with Jesus' historic mission for the sake of the kingdom of God.

There is a vital link between Jesus Christ and the church. The church has its origin in Jesus identified by his person and work. Jesus' mission was not to gather together the just or righteous but to go to the lost sheep of the house of Israel (Mt 8:11-12; 10:6; Lk 13:28-29). The whole of Israel, and no group or sect within it, is called to be God's people. Even the twelve disciples were to represent Jesus' call to all the twelve tribes of Israel, and they were entrusted with the mission to Israel as a whole as rulers and judges (Mt 19:28; Lk10:1-20; 22:30).

If the image of the people of God underlines the church's intimate correction with Israel and with God's call to a covenant relationship, the image of the body of Christ underlines the church's intimate connection with Jesus Christ and with God's call to a communal relationship one with another in Christ. The image is like that of the vine and the branches (Jn 15:1-8). The conception of the church as the body of Christ is grounded in the union that exists between the Christ and the risen body of Christ.

The union between Christ and the church lies behind the development from the notion of one body in Christ to one body of Christ. (Rom 12:4-21; 1 Cor 12:4-27; 12:13, 27; 6:15, 19). Christ is the head of the body, the church, and hence the principle of union and growth (Eph 4:12, 16; 5:23; Col 1:18; 2:19). The church, the body of Christ, is also the temple of the Holy Spirit (e.g., 1 Cor 15:45; Acts 1:8; 2:3-4, 38; 4:8, 31; 6:8; 9:17; 11:24; 13:52). Just as Jesus identified himself with the temple, so the body of Christ is the new temple (1 Cor 3:9, 16-17; 2 Cor 6:16; Eph 2:19-22). The church is God's dwelling place.

JANET NASAMBU KASSILLY

speaks to Israel rather than to Hosea's wife. Israel will be allowed to discover the consequences of its behavior. It would learn that the good gifts came from Yahweh rather than Baal. Defeat and exile will be part of the punishment. No allies will come to its aid.

Yahweh Woos Israel (Hos 2:14-23)

After destruction and exile come reconciliation and restoration for a remnant of Israel. After the harshness of judgment Yahweh seeks to woo Israel back. They will return to the wilderness, where the covenant was first forged and their relationship was at its most vibrant.

The Valley of Achor, the site of Israel's defeat because Achan had stolen spoils of war (Josh 7), became a place of disappointment and defeat during the early days in Canaan. This gateway of disappointment will turn into a gateway of hope. In a renewed relationship with Yahweh, Israel will respond to him as in their early days together.

The day of restoration will not be for Hosea's generation. Instead, the remnant of the northern kingdom will return to its allegiance to Yahweh, and their exclusive marriage relationship will be restored. This time it will be a perfect union and will last forever. Yahweh will be husband, and it will be as if Baal had never existed. A covenant will be crafted with all of creation in mind. All wars will cease, and there will be peace under the protection of Yahweh.

The names of Gomer's children are reversed. Jezreel plants instead of using aggression and military might. "No compassion" has compassion poured out on her, because now Israel is God's people for all time.

Hosea Buys Back His Wife (Hos 3)

Yahweh commands Hosea to love an adulteress, that is, to make a deep emotional investment that will leave him intensely vulnerable. There is debate as to whether this is Gomer restored to the marriage or whether Hosea marries yet another adulteress. The metaphor fits more precisely if it is understood that Gomer has been redeemed from prostitution and reconciled to Hosea. Hosea has to buy back Gomer, either because she is a slave or to pay the brothel keeper for loss of revenue. He can pay only part of the fee in money. The remainder has to be paid in grain and wine. It cost him dearly to take her back.

Conditions were placed on the wife. She must remain faithful and have no sexual relations with anyone—for a time, not even with her husband. Her lovers had used her as a sex object; her husband would not. After so many extramarital relations she also needed to undergo a period of cleansing (*see* Holiness and Wholeness). Hosea has bought her back, but she must do as he desires.

In parallel with Hosea's marriage, Israel would be deprived of its monarchy and pagan worship. The deprivations, which would occur during exile, would be followed by a return to Yahweh and a reinstatement of the Davidic kingdom. When Israel turns to Yahweh in true repentance they will find him full of goodness and forgiveness.

The Case Against Israel (Hos 4:1—5:7)

The case against Israel is constructed. Accusations are brought against various sections of society. The first three accusations are sins of omission: no faithfulness, no kindness or knowledge of God is found. Rather, there is infidelity, selfishness and no relationship with Yahweh.

Priests had a clear role in Israel: they were to lead the people and encourage them in their relationship with God. But Yahweh accuses the priests of corrupting the religious system and using it for financial gain. They lead the people astray so that they all stumble and fail to walk in God's ways. In Jerusalem priests and prophets served in a parallel role. Yahweh rejects them and their heirs.

Sacrifices and union with cult prostitutes were to ensure the fertility of the land. The women who prostitute themselves do so believing it is an act of devotion. The priests are to blame for encouraging the immoral practices. There is no double standard: males and females alike are held accountable.

The leaders of Israel are summoned to pay attention to God's prophet. The priests have already been chastised for their part in Israel's depravity, and now, with the other national leaders, they are accused of entrapping the people. The structure of government meant that state and religion were entwined; each supported the other to maintain stability and authority. Both corrupt ruling bodies encouraged the worship of Baal. An increased number of sacrifices led to larger taxes and tithes, of which they had a share. Priests and royalty are held accountable for Israel's infidelities.

Weary of their behavior, Yahweh has left them to their own devices. No longer legitimate offspring, they do not inherit and will be deported into exile. Evidence has been produced and judgment made.

Advancing Judgment (Hos 5:8—6:11)

Sound the alarm! The enemy advances from the south along the mountain passes from Jerusalem to Bethel and into the heart of Israel. Israel's punishment is upon them. Moth and dry rot destroy until the damage is too far advanced to be rectified. Israel's sickness and Judah's injuries are compared with the covenant plagues (Hos 5:13; cf. Deut 28:9, 61). The injuries are those inflicted by enemies during conflict, and the illnesses relate to captivity and exile. Ephraim appeals to Assyria for help, but the Assyrians were not to be trusted. Yahweh will tear Israel apart and destroy them as a lion tears its prey. It is Yahweh they should fear, not Assyria. No one can rescue them.

Yahweh abandons Israel and Judah. Thus they are given time to consider why he has left them and not come to their aid as on previous occasions. When they realize that they are guilty of sin and have brought this predicament on themselves, they search for Yahweh (*see* Sin). They go to him in the hope that their punishment may be reversed. They are convinced that Yahweh will come to their aid yet again sometime in the near future, not literally three days.

They have decided to strive to know God and accept his covenant and return to the relationship they had enjoyed before. His help and acceptance, they believe, is as certain as day follows night. But Yahweh knows their hearts. They express their love and perform their sacrifices, but their devotion is an act to save themselves. Like dew it will disappear as soon as the sun rises.

Corrupt and Half-Baked (Hos 7)

Passion for Corruption (Hos 7:1-7)

Hosea 7 starts a new section that demonstrates the dangerous game of Ephraim's alliances with other nations, particularly Egypt and Assyria. Israel's hope is that an alliance will protect them, create wealth and improve their position as a nation of worth. But without Yahweh at the center of these negotiations they face ruin.

The image of a baker's oven describes the heat of the Israelite leaders' passion for corruption. Bakers' ovens were dome-shaped, fired-clay structures with a door in the top and floor-level apertures. A fire was lit and tended until the inside walls glowed with heat. The dough was then pressed into the walls and the top door closed. The oven would retain sufficient heat to cook the bread.

The reference to the flat cake alludes to bread baked on hot stones (cf. 1 Kings 19:6); the cakes would need to be turned so they would bake on both sides. Some interpreters conclude that Hosea's knowledge of baking processes suggests that he was a baker by trade.

Leaders, inflamed by the excitement of political power, burn with intrigues. Like an oven smoldering overnight, they in their dreams and half-waking moments smoldered with political ambitions. In the morning they burn "like a flaming fire" (Hos 7:6), but in their quest for power they bring destruction to themselves and the nation. None have sought the advice of Yahweh. They are too arrogant and too sure of their own abilities to do that.

Israel as Male (Hos 7:8-10)

Ephraim has engaged in the forbidden practices of mixed marriages and religion. The time referred to is the reign of King Hoshea. When Hoshea came to power Israel was paying tribute to Assyria but had not yet come under its control. Before long Hoshea stopped the payments and formed an alliance with Egypt. In keeping with the baking analogy, Israel was mixed up and only half-baked. Bread not turned during the baking process would be crisp or even burned on one side and soft and doughy on the other. Israel was crusty, hard and unyielding toward Yahweh but soft and pliable toward the nations.

Flightiness and Deceit (Hos 7:11-16)
Israel's foreign policy is like a silly bird flitting from here to there. Birds that are a nuisance are caught and disposed of. As Israel flies between Assyria and Egypt for foreign aid they will be caught in Yahweh's net, and no amount of struggling will release them. They will be brought down in mid-flight—representing their downfall as a nation.

Yahweh cannot buy back his people because they still lie about him. They give no evidence of remorse or repentance for their actions. According to the laws of redemption an individual could buy someone back only if that person was worthy of redemption. Israel is not deemed worthy.

Trumpets and Whirlwinds (Hos 8)
The trumpet blasts warn that the enemy is so near that a vulture hovers over Israel waiting for its feast. In vain the people cry to Yahweh for help. They plead their knowledge of him, but their actions have proved them false.

"They sow the wind, and they shall reap the whirlwind" (Hos 8:7). A sower would scatter seed into the wind on a day with a light breeze so that the wind would carry the seed and distribute it evenly across a newly plowed field. A gentle breeze may be helpful, but if it develops into a whirlwind its power can destroy everything in its path. So too sin may appear harmless, but it destroys. The full force of Israel's disobedience will be shown them. The ears of grain will be blown off the stalks. If any of the crop survives, it will be eaten by foreign invaders, and Israel's work will be in vain.

Like "a wild ass wandering alone" (Hos 8:9), Israel, ridiculed by other nations and abandoned by Yahweh, turns in foolish desperation to Assyria. Their foreign allies will turn on them and take them captive into exile. As slaves they will do as their new masters command.

Festivals and Punishment (Hos 9)
Israel's jubilant mood coincides with the period around 732 B.C., when the Assyrians had temporarily withdrawn from the northern kingdom. They had survived, and life could return to normal. Even in their celebrations they forgot to thank Yahweh for their improved situation and immediately fell back into harlotry. The metaphor of prostitution is used here for the last time in Hosea.

Yahweh reminisces about the time he first found Israel alone in the wilderness. Israel responded, and the covenant was made at Sinai. This relationship was rare and precious, as would be finding grapes in the desert. Gradually the grapes lose their sweetness; the rare and lovely turns against Yahweh, and their unique relationship turns ugly and sour, marred by sin. Israel has not improved since the events at Baal-peor. There, at the instigation of Balaam the prophet, Moabite women seduced Israelite men into ritual prostitution in Baal worship (Num 25:1-4; 31:16).

In the coming devastation, children will die at the hands of the enemy. Punishment will affect not only the general population but also women specifically. If any conceive, they will miscarry. Their breasts will not produce milk because there will be no pregnancy. No longer will there be the joy of childbirth.

Punishment for False Hearts (Hos 10)
The Israelites' behavior is likened to that in the time when a man's concubine had been gang raped and dismembered (Judg 19—20). The book of Hosea is remarkable for its recurring recognition of and sympathy for the vulnerability of women.

Ephraim will be like a yoked cow rather than a stubborn heifer (Hos 4:16). Cattle were used to tread grain to separate it from the chaff. The owners' favorites were unyoked and unmuzzled so they could eat as they trod the grain. Ephraim was given freedom to roam, but because of its sin, it would be treated as any other nation, no longer Yahweh's favorite.

Israel and Judah will have the opportunity to turn and to make amends, to plow and sow righteousness to produce steadfast love. First they need to break up the unyielding ground of their hearts so that the grain of righteousness can germinate. Love and righteousness would be ideal crops, but instead they have sown the seeds of sin and harvested injustice. They reap what they sow—sin, evil, lies. Because they put their trust in military strength, by their own abilities they shall be destroyed. This war will be like the battle at Beth-arbel, where Shalman brutally defeated them. All kinds of atrocities occurred, and Israel knew what a similar war would mean. No one would survive it (2 Sam 8:12). The population, including women and children, will be treated mercilessly.

A Parent's Love (Hos 11)

This chapter reveals another aspect of Yahweh's character: a parent's love for his or her children.

God's Motherlike Love (Hos 11:1-4)

Teaching a child to walk, holding it in one's arms and lifting an infant to one's cheek are more frequently the activities of a mother rather than of a father. These actions are, however, appropriate to parents of either gender. Israel is portrayed as a male child. Like any infant it had certain requirements for survival and development into a well-adjusted adult. At the start of its life Yahweh was present, lovingly watching over it. In its developing state, weak and insignificant, Yahweh called Israel out of slavery in Egypt, where its growth had been stifled and stunted by unloving taskmasters.

A Wayward Child (Hos 11:5-7)

As time progressed Israel became rebellious, and as it grew, nurtured by Yahweh, it found other things more interesting. Yahweh called it back, but rebelliousness separated the two. God had led and guided the people; the metaphor adapts into one of an animal being led and controlled by a yoke. The animal is led by a gentle restraint. The yoke is removed to give more comfort. Yahweh reaches down and provides. But his loving kindness does not make an impact; they still prefer a life of anarchy and idols.

Hosea brings his audience to examine their current situation. Legally Yahweh could have the rebellious child put to death. They will be severely punished, sent into captivity under the rule of Assyria because they refused to repent and reject Baal. They continued further and deeper into sin and rebellion.

God's Strong Love (Hos 11:8-12)

Even after all their defiance and sin, Yahweh cannot continue with destruction. God's love is too strong. Justice, however, demanded that punishment be carried out but with leniency. Acting in keeping with the divine nature, one of eternal and steadfast love, Yahweh extends compassion and mercy to the undeserving.

Israel's Past (Hos 12)

The prophet reminds Israel of incidents from the life of Jacob (Gen 25:21-26; Gen 32:22-32), from whom the nation takes its name (Gen 35:9-15). He had worked to earn a wife, as had Hosea (Hos 3:4). The long years of labor seemed but a short time because of Jacob's love for Rachel. His continuing devotion to her is one of the few admirable characteristics of the trickster and cheat whose name meant "deceiver." The climax of this excursion into the life of the patriarch is his renaming at Bethel (Gen 35:1-10).

Hosea compares the role of Jacob (looking after his uncle's sheep, guiding and protecting them) with the actions of Moses (leading, guiding, protecting Israel) as he brought them out of Egypt. Generally the prophet's occupation was to watch over Israel and to warn them when they strayed.

Yahweh Alone Can Save (Hos 13)

Yahweh sets out his credentials as the one who brought Israel out of Egypt. God had guided them through the desert and provided what they needed in life and more. They forgot about Yahweh during the times of plenty, turning back only when they needed help. The Almighty gave; they took and kept taking.

The love and devotion of God's children has been stolen. Yahweh's anger is compared with that of a mother bear robbed of her cubs. The protective mother will defend her young at any price, tearing to pieces those who dare to take them from her. At significant points in the Hebrew Scriptures, God is portrayed in feminine imagery (Deut 32:11, 18; Ps 131:2-3; Is 42:13-14; 49:15; 66:9-13; Hos 13:8; *see* Images of God as Female).

Ephraim is pictured as a baby that has come to the time for birth but is not in the correct position to emerge from the birth canal (*see* Birth Pain Imagery). Without medical intervention baby and mother are at risk. Translators have understood Hosea 13:14 variously. In the NRSV rendering Yahweh asks, "Shall I ransom them from the power of Sheol? Shall I redeem them from Death?" If God does not assist, tragic loss of a new life and loss of mother will occur. Yahweh questions whether to rescue them from their fate and have compassion. There is no compassion now for them, and punishment is part of their future. God will have no mercy. All that the child could have been, all the potential of a newly formed life, is extinguished.

The NIV construes the questions as affirmations: "I will ransom them from the power of the grave; I will redeem them from death." Here, as in Isaiah 66:9, Yahweh is midwife, intervening in the life-threatening circumstance to bring deliverance (*see* Midwifery and Birthing Practices). Then follows the exaltation that is adopted in 1 Corinthians 15:55: "Where, O death, is your victory? Where, O death, is your sting?" Apparently Paul understood the original application to be that of joyful deliverance of a mother and child trapped in a dire circumstance of certain death.

Allusions to pregnancy and birthing have appeared throughout this prophecy, and the final one is the most terrifying. The sins of Samaria will unleash the scourge of the aggressor, including atrocities perpetrated on pregnant women (Hos 14:1). In the biblical record, their disembowelment represented the ultimate in vicious and senseless cruelty (2 Kings 8:12; 15:16; Is 13:16; Amos 1:13).

At Last Israel Returns (Hos 14)

Hosea urges Israel to return to the Lord. It may be too late for the current generation to escape punishment, but for a future generation there may be hope and restoration if they listen to the prophet's warning and return to the Lord in repentance. The sins against Yahweh would be forgiven, and they would be healed. They would remain faithful to each other. Hosea's generation would be destroyed, but a remnant would remain. A new generation of Israel would experience unconditional steadfast love. Where there had been death, desolation, dryness, all manner of beauty would spring forth. All the most beautiful plants would grow and develop. The land and people would be blessed. The fragrance of the flowers would overpower the stench of death and destruction. All would be fertile and filled with beauty.

KEREN E. MORRELL AND
CATHERINE CLARK KROEGER

JOEL

Introduction

The people of Judah were in a sorry state. Their faith had degenerated into mere duty. God never enjoys seeing his people like this, so to make their faith real again, first he sent a disaster, then he sent the prophet Joel (meaning "the Lord is God") to interpret it. Dating the book is difficult, but the content (e.g., interest in temple and cult but no mention of a king), suggests Joel lived around 500 B.C. He says little about himself; what mattered was the "word of the LORD" that came to him.

Outline

1:1-20	Responding to the Disaster
2:1-17	Responding to the Day of the Lord

Commentary

Responding to the Disaster (Joel 1)

Joel 1 begins by implying the disaster was the worst locust plague in living memory, compounded by drought. Joel likens the swarming insects to an invading army. They destroyed all vegetation, eating the vines, fig trees, cereal crops, and fruit trees. Food and drink were in short supply. Humans and animals alike suffered, and the economy was ruined. No wonder that "joy withers away among the people" (Joel 1:12). Joel especially encourages the drunkards, farmers and priests to "lament." They would be particularly affected, as would be one unidentified sufferer, possibly the land (in Joel 1:6, "land" is feminine singular, as are the verb and imagery in Joel 1:8).

Joel wants to convince everyone of the need to turn to God for help, for Joel saw beyond the immediate disaster to its spiritual and future significance. It was a sign of the coming "day of the LORD." Joel 1:15 links two earlier prophecies, Ezekiel 30:2-3 and Isaiah 13:6. There "the day of the LORD" threatened judgment for Judah's enemies; here it warns of judgment for Judah. It is rapidly heading for ultimate disaster, for the Lord is a holy God who demands holiness from his people. Years earlier, he had promised that if they walked with him, he would make their land fruitful (e.g., Deut 11:13-17), but if not, their harvests would fail. The prophecy has become a reality. Their faith has degenerated into mere ritual, and they suffer the results of God's wrath, spiritually as well as physically. The usual temple sacrifices have had to cease, and joy has gone out of worship.

Joel's task was to shock the people of Judah into thinking spiritually again: to help them see God's hand in their situation, hear what he was saying through it and respond rightly. The Lord is not interested in mere external response or mere emotional response. He seeks a deep, heart-based, inner response. Therefore lamentation alone wasn't enough. Even the animals seek God's help; his people must do the same. They must turn to him in prayer, cry to him in repentance for help and mercy. It was the priests' responsibility to set the example.

Though he is not a priest, Joel, like all good ministers, identifies with God's people. He laments and prays. He recognizes this disaster as a sign of the far worse "destruction from the Almighty" that on the day of the Lord would fall on all who had persistently refused to take him seriously. Much later, Jesus Christ would repeat the warning (Mk 13:35-36). But even in such dark words of judgment, there is the light of hope. Behind the emphasis on "my land . . . my vines . . . my fig trees" (Joel 1:6-7) is the truth that God cares, and the encouragement to believe he will answer their prayers favorably.

Responding to the Day of the Lord (Joel 2:1-17)

Joel 2 begins with a warning: "the day of the LORD is coming" (Joel 2:1), of which the locusts are a sign and forerunner. Both were days of inescapable "darkness and gloom" (Joel 2:2-3; cf. Ex 10:14-15; Zeph 1:15). Joel 2:4-11 poetically portrays the invading army of locusts aggressively bent on destruction (cf. Joel 1:6). They charged the city; they climbed into every home. "Peoples" who heard them coming were terrified (Joel 2:5-6). The day of the Lord will be similar, only even more terrifying and destructive. The earth and heavens will shake, and even the sun will fail to shine. The picture reaches a climax with the appearance of the army's commander: the Lord.

"Yet even now" (Joel 2:12) the situation could change if Judah would respond rightly. For those who take God seriously, the day brings good news of salvation. The first step is deep-seated, genuine repentance: "return to me with all your heart." "Heart" *(leb)* speaks not only of the emotions but also of the mind and will. Repentance will show itself outwardly in "fasting, . . . weeping, and . . . mourning," but the inner (heart) response must come first. The basis of this last-minute hope of forgiveness is in God's character. The "steadfast love" of "the LORD, your God" (Joel 2:13) inclines him to "turn and relent" from punishing his covenant people (Joel 2:14).

So for a third time Joel calls everyone to "a solemn assembly" (Joel 2:15), to urgent fasting and prayer. All must join in, whether they are aged or babies or newlywed, and again the priests must set the example. Joel even tells them what to pray.

The remedy for dried-up faith doesn't change. The only way to deal with sin is by repentance. The only way to overcome failure is by prayer.

The Lord Responds to His Penitent People (Joel 2:18-32)

Evidently Judah did repent and pray, for "in response" (Joel 2:19) comes a series of direct words from the Lord (Joel 2:18—3:21). First he promises that the immediate future will be one of blessing. He will repay "the years that the . . . locust has eaten" (Joel 2:25). He will undo all the suffering of Joel 1. Material blessings will return. His people will be "satisfied" (Joel 2:19). The locusts, which came from the north, will be driven away south, east and west, into the desert, the Dead Sea and the Mediterranean. The next harvest will be a full one, so land and animals need fear no more. Spiritual blessings will follow. Already the rains have started, and with them joy has returned. All this is a "vindication," (Joel 2:23), a sign that the Lord has returned to his people and restored his covenant favor.

But Joel knows how quickly God's people may again grow forgetful or complacent. Therefore land and people are called to remember that the Lord alone saves them and to praise him. The past tenses convey certainty. Salvation is sure, for two reasons: "the LORD became jealous for his land, and had pity on his people" (Joel 2:18). There are two faces to the Lord's steadfast covenant love: jealousy and pity. Both words convey an emotional involvement. His people, and even his land (see comment on Joel 1:8), may be full of deep emotion, but so, Joel believes, is the Lord. Jealousy means he is exclusively committed to Judah and cannot tolerate anything less than Judah's exclusive commitment in return. Nor can he tolerate seeing his people humiliated by their neighbors (Joel 2:17; cf. Ps 79:4, 10). Therefore, in answer to prayer (Joel 2:17), twice he adds, "my people shall never again be put to shame" (Joel 2:26-27).

Joel 2:28-32 (Joel 3 in Heb.) reveals even deeper blessings to come in the future. One day the Lord will pour out his Spirit "on all flesh" (Joel 2:28; cf. Is 44:3; Ezek 39:29; Zech 12:10). In the Old Testament, God's Spirit is active in creation and in equipping individuals for particular tasks (e.g., Judg 6:34; 1 Sam 10:10; Is 61:1), but never is it said that the Spirit is given to every believer, though Moses had longed for it (Num 11:29).

Now the Lord reveals that this is what he wants too. God's Spirit will be given to all his people. In Old Testament society, sons were often valued above daughters, older above younger, free above slave and men above women. But when it comes to receiving and manifesting the Spirit, all such distinctions are irrelevant. Acts 2:16-21 makes it clear that this prophecy was fulfilled at Pentecost.

All this is set in the context of that "great and terrible day of the LORD" (Joel 2:31). First comes the pouring out of God's Spirit. Then come terrible signs in heaven and on earth, signs that the Almighty is bringing this world to an end (cf. Mt 24). As they see these signs, says Joel, "everyone who calls on the name of the LORD shall be saved" (Joel 2:32; cf. Rom 10:13). He explains that they call on One who is already calling them. Salvation is offered to everyone but is received only by individuals humble enough to repent, believe and pray.

The Lord Restores His Penitent People (Joel 3)

Joel 3 (Joel 4 in Heb.) deals with the final

triumph of justice and good over sin and evil. For a long time, Judah's neighbors had been abusing the nation. Child slavery was bad enough, but they were selling Jewish children solely for cheap pleasure (*see* Ancient and Modern Slavery). Now the Lord promises to judge them for their crimes. Jehoshaphat (meaning "the Lord judges") is probably a symbolic valley rather than literal. The Philistines are especially condemned because they had stolen the temple treasures and sold God's covenant people into distant slavery (Joel 3:4-6; cf. Ezek 25:15—28:26). Notice the repeated personal pronouns, "my people . . . my land . . . my silver" (Joel 3:2-3, 5), and the indignant question (Joel 3:4). The Lord will retrieve his scattered people and sell the nations into their hands. Thus the punishment will fit the crime, and the mocking question of Joel 2:17 will be answered. History records that the Tyreans and Sidonians were sold into slavery in the mid-fourth century B.C.

There's a deliberate contrast between the summons to Jerusalem (Joel 1:14; 2:15) and the summons to Jehoshaphat (Joel 3:9-12). In both cases the summons is to every individual. All must share responsibility for what has happened; all must face up to the reality of God's wrath. But where Judah repented and the Lord responded with mercy (Joel 2), the nations remain arrogant ("ripe" for harvest, Joel 3:13), and the Lord brings down his warriors, presumably angels, to mete out judgment (Joel 3:11-13; cf. Zeph 3:8).

By now Joel is no longer speaking only of Judah's immediate neighbors but of "multitudes" (Joel 3:14). From Joel 3:15, he again describes the day of the Lord—the signs in the sky, a loud roar from Jerusalem—until at last the nations realize they have been abusing not only God's people but also God (cf. Mt 25:45). So the valley of judgment becomes the valley of final decision. Primarily God's decision, yet human decision too, because his final decision about people is related to their final attitude to him. He pours mercy on the penitent but wrath on the proud.

The day of the Lord therefore holds terror only for God's enemies; those who trust him have nothing to fear. Believers will be "survivors" (Joel 2:32), not because of what they are but because of what their Lord is (Joel 3:16, "a stronghold"). Better still, as he judges the nations of this world, so the Lord will establish his people as citizens of a purified, holy, new Jerusalem, center of a glorious new world (Joel 3:17-18; cf. Rev 21:1—22:5). The Lord will live there among them and allow them to know him. Joel describes it in language appropriate to his time. Even the driest valley, Wadi Shittim, would be watered. The contrast to the fate of Egypt and Edom highlights the abundance of blessing. Again it's a reversal of the devastation caused by the locusts. But much of this is yet to come. So Joel ends by reassuring those who still suffer that the Lord is always present and active on their behalf.

Bibliography. L. C. Allen, *The Books of Joel, Obadiah, Jonah and Micah,* New International Commentary on the Old Testament (Grand Rapids, MI: Eerdmans, 1976) 9-126.

GWYNNETH MARIAN NAPIER RAIKES

AMOS

Introduction

Amos's prophetic ministry can be dated to 750 B.C., two years before the earthquake that occurred during the reign of Jeroboam II (786-746 B.C.) and Uzziah (783-742 B.C.). Amos prophesied in the waning years of Jeroboam II's reign, when internal strife and external threats had returned after a brief period of peace and prosperity. For most of its history, the northern kingdom was embroiled in wars with Judah and its neighboring states over trade routes and territorial claims and over the forming and breaking of coalitions against Assyria. Toward the end of Jeroboam II's reign, Pekah (736-732 B.C.) may have already established himself as a rival king with Syrian support. 2 Kings 15:27 states he reigned for twenty years, making his claim to the throne overlap with Jeroboam's last years.

Political strife, however, was not the only concern; social and economic conditions in Israel were also deteriorating. The international trade begun by the Omride dynasty (ninth century B.C.) had been continued by Jehu's dynasty (ninth-eighth centuries B.C.) and had brought prosperity to the royal houses and their officials. Israel exported agricultural products such as wheat, olive oil and wine in exchange for luxury items like jewels, metal and ivory. The unquenchable demand for exotic imports required increased production of exportable cash crops. The combined market and sociopolitical pressures forced peasants to change their agricultural practices and subsistence strategy, resulting in dangerous exposure to production risks and market price fluctuations. These socioeconomic factors worked to the disadvantage of the peasants, who incurred debt, lost land and possessions and were forced into debt slavery. The rich and powerful exploited the poor and weak through legal, if unethical, means. These lamentable consequences are voiced not only by Amos but also by other eighth-century prophets (Is 5:8; Mic 2:2). Archaeological finds such as the Samaria ostraca in the north and the *lmlk* jar seal impressions in the south suggest the existence of large private and royal estates and the collection of "washed oil" and fine wine in storage or as taxation in kind. The gap between the rich and poor continued to widen in the eighth century B.C., with increasingly luxurious lifestyle and conspicuous consumption for the wealthy and worsening living conditions for the poor. To this society Amos delivered his message.

The oracles were directed primarily to a male audience, especially the wealthy and ruling class. Except for the attack on the rich women of Samaria, the oracles make only sporadic references to women in ancient Israel.

Amos was the first prophet to have his oracles and visions collected into a book. The authorship and date of the book, however, are much debated. While the possibility of a history of oral transmission and redaction of the oracles cannot be rejected, the present structure of the book argues favorably for a single author, whether it is Amos or a later redactor.

Amos's concern for the poor and oppressed included women, but his focus was not on women per se. Modern readers of Scripture, however, have benefited from recent research methods such as social scientific and anthropological studies of preindustrial, agrarian societies, which help in the recovery of women's experience and women's voices from the pages of Amos.

The book of Amos addresses the social ills of eighth-century B.C. Israel but provides little information about the prophet. Amos 1:1 states that the prophet was "among the shepherds of Tekoa," a town ten miles south of Jerusalem, situated on the border between arable land and the desert. The town was also known for its wise woman who reconciled Absalom to David (2 Sam 14:2).

Amos was probably a sheep breeder and owner of herds, because the term used to identify him as a "shepherd" is used in 2 Kings 3:4 to describe King Mesha of Moab. Amos was also a "dresser of sycamore trees" (Amos 7:14). Sycamore is a poor-quality fig that grows in the lowlands, the coastal plains and the Jordan Valley and requires the piercing of the fruit to speed its ripening. Perhaps Amos's work took him outside of the hill country of Judah and his business dealings with Israel revealed the abuses in the northern kingdom. His knowledge of international affairs and domestic conditions, as well as the language and structure of the book, suggests that Amos was not an ignorant, backwoods herdsman but one with a bright mind and a sensitive heart.

Outline

1:1—2:16	Oracles Against the Nations
3:1—6:14	Oracles Against Israel
7:1—9:6	The Visions of Amos and Confrontation
9:7-15	Judgment and Hope

Commentary

Oracles Against the Nations (Amos 1:1—2:16)

The Nations

Amos opened his indictments against the nations with an emphatic warning of the devastating effect of Yahweh's voice. Because the nations had exceeded the limit of offenses, God declared that "I will not revoke the punishment" (Amos 1:3), more precisely translated as "I will not cause it to turn back." The transgressions were not merely offenses but rebellions against Yahweh, and for the people's repeated rebellion, God would not turn back God's voice.

In Amos 1—2, the prophet indicted eight nations, including six non-Israelite nations, for crimes against their neighbors, Judah for rejecting the torah (instructions) of Yahweh and Israel for socioeconomic oppression against their own. The Syrians were accused of threshing Gilead with "sledges of iron" (Amos 1:3). The reference is not to threshing grain or plowing fields. 2 Samuel 12:31 uses the same phraseology to describe one form of punishment David exacted on the defeated Ammonites. In the Old Testament, *iron* evoked fear because of its association with weapons of aggression, brutality and torture from Israel's enemies, who used iron yokes, furnaces, chariots and sharp threshing instruments (Deut 4:20; 28:48; Jer 28:14).

The Philistines were indicted for wholesale deportation of communities, including young and old, male and female. The taking and selling of war captives was a common practice in the ancient world, but the "complete" (from *shalom*) exile may have been perpetrated on a peaceful *(shalom)* people. Even the Assyrians and Babylonians, who were infamous for their deportation of defeated enemies, did not usually remove entire communities. What the Philistines did is comparable to events in Kosovo in 1999, when tens of thousands of ethnic Albanians were forcibly removed from their homeland in an attempt to displace and erase the memory of a people.

The Phoenicians were also charged with selling whole communities into slavery (cf. Joel 3:4-8; Ezek 27:13) because of economic greed. They were charged, furthermore, with not honoring covenant relationships formed by treaties ("covenant of kinship," Amos 1:9).

If the Phoenicians were brothers by treaty, the Edomites were brothers by lineage (Gen 25:24-26). Yet Edom relentlessly "pursued his brother with the sword and cast off [destroyed] all pity" (Amos 1:11). The word *pity* comes etymologically from the word *womb (rhm)*. Pity is a "womb feeling," an expression of tenderness and compassion toward the weak. Based on the Moabite Mesha inscription, Ugaritic parallels and usage in Judges 5:30, the word *pity* can also be translated "young women," in which case the Edomites were killing their brother and his womenfolk.

The Ammonites likewise were indicted for ruthless slaughtering of women with the sword: "They have ripped open pregnant women in Gilead in order to enlarge their territory" (Amos 1:13). This horrific act of violence is not poetic exaggeration, as is evidenced by a perusal of biblical texts and ancient and modern incidents. In 2 Kings 8:12, Elisha wept for Hazael's future treatment of the Israelites. He will invade Israel and "dash in pieces their little ones, and rip up their pregnant women." 2 Kings 15:16 reported that after Menahem son of Gadi seized the throne, he retaliated against Tiphsah and the territory of Tirzah. Because these cities/regions refused to submit to him, "he ripped open all the pregnant women in it." If "Tiphsah" is read as "Tappuah" (with the Septuagint), Menahem's revenge was not directed toward women in a distant town on the Euphrates but against Israelite women in his kingdom! Hosea 13:16 also pairs the dashing of the little ones with the ripping open of pregnant women as part of the horrors of war that will be inflicted on Samaria as just punishment from Yahweh. Other ancient texts that mention such atrocities include a Middle Assyrian poem extolling Tiglath-pileser I's (1114-1076 B.C.) military victory, citing specifically the slitting of the wombs of pregnant women and the blinding of infants. Greek and Arabic texts also speak of killing the unborn of the enemy.

The ripping open of pregnant women is not limited to ancient times. During the Japanese occupation of the Chinese capital of Nanking (1937-1945), pregnant women, regardless of how late term, were not spared from being raped and killed. Some of these women had their bellies slashed open and the fetuses ripped from their wombs. As recently as late 1998, news pictures flashed across television screens showing war atrocities in former Yugoslavia, one of which was a pregnant woman with her belly ripped open.

The extreme brutality of ripping open pregnant women makes one recoil with disgust, but these violent crimes should be acknowledged for what they are and not relegated to a sociological phenomenon of war. Scholarly attempts to explain such atrocities have tended to focus on the effect on the male population. Ripping open pregnant women should not be explained as an unfortunate result of eliminating the male line or of emasculating the fathers. The atrocity is perpetrated most directly on the woman. The unborn that is torn from the mother's womb is not always an unborn son; she may be an unborn daughter. Whatever the rationale for such barbarity, the woman is the one slaughtered. This is not mutilation, like the cutting off of an ear or a nose. Ripping open pregnant women is the vicious murder of mothers and their children.

Women can also become the "spoil of war" (Judg 5:30). Deuteronomy allows the enjoyment of the spoil of the enemy (Deut 20:14) and the taking of beautiful captives as wives and concubines (Deut 21:10-14). The women captured were usually virgins, since nonvirgins would be killed along with boys and men (Num 31:18, 32; Judg 21:12). Whether they become servants, field hands, wives or slaves, it was a bitter fate to be torn from one's homeland, carried away as a war trophy and perhaps be forced to marry someone who had murdered one's father and mother.

The Old Testament recorded women's participation in times of crisis: Deborah and Jael (Judg 4—5), the woman who threw an upper millstone on Abimelech's head (Judg 9:52-55) and the wise woman of Abel of Beth-maacah (2 Sam 20:14-22). Judith in the Apocrypha saved her people by assassinating Holofernes, while Esther saved her people through her ingenious plan. The infrequent references to women's role in war in the Old Testament should not be read as an absence of resistance, since only exceptional feats are recorded. The norm of women's participation in war may well have been active evasion and resistance.

Israel

The real target of Amos's preaching was Israel, which was indicted for social injustice and for oppression and exploitation of the poor. For the sake of economic and territorial greed, persons were sold for insignificant sums, the poor were treated with contempt, and justice was perverted (Amos 2:6-7). Debt slavery was common in the ancient Near East, and ancient Israel was no exception (cf. Ex 21:7; Lev 25:39-40; 2 Kings 4:1-2; Neh 5:5). In a patriarchal society, with concerns of lineage and inheritance through the male line, a debtor who was forced to sell a dependent would more likely sell a daughter before selling a son. Even when females had less worth in society, the selling of a child was not necessarily out of disregard for the daughter but out of desperate poverty.

Amos cites a specific abuse of women in Amos 2:7: "a man and his father walk/go *(hlk)* to the girl *(n'rh)*." The use of an article with "girl" indicates that a specific young woman was in mind; thus some versions translated as "the same girl." The word *n'rh* refers to a virgin, a young woman of marriageable age or a high-ranking maidservant (Ex 2:5; 1 Sam 25:42; Esther 2:9; 4:4, 16). She was not necessarily a slave, nor was she a common or cultic prostitute. She was most likely a young female, dependent on and controlled by the males in her life. She represented a class of vulnerable and defenseless persons in society.

The activity of the father and son is described as "walk/go," but the exact nature of this offense is unclear. *Hlk* is not usually a euphemistic term for sexual intercourse. If it is so used, this would be the only occurrence in the Old Testament. Based on Akkadian parallels, however, Shalom Paul argued strongly for the possibility of reading this as sexual relation. His argument is strengthened by the literary connection to the indictment against Judah, in which sons "walked" in the same manner as their fathers did (Amos 2:4).

The question remains as to what sort of sexual relation Amos was referring. The legal codes provide ample regulations on sexual behavior, including prohibitions against father and son having sexual relations with

---

Yahweh's Concern for the Disenfranchised

Yahweh's concern for widows, orphans, slaves, women, sinners and the dispossessed permeates the biblical story. God's self-description is "the great God, . . . who is not partial and takes no bribe, who executes justice for the orphan and the widow, and who loves the strangers, providing them food and clothing" (Deut 10:17-18). The people who rightly reflect the image of this God do so by caring for these disenfranchised persons.

Torah gives explicit guidelines for such care in laws about gleaning, forbidding the charging of interest, forbidding the keeping of a pledge, or withholding of wages, overnight, for seeing that one's kin do not fall into slavery and for redemption for slaves and the land.

The prophets unrelentingly proclaim that Israel's failure to care for the dispossessed results in judgment and exile. Failing to practice mercy and justice (e.g., Amos 5:7; 6:12; Mic 6:1-12), Israel ground down the poor and needy (e.g., Jer 2:34; Ezek 22:29; Amos 2:6-7 cf. Job 24:9-14; Ps 37:14; 109:16).

Yahweh's concern for the disenfranchised comes to fullest expression in the life of Jesus. Throughout his ministry Jesus welcomes, heals and eats with prostitutes, tax collectors, sinners, the unclean. He speaks with women and heals them without regard to impure status or ethnic background. He proclaims good news to the poor and freedom for prisoners (e.g., Lk 4:18). He provides food for the hungry and healing for foreigners. He instructs his followers to do likewise.

This ministry comes to its climax in Jesus' death where, after taking on the form of a slave (Phil 2:1-13), he is enthroned on a cross, forsaken by followers and by his God. In Jesus' death, God's self is identified with the disenfranchised. After his resurrection, Jesus appeared first to the women, whose proclamation of his resurrection was thought unreliable and hence was disbelieved (but *see* Women as Witnesses).

Jesus' teachings and his enacting of those teachings seem to have been clearly understood in the early church. Hence in Acts we read that the community gathered together after Pentecost sold possessions to help those in need and responded to a concern about the neglect of Hebrew widows.

Throughout the Epistles, believers are called to continue to bear the image of their God in their practice of caring for those who have nothing (1 Cor 8—9). Moreover, it is clear that God's concern for the disenfranchised manifested itself in other ways: Paul's assertion that in Christ there is no longer Jew or Greek, slave or free, male and female (Gal 3:28; cf. Col 3:11); the household codes, which by addressing women, children and slaves subvert the oppressive hierarchies of first-century culture (Eph 5:21—6:9; Col 3:18—4:1); the call for concern for laborers and the poor (Jas 1:27; 2:1-7, 14-17; 5:1-6; 1 Jn 3:17).

Throughout the biblical story Yahweh's concern for the disenfranchised is linked with the righteousness of the people and God. Descriptions of the new heaven and new earth as the place where "righteousness is at home" (2 Pet 3:13) and where God will wipe away all tears (Rev 21:4) indicate that those who seek to hasten the coming of this kingdom will reflect the image of their God in their concern for the least as well.

Bibliography

B. C. Birch, *Let Justice Roll Down* (Louisville, KY: Westminster/John Knox, 1991); idem, "Hunger, Poverty and Biblical Religion," *Christian Century* 92: 593-99; G. Gutiérrez, *The Power of the Poor in History* (Maryknoll, N.Y.: Orbis, 1983); S. H. Ringe, *Jesus, Liberation and the Biblical Jubilee* (Philadelphia: Fortress, 1985); P. Trible, *God and the Rhetoric of Sexuality* (Philadelphia: Fortress, 1978); J. H. Yoder, *The Politics of Jesus* (Grand Rapids, MI: Eerdmans, 1972); R. J. Sider, *Rich Christians in an Age of Hunger* (Maryknoll, N.Y.: Paulist, 1987); M. D. Meeks, *God the Economist* (Philadelphia: Fortress, 1989).

SYLVIA C. KEESMAAT

---

each other's wife (Lev 18:8, 15), but the young woman's social status and familial relation were not specified in Amos 2:7. Extramarital relation was not a problem for the man as long as it did not involve a woman who belonged to another male (Ex 21:7-11; Deut 15:12, 17). If the female was not designated, no property right was violated; then where was the offense? The sexual abuse in this case may be legal but not ethical. The sexual exploitation of this young woman was a grave offense that profaned God's holy name.

In contrast to Israel's treatment of the poor and defenseless, Amos 2:9-11 presents God's gracious treatment when Israel was weak and oppressed. The imagery of God in this passage is not only of a warrior and savior but also of a mother who fiercely fought, protected and provided for her brood, though her children were callous and ungrateful. They even rejected God's provisions of prophets and Nazirites (Num 6:1-21). How unlike God the Israelites were!

The indictments against Israel paralleled those against the other nations. They were accused of economic and territorial greed and disregard for human life and decency. If God held the nations accountable for offenses against their neighbors, how much more would God hold the Israelites accountable for the same kind of offenses against their own? Israel was supposed to know God and the law of Yahweh (Amos 2:4). Their covenant relationship disallowed any claim of ignorance.

Oracles Against Israel (Amos 3:1—6:14)

Amos 3:1, Amos 4:1 and Amos 5:1 begin with "hear this word," a word of indictment from Yahweh. Most of the oracles in this unit were directed toward the rich and powerful because they were responsible for the oppressions and they had the power to correct the abuses.

The accused in Amos 3 is the entire clan of Israel, whose behavior indicated that they had forgotten their covenant relationship with one another and with God. Private greed and ambition had replaced communal concern and welfare. Out of all the nations, God had entered into a relationship only with Israel; yet Israel did not act like one who knew God. Therefore God will punish them for all their iniquities.

Amos 3 provides a synopsis of what was wrong with Israel and the judgment that God has rendered. The prophet summoned the Philistines and Egyptians, enemies known for their violence and oppression, to witness and to be astounded by the tumults and oppressions in Samaria (Amos 3:9-11; cf. Ezek 45:9). The ruling class had grown rich and powerful through crimes against persons ("violence") and property ("robbery"). As a result of their moral and ethical offenses, Yahweh would destroy the nation (Amos 3:11-12). The many references in Amos 3:13-15 to "house/houses" that will be torn down included the palaces, the house of God (Bethel), luxurious mansions and houses of ivory (1 Kings 22:39; Ps 45:8; Amos 6:4). The social structures in which they had placed their security and the fruit of their exploitation would be no more.

After the summary charges of Amos 3:9-11, the oracles of Amos 4:1, Amos 5:1 and Amos 6:1 focused on specific groups on the hill of Samaria. The first group named was the "cows of Bashan." Bashan is a fertile region in the Transjordan known for its lush pastures and prized cattle (Deut 32:14; Ps 22:12). Since the Hebrew Bible and Ugaritic literature are replete with the use of animal names as titles for leaders and dignitaries, the title "cows of Bashan" as the female counterpart to the "bulls" is a reference to the wealthy women of the royal household and its officials. The "cows of Bashan" may also be descriptive of the result of these women's indulgent, pampered lifestyle rather than as an insult. The phrase should not be read according to contemporary Euro-American ideals for women's figure. Slenderness was not a desired feature, since it spoke of hunger and sickliness, whereas plumpness was a sign of a blessed and well-provisioned life.

The wealthy women of Samaria were charged with the abuse and exploitation of the poor. They were oppressing the poor, crushing the needy and saying to their lords, "Bring so that we may drink." The use of the three participles suggests continuous action—their unquenchable demands for more were responsible for the injustice

Two Hittite dignitaries socializing with beer. (Amos 4:1)

and oppression in society. In Amos the frequent association of wine and excess feasting among the upper class suggests that the women were demanding wine and luxury items befitting their social status, items that wives and husbands would enjoy.

The wealthy women of Samaria, like other women in patriarchal societies, were relegated to the domestic realm while their men dominated the public arena; but women were not without power or influence in the families and indirectly in society. The rich women were in an advantaged position in comparison with women and men of lower socioeconomic status, but the power they had was borrowed power. They too were dependent upon and controlled by their husbands, and their desires and demands had to coalesce with those of the males. But the women were nevertheless responsible because they encouraged and participated in a lifestyle that perpetuated oppression. For Amos, the ethical implications of the covenant applied to women and men.

Amos 5:1-3 is a funeral lament directed at the house of Israel, bemoaning the fallen virgin of Israel. The virgin in this case is not a collective term for the unmarried young women of Israel but an appellative for the capital city of Samaria. The Old Testament frequently uses the feminine gender to denote cities. Jerusalem is called Daughter Zion, and the city of Abel of Beth-maacah is called "a mother in Israel" (2 Sam 20:19). Towns and villages surrounding a significant city were called its daughters.

From a patriarchal perspective, the city, like the woman, is an object of possession and protection by the male, while an enemy's city is an object of conquest and domination. The Old Testament combines the feminine designation of cities with language of violence to present metaphorically the fallen city as a raped woman, whether it is Nineveh, Babylon or Jerusalem, and in the case of Amos 5:1, Samaria. Samaria, like a raped woman, was ravished and abandoned, publicly violated and shamed. She was on her own land, but there was no one to help. Where were her warriors and defenders? Had she been grievously wounded? Was she dead? Samaria will be punished because the Israelites were guilty. When the day of disaster comes, the capital city will no longer be an object of desire but an object of pity and contempt.

The language in the Old Testament should not be used to claim that violence, including sexual violence, could be just punishment against another person. Callous, unreflective use of language will perpetuate the misconception that violence against women is divinely sanctioned.

Amos 6:1-7 consists of two woe oracles against the ruling house and leading citizens on the hill of Samaria. The prophet indicted them for their self-importance and false confidence, their violence and oppression without regard for consequence and their leisurely idleness and conspicuous consumption. The repeated use of participles indicates that these were repeated offenses.

Amos 6:4-6 describes the Israelites' participation in the *mrzh* institution ("revelry," Amos 6:7; cf. Jer 16:5), a funerary association, perhaps related to the cult of the dead, which was popular throughout the ancient Near East. Based on inscriptions and tesserae depictions, the *mrzh* was a clan or family association with social and religious significance to which only the upper class of society could belong. The primary activity of the gathering was feasting, and from Amos's descriptions, the Israelite banqueting was extravagant indeed. Reclining on couches and beds decorated with ivory inlay, the upper class of Samaria feasted on choice cuts of tender meat and improvised songs on musical instruments. Meat was a luxury that only the rich could afford, and they were enjoying lambs and calves from the stall. Wine and oil were among Israel's exported items, and they were lavishing wine and the finest oil on themselves. If this was a funerary association, how ironic that they did not see or grieve over Israel's last gasps.

God's judgment on the sinful nation was destruction, as God swore in Amos 6:8. The themes of destruction and exile have reverberated throughout Amos 3—6. Just as the leading women will go into exile (Amos 4:2-3), so will the leading men of Samaria (Amos 6:7) and the nation (Amos 5:27). Those who had regarded themselves as first will be the first to go into exile. Even the sanctuaries of Bethel and Gilgal and Beersheba will suffer the same fate. The destruction will affect everyone, rich or poor, male or female. It will be so devastating that nothing worthwhile will be left. The day will be so bitter that wailing and lamenting will be heard in all the squares and all the streets. Instead of celebrating the harvest of fields and vineyards, the farmers and the professional male and female mourners will mourn (Amos 5:16-17).

Amos's oracles against the rich and powerful challenged the popular theology of eighth-century Israel by reversing its claims and expectations. In a retributive theology, material wealth and prosperity are indicators of blessings and right relation with God while being poor and afflicted is

God's Call to Social Justice

Scripture teaches that "the LORD is a God of justice" (Is 30:18), that "righteousness and justice are the foundation of his throne" (Ps 97:2) and that God always acts justly (Gen 18:25). Underlying God's call to social justice is the biblical teaching that because our just God created a good world, with adequate resources for all, God cares deeply about the welfare of the unique life form created in his image (Gen 1:26-31; Ps 146).

Recognition that "the earth is the LORD's" (Ps 24:1) encourages responsible stewardship over creation by precluding any notion of absolute human ownership that would stifle a compassionate lifestyle (Deut 10:12-21; *see* Men and Women as Stewards of the Environment; Monotheism). Thus the prophet Micah challenged the faith community "to do justice, and to love kindness, and to walk humbly with your God" (Mic 6:8).

In harmony with the New Testament teaching that faith without works is dead (Jas 2:14-16), the Old Testament connects doing justice with faith in God and unjust actions with unbelief (Prov 14:31; Jer 22:13-17). The repentant heart expresses its love for God by concern for the poor and oppressed (Ps 15), whereas ingrained injustice indicates a hardened heart that separates an individual and a nation from God (Is 59:1-15). All of Scripture clearly links love of God with love for others (Ps 112; 1 Jn 3:16-17) and condemns the false piety of any who engage in outward religiosity while acting unjustly (Is 1:12-20; Amos 5:21-24; Lk 11:37-44).

The Old Testament prophets called God's people not only to turn to God from worthless idols and to renounce personal sin but also to demonstrate a new inner heart for God by outward acts of compassion for the needy. In particular, Micah and Amos warned against the delusion that would think God's people exempt from God's call to pursue social righteousness, and they indicted Israel for tolerating personal and institutionalized legal and religious discrimination (Amos 5:11-15; Mic 3:9-12).

In the New Testament, Jesus explicitly connected discipleship with social concern (Lk 6:27-36) and cited compassion for the needy as one measure by which he would recognize his followers (Mt 25:31-46). One of the somber biblical themes is that God's judgment will descend on individuals and nations who ignore social justice (Prov 22:8; Jer 5:20-29; Zech 7:8-14; Mt 23:23).

The specificity with which the Bible treats social justice indicates that God hates any injustice whatsoever because every sin against society or against an individual member of society harms God's good creation. The Ten Commandments instructed redeemed Israel how to live as "a holy nation" (Ex 19:6) in right relationship with their God and with each other. These instructions are expanded in detail elsewhere in Scripture to teach all God's people everywhere that a just lifestyle best witnesses to our Redeemer's holy and loving nature (Lev 19:1-18; Mt 7:12; Rom 13:9-10).

In line with the biblical truth that humankind exercises only delegated authority over creation (Gen 1:26-31; Ps 8; Rom 13:1), leaders are stewards who have special responsibility for equitable treatment of those in their care (Ps 72:1-4, 12-14). Rejecting any human notion that might makes right, God's Word places special emphasis on protecting the powerless, including orphans, aliens and widows (Deut 24:17-21; 27:19; Jer 22:3; Jas 1:27). Throughout recorded history, women have been among the poorest of the poor, and Scripture teaches society's obligation to meet their basic needs.

The Bible contains significant examples of women who exemplify God's justice. The capable wife in Proverbs is a timeless role model who "opens her hand to the poor, and reaches out her hands to the needy" (Prov 31:20). Tabitha was revered in the early church for being "devoted to good works and acts of charity" (Acts 9:36-41). Women gave generously to support Jesus' earthly needs (Lk 8:1-3), and Jesus' citation of the persistent widow who sued for justice encourages every unempowered person facing unjust treatment (Lk 18: l-8).

Although women have most often been among the disadvantaged, nevertheless women as well as men are accountable to God for their response to God's call to social justice. Amos predicts doom for idle, rich women who "oppress the poor, who crush the needy" (Amos 4:1-3). Sapphira and her husband were equally culpable for deceiving the faith community (Acts 5:1-11). Biblical justice rejects any special pleading that would in reality foster further discrimination against women by implying their inability to act as responsibly as men.

God's social ideal is a compassionate community in which all persons are equally valued as fellow image bearers. Isaiah describes the future Zion as "the city of righteousness . . . redeemed by justice" (Is 1:26-27) and declares that "the needy among his people will find refuge in her" (Is 14:32), while Ezekiel adds God's promise to the helpless that "I will feed them with justice" (Ezek 34:15-16). In the New Testament, Jesus uses powerful banquet imagery to depict the future faith community as a place where everyone's needs are met (Lk 13:29-30). Notably, the practice of the early church provides a practical model of active social concern that all generations can emulate in this world (Acts 2:44-46; Gal 6:10; Heb 13:16). GRETCHEN GAEBELEIN HULL

---

regarded as punishment for sin. Amos, however, called the poor righteous and the rich sinners. He scorned them for their fervent participation at cultic sites and their many offerings, for the sanctuaries cannot save. Amos urged them to seek God and not the house of God (Bethel, Amos 5:4-5). True worship requires integration of head and heart and hand. Genuine worship of God and ethical behavior toward one's neighbor are inseparable corollaries (cf. Mic 6:8; Jas 1:27). God cannot stand bloodshed and solemn assembly (Is 1:10-17). While the Israelites claimed that God was with them, that they were in the right, Amos claimed that this could be reality only if they dedicated themselves wholly to seeking God and what God desires and seeking good through a moral, ethical life (Amos 5:4-7, 14-15).

Amos impugned the Israelite belief of the day of Yahweh as well. The concept of the day of Yahweh may have developed from the holy war tradition in which God fought for Israel and destroyed their enemies. Amos was the first biblical author to use this term. The Israelites looked forward eagerly to that day, but Amos asked incredulously why they desired this for themselves (Amos 5:18). It will not be a day of light and glory, as anticipated, but an inescapable day of darkness and gloom (Amos 5:19-20). God will punish God's enemy on that day, and that enemy is Israel.

The purpose of Amos's preaching was not merely to deliver gloom and doom. A prophet is a sentinel who sounds warnings, announces what is on the heart and mind of God and urges repentance while it is still possible. The repeated calls to seek God, to love good and to choose life are calls of repentance. Just as God had raised up prophets and Nazirites and used various disasters in the past to try to get Israel's attention, so Amos's preaching was another attempt to turn Israel back to God.

What God desired of Israel was not extravagant rituals and manifold sacrifices (Amos 5:21-23) but that justice and righteousness may permeate every aspect of society (Amos 5:24). Justice and righteousness are practical expressions of life together as the people of God, demonstrated by right decisions and behavior based on right relationships. To establish justice and righteousness means the cessation of violence and robbery (cf. Ezek 45:9; Amos 3:9-11); it means to love good and hate evil and to correct what is crooked.

God's desire for justice and righteousness (Amos 5:24) is far from accomplished today. The people of God cannot be indifferent to the suffering that injustice and oppressions inflict. When taxation unfairly burdens the poor, when drawing of voting districts favors the powerful, when justice can be bought through highly paid lawyers, are these not exploitation and oppression? Nor can we claim ignorance when communication technology brings the needs of Rwandan and Kosovar refugees and the plight of Pakistani and Afghani women into our living rooms nightly. Neither can we feign powerlessness. Christians can work toward justice and righteousness by effecting structural changes in society, by altering personal lifestyle choices, by standing with the oppressed and needy, by promoting equality and dignity of all persons and by participating in programs that advance justice and equity.

What will God's people do so that "justice [will] roll down like waters, and righteousness like an ever-flowing stream" (Amos 5:24)?

The Visions of Amos and Confrontation (Amos 7:1—9:6)

All standard commentaries note the structure of Amos's visions and the parallels between the first two pairs of visions. The first vision relates an agricultural disaster in which locusts devour the newly sprouted crop that was planted after the king took the first crop. The second vision relates an ecological disaster in which fire devours the land and the water that supported the land ("the great deep"). Amos interceded in both cases, but his pleas only delayed judgment.

The third and fourth visions present objects that the prophet did not understand. Although divine interpretations were offered, the meaning of the third vision continues to elude modern interpreters. In the third vision, God was standing by a wall of *anak,* traditionally translated as "plumb line." *Anak,* however, is "tin," not "lead," making a plumb line an unlikely object in the vision. Tin is a soft metallic element with a low melting point that can be hammered and shaped at ordinary temperature. It can be mixed with copper to produce bronze but by itself is unsuitable for making tools or weapons. "Metal wall" as a figure of speech is not unknown in the Old Testament. Jeremiah's bronze wall (Jer 1:18) and Ezekiel's iron wall (Ezek 4:3) were symbols of strength and resistance, but a tin wall would be weak and flimsy and useless for defense. A curious note is Amos's choice of word. Why did he use *anak,* an Akkadian loanword for "tin," when a Hebrew word *(bədyl)* was available? Was *anak* an indication of the source of Israel's trouble?

The fourth vision is based on a wordplay of *qayiṣ,* a basket of overripe fruit, and *qeṣ,* the final hour. The end has come because God will no longer overlook Israel's transgressions (Amos 7:8; 8:2). The fifth vision confirmed that Yahweh's decision was final. The religious and political structures of Israel would be demolished (Amos 7:8-9; 8:3; 9:1).

Sandwiched between the third and fourth visions is Amaziah's confrontation with Amos. Amaziah challenged Amos's legitimacy to preach in the north and charged that his preaching was threatening the monarchy and social stability. Amos, however, countered the charge with the irresistible nature of the call of God (Amos 7:14-15). "The Lord GOD has spoken; who can but prophesy?" (Amos 3:8).

For his attempt to obstruct Amos's message, Amaziah was cursed with a fivefold curse, including a life of prostitution for his wife, a particularly harsh and degrading punishment for Amaziah because of the sanctity of the priesthood. According to Leviticus, priests are forbidden to marry prostitutes or divorced women (Lev 21:7-9,

13-15), and the daughter of a priest caught in adultery would be burned, not stoned (Lev 21:9). Like other women in war, Amaziah's wife would be victimized. Deprived of husband and children, her only means of survival was prostitution. She would bear a greater humiliation than other women, for she was the wife of the priest of Bethel.

Judgment and Hope (Amos 9:7-15)

Amos called into question Israel's arrogance and self-importance, for they were no different from other people whom God moved at will. If Yahweh can move the Arameans back to Kir, their place of origin (Amos 9:7; cf. Amos 1:5), Yahweh can move the Israelites back to their place of origin. Israel's election brought responsibility, not immunity. God will punish the sinful nation.

Though the destruction from God was sure, God will not utterly destroy Israel. Hope was extended to the remnant. God will restore them to the golden age of the Davidic kingdom; their territory will expand; the land will respond with agricultural abundance; they will live in peace and security; and the gift of the land will be their permanent possession.

Bibliography. H. S. Barstad, *The Religious Polemics of Amos*, Vetus Testamentum Supplements 34 (Leiden: E. J. Brill, 1984); C. V. Camp and C. R. Fontaine, eds., *Women, War and Metaphor: Language and Society in the Study of the Hebrew Bible* (Atlanta: Scholars Press, 1993; originally *Semeia* 61 [1993]); J. H. Hayes, *Amos the Eighth-Century Prophet: His Times and His Preaching* (Nashville: Abingdon, 1988); S. M. Paul, *Amos: A Commentary on the Book of Amos*, ed. F. M. Cross, Hermeneia (Minneapolis: Fortress, 1991).

LAI LING ELIZABETH NGAN

OBADIAH

Introduction

The book is attributed to Obadiah, whose name means "worshiper of Yah[weh]" or "servant of Yah[weh]." The name Obadiah appears twelve times in the Bible, but none of these men are identifiable as the prophet.

The time of composition is much debated, but internal and external evidence suggests the exilic period. First, Obadiah 11-14 likely alludes to the fall of Jerusalem (587 B.C.). Second, Obadiah 1-3 probably is dependent on Jeremiah 49:14-16, since Jeremiah speaks in the singular ("I have heard") as alone having received the word from the Lord, whereas Obadiah uses the plural ("we have heard"), grouping himself with the community that had heard Jeremiah's message (Barthelemy, 697). Third, Malachi's fifth-century B.C. description of Edom in ruins (Mal 1:2-5) makes it viable to link Obadiah 6-7 with the disaster Edom suffered at the hands of Babylonians (552 B.C.).

The judgment on Edom as a whole lacks obvious historical reference and is cast in the context of an eschatological oracle against all nations. This means that Obadiah should be interpreted within the prophetic tradition concerning "the day of the LORD" (Obad 15).

Isaac's words of blessings to Jacob and Esau (Gen 27) are determinative of the future political relationship between Israel and Edom as one of dominion and vassalage. Edom was subjugated by David and gained independence under Jehoram in 845

B.C. (2 Kings 8:20; Bartlett, 85). Despite the mutual national hostility, Edomites provided a partial refuge to Judean fugitives after the fall of Jerusalem (Jer 40:11).

Outline

1	Title and Introduction
2-9	Judgment on Edom
10-14	Prohibitions for Edom
15-21	The Day of the Lord

Commentary

Title and Introduction (Obad 1)

The word *vision* generally refers to the revelation or word of God (1 Sam 3:1; Is 1:1) and here might include a visual revelation (cf. Is 2:2; 13:1; Nahum 1:1). A messenger urges the nations to rise up against Edom along with Israel and Judah (hereafter, Israel), hence, "Let us rise."

Judgment on Edom (Obad 2-9)

Edom's pride (Obad 3) is reminiscent of Israel's preexilic presumption of its inviolability. The divine favor and protection offered to Edom in Deuteronomy 2:3-6 and Deuteronomy 23:6-7 may have contributed to its false sense of security.

God's reproach comes in the light of Edom's arrogance and violent actions against Israel. That Edom is Israel's brother but sided with Israel's enemies (Obad 11) emphasizes Edom's treachery (cf. Amos 1:9-10)—treachery by which Edom in turn will fall (Obad 7). Edom will be judged in the same manner as it abused Israel.

Scripture presents Edom as sharing a common religious heritage with Israel, beginning with Esau (Bartlett, 194-99). Job's friend Eliphaz, possibly Esau's descendant (Gen 36:10-11), is an Edomite worshiper of Yahweh who receives divine revelation and displays knowledge of God (Job 2:11; 4:1). Deuteronomy 33:2, Judges 5:4 and Habakkuk 3:3 strikingly describe God's glory as proceeding from Edom. Deuteronomy 23:8 states that Edomites from the fourth generation may be admitted to the assembly of the Lord. The Bible mentions no idolatry in Edom until 2 Chronicles 25:5-24. Rather like Israel, then, Edomites apparently mixed worship of Yahweh and idols. Edom's religious affinity with Israel underscores the odious nature of its offenses.

Obadiah assures us that God will bring just retribution on the enemies of God's people, for vengeance belongs to the Lord (Deut 32:35; Rom 12:19). This should produce in women and men humility, forgiveness and compassion rather than hypocritical judgment, vindictiveness or triumphalism when our adversaries or abusers (within and outside the faith or family) undergo God's judgment or endure misfortune, lest we ourselves be judged by God.

Prohibitions for Edom (Obad 10-14)

The series of Hebrew imperatives (Obad 12-14) should be rendered as prohibitions: "Do not look down," and so on. These function as words of indictment against Edom for its past actions and as a straightforward series of prohibitions for Edom to abstain from further offense against Israel. The whole oracle is not only an antagonistic message of judgment against Edom but also an urgent warning and call to repentance for a nation that rejoiced and would still rejoice over the misfortune of its enemy (cf. Prov 24:17).

The day of Jacob's trouble, disaster and so forth would point not only to the day of the fall of Jerusalem but also to the indefinite time during which Jacob is humbled as a dispossessed nation.

The Day of the Lord (Obad 15-21)

In oracles about "the day of the LORD," those nations that were familiar to Israel because of their geographical proximity and political relation are the usual targets and serve as tangible examples of God's judgment. In Obadiah, Edom is the prime example of the fate of the nations. Thus Edom is not being singled out for God's judgment. As Israel was judged, so all nations will be judged. Justice will be done as Edom, along with the nations, receives just recompense according to what it has done (Obad 15; cf. Joel 3:7).

In Obadiah 2-14, Edom is the sole addressee. But this last section addresses all Gentile nations, as well as Israel and Judah, whose final destiny is contrasted with that of the nations. Therefore, "you" (plural) in Obadiah 16 is best understood as referring to Israel and Judah. As "you," Israel and Judah, drank the cup of God's wrath (cf. Jer 49:12; 25:15-26), so will all the nations, including Edom, drink the same cup (Is 51:22-23).

The annihilation of Edom (Obad 18) is an event cast in eschatological language that may still await its final fulfillment. Furthermore, there a distinction between national and individual destiny that allows the holy remnant in Edom and all nations to be saved (Amos 9:12; Zech 14:16).

"In that day," all high places or nations will be lowered and every proud heart will be humiliated, for the Lord alone will be exalted as King (Obad 21; Is 2:1-5, 11; Mic 4:2-5).

Bibliography. D. Barthelemy, *Critique Textuelle de L'Ancien Testament,* (Fribourg: Presses Universitaires, 1982) 3:697-706; J. R. Bartlett, *Edom and the Edomites,* Journal for the Study of the Old Testament Supplement Series 77 (Sheffield: JSOT Press, 1989).

HYUNHYE JUNIA POKRIFKA-JOE

JONAH

Introduction

Jonah seems to be the ultimate patriarchal book in which women never appear, the main characters are one man and his God, and even the backdrop is masculine—sailors on the high seas, a king and his court. Yet for all its masculine characteristics this story transcends gender and implicitly attacks racism, sexism, ageism and any -ism that questions God's full acceptance of all human beings and God's freedom to bestow good gifts on anyone.

One of the main issues in studies of Jonah over the last century has concerned its historicity. The debates over whether this is history or a type of parable can be found in any of the larger commentaries. More recently scholars have laid aside these discussions to concentrate on the message and themes of Jonah, an approach that will be followed here. The current concerns now revolve around the genre and tone of the book. Is the story told didactically or satirically, ironically or sympathetically?

Clearly the author writes with a purpose. But he or she is also an expert storyteller who delights in playing with words to create suspense and heighten the twists in the tale. No wonder it has spawned so many children's storybooks. Unfortunately much of the author's art is often lost in translation. As an example, a major key word in the book is *gadol,* meaning "great." It occurs fourteen times, with many plays on its different nuances (great city, great storm, great fear, great fish), yet the translation *great* occurs only six times in the NRSV. This is a story about a great nation but an even greater God who creates great events to bring about salvation. Against this background the author seems to mock Jonah's great anger and great happiness as small-minded self-centeredness.

Perhaps one of the greatest skills of the narrator is to leave tantalizing gaps that require the reader's imagination and involvement in the plot. For many people, familiar with the story from Sunday school or sermons, these gaps, filled by teacher and preacher, are not readily obvious. Therefore the book, short as it is, repays careful rereading. One of the greatest enigmas of the book revolves around Jonah's behavior, and we receive little guidance until the end. Does he head for Joppa scared, rebellious, confused, or . . . ? The omission of motive by the narrator creates space for us to fill the gap creatively and imaginatively. If we place ourselves in Jonah's shoes and ponder the enigma anew, God is free to pinpoint our fears, rebellions or confusions and speak to us through the book.

The book gives no indication of either a date of composition or a date for the events, if they are historical. Second Kings 14:25 mentions a prophet named Jonah, son of Amittai, in the early eighth century, a time before Nineveh was a real threat to Israel; he may or may not be the same Jonah. Certain language and style factors suggest that the book was written in its current form after the exile, but this does not help in dating its origin. It seems that the typically anonymous author has deliberately omitted the normal time reference "in the days of . . . " in order to create a timeless narrative, relevant to all.

As a timeless narrative the story is understandable with minimal background information. Nevertheless it is a very Jewish tale. Gentile readers will need to recall the strict segregation that became an increasing part of Jewish life. This God-ordained separation was designed for Israel's protection, to lessen the temptation to apostasy and syncretism, to enable holiness (*see* Holiness and Wholeness). Yet the human tendency is so often to abuse and misuse God-given guidelines, to bend the rules or to apply them so rigidly that their purpose is defeated. Such legalistic application resulted in Ezra's banishment of foreign wives and Peter's reluctance to eat with Gentiles. Jonah, along with the stories of Ruth and Rahab, is part of the Old Testament's counterbalance to such application. They remind us that God's guidelines exist because of our weakness, and we must not duck the hard task of rightly discerning when they are not applicable. Similarly we need to recall that Nineveh was to Israel what Hitler was to the Jews and erase any notion that such divine punishment would be unjust.

The narrator's skills extend to a careful structuring of the book into two mirror halves. Many scholars wish to exclude Jonah 2 as an ancient hymn of praise inserted into the book at a later stage. If so, the psalm has been extremely well integrated and is now so essential to the structure that it cannot be excluded or passed over.

Outline

1:1-17	The Consequences of Disobedience
2:1-10	Jonah's Monologue of Praise
3:1-10	The Consequences of Obedience
4:1-11	Jonah's Monologue of Complaint

Commentary

The Consequences of Disobedience (Jon 1)

This book is full of surprises from the outset. It commences as an oracle of judgment like Joel or Obadiah, but this illusion of prophecy quickly gives way to narrative. The next surprise is Jonah's actions. We know of reluctant prophets and patriarchs prepared to argue back, but nowhere do we find such mute disobedience. Is Jonah God's rebellious teenage son, flagrantly insubordinate behind a stone wall of silence? Or is he too compassionate to declare judgment on a people he knows not? Or is he so petrified by Nineveh and the nature of the commission that he runs blindly in the opposite direction? As the story goes on we begin to wonder if he is callously uncaring or blindly self-absorbed. Is his affirmation of faith to the sailors (Jon 1:9) genuine belief or a parroting of religious formula? Is he suicidally depressed (prepared to be thrown overboard but not quite willing to jump) or magnanimously sacrificial (giving his life for the sailors)? At this stage we do not know how to read Jonah.

But one thing is clear: Jonah has a completely inadequate understanding of Yahweh. He seems to think that if Yahweh is up above, out there (Jon 1:2), he can go far enough down and in to escape the God of Israel—down to Joppa, into the ship, down into the hold, down into the sea (symbol of godless chaos) and even down into death (Sheol). He has yet to learn the truth of the psalmist that it is impossible to flee God's reach (Ps 139:8-10). He has also to discover, it seems, that God is preeminently a merciful God. In his utmost extremity he seems to have no concept that God might relent if he were to repent (Jon 1:6). Is this the ultimate in stubborn impenitence or a tragically faulty theology? Is the god he is running from not God at all?

In response God does not gently woo Jonah back but actively pursues him, engaged in a policy of tough love. God even encourages Jonah in his downward and inward flight. The sailors are prevented from carrying out anything that might spare Jonah's life, and when Jonah has gone as far down into chaos and destruction as he can, God provides a great fish to take Jonah further down and further in.

But Jonah's disobedience has consequences for others. The sailors suffer, the cargo owners suffer, even the inanimate ship suffers (she is personified as "reckoning herself to be broken into pieces," Jon 1:4, author's translation). Yet lest we despair, we should note that through Jonah's flight the sailors are brought to true fear of Yahweh. There is nothing God cannot redeem. And in Jonah 1:16 we get our first intimation that outsiders might be insiders, that pagan sailors may worship more genuinely than Jonah.

And even for Jonah, author of their misfortune, there is hope. Jonah has chosen, and Jonah has acted. Whatever the motives, Jonah has been in control of his life. But now that he has gone as far as he can, he finds his supposed control illusory. He has brought himself to the position where others now control his life: sailors pick him up and throw him overboard; a fish swallows him up. The self-absorbed subject becomes an object. But behind the sailors and the fish is an even bigger subject who is at last free to act directly. It may not yet be apparent, but a turning point has been reached.

Jonah's Monologue of Praise (Jon 2)

A psalm of praise is so surprising at this point that many scholars relegate it to a later addition. Not only is its effusive praise at odds with our taciturn Jonah but also Jonah is hardly high and dry yet. A lament of penitence perhaps, but not praise for past salvation. Yet in a text that delights in undermining readers' expectations this psalm is quite plausible. Structurally Jonah 2 balances Jonah 4; both involve a monologue concerning God's nature and center on the relationship between Jonah and God.

Jonah has been running from God, running to the point where Sheol seems to be his only escape. And what does he find but that God will not even allow him the luxury of death? Or is the fish Sheol for Jonah, and does he find that even there, God is?

In Jonah 2:1 (Jon 2:2 Heb.) an interesting and puzzling grammatical change occurs. In Jonah 1:17 (Jon 2:1 Heb.), Jonah is swallowed into the inner parts or belly (*m'h*, a masculine noun) of a masculine fish (*dag*), while in Jonah 2:1 he prays from the belly (*m'h*) of a very feminine fish (*dagah*). This change has caused much debate and speculation (Jon 2:10 [Jon 2:11 Heb.] returns to the masculine *dag*). In Jonah 2:3 (Jon 2:4 Heb.) Jonah cries out again from the belly of Sheol, but this time the word for belly is the feminine *beten*, a synonym with the added possible translation "womb." The image is incongruous. Sheol is the place of death, not birth, a barren womb (Prov 30:16) from which no one comes up (Job 7:9) and from whence none can praise Yahweh (Ps 6:5). Yet always in Jonah the impossible and the improbable are the reality. Jonah, who has sought death to escape God, discovers that death is his place of capture, his womb of rebirth.

Having come face to face with the death he sought and finding himself thankfully very much alive, Jonah is on the path to a proper understanding of God. He learns in a new way that the God who inhabits Israel's holy temple (Jon 2:7 [Jon 2:8 Heb.]) is a God of rescue and salvation. His response is, as it can only be, praise, worship and thanksgiving. Jonah's conversion and education have begun, but he has further lessons still to learn.

The Consequences of Obedience (Jon 3)

Yahweh is a God who never gives up on people, a God of second chances. So Jonah 3, mirroring Jonah 1, begins again with the call to Jonah. And again Jonah arises, but this time he hastens, obediently it seems, to Nineveh, where almost immediately upon entering he begins to call out his message of doom. His lesson is now learned, his conversion complete—or is it? Jonah 4 springs yet another twist to the story that suggests a different view. A trek of only one day into a city of three days' journey may not be eagerness in obedience but the bare minimum required to fulfill God's command. The king, as representative of the nation and the normal target for God's prophets, is left to hear the message secondhand.

If, by God's grace, Jonah's disobedience brings pagan sailors to true fear, how much more does God use his obedience, eager or reluctant. Such immediate response, such total repentance by the Ninevites, is little short of miraculous, and thus the storyteller springs the next surprise. Not even Israel in its best moments heeded the call of God's prophets so swiftly or so completely. The story begins to bite. The king's speech is a model of repentance of which any prophet would be proud. There is evidence of contrition; there is reform of lifestyle and finally a proper humility before the sovereignty of God (Joel 2:14).

For Jonah there is none of the scorn, derision, imprisonment or even simple apathy that most prophets face. The extent of faith and remorse borders on the unbelievable. The thought of the renowned king of Nineveh in sackcloth, Job-like among the ashes, while whole herds of Ninevite cattle cease grazing to cry to the God of Israel is preposterous. The writer is not averse to playing up the story with a little hyperbole and plenty of puns (e.g., in Hebrew "evil" and "feed" sound similar, as do "decree" and "taste") to make the point and bring the story to its unexpected climax.

In a fitting finale, Yahweh, the God of second chances, also repents of the evil intended. Yahweh is no aloof, remote deity but a God of relationship. Prayers are heard, and God is not above altering plans, particularly plans of judgment, as a result of repentance. We meet here another of the key words in the book: *ra'ah* ("evil"). The author of Jonah is not afraid to attribute evil to God: the evil of the storm (Jon 1:7; Jon 1:8, "calamity") and the evil of planned destruction (Jon 3:10). Such evil is a fitting, just and proper response to human evil. Jonah's disobedience endangers the lives of countless Ninevites who had in their turn created innumerable victims of their violence (Jon 3:8). God is not oblivious to the evil of the world. The cries of the oppressed (so often feminine!) rise up to Yahweh (Jon 1:1), and this story holds out for everyone hope of justice in this world. Yet paradoxically and thankfully the story also offers to all the assurance of a second chance, a new start.

Jonah's Monologue of Complaint (Jon 4)

So the story has reached a happy denouement. Jonah's task has been completed, the Ninevites have chosen faith, and God's great mercy has been revealed. A concluding chapter seems superfluous. But we would be wrong to see Jonah 4 as simply a moralistic afterword in case the message is overlooked. Yet again the author startles the readers, reminding them that there are three strands to this story: Jonah, God and the Gentiles. Not all is sewn up yet; the real climax is still to come.

Jonah, sidelined in Jonah 3, is the true center of the story. At last this enigmatic character will be revealed. Until now his motives have been masked, his actions ambiguous, his speech short and brusque. Nothing has prepared us for the sudden exposure of a deep, intense anger. Few English translations capture the vehemence of Jonah 4:1, which plays again on the key words. God's actions were in Jonah's mind a great evil. Only Jonah could turn the magnificent creed of Exodus (Ex 34:6; Ps 86:15; Joel 2:13) into a vindictive denunciation. Immediately the piety of Jonah 2 and the obedience of Jonah 3 come under serious question, and the negative evaluations of Jonah 1 resurface. Disaster brought forth praise in Jonah 2. Success brings forth lament. Everything in this book is turned on its head in dramatic overstatement.

What could be so bad as to provoke a death wish in Jonah? He has not been persecuted or ignored but has achieved a success the envy of any other prophet. Is he disgruntled because his reputation is tarnished—a false prophet whose word does not come true? Is he angry that God should show mercy on Gentiles, even on Israel's greatest oppressor? Does he feel let down, betrayed by an irrational God whose seemingly arbitrary mercy triumphs over justice and consistency? And what does he go out to see? Whether Nineveh will be destroyed? Or more subtly, how long the Ninevites will keep their change of heart—is repentance skin deep? Has God been conned? The author does not tell us, but the gap is worth pondering. In Jonah's shoes, what would make us so angry?

Yet Yahweh is indeed gracious and merciful, slow to anger, the God of third chances who will not leave Jonah to his self-pity. So God seeks to engage him in conversation. Jonah, however, is not ready for dialogue. Therefore God must again resort to tough love to turn Jonah from his evil, as the Ninevites (and God) have turned from theirs. God appoints a *qiqayon* to shelter Jonah. What sort of plant or bush this was is much disputed, but it brought relief from Jonah's distress ("evil" in Heb.). For the first time Jonah is happy, exceedingly happy; in the measure that he was angry so now he rejoices. But God has only just started appointing. Appointments for protection, a fish (Jon 1:17) and a bush are succeeded by appointments for destruction, a worm and an east wind.

So at last taciturn Jonah is goaded into dialogue, and the full extent of his self-centeredness is revealed. Jonah is not interested in others, certainly not Gentile sailors and Ninevites. His concern is himself and occasionally his God. "I" and "me" occur twelve times in the few sentences he speaks, and even his praise in chapter 2 has twice as much "me" as "you." But God has caught him in a trap that will bring him face to face with his selfishness. He must either answer God's insistent question in the negative and confirm that sovereign Yahweh may do what Yahweh pleases, or he must answer (as he does) in the positive and confirm that it is right for God to be compassionate.

What are we to make of Jonah? There are elements of caricature that support a pointed, satirical portrayal of Israel's self-righteous exclusivism. But such views overlook the positive aspects of Jonah 2 and Jonah 3. So too do those views that write Jonah off as a petulant and rebellious prophet. Jonah is sullen and self-centered, but he can also be obedient. He knows that God is his salvation and hope, and if at times he acts from mixed motives does that not make him more human? Above all he is a person struggling to understand a God who is far bigger than he ever conceived. He is a finite human being caught in the tension between justice and mercy, the paradox of a sovereign God who gives way before prayer, the reality of a God who asks of us outrageous things.

The book is about God's staggering compassion on all people everywhere, even those who seem furthest from love. Our

God delights to give gifts to those whom we think are beyond the pale. But this is only one strand of a multifaceted message. The center is Jonah, representative of Israel and every reader and his or her relationship with God. Even God's saved people can harbor ingrained prejudices, legalistic attitudes and unacknowledged self-centeredness. We can seek death rather than life and work from a far too small picture of God. But God pursues us, ever offering a bigger perspective. We do not know if Jonah needed a fourth chance, but we can respond to the writer's invitation to examine our response.

ELIZABETH A. HARPER

MICAH

Introduction

The book of Micah is typical of the prophetic books that stem from the eighth century (Isaiah, Hosea, Amos). The primary message of these books is despair and outrage at perceived social disintegration with dire warnings of the consequences. The prophets all felt they got short shrift from their comfortable, confident and unconcerned contemporaries, who saw them at best as reactionary scaremongers and at worst as dangerous political radicals. But their books, in the form we have them, are not just doom and gloom. The world that is is contrasted with a world that could be, indeed, God willing, a world that will be, in which all injustice will be righted, all aggression vanquished and all oppressed released.

Micah's particular contribution is concern for the policies and practices that create the poor. His ire is strongest against the political and economic actions (debt-inducing loans, land seizures, uncontrolled violence, extortionate prices, fraudulent payments) that impoverish the hardworking backbone of society. But he does not spare the religious establishment for its support of the wealthy, and he sees it all as a failure of true faith, true submission to the laws and worship of Israel's savior YHWH.

Micah is of particular interest to women for his championing of justice in the name of God for all people, including women and children. But he is also of interest for the extent of the female imagery he uses in his pregnant pictorial poetry. His imagery recognizes the good and bad in humanity, male and female, and overturns some common stereotypes.

Micah 1:1 suggests dates between 750 and 700 B.C. Many scholars have tried unsuccessfully to date individual prophecies more specifically. It would seem that a degree of generalization has taken place so that each era could identify in the book its besetting sins and God's discipline through current events. Moreover, while most scholars believe the core of Micah comes from this period, the extent of this core is hotly debated. Evidence suggests it was common practice for prophecies to be collected, added to and commented on over time. In this way God's living word was interpreted anew for each generation. For this commentary the canonical book in its final form is considered the Word of God to be interpreted today.

Micah the prophet is an enigmatic figure. This is perhaps deliberate, for the focus is on the word of YHWH, not the servant. We assume Micah is male from the use of the Hebrew masculine "you" in Micah 2:6, although the name could be feminine. We learn most about him by examining his concerns. His keen sense of social justice is everywhere evident. He feels deeply for ordinary people struggling to make ends meet, and he fights strongly against any unjust structures and activities that tip such people into poverty. He starts by championing the cause of rural citizens (Mic 2:2) who ought to be self-sufficient contributors to the economy. He then moves on to the oppressed townsfolk who lose their hard-earned profits to extortion (Mic 3:11). His courage to stand against the tide is glimpsed when he is goaded into rousing self-defense (Mic 2:6-7; 3:8), but it is at great personal cost (Mic 1:8).

The later part of the eighth century was an unsettled time. The cost of economic boom and social revolution during King Uzziah's golden era may have resulted in a growing gap between poor and prosperous attended by a disintegration of the traditional social order. On top of this, international peace was shattered by renewed aggression from Assyria. Samaria's fall in 722 B.C. sent shock waves through Judah as well as an influx of refugees to strain the economy. Judah's fear was justified, for in 701 B.C. Assyria marched on Jerusalem, ravaging Micah's region, the Shephelah. Although Jerusalem survived, Judah was a chastened, smaller and poorer nation in 700 B.C. The country struggled on for another century before defeat and exile. For pockets of time, life was doubtless settled and secure, and Micah's threats may have seemed alarmist, but as time wore on, instability increased.

We cannot be certain of the status of women in ancient Israel, although public society at least seems to have been male-dominated. Women's prime role was probably homemaking and child rearing in an extended family. This family was the only security, and widows, single and childless women were particularly at their mercy (*see* Widows; Singleness). In the unsettled times women were doubtless even more vulnerable than men, often victims of rape and slavery through warfare (*see* Violence). Micah recognizes women's vulnerability and in Micah 2:9 singles out women for special mention. Nevertheless, it is also likely that many women, especially those of wealth, had some freedom, authority and responsibility. Not all women were oppressed, and some were doubtless oppressors.

The seemingly rambling style of the prophetic genre is not easy to comprehend. The prophets have often been likened to anthologies, whose structure comes solely from the addition, over time, of small, distinct, unconnected prophecies. (Micah 1—3 is often considered original to the eighth century, while Micah 4—5 is dated to the exile, and Micah 6—7 is viewed as a postexilic afterword.) However, this analogy may overlook the poetical and rhetorical nature of Hebrew prophecy. For the prophet, forthtelling, or God's perspective on the world as it is, was as important as foretelling, or God's intentions as a result. Both issues are developed through the interweaving of imaginative, evocative and provocative poetry. As with all poetry, the normal rules of logic, grammar and transition could be flouted for effect. Recent attention to the rhetoric and poetry of Micah has highlighted how much these devices unite the book. There is a deliberate alternation of God's love-engendered judgment (or rather discipline) with reconciling restoration.

The book is aware that our world is not as it should be, especially for women. All who have power, wealth and authority (primarily men) are warned to take stock. Apathy, indifference and a blinkered parochialism are as sinful as outright wickedness if they fail to prevent injustice. Such is God's love for all people, oppressed and oppressors, that this old world must be overturned and wealth, power and authority redistributed, however painful such discipline may be. Only thus can a new world be born in which those who were once rich and poor, Israelite and Gentile, male and female might worship YHWH equally. Most chapters alternate between discipline and restoration, what is and what will be, but the pattern occurs on a larger scale in the structure of the book. Thus Micah 1 and Micah 7 mirror each other, as do Micah 2, Micah 3 and Micah 6; and Micah 4 and Micah 5.

Outline

1:1-16	Lament for a World Gone Wrong
2:1-13	Justice for Rural Citizens
3:1-12	Justice for Townspeople and Temple
4:1-13	A New World Through New Birth
5:1-15	A New World Through Reversal
6:1-16	Justice for YHWH
7:1-20	Second Lament for a World Gone Wrong

Commentary

Lament for a World Gone Wrong (Mic 1)

After the introductory formula the book opens with a theophany—an earth-shattering appearance of God—not to herald a glorious rescue, as the hearers may have expected, but rather to proclaim judgment and discipline. The rebuke of God is directed first at the northern kingdom (Israel) typified by its capital, Samaria. However, for Micah this is merely a preliminary warning shot for Judah and its capital, Jerusalem. As God's prophet Micah's task is to proclaim the verdict perhaps in the hope of provoking repentance (Jer 26:18-19). Micah's opening ploy is therefore a clever, humorous, attention-grabbing lament, full of untranslatable puns. ("Tell it not in Telham; wail, O inhabitants of Whaleton"). Yet underneath the black humor is heartfelt sorrow. Idolatry eventually brings destruction, and often it destroys the little people—the poor, the women, the children. The prophet has heard their cries, past and future, and laments in solidarity with them while provoking the complacent to fear and action.

As is typical of the prophets, Micah uses poetry and its attendant metaphors and imagery to announce his subversive, God-inspired protest against a world gone dreadfully wrong. His first image portrays Israel as a culpable defendant (Mic 1:2), but he moves swiftly on to Israel, the prostitute (Mic 1:7). Today this metaphor seems harsh and disturbing, portraying unfaithfulness as a feminine vice and suggesting subconsciously an association between women and evil in readers' imaginations. Aware now of such implicit messages we ask, "Why must Israel at its worst be portrayed as a female prostitute and not as, say, a greedy, fraudulent male trader or a selfish, wayward son?" The difficulty of the imagery must not be understated or ignored, and we must struggle with it while keeping it in perspective.

We need to be careful of reading our sensitivities back into the original meaning. Who knows, Micah may have been horrified by such an implication. From the context it is clear that Micah is using an image for idolatry. Male (Deut 23:7-18; 1 Kings 14:24; 22:46) as well as female prostitution seems to have existed in Israel and was linked, at least in the prophet's mind, with some of the Canaanite fertility religions. The prophets starting with Hosea see the covenant relationship of Israel and God through the metaphor of marriage (*see*

Marriage), a marriage not between Israel as passive, silent bride bought by God but a marriage between two parties elevated to a real partnership. Yahweh and Israel have entered freely into this relationship (Josh 24:15-23) and undertaken voluntarily the mutual obligations of loyalty, fidelity and commitment. For the prophets, both parties

Fertility goddess thought to assure agricultural and reproductive success. (Micah 1:7)

are accountable, YHWH (Mic 7:19-20) as well as Israel. However, for the eighth-century prophets Israel's betrayal of God is everywhere apparent in injustice and religious compromise. Yet no one else seems to see it. Their burning goal is to waken people to the hollowness of the marriage that they may return to mutual love before it ends in divorce (*see* Divorce). The prophets therefore deliberately use harsh, shocking, disturbing language to forestall a harsh, shocking, disturbing reality.

But while this might clear Micah of deliberate misogynism, it does not deal with the underlying patriarchalism and the problem of linking evil and femininity. Once again context can ease although not eradicate this difficulty. The Hebrew writers invariably use concrete cultural images where we would use abstract propositions. They paint vivid word pictures to communicate ideas, but they rarely stick long with one image. The prostituted feminine Samaria (Mic 1:7) is mirrored by the degenerate masculine Jacob (Mic 3:8) and the guilty masculine Israel (Mic 6:2). The nation in its injustice is likened not just to a prostitute but also to a butcher (Mic 3:2-3), a masculine aggressor (Mic 2:9), a bloodthirsty hunter (Mic 7:2) and a thorn bush (Mic 7:4). Nor are all the feminine images negative. If Israel is a prostitute, she is also a bereaved mother (Mic 1:16) and a woman in the pangs of labor (Mic 3:10) who brings forth salvation for the nation (Mic 5:3). She is a sovereign ruler (Mic 4:8) and an invincible female ox (Mic 4:13). She is beloved daughter destined for redemption in contrast to gloating masculine enemies destined for destruction (Mic 4:10-13). Micah used a mixture of good and bad, feminine and masculine imagery alongside many other pictures from his time.

Similarly, although YHWH is the humiliated husband, never the wronged wife, God is also shepherd (Mic 2:12), gentle teacher of peace (Mic 4:2) and compassionate gatherer of the afflicted (Mic 4:6; 7:19) who exhibits traditional masculine and feminine attributes. To talk of our relationship with God we are forced to use metaphors from our known world and culture. Micah's reality was in many ways a patriarchal society, and his metaphors cannot help but reflect that. In his world, the image of Israel as an unfaithful husband would never have had the same shock value.

God doesn't wait for us to get it fully right before using us, but rather in the midst of our and our culture's imperfections God communicates through us while still working on our redemption. In a changed world and a different culture, certain metaphors, such as Micah's image of a prostitute, must be used with care, as they fail to communicate as intended. The task for each believer is to redescribe those eternal characteristics of God in images fitting for today. In this we need to imitate Micah with a wide range of imagery—masculine, feminine and neutral.

From the indictment of Israel and Judah we move to Micah's heartfelt but witty rhetorical lament in which Judah remains personified as a woman—daughter, mother, mourner. There have been many debates as to the significance of feminine pronouns ("she," "her") for describing Jerusalem and Judah. All Hebrew nouns are gendered masculine or feminine (there is no neuter), and the designations may not be significant. Jerusalem may be "she" simply because the words for "city," "inhabitants" and "land" are feminine. This in turn may have led to villages being thought of as daughters to their mother cities. But each step in the process inevitably acquires deeper symbolism and significance. Did the designations stick because towns and villages were believed to provide stability, nurture and community, just like women? Is this a symbol of a positive regard for women in Israelite society? We can only surmise.

What is intriguing is the way Micah switches between masculine and feminine forms. In Micah 1 the majority of the words for "you" are feminine, as also in Micah 4, while Micah 5 is wholly masculine, but neither is more positive or negative than the other. Perhaps it is part of his policy to have a mixture of images.

For Christians there is an added dimension to this personification of Israel as woman as well as man. Too often the Christian church has portrayed Israel as an unmitigated failure, forgetting the great debt owed to her. Israel is our biblical role model: not a superhero we cannot emulate or a saint we should follow blindly but a model with whom we can empathize and from whom we take encouragement. Old Testament role models show life as it is. Israel struggled to be God's people in a fallen world, sometimes with success, sometimes with failure, and her struggle mirrors ours. She has walked this earth before us, and we would do well to learn from her, remembering that through her faithfulness salvation eventually came. She is our older sister and our older brother, a role model that is feminine as well as masculine, positive as well as negative. Therefore all of us, male and female, can find in her our experiences of faith and so learn faithfulness.

Justice for Rural Citizens (Mic 2)

Having softened his audience with a witty lament, Micah now justifies his condemnation, graphically highlighting the evil they refuse to see. He proclaims the harsh indictment the victims can never utter. In this chapter he speaks particularly for the villagers and small farmers of the countryside, those who have lost their land, lodgings and livelihood through violence or extortionate debt or both. In so doing he particularly highlights the plight of women (Mic 2:9) as casualties. God, Micah thunders, is not unaware of the injustice. The oppressed are to have hope. God may tarry, but the day of justice is coming. It will come in this world, not the next. The prophets hold out light in the darkness for all who suffer at the hands of others, a flame of hope that might seem small and distant but is nevertheless a promise of freedom.

But this flame of hope to the oppressed is a dangerous fire to the oppressors and especially to the complacent, to the secure and to the contented. Those who see injustice and do nothing or do not see it risk being burned. When the world gets turned upside down by the coming of God's justice, they may well find they were on the wrong side. Micah struggles with the interrelatedness of us all. He wants to affirm that we are each accountable for our deeds (Mic 2:1) or lack of them. Yet at the same time he is aware that the innocent bystander gets caught in sin's fallout. Punishment necessarily has effects far beyond the punished. Therefore, if for no other reason, we must not only act justly but also must actively seek justice for all.

Typical of the prophets, Micah's justice is strict justice—an eye for an eye, a tooth for a tooth. Those who seize fields (Mic 2:2) shall lose land (Mic 2:4); those who plot evil (Mic 2:1) will be the victims of an evil plot (Mic 2:3). To the Western Christian free of oppression and schooled in mercy, this seems rough justice and harsh punishment. For the oppressed victim it may seem too little and too late. It is direct justice, strict equality that counters our all-too-human desire for revenge and retaliation. In pain we often long to inflict more pain, to make others suffer. But this is not God's way. If there is to be punishment, it will be just, fair and equal. YHWH longs to grant mercy, but mercy without repentance rubber stamps evil. Therefore God must pronounce justice or at least threaten it. Those who oppress are warned that they risk becoming oppressed.

Such a subversive message wins Micah no friends in high places, and the chapter is punctuated by a terse argument between Micah and his opponents. The chapter then closes on an ambiguous note. Micah 2:12-13 appears to provide a note of postexilic hope, mercy and restoration in place of punishment, thus providing a rather star-

Land Ownership & Economic Justice in Israel

Private property is upheld in the Torah, but the ownership of land in Israel was not absolute. God is the ultimate landowner, and the rights of human ownership are limited by God's demands for justice. Since most families lived by farming and keeping herds, the law made sure that the poor were not denied property. After the exodus, God provided for an equitable distribution of land among the families and tribes. It was divided by lot, with the larger pieces going to the larger tribes. The land was to stay within the tribe. If there was no son to inherit the family plot, a daughter would inherit as long as she married within the tribe (Num 36:1-10). Land could be bought and sold by women as well as men (Prov 31:16), but not on a permanent basis. After a sale, property not in a walled city could be bought back any time by the original owner or a close relative. If it was not bought back, it had to be returned to the original owner in the year of jubilee. In addition to the laws on ownership, other provisions made sure the poor had means of livelihood: laws that allowed gleaning and restricted what could be taken as surety for loans. These laws showed particular concern for widows and orphans, who were especially vulnerable.

However, Israel failed to follow God's commands for economic justice. There is no evidence that the year of jubilee was ever implemented. And in the time of the monarchy, wealthy landowners and kings acquired, by force or sale, vast landholdings. God condemned the powerful who deprived the common people of their economic rights and their land (Is 3:14-15; 5:8; 10:1-2; Ezek 46:18; Amos 8:4-4; Mic 2:1-5).

PATRICIA B. BOYLAND

---

tling juxtaposition to the previous judgment speeches. The verses are, however, more nuanced than this. Their ambiguity threatens exile while promising restoration. For the book, discipline and reconciliation go hand in hand. Judgment is not the last word. For the punished too there is a flame of hope. The wayward child is chastised, not disinherited.

Justice for Townspeople and Temple (Mic 3)

Micah turns his attention to Jerusalem and the scandals within the walls of the sacred city. He commences a three-pronged attack on the unholy alliance of prophet, priest and prince, who out of greed butcher the people (Mic 3:1-3). All things come for a price, and a rip-off one at that. The image of butchery is among the most horrific in the book, used for its pure shock value. One can almost imagine the suffering crowds lapping it up and cheering Micah on in the face of official disgust at such coarse, crude language in the name of God. Micah is not afraid to work himself into a passion over the issue of justice. Exceedingly emotive language does not embarrass him. Micah's example affirms that it is right to be passionate about injustice, to speak out boldly against oppression, to fight for those who suffer.

As in Micah 2, Micah affirms that such injustice and oppression do not escape God's concern. Micah alone of the eighth-century prophets dares to prophesy the fall of Jerusalem (Mic 3:12). This chapter, however, is addressed not just to the political rulers but also to the religious leaders. Like Jesus (Mt 7:21), Micah claims that it is not enough to cry "Lord, Lord," to speak in God's name, to carry out the rituals, to trust in YHWH while practicing selfishness, complacency and self-interest. Those who truly speak for God are those who stand for what is right though it ruins their income and reputation. In Micah justice comes before piety, or rather, justice is the true sign of piety.

In all this, no self-effacing modesty prevents Micah from blowing his own trumpet (Mic 3:8). The lack of self-esteem that afflicts so many women (and men) does not inhibit Micah. He believes God has spoken to him personally, commissioned and empowered him for a task. But isn't this ironic hypocrisy? Having brazenly chastised his opponent's self-assurance, does he replace it with his own? If it is wrong for the false prophets to be assured, isn't Micah arrogant to claim it is right for him? In the light of so many examples of abuse of power and self-seeking in the name of God, is it possible for Micah to claim that God has endorsed his point of view and not theirs? How can he be sure?

Rather than hypocrisy, Micah's claim may evidence a deeper paradox. We must question our assurance, and yet we must also act boldly. Too often our motives are mixed, and we deceive ourselves into believing our views are God's views. Yet at the same time self-doubt, self-pity and low self-esteem can be selfish excuses to avoid the tasks we are commissioned for. Our certainties must be tested, as Micah's self-assurance is tested, by opposition, by doubt, by the reality of his own failings (Mic 7:1-10) in order to weed out any self-deception. But at the same time, this does not hinder the work of God as he understands it. So it is that God's people are called to walk in the paradox of humility (Mic 6:8) and boldness. We must question; we must let God question which side of the paradox is out of balance. Have we spent too long in humility or become overconfident?

A New World Through New Birth (Mic 4)

At Micah 4 a remarkable change of direction occurs, so remarkable that many want to see this chapter as a later exilic addition. It may have been a new word from God, but it now highlights the canonical book's juxtaposition of discipline and restoration. God's judgment is not vengefully destructive purely for the sake of it. The world is torn down in order to build up. Pain is a reality that in God's hands can become redemptive.

So far Micah has proclaimed God's opinion of the world as it is, an opinion greatly at odds with the official view. This opinion will lead, Micah says, to the destruction of all that is rotten, even, if necessary, Jerusalem (Mic 3:12), but it will be replaced by a world as it should be. It is to this vision that the book turns. It is a vision of a new Zion that was already well known (Is 2:2-4) but worth repeating, a vision in which the wrongs of the past are righted. Force is forsaken, fear is forbidden, and freedom is forever. In this new world, which is very much this-worldly, the roots of violence, envy and poverty have been tackled. All individuals are now sustained and satisfied by their own fig trees and vines, symbols of sufficiency, plenty, prosperity for everyone.

In this new world many things are reversed, and among them, it seems, the status of women. The lame, those driven away and those cast off whom God restores (Mic 4: 6-7) are all feminine, although normally masculine forms are used (e.g., in Deut 30:4; Is 11:12). The result is ambiguous. The feminine probably indicates that this is a metaphor for Israel personified now as a wounded woman. The Israelites no doubt thought of themselves as strong and masculine, but in exile they were to discover their weakness and vulnerability. They were womanlike in the face of their enemies. In the new world order, however, this weakness will be turned to strength. Yet this new, strong nation with power, dominion and sovereignty remains in feminine form. It is Zion pictured as a woman in leadership who will bring good government over the land.

Some interpreters argue that Zion portrayed as a daughter (Mic 4:8) is an insult to womankind, while others see it as a compliment, a symbol of elevation (compare Europe's concept of fatherland). At this distance from Israelite culture it is hard to decide whether the personification is a sign of incipient patriarchy or revolutionary equality. What is clear is that in this chapter daughter Zion becomes a positive image that does not fit the stereotypical roles for women.

The fact that the lame and outcasts can be understood as a metaphor for Israel should not stop us from us also taking them as a metaphor for suffering women generally. The ambiguity of the verse allows both meanings to hover on the horizon. Women, who in the old world have been weak, vulnerable and wounded, will now be restored, made a strong nation with God rather than man as their leader. In this context God makes what may seem a sacrilegious confession. God seems to admit to afflicting them, doing them evil or calamity (Mic 4:6). Micah is not afraid to lay evil at God's door (see also Mic 2:3), and in this he portrays the reality that in war and exile the innocent suffer with the guilty. Sin, in Micah's understanding, was so endemic that only the overthrow of all society could eradicate it. Inevitably the blameless would suffer too. Faith in God is rarely a foolproof protection from harm. But this does not mean that God is without compassion. Once again Micah asserts, God knows, God cares, and God is bringing about a new world.

But such a wonderful utopia is yet a far cry from the Jerusalem we have only just seen reduced to a pile of ruins. The final half of this chapter bridges the gap between old Jerusalem and new Jerusalem, and that bridge is exile, that bridge is Babylon. The delight of deliverance must be preceded by the distress of discipline.

Once again Micah turns to feminine imagery, this time to prepare the people for the unimaginable—exile. Only women can provide him with a comprehensive metaphor for life-giving pain.

Labor and childbirth have always been perceived with great fear and great joy. Without epidurals and caesareans, the pain and the danger of childbirth were even greater then than today, as the Bible honestly acknowledges (Gen 25:22; 35:17-19; Jer 4:31). Up to a third of women may have died in childbirth. To use the image was to paint a grim picture of the agony and fatalities of exile. Paradoxically, birth has also been a time of great joy. In a society in which children were a woman's social security and immortality, barrenness was a social stigma as well as a personal sorrow (Gen 30:1; 1 Sam 1:6; *see* Barrenness and Fertility) Children are the enduring symbol of hope, of life, of future. And this too is captured in the prophet's image. Zion is in travail under the hand of discipline, but it is a discipline that will give birth to new life. By exile, Jerusalem's inhabitants are pulled screaming out of the security of their womblike city that can no longer hold them into the open fields of the world, while midwife Micah urges on Mother Zion (Writhe! Bring forth! Push! Mic 4:10). Finally a remnant is born, carrying within it the future hopes of its parents, YHWH and Zion, and the new life of the utopia. Only through the pain can this new hope arise. No other image could capture this dual reality so completely (*see* Midwifery and Birthing Practices; Childbearing and Rearing; Birth Pain Imagery).

Micah equates the painful labor with exile and the new utopia with the restoration of a redeemed and transformed remnant. The reality of return did not live up to the dream; the vision promised more than humanity could fulfill. Yet the fact of restoration seemed assurance that the promise was God-inspired. In its partial fulfillment it became a symbol of a final, future fulfillment, an image for the end of time. The birth pangs were not yet over; the world was still in labor. Jesus took up this image and breathed new life into a jaded hope (Mk 13:8). As Christians we still live between the old world of which Micah despaired and the new world finally made possible in Christ. Maybe we need to resurrect Micah's metaphor as we struggle to see the kingdom brought to life in our world and us.

It may be that the thought of a woman flailing in childbirth gave rise to the image on which this chapter closes—Jerusalem the threshing ox, or rather heifer, for Micah maintains the feminine forms. Horns denote power (Deut 33:17; 2 Sam 22:3), iron symbolizes strength (Ps 2:9; 1 Kings 22:11), and bronze implies harshness (Is 48:4). God commands Israel to break the mold, to break the expectations of others (Mic 4:11). She who once had to "arise and go" (Mic 2:10) now is told to "arise and thresh" (Mic 4:13). Breaking stereotypes seems to be part of the new world order. In the new ideal, the land of God's promise (portrayed as a woman) has power, strength and sovereignty. Once more the old things are turned upside down. That which was lacking through injustice and oppression is now restored abundantly. As Christians who claim to live in that long-awaited new order we should not be surprised to see old stereotypes cast down.

And it must not be overlooked that at the center of this new world YHWH takes up residence and all are united in worship of the God of justice, the God of love.

A New World Through Reversal (Mic 5)

Micah 5 continues this theme of contrast that so characterizes the new world. The humiliation of the current leadership (Mic 5:1) is set against the new leadership that God will raise up (Mic 5:2). Under this new leader all will be reversed, the strong destroyed, the conquerors vanquished, the exiled restored. Micah seems to be envisaging one or perhaps several leaders—new, warlike kings still of the great line of David but of a fresh branch contrasting sharply with the degenerate descendants who now hold power. But Matthew 2:6 rightly sees that the superlatives Micah heaps on this new savior go beyond anything to which an ordinary mortal can aspire.

The new age in this chapter seems to be much more violent and warlike than the one found in Micah 4. It is perhaps not surprising that we return to masculine imagery for Israel—not perhaps to its credit. Such imagery is difficult and seems to go against the Christian ideals of mercy and forgiveness. The chapter reminds us that revenge is a basic human desire and forgiveness is more easily exhorted than executed. Those with nothing to forgive need to be slow to judge those for whom forgiveness is difficult. Our Christian concerns may be eased although not eradicated by viewing the chapter as a further example of the theme of reversal. Often the only way to break the abuse of power is by rendering the oppressors powerless and conversely empowering those who have been oppressed. This is what this chapter graphically portrays. The danger, as we see played out on too many stages of the world, is that those so empowered become abusers of power in their turn. So, having established that triumphant enemies will become shattered adversaries, the chapter moves swiftly to the reassertion that power, wealth and authority belong only to God. In the new world horses and chariots will be destroyed, fortresses that demonstrate superiority and invincibility will be torn down, for no longer will we need protection. But above all false religion will be rooted out. The pseudo-gods, which seem to offer security, wealth and sparkling promises of certainty without the need for submission to YHWH, will be unmasked as the human concoctions they are. False gods legitimate human domination, pride and greed. They manipulate and can be manipulated (*see* Manipulation). In the new world, power will no longer be invested in the works of our hands, the self, the created order. No more will one person play god over another.

Justice for YHWH (Mic 6)

Micah 6 is often considered a new and later section. Certainly it seems to start again with a new calling to order of the court of judgment. We return from the future of hope into the forlorn reality, a reality far removed from the justice and goodwill of God. Rather than the short, sharp shock of vivid metaphors (Mic 1), the prophet chooses this time an impassioned plea to shame the people into repentance. Recalling God's continuous salvation in the past, he questions in increasing hyperbole what might be a fitting response of gratitude. The answer, when it comes, makes plain the current running throughout the book—what the Lord requires is not proper worship or sound doctrine or even great sacrifice but justice, humility and *hesed,* the lovingkindness, mercy and faithfulness characteristic of God. But *hesed* is missing in the violent, greedy, deceitful streets of the city, and therefore God out of *hesed* for the poor and oppressed will reestablish it. The choice is offered: Give up your power voluntarily or run the risk of having it taken from you. It is already slipping through your fingers.

Here, as always in the Old Testament, obedience to the commands and requirements of God is considered a response to the grace of God, not a prerequisite for it. God has already superabundantly demonstrated *hesed* for Israel. YHWH has already redeemed them, already bought them out of the Egypt of slavery, already settled them in a land of freedom (*see* Ancient and Modern Slavery). They have been granted a special relationship, a unique calling; what more could be given? How could Israel do anything but bow in gratitude and return the *hesed* in thankfulness?

Among those mighty saving acts, says Micah, was the sending of Miriam (Mic

6:4). Micah alone of biblical writers thinks to include Miriam in the list of God's exodus-ordained leaders (cf. Josh 24:5; 1 Sam 12:6; Ps 77:20; *see* Women as Leaders). Yet her role and status as a leader of Israel was well enough known to need no justification, explanation or comment (unlike Balak, Mic 6:5).

As with most female biblical characters there is an elusiveness to Miriam. The exodus story leads us to assume, but does not state, that she is the sister who so skillfully masterminded Moses' survival from the waters of the Nile (Ex 2:7). We are told that as a prophet she led the celebrations by the waters of salvation (Ex 15:20) but also that she instigated a rebellion against Moses and suffered for it (Num 12:1-15) before dying in the wilderness (Num 20:1). This meager account was fleshed out in various ways by Hebrew traditions. Some relegated Miriam's leadership to the teaching of women. Other traditions elevated her as a national savior, the provider of a never-ending well—sustenance in the desert wanderings. It is this latter, positive strand that Micah picks up, granting her a high role in salvation and leadership. He accords her the honor of standing in her own right, unqualified by relationship to husband, father or brother that was so typical of his male-dominated society. Once again Micah is not ashamed to ascribe God-given leadership and authority to women.

Second Lament for a World Gone Wrong (Mic 7)

The book concludes as it began with lament, but lament turned inward almost in despair (Mic 7:1). There was something rhetorical, showy, dramatic in the puns of Micah 1 that is missing from the bitter personal lament of Micah 7. The prophet of this chapter collapses in feelings of failure and ostracism, the opposite of the fiery strength of Micah 3:8. Pioneering for justice is often a long and sometimes lonely road. The altruism that leads to eschewing an easy life, to siding with the oppressed is no protection from the weight of injustice and sense of futility. In a final but forlorn attempt to persuade he utters a personal lament for the decay of society. The prophet may have felt a failure, but history saw things differently. Micah's viewpoint would survive long after his popular opponents were dead and forgotten. Though nothing in the book suggests it, history would credit Micah with the salvation of Jerusalem (Jer 26:18-19). So often we have to walk in faith, trusting that God and history will vindicate our long and seemingly fruitless efforts at change.

Yet this chapter is much more than a personal lament. Micah has so identified himself with his nation that this lament is the lament of exiled Israel. His cry is her repentant crying in the wilderness, her despair at the disobedience that led to discipline and her hope against hope for restoration. Micah, who until now has disowned Israel's leadership, distanced himself from his people, is now portrayed as one with them in the pain, punishment and lament. To be a prophet, a God-appointed critic of God's people, is not to be separated from them. It is because he is within, it is because he is a member, that Micah is qualified to speak out in such a judgmental way. But such identification has a cost.

Yet even in despair, Micah and Israel assert their faith in an absent God (Mic 7:8) while inwardly pleading that this faith might be justified (Mic 7:14). In a way typical of the psalmist, Micah's lament becomes a bold assertion of the majesty of God despite all appearances. A cynic might label it wishful thinking, foolhardy faith, but Judaism and Christianity together proclaim their faith in things not yet seen. God's light will shine in dark places, the oppressed will be set free, women and men together will worship God in a world the same and yet so different from the one we now live in. ELIZABETH A. HARPER

NAHUM

Introduction

The book of Nahum is not a biblical writing with which the average Christian is familiar, probably because it has not been highly favored by those who select lectionary readings. Many who are acquainted with the contents of the book would probably say it is better so, for the tone of Nahum is one of unabashed glee in revenge for the defeat of Assyria and its capital city, Nineveh. Even more problematic from the point of view of a woman reader, Nineveh is portrayed as a prostitute whose punishment by a vengeful God is the humiliation of sexual violation. Yet Nahum is part of the Christian canon. What is a Christian reader, particularly a Christian woman, to make of this disturbing writing?

The book of Nahum consists of a prophecy of the downfall of Assyria, apparently generally recognized not only in Israel but also in the ancient Near East as a hated, abusive, tyrannical government. The reference to the fall of the great Egyptian city of Thebes (663 B.C.) in Nahum 3:8 and the graphic description of the impending doom of Nineveh, which fell in 612 B.C., provide the upper and lower limits for the time period of Nahum's activity. Some scholars would suggest that the prophet wrote closer to 612, but J. J. M. Roberts points out that by 616 Egypt had become the ally of Assyria, so the reference to the fall of Thebes would be more compelling closer to 663. Also, the need to reassure Judah of Assyria's fall would be greater if that event did not appear so imminent. By 625, the likelihood of Assyria's demise would probably not have required prophetic assurance.

Beginning with the end of Nahum 1 and through Nahum 2 the Hebrew and English chapter and verse divisions of the book do not totally agree, and there are several textually difficult passages. Nonetheless, the overall message is clear and unequivocal: God will soon deliver God's people from the hated oppressor, Assyria. God's judgment is certain; the evil nation will find no mercy. So single-minded is Nahum in this message that, unlike most of his prophetic colleagues, he makes little or no reference to the failings of Judah, depending on whether Nahum 1:9 is interpreted as being addressed to Judah or its foes. It is suggested that the name Nahum is not a proper name but is related to the word rendered in English as "comfort." Nahum gives consolation to Judah, but for Assyria there is no comfort, only destruction.

Outline

1:1	Superscription
1:2-9	Yahweh, Jealous and Avenging
1:10-15	Assurance of Assyria's Fall
2:1-13	An Oracle Against Assyria's King
3:1-17	An Oracle Against Nineveh
3:18-19	An Occasion for Rejoicing

Commentary

After the superscription (Nahum 1:1), Nahum 1:2-8 is generally recognized as an acrostic. In the extant text some letters are missing, and numerous attempts have been made to restore the full acrostic, but what is clear is the portrayal of Yahweh as a jealous God, filled with rage, who takes vengeance on enemies. The challenge in Nahum1:9 may be read as directed either toward Assyria or toward Judah for its lack of trust. The following section, Nahum 1:10-15 (Nahum 1:10—2:1 Heb.) reassures Judah that Assyria will fall, with the last verse abruptly switching to an irenic reference to the feet of the herald who proclaims peace on the mountains. Nahum 2:1-13 (Nahum 2:2-14 Heb.) constitutes an oracle against the king of Assyria, while Nahum 3:1-17 is an oracle against the city of Nineveh, represented as a prostitute who will be humiliated as was Thebes. There is a striking contrast between the portrayal of violence and the literary artistry of the description of that violence. The final two verses, Nahum 3:18-19, return to an oracle against the Assyrian king, whose downfall is seen as the occasion of rejoicing not only for Judah but for all the nations, who have without exception suffered at the hands of Assyria: "For who has ever escaped your endless cruelty?" (Nahum 3:19).

Some years ago at a meeting of the Catholic Theological Society of America, feminist scholar Sandra Schneiders was attempting to rethink the notion of revelation in an effort to deal with disturbing texts such as this one of Nahum, particularly those that appear to be oppressive toward women. She suggested that all of Scripture is revelation, but perhaps some of it is a revelation of what should not be, of what went wrong. In response, Donald Senior suggested that judicious use of the historical-critical method could often make it easier to deal with such passages by allowing them to be interpreted in their context. However, Schneiders's proposal has not met with enthusiasm in all quarters, and use of the historical-critical method in interpreting Nahum has yielded mixed results.

In his commentary, J. M. Powis Smith contrasts the approach of Nahum with that of preceding prophecy in Israel, as well as, most strikingly, with that of Nahum's contemporary Jeremiah, "the prophet of larger vision and deeper insight" (281). Jeremiah makes no reference to the fading of Assyrian domination, too overcome by anguish and fear for his people to take comfort from the downfall of another, which in any case could not alleviate the dire circumstances of Judah.

Though he refers to Nahum as part of the canon, Powis Smith views this book as "a representative of the old, narrow and shallow prophetism" (281) for which the bond between Yahweh and Israel was unbreakable, the recognition of Israel's ethical failings lacking and any thought of adapting the cult of Yahweh to new circumstances unthinkable. Insult to Yahweh's people was insult to Yahweh and could not be suffered unavenged. Thus Powis Smith can assert that the fall of Nineveh was not, for Nahum, satisfaction of a natural human desire for revenge but an objective demonstration of God's justice, which was essential to the validity of his theology. Nahum's rejoicing at the destruction of Nineveh "is not only and merely exultation over a fallen foe, it is also the glad cry of an assured faith in the God of the fathers" (282).

Despite acknowledgment of the canonical status of Nahum, therefore, Powis Smith is critical of the lack of ethical discernment and refusal to rethink old practices. Thus, one might ask, in what sense is Nahum meant to be revelation? Does the fact that Nahum is a cry of faith in the God of the "fathers" justify the vindictive glee over a fallen foe, to the extent that one rejoices at the prospect that children will be dashed to pieces on every street (Nahum 3:10)?

Ralph L. Smith, in his commentary on Nahum, characterizes the criticism of Nahum as too harsh and as indicating a failure to grasp or appreciate the real message of Nahum: God's sovereignty over history and the cosmos. God is good and just, the defender of the helpless and outraged who will by no means justify the guilty (Nahum 1:3). The threat against Nineveh "does not stem from personal hatred of the human author or some historical event in the seventh century B.C. but from the nature of God who is jealous for the right, wrathful toward his enemies, and claims dominion over the world" (68).

Despite the assertion that the threat against Nineveh does not stem from personal hatred, Smith goes on to argue that the delight of Nineveh's victims over its demise is understandable if one recalls the reaction of the victims of Adolf Hitler and Idi Amin. This would seem to imply at least some sense of "personal hatred." One might also object that if the author feels no personal hatred it would be difficult to tell from what is written. The historical-critical method generally seeks to determine the intention of the author, but after reading such a text, how can one justify the conclusion that there is no "personal hatred"?

The suggestion of J. D. W. Watts, which R. L. Smith considers as a possibility, at first reading appears more helpful. Watts proposes that for the prophet, Nineveh and Assyria represent not any ordinary city and depraved civilization but rather the ultimate supernatural evil that attempts to thwart and subdue the purposes and people of God. The defeat of Nineveh and Assyria is the basis for hope in God's ultimate victory over evil. It is true that in the wider context of the Bible as a whole, beginning with the story of Adam and Eve and the serpent and the forbidden fruit, there does seem to be a perception that the evil that exists in the world is greater than that which can be attributed to human beings. Again, however, the question arises, How can we be certain that this is what the author of the book of Nahum intended? Using a reader-response approach, one might suggest that the modern reader could view Nineveh and Assyria as representing ultimate supernatural evil, but even at that the imagery with which its downfall is depicted is troubling, particularly when God is the one portrayed as exercising sexual violence over the harlot city Nineveh (Nahum 3:5-6; *see* Violence). J. M. P. Smith hastens to remind us that God is not doing this; it is Nahum's vivid way of describing God as the ultimate agent of punishment (J. M. P. Smith, 339). This may be true in the sense that ultimately all human language about God must be metaphorical, but it is not so clear that this is the prophet's intention.

Roberts cautions that one should hesitate to disparage the whole of Nahum's theology on the basis of the restricted portion of it that is available to us. He notes that Nahum 1:12 indicates that the fate under which Judah languishes is due to Yahweh's punishment. Roberts disagrees with the efforts of George Mendenhall to discover a different, less negative, English translation for the Hebrew participle *nqm* than "[takes] vengeance," maintaining that the Hebrew root carries no suggestion of an illegal punitive misuse of power but does signify harsh punitive retribution for wrongs committed against one. He does not view this as problematic, since God's avenging of wrongdoing does not run the risk of human attempts at retribution that may involve abuse. By definition, if God does it, it is legal. For Roberts, the desire for vengeance, though it can be corrupted, arises from a sense of justice, and cannot be eliminated without also disposing of the concern for justice (49).

Roberts also points out, however, that "God's vengeance" is metaphorical language, which must be balanced by biblical metaphors that stress God's love, care and accessibility. Without this balance, God could be viewed as an irrational divine bully and yet as an undemanding dispenser of cheap grace. "The God of the cross remains an awe-inspiring, devouring fire" (50).

Irene Nowell, like Roberts, defends Nahum for his lack of criticism of Judah and his apparent glee at the demise of Assyria, stressing that the prophecy intends to make one assertion, that the faithful God has not deserted Judah. As in the past God delivered the Israelites from slavery in Egypt, God will now deliver Judah from the oppression of Assyria (*see* Ancient and Modern Slavery). Exodus 1—15, like Nahum, is not concerned with expressions of sympathy for the oppressors.

Judith Sanderson suggests that even though we can recognize that language about God is metaphorical, an attempt to express the inexpressible through human analogy, one cannot escape the pain of reading about God's judging activity in terms of sexual violence (Nahum 3:5-6). She maintains that for modern readers to understand and respond to these images, four issues must be raised: What situation in the Israelite society of Nahum's day made these images significant? In what manner did Nahum utilize these images to communicate something about Nineveh and about God? What situation in modern society affects our hearing of these images? What would such images communicate to modern society about God?

After discussing the first two questions, Sanderson expresses understanding for the rage the book of Nahum conveys in view of the ruthlessness of Assyria's treatment of those it had conquered. Likewise she can empathize with the prophet's urge to utilize the metaphor of the harlot Nineveh that so graphically depicts the biblical view that God's punishment fits the crime in appropriate fashion. She does not find the notion of God's (metaphorical) anger and punishment so problematic but insists that today it must be expressed in ways that neither demean women and their sexuality nor promote violence against women.

Whether this writing represents the whole of Nahum's theology, however, is not the most problematic issue for every Christian reader. The problem is that this book is part of the Christian canon, and it raises serious issues of what we understand by the notions of revelation and biblical inspiration. I would venture to suggest that the issue is not even the metaphorical brutality of God's punishment depicted here, but rather how we understand the notion of God's punishment in any sense. Does God consistently intervene in human history to punish evil, and if so, how do we explain the horrible evil that so often appears to go unpunished?

Ancient Israel had a diversified response to the problem of human suffering. Consciousness of guilt led to the idea of suffering as punishment, but what of the suffering of the innocent? Some inspired writers pondered the question and developed the notion of suffering as a test, something that could offer the possibility of growth. But some suffering is too appalling to be explained in either of these ways. The author of the book of Job ultimately gives no answer other than that humans cannot understand the ways of God. The author of the book of Wisdom looks for an answer beyond this life. Both ultimately have no answer other than to call for trust in God. Despite the culpability of God's people, Nahum seems to be likewise a call to trust at a time when the suffering of Judah seems out of proportion to its faults.

But in what kind of God does the Bible call us to trust? Is it the two-sided God depicted by Roberts, one whose vengeance is balanced by love, care and accessibility? What is the nature of the God of the cross who remains an awe-inspiring, devouring fire? The God of the Bible is one who is in some way in control of everything that happens in human history yet at the same time holds human beings responsible for their actions. God "inspires" David to take a census of Israel, then calls him to account for his pride in doing so. God hardens Pharaoh's heart, but nonetheless Pharaoh is held culpable. In another of those disturbing passages, God's mighty word leaps down from heaven to slaughter the firstborn of the Egyptians as "punishment" (Wis 18:14-16). Some interpreters would suggest that is the way God is, according to the Bible, and we have to accept such a God if we are believers. But perhaps there is another possibility.

Perhaps we must be careful in interpreting the language about God used in the Bible, being mindful that it is an attempt to describe the indescribable in human words. If God has given human beings free will, which involves responsibility, does God constantly intervene when evil seems to triumph? Experience, in the Bible and in human history, has shown that God does not always so intervene. So the question might be asked, Does God ever intervene? Or do the seeming fitting punishments of the guilty come about because of the interaction of human choices? In granting humans freedom, has God not limited God's ability to intervene? What then can this God, whom Christians understand as three in one (*see* The Trinity), do for those who suffer inconsolably, except to refuse to use equality with God for self-advantage and to empty self, to pour self out unto death, even death on a cross (Phil 2:5-11)?

Several exegetes, among them N. T. Wright, have begun to further develop not only christological but also theological significance from the references in Philippians 2:6 to Christ being in the form of God and possessing equality with God. Translations such as those of Gerald F. Hawthorne ("Precisely because he was in the form of God he did not consider being equal with God grounds for grasping") and Peter T. O'Brien ("Precisely because he was in the form of God, he did not regard this divine equality as something to be used for his own advantage") suggest that the self-emptying of Christ does not refer to the loss of divine attributes but to the fact that Christ made himself powerless. Gordon Fee likewise emphasizes the aspect of self-giving rather than giving up divine nature.

Thus the significance of the self-emptying of Christ, expressed in a citation of O'Brien from F. F. Bruce, asserts that in Philippians 2 something is being said not only about Jesus Christ but also about the nature of God: "Not that he *exchanged* the form of God for the form of a slave, but that he *manifested* the form of God in the form of a slave" (216). "The real theological emphasis of the hymn, therefore, is not simply a new view of Jesus. It is a new understanding of God" (345-46). It is not because Jesus is led by divine wisdom but because he is divine wisdom (1 Cor 1:24) that he could, in the words of Wright, regard equality with God as uniquely qualifying him for the vocation of redemptive suffering and death (345). The forceful christological assertion of Philippians 3:7-11, which is precisely concerned with knowing how to properly regard everything in relation to Christ, further supports and strengthens this conclusion.

The hymn in Philippians 2 makes clear that the one whom the Philippians know as Christ Jesus deliberately chose to empty himself and become obedient unto death. It is because of this free choice of Christ that the power of God becomes operative. Not only in Paul and in Jewish wisdom literature but throughout the Old Testament there is the awareness that God does not choose as do human beings, nor is God's perspective that of humans. God's power operates in the midst of apparent human weakness. The Israelites are exhorted to rely on God rather than on foreign armies. Women like Judith and Esther and Jael and young boys like David are chosen to become saviors of their people. Younger sons such as Saul, Moses, Jacob and Joseph are called to become leaders, whether they like it or not. Barren women like Rachel and Hannah are more loved than those who have children. The child of Ruth is known not as the son of Mahlon but as Naomi's heir. The righteous one who is mocked and set upon by enemies, condemned to an early grave, can expect justification beyond this life. The Wisdom of God teaches the righteous to view things from the divine perspective. Those who walk in the way of wisdom are empowered to overcome evil.

Perhaps the best way to read Nahum is as an anguished cry of the prophet on behalf of a suffering people whose agony appears out of all proportion to any guilt that might be theirs. In the midst of such anguish, it is difficult to trust that the ways of God are not human ways, and perhaps it is difficult as well to refrain from expressing a human desire for vengeance. But as modern readers we must keep in mind that God's ways are not human ways and that the kind of vengeance humans often crave is not what God offers. Perhaps the revelation that we can claim is that we, like Nahum's people, are called to trust in a God whose ways still often appear incomprehensible, to trust, in spite of enduring injustice so intolerable that it cries out for vengeance, that God is just, and God's justice may not involve the kind of vengeance for which we cry out in our pain. But in addition, as Christian readers of Scripture, we are called to trust that a God who came to share our suffering will one day turn that suffering into such a joy that it cannot enter into our hearts to conceive what has been prepared for us.

Bibliography. G. F. Hawthorne, *Philippians*, Word Biblical Commentary 43 (Waco, TX: Word, 1983); I. Nowell, "Nahum," in *The New Jerome Biblical Commentary*, ed. R. E. Brown, J. A. Fitzmyer and R. E. Murphy (Englewood Cliffs, N.J.: Prentice-Hall, 1990) 258-61; P. T. O'Brien, *The Epistle to the Philippi-*

ans: A Commentary on the Greek Text, New International Greek Testament Commentary (Grand Rapids, MI: Eerdmans, 1991); J. J. M. Roberts, *Nahum, Habakkuk, and Zephaniah,* Old Testament Library (Louisville, KY: Westminster John Knox, 1991); J. E. Sanderson, "Nahum," in *Women's Bible Commentary,* ed. C. A. Newsom and S. H. Ringe (Louisville, KY: Westminster John Knox, 1992) 217-21; J. M. Powis Smith, "Nahum," in *A Critical and Exegetical Commentary on Micah, Zephaniah, Nahum, Obadiah and Joel,* J. M. Powis Smith, W. H. Ward and J. A. Bewer, International Critical Commentary (Edinburgh: T & T Clark, 1985) 267-360; R. L. Smith, *Micah-Malachi,* Word Biblical Commentary 32 (Waco, TX: Word, 1984); N. T. Wright, "ἁρπαγμός and the Meaning of Phil. 2:5-11," *Journal of Theological Studies* 37 (1986) 321-52.

VERONICA KOPERSKI

HABAKKUK

Introduction

In Habakkuk 1:1 and Habakkuk 3:1, Habakkuk is identified as a prophet, but his book offers no further facts about him. The names of his parents are missing, as is his place of origin; there is nothing to indicate the circumstances of his life. Although Habakkuk is labeled a prophet, calls to repentance—a form usually associated with the role of prophets in ancient Israel—are missing from the book. Rather unconventionally there are no messages to a listening audience. The book is not apparently a record of oral sermons.

From the description of the Chaldeans, or neo-Babylonians (Hab 1:6), one can surmise that Habakkuk was ministering in Judah while the Babylonians were creating their empire toward the end of the seventh century B.C. The original core of the work presumably comes out of a historical situation in the life of the southern kingdom of Judah, and most of the evidence in the work seems to point to a date around 609-598. This corresponds to the reign of the Judean king Jehoiakim. He was extravagant with money, politically irresponsible and repressive (see Jer 22:13-19; 26:20-23; 36:20-31), so as to deepen the public moral and religious crisis in Judah.

Habakkuk is a book for faithful people of any era who live in the time between the revelation of God's promises and the fulfillment of those promises. Most of the book is in poetry, but in three very different genres: a dialogue between Habakkuk and Yahweh (Hab 1:2—2:5), a series of five woes (Hab 2:6-20) and a prayer psalm complete with liturgical instructions (Hab 3:2-19). A major point of the book is that while humans legitimately bemoan the lack of justice in human relations, God is aware and is responding, acting among nations, peoples and groups where one might not first expect God to be operating. The overarching theme of the book is that regardless of present appearances, human violence will ultimately be defeated by divine violence. Many people today may question the continuing appropriateness of biblical images depicting God as violent.

Elements of Jeremiah's confessions (Jer 11:18—12:6; 15:10-21; 17:14-18; 18:18-23; 20:7-18) but even more so the argumentative sounds of the Psalter's laments (e.g., Ps 44; 69) can be discerned in Habakkuk's complaint. Such contention occurs similarly in

Job's agonizing—how to understand the righteousness of God and to do so in a life-and-death struggle. Habakkuk was evidently a thoughtful and sensitive person. He was concerned about human suffering and helplessness before the powers of evil and was deeply troubled by God's apparent acquiescence in oppression. He shows us that it is acceptable to challenge and question God.

Habakkuk spoke for all the oppressed who had no or little voice. Women especially feel and suffer the effects of injustice. Women and children are disproportionately victims of drug wars, gun violence, domestic violence, inequities in the workplace, sexual harassment, powerlessness in government and so forth. They can relate to the prophet's description of lack of control.

Outline

1:1—2:5	Dialogue
2:6-20	Woes
3:1-19	Psalm

Commentary

Dialogue (Hab 1:1—2:5)

Protesting Injustice (Hab 1:1-4)

The strong in Judah, perpetrators of violence, oppress the weak. Habakkuk objects to the ill-treatment people have to undergo and the wrongs they have to endure from their fellow human beings. He also rejects the arbitrary power of the administrators of the law and the experience of suffering from the perversion of justice. The people of Judah have abandoned the righteous order intended by God for their society. Violence has become prevalent, and justice is warped.

Why must one regard helplessly the course of events in the life of the community when Yahweh could put a stop to it but does not? How long will Yahweh remain silent, when the patience of those who pray is gradually being exhausted under the load they carry? The prophet does not doubt God's might, as if God were unable to rescue; what agitates him is that he has received no answer to the cry he has raised so often. Habakkuk faces the dilemma that has confronted faithful people in every age: the dilemma of seemingly unanswered prayer for the healing of society.

The words of Habakkuk 1:2 can often be uttered by individuals, especially women and children, who suffer from domestic violence (*see* Violence, Abuse and Oppression; The Purpose and Value of Human Life). They may feel stuck in conditions of abuse without sensing either a divine or a human response to their pleas. Power differentials can result in abuse in other places, such as the work environment, with sexual harassment coming readily to mind. However, the cry does not exclude less obvious forms of disrespectful manipulation. Habakkuk's cry is a shout for help like "Robbery!" or "Rape!" or "Murder!"

Ordaining War (Hab 1:5-11)

After the complaint follows a response that gives evidence that the complaint has been heard. Yahweh's work will proceed on the level of world events according to his might and unsearchable wisdom. Swinging the scythe (i.e., Babylon)—using it for his purpose—will be Yahweh, the God over all nations. God endlessly rouses instruments throughout history and through them accomplishes God's service, including disciplinary and judicial activities.

But the crisis about which the prophet had complained and for which he sought punishment upon a repressive tyranny does not end. Instead, the Chaldeans will bring violence on a much larger scale while they plunder the region and punish for God the violence of those in Judah. The Babylonians arrogantly depend on their military strength. They strive only to accomplish their own mission: ransacking, confiscating, conquering, seizing, plundering and pillaging. Yahweh seems by having authorized such workers to be going in the contrary direction from pressing forward toward the realization of his peaceable kingdom on earth. Rather than peace, Yahweh ordains war; rather than security, violence. In place of good, Yahweh brings evil; and in place of life, death.

Among the countless captives (Hab 1:9) are undoubtedly women and girls who will be raped by the enemy troops, pressed into servitude as prostitutes or claimed as brides involuntarily. This is one of the sad features of wars. Why does the prophet not mention such detail? Perhaps he never thought of the women and girls, or maybe he was not concerned about them in this context. In any case civilian suffering is in view in the strophe: notice the seizure of homes "not their own" (Hab 1:6).

Objecting to Violence (Hab 1:12-17)

Habakkuk objects that violence within Judah should not be punished by worse violence from the Babylonians, for whom might makes right. Why does the One whose eyes are too pure to behold evil, the holy Yahweh, choose this instrument to accomplish his will? How can the God of law and of righteousness choose these means for the administration of justice? In his complaint Habakkuk appeals to God and awaits protection for humankind in their cruel state of helplessness and exploitation.

Can a God of overflowing life will first that there be destruction and death before abundant living is granted? If so, it is an enigma in the working of God that defies human understanding.

In Habakkuk 1:12-14 we observe the prophet currying favor with God while trying to hold God to account. We may compare how many women find themselves in circumstances in which they must appease men while trying to get them to stop their abuse. Both cases reflect a sizable power inequity. The analogy of the Lord as an abusive male is more than a little troubling. It may be that Habakkuk is truly and thoroughly perplexed by the Lord's actions or inactions and is not pretending a role.

In neither Habakkuk 1:2-4 nor Habakkuk 1:12-17 is there any expression of trust in God. These laments do not end with an expression of confidence (rather like the supplications in Ps 39; 88). Instead, a change of mood from despair to assurance occurs later, among the woes and in the psalm.

Living in Faithfulness (Hab 2:1-5)

Yahweh does not explain his compulsion to act in this strange manner; rather, as the Lord of world history, Yahweh proclaims his will in a sovereign manner. When God saw fit, then he would fulfill his plan.

The ethical appraisal of two poles—the "proud" and the "righteous"—is brought to the notice of the cultic community (Hab 2:4). The proud are vain, presumptuous, conceited persons, but the righteous fulfill the demands of relationship with God, people and the earth. Yahweh's final answer to the prophet's impatient complaint is that the proud will bear their punishment; the righteous will remain alive amid all their trials. Those who will have true life, those who will fully live, those who will blossom and flourish and bring forth their fruit in due season are the righteous people (cf. Hab 1:4) who live in faithfulness to God. The word *faithfulness* brings together passive and active aspects—confidence and obedience toward God, whose deeds and ways remain beyond human comprehension. To have faith means to believe God's promise and to act as if it is going to be fulfilled.

Woes (Hab 2:6-20)

This series of woes is evidently intended to reinforce the promise given in Habakkuk 2:4-5 by showing that those who rely on their own powers and not on God cannot sustain their self-contained life or find permanent satisfaction in it. The activities of the threatening great power that acts for

Yahweh are temporary; its deeds of greed and insatiability will not remain unpunished. God is at work in the world, and part

Babylonian inscription from the time of Habakkuk. (Habakkuk 2:2)

of that working is judgment on all who have been proud and mighty.

Habakkuk's five taunts confidently mock the oppressors, who will be penalized for their violence, since they achieved God's purpose in an excessive manner. It seems as if Yahweh must take some responsibility for that, since he picked them despite knowing their character. Yahweh was the one who had maintained the Babylonians as his instrument of punishment. Nevertheless, the Babylonians would be accounted responsible for their behavior and would have to accept their punishment. The fact that God had use for their oppression does not mean that their responsibility was removed.

Conquered Peoples Retaliate (Hab 2:6-8)

The Babylonians will have to listen to scorn and mockery from those whom they have oppressed and made to suffer in humiliation. The little peoples, among them Judah, who had been subjugated by the Babylonians will utter this. Those who have plundered will share in a like affliction. The lustful great power, which lawlessly confiscated belongings, becomes the prey of its creditors. It appears, moreover, that the conquered peoples retaliate.

Exploiters Seek Security (Hab 2:9-11)

The exploiters seek to secure their valuables along with their households. Habakkuk 2:9 sounds quite similar to the modern phenomenon of gated communities that are meant to protect their inhabitants. The less fortunate are left to reside in deteriorating neighborhoods. Habakkuk 2:11 reminds us of the hope that the suppressed voices of women will be heard. May they also gain full access to and participation in decision-making and power-brokering processes. While Habakkuk was not addressing these contemporary matters, nonetheless the passage does provide, by extension, helpful lessons for our time.

Two Kinds of Glory (Hab 2:12-14)

The aim is to create renown and glory for the days to come by building—with blood. It could refer to prisoners of war or other slaves doing forced labor. The attempts of human beings to gain glory for themselves by public works built on injustice are empty and vain endeavors that will fall. Contrarily, "the earth will be filled with the knowledge of the glory of the LORD" (Hab 2:14).

Lack of Restraint (Hab 2:15-17)

The host of a party goes to excess and ensures that his guests become drunk. He gets them to discard their clothes and seduce one another. Habakkuk 2:15 is reminiscent of reports from women who have been sexually assaulted while under the influence of a date-rape drug. The whole stanza speaks about lack of respect and no restraint. Lack of respect for women contributes to date rape besides encouraging abuse in general of people who appear to be weaker.

Habakkuk 2:17 is an insertion referring to Habakkuk 2:8. The Babylonians destroyed humans, animals, forests and other natural resources. The violence done to other nations will return upon the head of the violent and overwhelm them.

The Futility of Idols (Hab 2:18-20)

Beside Yahweh every divinity is born of human fantasy. God alone can uphold and guide. Despite how it might seem, the writer does not display a fundamental misunderstanding of idols. Habakkuk knows that the worshipers rely not on the image but the deity represented by the image. The mockery, however, is part of an idol parody. It is a conscious and polemic negation of ascriptions of creative power to images and their gods.

Yahweh, who is present for his people in his temple, is to be feared or at least honored. God is ruled by holiness, says the prophet, even though he surely knew that

God is also ruled by love.

Psalm (Hab 3)

Thus far God's judgment has operated through the violence of human beings; God was not portrayed as directly involved in the violence. In this psalm, Yahweh appears as a warrior conquering the earth, wreaking havoc in his path. A theophany generally includes two elements in the Old Testament: a description of the deity's approach and a description of the accompanying upheavals (e.g., Deut 33:2; Judg 5:4-5; Mic 1:3-4; Ps 68:7-8). God is depicted as a storm god whose lightning brings destruction (Hab 3:4, 9, 11). Arriving in the majesty of divine might, Yahweh engages in battle victoriously. It is not only the prophet who is dismayed in his whole being; all nature and people along Yahweh's route are profoundly upset.

The function of the hymn in Habakkuk is to give sufferers confidence that Yahweh can and will intervene to aid them as he did in the past. The prophet delineates in detail the vision that had come to him partially at Habakkuk 2:1-5.

Wrath and Mercy (Hab 3:1-2)

"In wrath may you remember mercy" signals a dreadful but compassionate Lord—wrath as when a person shakes with anger, mercy as when a parent expresses anxious solicitude. Before frightful wrath Habakkuk can only pray for mercy.

Afflictions (Hab 3:3-7)

Pestilence and plague, mythical gods subject to Yahweh, come in the military retinue. Pestilence is God's herald, while plague is God's rearguard. This personification refers to ancient Canaanite religion, to the power of those horrible divinities that oppressed mortal human beings with epidemics (perhaps burning fevers).

Enemies Confronted (Hab 3:8-15)

Confronting his enemies, Yahweh makes war for the liberation of his people. The enemies are trampled and pierced, exterminated and overthrown. Habakkuk pictures Yahweh's victorious means of granting release and salvation to his people in terms of a whirling tornado and a procession of war vehicles (Hab 3:8, 14-15; cf. an earthquake, Hab 3:6). Yahweh's flashing arrows and glittering spear have terrified even the heavenly bodies in his blinding stream of light. The mountains grow benumbed in convulsions as at the moment when a pregnant woman is in the pain of labor (Hab 3:10), labor being what the word *writhe* frequently indicates.

The militarism of Habakkuk 3:9, 11 more commonly characterizes the actions of men than of women. Yet the latter, counting civilians, suffer its consequences at least equally with the former.

Inner Harmony (Hab 3:16-19)

With dismay Habakkuk hears the report of and sees the execution of judgment, which will shake all humanity. The numbing situation of God's devouring and annihilating of everything produces a terrible tension within the prophet. A trembling body accompanies the prophet's great inner shock and fear. Yet from this shattering experience emerges an overflowing joy. Habakkuk's theophany ends with a trustful hope for the future. The theophany empowers the psalmist to find strength in God. Perhaps the image already used continues—although it involves pain, birthing brings great joy (*see* Birth Pain Imagery; Midwifery and Birthing Practices).

Habakkuk's final affirmation is that nothing can steal his joy in the God of his salvation. It is not a question of something casual or of mere human cheerfulness or enthusiasm but of a deep calm arising from an inner harmony placed there by Yahweh. Come what may—injustice and violence in Habakkuk's society, a desolating foreign invasion, God's destruction of the wicked in the world—he and the faithful like him can rejoice and even exult, because God is their salvation. Although Yahweh seemingly left Habakkuk alone in the world to deal with the problems of enduring evil and torture from another hand, the book gives a statement of faith that has few parallels in the Old Testament.

An early modern Habakkuk was a seventeenth-century minister named Martin Rinkart. Throughout the Thirty Years' War several waves of deadly pestilence and famine swept his city as various armies marched through the town, leaving death and destruction in their wake. Nevertheless Pastor Rinkart could still pen the words to the widely used and stately hymn "Now Thank We All Our God."

Bibliography. E. Achtemeier, *Nahum-Malachi* (Atlanta: John Knox, 1986); J. E. Sanderson, "Habakkuk," in *Women's Bible Commentary,* ed. C. A. Newsom and S. H. Ringe (Louisville, KY: Westminster John Knox, 1998) 237-39; M. E. Széles, *Wrath and Mercy: A Commentary on the Books of Habakkuk and Zephaniah,* trans. G. A. F. Knight (Grand Rapids, MI: Eerdmans, 1987).

EDWIN C. HOSTETTER

ZEPHANIAH

Introduction

The book of Zephaniah, permeated as it is by the theme of an apocalypse, is not for the faint of heart. Yet the work of God sometimes is a work of destruction before renewal and purifying can begin. The author, Zephaniah son of Cushi, was a prophet who traced his lineage to Hezekiah (Zeph 1:1). This mention of his genealogy suggests that it is important to know not only from whom Zephaniah had descended but also where he may have been from. The reference to Cushi either indicates the land of Zephaniah's birth in Africa (*Cush* is sometimes translated "Ethiopia") or the presence of Cushite people in Israel. The fact that the prophet was of African descent reminds us of the place of all peoples in the work, salvation and judgment of God (*see* Africans in Biblical History). In Zephaniah's text the whole known world faced judgment; those who had been exiled into regions of Africa would be the ones God brought back to Israel.

Zephaniah's ministry, about 640-609 B.C., was during the reign of Josiah, a reforming king who took advantage of the Assyrians' declining power. Zephaniah was possibly related to Josiah, so that gave additional force to his condemnation of Israel's leaders. Even though Josiah was king, Zephaniah, in prophetic fashion, did not curry favoritism. Leaders in the kingdom had been corrupted by their embrace of other gods. The people of Israel had forgotten portions of the law and intermingled worship of Yahweh with worship of gods appropriated from their captors. However, during Josiah's reign one of the Deuteronomic scrolls was found, and Josiah began a program of religious renewal. Zephaniah's prophetic words were spoken prior to this discovery. Interestingly, when the scroll of the law was found, it was not Zephaniah who was consulted, but Huldah (2 Kings 22:14-20). God's use of a woman to remind people how to apply and reinstate the divine law is significant. God did not make laws only for men to wield; the law applies to all and is able to be interpreted by all those to whom God speaks.

In Zephaniah's prophecy, the "day of the Lord" took on great importance in the face of Israel's idolatry. The day of the Lord, a day in which God pronounces judgment, is best known by most Christians from the New Testament passages of 1 Thessalonians 5:2 and 2 Peter 3:10. The message of Zephaniah, far from being a message for the past, is a message viable for people living in idolatrous societies that have separated themselves from Yahweh's presence and plan. For women especially, the message of destruction and renewal can provide hope in the midst of unjust and burdensome situations. When the day of the Lord comes, the injustices of inequality, subjugation and indifference to God will be destroyed.

Zephaniah's day was a time of turmoil not only for Israel but also for the kingdoms that surrounded it. The northern kingdom had been taken into captivity by the Assyrians, and in the southern kingdom, the people had forgotten most of the Jewish laws. Yet according to the law, interspersed worship of other deities with their worship of Yahweh was an abomination. Worship of some of these deities, creation goddesses such as Astarte, put women in charge of some idolatrous practices. But other idolatrous practices could cause them great grief. Their children could be sacrificed to Molech in a fiery ceremony. Women were abused sexually by the fertility rituals that worshipers engaged in. The current embrace of the goddess must be tempered by the reality that even though the female form and person were worshiped, women were not treated justly in these societies. They were often chattels with few rights and many perils.

In Zephaniah, the theme of destruction mirrored the historical setting, for when Josiah ascended to the throne, the Assyrians were in decline and in danger from the Babylonians, Arab tribes and peoples from the north. The power structure of the region was being rearranged. Within Josiah's reign, most of the nations surrounding Judah underwent war and upheaval. The focus of foreign enemies and incorporation of other gods into Jewish worship therefore was of paramount concern in Zephaniah's prophecies.

Outline

1:1-18	The Day of the Lord and the Ensuing Destruction
2:1—3:13	Prophecies Against the Nations and Jerusalem
3:14-20	Rejoicing and Restoration

Commentary

The Day of the Lord and the Ensuing Destruction (Zeph 1)

The book of Zephaniah begins by stating that the word of the Lord has come to Zephaniah, who gives his genealogy as a way to orient readers to the historical context. Including a genealogy in the prophetic introduction is unusual, and by informing the readers that he is of the royal line, as well as from Cush, Zephaniah's word from the Lord cannot be separated from the circumstances of his birth or nationality. Zephaniah's nationality has an integral role in the judgment that the Lord is about to pronounce on the peoples and nations that have not worshiped Yahweh, as well as the later salvific work of God.

The theme of destruction is a stark beginning to the prophetic word. God is doing destructive rather than creative work. From the land, sea and air, humans will be cut off from earth. The reversal of the created order through destruction suggests that there is an imbalance. Worship of other gods, such as Baal and Milcom, has upset the created order. The gods of the

Ammonites and the Assyrians have infiltrated worship in Judah because the people have forgotten the laws of Yahweh. The seriousness of the idolatry is evident in the worship of Milcom, which may be a reference to Molech, to whom children were sacrificed in a fiery ceremony. It is striking that the Israelites have taken to worshiping the gods of their oppressors, and even Yahweh's priests participate in these idolatrous ceremonies. The Israelites not only worship the foreign gods but also bow down to the stars in heaven and divide their worship between the Lord and Milcom. They have embraced the gods and practices of the pagan neighbors who have fought and enslaved them. Some of these gods, which represent fertility, also are invoked for creative or regenerative purposes. So when the creation is being destroyed, it may be a reference to the creations attempted by those who worship false gods. These times resemble our own, when Christians have embraced astrology and other religious means in order to enhance their spiritual experiences. Like their counterparts in Zephaniah, they have not sought the Lord in the matter of their worship practices.

In response the Lord will call for sacrifice, just as the Israelites have sacrificed to foreign gods. The sacrifice that God requires, however, is the sacrifice of those who have led the people astray. Those who have participated in the ceremonies, including the royal officials and the priests, will be punished. The reference to those who leap over the threshold and fill their master's house with violence and fraud are those who have brought the worship of foreign gods into the temple and have made sacrifices to other gods there instead of keeping the temple sacred to Yahweh (Zeph 1:9).

Zephaniah 1:10 shifts to the effect that the destruction will have on Jerusalem. From the Fish Gate, where the fish markets were, to the Second Quarter, the upper-class area where Huldah was reputed to have lived and that looked over the temple mount, "a cry will be heard." The cries of the people who witness the destruction will be from upper and lower classes. The Lord will search Jerusalem with a lamp, so that no one will be able to hide from God's wrath. All the material goods that the Israelites have coveted will be destroyed. Even the place where those who followed God lived would be destroyed.

The destruction is emphasized by sound; the Hebrew word *qwl* (Zeph. 1:14) emulates shrieking, a harsh sound of bitterness and wailing. Even the mighty will cry aloud at the destruction. Darkness, like a storm or an eclipse, will descend on the city. The trumpet, the ram's horn used to signify entrance into battle, will be used against God's people. The trumpet is also used in the New Testament as signaling the Lord's return (1 Cor 15:52) and indicates that the Lord's wrath and judgment are soon to come. Judgment will come upon the city, and the people will be ravaged.

Zephaniah 1 reminds us that there is a cost to engaging in the worship of idols. The whole earth will have felt the wrath of God's vengeance on unfaithful people.

Prophecies Against the Nations and Jerusalem (Zeph 2:1—3:13)

The theme of destruction is interrupted by a call to repentance. Those who are called to seek the Lord are the humble, perhaps the lower strata of society that have not had the opportunity or the funds to engage in the sinful practices of those with too much money and time. The theme of the day of the Lord is mentioned again; those who seek the Lord will be hidden from the Lord's wrath on that day. In Hebrew, Zephaniah 2:2-3 start with words that begin in B, sounding an almost rhythmic beat. The warning is strong, but the hope for those who repent and turn from wickedness is that the Lord will not harm them. Righteousness and humility will bring protection from the day of the Lord.

Zephaniah 2:4 begins the judgments against the nations. Gaza, Ashkelon, Ashdod and Ekron are all neighboring cities of the Philistines (with a south to north orientation). Each city has a punishment: Gaza, desertion; Ashkelon, desolation; Ashdod, driven out; and Ekron, uprooted. These four cities are viewed as women, and they suffer abandonment, or desertion; spinsterhood, or desolation; divorce, or being driven out; and barrenness, or being uprooted (*see* Barrenness and Fertility; Divorce; Singleness). For a woman of that time, any of these circumstances would diminish her status and jeopardize her ability to live. We may consider ourselves to be immune to such issues, but the pain of separation, loneliness, infertility or abandonment continues to press women. What is unique in this passage is that the Philistine cities, not the Israelite cities, are being compared with women. Usually the prophets use this analogy for Israel.

The focus of the Lord's attention moves to the seacoast. The prophet proclaims that the Canaanites, the Moabites, the Ammonites and the Ethiopians will feel the wrath of the day of the Lord. The coastal cities of the Canaanites will become pastureland, and the righteous remnant of Judah will reside in the houses of Ashkelon. Those who have lost possessions in Israel because of the wickedness of their kindred will have their possessions restored. This allusion is a precursor to the theme of restoration (Zeph 3). The Moabites and Ammonites are compared with Sodom and Gomorrah, the historically wicked cites God destroyed. The pride of the people of the land especially is an abomination to the Lord, and their mistreatment of the Israelites will not go unpunished. To make their subjugation complete, God will reduce their gods and make them bow down. Even the Ethiopians will be slain by the sword. Zephaniah is saying that even his homeland will feel the wrath on the day of the Lord.

Assyria, home to many of the gods that the Israelites worship and an especially vicious nation in its war against the Israelites, will have its prized city of canals, Nineveh, destroyed. The architecture and beauty of Nineveh were sources of pride to its people. The "city that lived secure," that said, "I am, and there is no one else," was to be destroyed so utterly that vultures, hedgehogs, owls, ravens and other creatures would inhabit the place where the wicked once lived. Nineveh, which exulted in its prominence among the nations, will be inhabited by scavengers that will eat the waste left from God's destruction.

Zephaniah 3 switches back the focus to Jerusalem. Like the other cities, Jerusalem and its inhabitants continue in their rebellion. Accepting no correction and not heeding God, the city's leaders are likened to roaring lions and evening wolves, beasts that stalk and devour prey. The prophets are wanton, longing after foreign gods, and they defile what is sacred. Even more frightening, they do violence to the law, a suggestion that they, like their leaders, subvert justice and attack those who are unable to defend themselves. They ignore God; the rebellion of their hearts has seeped out into the community, making it dangerous for those who are unable to protect themselves. Jerusalem's engagement with other religious practices has taken them away from the truth of the law given to them. Their behavior has modified itself to the behavior of those surrounding kingdoms that worship gods other than Yahweh. The corruption of Jerusalem seems complete.

Unlike the faithless in Jerusalem, God is righteous and does no wrong. Every morning God's justice shines forth as a beacon to the unjust, but they continue in their practices without shame. God reminds Jerusalem of the destruction that the surrounding nations have suffered because of rebelliousness toward God. Yet Jerusalem continues its corrupt activities, not accepting God's correction. God therefore resolves to bring witness (charges) against the nations and Jerusalem. Nations and kingdoms will be gathered in order that God may vent the full fury of the destruction that their misdeeds have wrought.

Even in the midst of this destruction, God still creates. The corrupted speech of the people will be changed into pure speech. The corrupted speech refers to the people's worship of other gods. The pure speech will be the speech that calls and serves the Lord. God will even reach far beyond the known nations, past Ethiopia, to bring those that have been dispersed so that they may bring offerings to the Lord. The reference in Zephaniah 3:10 is vague, but perhaps it refers to Judeans who had worshiped the Lord but had been scattered after the destruction of Jerusalem. An alternate interpretation could be in reference to the descendants of Sheba, residing in Ethiopia and beyond. The story of Solomon and Sheba is an important one for the history of Ethiopia. Although the biblical text indicates that Sheba brought gifts to Solomon and returned to Ethiopia, Ethiopian stories maintain she became pregnant by Solomon and bore a son, Menelek. He is considered to be the beginning of the dynastic line of Ethiopia that ended with Haile Selassie.

Those who have been prideful and haughty and have worshiped other gods will be removed from the midst of the people. Those who remain will not be put to shame; that is, they will not receive the punishments that will be accorded to those who rebelled. The humble and lowly can seek their refuge in the name of the Lord, and they will be protected. Those who remain after the destruction will be truthful. They will not lie about worshiping the Lord and then turning to other gods. They shall not go after other gods; rather, like sheep, they will be able to pasture and lie down and fear no retaliation from other kingdoms or internal enemies, because the Lord protects them.

Egyptian tomb figures depicting procession of offering bearers. (Zephaniah 3:10)

Rejoicing and Restoration (Zeph 3:14-20)

The salvation of God is always present for those who lay aside idolatry to serve God. Zephaniah 3:14 starts with a call for Jerusalem to sing, shout and rejoice, because the judgments that the Lord had pronounced have been taken away. Those who were enemies of the people of God, who worshiped the idols, have been cast out, and God's presence is in the midst of the people. The call to Jerusalem to rejoice is a call to acknowledge that God is present. The admonition in Zephaniah 3:16, "Do not fear, O Zion," suggests that Zion should not fear the nations that have plagued them in the past, nor should they fear the Lord. They are admonished not to let their hands grow weak because of what has come before. Rather, their resolve should be strengthened because Yahweh is taking care of them. The fear should be replaced by courageousness in the hope of the Lord's blessing.

The presence of the Lord in Israel and Jerusalem is likened to a warrior who gives victory, a reminder that they should not fear the enemies that have surrounded them. The image of the warrior is also an image of salvation of the peoples. The Lord has saved them from destruction because of their faithfulness. The people who are righteous are rejoiced over by God with a renewed love. Where the noise of destruction once reigned, the voice of God singing loudly, as though at a festival or celebration, prevails. The disasters that have come upon the unrighteous and the surrounding nations will be removed, so that they will not bear the blame for them. Whatever oppressors may remain will be dealt with and removed. Those who were oppressed, the lame and the outcast, will be brought back, and their shame exchanged for praise and fame throughout the earth. The final verse brings in those who have been exiled from Jerusalem and Israel, reuniting them with God's people. All that they have lost will be restored to them, and Israel will be restored to its former greatness in that region of the world. The blessings of God will restore the nation and its people.

Bibliography. A. Berlin, *Zephaniah, A New Translation with Introduction and Commentary*, Anchor Bible 25A (Garden City, NY: Doubleday, 1994); G. Emmerson, *Minor Prophets II: Nahum, Habbakuk, Zephaniah, Haggai, Zechariah, Malachi*, Doubleday Bible Commentary (Garden City, NY: Doubleday, 1998).

ANTHEA D. BUTLER

HAGGAI

Introduction

Little is known about the prophet Haggai beyond the fact that he delivered four oracles to encourage the Jewish returnees from Babylon to rebuild the Jerusalem temple and to restore their defiled relationships with God. We learn from Ezra 6:14 that the prophesying of Haggai and his contemporary Zechariah had prompted this remnant to rebuild the house of the Lord. These Jews had prospered, whereas previously they had suffered the loss of their material blessings (Hag 1:7-11). The restoration occurred during the second regnal year of the Persian emperor Darius I.

The history of the remnant of Jews (about forty-nine thousand) who returned to Palestine from the Babylonian captivity needs little repetition. Introductions to the historical books from 1 Samuel to Ezra and Nehemiah have told the story that forms the prelude to the prophecies of Haggai and Zechariah.

Four prophecies are given and set in an editorial format. Haggai's message is one that the people of God, past and present, most need to hear and heed. When other concerns precede the priority of doing God's will, human effort amounts to little. The matters that greatly disturbed those sixth-century Jews were financial, but they were to learn that there were rewards greater than they could ever have expected in an obedience of faith (cf. Mt 6:31, 33).

Outline

1:1-15	First Message: Consider How You Have Fared
2:1-9	Second Message: Unexpected Blessing
2:10-19	Third Message: Holiness as Precursor to God's Blessing
2:20-23	Fourth Message: Zerubabbel, a Kind of Messianic Figure

Commentary

First Message: Consider How You Have Fared (Hag 1)

In August 520 B.C. Haggai, on coming to Jerusalem, found a forlorn people hanging, as it were, on the horns of a dilemma.

The first settlers to return from Babylon to Palestine were filled with dedication. Even before the foundation of the new temple had been laid upon the old ruins, an altar was built and worship reinstituted (Ezra 3:1-6). While some rejoiced that praises were again being offered to God on the holy hill, others wept to compare the humble beginning with the grandeurs of the former temple (Ezra 3:8-13). Before the walls could rise, the work was halted by the Persian king at the instigation of jealous neighboring peoples. Discouragement and despondency ensued.

Yet Israel's cult demanded a centralization of worship in the place that the Lord had designated (Deut 12:5-7, 11-14; 2 Chron 7:16; 33:7). The one people of God must unite in solemn assembly at specific occasions to affirm solidarity of faith and commitment. To one sacred place they brought their tithes and offerings. Only in one shrine could sacrifice be offered and the priest make propitiation for their sins. There whole families were to join in the celebration of God's goodness and find a sense of meaning and cohesion (Deut 12:7, 12).

The forced deportation of Jews to Babylon had challenged the faith of many. The temple lay in ruins. How could they sing the Lord's song in a strange land (Ps 137)? Yet it was there that the faith of Israel had been revitalized. In Babylon had begun the establishment of synagogues, where there was prayer and the study of Scripture; but there could be only one temple, and that was on Mount Zion. In order to reestablish that revitalized faith in Jerusalem, priests and Levites had accompanied the returning band, expecting to build a strong community of faith with the temple at its center. In that prospect the women might have found consolation, but this too had been wrenched from them. Somehow the original mission had been forgotten.

Women who are forced to relocate their families suffer especially in adjusting to a new environment. It is they who maintain the greatest attachment to the old country and to the old ways. They mourn what has been left behind and may experience severe depression as they try to find meaning in a new context. Often men have more opportunity to learn the language and to socialize with the population in the new environment. Women tend to be more isolated, lonely and homesick. The hostility of the inhabitants was likely to be felt more keenly by the women.

Having abandoned the work of rebuilding the temple, the people had been left by God to their own devices. For sixteen years they had allowed the building materials to rot and rust while they entered, with great expectations, on a course designed to procure economic security and material comforts. Haggai 1:5-6 describes the futility of their efforts.

There was an intention to rebuild the temple at some point, but personal concerns took precedence. Those citizens of ancient Jerusalem had looked for much, but it had come to little. Their preoccupation with their houses had left the house of God still in ruins. What seemed to be natural calamities were disciplinary acts of God.

Among the women, the initial prosperity may have inspired bright hopes as they turned to a material vision rather than a spiritual one. In faraway Babylonia, mothers and grandmothers had told them of the family homesteads that had been theirs in the Promised Land from which they had been exiled. In contrast to the reality of the present ruins, memory would have tended to glorify the fields and gardens, the shady courtyards of the ancestral dwellings and the ample chambers within them.

The old orthodoxy of the two ways of blessings and cursings (the so-called Deuteronomic theology; *see* Blessing and Cursing) had been indelibly impressed on the minds of Israelite people of all classes. Catastrophic losses of basic necessities must surely have been related to the returned remnant's sins. The successful construction of their houses, embellished with cedar paneling, was taken as a sign of prosperity and favor with God. Now the prophet has announced that though they "looked for much, . . . lo, it came to little" (Hag 1:9). God had blown away their resources, a devastating thought to Jews who had ventured back to the land of promise. They had understood themselves to be God's special emissaries sent to rebuild the temple and to revive its worship.

Led by Zerubbabel and Joshua, the people had "obeyed the voice of the LORD their God" in returning to Jerusalem. Haggai 1:12 indicates that Haggai added words of interpretation and application to God's message. His hearers accepted his oracle as truly prophetic, believing that "the LORD their God had sent him."

Then came the confirmation of their change of heart and willingness to obey. "I am with you, says the LORD" (Hag 1:13). Immigrant women, far more isolated and lonely than their male counterparts as they settle into a strange environment, are given assurance of the companionship of the heavenly friend.

Beyond mere human emotion, the Spirit of the Lord "stirred up" the spirits of the leaders and the remnant of the people. "All the remnant of the people . . . came and worked on the house of the LORD of hosts, their God" (Hag 1:14). Women may have contributed their labor, as did the daughters of Shallum in constructing the walls (Neh 3:12). The criterion for service was not gender but willingness. Throughout the return from exile, Hebrew women were respected as members of the covenant during times of obedience (cf. Neh 8:2-3) and debased during lapses of faith (Mal 2:11, 14-15).

Second Message: Unexpected Blessing (Hag 2:1-9)

Again in Darius's second year, God spoke through Haggai. People of the older generations, who in their youth had seen the glories of Solomon's temple, complain that the structure and appointments of the new temple are "as nothing" (Hag 2:3; cf. Ezra 3:12).

Comparisons are odious, but here the comparison could be deadly. In light of the previous failures to further the work and the unfortunate consequences, this negative attitude could be disastrous. Many relocated people groups find meaning and perpetuation of their culture through their collective worship. Women in particular tend to preserve the language, culture and spiritual values of the lands from which they came, usually within their houses of worship.

Only the temple would now give meaning and cohesion to the new community that clung so tenuously to survival. If the reconstruction did not go forward, there might even be a threat to their lives and to those of their children. They might be overpowered by their hostile neighbors. God might blow away everything.

But again God intervened through Haggai, calling on the whole host of Israelites, from the leaders and elderly former leaders to the least of the people, to "take courage." First the instruction came to Zerubbabel, then to Joshua and then to all the *am ha-arets* (people of the land). Three times God exhorts them to "take courage" (cf. Josh 1:9) and reminds the remnant at Jerusalem that he is with them. God links the promise here with the Mosaic covenant and its history. God first reminds Haggai and through him the people of his attribute as Emmanuel, "God is with them."

The grousing of the older generations will suddenly cease in the face of Haggai's next overwhelming word. If the shaking of the earth at Sinai was God's answer, through Moses, to the complainers of that day, how much more will God's workings invest the second temple with a greater glory? The earthquake of Sinai was a symbol of God's intentions for great change. One cannot escape the sense that Haggai 2:9 anticipates glory and prosperity that were never literally realized even in the splendors of the Herodian structure. That the Messiah did come, and with his coming provided the full actualization of the goal of salvation history, would naturally move the ordinary reader to see the messianic undertones. The case here is mindful of God's promises that David's seed would reign eternally because the Messiah would come as Son of David.

Third Message: Holiness as Precursor to God's Blessing (Hag 2:10-19)

Two months after the second message, Haggai received another word from God: for the priests of Israel to define ritual holiness. "Every work of their hands" (i.e., work on the temple) "and what they offer there" (i.e., temple sacrifices) are "unclean" (Hag 2:14).

As the people sought a new holiness, the Lord had said, "I am with you" (Hag 1:13; 2:4). Haggai 2:15 speaks of "what will come to pass from this day on." There will be seed in their barns, and their vines, fig trees, pomegranates and olive trees will be abundant producers. The conclusion of the third message is an encouraging "From this day on I will bless you" (Hag 2:19).

Fourth Message: Zerubbabel, a Kind of Messianic Figure (Hag 2:20-23)

For displaced and disheartened women, there is a yet more glorious promise. God will give a charismatic leader who will bring God's people to a level of blessing and significance. They will gain a new understanding of themselves and their identity.

The chosen people will be a distinctive, for God's glory is as a signet ring especially designed for the hand of a ruler. Such a ring was pressed into hot wax by the king and left an impression of the image that had been carved into the ring. A document thus bore the seal and officially conveyed an unmistakable royal order. It was recognized for its authenticity and conveyed the official image to all peoples and nations.

Just so these chastened people were to become a distinctive of the working of God's love and power among the nations. Though they would lack political power, theirs would be a spiritual power that none could gainsay and a glory that could not be surpassed. Some commentators have considered this passage to vest Zerubbabel with messianic qualities. Many have seen in this text a prophecy that goes beyond Zerubbabel to the Messiah who was to come, bringing meaning and self-definition to all who are disenfranchised (*see* Yahweh's Concern for the Disenfranchised).

RICHARD CLARK KROEGER JR.

ZECHARIAH

Introduction

The Hebrew name Zechariah comprises two important words: "Yahweh remembers." In essence that is the theme of this book. The largest of the minor prophetic books, Zechariah is a great attestation that God cares about his people. The book continues to be an encouraging message to believers in every age.

The first verse of the book of Zechariah introduces the author as Zechariah, the son of Berechiah, the son of Iddo. Iddo was among the priestly families who returned from exile under Zerubbabel and Joshua in 536 B.C. (Neh 12:16; Ezra 5:1; 6:14). The precise date of Zechariah's ministry is recorded as the eighth month of the second year of Darius, king of Persia, or October 27, 520 B.C.

Along with the prophet Haggai, Zechariah encouraged the Jewish exiles who had returned from Babylon to Judah under Sheshbazzar and Zerubbabel in 538-536 B.C. If the designation "young man" in Zechariah 2:4 refers to Zechariah, he was probably a young assistant to Haggai and outlived him. Haggai and Zechariah urged the Jews to rebuild their community and temple (Ezra 5:1-2). In addition, the Jews sought these prophets for advice in daily affairs (Zech 7:3).

Most scholars agree that Zechariah wrote Zechariah 1—8, but there is considerable disagreement about Zechariah 9—14. The argument is that these later chapters contain a different vocabulary, style and content. The historical setting of each section too appears to be different. For example, the temple that is expected and encouraged in Zechariah 1—8 is a reality in Zechariah 9—14. Also, the Greeks are more evident on the world scene in Zechariah 9—14, as opposed to Persian dominance in Zechariah 1—8. In light of the most recent consensus, that the second part of Zechariah was written in the early fifth century B.C., it is possible that Zechariah wrote it late in his life. If he was a young man at the beginning of his ministry, this would account for the differences in style, vocabulary and historical setting between the two sections of the book.

The evidence for authorship is not conclusive. The book may have been written by one prophet, or it may include additional, anonymous prophecies. Some rabbis thought that sometimes inspired but anonymous prophecies were appended to known prophetic books in order to preserve them. Nevertheless, whether it is of single or multiple authorship, the full book of Zechariah has been recognized as authentic prophecy from very early times by Jews and Christians alike. Unity for this book, if not original, came early in its history. The text found in the Dead Sea Scrolls contains no seams, indicating multiple authorship. New Testament writers, too, regard Zechariah's prophecies as inspired. More than 30 percent of the Old Testament quotations in the passion narratives of the Gospels are from Zechariah 9—14 (cf. Zech 11:13 and Mt 27:9; Zech 13:7 and Mk 14:27; Zech 12:10 and Jn 19:37).

A unity of theology and purpose binds the book together. Both sections contain the following themes: the certainty of judgment (Zech 2:1-2; 14:6), the continuing divine covenant (Zech 8:8; 13:9), a glorious future under a messianic figure (Zech 3:8; 4:6; 9:6-7), concern for the renewal of Zion (Zech 2:5; 9:8; 14:11), the ultimate conversion of the nations (Zech 2:11; 8:22; 14:6), concern for leadership (Zech 4:9; 11:5), ingathering of exiles (Zech 8:7; 10:9-10), outpouring of the Spirit (Zech 4:6; 5:4; 12:10: 13:3) and expectation of peace and prosperity (Zech 8:6; 14:6-8). Both sections reveal the underlying tradition of the Mosaic law.

The prophecy of Zechariah concerns Judah under the Persian Empire. The first emperor of this regime, Cyrus, had allowed foreign captives, including the Jews of Babylon, to return to their homelands. He granted them a large measure of autonomy and allowed them freedom of religion. Approximately fifty thousand Jews returned from Babylon to Judah under the leadership of Sheshbazzar and Zerubbabel in 538 B.C. The trip was assisted by the Persians, and the temple vessels were restored (Ezra 1:3-11).

Although initially the returning exiles had been eager to work on the temple, they had become discouraged by the hardships they faced from hostile neighbors and economic depression. They had been opposed by the local populations who protested the newcomers' rights to property. The Samaritans even accused the Jews to the Persian authorities of planning a rebellion against the government. Unsurprisingly, the Persians halted all attempts to rebuild the temple. The return to the Jewish homeland had become a bitter disappointment.

In 520 B.C., Haggai and Zechariah began to prophesy and encourage the people to rebuild the temple. Haggai insisted that the Jews had used economic depression as an excuse for not finishing the work on the temple. He pointed to the fact that they had managed to finish their own "paneled" houses while God's house still lay in ruins (Hag 1:4). Zechariah promised that God's Spirit would assist them in the building effort (Zech 4:6). The Jews responded without delay, and in four years the temple was completed (Ezra 6:14-17).

Zechariah reveals more about the Jewish community in Judah at the end of the sixth century B.C. The eight night visions of Zechariah 1—8 address particular concerns among the people. These range from issues of community security (Zech 2) to guilt feelings (Zech 3). Each vision promises divine assistance to meet the physical and spiritual needs of the people.

The oracles at the end of Zechariah are of a different character from Zechariah 1—8 and probably reflect later circumstances. It appears that discouragement again plagued the Jewish community, this time in the early fifth century B.C. after the demise of Zerubbabel and Joshua. The apocalyptic oracles of Zechariah 9—14 speak to a people disillusioned with their present situation and promises hope for the more distant future.

Extrabiblical evidence from the Persian period supports this change in Jewish circumstances. In the early fifth century B.C. Persian control in the Mediterranean area tightened as a response to rising pressure from the Greeks. Forts were constructed on both sides of the Jordan River, in the coastal plain and in the hill country. Demographic charts reveal that Judah did not flourish in this period (538-450 B.C.). The Jews turned increasingly to eschatological thinking as a negation of their current, depressed situation.

To this disheartened community, Zechariah presents a picture of God who is in control of world history until the end of time. God had not forgotten; he was just not ready to act. Jewish autonomy would come eventually. The daughter of Zion was still the apple of God's eye.

Outline

1:1—8:23	Encouraging the Jewish Community
1:1-6	Introduction
1:7—6:15	Night Visions
7:1—8:23	Keeping the Covenant
9:1—14:21	Eschatological Oracles
9:1—11:17	The Messianic King
12:1—14:21	God's Final War

Commentary

Encouraging the Jewish Community (Zech 1—8)

Introduction (Zech 1:1-6)

God's love for his people, a central theme in Zechariah, is apparent in the introductory verses. God pleads with Israel, "Return to me, says the LORD of hosts, and I will return to you" (Zech 1:3). God promises to meet his people halfway, as it were. He is more than willing to mend their broken relationship. The tone of the book is not accusatory but encouraging. In the eight night visions (Zech 1:7—6:15) God pledges support to Judah. These visions address particular community problems and promise divine aid.

Night Visions (Zech 1:7—6:15)

In the first vision, that of the horses of the divine patrol, God is presented as a sort of universal watchman with a particular interest in Jerusalem. His love for the city is intense, and he declares, "I am very jealous for Jerusalem and for Zion" (Zech 1:14). God is angry that the nations he has used as a chastising agent against his people have punished them more than they had deserved. He promises to show compassion to the city in the future and enrich it.

Zechariah's language personifies Jerusalem as a woman. Words such as "comfort," "choose" and "jealous" reveal the depth of personal emotion God feels. The use of the root *kinah* ("jealous") is especially noteworthy. The word is probably related to the Arabic cognate, which means to become extremely red (or black) with dye. Thus God's love for Jerusalem is intense, strong enough to fight the whole world on its behalf. Other prophets describe God's intense feeling for Israel as a marriage relationship in which the husband, God, will not give up his wife, Israel, despite her unfaithfulness to him (Jer 3:1-14, 20-22; Ezek 16:8-14, 38, 60-63; Hos 11:8-9).

The third vision speaks to the Jews' anxiety because of lack of protection from their enemies. Archaeologists estimate the size of Jerusalem at this time to be four to five acres and to include no more than four hundred people. The size of Judah in the early Persian period has been compared with that of Rhode Island, and estimates of its population are well under ten thousand persons. Evidently the large group of Jewish exiles of the first return had dwindled considerably. In such a small, threatened community many Jews no doubt questioned the wisdom of the temple building project. How could the temple be protected, even if it could be built?

God encourages the Jews by promising to be a "wall of fire" around Jerusalem and "glory" within it (Zech 2:5). Again Zechariah portrays God as jealously protective of his people. He is like fire, powerful and dangerous, ready to blaze hotly against any enemy of his people.

Kabod, God's glory, is the almost tangible evidence of the divine presence. To experience God's glory is to sense his presence. Ezekiel states that God's glory abandoned Jerusalem just before the city's destruction (Ezek 10:18-19; 11:22-24) but would return in the future (Ezek 32:3; 33:3; 43:2-5). Zechariah claims that divine glory will permeate Jerusalem and extend throughout the land of Israel (Zech 2:12; 14:20-21).

Israel is described as the pupil or "apple of [God's] eye" (Zech 2:8 NRSV, KJV). Whoever harms Israel harms, as it were, the very pupil of God's eye. This radical imagery emphasizes the preciousness of God's people to him. They are as important as one of his eyes. Israel is compared with the vulnerable pupil of the eye, thus illustrating the sensitivity God feels toward his people. Moreover, it is as if he cannot see the world without first seeing his people and their concerns. They are always in front of him.

Zechariah calls the Jews "daughter Zion" and urges them to "sing and rejoice" (Zech 2:10). The phrase "daughter Zion" intensifies the personification of Jerusalem as a woman. In the ancient world daughters were dependent on their parents for financial support and for daily decision making. They had the least independence of anyone in society. This is just what God wants of his people: their complete dependence on him. God was once very angry with daughter Zion, causing the author of Lamentations to compare her with a lonely widow, a captured princess and a weeping woman deserted by her lovers and friends (Lam 1:1-2). Zechariah promises that laments like this one will be turned into joy, for God is coming to dwell among his people. He will again choose Jerusalem as the site of his house. The rabbinic translation of Zechariah interprets the word *bahar* ("choose") here as "taking pleasure in." One day God will again be proud of daughter Zion.

In Zechariah's fourth vision Judah's problem is the torment of guilt. Joshua the high priest officiates in the temple in filthy robes, and Satan, like a prosecuting attorney, accuses him before God. However, God rebukes Satan and declares Joshua to be innocent.

Joshua's filthy clothing represents a deeper problem than physical uncleanness. Clothing is often a symbol for a person's moral condition (*see* Purity Laws Related to Women; Leviticus). In this case the filthiness of Joshua's clothes represents his impurity and that of the people. First there is the ritual impurity of a priest born and reared in a foreign land and thus unfit to serve in the temple as the people's representative before God. Ezekiel implies that a ritual of water sprinkling was necessary in order for any returned exile to be cleansed from the impurity of foreign lands (Ezek 36:24-25). Second, the people had been guilty of various sins. The problem of foreign wives and their idolatrous ways had tainted the people and penetrated even to the priesthood and Joshua's family (Ezra 10:18; cf. Neh 13:23-27; Mal 2:11). The filthiness of Joshua's clothes contrasts starkly with the holiness of God's presence. Similarly the prophet Isaiah felt impure in the presence of God until an angel touched his lips with a burning coal and pronounced him pure (Is 6:5-7).

In Scripture clothing can also refer to righteousness or righteous deeds (1 Tim 2:9-10; Is 61:10; Job 29:14; Rev 19:8). Replacing Joshua's filthy clothes with clean garments symbolizes the change in his status before God and, by extension, the status of all of the returned exiles. The proclamation of innocence is accomplished by God as an executive decree. The angel, as the divine representative, pronounces, "See, I have taken your guilt away from you" (Zech 3:4). God rebukes Satan directly (Zech 3:2), and the divine declaration of innocence is more than sufficient to nullify Satan's accusation. God identifies himself as "the LORD who has chosen Jerusalem" (Zech 3:2). In other words, God has arbitrarily chosen Jerusalem, and even though Israel has sinned, God has not totally rejected the people and never intended to do so (Zech 1:17; 2:12). The feelings of guilt and inadequacy that were tormenting Joshua and the people were groundless.

In the fifth vision, God promises strength to overcome opposition and rebuild the temple. Zechariah sees a gold lampstand with a bowl on the top. Two olive trees flanking the lampstand supplied the bowl with oil via two gold pipes. Oil poured out of the bowl into the seven lamps of the lampstand. Through this vision God encouraged the people, represented by the lampstand, that the seeming mountain of opposition they faced would not be leveled by force but by his Spirit, represented by the oil and the light.

Opposition was from both within and outside of the community. The local Samaritans had opposed the Jews by accusing them of sedition to the Persian authorities (Ezra 4:1-16). Additionally the Jewish community was divided. Some Jews felt that the temple rebuilding effort was too large a task for the struggling community. Some of these people had even seen Solomon's magnificent temple (Hag 2:3; Ezra 3:12) and felt that its re-creation was impossible in light of the current economic hardships and foreign taxation. Any substitute would be viewed as a small thing (Zech 4:10).

The emphasis in this vision is on the oil representing God's Spirit as the agent of success (Zech 4:6; cf. Mt 25:1-12; 1 Jn 2:20, 27; Rev 4:5). The oil furnishes the light. Throughout the Old Testament oil was used to anoint kings, prophets and priests. When an individual was anointed, God conferred upon him the Holy Spirit, guaranteeing him support (1 Sam 16:13-14; 18:12), strength (Ps 89:21-25) and wisdom (Is 11:1-4). The idea was that people became God's representatives empowered by his Spirit. The Spirit was poured on God's servants, even as the anointing oil was poured on the candidate for service (cf. Acts 2:17-18). In this vision the two leaders, symbolized by olive branches, are channels of God's Spirit to the community. Zechariah's audience would have undoubtedly understood these anointed ones to be Joshua and Zerubbabel, their religious and civil (or priestly and Davidic) officials.

Zechariah's seventh vision concerns the removal of sin from the community. The prophet envisions a woman confined in a basket with a lid of lead. The interpreting angel explains that the woman represents wickedness and pushes the heavy lid down on her. Two women with wings like those of a stork lift up the basket and take it to the land of Shinar, where they will build a house for it.

The word *ephah,* translated "basket" (NRSV, NIV), "barrel" (NEB) or "tub" (NJPS), is not usually a term for a container but rather a measurement for dry goods. The exact size of an ephah, or a container large enough to contain an ephah, is unknown but ranges from approximately five to ten gallons. The problem is that even a ten-gallon container is not large enough to contain a woman. Thus the woman in the vision was stuffed into the basket and restrained only by its heavy lid from leaping out.

The woman in the basket represents evil. She may have looked like a fertility goddess or a genie in a jar. Like evil, she was hidden from sight but was a dangerous force difficult to contain. Indeed, wickedness cannot be confined but must be removed with divine aid (*see* Sin; Holiness and Wholeness).

Why does Zechariah personify wickedness as a woman? Some commentators suggest that the impurity of menstruation, a common metaphor used by the prophets for sin, is at the root of this analogy (cf. Ezek 36:17; *see* Menstruation). Others point out that sin, especially idolatry, is sometimes described as prostitution, an evil involving women (Hos 2:2; Jer 23:10; Ezek 16:15). One suggestion is that the woman in the basket represents the foreign women with whom many Jews had wrongfully intermarried. Some interpreters claim that women are inherently more susceptible to sin and so are an appropriate symbol for evil (*see* Genesis). This last view, however, is countered by the fact that in this vision women are also the agents of sin's removal. The winged women remove the evil creature from the land.

Probably the answer to the female gender of wickedness in this vision is grammatical. The term *wickedness (rish'ah)* is feminine and so must be represented by feminine pronouns, adjectives and verbs. It is worthy of note that the Hebrew letters of *rish'ah* form an anagram of the name Asherah, the Canaanite goddess whom so many Israelites had worshiped to their destruction. In any case, inherent female association with evil cannot be claimed on the basis of grammar, especially since the opposite of evil, righteousness *(tsedakah)*, is another feminine noun.

If the woman in the basket symbolizes a pagan goddess as the archrepresentative of evil, the symbolism of the shrine that is prepared for her in Babylon becomes clear. The goddess in a Babylonian temple was seated in a special chamber, or cella. She was the sole occupant of this room, considered to be the holiest room in the shrine. The transfer of the evil goddess, who represents the evil that had controlled Judah, to a shrine in Babylon is necessary for the countermovement of God to his temple in Jerusalem. In order for Yahweh to move into his house, other gods had to move out.

Syrian synagogue fresco depicting Aaron in temple. (Zechariah 6:11-13)

Keeping the Covenant (Zech 7—8)

After the night visions, Zechariah's focus shifts to the matter of Israel's obligation to the covenant with God, that is, obedience to God's laws of justice and mercy. Through Zechariah God reminds the Jews, positively, to render true judgment and show kindness and, negatively, not to oppress other human beings or devise evil against them in any way. Justice in society, as called for by the prophets, is not an abstract ideal but consists of daily, ethical transactions between individuals regardless of their social status (Amos 2:6-8; Mic 2:1-5; *see* God's Call to Social Justice). The way in which one Israelite treats another directly affects the larger covenant relationship between God and Israel.

Kindness and mercy follow justice here, as they do in other passages (Deut 10:18; Mic 6:8). Indeed, there can be no kindness without justice. *Hesed,* an attitude of love often translated "kindness," refers to close human relationships, especially between family members, friends and allies. *Hesed* also refers to loyalty and faithfulness. "Faithful love" may be a good translation of the term. *Rahamim* ("mercy" or "compassion") comes from the same root as *rehem,* which means "womb." It signifies compassion, the epitome of which is seen in a mother toward her child.

The exhortation includes warnings not to oppress the poor, orphans, fatherless, sojourners, widows and other unfortunate members of society. The term for widow, *almanah,* is a particular one that refers to a widow who has no means of financial support. All of the persons in this list are disadvantaged. God is warning Israel not to cater to those individuals who are financial contributors in society but to treat all Jews with respect as equal partners to the divine covenant.

Zechariah 1—8 concludes with God's promise that he will return to Jerusalem and cause it to flourish as never before. The elderly are living in peace and relaxation, and children are not forced into labor but are allowed to play. Not only will the citizens prosper but also God promises to bring Jews back to Jerusalem from all over the world. God reiterates his strong feelings for Zion (see above on Zech 1:14). The root *kinah* ("to be jealous") appears three times in Zechariah 8:2, again emphasizing God's absolute commitment to his people. Zechariah foresees that Jerusalem will one day reciprocate God's devotion and will even be called "the faithful city" (Zech 8:3). Since Jerusalem had been described as a prostitute more than once by the prophets (Is 1:21; Lam 1:8-9), this designation is striking.

In Zechariah's day Jerusalem was not the happy place pictured above. Archaeologists describe it as a congested cluster of buildings. Nevertheless God rebukes in advance any lack of faith in Zechariah's audience regarding the divine promises. He challenges them that they are measuring difficulty in their scales rather than in his: "If it is *yipale* ['impossible,' lit., 'too full of wonder'] in the sight of the remnant of this people in these days, should it also be *yipale*

Girls on seesaw. (Zechariah 8:5)

in my sight?" (Zech 8:6, author's translation). The language reminds the reader of God's challenge to Sarah, who did not believe that she could bear a child at her advanced age: "Is anything *yipale* for Yahweh?" (Gen 18:14; see also Jer 32:26). The Jews were to be encouraged that, although they were not enjoying these blessings at present, they were the sole link to Israel's glorious future. God promised to build up his future kingdom, which would attract even the Gentiles, upon their faithfulness.

Eschatological Oracles (Zech 9—14)

The Messianic King (Zech 9—11)

Zechariah 9—14 focuses on the future of Israel. Unlike the first part of the book, the second part makes no direct reference to present circumstances. It consists of two eschatological oracles, Zechariah 9—11 and Zechariah 12—14. Prominent themes include the future supremacy of Jerusalem and the messianic king.

Zechariah 9 brings good news. The daughter Zion is told to rejoice and shout because a wonderful king is coming to greet her (Zech 9:9). "Rejoice" *(gil)* refers to an expression of spontaneous joy and enthusiasm, generally without words and song. Shouting aloud *(rua')* often accompanies national celebrations, such as royal coronations (1 Sam 10:24), battle cries (Josh 6:10, 16, 20) and temple rejoicings (Ps 47:1; 66:1; 81:1). When God intervenes during times of desperation, his people break forth in shouts of joy.

The great king described in Zechariah 9:9-10 is like no other in history. He is triumphant but righteous. He is victorious but humble and gentle. Instead of riding a military horse, he rides on a lowly donkey. He brings world peace by destroying weapons of war. His reign will not be simply over Judah but will extend worldwide (cf. Ps 2:9; Is 11:4; Zech 14:17; Rev 19:15). New Testament writers identify the coming king as Jesus (Mt 21:5; Jn 12:15). The triumphal entry of Jesus riding into Jerusalem on a lowly donkey in the first century A.D. was hailed by crowds of Jews who expected in Jesus the fulfillment of prophecy.

On this day of national salvation, God promises that Israel will sparkle as jewels in a *nezer* ("crown," Zech 9:16). Isaiah makes a similar claim, "You shall be a crown of beauty in the hand of [Yahweh], and a royal diadem in the hand of your God" (Is 62:3). *Nezer* is used of the gold diadem on the high priest's turban (Ex 29:6) as well as of a royal crown (2 Kings 11:12). Both items are appropriate symbols for the future of God's people. Israel will finally fulfill its mission as a priestly nation, a people who are holy before God (Ex 29:6). They will also be political rulers over the rest of the world (Zech 14:12-16).

In the fifth century B.C., the political situation was bleak for Judah. In response to the rise of the Greeks in the west, the Persians had increased military domination along the Mediterranean coast. Nevertheless, in God's master plan his people would overcome all of their enemies under the banner of the messianic king who would rule the world in peace and righteousness.

Finding true leadership is a perennial problem for God's people. Jews in Zechariah's community were looking in the wrong places for guidance by resorting to diviners and household gods (*see* Household Gods). It was easy for false shepherds to lead the flock of Israel astray. Nevertheless God is aware of every need, including the problem of deceivers, and he urges total reliance on him. He promises to make the lowly sheep like a proud steed in battle (Zech 10:3).

Zechariah compares the messianic king

with a cornerstone, the stone that is laid between two walls to hold them together. Scripture occasionally uses this metaphor to describe Israel's leaders (Judg 20:2; 1 Sam 14:38). Both the Jewish targums and the New Testament identify Zechariah's cornerstone with the Messiah. Peter accuses the Sanhedrin of rejecting the cornerstone when it rejected Jesus Christ (Acts 4:11). First Peter identifies Jesus as the cornerstone on the basis of Old Testament prooftexts: "See, I am laying in Zion a stone, a cornerstone chosen and precious; and whoever believes in him will not be put to shame. . . . The stone that the builders rejected has become the very head of the corner" (1 Pet 2:6-7; cf. Ps 118:22; Is 28:16).

How is it possible to distinguish the true leader from the false one? Based on the divine model of leadership, Zechariah 10 reveals the quintessential ingredient that is present in the genuine shepherd but lacking in the false one: compassion. The reason God brings Israel back from exile, according to Zechariah, is compassion. By contrast, deceitful leaders will "tell false dreams and give empty consolation" (Zech 10:2). Jesus claims that the good shepherd would even be willing to lay down his life for the sheep (Jn 10:11).

The true prophet-shepherd is revealed in Zechariah 11. Several overtones throughout the chapter remind Christians of Jesus. Jesus presents himself as the good shepherd who is truly concerned about the sheep (Jn 10:11); he is bought for thirty pieces of silver, which are later cast into the temple (Mt 27:5); he breaks the exclusivity of the old covenant and gives the world a new one; and he is vindicated by the punishment of those who reject him. The divine Shepherd is not a new concept in Scripture, for God is often referred to as the Shepherd of his people (Ps 23:1; Ezek 34).

God's Final War (Zech 12—14)

Zechariah's final oracle could be titled "God and One Are a Majority" or "David and Goliath Revisited." It is a vivid description of the eschatological war against Judah. The nations of the world will eagerly muster troops for an expected easy victory over Jerusalem, but they will be destroyed by God.

Striking metaphors describe the battle. Jerusalem is described as a "cup of reeling" that the nations are quick to grab, but the potion causes them to become drunk and stagger. Jerusalem is also compared with a heavy, jagged stone (Zech 12:3). Those who try to lift it will only hurt themselves.

God can empower the weak who rely on him against strong opponents. Although Jerusalem appears weak on its own, God will, as in the days of Joshua, do most of the fighting, and the nations will have no chance against his weapons. In this battle God inflicts pain, panic, blindness and madness on the attackers (Zech 12:3-4). He will increase the strength of Judah so that they become like a blazing pot among wood and a flaming torch among sheaves of grain, in other words, invincible (Zech 12:6). Even the weakest of the people will be like the warrior king David, and the house of David will be like God (Zech 12:8).

After the military victory, the Jews mourn over the death of an anonymous hero for whom they feel responsible. Various suggestions have been raised for the identity of this martyr (lit., "pierced one"), from the martyrs of this battle to various prophets. However, it is important to note that the mourning over this individual is so intense that it brings about national repentance and purification. Whose death could bring about such a change?

New Testament authors identify the pierced one with Jesus Christ. John identifies the "one whom they have pierced" with Jesus (Jn 19:37). The phrase is used again in Revelation. The writer says that Christ will come in the clouds, and "every eye will see him, even those who pierced him; and on his account all the tribes of the earth will wail" (Rev 1:7; cf. Mt 24:30). The Revelator apparently interprets Zechariah's pierced one as Jesus.

Mourning over the pierced martyr will be intense. The term *mourning* appears five times in this passage and the word *grieve* twice. This grief will be equivalent to the sorrow over the death of an only child (Zech 12:10). In Israel mourners wore sackcloth and ashes, tore their garments and beard, wailed and prayed (*see* Grief and Bereavement). Sometimes professional mourners were employed as well. Public mourning lasted at least a week and could continue for a month. Mourning on this occasion will be done in groups of families, or clans (Zech 12:10). No professional mourners will be hired; rather, weeping will be done privately among one's kin.

Women will be separated from men during this mourning period. The visitor to modern Jerusalem will be reminded of the custom of separate prayer at the Western (or Wailing) Wall, the only remaining wall of the second temple courts. In accordance with rabbinic law, men pray on one side of the plaza and women on the other (*b. Sukk.* 51b, 52a). The point is to reduce distraction while communicating with God.

After a national cleansing, God will renew his covenant with Israel (Zech 13:9). God promises Zechariah, "I will say, 'They are my people'; and they will say, 'The LORD is our God' " (Zech 13:9). As in any marriage covenant, the responsibility of both parties is emphasized. Zechariah uses a call-and-response presentation to illustrate this mutual obligation: "They will call . . . and I will answer . . . I will say, 'They are my people,' and they will say, 'The LORD is our God.' " The reciprocal character of the covenant is evident even in the syntax Zechariah uses. The pronouns are arranged in chiastic symmetry: "they . . . I . . . I . . . they."

Zechariah 14 refers to the same eschatological battle described in the preceding chapters. However, this time the battle is presented from a different angle and its aftermath is included. The first scene is a shocking picture of God descending on the Mount of Olives, on the east side of Jerusalem, and splitting the mountain with his feet (Zech 14:4). The Mount of Olives, which faced the east side of the temple, was a place of worship in antiquity, whether for good (2 Sam 15:32) or evil (1 Kings 22:43). Jesus went to the Mount of Olives many times to pray, especially in the Garden of Gethsemane (Mt 26:30; Lk 19:37; Jn 8:1). The sense of holiness attached to the mountain continued throughout the Middle Ages, and the rabbis offered prayers regularly on it. Throughout history, many Jews have been buried on this mountain in order to ensure their resurrection when the feet of God burst open the mountain.

As a result of this battle, Jerusalem will become the capital of the world. Zechariah's emphasis on Jerusalem throughout the book reaches a climax in this final chapter. The kingdom will be spectacular. World peace will finally be achieved under divine rule. Changes in climate will be supernatural, including the elimination of cold, frost and even the cycle of day and night. Miraculously, water will flow out of Jerusalem, which has always depended on an outside water source. In addition, the city will be physically elevated so as to become an impregnable fortress visible to everyone.

The survivors of the nations will be forced to come to Jerusalem to worship God and keep the Feast of Booths *(Sukkot)*. This feast, also called the Feast of Ingathering or simply the feast, was one of the three pilgrimage festivals when the nation gathered together at the temple before God (Deut 16:16; cf. 1 Kings 8:2; Neh 8:14; Ps 81:3; Ezek 45:25). Great joy, for the ingathering of the harvest as well as for the continuance of the covenant, was characteristic of the feast (Ex 23:16; 34:2; Lev 23:40: Deut 16:14-15; Neh 8:17). The feast had universalistic and nationalistic elements. The feast was open to everyone, even the stranger (Ezra 3:4; Neh 8:14-18), but *Sukkot* was a time of renewing the covenant between God and Israel; the law was read publicly on this occasion. Zechariah describes a future ingathering of humanity when all nations will be assembled under the banner of the messianic King and will come at least once a year to Jerusalem to worship.

Jerusalem will be the epicenter of holiness in the eschatological kingdom. Holiness will extend outward from the temple to encompass the city and land. Ordinary cooking pots in Jerusalem will become sacred and fit to contain sacrificial meat. Pots in the temple will be as holy as those used at the altar. In fact, all food cooked in Jerusalem will have holy status (cf. Lev 17:3-4). Even the horse, heretofore used for war, will be drafted into the service of holiness. Its bells will be engraved with the words "Holy to the Lord," the same words that were engraved on the high priest's golden diadem. The biblical ideal that Israel would be a holy priesthood unto God and the land a center for divine activity will finally be realized.

Bibliography. J. Baldwin, *Haggai, Zechariah, Malachi: An Introduction and Commentary* (Downers Grove, IL: IVP, 1972); K. L. Barker, "Zechariah," in *Expositor's Bible Commen-*

tary, vol. 7, ed. F. E. Gabelein (Grand Rapids, MI: Zondervan, 1985) 593-697; C. L. and E. M. Meyers, *Haggai, Zechariah 1—8,* Anchor Bible 25B (Garden City, NY: Doubleday, 1987); D. L. Petersen, *Haggai and Zechariah 1—8: A Commentary* (Philadelphia: Westminster Press, 1984).

HANNAH K. HARRINGTON

MALACHI

Introduction

Malachi, the last of the twelve Minor Prophets, concludes a collection that spans the history of Israel from the mid-eighth century B.C. through at least the fifth century B.C. God's people had lost their status as nation-states, suffered conquest and exile, and survived as scattered communities in the Persian Empire. Under Persian rule the focus of Jewish life was the province of Yehud in the satrapy Beyond the River. The province was ruled by a Persian-appointed governor from Jerusalem, where the Lord's temple had been rebuilt with imperial sponsorship near the end of the sixth century.

The return from exile and the new temple began to fulfill earlier promises of restoration after judgment. Zechariah 9—14, however, reveal generations of further restoration, more internal dissension and external attack before the day Yahweh becomes King over all the earth and the nations go up to Jerusalem to worship. The book of Malachi reaffirms and supplements earlier eschatological prophecy, but its main purpose is to communicate God's word and will for the generations waiting for the Lord's coming. Through Malachi God urges repentance, obedience to the law, faithfulness within the covenant community and the fear of the Lord.

Malachi's ministry and the composition of the book cannot be dated precisely. The rebuilt temple, completed by 515 B.C., had been in operation long enough for Malachi's audience to become disillusioned and cynical about worship there. A governor administered Persian rule and accepted tribute. When Nehemiah held this office twice during the reign of Artaxerxes I (464-423 B.C.), he did not accept material support from the populace. Ezra taught and enforced covenant law in Jerusalem in the middle of the fifth century. Ezra and Nehemiah also dealt with the problem of mixed marriages, a recurring threat to the restoration community. These common concerns suggest a time in the fifth century for Malachi's ministry.

Although the Persian emperor had contributed to the temple building, the Jews worshiping there acknowledged the Lord as king. At the temple they remembered their history and maintained their identity as the Lord's people. In temple worship the Jews enjoyed more autonomy as a community than in any other area of life.

Six dispute speeches make up most of Malachi. Each speech has three basic parts. God makes an opening statement, either an announcement of good news or an accusation. Then a question arising from the opening statement is attributed to the audience. The question exposes the issues that may cause the audience to doubt or resist the divine word. God answers the question with examples and instruction for living faithfully while waiting for the Lord's coming.

Outline

Commentary

Superscription (Mal 1:1)

The book gives no personal information about Malachi. Even his name sounds more like a title than a personal name. Malachi, "my messenger," does not fit the practice of a parent naming a son as a testimony (e.g., Gen 27—28). Rather, God is the one who sends messengers. Messengers (also translated "angels") appear frequently in Haggai, Zechariah and Malachi; Haggai is called "the messenger of the LORD" (Hag 1:13). No call or naming account exists for Malachi, and no Old Testament prophet is given a new name at his or her call.

God's Love for Jacob (Mal 1:2-5)

The first word in Malachi is a declaration of God's enduring love. As evidence, the divine word reveals how God has loved Israel since before the birth of their ancestor, Jacob/Israel. The story of God's dealings with Esau and Jacob and the nations that came from them, Edom and Israel, shows the consequences of God's choice. Jacob is the bearer of the covenant and promises previously given to Abraham and Isaac (Gen 25:23; 28:13-15; Rom 9:10-13), but being loved and chosen did not give Jacob/Israel domestic security or political independence. Esau became wealthy and powerful in Edom; Jacob lived as a dependent in his father-in-law's household, far from the Promised Land. Jacob then went to Egypt, where his descendants became slaves, while Esau's descendants became chiefs in Edom.

God gave Israel and Edom their own land, but by Malachi's time both countries had been conquered. Malachi 1:3 reports fulfillment of the judgments against Edom in Isaiah 34:6, Ezekiel 35:3-4 and Joel 3:19. God's choice of and love for Jacob is evident because Israel by God's grace had been brought back to its land and had rebuilt the capital city and temple. When Edom tries to rebuild, however, God promises to thwart their efforts. Several bitter denunciations support the designation *wicked:* Edom had taken revenge and planned to devour Judah (Ezek 25:12-13; 35:1-15). The Edomites also were guilty of violence and shedding innocent blood (Joel 3:19). Obadiah accuses Esau of betraying his brother when the Babylonians took Jerusalem (Obad 10-14; Ps 137:7). God's anger against Edom is for just cause, and Malachi's audience will witness its effects.

The Priests Despise God's Name (Mal 1:6—2:9)

Terminology suited to a patriarchal household, "father" and "master" (Mal 1:6), applies to the function of the temple as a divine dwelling place. God had chosen Jerusalem "as a dwelling for his name"

(Deut 12:11). Priests ministered there in the Lord's name, responsible to live holy lives and carry out their duties so that the Lord's name would not be profaned. The altar as "table" and the offerings as "food" (Mal 1:7, 12) point to the temple communion meals and the provisions made for priests and their families.

Women participated in worship at the temple (*see* Women in Worship). Women sang in the temple choir (Ezra 2:65; Neh 7:67) and may also have played in the orchestra (1 Chron 25:5-6). Certain offerings were specifically required of women (Lev 12:6; 15:29), and other sacrificial obligations fell on women and men (e.g., Lev 14, the purification of lepers). Women could make vows, including the Nazirite vow, although their fathers or husbands could cancel the vows (*see* Numbers). Vows typically included an offering, so free-will offerings must have been performed by women. A person bringing a peace offering not only provided the sacrificial animal but also slaughtered it and then made a meal of the parts not reserved for God or the priests. Since pregnancies and prolonged breast-feeding occupied most of women's fertile years, ritual impurity due to menstruation probably restricted women's participation only a fraction of the time (*see* Menstruation; Leviticus; Purity Laws).

This second dispute speech accuses the priests of showing contempt for God by accepting forbidden animals for sacrifices. The priests have called their responsibilities a "burden" (NIV; Mal 1:13), a word used elsewhere to refer only to hardship suffered under Egypt, Assyria and Babylon (Ex 18:8; Num 20:14; Neh 9:32; Lam 3:5). The priests were privileged to bless the people, putting Yahweh's name upon them, but God had made those blessings ineffectual as a consequence of the priests' failure to honor the name of the Lord. The temple and its rituals constituted a gracious gift of access to the divine presence. God, however, remained free to shut the doors and, someday, to receive pure offerings everywhere.

The priests' faulty teaching and practice fostered falsehood, teaching the people that the Lord was less worthy of respect than the Persian-appointed governor. Whenever they accepted a blemished sacrifice in place of the perfect animal someone had vowed to give to God, they taught the people to cheat. And they destroyed the witness of temple worship to the truth that the Lord's name is to be feared among the nations.

God desired to preserve the priesthood. Malachi's profile of the ideal priest who reveres God's name, teaches the truth and turns many from iniquity condemns his priestly audience by comparison. Yet Malachi 2:1-4 introduces this condemnation as a command to be heeded. There is opportunity for priests to repent and follow the model of Levi.

Faithlessness Within the Covenant Community (Mal 2:10-16)

Malachi appeals again to the metaphor of the patriarchal household and to his audience's belief that members of the household

Marriage

Old Testament

In the Pentateuch

The union of a man and woman in an exclusive and procreative covenant of marriage is presented as God's creative intention in the two stories of creation with which the Old Testament begins. In Genesis 1, God creates humans male and female, blesses them and commands them to be fruitful and together to exercise dominion over the earth. In Genesis 2, God first creates the male and then determines that it is not good that the man should be alone. God remedies the solitariness of the man by creating the woman to be his "helper" (Gen 2:20), a word most commonly used in the Old Testament to refer to someone who rescues another from distress. The woman is one who corresponds to him and complements him, so that together they are complete.

When God brings the woman to the man, he exclaims, "This at last is bone of my bones and flesh of my flesh" (Gen 2:23), an evocative description of the covenantal unity and mutual dependence of marriage. The story ends with the observation, "Therefore a man leaves his father and his mother and clings to his wife, and they become one flesh" (Gen 2:24). The relationship between a husband and wife in marriage takes precedence over the relationship of children to their parents, not for the wife only, as might be expected in a patriarchal society, but for the husband as well.

Few marriages in the Old Testament conform to the pattern set out in Genesis 1—2. While there are examples in the Bible of marriages that are faithful, loving and in harmony with the purposes of God, there are many more examples of marriages that are disrupted by polygamy, concubinage, infidelity, divorce and infertility. Marriage in the Old Testament is just as untidy and complex as marriages in postbiblical societies. It is thus important "to distinguish between the divine will in marriages and O[ld] T[estament] marriages as they are illustrated. The latter may reflect the former, but not necessarily so" (Hamilton and Collins, 4:560).

There is no unified body of marriage law in the Old Testament. Scattered throughout the various legal codes in the Old Testament are laws that address such matters as whom one may not marry, the dissolution of marriage and remarriage. A person is not permitted to marry a variety of persons related to him or her by blood or by marriage (Lev 18:6-18). Marriage to a member of certain foreign peoples is prohibited (Deut 7:3), although other passages suggest that marriage to foreigners was not necessarily always evil. Examples are the permission given for Israelite men to marry foreign prisoners of war (Deut 21:10-14) and the account in the book of Ruth about the marriages of Ruth the Moabite to two Israelite men.

Some laws regulate situations that appear to be inconsistent with God's creative intent for marriage. For example, monogamy is presented as an ideal, but there is a law that requires fairness from a man who is married to two wives at the same time (Deut 21:15-17). Similarly, lifelong marriage is presented as an ideal, but there are laws regulating divorce. If a divorced and remarried woman is divorced again or widowed, the man who first divorced her may not marry her again (Deut 24:1-4).

Levirate Marriage

Deuteronomy 25:5-10 addresses the question what is to become of a childless widow. If a woman's husband dies without offspring, the brother of the deceased man is to perform "the duty of a husband's brother to her" by fathering a son with her. This is called levirate marriage, from the Latin *levir* ("brother-in-law"). As Leviticus 18:16 forbids sexual relations with one's sister-in-law, levirate marriage must be seen as an exception to this more general prohibition. Levirate marriage persisted into the New Testament period, as evidenced by the Sadducees' question to Jesus about the childless widow who was married in turn to each of seven brothers (Mt 22:23 pars. Mk 12:18-27; Lk 20:27-40).

Instances of levirate marriage are portrayed in Genesis 38 and Ruth. In neither story are the details in accord with the prescriptions of Deuteronomy 25. In Genesis 38, Tamar's father-in-law finally and unwittingly performs the duty of the levirate; in Ruth it is a distant relative. In addition, Deuteronomy 25 specifies that the child is to "succeed to the name of the deceased brother," but in the genealogies of the sons born to Tamar and to Ruth, the biological fathers are named, not the deceased husbands. This suggests that "levirate marriage in the O[ld] T[estament] is not simply concerned with producing a male child nor with producing an heir to the dead man's property. It is concerned just as much, if not more, with the support and protection of the widow" (Hamilton and Collins, 4:567).

The Prophets

The prophets use the metaphor of marriage to describe God's relationship to the covenant people, Israel. The prophet Hosea's tragically broken marriage to Gomer becomes in Hosea's prophetic utterances an illustration of Israel's unfaithfulness to God and God's consequent heartbrokenness over her infidelity. As Hosea anticipates his eventual reconciliation with his wife, this also becomes an illustration of God's reconciliation with his spouse, Israel. Hosea looks forward to the time when Israel will call God not "my Baal" ("owner, master") but "my husband" (Hos 2:16). This juxtaposition of "Baal" with "husband" constitutes a strong affirmation that a wife is not meant to be a slave but a trusted covenant partner and friend.

Jeremiah follows Hosea in using the language of infidelity to describe Judah's unfaithfulness to God (Jer 2:20-25; 3:1-3). Judah's political allies are called her "lovers" (Jer 22:20, 22; 30:14; see also Hos 8:9). Ezekiel 16:8 uses two expressions to speak of God's marriage to Judah: "I spread my skirt over you," that is, "I married you" (cf. Ruth 3:9); and "I made a covenant with you." The remainder of Ezekiel 16 is an extended description of Judah's unfaithfulness as shameless adultery and of God's efforts to call her back to fidelity and to reestablish his covenant with her (Ezek 16:60). Isaiah describes God's joy in Israel as that of a bridegroom for his bride (Is 61:10; 62:5). Malachi describes God's people as his "wife by covenant" and Israel's apostasy as "divorce" (Mal 2:14-16).

New Testament

The Gospels

Marriage is presented in the Gospels as an ordinary and unremarkable aspect of human life, like eating and drinking (cf. Mt 24:28 par. Lk 17:27). Within that context, Jesus calls all persons to follow him. The only person whose marital status Jesus addresses is the Samaritan woman (Jn 4:7-30), and the effect is to make her a disciple and an evangelist. When a woman calls out to Jesus, "Blessed is the womb that bore you" (Lk 11:27), Jesus replies, "Blessed rather are those who hear the word of God and obey it!" Discipleship is thus presented as more fundamental than marriage or parenthood.

Jesus emphasizes the importance of marital fidelity (Mk 10:19 par. Mt 19:3-9; Lk 18:20; see also Jn 8:11) and explains that the commandment "do not commit adultery" forbids lust as well (Mt 5:28). In Jesus' day there were disagreements between religious teachers about the circumstances under which divorce was permissible (Mk 10:2-12 par. Mt 19:3-9). Jesus refuses to specify circumstances under which divorce is legitimate and instead emphasizes God's intention that marriage be indissoluble and the serious moral consequences that attend divorce.

Marriage figures a number of times in illustrations of the coming of the kingdom. The kingdom of God is like a great (wedding) banquet; one should not cite one's own marriage as an excuse for not attending (Lk 14:20; Mt 22:2-14). In fact, people may be required to abandon family (Mt 19:29; Mk 10:29) or even spouse (Lk 14:26; 18:29) in order to follow Jesus. Jesus' relation to people is like that of a bridegroom to his bride (Mk 2:19 par. Lk 5:34).

People should await Jesus' coming eagerly, as a wedding party eagerly awaits the bridegroom (Mt 25:1-12). Marriage is not a prerequisite for entry into the kingdom of heaven (Mt 19:10-12). At the resurrection, marriage will no longer exist (Mt 22:23 pars. Mk 12:18-27; Lk 20:27-40).

The Epistles

A prominent emphasis in the Epistles is on the importance of sexual fidelity in marriage. Paul's first word of exhortation in what is probably his earliest epistle is that a Christian should "Abstain from unchastity . . . [and] take a wife for himself in holiness and honor" (1 Thess 4:3-4 RSV). Marital fidelity is a way in which Christians image the holiness and purity of God (1 Thess 4:7). Conversely, fornication and adultery are just as incompatible with the kingdom of God as is idolatry (Eph 5:5; Phil 3:5). This spiritual dimension of marriage makes it imperative that a Christian marry only another Christian (1 Cor 7:39; 2 Cor 6:14-18).

In light of the demands of God's kingdom, Paul expresses a preference for singleness (1 Cor 7:1, 8, 26, 32-35, 40) but acknowledges that most people will marry (1 Cor 7:2, 9, 28, 36-38). Twice Scripture speaks of the relationship of husband and wife in terms of headship and likens this to the relationships among the church, Christ and God (1 Cor 11:3; Eph 5:21-33). Given the perfect peace and mutuality obtained between Christ and his head, God (1 Cor 11:3), and the self-emptying love with which Christ poured out himself for the church, of which he is the head (Eph 5:25-33), the headship that a husband is to exercise with respect to his wife is presumably to be characterized by similar peace, mutuality and self-emptying love. Accordingly, a number of other texts speak of the mutual self-giving of husband and wife (1 Cor 7:4; Eph 5:21; 1 Pet 3:1-7).

Marriage is a practical as well as a spiritual reality, and all Christians are to take care that their marriages are in good order. Bishops and deacons are to be "married only once" (1 Tim 3:2, 12), a requirement that demonstrates the compatibility of marriage and ministerial office and the importance of a well-regulated household for those who would be leaders in the church. Older Christian women are to help younger women learn to love their husbands and children in ways that glorify God (Tit 2:3-5). All Christians are to honor marriage and to respect the covenant between husband and wife (Heb 13:4).

Bibliography

H. Anderson and R. C. Fite, *Becoming Married* (Philadelphia: Westminster/John Knox, 1993); M. E. Cavanagh, *Before the Wedding* (Philadelphia: Westminster/John Knox, 1994); V. P. Hamilton and R. F. Collins, "Marriage," *Anchor Bible Dictionary* 4:559-72; C. S. Keener, *Paul, Women and Wives: Marriage and Women's Ministry in the Letters of Paul* (Peabody, MA: Hendrickson, 1992); W. Wangerin Jr., *As for Me and My House* (Nashville: Thomas Nelson, 1990).

MARGARET KIM PETERSON

---

ought to honor their father and not betray one another. The head of this household is the Lord, who had brought Israel into being by means of the covenant made at Sinai. Malachi's charge of treachery requires that his audience acknowledge their unifying identity as one people under one God.

The first example of faithlessness is marriage of a Jewish man to a woman who worships another god. If Yahweh is the father of the Jewish husband, then the wife by analogy is a daughter of the deity she worships. Deuteronomy 7:3-4 forbids this type of intermarriage, as well as marrying one's daughters to non-Yahweh-worshipers, because the children would learn to follow other gods. Intermarriage that led to apostasy cut off individuals, but this choice also hurt the community. Malachi calls this intermarriage an "abomination," a term used for idolatry, cultic prostitution and other rites pertaining to the service of other gods. In this way the holy people and God's sanctuary (Mal 2:11) would be profaned by such marriages.

Malachi's second example of faithlessness is divorcing "the wife of your youth" (Mal 2:14). In the Old Testament a husband could divorce his wife by writing out and giving to her a bill of divorce (Deut 24:1-4; *see* Divorce). The verb is literally "send away," and the husband owned the land (i.e., the means of livelihood; *see* Numbers). The Old Testament associates "the wife of your youth" with the joys of mutual discovery and devotion (Prov 5:18; Jer 3:2). The next term, *companion*, is unique, a feminine noun from a verb meaning "unite, be joined." The masculine form of the noun denotes men who work together and have similar values (Ps 119:63; Prov 28:24; Song 1:7; Is 1:23). This Hebrew word is an apt designation for a wife who has labored with her husband to build their family and to achieve shared goals of survival and sufficiency.

Finally, Malachi introduces the insight that she is "your wife by covenant." Instead of using marriage to illustrate the covenant, Malachi uses the theology of the Lord's covenant with Israel to interpret marriage (*see* Marriage). Although there are no marriage ceremonies in the Old Testament and marriage arrangements are never called covenants, the notion of marriage as a covenant has clear antecedents. In Deuteronomy 7:1-4 forbidden covenants between Israel and foreign nations parallel forbidden marriages between Israelites and non-Israelites. Marriage serves as a metaphor for the covenant relationship between the Lord and Israel (e.g., Hos 1—3). If the covenant is like a marriage, then a marriage could be like a covenant.

Laws regarding the conduct of wives and husbands are part of Israel's obligations under the covenant (e.g., Ex 20:14; 21:10). Jeremiah 33 provides the earliest example of people making a covenant with God and one another to observe a particular aspect of the law. One can imagine the development of an analogous practice between marriage partners.

Wife and husband were members of God's covenant people. The Lord's role as witness to the covenant between wife and husband includes knowing the content of their promises, warning them to keep their word and bringing charges against them when they fail. In Malachi 2:14, 16 the Lord as witness speaks on behalf of the wife against the faithless husband. Divorcing one's Jewish wife is an act of violence, says God. It belongs to a category of malicious harm ranging from injustice created by false testimony to bloodshed. Violence leaves its mark on the perpetrator (*see* Violence, Abuse and Oppression), in this case likened to a stain on the husband's garment. Because a man might spread the corner of his garment over a woman as a gesture pledging marriage (Ruth 3:9; Ezek 16:8), the garment becomes a symbol of the relationship between husband and wife (Deut 22:30).

The Lord desires godly offspring, which may refer to children of the husband and his Jewish first wife. They may have been more likely to remain faithful to God if their father had not broken faith with their mother. The other possible meaning of "godly offspring" embraces Israel, daughters and sons of the one God who created them as a people. By keeping faith with their Jewish wives, (whether or not their marriages are blessed with children) husbands preserve the covenant with God and guard the unity of the covenant community (*see* Covenant and Community).

Where Is the God of Justice? (Mal 2:17—3:5)

Malachi's audience has wearied the Lord with their words to one another of doubt and complaint. Evil people appear to enjoy God's favor. Why doesn't God restore justice?

The God of justice is indeed coming for judgment. The messenger of the covenant will prepare the way by purifying the priests. Then the divine judge will arrive to condemn those who are guilty according to the law.

These promises for the future are related to what God is doing in the interim. By the prophetic word God is reforming the priests. Priests who fear the Lord will teach God's law and set people on the way to doing justice. The standard for the future judgment will be the law they already know and should obey. That law protects widows, orphans, day laborers and aliens from oppression by the powerful (*see* God's Call to Social Justice; Yahweh's Concern for the Disenfranchised; Widows). The law refutes the idea that God delights in evil.

How to Return to the Lord (Mal 3:6-12)

Because the Lord doesn't change, Israel hasn't perished. Indeed, for as long as they had been turning away, God had loved them (Mal 1:2; cf. Hos 11:1-11). Because of this enduring fidelity God calls on them to repent and be restored to relationship with God (Mal 3:7; cf. Zech 1:3; Hos 14:1-8).

When the people question, "How?" the response is severe but practical: "You are robbing me!" (Mal 3:8). They must bring their full tithes and offerings. Offerings supported priests and Levites at the temple. Every third year Deuteronomy required the tenth of crops to be stored in the towns to feed landless widows, orphans, resident foreigners and Levites. Tithes were paid in grain, wine and oil and from flocks and herds. Tithing in the first and second years required that a family make a pilgrimage to the temple, where they were to eat their tithed produce and rejoice. The spiritual purpose of tithing was to learn to fear the Lord and not transgress any divine commands.

God's invitation to "put me to the test" (Mal 3:10) is given in the context of the covenant. The nation stands under the curses of the covenant because the people have violated their covenant obligations in the matter of the tithe (*see* Deuteronomy). As a nation, Malachi's audience can prove God's faithfulness to the covenant by bringing the full 10 percent. If they do, curses on the crops will be turned back and bountiful blessings will be given, as listed in Deuteronomy 28:8-12. The covenant is not, however, a means for Israel to manipulate God to bless them. God's people have the opportunity to return because of God's unchanging mercy.

Choosing to Fear the Lord (Mal 3:13—4:3)

The sixth dispute speech, like the fourth, has to do with the people's theological conversation. Speaking among themselves they say that either the Lord doesn't care about unrighteousness or lacks the power to do anything about it. God responds by describing the Lord's day of judgment, when the arrogant will be eliminated and the righteous spared.

A unique verse of narrative (Mal 3:16) interrupts the speech and describes a group who separated themselves from the rest of the audience. God acknowledges them as "my special possession" whom "I will spare" (Mal 3:17). The distinguishing feature of these people is that they fear the Lord. In Malachi fearing the Lord epitomizes the response God desires. This fear is not panic at the prospect of punishment but a fitting response to God's holiness, power and love. As this relationship matures, increasing reverence nourishes a love for and desire to serve God. Malachi's audience in every generation can choose to follow the example of those who fear the Lord and receive the promise of healing and deliverance on the day that God acts.

Coda: Moses and Elijah (Mal 4:4-6)

An admonition and a promise conclude Malachi and serve as a coda to the prophetic books. In Malachi, women and men who accept God's invitation to return and who fear the Lord keep the commands of the law. They accept as covenant obligations the statutes and ordinances that God gave at Horeb. As Joshua commanded Israel and David advised Solomon, so Malachi 4:4 extends the admonition to remember the teaching *(torah)* of Moses to every generation of Israel waiting for the Lord's day.

Malachi stood in a long line of prophets like Moses who called Israel to repentance and covenant faithfulness. Elijah appears at the beginning and the end of this line. On the great and terrible day of the Lord the guilty will not escape, but God will provide a way to survive (e.g., Joel 2:32; Zeph 2:3; Zech 13:7-9). Elijah's ministry of restoration will be part of that provision, so that the land may avoid the curse of destruction. In the Hebrew Bible Psalm 1 follows Malachi, with a beatitude on those who delight in the law of God. In the Christian Bible Matthew follows Malachi. Moses and Elijah appear with Jesus when he is transfigured, and Jesus reveals that Elijah has already come, namely, John the Baptist (Mt 17:1-13).

Bibliography. J. G. Baldwin, *Haggai, Zechariah, Malachi: An Introduction and Commentary,* Tyndale Old Testament Commentaries (Downers Grove, IL: IVP, 1972); B. Glazier-McDonald, *Malachi: The Divine Messenger,* Society for Biblical Literature Dissertation Series 98 (Atlanta: Scholars Press, 1987); M. I. Gruber, "Women According to the Priestly Code," in *Judaic Perspectives on Ancient Israel,* ed. J. Neusner, B. A. Levine and E. S. Frerichs (Minneapolis: Fortress, 1987) 35-48; G. P. Hugenberger, *Marriage as a Covenant: A Study of Biblical Law and Ethics Governing Marriage Developed from the Perspective of Malachi,* Supplements to Vetus Testamentum, vol. 52 (Leiden: E. J. Brill, 1994).

PAMELA J. SCALISE

Intertestamental History & Literature

It has been said that the New Testament and Christianity can be understood only by being reviewed against the backdrop of the Old Testament (Metzger, 151). It should be added that insights about the intertestamental era are also critical for grasping the historical, cultural and social context of the New Testament. The literature of this time discloses the nature, history and thought world of the people and times leading to the coming of Christ. We will briefly consider this literature for a glimpse of the wealth of insight included in it: history, 1- 2 Maccabees; philosophy, the four great schools of thought (Plato, Aristotle, the Stoics and the Epicureans); apocalyptic literature, 4 Esdras, 1-3 Enoch and 2 Baruch; stories, Tobit, Judith, Susanna, and Bel and the Dragon; and wisdom literature, Ecclesiasticus and the Wisdom of Solomon.

History

Jewish writers have provided two historical works that record the religious and political struggle of the Jews for freedom during the second century B.C. Written by writers independent of one another, for different purposes, they reveal vastly different perspectives of one of the most complicated historical eras recounted in literature. 1 Maccabees is a clear attempt to recount the events surrounding the rise of the Hasmonean dynasty from the courageous deeds of the priest Mattathias and his five sons to the reign of John Hyrcanus and the death of Simon, the last of the Maccabean brothers (c. 175-132 B.C.). Apparently this author wanted to set out these historical events in a chronological sequence, detailing the deeds of the Maccabean brothers. The text provides the context from which emerged some of the most important groups of the New Testament: the Pharisees, the Sadducees and the Zealots. In style this text can be distinguished from the biblical historical material by two traits (Goldstein, 12-21), the lack of reference to prophecy and the absence of the name of God. Like the biblical book of Esther, I Maccabees possibly avoids any reference to God because the divine names were too sacred to be used (Goldstein, 13).

The straightforward and unadorned style is more reflective of Hebrew thinking and language than Greek and indicates the likelihood of a Hebrew original underlying the Greek copies that we have.

In contrast to 1 Maccabees, 2 Maccabees is written in an emotional and dramatic style, a literary style called pathetic history, in which the author uses sensational language to create empathy in readers. Some scholars suggest that the author rewrote 1 Maccabees in the more popular style of the Alexandrean period, although it does cover a slightly different time frame (1 Macc, 175 to 132 B.C.; 2 Macc, 175 to 160 B.C.).

Several characteristics of the text are notable. The reverence for the temple is an important theme; amplification of miraculous elements attempt to reveal God's intervention in times of crisis and stand in marked contrast to the lack of this element in 1 Maccabees. There is a considerably more negative view of the Maccabean brothers than in 1 Maccabees, as the author includes their shortcomings and mistakes. This text was written in elegant Greek, whereas 1 Maccabees was probably originally written in Hebrew.

Philosophy

The period between the Testaments, or the four hundred silent years, was anything but silent philosophically. This era birthed the major philosophical schools or systems of thought that not only changed the perspectives of the world at that time but also posed questions that were to influence the rest of Western civilization. These are the schools of Plato, Aristotle, Zeno (the Stoics) and Epicurus. Their main concerns can be briefly summarized.

Plato, born around 427 B.C., is best known for recording the words and deeds of Socrates. He did not originate philosophy as we know it; he addressed the issues and concerns raised by those before him, the pre-Socratics Thales, Anaximander, Anaximenes, Pythagoras and others who raised questions about the nature of the universe, why things were as they were and conjectured about the source of it all. Although they proposed different solutions to these questions, these philosophers had several significant presuppositions in common. They all assumed that there was some sort of common source for the material universe and that nature as a whole could be explained and exhibited an order that was comprehensible. Plato, primarily via Socrates' teaching, also addressed these concerns but expanded his system to include issues of ethics and politics. He grounded this in a metaphysical dualism that sharply contrasted the immortal and unchanging soul or intellect with the perishability and changeability of the material world around us. This dualism centered around two major ideas: knowledge is innate and the truth of all things is always found in the soul or intellect; reality cannot be found in the changing, perishable material world of the senses.

Aristotle built on these ideas at first but later began to shift to a more empirical position that posited that all knowledge is rooted in sense experience, although through logical reasoning the intellect can move to an understanding of concepts. He developed the system of logic as we know it in order to demonstrate this intricate process of reasoning. It is also interesting to note that Aristotle was Alexander the Great's tutor.

Meanwhile, two other philosophers were struggling to develop systems of thought that would more quickly give people answers to the questions of how we should live and what we should believe: Zeno, founder of Stoicism, and Epicurus, founder of the Epicurean school of thought. Zeno found the answers to life in the order of the universe ruled by the logos, or reason (cf. Jn 1), while Epicurus advocated that the key to tranquility is to avoid pain. Although the Stoics acknowledged the presence of the gods more than did Epicurus, both systems hoped to give answers to life's questions when the traditional religion of the times seemed to be failing. Both systems are reflected in the New Testament in the use of vocabulary (such as *logos*, a major Stoic term). Both are mentioned by name in Acts 17, Paul's sermon on Mars Hill, where Paul directly relates Christianity to the thought world of that day.

Apocalyptic Literature

In approximately 200 B.C. the social and political unrest of this period led to the emergence of another body of literature concerning human destiny. These literary works became known as apocalyptic and tended to vary in form and literary characteristics. In these books, writers recorded visionary experiences that had been communicated to them by God. The books of 4 Esdras, 2 Baruch and 2 Enoch as well as the Old Testament book of Daniel and the New Testament book of Revelation are also apocalyptic.

The term *apocalyptic* derives from the Greek *apokalyptō* ("to unveil" or "to reveal") and generally includes a wide variety of forms incorporating symbolic utterances, visions, blessings, wisdom sayings, sacred sayings and parenesis. The account is presented in the form of a vision or rapture and is usually pseudonymous, that is, written under the name of an ancient spiritual person (e.g., Enoch, Esdras, Baruch or Moses).

The apocalyptist's message includes such concepts as time and history, angels and demons, the messianic kingdom and life after death. In this literature the secrets of the world beyond are disclosed to a prophetlike figure and interpreted by a divine agent. Answers are given to such issues as why the righteous suffer (4 Esd), when the end time will be (2 Bar) or whether there is a sequence of history (Dan). It is often a dualistic message emphasizing opposing forces of good and evil struggling to exert control over the world and human destiny. A strong sense of determinism maintains that the world is preordained, moving forward according to a divine plan and schedule. This message provides comfort and hope to a group that typically feels oppressed socially and theologically. God knows about the situation and will bring vindication to the righteous in preordained time.

The origin of apocalyptic concepts is difficult to determine. Some scholars trace its roots to foreign ideas found in Babylonia and Persia. For example, as Israel experienced extreme persecution during the Seleucid oppression (200-100 B.C.), the Jewish prophets were stimulated to look for answers of God's justice, judgment and vindication in the future. There was also a need for secrecy. Therefore writers tended to cloak the divine message of retribution in symbolic code. Some of the mystical codes (i.e., symbolism, numerology, animals to represent empires) may have been borrowed from the Eastern peoples.

Other scholars see apocalyptic literature as a continuation of Jewish prophecy, an expression of folklore, esoteric Jewish literature or a product of wisdom tradition, in which symbolic language was accepted as a divine means of communicating a message. The fact that it was difficult to interpret only heightened the idea that humans cannot easily understand God.

Apocalyptists expand the scope of prophecy to encompass a broader concept of time and space, belief in a future life, the expectation of a new heaven and earth, and the catastrophic end of the present world. The apocalyptist's message offers encouragement that God's end time will break into the present without the typical prophetic rebuke of sin and ethical admonitions. While prophets preached a message that was later written down, the apocalyptists recorded their visions usually under the name of an ancient prophet.

Jewish apocalyptic literature can help us understand the spiritual and theological struggles that the religious remnant of Israel was experiencing under Seleucid and Roman domination during the intertestamental period. Unlike the Old Testament prophetic voice, which attributed oppression to Israel's constant tendency to sin, the apocalyptists address the even more difficult situation in which oppression occurs even when righteousness is vigorously observed. God's message that he controls human destiny gives a larger perspective to his work in creation. An understanding of this literature's use of symbolism and visionary experiences can help us to understand the motivating factors that brought about Revelation and other New Testament apocalyptic passages. In times of social, political and spiritual crisis people tend to turn to the hope of a new social order in which righteousness would reign.

Stories

Among this literature can be found four short stories that are written in a delightful style and reveal various aspects of Jewish culture and piety during this era. Women feature prominently in three of the four stories.

Tobit, written by a devout Jew (c. 190-170 B.C.), uses the form of an adventure story to address the issue of God's role in the suffering of the righteous. The author shows by the example of Tobit that although calamities befall the righteous, God is with them in their suffering and brings all the trials to an eventual happy ending. The key component is that throughout the trials, the righteous one remains faithful to God. Tobit, a Galilean Jew, is taken captive to Babylon with his wife, Anna, and their son, Tobias. In spite of the surrounding paganism and idolatry, Tobit remains faithful to God, not only keeping the Jewish laws but also helping his fellow captives. Eventually he is allowed to return to his homeland, where he continues his good works. One day when he returns from an especially selfless deed, through an accident he loses his sight.

In another country a kinswoman, Sarah, a pious and devout woman, has also been suffering. She has been married seven times, and each time her husband dies before their wedding night, killed by a demon, Asmodeus. She, however, like Tobit, remains faithful to God. God hears the prayers of both faithful people and sends his angel Raphael to help.

Tobit, in a state of despair and praying for death, sends Tobias on an errand to the town where Sarah lives. On the way God reveals to Tobias that he is to marry Sarah, an event for which he is understandably reticent. Yet Tobias follows the angel's directions and marries Sarah. He also fulfills the rituals prescribed by Raphael to get rid of the demon that has killed her previous husbands. Tobias completes the wedding celebration and returns with his bride to his home. Tobias applies to his father's eyes some of the same remedy that expelled the demon. Tobit receives his sight once again, and the family celebrates the happy events with rejoicing.

The story of Tobit provides delightful examples, one of a man and one of a woman, who remain faithful to God in spite of serious suffering. God in his mercy restores wholeness and happiness to the family. Also included are lessons of faithfulness in marriage and the hope that the grace of God will triumph in the end.

Judith is a dramatically different kind of story, set in a time of war, probably around the time immediately following the Maccabean war. Although the story is set in a historical context, the reader is quickly made aware of historical and geographical errors so that it is apparent that the purpose is other than the recounting of a historical episode (see Moore, 33).

The story centers around a beautiful and wealthy widow who combines an intense devotion and piety for God with a grim cunning and treachery in order to save her country. The story is told in two parts, the first detailing the war between Israel and the Assyrians (Jdt 1—7) and the second describing Israel's deliverance brought about by Judith's clever plan (Jdt 8—16). Judith's plan is similar to the biblical story of Jael (Judg 4:4-22; 5:2-31), where by seduction and deception a woman brings about the defeat and death of Israel's enemy. Judith represents an intriguing picture of womanhood. Although she is beautiful and intensely devoted to God, yet she plays the role of a flatterer (Jdt 11:7-8), an equivocator (Jdt 12:14, 18), a liar (Jdt 11:10, 12-14, 18-19) and a ruthless assassin (Jdt 13:7-8). Although she lives a celibate existence, filled with prayer and selflessness, she prays for a deceitful tongue (Jdt 9:13) and strength to cut off Holofernes' head (Jdt 13:7; Moore, 36). Ultimately this beautiful, godly woman carries out a grisly act for the deliverance of her country.

The third story, Susanna, is sometimes thought to be one of the best stories written in the world's literature (Metzger, 107). It is uncertain when or where it was written, but most likely the author was Judean. Again the central figure, Susanna, was an intensely devout and pious woman who risked her life to remain faithful to the laws of God. Unlike the story of Judith, this tale is set in a peaceful time in a lovely garden. Susanna, the beautiful wife of a prominent and wealthy Jew, was envied and lusted after by many. Two local elders were particularly taken by her beauty and determined to seduce her. When she rejected their advances, they accused her of adultery with a young man. Although everyone who knew of her piety was amazed, she was convicted by the court on the witness of her accusers and sentenced to death. Appeal for the verdict was granted, and Daniel as counsel for the defense was called to cross-examine the two accusers. He requested to be allowed to ask each of the accusers one question, and upon their answers was able to vindicate Susanna of their accusations. The question he asked was, "If you really saw her [with the young man], tell me this: Under what tree did you see them being intimate with each other?" (Sus 52-54). The first accuser stated that it was a mastic tree; the second called it an evergreen oak. Her accusers were put to death. Again, strong lessons about the result of piety, devotion and obedience to God are revealed: God protects those who trust and believe in him.

The fourth and final story is Bel and the Dragon. Written as a sort of detective story, this tale ridicules idolatry and heathen worship. Bel, also called Marduk, was the most popular Babylonian god from 2250 B.C. until the time of Christ (Metzger, 115). The story, whose hero is Daniel, is often seen as a companion text to the biblical book of Daniel. On account of a disagreement with the king, Daniel was commanded to ascertain whether the god Bel did indeed eat the food brought to the temple as offerings to him. Daniel's life was in question since if Bel did eat the food, then he had blasphemed the god.

Daniel set up the food as usual. The priests agreed, since they and their families ate the food each day. Daniel prepared one additional aspect, however—he sifted fine ashes on the floor of the temple.

During the night, the priests and their families came as usual and ate the food, so at first the king thought that Bel had been vindicated. The footprints left by the families in the ashes, however, showed beyond question that the priests, not the god, had come for the food. The king in response ordered the priests to be executed and allowed Daniel to destroy the image of Bel and the pagan temple (Bel 8-22).

The author follows this with a second episode in which Daniel confronts the Babylonians' belief in a dragon or serpent. Daniel refuses to worship this god and is therefore thrown to the lions. When the king finds Daniel unharmed, his accusers are executed and Daniel's God is exonerated (Bel 40-42).

Although delightful in themselves, these stories reveal cultural and religious insights into Jewish life and customs in the intertestamental era. They also indicate the position of reverence and respect held by the Jewish laws. All of the central characters were devoted to God and were intensely faithful to the laws even in the face of personal risk or death. Several points are notable about the presentation of women. Evidently women were accepted in roles other than the traditional ones of wife and mother. Judith, for example, although a widow, uses her cunning, beauty and intelligence to outwit and defeat the enemy of her people. Susanna also serves as an example of selfless devotion to God in the face of certain death. Finally, Sarah, in spite of the loss of her husbands and in the face of humiliating rumors, continues to trust in God. All of these stories make clear statements about God's grace and mercy to those who trust him even in times of suffering.

Wisdom Literature

The genre of wisdom literature was written by sages or wise men who functioned in ancient times in a role similar to that of the priests or prophets. However, the sages' main pursuit was to reflect on and instruct others in many practical aspects of daily life. Ecclesiasticus, or Wisdom of Ben Sira, is one of the earliest and longest of the apocryphal Old Testament books. It is similar to the book of Proverbs and contains a variety of literary forms: proverbs, psalms of praise and lament, ethical and cultic maxims, philosophical and theological reflections, exhortation and general comments on life and customs. The original work was written in Hebrew but was translated by Ben Sira's grandson into Greek (132 B.C.). The book appeals to those who long for intellectual respectability by using Hellenistic language, content and style. The main point is that true wisdom is found only in God as revealed in the law of Moses (Sir 24:23). Devotion to a life of study of Scripture is the best occupation of all (Sir 38:34; 39:1).

The Wisdom of Solomon (first century B.C.) also stresses that wisdom must be the first priority in a person's life and desires (Wis 7:7-14), that all things are acquired along with it and that God is its only source (Wis 7:15-21). For the author of the Wisdom of Solomon, wisdom is not merely proper behavior but represents the righteous life pulsating with a vibrant relationship with God. The individual who acquires true wisdom is promised a fulfilling life not only in the present but also for eternity (Wis 6:18; 8:13).

Both Ecclesiasticus and the Wisdom of Solomon personify wisdom as a woman. As the breath and power of God (Wis 7:25-27; 9:17), Wisdom participated in creation (Wis 6:22; 9:2) and continues to pervade and penetrate all things (Wis 7:22-24). Wisdom is sweeter than honey and ultimately satisfying (Sir 24:19-21). Those who obey her will not sin (Sir 24:22). She knows all things and eagerly instructs the willing student (Wis 7:17-22).

Like the important choice a young man must make in deliberating marriage with one of two women, the proverbial choice between Lady Wisdom and Dame Folly is critical. Both options are alluring, and the individual must use the utmost of intellect and will to make the right choice. Like a woman, Wisdom is attractive; she is more beautiful than the sun (Wis 7:29-30). She is a reflection of God and the image of God's goodness (Sir 7:26). Wisdom seeks to arouse the young man to pursue the godly life (cf. Sir 51:21, "My heart was stirred to seek her"). She desires friendship with human beings, promises joy and accepts love (Wis 6:12-17; 8:9-18).

In consideration of this glimpse into the literature of the intertestamental era, we can observe that there is a strong emphasis on the centrality of God and the laws in the lives of the Jewish people. Taken together, the literature includes references to a variety of kinds of people, careers, lifestyles and situations. The various types of literature address the issues in different styles and formats, yet all of them assert that although the righteous suffer, God will still be with them and will in the end vindicate them. Although the philosophers address difficult issues, all of them argue for something beyond human existence and expound strong ethical systems.

This literature is important because of its wealth of insight into Hellenistic as well as Jewish thought and customs. Although some of the topics reflect an ancient worldview that might be offensive to modern people (e.g., the consideration of women as property in Greek and Roman culture), much of the material provides insight and inspiration on topics such as God's role in human suffering and how one should behave in a variety of ethical situations in relation to surrounding pagan society.

Bibliography

J. L. Crenshaw, *Old Testament Wisdom: An Introduction* (Atlanta: John Knox, 1981); A. A. DiLella, "Wisdom of Ben-Sira," *Anchor Bible Dictionary* (Garden City, NY: Doubleday, 1976) 931-44; J. A. Goldstein, "1 Maccabees," *Anchor Bible Dictionary* (Garden City, NY: Doubleday,1976) 12-21; B. M. Metzger, *An Introduction to the Apocrypha* (New York: Oxford University Press, 1963); C. Moore, "The Case of the Pious Killer," *Bible Review* 4/1 (February 1990) 33; D. Winston, "Wisdom of Solomon," *Anchor Bible Dictionary* (Garden City, NY: Doubleday, 1979) 120-27.

PRISCILLA BENHAM, HANNAH K. HARRINGTON AND REBECCA SKAGGS

New Testament Use of Old Testament Quotations Referring to Women

Today when we want to quote from the Bible, we are apt to grab it off our shelf. In the ancient world, however, scrolls of biblical books (and in the second century A.D., codices or books) were the property of libraries (which were scarce) or the wealthy few. Both Jewish and Christian groups created groupings of biblical quotations or testimonies, thereby greatly reducing the "paper" used and the cost of scribal copying. Many Old Testament quotations found in the New Testament, therefore, were likely taken from a testimony source rather than a particular biblical book.

Also, because Greek was the language of commerce, many quotations cite a testimony source based on the Septuagint (LXX), a Greek translation of the Hebrew Bible, or they cite the LXX directly. Translation of the Old Testament into Greek began about 250 B.C. by Jews living in Alexandria, Egypt. For the most part, the Hebrew and Greek texts are similar, but there are important differences on which some early Christians capitalized to explain Christian beliefs. For example, the phrase "a virgin shall conceive and bear a son" (Mt 1:23) is taken from the LXX of Isaiah 7:14. The Hebrew rendering reads, "a young woman shall conceive and bear a son." Clearly the Greek text strengthens Matthew's argument concerning the virgin birth of Jesus, though the Hebrew reading in no way disqualifies Matthew's argument.

A brief but thorough (though not exhaustive) listing of quotations focusing on women can be grouped into four categories.

Childbearing
Matthew 1:23 (Isaiah 7:14)
Matthew 2:18 (Jeremiah 31:15)
Romans 9:9 (Genesis 18:10)
Romans 9:12 (Genesis 25:23)
Galatians 4:27 (Isaiah 54:1)
Galatians 4:30 (Genesis 21:10)

Motherhood
Matthew 15:4 (Exodus 20:12; 21:17; Deuteronomy 5:16)
Matthew 19:19 (Exodus 20:12; Deuteronomy 5:16)
Mark 7:10 (Exodus 20:12; 21:17; Deuteronomy 5:16)
Mark 10:19 (Exodus 20:12; Deuteronomy 5:16)
Ephesians 6:2-3 (Exodus 20:12; Deuteronomy 5:16)

Marriage
Matthew 19:4-5 (Genesis 1:27; 2:24)
Mark 10:6-8 (Genesis 1:27; 2:24)
1 Corinthians 6:16 (Genesis 2:24)
Ephesians 5:31 (Genesis 2:24)

Christian Living

Acts 2:17-21 (Joel 2:28-32)

At first reading, one would think that the New Testament authors' primary emphases when quoting from the Jewish Scriptures were women's domestic roles and relationships within the home. While this is sometimes the case, text citations in fact often served to highlight God's redemptive plan in history.

Childbearing

Paul uses various interpretative methods with the Jewish Scripture quotations to support his overall argument to the Galatian churches. In Galatians 4:27-30, Paul interprets allegorically both Isaiah 54:1 ("Rejoice, you childless one") and Genesis 21:10 ("Drive out the slave and her child"). These texts symbolize for Paul the future triumph of his Galatian Christian communities. Paul shows that the women in these Hebrew Scriptures model the Galatian church's experience as well as appropriate Christian behavior. The reference of barrenness turning into joy in Isaiah 54:1 uses a common female experience as a way to understand God's working in the world and in the church. What the world may judge as failure (the barren one), God uses to provide abundance for his people.

Genesis 21:10 is more problematic in its context, which depicts two women pitted against each other over their sons' rights of inheritance. God chooses Isaac, the child of the promise, and rejects Ishmael, the child born in the natural way through Hagar. These women anticipate for Paul the situation of the church, which relies on God's promised Son, Jesus. Even as Sarah sends Hagar and Ishmael away, so too Paul calls on the Galatian believers to make hard choices for freedom in Christ. Sarah serves as an example of staying with God's promise, thus she is an example to all believers.

Unlike the allegorical interpretation given in Galatians, Paul points the Roman churches (Rom 9:9-12) to Sarah's having a son (Gen 18:10) and the words to Rebekah concerning her twins (Gen 25:23) as examples of God's activity in history. Both these verses highlight God's working in a woman's life for purposes of salvation. Sarah's son is born because God opens her womb when she is postmenopausal. Rebekah inquires of God about her pregnancy, and God answers, explaining how Israel's salvation will be worked out through her twin sons. Not only does God fulfill promises through women, but he also reveals to them his intentions and plans.

Matthew uses Jewish Scripture texts on childbearing, but his purpose is different from either of Paul's uses, for Matthew is interested in prophecy. One well-known citation, noted above, is Isaiah 7:14, "a virgin shall conceive and bear a son" (Mt 1:23). This quotation and one from Jeremiah 31:15 about Rachel weeping for her children (Mt 2:18) are included in Matthew's birth narrative to highlight fulfilled prophetic statements.

Though Matthew's quotations spotlight Jesus' unique birth, the individual passages themselves could not be less similar. Isaiah 7:14 rejoices with a mother on the promised birth of her child, celebrating the gift of life from God. Jeremiah 31:15 forcefully presents the opposite of birth—death. Women bear much sorrow when the promised life in their womb is destroyed. Matthew, in stressing the incarnation, affirms the relevant connections in female experiences of a child's birth and a baby's death.

Motherhood

Most often when discussing motherhood the New Testament calls on its audience to honor father and mother. Honoring one's father would have seemed self-evident to ancient ears, as both Jewish and Greco-Roman cultures were structured around the *paterfamilias*—the male headship of the family. Thus the injunction to honor one's mother would have caught listeners' attention. Paul uses the commandment in Ephesians 6:2-3, advocating a deference to parents within the household that may have elevated mothers' positions. Elsewhere Paul honors motherhood as he praises Timothy's mother and grandmother for teaching spiritual lessons to Timothy (2 Tim 1:5).

A slightly different slant to this quotation is found in Mark 10:19 and the parallel passage in Matthew 19:19. Jesus, in response to a question about attaining eternal life, includes honoring one's parents in his list of commandments to follow. While the specific commandment to honor one's parents is intended as an example of a larger category, that of obeying all the commandments, it is likely mentioned because it is so important. Proof of its importance is found in Mark 7:10 and Matthew 15:4; Jesus cites this commandment to highlight its misinterpretation by some Pharisees. Jesus speaks against the developing tradition of sons pledging to the temple monies which would help support their aging parents. Such a trend was especially harmful to widowed mothers, as they were socially the most vulnerable. Jesus, in his insistence on honoring both father and mother, was protecting women who had little recourse for support.

Marriage

Genesis 2:24 ("Therefore . . . they become one flesh") is the only passage regarding marriage to be quoted directly, both by Paul and by Jesus (who includes Gen 1:27: "male and female he created them"). The discussion in Mark 10:6-8 (par. Mt 19:4-5) springs from a question on the proper procedure for divorce. Jesus' answer suggests that such a focus is skewed, for God never intended marriage to end in divorce.

Paul, however, speaks not about divorce but about the proper physical relationship within marriage. Ephesians 5:31, in its context, emphasizes the appropriate perspective a husband should have toward his wife, treating her as he does his own body. In the ancient world Demosthenes (fourth century B.C.) expressed a common Gentile sentiment for male sexuality: "Mistresses we keep for the sake of pleasure, concubines for the daily care of our persons, but wives to bear us legitimate children and to be faithful guardians of our households" (*Speeches* 59.122). Once a son/heir was produced, there would be no further need for physical relations with one's wife. Assuming Paul is not just spouting platitudes here, he may be reacting to a situation of domestic abuse in his call to treat a wife as one's own body. That is, Paul speaks of feeding and clothing one's own body as a standard which should be applied by husbands toward wives, which suggests that some Christian husbands neglected the needs of their wives. Paul responds by pointing to God's original purpose in marriage (citing Gen 2:24).

In 1 Corinthians 6:12-20 Paul corrects the Corinthians' view that sexual relations with a prostitute are of no consequence because the body has no relevance to the Spirit-led life. Paul advises firmly that sexual relations are much more than simple biological functions (as the Corinthians seemed to believe), for a Christian's body is the temple of the Holy Spirit (1 Cor 6:19). Given that the majority of prostitutes then and now are women, this teaching (supported by Gen 2:24) serves to protect women. Even more, Paul's proclamation promotes the truth that a woman fully represents the dwelling place of the Holy Spirit in her body, a temple.

However one may interpret the New Testament passages on marriage, it should be noted that Genesis 2:24 says nothing about specific roles or duties for the wife or husband, and certainly nothing about "headship" within marriage. Instead this text stresses the permanent joining of two equal persons to become one.

Christian Living

Peter quotes from Joel 2:28-32 in a discussion of Christian living in Acts 2:17-21. Peter notes that men *and* women of all backgrounds were experiencing the Holy Spirit, as prophesied by Joel ("your sons and your daughters shall prophesy"; "even upon my slaves, both men and women, / in those days I will pour out my Spirit; / and they shall prophesy"). This text portrays both women and men as active participants in the life of the church, outside any cultural or familial roles. There are quite a few other places in the New Testament where women function without regard to their social-familial roles (well-known names include Phoebe, Prisca and Junia in Rom 16:1-7, Euodia and Syntyche in Phil 4:2, Lydia in Acts 16:14-15); Acts 2:17-21 highlights this common experience.

In summary, the New Testament authors chose texts from the Jewish Scriptures that emphasized women's domestic roles as wife and mother, but these roles were expanded as examples or allegories of God's plan of salvation throughout history. God's promises and provisions were extended as much to women as to men.

LYNN H. COHICK

MATTHEW

Introduction

Matthew's Gospel takes us leaping and dancing straight into the heart of the good news about the Lord Jesus Christ. A mere seventeen verses (Mt 1:1-17) provide the bridge between the Old Testament and the New. For centuries there had been an accumulating collection of God-breathed Scriptures, followed by a period of silent anticipation, puzzlement or lethargy. Then, within a few short decades, the New Testament documents all came tumbling into life, marking the radical transition from the old dispensation to the new. It is not possible to date exactly when Matthew's Gospel took its place in that process, but it probably appeared in the sixties, or possibly in the early seventies, of the first century.

In the twentieth century, scholars have come up with a variety of theories as to who wrote the first Gospel and when. But detailed though those discussions have been, there is no convincing reason to quarrel with the traditional belief of the church, traceable from early in the second century, that Matthew, called by Jesus to leave his tax-collecting to become one of the original twelve disciples (Mt 9:9; 10:3), was the author. He would have seen and heard firsthand most of what he writes about and would have had direct access to others, such as Mary, the Savior's mother, for further information. Perhaps he and Mark and Luke compared notes as they wrote their complementary biographies.

Not that the Gospels are historical biographies in quite the form to which we are accustomed in the contemporary West. In the accepted genre of the day, strict chronological accuracy could give way to topical rearrangement where that better served to highlight an emphasis or to underscore an interpretation of meaning and significance. This accounts for the variety in order and details among the Gospels. In the same way, at that time nobody would have thought it in the least bit unacceptable to have Matthew and Luke draw heavily from Mark's version, if, as many think, his was the first Gospel to be written. In any event, they would all have quoted freely from a much-repeated and well-known oral tradition, rearranging the pieces and adding commentary to suit their purposes.

In the print-oriented West, repeated stories tend to be quickly distorted or embellished: oral accuracy is low compared with transmission through print. But in oral cultures enormous bodies of information can be passed through many generations and repeated by and among many people with astonishing accuracy. To the present day, there are many African and Asian cultures in which people commit to memory, and retell with absolute accuracy, amazing volumes of folklore and history. Almost certainly the sayings of Jesus and accounts of his life would have circulated widely in this way and may well have been the basis for the Gospels before any of them was committed to writing. Perhaps, had more scholars paid sufficient attention to the characteristics of oral cultures, many of the discussions about sources, dates, who wrote which document first and who plagiarized from whom would have never taken place.

Central to all four Gospels is the question Who is this Jesus? Individuals and groups within the texts face that question, usually needing to shed misconceptions along the way. But the question and its answer lie at the heart of the purpose of these pen portraits of the life and work and teaching of Jesus of Nazareth, real historical figure, the one on whom the Christian faith rests. Nonetheless the Gospels each address the question differently.

Matthew seems to have written primarily for a Jewish audience, repeatedly and painstakingly showing how the events he records are the fulfillment of Old Testament prophecy and promise (e.g., Mt 1:22; 2:17; 4:14). He regularly echoes or quotes from the Old Testament, drawing on many different parts of the Scriptures (e.g., Gen, Ex, Lev, Deut, Ps, Is, Jer, Dan, Hos, Zech, Mal: this is an extraordinary breadth of textual familiarity). He points to Jesus as long-awaited Messiah and promised King of the kingdom. He frequently shows how familiar interpretations of the Old Testament were mistaken and that Jesus' teaching did not contradict the Scriptures but rather illuminated their true meaning. He writes about judgment in style and language familiar to Jews from the prophets and intertestamental writings. He conveys Jesus' great love for his nation. He writes as a Jewish insider.

And yet, at the same time, Matthew weaves throughout his Gospel Gentile threads. It is Matthew, not Luke the Greek, who includes Gentiles and women in his prologue genealogy of Jesus. It is Matthew, not Luke, who tells us of the Gentile Magi coming to worship the infant Christ (Mt 2:1-12). It is Matthew who gives us the most familiar version of the Great Commission (Mt 28:16-20) with its resounding call to make disciples of all the nations. In many details, he hints at the universal scope of that great finale as he selects material for his biography. Yet here too Matthew is steadily asking his Jewish audience to revisit the way in which they had grown accustomed to understanding their Scriptures: "Look! Abraham's descendants, the Jewish nation, are called to bless and bring in the nations, to be a dynamic visual aid to help the Gentiles come to know and love and serve the living God! You've read the story in terms of exclusion; but God wanted you to read it in terms of inclusion!"

It is perhaps above all else Matthew's theme of the kingdom that would have resonated with a Jewish reader or listener. For, from the days of David onwards, the kingdom had crumbled and never yet been fully restored. Through civil war, exile and occupation, the dream had grown more precious, its realization apparently ever more elusive. By the time of Christ, no wonder that first the Greek, then the Roman, imperial might had seemed to squeeze out the last drop of probability that the kingdom should be restored. At the same time, there were those who looked for it passionately, convinced that the Messiah would come and establish kingly rule over a freed and united kingdom.

It is against this background that Matthew's portrait of Jesus fits. At the outset

Jesus is established as one descended from the royal line, great King David's greater kingly Son, the one to whom, newborn, both the great and the humble come to pay homage. The Gospel is arranged around five major discourses on the theme of the kingdom, a kingdom far different from the sociopolitical aspirations of many a Jew. Jesus enters Jerusalem to the excited welcome by the crowds who name him their king; but so deeply ingrained are their mistaken expectations and so dismayed are they that he does not make moves to evict the Romans, in no time at all they are baying for his blood. Tacked to the cross as the Lord hung dying was the label "Jesus, king of the Jews," while the chief priests sneeringly called him king of Israel. The irony was that such labels made claims too small, not too great. For the risen Christ's last command claims kingly authority over all the nations of the world, for time and eternity. Who is Jesus? An amazing King, declares Matthew.

Clearly none of the Gospels was written as a feminist tract, and it is inappropriate to judge them from such a framework. Nor were many of the questions that exercise us about the role of women in home, society and church issues that Matthew could have dreamed of. Yet, given the male domination of the culture at that time and the wholly male worldview of most contemporary literature, the extraordinary thing is how much Matthew draws attention to women as well as men from start to finish of his Gospel. Of course he is reflecting the radical way in which Jesus included women, dignifying them with value equal to that of men. This is evident in all four Gospels. But it is striking that Matthew did not edit this out as he selected material for his biography: after all, he summarizes thirty-three years in a few thousand words, and much must be left out.

On the contrary, Matthew must have stunned many a Jew (and, indeed, many a Gentile) by his inclusion of women in his introductory genealogy. That two of them were not Jewish, and four of the five women were with a history, while the fifth claimed to have conceived and given birth while still a virgin, must have added to the shock for any alert reader or listener. Was Matthew out to shock? No. But, under the inspiration of the Holy Spirit, he draws attention, right from the start, to the fact that the Gospel is good news for all the human race, not just for Jewish men.

With the conclusion of the genealogy, Matthew introduces us to Mary. While some Christians have given her greater status than is warranted from Scripture, others, especially evangelical Protestants, have treated this remarkable woman with less respect than she deserves. Matthew tells us less than does Luke but more than either Mark or John. It is hard to see how anyone other than Mary could have been the source of much of the information contained in the opening chapters of Matthew's and Luke's Gospels. The inclusion of the material, woven into the biographies on exactly the same terms as anything else, indicates the highest value put on Mary's testimony, whether it came to Matthew directly or through others. This in itself is indicative of a lesson well learned from the Lord Jesus, for while he treated women with revolutionary respect, rather few men of his time would have been anything other than scathing about trusting a woman's word. Yet the Gospel writers depend on women's testimony for key events. Mary and Elizabeth must have told the story of the conception and birth of Jesus and of John the Baptist (Joseph at least, and probably Zechariah, were long dead). But apart from John, we are told that it was the women who stayed close enough to witness the crucifixion, while the men slunk away; and it was the women who discovered the empty tomb and first met the risen Lord. By the time Matthew came to write down his Gospel, he must have pondered the significance of God's sovereign dealings, because he is matter-of-fact and without apology in asking us to stake our lives on the word of women. Why? Because God himself entrusts the key testimony to those breathtaking, world-changing events of his Son's birth, death and resurrection to women!

There is a further pervasive reason why Matthew's Gospel is good news for women.

It is difficult to put ourselves into the shoes of first-century Jewish women. Yet the more we attempt to do that, the more liberating and extraordinary Christ's message is seen to be. Much of the religious life of Judaism revolved around the temple and the synagogues. In both, women were tolerated but marginalized. In the temple a woman could find a corner in which to pray, she could put her pennies in the collecting box, but with few exceptions (e.g., Anna, Lk 2:36-38) it was men who conducted the real business of temple life and public worship. In the synagogue, women were seldom more than silent onlookers, if they were there at all.

Yet Matthew matter-of-factly shows Jesus breaking all the conventions. This teacher, unlike any self-respecting rabbi, scribe or Pharisee, delights to teach women and children along with the men (e.g., Mt 14:21; 15:38). When the Twelve become impatient, almost certainly with women, Jesus is insistently welcoming and compassionate (e.g., Mt 19:13-15). He tackles the exploitative way in which many men treat women over divorce or as sex objects (Mt 5:27-32; 19:3-12). His teaching, the parables and stories he tells, the illustrations he uses, the way in which he teaches his disciples to pray to the Father in heaven, are as accessible to women as to men. Women listening to him must have been riveted by the sense of acceptance and inclusion they felt, the dignity bestowed, the courtesy extended. Here is a life of faith as open to them as to their fathers and husbands! Here is a life of faith wholly compatible with the domestic sphere and not dependent on the ritual that was largely the province of males.

Many contemporary preachers were urging armed resistance to throw off the Roman occupation: what hope could there be while their present political situation continued? By contrast, here was a man teaching transformed relationships, integrity, kindness, religion that engaged the heart and every part of everyday life. While the former excluded women, except in requiring them to give up their husbands and sons to violence and possible death, the latter included them fully alongside their men, with a message that offered hope and change, even within the current political framework, and grounded in the practical realities of ordinary life. It is hard, from the standpoint of a modern Western woman with open access to so much information of every kind, to grasp quite how amazing this must all have been to many of the women who heard Jesus or, later, heard or read Matthew's account.

Any division of that account is a little artificial, and in any case the Gospel, like any good story, gains greatly from being read, sometimes at least, at one sitting. But the following outline may provide a working structure.

Outline

1:1-17	Prologue: The Genealogy of Jesus
1:18—2:23	The Birth and Infancy of Jesus
3:1—4:25	Narrative: Preparation and the Beginnings of Public Ministry
5:1—7:29	Discourse: Living the Life of the Kingdom
8:1—10:4	Narrative: Demonstrating the Life of the Kingdom
10:5-42	Discourse: The Mission of the Kingdom
11:1—12:50	Narrative: Opposition to the Kingdom
13:1-52	Discourse: Parables of the Kingdom
13:53—17:27	Narrative: The King Recognized, the King Rejected
18:1-35	Discourse: The Upside-Down Kingdom
19:1—23:29	Narrative: The King Must Die
24:1—25:46	Discourse: And the King Shall Come Again
26:1—28:20	Narrative: Tragedy—and Triumph!

Commentary

Prologue: The Genealogy of Jesus (Mt 1:1-17)

Who is this Jesus?

Any Jew would perfectly well have understood that the genealogy at the start of his Gospel is Matthew's first answer to exactly this question, unstated though it is.

In the contemporary West, our identity is usually tied to what we do: "I'm a doctor/teacher/secretary," we might say, introducing ourselves to a new acquaintance. In cultures where importance is gauged by salary earned, that has often made most women look insignificant beside men. But in biblical culture and in many African and Asian cultures today, identity is more often linked to birthplace and family relationships: "I'm Rachel's mother, William's granddaughter, Dick's wife . . . from Bristol." Where filial piety or ancestor worship is practiced, genealogies are of the utmost importance: that's who I am, where I come from. I am who I am because of the place I take in the stream of human life.

So Matthew begins with Jesus' family tree. It's slightly adjusted, to make three neat blocks of fourteen generations, and it begins with Abraham, to demonstrate that Jesus is truly in the line of promise, a true Jew who could genuinely claim Abraham as his forefather.

No sanitized family tree, this. Saint and sinner, illustrious king and obscure nobody, are all included. Humanly speaking, Jesus came from a line that had quite as many skeletons in the family cupboard as any of us might have.

Yet even more intriguing is the inclusion of five women, five mothers, each of whom, in a beautiful way, is a sign of the grace of the gospel: God's good news for sinners.

Widowed Tamar (Mt 1:3), whose sad story is told for us in Genesis 38, plotted to lure her father-in-law, Judah, to mistake her for a prostitute and use her in order that she might have the child she needed for identity and security. Under levirate law, Judah and his sons had sinned against Tamar, and in this sense she was seeking what was hers by right. Perez, the first-born twin of this incestuous union, thus finds himself in the family tree of Jesus.

Rahab (Mt 1:5) too was a prostitute but became the mother of godly Boaz. She was a foreigner, a citizen in Jericho, whose story is told in Joshua 2. Having put her faith in the living God ("The LORD your God is indeed God in heaven above and on earth below," Josh 2:11) and risked her life to save the lives of the Israelite spies, in turn she is spared the destruction that falls on all her fellow citizens. Even in the hall of fame of Hebrews 11, she is still known as "Rahab the prostitute" (Heb 11:31). But most beautifully, she stands among those of whom "God is not ashamed to be called their God" (Heb 11:16).

In time Rahab was to become mother-in-law, with Naomi, to Ruth. The book of Ruth is in some ways the loveliest of all pictures of the gospel in the Old Testament. Widowed and childless like Tamar, and therefore with no ongoing identity, no future, no significance in a patriarchal scheme of things, this woman lives with the awesome reminder every time her name—Ruth the Moabitess—is uttered that her origin is in the gutter. The story of the origin of the Moabites is among the seediest of all in Scripture (Gen 19:30-38). In terms of public perception, Ruth might almost as well have carried a placard "Shameful Woman" when she accompanied her broken mother-in-law to Bethlehem. Boaz was probably almost unique in recognizing that "the LORD, the God of Israel, under whose wings you have come for refuge" (Ruth 2:12) in his loving grace could wipe out the shame of the past and give her a new beginning and an undreamed-of future. And in Boaz God provides Ruth with the kinsman-redeemer through whom the childless widow becomes a cherished wife and fruitful mother, the celebrated ancestor of King David—and King Jesus.

The fourth woman to appear in this extraordinary list is Bathsheba, whose story is told in 2 Samuel 11—12. Like Tamar, Rahab and Ruth before her, Bathsheba could be seen as the hapless victim of a society whose rules were heavily biased in favor of men. When David, lustful, sends "messengers to get her" (2 Sam 11:4), she could hardly choose whether or not to comply: a subject, especially a woman whose husband was away from home, would have no option but to obey the king. The story is usually retold as one of adultery, implying mutual consent. In today's terms, it was probably closer to rape. Indeed, when David has brought about Uriah's murder, we are told that Bathsheba mourned for him (2 Sam 11:26). Yet, out of the whole sorry tale, the God of grace brings a new future: a repentant David, a genuine marriage, a dearly loved son, Solomon. For Tamar and Rahab, Ruth and Bathsheba are not merely hapless victims of exploitative men. They are wonderfully loved and cared for by God. Out of sin and suffering, however bleak and black, God can bring transformed new life.

What is Matthew doing in including these women in the genealogy of Jesus? He is celebrating the thread of God's grace in the Old Testament, a thread that is quite as much in evidence in the lives of women as in those of men. He is showing how God turns tragedy into triumph, even as he does with his Son. No one, man or woman, is condemned beyond hope, no one need feel so dirty, so worthless, so powerless, that there is no possibility of being drawn within the circle of the Lord's compassion and merciful concern. Women as well as men are of such immeasurable value to him that he will go to any lengths to give us a hope and a future, to bring good from evil, to give the grace of a new beginning with the slate of the past wiped clean.

This is Matthew's first answer to Who is this Jesus? He is the one who fits into the line of God's redeeming love, not ashamed to be identified with those who sin and those who have been sinned against.

This is an electrifying introduction to his Gospel for anyone listening closely.

The Birth and Infancy of Jesus (Mt 1:18—2:23)

The fifth woman whose name appears in the genealogy is Mary. Matthew does not give us the extended details about the annunciation, the pregnancy and birth, so beautifully recorded for us by Luke. But Matthew tells us considerably more about Joseph and God's dealings with this godly man who became Jesus' earthly father. Four times (Mt 1:20; 2:13, 19, 22), we are told, the Lord or his angel appears to Joseph in a dream, and on each occasion Joseph does exactly what he is told. In each case, he is to act to protect Mary and the child she bears, the child of whom Joseph is not the father.

At the time of their betrothal, neither Joseph nor Mary could have had any inkling of what lay ahead. Perhaps they looked forward to a quiet, ordinary village life, probably remaining all their lives in the community where they had been born and reared, among their families. For a very young couple (Mary would probably have been a young teenager, Joseph maybe a few years older), such an arrangement would have been both normal and a source of security. Yet all at once they find themselves embarking on a journey of faith quite as extraordinary as Abraham's when he set off from Ur.

It is hard to begin to imagine how first Mary, then Joseph, felt as events unfolded. Betrothal commonly lasted a year and was a serious contract between two families, not just between two young people. A long betrothal was not just to ensure that a young girl was physically and emotionally ready for marriage; it was also designed to ensure that the first child born of the marriage was without doubt the child of the new husband. During the period of engagement, both young people would be watched closely by both families. Everybody knew the penalties for sexual misconduct.

How did Mary find the courage to tell Joseph she was pregnant? How did he react when she told her story? Clearly he could not initially take it in. He loved her too much to want to expose her to public disgrace, which could include being stoned to death, yet he would be under enormous pressure from his culture and his family to wash his hands of her, certainly to disown the child. And however well he may have known and trusted Mary, he must surely have found it almost impossible to believe that her child was not fathered by some other man. Virgin births don't happen. Was it while he was wondering what to do that Mary spent three months with her cousin Elizabeth? However reassuring events there must have been to Mary, Joseph wasn't there, and she must still have wondered what he would decide. If he were to divorce her, what kind of a future must she and her precious child face?

How gracious God is! His direct words to Joseph on four separate occasions must have given Joseph the courage to dare to trust God for an uncharted future, to dare to run the gauntlet of his family's almost certain outrage and the neighbors' gossip ("It must be Joseph's after all, otherwise he'd have divorced her. Who'd have thought that of him?"), to dare to cope with all the demands of travel and exile and danger on behalf of this child who was not his. And what tender grace to marry Mary, to protect her and live with her, without seeking sexual consummation until after the birth of Jesus. Later, from their marriage, were to come at least four sons and several daughters (Mt 13:55-56).

So Matthew's second answer to the question Who is this Jesus? is that he is the son of Mary, born from her body, and the foster son of God-fearing Joseph: fully human, fully Jewish, a precious firstborn, a child in a family, nothing unusual.

But the third answer is rather different. For this child is "from the Holy Spirit," and from before birth he is declared to have both a unique origin and a unique destiny. He is to be given the name "Jesus, for he will save his people from their sins" (Mt 1:21), a name and a future determined by God, not by Mary or Joseph. How did this young couple, inexperienced in parenthood, feel as they undertook the task of rearing this child, so different from any other? In a world where infant mortality was very high, did they experience a wave of panic every time he fell over or put dirt in his mouth or ran a fever? Or did their confidence that he must fulfill his destiny give them unshakeable faith that he must survive? Many a Christian mother dedicates her child to God from within her womb, recognizing that he or she is a gift from the Lord. But Mary and Joseph's experience was very different, for this child was not simply a gift from God. He was conceived through the Holy Spirit and singled out to be Savior and Messiah.

Perhaps, in the circumstances, it was a relief to Mary that her baby was born away from home, where the busybodies could not be counting dates on their fingers. Yet she must have longed for familiar surroundings and familiar women's hands to help deliver her baby and steady her through that first experience of childbirth. Instead of which, she finds herself adjusting to new motherhood (itself overwhelming), playing hostess to a group of "wise men from the East" (Mt 2:1) who pay homage to her baby son with gifts that might have left a seasoned king gasping, let alone a young peasant girl.

It is hard to believe that, having traveled so far, perhaps for many weeks or even months, these men called in for a five-minute, welcome-the-new-baby visit. How did Mary and Joseph feel as these educated foreigners poured their worship and their precious gifts at Jesus' feet? Did the Magi explain their coming in the same terms they had to Herod? Did they tell Mary why they believed her son to be "the king of the Jews"? Was this the first time that the parents linked that title to their child, special though they knew him to be? All down the years, did that title ring in Mary's ears, until that terrible day when she saw it written above her dying son's head? "Me? The mother of a king?" And in their turn, did Joseph and Mary tell the Magi how the angel of the Lord had spoken to each of them? Did they speculate together as to how it would all be fulfilled? And did the crowds gather at the door, curious to learn why travel-stained visitors should take so much trouble to seek out a baby boy who happened to be born away from home because of a national census?

No sooner had the wise men set off for home than the family was in danger. Once again, Matthew tells us, Joseph is guided as an angel appears to him in a dream (Mt 2:13). Alongside the threat of harm is the assurance that God's loving protection surrounds them. All the scheming of the insecure puppet king, Herod, is powerless in the face of the authority over life and death of the true King. Yet, as Joseph and Mary made their way to Egypt and as they heard of Herod's awful retribution on many other innocent families in Bethlehem, how heavy their hearts must have been. Did Mary grieve for all those mothers bereaved of their sons, innocent children dying in the place of her son, as one day, and far more profoundly, he was to die in the place of all guilty humanity? Surely her joy at escape must have been tempered by the agonized question other mothers down through history have asked: "Why should my child's life be spared, and these other mothers' children taken?" And perhaps, while obedient to their heavenly instruction, they must have pondered the strangeness of being delivered into safety *in* Egypt, the scene centuries before of another slaughter of the innocents, from which another baby, Moses, had escaped, later to lead his people to safety *out of* Egypt. As in Moses' day, the Jewish population in Egypt was very considerable: maybe as many as a million in Alexandria alone, for example. One more family coming or going would scarcely draw much attention to itself; the Name above all other names becomes an anonymous migrant.

Twice more Joseph is guided through a dream, and the family treks north again to settle in Nazareth. Mindful of potential danger, did Joseph and Mary keep silent about their strange past? Or as Mary fetched water from the well along with the other women, or as friends watched Joseph crafting a piece of furniture in his shop, did their faith-rooted hopes and dreams for their first son pour out in recounting what had happened? Who is this Jesus? The vulnerable child, recognizable as to his true identity only by revelation responded to by faith, is kept safe by the sovereign power of the Father for the fulfillment of his special destiny as Savior, King of the Jews—and of the nations beyond. The one who is fully human is also paradoxically in a quite different category altogether.

Narrative: Preparation and the Beginnings of Public Ministry (Mt 3—4)

Luke tells us that Jesus was about thirty years old when he began his public ministry (Lk 3:23). It was ushered in by that of his cousin, John the Baptist. Matthew gives us no explanation about John's background, though Luke does, but he presents John firmly in the tradition of an authentic Jewish prophet (Mt 3:1-12), someone to whom people from far and wide came to listen (Mt 3:5). His message was calculated to cause excitement, for any good Jew would interpret "the kingdom of heaven has come near" (Mt 3:2) as a prophetic word that God was about to put his people back at the center of the universe, for all the world to see, in contrast to their current shame as a subjugated nation under Roman occupation.

Yet John's message is unpalatable too. In asking his audience to repent and be baptized, he is treating them as pagans wishing to convert to Judaism rather than as bona fide Jews. Perhaps Matthew's inclusion of this, recorded this side of the resurrection and Pentecost, points to the way in which Jew and Gentile without distinction need the one who "will baptize you with the Holy Spirit and fire" (Mt 3:11), and that would be reinforced by the pointedness of John's brushing aside the importance of blood descent from Abraham (Mt 3:9). John's message and actions would have greatly offended the Pharisees and Sadducees who came out to see what all the fuss was about. Were they not the appointed guardians of religious purity and of Jewish superiority? In asserting that repentance was necessary, rather than mere tradition keeping, and in dismissing automatic acceptance by God if you were Jewish, John is striking at the heart of the Pharisees' and Sadducees' self-perception. No wonder that they were soon to be Jesus' bitter enemies. For all, there is a message of fearsome and imminent judgment, rather than the immediately comforting message of imminent deliverance from their political masters.

We do not know how much John and Jesus may have seen of one another while they were growing up, though their mothers knew that their lives would be intertwined. Nor do we know how much either mother may have tried to shape her son's life by talking to him about the circumstances of his birth. But by Matthew 3:13-17 each has a conviction of what he must do, Jesus has deliberately sought out John, and both know that the moment has come for Jesus' ministry to begin. If either had any shadow of doubt, the voice from heaven and the visible manifestation of the Spirit resting on Jesus were unmistakable. Who is this Jesus? "My Son, the Beloved, with whom I am well pleased" (Mt 3:17). Here is the Father's loving affirmation, not for works achieved (Jesus' ministry is not yet begun) but in sheer delight in his Son.

Matthew then shapes the account of Jesus' temptation in the desert as a deliberate echo of the experience of the children of

Israel in the wilderness centuries before. They had been there for forty years, Jesus for forty days. They had been disobedient and unfaithful; Jesus remained utterly faithful to his Father. They had disregarded God's word; Jesus rebuffed Satan with it.

In Matthew's account it is at this point that John is imprisoned. Then, the period in the wilderness completed, Jesus travels back to the north of the country to fulfill prophecy (Mt 4:14) and to proclaim the same message as John had boldly declared: "Repent, for the kingdom of heaven has come near" (Mt 4:17). When Elizabeth heard of her son's imprisonment, through her tears and fears could she see that his appointed task as forerunner to Jesus (Lk 1:76-79) was already completed, and be comforted?

For Jesus' public ministry is now well and truly launched. He begins to gather his close associates, the Twelve, starting with Peter and Andrew (Mt 4:18-20) and James and John (Mt 4:21-22). Were their families outraged at this abrupt upheaval in their way of life, the removal without consultation of their strong young men from what were probably lucrative family businesses? Perhaps anger turns to awe as Jesus, newcomer in their midst, begins to draw crowds from many miles away, including Gentile territory, for word spreads quickly of his teaching, his preaching, his power to heal the sick and to deliver the demon possessed. Maybe he does have the authority to command their sons' loyalty after all.

Discourse: Living the Life of the Kingdom (Mt 5—7)

John had told the Pharisees (Mt 3:8) that they must "bear fruit worthy of repentance." Now Jesus, in the Sermon on the Mount, this first great discourse of the Gospel, spells out in practical ways what that fruit-bearing life looks like. The teaching may have taken place over many hours or even more than one day, and apparently a sizeable crowd of genuinely serious listeners ("disciples," Mt 5:1; astounded "crowds," Mt 7:28) stayed to hear.

Matthew does not specify here, as he does elsewhere, that there were women and children as well as men among the crowd, but it seems safe to assume so. This is no list of instructions for men to perform religious ritual reserved to them, no abstruse discussion or esoteric argument from which most (men as well as women) would be excluded. This is rooted in the down-to-earthness of everyday life and experience of old and young, male and female, educated and uneducated. Here was teaching of which a woman could say, "This is for me! I really see how this relates to my life!" Prayer is quiet conversation in ordinary language in the privacy of one's own home (Mt 6:6-14). Principles are expressed in images of yeast and lamps and keeping the moths out of the clothes closet. Images of the home, to be sure, but among Jesus' audience perhaps especially from a woman's world. One can't help thinking that Mary reared her son to help with domestic chores. He appears to be as at home in the language of the kitchen as in that of the carpenter's shop.

Jesus sets the scene for all he has to say against the background of the Beatitudes, following the Old Testament formula of "Blessed is the one who . . . " (e.g., Ps 1:1; Prov 3:13 NIV). Not one of the blessings is associated with being a strong man or with the characteristics of those who plotted to recapture Israel by violent overthrow of the Romans. The promise of the kingdom, future or present, is to those who exemplify what in the world's eyes might often be mistaken for weakness. Not that there is anything flabby about any of the qualities Jesus commends. On the contrary, it may take great strength of character to persist in making them our aim. Yet in many cultures these characteristics may be seen as more womanly than manly.

Jesus' message, like that of the prophets before him (Mt 5:12), would cause a storm of trouble, not least for those who threw their lot in with him. To the Zealots, his message would be subversive and traitorous, for he was challenging head-on their commitment to violence when the moment came. To the religious leaders, he was an offensive menace, challenging as he did time-honored interpretations and the enormous superstructure of requirements to keep the law and to satisfy God. Who likes to have their credibility undermined? To many ordinary folk, he spelled trouble, upsetting the status quo, causing family members to disappear in his wake, causing a sudden surge of people into a village—eating everyone out of house and home and disrupting everyday rhythms before they moved on again. With religious, political and community opinion makers all speedily ranged against Jesus, his followers could expect opposition, especially since they were to live out their commitment to him openly (Mt 5:14-16). They must live lives of such transparent goodness that those looking on would be won over in spite of themselves.

Yet, says Jesus, the truth of the matter was that, contrary to accusation, he was asking them to be more truly Jewish, not less so (Mt 5:17-20), to take God's word more seriously, not less so. He illustrates this with six examples, in the areas of murder, adultery, divorce, oaths, retribution and relating to one's enemies. For the men and women gathered on the hillside, if the Beatitudes had been arresting, the application of the law to inner spirit and motivation, not just outward action, must have been breathtaking. No wonder Jesus completes this part of his teaching with the extraordinary admonition "Be perfect, therefore, as your heavenly Father is perfect" (Mt 5:48), for what lesser standard could meet the need? Well, implies Jesus, if you really want to see the restoration of the kingdom, it's not about kicking out the Romans, it's about living according to the mandate of the King, reflecting his total loveliness. The kingdom of heaven is at hand. This is what it means. Are you prepared to live like this? Repentance is about turning your backs on anything less.

It's hard to overestimate how shocking Jesus' teaching must have been to the crowd on the hillside. Man, woman or child, how could you possibly attain to such standards? Among modern Christians, the Sermon on the Mount is usually regarded as inspiring and comforting, but most of it is profoundly disturbing. And so it must have been to the original audience. A woman might be less likely than a man to commit murder, but she could not wriggle out of conviction on the charge of anger (Mt 5:21-26). She might not be able to take the initiative in divorce; but she might quite as easily as a man fantasize about someone else's spouse (Mt 5:27-30). She could not blame her circumstances or her powerlessness in a patriarchal society when things went wrong; for Jesus shows how sin bubbles up from the deepest recesses of human motivation, for which circumstance merely provides a context.

Had I been among the crowd that day when the Lord came to the close of Matthew 5, I think I would have been horrified

Divorce

Under Mosaic law a man was allowed to divorce his wife by giving her a bill of divorce bearing the words "you are free to marry any man." A husband did not need a bill because male polygamy was tolerated (*see* Polygamy). A woman might possibly petition a rabbinic court to put pressure on her husband to divorce her but only if she could prove he was depriving her of the basic necessities that were held to be the basis of his covenant with her (Ex 21:10-11). Isaiah 54:4-8 reveals God's tender concern for women who suffered rejection and impoverishment in this unequal situation, and Malachi 2:14-16 shows God haranguing those who "broke faith" with their wives.

The principal Old Testament reference to divorce (Deut 24:1-4) prohibits a man from remarrying a woman whom he has already divorced if she has been married again in the meantime. It implies that there is something adulterous about the intervening marriage and protected wives from being used for adulterous purposes in temporary marriages (as in a form of legalized wife swapping still found in some Middle Eastern countries). The law prohibiting remarriage of the same wife may explain why a compassionate God, having justly divorced Israel for unfaithfulness to the covenant, refuses to divorce unfaithful Judah (Is 50:1).

In Jesus' day the grounds on which a man could lawfully divorce his wife were the subject of rabbinic debate. The Deuteronomic ground (Deut 21:1) literally, "uncleanness, a thing," was interpreted by Shammai to mean only some form of sexual indecency and by Hillel to mean that and virtually anything—"even if she burns a dish for him" (Mishnah, *Gittin* 10).

In the context of the divorce scandal that cost John the Baptist his life, Jesus entered the Pharisees' debate with sharp moral condemnation of easy divorces (Mt 19:1-9; Mk 10:1-9). The story in Mark uses Mishnaic brevity to refer to the debate (Mk 10:2) and reveals Jesus referring his hearers to God's original intentions in creation, endorsing monogamy for all and gender equality (Mk 10:8, 12).

Jesus' proverb on the issue (Mt 5:31, 19:9; Mk 10:11-12; Lk 16:18; 1 Cor 7:10-11) is presented in a quasi-legal biblical form used for emphatic moral teaching: Whoever does *x* will receive the penalty *y*. A first-century Jew would have understood it to say, "Whoever breaks the marriage covenant with the spouse is [acting as immorally as if he or she were] committing adultery [and deserves similar punishment]" (cf. Mt 5:28).

As with all issues that deeply affect women, this shows Jesus exhorting his followers to exercise moral integrity with regard to divorce. Paul writes in a similar vein, deploring divorce though recognizing it as a way of escape from a pastorally intolerable situation (e.g., 1 Cor 7:15). In view of the coming apocalypse he counsels against all marriage, including remarriage, particularly against the latter where the divorce has been for an adulterous purpose (i.e., in order to remarry, 1 Cor 7:12-13).

LISA KATHERINE BATTYE

---

as well as astounded. And yet I think, too, there would have been born within me a deep wistfulness for the kingdom life being described: a life where people did not hurt and exploit each other, where loving relationships prevailed, where faith transformed present adversity into a highway to God-rooted happiness.

In Matthew 6:1-18, Jesus turns to more obvious religious observance. Again it may have seemed at first that Jesus' stringent criticisms were directed at men rather than women, because it would have been men rather than women who were in a position to ensure a fanfare to announce their generous almsgiving or to indulge in very public praying or fasting. Yet women, then as now, had ways of drawing attention to themselves when they wished for recognition of their virtues; quite as much as men, women could have very sinful motives for their religious observances. So Jesus' words would have challenged the integrity of anyone with ears to hear.

But at the same time there may have been special comfort for women. For the practices of almsgiving, prayer and fasting Jesus commended were as open to women as to men and compatible with a more restricted and domestic life. In many cultures of the world even today, the role of women still is more restricted and confined to the domestic sphere than that of men. It is estimated that the majority of secret believers in hostile contexts are women. What a comfort that, with or without the approval of those around for one's Christian faith, with or without access to a place of worship and public Christian life, a woman may find many quiet ways of being generous to those in need, of concentrating deep within on the Lord and of praying in the simplest of words directly to her Father in heaven. "Your Father who sees in secret will reward you" (Mt 6:4, 6, 18).

From here to the end of the sermon, with the exception of Matthew 7:22-27, every injunction, every illustration, is as inescapably directed to women as to men. For every principle is couched in language of home and garden: concern over food and drink and clothing, issues of values by which to live, straightforward dealings with God and with the people around one, recognition that it is all too easy to be critical of others while woefully deluded about ourselves. And even in the more male preserves (at least at that time and in that culture) of public ministry (Mt 7:22-23) and house building (Mt 7:24-27), the principle at stake could easily be illustrated in women's terms. The master Teacher's lessons connect absolutely with the daily realities of his audience's lives. What an example to copy as we try to communicate Christian truth today.

Who is this Jesus? The one who "astounded [the crowd] at his teaching, for he taught them as one having authority, and not as their scribes" (Mt 7:28).

As Jesus' reputation grew, what did his mother, Mary, make of the reports that came back to her? Did she see the connection between the Beatitudes and the song she had sung before his birth (Lk 1:46-55)? Did she wonder how what was happening now fulfilled the word of the angel of the Lord to Joseph, "you are to name him Jesus, for he will save his people from their sins" (Mt 1:21)?

Narrative: Demonstrating the Life of the Kingdom (Mt 8:1—10:4)

Much of this section describes Jesus engaged in healing the sick, either in general terms Mt (9:35) or in thumbnail sketches of particular individuals. In some instances, healing was accomplished by word of command (e.g., the healing of the centurion's servant in Mt 8:5-13, or that of the two demon-possessed men in Mt 8:28-34), but repeatedly Matthew records that Jesus touched those he healed. This must have caused quite a stir, for at least some of those he touched would have been regarded as unclean: the leper (Mt 8:2-4), the dead child (Mt 9:18-26) and the hemorrhaging woman (Mt 9:20-22). In some but not all cultures, females are much more tactile than men, though men may hug young children; and in many cultures, for a man to touch a woman, other than those of his very closest family, would be scandalous. Yet all around the world, healing and compassionate touch are closely associated, and it may be no accident that the majority of nurses, whose gentle touch is often crucial to patients' recovery, are women. Why is touch so important? Perhaps because it communicates security and love, which is why abusive touch is experienced as betrayal (*see* Violence, Abuse and Oppression). It is important to note that Jesus' touch is that of divine authority, not that of magic, and his authority was an incontrovertible fact whether or not he touched the person being healed.

The encounter with the centurion is especially important in the light of Jesus' later instruction to the disciples in Matthew 10:5-6, where, sending them out on their own, he bids them "Go nowhere among the Gentiles, and enter no town of the Samaritans, but go rather to the lost sheep of the house of Israel." Some have assumed the latter to mean that Jesus saw his mission, and subsequently that of his disciples, to be limited to Jews. But in Matthew 8:5-13 Jesus is clearly commending the centurion's faith and recognition of the Lord's authority, and he goes on to state that while many of the "heirs of the kingdom" (Mt 8:12; i.e., Jews) will be excluded, many "from east and west" (Mt 8:11; i.e., Gentiles) will take their place in eternal fellowship with Abraham and Isaac and Jacob. This must have been shocking to some of those who heard him, but Matthew is deliberately selecting teaching that undergirds the great conclusion of his Gospel.

It appears that however disruptive Jesus' claims upon their sons' lives may have been, both Peter's family and James and John's family (Mt 20:20) still welcomed Jesus among them and recognized the honor of his company. They would have been aware of his growing following and that he was the center of a great deal of attention. Since she was the one to serve him (Mt 8:15), the implication is that Peter's mother-in-law must have been the woman in charge of the domestic arrangements of the household. A woman expecting guests is usually quite sick before she takes to her bed. So the fever of which Jesus healed her may have been severe.

But Jesus was not just a healer, doing kindnesses. He is one who has sovereign rights over people, demons and creation. Matthew persistently points beyond the events themselves, however briefly recounted, to levels of significance. So Jesus responds to a cautious volunteer (Mt 8:21-22) by demanding unconditional and immediate discipleship in terms that would have been shocking in that culture. ("He's putting his claims above the most important duty any man has! Who does he think he is?") He responds to an effusive volunteer

(Mt 8:18-20) by warning that discipleship strips away all other security. ("Can't this king even guarantee a bed for his entourage?") For the first time in Matthew's Gospel, where there are a further twenty-nine usages, Jesus appears to lay claim to the title "Son of Man" (Mt 8:20), which would have raised goose bumps for any Jew: here was a title resonating with Old Testament content (see, for example, Dan 7:13-14). It is immediately followed by the stilling of the storm and the response of the disciples, "What sort of man is this . . . ?" (Mt 8:27), a most telling juxtaposition.

Further, in the healing of the two demon-possessed men (Mt 8:28-34) and then the paralytic (Mt 9:2-8), Jesus demonstrates authority over the powers of darkness and the spirit world and power to deal with sin and all its consequences. The demons recognize his true identity and call him "Son of God" (Mt 8:29); the outraged scribes cannot recognize his true identity, and thus the authority that flows from it, and call him a blasphemer (Mt 9:3). The crowds assume he is a special human, but human nonetheless, but at least they "glorified God" (Mt 9:8). The Pharisees concede he is a teacher (Mt 9:11) but think his powers are satanic in origin ("By the ruler of the demons he casts out demons," Mt 9:34). Two blind men call him "Son of David" (Mt 9:27), another title loaded with Old Testament overtones—and ambiguities: from David's enormous number of descendants, or a specially anointed king, as was David?

As Jesus' ministry gathers pace, the answers to the question Who is this Jesus? multiply. It's as if Matthew is saying to us, "And which way do you believe the evidence points?"

It is following the healing of the paralytic (Mt 9:2-8) and the rumpus that ensued because Jesus chose to say "Your sins are forgiven" rather than "Stand up and walk" that Matthew describes his own summons to follow the Lord (Mt 9:9). Here Matthew deliberately emphasizes that it is the excluded who become the included, one of the motifs of his Gospel. Jesus is in the business of healing at a level far deeper than the physical. The tax collector, marked out by society as a specially wicked kind of sinner, is transformed by encounter with the One who was not ashamed to be known as the friend of sinners. And the friend of sinners, to the scandal of the Pharisees, rubs in the futility of their system of self-righteousness by making himself at home at Matthew's dinner table. (Whom do I welcome to mine?)

The way in which Jesus reacts to the hemorrhaging woman and his touching of the dead child (Mt 9:18-26) challenges again misunderstandings about sin and uncleanness. Instructions originally given for protection and hygiene had become grounds of cruel rejection. Sexual intercourse during a woman's menstruation is unwise less because it is messy and distasteful for the man than because the woman's internal tissues are especially vulnerable at such a time to infection (*see also* Leviticus). In other words, God's instructions are compassionate and for the protection of women. But instead women had come to be treated as dirty and polluting during menstruation, and should they so much as brush against a man at such a time they could be treated to a torrent of abuse and anger (*see* Menstruation). It was her responsibility to keep her contaminating self at a distance. It was a short step for many men to regard all women as a source of danger. But here is a poor woman who has had hemorrhages for twelve long years, which must have devastated her life physically and socially, not to mention financially, as Mark 5:26 tells us. Desperation and faith drive her to risk deliberately touching Jesus' cloak. Her faith is not misplaced. Instead of the rejection she must have experienced every day all those long years, here is a loving welcome and total healing. The excluded finds herself among the included.

Jesus himself is ambiguous about the dead little girl, saying she "is not dead but sleeping" (Mt 9:24). Yet her father, a man of standing as the leader of the synagogue (Mt 9:18), and the crowd outside all believe her to be dead. So sure are those gathered that the child is dead, the mourning rites have already begun, and the crowd's response to Jesus' assertion is one of scornful laughter. Who does this insane man think he is, denying the reality of death? But in raising the little girl from the dead, Jesus graphically demonstrates that there is life beyond death—and he is Lord of it. Who is this Jesus? The one who holds power over life and death in his hands.

Discourse: The Mission of the Kingdom (Mt 10:5-42)

At the close of the previous section (Mt 9:36-38), Jesus, says Matthew, likens the people to sheep without a shepherd, an allusion to Ezekiel 34 and the failure of current religious leaders to fulfill their calling. Against that background, he insists that there is genuine spiritual responsiveness if only there were those to harvest it and that the disciples must pray for the Lord to commission harvesters. Perhaps, as has happened frequently in the history of Christian mission, the disciples prayed as told and then found themselves being called to be the answer. For Matthew 10 opens with Jesus summoning the inner circle of twelve disciples and investing in them the authority over sickness and demons he has just been demonstrating.

Matthew lists for us the Twelve by name. They are, of course, all men. Some interpreters have used this as a definitive plank in their argument that all Christian leadership must be vested in men (though they do not also insist that they must all be

---

Faith Development

Faith is a concept present throughout the Bible, from the first family (Heb 11:4) to the saints who "hold fast to the faith of Jesus" (Rev 14:12). In the Old Testament God's faithfulness is a continuing theme (Deut 7:9), and the men and women who hoped and trusted in him were considered to have faith (Ps 26:1; 42:5). His great promise was that "the righteous live by their faith" (Hab 2:4). In the New Testament the basic meaning of faith is that of trust or confidence in God; God in Christ initiated and developed the faith of God's people (Heb 12:2).

Growth in faith involves growth in knowing and experiencing God, relying on the Son for salvation, believing God's promises and finding daily strength to obey his will through the power of the Holy Spirit.

Jesus Nurtured His Followers' Faith

Jesus desired to nurture faith among his hearers. He refused to perform his deeds of power for the unbelieving (Mt 13:58; 17:17) but used a variety of experiences to develop believers' faith. He recognized the faith of those who came for healing and so ensured that their example was observed (Mt 9:2, 22, 29). Jesus did not minister to physical needs alone but helped people experiencing major crises to understand and trust in God's faithfulness (Jn 9; 11:21-27). By his parabolic teaching Jesus entertained the crowds, but genuine seekers found sustenance and were satisfied (Mk 4:9-12). His miracles were dramatic enactments of his power and person for those who would believe (Jn 2:11). Jesus' encounter with the Samaritan woman (Jn 4) is paradigmatic for the encouragement of faith development through questioning and shows Jesus reaching out across gender and ethnic barriers.

Jesus selected men and women who formed a group of learners committed to close, personal, long-term relationships with him and with one another. At his call they left home, family, employment and their communities (Lk 5:10-11; 9:58), met different people and faced conflict with the religious authority figures (Mk 2:23; 7:1-13; Lk 19:39). Jesus gave them power and sent them out in pairs to preach, heal and exorcise (Lk 9:1-6; 10:1, 17). Their resultant successes and failures led to reflection and further learning (Mt 14:16; 15:33; 16:12; 17:16). Jesus structured their experiences so that their relationships and active involvements forced them into critical reflection concerning their beliefs and values and led them to relate to him with increasing faith.

Matthew's Gospel gives insight into three distinct stages of faith that Jesus identified among those he encountered. First was the "little faith" of his disciples. Jesus drew attention to their need for faith development when they feared the storm even though he was with them; when Peter began to sink and doubted Jesus' calling; when they missed the spiritual dimensions of his teaching because they were too busy discussing food; and when they failed to use his imparted authority to heal and deliver (Mt 8:26; 10:1; 14:31; 16:8; 17:20). The second level of faith was described as "small as a mustard seed." This does not appear to be very different from little faith, but its identifying characteristic is believing prayer in the face of humanly impossible situations (Mt 17:21; 21:21). The third level and highest commendation for "great faith" was reserved for two Gentiles—a Roman centurion and a Canaanite woman (Mt 8:10; 15:28). By praising them Jesus demonstrated that faith in God is greater than observing the law.

The event with the greatest impact on the faith of Jesus' followers was the crisis precipitated by his death and resurrection (Mt 28:17). When it was obvious that their master would no longer be present among them, they were forced to accept responsibility for their lives, beliefs, commitments and values. He supported them in their struggles by a number of resurrection appearances (Acts 1:3-9), but when the Spirit came at Pentecost they were ready to declare themselves and their belief in Christ before thousands of listeners, hostile and sympathetic (Acts 2:14).

Faith Nurture in the Early Church

Acts and the Epistles record how the early faith communities took up the task of bringing others to a growing faith relationship with Christ. They taught that faith is a trusting relationship with God as Father, Son and Spirit and expresses itself in action within a person's daily life and in a continuing struggle between flesh and Spirit (Jn 20:31; Jas 2:14-17; Rom 5—8). They proclaimed the message of Jesus and told the stories of great heroes and heroines of the past whose trust in God developed as a result of their troubled circumstances (Heb 11). They carried their message across the Roman Empire; they planted and taught new churches so that the different members would use their spiritual gifts to build up Christ's body and develop faith (Eph 4:11-16). Then all received spiritual nourishment to bring about a maturity that enabled them to share the faith with neighbors and succeeding generations (Heb 5:11-14; 2 Tim 2:2). Women may have had a special part to play in faith nurturing as Lois and Eunice did with Timothy (2 Tim 1:5).

Faith Nurture Today

In recent years James Fowler and others have proposed various theories of faith development and stages of faith. Some of the factors that have been identified as enabling development of faith today were evident in Jesus' methods and were implemented by New Testament communities. One factor is developing trusting relationships with others and with God within a community of faith. Other factors include leaving the familiar and moving into new places and experiences; encountering those with different perspectives and sometimes clashing with previous authority figures as new truths begin to emerge. Or one may struggle to find hope in life crises, accept responsibility for one's beliefs and actions, operate as an individual and a fully participating group member and critically reflect on one's self. One may spend and be spent in service for others and work toward the transformation of this world.

Bibliography

J. W. Fowler, *Stages of Faith* (San Francisco: Harper & Row, 1981); O. Michel, "Faith," in *The New International Dictionary of New Testament Theology*, ed. C. Brown, 3 vols. (Grand Rapids, MI: Zondervan, 1975) 1:593-606.

SYLVIA WILKEY COLLINSON

Jewish and that there must be twelve of them). It is extremely unlikely that Jesus was making such a point. He is picking up the powerful symbolism, adopted by others before him, that this group represented the whole of Israel (the twelve tribes) but also the true spiritual Israel, the faithful remnant. "Look well at this new beginning," he is saying.

God had promised (Ezek 34:11-31) to shepherd the unshepherded sheep of God's people, and it is perhaps for this reason that Jesus instructs the Twelve initially to go only to "the house of Israel" (Mt 10:5-6). The message ("The kingdom of heaven has come near," Mt 10:7) and the accompanying signs ("cure the sick, raise the dead, cleanse the lepers, cast out demons," Mt 10:8) are exactly those that they have just seen and heard in the Lord's ministry.

But the hostile response and suffering the disciples can expect is repeatedly brought to their attention (e.g., Mt 10:14, 16-17, 21-23, 28, 31, 34, 38). This is no promise of easy success and of people tumbling over themselves to accept the message. However plentiful the harvest may be, that may not be the dominant experience of the harvesters. They may be more aware of rejection, persecution, vulnerability, getting hurt, being frightened and hated, of families being set at loggerheads among themselves even to the extent of betrayal to death.

Perhaps Jesus had experienced these much more than Matthew records up to this point, or perhaps he knows that from now on it will all steadily intensify. However it is, it is at this moment that Matthew first records Jesus speaking of the cross (Mt 10:38). If ever there had been a moment of romantic idealism in the heads of any of the disciples, it should surely have been banished now.

Not that there are no encouragements along with all those sober warnings. For, says Jesus, there will be those who will welcome them and feed and house them. When they are hauled before the authorities, "the Spirit of your Father" (Mt 10:20) will give them words to speak in self-defense. They will not be asked to bear what Jesus does not suffer. Jesus will be their advocate in heaven (Mt 10:32).

It may have been twelve men who first received these awesome instructions. But in the cause of the mission of the kingdom down through the centuries, many a woman has been commissioned too. And so many a woman has experienced firsthand the suffering but also the promises Jesus spoke of that day, as she has taken up her cross and followed.

Narrative: Opposition to the Kingdom (Mt 11—12)

There is a world of difference between knowing in theory that suffering is part and parcel of following Christ and experiencing it. John the Baptist, incarcerated in the desperate circumstances of a first-century prison, perhaps expecting a rather different unfolding of events once Jesus began his public ministry, begins to entertain doubts. Had he staked his life on the wrong person? Is Jesus only another forerunner, pointing to someone yet again still to come?

In the face of Satan, Jesus hadn't argued, simply responded with Scripture (Mt 4:1-11). Now again he echoes God's word, this time the messianic prophecy of Isaiah 35:4-6 and Isaiah 61:1. "This is what the Lord's Anointed was to do. You know the prophecy, John. That's being fulfilled in me. So, who am I, John?"

It isn't only John who is puzzled by his imprisonment. The crowds too wonder why, if Jesus is who John said he was, he hasn't stepped in to free him. This failure to meet their expectations makes them wary of John and Jesus. They have been happy to have him heal the sick and exorcise the demonized. But what about the rest of their agenda? Presuppositions can prevent us from recognizing the truth when it is in front of us. Jesus has to tell the crowds that they were right to believe that John was a prophet; but prophets are like this, not like that.

Indeed, Jesus says, failure to understand what is going on is not just unfortunate, it is profoundly culpable; and many of those communities that have seen and heard John, and now Jesus, can look forward only to the most fearful judgment. God had said in the past with the utmost clarity what he would do, and now he has done it or is doing it. They have had many privileges, they have seen "the deeds of power" (Mt 11:23) which, had *they* seen it, would have brought the city of Sodom to repentance. But the people of Chorazin and of Bethsaida and of Capernaum have chosen not to respond with the changed lives about which Jesus has so explicitly taught. They must live with the consequences. And the reference to Sodom reminds them that judgment brings destruction.

For the first time in Matthew's record, Jesus speaks directly with his Father (Mt 11:25-30). Who is this Jesus? The one who exclusively completely knows, and is known by, the Father in heaven, God. It is from God, Jesus says, that his authority comes. A little later (Mt 12:8), he claims that "the Son of Man is lord of the sabbath," putting himself at the heart of what the law and worship are all about. Matthew makes the connection between what is happening and messianic prophecy from the Old Testament (Mt 12:17-21), but the Pharisees, by now determined to destroy Jesus (Mt 12:14), insist that he is empowered by Satan (Mt 12:24).

It is into this hotbed of intrigue, and the obvious danger to Jesus and his close followers, that Mary and Jesus' brothers come (Mt 12:46-50). Perhaps they had come to beg him to come home to quiet and safety. Perhaps they were afraid that they too would be in danger if he continued: guilt by association. Perhaps they had come to affirm their support and belief in him. We are not told. But they must surely have felt rather hurt, and perhaps offended, when he apparently played down their unique place in his life. And yet Jesus is saying something immensely important. It is the family of faith (to which we have access), rather than the family of his birth (to which we do not have access), who are his true family. Once more the excluded become the included.

Discourse: Parables of the Kingdom (Mt 13:1-52)

Again Jesus teaches great crowds, which must have included women and children as well as men. Again he draws on themes familiar to them all. Most of the parables revolve around the sowing of seed, but Matthew included a brief parable likening the kingdom of heaven to yeast mixed with flour until all is affected. After that, each time she made bread at home, did every woman who heard him recall his words?

Narrative: The King Recognized, the King Rejected (Mt 13:53—17:27)

For the people of Nazareth, the answer to the question Who is this Jesus? was easy; he was Joseph and Mary's son and brother to four local young men and to an unnamed number of sisters (Mt 13:55-56). It was a correct answer. But at the same time, it was a wrong answer, for they ruled out the possibility of anything more. Were Jesus' family proud of him, embarrassed by him, jealous of him, glad to see him go again? Did Mary remind him of all that happened when he was born? Urge him to take care? We are not told.

But we are told that it was "at that time" (Mt 14:1) that Jesus heard of the murder of John the Baptist, and of Herod Antipas's superstitious fear that Jesus was John raised from the dead. This was not the outcome Zechariah and Elizabeth had dreamed of, all those years ago, as they had held their baby in their arms. Did Mary, too, feel betrayed? Fear for her son must have come gnawing at her heart.

Jesus craved solitude, probably to grieve and to pray. Instead he finds himself pursued by an enormous crowd of needy and then hungry people. It was many hours before he could be alone and quiet (Mt 14:23), and he must have been emotionally and physically exhausted. And yet it is in the aftermath of these events and the storm that followed that the disciples take a giant step forward in acknowledging Jesus' true identity: "Truly you are the Son of God," they say—and worship him (Mt 14:33).

By contrast, the Pharisees, sufficiently concerned to challenge Jesus to have walked for several days from Jerusalem to Gennesaret (Mt 15:1-9), are blind to his true identity because of their tenacious commitment to their religious system, sincerely held. A particular cultural form of worship may displace the one in whose honor the worship is undertaken. In many cultures, girls even more than boys are schooled to tight patterns of conformity from a very young age, in which case, like the Pharisees, they may find Jesus' insistence on inner transformation rather than outward conformity profoundly disturbing (Mt 15:17-20) before they discover its liberating power.

Matthew does not tell us why Jesus then headed west, beyond the boundaries of Palestine. But like Elijah many centuries before, here Jesus encounters a woman in great distress and heals her precious child.

The Canaanite woman, pagan and foreigner though she would have been contemptuously labeled by many a Jew, nonetheless in simple but persistent faith has deep insight into his true identity ("Son of David" = the king, Mt 15:22) and his authority over the powers of darkness. The disciples dismiss her as a nuisance: wrong race, wrong gender, perhaps. But the Lord draws her into the circle of his grace. The excluded takes her place among the included.

A round trip of a hundred miles, perhaps, for one woman. Then, back to the crowds beside Galilee, to heal, to love, to feed (Mt 15:29-31); to be haunted and taunted yet again by the Pharisees trying to discredit him (Mt 16:1-11); to press the disciples to recognize the Pharisees' and Sadducees' teaching for the error that it was (Mt 16:12). And then in Caesarea Philippi—a city of religious pluralism if ever there was one, with temples to Baal, a great temple to Caesar, the headwaters of the Jordan (so important in Jewish history and identity) and claimed as the birthplace of the Greek god Pan—Jesus forces the disciples to face up to his identity (Mt 16:15). "Simon Peter answered, 'You are the Messiah, the Son of the living God'" (Mt 16:16). Among all the gods, there is only one God.

This is the turning point of the Gospel. Everything else, from here to the end, weaves around the central theme of the cross. The King must die.

Not only must the King die, but his subjects also must be willing to take up the cross. From now until Pentecost, the disciples will struggle over and over again with the fact that humanly speaking they are walking into disaster. Any possible last vestiges of hope that they would be at the center of a triumphant, imminent restoration of Israel should surely have been swept away. Shaken they must have been, probably still tempted to abandon Jesus, struggling over the price tag attached to staying with him. But God in his tender grace takes Peter, James and John to the Mount of Transfiguration (Mt 17:1-13) and allows them to see and hear that in eternal terms, if not in earthly terms, Jesus has glory far beyond anything they could have dreamed of. They were right to look for a glorious king; they were wrong, and their vision myopic, to look for that in terms of an insecure throne in a small and impoverished Mediterranean country.

What irony, then, that the King of the whole earth should pay tax (Mt 17:24-27) of any kind. That it should be temple tax is almost beyond belief, except that this King is the one who stands in the place of, is substitution for, his sinner subjects. Then it makes most beautiful sense.

Discourse: The Upside-Down Kingdom (Mt 18)

Perhaps ambition for the immediate future is fading, but apparently it has been projected into the more distant future. If they can't have status here and now, well, who's going to be promoted to the greatest honor in the kingdom of heaven (Mt 18:1)?

Some cultures today have gravely distorted their children, encouraging them to become arrogant, manipulative and selfish. But Jesus could use a small child as a visual aid, not to draw attention to childish innocence and purity (even the smallest child is neither pure nor innocent) but because in his culture a child might be cherished but nonetheless had the lowliest of status in the pecking order. Children knew their dependence and expected to be able to trust the adults around them. They did not claim inflated rights but received what was given and were expected to be grateful, not grasping. This fundamental humility, Jesus says, is the childlike characteristic that should mark his disciples. Further, the humble disciple will gladly welcome and respect children and in so doing will be welcoming Christ. What a lovely affirmation of the dignity of child rearing, much of which falls to women (*see* Childbearing and Rearing).

To Jesus, the important people are not those who have worldly status: God cares so deeply about the most insignificant child that anyone who causes him or her to sin deserves utter destruction for such a terrible sin (Mt 18:6); God cares so deeply that he hunts high and low for the child who strays (Mt 18:10-14).

If this seems upside down in terms of who is important, so must the way Jesus tells his disciples to respond to those who hurt them (Mt 18:15-35). The world says, "Grab your revenge!" Even the law speaks of retaliation. But, says Jesus, instead show mercy, seek reconciliation, seek to restore the sinner to fellowship, forgive deeply and over and over again. These are the practical evidences of genuine humility in adults. As we deal with hurt in the context of prayer (Mt 18:17, 19-20), we are humbled in the presence of our Father who has forgiven us so much.

Narrative: The King Must Die (Mt 19—23)

The Pharisees are bent on trapping Jesus, and the subject of divorce was a minefield (*see* Divorce). Schools of Pharisees disagreed among themselves on the grounds, from the very strict to the very lax, for divorce. Jesus restates the creation principle (Gen 2:23-24): marriage should be permanent, dissolved only by death; it is a profound union—two becoming one—of a man and woman equally; it is for mutual good; the woman is not to be at the mercy of her parents-in-law. This principle, rightly understood, gives great dignity and protection to women. Further, Moses' instructions (Deut 24:1), frequently used to justify a man divorcing a woman on the most trivial of grounds, Jesus insists on the contrary, are a concession, an attempt to protect women from arbitrary divorce on the one hand or abusive captivity on the other. The law had become so twisted down through the centuries that a woman was a thing, a possession of her father, then her husband. She could not initiate divorce, however cruel her husband; she could not protect herself if her husband chose to evict her. Jesus is challenging this particular manifestation of male sin at the time and firmly asserting the preciousness of women in their Creator's sight. No wonder that the Pharisees were left speechless.

Despite Jesus' recent teaching, the disciples apparently see faith as a very adult thing and want to turn away little children too young to understand. There is more important adult business to attend to. Jesus' rebuke to the disciples and welcome to the children (mostly perhaps brought by their mothers) topples the assumed men-women-children hierarchy. Each individual, male or female, old or young, Jew or Gentile, is profoundly valuable to the King. It is on the grounds of the character of God, not the status of the person, that there is entry to the kingdom of heaven (Mt 19:17, 25-26). Indeed, so deeply ingrained is the belief that one's status, wealth and attempts at morality unlock heaven's door that these things are a hindrance (Mt 19:20, 23-24).

The parable of the workers in the vineyard (Mt 20:1-16) underlines the same point. The payment or reward is not calculated on the number of hours different workers have completed but on the generosity of the owner. The gift of eternal life does not come in incremental degrees based on the believer's length of service. The disciples will have a special role in heaven (Mt 19:28), but it will be in the gift of the Father, not a reward for superior status.

Perhaps, despite everything, the disciples boasted to their families about that role, because James and John's mother is eager to ensure the places of the highest honor for her sons (Mt 20:20-28). She may possibly have been Jesus' aunt, Mary's sister, Salome (cf. Mt 27:56; Mk 15:40; Jn 19:25), and she speaks with the full connivance of her sons. Jesus refuses her request: it is not his to grant, but his Father's. Maternal ambition can be sadly out of line with God's ways. Jesus pulls the focus back to the cross and resurrection, now close at hand; there is no future glory, for him or for them, without deep suffering first (Mt 20:18-19, 22-23).

The reaction of the other disciples is not commendable either. Their anger (Mt 20:24) appears to be that of jealousy that James and John had even put them at risk of taking a position inferior to theirs. They are still jockeying for positions in the hierarchy model. No, says Jesus, godly leadership is not about giving orders and being in charge; it's about humble service, about voluntarily adopting the role of the slave who has no rights (Mt 20:25-28; *see* Ancient and Modern Slavery). Feminism that is assertive and domineering is as sinful, as much a product of the Fall, as any patriarchalism that it seeks to redress. The pattern for men and women alike must be that of "the Son of Man [who] came not to be served but to serve, and to give his life a ransom for many" (Mt 20:28). Our sacrificial service cannot be salvific in the way that Jesus' was; it is nonetheless the model from which flows spiritual fruitfulness and spiritual authority. It is as countercultural today as ever it was.

It was not that Jesus was any the less of a King for being the Servant. And in fulfillment of Isaiah 62:11 and Zechariah 9:9, Jesus borrows a donkey and a colt (Mt 21:2-7) and deliberately displays himself as the awaited Savior-King coming to Zion. Passover is only days away, that great festival that commemorates a historic deliverance and acts as a powerful symbol of salvation through the blood of a lamb shed in substitution for one's own. The crowds had gathered many times before, but this time they respond to symbol with symbol, cutting down palm branches as token that the one they greet is conquering hero, a king entering his rightful kingdom (Mt 21:8). As they shout "Hosanna!" (Mt 21:9), they identify him as the one who is to save now. For this brief moment, they echo the angel of the Lord (Mt 1:21). Yet, as others ask them "Who is this?" (Mt 21:10), they can only say, "This is the prophet Jesus from Nazareth in Galilee" (Mt 21:11): true but inadequate. Down through the centuries, people have said, "Good man, great example, great teacher." That too is true but inadequate.

The adulation of the crowds must have made the Pharisees incandescent. Yet Jesus' next action, the clearing of the temple (Mt 21:12-17), ensured that the priests too were raging with anger against him. Jesus was tangling with their vested interests: the money changers and the dove sellers made the most of their monopoly, shamefully exploiting rather than serving travelers coming to the temple to make their sacrifices. They had them at their mercy, and they made the most of their power. Excited bartering would make the place more like a street market than the place it was meant to be, a place of worship and awed encounter with God and a place of prayer for all nations (Is 56:7). Abuse of power greatly angers God.

Moreover, the priests, the so-called experts in doing business with God, are, says Jesus, ignorant in comparison with the little children who sing "Hosanna." A tiny child may not be able to articulate his or her faith in adult terms, but even one so young as to be nursing at the breast can give beautiful praise to the Lord (Mt 21:16). Matthew has repeatedly recorded Jesus' great delight in young children. In a context where infant mortality was high and where in many parts of the Roman Empire unwanted infants—mostly girls—were left out to die (not normally practiced by Jews), perhaps many a mother would have been comforted at this living out of "the promise [that] is for you [and] for your children" (Acts 2:39).

The chief priests are eager to trap Jesus so as to be able to bring a charge against him. So they ask him about the source of his authority (Mt 21:23). If he answers, "God," he can be accused of blasphemy. If he answers, "Myself," he can still be accused of the same. But Jesus turns the tables on them. Moreover, he says that tax collectors and prostitutes (Mt 21:31) showed proper response to John's prophetic message from God and repented and "are going into the kingdom of God ahead of you," because the priests have shown no evidence of repentance. The priests would have been outraged at the suggestion that repentant prostitutes were more welcome to God than they. They despised prostitutes, blaming them for their lifestyle and conveniently overlooking the fact that men's demand for sexual gratification, or men's failure to provide for widows and desperately poor women, drove them to the trade. The parable of the killing of the vineyard owner's son (Mt 21:33-46) is a scarcely veiled challenge: "You can kill me, but the kingdom of God will be given instead to those you despise, the repentant ones, whatever their previous background."

The parable of the wedding banquet (Mt 22:2-14) rubs in the same warning. The priests and the Pharisees had ignored the invitation, "Repent, for the kingdom of heaven is at hand," brought by first John and then Jesus. So now the invitation has been given instead to those whom they would regard as unworthy. Those who didn't respond appropriately (Mt 22:5-7, 11) faced destruction.

Jesus in turn exposes the wicked motives of the Pharisees and the Sadducees, cutting through their trick questions about paying taxes to the emperor (Mt 22:15-22), the resurrection (Mt 22:23-33) and the core of the commandments (Mt 22:34-40). He asks them a question that exposes their lack of understanding of the Scriptures (Mt 22:41-46). He tells the crowd and his disciples that the scribes and Pharisees are hypocrites who do not practice what they preach (Mt 23:1-12).

And then Jesus addresses the scribes and Pharisees again with a series of blistering charges (Mt 23:13-36). Repeatedly he calls them hypocrites. He batters them with their culpability, their awesome responsibility not only in shutting themselves out of the kingdom but, even more damning, locking others out too (Mt 23:13). They have twisted God's law over and over again and totally missed the things that matter (Mt 23:23). They show religious rectitude on the outside, but God, who sees on the inside, sees only filth and sin (Mt 23:25, 27). They set themselves up self-righteously (Mt 23:29-30), but their assured destination is hell (Mt 23:33). There is nothing to look forward to but the most fearsome judgment.

Jesus could not have more surely signed his death warrant.

It is not that Jesus delights in his message of condemnation and destruction. It is simply that it is the truth. He turns to the city and shares his heartache for all that lies ahead. He likens himself to a mother hen, spreading her wings so that her chicks may scurry for shelter beneath her when danger looms. It is a beautiful, tender, powerful image. But if the chicks won't come, what can she do?

It is not only the King who will die.

Discourse: And the King Shall Come Again (Mt 24—25)

It must have been inescapable that events were reaching a climax. Jesus foretells the coming destruction of the temple, which would have horrified the disciples as well as the religious authorities. So the disciples ask him not only when this will happen but also what signs will warn them it is about to happen and that Jesus is about to return, both events which they expect to accompany the end of the present age (Mt 24:3).

Jesus gives no timetable, in the sense of naming dates. Rather, he speaks first of a lengthy period of suffering, of wars and of natural disasters. He warns of those who will come claiming to be the returning Mes-

---

Birth Pain Imagery

Because of their intensity and the peril associated with them, yet the positive result that is hoped for, birth pains are a potent theological metaphor.

The intensity and the peril are in view in Genesis 35:16-18, the story of Rachel's death in childbirth. These aspects are also in view in many other passages (e.g., Jer 4:31; 30:12-15) where pain is a symbol for God's judgment. In 1 Enoch 62:4-6 and other passages the process of childbirth is the focus, and the birth is omitted. The metaphor does not extend to birth: no metaphorical child is born to the kings and governors who are being judged; they have the intense pain and nothing more.

This narrow focus is present also in some of the New Testament passages (Mk 13, surprisingly, and 1 Thess 5:3). It is important not to read in the birth event when the passage does not contain it.

Birth pains are not only intense and dangerous, however; they are also helpless pains. The biblical authors capitalize on this aspect in passages such as Jeremiah 48:41 or Isaiah 13:4-8. Again, facets such as birth and hope are out of the picture; what is in view is the pain, ineffectuality and humiliation. This is probably the background of Romans 8, where the frustration and pain is rather remarkably featured alongside not birth but adoption. When Paul feels birth pains for the Galatians "until Christ is *formed* in you," the birth is implied, but the metaphor mostly speaks about helplessness and frustration: "for I am perplexed about you" (Gal 4:19-20, emphasis added).

Some passages refer more directly to the implied birth, and for some authors, therefore, birth pains are productive pains. In John 16:20-22, the pain is real but not final. Judgment and restoration are apocalyptic symbols (Is 66:6-9; Mic 4:10; 5:3-4; cf. Rev 12:1-6).

The biblical authors make use of one more aspect of birth pains: they are a type of pain that must run its course. This pain is not just sharp; it involves a period of time rather than a point in time. It recurs within that period of time, and once begun, there is no escape until it runs to completion. For the Scriptures, this is a perfect analogy for the eschaton: the onset of birth pains is not yet the end but the beginning of a process that must surely culminate (4 Ezra 16:37-39; Mk 13 and par.).

From the curse in Genesis to the birth of the holy one in Revelation, birth pains are an important image. In the Christian writings, such as Revelation, however, the image has been turned upside down. In the prophets, the mighty God causes his enemies to swoon like women in labor. In Revelation 12, it is the enemy who seems mighty, while salvation arrives through the humility of birth pains and childbirth.

CONRAD GEMPF

---

siah and of many false prophets who will successfully deceive many people. The waiting and the suffering will make many fall away. There are terrible days yet to be endured.

But when he comes again, it will be no hidden event. Rather, the whole world from east to west will see him in his glory (Mt 24:30). The whole world will have heard the "good news of the kingdom" (Mt 24:14), because the gospel is truly universal. There will be no warning, and response must be immediate (Mt 24:17-31).

And yet there are signs: signs that are seen in every generation, signs to ensure that down through the centuries the alert will always be ready and expectant, waiting for the King to return at any moment (Mt 24:32-35, 44; 25:1-13). The exact moment is known only to the Father (Mt 24:36), but this will not be the moment to change your fate (Mt 24:40-41).

The whole discourse is couched in vivid, dramatic picture language. For example, the illustrations taken from the days of Noah, the people in the field, the women side by side grinding corn, are dramatic sketches that grab the imagination. Again, the story of the ten bridesmaids (Mt 25:1-13) heightens the sense of drama, the spine-tingling truth that if you are not ready at the right moment, it is too late. If Matthew has often shown the excluded becoming the included, here the reverse is true: like the religious experts, some who are sure of their inclusion will find they are among the excluded.

The Master will return. This insistent motif comes over and over again throughout this section. His return will be without warning, and it will be a moment of inescapable accountability and judgment. The parable of the talents (Mt 25:14-30) highlights the way in which God sovereignly entrusts different gifts and resources to different people "to each according to his ability" (Mt 25:15). The question is not what we might have done in different circumstances or with someone else's opportunities but how we have used to the full what we do have for the benefit of the Lord. Lack of freedom to choose our circumstances is no excuse.

It will be a moment where all the nations of the world will see Jesus in his full glory (Mt 25:32) and the whole human race will be judged by him. Most people will have never seen Jesus in the flesh, but practical, compassionate goodness is seen as being as unto the Lord. It is not that good works save us, but that the picture given (Mt 25:34-40) is of those living out the reality of repentance, for the kingdom of heaven is at hand, and echoing the ministry of the Servant (Is 61:1-2). Such mercy and kindness is open to old and young, male and female, rich and poor. Within your circumstances and abilities (Mt 25:14-30), says Jesus, live like this (Mt 25:34-46). That is the evidence that you belong in the kingdom. When the King returns, he will know where you belong for eternity.

Narrative: Tragedy—and Triumph! (Mt 26—28)

Passover was not only the focal point of the

Jewish religious year, recalling the dramatic intervention of God to deliver his people from judgment and oppression (Ex 12). It had also become, by extension, the powerful focal point for nationalism. God who had delivered in the past must surely intervene again, and he had promised to do so through his Messiah. Many people believed that this year and this charismatic figure, Jesus, meant that now was the time.

They were right. But all the assumptions that went along with it, supremely throwing out the Romans, were painfully wrong. Nonetheless the chief priests and religious leaders know they cannot wait a moment longer to get rid of Jesus (Mt 26:3-5).

Jesus warns his disciples that, despite the triumphal entry into Jerusalem of only a few days before, he will be crucified—killed barbarically as the most despised of criminals—in a couple of days' time (Mt 26:2). The anointing with costly ointment by an unnamed woman (Mt 26:6-13) is especially symbolic, for the body of an executed criminal was forbidden anointing, a sacred symbol. So in this act, Jesus says, "She has prepared me for burial" (Mt 26:12), dramatically acting out that though he became sin for us, he was truly the righteous One and did not deserve to die a criminal's death. Matthew does not tell us what prompted this woman's extravagant gesture. She was probably lavishing on him her most costly possession. While the disciples express anger over what seems to them illogical wastefulness and perhaps excessive emotion, Jesus affirms the pricelessness of the woman's love and the accuracy of her intuition.

The ointment was costly, the love beyond price—but Jesus' life can be bought with a mere thirty pieces of silver (Mt 26:15), the price of a slave accidentally killed (Ex 21:32). No wonder Jesus declares that "wherever this good news is proclaimed in the whole world, what she has done will be told in remembrance of her" (Mt 26:13).

As Jesus and his disciples keep the Passover meal (Mt 26:17-29), it is on the one hand totally in the shadow of betrayal and death and on the other a triumphant reformulation of what it is all about (Mt 26:27-28). Jesus could not more explicitly state the reason for his death: "for the forgiveness of sins." The angel's promise to Joseph (Mt 1:21) is about to be fulfilled.

In different ways all the disciples, not just Judas, betray Jesus. Even Peter, effusive to the last (Mt 26:33, 35), first sleeps when his watchful company is most badly needed, then runs away (26:56), then denies ever knowing Jesus (Mt 26:74). Jesus faces his ordeal alone, even when surrounded by people. Only his Father stands by him, as he agonizes in prayer, and even his Father has no comforting word of reprieve. There is no other way (Mt 26:54).

It is impossible to begin to fathom the desolation of desertion by all his friends, the pain of having the crowds, over whom he had wept and mourned and for whom he had done so many compassionate acts, turn in abrupt fickleness from adulation to hatred. They come, a hostile army, prepared to fight to capture him (Mt 26:47). But there is no fight: Jesus gives himself up.

There was no legitimate charge to be brought against Jesus. The chief priests, appointed guardians of truth and righteousness, deliberately seek false witnesses, purveyors of untruth and wickedness (Mt 26:59), to justify their unlawful actions. Finally it is that central question, Who is this Jesus? addressed directly to Jesus by the high priest, that leads to the charge: blasphemy (Mt 26:65-66).

It is this same question, "Who are you?" that Pilate in his turn puts to Jesus (Mt 27:11). The high priest had posed the question in Jewish religious terms: "Are you the Messiah?" (Mt 26:64); Pilate poses it in Gentile terms: "Are you the King of the Jews?" (Mt 27:11). Shrewd enough to know that Jesus has been framed (Mt 27:18), Pilate nonetheless gives way to popular demand in order to prevent a riot (Mt 27:17, 24). After all, he might pay with his life if there is an insurrection. His wife's dream (Mt 27:19) may have filled him with superstitious dread, and he protests Jesus' innocence (Mt 27:23); he takes pains to show that he disclaims responsibility for Jesus' death (Mt 27:22, 24). And the crowd, incited by the chief priests (Mt 27:20), shout, "His blood be on us and on our children!" (Mt 27:25). They speak more truly than they know.

Sentence passed, Jesus is fair game for abuse by the Roman soldiers (Mt 27:27-31). To them, holed up in a hostile foreign country, nervous because this was the most volatile point of the year, this is an opportunity for legalized violence, an occasion to open the valve on their pent-up emotions. Perhaps for them it was routine cruelty in a cruel age. After brutal torture, Jesus is taken to Golgotha and crucified.

Even in these last, terrible, pain-wracked hours, shame upon shame is heaped on Jesus. He is stripped. The soldiers gamble for his clothes, then settle down to watch until he dies, their callous job. They contemptuously label him: "This is Jesus, the King of the Jews" (Mt 27:37). The passing crowds (Mt 27:39), the chief priests who have come to gloat (Mt 27:41), the two bandits dying alongside him (Mt 27:44) all mock and taunt.

Yet at the moment of Jesus' death, the unnatural darkness (Mt 27:45), the earthquake (Mt 27:51) and the tearing of the great temple curtain, symbolizing the opening up of access to God, brought transformed understanding. "Truly this man was God's Son!" (Mt 27:54). Gentiles, Romans at that, grasp who Jesus is.

Sarcophagus detail with a woman seated at tomb. (Matthew 27:61)

It was the women who stayed with Jesus to the end. Matthew tells us they were "many" (Mt 27:55), though he names only three. Mary the mother of James and Joseph is probably Jesus' mother. Matthew tells us that these women had traveled with Jesus and "provided for him." Perhaps even now they hoped to perform one last service for their loved one, though the bodies of the crucified were normally not returned to their families but tossed into a common grave. What must Mary have felt as she watched her beloved son die? Moreover, watched him die in excruciating agony and utter disgrace? Could she even remotely begin to understand? Did she feel most of her life had been built around a lie, that she had been betrayed by God?

Wonderfully, Joseph of Arimathea, apparently a man of influence as well as wealth (Mt 27:57-60), obtains the body for dignified and proper burial, a tiny shaft of light on that bleak day. Did Mary help bathe the bloodied body, torn flesh of her flesh? At last there is nobody left but the two Marys (Mt 27:61). His mother is the only one to have been there from the very beginning to the very end.

As soon as the sabbath is over, at dawn the Marys return. The soldiers sent meanwhile to guard the tomb are no match for divine intervention (Mt 27:62-66; 28:4). A glorious angelic being tells the women not to be afraid: just as he had promised, Jesus has risen from the dead. They are told to look for themselves to see the tomb is empty and then to go and tell the disciples. As they turn to go "with fear and great joy" (Mt 28:8), Jesus appears to them. Jesus' love for his mother is very tender at this point. So God entrusts to these women the key role of testimony to Jesus' death and resurrection. Every last detail must have been etched on Mary's mind and heart. God entrusted her with being the mother of his Son. Now he has entrusted her with that first revelation of Jesus' triumph over death and disaster. God has kept his word. Jesus is the one whom the angel said he would be: the Savior.

And because the answer to the question Who is this Jesus? is what it is—Savior, King, Messiah, God's beloved Son—as Matthew has vividly shown, so "all authority in heaven and on earth has been given to me" (Mt 28:18). The King reigns. And because "King of the Jews," though true, is too small a title for the one who is King of the whole earth, it is now the whole earth, all the nations, all the peoples, who are to be discipled. It is now the Lord's people who are to go, in the name of the Father, Son and Holy Spirit (in other words, with all the conjoint authority and equipping of the full Trinity [*see* The Trinity]), to every community of the globe, to declare the good news of the kingdom and to prepare for Jesus' promised visible return. And in the going, unseen but in abiding grace, "remember, I am with you always, to the end of the age" (Mt 28:20).

Bibliography. D. A. Carson, *The Bible Expositor's Commentary: Vol. 1, Matthew 1-12* (Grand Rapids, MI: Zondervan, 1995); idem, *The Bible Expositor's Commentary: Vol. 2, Matthew 13-28* (Grand Rapids, MI: Zondervan, 1995); J. R. W. Stott, *The Message of the Sermon on the Mount* (Downers Grove, IL: IVP, 1978).

ROSEMARY M. DOWSETT

The Trinity

Theological study of the doctrine of the Trinity experienced a renaissance in the latter half of the twentieth century. The Trinity reveals a distinctive Christian perspective not only about God but also about the nature of the universe and of humankind. Although the term *Trinity* cannot be found in the Bible, its Latin form was coined by Tertullian and the early church viewed the Trinity as a foundational Christian belief. This article will explore what is meant by the Trinity, with acknowledgment that this doctrine is steeped in mystery and that the mystery eludes precise definition. Of particular relevance are three specific questions about this doctrine. Why historically has this been at times such a neglected doctrine when it is fundamental to the Christian understanding of God? What is the relationship of the neglect of this doctrine to attitudes and understanding of the feminine? How does belief in the triune nature of God shape understanding of the nature of humankind—creatures who have been created in the image of God as both male and female?

The Meaning of the Trinity: God as One Being in Three Persons

The Nicene definition of the Trinity affirms that God exists eternally both as one in essential being and as three persons in loving communion. Throughout history the emphasis of the Western church has been more on the oneness of the triune persons, whereas in the Eastern church, the tripersonalness of God has been more prominent. Both emphases are fundamental in Scripture and express fuller apprehension of the Trinity when they are held in a mutually informing relationship.

The oneness of God is a consistent theme throughout the Bible. A triune understanding of God holds fast to the central affirmation of the Old Testament known as the Shema, "Hear, O Israel: The LORD our God, the LORD is one" (Deut 6:4 NIV; cf. Mark 12:29). The affirmation of Jesus' divinity by New Testament authors in no way implies God is not one, for as James so dramatically expresses, "Even the demons believe [there is one God]—and shudder" (Jas 2:19). Paul's words in Romans 3:30, that God is one, make clear that Paul was no tritheist, a believer in three gods, although he affirmed the threefold nature of God throughout his epistles by using variations of a threefold formula or pattern (cf. 2 Thess 2:13-14; 1 Cor 12:4-6; 2 Cor 1:21-22; 3:3; 13:13; Gal 3:11-14; 4:6; Rom 5:1-5; 8:9-11; 14:17-18; 15:16, 30; Eph 3:14-16; see also Gregory of Nyssa's treatise *On Not Three Gods*).

The early church's reflections on the Trinity constantly emphasized God's oneness. The affirmation that the Father, Son and Spirit may not be separated or divided derived from the fourth-century councils of Nicea (325) and Constantinople (381), along with the fifth-century Chalcedonian definition. The triune persons are of one substance *(ousia)*. Therefore no superiority or inferiority exists within the triune relationship, and no discrepancy in character, will or purpose. Traditionally God the Father has been correlated with creation, God the Son with redemption and God the

Spirit with sanctification. However, serious distortions have resulted when the mutual involvement of all three persons of the Trinity in some sense in each domain has been ignored or denied. Marcionism, which posited an inferior and unworthy God of creation over against the entirely new revelation of Jesus Christ, is one extreme example. The temptation to distinguish too much between the Father and the Son has been a tendency throughout history that has militated against maintaining the complete unity of the Father and the Son, a unity pivotal in Jesus' own teaching (Jn 14:9; 17:21-22). The Athanasian Creed articulates the unity of God in the statement, "the Godhead of the Father, of the Son, and of the Holy Ghost, is all one, the Glory equal, the Majesty co-eternal. Such as the Father is, such is the Son, and such is the Holy Ghost. . . . So are we forbidden by the Catholic religion, to say, There be three Gods or three Lords."

Christian orthodoxy has understood Scripture to convey that Jesus Christ does not reveal a secondary God. He is "the image of the invisible God" (Col 1:15), such that when one sees the face of Christ, one sees the face of God. Christ is able to be the true Mediator, because he is the very Word of God. "In the beginning was the Word, and the Word was with God, and the Word was God" (Jn 1:1). This is the basis of Jesus' ability to forgive, to save, to recreate and to unite humanity with God, for truly Jesus is God. Therefore any tendency to suggest a dichotomy in character, in being or in purpose between the God of the Old Testament and the God of the New Testament cuts off Christian doctrine from its roots of God's longsuffering self-revelation, roots that are deeply embedded in the oneness of God. Christian theology has historically insisted that it is necessary to maintain continuity between the Old and New Testament, between God the Father and God the Son, for "God is not mediated by that which is not God" (Torrance, 102).

Furthermore, holding to the oneness of God includes acknowledgment that the scope of the Spirit in action and gifts is as large as the scope of the Father and the Son. The Spirit of God is involved in creation, in the birth, life, death and resurrection of Jesus, and in the birth and equipping of the body of Christ. In Acts 2:17 Peter quotes Joel, saying, " 'In the last days it will be, God declares that, I will pour out my Spirit upon all flesh.' " Again, biblical emphasis on God as one requires affirmation that there is no superiority or inferiority within the triune relationship and no discrepancy in character, will or purpose.

Whereas there is unity between the New and Old Testaments in affirming the oneness of God, a measure of discontinuity seems to exist when one introduces the idea of God existing as three persons in triune communion. In the Gospel of John some Jewish leaders are portrayed as considering Jesus' identification of himself with God as a blasphemy worthy of death. They did not expect that the Messiah would be literally God with us, although Immanuel was one of the prophetic messianic titles. Jesus' divinity has continued to provoke controversy throughout the ages. Some theologians have attempted to explain this mystery, along with the mystery of the divinity of the Holy Spirit, by describing the three persons of God as three modes of presence of the one God. This view, called modalism or Sabellianism, asserts that the names Father, Son and Spirit are references to the modes of God—something like masks of God—rather than descriptive of God's inmost being. Christ's life, death and resurrection and the outpouring of the Holy Spirit thus understood may reveal nothing of the true character of God. The idea that the three persons are only manifestations of a Being that is something other and higher implies that we deal with a God of appearances and not of reality. A parallel may be seen with Greek actors who would hide their own personality and character behind the masks worn to act out particular parts. With this view of the Trinity, according to Karl Barth, "belief in revelation necessarily becomes idolatry," for to embrace the mask of the Son or the Spirit and worship this would not be to worship the real Being behind it (I/1, 353).

In order to apprehend the essential nature of God's threeness without collapsing it into modalism or fragmenting it into tritheism, the early church labored to develop a deeper understanding of the very nature of personhood. *Person,* when applied to God, was distinguished by early Christians from the Greek notion of mask and its Latin parallel, *persona.* The term *hypostasis* was adopted instead of *prosōpon* (Gk. for *persona*) to convey the idea that person is something more intrinsic to God, which must be understood in terms of the very tripersonal nature of God's being. Just as *person* or *hypostasis* is not used to speak about personhood as a mere mask, so it is also not used to denote separateness of being or individual centers of subjectivity. The Christian faith does not have three objects, which would mean three gods. Rather there is consistency between the identity of God implied by the statement "I am" and that which Jesus reveals in his affirmation that "The Father and I are one." Furthermore, Jesus identifies himself with the Spirit whom he refers to as another "Comforter" or "Advocate" (Jn 14:16). Divine personhood or *hypostasis* is understood, particularly in the Eastern church, as the combination of both God's being and God's relatedness. The radical revelation in Christ is that God exists in communion, that relationships are at the heart of the universe and being, not autonomous isolation. The particular nature of this divine communion is revealed most profoundly on the cross, which offers a window into the unity within the Trinity: a unity of self-relatedness that overflows in selflessness. The relationship between the triune persons is one of reciprocal interpenetration in which "Father, Son and Spirit mutually indwell and contain one another, while remaining what they are" (Cyril of Alexandria). A musical chord provides a partial analogy to this understanding of God, for in a chord three notes remain as they are but interpenetrate one another to convey a harmonious and unified sound.

The Neglect of the Trinity and of the Feminine

Western theological development has at times reflected a movement away from the mysterious tension of God as both one and three. This movement derives rather early on from the Augustinian-Western conception of the Trinity, which exalts the oneness of God above the triunity of God and which leads to philosophical and abstract treatises about God with diminished reflection on God as experienced in salvation history (Rahner, 19). Neglect of the Son and Spirit as conveying essential understanding about the character of God is one result of this movement. A heightened expression of this neglect is evident in the modern period from the eighteenth through the early twentieth centuries. The supremacy of rationalism and the lingering influence of Platonic dualism further impaired understanding of the biblical revelation that Jesus offers in shaping perceptions of the one God.

One expression of this philosophical dualism is evident in the Kantian philosophical chasm between the noumenal, or spiritual realm, and the phenomenal, or material realm. This framework created a context in which to affirm the trinitarian faith that the eternal divine Word became human flesh and now dwells with us as the Spirit was not seen as academically credible. Responses to a perceived threat to the credibility of Christian faith took numerous routes. On the one hand were efforts, like Bultmann's, to demythologize Christian belief and Scripture such that Jesus could be recognized as an eminent leader and teacher without having to violate Newtonian laws of physics, historical criticism or this philosophical dualism by affirming his divinity or miracle-working power. On the other hand certain doctrinal schools developed rigid logical systems to accommodate the demand for greater intellectual mastery and consistency. Federal Calvinism is an example of such an endeavor in which the logic of particular notions of the sovereignty of God created one sphere for the Father, that of lawgiver, and another for the Son, that of the fulfillment of a legal transaction. The Son does not reveal the character of God the Father who has decreed to elect some and damn others for eternity. In this system, Jesus Christ reveals the Father's decision to be gracious to the elect. Similarly the Spirit has often been limited to a particular sphere of involvement, either depersonalized and attached to the world historical movement, consigned to a particular class or gender within the church or neglected as a part of the unknowable noumenal realm. In this subordinated scope, the biblical teaching about the abiding, nurturing presence of God's Spirit is also allowed little role in illuminating understanding of the character of God.

Emphasis on the oneness of God in fatherly or kingly conceptions that are separate from the Son and the Spirit has been part of a larger dichotomization of life that has prevented that which is mysterious and relational from being held organically together with that which is logical and reasonable. "Western culture has been oriented towards masculine values—power, reason, technology," writes Swiss psychiatrist Paul Tournier. He traces this movement to the Renaissance, which he claims "made a resolute choice of the rational as against the irrational, of the 'I-it' as against the 'I-thou', of objectivity as against affective and mystical communion, of physics as against metaphysics" (16). In this way the neglect of the doctrine of the Trinity has been at times interrelated with the neglect of the value of the feminine. The exaltation of reason meant a diminished emphasis on relationships, both inner, triune relationships and relationships between males and females created in the image of God as beings for communion. The ensuing imbalance led at times to a preoccupation with culturally defined masculine aspects of God's character and a diminishment of culturally defined feminine aspects. The imago Dei was often equated with being rational, autonomous, self-determining, qualities prized as real by the Age of Enlightenment. The feminine principle of relationships, of imaginative and intuitive connectedness, was often associated with that which is less real.

This masculinized view of God contributed to the perspective that only a man could represent God before the church, for God is supremely rational, initiating, sovereign. Because the image of God was associated primarily with rationality and autonomy, men were somehow more representative of that image of God than women were. Women have been caricatured as emotional (often seen as synonymous with irrational) and dependent beings. Although Jesus, "the image of the invisible God" (Col 1:15), was not autonomous, unemotional or coercive, the fact that he was male has been used as one more sanction against female leadership and the concrete value of the feminine by such writers as J. I. Packer and C. S. Lewis. An idea of Jesus the man's revelation of the masculinity of God was implicitly accepted, but Jesus' revelation of the character and nature of God, the radiance of God's glory (Heb 1:3), was subsumed under ancient philosophical notions of sovereignty, power and rationality. Similarly the Spirit's subordination theologically paralleled women's subordination ecclesiastically. Any nurturing, abiding motherly character of God that the Spirit would convey was veiled by philosophical and theological preoccupations with the one God, Father and King. How could a woman ever represent a God who is predominantly Father and King?

As a result, throughout history there have been streams of thought that have reduced the oneness of God to a unitarian view of a god who looked a great deal more like human monarchs than like Jesus Christ. God was often perceived as deistically removed from the material world, managing human life, sin and redemption from a distance. A deepening theological fracture occurred that lost sight both of the unity of the Father, Son and Spirit and of the loving nature of that community of divine persons as supremely revealed in Jesus Christ. Furthermore, this created a weakened understanding of God's purposes to heal humanity through uniting humanity to God. On one hand the rift between the divine and the human was perceived as too immense to conceive of such a union, as in schools of thought influenced by Kantian dualism. On the other hand the logic of divine holiness and human sinfulness often accommodated only legal transactional understanding of reconciliation, which was perceived as external to God and to humankind. Predominant emphasis on salvation as Christ's payment of the human debt to God, the Lawgiver, obscured the biblical idea of the coming of the living Word as flesh to re-create and unite creation with God (*see* Atonement). In giving priority to external notions of salvation, it also veiled God's purposes to transform people from within and to fill them with God's own Spirit that they might exist within and reveal the very glory of God's own divine communion.

Implications of the Trinity for Understanding the Image of God

We live in the midst of a movement to recover a more biblical model of the Trinity that honors God as both one and three. A scriptural understanding of the trinitarian nature of God has significant implications in at least three areas: the character of God, the nature of male-female relationships and the nature of community. If one takes seriously the triune nature of God as revealed through Jesus Christ, one will have to abandon the masculinized idea of God as supremely solitary and sovereign. The feminine principle of creative, sacrificial and nurturing love will be harmonized with affirmations of God's reign and sovereignty. This kind of love is of the essence of God the Creator, who would give life and new birth to humans that they might exist in relationship as male and female with one another and with God. Furthermore, such nurturing love is at the heart of the life, death and resurrection of Christ and of the ongoing work of the Holy Spirit to inspire, comfort and empower.

Jesus reveals the communion of the triune persons to be one of mutual self-giving without domination and hierarchy. The triune persons are understood to be mutually interpenetrating as in a divine dance. The technical theological term for this is *perichoresis*. Each of the divine persons expresses on the one hand an openness of being and on the other hand a form of existence *(hypostasis)* that is unique and unrepeatable. There is both self-relatedness and selflessness. The triune persons are not each subsumed in mutual interpenetration but are each expressed and realized within the mutual relationship (Torrance, 256). The overflowing of this self-relatedness in self-offering to humanity and the created order retains both the nature of openness of being and absolute unrepeatability. The deeply personal nature of the triune God reinforces the use of the biblically warranted names of Father,[1] Son and Spirit, and challenges the exclusive use of impersonal terms like Creator, Redeemer and Sustainer that fail to convey the relational glory of the Trinity. However, the self-accommodation of God to the names Father, Son and Spirit must be informed by God's self-revelation and thus not reduced to human notions of individuation or sexuality. For a redeemed understanding of these terms they must be filled and transformed through the revelatory reconfiguring of them in Christ, lest projections of our broken experiences with our fathers create distortions and diminishment of the unconditional love and intimacy that these terms connote in Christ and the Spirit.

Such revelation of the nature of the personhood of God is helpful also in informing understanding of human personhood, created in the image of God. Human personhood should not be viewed reductionistically either in terms of individuation or sexuality. Rather, it is best understood theocentrically as both openness of being and unrepeatable uniqueness. Sexuality is a gift through which self-transcendence may be experienced in union with the other. It should not be used in an antipersonal way as an attempt to contain and delimit another human being. To place artificial boundaries and

[1]There is also biblical and theological justification for arguing that God's self-revelation includes warrant for maternal appellations (Is 42:1-14; 49:15-16; 66:8-9, 13; Jn 1:12-13). For three expressions of theological justification among many, note: the Council of Toledo affirmed in 675 that the Son was begotten "from the womb of the Father [de utero Patris]," J. Neuner and J. Dupuis, *The Christian Faith in the Doctrinal Documents of the Catholic Church* (New York: Alba House, 1982), 102-6 (306) [The Denzinger Schoenmetzer equivalents, 526]; Julian of Norwich wrote of "Christ our Mother" and that "the deep wisdom of the Trinity is our Mother," *Showings*, trans. E. Colledge (New York: Paulist, 1978); and Calvin asserted that God "did not satisfy himself with proposing the example of the father, (which on other occasions he very frequently employs), but in order to express his very strong affection, he chose to liken himself to a mother," *The Book of the Prophet Isaiah*, trans. W. Pringle (Grand Rapids, MI: Eerdmans, 1958) 4:30.

limits around persons by reducing personhood to function and gender is to regard such persons as static objects rather than full human beings. In Martin Buber's terms, it is to reduce the other to the status of an it that denies his or her unbounded nature and one's own responsibility toward the other. We are created for I-Thou relationships in which love frees the other to be a subject who is fully realized through self-transcendence and communion with God and with others.

If one takes seriously a trinitarian understanding of the creation of humans in the image of God, a number of implications for male-female relationships emerge. Male-female relationships are to be patterned after the relationality of the Trinity in whose image human beings have been created. Unity and diversity should be held together without dominance and hierarchy. Authority structures, which derive from the entrance of sin into the world, should no longer be determinative of human relations. Rather, the embrace of the Father through the Son and the Spirit should enable relationships in Christ to be taken into the life of God in which personhood is preeminent, not gender. "Human persons can be fully mutual, reciprocal, equal because we see in the proclamation and life of Jesus that the summit of personhood is to transcend (not escape from) every limit condition, including or especially gender, where gender means sex-role. In the reign of God human beings are judged on how they love others, not on whether they are male or female, white or black, bright or mediocre" (LaCugna, 282). Differences do not create the basis for hierarchical categories but the context for equal and interdependent relationships in Christ. Paul encapsulated this in Galatians 3:28: "There is no longer Jew or Greek, there is no longer slave or free, there is no longer male or female; for all of you are one in Christ Jesus."

In trinitarian understanding community, not isolated individuality, is constitutive of human life. To be fully human is to be free for one another and given space to be, by one another. Jesus Christ is both the foundation and the exemplar of life lived in community. Through Jesus' recreation of humanity the Spirit has been poured out on all people equipping Christ's followers to experience the loving and gracious reign of God. "Jesus' own sexuality—his free and perfect relationality—shows that maleness and femaleness, which are the vehicles of self-transcendence through union with another person, have the potential to become free and mutual when persons meet and unite with each other *in Christ*" through his Spirit (LaCugna, 282).

Community life that radiates from the light of the Trinity challenges many contemporary understandings of human relationships and creates a quality of community life for which humankind hungers. It challenges the deprecation of the feminine gifts of relationality. It obviates demoting that which is traditionally associated with the feminine—emotion, imagination, the created order—and rather sees all of these as rooted and established in Christ and born with him into the triune and eternal nature of God. It challenges the destructive tendency to divide and dichotomize that which God has united in Christ through the Spirit. Instead it offers a way of life that is not static and conveniently categorized but overflowing in creativity from the dynamism of bringing diverse gifts and self-expressions together. It rejects the idea that to be fully human is to be autonomous and self-made. Furthermore, it offers the possibility of fellowship based on the communion that constitutes the Trinity. As Jesus prayed, "that they may be all one. As you, Father, are in me and I am in you, may they also be in us, so that the world may believe that you have sent me" (Jn 17:21). Such community is an eschatological gift that will be fully realized only when God is all in all. Yet the kingdom of God is in our midst, and in this kingdom we are called and empowered to begin to express that which we one day will be. This life of loving communion is extended to creation now in the Spirit as the very love with which the Father eternally loves the Son (Jn 17:26).

Bibliography

K. Barth, *Church Dogmatics*, 4 vols. (Edinburgh: T & T Clark, 1936-1969); C. M. LaCugna,

God for Us (San Francisco: HarperSanFrancisco, 1991); C. E. Gunton, *The Promise of Trinitarian Theology* (Edinburgh: T & T Clark, 1991); J. Moltmann, *The Trinity and the Kingdom* (London: SCM, 1981); A. J. Torrance, *Persons in Communion* (Edinburgh: T & T Clark, 1996); K. Rahner, *The Trinity* (New York: Herder & Herder, 1970); P. Tournier, *The Gift of Feeling,* trans. E. Hudson (Atlanta: John Knox Press, 1981). KERRY L. DEARBORN

MARK

Introduction

The first canonical Gospel, Mark is a popular work written to evoke faith that Jesus is the Messiah and Son of God. Scholars have compared it with Hellenistic biographies like Xenophon's *Memorabilia* and Plato's *Apology of Socrates* and have called it eschatological history. Its literary form is also reminiscent of folktale, a realistic narrative meant to be told or read aloud. If, as many scholars suggest, the social location of the Gospel is the lower classes, this genre designation is consistent. It means that Mark's story was first told among people who would have delighted in the fact that in the Gospel, nothing good is said about officialdom, whether Roman, Jewish or apostolic.

But although Mark is almost certainly the first written Gospel, much of the material about Jesus predated it. Scholarly consensus suggests that before canonical Mark there existed an oral proclamation of Jesus, probably a written account of his passion and a number of collections of narratives of the same literary type (for example, a collection of parables, of miracle stories and of sayings of Jesus, the Q or sayings source material). Some scholars think that there was an earlier version of Mark than canonical Mark, that this earlier draft accounts for the many textual variants in the manuscript of Mark and that this so-called Ur-Mark was used by Matthew and Luke in writing their Gospels. Ur-Mark is by no means certain, but Matthew and Luke do seem to have patterned their Gospels on some version of Mark's. (Note that primacy of Matthew's Gospel is still held by some serious scholars like William Farmer and C. S. Mann.)

Several factors led the early Christians to transfer their oral material to written form, to begin to write Gospels in the second half of the first century. The anticipated return of Jesus in glory, the parousia, was delayed; the eyewitnesses of his ministry were dying or being martyred. Within the church there was need for authoritative versions of Jesus' life and teachings, and in the Gentile mission, Gospels met evangelistic needs. Mark was probably written between A.D. 65 and 70. The only internal evidence for dating is Mark 13:14, which may be a reference to the siege of Jerusalem in 70. Toward the end of Nero's reign (A.D. 54-68) Christians in Rome suffered terrible persecution, and with the Jewish war of 66-70, their apocalyptic expectations surged. Both seem to be reflected in Mark, a Gospel for a suffering church. The text suggests the Gospel was written for a predominantly but not exclusively Gentile community. For example, it explains Jewish customs and beliefs and contains many Latinisms. It came from a location prominent enough that it was known and used in the writing of subsequent Gospels. Suggested locations for Mark's community include Rome, Galilee and Syria or points east. John Chrysostom suggested Egypt.

Ancient tradition associates Mark the Evangelist with the John Mark of Acts in whose mother's home the Last Supper was said to have been held (see Acts 12:12, 25; 13:13; 15:37, 39; 1 Peter 5:13; Col 4:10; Philem 24). If this is correct, the author was a companion of Peter and Paul. The earliest church fathers associate Mark with the apostle Peter and the city of Rome. Eusebius's *Ecclesiastical History* 3.39.15 quotes Papias, who in the first half of the second century wrote the five-volume *Interpretation of the Lord's Sayings,* that Mark was Peter's interpreter: "This also the Elder said: Mark, who became Peter's interpreter, wrote accurately, though not in order, all that he remembered of the things said and done by the Lord. For he had neither heard the Lord nor been one of his followers, but afterwards . . . he had followed Peter, who used to compose his discourses with a view to the need [of his hearers], but not as if he were composing a systematic account of the Lord's sayings. So Mark did nothing blameworthy in thus writing some things just as he remembered them; for he was careful of this one thing, to omit none of the things he had heard and to state no untruth therein."

In addition to providing helpful comments about how Gospels were written, this long quotation from Eusebius describes the connection between Mark and Peter. Papias's, or a similar view, was held by Justin Martyr (*Dialogue with Trypho* 100), Origen, Tertullian and Jerome, who said that Mark wrote what Peter dictated. Clement of Alexandria located Mark in Rome during Peter's ministry. Many modern scholars, however, doubt the connection with Peter and Rome, although some, like John Donahue support it. While it must be admitted that the writer of the Gospel is unknown, the inelegant Greek of the text suggests that language was not his native tongue.

Although his Greek style is rough, Mark's Gospel is a remarkably carefully crafted narrative. It moves steadily forward toward the passion narrative and is structured by means of geographical references that have theological significance: Galilee (Mk 1:14—6:13); beyond Galilee (Mk 6:14—8:26); Caesarea Philippi to Jerusalem (Mk 8:27—10:52); Jerusalem (Mk 11:1—16:8). Note that about half of Jesus' public ministry is in northern Palestine and half in the environs of Jerusalem. The Gospel also contains periodic summaries of Jesus' ministry (Mk 1:14-15, 21-22, 39; 2:13; 3:7-12; 5:21; 6:6, 12-13, 30-33, 53-56; 10:1). (For another helpful outline of Mark's Gospel, see R. A. Guelich, "Mark, Gospel of" in *Dictionary of Jesus and the Gospels* [Downers Grove, IL: IVP, 1992] 516-17.) Mark's tendency is to group together similar forms of material (e.g., Mk 4:1-34 is a collection of parables; Mk 4:35—5:43 is a collection of miracle stories; Mk 11:27—12:37 are controversy dialogues), a fact that has suggested to some students of the Gospel that he might have had such collections at hand when he wrote. Mark is particularly fond of the technique of intercalation, that is, story-within-a-story construction. For example, he begins the story of Jairus's daughter (Mk 5:21-24), interrupts it with the account of the hemorrhaging woman (Mk 5:25-34) and then returns to the original narrative (Mk 5:35-43). Mark uses this device repeatedly, and it effectively propels the reader toward Mark's central concern, Jesus' passion.

Other literary characteristics of Mark the writer include his interest in vivid, eyewitness touches (Mk 4:37; 5:5; 6:40; 10:21), his tendency to preserve important words of Jesus in the original Aramaic (Mk 3:17; 5:41; 7:11, 34; 14:36; 15:22, 34; some scholars have suggested this reflects the oral memory of Peter) and his use of the historic present, which gives the narrative its rapid, dramatic character. Mark is fond of the words *immediately* (it occurs forty-one times in the Gospel) and *again* (twenty-five occurrences), of diminutives (Mk 5:23; 7:25; 10:13) and of repetition, to the degree that the later Evangelists often edited out these redundancies.

But Mark was not only a literary stylist; he was a theologian of some sophistication. Two examples will have to suffice: Mark's use of what has been called the messianic secret and his special interest in discipleship. In *Das Messiasgeheimnis in den Evangelien* (*The Messianic Secret,* 1901) William Wrede noticed the following about Mark's Gospel: demons recognize Jesus and are commanded to be silent; the healed are enjoined not to reveal who healed them; the disciples are initially forbidden to make Jesus' messiahship public; and Jesus frequently withdraws to teach his disciples privately.

Wrede suggests that Jesus' messiahship could not be kept secret. He argues that no one thought of Jesus as Messiah until after the resurrection and that Mark or one of his sources invented this motif of secrecy. While Wrede's point is that the secrecy passages are not from the life of Jesus, there are other ways to explain this important theological motif in the Gospel. It is clear, for example, that Jesus wanted to avoid being known as a thaumaturge, a wonder worker. Furthermore, he had a very different understanding of Messiah than was current at the time, and his refusal to allow his messiahship to be proclaimed was an attempt to avoid violence in already violent Palestine. In any case, the resurrection would only validate the claim of Jesus' messiahship if it had already been made.

In a helpful article J. D. Kingsbury suggests that the purpose of secrecy in Mark is gradually to bring the reader of the Gospel to recognize that to confess Jesus as Son of God is to confess him as the one appointed to die on the cross. (See J. D. Kingsbury, "The 'Divine Man' as the Key to Mark's Christology? The End of an Era?" *Interpretation* 35 [1981] 243-57.) The reader is to have a more profound understanding of the meaning of Jesus' messiahship than did Peter at his confession in Mark 8. The messianic secret motif in Mark is to fix our attention squarely on the importance of the cross and its witness that God's most perfect revelation in history is not that of triumphant glory but of his death on the cross. Mark may well have been written, as R. H. Gundry argues, as an apology for the cross. The messianic secret motif in Mark points to the fact that the messiahship of Jesus can be understood only in light of his cross.

Second, Mark as a theologian had a distinctive view of discipleship. It is found in his use of two Greek words, *paradidomi* ("handed over") and *akoloutheō* ("to follow"). In Mark's Gospel, John the Baptist preached, was handed over and then killed. Jesus too preached, was handed over and then killed. If the disciples are to follow their master, this will probably be their fate as well. This theme of being handed over is also related to Mark's main theological insight, the necessity of the cross. It is helpful to trace carefully the use of *follow* in the Gospel. Those who are healed or exorcised follow as a mark of their restoration. The central portion of Mark (Mk 8:22—10:52, which is framed by the healing of two blind men, making the whole section about seeing or understanding) is largely devoted to discipleship, to showing what it means to follow Jesus.

For Mark, to follow Jesus is to be identified with the Lord and his passion. The disciples therefore are often depicted in the narrative has having a faulty or partial understanding of Jesus. Mark uses their inadequate christology as an occasion to instruct his readers. The disciples' incomprehension helps our comprehension as Mark seeks to show how, in the life of discipleship, there is no shortcut around the cross. In Mark's Gospel, Jesus' women disciples seem to be the first to understand his message.

Roughly one-fourth of the characters in Mark's narrative are women. In the Gospel's sixteen chapters, thirteen pericopes center around women (Mk 1:30-31; 3:31-35; 5:21-24, 35-43; 5:24-34; 6:3, 14-29; 7:24-30; 12:41-44; 14:3-9, 66-69; 15:40-41, 47; 16:1-8). However, only five named women appear: Mary the mother of Jesus (Mk 6:3); Herodias (Mk 6:19); Mary of Magdala, Mary the mother of James and Joses, and Salome (Mk 15:40, 47). Mary Magdalene, Mary the mother of James and Joses, and Salome seem to parallel Jesus' inner circle of male disciples, Peter, James and John. Other women in the Gospel are designated in relation to men (Simon's mother-in-law, Mk 1:30; Jesus' mother and sisters, Mk 3:31-35; 6:3; Jairus's daughter, Mk 5:23; a widow, Mk 12:41-44; and a servant girl of the high priest, Mk 14:66-69) or to their nationality (the Syro-Phoenician woman, Mk 7:24-30). Only the hemorrhaging woman (Mk 5:24-34) and the anointing woman (Mk 14:3-9) stand independently.

Although this point is frequently overlooked, it is important to remember that the many crowds in Mark would have been made up of both men and women. This is demonstrated in Mark 5 by the woman who emerges from the crowd for healing. Thus women too experienced Jesus as teacher and miracle worker. They too would have been amazed and would have followed (the technical term for discipleship in Mark), participated in the triumphal entry into Jerusalem and called for his crucifixion. Mark 15:40-41 reports that Mary Magdalene, Mary and Salome "used to follow him and provided for him when he was in Galilee." As noted, "follow" (*hēkolouthoun)* in Mark 15:41 is a technical term and the exact word used for the responses to Jesus of Andrew and Simon (Mk 1:18) and Levi (Mk 2:14) to Jesus. The word here translated "provided" (*diēkonoun*) is probably more accurately rendered "ministered" or "served." It is the word used to describe the central aspect of Jesus' ministry and that required of all his disciples. So at least two technical terms related to discipleship are used of women in Mark's Gospel.

Mark 15:41 also notes that "there were many other women who had come up with him to Jerusalem," indicating that the original circle of Galilean disciples included women (cf. Lk 8:1-3). Thus when Mark 4:10-34, Mark 7:17, Mark 9:28 and Mark 10:10 describe the special instruction that Jesus gave to the disciples, women should probably be numbered among them. "Those who were around him along with the twelve" (Mk 4:10) and "he explained everything in private to his disciples" (Mk 4:34) make clear that Jesus' inner circle included more than twelve males. "His disciples" (*tois mathētais*) occurs forty-three times in Mark for Jesus' followers, suggesting that Mark is more interested in the larger issue of discipleship rather than of apostleship (if the Twelve can be equated with the term *apostle*), which by the time of Mark's Gospel would have been connected with issues of tradition and authority.

In the narrative, these women disciples appear more positively than many of their male counterparts. The male disciples misunderstand Jesus' person, mission and message (Mk 6:35-36, 49; 8:16-21; 9:32-36; 10:35-45), are sharp with their teacher (Mk 4:38; 5:31; 8:4; 14:4) and disobey him (Mk 7:36). Peter confesses Jesus as Messiah in the central pericope of the Gospel (Mk 8:27—9:1), but his subsequent behavior indicates he does not understand what Jesus means by *messiah*. And Jesus rebukes that misunderstanding (Mk 8:32). Judas Iscariot betrays Jesus (Mk 14:10-22); his male disciples flee (Mk 14:50-52). Or were there females there in the Garden of Gethsemane? In Mark 14:12-13 the disciples prepare the Passover; the meal is eaten with "the twelve" (Mk 14:17). But when the company repairs to Gethsemane, they are called "disciples" again at Mark 14:32. While "the twelve" excludes women, the more general term *disciples* does not. In any case, thereafter Peter repeatedly denies knowing Jesus (Mk 14:53-72). The only males specifically noted at the crucifixion other than those in the crowd and among the chief priests and scribes are the soldiers who execute Jesus; the two bandits crucified at his side; Simon of Cyrene, who carried his cross; Joseph of Arimathea; and the centurion who confesses Jesus. This confession by a Gentile is theologically significant for Mark. It suggests that Jesus can be understood only in light of the cross, and that a Gentile does so probably reflects the Evangelist's audience and his understanding that Jesus intended the reign of God to include Gentiles.

Mark's women, however, are usually model disciples. Simon's mother-in-law "serves" when she is healed (Mk 1:30-31). Service or ministry *(diakonia)* is the prototypical act of discipleship. The woman with the flow of blood had the faith and initiative necessary to approach Jesus. The Syro-Phoenician woman not only bests Jesus in debate but also reveals something about the extent of his mission. Mark 13 is framed by stories of exemplary women in contrast to men who are less than model disciples. An anonymous widow exemplifies religious devotion and self-giving, although in the context of Mark 12:38-40, especially Mark 12:40, one wonders how Jesus felt about a religious system that demanded such sacrifice from its most at-risk and marginalized members (see E. S. Malbon, "The Poor Widow in Mark," *Catholic Biblical Quarterly* 53/4 [1991] 589-604). And an anonymous woman anoints Jesus in Bethany. Her anointing is understood prophetically as it leads Jesus to speak of his impending martyrdom (Mk 14:3-9). The faithful women disciples witness the crucifixion (Mk 15:40-41), follow to see where Jesus' body is buried (Mk 15:47) and set out early the first day of the week to anoint that body (Mk 16:1-8), thereby becoming the first witnesses to the resurrection and the first to be told to proclaim it.

Outline

1:1-15	Prologue
1:16—6:6a	Ministry in and Around Galilee
1:16-39	Typical Features of Jesus' Ministry
1:40—3:35	Opposition to Jesus
4:1-34	Teaching in Parables
4:35—6:6a	Miracles
6:6b—8:21	Ministry Around Capernaum
8:22—10:52	Journey to Jerusalem and Discipleship Teaching
11:1—16:8	Ministry in and Around Jerusalem
11:1-26	Triumphal Entry and Temple Teaching
11:17—12:44	Controversy in the Temple Precincts
13:1-36	Apocalyptic Discourse
14:1—16:8	Passion and Resurrection

Commentary

Commentary on Mark's Gospel appears relatively late in church history. The first commentators were apparently Victor of Antioch in the sixth century and the Venerable Bede in England in the eighth. This suggests the theological primacy of the other Gospels, especially Matthew (which Irenaeus thought was written first), in the early church. Space constraints prevent a full exposition of Mark's Gospel, but by commenting on representative general passages, several dealing with women, an understanding of the Evangelist's methods, theology and view of women emerges. Chosen for commentary are Mark's introduction and first chapter; the woman with a flow of blood; the Syro-Phoenician woman; Mark's section about discipleship; the stories of the generous widow and the anointing woman; and the Gospel's ending.

Beginnings (Mk 1)

Although there is little consensus about its exact length, most students of Mark agree that the book has an introduction or prologue. Mark 1:1 is generally taken to be the title of the book. It gives the reader information that no one in the story has, namely, that Jesus is Christ and Son of God. "The beginning" echoes the opening verse of Genesis, suggesting that with Jesus, God is making a new beginning. His story is "good news," a message of salvation. In short, the substance of Mark's Gospel is that Jesus is the Christ.

Immediately the reader is introduced to John the Baptizer with a quotation conflating Malachi 3:1 and Isaiah 40:3. We are told that Jesus fulfills prophecy. John, as forerunner and proclaimer, is a prophetic figure reminiscent of Elijah. His desert locale reminds us that in Hebrew Scripture, the desert is the place where God prepares people for salvation and where those expectations are fulfilled. John's message is that the Jews must repent; therefore the common assumption that God's chosen people and visible Israel are one is incorrect. Thus the Messiah is not to be a fulfiller of political expectations. Mark's Gospel begins with one in service to another and with a message of repentance rooted in Israel's history. By means of allusions to Hebrew Scripture, John has been presented as having prophetic authority, but he stoops to untie sandals, the work of a slave (*see* Ancient and Modern Slavery). Already Mark's understanding that for Jesus' disciples authority comes via service is evident.

With the baptism of Jesus (Mk 1:9-11) we learn more of Jesus' unique Sonship. This is the beginning of the ministry of Jesus, his commissioning by God. The theological problem is why Jesus was baptized, since we know he was without sin. In Mark, Jesus' baptism carries with it something of the sign acts of the prophets in Hebrew Scripture. It expresses his solidarity with sinners (whom, the meaning of his name tells us, he came to save) and unifies Jesus with the movement toward repentance, the new thing. It solidifies his unity with the repentant, sets an example for his followers, sanctifies water and reveals his divine nature (Mk 1:11). Here all three persons of the Trinity are present, the Son, the Spirit as dove, the Father as speaker (*see* The Trinity). Again, Mark 1:11 provides many ties with Israel's history. In Psalm 2:6-7 God has promised to crown a messianic Son. In Isaiah 42:1 God has promised to commission a servant by the divine spirit. The echo of Genesis 22:2 associates Jesus the beloved Son and Isaac whom Abraham loved, perhaps providing a veiled foreshadowing of another sacrifice.

In Mark's Gospel the temptation narrative is brief (Mk 1:12-13), perhaps because the Evangelist views the whole ministry of Jesus as his temptation, his temptation to be a messiah in terms other than those of God. Later in the Gospel the demons recognize Jesus because he has contended with and overcome them in the wilderness. It is important to note that Moses and Elijah, who appear later on the mount of transfiguration, spent "forty periods of time" in the wilderness. From the outset, Jesus is presented in the mode of the great leaders of Israel, of lawgivers and prophets.

Mark 1:14-15 completes the Evangelist's prologue by proclaiming the gospel in miniature. History is dealt with summarily; the forerunner, John, is imprisoned and handed over (thus introducing the apocalyptic drama of preaching, being handed over, being martyred). Jesus' message is also presented summarily with two indicatives ("the time is fulfilled," "the kingdom of God has come near") and two imperatives ("repent," "believe in the good news"), the two facts and the two acts that are required as a result of them. God's reign is revealed in the gift of a new relationship to God.

Mark's prologue is an example of his careful compositional techniques. It begins and ends with a focus on the gospel (Mk 1:1, 14-15) and within that frame alternates material about Jesus and John the Baptist (Jesus, Mk 1:1; John, Mk 1:2-8; Jesus, Mk 1:9-13; John, Mk 1:14; Jesus, Mk 1:14-15). At the end of Mark's prologue, the heavenly word has been revealed; God has spoken, and Jesus has preached. Mark has attempted to communicate that the ministry of Jesus is about the inauguration of the reign of God. A number of interesting features have been presented that will be repeated at the end of the Gospel and that form a variety of inclusions. Mark 1:1 has announced Jesus as "the Son of God," an ascription echoed by the centurion at the foot of the cross (Mk 15:39). The heavens are opened at baptism (Mk 1:10), and the temple curtain is rent at the crucifixion (Mk 15:38), both events signaling the availability of God to people, "God with." Finally, Jesus begins his ministry in Galilee (Mk 1:14) and promises to meet his disciples there after the resurrection (Mk 16:7). Jesus' identity is established; God's presence is promised in the ordinary circumstance (Galilee), so the reader is ready for the story of Jesus proper.

Mark 1:16-45 presents a sort of typical day in the ministry of Jesus. He calls disciples, teaches, heals and withdraws for prayer. In Mark 1:16-20, Jesus calls disciples. As noted, *follow* is a technical term for discipleship. The manner of this call emphasizes the radical nature of discipleship as Simon, Andrew, James and John leave livelihood and family to follow Jesus. If Mark 1:14-15 summarizes the message of Jesus, Mark 1:16-20 depicts the appropriate response to it. In Mark 1:21-22, 38-39 Jesus is depicted as teaching ("teacher" is Mark's favorite designation for Jesus, although he presents fewer of his words than do the other Evangelists), and Capernaum is established as his Galilean headquarters. In Jesus, people experience a new sort of authority. This causes problems because the religious authorities do not know its origin (*they* didn't authorize it).

The exorcism (Mk 1:23-28), the healing of Peter's mother-in-law and general healings (Mk 1:29-34) and the healing of the leper (Mk 1:40-45) establish the fact that Jesus doesn't just talk; he is empowered to heal. The healing miracles are proof of Jesus' authority as a teacher. (Note that about half of the narrative in Mark 1—8 is healing miracles.) The exorcism introduces more apocalyptic elements as the spirit world recognizes Jesus' identity. The messianic secret is introduced clearly (Mk 1:44). Finally, in Mark 1:35-39 Jesus withdraws for prayer. Thus in Mark 1:16-45, the reader understands Jesus' ministry to be composed of calling disciples, teaching, healing and prayer. And the two great conflicts of the Gospel are prefigured as the Son of Man destroys the powers of evil and the authority of Jesus faces the authorities of Judaism. In some ways the rest of the Gospel is the working out of these two strands of conflict. (See also F. Matera, "The Prologue as the Interpretive Key to Mark's Gospel," *Journal for the Study of the New Testament* 34 [1988] 3-20.)

Healings (Mk 4:35—5:43)

The block of healing miracles in Mark 4:35—5:43 is characteristic of Mark's compositional technique of gathering together units of material by genre, but these miracle stories are richer in detail than the typical Greco-Roman miracle stories. It is important to recall that reports of miracles were common in the first century and readily accepted by many Greeks and Romans, assuming, as they did, a cosmology in which gods intervened in the human world in the ordinary course of things. While in a sense all four miracles—the stilling of the storm (Mk 4:35-41), the exorcism of the Gerasene demoniac (Mk 5:1-20) and the healing of Jairus's daughter and the woman with a

---

Biblical Images of Women

There's Eve, Ruth, Deborah and Esther from the Old Testament; Mary, Dorcas, Priscilla and Eunice from the New Testament. We have stories of women leading troops into battle, hiding spies in their homes, sewing for widows and living with animals on an ark. A woman poured expensive perfume on Jesus as a love offering, and women took spices to the empty tomb. Sometimes women were portrayed as evil, sometimes as holy. Women were healed, forgiven and taught spiritual truth. And women were commissioned to spread the gospel of Christ.

Notwithstanding the variety of biblical images of women, some themes are common to the Old Testament, and others emerge with the coming of Christ. The Old Testament records the status of woman as dependent, first on her father and later on her husband (Deut 22:13-21). Sexual purity and faithfulness to one husband were the demands of the law on her life, ensuring that her main function, childbearing, would not be compromised (Gen 30:23; Num 5). In many ways she was considered subordinate to men, with a father or a husband bearing responsibility or offering consent for her actions (Num 30). Her life was valued at less than a man's (Lev 27:2-8), and cleanliness codes were more stringent for the birth of a female than a male child (Lev 12:1-5).

While priesthood was outside women's domain, the office of prophet was open to them, as were the roles of professional mourner and temple server (Jer 9:17-22; Ezra 2:65). In part, the Old Testament paints a picture of men being primarily involved with conquering nature; women's roles revolved around the burdens and joys of reproduction. In ancient Israel, shame was attached to being without land (for men) or without child (for women).

Jesus entered a society in which the rabbinic custom was to thank God daily as a man that you had not been born a woman, slave or foreigner. Rabbis were not permitted to speak to women in public, and the words of the Torah were not taught to female students. By his words and by his example, Jesus of Nazareth challenged these practices.

Women played a vital role in the earthly life of Christ: from his mother Mary, to women followers who gave of their financial resources and their hearts to follow the teachings of Jesus, to women in the first-century church who opened their homes so that the early Christians had a place to gather for worship and study. Jesus' tenderness toward women is displayed in his actions toward the Samaritan woman (Jn 4:1-42), the woman with the issue of blood (Mk 5:21-43), Mary and Martha (Lk 10:38-42) and the women who first carried the message of the resurrection (Mt 28:5-8). His behavior toward women followers confirmed the authenticity of his words, "whoever does the will of God is my brother and sister and mother" (Mk 3:35).

What a rich heritage we have as Christian women! Whether we are serving God and our families at home, at church, through the workplace or in the community, we can be assured of God's blessing if our hearts have been set ablaze with the truth.

NANCY NASON-CLARK

---

hemorrhage (Mk 5:21-43)—are about fear, Mark probably inserts the accounts here for two reasons.

First, the miracle unit (Mk 4:35—5:43) follows a parable unit (Mk 4:1-34). By having Jesus perform miracles, Mark is demonstrating that he has the authority to teach as he did. When, for example, Jesus stills the storm (Mk 4:39), Mark attributes to him an authority the Old Testament gives only to God. Second, then, the set of miracle stories shows the extent of Jesus' authority. He has authority over the natural world (the sea), over the spirit world (unclean spirits), over the human body (the hemorrhage) and over life and death (Jairus's daughter). Mark suggests that nothing in creation is outside the sphere of Jesus' authority (cf. Col 1:15-20).

The story of the woman with the flow of blood is intercalated with the healing of Jairus's daughter (Mk 5:24-34 in Mk 5:21-43). Jesus interrupts one act of mercy to accomplish another. This woman is without a male relative to be her advocate, without financial resources and subject to blood taboo. The Levitical restrictions on menstruating women (Lev 15:19-30) indicate that the woman would not only be considered unclean; she would make anything she touched unclean. Her "flow of blood" or "hemorrhages" excluded her from normal social contact and religious or cultic activity. She has effectively been excluded from society for twelve years.

Unique in the healings in Mark, this woman takes the initiative to go to Jesus, ignoring the social custom that would have prevented her from speaking to a male in public and the cultic, blood taboos that would prevent physical contact. Jesus responds verbally to her, acknowledging her existence. He calls her "daughter" (Mk 5:34), establishing kinship within the family (cf. Mk 3:31-35), and acknowledges that her complete healing is because of her faith. The hemorrhaging woman depicts the faith that Jairus must have for his daughter's healing, and Jesus breaks social and religious custom to liberate a bound woman by restoring the wholeness of her body and consequently her social functioning. In the intercalation Jesus is depicted as Lord of every situation, even apparently hopeless ones.

The Syro-Phoenician Woman (Mk 7:24-30)

Ironically the Syro-Phoenician woman restores Jesus to himself. Again he is approached by a marginalized woman, a Gentile of Greek heritage and Syro-Phoenician by birth. There is an implied comparison in Mark between the way the religious officials have approached Jesus (Mk 7:1-23) and the woman's approach. Hers is to be preferred. The single parent of a demon-possessed daughter, a triple liability, this woman throws herself at Jesus' feet with a request for her daughter. Jesus' response to her (Mk 7:27) is troubling, reflecting as it does the Jews' contempt for the heathen, the *ethnē*. While some scholars want to soften Jesus' response, I think Mark's preservation of the story shows remarkable candor. Here is the human Jesus, responding sharply and reflecting his religious background.

But the woman persists. First she agrees with Jesus and addresses him as "Lord," the only time he is so addressed in Mark. Then she points out that when the children (the Jews) are fed, the dogs (Gentiles) get the leftovers. Jesus, perhaps remembering his teaching that custom should not stand in the way of helping others (Mk 2:23-28; 3:1-6), realizes the wisdom of the woman and in a long-distance exorcism frees her daughter from the demon. Mark probably preserved the story as part of his interest in the Gentile mission of the church. This does not lessen its impact as we see a sharp-witted Gentile woman, one who is altruistic, persistent and inventive, who does not hesitate to approach Jesus, and a Jesus who learns from a woman, who transcends the racist and sexist boundaries of his culture, who recognizes insights from outside the pale and acknowledges that faith can be found there too.

Discipleship (Mk 8:22—10:52)

Moving ahead in the narrative to the central section, the reader finds a body of material devoted primarily to discipleship and framed by two stories of the healing of blind persons (Mk 8:22-26; 10:46-52). Into this inclusion Mark has inserted three passion predictions by Jesus that are misunderstood by his disciples. Their incomprehension gives Jesus the opportunity for further instruction on the nature of discipleship. (My understanding of this section was shaped by Norman Perrin's *What Is Redaction Criticism?* [Philadelphia: Fortress, 1969] 40-63.)

Many commentators divide the gospel at Mark 8:22-26, the healing of the blind man at Bethsaida. From here, Jesus is on the way to the cross. He and his disciples are outside Galilee, in Gentile territory, and his teaching is directed more narrowly to his disciples, with suffering a prominent theme. (A careful reading of the Gospel reveals that as the narrative progresses, the group around Jesus constricts from crowds, to disciples, to the Twelve, to Peter, James and John, until Jesus is left alone on the cross.) The healing happens by degrees, leading some interpreters to suggest that when it comes to human regeneration, Jesus is not satisfied with second best; he works in human life until grace is complete.

Mark 8:27—9:1 is a long unit of material that sets forth a pattern that will be repeated twice more in this section of the Gospel. At Jesus' prompting, Peter confesses Jesus at Caesarea Philippi (Mk 8:27-33). Peter has said the correct thing; Jesus has responded with a passion prediction (Mk 8:31); and Peter's rebuke (Mk 8:32) indicates that he has not understood what his confession meant. Thus the way is open for Jesus to give further instruction on discipleship (Mk 8:34—9:1). These verses encapsulate discipleship; it is an active taking up of what could be avoided for the sake of Jesus and his gospel.

The pattern in Mark 8:27—9:1 is repeated twice in this section of the Gospel, which is preparing for the events of the passion by defining discipleship. A geographical reference (Mk 8:27; 9:30; 10:1) is followed by a passion prediction by Jesus (Mk 8:31; 9:31; 10:33), which is misunderstood by the disciples (Mk 8:32-33; 9:34; 10:42). This misunderstanding gives Jesus the opportunity for further teaching (Mk 8:34-38; 9:35; 10:43-45). Mark's apparent purpose in structuring his material this way is to link the sufferings of Jesus with those of his disciples (Mark's Christian community?). Disciples follow Jesus. Jesus is delivered up to his passion. Disciples therefore will also suffer persecutions and death and, as we know, ultimately resurrection.

In the midst of this rather dark scenario is one of the most perplexing stories in the Gospels, the transfiguration (Mk 9:2-13). Some scholars understand it as a misplaced postresurrection appearance; others that it is the fulfillment of the prediction made in Mark 9:1 or that it anticipates the parousia. Still others argue it serves as the disciples' counterpart of Jesus' baptismal revelation; it is the disciples' "voice from heaven." The image in the narrative is of a glorified Jesus with Moses, representing the Torah, and Elijah, representing the prophets, who in Jewish and Samaritan tradition were associated with the Messiah. Jesus' inner circle of Peter, James and John are clearly told to "listen to *him*" (emphasis added). In Mark's narrative the event fits here after Peter's confession that Jesus is the Messiah, confirming its truth and, in the context of discipleship, showing what it means as Jesus is given precedence over the law and the prophets.

The theme of discipleship continues in Mark 10:1-31 in relationship to external things: marriage, children and possessions. The discussion of divorce in Mark 10:1-12 (*see* Divorce) reflects a lively conflict in Judaism between the school of Shammai, which taught that divorce was to be sought only in response to infidelity (*see* Adultery), and that of Hillel, which was more lenient and allowed divorce for other reasons. The legal right to divorce is assumed (probably from Deut 24:1-3); what is at issue are the grounds for divorce. Jesus is more stringent than the rabbis; he appeals to what God wills, not to what the law allows. In Mark 10:5-9 Jesus speaks a governing principle, not a law. Rather than ruling out divorce, he elevates marriage (*see* Marriage). Note that Mark 10:12 reflects the situation of Mark's audience rather than Jesus' environment, since in Jewish Palestine women could not sue for divorce.

In this carefully constructed section of the Gospel, the story of the rich man (Mk 10:17-31) parallels that of Peter's confession. Just as Jesus was interested in what Peter thought of Jesus (Mk 8:29, "who do *you* say that I am?"), here Jesus is interested in what this particular man needs to do to enter the kingdom. Some see the rich man as wrong in his priorities, his flattery and superficiality, but Jesus looks at him, presumably knows him and loves him. Here is a man who has done the right things but who cannot accept the radical demands of discipleship (Mk 9:21-22). The story fits smoothly into the larger context of the section that is shaped by Mark.

The penultimate unit in this section, the third passion prediction (Mk 10:32-45) is sadly indicative that the male disciples, even those of the inner circle (James and John) still do not understand. Mark 10:35-42 indicates that they understand neither Jesus as the suffering Messiah nor discipleship as a matter of service rather than honor or prestige. The disciple must be like the master, who "came not to be served but to serve, and to give his life as a ransom for many" (Mk 10:45). By the time the narrative reaches Mark 10:46-52, the healing of blind Bartimaeus, we have a man taking the initiative to be known by Jesus. This is the last healing miracle in the Gospel. The story illustrates Markan irony in that the blind man who uses a messianic title for Jesus *sees* more than the sighted, and the story picks up the theme of faith where it is least expected (cf. Mk 7:24-30; 9:14-27). Jesus offers Bartimaeus three things that all people need: recognition, sight and purpose. A nobody on the road of life has confessed Jesus and followed. Discipleship has symbolically been understood. In the terms of the narrative it is time for Jesus to go on to Jerusalem and the violence awaiting him there.

Road to the Passion (Mk 11—14)

As previously noted, Mark is often understood as a passion narrative with an extended introduction. This seems evident in the fact that six of the Gospel's sixteen chapters (Mk 11—16) relate the events of the last week of Jesus' life. Mark 11:1—14:9 chronicles Jesus' last week in Jerusalem, Mark 14:10—16:8 the passion and resurrection. Mark carefully keeps time with references that indicate the passing of the week (Mk 11:12, 20; 14:1, 12; 15:1, 42; 16:1). The day of the crucifixion is divided into Roman watches (Mk 15:1, 25, 33, 34, 42).

Immediately after the triumphal entry (Mk 11:1-11) we encounter the curious lesson of the fig tree (Mk 11:12-26), another example of Markan intercalation. Jesus curses a tree that has no figs (Mk 11:12-

14), cleanses the temple (Mk 11:15-19) and uses the example of the fig tree in a teaching about faith and forgiveness (Mk 11:20-26). It is the only miracle of destruction that Jesus performs and seems uncharacteristic of him, especially since figs were out of season (Mk 11:13). At this point the device of intercalation becomes extremely important, for the lesson is not about figs but about the temple in Jerusalem. The symbol of the temple and the conflict with Jewish authorities there dominates this section of Mark: Jesus enters Jerusalem and visits the temple (Mk 11:1-11); the fig tree inclusion (Mk 11:12-26); controversies in the temple (Mk 11:27—12:27); Jesus anointed (as priests in the temple were anointed? Mk 11:41-44); a view of the temple leads to the apocalyptic discourse (Mk 13).

The first commentator on Mark 11:12-26, Victor of Antioch in the fifth century, recognized that the fig tree was used to set forth the judgment that was about to fall on Jerusalem. While it is true that Mark 11:17-18 set the stage for the following controversies, the point is that Jesus' temple cleansing and his cursing the fig tree are powerful sign acts in the tradition of the prophets. Both presage the destruction of Jerusalem and the temple. That the fig tree is "withered away to its roots" (Mk 11:20) represents what happens to the temple. Jesus' injunction to "have faith in God" becomes the frame on which Mark hangs sayings on prayer and forgiveness. In *Prayer, Power and the Problem of Suffering* (Atlanta: Scholars Press, 1988), Sharyn Dowd explains that the teaching on prayer follows the destruction of the temple because in the ancient world prayer was associated with a place. The question in the minds of Mark's readers would be, If there is no temple, does God hear? Jesus responds that prayer is a matter of faith, of attitude, and not of geography. Once again the text reflects the situation of Mark's audience.

After a series of conflict stories (Mk 11:27—12:27) intended to demonstrate Jesus' superiority within Judaism (Jesus wins a debate with chief priests, scribes and elders [Mk 11:27—12:12], Pharisees and Herodians [enemies who have come together in the face of the threat that Jesus poses, Mk 12:13-17] and Sadducees [Mk 12:18-44]), the reader encounters in Jerusalem and its environs two more women, the generous widow and the anointing woman.

The story of the generous widow (Mk 12:41-44) is a prime example of how a familiar interpretation can obscure the implications of a Gospel text. The usual reading of the text is that Mark is closing the conflictual temple-teaching account (Mk 11:27—12:44) with a contrast between outward religiosity and inward conviction; the widow

Arch of Titus depicting the destruction of Jerusalem. (Mark 13)

is contrasted to the scribes (Mk 12:38-40). The widow, the one without legal protection or economic security, the one whose social vulnerability makes her a special object of God's concern, gives all she has to support the temple and is commended by Jesus for doing so (*see* Widows; Yahweh's Concern for the Disenfranchised; God's Call to Social Justice).

But this is problematic. In Mark 12:38-40 Jesus has condemned the scribes who "devour widows' houses." Is Mark 12:44 praise for the widow or lament over a system that would lead her to give away her security? Shouldn't the religious establishment be supporting the widow? In the narrative, the next words of Jesus (Mk 13:2) predict the destruction of the temple. The account does indicate that complete surrender to God is what counts, not outward ostentation, and it underlines Mark's understanding that discipleship implies such complete surrender. But while Jesus may have been moved by the widow's offering, he can hardly have approved of the religious system that explicitly or implicitly asked it of her. (For more on this subject see A. Wright, "The Widow's Mite: Praise or Lament?" *Catholic Biblical Quarterly* 44 [1982] 256-65.)

Along with Mark 4, the Markan apocalypse (Mk 13) is the largest block of Jesus' teaching in Mark. Mark 4 and Mark 13 form an inclusion around the active ministry of Jesus. Both demonstrate Mark's compositional technique of giving a general teaching to a crowd and then a more detailed private instruction to the disciples. The placement of the material in Mark 13 is important. The narrative has moved rapidly toward the passion; the preceding conflict stories make it inevitable. The insertion of a speech into the narrative slows it down and gives special emphasis to the contents of the teaching.

To interpret Mark 13 properly, the reader must become familiar with apocalyptic as a literary form and a theological position. As a form, apocalyptic usually arises when a minority group feels alienated from the values of the dominant culture. Thus it usually appears in times of persecution or catastrophe. (For example, the Revelation of John probably appeared during the persecution of Domitian.) The word *apocalyptic* means "uncovering," and thus apocalypses uncover or reveal what will ultimately happen; their subject is eschatology.

While Mark presents Mark 13 as a teaching on the lips of Jesus, some scholars think it was a pamphlet, written during the Jewish war of A.D. 66-70 to encourage Christians in Judea, that Mark incorporated into his Gospel. It sets forth the conviction that God's plans as foretold in Scripture will be fulfilled, specifically against the enemies of God's elect. (And note the reappearance of the metaphor of the fig tree in Mark 13:28-31.) Mark 13 contains several exegetical cruxes (e.g., what was the "desolating sacrilege" that the reader is to "understand" [Mk 13:14], or what are the limits on the Son's knowledge [Mk 13:32]) that bear closer examination than can be given here. (For particularly helpful material on Mark 13, see the work of George Beasley-Murray and Adela Yarbro Collins.)

The Markan apocalypse (which is meant to encourage the persecuted faithful to endure in hope because God will ultimately intervene and prevail) is framed by stories of two anonymous and generous women who are contrasted to named and venal men: the scribes and Judas. In contrast to the plots against Jesus by men (Mk 14:1-2, 10-11), Mark 14:3-9 narrates the extravagant love of a woman for him. (Note that Mk 14:1-11 is another example of intercalation.) It is one of the few stories recorded by all four Evangelists.

The Markan Passion (Mk 14—15)

In Mark 14:3-9 Jesus is reclining at table, indicating a festive occasion, in the home of Simon the leper; Jesus' followers routinely met in private homes (Mk 1:29; 2:1, 15; 7:24; 9:33; 14:3, 15, 17). In this one, Jesus breaks cultural and religious taboo by keeping table fellowship with a leper (see Lev 13—14). Mark notes that the woman came (*ēlthen*) with a jar of costly ointment, not that she came in, which suggests she was one of the dinner guests or part of the household, another indication that the group around Jesus routinely included women. This woman anoints Jesus' head with an expensive perfume that represents a year's wages. That some with Jesus grumble about the waste involved in this anointing is another indication that they do not understand either Jesus or what is imminent.

In the history of Israel, anointing of the head signified selection for a special task, like priesthood or kingship. During the period of the united kingdom, a primary function of the prophet was to anoint kings with oil. The woman's anointing is her symbolic confession that Jesus is Messiah, the Anointed One. Mark's addition (Mk 14:8-9) indicates that Jesus understood her action as prophetic of his crucifixion. Thus she is the first person in the Gospel to understand Jesus as the crucified Messiah, and she anticipates the spice-bearing women who are the first to go to the tomb and the first to receive the charge to declare the resurrection.

Mark's treatment of women in the passion narrative is fascinating. Whereas the named male disciples sleep when charged to watch (Mk 14:37), betray Jesus (Mk 14:43) and deny having known him (Mk 14:68, 70-71), women appear as astute bystanders and as loyal disciples. The servant girl of the high priest recognizes Peter as a follower of Jesus (Mk 14:67, 69). At the crucifixion, no male disciples seem to be in attendance, but Mary Magdalene, Mary the mother of James and Joses, and Salome are there, apparently with many other women who had followed Jesus in Galilee and ministered to him (Mk 15:40-41). The fact that Mary Magdalene and the other Mary witnessed the crucifixion, Jesus' death and the manner of his burial (Mk 15:47) make them credible witnesses to the resurrection. In what may be the greatest Markan irony of all, the veracity of the resurrection is dependent on the witness of women (*see* Women as Witnesses).

The Gospel's Ending (Mk 16:1-8)

The apostolic charge to the two Marys comes at Mark 16:1-8. Since women are so positively portrayed in Mark, it is especially interesting that they do not immediately obey the angelic charge in this final pericope of the Gospel. Most scholars concur that Mark 16:8 is the original ending of Mark. Ancient witnesses show no knowledge of Mark 16:9-20, and its content, vocabulary and style are distinctively non-Markan. So the narrative ends with the words "they were afraid." This ending has troubled some scholars, who have suggested variously that Mark was for some reason prevented from finishing the Gospel or that the real conclusion was lost or destroyed or that it was suppressed.

But there is strong reason to think that Mark 16:8 was the intended conclusion. The empty tomb is the signpost toward a new encounter with the risen Jesus. The angel has declared that Jesus is no longer dead, and the silence at the end suggests reverence in the face of the realization that the new day of God has dawned. However, that fear, awe and wonder are standard features of epiphanies in Hellenistic literature hardly solves the problem of the women's silence. They stand as representatives of human inadequacy in the presence of divine action. The fact that the women in Mark 16:8 "said nothing to anyone" forms in inverted inclusion with Mark 1:45, where a leper who is charged not to speak begins to "proclaim . . . freely." Here those charged to speak are initially silent, but only initially.

This ending is consistent with Mark's view of Jesus in the Gospel; faith has been generated by the word of Jesus, by message and not miracle. It also serves to illuminate Mark's view of discipleship. In his Gospel, no disciples, female or male, are perfect; all are in process. The ending of the Gospel shows us how fragile the message of Jesus is: will the reader respond to it, proclaim it or remain silently in fear? Mark's Gospel has depicted John the Baptist as having preached, been delivered up and martyred. Jesus too preaches, is delivered up and is martyred. Disciples are not greater than their masters. They are to take up their crosses and follow, to lose their lives for the gospel (Mk 8:34-35), to be "last of all and servant of all" (Mk 9:35).

For the women to be commanded to proclaim the resurrection is to place them firmly on this same path. No wonder they hesitate in silence before taking up the task! In the ethos of the narrative and in the Greco-Roman culture to which Mark was introducing it, for women to become prominent disciples and witnesses of Jesus is a dramatic example of the last becoming first. In fact, the rehabilitation of the Twelve and the male disciples depend on their accepting the testimony of women. Surely this is among Mark's most surprising understandings of the reign of God and the changes it will entail.

Conclusions

The enormous problem faced by Mark and the other Gospel writers was the question of why, if Jesus were the Messiah, he died as a criminal on a cross. The simplest answer is that is what happened, but for the Evangelist Mark, three more specific answers present themselves. First, Jesus' death was a result of his choice; Jesus chooses to go to Jerusalem, even when his disciples fear that choice (Mk 10:32). Jesus dies on a cross because he knows it is God's will for him (Mk 8:31; 9:31; 10:33); He goes his appointed way (Mk 14:21) to fulfill God's will for his messiahship. Second, Mark presents two conflicting views of religion in his Gospel, a rigid code of outward observance and a flexible law of love, social responsibility and mercy. The conflict between the two arises early in the narrative and culminates at Mark 15:10. Historians of religion tell us that Mark's view is oversimplified, and that is probably so, but we must still note that it was Mark's view. Thus Jesus died on a cross because his view of religion apparently lost out. But the cross was not the last word.

Finally, in Mark's Gospel, that Jesus dies on a cross is consistent with the Evangelist's view of discipleship. He apparently lives in and writes for a community that has, is or shortly will be experiencing persecution. Pastorally Mark must make the connection between the suffering of his community and the suffering of Jesus. In

Women as Witnesses

Israel's jurisprudence relied heavily on witnesses and regarded testimony seriously. The law obligates witnesses to testify and requires at least two or three witnesses in any given case (Lev 5:1; Deut 19:15). The Decalogue forbids perjury along with other serious transgressions such as idolatry, murder, adultery and theft (Ex 20:16; Deut 5:20). Perjurers were subject to the *lex talionis* (the "eye for an eye" law), meaning that a perjurer might be put to death (Deut 19:16-21). In the story of Susanna, for example, two men who testify falsely that she has committed the capital offense of adultery are themselves executed (Sus 61-62). Indeed, it became proverbial in Israel that "a false witness will not go unpunished, and the liar will perish" (Prov 19:9).

The Old Testament records no instances of women giving legal testimony, but neither does it legislate against women being witnesses. This presumably reflects that in preexilic Israel, women's testimony was excluded not by law but in practice. In postexilic times, rabbinic codes make comprehensive but not categorical prohibitions against women's testimony. Although most rabbis probably concurred that "the law concerning an oath of testimony applies to men but not to women" (*m. Šebu.* 4.1), some rabbis disagreed. Ambivalence toward women as witnesses is evidenced by opposition to the opinion that "one might perhaps hold that a woman also is fit to bear testimony" (*Sifre Deut.* 190).

In nonlegal contexts, women's testimony in religious confession and prophecy is common and accepted. Testimony to God's nature and deeds comes, for example, from Miriam (Ex 15:20-21), Deborah (Judg 5:1-31), Hannah (1 Sam 2:1-10), Huldah (2 Kings 22:14-20), Judith (Jdt 16:1-17), Mary (Lk 1:46-55) and Anna (Lk 2:36-38). Women also were competent to swear religious vows and oaths (Deut 29:9-15; 1 Sam 1:11; Jer 44:24-25).

Biblical and apocryphal writings record women giving eyewitness testimony to Jesus' resurrection. In Luke, disbelief is directed not against the gender of the witnesses but the content of their testimony: "But these words seemed to them an idle tale, and they did not believe them" (Lk 24:11). In the longer ending of Mark, Jesus rebukes the apostles "because they had not believed those who saw him after he had risen" (Mk 16:14)—a clear endorsement of the women's testimony. The ambivalence toward women's testimony is encapsulated in the Gospel of Mary 17, where Mary Magdalene's testimony to a revelation she received from the risen Jesus is rejected by Andrew because of its strange content and by Peter because of its female agent.

Exceptions to the rabbinic prohibitions against women's testimony are intriguing when read against the Gospels, especially John. For example, the rabbis allowed the testimony of women to establish the fact of a man's death: "Even if a man only heard women saying, 'Such-a-one is dead,' that suffices" (*m. Yeb.* 16.5). Thus, Mary and Martha are qualified to testify to their brother Lazarus's death, and their dual witness to his death is crucial evidence that he was raised from the dead, not resuscitated from unconsciousness (Jn 11:1-44). Similarly, the women at Jesus' cross are eligible to provide multiple attestation to his death (John 19:25-30). Mary Magdalene's testimony serves to support that Jesus' body was not in the tomb, that it had not been removed, that it had not been resuscitated, and that his bodily appearances were not phantasms (Jn 20:1-18)—crucial evidence in support of the resurrection.

Paul's inherited list of resurrection witnesses does not include the women (1 Cor 15:5-8). Assuming that Paul knew about the women witnesses, why, when citing the list, would he either omit them or fail to add them? It has been argued that Paul excluded them because they were not credible witnesses. But if Paul were trying to maintain control over charismatic women leaders in the Corinthian church (Wire), it may be that he excluded them precisely because they were credible, and such credibility helped to invest the Corinthian women with authority and autonomy. Although Paul's letters do not record detailed cases of women acting as witnesses, his references to women as colleagues in his mission point to their active involvement in the witnessing of the earliest church (Rom 16:1-12; Phil 4:3).

Bibliography

R. G. Maccini, *Her Testimony Is True: Women as Witnesses According to John,* JSNTSup 125 (Sheffield: Sheffield Academic Press, 1996), esp. chaps. 3, 11; A. C. Wire, *The Corinthian Women Prophets* (Minneapolis: Fortress, 1990).

ROBERT GORDON MACCINI

---

short, Mark shapes his Gospel to be a word of encouragement and hope. In this divine human drama that began with Israel's election, continues in the ministry of John the Baptist and comes to a head in the life of Jesus of Nazareth, those who align themselves with God suffer but are ultimately vindicated by God, raised to new life. What is, is not what always will be. Mark's is preeminently the Gospel of hope for the suffering.

In the Evangelist's scheme, we find that women are remarkably prominent. As the narrative progresses they move from being passive recipients of miracles, to active examples of discipleship, to being given the apostolic commission to "go, tell his disciples and Peter" (Mk 16:7). In fact, named women appear more prominently in the passion narrative than in any other section of the Gospel. Mark understands that discipleship is a matter of following, serving and suffering, and in his Gospel women do all three. The text of the Gospel as we have it suggests that the community for which Mark wrote also must have had strong women leaders. Some scholars have suggested it might have included some of the prominent women in the later chapters of the Gospel. Compared with the prevailing attitudes in the Greco-Roman world, Mark's Gospel assigns to women high value. They are vital participants in the public ministry of Jesus, examples of his understanding of discipleship and witnesses, the crucial witnesses, of his death and resurrection.

Bibliography. A. Y Collins, *The Beginning of the Gospel: Probings of Mark in Context* (Minneapolis: Fortress, 1992); R. H. Gundry, *Mark: A Commentary on His Apology for the Cross* (Grand Rapids, MI: Eerdmans, 1993); M. D. Hooker, *The Gospel According to Saint Mark* (Peabody, MA: Hendrickson, 1997); E. S. Malbon, "Fallible Followers: Women and Men in the Gospel of Mark," *Semeia* 28 (1983) 20-48; W. Munro, "Women Disciples in Mark?" *Catholic Biblical Quarterly* 42 (1982) 225-41; B. Thurston, *Preaching Mark* (Minneapolis: Fortress, 2001).

BONNIE BOWMAN THURSTON

LUKE

Introduction

No book of the Bible is more dependent on the witness of women or more concerned with their welfare and work than the Gospel of Luke. The author freely admits that others have made various attempts to recount the significant events and trends in the life of Jesus, but none has given the perspective that he seeks. As a methodical historian he interviews those best in a position to give him firsthand information.

Luke's Gospel recognizes the major role played by women in key salvation events. It appropriately has been called a Gospel of women. They are the major witnesses of the birth, crucifixion, burial and resurrection of Jesus. They follow him on his mission trips, offer him care and concern, and interact with him in startling ways. Women, whether affluent and influential or poor and disadvantaged, are persons of great interest and importance to Luke. Step by step he builds the picture of women as followers, believers, transformed sinners and credible witnesses in the remarkable narrative that he tells. It is not that women are emphasized at the expense of men or to the exclusion of men. Luke takes care to balance a story or a parable about a woman with one about a man or vice versa. Luke's equal stress on the part of women and men stands in contrast to other accounts and is therefore particularly noteworthy.

Luke, a physician (2 Tim 4:11) and an associate of the apostle Paul (Col 4:14; Philem 24), is the author of the Gospel of Luke and the Acts of the Apostles. Both books are addressed to Theophilus, perhaps a personal name or an honorific title. The addressee is also called "most excellent," a manner of address ordinarily reserved for high-ranking public officials (cf. Acts 23:26; 26:25). Some scholars have suggested that the two-part document was intended to present the activities of Jesus and his followers in an orderly and lucid fashion to those who might sit in judgment upon them. The presence of women during the interrogation of Paul (Acts 24:24; 25:23; 26:30, cf. Mt 27:19) and their interest in his defense are noted by Luke. A public official might well read with interest the careful delineation of the trial proceedings and charges brought against Jesus and Paul. But the treatise is aimed at other audiences as well, especially women. More were learning to read and were seeking stories that they could treasure.

Luke is a consummate storyteller, and in his writing we find the story of the good Samaritan and of the prodigal son. He is at his best in his telling of the Christmas story, and his depictions of the pious elderly are superb. The Third Gospel is rich in songs: those of hope and prophetic expectation, those of exaltation at the fulfillment of God's promises (Lk 1:42-45, 46-55, 68-79; 2:14, 29-32; 19:38), those of the angels (Lk 1:13-17, 30-33, 35-37; 2:14). There are as well snatches of prophetic poetry that become songs in Luke's handling of the material (Lk 3:4; 4:18-19).

Luke's is a Gospel of touch. Jesus touches and is touched by those whom we would not expect to find in such proximity to him. He reaches out to touch a leper (Lk 5:13) and two dead persons (Lk 7:14; 8:54), both actions causing uncleanness in Hebrew law. Parents seek his touch for their infants (Lk 18:15). He allows a sinful woman and one with an issue of blood to touch him (Lk 7:39; 8:44-47). With his touch, he performs a healing on the ear of his captor (Lk 22:51). In each of these cases, there is an affirmation of solidarity and sympathy for those with desperate needs of body and soul. After he has risen from the grave, Jesus calls his disciples to touch him and thereby to discern for themselves the reality of his resurrection (Lk 24:39).

The dating of the Third Gospel has ranged from A.D. 59 to the 70s or 80s. Clearly other accounts of the life of Jesus were already circulating, and Luke availed himself of some of these while incorporating much material that was exclusively his.

In writing his Gospel, Luke's purpose and method of composition are carefully defined. He wished to interview firsthand witnesses and to construct their concerted testimony into an "orderly account." The witness of women is clear throughout, and particularly that of Mary the mother of Jesus. She must have provided him with much of the information that fills the first two chapters. Only she or someone who knew her well would have been in a position to recount the details of her visit to Elizabeth, the dedication in the temple and the search for the adolescent Jesus.

The reader is led to suppose that Mary, who "treasured all these things" and "pondered them in her heart" (Lk 2:19, 51), had previously been reticent to divulge much of this information. It may well have been to Luke that she was able to give her own orderly account, a process that may have been helpful in integrating her memories. There had been so many perplexing experiences that were so contrary to what she might have expected: the supernatural pregnancy and birth, the necessity of bearing the heralded child in less than ideal conditions and utilizing a cattle trough as crib. There was as well her difficulty in understanding the mission and priorities of her son, the ignominious execution, despairing grief snatched away by the resurrection. Luke, the empathic Gentile, may have been the perfect auditor for whom she could review all that had passed and find in their integration a fuller and more satisfying meaning.

Outline

1:1—2:52	The Birth and Childhood of Jesus
3:1—6:19	The Beginning of Jesus' Ministry
6:20—9:17	Good News for the Poor and Disadvantaged
9:18—19:27	On the Way to Jerusalem
19:28—22:46	Mounting Tensions in Jerusalem
22:47—23:56	Trial, Arrest and Execution
24:1-53	The Disciples' Recognition of the Risen Jesus

Commentary

The Announcement to Zechariah (Lk 1:5-25)

The first announcement that the time has come at last for the birth of the Messiah is made in Jerusalem's temple to a righteous priest as he performs his appointed duty. As the archangel Gabriel had appeared to Daniel "at the time of the evening sacrifice" (Dan 9:21), so now he appeared to Zechariah. The archangel Michael is said to have charge of the people of Israel (Dan 12:1), while the domain of Gabriel appears to be that of proclamation and interpretation of God's salvific intentions and actions (Dan 8:17; 9:21-23; 10:13-14). Gabriel had brought to Daniel eschatological messages dealing with Israel's destiny and the events that must precede Messiah's coming (Dan 8:15-26; 9:20-27; 10:5-14). Now the mysterious schedule of weeks (Dan 8:14) has run its course. The celestial being who foretold the rise and fall of mighty empires now communicates the preliminaries of a new stage in God's redemptive plan. The focus is an intensely personal one, on a pregnancy and the answered prayer of two devout people who longed not only for a child of their own but also for the deliverance of Israel.

Although the message is addressed to the priest Zechariah, it deals intimately with the pregnancy of his pious wife. Elizabeth the barren, though advanced in years, will bear a son who will be great in the sight of the Lord. Even in her womb, the child, who is to be named John, will be filled with the Holy Spirit. The scene is reminiscent of the birth announcement to the mother of Samson (Judg 13:3-5). Both children were to be reared as Nazirites without wine or strong drink.

The archangel bursts into a song foretelling not only the joy that the parents will find in this child but also the gladness of those who will heed his message (Lk 1:13-17). He will come in the spirit of Elijah to turn an unready and unrepentant people back to the Lord. To this child is assigned the role of precursor for the anointed One. If Gabriel proclaims a time of divine fulfillment for God's plan, Zechariah sees that Elizabeth's biological time for conception and birth is long gone. Overwhelmed with amazement, shock, hope and fear, he asks for a sign. His request bespeaks the many disappointments he must have known in his hope for a child. He dare not entertain another cruel hope.

Of course he has not recognized the identity of the emissary entrusted with the astounding proclamation. Gabriel, whose name means the "Strength of God," stands before the Lord and is entrusted with the most solemn of divine messages. The sign of Zechariah's silence is not so much punishment for unbelief as it is confirmation of the promised event. During the remarkable pregnancies of his wife, Elizabeth, and her young protégé, Mary, the old man will be unable to offer advice, no matter how well intended. Although he has been first to hear the news as official representative of God's people, the two women must develop their own concepts of preparation for motherhood. As they enter a new sphere of women's experience, they must lean on each other and on God.

Zechariah's silence is also protection against the curiosity and concern of those who wait outside. He cannot communicate what must not yet be made public. How did he convey the joyous news to his faithful wife of so many years? Apparently by writing, by signs and by the tenderness of his embrace. The newly expectant mother is reluctant to reveal her condition to others. Her reticence may have sprung from many conflicting emotions and concerns.

Luke evinces a ready sympathy for Elizabeth's formerly devastating circumstance. Barrenness was considered a disgrace for a woman (*see* Barrenness and Fertility). She had failed at the most basic level in what is expected of her as a woman. In Luke's view of the kingdom of God, personal piety has far more relevance than reproductive capacity. The Evangelist understands that Elizabeth experiences joy in anticipating the arrival of her child and relief at being delivered from the opprobrium that she has endured. The disgraced wife was to bear a son divinely appointed to proclaim the redemption of Israel. She delights in God, who has removed her humiliation, and in seclusion she ponders the working of God's power in her life. Better to savor in private her precious secret rather than to attempt explanations that no one would accept.

Annunciation to Mary (Lk 1:26-38)

Gabriel's next recorded mission is again to proclaim a pregnancy that defied belief. This time he comes neither to Daniel, prime minister of the vast Persian Empire, nor to the priestly Zechariah, but to a peasant girl in a city of dubious distinction. She is denoted a virgin *(parthenos)*. Although she is betrothed to Joseph, the engagement period was often a long one, and they are not yet living together.

Gabriel declares that Mary has found favor *(charis)* with God, as did Noah (Gen 6:8) and Moses (Ex 33:12-13) when they were called to salvific tasks. The angel declares that Mary will conceive and bear a son and that his name will be Jesus. There is again a paean of praise, one that identifies Jesus as the Davidic Messiah and the Son of God. The coming one will bring in the unending kingdom of which Gabriel had spoken to Daniel.

The pronouncement immediately prompts a question in Mary's mind. How can this be, since she has not yet experienced sexual congress with a man? Her response differs from that of Zechariah in that she requests clarification rather than a sign. The conception is to occur by the coming of the Holy Spirit on Mary and the power of the Most High overshadowing her. The child whom she will bear shall be called the Son of God.

Mary is, however, given a sign as well as an avenue for support during the months that would lie ahead. Gabriel announces the miracle in Elizabeth's life as proof of God's power to do the impossible. Just as Sarah was able to conceive in her old age (Gen 18:12-14), so too Elizabeth will discover that God can open the wombs of barren women. Mary is also thus provided with a confidante with whom she can share the uncertainties, discomforts and perplexities of incipient motherhood. Elizabeth, her cousin, has also been called to a mystifying and magnificent mission.

At this point the story of the virgin birth

differs markedly from the mythological tales of heroines who were impregnated by the gods. In each case, the woman is tricked, seduced or raped to satisfy the lust of one or another of the traditional deities. Zeus in particular made a practice of deceiving his unsuspecting victims with the use of disguises. Here Mary is provided with an honest explanation and given the opportunity to accept the mission or to decline it. This is not a matter of sexual exploitation but of a maiden consciously and willingly joining with the purpose of God to bring salvation to the world.

Mary Visits Elizabeth (Lk 1:39-56)

In her sixth month of gestation, Elizabeth received her relative Mary into her home. As Mary calls out a greeting upon her arrival, the child in Elizabeth's womb leaps for joy. There came an exultant response from one yet unborn who was already attuned to intimations of the coming Messiah.

Surely this text contains the pinnacle of expressions of jubilation over a pregnancy. Usually there is a tendency to dwell on the dangers, discomforts, uncertainties and unpleasantness of the condition. Here the focus is on the glory of the anticipation. The exultation of the two women arises not only from the sheer joy of carrying a child within them but also from their knowledge of the mission destined for their unborn children. They will transform the world into which they will come.

Now a prophetic utterance rises to the lips of Elizabeth. Gabriel had sung of the two children and of their mission, but Elizabeth sings of a young mother's faith and courage. As a pregnant and unmarried woman, she had made her way to the home of a priestly couple distinguished by their scrupulous observance of the law. Surely she must have pondered how best to explain to them her situation, how to point to the angel's promise rather than her predicament. Beyond such immediate considerations lay the knowledge that a woman pregnant outside of wedlock could be stoned to death at worst, dishonored and disgraced at best.

Elizabeth's recognition of Mary's faith has brought to expression what has been lying unsaid in the young mother's heart. Her response is that of a faithful disciple as she faces her unknown and surely hazardous future. Now Mary's reticence and hesitancies are dispelled in a rush of praise to God, who is working such great miracles.

Each woman appears to have waited for the other to give full expression to the emotions that sweep through them. Elizabeth had hidden the happy news from her neighbors and only now is freed to voice her praise, while Mary need no longer conceal what God is bringing to pass within her.

The young mother-to-be bursts into a song that harks back to that of Hannah (1 Sam 2:1-10; *see* Women as Psalmists), though it is also reminiscent of certain of the psalms (Ps 33; 47; 48; 117; 135; 136). The concepts are deeply rooted in Scripture and provide us with remarkable insights into Mary's character.

The Magnificat requires readers to adopt a new set of values if they are to understand the significance of Luke's story. Mary's emphasis is on God's ability to create a new order. The kingdom belongs to those who are rich in faith but humble enough to see God's work in ordinary humanity. Pride and power become disqualifications for participation in the kingdom of God, and right attitude far outweighs the trappings of the establishment. The poor are filled, the rich are emptied, the despairing given hope and the abject accorded a status of dignity.

Mary will impart this concern for social justice to her sons (*see* God's Call to Social Justice). Not only will Jesus sound the same notes as those found in the Magnificat, but James his brother will likewise insist on equality of treatment and respect for all persons. Jude, possibly another brother, will emphasize the fundamental justice of God.

Elizabeth's special legacy to Mary is guidance on the path of faith. The seclusion to which the older woman has consigned herself during the early part of her pregnancy has protected her from manifold pieces of advice frequently provided at such times by friends and neighbors. The fruit of her meditations and conclusions is available to Mary. During their time together, the two work their way through delicate issues of faith and steadfastness against unbelievable odds.

At the end of three months, Mary returns to Nazareth: perhaps because she has found the perspective that she had come to seek, perhaps because she is feeling well enough to travel after the nausea of the first trimester, perhaps to prevent an unnecessary burden on the household during the upcoming birth, perhaps to avoid difficult questions from meddlesome relatives.

Elizabeth Gives Birth to John the Baptist (Lk 1:57-80)

When the moment of birth comes, Elizabeth is surrounded with well-meaning friends, neighbors and relatives. It is at such rites of passage that women excel. Those well experienced take charge, direct and anticipate all the needs before they are even felt.

In their excitement over the unexpected and most welcome event, they rejoice with the mother and recognize the birth as the work of God's kindness (*see* Midwifery and Birthing Practices). Their support has been most important as Elizabeth goes through the process of parturition, but their attendance at the circumcision is less fortuitous. The women, now becoming meddlesome, insist on selecting a name, specifically that of the child's father.

When Elizabeth protests that the name is to be John, the neighbors and kinsfolk carry the matter directly to Zechariah. Confident in their knowledge of what is right and proper, they convey writing materials to the stricken priest so that he may countermand the wishes of his wife. No sooner has he penned a confirmation of the angel's instruction that his son be named John than the father's tongue is unloosed. He too bursts into a prophetic song, glorifying God for bringing salvation to Israel. His promises are being fulfilled, and the newborn child will be the precursor of the Messiah, to make ready the road before him. Hope has been kindled because a seemingly impossible birth has occurred, to parents who earnestly desire the consummation of God's promises for Israel. They recognize, however dimly, that they are to be agents in the development of that deliverance.

Here we see birthing as involving not merely the realm of women, but rather as the focus of God's providence and provision for the world. It is the concern of a devout priest and of a mighty archangel. Bringing a child into the world is as significant a piece of work as is the administration of an empire, the defeat of an army or the establishment of temple worship. Luke's treatment of the birth narratives brings affirmation of the intrinsic dignity, honor and significance of childbearing for all women (*see* Childbearing and Rearing).

Mary the Mother of Jesus Christ (Lk 2:1-20)

Mary's perceptions are the center of the telling of the miraculous birth of Jesus Christ. The pregnant virgin returns to Joseph in Nazareth after her three-month stay with Elizabeth. Luke tells us nothing of her betrothed's reaction to her news as it was related by Matthew (Mt 1:18-22). Rather, the emphasis is centered on the perspective of Mary (*see* Mary the Mother of Jesus).

The facilities in Bethlehem are overcrowded and inappropriate for the upcoming delivery. The only accommodation is also occupied by animals. Thus the manger is readily at hand for use as a crib, safe, sturdy and raised above the animals' hooves. If there was any particular concern in Bethlehem to meet the needs of a woman in labor or the newborn infant, it is not noted. There will be rejections of many sorts throughout Luke's Gospel (e.g., Lk 2:7; 4:16-30; 5:21, 30; 6:11; 9:52-56; 10:12-16; 13:34).

Few amenities are available to the holy family. The circumstances are those that prevail at the humblest of human births. As Mary has sung, she and her child take their position alongside the world's poor and unempowered (*see* Yahweh's Concern for the Disenfranchised). The world's most momentous birth is also one of its lowliest and least pretentious. Jesus is born as a homeless person and will retain this identity in his adult life (Lk 9:58). The event has not caught Joseph and Mary by surprise, however. The swaddling bands, linen strips that are absorbent and enveloping, have been carefully prepared.

Angels are again employed to announce the birth, not to the political or ecclesiastical establishment but to those who cared for the temple flocks. Again there is singing, the giving of a sign and joy promised to the world. Rather than the lordly wise men of Matthew's account, the visitants are simple folk of the field and fold. The shepherds share the words that they have heard from the angel, most notably that the newborn child in the manger is the Son of God. Just as Elizabeth had ruminated on all that God was doing, so Mary too keeps her counsel and ponders the revelation in her heart. Although her subsequent relations with her son will not always be harmonious, she retains a conviction of a divine purpose. The motif of her quiet contemplation will recur in Luke 2:51.

The Presentation in the Temple (Lk 2:21-38)

As faithful Jews, the parents observe not only the rite of circumcision for their infant son eight days after the birth but also after forty days the purification ritual of the mother from the pollution of childbirth. Until the beginning of the twentieth century, infection of puerperal fever was the scourge of new mothers. The purity laws of Israel did much to safeguard maternal health (*see* Leviticus; Purity Laws Related to Women).

The ritual marking the end of the period required that Mary would bring a sacrifice to the Court of Women in the temple. The couple can afford only two doves, as prescribed for the poor (Lk 2:24; Lev 12:8). One of the riddles with which Mary must wrestle is that of the exalted promises concerning her child and the impoverished circumstances attendant to the birth.

Luke couples an aged man and woman, both of whom have prophetic insight, to discern the Messiah in the babe carried to the temple by a humble and unprepossessing couple. Simeon not only thanks God for

Mary the Mother of Jesus

In the New Testament, the four Gospels and Acts are the only sources for information about the life and the role of Mary (cf. Gal 4:4, where Jesus' birth via a woman is simply mentioned). There are approximately thirty references. Before the birth of Jesus, Mary is depicted as a virgin (*parthenos,* Mt 1:23; Lk 1:27) living in Nazareth (Lk 1:26-27), a woman betrothed to Joseph (Mt 1:20; Lk 2:5) and a relative of Elizabeth (Lk 1:36). During Jesus' public ministry, she is also called the mother of James and Joseph or Joses (Mt 27:56; Mk 15:40; Lk 24:10) and has some daughters (Mk 6:3). More frequently, however, she is known as the mother of Jesus.

Mary's appearances in the biblical accounts are always in relation to Jesus, whether in his birth, his public ministry, his death, his resurrection or after his ascension. She is hardly mentioned on her own. Yet behind the scenes we can trace a composite portrait of Mary through the pens of the four Evangelists.

A genuine servant of God. The birth of Jesus marks the turning point of human history, inaugurating the New Testament era. When God commissioned Mary to be Jesus' earthly mother prior to her formal marriage to Joseph (*see* Marriage), a genuine spirit of servanthood was manifested as she said, "Here am I the servant *(hē doulē)* of the Lord; let it be with me according to your word" (Lk 1:38).

A faithful follower of Jesus. During Jesus' public ministry, Mary was at the scene from place to place (Mt 12:46; Mk 3:31-32; Lk 8:19; Jn 2:1, 12). Sometimes her presence seems to shed a negative light (if Mk 3:21 ["his family"] and Mk 6:4 ["his kinspeople"] include Mary), but often she was there to offer support and services (see Mk 15:40-41; Jn 2:1-12). And she bravely followed Jesus even to the foot of the cross (Mt 27:56, 61; Mk 15:40, 47; Jn 19:25, contra the disciples). The mark of discipleship (Mk 8:34-35;

Lk 9:23) finds its true expression in Mary.

A believer filled by the Holy Spirit. After Jesus' ascension, Mary was listed among the first group of disciples who gathered in Jerusalem to pray (Acts 1:14). When the Holy Spirit came upon all the disciples at Pentecost (Acts 2:1-4), Mary also must have encountered the power and impact of the Holy Spirit firsthand and was probably one of the active members of the early Christian community that continued to witness the indwelling presence of the Spirit (Acts 4:31). The Holy Spirit who had once come upon her for a special assignment—to bring the Savior to the world (Lk 1:35)—eventually came upon her and upon all believers for a lifelong assignment, which was to be a witness for the risen Lord (Acts 1:8).

Although Mary played a supporting role, yet an indispensable one, in the story of Jesus' life, she was one of the leading characters in the drama of early Christian history. She played her role well and subsequently became an inspiration for many. Her need of a savior (Lk 1:47) is also reflected in her song (Lk 1:46-55, the Magnificat, a liturgical praise quickly recognized by the early church; *see* Women as Psalmists). Mary's life exemplifies the essence of Christian faith.

Bibliography

A. Carr, "Mary, Model of Faith," in *Mary, Woman of Nazareth: Biblical and Theological Perspectives,* ed. D. Donnelly (New York: Paulist, 1989) 7-24; B. R. Gaventa, *Mary, Glimpses of the Mother of Jesus* (Columbia: University of South Carolina, 1995); J. M. Liu, "The Mother of the Son in the Fourth Gospel," *Journal of Biblical Literature* 117 (1998) 61-77; J. L. Wu, "Mary," in *Dictionary of the Later New Testament and Its Developments,* ed. R. P. Martin and P. H. Davids (Downers Grove, IL: IVP, 1997) 722-24.

JULIE LEE WU

---

the advent of the child but also addresses Mary directly. Her anguish at the crucifixion is foretold with powerful insight. As in other places in the birth narrative, Luke is keenly sensitive to the emotions and reactions of Jesus' mother. One can only suppose that in her narration she was not reticent to share the feelings that had at first been concealed from the world around her.

Simeon has been described as a devout man who looks for the consolation of Israel. In contrast, Anna is called a prophet. As such, she will announce the arrival of the Messiah to all who await the redemption of Jerusalem. In the narrative that so strongly features the activities and perceptions of women, it is in keeping that the role of prophet is also filled by a woman. As the only prophet named in the birth narrative, she is both heir and precursor of women in prophetic ministry (Ex 15:20; Judg 4:4; 2 Kings 22:14; Neh 6:14; Is 8:3; Acts 21:9).

The text makes it difficult to determine whether Anna had been married for seven years and a widow for the remainder of the eighty-four years, or whether she had been a widow for eighty-four years. Hers has been a life of fasting and prayer and watching for the redemption of Israel. In her mission as prophet, she makes known the birth of the Messiah to all in Jerusalem who await the long-promised event. While angels make the annunciation to Zechariah, Mary and the shepherds, Anna makes the proclamation to the pious of the holy city.

Mary's Anxiety: Jesus Lost (Lk 2:39-52)

Few experiences are as harrowing for women as that of a losing a child. Mary's fear and anxiety are palpable throughout the story. Of all the stories that she may have told Luke about the childhood of Jesus, this may have been the one most sharply etched on her memory. Her young son as he approaches adolescence has traveled with her and Joseph to make his bar mitzvah in the temple, to become a man in the eyes of the law. Never was there a mother more justifiably confident in her son's readiness to demonstrate mature and responsible behavior. But there has been a breakdown in communication between her and the child she knew so well.

The narrative implies that Mary considered Jesus to be well aware of the time appointed for the group of family and friends to travel back to Galilee. Her remark upon finding him indicates her dismay at his lack of consideration for her, while his response reveals that his overriding concern was to comply with the will of his heavenly Father. Although Jesus will return home with her, her son has set out on a journey that she cannot as yet fathom. Mary's understanding of Jesus' identity will advance slowly as she ponders these things in her heart. Until she stands at the foot of the cross, the relationship between mother and son will be an uneasy one.

We are told that Jesus was subject (*hypotassō*) to his parents. The Greek term does not necessarily imply obedience or submission but can denote association, loyalty or adherence—even the responsible discharge of a duty. Harold Moulton pointed out that it can also have the value of coming under the influence of someone or something (*Analytical Greek Lexicon,* s.v.). Jesus leaves the brilliant world of the temple, where the disciples of Shammai and Hillel argue the intricacies of the law. He forsakes the intellectual excitement of Israel's finest schools to take up his father's trade in a humble village. He will adhere to the world of common people with real concerns and real needs.

Rejection in Nazareth (Lk 4:14-30)

To this real world Jesus returns after his baptismal and wilderness experience to proclaim his mission to those with the deepest needs. His mission is pointedly directed to reach the disadvantaged, the marginalized and the oppressed. His townspeople can accept neither his messianic role nor its stated purpose.

In response, Jesus alludes to the stories of two Gentiles, a man and woman who participated in the faith and blessings of Israel. Naaman the Syrian was healed of his leprosy because of the witness of a young servant maid (2 Kings 5:1-19), while the widow of Zarephath received the prophet Elijah into her home even when she did not have enough food for her child and herself. Her provisions were miraculously extended as she shared with her guest; and when her young son died, Elijah restored him to life. Then it was that she understood that Elijah was a prophet of God whose message she gladly received (1 Kings 17:24). Thus the impoverished Gentile widow stands as a witness against the unreceptive inhabitants of Nazareth.

The Healing of Simon Peter's Mother-in-Law (Lk 4:38-39)

Here we are given a glimpse of the home life of Peter. He is married, with a mother-in-law who lives in his home at Capernaum. She appears to have provided significant assistance about the house to Peter's wife while he was itinerating with Jesus. Immediately upon her healing she rises to minister (*diakoneō*) to the guests.

In contrast to the accounts in the other Synoptics (Mt 8:14-15; Mk 1:29-31), Luke the physician gives a more detailed description of the "high fever" (Lk 4:38; cf. Mk 1:30) that rages within her. Jesus heals by a command alone in Luke, but in Mark he touches her hand (Mk 1:31). Here Luke begins the motif of women who are healed and enabled to minister to Jesus.

Raising the Son of the Widow of Nain (Lk 7:11-17)

The death of a child is one of the most devastating losses a parent can suffer. Jesus' sympathy is aroused by a mother who walks before the bier of her dead son. He is aware not only of her grief but also of the destitution that will be occasioned by the son's demise. With him gone, this widow is now the poorest of the poor, alone and destitute (*see* Widows).

Jewish tradition required the female relatives to walk in front of the corpse in funeral processions. The custom was said to have been established as a reminder of Eve's defection in bringing death into the world. Just as women light the sabbath candles because Eve brought darkness to humanity, so there is a reminder at this moment of deepest woe (*see* Grief and Bereavement).

As Jesus came face to face with this widow, he stopped the funeral cortege and stretched out his hand to the figure on the bier. To touch the corpse would render him unclean for a week (Num 19:11). Jesus, however, is more concerned with alleviating the woman's grief than with his own impurity. The son is no longer dead but restored to life and to the arms of his joyous mother. Before the town's gate, life has met death and overcome it.

Disparate Patterns and Paths to Doing God's Will (Lk 7:31-35)

Jesus demonstrates that different lifestyles may be appropriate for the servants of God. John the Baptist lived on desert fare readily available to him, while Jesus joined rich and poor in their meals and in their homes. Both styles were suitable for the situations in which they ministered. Paul too takes up the matter of dietary differences and affirms that all may promote spiritual welfare. One pattern of eating or fasting does not make one more spiritual than others. It is only when the ingestion of food creates an offense for others that harm is done (*see* 1 Corinthians).

The wise can perceive the fundamental purposes even if there are wide varieties of practice among God's saints. Adaptation to a particular set of circumstances is often the most productive path in the kingdom of heaven. Wisdom, an abstraction, is personified as a mother whose children achieve their ends through varying routes along life's way.

The Sinful Woman Who Anoints Jesus (Lk 7:36-50)

While Jesus is being entertained at a private dinner, a woman of ill repute enters the room. She approaches the table where he is reclining, his head toward the center of the room and his feet toward the wall. He is not aware of her presence until she has poured the contents of her alabaster vial on him.

Luke affords us here the clearest affirmation of Christ's acceptance of women with dubious sexual histories. The sinful woman is accepted while the judgmental stance of her critics is condemned. Jesus receives her ministrations and recognizes them as indicative of a profoundly altered attitude. Her act of devotion represents her best effort to express her newly awakened response to God's grace. Whether her past actions have been the result of lust, need, manipulation or defiance, she has been transformed by the power of divine love. Before hostile onlookers (who are perhaps also former lovers) she renounces the former liaisons and moves into a new life of freedom and holiness (*see* Holiness and Wholeness; Sin).

There appear to be two distinct anointing stories recorded in the Gospels; that of Luke differs in a number of points from the rendering given by the other Evangelists. In Luke's version, the anointing takes place in Galilee at the home of a Pharisee, while Matthew and Mark designate Simon the leper's house in Bethany as the location. In Luke's Gospel the woman is unnamed, identified only as a sinner; and only John gives the woman of Bethany a name: Mary the sister of Lazarus and Martha. There are no allusions to a sinful past in the accounts of Matthew, Mark and John.

The most marked difference in the treatment of the two episodes is that of Jesus' response. In Luke's Gospel the incident takes place earlier in the ministry of Jesus and emphasizes the importance of repentance and humility toward God. He reminds the host that he has failed in the simple courtesy of providing wash water to bathe Jesus' dusty feet, and this the woman has supplied abundantly with her tears. The dinner guests are horrified that a sinful woman is allowed to touch this controversial rabbi, and Jesus is critical of their ungracious and inhospitable attitude. Implicit is his welcome of prostitutes and tax gatherers who walked into heaven before the high priests and elders of the people (Mt 21:31).

In the accounts from Matthew, Mark and John, Jesus declares that the action is an anointing in anticipation of his burial and that her perceptive and priestly unction is a "good work" that will be told as a memorial to her wherever the gospel is preached. Elisabeth Schüssler Fiorenza, noting her anointing of Christ's head and his affirmation of the "good service" (Mt 26:10), declares the woman's deed one of messianic importance.

John identifies Mary of Bethany as the sister of Lazarus, "the one who anointed the Lord with perfume and wiped his feet with her hair" (Jn 11:2). In John's account, Jesus again recognizes the act as an anticipation of his burial. In the three Bethany renderings, the woman is defended against the charge of having wasted the precious ointment on a futile gesture. Jesus maintains the legitimacy of the extravagant expression and indicates that there is a place for devotion and for altruism. The poor are rightfully the concern of the faithful, but there must also be room for worship. In both anointing episodes, women pour forth their most precious possession, impelled by a consuming dedication of heart and life.

Jesus' Female Followers (Lk 8:1-3)

There has been a listing of the male disciples in Luke 6:12-19. In Luke 8:1-3 there is an abbreviated listing of named and identifiable women followers. They are said to be persons healed of various diseases and afflictions. Perhaps because of their previously marginalized status, they had been given permission by their families to leave their homes and follow Jesus. A case in point would be that of Joanna, wife of Chuza, Herod's steward. Despite her husband's prominent political position, she travels with Jesus, supports his mission monetarily and is named as a witness of the resurrection.

The most conspicuous of the group is Mary Magdalene. Contrary to popular supposition, she is never mentioned as a prostitute. Rather, she has borne a spiritual and mental affliction—that of possession by seven evil spirits. Today we might well identify these as multiple personalities, often the result of abuse (*see* Violence, Abuse and Oppression). She has known the healing of Jesus and will assume the title "apostle to the apostles" as she is the first to see the risen Christ and to give testimony to the Easter event (Mk 16:9-10; Jn 20:1).

Of Susanna we are told nothing more than her name, followed by the observation that many other women followed Jesus as well. This is in marked contrast to the identification of each of the male disciples and may indicate a reticence to reveal their names in a public record. Pericles had declared that the greatest honor belonged to the woman whose name was never mentioned outside her home, whether for good or evil. Even in Palestine such attitudes were not wholly lacking.

These women traveled as part of the retinue of Jesus. So far as we know, they were

---

Women Disciples

In the ancient world, teachers were seen as possessing superior knowledge that they would impart to disciples who gathered around them to learn from their life, words and actions. Close relationships developed between teacher and learners over time as they committed themselves to one another and to their shared beliefs. Many teachers developed a peripatetic lifestyle, propagating their beliefs or philosophy in many places, assisted by their disciples.

It is uncertain how many Old Testament relationships could be described as discipling in intention. Elijah's and Elisha's interaction may be one. However, by New Testament times it was a widely recognized method of teaching; Jesus used it to train the future leaders of his church. During his public ministry Jesus' disciple-assistants numbered between twelve and seventy individuals (Lk 6:13-16; 10:1).

The Gospels never refer to any woman as a disciple, and the feminine word *mathētria* is used once only in the New Testament and describes Tabitha, a disciple in Joppa (Acts 9:36). In the first century women usually had no part in organized education. Few were literate. Their education was confined to domestic and family matters. Thus the considerable evidence that women were followers of Jesus and played a significant part in the disciple band is in contrast to the accepted practices of the day.

The verb *akoloutheō* ("to follow") can mean "to accompany or go along with," but it is also a technical term for following someone as a disciple. It appears that the women mentioned in Luke 8:1-3 were Jesus' disciples who followed with him and his disciple band and provided for Jesus from their resources.

At the end of the Gospel accounts we discover many women whose following (a continuous action, Mk 15:41) of Jesus had begun in Galilee and continued to Jerusalem and the cross. There they maintained their faithful vigil even though all others had "deserted him and fled" (Mk 14:50). The women watched where he was laid and prepared to anoint his body for burial, which was the customary way disciples demonstrated their final respect for their master (Mt 28:13; Mk 15:47—16:1).

Jesus welcomed many different women as learners (Mary of Bethany, Lk 10:39, 42) and encouraged them to engage with him in theological conversations (Martha, Jn 11:21-27; Canaanite woman, Mt 15:24-28; Samaritan woman, Jn 4:7-26). This was in contrast to the rabbinic practice of excluding women. Mary of Bethany was alone among his followers in her understanding that he was about to die (Jn 12:7). On the resurrection morning Jesus and the angelic messengers asked the women at the tomb to "remember" his previous instructions about their meeting in Galilee and commissioned them to remind the absent disciples of this arrangement when they conveyed the resurrection news (Mt 28:6-10; Mk 16:7; Lk 24:6-9). Being entrusted with that task indicated a divine endorsement of their role in sharing the good news and teaching others to obey Jesus' commands and placed them under the same obligation as the other disciples (Mt 28:19-20). Their access to the disciples, behind locked doors, on the day of resurrection shows their acceptance as welcome members of the disciple band (Jn 20:18-19).

Jesus was not unique in gathering female as well as male disciples, as seen in this depiction of Plotinus's disciples. (Luke 8:1-3)

Among the women followers named in the Gospels Mary Magdalene's name heads all but one list (Mt 27:56; 28:1; Mk 15:40-41; 16:1; Lk 8:2; 24:10; Jn 19:25; 20:1). Many scholars conclude this indicates her leadership among the women. The mention of the women's names probably indicates they were well known in the Christian community at the time of writing.

Jewish law required men's attendance at three temple-based festivals every year (Ex 23:17), but women were free to remain at home and attend to family duties. Maybe women were not included among the Twelve because Jesus gave them the choice of traveling with his band or remaining at home (Lk 10:38-42), but the Gospels do not indicate a different expectation for men and women in the life of discipleship. All were called to put God's kingdom first and to commit themselves to hear and do his will whatever the cost (Mt 6:33; Lk 8:19-21; 11:27-28).

It is possible that women were among the seventy Jesus sent in pairs to the towns of Galilee to prepare for his later visits by curing the sick, casting out demons and announcing the coming kingdom (Lk 10:1-12, 17-20). The male disciples and Jesus had female relatives who were members of the disciple band. These included Jesus' mother and aunt (Jn 19:25), the mother of James and John (Mt 27:56), the mother of James the younger and Joses (Mk 15:40) and the wife of Clopas (Jn 19:25; see also Lk 24:18). They may have ministered in partnership with a male relative. The believing wives of apostles and brothers of the Lord accompanied their husbands in traveling ministry two decades later (1 Cor 9:5).

Following the ascension of Jesus, the teacher-disciple function of the followers of Jesus changed. Although his physical presence was withdrawn, he remained their Lord and master, and they continued part of his disciple band. In Acts the word *mathētēs* ("disciple") is used as a general term denoting all believers or members of the new Christian community. Acts nominates four individuals by the singular (Ananias,

Acts 9:10; Timothy, Acts 16:1; Mnason, Acts 21:16; and Tabitha, Acts 9:36). All other occurrences are in the plural and include men and women living in Damascus, Jerusalem, Joppa, Antioch, Lystra, Derbe, Galatia and Phrygia, Ephesus, Tyre and Caesarea. They took part in major church decisions (Acts 6:2), performed acts of service for others and suffered persecution for their faith (Acts 9:1-2). Their service included charitable good works (Acts 9:36, 39), famine relief (Acts 11:29), providing spiritual and physical deliverance to Paul (Acts 9:17, 25; 14:20), and hospitality and advice concerning his well-being (Acts 19:30; 21:4, 16).

Consequently women were present among the disciple band for a large proportion of Jesus' public ministry and from the beginning of the Christian church. They were regarded as significant learners capable of theological understanding and maintaining a loving, obedient relationship with Jesus as Lord. They were expected to put into practice all his teachings and to give priority to serving him with others of his followers, by sharing the good news of the kingdom of God and ministering to all those they encountered who were in physical or spiritual need. SYLVIA WILKEY COLLINSON

---

not sent out two by two on missions away from the safety of the main group. They remained faithful followers and witnesses of the cross, burial and resurrection. They had been instructed in the significance of these events during their close association with Jesus so that they might serve as carefully briefed witnesses (*see* Women as Witnesses). Like the women who financed the exodus (Ex 3:22; 11:2-3), these women provided much-needed resources for the ministry of Jesus.

The names of these women will be given in the other Gospels as they stand watching the crucifixion (Mk 15:40-41; Mt 27:55-56; cf. Lk 23:49; Jn 19:25). The majority, however, will again be the nameless "many women." Their longstanding and faithful discipleship will be noted at the time of Jesus' death, but Luke is careful to give us this information at the beginning of his ministry (*see* Women Disciples).

The Visit of Jesus' Mother and Brothers (Lk 8:19-21)

Other accounts mention the presence of sisters as well as Jesus' mother and brothers (Mt 13:54-55; Mk 6:3-5). *Adelphoi,* however, can include male and female siblings. This pericope lets us see the rift that is growing between Jesus and his family. They have come to claim his time and his attention. They assume that he will send away the crowds and devote himself exclusively to them. Jesus maintains that those who are truly his family are those who prize the word of God and act on it (Lk 8:21; cf. Mt 13:54-58; Mk 3:20-21). This reaction could not fail to have been a challenge to Mary in her role as mother of a son whom she could not understand.

Jairus's Daughter Raised and the Woman with a Flow of Blood Healed (Lk 8:40-56)

In balance with the story of the healing of the male demoniac, Luke presents two episodes of Jesus' outreach to women in desperate straits.

Jairus, father of a twelve-year-old daughter and chief official in the synagogue, begs Jesus to attend the young girl, who is close to death. If at other points his position in the synagogue may have afforded Jairus some security, he must in this dire circumstance seek the aid of the controversial Jesus.

The road to Jairus's house is obstructed by a large crowd, however, and progress is further impeded by the presence of a woman afflicted with a flow of blood. For twelve years the condition has persisted, and medical intervention has only worsened her plight. In her extremity, she risks approaching Jesus to touch the *kraspedon,* the fringe of his prayer shawl, the holiest of his garments (Lk 8:44; Mt 9:20; Mk 5:27). Her discharge rendered her unclean according to levitical law (Lev 15:19-33), and any whom she touched would also become unclean. She was therefore a social outcast. Her many years of constant menstrual discharge are juxtaposed with the story of a young girl who hovers at the point of death just as she comes to the age for the onset of menstruation (*see* Menstruation).

Jesus' concern is not for the woman's impurity but for her faith. He shows no repugnance for the bodily function that is a recurrent feature of all women's experience. In contrast to Mark's account, in which the woman speaks privately to Jesus (Mk 5:33), Jesus asks her to make a public confession. While this might seem to expose her to embarrassment, her condition could scarcely have remained a secret for twelve years; and the declaration along with Jesus' affirmation marks the definitive end of her devastating affliction and her reentry into human society as an acceptable person.

Jesus affirms her as "daughter" (Lk 8:48; Mt 9:20-22; Mk 5:34), an indication of her full membership of the covenant community (*see* Covenant and Community). Her faith has effected the healing: "Daughter, your faith has made you well" (Lk 8:48).

But the delay has ostensibly proven fatal for Jairus's daughter. Despite the announcement brought to him that the child is dead, Jesus continues his progress to her bedside. His entrance to the house is blocked by highly experienced professional mourners, women who led the family in expressions of grief at the time of death. Jesus elicits from them laughter of derision when he announces that the young girl is not dead but sleeping. Their unbelief stands in stark contrast to the faith of the woman who has been healed and of Jairus's family.

In defiance of the ritual prohibition against touching the dead, Jesus takes the girl's hand and commands, "Child, get up!" (Lk 8:54). The restoration to life is immediate, and the astounded parents are bidden to provide her with nourishment—an intensely practical step to augment the mighty miracle.

Mary and Martha (Lk 10:38-42)

This vignette gives us another view of the home life of women, with its potential and its frustrations. Luke has obtained distinctive material, ostensibly from a woman in some way acquainted with the episode. The Gospel of John tells of Jesus raising from the dead Lazarus, the brother of Mary and Martha (Jn 11:1-45), and of Mary's anointng Jesus at Bethany (Jn 12:1-8). Here, however, we see the full-orbed nature of the support of Jesus' mission by his female followers. To this Luke has already alluded as ihe speaks of the discipleship and material support of the women who itinerate with him.

Luke is a book of journeys, but it is also a book that recognizes the importance of hospitality. The homeless and the travelers have need of shelter and of a caring reception at the end of the day (Lk 9:4; 10:5-8; Mt 10:11-12; Mk 6:10). In accounts of the early church we are made especially aware of the women who received traveling evangelists into their homes (Acts 16:15, 40; 18:2-3). More often than those of men, we are told the names women in whose houses the early churches met (Acts 12:12; 16:13-15, 40; Rom 16:3-5; 1 Cor 16:19; Col 4:15). Theirs was the responsibility not only to provide food and housing for the itinerant missionary but also to assess the message that was brought (*see* 2 John; 3 John). This required that the women must be carefully taught and possess a strong understanding of the fundamentals of the gospel. If the visitor came with a faithful witness to Christ, the leaders were to aid in its dissemination within their communities (2 Jn 7-11; cf. 3 Jn 5-8). The story before us presents a paradigm of the attitudes and activities of women who open their homes for gospel ministry.

Catacomb painting of the woman with a hemorrhage. (Luke 8:44)

Jesus has no home of his own but can be comfortable in the houses of those who welcome him. Here his visit exposes the possibilities for service and personal growth of Mary and Martha. Thus it is that we find the sisters occupied with two different aspects of the total mission. Martha energetically plunges into the task of preparing a lavish meal and seeks to outdo herself in the hospitality that she offers. She becomes overwhelmed by the arrangements that she has deemed necessary. There are too few hands and too much to do. "Many tasks" refers to much service *(diakonia).* The pressure of these tasks did not permit Martha to learn from Jesus. Her strategy is to shame her sister into sharing the burden.

Mary has seated herself at the feet of Jesus in the position of a learner (cf. Acts 22:3). In Jewish tradition, this was ordinarily not an option for women. A much-quoted proverb declared that it was better to give the Torah to be burned than to teach it to a woman. Martha's demand may be based as much on her discomfort at her sister's unconventional behavior as on her need for assistance. We may suppose that there may also have been an element of jealousy. While she fulfilled the appropriate role of a traditional woman, her sister was seated with the male disciples. Mary was afforded an opportunity to learn that was denied to Martha. Luke will later demonstrate the importance of instructing women in order to make them faithful witnesses.

When Martha appeals to him for the assistance of her sister, Jesus replies that he seeks a simple repast so that the harried hostess will not spend all her time in catering a sumptuous feast. He does not decry the faithful discharge of necessary household tasks, but he points to a higher priority. In no way is this a denigration of the physical labor that is necessary for the enablement of ministry, for Luke records that the apostle Paul took great pride in the toil wrought with his hands in order to support his mission (Acts 18:3; 20:34; cf. 1 Cor 4:12; 1 Thess 2:9).

The Third Evangelist's story is about fundamental priorities. A woman may find great satisfaction and much appreciation for her skill in the culinary arts. Nevertheless she is not ultimately defined by the excellence of the table she spreads but on spreading her heart open to God's Word (cf. 2 Cor 6:11). The perfect housekeeper may not be the one most receptive to the voice of God. Jesus supports Mary in her role as disciple and invites Martha also to hear his teaching. How often narrowly prescribed roles have obstructed the calling of women! Neither social custom nor rabbinic tradition can be allowed to deprive them of their divinely ordained and courageously chosen right to learn.

Motherhood and Mission (Lk 11:27-28)

In this pericope, sexual identity is pitted against the spiritual identity of women. A woman from the crowd shouts out a bless-

---

Martha & Mary

These women are not named in Matthew or Mark, but for Luke and John they have an important place as sisters who were friends and disciples of Jesus. As Jesus' friends, they give an insight into his genuine humanity. Although his mission involves love for the world, he has specific friends he can relax with. He stays with them in Bethany, near Jerusalem (Lk 10:38; Jn 11:1); when their brother is sick, they expect him to come. John specifies that Jesus loved each of them (Jn 10:5). We see him with them, individually and together, affirming or challenging as the situation demands.

The apostle Paul described Christians as brothers and sisters, adopted into a new family in Christ. Yet learning to respect each other's differences can be hard (Gal 4:4-7;

1 Cor 12:21-26). The sisters illustrate this theme.

Martha's strength is taking the lead where action is required. She wants to serve Jesus well. After Lazarus's death, she steps out to meet Jesus and question his delay. In the process she becomes a key witness to Jesus as Christ, the Son of God, and to hope in the resurrection (Jn 11:24-27). Yet her strength is allied to her weakness. Anguish wells up when she gets overanxious about achieving her goals. She cannot bear Mary's apparent inactivity (Lk 10:40).

Mary's strength is to pay close attention to Jesus. She discerns the weight on Jesus' heart as the cross approaches. She anoints his body in advance of his burial. This sign, Mark adds, will always be included when the message of Jesus is told to the world (Mk 14:9).

Each of these women, in her own way, is an evangelist. Both their gifts are needed if the death and resurrection of Jesus is to be made known. VERA M. SINTON

---

ing upon the womb and breasts that had produced and nourished so remarkable a son. This was, to be sure, a traditional form of praise for son and mother (cf. Gen 49:25). Though to this day many societies value women chiefly as childbearers, Jesus viewed them as total beings. Reproduction is not their highest calling. The childless woman is of equal value in God's economy (*see* Singleness). Here Jesus affirms those who hear and obey his Word.

This passage marks one of the final stages of the severing of the umbilical cord between Jesus and Mary, his mother. The woman in the crowd has praised the reproductive organs of Mary. As the one who bore the child within her body and nourished him at her breast, her ties of maternal relationship have been strong. However, Jesus summons the crowd and his mother to move onto a higher plane. Elizabeth had declared that Mary was blessed not just because she was to be Messiah's mother but also because she had believed.

Throughout Jesus' life, Mary is there (Lk 8:19-21; Mt 12:46-50; Mk 3:31-35), struggling to understand her son though not always succeeding (Lk 2:49-50; Jn 2:3-4; Mk 3:21). Now her specific role as childbearer is deemphasized, replaced by that of believing disciple. As such, she stands in Luke's account among the company of Jesus' followers. Her presence is presumed along with the other woman disciples as one who hears and obeys the Word of God.

For this reason Luke will no longer single out Mary for special reference until he notes that she was in the upper room involved in the decision making of the early church (Acts 1:14). In that context, she is mentioned in the company with the other women.

The transition for Mary cannot have been an easy one. She who had been honored for her willing role in bringing Messiah into the world was now called to be follower. She whose maternal functions had been memorialized (Lk 1:31, 42, 48; 2:5-7) must now recollect that she has been affirmed most of all for her faith and her walk with God (Lk 1:28, 45). Throughout the trying and perplexing circumstances of her son's life, she has maintained a confidence in God's promises and power. If she cannot comprehend, she can still trust.

Luke demonstrates a rare sympathy in describing Mary's experience of motherhood, and clearly he had drawn on her heavily as a source for his story. Was it Luke or Mary who now perceived the change of role? In this she is a model to all mothers who must come to view their children as fellow adults to whom they must relate in a new way.

The Queen of Sheba (Lk 11:29-32)

Jesus' hearers ask for a sign, and he points to an important character in the Old Testament. In balance to Jonah and the people of Nineveh (see also Mt 12:38-42), he cites the Queen of the South, apparently the Queen of Sheba. Like the Ninevites, she underwent a profound spiritual change (1 Kings 10:1-29; 2 Chron 9:1-12). When Jesus' critics demand a sign, Jesus uses the Queen of Sheba as a prophetic figure. She is thought to have hailed from the southernmost part of the known world on either the African or Arabian coast of the Red Sea. Powerful queens are historically attested in the Yemen and in Ethiopia. In Isaiah 43:3, Ethiopia and Sheba are mentioned in the same context, augmenting the ancient tradition that it was an Abyssinian queen who visited Solomon (*see* Africans in Biblical History).

The initial contact may have arisen from the queen's curiosity as to the famed wisdom of Solomon as well as her desire for maritime negotiations. The entrance and expansion of his merchant fleet (1 Kings 9:26; 2 Chron 8:17-18) into the Red Sea would necessitate skillful diplomacy in order to forge trade agreements characterized by wisdom and justice. In this Solomon did not disappoint her. But if he was fair in his business dealings and splendid in his program of magnificent public works, she found far more to admire in the faith that he espoused (1 Kings 10:1-29; 2 Chron 9:1-12). It was this that she carried back with her. Jesus maintained that her perception of Solomon's grandeur was a condemnation of those who could not perceive one greater than Solomon in their midst. To allude to her in this manner is a powerful statement about the significance of this woman and of all women of faith. They are respected for their initiative in searching for the truth, their courage and their integrity.

The Voice of Wisdom (Lk 11:45-54)

This is the only point in the New Testament at which personified Wisdom is given her own voice. Because God's message has not been heeded, a decision is made that prophets and apostles will be sent even though their lives may be at risk. Those who hear will gain insight, but those who resist the messengers must bear the guilt. Wisdom is set in direct antithesis to the male lawyers who "have taken away the key of knowledge" and hinder others from gaining admission to its halls.

Priorities Within the Household (Lk 12:49-53)

Women often set great store by relationships and will sometimes sacrifice everything else to preserve them, even when the ties are unhealthy. Jesus declared that he had not come to ensure unruffled households. He saw the family not as a fetish but as a union of persons who might have different values. Commitment of his followers must take precedence over domestic peace. In particular he prophesies friction among the women of a household: mother against daughter and mother-in-law against daughter-in-law. Those who are willing to give first loyalty to the cause of Christ may encounter difficult circumstances and lack of understanding at home. He had come to bring fire upon the earth, a consuming passion that would stretch and strain families to the utmost.

The Bound Woman Set Free (Lk 13:10-17)

This episode is recorded only in Luke and stands as a monument to the rights and dignity of women. For eighteen years the woman has been unable to stand upright, bent nearly double. Her affliction may have been spondylitis ankylopoeitica or a severe case of osteoporosis, a condition that besets women more commonly than men. Marginalized women are objects of consistent concern to Jesus. With no request made of him, Jesus undertakes her healing. Its instant effect is contrasted with the long years that she has spent with her affliction. "Woman, you are set free from your ailment" (Lk 13:12).

Jesus addresses her as "daughter of Abraham" (Lk 13:16), thereby giving her value as a person of worth and dignity in the kingdom of God. His opponents, however, viewed her as less than human and unworthy of healing on the sabbath. Jesus points out that any of them on the sabbath would loose *(lyō)* the tethers of their livestock and lead them to water. How much more should this woman be loosed from her bonds on the sabbath? He has identified her as a member of the covenant people of Israel. Although her prayers had been unanswered for eighteen years, she was still faithful in synagogue worship. Her previous condition was not the result of any misdemeanor on her part but rather was due to the malice of Satan. As a liberated member of the covenant community, she may now stand erect and look people in the face. Those who must hide their faces in shame are they who would deny her this right.

The Woman with the Yeast (Lk 13:18-21)

In this text we can see Jesus' acute perception of the ordinary household tasks of women and his valuation of the labor. In balance with the parable of a man planting mustard seed is the parable of a woman kneading yeast into dough. The paired parables affirm male and female participation as necessary to understand growth of the kingdom of God.

Kneading the dough requires vigorous use of the hands, persistence and sensitivity to the texture. Yeast, the leavening agent, is a living organism that does not always respond in precisely the same way. No two batches of dough are ever alike. Quantity of flour, temperature and environment must all be controlled by the skilled breadmaker for the yeast to raise a mass to many times its weight. The parable suggests the influence and sensitivity of women in promoting the kingdom. Their hands-on ministry of positive nurture and practical outreach permeates society far beyond their numerical strength.

Jesus' Yearning over Jerusalem (Lk 13:31-35)

Here we find an image that had been developed in the Hebrew Scriptures. It is that of God as a mother bird protecting the young with her wings. The eagle bears her young on her wings as they learn to fly (Ex 19:4; Deut 32:11-12), though the more common figure is of God as a bird offering protective shelter under her wings (Ps 17:8; 36:7; 57:1; 61:4; 63:7; 91:4; cf. Ruth 2:12). The repeated references to resting under the shadow of God's wings evoke a concept of shade that could shield from the blistering sun. All of these metaphors are those of loving nurturance, stability and safety. Other maternal images are Deuteronomy 32:18, Isaiah 42:14; 49:15; 66:9, 13, Psalm 22:10-11 and Psalm131:2-3 (*see* Images of God as Female). Jesus is actually depicted as a hen with a brood of chicks. What could be more emblematic of solicitous maternal care?

The Woman and the Lost Coin (Lk 15:8-10)

Grouped together are the parables of the lost sheep, the lost coin and the lost son. Readers readily identify God in the figures of the seeking shepherd and of the waiting father. The image of God as housewife is more difficult for some readers to recognize.

The woman is seeking a valuable coin that represents one-tenth of her dowry. Ordinarily the coins were sewn into a woman's headdress, thus becoming her adornment as well as her security against future adversity (*see* Numbers). But the thread by which one of the precious coins was attached became loose, and the coin rolled away onto the ground, where the woman fumbles to pick it up. Since Palestinian houses had little light, she is unable to locate it in the darkness.

The woman lights one of the tiny lamps that gave a flickering light and begins a more comprehensive search. With a broom, she sweeps the floor repeatedly until her diligent persistence is rewarded. The lost is found. In relief and joy she calls the good news to the other women of the neighborhood; they hasten to join in the jubilation. Just so, Jesus insists, the angels rejoice before God at the reclamation of a sinner.

Jesus and Divorce (Lk 16:18)

In Luke's account we may discern in Jesus' teaching a desire to protect women against capricious divorce action that could leave them without protection (*see* Divorce). A man might put away his wife for a wide variety of frivolous reasons and remarry at will. The wife, having no such rights, was vulnerable and at his mercy. She might be easily discarded in favor of another woman, with little provision made for her continued survival. In first-century Judaism divorce and remarriage were so widespread that there was a proverb: "Even the altar weeps when a man puts away his first wife, but only for the first wife." Polygamy was still practiced by some Jewish males until the time of Justinian, but this entailed the expense of supporting more than one woman. Divorce was a more economical option.

Pharisaic debates centered on the causes for which a man might divorce a wife without having to return her dowry, thereby making her situation even more desperate. Among the offenses listed as justifying divorce were burning a man's dinner, spinning in the street or suffering a dog bite that did not heal properly. In response to the Pharisees' mockery, Jesus insists upon a morality propounded by the law and the prophets. He declares that if a man divorces his wife and remarries, it is adultery against the wife. This is a memorable statement given that adultery was normally seen as a crime against a man (*see* Adultery). Also, if a man marries a divorced woman, it is adultery, for both actions perpetuate the widespread and irresponsible practice that destroyed the security and stability of so many women.

The Image of Lot's Wife (Lk 17:28-33)

Lot's wife is an unusual instance in which Luke employs a figure of a woman as a negative example. The reference occurs in Jesus' teaching on future judgment as he recalls the fate of Sodom and Gomorrah (Gen 19:15-28). Women often have a particularly difficult time in leaving a familiar environment and moving on to a strange and alien location. Although the family had been commanded not to look back, she could not resist a last look at so much that had made her life meaningful (Gen 19:26). In this she evinced her willingness to cling to her attachment to the corrupt society she had known rather than to the commands of God. The wrong choice cost her life, possibly as she was engulfed in the fumes of the burning city.

Jesus speaks of this woman when he cautions those on the housetop and in the field not to turn back when the Son of Man is revealed. She is here a symbol of the resistant and unbelieving soul, free to make her own decision but choosing an action that led to her death. Luke's Gospel gives women significance, but there is no idealization.

Women at the Mill (Lk 17:35)

Jesus shows sensitivity to the disparate work schedules of women and men. On the day of judgment, two men will be still sleeping while two women will be grinding grain, a task usually done early in the morning to prepare flour for the family's daily bread. The stone mill needed to crush the grain was heavy, and so the work was often shared by two women. Each would seize one of the wooden handles that protruded from the upper millstone and rotate it back and forth in rhythm. An animal might be used, but here the reference is to the arduous work of women. Of the two, one is caught away to heaven while the other remains on earth. Believing and unbelieving women share common tasks until the final day when faith will make a clear distinction between them.

The Widow and the Unjust Judge (Lk 18:1-8)

The widow was a focus of particular concern in the Hebrew Scriptures (Ex 22:22-24; Ps 68:5; 146:9; Is 1:17; Jer 7:6-7). The heroine of Jesus' parable is apparently threatened with dispossession, perhaps in payment of a debt (cf. 2 Kings 4:1-7). She must seek to represent herself in her claim for what is rightfully hers, and she has pleaded in vain with the local judge. Although he is legally required to do so, he refuses to give her a hearing. However, he alone has the power to grant her petition. The judge "neither feared God nor had respect for people" (Lk 18:2); he was a corrupt public official who withheld his power to dispense justice. Nevertheless, the widow continues to seek redress of the wrong that is being done her. At last her persistence drives the judge to give her a fair hearing. The woman is rewarded not for her passive acquiescence but for her insistence on receiving justice. Her assertiveness is commended.

Jesus points out that God's character is the opposite from that of the unrighteous judge. In response to persistent prayer, there will be an answer even if it is not given immediately. This parable has parallels to that of the male householder who is granted his petition because of his refusal to desist in his requests for food for his friend (Lk 11:5-9). He and the widow are commended for their steadfastness despite seemingly unanswered prayer.

Jesus Receives Mothers and Children (Lk 18:15-17)

A Western text variant states that mothers brought their little children to Jesus. If the fathers came too, surely the mothers played a key role in seeking the touch of Jesus for their children. The little ones are called *brephē,* usually applied to infants who are still nursing and cannot be separated from their mothers. Presumably they would be too young to understand Jesus' teaching or afterward to remember the event. They are at that stage of life when they are most demanding, especially of their mothers.

Understandably the disciples felt that the intrusion of crying infants was disruptive of the orderly conduct of Jesus' mission. They are not only refused access to Jesus but rebuked as well. Running noses, sticky hands and undergarments in need of change would not make them more attractive. The rebuke that the disciples issued cannot have been directed toward the infants but toward those who brought them. Few things are so painful to a mother as the feeling that she and her brood are unwanted. The care of young children is enormously consuming of time, effort, patience and endurance. Sleep is broken, schedules ruined, rest nonexistent and tempers strained. Worse yet, her unending labor is seen as essentially worthless, and her status as a human being compromised (*see* The Purpose and Value of Human Life).

The women and the children that they bring have been devalued by the callous reception of the disciples. They are not welcome in the mission of Jesus. He, however, insists that the children, as well as their caregivers, be brought to him and that they are of major importance. It is of such that the kingdom of God is comprised. Despite the hardships and ignominy, mothers play a key role in building this kingdom and in instilling within their children attitudes of faith and receptivity.

To Which Husband Is She to Be Assigned? (Lk 20:27-40)

The Sadducees have contrived a trap to ridicule the doctrine of the resurrection. They narrate a hypothetical case in which, according to the law of levirate marriage, a man marries the widow of his deceased brother. The arrangement provided the woman with support and hope of a son who could provide for her (Deut 25:5; *see* Marriage).

The widow's second husband dies as well, and in the end seven husbands predecease the woman. The tale is a preposterous one, perhaps inspired by a story from the book of Tobit, in which seven successive husbands are slain by a wicked demon. In the case propounded by the Sadducees, the woman too dies, and they ask to which of the seven husbands she shall belong in paradise. Their concern is not about the woman in the afterlife but rather about how they may discredit Jesus' belief in the resurrection.

Essentially the Sadducees view the woman as the property of her husband, with no autonomy. Jesus, however, perceives women as full persons here and hereafter, by no means the possession of another. He replies that the new relationships in heaven will no longer emphasize physical sexuality, marriage or death. The spiritual bonding to God supersedes bonding in the flesh (cf. Jn 3:6).

The Widow's Offering (Lk 20:45—21:4)

The theme of Jesus' concern for widows is a recurring one. Immediately before the temple episode, he had scathingly denounced their exploitation at the hands of the scribes (Lk 20:47). Now his attention turns to those who are making contributions to the temple treasury. The rich make conspicuous donations, but Jesus observes an impoverished widow whose offering consists of two minuscule coins worth about a hundred-and-twenty-eighth part of a drachma. In so doing, she cast in all the money she had. The gift is far beyond her means. Yet it is given not to gain recognition but to maintain the temple and its services for all who desire to worship God.

Again Jesus singles out a disadvantaged woman as a spiritual and practical model. She stands in direct contrast to the affluent who give only after their needs and gratification have been met.

Issues of Power and Dominance (Lk 22:24-27)

Even at the Last Supper the disciples are not immune from petty wrangling. Earlier they had argued over who held the foremost position among Christ's followers. As they anticipated the beginning of the kingdom, the potential for power began to pull them toward self-aggrandizement. Now the dispute has grown more intense. Jesus' remark about kings of the Gentiles reveals that their thinking had taken a political turn. The title of benefactor *(euergetēs)* appears repeatedly in the honorific inscriptions of many regions and cities. Behind the benign ascription of generosity lay the financial and political might of those who, while ostensibly benefiting the citizens, were working their will upon them. They lorded it over *(kyrieuō)* the citizens and brought power to bear on *(exousiazō)* them. Jesus repudiates such manipulation of power and privilege. He declares it antithetical to the values of the kingdom and to those who are truly great in God's eyes.

The Slave Girl (Lk 22:56-57)

On the night of Jesus' arrest by the temple guard, he is led first to the high priest's house. A slave girl is present in the courtyard, though she is not mentioned in the other Gospels (cf. Mk 14:54). She is one of the few female figures in Luke's Gospel who does not have a sympathetic attitude toward Jesus and his mission. She made up one of the large number of slaves owned by the priestly establishment (*see* Ancient and Modern Slavery).

Perhaps wishing to demonstrate her importance as a clever informer in the high priest's service, she challenges Peter, who has seated himself by the fire outside in the courtyard. He had hoped to escape notice in the midst of a crowd of bystanders, but the quick-witted girl recognizes that she has seen him in the temple with Jesus. She is the first one, after personal association has become so dangerous, to call Peter to an honest confession of his relationship to Jesus. John identifies her or her counterpart as the doorkeeper (Jn 18:17). Like the other slave woman whom Luke mentions, she has a shrewd perception as to who may appropriately be admitted and who should be excluded (Acts 12:12-16).

Peter's inconsistency and ineffectiveness become a foil for the faithfulness of the women who will follow Jesus to the cross and tomb. Although he has promised to accompany Jesus to prison and death, Peter fails egregiously. In the Gospel of John he shows more desire than the other disciples to stage a defense and is identified as the one who severs the ear of the high priest's servant (Jn 18:10, 11, 26). Luke, however, leaves him nameless and mentions only that one of the disciples took the action.

Daughters of Jerusalem (Lk 23:26-31)

Peter abandons the scene to weep bitterly. He has failed not only to render assistance but even to stand by Jesus in his need. There are others, however, who will stand alongside the way of Jesus and weep openly. On the way to the cross a large crowd of people followed Jesus, including many women who mourned and lamented him. In the joyful Palm Sunday entry into Jerusalem, the children were prominent, but on Good Friday it is their mothers who line the way.

In the next few verses, women will three times be mentioned as those who followed Jesus to the cross and to the tomb. If they cannot defend him, they will at least attend him. They are determined to give Jesus the proper observances due him at his death. Roman law forbade women to prepare the body of an executed criminal for burial. If they will be denied access later, they will give Jesus his fitting funereal due as he walks past.

The observance of rites of passage was usually entrusted to the hands of women. Women were the ones who washed the body for burial and wrapped it in grave clothes. It was they who raised their voices in lament as professional mourners and as those deeply devoted to the deceased. A funeral was not complete without the hands and voices of women. The spontaneously composed dirge was a form of literary expression in which women excelled. It is to this lament over his fate that Jesus responded.

Luke's treatment of the mourning women is evocative of the motifs of Zechariah 12:10-14, where Jerusalem mourns the death of a king. A repeated theme in the passage is that the women shall mourn by themselves. Thus it is that Jesus responds, not as to devout women bewailing his execution but as to daughters of Jerusalem who must soon face their impending fate. The address "daughters of Jerusalem" is used in the Old Testament (Is 37:22; Zeph 3:14; Zech 9:9) and is generally intended to include all of the inhabitants. Jesus tells these women not to weep for him but for themselves and for their children. It is far easier for women to express compassion for another than to identify and acknowledge their sufferings.

On the way to his passion, Jesus is mindful of the burden that women bear. Already severely beaten and humiliated, he turns his attention to those who are even more marginalized than he. In Luke 21:23, he had already spoken of the horrors that might befall pregnant and nursing mothers when the city would be crushed by the Rome in retaliation for Jerusalem's insurrection. Here his concern is not merely for the plight of the city but also for the vulnerability of women. He identifies with the experiences that are peculiarly theirs: childbearing and nursing. These are the times when a woman can least protect herself and her young, when she suffers the most from maltreatment and can be most cruelly subjected to the vicissitudes of war.

The prophet Jeremiah employed the term "daughter of Jerusalem" in an extended metaphor of a woman abused by her former lovers (Jer 4:30-31; 8:20—9:1). In his crisis, the disenfranchised, dehumanized and disempowered Son of Man expresses his solidarity and sympathy with those who have come to mourn him. Luke makes Jesus a fellow sufferer with the lot of women, willing to have them weep for themselves rather than for him. With them, he has known beating, vilification, insult, ridicule, mockery, demeaning trivialization, the twisting of words, emotional abuse and ultimately death. He too was deprived of justice even though the Roman governor declared him to be innocent of all the charges brought against him. Thus he is equipped to be the Savior of women because he, although a male, has undergone similar outrage and afflictions.

It was precisely Jesus' sufferings that made this a supreme opportunity to address himself so clearly to the abuse of women and children. Surely this concern must be understood as encompassing a universal concern for violence against women and children, wherever and whenever it occurs (*see* Violence, Abuse and Oppression). Unlike Luke 21:20-21, this text does not speak specifically of Jerusalem's fall. It does speak, however, of the intense depression that can engulf abused women and children so that they long only for death (*see* Depression).

But Jesus is also mindful of those who have never borne children or suckled them at their breasts (cf. Lk 11:27-28). In a reprise of Isaiah 54:1-10, he declares that the childless woman will be blessed, as will she who has never nursed an infant. While surely the destruction of Jerusalem is in view, along with the terrors that it would hold for women, there is a wider meaning. Childless women can more easily escape in time of danger. They are less bound to the old than was Lot's wife, more able to forsake all for the sake of the gospel, less hampered with the cares of this world (cf. 1 Cor 7:35). In challenging times their worth is the greatest. Often it has been women who have carried the gospel farthest in the most dangerous circumstances.

Women Witnesses (Lk 23:44-56)

The crowd that has gathered to view the spectacle is stricken as they view the death of Jesus. They beat their breasts and return to Jerusalem. Those who remain at the cross are identified as the acquaintances *(gnōstoi)* of Jesus. They stand afar, unwilling witnesses of earth's greatest tragedy. The readily identified male disciples are no longer visible. Their place is taken by equally dedicated followers, the women who have accompanied Jesus from Galilee. We are told that they followed along in the company of *(synakoloutheō)* Jesus, and we recognize in them the women followers of Luke 8:2-3. The author does not name the women in this account as do Matthew (Mt 27:55-56) and Mark (Mk 15:40, 47). Luke will again give their names in his narrative of the resurrection.

While the acquaintances "stood at a distance," the female followers "saw." The latter verb implies to see and to know or gain understanding by the seeing. They will prove to be the major witnesses of the resurrection. A second group of women, along with the Beloved Disciple, stand at the foot of the cross in John's Gospel (Jn 19:25). They are named as Mary the mother of Jesus, his mother's sister, Mary the wife of Clopas and Mary Magdalene. Mary Magdalene is placed by Matthew and Mark in the group that is further removed (Mt 27:55-56; Mk 15:40-41). This is not necessarily inconsistent, as she may have paced between the two groups, as in often the case with someone who is watching a loved one die.

Although they are not allowed to assist in the removal of Jesus' body, the women follow along *(katakaloutheō)* as Joseph of Arimathea and Nicodemus transport the corpse to its grave. Luke adds a point that will be an important corroborative witness to his story: they carefully observed the location of the tomb and "how his body was laid." Mark identifies those who made the observation (Mary Magdalene and Mary the wife of Justus, Mk 15:47), and Matthew (Mt 27:61) names those who sat beside the tomb—apparently until they were frightened away by the Roman guard (Mary Magdalene and the other Mary). Their witness will be critical in the establishment of the facts concerning the raising of Christ from the dead.

Women at the Tomb (Lk 24:1-12)

Before sundown on the day of preparation, the women purchase spices that they will bring to the tomb at the dawning of the first day of the week. As devout Jewish women they rest on the sabbath in conformity with the law. Here the verb *hesychiazō* is employed not for refraining from speech, but rather for observing the sabbath strictures for rest. The noun form *hēsychia* is applied to women in 1 Timothy 2:11 in conjunction with *hypotagē* in a formula implying readiness to hear the word of God and to do it (see *ANET*).

The women are obedient to the Jewish laws but are willing to brave the Roman guard and the prohibition against women officiating at the burial of an executed criminal. They are also willing to take on the challenge of rolling back an exceedingly heavy stone that had been placed at the mouth of the tomb.

The account becomes a succession of electrifying images impressed on the memories of the startled women. The records of the four resurrection accounts are not entirely congruent, a phenomenon that often occurs after a highly emotional, confusing and terrifying event. There is agreement on the main points, with each contributing individual recollections of what must have been a wider picture than any of the narratives reflect. All of the accounts insist that women were the first witnesses of the risen Christ, and all contain the instruction that they were to proclaim the news to the male disciples.

In Luke's account the women enter the tomb that lies open before them and discover that the body of Jesus is missing, though they had observed its placement there. At the appearance of the angels, the women "lower their eyes" (JB) or "bowed their faces to the ground" (Lk 24:5).

There is no encounter between Jesus and the women. Rather, the angel reminds the women that Jesus has prepared them to be the witnesses of the resurrection. While they were still in Galilee, he had taught them of the necessity of his death and rising again on the third day. Then it was that the women remembered. Like the male disciples, they had apparently found Jesus' prophecies of his death too painful, and they had put them from their minds (cf. Lk 9:21-22, 44-45; 18:31-34). Now, comprehending what it was that he had foretold, they hurry off to make their joyful announcement to the Eleven and to those gathered with them.

The women accomplish the mission of declaring the news that the men refuse to accept. Just as they had resisted the threefold prediction of Jesus, so now they repudiate the news that the women bring. Peter is able to substantiate the fact that the tomb is empty of the body although the grave clothes remain. He returns incredulous but unwilling to accept the angels' testimony that the women have relayed to him.

The Visitation on the Way to Emmaus (Lk 24:13-35)

In the afternoon of the same day, two disciples are traveling along the road to the nearby town of Emmaus. The walk is not a pleasant one, for they are arguing bitterly. A stranger overtakes them and asks about what subject they were hurling speeches back and forth at each other *(antiballō)*. They cease the dispute, but their expressions remain sullen *(skythrōpoi)*.

Still in a resentful mood, Cleopas begins to explain to the uninformed stranger the improbable state of affairs that has developed over the death of Jesus of Nazareth. If this Cleopas is the same person as Clopas whose wife observed the crucifixion (Jn 19:25), then it may well be that the person with whom he was quarreling was his wife. As he relates the report of the women and the corroboration of their story by the men who later visited the empty tomb, his skepticism shows through.

At this point the stranger bursts in with a rebuke for the failure to accept the word of the women. Their testimony reveals the fulfillment of all that the prophets have foretold of God's design for human redemption through the death and resurrection of Messiah. Jesus, the unidentified stranger, launches into a confirmation of the women's report by an exposition of the

Scriptures concerning himself. The issue is one of God's promises, conveyed first by the ancient prophets and then by the terrified but faithful women.

Luke's account has presented women as the primary witnesses of the birth, crucifixion and resurrection of Jesus Christ. They are followers who accompany his ministry and faithful friends who attend him even in death. When the qualifications for an apostle are listed, it is clear that Jesus' women disciples possess the necessary qualifications (Acts 1:21-22).

Bibliography. C. Keener, *The IVP Bible Background Commentary: New Testament* (Downers Grove, IL: IVP, 1993); I. H. Marshall, *Commentary on Luke,* NIGTC (Grand Rapids, MI: Eerdmans, 1978); B. E. Reid, *Choosing the Better Part? Women in the Gospel of Luke* (Collegeville, MN: Michael Glazier/Liturgical Press, 1996).

CATHERINE CLARK KROEGER

JOHN

Introduction

Reading the Gospel of John is like standing between two full-length mirrors: the view is infinite before and behind. The ever-repeated reflections of reflections strongly impel you to that conclusion, even though the images eventually become too small to be seen. Somehow, you know that that is not all there is; it is only the limit of your physical vision. The Gospel of John is just such an image of Jesus, in several senses. First, the Gospel writer (hereafter called John) literally takes infinity as the temporal scope of the story. The earthly life and ministry of Jesus are recounted, but the narrative is not limited to those years. John tells this story against the backdrop of the history of Israel, particularly Moses and the prophets. Thus the author keeps the historical past always in view. Beyond this, John also gazes continually toward prehistory: "In the beginning was the Word" (Jn 1:1). Before the creation, Jesus was God's Word, God's self-revelation.

The Gospel also addresses the problems that have arisen in the author's time, when the Gospel was being written, well after the crucifixion. It looks over that horizon, however, across geography and time, to speak to the modern reader. The story does not stop even there but maintains a continual awareness of the risen Christ, the Jesus who lives from eternity, for eternity and for the eternal life of the believer.

There is yet more to the double mirror. This Gospel is multilayered in time and in meaning. Jesus' actions and teachings give an earthly account, a spiritual account and a reflection on the impact of both on the current reader. For example, we are given a traditional account of Jesus conversing with the woman at the well. The larger subject of the story is the way in which any person might obtain eternal life (symbolized by "living water"), thereby informing the modern reader that Jesus is the source. Each such narrative is punctuated by the use of double and triple entendres in the vocabulary. Although these terms are often evident in English, they are more striking in the original Greek. For example, in John 4:11-14, the word for the source of water used by the woman means "artificial well" and emphasizes the seemingly still water into which one lowers a jar. However, the word used by Jesus means "spring," or running water, and symbolically, the Holy Spirit and eternal life. The multilevel nature of terms and of narratives makes this Gospel available to any reader, however theologically (un)sophisticated. But such a complex literary and theological style is the result of the author's long and deep incubation rather than of literary skill alone.

The Purpose of the Fourth Gospel

The totality of the Gospel, however complex, serves a single purpose. This purpose is announced in John 1:12: "To all who . . . believed in his name, [Jesus] gave power to become children of God." It is restated in John 20:31 as the capstone of the narrative: these things have been written "that you may come to believe that Jesus is the Messiah, the Son of God, and that through believing you may have life in his name." Becoming God's child is not like being given life through natural birth. It is a matter of birth from above, spiritual nurture and an eternal heritage. The theme of birth is of central importance as a metaphor for the purpose of the book.

To accomplish this purpose, John builds and shapes the reader's knowledge of what does and does not constitute true faith and discipleship. In part this is done by contrasting the reactions of various characters with one another. In part it is done by a series of powerful literary devices, in particular ironies, misunderstandings, comments directed specifically to the reader and insider language, theological meanings known only to the community of the faithful. Often these four devices are combined. One example is John 11:49-53. The high priest explains why Jesus must die without realizing that he is stating God's purpose in it. The author then explains the real meaning to the reader, and the irony of the story becomes self-evident. A prominent insider term in John is that Jesus must be "lifted up." The faith community, unlike those in the story, know that the phrase refers to Jesus lifted up physically on the cross, and lifted up spiritually, since his death is inseparable from his glorification by God. The phrase also has another sense that transcends this distinction: lifted up in his resurrection. All of these literary devices contribute to the reader's sense of being an insider in the company of this great witness to Jesus and thus superior in faith to those who lack understanding. The reader thus is given ownership in the true faith.

Author, Date, Place of Writing and Audience

The author is never named in the Gospel. The long-held traditional view is that the author was the Beloved Disciple, and that he was the apostle John. These assumptions are at least as old as the letters of the second-century bishop Irenaeus. A consensus about authorship no longer exists, however. Among the many views is that the author was a woman because of the treatment of women in the Gospel. In any case, the material in John bears traces of an eyewitness, such as its details of geography and conversation. For example, Jesus addresses his mother solely as "woman." Since these passages are unique in ancient Greek-language literature, the recorder of Jesus' words is unlikely to have invented this detail or made a mistake in this way.

It is virtually certain that John 21 was added later. John 21:20-23 answers a rumor that the Beloved Disciple would never die, implying that he had died by the time John 21 was written. The primary thematic element of John that is often thought to be late is the characterization of Jesus' divinity. This high christology is, however, the logical conclusion of such central elements as the author's opening statements of Jesus' true nature and the resurrection. The divine and human Jesus, the saving Christ, is the central revelation of Christianity. No matter when a particular christological phrase arrived in this Gospel, it cannot easily be dismissed (as often, in some branches of the modern church).

This Gospel was probably written in its present form at the end of the first century, after a period of oral transmission or transmission in segments. The concern about the disciples' conflict with "the Jews," for example, echoes the most pressing concern of the

Christian community in the 80s and 90s, when believers in Jesus were being thrown out of the synagogues and were becoming a distinct religious group. Other passages indicate that the temple had been destroyed, dating the writing after A.D. 70. However, the author's concern with this event does not imply that Jesus never prophesied the destruction of the temple (one possible implication of Jn 2:19, "destroy this temple, and . . . I will raise it up"). John's narrative reflects real disputes between Jesus and other Jews. However, this aspect of Jesus' ministry is highlighted all the more because of the circumstances of the Johannine community in the late first century, particularly the strife caused by their belief, voiced in the synagogues, that Jesus is divine.

The place of writing is not indicated in John. However, the way in which the locations are described indicates that the writer knew Jerusalem in detail but the readers did not. Hence the readers are outside of Jerusalem. The translation in the text of certain Hebrew or Aramaic terms indicates that the audience spoke Greek or Latin but not Hebrew or Aramaic. A traditionally accepted place of origin is Ephesus in Asia Minor. The audience for which the author wrote was distinctive among Christians of the time. This is evidenced by John's high christology, unique to this Gospel—the emphasis on the person of Jesus as the sole source of salvation. In addition, much of the material in John is different from that in the Synoptics, indicating a distinct set of traditions and sources.

Differences Between John and the Synoptics

Over the centuries, readers have attempted to harmonize Matthew, Mark and Luke with John. They cannot be harmonized because John differs in overall material, in the length and sequence of events, and especially in the nature of the Christ as preexistent Son of God rather than simply the one raised from the tomb. The need to reconcile the various Gospels is a modern problem and a misunderstanding of the nature of ancient writings. For the first-century writer or reader, differences do not imply that one or the other must be wrong or that the story as a whole must be fictional.

There are several reasons for this different attitude. History and the teachings of a great man or woman were passed down orally, but the keepers of the tradition—particularly the Jews—were extremely careful that the oral narrative be faithfully preserved. However, it was customary for additional traditions to be added alongside the old, even if they differed. Look, for example, at the two different yet complementary creation stories in Genesis 1 and Genesis 2. Also, with the passage of time, the communities that depended on these traditions placed the emphases differently to answer the new questions presented by their situation. Finally, as John 20:30 says, "Jesus did many other signs . . . which are not written in this book." The tradition about Jesus that is preserved in John should be seen as complementary to that of the Synoptics. Each Gospel is a theological representation of the person and work of Christ. With this point of view, the reader can savor all of the Gospels as contributions to the question Who is Jesus?

The particular differences between John and the Synoptics include the following. Unlike the Synoptics, John's christology renders belief in eternal life or other promises secondary to the person of Jesus. In John the appearance of the Son of God on earth, in mortal as well as resurrected form, is the evidence that the kingdom is already being realized for believers. This stance is alluded to in Luke, but it is everywhere in John.

In John, Jesus' ministry extends for three years as opposed to the one implied in the Synoptics. Also, in John, most of his ministry is conducted in and around Jerusalem rather than in Galilee. Unique to John are the designation of the miracles as "signs"; the "I am" statements of Jesus; places and people such as Cana, Nicodemus, the Samaritan woman, Lazarus and the Beloved Disciple; the association of Jesus with the paschal lamb; the appearance of the mother of Jesus at the cross; and Mary Magdalene in the garden after the resurrection. Unlike Matthew and Luke, John contains no birth story of Jesus, although the reader is expected to know of Jesus' birth.

John contains no exorcisms, no mystical experiences such as the transfiguration, no Sermon on the Mount (Matthew) or on the plain (Luke), no explicit establishment of sacraments and no messianic prophecies. The mother of Jesus is never named, and Jesus is never addressed by name by another person in the story. Most of the conversations and healings in John do not appear in the Synoptics, although all of the Gospels share the story of the passion. The command to love one another as Jesus has loved the believers is nowhere so prominent as in John. Love is the way in which the believers will be known.

Unlike the Synoptics, John contains no explicit reference to the Sadducees, the priestly party whose power was based in the temple. However, the Pharisees (the legal experts) are prominent. Further, the crucifixion is blamed on "the chief priests and Pharisees." John refers to "the Pharisees" eighteen times—sixteen of which show them driving the crucifixion and directly influencing those called "the Jews" against Jesus. The significance of this emphasis is twofold. First, it supports the assumption that the Gospel was written after the destruction of the temple; then the base of the Sadducees' power was gone. At that time, the Pharisees had become the leaders of Judaism, reformulating Judaism around the law and the synagogue.

Second, John has made an explicit distinction between "the Jews" in general and "the Pharisees." If we include Nathanael ("an Israelite") and Nicodemus ("a ruler of the Jews"), John has nine references to "the Jews" that show them believing in Jesus, and only nine or ten showing them against Jesus. Two other passages show "the Jews" in favor of the crucifixion, but only under the strong domination of the Pharisees. The rest of the references to "the Jews" show them asking neutral or challenging questions of Jesus—a time-honored manner of engaging in theological debate, preserved for us in the Talmud (Jewish law as it was later put into writing). Thus, unlike the Synoptics, John makes a strong distinction: some particular leaders of the Jews determined to kill Jesus, but the Jews in general, including their customs and feasts, are affirmed.

John and Women

Commentaries on the Fourth Gospel as a document of significance for women tend to focus on Jesus' interactions with women. The major insights from this type of work have included the following. Women's inclusion in the narrative, especially in conversation with Jesus, bestows on them an importance beyond their status in the cultures of the first century. Each woman appears at a point in the narrative where the author is bringing Jesus' ministry to a new level. For example, the conversation with the Samaritan woman becomes the occasion for Jesus' revelation that he is the Messiah. Women are given a unique place in the Johannine community, as exemplary disciples and as full-fledged apostles. Mary Magdalene is the premier example. In Paul's letters (written several decades before John), the two criteria of apostleship are to have seen the risen Jesus and to have been sent to proclaim him. John 20:17-18 presents Mary Magdalene as the one person in John who most closely fits these criteria. Further, she makes the prototypical apostolic announcement of the resurrection: "I have seen the Lord."

Apart from these special roles given to women in John, it is probable that modern readers undervalue the traditional roles of women seen in John and in ancient Jewish society. Although women's sphere of action was usually the family, their role as the bearers of children—regarded by many as the means to immortality—was highly valued. In the Ten Commandments, father and mother are to be honored equally. The woman in the home also had a spiritual significance, one that is foreign to moderns. For example, as recorded in the Mishnah (an early, authoritative form of Jewish law expanding on the Pentateuch), Rabbi Phineas ben Hannah held that the woman in the home has an atoning force not inferior to the altar of sacrifice. Thus what the Johannine community bestows upon women is not good exchanged for bad, but one type of honor given along with another.

There is yet deeper significance for women in John's Gospel, however. A closer look at the Gospel will lead to further conclusions in this domain. Suffice it to say here that Jesus takes on, in deeply symbolic fashion, the roles of birthing mother and midwife. (For the characteristics associated with these roles in the ancient Near East, *see* Midwifery and Birthing Practices.) One striking example occurs in the raising of Lazarus, where Jesus employs the formula used by a midwife to bring to fruition a particularly difficult birth: "[Name], come forth!" Thus in John 11:43, Jesus commands, "Lazarus, come out!" and a man is born again from above (by divine power) and from below as well (from the grave). The inclusion of such an image in the Gospel makes the allusion highly pointed, particularly in view of the importance of John's theme of new birth.

No greater affirmation of womanhood can be given than for Jesus to take on a role that in the first century is strictly the province of women—and to do so as a part of his essential nature, being one with the Creator. Such imagery is not new with John, however. Romans, written several decades earlier, has the whole creation "groaning in labor pains" (Rom 8:22). In this text, the Holy Spirit is the midwife (Rom 8:26): "The Spirit helps us [i.e., to give birth; or, to be reborn] in our weakness." This image of God would have been clear to the first-century reader. For the modern reader, it is especially significant in juxtaposition with what may appear to be John's exclusive characterization of God as Father.

Before proceeding, we note that the modern feminist theologies have much to offer. However, theological conclusions from the use of the feminine in John are left to the reader. The task here is to present, as faithfully as possible, the content of John and its meaning in its first-century cultural context.

The Structure of the Fourth Gospel

Most commentaries today divide John into four sections: the prologue (Jn 1:1-18), a testimony to Jesus' true identity; the book of signs (Jn 1:19—2:25); the book of glory (Jn 13—20); and the epilogue (Jn 21). While this division is useful, it obscures structures that may indicate a point of connection with the Synoptics (to be discussed later). This structure is indicated below in the outline.

The book of signs is named for the seven signs or mighty works of Jesus recorded therein. Other genres of John that are commonly discussed in commentaries are the seven "I am" statements of Jesus, a number of controversies with a group called "the Jews" and several one-to-one conversations between Jesus and a character in the narrative.

Another genre, however, has received far too little attention—the confession of faith in Jesus. The confession is defined here as any statement by one or more persons that Jesus demonstrates divine attributes such as performing miracles (signs) or any statement by the author that someone believed in Jesus (thus must have confessed faith in him). Confessions can be seen as the skeleton of the narrative. The beginning and ending of John are confessions by the author. They are written specifically to propel the reader to confess Jesus as well. In between, the Fourth Gospel contains more than forty confessions by people in the story. These confessions represent the spectrum of belief, and cumulatively they form a paradigm of the purest type of confession.

Confessions are attributed to every group in the Gospel or their representatives. Almost all of the confessions are made by Jews, either called "Jews" in the immediate context or understood to be Jews, such as Jesus' disciples. This observation may seem to beg the question; nearly everyone in the Gospel is a Jew. The point is that in John, condemning the whole of "the Jews" is not the author's intent; probably the intent is to honor the Jewish roots of Christianity.

Tables 7 and 8 show where the confessions occur in relation to the signs, the one-to-one conversations, the controversies and the "I am" statements. (The list of confessions in the tables is intended to be comprehensive but not exhaustive.) The confessions in John 11:45—19:24 are shown in table 8. Separating this portion allows us to highlight the literary and theological patterns of the other sections, in which Jesus is engaged with a variety of present and potential disciples and enemies. The tables are to be read from left to right and downward, so as to reveal the placement in John of the various genres. The confessions merit a separate section; they will be discussed after a consideration of the way in which the tables reveal the overall structure of John.

Several great sweeps of John's argument can be discerned upon noticing the relationships among the texts listed in the tables. Among the signs, the changing of water to wine at Cana is the overall introduction of Jesus as Lord over all and as the real master of the wedding feast, that is, the marriage of God and God's people. The healing of the official's son and the healing of the invalid at the pool present Jesus as the healer of the present human condition. The next two signs, feeding the five thousand and walking on water, present Jesus as the Lord over nature and over earthly life. The healing of the man born blind and the raising of Lazarus demonstrate Jesus as the author of life (sight/blindness being considered a symbol of life). The "I ams" reveal Jesus metaphorically as the source of all things that are essential to human life—bread, light, security, life ("the resurrection and the life"; also the true vine, whose life flows out to its tendrils) and truth.

Further, the signs and the "I ams" interact with the controversies to create a series of larger images of Jesus' identity. Jesus' healing at the pool (the third sign) incites the first controversy. The controversy begins because the healing was on the sabbath but continues because the Jews are angry that Jesus makes himself equal with God. Ironically the first three signs have shown that he is. The next controversy begins with the feeding of the five thousand. The theme of bread continues through the great controversy in which Jesus offers his flesh and blood for the life of the world. The section concludes when many disciples decide no longer to follow him, specifically because of the first "I am": "I am the bread of life."

"I am the light of the world" incites further controversy about Jesus' identity and particularly his origin (with the Father). The controversy escalates and ends abruptly with Jesus' answer to the Jews at John 8:58: "Before Abraham was, I am." Jesus has used the name of God by implication as his identity while also saying that his origins are even greater than the man regarded as the earthly father of the Jews. This self-revelation is intended as spiritual light given to those who are ready to receive it. John returns explicitly to the theme of light in the sixth sign, the healing of the man born blind. This section ends with a powerful argument in which Jesus accuses the Pharisees of spiritual blindness, the opposite of Jesus' nature, light (true revelation).

In John 10, the theme changes to that of the gate of the sheep and the good shepherd. These images are central to the next controversy, which strongly implies that the Jews who challenge him may not be of his and God's flock. The controversy ends with Jesus' declaration of the purpose of the signs (Jn 10:37-38): "If I am not doing the works of my Father, then do not believe me. But if I do them, even though you do not believe me, believe the works, so that you may know and understand that the Father is in me and I am in the Father."

The final sign is preceded by the fifth "I am": "I am the resurrection and the life." Upon the demonstration that this is so—the raising of Lazarus—the ultimate controversy occurs, wherein Jesus' opponents cease debating with him and plan his death, fearing the political implications of the large group of people who have seen and believed this sign. The final two "I ams" are reserved for the disciples in private and contribute to the disciples' corporate confession of faith. But all discussion is over; the disciples and the enemies of Jesus have set their differing courses.

The Meaning and Character of the Confessions in John

Confessions occur in every chapter except John 13—15 and John 17. The confession is defined broadly, in part so that this list will include the ones Jesus acknowledges as such. The disciples' confession in John 16:29-31 is a good example: " 'By this [that

Table 7. Confessions in 1 John 1:1—11:44; 19:25—21:24

Chapter	Signs	Conversations	Confessions of Faith in Jesus and Implied Confessions	Controversy	"I Am"
1			[D1] 1:1, 14, 29, Evangelist: "the Word was God" . . . Jesus is the Son of God (the Word) [D1] 1:29, John the Baptist ("Lamb of God"); 1:34 ("Son of God); cf. 3:22-26 [D1] 1:49, Nathanael ("Son of God," "King of Israel")		
2	2:1-11, water to wine at Cana		[I1] 2:11, "his disciples believed in him" because of the wine		
3		3:1-21, Nicodemus	Nicodemus never confesses Jesus as Christ, though he acknowledges that Jesus must have come from God, 3:2; cf. 7:50 [D1] 3:22-26, John the Baptist ("given from heaven")		
4	4:43-54, healing of official's son	4:4-26, Samaritan woman	[D1] 4:19, woman, "a prophet" [U] 4:26, Jesus confesses his messiahship to the woman [D1] 4:39-42, the other Samaritans ("Savior of the world")		
5	5:1-15, healing, pool of Bethesda		[D2] 5:15, man tells the Jews it was Jesus who healed him	5:16-47, "the Jews" are angry because Jesus made himself equal with God; Jesus answers that all that he does and says is from God	
6	6:1-15, feeding five thousand 6:16-24, walking on water		[I1] 6:14, people who want to "make" Jesus king because of the bread—a parallel and precursor of "King of the Jews" (18—19). Both "confess" Jesus as a solely earthly king (cf. 18:36, "my kingdom is not from this world") 6:66, "Because of this many of his disciples . . . no longer" followed Jesus [D1] 6:69, Peter, "Holy One of God"; however, in 18, he denies Jesus three times.	6:25-65, "the crowd"; "the Jews" dispute Jesus' offer of true bread	6:35, "I am the bread of life"

7			[I2] 7:12-13, "the crowds" are divided but did not speak publicly "for fear of the Jews" Ironic, 7:25-27 ("the people of Jerusalem"): "Can it be that the authorities really know that this is the Messiah? Yet we know where this man is from; but when the Messiah comes, no one will know where he is from." They do not know where Jesus comes from, heaven or Bethlehem. [I1] 7:40-41, the Jews, "prophet," "Messiah"; Jews divided Ironic, 7:42, "But some asked, . . . 'Has not the scripture said that the Messiah is descended from David and comes from Bethlehem . . . ?" (so how can Jesus be the Christ? cf. 7:52)	7:14-24, Jesus tells "the Jews" that all that he does is from the Father 7:25-31, "the people of Jerusalem" ask if Jesus can be the Christ 7:32-39, "the Pharisees" are hostile; Jesus tells them they cannot come where he is going	
8			[I1] 8:30, many of the Jews put their faith in Jesus	8:13-59, "the Pharisees" and some of the Jews dispute who are children of Abraham versus the devil	8:12, "I am the light of the world"
9	9:1-12, healing the man born blind		[I1] 9:16, Pharisees divided; some believed [D1] man born blind: 9:17, "prophet" 9:33, "if this man were not from God, he could do nothing" 9:38, to Jesus: "I believe" (in you, the Son of Man)	9:40-41, Jesus accuses "the Pharisees" of spiritual blindness	
10			[I1] 10: 40-42, many of the people believed in Jesus (all that John the Baptist had said about him)	10:22-39, "the Jews" want to know whether Jesus is the Christ; Jesus uses the shepherd metaphor	10:9, "I am the gate" 10:11, 14, "I am the good shepherd"
11	11:38-44, Lazarus's resurrection	11:17-44, Martha, sister of Lazarus	[D1] 11:27, Martha, "I believe that you are the Messiah" [I1] 11:45, many of "the Jews" put their faith in Jesus after Lazarus was raised		11:25, "I am the resurrection and the life"

Table 7—*Continued*

Chapter	Signs	Conversations	Confessions of Faith in Jesus and Implied Confessions	Controversy
19:25-42			[U] 19:35, "he who saw this": "His testimony is true," and "he has testified so that you also may believe" [I2] 19:38, Joseph of Arimathea, "who was a disciple of Jesus, though a secret one because of his fear of the Jews"	
20	20:1-29, Jesus' resurrection	20:1-2, 10-18, Mary Magdalene 20:26-29, Thomas	[I1] 20:8, Beloved Disciple "saw and believed," but he and Peter still did not understand [D1] 20:18, Mary Magdalene, "I have seen the Lord" [I1] 20:20, Disciples acknowledge Jesus after seeing his wounds [D1] 20:28, Thomas, "My Lord and my God" [D1 or 2] 20:29-31, author, prompting readers' confession	
21		21:13-19, Peter	[D1 or 2] 21:15-17, Peter makes threefold confession that he loves the Lord [U] 21:24, the writer of 21 about the writer/witness of 1—20: "This [the Beloved Disciple] is the disciple who is testifying to these things. . . . We know that his testimony is true"	

Types of Confessions (see descriptions p. 594):
D1 = Direct type 1
D2 = Direct type 2
I1 = Indirect type 1
I2 = Indirect type 2
Ironic
U = unique

Table 8. Confessions in John 11:45—19:24

Chapter	Signs	Conversations	Confessions of Faith in Jesus and Implied Confessions	Controversy	"I Am"
11:45-57			Ironic, 11:47-48, Pharisees acknowledge Jesus' miraculous signs and that everyone will believe in him		
12			Ironic, 12:10-11, plot to kill Lazarus as well as Jesus because so many put their faith in Jesus [I1] 12:17-18, the crowd vote with their feet and come out to greet Jesus [I2] 12:42, despite unbelief of the Pharisees, "many [of the Jews] believed in [Jesus]" but would not say so openly		
13—17			[D1] 16:29-30, the disciples, "You came from God" (with 16:31, "Do you now believe?")		
18:1—19:24			Ironic, 18:33, 38-39; 19:14-16, 19-21, repeated "King of the Jews"		

Jesus knows all things] we believe that you came from God.' Jesus answered them, 'Do you now believe?' " Jesus immediately tells them that they are about to desert him, which might seem to negate their confession except that Jesus does not reject the confession per se. To understand the power and purpose of the confession genre, the various types of confession must be made clear. There are six types of confession; the tables contain an indication of each type. The types are defined as follows.

Direct type 1 consists of a quotation that ascribes a messianic title to Jesus or contains the words "I believe." The titles are usually "Christ," "Son of God," "King of Israel," "King of the Jews" or "the [or a] prophet."

Direct type 2 consists of a statement in which an individual is reported to have testified about Jesus. In Greek grammar, there is no formal difference between a direct quotation ("he said, 'X' ") and an indirect one ("he said that . . . "). The major difference from direct type 1 is that type 2 is often stated to people other than Jesus.

Indirect type 1 consists of a collective subject ("the crowd," "the Jews," "the people," "the disciples") plus a statement that the subjects believed or the equivalent.

Indirect type 2 confessions are distinguished by the fact that the person or group who believed did not admit faith publicly because of fear, usually of the Jews. Note that sometimes the Jews hold back their testimony for fear of a subgroup of the Jews, "the Pharisees" (e.g., Jn 12:42).

Ironic confessions are true statements indicating sincere belief in the divine attributes or actions of Jesus. However, they occur in the course of explaining why Jesus should be killed or in the argument over the sign on the cross that calls Jesus "the King of the Jews." John uses these ironies systematically and forcefully to proclaim a truth about Jesus.

In unique confessions Jesus confesses his messiahship (Jn 4:26) and the author looks back upon the Gospel and expresses belief (Jn 19:35; 21:24).

Considering the entire pattern of confessions, one particular literary structure becomes visible. In John 6:68-69, Peter confesses that Jesus has "the words of eternal life" and is "the Holy One of God." The author has placed this statement and its immediate context at the virtual center of the presentation of Jesus' public ministry. Although verse numbers are not original to the text, verse counts yield a reasonable approximation of how much of the text occurs before and after the passage. In John 1:19—11:57, there are 253 verses before the passage containing Peter's confession and 253 after it (through Jn 11:44, 240 verses). This verse count supports the thesis that the author placed Peter's confession in a highly deliberate way.

The book of signs therefore bears a literary affinity with the Synoptics, which is of considerable interest to Bible scholars. In each of the Synoptics, Peter's confession is at the center of the book. Jesus' public ministry ends with it, and the passion narrative follows almost immediately. In John, Peter's confession occurs at the center also, but at the center of the book of signs only (that is, of Jn 1—11). In the immediate context (Jn 6:67-68), Peter is upheld, as in the Synoptics, as the one true believer. However, he is divided within himself, later denying Jesus three times. Further, Peter's confession is ultimately portrayed as inferior in John's theology to that of Martha (see below).

Peter's confession in John further symbolizes division among the community. His confession immediately follows a unique statement: After Jesus had declared himself the bread of life, "many of his disciples turned back and no longer went about with him" (Jn 6:66). Thus new and sharp division among the disciples is the occasion of Peter's confession. The divisions among the other characters in the narrative can be seen from the placement of the various types of confession (see tables 7 and 8). The direct type 1 confessions are about equally divided on either side of Peter's confession. However, the indirect types 1 and 2 occur almost exclusively after Peter's confession; almost all of them state explicitly that the believers represent one faction of a sharply divided group. The divisions reach their peak with the ironic confessions, all of which occur after Peter's confession. These statements, condemning Jesus for his acknowledged divine attributes and actions, represent a powerful spiritual division in the hearts of those who pronounce the worst condemnations. Thus the placement of Peter's confession ultimately makes Peter the symbol and signpost of division.

Could it be that John had read one or more of the Synoptics and is responding or completing the story by echoing their literary device of centering Peter's confession with this particular twist? Even if John is not intentionally commenting on the Synoptics, Peter's confession and the distribution of confessions around it ultimately render what constitutes the purest form of confession in John. The disciples are seen to represent the spectrum from outright betrayal (Judas) to belief, denial and return (Peter), all the way to simple, loving presence with the person of Jesus (the Beloved Disciple at the Last Supper).

Another type of spectrum is represented in the pattern of confessions as well. After the prologue, John the Baptist's confessions (Jn 1:29, 34) provide a firm anchor by which other confessions may be judged. (Many scholars believe that the Johannine—John the apostle's—community was originally the followers of John the Baptist.) His confessions are matched only by that of Martha (Jn 11:27). Between John 1:29 and John 11:27, however, there is a general progression in the confessions. They begin with faith in Jesus occasioned by his works (seeing Nathanael under the fig tree; the changing of water to wine at Cana; the feeding of the five thousand). Then they begin to center on Jesus' promise of eternal life (Peter). Martha's confession is exemplary because she declares, "I believe that you are the Christ" before the resurrection of Lazarus. Hers is a faith in the person of Jesus; miracles and eternal life are neither the occasion nor the condition of her faith.

This crescendo of confessions is masterfully punctuated by the placement of the one-to-one conversations and the way in which they contrast with each other. These conversations also bring into high relief the role of women as disciples. In John, apart from John the Baptist's confessions, the women's confessions most consistently represent ideal statements of faith. For this reason, most of this commentary will dwell on the relationships among the conversations, particularly conversations with men versus women. Since exactly half of the conversations are with women, this analysis will provide some insight into the place of women among the Johannine community.

Outline

1:1-18	Prologue
1:19—11:44	Book of Signs
11:45—12:50	Transition, Physical and Symbolic
11:45-57	Final Plot to Kill Jesus
12:1-11	Jesus' Anointing
12:12-19	The Triumphal Entry into Jerusalem
12:20-36	Jesus' Prediction of His Death
12:37-50	Reaction and Response
13:1—20:31	Book of Glory
13:1—17:26	Jesus Speaks with His Disciples
18:1—19:24	Jesus' Trial and Crucifixion
19:25—20:31	Jesus Returns to His Disciples
21:1-25	Epilogue

Commentary

The Conversations in Relation to the Confessions

A conversation, for the purposes of this commentary, is a passage in which Jesus talks principally with one other person. Other people may be present but do not take part in the main conversation. An occasion and place are usually given. The person is usually named; one significant departure is when the mother of Jesus and the Samaritan woman are addressed, or referred to by John, only as "woman." This is often read as a distancing or deprecating title. However, it bears one of John's pregnant double meanings; it is part of an extended reference to the object of Jesus' coming, the new birth of the people of God. Conversations may be distinguished from controversies; in the controversies, usually a question is posed and Jesus answers in what is essentially a monologue. In the conversation, however, a statement or question begins the section, followed by a series of misunderstandings by the other person. Through his statements combined with the misunderstandings, Jesus reveals to the reader something essential about himself.

It is therefore important to understand the Johannine concept of the believer as disciple. By this concept we may judge how closely each conversant approaches ideal discipleship. Discipleship is based upon love of Jesus and of one another—and upon service begotten of love, the peak of which is to lay down one's life for one's friend. Disciples are further appointed to continue Jesus' mission to the world.

While there are criteria for human response to Jesus, the variety of confessions shows also that human virtue does not determine eligibility for the love of God. In the Old Testament, Zion is given its place of honor despite its frequent unfaithfulness. The Samaritan woman is accepted even in her earthly unfaithful state. Think of the story of the woman caught in adultery (Jn 8:1-11). Or think of Peter: he is to become the shepherd for the Shepherd despite his periodic unfaithfulness (Jn 21). God will bless faithfulness wherever it is offered.

Nicodemus and the Samaritan Woman

The first two conversations occur in John 3:1-21 (Nicodemus) and John 4:1-42 (the Samaritan woman). Among the conversants, Nicodemus is the only one who never expresses belief in Jesus as a result of the conversation. The scene begins with Nicodemus coming to see Jesus "at night." Nicodemus announces the seeker's faith: Jesus' miraculous signs must mean that he is "from God." This in itself is not unacceptable. Jesus' reply introduces the major theme of the conversation, that of being "born from above," "born again" or both. Jesus states further that to see the kingdom of God, a person must be born "by water and the Spirit." Nicodemus misunderstands each of these statements, seeing only the material, reductionistic sense of Jesus' words.

Jesus goes on to explain that only with the spiritual view of himself will the world understand and follow him. This passage contains the statement, so cherished by Christians, of God's purpose in sending Jesus (Jn 3:16): "For God so loved the world that he gave his only Son, so that everyone who believes in him may not perish but may have eternal life." This stunning pronouncement, juxtaposed with the lack of further response by Nicodemus, is intended to arouse the reader to a greater identification with the spiritual believer, the one who loves the light. This is opposed, by implication, to Nicodemus, who comes to Jesus in the darkness.

As the Gospel goes on, Nicodemus's lack of response to Jesus becomes the more meaningful. He appears only twice more. In John 7:45-52, soldiers sent by the Pharisees to arrest Jesus have returned without him, saying that no one has ever spoken as Jesus has. The Pharisees ask ironically, "Has any of the authorities or the Pharisees believed in him?" Nicodemus, "who was one of them," pointedly does not correct them but poses a question: Should we not hear him out before condemning him? The Pharisees reply with a taunt: "Surely you are not also from Galilee, are you?" Nicodemus remains silent. The second passage is John 20:39-40; Nicodemus and Joseph of Arimathea, who also has hidden his faith "because of his fear of the Jews" (Jn 19:38), claim and bury Jesus' body. Thus Nicodemus's faith in Jesus does not bring others to Jesus physically or religiously. He will not endanger his life or status by acknowledging Jesus. He thus fails the criterion in John 15:13 of giving one's life for a friend. Yet Nicodemus is of the most acceptable and honored social group. He is named, male, a Jew, a Pharisee, and a ruler and teacher of Israel.

The conversation with the Samaritan woman (Jn 4:1-30, 39-42) also revolves around a misunderstanding about water and the spirit. However, the woman could not contrast more sharply with Nicodemus. She is thoroughly unworthy in the view of the first-century Jews. A Jewish man did not engage in conversation with a woman to whom he was not related, a non-Jewish woman, anyone of disrepute or any Samaritan. Thus her status is as low as it can be. The lack of a name further emphasizes her apparent unimportance.

In the passage, Jesus is passing through Samaria at about noon and sits down to rest at the well of the patriarch Jacob. When the woman comes to draw water, he asks her for a drink. She expresses amazement that a Jewish man asks her for water. Jesus

Wells

For millennia, wells have provided water for communities, travelers and animals. A sign of prosperity and abundance in the biblical narrative (e.g., 2 Chron 26:10; Neh 9:25), wells have also proven to be significant meeting grounds, giving relief to emotionally and spiritually parched people.

In Genesis 16, the angel of the Lord discovers Sarai's runaway slave, Hagar, by a well (Heb. *beer*) in the desert. While ordering Hagar to return to her mistress, God simultaneously promises to multiply her descendents. In her pain and bewilderment, Hagar recognizes that God has not abandoned her but singled her out for blessing. Acknowledging God's mercy, she calls God "the living One who sees me" (Gen 16:13, authors' translation), the God who understands and meets her. The author of Genesis depicts Hagar relying on the same Hebrew naming formula as Adam and others, with the distinction being that she is naming God.

In Genesis 24, Abraham entrusts his oldest servant, presumably his most loyal and trustworthy helper, with finding Isaac a non-Canaanite wife. The servant turns to the God of his master for success in the mission. Arriving at a well in the town of Nahor, the servant prays that the woman who responds to his request for water by offering water to his camels as well as to him be God's choice for Isaac. Providentially, when the servant approaches Rebekah, she gives him a drink and waters his beasts of burden. The servant then discovers that Rebekah is a daughter of Abraham's nephew and eagerly returns with Isaac's future bride.

Fleeing for his life, Rebakah's son Jacob arrives at a well where flocks are waiting to be watered. The assembled shepherds point out to him the approach of his uncle Laban's daughter Rachel with her flocks. Jacob rolls back the stone, waters her sheep and is welcomed into Laban's home, where he ultimately claims Rachel as his bride (Gen 29:1-14).

In a similar vein, Exodus 2:15-21 tells the story of Moses fleeing Egypt and meeting his future wife, Zipporah, at a well in Midian. The day that Zipporah meets Moses, some local shepherds chase Zipporah and her sisters away. To the women's surprise, Moses then waters their flocks for them. When their father hears the news, Reuel (also known as Jethro) insists on inviting Moses to eat with them and ultimately gives his daughter Zipporah to Moses in marriage. While Moses is in exile, God begins to groom Moses for leadership by entrusting him with a family.

Catacomb fresco of the woman at the well. (John 4)

The New Testament builds on the Old Testament imagery. In John 4, wells once again serve as a place of meeting and rescue. In the heat of the noonday sun, Jesus sits by a well (Gk. *pēgē*) in Sychar and encounters a Samaritan woman who has come to fetch some water. In the course of the conversation, Jesus points to himself as the source of living water and draws out the spiritual thirst of a woman with a history of failed relationships. As they engage in a discussion of true worship, Jesus reveals that he is the Messiah, a truth she not only embraces but also shares with all of Sychar. On account of her witness, the whole town hears Jesus and many believe.

From Beer Lahai Roi ("The Well of the Living One Who Sees") to Jacob's well, God meets seekers and quenches their thirst in surprising ways.

GRACE YING MAY AND HYUNHYE JUNIA POKRIFKA-JOE

---

tells her that she should be asking him for water. Throughout, the woman understands and responds to Jesus on the most material level. However, upon hearing that he is offering eternal life, she responds by asking for some of it—albeit so that she can avoid the human task of drawing and carrying. Finally Jesus correctly tells her her marital status. She responds, "I see that you are a prophet," a high affirmation (Jn 4:19).

The subject then changes to a central point of contention between Jews and Samaritans: the place of true worship. Jesus responds that God will be worshiped neither in Jerusalem nor at the Samaritans' mountain, Gerizim. Rather, "the hour is coming, and is now here, when the true worshipers will worship the Father in spirit and truth" (Jn 4:23). Here we see a theological parallel with the cleansing of the temple. In that passage, upon being challenged by the Jews for disrupting the commercial activity there, Jesus answers, "Destroy this temple, and in three days I will raise it up"—at which the onlookers scoff (Jn 2:19). The author explains, "But he was speaking of the temple of his body" (Jn 2:21, and the raising of it, the resurrection). In John 2 and in the story of the Samaritan woman, Jesus is declaring that from his time on, no physical temple will be able to hold the Spirit. Jesus' body is the true locus of the Spirit of God and the appropriate object of worship.

In the temple cleansing, even the disciples fail to understand. In contrast, the Samaritan woman responds with heartfelt longing: "When [Messiah] comes, he will proclaim all things to us" (Jn 4:25). Jesus then declares, "I am he" (Jn 4:26). Literally this is, "I am, the one speaking to you," or "I am; the one speaking to you [is the 'I am']," using the name of God given to Moses (Ex 3:14). Thus the only pronouncement of Jesus' messiahship and an implicit identification of the Messiah with God is made to a woman, a non-Jew and a person of earthly disrepute, rather than to one of his own—because she is thirsty for that knowledge.

In contrast to Nicodemus, the Samaritan woman goes into the city and brings her fellow Samaritans to faith in Jesus. The story closes with the Samaritans' declaration that they now believe because of Jesus rather than the woman's testimony alone. They alone in this Gospel call him "the Savior of the world." The expanding awareness of Jesus' true identity—within one person, then within the community—is replicated for and in the reader by means of a literary device. This device, however, is also the author's witness to the reader; it is the escalation of christological titles throughout John 4:1-42. Jesus is first a Jew, then Lord, greater than Jacob, prophet, Messiah, Christ, the "I am" and "Savior of the world." In the structure of the narrative, the Samaritan woman has been used by the Lord to bring the reader along in faith. There is a similar escalation of christological titles by Jewish, male disciples in John 1:19-51. Perhaps John 4:1-42 also serves to show that the unacceptable woman and her people can be as spiritually perceptive and devout as those of whom it would be expected.

Thus this woman is fruitful for Christ, whereas Nicodemus is not. She contrasts with other disciples also because she enters into a theological discussion with Jesus. Characteristically in John, the male disciples are passively present; they fail in persistence; they leave the tomb upon finding it empty; and they fail to speak their mind to Jesus. This woman may be regarded as one of the sowers whose planting the other disciples are to reap. In a powerful way, one that defies social convention, she carries out the functions of a true disciple.

One other dimension of this story must be addressed: it incorporates Jewish imagery of sexuality and marriage (*see* Marriage). Each of the conversations with women contains such imagery. In this short study, there is not room to make all of this imagery explicit, but John 4:1-26 will serve as an example. In this story, "well" refers to the female (*see* Wells). In the Old Testament, the imagery of wells often refers to God's relationship with Israel (e.g., Prov 5:15-18; Song 4:12; Jer 2:1-15). Jesus' spring of living water (Jn 4:14) recalls God as "the fountain of living water" (Jer 2:13). Living water may also be construed as semen. (In ancient Jewish Palestinian culture, the male's semen was not considered to have greater value than the woman's equivalent contribution in procreation. It is Jesus' unique spiritual gift that is greater, and it is greater than the contribution of male and female alike.) In these terms, the Samaritan woman is a symbolic wife who brings to Jesus many offspring. Her disciple love for him is the love of the bride of Christ. Thus she is not only a woman, in the sense of being lowly. She is an active part of the rebirth by faith of God's new people. As a representative of the Samaritan community, she becomes a paradigm for any true disciple, man or woman.

Martha and Mary Magdalene, Thomas and Peter

Jesus' conversations with Martha (Jn 11:21-27, 38-40), Mary Magdalene (Jn 20:10-18), Thomas (Jn 20:24-29) and Peter (Jn 21:15-19) bear a complex relationship with one another. If we take the text as we have it, the Martha-Mary Magdalene pair forms a sharp contrast with the Thomas-Peter pair of conversations. A perusal of table *7* shows that these four conversations and those with Nicodemus and the Samaritan woman form brackets around the bulk of the confessions and punctuate them by demonstrating good faith and good praxis.

However, let us begin with the three conversations in the original ending of the Gospel. There is a definite progression among Martha, Mary and Thomas, with the purpose of specifying the truest form of faith. Martha accuses Jesus, "Lord, if you had been here, my brother would not have died" (Jn 11:21). Upon being told by Jesus that her brother will rise again, she acknowledges the resurrection on the last day. Jesus replies, "I am the resurrection and the life. . . . Do you believe this?" (Jn 11:25-26). Without hesitation and without requesting a miracle, Martha confesses, "I believe that you are the Messiah, the Son of God, the one coming into the world" (Jn 11:27). Thus she expresses the ideal faith in the person of Jesus, apart from any promise or miracle. This is, of course, the Jesus whose body is still mortal.

Mary Magdalene too is centered wholeheartedly on the person of Jesus, seeking his body. She will not desist, despite the other disciples' having left in confusion after seeing the empty tomb. Her tearful persistence is an embodiment of Jeremiah's prophecy: "If you seek me with all your heart, I will let you find me, says the LORD" (Jer 29:13-14). Having been called by name by the man she thought was the gardener, she recognizes him as the risen Jesus. When he commands her, she obeys immediately, going to tell all of the disciples, "I have seen the Lord" (Jn 20:18). She thus becomes the first to be sent by Jesus to witness to the resurrection and the first to witness to the other disciples (*see* Women as Witnesses). For this reason, she is often called the apostle of the apostles. Where Martha is considered the model of ideal faith, Mary Magdalene is considered to be the model of Christian praxis.

John contrasts Thomas with the two women who have looked so long for Jesus without asking for any personal demonstration. Thomas, having missed the appearance of the risen Christ to the other disciples, declares, "Unless I see the mark of the nails in his hands, and put my finger in the mark of the nails and my hand in his side, I will not believe" (Jn 20:25). This turns the paradigm of seeking Jesus upside down. Thomas has good reason to believe that Jesus is risen, but he puts a condition on his faith. The reader is thus predisposed by the author to recoil from Thomas's manner of expressing his faith. Nevertheless, Jesus accommodates Thomas, even using Thomas's words in granting his desire. Thus Jesus heals Thomas's petulantly expressed fear of disappointment and confirms his demand for a personal visitation. This is paradoxical; but with it, John has set in place everything that is required for his conclusion.

John wants the reader to believe all of the signs Jesus performs, including the resurrection. The reader's faith is to be based in large part upon the signs. For this reason John 20:31 says, "These [signs] are written so that you may come to believe that Jesus is the Messiah . . . and that through believing you may have life in his name." Beyond this, John wants the reader to know Jesus' boundless love for the believer, even when, like Thomas, the believer is not perfect in faith. However, John wants the reader to confess Jesus even in the absence of signs. If this point is not made, Martha's reward of Lazarus's resurrection and the appearance to Mary Magdalene might seem to foster a dependence on signs. In John's time, evidently this was becoming a problem for even the most ardent disciples.

This is the reason for Jesus' strangely formulated final word to Thomas: "Have you believed because you have seen me? Blessed are those who have not seen and yet have come to believe" (Jn 20:29). The disciple who will not believe without a sign is not disconfirmed. Thomas's ultimate recognition of Jesus is in fact a model for the reader: "My Lord and my God!" (Jn 20:28). John hopes that the reader will rise

Changing Life Circumstances

Women often have to change the circumstances of their lives. Some of these changes come because of personal tragedies, because children bring about much change in their lives or because their nurturing natures wish to meet the needs of those dependent on their love and care. As we face the need or desire to change the circumstances of our lives, we can look to role models in the Bible to give us the courage and the wisdom to handle the necessary changes.

A primary example of a biblical character who changed her life's circumstances is Mary Magdalene. Mary was from a small town south of the Plain of Gennesaret, Magdala. She was afflicted with either a mental disorder or was demon-possessed, a phenomenon that has been verified by medical science in modern times. There is little doubt that she must have been a reviled and ostracized woman in her hometown prior to her healing. When she came to Jesus for healing, she changed her life's circumstances. She became a powerful and poised figure who gave of her means as well as of herself to his ministry. Mary is mentioned fourteen times in the Gospels, and she holds the distinction of being the first to witness Jesus' resurrection. Mary didn't let her past deter her from developing into one of the Christian church's first woman leaders. As Edith Deen describes Mary, "We see a Mary Magdalene who displayed the highest qualities of fortitude in moments of anxiety, courage under trying circumstances, love that could not fail, and humility and unselfish devotion to the Saviour who had been crucified" (Deen, 204; many Bible scholars, Deen among them, have pointed out the erroneous identifications of Mary as the sinful woman described by Luke). As a result of her witness about Jesus' resurrection, she experienced a transformation in her life, from material to spiritual.

Other women of the Bible hold a valued place in the honor roll of courageous women who effectively changed their life's circumstances.

Rahab, the prostitute of Jericho, was wise enough to understand that the spies were sent by God—the God she didn't know but believed existed—and by assisting them she assured her survival in a turbulent and dangerous time (Josh 2).

The widow of Nain had the courage to step out of her subservient and maligned role and implore Jesus to heal her son, her only means of keeping her from destitution (Lk 7).

The Syrophoenician woman approached Jesus on behalf of her daughter. Jesus not only used her as an example of faith in action but also admired her courage to act out of character and therefore gain Jesus' blessing, resulting in the healing of her child (Mk 7).

Hagar may have been inappropriately and unjustifiably proud when she appeared to replace Sarah as the favored mother of a nation, but when she was cast out, she determined to find a place for herself and her son. Her will to survive adverse circumstances and change them serves as an example for all women who find themselves in a dilemma, even if the dilemma is partly a result of their actions (Gen 16).

Naomi and Ruth changed their life's circumstances. The loss of their husbands caused them to bond not just in their relationship as mother-in-law and daughter-in-law but as loyal, supportive friends. They overcame their sorrow and created new lives. Each encouraged the other, and they found new interests and expressions for their talents and exceptional characteristics. Therefore Ruth became an ancestor of Jesus, and Naomi found fulfillment in a new family.

Esther was an orphan who became the favored of the king in her land of captivity. She took a great risk in making her plea on behalf of her people, therefore changing not only her circumstances but also those of her people. Hers is a dramatic story of a woman who saw opportunities and had the will to change until she became revered in her time and throughout biblical and secular history.

This short honor roll is only a sampling of women who deserve to be listed because they overcame some of life's greatest difficulties and had the will to change their circumstances. Women of our time who find their lives restricted, hampered, even destroyed, can find no better role models than our spiritual, biblical ancestors.

Bibliography

E. Deen, *All the Women of the Bible* (San Francisco: Harper, 1955).

LILYA WAGNER

and say these resounding words along with Thomas, albeit without seeing signs beyond those that are written in this book.

If we add the conversation with Peter, additional dimensions of the message emerge. Martha and Mary Magdalene represent two stages of the nascent church's relationship with Jesus: when he has not yet died, and when he has risen. Thomas and Peter see the risen Jesus. However, Thomas is confronted against his unbelief, and Peter is in the convicting situation of having denied Jesus three times. Further, Thomas and Peter are related by their bravado; both have proclaimed that they will willingly die with Jesus. While this appears to be bravery, it expresses gloomy expectations and highlights their unfaithfulness. The two men—because of their explicit promise to die for Jesus—in the end explicitly deny to Jesus the most valued form of love (recall Jn 15:13). Thus Thomas and Peter contrast with the simple, acted-out devotion of Martha and Mary Magdalene.

Mary Magdalene contrasts with Peter in another way. When Jesus calls her by name (Jn 20:16), causing her to recognize him at last, the two act out the parable of the good shepherd (Jn 10). John 10:1-5 forms a metaphorical definition of discipleship: The good shepherd "calls his own sheep by name and leads them out. . . . The sheep follow him because they know his voice." As a true lamb of Jesus, Mary knows him because of his voice calling her by name—and she proceeds to feed his other sheep by declaring his resurrection. Peter, however, must be commanded three times to feed Jesus' sheep—after all of the opportunities for spontaneous imitation of the good shepherd, when the disciples had him to themselves, have passed. Thus Mary Magdalene implicitly becomes a lamb of God reflecting Jesus' true nature. This highly symbolic touch forms a closing bracket to the declaration of John the Baptist: "Here is the Lamb of God" (Jn 1:29). The lambs of God after the resurrection are to be God's people, and Mary Magdalene is their standard.

Martha, Mary Magdalene and the Twelve

The above brings us to a refinement of the definition of discipleship. It is a hallmark of John that the Twelve as such are not accorded singular status. The phrase occurs in only two passages. Peter and his confession are immediately juxtaposed with Judas, who "though one of the twelve, was going to betray [Jesus]" (Jn 6:67-71). The other reference is to Thomas, "one of the twelve" (Jn 20:24), just as he is about to state his conditional belief. Thus uniquely in John, "the twelve" represents the gamut of confessional stances. These stances are those of Judas, who betrays Jesus; Peter, who denies him; Thomas; and the other male disciples, who, though largely silent, remain with Jesus throughout his earthly ministry but desert him at the crucifixion. At the virtuous end of the spectrum is the Beloved Disciple, who represents the peak of true discipleship among the men. Though he is introduced only at the Last Supper, he is as much centered on the person of Jesus as Martha is—his only recorded acts being to lie against Jesus' breast at the Last Supper and to stand under the cross with Jesus' mother and other women. Thus "the twelve" are a symbol of division as well as of discipleship.

In respect of being true disciples in every sense, the women not only carry out the role but also are consistent, vocal and proactive in it. Yet this is not intended to portray men per se as of lesser faith. Recalling the bridal imagery of the passage about the Samaritan woman and noting that there is similar imagery elsewhere in connection with the women disciples, the import is this: The women are the bride of Christ, "the new Jerusalem . . . prepared as a bride adorned for her husband" (Rev 21:2). The women represent all true discipleship in the metaphor of the ancient prophets: God's people as God's true love. Hence the carefully placed references to certain disciples solely as "woman" (Jn 4:1-42; 2:4; 19:26) evoke the image of all who are devoted to Christ.

Nevertheless, a great honor has been bestowed upon women in John's use of the woman as disciple. This honor is intentional and is in direct line with the prophets, who made such a point of the unique place accorded to Jerusalem (Zion) as God's wife (*see* Israel as the Wife of Yahweh). It may be objected that this symbolic schema still leaves God in the image of the male. There is a strong theme in John of God as the Father of Jesus and of the believer. One of the most subtle but powerful messages in John for women derives directly from this fact, however. First, it should be said that none of the writers of the Bible intended us to use "Father" reductionistically, as if the Deity could be completely described in human terms. But further, in the culture out of which this Gospel comes, for John to use feminine imagery to define any of the functions of Jesus, who is one with the Father, is extraordinary. He does so in few but crucially placed instances. Besides the one where he is midwife to Lazarus, the most powerful of these are the imagery of birth and death relating to Jesus.

Jesus' Mother and Jesus as Mother

Jesus' two encounters with his mother, who is never named in John, contain John's most striking uses of the term *woman*. Unique in ancient Greek-language literature, Jesus' addressing his mother as "woman" can be understood only against the backdrop of the overall meaning of the woman as a metaphor for true discipleship. These encounters involve no real conversation and no misunderstandings and so do not fit our definition of a one-on-one conversation. However, they overlay the structure of confessions and conversations with another structure: the two exchanges bracket Jesus' ministry before his death on the cross.

The first encounter is part of the first sign, the provision of wine at the wedding in Cana (Jn 2:3-4). The passage says that when the wine provided by the host was gone, Jesus' mother "said to him, 'They have no wine.' " This statement of need without a direct request is a typical courteous form in which a Jewish woman of the time might ask a man for something (cf. Jn 11:3). From this point in the story, however, almost all translations confuse Jesus' answer in one way or another, attempting a nearly impossible idiomatic translation. Literally what Jesus says is, "What [is that] to me and to you, woman? My hour has not come."

If the reader takes the first part of the reply literally, it makes sense. Jesus is a guest, and in that culture a guest is not called on for such things; it is a matter of honor for the groom's family to provide wine. One might dishonor them by presuming that they could not do so. Against this cultural backdrop, however, if Jesus does provide the wine, he must be the bridegroom. This is one of John's two-story stories, as may be seen in the use of "woman" and "my hour." Each term has at least two meanings, and John uses them with literary precision. They open for us an alternative reading, without denying that just given.

Let us take first the direct address, "woman." John is uniquely marked by his direct address to the reader, and such direct address might occur anywhere in a narrative. Given that *woman* is a term that, by the end of the Gospel, means the true believer of either gender, it is possible that the author records Jesus speaking to his mother and, as the author, addresses all believers. If so, John is asking the believer a pointed and highly charged question: What *is* this to you and to me? Thereby he says, Notice this! "This" is the lack of wine and the miracle that is about to happen. The real question is What is the significance of these things in Jesus' life and in yours? If you cannot answer, you have not understood; you are not an insider. The correct answer is In this sign, I, Jesus, show you my identity. (Hence through this miracle, Jesus "revealed his glory; and his disciples believed in him," Jn 2:11.)

Such a communication to the reader is the more likely because of the presence of the phrase "my hour." This phrase is used in only two ways in John. It refers to Jesus' ultimate purpose, his death and new birth for the sake of the believer's rebirth. It also refers to the woman's hour, the hour of giving birth. The latter, however, is a metaphor for Jesus' leaving (his death) and its effect on the disciples (Jn 16:21). This usage is further interpreted in John as the hour in which God will glorify Jesus and in which God is glorified. Jesus' glory will be ironically reflected in the sign over the cross, The King of the Jews. However, the theme of glorification is most poignant in John 12:27-28, the closest passage in John to the scene at Gethsemane. Jesus says, "Now my soul is troubled. And what should I say—'Father, save me from this hour'? No, it is for this reason that I have come to this hour. Father, glorify your name." Thus the seemingly incongruous mention of his hour during the wedding at Cana is an example of familiar insiders' language. It tells us that Jesus' death and resurrection are the theological subject of the wedding story.

As the story goes on, Jesus' mother says, "Do whatever he tells you"—another word to characters in the story but also to the reader (Jn 2:4). Upon Jesus' command, the servants fill stone jars with water and present some of it to the master of the banquet. The master calls the bridegroom and says, unlike everyone else "you have kept the good wine until now," that is, until the end (Jn 2:10). This is the end of the banquet and the end of the Gospel story, the crucifixion and resurrection. The water and wine, usually assumed to be red wine, serve a double purpose. One of John's purposes in writing was to dispel the Gnostic heresy that Jesus seemed to be human but was solely spirit from the beginning. The water and wine are symbols of the genuine, earthly water and blood that are shed during earthly birth. They also foreshadow the blood and water that will flow from Jesus' earthly body on the cross. The presence of Jesus' mother, addressed as "woman," reinforces the reader's association of the wedding at Cana with Jesus' natural birth, even while he is performing the first sign that will evidence his divinity. This complex of symbols thus affirms the incarnation. The Christian doctrine that Jesus is fully divine and fully human is strongly defended in these texts. Also, in Jesus' first miracle the story of God's purpose, worked out through Jesus' birth, death and resurrection, is presented *in nuce.*

In the other appearance of Jesus' mother (Jn 19:25-27), we read that only she, three other women, including Mary Magdalene, and the Beloved Disciple stayed with Jesus at the cross. Jesus presents his mother and the Beloved Disciple with each other as a new family. It is significant that literally Jesus "says to the [not his] mother, 'Woman, behold your son' . . . [and] to the disciple, 'Behold your mother.'" "Behold" is a revelatory formula; it is not simply "here is," as in many translations. These commands to Mary and the Beloved Disciple double as prophetic pronouncements for the reader. To Jesus' mother and to the believer (the symbolic mother, the one who bears fruit for God), Jesus is also saying, "Behold your Son—behold me on the cross." He reinforces this by a command to the disciple, including the reader, to behold his new mother—*also* Jesus on the cross, about to shed his blood for the new birth of the world.

Now comes the climax: Jesus gives up his spirit (Jn 19:30). Then a soldier pierces his side with a spear, "and at once blood and water came out" (Jn 19:34). This text is the mirror image, in a sense, of the miracle at Cana. The blood and water at his death are commonly taken as a reference to Jesus' natural birth as well as to his natural death, reinforcing the theological point already made. However, if this is birth imagery, it is that in the fullest sense (*see* Birth Pain Imagery). Jesus understood his death, its manner and its effect on the believer in this way (Jn 16:21-22): "When a woman is in labor, she has pain because her hour has come. But when her child is born, she no longer remembers the anguish because of the joy of having brought a human being into the world." The crucifixion is thus presented metaphorically as Jesus' going away to give birth to God's people. Like a woman in labor, he pours out his blood for the life of the world. This is why, just after the flow of water and blood, the author stops the story to reinforce its importance: "(He who saw this has testified that you also may believe. His testimony is true, and he knows that he tells the truth.)" (Jn 19:35). The theological point of Jesus as birthgiver could not be made more strongly than in the repetition of this imagery in the two pericopes involving Jesus' mother.

There is one more element in the death of Jesus. This is symbolically the last birth in which the mother will experience anguish and pain. John may be alluding in this imagery to Isaiah 66:7-11, one of the most graphic prophecies of the new creation in the Old Testament. Isaiah 66 is one of two passages (along with Ps 22) in which God is described as midwife (*see* Midwifery and Birthing Practices). It is also a promise that when the new creation is complete—for John's community, that means in the resurrection—it will be as it was before the Fall of humankind. Isaiah 66:7 says, "Before she [God's people, Zion] was in labor she gave birth." The curse of painful birth will be reversed; God's people are freed from the effects of the Fall. Thus in the manner of Jesus' death, he takes on the ultimate and most deeply honored role of the woman, that of birthgiver. He takes on and incipiently takes away the pain, the curse of disobedience to God, not only for women but also for the whole world.

Since God is the author and presider over this death and birth (e.g., Jn 19:11), further Old Testament allusion may be present here. Psalm 22:9 says, "You [God] . . . took me from the womb; you kept me safe on my mother's breast." It is notable in this context that in Matthew 27:46 and Mark 15:34, Jesus on the cross quotes Psalm 22:1, "My God, my God, why have you forsaken me?" Matthew and Mark thus make Jesus the speaker of this psalm—the one who is brought forth from the womb by God. There are further complex quotes and allusions to Psalm 22 in these three Gospels' account of the passion. For example, in John, Jesus' flow of blood and water alludes to Psalm 22:14, "I am poured out like water." Thus John, perhaps having read these other Gospels, may be naming God as the midwife of the new creation birthed by Jesus on the cross and of Jesus, reborn from the tomb.

The image of God as midwife to the one who is simultaneously dying, giving birth and about to be reborn is striking, particularly to the reader who knows the Old Testament. Much of John's language is metaphorical, but being so, is the more true than what is humanly inexpressible. God is Father, but to limit God to the role of an earthly man is reductionistic, almost blasphemous: God is Creator. God therefore is also midwife and birthgiver, and these roles are far from incidental. Thus John punctuates the male images of Jesus and the Father with profound images of the feminine—the more powerful because of their placement at the beginning and end of Jesus' earthly ministry.

Conclusions

Several general statements may now be made about the theology of the Fourth Gospel. First, belief in Jesus Christ will produce divisions in the community of which the faithful are a part. John is particularly concerned to tell the faithful: Do not give up. God is with you, and Jesus Christ has already brought you to the door of the kingdom (that is, to himself).

Second, from the time of the earthly Jesus on, no temple or other physical location will be able to hold the Lord or be sufficient for true spiritual worship. The cleansing of the temple, the discussion with the Samaritan woman and the story of the man born blind being outcast from the synagogue all attest to this point. Similarly, ideal faith does not reside exclusively in any one ethnic or social group or stratum—Jews, Samaritans, Gentiles, men, women, faithful, sinful, well or sick. All who believe in his name have the right to become the children of God.

Third, the Fourth Gospel is not anti-Semitic, since the full range of unbelief and belief in Jesus Christ is shown in Jews and non-Jews alike. It is also not nearly so exclusively male-dominated as it may seem on first glance. Women's roles in the Fourth Gospel as well as the feminine imagery used to describe Jesus show that the feminine response to God, as well as women's contributions to the community of the faithful, are to be greatly honored. Given the roles of Jesus' women disciples in John, bias against women's leadership in the church is not an appropriate response to John's Gospel. However, Jesus transcends the birth processes of men and women. The believer is to be born of God; next to that, human birth and human gender are secondary as a source of worth. Thus the spiritual potential of all humankind is affirmed, and this is the greatest reason to affirm the spiritual callings of all believers.

Bibliography. R. E. Brown, *The Community of the Beloved Disciple: The Life, Loves and Hates of an Individual Church in New Testament Times* (New York: Paulist, 1979); E. Schüssler Fiorenza, *In Memory of Her: A Feminist Theological Reconstruction of Christian Origins* (New York: Crossroad, 1983), particularly "The Gospel of John," 323-34. This book also contains a detailed description of the many social and religious roles of women in the ancient Mediterranean area. L. Morris, *The Gospel According to John,* New International Commentary on the New Testament, rev. ed. (Grand Rapids, MI: Eerdmans, 1995); D. M. Smith, *John,* Abingdon New Testament Commentaries (Nashville: Abingdon, 1999); B. Witherington III, *Women in the Ministry of Jesus: A Study of Jesus' Attitudes to Women and Their Roles As Reflected in His Earthly Life* (Cambridge: Cambridge University Press, 1984).

KAMILA A. BLESSING

ACTS OF THE APOSTLES

Introduction

If Acts were a novel, it would be a blockbuster thriller. It has all the ingredients of a gripping tale: intrigue and suspense; dramatic escapes; exotic travel; the extraordinary and the bizarre rubbing shoulders with the mundane; and the ultimate triumph, against all the odds, of the heroes and heroines of the piece.

Of course, Acts isn't a novel—it's an extraordinary, remarkably accurate historical record. It covers the period from around A.D. 33 to around A.D. 65, and it was probably written sometime in the early 70s or possibly a little later. But like a novel, Acts well repays reading straight through or at least in satisfying, long sections, so that the reader is immersed in the drama and the flow of the story. Reading disjointed snippets dulls our senses and leaves us unaware of how amazing is the tale that is unfolding.

This story, which spans a mere thirty years, takes us from the ascension of the Lord Jesus Christ into heaven to a point at which the fledgling church has turned the world upside down. It takes us from a small, dejected and fearful band of disciples hidden behind locked doors in Jerusalem to many thousands of believers established in worshiping congregations throughout Palestine, Asia Minor and Greece, and even as far away as Rome, the center of the great empire. It takes us from a group bewildered at the absence of their human companion and leader, Jesus, to a vast community confident in the constant presence of the Holy Spirit. And it takes us from a fundamentally monocultural Jewish sect to a multicultural predominantly Gentile religion.

Moreover, it records that all this happened in the context of growing persecution and resistance. This hostility was primarily because the early Christians in general, and the apostles in particular, insisted that Jesus Christ had been raised by God from the dead, thereby proving his unique right to offer salvation on the one hand and judgment on the other. This Jesus was no less than sovereign Lord of the whole earth, before whom every person and every religion must give way. Even Caesar came under his authority. No wonder there was opposition!

Luke, the author, tells us (Acts 1:1-2) that Acts is the sequel to his Gospel; but, whereas we have four Gospels, this is the only historical record of the birth and early growth of the church. It is crucial not only for the history that it is but also in setting the context for the Epistles that follow. It shows us, for example, how the churches to which the Epistles are addressed began and against what background; it tells us who Timothy was; and it describes the persecution experienced by congregations such as those to which Peter wrote. It is crucial in showing us how the church, led by the Holy Spirit, made the huge transitions mentioned above. And it is crucial in establishing for us many important principles as we too seek to live for Jesus Christ in our diverse contexts. But most of all it is crucial in demonstrating that Jesus Christ, crucified, risen and ascended, is the fulfillment of all past history and promise and the pivotal figure for all humanity in the present and the future.

At first glance it might seem that Luke is not interested in women, inside or outside the church. Certainly men—Peter, John, James, Philip, Barnabas, Paul, Festus and

Agrippa—stride through the story. Yet to conclude that Acts marginalizes women would be to be guilty of superficial judgment. In the world in which the events of Acts take place, and especially in the public world of debating in the marketplace or standing up and teaching in the synagogue, it could not be otherwise than that men hold the stage. In any case, Luke's primary purpose is not to provide an apologetic for women's equality in the church but to continue the "orderly account [begun in the Gospel] . . . so that you may know the truth concerning the things about which you have been instructed" (Lk 1:3-4 NRSV). The central concern of that account is to establish the identity and credentials of the Lord Jesus Christ and the reliability of the apostolic teaching about him.

Nonetheless Luke repeatedly draws attention to the full involvement of women in the emerging Christian community. We encounter women praying (Acts 1:14; 12:12; 16:13) and prophesying (Acts 2:17; 21:9), coming to faith and being baptized (Acts 5:14; 8:12) and being persecuted alongside their men folk (Acts 8:3; 9:2; 22:4). In the terrible story of Ananias and Sapphira (Acts 5:1-11), Luke makes clear that women are answerable to God in their own right and may not devolve responsibility on their husbands. Through the story of Tabitha (also known as Dorcas, Acts 9:36-42), we are left in no doubt that a godly woman can have a powerful testimony to the grace of God, affecting a whole community. In Priscilla (Acts 18:2, 26), we meet a woman discipling a man, recorded with approval. And in Lydia (Acts 16:14-15, 40) we are introduced to the first convert on the European mainland through Paul's ministry, who became the linchpin of the church at Philippi.

These records are neither sentimental nor apologetic but quietly matter-of-fact. Given the absence of parables and the limited number of encounters with individuals, in both of which many of the Gospel references to women appear, and given the focus of Acts (e.g., establishing the facts about Jesus through many public sermons, or describing pioneer evangelism into new areas, or explaining how God was insisting the church must be universal and not Jewish), our surprise should be at how much, not how little, is said specifically about women.

Many commentators have divided Acts into six main sections. Each section focuses on one key phase in the establishing and expansion of the church, and each concludes with a summary statement indicating progress for the word of God and for the church. This simple outline is helpful and is therefore adopted here, though with fresh headings.

Outline

1:1—6:7	The Church Is Born: Beginnings in Jerusalem
6:8—9:31	Beyond Jerusalem: Persecution and the Scattering of God's People
9:32—12:24	Further Still: Bridgehead into the Gentile World
12:25—16:5	The Asian World: Good News for Gentiles
16:6—19:20	Across the Sea: The Gospel for Europe
19:21—28:31	At Great Cost: Rome at Last

Commentary

The Church Is Born: Beginnings in Jerusalem (Acts 1:1—6:7)

In the concluding chapter of his Gospel, Luke tells us (Lk 24:10) that "Mary Magdalene, Joanna, Mary the mother of James, and the other women with them" were the first witnesses of the resurrection. But when they reported back to the apostles, "these words seemed to them an idle tale, and they did not believe them" (Lk 24:11). After this, in Luke's account it seems that Jesus appeared only to men between the resurrection and the ascension. Perhaps he was content that the women needed no further convincing.

Acts begins with a recapitulation of the final verses of the Gospel, including the promise of the Holy Spirit, so soon to be given, and the anticipation of the worldwide mission of the church. It seems that even now, some among them still had their hearts set on political deliverance and an earthly kingdom (Acts 1:6); numerous Old Testament references to the outpouring of the Spirit were understood to be referring to the restoration of exiles to their land and a new beginning for Israel (e.g., Is 32:12-20; Ezek 36:25-28). But here the King returns to heaven rather than arrives on earth, and the angels who appear (Acts 1:10) seem to imply that he won't be coming back soon. In the meantime, the disciples must carry on the work Jesus has begun.

It is unclear whether it was only the Eleven together with the women who "were constantly devoting themselves to prayer" (Acts 1:14) or whether the "one hundred twenty persons" (Acts 1:15) were all so engaged. However it was, this was no idle waiting "for the promise of the Father" (Acts 1:4) but a sustained, prayerful watchfulness extending from the fortieth day since Passover to Pentecost, the fiftieth day. Contrary to common but not exclusive synagogue practice, it seems that the women joined the men for prayer, and over such a period some of them must have been also occupied with preparing food and caring for children and other domestic tasks (*see* Food and Water; Occupations, Skills and Crafts of Women). Were the men and women still a little uncomfortable in mixed company beyond the boundaries of their extended families, or were they already deeply bonded together as the family of God? Did some of them have long-suffering (unwilling even?) relatives living in Jerusalem, with whom they could stay long week after long week? How many relationships were strained in the process?

Conscious of the symbolic importance of having twelve apostles to represent the whole of Israel, Peter urges the company, in the context of prayer, to appoint someone to take Judas's place (Acts 1:15-26). Here is an intriguing bringing together of Scripture (which must be fulfilled), divine sovereignty (God could overrule the outcome of the lot) and human responsibility (choosing two people who met the criteria). The key qualification was that the candidates must have been with Jesus from his baptism until his ascension and thus be able to bear witness to the resurrection in the context of Jesus' complete earthly ministry. The implication is that an unknown number beyond the Twelve accompanied Jesus for a significant part of the time and, much more importantly, that the apostles recognized that the resurrection was the ultimate proof that Jesus Christ is truly Lord and God. There were certainly women who met the criteria set out here (cf. Lk 8:2-3), but for whatever reason, none of these made the short list.

Pentecost, also known as the Feast of Weeks, was a celebration and thanksgiving for the barley harvest (see Lev 23:16; Ex 34:22; Deut 16:9, 16) to be held fifty days after Passover. It was an acknowledgment that God is not only the one who saves and delivers (Passover and exodus) but also the one who provides food and daily life. Many pilgrims, especially those of the Jewish diaspora, who came to Jerusalem for Passover in the time of Christ stayed on for Pentecost as well, so that the city would have been crowded with men and women from far and wide, in a celebratory mood.

This was the great party before heading home.

In this highly charged setting the promised Holy Spirit is poured out on the disciples. They were "all together" (Acts 2:1), men and women, presumably still prayerfully waiting, as the Spirit made his dramatic entrance. The birth of the Lord Jesus was accompanied by a heavenly angelic choir. At the baptism of the Lord Jesus, the Spirit came visibly "in bodily form like a dove" (Lk 3:22) and the Father spoke. Here, at another great beginning, sound and visible sign converge. The coming of the Spirit is accompanied by "a sound like the rush of a violent wind" (Acts 2:2), a visible sign "as of fire" (Acts 2:3) and the gift of languages with which to declare "God's deeds of power" (Acts 2:11).

Such a hubbub resulted that an astonished crowd swiftly gathers and demands an explanation. Luke records that there were visitors from many different countries and of many different language groups—he lists fifteen distinct ones—each of whom heard disciples joyfully speaking about God in his or her native tongue. While no one would be foolish enough to come to Jerusalem and battle with the crowds at festival time unless he or she was a devout (or partying) Jew, many came from communities exiled generations before, so that they tended to have lost their Hebrew language and taken on the language of their adopted country.

While some assumed the worst—that the disciples were drunk, early morning though it still was (Acts 2:15)—Peter, bold with the dynamic life of the Spirit, seizes the opportunity to explain the true meaning of these momentous events. "This is that!" he says, quoting Joel's prophecy (Joel 2:28-32). Joel had prophesied that women and men, young and old, slave and free, would experience such an overwhelming outpouring of the Spirit of God that all would prophesy, see visions or dream dreams; no one would be excluded by gender or age or civil status. There would be signs in the sky and on the earth. All this would be a prelude to "the coming of the Lord's great and glorious day" (Acts 2:20), a day when "everyone who calls on the name of the Lord shall be saved" (Acts 2:21).

The emphatic inclusion of women on equal terms with men is especially instructive. For prophecy was less to do with prediction of the future and more to do with acting as the mouthpiece of God. Prophecy was a teaching ministry in which the prophet declared the word of the Lord. Women, equally with men, are equipped by the Spirit in this new phase of the kingdom for prophetic teaching ministry. And here at least there is no hint that this ministry must be exercised only among women, any more than men only among men.

If the Spirit had been poured out in this dramatic and definitive fashion, in fulfillment of the promise—the explanation for this large crowd of men and women declaring the word of God—then it must be of the utmost importance that all should grasp the identity of the Lord upon whose name they must now call for salvation. So Peter shows how Jesus of Nazareth, in his life and death and resurrection, is the fulfillment of the warp and weft of Scripture. "You crucified him!" Peter insists twice (Acts 2:23, 36), but "God raised him up. . . . God has made him both Lord and Messiah" (Acts 2:24, 36).

The response was overwhelming. "About three thousand persons" (Acts 2:41) were baptized and added to the apostolic community. How would we cope if we suddenly found ourselves one afternoon with a flood of new converts, outnumbering church members twenty-five to one? In this potentially chaotic situation, and led by the Spirit, the apostles set about teaching everything they knew about Jesus: how he fulfilled Scripture, what he had taught and done so recently among them, the facts about his death and resurrection and ascension. Whatever other plans people had had for travel or business were swept aside. They gave themselves totally to this radical new life as Jesus' disciples. Strangers became family in the intimacy of shared meals.

Luke is practical. Such an emergency, happy though it was, must have been extremely disruptive. Ordinary daily work came to a standstill. Pilgrims, unexpectedly delayed, would run out of funds. The apostles, possibly most of the 120, were from Galilee, and therefore several days' journey from their homes. Day after day, thousands must be accommodated and fed in a culture in which hospitality was important. (How busy the women must have been! Did the prices in the market soar? How many jars of water did they have to carry every day?) The only possible solution was to pool resources (Acts 2:44-45), and it seems they did so gladly (Acts 2:46). All other affairs paled into insignificance.

We do not know for how many weeks or months this state of affairs continued, but it seems that in addition to meeting in smaller groups in homes the apostles and the new converts converged daily on the temple. They came for the twice daily hours of prayer, associated with morning and evening offerings, and also because the outer court would have been one of the few spaces large enough to accommodate several thousand people at any one time for public teaching by the apostles.

One day, as Peter and John went to pass through the Beautiful Gate that led from the Court of Women into the inner area of the temple, a cripple (lame enough from birth to need to be carried in, Acts 3:2) begged them for money. Males with disabilities, along with women, were excluded from the Court of Israel on the grounds that nothing imperfect could pollute such a hallowed place; so the crippled man was as close as he was permitted to go. The apostles had no money to give, "but what I have I give you; in the name of Jesus Christ of Nazareth, stand up and walk," says Peter (Acts 3:6). The effect is immediate: full physical healing (the man does not just walk but jumps and leaps!) and a torrent of thanksgiving to God. The significance is deeper than we might think. Not only for the first time in more than forty years (Acts 4:22) could this man walk but also for the first time he could enter that inner sanctum of the Court of Israel and worship at the altar. The Lord Jesus gives access to the presence of God.

No wonder that at once a large and curious crowd gathers—and no wonder that Peter, by now back in the huge outer court, accessible to both men and women, Jews and Gentiles, hastens to seize the opportunity to explain that it is not he but Jesus who has so wonderfully healed the man. Once again Peter insists that his listeners have been guilty of killing "the Author of life, whom God raised from the dead" (Acts 3:15) and urges them to repent. Once again there is a massive response, though it is not clear whether the five thousand (Acts 4:4) are all fresh converts or whether this represents a running total.

However that may be, now, for the first time since the resurrection, we are told of active hostility toward the apostles. Not surprisingly, it comes from the temple authorities, dominated by the Sadducean party. The particular issue that raised their anger, Luke records (Acts 4:2), was that the apostles "were teaching the people and proclaiming that in Jesus is the resurrection of the dead." This was at the heart of their message. By contrast, the Sadducees denied the possibility of resurrection, so should many people come to believe what the apostles were saying, their credibility and power would be undermined.

There was no legally sustainable charge; the lame man had beyond question been healed (Acts 4:14, 16), and, however briefly, the apostles were enjoying widespread popular support (Acts 4:21). The religious authorities could do little, but they imprisoned Peter and John overnight, threatened them before letting them go the following day and ordered them "not to speak or teach at all in the name of Jesus" (Acts 4:18). Far from being cowed, Peter and John insist not only that the religious leaders were guilty of failing to see Jesus' divine credentials (Acts 4:11) but also that salvation is exclusively to be found in Jesus Christ (Acts 4:12). Only months before, Peter had denied all association with Jesus (Lk 22:54-62). Now, filled with the Holy Spirit, he throws down the gauntlet in the most unmistakable manner possible.

The response of the newborn church is united and decisive. They interpret the opposition as the fulfillment of prophecy (Ps 2:1-2), and they affirm their faith in the Lord as sovereign (Acts 4:24). They pray that they might witness boldly, while asking the Lord to perform unequivocal healings and signs to confirm their message. Not only does the Holy Spirit shake the place where they are gathered—which in itself must have been an awesome experience—but their commitment to one another is profoundly reinforced, so that "everything they owned was held in common" (Acts 4:32), that is, was available to the Christian community rather than just to the legal owners.

This included revenue raised by the sale of property, both land and houses. It is important to note that there was no compulsion about this. Nor would it seem that it was total or universal, because, for example in Acts 12:12, Luke without need for explanation refers to a private home belonging to an early believer. So this is not a charter for Marxist public ownership. Rather, it seems that under the compulsion of the Spirit different people sold property to meet the needs of the church as they arose.

In this context we first meet Barnabas, "which means 'son of encouragement' " (Acts 4:36). Barnabas was a member of the sizeable Jewish community in Cyprus at that time. Among the thousands, Barnabas apparently stood out as an individual to the apostles, for it was they who gave him his nickname. He sold a field and gave the proceeds to the apostles for careful distribution. Luke deliberately contrasts his noble example with the actions of Ananias and Sapphira. They too sold property, but they gave only a part of the proceeds to the apostles. That in itself would not have mattered; Peter makes it clear that they had the right to sell or not to sell the property, just as they had the right to give or not to give the proceeds (Acts 5:3-4). What mattered was that they deliberately lied, saying they had handed over the full value when they had not done so. Judgment comes swiftly and dramatically: first Ananias (Acts 5:5), then Sapphira (Acts 5:10), falls dead at Peter's feet.

Perhaps it seems rather a horrifying punishment for telling a lie. But what is at stake is integrity and truthfulness within the young Christian community, hypocrisy about commitment and, as Peter puts it, the attempt to lie to the Holy Spirit (Acts 5:3, 9). What is also of great significance is that

Women in Mission

Women were part of God's plan for mission from the creation of humanity. In the Old and New Testaments women were partners in God's kingdom plan. Half of humanity, and half of the church, the body of Christ, are women. It is clear that men and women need to work together to accomplish God's mission.

Women, like men, are created in God's image. God asserted the goodness of creation, including women. There was no impurity or weakness in women as such, nothing to prevent them from being involved in God's plans for mission and the salvation of humanity after the Fall. When sin came into the world, the relationship between men and women changed. Separation between God and humanity and enmity between men and women were inevitable.

Jesus' coming into the world through a woman made possible a change in these relationships. Many times women are not allowed to engage in mission activities because they are considered weak and impure. But God has shown through his selection of a woman to be involved in his greatest action in mission, salvation itself, that he does not consider women impure. It is her humanity God used to be part of Jesus' humanity.

Jesus demonstrated through his life and teachings that the male-female relationship is redeemed and restored through his atonement for our sins. Jesus gave women equal standing and responsibilities (Lk 8:1-3). He encouraged them to learn and grow as his disciples and challenged them to deeper life and faith (Lk 11:28). He commissioned women to witness to the good news of salvation (Mt 28:10; Jn 20:17). The encounter between Jesus and the Samaritan shows how women can play a critical role in reaching the unreached. The importance of women as a responsive entry point to resistant people groups is worth considering in today's world.

Lydia started a church in her home when she accepted Jesus as her Savior (Acts 16:15, 40). Women spread the gospel wherever they went. Women suffered persecution alongside men (Acts 8:1-3). Women, like men, received the Holy Spirit on Pentecost, and they used their gifts for God's kingdom (Acts 2:17-18). A great army of women did God's mission in the early church. Priscilla was a great teacher of the word, Philip's daughters prophesied, Phoebe was a deaconess, Junia was an apostle, Dorcas was a social worker. Paul called women fellow workers in the gospel (Phil 4:3; Rom 16:3). Many women were uneducated because their society did not allow them to learn, but Paul encouraged them to learn the word of God well and use their gifts for God.

When we look at the Bible as a whole we can conclude that men and women were called for radical discipleship. Both were called to mission for the expansion of God's kingdom. They are equally accountable for the gifts God has given to them (Acts 5:9-10). Women need to come forward and do their share of mission.

Bibliography

S. Athyal, *Indian Women in Mission* (Bihar, India: Lalgarh Madhupur, 1995); R. Tucker, *Guardians of the Great Commission* (Grand Rapids, MI: Zondervan, Academie Books, 1988). SAKHI M. ATHYAL

Sapphira has to take full responsibility for her dishonesty. In a day when almost any wife could excuse herself on the grounds that she had no freedom to do other than obey her husband, Peter insists that she may not hide behind her husband's leadership. When it comes to moral and spiritual issues, a wife must put the Lord's requirements before her husband's.

No wonder that "great fear seized the whole church and all who heard of these things" (Acts 5:11). Yet at the same time "great numbers of both men and women" (Acts 5:14) became believers, and many people were healed or exorcised of demons (Acts 5:16). Again Luke does not give us a time frame, but it seems that this time of consolidation and growth extended for quite some while.

Eventually, as the numbers swelled and people began traveling from farther and farther afield to Jerusalem, the high priest could contain himself no longer. Luke tells us that he and the Sadducees were "filled with jealousy" (Acts 5:17), perhaps because of the numbers who flocked to hear the apostles and also because of the extraordinary events occurring. Sadducees were antisupernaturalist, so that the constant preaching about the resurrection of Jesus and the repeated healings, signs and wonders taking place through the Christian community called in question everything that they stood for. Moreover, the Sadducees were powerful but not popular. No wonder they seethed with bitter jealousy.

The apostles (Luke does not tell us how many or specifically who) are thrown into prison. "During the night an angel of the Lord opened the prison doors" (Acts 5:19) and led them out, though the next morning the prison was found to be securely locked and the guards still on duty (Acts 5:23). The angel tells the apostles to go straight back to bold preaching in the temple, that most public of places. No prudent pause or withdrawing to some secluded spot: the Holy Spirit seems to be pressing the apostles into increasingly deliberate confrontation with the religious authorities.

When only a few hours later the apostles are brought before the council, Peter's preaching is again inflammatory. Without any doubt, Peter is accusing those whose calling it is to be spiritual leaders of being the greatest barrier to the people coming to salvation. Further, he is claiming that he and the apostles are the ones who are obedient to the Holy Spirit, not the high priest or the council or the religious bureaucracy. Had it not been for the intervention of Gamaliel—a Pharisee, and thus possibly less opposed to everything the apostles were teaching and doing, and a man highly respected—Peter and the others with him would surely have been killed there and then. Gamaliel is not convinced about whether the Christians are right (Acts 5:38-39) but is pragmatic enough to urge a wait-and-see policy. Moreover, for the council to kill them would be beyond their legal rights under the Roman administration, but if Peter and the rest were spearheading another nationalist uprising the Romans would soon deal with them as they had former rebellions.

So the council has the apostles flogged instead. This was brutal (up to thirty-nine lashes, which could lay flesh open to the bone) but commonplace enough and within the rights of the Jewish authorities. Luke does not dwell on the apostles' injuries, focusing instead on the fact that "they rejoiced that they were considered worthy to suffer dishonor for the sake of the name" (Acts 5:41), a remarkable response that has been repeated in many places down through the years of church history. In fact much of the New Testament reflects the fact that suffering is a normal part of discipleship, not an infrequent aberration. In this case, the apostles immediately return to teaching and preaching in the temple, demonstrating what they had claimed: they must obey God rather than human authorities (Acts 4:19; 5:29).

Luke gives us no clue as to how these events were perceived by the ordinary believers. Some must have been fearful, but overall faith and morale must have been high because there continued to be a steady growth in numbers (Acts 6:1). In fact the next difficulty came from within rather than outside the church. Judaism had a well-established tradition of caring for widows and other vulnerable members of society, even if the practice didn't always live up to the theory. And Jerusalem had more than its fair share of widows, since there was a custom for elderly Jews of the diaspora, if they could, to return to the city at the heart of their faith and identity as they awaited death. If their wives outlived them, they were needy indeed, far from their families and friends and isolated in terms of supportive relationships. It seems that some of these women had come to faith in Jesus and were now part of the church. Probably they could be more easily overlooked because they would be less well known to the mainstream community. It is hard to be on the fringes.

For the first time in Luke's record, we are given a glimpse of tension within the church, a sense of unfairness that some do better than others. The apostles see the grave potential of such resentment left to fester, and they do not brush off the needs of these women as only widows but insist that they themselves are called to "prayer and to serving the word" (Acts 6:4). Their respect for these vulnerable women is such that only the best care is appropriate, and so "seven men of good standing, full of the Spirit and of wisdom" (Acts 6:3), are appointed. These men all have Greek names (Acts 6:5), suggesting that they probably had strong links with the diaspora community and would thus be especially sympathetic advocates for the widows. The apostles see their ministry as so significant that Luke records for the first time formal appointment through prayer and laying on of hands.

The section concludes with a summary statement about this first phase of the church, revolving around Jerusalem. The church was still growing steadily, and even "a great many priests became obedient to the faith" (Acts 6:7). At last, it seems, even some of the religious establishment was recognizing the truth of the apostolic message.

Beyond Jerusalem: Persecution and the Scattering of God's People (Acts 6:8—9:31)

It is Stephen, one of the seven appointed to care for the widows, rather than one of the apostles who becomes the first martyr in the church. Luke describes Stephen as "full of faith and the Holy Spirit" (Acts 6:5) and "full of grace and power" (Acts 6:8). This is the portrait of a remarkable, winsome and godly man. He is also the first besides the apostles whom Luke specifically tells us "did great wonders and signs" (Acts 6:8).

Trouble comes from "some of those who belonged to the synagogue of the Freedmen" (Acts 6:9). Luke does not tell us why they should take this initiative, but the explanation may be like this. Stephen's name and appointment (Acts 6:5) imply that he was not a native Hebrew Jew but one who had been born in a Greek-speaking family somewhere in the dispersion. The synagogue of the Freedmen was a synagogue for those who either themselves prior to coming to Jerusalem or their forebears had once been slaves (Jews within Palestine could not be enslaved). The mainstream Jewish community, conveniently overlooking its own history of exile, regarded them as inferior. Stephen may have been converted from among them or could easily be identified with them, mistakenly or not. In their desire to be accepted by the Hebrew Jews, the Freedmen would wish to make clear their disassociation from Stephen. Moreover, by discrediting the Christians they could curry favor with the Jewish leaders.

Whether this is what lay behind their subsequent actions or not, they could lay charges against Stephen only by being dishonest. They resorted to false witnesses. But the trumped-up charges of these men ensured that Stephen was taken before the high priest and Sanhedrin (Acts 6:12; 7:1). Stephen's defense is a masterly review of Old Testament history that tellingly highlights the experience of slavery in Egypt and the frequent failure of God's people to recognize what God was doing among them. Stephen is accused of dishonoring Moses; on the contrary, how much more did their forebears do just that. Stephen is accused of "saying things against this holy place," the temple (Acts 6:13); on the contrary, "the Most High does not dwell in houses made with human hands" (Acts 7:48). Now, says Stephen, "You stiff-necked people, uncircumcised in heart and ears, you are forever opposing the Holy Spirit, just as your ancestors used to do. . . . You are the ones that received the law as ordained by angels, and yet you have not kept it" (Acts 7:51, 53).

It would have been hard for Stephen to have been more provocative, though this is the provocation of the impassioned evangelist and apologist for truth rather than insult for insult's sake. The last straw is when Stephen claims to "see the heavens opened and the Son of Man standing at the right hand of God" (Acts 7:56). The crowd would have picked up the allusion at once: Daniel (Dan 7:13-14) spoke of the Son of Man as the one who would come with direct and eternal authority from God, and Jesus had frequently taken the title upon himself. Further, the position of standing indicated a judge declaring judgment. Stephen is saying, "God is judging you at this very moment, and it's not I who am found guilty!"

The outcome could scarcely have been different. The enraged crowd drags him outside the city walls and stones him, the traditional punishment for blasphemy. That they did so is the measure of their anger, for capital punishment could legally be sanctioned only by the Roman authorities, and there were severe penalties for those who took the law into their own hands. In the heat of anger we do not always stop to consider consequences. As he dies, Stephen echoes the Lord Jesus on the cross—"Lord Jesus, receive my spirit"(Acts 7:59)—and prays that his murderers may be forgiven.

Stephen's death marks a critical turning point in the life of the church. That day severe and widespread persecution broke out, affecting the whole Christian community, not just the leaders, so that many disciples were scattered throughout Judea and Samaria. The attacks were spearheaded by Saul, who had witnessed approvingly Stephen's stoning (Acts 8:1). So dedicated was he that he pursued the believers from home to home, "ravaging the church" (Acts 8:3) and throwing all he caught into prison. It is highly significant that Luke tells us Saul arrested women and men; normally women would not have been imprisoned. Saul recognizes that women are as committed to the cause as men and that to stamp out the church must involve destroying everybody associated with it. If women were to be members of this new religion in their own right, so be it. They must take the full consequences—the responsibilities along with the privileges.

Meanwhile, those who escaped proclaimed the word wherever they traveled (Acts 8:4), a direct fulfillment of Matthew 28:19. Among them was Philip, another who like Stephen had been appointed to care for the Hellenist widows. Probably the fact that he was not a Palestinian Jew made it easier for him to overcome prejudice and go to Samaria (Acts 8:5), and by the same token it probably made it easier for the Samaritans to listen to what he had to say. It is intriguing to wonder whether the Lord Jesus' encounter (Jn 4) with the woman at the well and the subsequent belief in him of "many Samaritans from that city" (Jn 4:39), perhaps three years previously, significantly affected their response now. However that may be, confronted with healings and deliverance from demons, the Samaritans listened attentively (Acts 8:6) and responded joyfully (Acts 8:8), and many were baptized, both men and women. Among them was Simon, who had prior to this had a great following as a powerful magician.

Word came back to the apostles in Jerusalem, and so improbable did it sound to them that Samaritans should come to true faith—moreover faith that had at its heart Jesus the Jew—that Peter and John are dispatched to Samaria. Had Philip in some way changed the message to make it more palatable to Samaritans? Luke does not suggest in any way that he had; rather, he writes positively about what had happened. But that must have been in the minds of the apostles, the more so because there was no evidence yet that the Samaritans had received the Holy Spirit. What was God doing?

When Peter and John laid hands on the Samaritan converts, "they receive[d] the Holy Spirit" (Acts 8:19), though Luke does not elaborate on that. Could it be that God was determined that, despite this radical new departure, everybody must see the essential unity of the true church? Had the apostles not come, the Samaritans might have continued on their separatist way, refused to acknowledge the Jewishness of Jesus and have sought to establish an independent Samaritan church. Had Peter and John not come, they and the Jerusalem church might have continued in their historic rejection of the Samaritans and refused to accept them as true brothers and sisters in Christ. In this event, the Holy Spirit is underlining their interdependence.

If the Samaritans needed to acknowledge that Jesus was king of the Jews, the Jews needed to acknowledge that Jesus was king of the Samaritans and indeed of the Gentiles. The Holy Spirit is gently nudging them closer to the true meaning of the universal lordship of Christ. Further, Peter's and John's decisive intervention underscores the profound difference between Simon's magic and the authentic work of the Spirit, who cannot be bought either by money or technique. He is truly the gift of God's grace.

Not only so, the Spirit is steadily reinforcing his lesson. Peter and John proclaim "the good news to many villages of the Samaritans" (Acts 8:25) on their way back to Jerusalem, while Philip is perhaps unexpectedly removed from the buzz of Samaria—where, it could be argued, there must be plenty of ongoing teaching to be done and he would seem to be sorely needed—to trudge down a desert road many miles away in obedience to an angel (Acts 8:26). There is no hint that Philip knew in advance why he must go; this is raw obedience, walking by faith and not by human reason.

But what an amazing encounter the Spirit has organized! We know nothing about Philip's social status, but he is chosen by God to lead to faith one of the highest in the land from one of the great ancient king-

---

Africans in Biblical History

While the Israelites hold center stage throughout much of biblical history, Africans play a noteworthy role in the unfolding story of God's salvation. Lack of adequate acknowledgment stems from confusion regarding terminology and location. The term *Africa* does not appear in the Bible, yet its lands and peoples do. Egypt features as Israel's powerful neighbor; Hebrew *Cush* or Greek *Ethiopia* (not modern Ethiopia/Abyssinia) or *Nubia* refers to the upper Nile region, and Libya and Put occupy the northern coast. Disagreement exists concerning the ethnographic classification of these peoples, and racial attitudes color scholarship, particularly when traditions of perverted exegesis attribute the curse of Canaan (Gen 9:25; not Ham) to Negroids.

Despite these problems, African presence in biblical history is unequivocal. Although the identity of Cush in the primeval narrative remains uncertain, some claim an African location. The table of nations records Africans among ancient peoples. Moses bears an Egyptian name, as do several Israelite priests (e.g., Aaron's grandson Phinehas, or "the Nubian," Ex 6:25), and Moses "was instructed in all the wisdom of the Egyptians" (Acts 7:22). Reference is made to Cushites in a proverbial expression concerning their skin color (Jer 13:23).

Examples of African figures in the Old Testament include David's Cushite soldier who brought news of Absalom's death. A Cushite court official, Ebed-melech, confronted King Zedekiah and rescued Jeremiah from the muddy cistern where he'd been cast. Cushite leaders Zerah (2 Chron 14:9-13) and King Tirhakah (Is 37:9) are noted. Among African women are the Egyptian slave Hagar, the high-ranking Egyptian wives of Joseph and Solomon, and likely the Cushite wife of Moses.

Africans in the New Testament include Simon from Cyrene, who carried Jesus' cross, and Apollos from Alexandria. Egyptian and Libyan Jews were present at Pentecost, and Cyrenian Christians were among those who took the momentous step of preaching to Gentiles in Antioch (Acts 11:20). Best known is the Ethiopian eunuch, an official of Candace, title for the queen of Meroë.

Africa and its peoples play various roles in biblical history. Egypt represents a place of refuge for the patriarchs during famine and for the infant Jesus during persecution from Herod. In contrast, Egypt signifies oppression or "the house of slavery" (Ex 20:2), from which God delivered his people in the exodus. As major players in the geopolitical world of the ancient Near East, Egypt and Cush are among those nations under God's judgement in the prophetic books (Is 18—20; Jer 46; Ezek 29—32; Zeph 2:12). Most significantly, however, these African peoples symbolize foreigners who will ultimately worship the God of Israel (Ps 68:31; 87:4; Is 45:14; Zeph 3:10). Herein lies the theological import of Acts 8:26-40, for the Ethiopian eunuch's conversion to Christ marks the fulfillment of these Old Testament prophecies. Africans are not recent additions to the story of God's salvation; rather, they have been actively present in biblical history from the earliest chapters of Genesis to the earliest expansion of the gospel.

Bibliography

R. A. Bennett Jr. "Africa and the Biblical Period," *Harvard Theological Review* 64 (1971) 483-500; C. B. Copher, "Blacks/Negroes: Participants in the Development of Civilization in the Ancient World and their Presence in the Bible," *Journal of the Interdenominational Theological Center* 23 (fall 1995) 3-47; J. D. Hays, "The Cushites: A Black Nation in the Bible," *Bibliotheca Sacra* 153 (October-December 1996) 396-409; E. Ullendorff, *Ethiopia and the Bible* (London: Oxford University Press, 1968).

DIANE B. STINTON

---

doms. The man in charge of the treasury of Ethiopia (Acts 8:27), undoubtedly a black African, probably came from Meroe, which is located in modern-day Sudan. He may have been a Jew, but as a eunuch he was more probably a Gentile Jewish proselyte or God-fearer. Devout he must have been to have made the long and expensive journey to Jerusalem in order to worship (Acts 8:27), especially when few Jews would have anything to do with a castrated male. And he must have been wealthy in his own right to be traveling in a chariot, the Rolls Royce of the day, and to possess his own scroll of Isaiah.

It was not hard for Philip to start from Isaiah 53 and lead to Jesus Christ (Acts 8:35), and the Ethiopian is clearly prepared by the Holy Spirit to come to believing faith. He eagerly asks for baptism, following which Philip is once more whisked away. We know no more about the Ethiopian eunuch, but it is possible that he was the first to take the gospel into Africa south beyond Alexandria. Philip is led by the Spirit up the coast through Azotus to Caesarea, the seat of the Roman governor of Judea and home to a large Roman garrison.

Luke moves from the story of Philip to pick up the story of Saul. We are not told what became of the believers thrown into prison in Jerusalem, but it may well be that many of them, men and women, were flogged if not put to death. Now Saul turns his attention further afield and asks the high priest for letters to the leaders of the synagogues in Damascus. These would less likely have been letters of introduction for Saul personally than letters urging the synagogue leaders to help in the hunt for Christians, again both men and women, and to arrange for their extradition to Jerusalem. Damascus in Syria, about 140 miles north of Jerusalem, had many thousands of Jewish inhabitants; perhaps as many as eighteen thousand were later to die in the Jewish revolt of 66. We do not know how the gospel came to Damascus, but Luke tells us that disciples were established there (Acts 9:19).

Centuries before, Moses had come face to face with the blazing glory of God in the burning bush and heard God speak directly to him (Ex 3). Now Saul too is overwhelmed by blazing light and God's direct word (Acts 9:3-9). There can be no mistaking now the identity of Jesus. Saul's world is turned upside down. Blind, stunned, prayerfully fasting, he waits in Damascus for the Lord to show him what to do next.

In visions, the Lord instructs Ananias to go to Saul, and Saul to expect Ananias. Ananias knows about Saul's reputation and his purpose for coming to Damascus, but the Lord insists that "he is an instrument whom I have chosen to bring my name before Gentiles and kings and before the people of Israel" (Acts 9:15). Ananias obeys and greets Saul with those memorable words, "Brother Saul"! Here is a glimpse into how radical a new life Ananias believed Saul's to be. The fanatical persecutor has been transformed into one of the family.

Baptized, filled with the Spirit and with sight restored, Saul immediately becomes as passionate an advocate for Jesus Christ as before he had been implacable enemy. As he declares in the synagogues that Jesus is the Son of God (Acts 9:20), no wonder "all who heard him were amazed" (Acts 9:21) and "confounded" that he should prove "that Jesus was the Messiah" (Acts 9:22).

Luke does not tell us how long Saul remained in Damascus, though Paul (Gal 1:17) tells us that after a brief period of reflection in Arabia he returned and spent three years in Damascus. This was long enough for him to attract quite a following as a Christian rabbi (Acts 9:25), but eventually his life is in danger and he escapes to Jerusalem. There, perhaps because they had suffered so greatly at his hands in the past, the disciples "were all afraid of him, for they did not believe that he was a disciple" (Acts 9:26). It is Barnabas, the son of encouragement, who persuades the apostles of the genuineness of Saul's conversion. Before long, Saul's life is in danger again, this time from the Hellenists (Acts 9:29), and he is escorted to Caesarea to board a ship to Tarsus, his home city several hundred miles away to the north.

Luke does not tell us why the persecution died down at this point, but the church grew quietly and in peace "throughout Judea, Galilee, and Samaria" (Acts 9:31) during the period of respite.

Further Still: Bridgehead into the Gentile World (Acts 9:32—12:24)

Peter, still the key leader in Jerusalem, apparently also visited groups of believers elsewhere. On such a journey he comes to Lydda, twenty miles northwest of Jerusalem, where a bedridden man is healed through his ministry. As a result many people in the district turn to the Lord (Acts 9:35). The news traveled, and ten miles away in Joppa, when a greatly cherished disciple died, the believers immediately want Peter to come to them. It is hard to tell whether they hoped he would raise Tabitha from the dead or whether they wanted him to conduct the funeral. Perhaps the old Peter would have brushed off the request; after all, what value was a widow, especially a dead widow, in traditional culture (*see* Widows)? But the Lord Jesus had demonstrated tender care for widows, and now Peter does too.

Luke's portrait of Tabitha (also known as Dorcas, both meaning "gazelle") is of a much-loved and compassionate woman, greatly mourned (Acts 9:39). She had already been prepared for burial, but Peter prays and then commands her to get up (Acts 9:40). We do not know whether some of the signs and wonders to which Luke refers earlier in his narrative included people being raised from the dead; this is the first specific account. As word spreads of this extraordinary event, "many believed in the Lord" (Acts 9:42). Peter makes it plain that the Lord, not Peter, has brought Tabitha back to life.

Thirty miles farther north, in Caesarea, lived the Roman centurion Cornelius. As a centurion on active service, he was not entitled to be married, but the household to which Luke refers (Acts 10:2, 24; 11:14) could have included extended family, servants and friends. Cornelius was a God-fearer rather than a proselyte (Acts 10:2, 28) but took his religion seriously and observed the temple hours of prayer (Acts 10:3). As with Saul and Ananias, the Lord appears in visions to Peter and Cornelius in order to ensure that they are brought together. Cornelius's vision is straightforward enough, terrifying though he found it to see and hear an angel (Acts 10:4), but Peter's vision is far more enigmatic, at least at the time (Acts 10:17). It would have been shocking, for every Jewish household knew and lived by the ancient food laws. Perhaps Peter thinks at first that the Lord is testing his resistance to temptation—whether hunger would make him justify disobedience. What a lot hinged on waiting for lunch.

Cornelius's messengers' arrival quickly provides the first clue to understanding the vision, for the slaves and the soldier would have been Gentiles, not welcome to stay in a Jewish home. When they arrive in Caesarea, Luke records Peter's opening remarks, which must stand among the most gauche comments in Scripture: "You yourselves know that it is unlawful for a Jew to associate with or to visit a Gentile; but God has shown me that I should not call anyone profane or unclean" (Acts 10:28). Yet, when Peter was later challenged over what happened next, how important that he could show how clearly he realized this was a defining moment.

Luke underlines this firmly: "I truly understand that God shows no partiality, but in every nation anyone who fears him and does what is right is acceptable to him" (Acts 10:34-35). The careful repetition of how God had dealt first with Cornelius, then with Peter, emphatically shows that this was no coincidence invested with meaning God had never intended.

Peter's sermon is different from earlier ones: his audience is different, and he does not blame them for Jesus' death. Even as he speaks, the Holy Spirit falls on them, and they speak in tongues and praise God (Acts 10:44-46). If the Spirit has been so manifestly given in exactly the same way as he had come to the disciples at Pentecost, there can be no grounds for excluding them. Peter baptizes them. They are fully identified with the Christian community.

Predictably, when Peter returns to Jerusalem, he is taken to task. "Why did you go to uncircumcised men and eat with them?" (Acts 11:3). Patiently, step by step, Peter tells his story and Cornelius's story. The crux of the matter for him is this: "If then God gave them the same gift that he gave us when we believed in the Lord Jesus Christ, who was I that I could hinder God?" (Acts 11:17). We should not underestimate how painfully hard it must have been for many there to think outside of the categories of deeply rooted traditional Judaism. If circumcision was the sign of the covenant, how could the uncircumcised be included in God's promises? And if the Jews were God's chosen people, how could the Gentiles be numbered among the chosen, unless they submitted to circumcision and became as Jews? It was a huge psychological hurdle for them to say, "Then God has given even to the Gentiles the repentance that leads to life" (Acts 11:18).

The persistence of the orientation toward Jews rather than Gentiles was not an issue just in Jerusalem. Believers scattered after Stephen's martyrdom went up the coast beyond Palestinian territory to Phoenicia, across to Cyprus and far away up to Antioch, which at the time was the third largest city in the Roman world. Most concentrated on witnessing to Jews, but among those who went to Antioch were some men who came from Cyprus and from Cyrene, on the Mediterranean coast in modern-day Libya. We are not told why they went to Antioch rather than back home, but their background may well have made them more at home in the Greek-speaking communities than in the traditional Jewish synagogues. They proclaimed the Lord Jesus among the Greek speakers, many of whom came to faith (Acts 11:21).

Perhaps fearful of what could go wrong with an ingathering of Gentiles far from the watchful eye of the apostles, the church in Jerusalem dispatched the trusted Barnabas to investigate. It was an inspired choice, for Barnabas appears to have had the humble flexibility that was more alert to what God might be doing, however unexpectedly, than bound by expectation. He quickly realized help was needed and went to Tarsus to enlist Saul. "For an entire year they met with the church and taught a great many people" (Acts 11:26). It was here too that "the disciples were first called 'Christians' " (Acts 11:26). From this point on, Christianity would increasingly be seen as a distinct faith rather than as merely a messianic sect within Judaism.

Following a prophecy of widespread famine soon to come, Barnabas and Saul are sent to take a love gift from the believers in Antioch to the believers in Judea (Acts 11:27-30). They arrived at a time of great trouble for the church in Jerusalem, for King Herod (Agrippa I), himself part Jewish, unleashed persecution in order to curry favor with the Jews. He had James killed (Acts 12:2), and he arrested Peter. Herod was taking no chances, for he has Peter put in the charge of sixteen soldiers, two of them chained to him (Acts 12:4, 6).

Once more Peter finds himself miraculously rescued, though at first he can only think he is having a vivid dream (Acts 12:9). He makes his way to the house of John Mark's mother, Mary. She must have been a wealthy and unusually fortunate woman, and probably a widow, to have a house in her name and with an outer gate. Despite the fact that the disciples were all earnestly praying for Peter's safety (Acts 12:5, 12), they did not presume that he must be miraculously delivered from prison. The maid, Rhoda (Acts 12:13), may have been little more than a child and reacts with the delighted excitement of a surprised youngster. After testifying to what the Lord had done, Peter leaves, probably concerned for his friends' security. Shortly afterwards, he slips away to Caesarea (Acts 12:19).

Herod meanwhile executes the guards. Soon afterward "the Lord struck him down" (Acts 12:23) because he allowed himself to be worshiped as a god. Such is God's jealousy for his glory.

The Asian World: Good News for Gentiles (Acts 12:25—16:5)

Barnabas and Saul returned to Antioch, taking with them from Jerusalem John Mark. The apostles had never stirred far from Jerusalem, and despite Peter's experience with Cornelius they did not show any signs of seriously undertaking mission to the Gentiles. But the Antioch church, by now well supplied with gifted leaders (Acts 13:1), is prompted by the Spirit to "set apart for me Barnabas and Saul for the work to which I have called them" (Acts 13:2). The Lord had made clear at the time of Saul's conversion that he was to be an apostle to the Gentiles as well as to Jews.

Together with John Mark, Saul (from now on called Paul, his Roman name, Acts 13:9) and Barnabas went first to Cyprus, Barnabas's home territory, working their way across the island. In Paphos they were summoned by the proconsul, Sergius Paulus (Acts 13:7), to explain the Christian message. Despite the opposition of a Jewish magician, doubtless afraid of losing his hold over people, the word of God prevails and the proconsul comes to faith.

Paul, Barnabas and John Mark return to the mainland, where John Mark leaves them to go back to Jerusalem. Luke does not tell us why John Mark left (was he concerned about his mother?), but Paul must have disapproved, because later (Acts 15:37-40) he and Barnabas disagreed so deeply about him that they parted company. However, for the moment Paul and Barnabas press on to Antioch in Pisidia, far inland in today's Turkey. Once more they first make their way to the synagogue, where as visitors they are courteously invited to speak. Apparently their reputation had not gone before them. As with other recorded sermons to Jews, Paul first traces Jewish history, showing how Jesus is the fulfillment of the Old Testament law and prophets. He is the promised one. Again there is an emphasis on the resurrection and on the need to respond in repentance and faith for the forgiveness of sins.

Soon public opinion is polarized between those (especially Gentiles, Acts 13:48) who respond in faith and those (especially Jews,

Acts 13:45, 50) who reject them in great anger. Paul and Barnabas tell the crowds that since the Jews, who should hear first, have rejected the word of the Lord, they are free to turn their attention to the Gentiles. This becomes the normal pattern of their ministry: to the Jews first, then to the Gentiles. The Jews incite civic leaders, including "devout women of high standing" (Acts 13:50), to drive them out of the city. Ancient sources note that a number of wealthy and politically important women were interested in Judaism; thus the Jews successfully solicited their support in driving Paul and Barnabas out of the city.

A similar pattern emerges at Iconium and Lystra, though in the former Jews and Greeks became believers (Acts 14:1), and it was some time before Paul and Barnabas were forced to flee. In Lystra, following the healing of a cripple, the crowds misinterpret what is going on and try to worship Paul and Barnabas as a visitation of Zeus and Hermes. Paul and Barnabas are dismayed (Acts 14:14). Such a misunderstanding could not have occurred when they were preaching to Jews, and the reality of reaching the pagan Gentile world perhaps registered more sharply than ever before. It is significant that here the preaching does not presuppose any familiarity with Jewish Scriptures.

Despite being driven out of Lystra, after visiting Derbe Paul and Barnabas retrace their steps through all the towns and cities where they have been in order to strengthen "the souls of the disciples" (Acts 14:22), to warn them of the inevitability of suffering and to appoint elders. Only then do they return to Antioch, reporting to the church that had sent them on their missionary journey.

It was timely that they should be in Antioch then, for some disciples came from Judea teaching that salvation was not possible without circumcision (Acts 15:1). Soon Paul and Barnabas and some others are sent to Jerusalem to consult with the apostles. This is a matter of the gravest significance. Paul and Barnabas are able to tell of all God had been doing among Jews and Gentiles alike, but then "some believers who belonged to the sect of the Pharisees" (Acts 15:5) try to insist that the Gentiles must be circumcised and keep the law of Moses.

After extensive debate between the apostles and elders, in turn Peter, Paul and Barnabas and finally James appeal to a combination of Scripture and events. They show how God is welcoming Gentiles into the church and that for Jew and Gentile alike the basis of salvation is not circumcision but "the grace of the Lord Jesus" (Acts 15:11). James suggests that a handful of directives (Acts 15:20), which by tradition predated Mosaic law or even Abraham and were believed to have been given to Noah (Gen 9:3-4), should be urged upon everyone. Keeping them was not for salvation but as a matter of basic upright living. This becomes the substance of a letter sent by the apostles to Antioch, conveyed not only by Paul and Barnabas but also by two senior leaders from Jerusalem (Acts 15:22).

After the peaceful resolution of affairs in Jerusalem, Paul and Barnabas soon have such a bitter argument that they never work together again (Acts 15:39). Yet, out of even this tragedy, God brought blessing, for Paul teamed up with Silas, and Barnabas with John Mark, and all had effective ministry, revisiting and strengthening existing churches and planting new ones.

It was on such a journey, revisiting Lystra, that Paul recruits Timothy to travel with him and Silas. Luke tells us that Timothy's mother was a Jewish believer (Acts 16:1), but because his father was Greek, Timothy had not been circumcised. Paul has him circumcised not as an issue of salvation (which would have repudiated the recent decision in Jerusalem) but in order to make him less offensive to Jews as they go to new areas, beginning with the synagogues, on their missionary journeys.

Across the Sea: The Gospel for Europe (Acts 16:6—19:20)

Paul, Silas and Timothy, shortly to be joined by Luke, had no liberty to preach as they traveled through Asia, and puzzled, found themselves at Troas. Troas was the major port linking Asia Minor and Macedonia, now northern Greece, and linking with the splendid Egnatian Way leading to Rome. The Holy Spirit convinces Paul through a vision that they should sail for Macedonia, and they disembark at Neapolis and proceed to the Roman colony of Philippi.

In his days as a Pharisee, possibly even

from childhood, Paul would have been trained to say each day, "I thank you, Lord, that you did not create me a slave, a woman or a Gentile." In the gentle humor of the Lord, the first three converts (as recorded by Luke) through Paul's ministry in today's European mainland were a woman, a slave girl and a Gentile.

There was no synagogue in Philippi, which probably means that the Jewish community was too small for there to be the requisite minimum of ten Jewish males. There is no mention of observant men at all. But a group of women met by the river to pray, among them Lydia, "worshiper of God" (Acts 16:14), spiritually alert. She was a native of Thyatira and by trade a dealer in purple cloth, a luxury fabric for which the dye was extracted not from plants but from shellfish (*see* Occupations, Skills and Crafts of Women). "The Lord opened her heart to listen eagerly" (Acts 16:14), and soon she and her household are baptized. She may have been a widow or a married woman with an absent husband (*see* Marriage), and there is no hint as to the size of her household. She urges Paul and the others to become her guests, and this would give plenty of opportunity to disciple these new believers.

Soon afterward Paul and Silas cast out a spirit of divination from a slave girl. Although she tells people that Paul and Silas are "slaves of the Most High God" (Acts 16:17; *see* Ancient and Modern Slavery), which is true, the disciples do not wish to accept testimony from a demonic source. The girl's exploitative owners are furious, for her supernatural powers have been lucrative for them, however distressing they may have been to her. They stir up the mob and cunningly appeal to the magistrates, so that Paul and Silas are flogged and thrown into prison. Even here they bear witness to Jesus Christ through prayer and singing.

In the night a violent earthquake shakes all the prisoners' shackles free from the wall, and the jailer assumes they will all have escaped. Rather than face execution for losing his prisoners, he is about to attempt suicide when Paul assures him that nobody has left (Acts 16:28). The jailer attributes this extraordinary turn of events to divine intervention and immediately asks, "'Sirs, what must I do to be saved?' " (Acts 16:30). Soon the jailer and his household are believing, baptized and rejoicing.

Perhaps superstitious about the earthquake, the magistrates are eager to be rid of Paul and Silas. But Paul reveals that, Jew notwithstanding, he is a Roman citizen, and the authorities apologize, afraid of retribution. The disciples spend some more time with this new little church family—to whom later Paul was to write one of his most tender letters—before walking on to Thessalonica.

Paul and Silas were to spend only three weeks in Thessalonica, which makes the Thessalonian epistles all the more remarkable (see, e.g., 1 Thess 1:2-10). Jews and Gentiles, including "not a few of the leading women" (Acts 17:4), believed. This time the charge brought against them by enraged Jews is one of sedition. They are accused of

Expectations of Women

The expectations of women in the Bible are diverse. It might be assumed that, given the ancient and Middle Eastern character of these texts, the place of women would be circumscribed by the expectations of that society. These expectations are evident in much of the law code of ancient Israel described in Leviticus and Numbers. It might also be argued that cultural assumptions account to some degree for the apostle Paul's restrictions on the role of women (1 Cor 14:35; 1 Tim 2:11-14).

Despite this, there is in God's dealings with the people of God a radical inclusivity.

The Bible begins with an affirmation that the image of God is borne in the whole of humanity, male and female (Gen 1:27-31), and responsibility for stewardship of the earth is given to men and women (*see* Men and Women as Stewards of the Environment; Monotheism). Likewise God covenants with all Israel, men and women. The women of Israel are freely accountable for their actions in relation to God (Num 6:2; 30:3-9; Deut 17:2-7). Women feature prominently in the ministry of Jesus as supporters and recipients of his ministry. Subsequently the gospel is preached specifically to women (Acts 16:11-15), and women play an active role in the life of the church (1 Cor 11:2-15; Acts 16). In general it can be argued that women are expected to engage in a full and active life of faith, responding to the call of God in their lives.

Close consideration of the women we meet in the pages of Scripture invites us to ask some new questions. Women are key to the execution of God's plans on many occasions. Many of these women are in some way or other on the margins of society. Sarah's advanced years and infertility set her apart from other women (Gen 18:9-15). Rahab (Josh 2; 6:22-25) was a prostitute in Jericho, and Ruth, a Moabite, ethnically an enemy of Israel (Deut 23:3). Yet all play key roles in bringing about God's purposes for humanity.

The women we meet in the Gospels are equally intriguing. The Syro-Phoenician woman who debates with Jesus (Mk 7:24-30), the woman who risks her reputation to anoint Jesus (Lk 7:36-50) and the Samaritan woman (Jn 4) stand on the margins of society. Others, such as the women disciples who followed Jesus from Galilee (Lk 23:49-56), have deliberately stepped outside of their social roles to do so. God calls women, no less than men, to give their lives in divine service. Some are freed to do so by their circumstances. For others it is a conscious choice, like that of Abigail (1 Sam 25), to defy the expectations of others. The Scriptures declare God's expectation that women, whether as wives and mothers, prophetic voices (2 Sam 14:1-20), hosts (2 Kings 4:8-37; Acts 16:14-15, 40) or explicit proclaimers of the gospel (Jn 4:39; 20:18), will respond boldly to God's call on their lives and give themselves in loving service to God, regardless of the expectations of the world around them. JILL MCCOY

"saying there is another king named Jesus" (Acts 17:7), that is, a rival to the emperor. Paul and Silas slip away to Beroea, where the Jews were "more receptive than those in Thessalonica" (Acts 17:11), checking the Scriptures for verification of the message. Once again Jews and Gentiles, including "not a few Greek women and men of high standing" (Acts 17:12), come to faith before Paul has to move on for safety's sake, this time to Athens, several hundred miles to the south. Within the pluralism of the Greco-Roman world, women, especially wealthy women, had greater religious freedom than their Jewish sisters, and it may have been easier for them to convert even when their husbands did not. The Thessalonian and Beroean women respond positively in contrast to the women of Pisidian Antioch (Acts 13:50).

Athens's greatest glory had faded, but it was still buzzing with philosophers and debaters—and idolatry. Paul is deeply distressed by the latter (Acts 17:16), but it became the stimulus to profound apologetics into the pagan world. Starting from the altar to the unknown god—the Athenians' attempt to cover all possibilities—Paul declares that their "unknown" is knowable and revealed in the God and Father of the Lord Jesus Christ, the one who made the world, who is close at hand and who will judge all humankind through Jesus, raised from the dead (Acts 17:22-31). Among those who come to believe are the intellectual Dionysius and Damaris, a woman about whom we know nothing further.

Paul moves on to Corinth, where he stays with Aquila and Priscilla, Jewish believers recently expelled from Rome by the emperor Claudius and by trade tentmakers like Paul. Initially Paul again tries to win a hearing at the synagogue, and some believe, including Crispus, "the official of the synagogue" (Acts 18:8)—that is, the person responsible for the services. Following a vision, Paul stays in Corinth for eighteen months, as many Gentiles come to faith. Finally the Jews try to accuse him to the proconsul of stepping outside the boundaries of Judaism and thus putting himself beyond the protection offered to Jews. Gallio dismisses the charge as petty insquabbling over trivia and refuses to intervene (Acts 18:15).

Paul sails back to Asia Minor, taking Priscilla and Aquila with him. He leaves them at Ephesus, going to Jerusalem via Caesarea and then to Antioch. It had been a long journey.

Meantime, in Ephesus Priscilla and Aquila share the discipling of Apollos, an Alexandrian Jewish believer whose grasp of the faith had considerable gaps (Acts 18:24-28). It appears that there was no bar to Priscilla teaching a man. When Paul comes to Ephesus, he finds another group who have received the baptism of John but not of the Holy Spirit. As the church grew and sometimes small groups of new believers had to be left without well-instructed leadership, it was inevitable that occasionally teaching was defective. It highlighted the need for the New Testament written Scriptures, at this time still almost all in the future.

Ephesus was the key city of a strategic province, and Paul spends three months witnessing to Jews (Acts 19:8) followed by two years of daily teaching in a public hall, in the pattern of philosophers with their students. Through word and miracle the gospel spread extensively, clearly distinguishable from charlatans (Acts 19:13-17) and leading to one of the most expensive bonfires of all time, in which vast quantities of magic paraphernalia were burned. Breaking with one's unregenerate past can be costly and must be decisive.

Ephesian magic consisted in mystic arrangements of six magic words. Books of these incantations brought a handsome price, for the spells could supposedly affect fate, fortune, family, fertility and affections.

At Great Cost: Rome at Last (Acts 19:21—28:31)

Perhaps sensing that his work in Ephesus was coming to an end, Paul planned to retrace his steps from Philippi to Athens and Corinth, then to visit Jerusalem again, and after that to set off for Rome. These names trip easily off our tongues, but the distances are enormous, overwhelmingly so when one remembers that Paul was no longer a young man, the fastest ship was under sail, and land journeys must be walked. It is not Luke's purpose to focus on these practical issues, and therefore it should not be ours. But it is humbling to realize the sheer hard work, often compounded by danger and rejection, that from the beginning has been the human price to be paid in order that the gospel should be heard.

Before Paul could leave, trouble erupted in Ephesus. Beneath the city on a marshy plain was the great temple of Artemis (in Latin, Diana), whose cult had a massive following all around the Mediterranean. Dominant among the powerful mother goddesses of Asia Minor was the Ephesian Artemis.

Fertility of people, animals and crops was believed to be dependent on acceptable worship at Artemis's shrine, so that associated trade was the bedrock of the economy for miles around. To make offerings to Diana was the closest to an insurance policy anyone could have. But so effective has been Paul's preaching that financial vested interests are severely challenged (Acts 19:23-27). Demetrius stirs up a mob, many of whom have no idea what all the rumpus is about but join in anyway (Acts 19:32), and two of Paul's companions are dragged away to the theater. This impressive structure, evidence of wealth generated by the Artemis cult, could seat twenty-five thousand people. Finally the town clerk quiets them, urging due procedure rather than mob rule, which can only bring down the wrath of the Roman authorities. Luke wants us to understand that opposition is because of the offense of the gospel and not because Paul and his friends wantonly flout the law.

We are told next to nothing about Paul's return visit to Greece (Macedonia and Achaia), other than that for some of the time he is accompanied by believers from various cities. Among them is Timothy, who reappears in Acts 19:22 and Acts 20:4 without explanation. While in the south of Greece, perhaps in Corinth, Paul's life is threatened, and instead of sailing back toward Antioch in Syria, he takes the long land journey back to Philippi. After celebrating Passover there (Acts 20:6), they sail to Troas. A week later, on the eve of departure, Paul talks through the night with some of the believers. Overpowered by weariness and the smokiness from the lamps, a lad named Eutychus falls asleep and crashes through the window to the courtyard three floors below (Acts 20:9). Luke implies that Paul brings him back to life and then goes on talking. One can't help wondering whether the women would not have been far too concerned about whether Eutychus was truly fully recovered to have paid close attention to more apostolic discussion at this point.

Artemis of Ephesus bursting with fecundity. (Acts 19:23-41)

Paul is eager to reach Jerusalem in time to celebrate Pentecost with the church there, but he breaks his journey long enough to have the elders of the Ephesian church come to him in Miletus (Acts 20:17). Here Paul delivers his moving farewell speech (Acts 20:18-35). Such speeches were customarily recorded following a well-established literary pattern, but that does not mean that Luke invents empty rhetoric. As with all the speeches and sermons in Acts, Luke gives us a summary, but a summary that carefully captures the essence of what was said.

Paul reviews his ministry among them: he has a clear conscience. It is a poignant glimpse into the way in which Paul reflected on his missionary service. Now the Spirit convinces him that he faces suffering and death, though he does not as yet know where or when, and that he will not see the Ephesians again. He urges them to "shepherd the church of God that he obtained with the blood of his own Son" (Acts 20:28) and commends them "to God and to the message of his grace" (Acts 20:32).

Leaving the coast, they sail across the open sea to Tyre (Acts 21:3). The disciples there beg Paul not to go to Jerusalem but cannot deter him. So they too, "all of them, with wives and children" (Acts 21:5), bid him farewell. Paul and his party continue to Caesarea, where they stay with Philip (Acts 21:8; cf. Acts 6:5; 8:5-9). Luke tells us that Philip had "four unmarried daughters who had the gift of prophecy" (Acts 21:9). That they were all unmarried probably means that they were below marriageable age, that is, younger than about sixteen. This is surely an example of the fulfillment of Joel's prophecy, quoted by Peter at Pentecost (Acts 2:17-18). Yet again, this time through the prophet Agabus, Paul is warned that he will be taken prisoner in Jerusalem (Acts 21:11), and this time even his companions try, without success, to dissuade him from going on.

Paul and his companions, some of whom were Gentile believers (Acts 20:4), are warmly welcomed, given hospitality and given the opportunity to report on all that God had graciously been doing. At the same time, the leaders of the Jerusalem church are still nervous about Hebrew believers' perceptions of Gentile believers, especially the ongoing unhappiness that the latter practiced neither circumcision nor all the requirements of the Mosaic law (Acts 21:20-21). The council of Acts 15 had not settled the question decisively enough, at least for some of the rank-and-file Hebrew Christians. Perhaps there were those who were willing to turn a blind eye to what happened far away but could not cope with the decision being implemented under their noses. There are sensitivities about what is appropriate in different cultural contexts and a struggle to discern what is acceptable cultural contextualization and what is syncretism, violating principles.

Paul is still a Jew, albeit a Christian Jew, and the leaders urge him to observe the rites of purification and to support four men who will also undertake them. This he is happy to do, apparently convinced that to do so does not compromise the gospel fundamental that salvation is by grace through faith, and not through circumcision or law keeping. However, some Jews whip up trouble, accusing Paul of bringing Mosaic teaching into disrepute and of bringing Gentiles into areas of the temple forbidden to them. Paul is seized, and the crowd would probably have torn him limb

Martyrion of Philip at Hierapolis, where Philip's four prophesying daughters were buried. (Acts 21:8-9)

from limb had it not been for the intervention of soldiers from the Roman garrison close by (Acts 21:32). The commander of the garrison mistakenly assumes that Paul is a notorious wanted Egyptian assassin (Acts 21:38), but when Paul explains his identity the tribune gives him permission to speak to the crowd.

Paul speaks in Hebrew (Acts 22:2), reminds the crowd of his impeccable Jewish background and then describes in detail how, in the midst of his persecution of Christians, he had been overwhelmed by the risen Christ on the Damascus road. The crowd listens attentively—until Paul says that the Lord commissioned him to go to the Gentiles. Immediately the uproar breaks out again, so deep is the outrage that Paul should claim God could possibly say such a terrible thing (Acts 22:22). That God should be equally concerned for the Gentiles is as unacceptable to them as it had been to the Lord Jesus' audience in Nazareth (Lk 4:16-30). Paul touches a raw nerve, but he cannot and will not compromise on the universal lordship of Christ.

Paul is whisked into the garrison, where, following common custom, the tribune orders him to be flogged as a means of frightening him into confessing whatever he may have done (Acts 22:24). But Paul tells him that he is by birth a Roman citizen, and the tribune dare not proceed. Instead he orders the Jewish council to assemble so that he can cross-examine them and Paul. When, contrary to Jewish law, the high priest orders Paul to be struck on the mouth while still unconvicted, Paul challenges him (Acts 23:3). Later, by appealing to the resurrection, Paul succeeds in dividing Pharisees against Sadducees, and as pandemonium breaks out he is again taken to the garrison for safety's sake.

The Lord assures Paul that he must bear witness to him in Rome (Acts 23:11), so Paul must have known that he could not be killed in Jerusalem. When a plot is hatched to capture him by trickery in order to kill him, Paul's nephew comes to hear of it and reports it. The tribune does not wish to risk being answerable for the death of a Roman citizen in such a fashion and hastens to shift the responsibility for his fate to someone else. He arranges for Paul to be taken with a formidable escort—nearly five hundred strong—to the much more secure garrison at Caesarea, where he can also be turned over to the governor, Felix. The size of the escort reflects recognition of the desperate lengths to which the tribune fears the Jewish leaders might go to murder Paul and the fact that at the time there were growing bands of national dissidents who might attack a small Roman detachment.

A few days later, the high priest and various supporters arrive in Caesarea to lodge their case against Paul. Their spokesman, Tertullus, begins with blatant flattery of Felix (Acts 24:2-4), who had been a corrupt governor. Tertullus then accuses Paul of being a political agitator, which would be of far more significance to the Roman authorities than religious squabbles. He also accuses Paul of profaning the temple; the Roman authorities, aware of the extreme sensitivities of the Jews in respect of their holy place, would be nervous of the destabilizing impact of such an act.

Paul defends himself simply, claiming to have been scrupulous in every way during his visit to Jerusalem, doing nothing to cause offense or trouble. Further, after a long absence, he had come to bring gifts and alms to his people. He insists that he endorses the Scriptures and Jewish customs. The only thing that he could be accused of was his "one sentence" about the resurrection (Acts 24:21).

Felix remands Paul in custody but defers sentence. Permission is given for Paul to be cared for by his friends; they would bring him food and other necessities as well as company. This implies that Felix knows Paul is not guilty but that ongoing imprisonment is the best guarantee of his safety. Frequently Felix and his wife, Drusilla, who was Jewish, summoned Paul to talk with them, Felix hoping that Paul would pay a bribe for his freedom. But Paul must have touched Felix's conscience, because he "became frightened" when Paul "discussed justice, self-control, and the coming judgment" (Acts 24:25).

For two years Paul was left in prison, until Felix was replaced as governor by Porcius Festus. Within days the Jewish leaders in Jerusalem were urging Festus to transfer Paul there, since they hoped to be able to ambush and kill him. This is an extraordinary comment on the festering sore Paul's survival was to them and also probably a measure of his continuing influence despite his imprisonment, perhaps because friends were allowed to visit him.

Festus was willing to do the Jews a favor—it would make them much more easily governable to have them positive toward him—and invites some Jewish leaders to come at once to Caesarea, where he will hear Paul's case. They bring many serious charges against Paul but cannot prove them (Acts 25:7), and Festus is far too prudent to permit a Roman citizen to be lynched without good grounds. He offers Paul the chance to go to Jerusalem, but Paul instead appeals to his right to go before the emperor. Maybe during his long imprisonment he has concluded that this is the only way he will get to Rome.

A few days later, the young King Agrippa II (who had succeeded his father, also Agrippa), and his sister, Bernice, come to pay their respects to Festus. Festus asks Agrippa for advice, because the latter was conversant with Jewish and Roman law. Soon Paul appears before Agrippa, Bernice and Festus and a large military and civic audience. Once again Paul is permitted to explain himself. Once again he insists that his Jewish credentials are impeccable. The pivotal issue, he says, is the resurrection (Acts 26:6-8). He tells once again the story of his conversion and of the risen Christ's commission to him to preach to the Gentiles. Aware of Agrippa's familiarity with the Scriptures, Paul takes trouble to explain how Jesus is the key to their rightful meaning.

Agrippa's evaluation is that Paul has done nothing justifying imprisonment under Roman law and could have been set free had he not already appealed to the emperor (Acts 26:31-32). However, since he had, he must go to Rome. That is exactly where Paul wishes to go, and he believes God is sovereignly overruling his circumstances to take him there.

Luke is among Paul's companions as they set sail for Italy (Acts 27:1), accompanied by other prisoners and all under the guard of a centurion and his detachment of about eighty men. Sailing against the prevailing winds, they made slow progress, and the wiser course would have been to have wintered in Crete (Acts 27:12). However, instead they are caught in a terrible storm, and despite throwing the cargo overboard to lighten the load, the crew and their passengers lose hope of surviving (Acts 27:20). The ship must have been large, for Luke tells us that there were 276 people on board (Acts 27:37).

Paul has again been reassured in a dream that he must appear before the emperor, and therefore he is confident that he and his companions will survive and reach dry land. He encourages the desperate men with his calm assurance, and after two terrifying weeks they run aground on Malta (Acts 28:1). Luke gives us a vivid description, complete with many specific details, about the final frightening days of the voyage and then the dramatic process of getting to shore. By the grace of God, not one person is drowned. Even on a calm voyage that would have been unusual; in such circumstances it is miraculous.

Luke emphasizes the way in which God is protecting Paul in order that his word might be fulfilled. At one point the soldiers wish to kill all the prisoners, Paul included (Acts 27:42). Again, after they reach Malta, warming themselves with a bonfire on the beach, Paul is bitten by a snake. Those around him superstitiously assume this is judgment for wickedness: he should not have cheated death at sea. When Paul is none the worse for his snakebite, their superstition swings to the opposite extreme: he must be not a criminal but a god (Acts 28:6).

Even in the midst of such turmoil, Paul loses no opportunity to preach about Jesus through word and deed, healing the sick father of the leading man of the island (Acts 28:8) and subsequently others. In gratitude, when spring comes and Paul and the others are able to continue their journey, the people provision the ship. They sail past Sicily and come to the port of Puteoli, where they are able to spend a week with believers (Acts 28:14).

Finally they come to Rome, the destination Paul has had his heart set on for so many years. Perhaps he would never have chosen to come through such painful suffering, but he is convinced that God has mercifully ordained his circumstances every step of the way. At Rome he is able to meet with believers and fellowship with them (Acts 28:15). Further, he is permitted amazing freedom to come and go, to live in his own home rather than in prison, with only one guard (Acts 28:16).

Despite being called to take the gospel to the Gentiles, Paul never lost his great longing to see his own people come to faith in Christ. At once he gathers the Jewish leaders (Acts 28:17) and insists that he is guilty of no offense against the Jews. His one great desire is to be able to convince them that Jesus is their Messiah and that truly he has risen from the dead. When most refuse to believe, he says that this is but the Scripture being fulfilled yet again (Acts 28:25-28).

Luke's marvelous account ends on a triumphant note. For two years Paul had a full and fruitful ministry, without any problems from the Roman authorities. His desire to carry the gospel of Jesus, the risen Messiah, to the heart of the Gentile world is granted by the grace of God.

Luke does not tell us the end of Paul's story. Perhaps in the mind of God it is of little significance, at least in the grand scheme of things. We may be curious, but we do not need to know. After all, we do not follow Paul but Jesus Christ, and it is Christ's death, not Paul's, that is the foundation of the church. Though Paul strides across so much of the story Luke tells, it is not ultimately his story. In the same way, we do not know the end of Peter's story, or Barnabas's, or Luke's. Luke does not tell us about the terrible persecution that broke out in Rome a year or so later, though it almost certainly occurred well before he wrote. He does not tell us of the gathering storm in Jerusalem that was to leave the Jewish church in tatters and the gulf between Jewish and Gentile believers wider than ever. These too it seems we do not need to know, at least not as part of this particular story.

What Luke, under the inspiration of the Spirit, has set out to record does not need these things. Rather, he leaves us worshiping the Lord who could take that frightened, defeated handful of disciples at the start of his account and bring us at the end to a church established all over the Mediterranean world, a church of countless thousands and of many races. The Holy Spirit wants us to see the sovereign grace of God, the inevitability of his coming kingdom, the power that is above all the machinations of mere human opponents.

It is this triumphant story Luke tells. Truly Jesus Christ is Lord, King of the whole earth, the whole of humanity.

Bibliography. I. H. Marshall, *The Acts of the Apostles,* TNTC (Grand Rapids, MI: Eerdmans, 1980); J. R. W. Stott, *The Message of Acts,* BST (Downers Grove, IL: IVP, 1990).

ROSEMARY M. DOWSETT

ROMANS

Introduction

No other epistle of Paul has had such an impact on the Christian faith throughout history. In a comprehensive way, the letter to the Romans addresses the concepts of sin, salvation and sanctification. Paul's goal is to explain God's salvation plan in relation to Jews and Gentiles as groups, thereby strengthening and reassuring individual believers.

The epistle has relevance for women, especially in its explication of sin and forgiving grace. This good news is urgently needed by many women, some of whom are willing to accept abuse because they are under the delusion that they deserve punishment for some misdeed in their past. Romans tells of universal sin and the free offer of forgiveness through the atoning work of Christ. For women struggling under a load of guilt, how blessed is the affirmation that there is now no condemnation for those who believe! Paul offers profound insight into the reality of a life liberated from besetting sin. Each believer is summoned to utilize her or his gift in ministry to the body of Christ and to those outside of it (Rom 12). The letters ends with the most extensive list of Christian women known in the New Testament.

Throughout the centuries, women have been defined as daughters, wives and mothers first and as disciples second. Or perhaps more accurately, women have been told that their Christian behavior is best defined as being a good daughter, wife and mother. Romans challenges that position by requiring each woman to take seriously her call before God. Paul asserts that all believers, women and men, must first be disciples. That self-identity then informs the various roles a woman might play in her community, including daughter, wife and mother, but perhaps extending to church, community and occupational leadership service.

There is no dispute concerning the authorship of this letter; all scholars agree that Paul composed this letter. This conclusion is based on the familiar style and language as well as the theology and ethics found in other works by the apostle.

It is likely that Paul wrote Romans from Corinth in about A.D. 57-58. This dating is supported by Acts 20:2-3, which says that Paul spent some time in Corinth before traveling to Jerusalem with his financial gift collected from his churches (1 Cor 16:1; 2 Cor 8—9). He wrote Romans before delivering the gift (Rom 15:25-28), in anticipation of coming to Rome and then going on to Spain.

Paul explains that he is writing to the church at Rome, addressing those from among the nations (Rom 1:5-6, 13; see also Rom 6:17-22; 11:13; 15:14-21). Some interpreters argue that he is also speaking to Jewish believers in the church, citing Paul's discussion about the place of Israel in God's salvation plan (especially Rom 9:1—11:16; 7:1). They add that Romans 16 greets several Jewish believers who are in Rome. Probably these Jewish believers were returning members of the Christian community in Rome. Many Jews and Jewish Christians who had been expelled by Claudius in A.D. 49 returned to Rome after his death in 54. Paul met these expelled Jewish believers in other cities, most notably Prisca and Aquila in Corinth and later Ephesus (Acts 18:2).

Aside from Romans 16, where Paul greets old friends, it is likely that Gentiles are his intended readers. Some of these Gentiles might have been sympathetic to and familiar with Judaism and the synagogue (see Acts 10:1-2; 17:4; 18:7). In addition, the

Greek translation of the Jewish Bible became the Gentile Christians' Bible. It is reasonable to assume a recently returned Jewish Christian presence along with Gentiles in the Roman church. A significant number of women converted to Judaism in this time, and their activities and enthusiastic adherence aroused literary comment.

While no one seriously questions that Paul wrote Romans, there is no consensus as to why he wrote it. Paul is hopeful that the Romans will fellowship with him for a time (Rom 1:11-13) and then send him on his way to Spain (Rom 15:23-24). Because he is not personally known to the Roman church, it is possible that he explains much about his mission and teachings by way of introducing himself. It is less likely that Paul wanted to write a summary of his theology, a sort of last will and testament. This theory does not explain the ethical instructions of Romans 14—15. Moreover, not all of his theology is addressed in Romans. For example, he does not speak on communion, on the makeup of the church or on the second coming of Jesus Christ, each a crucial component of Paul's theology. It is important to keep in mind that this is not a sermon or systematic theology lecture but rather a well-composed and articulated letter, one directed to a particular church that Paul had not visited (Rom 1:8).

The problems faced by the Roman church seem to concern the relationship between Jews and Gentiles, especially as that relates to God's overall plan of salvation for humankind. There is no hint of a group stirring up discord, but there is evidence that the relationship between the law given to Moses and the work of Christ, especially as it pertains to Gentiles, was a live issue. This explains why Paul placed so much emphasis on the proper interpretation of the law (Rom 3:1—4:25), as well as the place of Gentiles and Israel in God's salvation plan (Rom 9:1—11:32).

There has been a tendency in the interpretation of this letter to minimize the historic situation of the Gentiles' grappling for a proper understanding of a right relationship with God through Christ and the Jews' struggle for an understanding of Jesus' work as Messiah within the church. Romans is often read as though it spoke primarily to the individual, answering the question "How can I be saved?" It is true that Romans 5—6 stresses individual responsibility to God in Christ, but that is done in a context of explaining how God, from the beginning of creation, has worked out his salvation plan. It has always been by faith that one is made right with God, and God has always desired that the Gentiles share in his love. Paul wants the entire picture developed, including the work of Jesus that opened the way for Gentiles, as Gentiles, to be part of God's family.

Rome at this time was the center of the Mediterranean world. The city included people from all parts of the empire and boasted about thirteen congregations. Later Christian tradition claims that Peter began the church there and that Paul was martyred there under Nero in the early sixties. No concrete evidence supports these claims, and it is possible that Roman Jews who were in Jerusalem for the first Christian Pentecost took their new faith with them when they returned to Rome.

There is concern about the last two chapters of the letter, as some ancient manuscript and commentary evidence indicates that certain writers knew only the first fourteen chapters of Romans. Marcion, a second-century heretic, was the first person to make a collection of several of Paul's letters, and his Romans letter was reported to end with Romans 14:23. Irenaeus, Cyprian and Tertullian, notable church fathers, do not quote from Romans 15—16 in their writings. But this argument from silence is not convincing proof that Romans was expanded, especially as "every extant Greek MS of the letter . . . contains the full text" (Fitzmyer, 50). Moreover, from a literary standpoint, Paul's argument in Romans 14 is clearly continued in Romans 15. Again, there is some speculation that Romans 16 was a personal letter intended to be sent to Ephesus. This theory is fueled by the fact that the oldest evidence of Romans, $\mathbf{p}^{46}$ (c. 200), includes the doxology of Romans 16:25-27 between Romans 15:33 and Romans 16:1 and then adds the rest of Romans 16. It is more likely, however, that the Jews whom

Paul knew and greeted in this chapter had moved or returned to Rome. Thus it is best to view Romans as originally including sixteen chapters penned by Paul from Corinth to Rome.

Outline

1:1-17	Introduction by Paul to the Romans
1:18—2:16	Gentiles Sin Against God
2:17—4:25	Jews Sin Against God
5:1-21	Jesus Reconciles Believers to God
6:1—7:25	Sin and the Law Work Against Faith
8:1-39	The Holy Spirit Indwells the Believer
9:1—11:36	Jews and Gentiles in God's Salvation Plan
12:1—15:13	Transformed Behavior for the Believer
15:14—16:27	Personal Greetings

Commentary

Introduction by Paul to the Romans (Rom 1:1-17)

Paul understands himself as a slave or servant belonging to Jesus. In the Greek translation of the Hebrew Bible, the Septuagint, done by Jews about two hundred years before the birth of Jesus, many prophets are described as slaves, such as Moses (2 Kings 18:12), Joshua (Judg 2:8) and David (2 Sam 7:5). In Romans 6:16 Paul notes that each human is a slave to sin or to righteousness. There is no middle ground, no third, independent option, nothing that allows for the secular, self-made woman or man. Paul also identifies himself as an apostle, set apart for God's special purpose (see also Gal 1:15). The phrase "set apart" reflects prophetic language like that spoken in Isaiah 49:1 and Jeremiah 1:4-5. This is important to note, as not every person will have a "Damascus road" call to follow Jesus (Acts 9:1-9). Paul is not writing as a Christian per se but with the authority given him by God for a specific purpose, to tell Gentiles the good news of salvation in Jesus. Paul composed this letter on his own; there are no other names accompanying his, such as Timothy (2 Cor 1:1, 1 Thess 1:1), Sosthenes (1 Cor 1:1) or Silvanus (1 Thess 1:1). This fact fits well with one of the purposes of the letter, which is to introduce himself to the Romans.

Paul understands the gospel to be the message of salvation. He asserts that the Messiah was foretold by the prophets, thereby reassuring the reader that God's plan was outlined in advance. Jesus was born a descendent of David, according to the flesh. This word *flesh* is important to Paul, because it is the opposite of spirit. Generally it has a negative connotation, as in Romans 7:14, but here Paul is juxtaposing the ideas of humanness (of David) and divine working (raised by God). The resurrection begins the clock ticking toward the end of the age. Although Paul rarely spends time talking about the earthly life of Jesus, he makes it clear that Jesus was completely human, and thus his resurrection stands as a signal of hope that all believers will likewise be raised.

While Paul is called to be an apostle, those to whom he is writing are called to be saints, that is, "holy ones," as a literal translation of the Greek would read. When asked regarding God's plan for a person's life, a believer can answer confidently that at the least, God has asked (called) all his children to be holy. Whenever life presents a choice and a believer needs direction, an important question to ask is how that choice would promote personal holiness.

Why does Paul state emphatically that he bears no shame concerning the gospel; of what would he be ashamed? This question might be answered by looking at 1 Corinthians 1:18-23, where he points out that the gospel is foolishness to Greeks and a stumbling block to the Jews. Romans were heavily influenced by Greek thought and culture, so that the allusion to Greek opinion is a clever one. Jesus' execution as a criminal was shameful by Roman standards and seemed utterly ridiculous to Greeks (Gentiles). Moreover, it was so contrary to Jewish messianic expectation that many Jews also rejected Jesus as Messiah. Even if others, Jews or Greeks, mock the gospel, Paul will proclaim it as the power to save.

The term *faith* in Paul's writings is critical. He is not speaking of some subjective experience, some warm feeling, nor does he mean a set of principles. Rather, he is referring to God's objective work in raising Christ. It is Christ's faithfulness and God's righteousness that are important. Believers are to live on the basis of Jesus' faithfulness to God's purposes and promises. Because Jesus lived faithfully (through faith), believers live faithfully (for faith).

Gentiles Sin Against God (Rom 1:18—2:16)

Paul begins to speak about the wrath of God as the flip side of salvation. He preaches salvation by faith, but he recognizes that humanity has turned from God to follow wickedness. "They" in this passage are Gentiles—that is, humanity prior to the calling of the Jewish people and those since who refuse to heed God's voice. Paul is describing the devolution of pagan religion, where humans choose to turn from God and follow their own sensual desires. The resultant sexual immorality includes homosexuality, which Paul decries as "unnatural." Lesbianism seems to be directly addressed here by Paul, though a few scholars disagree with this reading of the Greek.

While male homosexuality is documented widely in literature and archaeology, little is written about lesbianism. However, same-sex intercourse among women is attested in artistic representations and in literary testimonia. The observance of the Festival of the Good Goddess in Rome and in that of Demeter at Haloa required homoerotic action, while the introduction into Italy of the cult of Dionysus by women was said to have been accompanied by homosexual activity for men and women.

Some suggest that Paul's antihomosexual stance can be understood as a product of his culture. They argue that humans are born with a particular orientation (heterosexual or homosexual), an anachronistic concept to Paul's day. The theory states that one's sexual orientation has little to do with specific behaviors but is rather an unchanging part of one's personality. Paul's attack against specific homosexual behavior, therefore, is inadequate or irrelevant when speaking about a person's essential makeup.

There are important points to be emphasized in this position, including the fact that Paul lived in a period that undervalued women and proclaimed male dominance and female submission as the rule of law and nature. But there are specific indications that Paul challenged those presuppositions; for example, Romans 16 lists several women who held authority in the church. One cannot conclude that Paul condemned homosexuality out of unconscious deference to his culture. Moreover, in Paul's day homosexuality was, generally speaking, practiced and accepted, though Rome established laws against pederasty (which may not have been enforced with vigor). Paul's injunction against this behavior was more in line with his Jewish heritage and the specific laws in Leviticus 18 and 20 than with any general adherence to broad cultural norms.

Examining Paul's specific language helps illuminate his intent. Paul uses unusual terms for women *(thēlys)* and man *(arsēn),* likely citing the creation account in Genesis 1:27 (see also Gal 3:28; Jesus quotes Gen 1:27 in Mt 19:4 and Mk 10:6). In creating male and female, God's desire was to reveal the Godhead's own unity and creativity. The unity of wife and husband, Paul declares (Eph 5), is a visible symbol of

Christ's union with his church. Sexuality should be expressed within a covenant relationship between two different (female and male) and yet essentially similar (human) beings, paralleling the covenant relationship between Christ and the church or God and Israel. As a pair, male and female witness to the unity of the Trinity, the community of the Godhead. Human society is not complete without both male and female; this means not that each human being must be married to be complete but that humanity must be both female and male to reflect completely the image of God.

The law is written on the human conscience, an innate sense possessed by humans to determine right from wrong or to discover the natural law. Here Paul differs directly from Aristotle, who maintained that women were not endowed with a conscience. Paul can say in Romans 1:32 that humans knew God's law, since it was part of the human constitution, but what they can know about God is limited to his creative acts.

The argument against Gentiles from Romans 1 continues to Roman 2:16; thus the traditional chapter break can be misleading. In Romans 2:1-4 Paul shifts from addressing the audience in third person plural to second person singular as he creates an interlocutor against whom to argue. This method of argument in which the writer engages in a dialogue with a fictitious opponent is known as diatribe and was common in the ancient world. The hypothetical Gentile (Rom 2:1-16) is one who believes he or she has mastered the passions and thus despises those Gentiles who are ruled by their obsessions. Such critics do not realize that their judgmental attitude is just as hateful to God as the sins listed in Romans 1.

God is described (Rom 2:5-16) as the God of Jews and Gentiles. There is no distinction made in favor of Jews in the context of salvation. All will be judged by their actions. It is likely that Paul is arguing against the assumption that Jews will have some special benefit toward salvation. Rather, Gentiles will be judged on the revelation given them, as will the Jews. Because the Jews were given the law through Moses, they will be held to that standard. The Gentiles are accountable to the law of their conscience.

Jews Sin Against God (Rom 2:17—4:25)

Paul turns from the proud Gentiles to the Jewish teacher of Gentiles as he introduces a new interlocutor (Rom 2:17-29). The issue is boasting, and Paul will talk of this for the next two chapters. Some Jews believed that their circumcision protected them from God's wrath and that their obedience to the

Homosexuality

Homosexual activity was not widespread in the ancient world, but where it existed, it was either accepted as one of the noblest forms of love or rejected as one of the basest forms of human vice. Jews without exception viewed it as the latter. Josephus sums up the prevailing attitude: "Our laws own no other mixture of the sexes but that which nature has appointed of a man with his wife. . . . But it abhors the mixture of a male with a male" (*Against Apion* 2.199).

Greek and Roman moralists generally followed suit. Plutarch, for example, called homosexual activity "contrary to nature" and "a completely ill-favored favor, indecent, an unlovely affront to Aphrodite" (*Dialogue on Love* 751D-752B). Upper-class Greeks, on the other hand, accepted homosexual liaisons; some even considered them to be the ideal. Such liaisons were common enough to the educational curricula of upper-class male youth (with an older male mentor; Plutarch *Lycurgus* 17-18) and were not unheard of among upper-class adult males (see Alcibiades' courting of Socrates [*Symposium* 217]; cf. Xenophon *Symposium* 8.32, 37). They were commonplace in situations where men were isolated together for extended periods of time (e.g., soldiers, diplomats; Plutarch *Dialogue on Love* 760D-761E; Xenophon *Symposium* 8.32-34).

Male-with-male sexual relations date at least as far back as patriarchal times. Philo identifies the sin of Sodom as "men discarding the laws of nature" and "lusting after one another" (*On Abraham* 135-36; cf. 2 Pet 2:7-10; Jude 7). Leviticus 18:6-27 names homosexual relations among the abominable practices of the indigenous peoples of Canaan. Specific mention of them in Paul's vice lists indicates that they were a live issue in the Gentile congregations of Greece and Asia Minor during the first century A.D. (1 Cor 6:9; 1 Tim 1:10). And male-male prohibitions from Paul's contemporaries bespeak a needful warning to Jews living abroad (*Pseudo-Phocylides* 3-5: "Do not . . . rouse homosexual passion" [*arsena kyprin orinein*]; *Sibylline Oracles* 2.73: "Do not practice homosexuality" [*mē arsenokoitein*]).

Female-with-female (or "lesbian") sexual relations, by contrast, appear to have been comparatively rare in antiquity. Apart from Romans 1:26, there is no acknowledgment of them in the biblical record, and they receive very little attention in extrabiblical materials. Classical Greece is one exception. Communities of Greek women did exist (for example, on the island of Lesbos). There is also some evidence that sexual encounters were part of the educational process for young females in these communal settings. Plutarch, for instance, claims that in Sparta young females paired up with older women of "good and noble character" (*Lycurgus* 18.9). Sexual activity between adult women seems likewise to have occurred. Plato (fifth-fourth centuries B.C.) treats it merely in theory (*Symposium* 189D-191E), but the earlier love poems of Sappho (sixth century B.C.) show its reality.

Beyond classical times, only a handful of Greco-Roman sources mention lesbian activity, all in a disapproving fashion (e.g., Lucian *Affairs of the Heart* 28; Marcus Valerius Martialis *Epigram* 1.90; 7.67, 70 [late first-early second centuries A.D.]). Yet, the fact that the first-century Jewish work *Pseudo-Phocylides* forbids lesbian activity ("Let women not imitate the sexual role of men," 192) shows that although it may have been rare (or not widely publicized), it nonetheless existed. Paul's reference to women who "exchanged natural intercourse for unnatural" suggests the same (Rom 1:26).

Biblical teaching mirrors Jewish sentiments toward homosexual activity. The created order of male and female without exception is lifted up as normative for God's people. Lot's offer of his own virgin daughters to the men of Sodom (Gen 19:7-8) and the Levite's offer of his concubine to the men of Gibeah (Judg 19:23-24) show just how wrong homosexual activity was thought to be ("wicked," "vile"). Departures from a male-female pairing are condemned in the severest fashion in Mosaic law: To "lie with a male as with a woman" is to commit an "abomination" (a term for particularly heinous wrongs in God's sight; Lev 18:22) and warrants—along with adultery, bestiality and incest—the death penalty (Lev 20:10-13, 15-16). This makes homosexual activity a moral wrong, not merely a ritual or cultic offense (as some feminists claim).

Homosexual activity is just as strongly condemned in the New Testament. Twice Paul warns a largely Greek congregation that "men who sleep with men" (*arsenokoitai*; not *pornoi* ["male prostitutes"] or *paiderastai* ["lovers of boys"]) are enmeshed in a lifestyle that not only is contrary to the sound teaching of both law and gospel (1 Tim 1:8-11) but will prevent entrance into God's kingdom (1 Cor 6:9-10).

Romans 1:24-27 alone treats female-female sexual activity. In this critical text Paul identifies rejection of the created sexual order (male-female) as the direct result of idolatrous thinking and practice. "Ever since the creation of the world," he states, human beings have "exchanged the truth about God for a lie and worshiped and served the creature rather than the Creator. . . . Women exchanged natural intercourse for unnatural and . . . men, giving up natural intercourse with women, . . . committed shameless acts with men" (Rom 1:20-27). While Paul does list other sins that follow from idolatry (Rom 1:29-32), his highlighting of same-sex activity is to be closely noted, as it says something about the intrinsic character of male and female sexual distinctions. This is clear from Paul's use of the Genesis 1:27 terms for "male" *(arsēn)* and "female" (*thēlys* only here and in Gal 3:28) and from his statement that same-sex encounters are "contrary to nature" *(para physin)*—thereby recalling the gender distinctions basic to God's creative design. This is not to say that same-sex sins are greater than other sins, but it does say that sexual aberrations of this sort strike at our humanness in a way that other sins do not (cf. Philo *On Abraham* 135; Plato *Laws* 636B-C; 836A-C; 841D-E).

Bibliography

L. L. Belleville, *A Biblical Perspective on Sexuality* (1997; reprint, Chicago: Covenant, 2001); K. J. Dover, *Greek Homosexuality*, rev. ed. (Cambridge, MA: Harvard University Press, 1989); R. Hays, "Awaiting the Redemption of Our Bodies," *Sojourners* 20 (1991) 17-21; U. W. Mauser, "Creation, Sexuality and Homosexuality in the New Testament," in *Homosexuality and Christian Community*, ed. C.-L. Seow (Louisville: Westminster John Knox, 1996) 39-49; T. Schmidt, *Straight and Narrow?* (Downers Grove, IL: IVP, 1995); G. Wenham, "The Old Testament Attitude to Homosexuality," *The Expository Times* 102 (1991) 359-63. LINDA L. BELLEVILLE

law was only secondary to their circumcision. Paul claims that circumcision is of no value if one's behavior does not match the obedience to the law that circumcision symbolizes. The law that the uncircumcised (Gentiles) followed is the law imprinted on their conscience, which supported the Mosaic law but was not identical to it. The lawbreaker is not a sinner who recognizes her or his sinfulness and repents but rather is one who does not repent even in the face of the evidence against her or him. The one whom God will praise is the one who serves the Lord from a heart of obedience.

This teaching was relevant to Paul because it allowed for the inclusion of Gentiles in the church, but today it may also be relevant to women. The rite of Jewish circumcision identified males as part of God's chosen ones, but there was no special rite that initiated women. In removing that male distinction of circumcision, Paul has leveled the ground not only between Jews and Gentiles but also between male and female.

What advantage is there to being a Jew, and why do they not believe in Jesus? Paul responds that their lack of faith should not determine the truth about God (Rom 3:1-8).

The apostle refuses to entertain the notion that sin is acceptable because it shows God is right. It is preposterous that anyone would wish to take advantage of God's favor. Paul presupposes a moral perspective whereby a person longs to be holy before God. In his letters, however, we find that he meets many people who would sooner justify their sin than consider its consequences for God's honor. How could anyone ever have spread the rumor (Rom 3:8) that Paul advocated evil? Perhaps it is because he allowed Gentiles to enter the church as Gentiles (uncircumcised), hence as "sinners" in some people's eyes (see Gal 2:15).

Jews and Gentiles are under the power of sin (Rom 3:9-31). This sin is more than the sum total of bad deeds done by humans; it is a cosmic force that has great influence over the earth for the present (see Rom 5—6). Every human, Gentile and Jew, is sinful before God. The law brings knowledge of sin, not protection from it.

Though Paul does claim in Romans 2 that each person will be judged by what she or he does, the point is that the moral code of ethics is known even to Gentiles. This law or moral code is the yardstick used by God to judge deeds but not to impute salvation. Jews and Gentiles are on equal footing, because the scales of justice are modified or personalized to reflect the person's background. Jews will not have an advantage based on simply acknowledging the Mosaic law.

With the phrase "apart from the law," Paul has clarified the place of the law in God's overall plan of salvation. The law served its purpose in pointing to God's work in the Messiah. Believers uphold the law, not as a means of salvation but because the law reveals God's holiness and moral expectations.

How could the overlooking or passing over of previous sins reveal the justice of God? The term does not indicate forgiveness. Rather, God is saving up his wrath until the full measure is reached. He does not discipline Gentiles regularly as he does his people, Israel. What might look like a passing over is a delay of judgment and also a display of God's mercy as he gives time and opportunity for all people to repent. Where the Jewish teacher and Paul would part company is with the conclusion that the way to God is through faith, not circumcision and obedience to the Mosaic law.

Abraham is one of the most important figures in Judaism at this time (Rom 4:1-8; see Gen 15:1—17:27). Many Jewish males defined themselves as sons of Abraham as a way of securing their relationship with God. It appears that some Gentiles in the early church were troubled because they were not technically children of Abraham. The issue is boasting, and Paul says that no humans have room to boast in their salvation, because they did nothing to earn it.

Although Abraham lived before the law of Moses and had only the covenant of circumcision, nothing that Abraham did earned him favor with God. Rather, he had faith in God, who justifies the ungodly. Abraham was declared upright before he was circumcised, because salvation was a gift from God even in Abraham's time. God has not changed the plan or mode of salvation.

Circumcision was never intended to save, but it was a distinction that separated those who believed (ancient Israel) from those who did not (Rom 4:9-25). God's promise, not the contractual agreement (the law) established between Israel and God, has the power to save. "Promise" is a key concept for Paul (see also Gal 3), here that God will bring blessing (salvation) to many peoples (nations) through Abraham (Gen 17).

The law reveals the importance of being holy before God, and thus it can be said to bring wrath. There is no transgression without the law (Rom 4:15). In other words, there is no accountability if there is no responsibility given.

The discussion of Abraham concludes by pointing out the necessity of the sort of faith that Abraham displayed. Paul mentions two distinctive aspects of Jesus' role in God's salvation plan: his death and his resurrection. Both are equally necessary to effect salvation. The death of Jesus is what satisfies for the punishment of sin, and the resurrection is what establishes a believer as righteous before God.

Jesus Reconciles Believers to God (Rom 5)

The last four chapters explained that justification by faith in God's promise makes a believer righteous in God's sight. Romans 5 builds on that specific fact to explain life in this new, justified state. Believers have peace and complete acceptance before God, because he has declared Jesus' death an acceptable substitution for human sinfulness.

Paul mentions boasting and uses "we" now to mean Christians. He is boasting in the Lord, exclaiming at God's great power and righteousness in saving him. He is boasting in hope, not in works. He is boasting that God has done a great thing, and he, Paul, is part of that thing, based on God's grace. That great thing is the salvation of Gentiles as well as Jews by their faith alone in God's promise of justification in Jesus Christ. Paul is contrasting the boasting of some who rely on their adherence to the law of Moses as a means of becoming righteous before God and the proper boasting that depends solely on what God has done in Jesus to provide righteousness to believers.

Paul will boast in the situations of suffering brought about by his choices to live for God. This is a direct challenge to those who proclaim that an outwardly comfortable life, relatively free of suffering, marks a true, beloved disciple of the Lord.

Suffering focuses attention on God's love, and hope is confirmed by the Holy Spirit. God's love becomes even clearer as sufferings produce hope. A believer does not create hope any more than a apple blossom works at becoming a fruit. The proof of God's love is the presence of the Holy Spirit in a believer's heart.

In writing that Christ died at the "right time" (Rom 5:6), Paul emphasizes God's sovereignty and astounding love. As evidence of that love, believers in Jesus will receive through him justification and reconciliation with God.

The wrath that Paul mentions in Romans 5:9 is likely the final judgment when God will judge the secret thoughts of all people. Paul sees two parts to Jesus' death and resurrection: his death bringing forgiveness of sins and thus reconciliation, and his resurrection confirming the hope of life eternal with God. Salvation does not mean only an escape from damnation but also offers a relationship with God through Jesus Christ.

The comparison of the first Adam to Jesus is not a one-to-one correspondence, but at least it highlights some specific differences.

Adam sinned, and thus sin was given access to the world of humanity. Sin took root in this world when Adam sinned, and so every human consequently dies, because death is the natural outcome of sin. Here, as in 1 Corinthians 15:22, responsibility for the first sin is attributed to Adam rather than Eve (cf. 2 Cor 11:3; 1 Tim 2:14).

In two other places in the Pauline corpus Eve is mentioned in reference to the Fall. In both places (2 Cor 11:3; 1 Tim 2:14) Eve is said to have been deceived. This refers to Genesis 3:13, where Eve answers God that she was *deceived* by the serpent and so ate the forbidden fruit. It must be noted that the serpent addressed *both* Eve and Adam (the serpent uses the plural *you* when speaking, and the text says "she gave some to her husband, who was with her"). God does not correct Eve's interpretation but agrees that she was deceived.

Eve, in her naiveté, does not represent all women; she has not rendered all women incapable of leading or making decisions. Wisdom itself is portrayed as female in Proverbs. The Old Testament identifies several women as prophets, including Miriam (Ex 15:20; cf. Mic 6:4), Deborah (Judg 4:4), Huldah (2 Kings 22:11-20) and Isaiah's wife (Is 8:3). Strength of character, courage and wisdom in difficult situations were shown by Esther, Abigail (1 Sam 25:14-35) and Jael (Judg 4:17-22; 5:24-27). The New Testament offers as women leaders Phoebe (Rom 16:1-2), Junia (Rom 16:7), Prisca (Rom 16:3-5; cf. Acts 18:1-26), Euodia and Syntyche (Phil 4:2-3), the elect woman of 2 John, and others. New Testament prophets include Anna (Lk 2:36) and Philip's four daughters (Acts 21:8-9).

Adam and Eve both, however, represent all subsequent *humans,* male and female, in their disobedience. Adam (Rom 5:14) and Eve (1 Tim 2:14) are each identified as transgressors (the same Greek word, *parabasis,* is found in both verses).

Humans can sin apart from the existence of the law given to Moses on Mount Sinai. Gentiles have a law in their conscience that condemns or vindicates them. For example, one cannot disobey the speed limit if there is no speed limit. Yet a person might drive recklessly and strike a pedestrian. That driver would still be guilty because she knew that she was being reckless (or at least those who saw the incident could determine that), but one could not charge the driver with breaking the speed limit.

In Romans 5:18 the gift of salvation, brought about solely by God's grace, is contrasted with Adam's "gift" to humanity, which was death. In essence, Jesus' death on the cross and his resurrection reversed the process Adam set in motion. Jesus' gift of salvation breaks the vicious cycle and allows for righteous living. Jesus' act is able to reverse, supersede and overthrow the work of the first man, Adam.

Adam's sin was not reversed by the law; in fact, the law served to increase the various things that Israel could do wrong. Sin, while powerful enough to have death as its consequence, is no match for the power of God's grace shown in Jesus Christ. That grace is the controlling factor in a believer's life.

Sin and the Law Work Against Faith (Rom 6:1—7:25)

Paul asks rhetorically whether God's grace gives a believer the license to sin (Rom 6:1-4). The answer fits logically with his discussion in Romans 5. In God's grace in Christ, sin no longer has any power; thus believers can resist sin.

Baptism connects the believer with Jesus' death on the cross, and by killing the old self which was in Adam, a believer is now "born from above" (Jn 3:3) and is a "new creation" (2 Cor 5:17). The faithfulness of God working through the faith of the believer secures this new life.

Paul urges believers to behave as members of the new reality of grace that Christ has brought. They now have the power to resist sin, as they have moved out of its sphere of influence.

In answer to a second rhetorical question about a believer continuing in sin, Paul responds to those who would take advantage of God's grace (Rom 6:15-23). All humans are slaves to sin or to God. As such, people are not on their own, in some middle ground, independent from God and from sin. In Christ, believers can live the life they have always wanted to, a life pleasing to God, outside the debilitating power of sin.

Here we see slavery as a metaphor for bondage and for meaningful commitment (*see* Ancient and Modern Slavery). Paul may have been the son of former slaves. He may have been attached to the synagogue of freedpersons and those from Cilicia, his home province, for this group spearheaded the persecution of Stephen (Acts 6—9). Freed slaves of Roman citizens received citizenship upon their manumission. Paul may well have thus inherited his citizenship (Acts 22:27—28). Many a freed slave advanced to positions of power and prominence. Thus Paul could see the degradation and dehumanization of slavery but also the opportunities that it might bring for advancement and propagation of the gospel.

Romans 7 begins with an analogy from marriage, assuming rightly that the readers, though Gentiles, will have enough understanding of the Jewish law to follow his argument. Though Paul is not engaged in a discussion of marriage per se, what he assumes about this institution is worth noting, especially for women and men today. Paul does not mention divorce but assumes that a woman cannot live with another man other than her husband. In 1 Corinthians 7, Paul discusses marriage, and there he states that believers should not separate from each other, but that if they do, they should remain single or reunite with each other. A wife is bound to her husband as long as he lives and is free to remarry when he dies, though Paul asks that the second husband be a believer. On the surface, there seems little room for divorce and even less for remarriage after divorce (*see* Divorce; Marriage). This understanding has been used as a weapon against women trapped in abusive situations.

A more careful reading of Paul's teachings on marriage, including Ephesians 5, and Peter's message (1 Pet 3), placed in the context of suffering in general in the New Testament, offers hope to those in an abusive situations. While neither Jesus, Paul nor Peter has sympathy for a couple who decide to explore greener pastures, it is clear that suffering at the hands of a husband or wife is not the kind of suffering that a disciple is called to endure. The wife is to love her husband (Tit 2:4). Paul and Peter make it clear that the husband is to love his wife, to treat her body as his own (Eph 5:25-33) and to honor it (1 Pet 3:7). Considering that these men wrote to real situations, it likely means that some husbands in the first century scorned their wives. But abuse is not acceptable in God's sight. Spousal abuse is not in the category of redemptive suffering.

In summary, then, Paul believes that marriage is a lifelong commitment, and both believers are to honor and support each other. Divorce is not an option between two believers, unless abuse or unfaithfulness is involved (Mt 19:9). Paul's hope in 1 Corinthians 7, that the two believers will reunite, is based on the assumption that the believers were separating because they thought it was more holy to live a single, celibate lifestyle. In Corinth they were separating for an unhealthy reason, much as today people separate because they are falling out of love. In that case, Paul wants them reunited. In the case of abuse, however, we might look to Jesus' words that divorce is allowed because of unfaithfulness.

In Romans 7:7-25 Paul uses *I,* and many commentators have understood him to be speaking biographically about his life before believing in Jesus as Savior. The two main reasons for this interpretation are (1) Paul's admission that with his will, he knows that the law is good and he delights in it, and (2) the use of the present tense in Romans 7:14-25. This theory presupposes that the human is so depraved that even the will is marred beyond any capacity to recognize good. Therefore Paul must be speaking as a believer in the later verses, with a new will that can appreciate God's goodness.

A better way to understand this passage is to suggest that Paul is using *I* as a representative of humanity before the coming of Jesus. He is writing a history of God's salvation work in the world, especially as it relates to Gentiles becoming part of God's people. He will use *I* other places to represent all humans, as in 1 Corinthians 13 and Galatians 2:20 (Fitzmyer, 463-65).

The theory also makes sense of Paul's distinctions between his flesh and will. He notes that nothing good dwells in his flesh, but then he exclaims that his will and his inmost self delight in God and desire good. This theory keeps Paul consistent with his statements that believers are dead to sin. Thus he cannot be speaking about a typical Christian experience in Romans 7, one of defeat and frustration. In this chapter we see the experience of a person who knows the law but has no power to put the law into practice. As he explains the divine value of the law, Paul needs to use the present tense. Paul, representing a seeker, cries out for help from this desperate situation. And he praises God that Jesus rescues those who call out to him.

The Holy Spirit Indwells the Believer (Rom 8)

The flesh, though powerless to resist sin, has been condemned by Christ's work on the cross. Jesus was able to fulfill all the just requirements of the law, and so believers too fulfill them in Christ, living in the Spirit. There is a marked contrast made between the flesh and the Spirit. "In the Spirit" ethics means living by faith in the power and reality of God's perfect gift of salvation. It means recognizing that the power of sin has been defeated in one's life. Paul's ethics are deceptively easy; he asks that believers listen to the Holy Spirit.

A believer's relationship to God is a familial one. Believers are children. As such, they have nothing to fear. Their adoption is secure because God has done it. The cry uttered in the Spirit, "Abba, Father," is confirmation to the believer that they belong to God. The Aramaic word *Abba* was thought to mean "daddy," suggesting a new intimacy that Jesus brought; however, further study has proved that Jesus did not introduce this new use of Abba. It is Aramaic for "Father."

Our heritage in Christ will include a glorious end but will involve suffering in this lifetime. The sufferings, however, are not the defining aspect of the Christian life, because they pale in significance next to the goal: life with God. The earth itself was damaged in the Fall and is itself longing for the end of sin's control (Rom 8:19-22). In this we can see Paul's appreciation for the magnitude of Christ's redemptive work. He suggests that the earth is going through just what each believer goes through—waiting. In both cases, it is waiting for God to make all things new.

The Romans' feeble prayers are magnified by the Spirit, who presents their needs (intercedes) to God in an effective way. They are not abandoned children but are cared for even beyond what words can express.

Romans 8:28-30 is quoted often as a comfort to those suffering, as it should be. But Paul did not say that all things are good that happen to a believer. In fact, one could argue that he says the opposite, that lots of things are bad. But he assures the believer that God uses them for his purpose. Those who love God will triumph ultimately, because God will work out his purpose. The love of Jesus Christ will conquer all the perils faced by humanity, including the ultimate one, death (listed first in Rom 8:38).

Jews and Gentiles in God's Salvation Plan (Rom 9:1—11:36)

One of Paul's deepest hurts is that not all of his people, the Jews, have taken advantage of God's gift (Rom 9:1-5). His sorrow is reflected in his bold and brash statement: he is willing to give up his salvation for their sake. He acknowledges that the Jews of his day are recipients of such wonders from God, including being claimed by God, rescued gloriously from Egypt, given the law, the temple and the prophets' promises, which are fulfilled in the Messiah. This completes the question raised in Romans 3:1, the advantage of being a Jew.

How could Jesus be the Messiah if many Jews, the chosen ones of God, did not accept him as such (Rom 9:6-13)? Would not that preclude Jesus from being the Messiah? Paul argues that not all those who call themselves Jews are truly chosen. He points to Abraham's sons, Isaac and Ishmael, as examples, noting that only through Isaac do God's promises come (Gen 21:1-7). He also cites Rebekah's experience, that one of her twin sons was chosen by God even before he was born, because God's promise, not human designs, effects salvation.

In these examples, the fathers (Abraham and Isaac) and the mothers (Sarah and Rebekah) are given equal billing. It was more common in the ancient world to note just the father, but Paul's point can be made only using Sarah (not Hagar) and Rebekah (see Gen 24—27). God chose these women to further his purpose and to make the crucial point that Israel is called by God, not because of anything Israel did or would do. Sarah learned firsthand the dangers of trying to manufacture God's will by giving her slave, Hagar, to Abraham to have a child for her. Ishmael was born, and dissension settled upon their house (Gen 16:1-16; 21:8-21). Abraham's and Sarah's faith was stretched in trusting that God would place a child in her womb (Gen 17:15-22; 18:1-16). It was God's doing, not any man or woman's efforts, that brought Israel into being. In answer to her request, God explained to Rebekah that the struggle she felt in her womb would continue during the two sons' lives, and that the younger one (Jacob/Israel, Gen 32:28) would be served by the elder (Esau). God revealed to her part of his plan to build a people dedicated to him.

God alone accomplishes salvation (Rom 9:14-29). God is merciful and patient and desires his glory be known. Pharaoh, the god-king of the Egyptians, was given his kingdom by God so that God could show the Egyptians and the Hebrews that he is more powerful than the Egyptian gods, including Pharaoh. If Pharaoh had accepted that truth, perhaps the exodus would have happened differently. The point is, Pharaoh refused to acknowledge the one true God and so sinned. In Exodus 7, Pharaoh turned from God and hardened himself against God's plan. God, knowing Pharaoh's response, is said to have hardened Pharaoh's heart. The Lord forewarned Moses and Aaron of Pharaoh's response so that they would not become disheartened. The point here and in Romans is that God is sovereign over history, and no human, not even the god-man Pharaoh, can thwart God's plans. No human has the right to argue with God on how God proceeds with his plan.

God's plan of salvation is by faith alone (Rom 9:30—10:13). Gentiles are invited, even though in their history they did not strive for a close relationship with the one true God. And Israel, though it had advantages over Gentiles, was tripped up over its understanding of faith. Christ's death and resurrection ended the separation of Jew and Gentile and fulfilled the law, so that all people might be made righteous before God.

A series of questions serves to highlight the disobedience of Israel to God's message, a pattern seen in the prophets, especially Isaiah (Rom 10:14-21). The first question, "How are they to call on one in whom they have not believed?" is directly related to the quotation preceding it, which promises that everyone who calls on the name of the Lord will be saved. Paul notes that a person cannot call on someone in whom she or he has no belief. Lack of belief may stem from not hearing about Christ.

But Paul seems to suppose that Israel has heard; he notes that not all have obeyed the good news (Rom 10:16) and that "they" (the Jews) have indeed heard (Rom 10:18). Moreover, Israel has the potential to understand what God is doing in Christ because the prophets have predicted as much: the nations will turn to God. But Israel has not accepted God's offer of salvation in Chirst.

Often Romans 10:14-15 is used as a missionary call, encouraging believers to travel to faraway places with the gospel. This is perhaps part of Paul's intention, as he was an apostle (similar to a missionary) to the Gentiles. But those Gentiles Paul sought lived in cities also inhabited by Jews, and many of those Gentiles heard the message of the one true God from the synagogue. Thus it would be inaccurate to label Paul as a crosscultural missionary. It is important to keep in mind Paul's original question: why all Israel is not saved if this Jesus is the Jewish Messiah. Isaiah's experience helps to answer the question: he was sent but not believed.

Has God rejected his people, the Jews (Rom 11:1-6)? God has been faithful to Israel and has consistantly desired a relationship based on faith. The idea of a faithful remnant is developed to explain how God has dealt with Israel. There have always been those who have followed God by faith, and Paul includes himself in that number. God had assured Elijah that he was not the only person alive who followed the Lord. There were seven thousand others who had not followed idols. God works through grace, accepting people not based on their deeds but because of God's mercy.

The elect, or the remnant, have gained what they sought: salvation (Rom 11:7-10). There is nothing left to chance, no human is buying off God, no deals being made. God established the way of salvation, which was by faith from first to last. The law given to Moses was to be lived out of faith that God would keep his promises of protection and care. The Gentiles accept Jesus by faith that God will raise them even as Christ was raised (1 Cor 15). With Jews and Gentiles, God has always accepted the heart that trusts him.

The analogy of an olive tree with branches broken off and grafted in is a visual lesson for the Gentile believers that their inclusion into God's family is by grace, completely (Rom 11:11-24). Paul stresses that Israel can be reattached to the olive tree and hopes that his ministry might save some Jews.

Paul expresses his belief that Israel is for a time hardened, or has turned from God (Rom 11:25-32). During this time, many Gentiles will come into a saving relationship with God through Jesus. This is a *mystery,* a word Paul used elsewhere in speaking about the wonderful plan of salvation, the inclusion of Gentiles in Israel as one large family. This does not suppose that in this family, every individual member will be saved. The phrase "all Israel" is likely parallel in meaning to the "full number" of Gentiles.

God is fundamentally responsible for all that happens and controls everything in the ultimate sense. Humans choose sin, but God has chosen to use such disobedience to show his mercy. Joy springs from knowing that God is acting mercifully to Jews and Gentiles (Rom 11:33-36).

Transformed Behavior for the Believer (Rom 12:1—15:13)

The Jews still offered sacrifices at the Jerusalem temple, and pagans continued to offer sacrifices in their various temples, so the image of animal sacrifice is a real one for the Romans (Rom 12:1-8). A living sacrifice, however, is a contradiction in terms. A believer is to be a living sacrifice, one who turns her mind completely to the will of God and thus knows what is good and perfect in God's sight.

Part of being a living sacrifice and renewing one's mind is recognizing soberly one's talents and abilities as given by God. Paul enjoins the Romans not to be boastful, but he does not encourage false modesty. Instead, he asks the believers to present themselves before God and let the talents and gifts given to them by God be used to God's glory and the upbuilding of the church, the body of Christ.

God determines the role for each believer to play in the church, and there are no small parts in this play. The gifts listed in Romans 12 are not to be seen as exclusive, for Paul lists other gifts elsewhere; rather, they are examples of how God might prepare a person to be used in the church. Nor are the gifts related to one's gender; there are no female gifts and male gifts. Within the church, there is functional equality (Gal 3:28).

Genuine love hates evil and seeks good (Rom 12:9-21). Hating evil does not mean that one can take revenge, nor does one have the luxury of hating one's enemy. Instead, the believer is to own God's perspective on what is ethical and exemplary and what is unjust and wicked.

In Palestine, many Jews thought that Rome was evil (Rom 13:1-7). Their assumption was that the Messiah would overthrow Rome and set up God's political rule on earth. The anti-Roman sentiment was based in part on a belief that a pagan empire should not rule the people of God. Paul does not sanction such beliefs, for he does not believe that Christians must be politically self-determining. The higher love of God is demonstrated when the civil laws of the larger community are practiced. Paul defines what he means by being subject to authorities when he discourages disobeying current laws set up by the government. He assumes that the government will keep the community peace and allow Christians the same freedoms the Jews enjoyed in the empire (cf. 1 Thess 4:9-12).

Does Paul then advocate peace at any price with the government? Paul is never willing to give an inch when it comes to a correct and clear understanding of the gospel. He will stand up to other apostles (Gal 2) and will speak harshly to false apostles (2 Cor 10—12) when his core belief in the sufficiency of Christ for Jew and Gentile is threatened. He is willing to accept all manner of beatings if they are done because he is a Christian. Yet he demands respect as a Roman citizen and will not accept mistreatment if people are against him personally. He insists on an escort out of Philippi because he is a Roman citizen (Acts 16:37). He forcefully requests to see Caesar (hoping to present the gospel to him) because he is a Roman citizen (Acts 22:25-29; 25:11-12). This teaching is especially important for women.

If a woman is persecuted because she is a Christian, then God will be glorified by her obedience. But she need not accept punishment or poor treatment because she is a woman. Often women are asked to sacrifice all, claiming this is the Christian way. No believer, however, is called to be insulted in her person, although a believer might be called to give her life for the sake of God. Specifically, for example, no man (husband) has the right to discipline a woman (wife). Domestic violence is never acceptable and can never be excused based on a false notion that a woman is suffering for Christ in such a situation.

At the second coming, Christ will judge the world and reward all according to their deeds and will embrace those who by faith have accepted his work on the cross for their sins (Rom 13:8-14).

Women dropping from exhaustion during pagan ritual forbidden to Christians. (Romans 13:13)

Paul uses the phrase "weak in faith" to connote a believer who is following the food laws and sabbath practices closely, rather than someone who is behaving sinfully (Rom 14:1-15). He encourages believers not to judge other believers on incidental matters of practice that are not sinful but are based on local custom or interpretation of the Jewish law.

Some believers in Paul's time set aside a day as special, and it is likely that Paul is speaking of the sabbath that Jewish believers or those Gentiles who connected themselves with the synagogue (God-fearers) might be setting aside as holy. Gentiles might not think any day of the week more special, as their background would not include such convictions. It might also be that some in Rome are meeting on Sunday, the Lord's day (1 Cor 16:2 may be relevant), though little is known about early Christian worship habits. Paul is revolutionary in declaring that Gentiles do not have to follow the same requirements before God as did Jews.

Some connected meat with idol worship and sacrifice. Most people in the ancient world rarely ate meat because it was so expensive. But during a festival for the city and state gods and goddesses, the wealthy patrons of the city would sponsor meals that often included meat. Thus eating meat was associated in some believers' minds with pagan festivals. Moreover, since much of the meat sold at markets had been previously sacrificed in a pagan temple, some believers thought that eating it would tarnish them or their witness (see 1 Cor 8; 10). Paul makes it clear that a believer who eats meat must not condemn one who does not.

Food issues were very important in the first-century Jewish community. Jesus spent much time teaching about food laws in the Gospels (Mk 2:23-28; 7:18-19 and par.), and Peter in Acts 10 receives revelational teachings about clean and unclean food.

One believer has no right to challenge another believer's eating practices, nor should one flaunt one's freedom to eat meat before those who abstain. Paul's guiding principle, placing the well-being of others above one's rights, is relevant. Paul is speaking about actions that are matters of conscience and culture. Believers should be confident that their behavior will bring honor to God. Respect for others in the body of Christ is of paramount importance.

If believers use their freedom to eat meat but cause pain to another believer by so eating, the good has been rendered bad (Rom 14:16-23). God is most pleased with believers who consider others before their own legitimate privileges. Consideration of others interests God, not whether a believer has the right or best insight into proper Christian behavior.

Paul identifies himself with those who are strong, those who can eat meat with a clean conscience (Rom 15:1-13). The weak are those who adhere to food laws. It is possible that some Gentiles were weak if they had been following food laws learned from the synagogue or if they had concerns about sacrificed meat and its connection to pagan worship. The primary responsibility is not to make the weak strong but to accept them as they are and respect them for their love of Christ. The goal of a strong believer is to build up the body, not challenge a weak believer's faith on a particular issue.

All believers are exhorted to welcome one another as neighbors. This message might have special relevance for women, who traditionally are responsible for the hospitality of the family and the church. In welcoming visitors, in preparing meals, in caring for those in need, a believer is performing acts similar to Christ Jesus. The servant Jesus declared that when anyone helps another, it is as though that person were helping him (Mt 10:40-42). This model of servanthood casts a holy light on deeds that society tends to devalue. It encourages women, the typical servers, to recognize the incredible value their deeds have in God's kingdom.

Personal Greetings (Rom 15:14—16:27)

Paul defines his mission from God as that of preaching to Gentiles, especially those who have not yet heard the gospel. He will not boast about another's ministry and claim it for his own. His preaching in other regions has been accomplished, and thus he is free to journey to Rome. Yet he will not stay long but hopes to travel to Spain to preach the gospel there. He recognizes that he will be in some danger personally when he takes the offering to "the poor saints" in Jerusalem. He requests that the Romans pray for his safety and that his offering is acceptable to the believers in Jerusalem.

Although Paul has never visited Rome, he is able to send greetings to named individuals whom he has known elsewhere in his travels. The greetings constitute a remarkable attestation of the involvement of Christian women in the church. We are given not only their names but also their ministries.

As with other emissaries unknown to a congregation, Phoebe is sent with a letter of commendation (Rom 16:1-2; cf. Acts 18:20; 2 Cor 3:1). These letters gave not only the name of the person being sent but also the qualifications for ministry (cf. 1 Cor 4:17; Phil 2:19-30). She is introduced to the Ro-

---

Women as Leaders

Leadership in the Old and New Testaments is based on the calling and spiritual gifting of God and the recognition of this by his people (Ex 3:10; 4:12; Judg 6:14, 34; 1 Sam 16:13; 18:6-7; Acts 6:3; Rom 12:3-8; 1 Pet 4:10).

The Bible accurately reflects the patriarchal background of the period, when leadership was predominantly male. But at the same time it establishes principles that critique that situation. Miriam, a prophet, led the women in celebration and worship after the deliverance from Egypt. Five hundred years later she was included as one of the three great national leaders of the exodus, when God said, "I sent before you Moses, Aaron, and Miriam" (Mic 6:4; Ex 15:20-21). In the time of the judges, a married woman, Deborah, was already acknowledged as a prophet and a judge when she was called to summon Barak to lead the nation against the enemy. The text does not suggest that Barak was weak (Judg 4:4-9); he recognized that the Lord had chosen to speak through Deborah, and with spiritual insight he insisted that she should accompany him to battle.

There were several prophets in Judah, including Jeremiah, when the book of the law was found in the temple (621 B.C.). But Josiah, the king, turned to the married prophet Huldah, and on her authority the newly discovered book was recognized as the word of God to the nation (2 Kings 22:11-20). Mordecai suggested that Esther had reached her unique position in order to save the nation, and she emerged with unusual authority, even for a queen (Esther 4:14; 8:7-8; 9:29).

God clearly called the first three women and overruled Esther's circumstances to use them as national leaders over both men and women. If they had refused, they would have disobeyed God.

Jesus also confronted contemporary culture. He rejected lording it over one another in relationships among his followers; by word and action, he modeled servanthood (Mt 20:25-28; Lk 22:25-27; Jn 13:12-16). He treated women with the utmost respect, included them among his closest friends and followers, and finally, in a culture that rejected women as witnesses, called them to proclaim the news of his resurrection (Lk 24:5-11; *see* Women as Witnesses). His example influenced the early church as women and men worshiped, prayed and worked together. Phoebe was a leader who helped Paul and served as a deacon in the church. Lydia, Priscilla, Phoebe, Apphia and Nympha are mentioned as women of stature in the church, with homes large enough to accommodate the local congregation at a time when most homes were far too small. Women received the same spiritual gifts, including those of teaching and evangelism, as did men. These gifts were to be used for the strengthening of the churches (Eph 4:7-13; Acts 18:26). Junia, although thought to be a man (Junias) by some scholars, was described as an apostle (a description which even Chrysostom found startling), and other women worked alongside Paul as colleagues (Acts 1:14; 16:40; Rom 16:1-16; Phil 4:3; Col 4:15; Philem 1-2).

The use of women as leaders even in the patriarchal societies of the Bible should make us critique our own culture. Women have shown that they possess gifts of leadership, but these are often undeveloped and lack public recognition in churches. Both women and men were created equally in the image of God and called to increase and have dominion over creation together (Gen 1:26-28). Jesus' example reinforced this. At Pentecost Joel's prophecy served to lay the foundation for the ministry of both women and men (Acts 2:17-18). Our task is to discover how God intends us to use these gifts in the redeemed community on earth.

VALERIE GRIFFITHS

---

mans as a deacon *(diakonos)* and they are asked to receive her (cf. Acts 18:27; Phil 2:29; 3 Jn 10-12). Many English translations change the Greek term to the feminine "deaconess," but Paul is not making any functional distinction based on Phoebe's gender. Thus she carries the same responsibilities and authority as anyone else who shares that title. Paul identifies himself as a *diakonos* (1 Cor 3:5; 2 Cor 3:6; Eph 3:7; Phi.1:1) as well as Timothy (1 Thess 3:2; 1 Tim 4:7), Tychicus (Eph 6:21; Col 4:7), Apollos (1 Cor 3:5) and Epaphras (Col 1:7). Christ too is a *diakonos* (Rom 15:8; Gal 2:17). The term is often translated correctly as "servant" or "minister" because it carries the meaning of someone serving or ministering to a ruler. As such, it would be correct to identify Phoebe as a minister in the Cenchrean church, located about nine miles from Corinth.

Phoebe has come to Rome on the business of the church, and Paul asks that she be given whatever assistance is necessary for her task. Apart from delivering the letter that has been entrusted to her, she has been given a particular mission. There is speculation that this may have been to raise support for the projected visit to Spain, as the word *propempō* is one used for promotion of a missionary endeavor (Acts 20:38; 21:5). Phoebe appears to have traveled independently and may have been able to make important contacts and to secure official permissions that would be necessary for the expedition to Spain.

Teaching center of Thecla, legendary associate of Paul, apostle to Seleucia. (Cf. Romans 16:7)

Paul describes Phoebe as his benefactor *(prostatis)*. The literal meaning is "one who presides" or "a woman who is set over others" (Thayer's *Greek-English Lexicon,* s.v.). This noun is found only here in the New Testament, but the masculine form *(prostatēs)* is employed by Justin Martyr to denote the person presiding at Communion (*First Apology* 65). Paul uses the verbal form of the word in several places, certainly a help in determining the meaning here. In 1 Thessalonians 5:12, the Thessalonians are encouraged to respect those who are over them in the Lord, and in Romans 12:8, Paul uses the participial form to describe the gift of leadership. The term also carries with it a sense of caring or giving aid, though in Paul's use supervisory leadership is emphasized. In the Pastoral Epistles, the word is used of church officials who preside over the congregation (1 Tim 3:4-5; 5:17).

The passive form of "has become" *(ginomai)* has in certain other New Testament passages the sense of appointment to an office, especially in relationship to the apostle Paul (cf. Col 1:23, 25; Eph 3:7). The passive is used in Hebrews 5:5 of Christ being made a high priest, a minister of circumcision (Rom 15:8) and of his being made unto us wisdom and righteousness and sanctification and deliverance (1 Cor 1:30).

The significant contribution of Prisca and Aquila to the advancement of the gospel is noted (Rom 16:3-4). In some dangerous situation, they risked their lives for Paul's sake, thereby putting not only Paul but all the churches of the Gentiles in their debt. In Corinth they had shared with him their home, their business and their common faith. Prisca's (or its diminutive, Priscilla's) name is mentioned first here (as in Acts 18:18, 26; 2 Tim 4:19, though in Acts 18:2 and 1 Cor 16:19 Aquila's name comes first). In the ancient world, the first named in a pair carried the greater honor. Thus it is likely that Prisca was gifted as a teacher and speaker, yet both share equally in their ministry. After sojourns in Corinth and Ephesus, they are back in Rome, leading a house church. They are "coworkers" of Paul; this term *(synergos)* is used by Paul to describe himself and many of his colleagues, including Urbanus (Rom 16:9), Timothy (Rom 16:21; 1 Thess 3:2), Priscilla and Aquila (Rom 16:3), Tychicus (Col 4:7), Philemon (Philem 1), Euodias and Syntyche (Phil 4:3), Mark, Aristarchus, Demas and Luke (Philem 24), and members of the household of Stephanas (1 Cor 16:15-16). To such, says Paul, the church ought to be subject (1 Cor 16:16).

Mary is applauded for her arduous work (Rom 16:6). Paul describes her efforts with the same term that he applies to himself (1 Cor 15:10; Gal 4:11; Phil 2:16; Col 1:29; 1 Tim 4:10). 1 Timothy 5:17 offers the injunction "Let the elders who rule well be considered worthy of double honor, especially those who labor in preaching and in teaching." Other examples of the verb as indicating labor for the gospel may be found at John 4:38, 1 Corinthians 16:16 and 1 Thessalonians 5:12. Each time that the verb is used in Romans 16, it is applied to a woman: Mary, Tryphaena, Tryphosa and Persis.

The name Junia is a Latin one and follows a specific, common pattern in transliterating it into Greek (Rom 16:7). The male form of this name in Latin is Junius (Gk. *Iounios*), while the female form in Latin is Junia (Gk. *Iounia*). In the fourth century, John Chrysostom noted that it is a woman about whom Paul is speaking: "Indeed to be apostles at all is a great thing. . . . But to be even amongst these of note, just consider what an enconium this is! . . . Oh, how great is the devotion of this woman, that she should be counted worthy of the appellation of apostle!" (NPNF 1st series, 11:555).

Later church leaders, uncomfortable with a woman apostle who had leadership within the church, changed her name and created one that is unknown in Greek sources—Junias. The name is nowhere attested in any inscription, public monument, graffito or literary document (for a brief, detailed discussion on this issue, see Cervin).

Junia and Andronicus are notable among the apostles. The term *apostle* as used in the New Testament could refer to the Twelve, but Paul explains his qualification as one who had seen Jesus (1 Cor 9:1; cf. Rom 1:1; 1 Cor 1:1; 9:1-2; 15:9; 2 Cor 1:1; 12:11; Gal 1:1; Eph 1:1; Col 1:1; 1 Tim 1:1; 2 Tim 1:1; Tit 1:1). Acts 1:21-22 also suggests that another criterion for an apostle was someone who had followed Jesus in his earthly ministry. Such a person was qualified, Peter explains, to be a "witness with us to his resurrection." Others called apostles include Barnabas (Acts 14:14), James the Lord's brother (Gal 1:19), Matthias (Acts 1:26), Epaphroditus (Phil 2:25) and unnamed brothers or sisters (2 Cor 8:23). There is no reason to assume the gift/call of apostleship should be restricted to males. Junia is a clear example that it was not. She and Andronicus may have planted the gospel in Rome much as Paul did in Corinth.

Besides Tryphaena, Tryphosa, Persis and Julia, there are two unnamed women (Rom 16:12-15). These are the sister of Nereus and the mother of Rufus. Of Rufus we may perhaps read in Mark 15:21, but the object of Paul's greeting is now in Rome. In a previous location his mother has shown a kindness and concern for Paul that cause him to consider her as a mother to him. The ministry of mothering those who are not of a woman's own blood is one that God has blessed throughout the ages.

Tertius identifies himself as the writer of the letter (Rom 16:17-23). It was quite common to use scribes to write letters or take dictation. Paul hints at this same procedure in Galatians 6:11 and 1 Corinthians 16:21, where he seems to be distinguishing his handwriting from that of the scribe.

The mystery of how God in Christ will save Gentiles has been revealed and completed (Rom 16:25-27). Even the prophets attest to this mystery, resting as it does on the wisdom of God and the faith of the people in Jesus Christ.

Bibliography. R. S. Cervin, "A Note Regarding the Name 'Junia(s)' in Romans 16.7," *New Testament Studies* 40 (1994) 464-70; J. A. Fitzmyer, *Romans, a New Translation with Introduction and Commentary,* Anchor Bible 33 (New York: Doubleday, 1993); P. Jewett, "Paul, Phoebe and the Spanish Mission," in *The Social World of Formative Christianity and Judaism: Essays in Tribute to Howard Clark Kee,* ed. J. Neusner et al. (Philadelphia: Fortress, 1988) 142-61; D. J. Moo, *The Epistle to the Romans,* New International Commentary on the New Testament (Grand Rapids, MI: Eerdmans, 1996); S. K. Stowers, *A Rereading of Romans: Justice, Jews and Gentiles* (New Haven, CT: Yale University Press, 1994).

LYNN H. COHICK

1 CORINTHIANS

Introduction

1 Corinthians is one of the earliest New Testament documents and attests to the skill of the apostle Paul in addressing a multiplicity of church problems. The epistle contains a tacit admission that it was not easy for persons from one religious tradition to find their way into a new realm of belief and practice. The audience appears to have consisted of a mix of highborn and lowborn, of highly educated and illiterate, of Jew, Greek and barbarian. Some converts had little status, education or illustrious family background, while others maintained an exalted opinion of themselves and their spiritual gifts. Snobbery in various forms was rampant.

Formerly some had been idol worshipers and had exhibited a dissolute, promiscuous lifestyle. Addressed to a community in the midst of profound social, political and philosophical change, the letter contains directives to this diverse congregation, all of whom had come to faith in Christ amid difficult circumstances. Mutual accommodation required new patterns and new understandings of one another.

The document offers a portrait of the perplexities and adversities endured by the early saints. Far from the purity often thought to have existed in the early church, we are confronted with the reality of divisions, depravity, debauchery and rancor.

1 Corinthians, almost universally regarded as Pauline, is the prime example of an occasional epistle, written in response to specific inquiries. There is considerable debate as to whether the letter as it now stands is a cohesive document or whether it is two or more different communications combined into one treatise. Although it lacks a sustained argument, the letter is not the patchwork that it may at first seem. The theme most consistently running through this epistle is an appeal to respect the unity of the church and to preserve it from doctrinal and moral corruption.

The adherents of Chloe had reported animosities and factions in the church. "Chloe's people" probably indicates a worshiping community with a female leader. A number of New Testament house churches appear to have been led by women (Acts 12:5-17; 16:40; Col 4:15; Rom 16:3-5; 1 Cor 1:11; 16:19; 2 Jn). Under this leadership, the group had taken the responsibility to inform the apostle of troubling factors and to solicit his help. Here we may gain a glimpse of the significant, if often unheralded, roles that women played in the early church. The initiative of a woman lies behind the letter's composition.

Paul's response deals primarily with issues of particular interest to women. Although Corinth was located at the crossroads of the Mediterranean, nothing is said of commerce or trade. Certain aspects of city life are addressed, but typically male interests, such as law and philosophy, are downplayed.

Though Corinth was the site of the Isthmian Games, the lone athletic image occupies a scant three verses (1 Cor 9:26-27). With the exception of this and construction, the imagery deals with feminine concerns such as wet nursing, child care, bread making, Passover housecleaning and the use of domestic vessels. Images of agriculture and shepherding, known to have involved heavy female participation in antiquity, are introduced. There is an allusion to the cost of a military expedition, an issue that Aristophanes maintained had been of intense female concern three centuries earlier.

The emphasis is on the social and relational aspects of the life of the congregation.

Peace making, an endeavor often espoused by women, is of major importance in the letter. Slavery, prostitution and social responsibility are given consideration, along with cultic activities that held a special attraction for women. Intimate issues concerning women, such as concepts of body, sexuality, puberty, marriage, divorce, feminine attire and conduct, foods and household management, come to the fore.

There are indications that the apostle is responding to messages and inquiries that have been sent to him at Ephesus. At points, usually in rebuttal, he quotes directly from his informants. They appear to have asked about several issues, though the letter may also include responses to other groups within the Corinthian congregation.

Although Paul writes in response to queries, it is not possible to reconstruct these questions in their entirety. Apparently he been asked about sex, virgins, meat offered to idols, spiritual gifts and a collection for the saints. There had been at least one previous letter about sexual problems at Corinth (1 Cor 5:9).

Outline

- 1:1—4:21 Laying Out the Issues
  - 1:1-9 Loving and Affirming Greeting
  - 1:10-17 Divided Loyalties
  - 1:18-31 The Centrality of Christ Crucified
  - 2:1-16 God's Power in Weakness and Simplicity
  - 3:1-23 The Folly and Immaturity of Personality Cults
  - 4:1-21 Buffoons for Christ's Sake
- 5:1—7:40 Sexual Matters
  - 5:1-8 Dealing with Abuse
  - 5:9-13 Maintaining Standards of Sexual Purity
  - 6:1-8 Excursus on Going to Law before Unbelievers
  - 6:9-20 The Transforming and Purifying Power of Christ
  - 7:1-40 Marriage, Singleness, Divorce and Widowhood
- 8:1—11:1 Ethical Matters
  - 8:1-13 Avoidance of Stumbling Blocks
  - 9:1-27 The Identity and Rights of an Apostle
  - 10:1—11:1 Idolatry, Allegory and Application
- 11:2—14:40 Worship and Congregational Life
  - 11:2-16 Male and Female Together in Christ
  - 11:17-34 The Integrity of the Body Destroyed
  - 12:1-31 Harmonizing the Spiritual Gifts
  - 13:1-13 The Superiority of Love
  - 14:1-40 The Orderly Conduct of Worship
- 15:1-58 Resurrection and Immortality
- 16:1-24 Closing Instructions

Commentary

Laying Out the Issues (1 Cor 1—4)

Loving and Affirming Greeting (1 Cor 1:1-9)

In view of the manifold problems facing the congregation, the term *sanctified* is surprising (1 Cor 1:2). Yet *hagiazō* ("sanctified") is used throughout the epistle of some unlikely people, including those who have previously embraced a reprehensible lifestyle and the nonbelieving spouse and children of a Christian. The transforming agent is Christ, who has become for them "wisdom from God, and righteousness and sanctification and redemption" (1 Cor 1:30). A recurring theme will be the need for unity and purity within the body of believers. Here their inheritance in Christ is laid out in positive, glorious terms. They are enriched in him and will be established as blameless by the grace of the God who has called them into fellowship with his Son.

Divided Loyalties (1 Cor 1:10-17)

The earthly reality is less happy. The congregation is riven with factions, dependent on human personality rather than the Holy Spirit's guidance. Those who followed Apollos must have been swayed by the brilliance of the Alexandrian school (Acts 18:24); the adherents of Peter were probably from a Jewish background (Gal 2:7-8); those who maintained that they were of Christ's party appear to have been as factious as the rest. They seem to have adopted a spirituality that placed little importance on matters of everyday life or the human condition. Such individuals displayed complacency toward the sins of the flesh and negativity toward the resurrection of the physical body.

The Centrality of Christ Crucified (1 Cor 1:18-31)

One area of debate was that of epistemology. How did one know truth? On what precepts was such knowledge built? The Athenian Academy had influenced some of the Corinthian Christians, but Paul argues that there is more than one way of knowing and more than one way of perceiving the mind of God.

Patterns of knowing have been a point of dissension. Does one turn backward to the intellectual foundation of the Greeks, or does one look forward to a new and spiritual sort of wisdom? Does one use typical Jewish reasoning or Aristotelian logic, or are there new patterns of thought that Christians may follow? The old ways of thinking had been male-dominated, rational rather than intuitive. Plato had been well aware of the dichotomy between the contemplative life with its philosophical musings and the life of the active individual involved in human society. If Athens typified the retreat of the philosopher from ordinary affairs, Corinth represented immersion in the real world. Likewise Jesus repeatedly pointed to the casuistry of rabbinic thinking that ignored the basic human needs of the faithful.

Women's insights and perspectives are not necessarily the same as those of men, but they may afford significant access to truth. While privileged males had been schooled in certain methods of intellectual inquiry, Paul offers a more universal avenue. The majority of the Corinthian congregation lacked the social, political and financial resources necessary to have command of these esoteric thought processes. Gender further disbarred most women from a comprehension of the academy.

The entry to God's truth is open to the poor, the uneducated, even those without superior mental endowment. To the humble seeker, Christ is made wisdom from God, righteousness, sanctification and redemption. Wisdom is not an abstraction or personification of God to be worshiped. Rather, it is an attribute of God that is bestowed on those open to receive it.

God's Power in Weakness and Simplicity (1 Cor 2)

God's wisdom is more profound than the brightest of human ideas. Here we have not a repudiation of higher education but recognition that the Holy Spirit's power is mightier. Though well trained in the rabbinic and philosophical traditions of his world, Paul acknowledges that spiritual perceptions are communicated by other paths. Individuals denied an opportunity to be schooled in the niceties of a theological education might be empowered by calling, conviction and commitment.

Paul's mission strategy had taken him to Athens, the intellectual capital of the ancient world, to Ephesus, the religious capital, to Rome, the political capital, and to Corinth, the commercial capital. He had dared to come to Corinth to assert the seemingly ridiculous claims of the gospel. His address would focus on straightforward promulgation of the gospel's content, without the highly polished rhetoric that composed so large a part of Greek education.

At the dawn of an era known as the Second Sophistic, rhetoric was queen of the literary arts. Skill in oratory was admired enormously and required intricate training. The results could be dazzling, though content was sacrificed to form. Indeed, one could argue brilliantly for a position that one did not endorse. Paul's commitment was to the truth of his message rather than to its style.

Insistence upon form as more important than substance placed women at a serious disadvantage in terms of communication. Their manner of expression betrayed their lack of formal education and of contact with the cultural bastions of ancient society. Yet theirs was the promise of enrichment in knowledge and in utterance.

The apostle wrote not to sophisticates but to those familiar with mystery religion, the cults of the disadvantaged, and with these images he fashioned his proclamation. These mystery cults filled a need in the life of marginalized persons, especially women; and women flocked to Christianity. It was said that Christianity drew women, slaves and children. To these Paul brought an unsophisticated message that depended not on rhetoric but on the power of God.

The Folly and Immaturity of Personality Cults (1 Cor 3)

Breast milk was sometimes given to initiates of the mystery cults, and Paul depicts himself as wet nurse for infants too immature to be nourished with table food (cf. 1 Thess 2:7; for image of Paul as birthing mother, see Gal 4:19; Philem 10). The nursing relationship between mother and child is one of tenderness and deep intimacy. But in order to grow adequately and develop into maturity, an infant must be weaned onto stronger food. As a mother, Paul must make harmony among squabbling children who each prefer dependence on their own leader.

Women who feel inadequate tend to gravitate to a dominant personality whom they consider more knowledgeable than themselves. For some, it is easier to accept the work of a recognized leader than to think seriously for oneself. The objective, however, is not to take pride in following the deductions of another but in reaching one's own conclusion by mature reasoning.

The imagery changes from nursing to that of cultivation and the importance of cooperation. Jesus too uses the image when he speaks of agricultural teamwork in connection with the ministry of the Samaritan woman (Jn 4:31-42). The motif of collaboration is a recurring one in the Pauline epistles. After a long image about building, the thought of believers as the temple of God is introduced, but in the plural. The use of the plural *hymin* indicates that he is not speaking of the individual believers' bodies (as in 1 Cor 6:19) but of the corporate body, the church: we are together the temple of God, and God dwells among us. Though women were excluded from worship in some of the most important Greco-Roman temples, they not only have access to but also are part of the temple of God. Factionalism threatens the temple of God.

Buffoons for Christ's Sake (1 Cor 4)

Paul and his ministry appear to have been disparaged by some of the factions attached to other leaders. Although he had first brought the gospel to their city, Paul's relationship with the Corinthians had not always been harmonious. If he was revered by some, he had been repudiated by others. At some point he had been treated shabbily by them, and on at least one of Paul's visits, he was rejected (2 Cor 2:1).

Paul writes poignantly of his marginalization. In the midst of his rejection by others, Chloe's people have sought him out and look to him for mediation. Apparently they consider him to be the individual who could most effectively bring unity into their divided midst. Paul counters that it can only be at the cost of personal sacrifice. He notes that he and Apollos are being treated like "scum," literally the sweat and dirt that was scraped off the bodies of athletes after competition. Perhaps the followers of Chloe have been drawn to him by this identification with those who are most unacceptable socially. Chloe's disadvantaged position as a woman may have given her a perception quite different from those of the other factions. Despite the scorn and humiliation that he endured, Paul persevered. His personal concerns were secondary to the urgency of the gospel.

Paul and Apollos have become a theater to the world. He has become a clown for Christ's sake, ridiculed and disgraced as a buffoon. He has taken on the persona of a *mimētēs,* a low-class character or fool in the farcical mime that was much in vogue at this period. Paul exhorts his followers to adopt a similar stance as fellow actors on the stage. Though the role of actor was forbidden respectable women, in the church they might play a role for the advancement of the gospel. Paul the fool is for them father and mother, able to nurture gently or to admonish sternly.

Sexual Matters (1 Cor 5—7)

Dealing with Abuse (1 Cor 5:1-8)

Paul considered the private sexual conduct of an individual to be the business of the believing community. In the case of known immorality in the Corinthian church, he demands that the congregation take responsibility for what they had so complacently accepted.

1 Corinthians 5:1 plunges into a dismaying problem, especially among those who are "called to be saints" (1 Cor 1:2). There is a shocking case of incest: a man makes no secret of the affair that he is carrying on with his father's wife. The case is one that Paul maintains would fill even the pagans with horror. There were traditions of similar alliances (consider Oedipus), but they were mentioned as the direst of human sacrileges. Although the horror that Paul expresses is restrained compared with that of the ancient playwrights, he understands the specific union as a threat to the community of faith.

The text does not tell us whether the Corinthian man was having an affair with his mother or with a subsequent wife of his father. She may have been a girl, for brides were usually between the ages of ten and fourteen. Only the man is condemned, whether because the woman was not within the fold of the church or whether she was too young and powerless to prevent what was happening. In that case, she would be vulnerable and must be regarded as a victim rather than an accomplice.

It seems unlikely that this was a marriage with the father's widow, since Roman law forbade that. The Hebrew Scriptures also prohibited such unions (Lev 18:7-8; 20:11; Deut 22:30), and Reuben lost his position as firstborn because he lay with his father's concubine (Gen 35:22; 49:3-4; 1 Chron 5:1; cf. 1 Sam 16:20-22; 1 Kings 2:19-25).

Buffoons on stage in a theatrical farce known as a phlyax. (1 Corinthians 4:9-10)

By contrast, the Corinthian Christians view the situation with complacency. They take pride in their permissive attitude, "arrogant" when they ought to be devastated by this infraction of God's law. Their acceptance has perpetuated the problem.

The misconduct of one has polluted the covenant community like the pervasive action of yeast. All have been permeated and betrayed. Here the apostle refers to the duties of women at Passover. Before the preparation of the meal and the baking of unleavened bread, there must be intensive housecleaning that is to this day incumbent on Jewish women. They must sweep and scour the house to ensure that even the tiniest speck of yeast has been ferreted out and removed.

Paul lays the responsibility for restoring purity on the offending church member and on the body of believers who have countenanced the conduct. They must neither ignore the outrage nor condone it by their tolerance. After a stinging rebuke, he calls on the faith community to treat the individual redemptively but to repudiate the behavior. The offender is not entitled to full fellowship until he repents and lives a transformed life. The mandate that he should be handed over to Satan is puzzling, but sometimes the world outside the church can best address a problem and bring the sinner to his senses. It is the duty of the church to deal with the abuse, to exclude the offender from full fellowship until he has a chance to reconsider and amend his ways.

Maintaining Standards of Sexual Purity (1 Cor 5:9-13)

While Jesus had dealt with overly judgmental Pharisees, Paul addresses those who were willing to countenance any sort of misconduct within the church. He spells out the sorts of behaviors that are not acceptable, for the most part involving abuse, sexual manipulation and exploitation. Upon these the church must act; what lies outside must be left to God.

There is a distinction regarding the responsibility of Christians to judge the conduct of others. Those outside the church are not within the purview of the body of Christ, and their judgment must lie in the hands of God. Neither should one believer pass judgment on another in petty matters that should be left to the individual conscience (cf. Rom 14:1-12; Col 2:16-17).

Paul lays out a rubric under which the congregation must apply its standards to all of its members. It is the obligation of the body of Christ to deal with flagrant immorality when it arises within its ranks. The apostle's twin concerns are for the unity and purity of the church, and he condemns all that may threaten it.

Those who display serious breaches of Christian behavior are not to be tolerated at table fellowship. The vice lists (1 Cor 5:10-11) contain some of the disqualifying offenses. Many are components of crimes against women. Idolatrous worship frequently required women to engage in ritual prostitution, fertility rites and sexual surrender.

Verbal abuse is specifically condemned, as is sexual immorality, substance abuse and rape. Though often translated as "rapacious" or "grasping," *harpax* is the technical word for a rapist (1 Cor 5:10-11; see also 1 Cor 6:10). One can only speculate about why this condemnation of rape does not find its way into our translations. Rape, even in marriage, is a horrendous crime that leaves severe trauma.

Excursus on Going to Law Before Unbelievers (1 Cor 6:1-8)

Paul moves to the seemingly unrelated matter of judgment and responsibility within the household of faith. Members were going to civil courts of law to have their internal disputes settled. Animosities had risen to such a level that Christians applied for arbitration to those who had only contempt for the church. Although the problems were apparent to everyone inside and outside the congregation, the Christians were not actively seeking a remedy. There was great reluctance to become involved either in the hostilities that flared or in addressing violations of basic moral code. No one within the church may have been willing to mediate in such disagreeable circumstances.

The church must find a suitable judge to arbitrate disputes without appealing to those outside the faith. They have a responsibility not only in this life but also in the one beyond. Those who belong to Christ will judge both this world and heaven's angels. Now is the time to begin the duties that will be theirs in the life to come. Paul's use of the indefinite *tis* indicates that a wise person of either gender might be used as arbitrator (a tradition known in early Israel; cf. Judg 4—5). The role of peacemaker is often congenial to women (cf. 1 Sam 25:14-22). Furthermore, there was hope that a woman would more easily obtain justice within the church rather than in a secular legal system, where female litigants had fewer rights.

The Transforming and Purifying Power of Christ (1 Cor 6:9-20)

In his endeavor to protect the purity of the church, the apostle for a third time turns to a vice list. It again concerns those who are within the faith. As in the Old Testament covenant community, certain behaviors jeopardized the welfare of the group (cf. Lev 18; 20). For the most part, these are sexual misdemeanors. Paul's diatribe employs vocabulary that denotes the agents who do these deeds—though their identity will change.

First come those who are sexually immoral. The word *pornoi* refers to prostitutes of both genders and to those who engage in other sorts of sexual impropriety. Then follows the mention of idolaters and adulterers, an association often made in Hebrew literature. Throughout the Bible there are repeated condemnations of adultery and fornication, but seldom is there a mention of the next two behaviors. *Malakoi* refers to one who is soft or effeminate, or the one penetrated in homosexual intercourse. *Arsenokoitēs*, apparently coined from the Septuagintal language of Leviticus 18:22 and Leviticus 21:13, denotes the penetrator or active partner in same-sex union.

Here we find one of the early suggestions of what will later be stated directly: some of the Corinthians had formerly been pagans who had not left behind all of their old practices. Homosexual acts were sometimes performed in certain religious rites, for Dionysus and Orpheus were said to have introduced the practice. Thus the behavior had been sacralized, as were rape, fornication, prostitution, abuse and drunkenness. All found a place in the ancient myths and their ritual reenactments. What was expected in pagans' modes of life and worship could not be tolerated by the Christian community.

All these, along with the exploitive, drunkards, verbal abusers and rapists, will not inherit the kingdom. Those whose deeds have been unacceptable in the community may find a new identity, however, as those who are washed and sanctified and justified. Regardless of their past, they are joyfully received as part of God's new family. Paul's willingness to accept even prostitutes is perhaps demonstrated by his quotation (1 Cor 15:33) of a snippet from a play about a famous courtesan, Menander's *Thais* (218).

Of Liberty and Its Loss (1 Cor 6:12-14). In 1 Corinthians 6:12 there appears to be a quotation in vogue among the dissidents: "All things are lawful for me." Paul takes up the saying and executes a play on words. *Existi* is usually translated as "it is permitted" or "it is lawful." It may also be rendered as "it is right, possible, fitting or permitted." The root form will occur as well in a substantive noun, *exousia* (often "power" or "potential" but used in 1 Cor to denote the right or freedom to make certain choices; 1 Cor 7:37; 8:9; 9:4-6, 12, 18), and in a verbal form, *exousiazō* (here and in 1 Cor 7:4), meaning "to have mastery" or the right of decision over another. The passive form used here indicates that Paul would no longer have control of his choices. He argues that though all things may be licit, they do not benefit the church or even his well-being. He might well be entrapped and coerced by the indulgence of his desires.

The Bonding Power of Sex (1 Cor 6:13-18). The body and its parts are given for appropriate use. In order to promote health and proper functioning, these uses must be respected. The body (involving the physical, emotional and spiritual nature) had never been designed for impurity, obscenity, fornication or adultery. The personality is intended for God and can only thus know its ultimate fulfillment. Other paths mean prostitution of the soul.

The physical aspects of the body are in view as well. Meat serves the *koilia* ("belly," though the term also meant "vagina"). The double meaning fits well into the next statement that the body is not for *porneia*. The body, no less than the soul, of a believer is bound to God in a covenantal relationship. The union of human bodies is sexual and spiritual, intended to enrich and bless. Here, as at 1 Corinthians 15:35-44, we see the body as vehicle of the soul, an arrangement that is intended to last into eternity.

The apostle to the Gentiles addresses sexual behavior and its implications in a radically new way. With a profound understanding of the nature and power of sexual union, he follows Jesus in viewing sex as glue that bonds two disparate personalities into a powerful and indissoluble unity. When Paul speaks of being joined to a prostitute, he uses the word *kollaō* (1 Cor 6:16, lit., "he that is glued to a prostitute is one body"; *kollaō* is also used in Mt 19:5, a Septuagintal rendering of Gen 2:24; for a sexual use, see *Anthologia Palatina* 1.73). The term means in the first instance to glue or cement something but also to bind one thing, element or person to another, to join fast, to unite or to bond indissolubly. Those of us who have struggled to pull apart what has been joined with some of the modern glues know that it is sometimes easier to break the fabric rather than to undo the cemented joint.

Paul recognizes sex as having power to sanctify an unbelieving partner and the resultant offspring in a marriage. It gives each power over the other's body. As Derrick Sherwin Bailey writes, "He [Paul] insists that it is an act which, by reason of its very nature, engages and expresses the whole personality in such a way as to constitute an unique mode of self-disclosure and self-commitment." Sexual congress unites not only the two individuals but also the believing community to the sexual partner of a Christian. The sin is against both the individual body and the corporate body.

The text advises, "Shun fornication *[porneia]!* Every sin that a person commits is outside the body; but the fornicator sins against the body itself" (1 Cor 6:18). The implication is that one inflicts upon oneself a spiritual, pychological or even physical injury. This thread is taken up by Paul's question, "Should I therefore take the members of Christ and make them members of a prostitute?" (1 Cor 6:15). Perhaps the answer is found in the previous comment that a little leaven exerts its influence on the mass of dough. An ungodly sexual union on the part of one member affects all.

Sexuality, according to Paul, lies far closer to our spirituality than we might imagine. The powerful bonding force may join us appropriately or inappropriately. Such union can do great harm to the other, but it can also do great harm to ourselves. We have come to realize that one person's sexual conduct can put a whole society at risk.

A recurring motif is that of the body: body as representing the personality, body as representing the believing community, body as the temple of the Holy Spirit. Twice in this section Paul repeats, "You are not your own. For you were bought with a price; therefore glorify God in your body" (1 Cor 6:19-20; 7:23). Sexual expression must first glorify God and then respect the unity of the covenant community.

Marriage, Singleness, Divorce and Widowhood (1 Cor 7)

The apostle has some remarkable things to say about legitimate sexual union. He calls for equality in the bedroom. The husband does not have power over his body but the wife, and the wife does not have power over her body but the husband. Furthermore, each is to give the other his or her marital due. Sex is an integral part of marriage between believers, and no one is to deprive anybody in this respect. There is to be mutuality in the marriage bed.

This entails not only sharing one's body but also the right to have one's body respected. In sexual union, believers are to be considerate of one another. The injunction not to defraud one's partner has often been interpreted to justify inappropriate demands on a woman's body. Practices that are repugnant to one member of the union constitute a deprivation of a meaningful and satisfying experience. According to 1 Thessalonians 4:3-6, sexual expression must be made in holiness and honor, without violation or exploitation. A believer's body is the temple of the Holy Spirit, and God will execute vengeance against anyone who debases this temple of God.

Paul maintains that it is a gift to be married and a gift to be single, and sex is basic to marriage. Only mutual consent might, for a time, remit the obligation of each partner to meet the other's sexual need. If sex is power, it also demands responsibility. Neither partner is to deny the other its joy and fulfillment.

This was an unusual viewpoint in a society in which women were often socially, emotionally and sexually deprived, nor was any need seen to rectify the situation. The remark of Demosthenes (*Against Neara* 59.122) was frequently quoted: courtesans were for companionship, concubines to meet everyday sexual needs and wives to tend the house and bear legitimate children. In an effort to raise the birth rate among citizens, Solomon had decreed that a husband, however reluctantly, must visit his wife's couch at least three times a month. By contrast, Paul understood sex as a drive that is not to be denied but recognized and channeled in meaningful ways.

Paul's permission to remain unmarried stood in direct opposition to the demands of the Rome state. Cicero tells of a fine that was imposed on the celibate (*De Legibus* 3.3). Two pieces of legislation, the *Lex Julia de Maritandis Ordinibus* (18 B.C.) and the *Lex Papia Poppaea* (A.D. 9), were designed to prevent celibacy and consequent childlessness. Widowers were allowed six months before they were expected to remarry, and widows were given an eighteen-month respite from marriage. Sensibilities were of little regard compared with the necessity of raising the birth rate. Those who procreated at least three children were given special privileges by the state. Plutarch noted that many persons married and had children to reap the legal benefits rather than from a genuine desire to build a devoted and caring family (*Amore Prolis* 493E), but Paul encouraged marriage only when there is a true yearning for conjugal union.

The apostle felt that in at least one situation other than infidelity, divorce could be countenanced (*see* Divorce). Jesus had responded to the debate among his contemporaries over legitimate issues for which there might be dissolution of a marriage (Mt 19:9; Mk 10:11-12; Lk 16:18). Even the treatment in the Sermon on the Mount appears to have been a repudiation of rabbinic casuistry (Mt 5:31-32). The school of Hillel proliferated excuses for which a woman might be put away, preferably without the return of her dowry. If her family could not arrange another marriage for her, she was left with few choices for survival other than prostitution. Opportunistic, male-dominated patterns of divorce and remarriage destroyed lifelong commitment in Jewish and Greco-Roman society (*see* Marriage). Jesus condemned a system in which the man made the decision and the woman was left vulnerable.

The situation in 1 Corinthians 7 has some parallels to the stark days of the Jewish return from the exile in Babylon, when many men found it expedient to divorce their Israelite wives and to marry instead the pagan daughters of wealthy landowners (Mal 2:11-16). Spiritual values had been exchanged for material ones. Unlike Ruth and Rahab, the Gentile wives did not appear to have developed any connection with the faith community. The husbands had invested so little in their home lives that half of the children could not even speak Hebrew (Neh 13:24). These marriages had drawn people, including religious leaders, away from the covenant community and concomitantly produced children who had no knowledge of God's ways or of Israel's distinctive role among the nations. Levites and priests had forgotten their sacred trust to preserve the ways and worship of the true and living God. In their dual role as priests and public health officers, theirs was a responsibility to the community (Num 1:53; 3:7; 8:19). Divorce was necessary to reestablish themselves in the covenant (Ezra 10:1-3).

The issue in 1 Corinthians 7 is one of relationship not only to an unbelieving spouse but also to a community of faith. In this case, the issue is not that of having divorced a believer but of an individual coming to Christ after the marriage. Paul cautions the believer not to leave the mar-

Singleness

How do we live in society? How do we ensure that life continues into future generations? These two questions are as relevant today as they were in Old and New Testament times. They encompass issues such as the public and permanent commitment of a man and a woman to each other (*see* Marriage), sexual intercourse and procreation, as well as the outworking of one's service to the Lord. Traditionally *singleness* has been an umbrella term to indicate either no or a yet-to-occur lifelong commitment to one person of the opposite sex and therefore by implication a celibate and childless life. Nevertheless the boundaries are quickly stretched in instances of widowhood, nonconsummation of marriage and deliberate abstinence from sexual intercourse within marriage (generally for a limited period of time and motivated by a spiritual impulse, 1 Cor 7:5).

At the core of the discussion lies the question of uncompromising, loving commitment, attested to throughout the Bible as being fundamental to the growth and dignity of the person. Unworthy commitment is degrading to the person and dishonoring to God, however, and Scripture presents a hierarchical order in which Yahweh is to be loved above all (Ex 20:3) and in which commitment to a spouse may mirror but not supersede this heavenly relationship (2 Cor 11:2; Rev 21:2). Marriage is the norm in human life, yet Scripture does not affirm it as necessarily better. Old and New Testament examples of singleness include Jeremiah (Jer 16:2), John the Baptist and Jesus; Paul too declares his singleness and sees this as a gift from God through whose grace it is maintained (1 Cor 7:7-8). The exalted status of these men in biblical terms has inspired many since to embrace the same state.

Scripture affirms the life so completely committed to God that commitment to another would risk introducing a diversion and distraction (Lk 17:27-30; 1 Cor 7:28). Singleness is portrayed as a positive choice of joyous, willed and willing obedience that ultimately liberates the bearer both emotionally and practically (1 Cor 7:32-35). Single people can be dedicated totally to the kingdom of God and widely able to practice the command to love their neighbor. It is unfortunate that lived examples of undivided devotion to and service for the Lord have all too easily been both awkwardly lived and scorned. Often single people find the privilege of their singleness deprecated and the outworking of Jesus' teaching emphasizing the need to value a relationship with him above all others (Mt 19:29; Lk 14:26-27) considered at best only second best and at worst unattainable or undesirable. Those who actively choose singleness are accompanied by those challenged to accept the state through force of circumstance (Mt 19:12). Within Christianity these are often women, due to both longevity of life and faith commitment; these women nevertheless have throughout the centuries radiated the truth of God's Word through their lives, witness, work and achievements.

For some, however, singleness remains an unwelcome position in which pain may well outweigh the pleasure of privilege. As so often in Scripture, ultimate reassurance is found in eschatological hope: those of the life to come "neither marry nor are given in marriage" (Lk 20:35 NRSV). Human wholeness and completeness, epitomized on earth by the single Jesus, will be expressed once again through singleness in heaven.

Bibliography

W. Deming, *Paul on Marriage and Celibacy,* Society for New Testament Studies Monograph Series 83 (Cambridge: Cambridge University Press, 1995); T. Partridge, *The Challenge of Singleness* (London: Marshall, Morgan & Scott, 1982); V. M. Sinton, "Singleness," in *New Dictionary of Christian Ethics and Pastoral Theology,* ed. D. Atkinson and D. Field (Leicester, UK: Inter-Varsity Press, 1995), 790-92.

ALISON LE CORNU

riage because of the new commitment to Christ. Continuance in the marital bond may lead the unbeliever to faith. If even a liaison with a prostitute makes her one with the body of Christ, how much more is effected by a bona fide marriage? The unbelieving spouse is recognized as a legitimate appendage to the faith community; and the children, apparently being reared in the nurture and admonition of the Lord, are considered holy, as the Corinthians are considered holy.

This might, however, place unwelcome constrictions on the unbelieving spouse. Christian commitment of necessity infringes on the ordering of the household and might rouse the ire of an unsympathetic spouse. Tertullian advised his wife that, were he to die, she should not marry a non-Christian, lest he refuse to countenance her rising in the night to pray, taking food from the larder to feed missionaries or walking through the poorer streets of the city to visit the sick.

If the unbelieving partner cannot accept the spiritual values of the believer, he or she may leave the marriage without any onus being placed on the remaining partner. "In such a case the brother or sister is not bound" (1 Cor 7:15; *douleuō* has the sense of bondage or enslavement) to hold the spouse in the marriage or in the confines of the believing community. Rather, believers are called to peace.

Paul argues that people have the right to remain single. In particular, he addresses the plight of the daughter who was married off at far too young an age. Even Aristotle remarked that fewer young mothers would die in childbirth if they were allowed to pass through puberty before marriage (*Politics* 1335A 19). And the Spartans refused to marry off their daughters when they were "too young or unready."

The young woman usually was married to a much older man whom she did not know and did not want. Juvenal described how a girl might scream and cling to her mother as she was forcibly removed and borne to her husband's home. Frequently a girl's first sexual experience was an unhappy one. Plutarch advised husbands to be patient with brides who have been alienated from them by their first experiences in marriage (*Moralia* 138C-E.).

1 Corinthians 7:36-38 may be understood either as speaking against marriage or against giving a young girl in a marriage for which she was not willing or ready. Helen Barrett Montgomery, in *The New Testament in Modern Speech,* translates it thus: "If, however, a father feels that he is not treating his virgin daughter in a seemly manner, in leaving her unmarried beyond the flower of her age, and so the matter is urgent, let him do what she desires; he commits no sin. Let the marriage take place. On the other hand, he who is firm in his purpose and is under no compulsion, but is free to carry out his own wishes, and who has determined to keep his daughter unmarried, does well. So he that gives his daughter in marriage is doing right, and he who keeps her unmarried will be doing better." Thus understood, the text gives the woman a chance to marry if she wishes once she has passed through puberty. This was far more humane than forcing marriage on an immature girl.

In Paul's view, freedom from the obligations of marriage was freedom to serve Christ. Nevertheless, he defended the right of the apostles to be married and to travel with their wives and specifically mentions Peter in this regard. Paul was not blind to the complications that marriage could bring and pointed out that he preferred to remain single. Thus he was more able to give himself to the exigencies of a traveling missionary.

Excursus on Slavery (1 Cor 7:21-23)

In the main, it is best to remain in the condition where one first made a commitment to Christ, whether married or single. This is expanded with the recommendation that those who came to Christ as slaves should not now seek their freedom. Yet Paul, who was free, maintains that he enslaved himself to all in order to win all. In his thinking, the metaphor of slavery has positive and negative aspects. Slavery under the Romans sometimes offered excellent prospects for education, a trade, career advancement and promotion to a responsible position (*see* Ancient and Modern Slavery). A case in point is the freed slave Felix, the Roman procurator before whom Paul was tried (Acts 24:22).

There have been scholarly suggestions that Paul may have been the son of freed slaves and had in this way received Roman citizenship. He was a leader in the persecution of Stephen, whose main opponents appear to have come from the synagogue of freedmen (Acts 6:9). If such was his background, his ambiguous stance on slavery might be better understood.

Ethical Matters (1 Cor 8:1—11:1)

Avoidance of Stumbling Blocks (1 Cor 8)

1 Corinthians 8 brings us to a subject of concern for women because it touches on relationships. Former idol worshipers found themselves at an unexpected juncture because animal sacrifice was a major component of Greek religion as well as opportunity for socialization. Meat was not a staple of the ordinary diet, and sacrifice provided an opportunity for enjoying a meal of roasted flesh. Excavations of the temple of Dionysos at Corinth reveal the remains of several private rooms for the accommodation of small dinner parties.

Thus Paul may appropriately ask what others are to think if they see a Christian participating in a feast in the idol's temple. Some believers would say that the idol meant nothing to them and that they viewed the occasion as an opportunity to maintain business or social ties with their old friends. For socially disadvantaged women, this convivial setting may have been the most difficult aspect of the old religion to renounce.

Paul agrees that an idol has no reality as a deity, but the conscience of other believers is another matter. In essence the question is whether offense should be given to old friends, who may feel snubbed by Christians' refusal to attend their banquets, or whether instead to offend believers who were struggling to break free from a strong bond with the old cult. The latter could not comprehend the attendance of other Christians at a gathering that so smacked of heathenism and all its accoutrements.

In this case, the first loyalty must be to the body of Christ and to the sensitivities of its members. Nothing should be done to confuse or impede those coming to faith in Christ. Even if their enlightenment enabled some to attend a sacrifice without a twinge of religious conscience, this was not the path of a love that built up others in their faith.

The Identity and Rights of an Apostle (1 Cor 9)

Paul moves to a defense of his methods of ministry. He declares the Corinthians to be "the seal of my apostleship in the Lord" (1 Cor 9:2). If he chooses to be self-supporting, that is his right. It is also his right to travel with a wife, as do Peter and the other disciples. The early church retained a memory of these traveling husband-wife teams, and especially of the devotion of Peter to his wife, even at the moment of her martyrdom. The wives were involved in ministry and were said by Clement of Alexandria to have gained entrance to the secluded quarters of women (*see* Women in Mission).

In 1 Corinthians 9:16-18 Paul expresses a compulsion to proclaim the gospel by word and deed. He maintains that he deserves no thanks for performing what he is impelled to do. He must not only preach Christ but must do so in a way that is freely available to all. No financial expectation is placed upon his hearers.

This same passion drove women in the early church to share the gospel with the poor. They studied the Bible avidly and commissioned Jerome to render the Bible into the vernacular so that the poor might understand it. They founded teaching centers and hospices for refuge and for healing. They supported orphans and educated them, visited households in need and tended the dying. All this they did at their own expense, even to purchasing gravesites in which to bury paupers. When Paula was reproved for her immense generosity, she was asked what she would leave to her children for an inheritance. She replied, "Jesus Christ."

Not only is Paul free to proclaim the gospel at his own expense, but he is free of other constraints as well. Rather than adopting a libertarian stance, he curtails this liberty in order to gain others for Christ. He will move among varying cultures and traditions in order to win persons of every sort and condition. He is willing to adopt their culture and their modes of expression. Just so did Gladys Aylward and Mary Slessor adapt their lifestyle to those whom they served, and just so did they reach their hearts.

The chapter ends with an athletic image, one that might have appealed to a city that hosted the Isthmian Games every second year. Here is one of the few allusions to activities that would be of interest to women only as spectators, although Spartan women did participate in running races. Paul ends by saying that he beats his body under and places it in bondage. This curious use of *body* apparently refers to bodily lusts and needs rather than to the body as personality. The bodies of athletes were subjected to enormous discipline. The prize for Paul's training is not the laurel wreath, however, but approval with God.

Idolatry, Allegory and Application (1 Cor 10:1—11:1)

Storytelling has always been a domain in which women excel. Whether as mothers, nurses or household attendants, women preserved the ancient myths and gave them new life in the telling. Plato remarked that by their stories nursemaids shaped the souls of their charges (*Republic* 2.377C). Thus we see a paradigm developed that had particular significance for women. By their selection and interpretation of Bible stories, mothers and nurses influenced spiritual formation of the young. The interpretation of the early Christian exegete might be profoundly relevant and instructional to the congregation (cf. 2 Tim 1:5). All good storytellers put their direction and embellishment on the basic material.

Just so we may observe Paul's shaping of an ancient story. His objective is to warn against idolatry, but he stops to allegorize other wilderness experiences of Israel. From these he draws out spiritual lessons that are not apparent in the text. In this he stands in a vigorous tradition embraced by monotheist and pagan alike. Paul's Jewish contemporary, Philo of Alexandria, was the most adroit at drawing spiritualized meanings from episodes that are told straightforwardly in the Hebrew Scriptures.

The most basic need in the desert was for water. Twice water flowed forth from a rock to meet the wanderers' need (cf. Ex 17:6; Num 20:11; Ps 78:15-16). In Paul's rendering the two rocks are merged into one and interpreted as Christ from whom life-giving water flows. The supply of water has special significance for women, who must assume the responsibility for the family's need of drinking, cooking, washing and watering livestock (cf. Jn 4:13-15).

After his flight into spiritualization, Paul's argument moves to a more basic application to a present situation. The exodus events were intended as examples *(typoi)* to present-day Christians to warn them against yielding to their lusts. The Israelites going astray after idols prefigured the defections of Corinthian converts, especially the worship of idols. Paul warns believers against those practices that accompanied pagan rites—feasting, promiscuity and sacred prostitution. He moves to the story of the seduction of Israelite men by Moabite cult prostitutes (Num 25:1-3; 31:16) and then to those who were afflicted by serpent bites because of their murmuring and complaining (Num 21:5-6). Just so those who complained of the demands of Christ on their lives were guilty of tempting Christ. Renunciation of pagan ways was not easy. The ancient stories were given as spiritual "examples" for guidance, encouragement and warning.

The import of the wilderness wanderings must call the Corinthians to the paths of the true and living God. They could no more embrace God and idols than could the ancient Israelites. To share the body and blood of Christ brought one into the fellowship of the body. Here for the first time, *body* implied the church, the body of believers. Table fellowship was not possible with Christ and with false gods. Although the latter had no reality, those at their banquets venerated them as a living and powerful presence. Participation in the ritual feast, whether pagan or Christian, is an act of worship.

The importance of sharing a common meal will recur. Breaking of bread is part of the Eucharist, but also part of congregational meals. Women, traditionally those who prepare and serve such communal meals, are the chief ministrants of a spiritual grace. They welcome the disparate members and lead them to the tables where emotional and spiritual bonds are created. Ties are formed, joys and concerns shared, needs understood and discussion of aspirations promoted. Such fellowship remains one of the major sources of the bonding and development of the church as body of Christ.

To share the meal as an act of pagan worship is unthinkable. Like a parent arbitrating between bickering children, Paul has addressed the dissidents who are weak and who are strong. It is important for each group to understand what he says to the other so that they may understand their respective concerns and viewpoint. He cautions against exasperating the Lord and asks, "Are you stronger than [God]?" They are free as Paul is free, but freedom must be a blessing rather than a stumbling block to others.

Worship and Congregational Life (1 Cor 11:2—14:40)

Male and Female Together in Christ (1 Cor 11:2-16)

The beginning of 1 Corinthians 11 brings us to a Scripture portion that is fraught with theological, social and ethical significance. Interwoven in the text are issues of relationships within the Trinity (*see* The Trinity), between men and women, and within the worshiping community.

We are first told that Christ is head of every man. This would have great relevance for the new Christian, torn between loyalty to family and to Christ. In the Roman legal system, only the oldest male agnate (whether father, grandfather or even great-grandfather) was the recognized person (i.e., head) of the family. As such he made domestic, financial and legal decisions for the family. He arranged marriages and also made religious choices for the family, expecting those under his control to participate in the worship of the ancestors and to make the appropriate offerings. This control, known as *patria potestas,* was not only onerous but in many instances stifling. The Greek system, though less stringent than the Roman, still deprived grown children of full personhood.

Thus Christ as head is good news for those who struggled with pagan ways. We must understand that the Greek and Latin words for "head" frequently indicated "source" or "beginning." Tiberius calls Augustus "your head and a father of the people" (Dio Cassius *Annals* 56.41), while Ulpian declares that "every woman is both the head [beginning] and end of the family." In Greek poetry, Zeus is called "head" and "beginning" of all things. Esau is "head and progenitor" of the Edomites. Men might look to Christ as their source and progenitor in the new birth, and their essential loyalty belonged to him.

The text follows the initial statement with a concomitant concept: that man is head of woman. *Kephalē* ("head") did not ordinarily imply a metaphor of authority; more often it had the sense of source or point of beginning. This refers in part to Eve being drawn from Adam (1 Cor 11:8, 12), though it also serves to define the status of a married woman. In some forms of marriage in the Roman Empire, a woman passed under the *patria potestas* of her husband's family, but more frequently she remained under the structures of her own.

In either case a woman's ability to serve Christ was restricted. A wife who was transferred into her husband's family assumed the legal status of a daughter in relationship to him. Nevertheless, she might thereby gain an independence from male agnates who had no understanding of the gospel. As the text proceeds, it will offer the believing wife greater status than the subordinate role of daughter.

The final part of the statement declares that the head of Christ is God. If we are to assign to "head" a metaphorical value commonly used in English, then God becomes chief or superior of Christ. This does violence to the concept of Father, Son and Holy Spirit as equal in goodness, power and love. The notion of any subordination within the Godhead drew repeated condemnation from church councils. It is more logically and theologically consistent to understand the Father as Source, sending forth the Son, the Son as source of every man, and man as source of woman.

Clothing Exchange and Gender Identity. The thought shifts to propriety of dress in worship. The directions to men are often overlooked, but they are important. In the religions known to have existed at Corinth, especially in Dionysiac celebrations, the exchange of male and female garments was a ritual act. Men in the cult of Cybele castrated themselves to become she priests. For women too, donning male personae was a part of worship. In a painted vessel recovered at Corinth a woman dances before Dionysos with a false phallus.

While there was deliberate clothing exchange in cults, it could not mask the deeper problems with sexual identity that were addressed by such moral philosophers as Epictetus: "Therefore we ought to preserve the marks God has given us; we ought not to give them up, nor, as far as we can prevent it, confuse the sexes which have been thus distinguished" (*Discourses* 1.16, 155). In a similar vein, Paul calls for Christians to assume the gender that nature had assigned them.

The Veiling of Women. The unveiling of women posed another set of problems. Arrangement of the hair and its covering were paramount issues for the status and respectability of women. Correct adornment of the head became especially critical at moments of transition, and adoption of a new religious faith was such a point in a woman's life.

The apostle decries the practice of a woman praying or prophesying with her head uncovered *(akatakalyptos)*. Since the word *veil* is not used in the passage, there is much scholarly debate as to whether this is a denunciation of a praying or prophesying woman's unveiled head or of her unbound hair. Both were considered dangerous and out of order. By the New Testament era, in some Jewish circles divorce was obligatory for a woman who appeared unveiled in the street. For a woman so to appear was a disgrace to her husband, her family and herself.

Greeks viewed a woman's uncovered hair with the same distaste. Unbound hair was a characteristic of female worshipers of Dionysos, those uncontrolled creatures called maenads, or "mad ones." 1 Corinthians 14:23 may refer to such ritual madness, for there are other indications that the members of the congregation who had previously been led astray by idols carried with them remnants of the Dionysiac cult. These include eating food sacrificed to idols, returning to the idol's temple for ceremonial feasts and ritual intoxication. In any case, unbound hair denoted the wild, uncivilized state of women and was affected only by maenads and prostitutes. Virgil's Amata unbinds her hair and calls on her female associates to join her in a Dionysiac rite of rebellion against their husbands (Aeneid).

The attitude that had been expressed by Sappho still prevailed: a woman without a headbinder suggests loss of civic status and liability to exile. Furthermore she is abhorred by the Graces (98b LP; 81b LP). The respectable woman was veiled, and the critical point of the marriage ceremony lay in unveiling the maiden and subjecting her to the view of her bridegroom and his relatives. This was called the *anakalypteria*. At this point, she was vulnerable until her husband, after removing her veil, bestowed gifts on her in exchange for the sacrifice of her virginity.

The moment of unveiling was considered the critical part of the marriage ceremony. Thereafter the woman was no longer considered a virgin, though the union had not yet been consummated. The unloosed locks of a girl must now be bound as those of a respectable married woman. When the bride entered her husband's house, her head was covered with the matron's veil and was showered with hazelnuts. This symbolized the transition from her father's house and inclusion into the new household.

Small wonder if lack of appropriate headgear loomed as a problem in the Corinthian congregation. It might bespeak not only moral looseness but also marital renunciation. As such, it constituted blatant disregard for accepted social convention. Women would again place themselves in the vulnerable position of the *anakalypteria*, a position from which their husbands had redeemed them and given them respectable status within the community.

The *angeloi*, perhaps messengers or talebearers who would report the proceedings of Christian worship to outsiders, might well misconstrue the situation. Just as Paul in 1 Corinthians 14:23 asks what outsiders might think, so here too he calls for propriety. Though affirming that women have power over their heads, he declares that neither is the man without the woman nor the woman without the man in the Lord. The deportment of each must show consideration for the other.

1 Corinthians 11:1-16 appears to concern appropriate headgear for women or perhaps propriety in worship. There are, however, layers of meaning in this section. At a far deeper level it has to do with the relationship of man and woman. The basis for all that Paul says is found in the Genesis account of man and woman being made in the image of God. The apostle begins, as does Genesis, with a statement of God's being and of the relationality within the Godhead. Humanity as male and female draws its reality and meaning from a reflection of God's being. Man's aloneness had been "not good," and so woman was created as partner and companion

Embedded in the text is the question of relationships between the sexes and of where one might look to find a true soul mate. The typical Greek view was that the gods had created womankind as a deliberate curse upon men. Revulsion against women and dread of female sexuality had led to widespread homosexuality in the Greek world. Though marriage might be available to all, the noble soul turned to another male and found thereby perfect companionship (*see* Homosexuality).

Paul, however, argues for woman as the glory of man, needed to complete the image of God. To do so he turns to Genesis, which tells of woman as a blessed gift created "for the sake of man" (1 Cor 11:9). The term *dia* is often used to designate an objective of ministry (1 Cor 4:10; 9:10 [twice], 23; 2 Cor 2:10; 4:11, 15). Christ was made poor for our sakes (2 Cor 8:9; see also Jn 12:30); Paul proclaimed himself a slave "for Jesus' sake" (2 Cor 4:5). Woman was given to complete and fulfill man, to minister to his aloneness (Gen 2:18).

While the Greek myths maintained that woman was created of inferior substance and incapable of true grandeur in her soul, Genesis tells of woman drawn from man's side, bone of his bone and flesh of his flesh.

She was endowed with the same spiritual aspirations, the same emotions, the capacity for the same moral virtues. She was worthy to be bound to man, his soul mate and complement.

That woman is called "the glory of man" is not a diminution of her glory, for she is equally made in the image of God (Gen 1:27; 5:2-3). Glory augments the reputation, wealth or status of another (cf. 2 Cor 3:7-11, 18). Paul declares that the Thessalonians were his "glory and joy" (1 Thess 2:20, surely not a pejorative term). They are the fulfillment of his aspirations, and his pride and happiness in them know no bounds. Thus it is that Paul sets forth the interdependence of man and woman and their need for one another.

The concept of woman out of man and man out of woman may be intended to deflect the discomfort felt by some males that they had ever passed through the birth canal of a woman. No fewer than three of the great gods of the pantheon were said to have come into being in other manners than through the reproductive anatomy of a woman.

The Integrity of the Body Destroyed (1 Cor 11:17-34)

The common meal has proved blessed and distressing. Paul's words of institution are followed by reproof for lack of the fellowship that constitutes the nature of communion. It is intended as a sacred tryst of penitents who together experience the joy of forgiven sin and an assurance of pardon. Instead the gathering is characterized by gluttony, drunkenness and callous insensitivity. The poor leave hungry and humiliated, while the affluent are gorged, inebriate and unable to recognize another's need.

In the institution of the Lord's Supper we are given words of the earthly Jesus that are not found in the Gospels. The only other instance is in his observation that it is more blessed to give than to receive (Acts 20:35). One cannot worthily partake of the Eucharist without a concern for others.

Harmonizing the Spiritual Gifts (1 Cor 12)

If some have utilized their economic resources to embarrass others, the use of spiritual gifts is no less of a problem. The owners of certain gifts disparage those of others. Paul maintained that believers were a body, each part interdependent with the others. No gift or member is dispensable, though the functions differ. Interdependence of the head appears as a bodily member that cannot do without the foot. Relationality, not dominance, is stressed.

Then comes another of Paul's surprising statements about sex: the genitals are worthy of the most profound honor and respect. Private parts were called *aidoia*, "shameful members," though the term also implied a shame that led to modesty. *Aidōs*, the root word, implied shame and reverence. New meaning is given to those parts of the body that distinguish a woman's gender identity. The bodily members that remain hidden are intended not only for sexual distinction but also for delight, intimacy, communion and the engendering of human life. These organs play a major role in God's purposes of covenant and communion.

The Superiority of Love (1 Cor 13)

In the midst of his efforts to heal bitter altercations and rivalries, Paul bursts into an unparalleled paean in praise of love. Love might resolve the specific abuses that vexed

Fresco depicting a group of women celebrating a Eucharistic meal. (1 Corinthians 11:25)

the Corinthian church. Charismatic gifts are useful to build and uplift the church, but none can compare with the gift of love. It lends itself not to rivalry but to peace, not to pride but to humility, not to aggrandizement but to leveling. Love binds where there has been division, heals where there has been hate, believes the best of others instead of the worst. It enables the ministry of others rather than the promotion of selfish interests or persuasions. Within love there is abundant place for grace, patience and harmony. Without love there can be no unity. Love does not harm others by its inappropriate actions. Love does not claim superiority over the opinion or status of others, love does not satisfy its own needs while ignoring those of others, love does not easily take offense. Love is more to be prized than the accoutrements of mystery religion: the gongs and cymbals, the acquisition of arcane knowledge, the mystic mirrors, the comprehension of mysteries.

This magnificent treatise is placed at the climax of the argument for the unity and purity of the Corinthian congregation. All that precedes has been build-up, all that follows a winding down.

The Orderly Conduct of Worship (1 Cor 14) One of the most remarkable glimpses of worship in the early church is afforded by the description in 1 Corinthians 14. The devotees have been so swept away with enthusiasm that they must be reminded that God is a God of order rather than of confusion and that all things must be done decently and in order.

The first concern is that of the need to convey meaning in worship. While tongues are frequently an accompaniment of ecstatic devotion, communication through prophecy is more necessary. Prophesying is here defined as speech that is intended to upbuild, comfort and exhort. This definition is useful in understanding other New Testament references to women as prophets (Lk 2:36-38; Acts 2:17-18; 21:9; 1 Cor 11:4, 13).

The word that is used in the prohibition for women is *laleō*, a term used by Aristophanes for the frivolous chatter of women. Differentiation is made in the text between nonintelligible speech, frequently designated in this chapter by the verb *laleō*, and communication that conveys meaning to its hearers *(legō)*. The apostle places a far higher valuation on meaningful speech than on *glossalalia*, and there is an insistence that all ecstatic utterance should be interpreted so that all may be edified. Only one person may speak at a time, and others must be allowed to take their turn.

This contrasts with many of the mystery cults in which there was a jangling of musical instruments along with confused outcries, a phenomenon know as *clamor*. The worship of Cybele and Dionysos required the simultaneous use of diverse and unstructured sounds. In the orgies, women in particular were swept along into an altered state of consciousness. Dionysos was known as "the lord of the loud cry, the mad exciter of women." Their abandoned state of mind led to raving and uncontrolled actions, as well as to ceremonial cries known as ululation. Even in more orderly cults, the cries of women were part of the ritual at properly appointed moments. At Corinth, in a temple used primarily by women, a series of plaques have been excavated. One is dedicated to the sacred shouts of women. In this vein, Paul asks whether observers might not consider the Corinthian congregation to be mad—probably a reference to the ritual madness of these cults rather than to insanity.

In response the apostle asks for noise control. A person who speaks in tongues must be silent if there is no interpreter; a person who is prophesying must desist if another wishes a turn. The third injunction to silence is directed to women. Some have suggested that this referred to interrupting the service by asking questions at inappropriate times, others that women were buzzing with their private conversations when they should instead have attended to the Word of God. If the women found the material difficult to understand, they might have a profitable conversation with their husbands at home, where there was frequently little communication between marital partners.

Women are enjoined to silence in exactly the same way as the one who has no interpreter and the one who must yield a turn at prophesying to another. All are given the right to prophesy, so that it does not seem to be a prohibition against contributing a message of spiritual significance to the service of worship. Rather, it is a prohibition against a disruption of some sort. It is possible that the injunction is meant to curb the ululations that women had been taught were their contribution to ritual.

A command for submission *(hypotassō)* had been issued to ecstatic prophets as part of an instruction to allow only one person to speak at a time. In the same manner, women are instructed to be subject—again implying restraint, responsibility and responsivity to the worshiping community. The reference to a law requiring the silence or submission of women is a puzzle, since such a command is not found in the Mishnah or the Talmud. Greek and Roman laws, however, sought to restrain disorderly and irresponsible conduct of women in the practice of religion. A number of literary references make plain the marked distaste with which men viewed the religious behavior of women. By contrast, Christian worship must be distinguished by its decency and order.

We should note that silence was the attitude of the learner in rabbinic and Orphic tradition. In the ancient Near East, silence and submission represented a formula denoting willingness to heed and obey the divine voice.

Many scholars have argued that 1 Corinthians 14:34-35 is an interpolation, perhaps a gloss that slipped into the text, appearing sometimes in its current location and sometimes after 1 Corinthians 14:40. But 1 Corinthians 14:36 continues the argument of 1 Corinthians 14:33. Philip Barton Payne has discovered an early manuscript in which the supervising bishop demanded that the monk recopy the passage, omitting 1 Corinthians 14:34-35.

Resurrection and Immortality (1 Cor 15)

1 Corinthians 15 contains a remarkable affirmation of the body as vehicle for the immortal soul. The discussion begins with the events of Christ's passion and moves on to his resurrection appearances. The mention of his encounter with Mary Magdalene and the other women is conspicuously absent, while two of the noted appearances are undocumented elsewhere in Scripture: the appearance to James and to five hundred at once. Paul may be dealing with a different set of early traditions, or he may have been handling the material selectively. The references to the witness of leaders of the church (Peter and James and the Twelve) may be intended to fortify the insistence on the bodily resurrection of Christ. These are the very ones whose Corinthian followers now claim an inappropriate authority.

Against those who would deny the validity of the resurrection, Paul argues for the body as seed for the immortal vehicle of the soul. Greek philosophers viewed the body as a tomb and prison. In the same train, Gnostics despised their corporeal existence and longed to be liberated from all that chained them to this world. They hated their material bodies no less than do many contemporary women. But Paul affirms a glorious existence in the transformed bodies that spring from the old.

Within this epistle, references to the body fall into various categories, sometimes with a deliberate overlap in meanings:

- body as physical presence (1 Cor 5:3)
- physical body as vehicle for serving God (1 Cor 5:3; 6:13, 15, 20; 7:34)
- body as including personality, emotion, sexuality and spirituality (1 Cor 6:16, 18)
- body as instrument of sexuality (1 Cor 7:4)
- body as temple of indwelling Holy Spirit (1 Cor 6:19)
- body as having needs, lusts and appetites (1 Cor 9:27)
- body of Christ, represented in communion (1 Cor 10:16; 11:24, 27, 29)
- body of Christ made up of believers (1 Cor 10:17; 11:29; 12:12, 13, 27)
- physical body made up of many members (1 Cor 12:12, 14, 15, 16, 17, 28, 19, 20, 22, 23, 24, 25)
- physical body as living sacrifice (1 Cor 13:3)
- body as vehicle of resurrected soul (1 Cor 15:27, 35, 38)
- bodies celestial and terrestrial (1 Cor 15:40, 44)

The forty-five usages evoke overwhelmingly constructive and creative images and constitute an answer to those who disparaged the body. Ultimately the body is linked to Paul's concept of immortality. The soul after death is not disembodied but clothed (1 Cor 15:53), an image employed by Jews and pagans.

For those who hold Eve accountable for initiating the sin leading to the Fall, one should notice the statement that in Adam all die (1 Cor 15:22) as well as that in Romans 5:12-14, 18 ascribing the primary fault to Adam. The biblical account is evenhanded in its attribution of responsibility for humanity's original sin. Paul's point is not to dwell on the effects of sin but rather to insist on the promised results of Christ's resurrection.

A particular perplexity to women is the affirmation that the Son will "be subject" *(hypotassō)* to the Father. This statement has been used to argue for subordination within the Godhead and for the subordination of women to their husbands. The early church did not understand 1 Corinthians 15:24-28 as implying such a concept. As we have noted, the verb can be used in various senses beside that of submission: to unite with, join, adhere to, behave responsibly toward or to make a meaningful relationship with. The verb occurs six times in 1 Corinthians 15:27-28, with a diversity of meanings. Eusebius declared (*De Ecclesiastica Theologica* 3.15) that the "submission" of the Son was that of union with the Father after his task of ruling the universe was at an end. His role completed as destroyer of all enemies, he might return to the relationship that had originally been his with the Father.

Closing Instructions (1 Cor 16)

The conclusion is conciliatory. If Paul has previously been harsh, he now speaks of his visit and suggests a plan of systematic giving so that a contribution may be ready for Jerusalem at his coming. Among those who send greetings are Aquila, here named first, and Priscilla, whom he regarded as fellow laborers (Rom 16:3) and to whom he asks the Corinthians to be subject. By heeding the patterns that Paul and his associates have instilled, the Corinthians may grow from factious children into those mature in the faith. His love remains with even the most difficult of them.

Bibliography. D. S. Bailey, *Sexual Relation in Christian Thought* (New York: Harper & Row, 1959); Epictetus, *Discourses*, trans. F. C. Grant in F. C. Grant, *Hellenistic Religions: The Age of Syncretism* (Indianapolis, IN: Bobbs Merrill, 1953); P. B. Payne, "Fuldensis, Sigla for Variants in Vaticanus and 1 Cor 14:34-35," *New Testament Studies* 41 (1995/2).

CATHERINE CLARK KROEGER

2 CORINTHIANS

Introduction

2 Corinthians is in many ways Paul's most personal letter. Written to the congregation already known to us from 1 Corinthians, this letter has less to do with the struggles experienced by that group than with Paul's understanding of his ministry, particularly as that ministry is the subject of criticism. Some readers treasure 2 Corinthians because Paul speaks eloquently of strength in weakness; others find it difficult to accept what they see as Paul's forward and overbearing manner. It may well be argued that 2 Corinthians presents a feminine side of Paul, a Paul who is openly emotional, who rejects games of spiritual one-upmanship, who talks about his feelings and concerns. Yet the personality who emerges from these pages is no weakling. Paul proclaims that in his weakness God's power is demonstrated, but he does not use his weakness as an excuse to do nothing. Rather, in 2 Corinthians Paul remains engaged in ministry, even as he refuses to let ministry become a vehicle for vaunting human achievement.

While Paul's authorship of 2 Corinthians is widely accepted, the letter's unity has frequently been questioned. Paul's proclivity to shift topics in midstream, to make long digressions and then to return unannounced to the previous subject seems in 2 Corinthians to reach beyond the breaking point, suggesting to many that the present letter is an edited collection of his correspondence with the church at Corinth. Paul wrote to the Corinthians more than twice: references to a previous letter (1 Cor 5:9) and a tearful letter (2 Cor 2:4) point to a complicated history. Too, it is difficult to reconcile the conciliatory, joyful tone of 2 Corinthians 1—2 with the angry outbursts of 2 Corinthians 10—13. The shift in subject of 2 Corinthians 8—9, which deal with the offering for the church at Jerusalem, seems to fit uneasily with what has gone before, and some scholars see a possible interpolation in 2 Corinthians 6:14—7:1.

Given Paul's penchant for changing the subject, only the division between chapters 1—9 and 10—13 demands further consideration. It has been suggested that 2 Corinthians 10—13 constitute the tearful letter referred to in 2 Corinthians 2:4; the existence of chapters 1—9 would be evidence that Paul's emotional outburst had its intended effect, and our story of the Corinthian church ends on a high note of reconciliation with Paul, their apostle and founder. The objection that chapters 10—13 are less distressed, anguished and tearful than angry and defensive does not seem a solid one, since personal pain, tears, deep anger and heated defensiveness can easily occur at once. It is possible, though, that the tendency to place 2 Corinthians 10—13 prior to chapters 1—9 stems less from the textual evidence than from a wish to see the story have a peaceful conclusion. Paul may need to speak sternly (2 Cor 10—13), but the church finally listens to him, and the end of the story is the confident thanksgiving at the end of 2 Corinthians 9. It is painful to imagine the alternate scenario for 2 Corinthians. After a humiliating visit from Paul, a tearful letter from him and reconciliation with the apostle, the church fell back into old ways, so that Paul was forced to write an even more scathing letter, with uncertain results. The early church document known as 1 Clement, probably written around the close of the first century, chastises the Corinthian church for dissension (apparently it had deposed and replaced its leaders), so we can easily imagine that they rebelled against Paul earlier.

Difficult though this scenario may be, it is not uncharacteristic of the ebb and flow of church life, of spiritual highs and divisive squabbles. We must admit that we read Paul's Corinthian correspondence without knowing whether the apostle was finally successful in keeping his beloved congregation loyal to himself. Since our congregational life is necessarily lived without knowing the ultimate consequences of our actions, perhaps Paul's relationship to the Corinthians is the more instructive for its uncertain ending.

For the purposes of this commentary we will take 2 Corinthians as it now appears and treat Paul's shifts of subject as separate topics and moods. The letter (or letters, if edited) clearly comes after 1 Corinthians and from somewhere far enough away from Corinth that Paul could not travel there on a whim, but near enough to keep up a complicated correspondence. The place of writing was likely Macedonia (see 2 Cor 2:13); the date, the mid to late 50s.

The focused attention given to the collection for Jerusalem (2 Cor 8—9) clues us in to the economic dynamics that underlie this letter. Apparently some of the Corinthians were people of means (Gaius, 1 Cor 1:14, hosts the whole church in his home, Rom 16:23; Crispus was, according to Acts 18:8, the synagogue ruler). Paul's argument in 1 Corinthians 1:26 that "not many of you" were powerful or nobly born implies that some members of his audience were of the higher classes. In addition, it appears that some of the wealthier members of the Corinthian church may have been its women. Chloe (1 Cor 1:11) is responsible for sending a delegation to Paul. Prisca (or Priscilla) and Aquila, in whose home a church meets (1 Cor 16:19), appear from other New Testament evidence to have been fairly wealthy artisans. The fact that Prisca's name is mentioned first in four out of the six New Testament occurrences (Acts 18:18, 26; Rom 16:3; 2 Tim 4:19) suggests that she was the spouse with the higher social status.

The apparent wealth of some of the Corinthian church's members, including some of its women, also signals us to other social dynamics underlying 2 Corinthians. In the cities of the Roman Empire, social status was determined by a number of factors, such as wealth, gender, occupational prestige, family, religion, liberty or servitude, and so forth. An individual's overall social status was in a sense the sum of the varying places he or she held in these hierarchies. Some individuals would occupy strikingly different positions on different scales: a slave with a high-status occupation, for example, or a female head of a well-to-do household. Such status inconsistency, as sociologists call it, may have contributed to a heightened concern about status and social role. Such individuals would be particularly concerned with comparing themselves with others and being certain that they preserved their place in society. When Paul refused to take the position of client to his wealthy Corinthian would-be patrons, insisting instead on the relatively degrading occupation of small-time artisan, some members of the Corinthian congregation distrusted his actions and questioned his motives.

The history of Paul's relationships with the Corinthian church, as we can reconstruct it from the letters and Acts, is complicated. Acts 18:8 attests, and the letters confirm, that Paul founded the church in Corinth, spending a year and a half there according to Acts 18:11. The first piece of Corinthian correspondence of which we have knowledge is that letter described in 1 Corinthians 5:9, in which Paul warns the church not to allow immorality among its membership. Apparently this directive was misunderstood by some members of the congregation, and Paul mentions the previous letter by way of correcting them. Our 1 Corinthians, then, is the second piece of correspondence from Paul to the Corinthian congregation; it is prompted by written communication from the church (1 Cor 7:1) and messengers to Paul from Chloe (1 Cor 1:11). Paul then visited Corinth, but the visit did not go well, and Paul wrote "with many tears" rather than returning to risk such pain again (2 Cor 2:1-4, 9; some scholars think that the tearful letter is 2 Cor 10—13). This letter had its desired effect, as reported by Titus (2 Cor 7:6-9); thus the beginning of our 2 Corinthians reflects Paul's great joy and relief at his "consolation" in being reconciled with the Corinthians. Yet this period of peace apparently did not last, if the canonical order reflects the order of writing of Paul's letters. 2 Corinthians 10—13 gives evidence that the opposition to Paul's person and message in Corinth are even greater than before, causing many scholars to believe that 2 Corinthians 1—9 and 10—13 were originally letters written on separate occasions. If this is not the case, we must imagine that Paul received some devastating news about Corinth while the letter was in process and shifted his tone to address the new concerns.

Much of the letter deals with various questions regarding Paul's ministry. His means of support has been questioned, as have his motives in taking up a collection from his Gentile congregations for the church in Jerusalem. The disciplinary measures he has advised for his Corinthian congregation have not met with universal support, and other preachers of the gospel have come to Corinth with great shows of spiritual prowess, undermining Paul's message and his authority. 2 Corinthians addresses all of these issues, as Paul defends and continues to proclaim his gospel.

Outline

- 1:1-11 Salutation and Thanksgiving
- 1:12—7:16 Paul's Ministry
  - 1:12—2:13 Issues of Past Concern
  - 2:14—5:21 Paul Describes His Ministry
  - 6:1-13 A Call for Reconciliation
  - 6:14—7:1 A Call for Separation
  - 7:2-16 Paul's Confidence in the Corinthians
- 8:1—9:15 The Offering for Jerusalem
  - 8:1-15 Appeal for the Offering
  - 8:16—9:5 Approved Coworkers

9:6-15 Results of Generous Giving
10:1—13:10 Paul's Response to His Opponents
10:1-18 Paul Lays Out His Claim
11:1—12:10 The Fool's Speech
12:11—13:10 Summary Appeal and Warnings
13:11-13 Final Greetings and Benediction

Commentary

Salutation and Thanksgiving (2 Cor 1:1-11)

The opening section of ancient letters followed a set pattern: the names of the sender and receiver, greetings and some form of thanksgiving to the gods for the sender's or receiver's health, safe travel in a recent journey and so forth. Paul follows this familiar formula but in every respect makes it reflect Christ. He identifies himself as Christ's apostle, Timothy as "our brother" and his recipients as the "church" and the "saints" (2 Cor 1:1). Instead of "greetings," Paul addresses them with "grace," adds the familiar Jewish blessing "peace" and reminds them that these are not simply wishes from himself but gifts of God. As is typical in Paul's letters, the thanksgiving is also a clue to the letter's important themes. Paul speaks forthrightly of affliction, reminds his readers of God's consolation and emphasizes that divine consolation has as its end the shared comfort of the community. The incessant repetition of the language of comfort or "consolation" (2 Cor 1:3-7) may seem to some readers a bit cloying, except that in 2 Corinthians 1:8 the tone changes drastically. Paul makes it clear to his readers that this is no shallow theology but an expression of deep joy arising from the experience of deep suffering. In speaking of God's consolation Paul speaks of what he knows. The report of his perilous experience does not provide details; Paul is less concerned with the readers' being able to retell his story than their knowing its outcome and understanding his emotions. His interest is primarily in their relationship to him, since in the rest of the letter this relationship is at stake.

Paul's Ministry (2 Cor 1:12—7:16)

Issues of Past Concern (2 Cor 1:12—2:13)

From the recounting of his recent experiences, Paul turns to the history of his relationship with the Corinthian church. Twenty of thirty-five occurrences of the verb *kauchaomai* ("I boast") in the Pauline literature appear in 2 Corinthians; the related nouns *kauchēma* ("boast, object of boasting") and *kauchēsis* ("boasting, pride") are prominent in this letter as well (three of ten and six of ten Pauline occurrences, respectively). As in English, the Greek concept of boasting or pride may carry positive or negative connotations, and in the last part of this letter Paul repeatedly protests that boasting, including his boasting, is unnecessary and unbecoming of a believer in Christ. Yet the boasting or pride that Paul expresses here is positive. An appropriate analogy might be the pride a mother feels in her children. Such pride includes an element of self-satisfaction, that she has done a good job in rearing them and shares in their accomplishments; it is not selfish or self-serving pride but deep delight in their development as persons, even as that development signals a change in her relationship with them. This is boasting in its best sense and the news Paul longs to tell about the Corinthian church, as he continues to chide them that another kind of boasting is divisive and dangerous.

While we are the beneficiaries of Paul's inability to oversee his churches personally, since the letters he wrote to them have become our Scripture, we can easily comprehend that supervision from a distance was difficult and somewhat inadequate. Paul would want to visit a congregation such as the one at Corinth as often as possible, and we deduce that he had communicated to them his plans to do so. When the first of two planned visits went badly, however, Paul canceled his return trip, writing instead an anguished letter to express his outrage and insist on congregational discipline. At the writing of the current letter, Paul has received word of the results of that previous communication. With relief he reminds them that even church discipline should be restrained when it has served its purpose, so that consolation may abound.

Paul writes openly of his feelings in having to discipline the Corinthian church, and the parental nature of his love is evident. He caused them pain by his disciplinary action—today we might call it tough love—and their pain grieved him deeply; yet he is glad that their pain led to reform and reconciliation, so he cannot say that he regrets having been its cause. He is not ashamed to let his feelings be known or to admit that he avoided unpleasant and unproductive conflict. He reminds them that his love for them remains constant. He is not even willing that the church member whose action precipitated the crisis be permanently exiled from the community; he encourages them to welcome this repentant brother.

Paul Describes His Ministry (2 Cor 2:14—5:21)

Introduction (2 Cor 2:14—3:6). Paul abruptly interrupts his narrative (it will resume in 2 Cor 7:5) to reflect theologically on the ministry in which he is engaged. The description begins with a military metaphor, that of a victory procession—although it is not clear whether the "us" who are being led are soldiers of the victorious Christ or his prisoners. The most vivid part of the metaphor is the olfactory image: the smell of incense that permeates the scene, sweetly fragrant to the victors but a putrid reminder to the prisoners of their defeat and, quite likely, approaching death. Smells often recall emotions to us, and the fragrance that to one person is the family holiday dinner or the beloved's cologne is to another person a reminder of painful past events. Similarly those who proclaim God's message are likely to be treated rudely by those who reject the message, even as they are welcomed by those who are glad to hear the word.

Focus on the proclaimers leads Paul to a related topic and a different metaphor. Those who are worthy to proclaim Christ, he says, are persons of sincerity like himself, not "peddlers" out to make a profit. Here we see a hint of one of the recurring themes of 2 Corinthians: Paul's contrast between himself and the rival preachers, to whom he later refers as "false apostles" or (sarcastically) "super-apostles." Apparently these rivals, eager to ingratiate themselves to the Corinthians at Paul's expense, made a great deal of their glowing letters of recommendation, perhaps even from the Jerusalem church. The early church, functioning as small and scattered cells throughout the far-flung Roman Empire, relied on such letters to distinguish true preachers of the gospel, who deserved hospitality, from hucksters or worse. 3 John 5-8 is a New Testament example of such a recommendation letter, and the early church manual called the *Didache* gives specific instructions regarding the reception of traveling prophets (*Didache* 11—12). For Paul and the Corinthian congregation, though, the requirement of written credentials was ridiculous. Paul was the church's founder! If the Corinthians were of a mind to require credentials, they should look to themselves; their Christian existence was Paul's letter of recommendation, written neither on parchment nor "on tablets of stone but on tablets of human hearts" (2 Cor 3:3).

The Glory of the New Covenant (2 Cor 3:7-18). The comparison between stone tablets and living hearts leads Paul to the deeper theological significance of his metaphor, and he reminds the Corinthians that he is involved in the ministry of a new, life-giving covenant. He develops this idea by a rather convoluted interpretation of Scripture, namely, the account in Exodus 34:29-35 of Moses' shining face and the veil he used to cover his face. Exodus has nothing of the detail on which Paul's interpretation is centered: that Moses covered his face because he knew that the shining glory of

God was fading. But neither does Exodus say that Moses continued to wear a veil, and Paul seizes on this omission to surmise that the glow eventually faded—a conclusion founded on his conviction that the divine glory given to Moses and represented in Israel's law, while great, has been surpassed by the even greater glory shown forth in Christ.

Women have been too frequently the victims of an "at least we're better than they are" attitude to accept the interpretation of this text that elevates Christian viewpoints at Jewish expense. Paul is distressed that his Jewish brothers and sisters fail to see the fullness of God's glory—that shocking, scandalous glory that has made divine grace available even to Gentiles. But he will not compromise God's trustworthiness in order to prove Jewish interpretation wrong. Rather, he takes his argument from Scripture, demonstrating from God's acts in history the promise that now reaches its fulfillment. The remarkable work of God today, Paul asserts, is best understood by affirming God's past work; and now, "how much more" (2 Cor 3:8).

A New Covenant Ministry (2 Cor 4:1—5:15). This remarkable gift of divine glory requires complete openness on the part of its ministers: they are to veil nothing. Paul ties together the theological insight, that God gives the ability to recognize the truth of the gospel, with the ministerial insight, that it is the responsibility of those who proclaim the gospel to do so openly and without deceit. Here we see the first development of the strength-in-weakness theme that is so important in 2 Corinthians. Paul will fall prey neither to the temptation to self-aggrandizement nor to the tendency to understate God's power. Metaphorically this is a priceless treasure stored in a common clay pot; if such a practice seems odd, it is additional evidence that God's ways are not human ways.

Indeed, the life of the apostle is not an easy one. On three separate occasions in 2 Corinthians Paul recites a résumé of sorts, each time focusing not on his accomplishments but on his sufferings and hardships. In this first list (2 Cor 4:8-12), Paul uses antitheses, paradoxes and word play to emphasize the reality of the hardship he faces and the depth of the hope that sustains him. Again, the underlying contrast is that of death and life.

We should not let the fact that Paul speaks almost offhandedly of the mortal dangers he has faced distract us from the reality of those dangers. There is no reason to think Paul exaggerates when he says that he has faced life-threatening situations in his ministry and that his physical suffering and material deprivation have been serious. Yet Paul mentions such experiences on the way to speaking of the surpassing greatness of God's grace, often using metaphors that he reveals piece by piece (2 Cor 4:16—5:5). With this complicated figurative language Paul makes several points at once. He is constantly on guard against the religious-philosophical view popular in the Greco-Roman world that the body and things of this world are evil and should be cast away. Paul's theology, rooted deeply in a concept of a good creation, rejected such notions, even as he recognized the power of sin in the material world and longed for the transformation of the physical body, so prone to suffering. At the same time, he is developing an image suggested by a word play: the Hebrew *kabod,* meaning "weight" and "glory." Although Paul is writing in Greek, the idea of weight of glory suggests a helpful concept to him: the burdens we now bear are a sort of strength training to prepare us for the wonderful weight of divine glory to be given to us one day. The metaphors of clothing and the house suggest protection for the individual, and Paul mixes them in developing his argument.

It may be disconcerting to read of Paul seemingly taking earthly life so lightly, speaking of it as nothing more than a rather interesting journey from which he will be glad to return "home" (2 Cor 5:6-9). Anyone who has been close to an aged or ill friend or relative who has made peace with his or her approaching death will have a clearer perspective on this sentiment. For such a person, the thought of death is not morbid or dismal; rather, such a person typically spreads peace and even joy to those around him or her, so contagious is the confidence in God's loving providence through death and beyond. While Paul is still engaged in active ministry, he has reached this same state of peace and confidence.

Indeed, Paul offers in this context a most interesting interpretation of the meaning of salvation (2 Cor 5:14-15). "One

[Christ] died for all," he says; but he does not follow with the conclusion we might expect, namely, that no one else has to die. Rather, he makes the opposite, surprising statement: "therefore all have died." Death is no less a fact of human life than it ever was—except that, for those who are in Christ, that most difficult and frightful experience is already behind us, accomplished in Christ for us. Thus we are freed from life lived under the shadow of death to live not for ourselves but for Christ.

New Creation (2 Cor 5:16-21). Paul is not, however, simply interested in promising his readers a better tomorrow. While he is concerned with eschatological matters, the driving force for that concern is his conviction that the God who will bring all to completion in the end is at work now, in those who are in Christ, and is already accomplishing the work of renewal. This is Paul's familiar dynamic between already and not yet. Paul expresses the idea briefly, almost cryptically but with undoubtable joy: "If anyone is in Christ—new creation!" (2 Cor 5:17, literal translation). English translations inevitably muddy the meaning when they attempt to correct the grammar; nonetheless the better choice is "there is a new creation," not "he (or she) is a new creation," since it more effectively communicates the idea that not just the individual's interior attitude is being changed by God. As Paul goes on to say, this renewal includes the believer's becoming a part of the divine work of reconciliation. The intimate, relationship-focused notion of reconciliation is a way of imaging God's work to which many women can relate. True reconciliation cannot be coerced; it requires willingness to become involved in the life of the other, to see things from the other's point of view. And, as many women and men can attest, reconciliation is arduous work. Yet we are made reconcilers by none other than the one who reconciled us; we speak not on our own behalf but that of Christ.

A Call for Reconciliation (2 Cor 6:1-13)

Paul has made himself and his coworkers examples of reconciling messengers; now he enlarges his message of reconciliation with his second list of experiences (2 Cor 6:4-10). It is an odd sort of appeal if we imagine that Paul is inviting his readers to share his ministry—who would willingly choose such a life? Paul does not shy away from the difficult details of his story but uses the paradoxes to further his argument. "Are we mistreated, misunderstood, burdened with care? Yes, but in those experiences God is most at work in us." The list recalls the "treasure in clay jars" (2 Cor 4:7-12) and continues to advance the theme of divine strength in human weakness. Paul concludes the appeal by addressing the Corinthians as his "children"; they should not be calculating in their affections but generous, as befits members of a family.

A Call for Separation (2 Cor 6:14—7:1)

The emphasis on the divine work as reconciliation fails to stress part of the message of the gospel that was particularly important in cosmopolitan Corinth. The Corinthian believers were converts from various Greco-Roman religions, and their culture tended to encourage individuals to construct religion from various sources; from 1 Corinthians we learn that some of them found it difficult to leave old religious practices and beliefs behind. Reconciliation, Paul insists, is not the same thing as syncretism. It is appropriate that Paul buttresses his point with quotations of Scripture, reminding the Corinthians that they now stand in a monotheistic tradition with clear practical and ethical expectations. The Torah and several different prophetic books are represented in this string of quotations. The promise in 2 Corinthians 6:18 is that originally made to David in 2 Samuel 7:14; Paul expands it in number and gender, changing the original "you shall be my son" to "you shall be my sons and daughters" *(hyious kai thygateras)* to emphasize that the promise is to all believers.

Paul's Confidence in the Corinthians (2 Cor 7:2-16)

In 2 Corinthians 7:5 Paul resumes the story he left in 2 Corinthians 2:13. The consolation language of the thanksgiving recurs, again with the reminder that Paul's comfort is great because his suffering has been great as well. Paul makes it clear that his grief was caused by the pain the church felt, even though he knew that discipline was the right thing to do. It is important to Paul that the Corinthians know the emotions he experienced and recognize that he did not enjoy causing them to grieve—traits that are often described as feminine. Once again Paul speaks of boasting in a positive, parental sense. The language is exuberant, even exaggerated; Paul's relief at his reconciliation with his beloved congregation spills out in his "complete confidence" in them (2 Cor 7:16).

The Offering for Jerusalem (2 Cor 8:1—9:15)

Appeal for the Offering (2 Cor 8:1-15)

On the heels of this joyfully confident exclamation, Paul broaches with the Corinthians the ever-delicate subject of money. Throughout his ministry, Paul promoted the collection of an offering for the church at Jerusalem, to whom he refers as the "saints." Understandably this practice raised a number of questions. As Paul's letters and the book of Acts demonstrate, relationships between Jews and Gentiles, even between Jewish Christians and Gentile Christians, were frequently strained. Gentiles of modest means, and those who experienced ostracism and persecution for their expression of Christian faith, may well have hesitated to contribute to a fund for persecuted Jewish Christians in far-off Jerusalem. Others wondered whether Paul took some of these funds for his use, and such speculation seems to have been encouraged by some of Paul's rivals. Roman social custom encouraged the wealthy to act as patrons who would expect certain services and behavior from their clients; Paul's refusal to participate in the patronage system, preferring to support his ministry by manual labor, mirrored his refusal to treat the wealthy among his congregations with special deference. Small wonder that the subject of money should be a matter to be handled carefully.

Paul, however, demonstrates that he is not squeamish about this practical matter of ministry. Nor does he treat it as something beneath his purview as an apostle; rather, he addresses the subject squarely as a theological issue. He refers to the offering as a *charis* ("grace," 2 Cor 8:4, 6-7; translated variously as "service," "gracious work," "act of grace," "generous undertaking") and connects it to the "grace of God" (2 Cor 8:1). Paul points not only to the Macedonian churches, who were likely financially less well off than the Corinthians, but also to Christ as an example of sacrificial giving: "though he was rich, yet for your sakes he became poor" (2 Cor 8:9). Yet Paul recognizes that rivalry is not always, or solely, an appropriate motivator to action, and he appeals to the Corinthians' fundamental sense of fairness, not just their competitive spirit, to urge their cooperation.

Approved Coworkers (2 Cor 8:16—9:5)

Paul recognizes that the trustworthiness of his ministry requires forthrightness in handling financial matters, and he recites the credentials of his coworkers who will see to the transfer of funds. While we frequently think of Paul working alone in ministry, texts such as this one reveal the depth of his reliance on others. Taking Paul as a ministry model should not cause us to neglect our cooperation with partners in ministry or denigrate the value of their service.

Again Paul speaks of boasting in its positive sense, with a suggestion of the familial relationship between himself and the Corinthian congregation. He has spoken of them in such glowing terms that their failure to do what he has promised would reflect badly not just on themselves but on him as well, as when children fail to meet the expectations of their parents. Paul walks a thin line between encouragement and coercion, so eager is he for the Corinthians to do what he has asked. He uses every tool of persuasion, including comparing them with others, appealing to the Corinthians' heightened sense of status consciousness; yet he continues to insist that the offering is voluntary.

Results of Generous Giving (2 Cor 9:6-15)

The voluntary nature of the Corinthians' gift has theological ramifications. Their freewill offering is a fitting response to God's blessings freely offered to them. Paul makes it clear that financial matters are not a subject apart from theological reflection. Rather, stewardship and generosity are themes intimately related to gratitude and thanksgiving for the abundance of the divine blessing. The act of giving increases fellowship among members and between churches, with the ultimate result being glory to God.

Paul's Response to His Opponents (2 Cor 10:1—13:10)

Paul Lays Out His Claim (2 Cor 10:1-18)

With the beginning of 2 Corinthians 10

Paul's tone shifts markedly. Does this, as many commentators have suggested, signal a separate letter? If this is not the tearful letter, then it seems that Paul's beloved Corinthians have again turned against him, and he must resume his self-defense anew. Yet there is no textual evidence (e.g., an extant copy of 2 Cor 1—9 or 10—13 without the other) to suggest that these were originally two separate pieces of correspondence. Perhaps Paul has received new information as 2 Corinthians 1—9 was being dictated, and he shifts his tone to address the changed situation. It is possible that the complexity of the Corinthian situation, inaccessible to us centuries later, justified to Paul the writing of a letter that praised (some of?) his recipients' renewed loyalty to him and castigated those who remained his opponents. While we cannot reconstruct the situation with certainty, we can sense the outrage the apostle expresses in these chapters.

By reading between the lines of Paul's opening defense, we are able to sketch the outlines of the charges brought against him. We recognize the rhetorical power and confident authority of Paul's letters that are part of our canon. It is not infrequently the case, though, that outstanding writers are less impressive as speakers; and apparently those who would challenge Paul's authority are seeking to portray this discrepancy as a fault. According to Paul, his opponents insinuate that he is a cowardly bully, threatening from afar what he cannot carry out in their presence.

Paul, ever self-confident, is loath to admit that his opponents even have a case. If his demeanor is meek and gentle, he says, he is reflecting the meekness and gentleness of Christ; if he does not have a ready answer for his opponents' verbal barbs, it is because he does not wage a war of words according to merely human standards. He does not hesitate to turn any alleged deficiency into a positive quality. But as it becomes increasingly clear in these chapters, Paul does have to contend with rivals who put on a better show than he does and openly cast aspersions on him by comparison. Paul does not dignify their charges with a direct reply—with the result that we, reading twenty centuries later, cannot be sure what the rivals' teaching was. Paul denounces their methods, charging that their tactics of self-commendation "do not show good sense" (2 Cor 10:12). Paul will limit his boasting to the strengths God has given him and seek to work within the limits God has imposed.

We are no less prone than the Corinthians to seek supercompetency in our leaders, particularly in the religious sphere. We respect authority, often to the extent that we tolerate an autocratic exercise of authority better than we understand someone who does not exercise his or her full authority. Personal charisma attracts us, and we fail to appreciate other strengths in its absence. Many a woman has neglected the exercise of her spiritual gifts because she did not possess the desired qualities of a strong speaking voice or an outgoing personality. Paul's words are a powerful reminder that our responsibility lies in cultivating the gifts we have.

The Fool's Speech (2 Cor 11:1—12:10)

Paul begins an extraordinary protestation by asking his readers to indulge him in "a little foolishness" (2 Cor 11:1). What Paul is about to say, he suggests, he would rather not; he is stooping to his opponents' tactics, much against his will, and he wants it to be understood that this is not his normal mode of operation. Yet what Paul reveals about himself in the following verses, often termed the fool's speech, has been found helpful by Christians through the ages who have experienced similar struggles. We may be tempted even to dismiss Paul's self-qualification; nonetheless we should take Paul's hesitation seriously enough to recognize that it is always a dangerous tactic to praise one's self by way of example to others. As these texts show, however, it may also be a tactic of enormous benefit to hearers or readers.

Paul opens this section with a metaphor that trades on a pair of stereotypes: the virgin bride and the sinful Eve (2 Cor 11:2–3). Paul images himself as father of the bride, eager to present her to her husband chaste and unviolated. By contrast, he points to the story of Eve's deception by the serpent, perhaps alluding to the later Jewish tradition that the serpent's seduction was of a sexual nature and neglecting to mention Adam's culpability. Women readers may be uncomfortable with the use of these stereotypes, which reduce women's identity to their sexual status. Nonetheless it is important to notice that Paul is not speaking merely of the women in the Corinthian congregation, as if he were singling them out as particularly prone to deception. Rather, he encourages the entire congregation, men and women, to identify themselves in these female metaphors. The sexual imagery, while blunt, is apt in the context of Paul's concern about his opponents, whom he sees as seducing the Corinthians' hearts and minds.

Paul must explain what he has refused to do and what has happened to him. In both cases, his opponents have leveled charges against him. His refusal to be supported by the Corinthians (who likely would have misunderstood any acceptance of support as a signal of a patron-client relationship) has been interpreted as a lack of love for them; his opponents may have pointed to his many tribulations as evidence that God has not given divine support and protection to his ministry. Paul is angered by these deceptions and levels harsh countercharges at his opponents, calling them "false apostles" and "deceitful workers" (2 Cor 11:13) and implying that they are in league with Satan. He addresses the Corinthians with sarcasm: although they think of themselves as "wise" (2 Cor 11:19; see also 1 Cor 1:18—2:16), they foolishly accept abuse from the rival apostles whose true concern is only for their own advantage.

Again, this indictment from Paul sounds strikingly like a description of modern church situations. Not only are leaders who abuse their power a problem in the congregation, says Paul; just as problematic are members who allow themselves to be taken advantage of, who are unwilling to challenge their spiritual leaders on grounds of mistreatment, who accept suffering within the congregation either as deserved or as an appropriate mirror of Christ's suffering. Paul is about to recite his sufferings for Christ's sake, and he recognizes that hardship is part of the life of the disciple. Still, he categorically rejects the acceptance of abuse from leaders of the congregation as Christian suffering. Such suffering, he says, is not to be tolerated, no matter how spiritually strong the leaders might seem.

While Paul speaks of others' behavior in this section, his main focus is on himself and his experience as example to the Corinthians. This sort of boasting, Paul says, is inappropriate—"I am talking like a madman" (2 Cor 11:23)—but necessary to demonstrate God's power at work in him. Almost casually Paul rattles off the list of calamities that have befallen him; some of these we are familiar with from stories in Acts, but in other cases this list is our only indication of the extent of Paul's tribulations. These dangerous, frightening and often humiliating experiences Paul lists as a badge of honor, not omitting the fact that in all these life-threatening circumstances his concern is not only for himself but also for his churches. The culminating story paints a comically pathetic scene: Paul escaping from Damascus by huddling in a basket as it is lowered down the city wall by his friends. The Corinthians would have known well the Roman practices of war against walled cities and how the first soldier to accomplish the risky feat of scaling the wall of a besieged town was treated with special honor. Paul is the comic antihero, descending the wall by the power of others in order to scurry away. By making such an experience his "boast" (2 Cor 11:30), Paul drastically redefines apostolic honor.

Presumably Paul's rivals have demonstrated their spiritual prowess by speaking extensively of their visions and special revelations. Once again, Paul is apparently torn by opposite impulses: he too has had ecstatic religious experiences (characteristically, he describes them as "exceptional," better than the experiences of others), but he does not find it appropriate to use these experiences as proof of his apostleship. The circumlocution he employs, "I know a person in Christ" (2 Cor 12:2), is patently transparent; he is speaking of himself but in such a way as to avoid at least the baldest form of self-aggrandizement. It is worth noting that Paul does think of ecstatic visions and revelations as valid spiritual experiences. He does not consider it appropriate to use such experiences as a yardstick of one's spiritual maturity or to compare such experiences or lack of them with those of others.

In the midst of this spiritual high, Paul says, he was given what he refers to as "a thorn . . . in the flesh *(skolops tē sarki)*, a messenger of Satan to torment me" (2 Cor 12:7). The cryptic nature of this passage has elicited volumes of commentary. "I was given" *(edothē)* is in the passive voice; Paul does not directly charge God with being the source of his torment, and he refers to it as "a messenger of Satan" (the word here translated "messenger," *angelos,* also means "angel"). Yet God is responsible for the negative answer to Paul's prayer that the thorn be removed. Paul well mirrors our experiences with evil and suffering; while we are uneasy about accusing God of being suffering's cause, we find to our dismay that God says no to our earnest pleas for removal of the suffering. The mention of praying "three times" (2 Cor 12:8) probably should not be taken literally, since Paul likely prayed more often about this besetting problem. Rather, the sense is likely closer to our expression "again and again."

If the verb "was given" is enigmatic, the phrase "a thorn in the flesh" is even more so. What was the nature of Paul's thorn? *Skolops* means something that is sharp and pointed, and the word can denote anything from a fishhook to a stake. This is Paul's only direct reference to it, and the imagination of interpreters over the ages has run wild. Some have suggested that it was some psychological or emotional problem, such as depression, or perhaps some persistent temptation (*see* Depression). The occasionally encountered view that Paul's tormentor was a woman or an uncontrollable urge to lustfulness on Paul's part arises more from the fancy of interpreters who try to find a way to blame women for all sin than from any evidence in the Scriptures. Nor is there any scriptural evidence for the assertion that Paul's thorn was a homosexual tendency (*see* Homosexuality). Since Paul says that the thorn is in his flesh, many interpreters have argued that Paul suffered from some sort of physical ailment, although Paul also uses the term *flesh (sarx)* to speak of human life apart from the Spirit (see, e.g., Gal 5:16-21). At the end of Galatians, Paul comments on what large letters he makes when he writes with his own hand (Gal 6:11). Professional scribes were trained to write in a small hand to save expensive parchment, so Paul's comment may signal that he is afflicted with poor eyesight (cf. Gal 4:15) or crippling arthritis—either of which would have materially affected his ministry, particularly his letter writing and his ability to make a living as a craftsman. The reference to Paul's coworker Luke as "the beloved physician" (Col 4:14; cf. Philem 24; 2 Tim 4:11) may provide additional evidence that Paul required frequent medical care during his ministry. Other interpreters have pointed to the illness or "physical infirmity" (*astheneian tēs sarkos,* "weakness of flesh") that Paul says brought him to Galatia (Gal 4:13). This description would well fit a condition such as epilepsy, from which Paul might suffer no ill effects for long periods of time, then suddenly and without warning be overtaken by symptoms that likely would have been interpreted by others as possession by an evil spirit. Such a condition, with its episodic nature, frightening and dangerous symptoms and demonic overtones, would cause Paul untold worry and grief.

Perhaps it is instructive, however, that we do not have a more specific definition of Paul's thorn in the flesh. Over the centuries countless Christians have each found their varied sufferings mirrored in Paul's description of his thorn and heard the divine response as words spoken directly to them. The Lord's answer does not explain suffering or remove its source but provides assurance of divine presence and care in the midst of suffering. Human weakness is a fact of life, but it need not engender helplessness. Oppression is real, but this is not a divine counsel to accept oppression passively. God does not tell Paul—and us—to quiet down and be content with weakness; rather, God offers the remarkable revelation that divine power dwells within human weakness. The cross is a paradoxical symbol of a paradoxical faith: in human terms it can mean only defeat, humiliation and suffering, but transformed by Christ it represents victory and life. Paul is no passive recipient of abuse or tolerator of injustice. He lashes out at his rivals, defends his reputation and brooks no compromise with sin. Yet he is able to continue to fight these battles because he knows that God's strength is at work in his weakness. Thus he can say, "whenever I am weak, then I am strong" (2 Cor 12:10). Perhaps women, who were often perceived as weak, could take particular encouragement from this thought.

Summary Appeal and Warnings (2 Cor 12:11—13:10)

Paul prepares to sum up his letter by reminding the Corinthians that he has been forced to say what he has said to them by the tactics of the superapostles and by the Corinthians' obstinacy to hear the voices of reason. Again he defends his practice of not accepting support from them, which must have been a major obstacle to some members of the congregation, by appealing to a metaphor implied and stated throughout this letter: Paul as the parent, the Corinthians as the children (2 Cor 12:14; cf. 6:13). The Corinthians are frustrated that Paul will not deal with them in a business-like way; he longs for them to love one another as family.

Familial affection does not, however, obviate the need for discipline. Indeed, moral failures are more serious within familial bonds than among business associates. Perhaps with the "painful visit" (2 Cor 2:1) still in mind, Paul warns that he will discipline the congregation, when he returns, if he finds sin still among them. While Paul is concerned about sexual immorality (apparently with good reason, given the Corinthian congregation's history; see 1 Cor 5:1-2; 6:13-20), the longer list of sinful behaviors he cites in this context has to do with the way members of the community treat one another: "quarreling, jealousy, anger, selfishness, slander, gossip, conceit, and disorder" (2 Cor 12:20). These, in addition to sexual sins, are the faults regarding which the Corinthians are to "examine" themselves (2 Cor 13:5) and correct before Paul arrives. Such a list ought to sober today's church members; while we may be quick to point a finger regarding acts we consider immoral, too many of us tolerate or even participate in the community-destroying behaviors Paul lists.

Final Greetings and Benediction (2 Cor 13:11–13)

Paul's farewell is accompanied by a list of brief exhortations. The word usually translated "farewell" or "goodbye" in this context is the word Paul uses more commonly to mean "rejoice." Even as he closes this often-stern letter, Paul wants his last word to be not one of scolding but one of encouragement. He urges them to community harmony and reminds them that they are not a lone band of believers, but connected with "all the saints" (2 Cor 13:12). The brief benediction, trinitarian in form, with which Paul closes this letter has long been a favorite of preachers and worship leaders. Perhaps we should learn, when we hear it at the close of our worship services, to recognize it as coming from 2 Corinthians and be reminded that this gifted, troubled, beloved congregation has much to teach us as well.

Bibliography. P. Barnett, *The Second Epistle to the Corinthians*, New International Commentary on the New Testament (Grand Rapids, MI: Eerdmans, 1997); L. L. Belleville, *2 Corinthians*, IVP New Testament Commentary 8 (Downers Grove, IL: IVP, 1996); E. Best, *2 Corinthians*, Interpretation (Louisville, KY: John Knox Press, 1987); V. P. Furnish, *2 Corinthians*, Anchor Bible 32A (Garden City, NY: Doubleday, 1984).

SANDRA HACK POLASKI

The Purpose & Value of Human Life

Ellen, a student in my systematic theology class, seemed especially melancholy as she entered my office for the appointment she had urgently requested two days earlier. A successful educator in her late thirties, Ellen had taken a leave of absence to engage in theological education, hoping thereby to find answers to the questions that plagued her. Suddenly she interrupted her recounting of her life's narrative. Unable to hold back her tears, she blurted out, "My problem is I no longer know who I really am. And I am afraid that if I find out, there won't be a place for me."

In her short statement, Ellen articulated what many people feel. We have lost our sense of purpose, and we wonder if we are of any value. Into this situation, the Bible speaks with good news: God has a purpose for human life, and God bestows value on all humans.

Our Human Purpose

The biblical writers repeatedly tackle the question of our purpose. After contemplating the wonder that God cares for humans who seem so puny compared with the vastness of the universe, the psalmist offered this response to the perplexing question about human existence: "You made them a little lower than God, and crowned them with glory and honor. You have given them dominion over the works of your hands; you have put all things under their feet" (Ps 8:5-6). The sage's declaration echoes the announcement that forms the climax to the first creation story: "So God created humankind in his image, in the image of God he created them; male and female he created them" (Gen 1:27). As these two texts suggest, the biblical view of our purpose is closely connected to the idea that we are created in the divine image.

Theologians offer a variety of suggestions as to what the imago Dei entails. Perhaps the most prominent theory links the image of God to some capability that the Creator placed within each person, especially the power of reason (or alternately the power of will), which constitutes us as humans. Our purpose becomes that of actualizing this aspect of our creaturely giftedness, ultimately, according to the medieval thinkers, by contemplating eternal truths.

The suggestion that the image of God involves primarily our rationality implies that we can best fulfill our purpose as individual knowers. Further, it means that the highest exemplars of the imago Dei are those persons who have developed our supposedly innate power of reason most completely. It is not surprising that historically the connection between the image of God and an innate power (such as reason) has been paralleled by a focus on the adult male as the model human.

In the Reformation a more relational view of the imago Dei became prominent. Rather than being primarily a power connected to our essential humanness, according to the Reformers the image of God consists in our standing as creatures before God. It refers to the special relationship to the Creator that was ours by creation but that Adam lost in the Fall. The Reformation focus on relationship marks a step in the right direction. If the imago Dei entails our relationality rather than our rationality, then all persons—male and female, young and old, able and disabled—are equally created in the divine image. Yet the relational understanding does not capture the fullness of the biblical concept of the imago Dei. Nor does the Reformation view go far enough in the direction of shifting the focus away from the individual.

Viewed from the perspective of the Genesis creation accounts, ultimately our being created in the image of God is connected with God's purpose for us. We are created in the image of God in that we have received from God a special vocation, a specific task to complete, a unique role to play in creation. The imago Dei is our human calling—a calling that we all share and that we share together.

The Bible speaks of our purpose as that of exercising dominion within creation (Gen 1:26; Ps 8:6). Exercising dominion does not mean, however, that we treat the universe as if it exists solely for our benefit. The Bible does not provide license for human exploitation of the world. Instead, the backdrop for the biblical idea of dominion as God's image bearers lies in the practice of the kings of the ancient Near East who often left images of themselves in territories where they could not be present in person. Such images served to represent the kings' majesty and power. In a similar manner, God created humans as representatives of the Creator.

According to the second creation narrative, central to our role as God's representatives is the responsibility of managing creation. The Genesis narrator declares, "The LORD God took the man and put him in the garden of Eden to till it and keep it" (Gen 2:15). This managerial role entails caring for creation after God's example of care. As we do so, we mirror the compassionate, loving character of the Creator. Thus, by caring for creation after the manner of the Creator, we exercise true dominion and live out our human purpose.

But even the idea of dominion does not bring us to the heart of the imago Dei. According to Genesis 1, God's resolve to make humans in the divine image led to the fashioning of humankind as male and female. This indicates that in addition to the task of exercising dominion, the imago Dei is connected to human life in relationship; it is related to community.

The story of Adam and Eve in Genesis 2 deepens this theme. God creates the first human pair so that humans might enjoy community with each other. More specifically, God creates the female to deliver the male from his isolation. In the subsequent biblical narrative, this primal community of man and woman produces the offspring that arise from the sexual union of husband and wife and eventually gives rise to the development of societies. What began in the Garden of Eden finds its completion at the end of history. One day God will bring to pass a human society in which God's children enjoy perfect fellowship with each other, the created world and the Creator (Rev 22:1-4).

Like the statement that concludes the first creation narrative, "male and female he created them" (Gen 1:27), the narrative of the formation of the woman from the man (Gen 2) is a poignant reminder that the imago Dei—and thus our human purpose—is not the exclusive property or prerogative of either gender. Nor is the isolated and solitary Adam the complete image of God. If anything, the narrative focuses attention on male and female in relationship. This does not mean that all persons must be married to live out their divinely given purpose. Jesus' life and teaching stand as a clear counterexample to this erroneous idea. But it does indicate that being created in the divine image entails an inherently relational aspect.

The statement in the first creation account, "Let us make humankind in our image" (Gen 1:26), hints at why the imago Dei involves humans in relationship or community. The God of the Bible is the triune one, the three persons united together in perfect love (*see* The Trinity). Because God is community—the Father, Son and Spirit in fellowship—the creation of humankind in the divine image is connected to humans in fellowship with each other. As we live in love—that is, as we give expression to true community—we reflect the love that characterizes the Creator and we indicate what God is like. In short, as persons in community we fulfill our divinely given human purpose.

According to the New Testament perspective, we discover that living as persons in community entails participating in the community of Christ's disciples. Our Lord articulated this truth in his call to radical discipleship: "For those who want to save their life will lose it, and those who lose their life for my sake will find it" (Mt 16:25). The way to true life leads through the giving of one's life in relationship to Christ and, by extension, to others. We come to find our true human purpose as we participate together with one another in the believing community. And according to the New Testament, Christ's fellowship is an inclusive community. It envelops Jew and Gentile, slave and free, male and female (Gal 3:28). It welcomes adult and child, rich and poor, able and disabled. All are gifts to each other, and all are to serve each other together using whatever spiritual gifts the sovereign Spirit has provided (1 Cor 12:5; 1 Pet 4:10).

People are desperately seeking to bring some measure of meaning into their fragmented, seemingly purposeless existence. The good news of the Bible is that we have a divinely given purpose, namely, to reflect God's character in our relationships with others and toward creation around us. As a result, our lives need not remain the meaningless collections of purposeless events they so often appear to be. Rather than being devoid of purpose, the various dimensions of our existence can fit together into a meaningful whole. And the pattern whereby we can weave the aspects of our lives together and that thereby gives meaning to our lives lies in the purpose God intends for us. As we acknowledge that we are to be God's image bearers, we can come out of our isolation and enter into relationships. By living in right relationship with God, each other and the created world around us, we discover our purpose for existing. And in this discovery of purpose as God's image bearers, our lives begin to take on an eternal meaning.

Our Human Value

The biblical teaching about God creating us in the divine image points toward the answer to our human quest for purpose. It reminds us that God graciously gives purpose to our lives. But the Bible also speaks to our longing for a sense of value. The good news is that God likewise graciously bestows value on us.

The question of value—what humans ought to value, as well as the value of the human person—has been a topic of conversation at least since the ancient Greek philosophers. Yet this question has become acute as society debates complex ethical issues, including abortion, euthanasia, doctor-assisted suicide and genetic engineering.

Some discussion participants approach these issues with the assumption that a person's value is derived from the human community. Proponents suggest that anyone is a person with value insofar as she is enjoying a meaningful existence as measured according to certain socially agreed-upon standards or insofar as he is acknowledged as a person by others. Thereby the final court of appeal becomes merely human conceptions of the good life. This outlook allows abortion, for example, to become a "pregnancy interruption" or a "pregnancy reduction." This assumption likewise allows us conveniently to institutionalize and then forget those whom we consider to be of minimal value—the poor, the disabled, the dying.

Other participants appeal to what they see as the intrinsic or innate rights of all humans. On this basis, proponents may champion the cause of the marginalized. But they do so by appeal to what they see as the intrinsic value of the human person. Like the focus on the good life, in the end this view with its appeal solely to the human person rises no higher than the anthropological level.

The Bible clearly sets forth a high view of human life. Every human being has value and is to be seen as a person of value. In contrast to many contemporary outlooks, however, the Scriptures ground this evaluation neither in society nor in the human person but squarely in God. The Bible opens with the ringing statement, "In the beginning . . . God created the heavens and the earth" (Gen 1:1), an assertion that finds echo in the Apostles' Creed, which rightly commences with the words, "I believe in God the Father Almighty, the Creator of the heavens and the earth." We could conclude that the term *Creator* capsulizes the fundamental relationship between God and the world. To confess God as Creator is to acknowledge that everything owes its existence and being to, and everyone derives her existence and being from, the God of the Bible: "For 'In him we live and move and have our being' " (Acts 17:28).

The declaration God is Creator provides the ultimate answer to our quest for value. To acknowledge God as Creator is to set forth a theological foundation for understanding and affirming value. If God is Creator, then questions of value must be approached from the perspective of the divine Valuer. If God is Creator, God alone ultimately determines what value is. Further, as the one who values truly, God is the standard for value. And this God calls us to value after the manner by which our Creator values.

What does God value? The first answer must be all creation. God values everything

God made. Consequently God calls us to view all creatures as valuable. But in acknowledging the value of creation, we must avoid falling into the widely held idea that we are the ones who determine this value. The value of anything does not arise from its utility for us. Nor are other creatures valuable merely insofar as they serve our ends. Instead, all creatures are valuable because God values them. And the loving Creator desires that we—as those created in the divine image—show God's loving character toward all by valuing them after the divine pattern.

Although God values all creation, God places special value on humans. Jesus pointed to this special value when he encouraged his disciples to trust in the gracious heavenly Father rather than to worry about the cares of physical life: "Look at the birds of the air; they neither sow nor reap nor gather into barns, and yet your heavenly Father feeds them. Are you not of more value than they?" (Mt 6:26). Jesus' rhetorical question leads naturally to the inquiry, Valuable to whom? Here the answer can only be to the Father. God values every human being.

We must note, however, that this assertion brings us again to the theological foundation of value. Contrary to the human-centered appeals widely espoused today, humans do not possess intrinsic value. The basis of our value does not lie in ourselves, in anything we might possess or even in anything we might do or accomplish. Rather, because we are God's creation, whatever value we have is derived value. Our value arises solely from the gracious judgment of the divine Valuer who values us. As a result, we can never dictate the value of any human, not even ourselves. Instead, God calls us to value one another and ourselves as God does.

The realization that we possess derived value ought to foster true humility in us. None of us can extol our value, as if we were the authors of our personal worth. Nor can we appeal to any value we claim to possess as the foundation for making demands on either God or others. At the same time, God's valuation should foster in us a true sense of worth. Rather than looking to others to determine our value, we can lift our heads high and boldly declare, "I am valuable, because God values me." In the same way, the awareness that each person is someone whom God values ought to lead us to treat everyone with the dignity befitting those whom God values so highly.

The biblical writers draw a connection between our calling to value all other humans and the imago Dei. The divine image in humans means that each person ought to be treated with respect. God's covenant with Noah after the flood, for example, stipulates a serious penalty for murder, because humans are created in the divine image (Gen 9:6). So ingrained was this idea in the Jewish mind that James could matter-of-factly state, "With [the tongue] we bless the Lord and Father, and with it we curse those who are made in the likeness of God" (Jas 3:9). Hence the scriptural writer appeals to creation in the divine image as a basis for respecting other humans even in our speaking to and about each other.

The value of human life is incomplete, however, without the future orientation the New Testament affords the imago Dei. Paul declares that Jesus Christ is preeminently the image of God (2 Cor 4:4; Col 1:15). Believers participate in the image in that they are being transformed into Christ's likeness (2 Cor 3:18), a process directed toward the new creation at Christ's return (1 Jn 3:2). As a result, the value of human life is ultimately based on God's salvation purpose, which will reach its goal only in the future in the new community that God will share with redeemed humankind in the renewed creation (Rev 21:1-4; 22:1-6). Because every person—from fetus to old age, whether male or female, regardless of national identity or socioeconomic standing—is potentially a participant in God's future community, each human is valuable in God's sight. The God who promises to make all things new one glorious future day (Rev 21:5) calls us even in the midst of the brokenness of our present to value all persons after the manner that God values.

For Ellen, as for each of us, knowing that God has a purpose for our existence and that God values us ought to give us a sense of who we truly are and to cause us to realize that there truly is a God-given place for us. And with this in view, we can devote our energies to cultivating relationships that because they are built on the good news of the Bible truly reflect the character of the God who created and redeemed us.

STANLEY J. GRENZ

GALATIANS

Introduction

During his career as a missionary in the urban centers of the eastern Roman Empire Paul of Tarsus had an experience familiar to numerous Christian workers since: he fell ill in the middle of a crucial missionary effort. As a result of his poor health, Paul spent some time with a group of pagan Celts (also called Gauls) in what is now north-central Turkey and preached Christ to them. They responded by placing their trust in God's Messiah Jesus, and the communities of new believers experienced the joy and miracle-working power of the Holy Spirit.

Not long after he moved on to a new mission station Paul learned that other teachers had come into the Galatian churches. These people had begun to teach the new believers that in addition to trusting Christ it was necessary for them to be circumcised, to participate in the religious observances of the Jewish calendar and to observe the biblical food laws. Since Paul had taught them that the God of Israel had sent the Messiah, the new converts naturally wanted to obey the God to whom they now belonged. If God's Torah said that the men of every family had to be circumcised, these eager new believers were ready to schedule themselves for surgery.

The letter before us is Paul's response to this situation. Apparently unable to come in person, he does the next best thing: he entrusts a written communication to a messenger, perhaps one of his associates, whom he instructs to read the letter to the believers gathered for worship.

Outline

- 1:1-5 Opening of the Letter
- 1:6-10 The Galatians' Defection
- 1:11—2:21 The Divine Origin of the Good News
- 3:1—5:12 Paul Presents His Arguments
  - 3:1-18 Claiming the Inheritance of Faith
  - 3:19—4:11 The Law as a Substitute Teacher
  - 4:12-20 The Personal Appeal of a Mother
  - 4:21—5:1 Born Free
  - 5:2-12 A Direct Assault on Circumcision

5:13–6:10	The Way of Life in the Spirit
6:11-18	Closing of the Letter

Commentary

Opening of the Letter (Gal 1:1-5)

Paul begins all his letters with a formula common to letter writers in antiquity: Sender to recipient(s), greetings! For the usual greetings Paul substitutes "grace . . . and peace," important concepts in his preaching. At the beginning of this letter Paul makes it clear that the good news that he had brought to the Galatians was not a new human way of being religious but a word from God. He stresses that he is an apostle, or missionary or emissary, from God.

In Galatians 1:1 the Greek word *anthrōpos* is used meaning "human being," in contrast to the divine being, God. It does not mean "male" in contrast to female. Another Greek word, *anēr,* means "man," "male" or "husband," but that word is not used here. Similarly, when Paul refers to his associates or to believers in general as *adelphoi* ("brothers"), he does not intend to exclude women believers. Romans 16 shows that many women worked with Paul in the spread of the gospel, and Acts confirms the participation of women in the early churches. That is why the NRSV translates *adelphoi* as "members of God's family" (Gal 1:2), or "friends" (Gal 4:12, 31; 5:11; 6:1).

The grace and peace offered to the Galatians come not from Paul but from "God our Father and the Lord Jesus Christ," whose death "for our sins" had the purpose not merely of forgiveness but of freedom from the evil powers of "the present evil age." Paul implies a contrast with the age to come, or the reign of God, in which the corrupt values and standards of the present world will be overturned. The fatherhood of the God who raised Jesus from the dead is unlike any parenthood experienced or even imaginable in the "present evil age."

The Galatians' Defection (Gal 1:6-10)

The other Pauline letters preserved in the New Testament include an expression of thanksgiving for the faithfulness of the recipients immediately after the letter opening. In writing to the Galatians, however, Paul sees little cause for thanksgiving. The "one who called" the Galatian believers was not Paul but God, and it is God whom they have deserted by turning to a gospel that is not good news (Gal 1:6-7). How could it be when human efforts are being substituted for the free gift (grace) available in Christ? This theme appears again in Galatians 5:4.

The contrast between God and human beings introduced in Galatians 1:1 appears again in Galatians 1:10, which serves as a transition into Paul's account of his call. He claims that his primary obligation is to God. All Christians, but perhaps especially women, need Paul's reminder. The problem with conforming to human or cultural expectations is not only that it is impossible to please all of the people all of the time but also that such a posture rules out the possibility of being the slave (*doulos,* Gal 1:10) of Christ, "whom to serve is perfect freedom" (Augustine).

The Divine Origin of the Good News (Gal 1:11–2:21)

In dealing with the situation in the Galatian churches, Paul emphasizes that the good news that he proclaimed was a revelation directly from God. And by revelation (*apokalypsis,* Gal 1:12) he does not mean a private religious experience so much as a lifting of the veil that obscures the purposes of God from humans caught in the "present evil age" that is rapidly coming to a close. God has done a new and unexpected thing in the death and resurrection of Jesus that cannot be comprehended in the traditional categories used by the teachers who supplanted Paul in Galatia.

These teachers apparently emphasize the importance of descent from Abraham for membership in the covenant people. This status is available to Gentiles only through the circumcision of males, they argue; and they have good scriptural backing for their claim. It is important to recall that although Mark records a saying of Jesus that relativized the biblical food regulations (Mk 7:14-19), the Gospel of Mark had not yet been written when Paul wrote to the Galatians. In addition, Jesus is not recorded as saying anything about circumcision. That means that Paul has to find some way to persuade the Galatian believers that the teachers who are urging them to accept circumcision as the sign of their entry into God's family are wrong, even though those teachers appear to observe the dictates of Scripture more assiduously than Paul does. The teachers' appeal to Scripture is the reason that so much of Galatians is an attempt to argue from Scripture for the inclusion of the Gentiles into the community of Israel's Messiah without the necessity of circumcision or any other mark of conversion to Judaism. But before he gets into his biblical argument, Paul trumps the teachers' appeal to Scripture by claiming that the good news that he preached in Galatia came to him by revelation from the Author of Scripture.

Galatians 1:13—2:10 consists of an autobiographical statement by Paul designed to show that he is not dependent on the Jerusalem church for the authority of his mission but that the "pillars" (Gal 2:9) of the original Christian community had given full approval to his preaching. He begins, as he does in Philippians 3:5, with his credentials as an observant Jew. He says that he was zealous "of the traditions of my ancestors" *(patrikōn)*. Having referred to God as "father" three times in the first sentence of the letter, Paul is making it clear whose authority matters, as well as suggesting that the teachers with whom he disagrees are relying on the traditions of their ancestors rather than on the revelation of the Father.

God's choice of Paul was "before [he] was born," and his call was motivated by grace (Gal 1:15). By this testimony Paul echoes the Old Testament prophets (Jer 1:4-5; Is 49:1-6) and dates God's gracious call prior to his circumcision, because it was prior to his birth. Keeping the focus on the God of Israel, Paul reports the experience that changed his life as an apocalyptic act by God, "who was pleased to reveal his Son to me" (not, as in 1 Cor 15:8, "[Christ] appeared also to me"). The purpose of God's revelation of Christ to Paul was "so that I might proclaim him among the Gentiles" (Gal 1:16). His mission to pagan Galatia began at that moment and was initiated by God.

Paul's independence of human authorities is emphasized by his not consulting "with any human being" and by his visiting Peter and James the brother of Jesus only after three years, still being a stranger to the Jerusalem church in general (Gal 1:17-24). On this issue and others, space does not permit a discussion of the difficulties encountered in attempting to harmonize Paul's account with the narratives of Acts. The focus here is on Galatians alone.

When it became necessary to consult with Jerusalem, Paul did not go because he was summoned "in response to a revelation" (Gal 2:2). It was God's idea that the church should be unified, and Paul remained committed to that unity throughout his ministry, though he must often have been tempted to lead his churches out of the orbit of Jerusalem. That he did not do so is because he knew that they were not his churches.

Four times in his account of this consultation Paul refers to "the acknowledged leaders" (*hoi dokountes;* Gal 2:2, 6 [twice], 9) of the Jerusalem church, and in the fourth instance he names Peter, James and John and calls them "pillars" (Gal 2:9). This must be a response to the teachers' claim that they represent the views of the Jerusalem leaders and Paul does not. Not so, Paul insists; although his gospel came directly from God, it had the approval of the apostles in Jerusalem, who acknowledged Titus, an uncircumcised believer, as a full member of the community of Messiah Jesus. For Paul, the meeting in Jerusalem confirmed what he knew: what God had done in Christ had changed everything, including God's definition of the covenant community. The trouble was that not everyone saw it as Paul did.

The incident at Antioch (Gal 2:11-14) made that painfully evident. The issue is not mere table fellowship, in the sense of sitting beside someone unpleasant at the church potluck dinner. When people in antiquity ate together, they ate the same food, and in Antioch it was obviously not fully kosher food. But Peter, Paul, Barnabas and the other Jewish believers were in the habit of eating the same food the Gentiles ate when they met together because God had done a new thing by bringing them into one body in Christ. When Peter and the other Jews "kept [themselves] separate" because they feared censure from representatives of the Jerusalem church, they were denying that Jesus' death on the cross was enough to bring them together. Further, they were in effect saying to the Gentile believers that if they wanted to continue to share meals, the Gentiles would have to learn to cook and eat kosher. They were saying, "Do it our way or you aren't part of God's people."

When Paul thought something he was likely to say it, this occasion being no exception. It is clear that "the people . . . from James" are guilty of the same offense as the teachers now disturbing the Galatian churches. That is why Paul relates the incident in Antioch. It is the climax of his account of how he came to preach good news to the Gentiles and what that good news means for Jewish believers in Christ. It means that God has changed the rules and it is the old guard who has to change to get in step with God, not the Gentiles who have to change to line up with the old rules.

Paul allows his speech to Peter to slide imperceptibly into a speech addressed to the Jewish teachers now influencing the Galatians. Including himself, Peter and the teachers with the pronoun *we* (Gal 2:15), Paul assumes that all Jewish Christians would agree that Jesus' death and resurrection make it possible for human beings to be in right relationship with God ("justified," Gal 2:16). That is what makes them different from Jews who do not believe in Jesus. But Paul draws a conclusion from this that makes his preaching and his practice more radical: because of Jesus' faithful death in response to God's will, Gentiles can be included in the covenant people without Torah observance ("works of the law").

It is not what people do that makes possible right relationship with God; it is what God has done in Christ's faithful death. The phrases *pistis Iēsou Christou* and *pistis Christou* in Galatians 2:16 should be translated "faith(fulness) of Jesus Christ" and "faith(fulness) of Christ." When Paul speaks about the necessity for humans to respond to God's gift in Christ he uses the phrase "believe in Christ," using the Greek preposition *en* ("in"), as he does in this same verse. Thus in one verse Paul uses two different phrases to speak about what God has done (the faithful death of Christ) and what humans do in response (believe in Christ).

For Paul, the good news is that Jesus was faithful and obedient, "even [to] death on a cross" (Phil 2:8), and that faithfulness is the source of our relationship with God, whether we are Jews or Gentiles. But no human being, Jew or Gentile, is put right with God by Torah observance. The corollary is that Torah observance cannot and must not separate Jewish and Gentile believers in Christ, at the table or anywhere else, because, as Paul will go on to say in Galatians 3:28, "all of you are one in Christ Jesus."

In Galatians 2:17-18 Paul responds to a criticism that must have been leveled against him by the teachers now influencing his Galatian converts. Their argument would be, "Not only is Paul a sinner because he rejects God's scriptural rules, but by substituting Christ for the rules and telling the Gentiles that they can ignore God's rules and trust only Christ, Paul makes Christ a servant of sin as well!" The teachers in Galatia are concerned about the possible consequences of destroying the connection between law keeping and relationship with God. What will motivate people to live moral lives if they are told that trusting Christ's faithfulness is all that matters? In response to the accusation that he has made Christ a promoter of sinful behavior, Paul exclaims, "Certainly not!" On the contrary, Paul says, if he were to try to add anything to God's straightforward, law-free gospel, that would make him a sinner. Then he goes on to explain why there is no going back and no need to go back.

Paul, a former Torah-observant Jew, has, by trusting Christ, died to the Torah in order to live in relationship with God, and he regards it as better than a fair trade. The teachers would not agree that God's Torah could be separated from relationship with God, but Paul has identified with the crucified Christ in such a way that he can say, "I have been crucified with Christ" (Gal 2:19).

Galatians 2:20 is a preview of Galatians 5:13—6:10 in that it explains why Paul's law-free gospel is not the lawless message that the teachers accuse him of preaching. The faithful and obedient Christ who lives within and through Paul empowers Paul's faithful obedience to God. The gracious gift of Torah to the people of Israel, symbolized by circumcision of the males of Israel, has been universalized into the gracious gift of the indwelling Christ to all human beings, Jews and Gentiles, females as well as males. And the gift is personal: "who loved me and gave himself for me." From Paul's point of view, to add anything to this gift would be to act as though Christ's self-giving death were unnecessary, and that Paul is not willing to do.

Paul Presents His Arguments (Gal 3:1—5:12)

At Galatians 3:1 Paul begins an urgent and well-planned series of arguments intended to convince the believers that their faith relationship with Christ is the whole truth of the gospel and to remind them that they are part of the new thing God has done through Jesus Christ. In this section Paul outlines the role of the law and sets out to show the Galatians that while circumcision may seem to be a minor issue, it is not. Not only is circumcision unnecessary for the Galatian believers because they already have been made part of God's new covenant people, but also undergoing circumcision would undercut the core of the message of God's gracious gift. To convince them of this, Paul uses arguments that target the emotions and the intellect.

Claiming the Inheritance of Faith (Gal 3:1-18)

Paul's first task is to show the Galatians that faith in Christ is the full story, not merely the prologue to something else. There are three parts to this argument. Paul first calls them to focus on their spiritual experience (Gal 3:1-5); then he appeals to Scripture and the historical example of Abraham (Gal 3:6-14); finally he argues from common legal practice (Gal 3:15-18).

Evidently Paul had overestimated the Galatians' grasp of the good news he had preached to them. Yet they were eyewitnesses to their conversion, and he cannot believe that they are prepared to deny the powerful spiritual experience that they had then. He wants them to remember that their birth in the Spirit had nothing to do with "works of the law" (Gal 3:2) but had everything to do with a response to Christ. So he confronts them with a series of stinging questions, accusing them of being "bewitched" and "foolish." The word *anoētoi* is translated "foolish" in the NRSV and the NIV (Gal 3:1, 3), and this is a better translation than "stupid" (CEV). It is clear from the context that Paul does not consider the Galatian converts to be slow to grasp an intellectual concept or an important facet of belief. Rather, he is accusing them of abandoning something of which they once were convinced—their authentic experience with God's Holy Spirit. The teachers have used their superior ability to quote Scripture to intimidate the Galatians into doubting their experience. Paul will have none of it.

In Galatians 3:6-14 Paul moves to refute what the teachers have been saying to the Galatians in his absence. He turns to the teachers' source of authority, Torah, and uses the example of their ancestor Abraham to make the radical claim that the blessing promised by God to the people of Israel now belongs to the Gentiles as well. Paul tells the Galatians that because of their faith response to what God has done in Christ, they are Abraham's true descendants even without circumcision.

To convince them, Paul first takes a positive approach, claiming that since the Galatian believers trusted God rather than performing works of the law, they are *hoi ek pisteōs* ("people of faith") and are like Abraham, who was given a right relationship with God on the basis of his trustful response to God. Like Abraham, they had turned to God from other beliefs and responded in trust, and it was "reckoned" or credited or counted to them as righteousness just as it had been to Abraham (Gal 3:6). The passive voice emphasizes that God, not Abraham, is the one who is acting.

Similarly God has acted to accept the Gentiles on the basis of faith. This blessing was promised "beforehand" to Abraham in Genesis 12:3, Paul argues.

Paul follows this positive argument with a negative one as he explains in Galatians 3:10-13 that getting involved with Torah involves hidden costs for the Galatians. If they are going to live a life centered on the law, then according to what Torah teaches, they are "under a curse," because "Cursed be anyone who does not uphold the words of this law by observing them" (Deut 27:26). As one who "hangs on a tree" (or cross), Jesus was also under a Torah curse (Deut 21:23), but by his faithful death "for us" (Gal 3:13; cf. Gal 1:4; 3:20), he initiated a new kind of living, one that is redeemed from the curse.

Turning from the negative (curse) and returning to the positive (blessing), Paul reminds the Galatians that the purpose of Christ's death was to extend the blessing of Abraham to the Gentiles (the *ethnē,* Gen 12:3 LXX). The blessing and the promise have come from God to those who are "in Christ Jesus"; faith is not the cause of the blessing but the mode of its reception (Gal 3:14). Identifying with his Gentile converts, Paul, the circumcised descendant of Abraham, uses the first person plural: "so that we might receive the promise of the Spirit through faith" (Gal 3:14). He makes it clear that his Jewishness does not make him any more a descendant of Abraham than the most recent convert from paganism to Christ. As people who are already part of the covenant with Abraham because of their Abrahamlike trust, the Galatian believers have no need to consider circumcision. What can they gain if they already have everything?

This is not the conclusion that the teachers would have drawn from these same passages of Scripture. In Paul's time, as since, Scripture could be used to argue opposing positions. What is important is that Paul's use of the Bible was appropriate for his time. In later Jewish writings we find exegetes interpreting one passage by another on the basis of commonly shared words. By using the methods of interpreting Scripture that would have been familiar to the teachers who were upsetting the Galatian churches, Paul manages to co-opt the example of their father figure Abraham and to turn the traditional teaching on its head, underscoring the radical nature of what God has done in Christ.

In case the Galatian believers are worried that the covenant of faith established through Abraham and guaranteed through Christ is invalidated by their failure to observe circumcision and food laws, Paul refers to the common legal practice of the time. He explains that God's covenant, like a will, is not annulled through something that comes later. Since the law came later than the promise to Abraham, the promise is still valid. The Galatians, like all Gentile believers in Christ, have been gratuitously included within the covenant alongside Abraham's descendants. Therefore they have no reason to worry about their rightful claim to the inheritance of faith.

The Law as a Substitute Teacher (Gal 3:19—4:11)

At this point Paul needs to redirect his argument slightly. Otherwise the Galatians could draw the conclusion that the law has no value. So he continues his argument using questions the Galatians might have at this point: "Why then the law?" (Gal 3:19) and "Is the law opposed to the promises of God?" (Gal 3:21). To answer these questions Paul explains that within God's plan for creation, the law had played a necessary role as a teacher (*paidagōgos,* Gal 3:24) during the interim period before God's promised fulfillment of time. As generations of people waited for God to fulfill the promise, they needed to know how to live; also, the law served to show people their sinfulness.

That interim time is now past. In Galatians 3:19—4:11, Paul explains that Christ's coming, "born of a woman" and "born under the law" (Gal 4:4), marks the fulfillment of God's time. This is good news for the Jews and Gentiles in Paul's time as well as for all people of our time. Previously people were waiting under guardians, either as minor heirs or as slaves (Gal 4:1-3). Now all are living in a new time and a new situation. Through Christ a new family is being born in the world; it is a community in which all people, despite their former distinctions, may join together in crying out, "Abba!" to the one Father who is like no other.

A picture of the relationships between people in this new community is given in

Galatians 3:26-29, where Paul draws on baptismal language (cf. 1 Cor 12:13; Col 3:9-11) to remind the Galatians that they had "clothed" themselves "with Christ" at their baptism (Gal 3:27). Paul's words reflect early baptismal practice. New believers took off their old clothes when entering the waters of baptism and put on new garments after coming up out of the waters. This symbolized the reality that the believers had cast off their old lives and were now new creations in Christ, alive to a new kind of existence.

As the act that marked a person's entrance into this new covenant community, baptism was a unifying act. Unlike circumcision, which involved only males, this sign of membership was one that touched all human beings, leaving its mark on men and women, who, because they have been baptized into Christ, are now "all . . . one in Christ Jesus" (Gal 3:28). Since they are all one person, their former claims based on race, gender or station in life no longer matter. The role and status distinctions of the "present evil age" are transcended in the faith community, even though the reign of God is not yet present in all its fullness, as it will be when Christ returns.

It is clear from Galatians 3:28, "no longer male and female," that Paul's use of the word *son (hyios)* in Galatians 3:26 and Galatians 4:7 (twice) is meant to include male and female Christians as children of God. His use of male language in this context reflects the legal practice of the time; property was passed down from father to son. In the new community created by the Spirit, women and men inherit the promises. Inheritance is not limited to males; rather, "all" are now "sons" in Christ Jesus.

The Personal Appeal of a Mother (Gal 4:12-20)

At Galatians 4:19, Paul uses the word *ōdinō,* which is correctly translated as "to endure birth pangs" or "to labor in childbirth" to describe how he suffers for the Galatians' mature growth in Christ (*see* Birth Pain Imagery). At first glance this seems to be a strange statement. Since he is male, it would have made more sense for Paul to have referred to himself as a father to the Galatians; he describes himself as a father to other believers in 1 Corinthians 4:14-15 and Philemon 10. Yet that would not have served his purpose; begetting a child is a wholly different experience from giving birth to a child. Birthing a child involves a passage of time, a hidden promise and a suffering in anticipation of new life in the future, none of which are part of the experience of begetting. While his reference to himself as the mother of the Galatians is odd, it is one with which the Galatians could agree. After all, they remember their close relationship with Paul.

However, Paul is doing more here under the guise of a simple personal appeal. In this verse, Paul is calling the Galatians to remember their spiritual birth (cf. Gal 3:1-5) while communicating that his work as an apostle is set within the larger framework of God's work in bringing forth the reign of God in the midst of this present evil age. In Romans 8:22 also, Paul uses the language of birth in the larger context of God's reign: the "whole creation has been groaning in labor pains" while it awaits its redemption. Here, although Paul is experiencing the labor pains, it is Christ who is being formed in the whole community of believers.

Born Free (Gal 4:21—5:1)

Paul continues using birth language while challenging those whom he addresses as "you who desire to be subject to the law." He embarks on a second argument from the law. Again he turns to the figure of Abraham (see also Gal 3:6-18), only now Paul traces the Galatians' spiritual lineage to their mother, rather than to their father, Abraham. He uses parts of the stories of Abraham, Hagar and Sarah (Gen 16:1—17:15; 21:1-21), though Sarah is never mentioned by name; she is referred to as the "free woman."

Though Paul compares a free woman with a slave woman in this section, he is not making a judgment about historical women or encouraging the mistreatment of slaves or children. Neither is he condoning slavery by writing about a slave (*see* Ancient and Modern Slavery). He contrasts the free woman with the slave woman in order to contrast the covenant of God's promise and faith in Christ with the Mosaic covenant. For rhetorical purposes he associates freedom with the former and slavery with the latter.

By telling the Gentile Galatians that they are the children of the "free woman" when he explains his allegory (Gal 4:28),

Paul is rejecting the position of the teachers that Jews trace their lineage to Sarah and Gentiles to Hagar. He is also answering the question he posed in Galatians 3:2-5 and reminding his listeners that the source of their spiritual experience was "believing what you heard" not "works of the law" (Gal 3:2), the "Spirit" and not the "flesh" (Gal 3:3). Those who teach the Galatian believers otherwise are guilty of "persecuting" those who were "born according to the Spirit," and Torah tells the believers what they must do to those teachers: Cast them out (Gal 4:30; cf. Gen 21:10).

Paul wants the Galatians to hear that they are connected to that which is their source, to that which gave them birth. The Gentile converts' birth was to a new creation (cf. Gal 6:15). Their birth waters were the waters of baptism and God's free outpouring of the Spirit on the Gentile converts. They began their relationship with the Spirit rather than with the law, and Paul hopes that they will no longer deny their true birth mother.

A Direct Assault on Circumcision (Gal 5:2-12)

With this powerful imagery behind him, Paul makes a direct assault on circumcision, the most pressing issue at hand. Paul repeats what he said earlier: once male members undergo circumcision, they are doing more than cutting off a piece of flesh; they are also obligating themselves to the Mosaic covenant and cutting themselves off from the covenant of faith.

As in the beginning of his arguments in Galatians 3:1-5, Paul uses sharp language. He ends with a graphic exclamation that he wishes those who support circumcision "would cut themselves off" or "castrate themselves" (*apokopsontai,* Gal 5:12). No doubt Paul truly wished that those teachers would cut themselves off from the Galatian communities rather than misleading these new believers and "cutting in" *(enkoptō)* on the race they were running so well (Gal 5:7).

The Way of Life in the Spirit (Gal 5:13—6:10)

New Testament scholars label the section of a letter in which Paul turns from his theological arguments to the ethical advice that follows from those arguments the parenesis section of the letter. The exact demarcation of that section of Galatians is disputed, but there are good reasons for regarding Galatians 5:2-12 as the last formal argument and reading Galatians 5:13-15 as a transitional passage that links the body of the argument with the exhortation to live in the Spirit that begins in Galatians 5:16.

In this transitional passage Paul repeats the central metaphors of Galatians 4:1—5:12 with a new twist. From the introduction of the motif of slavery in Galatians 4:1 all the way through the ringing conclusion of the allegorical argument in Galatians 5:1,

---

Sin

Christian ideas about sin have been a focus of feminist discussion from the outset. This is a doctrine embedded at the center of Christian faith—faith in salvation presupposes a need for salvation—and yet it has developed in ways that have been extremely harmful for women.

Sin: The Range of Meanings

Although the Bible does not spend much time theorizing about the nature and origins of sin, it is a fundamental concept and is presented in graphic and concrete ways. The important thing is the reality of sin and how to deal with it. In the Old Testament sin is seen in relationship to the law and in the New Testament to the redemption achieved by Christ. Sin is seen, broadly speaking, as deviation from some required pattern, as a going wrong, and it is described in the Old Testament through a multitude of terms carrying a range of shades of meaning. For example, sin may be transgression of a specific law, missing the mark or wandering astray or rebellion or error.

The Nature of Sin

Sin is objective and subjective. It is objective in relation to the law, having to do with specific acts that are measurable against this standard. The ultimate standard for judging wrongdoing is the character and will of God, the source of law. There is a repeated pattern whereby confrontation with the holy God leads to a sense of sin (Gen 3:8-10; Is 6:1-5). The same pattern is seen in the New Testament, for example after the great catch of fish, when Peter's response to Jesus is a confession of sinfulness (Lk 5:8).

Sin is subjective; it has to do with intention—pride, unbelief, unfaithfulness. And the objective and the subjective, the act and the intention, are linked. A wrong heart leads to sinful acts, and both are in need of atonement (*see* Atonement). Amos declares to the people that God will not accept their assemblies, offerings and songs because of their unrighteousness. Inward purity and social justice are both necessary (*see* God's Call to Social Justice). Jesus talks of purity as internal, not external: what comes out of a person defiles (Mk 7:15-23).

Sin is also religious (a breakdown between humanity and God) and social and moral (a breakdown between human beings and between human beings and their environment). So it is related to every level and aspect of human interrelationality and behavior within the created order.

Sin is individual and corporate. Individuals are held responsible for their actions. The righteous person who does what is right shall live; the soul that sins shall die (Ezek 20). Yet there is also corporate responsibility and liability. Daniel in exile, a righteous man, confesses for the sin of Israel identifying himself with his people (Dan 9; cf. Ezra 9—10).

The Consequences of Sin

Sin also has clear consequences. This was a particular concern of the prophets, who emphasized that sin leads to guilt, punishment, death and destruction. Here we see the ways sin works on a multitude of levels. Guilt is not merely a subjective feeling; it is an objective state of being wrong and liable. The effects of sin are not purely individual but corporate, and sin breaks down relationship not only between individuals and God and within the human community but also within the created order. This latter point has been greatly neglected in much Christian thought, although it has been partially recovered during recent decades (*see* Men and Women as Stewards of the Environment; Monotheism). For the Bible the physical environment is included in sin and redemption, and our abuse of the environment must be included in the catalogue of human sin. The covenant after the flood is between God, humanity and every living creature (Gen 9:8-11), and Isaiah 24 links human evils with the desolation of the earth, defiled because of the broken covenant between the people and God. Paul talks of the whole creation as groaning, in bondage to decay and futility and as eagerly anticipating the redemption that will include it (Rom 8).

This range of consequences is seen in Genesis, which carries through some of these themes. The act of disobedience results in broken relationship with God: Adam and Eve feel shame, they hide and they are excluded from the garden where God walked with them. It also results in breakdown of relationship between human beings: Adam blames Eve, and they are ashamed before each other. It is after the Fall that women will be subordinate to the domination of men and will suffer in childbirth. It has been a vital argument of feminist theology to point out the distinction between the original creation and creation affected by sin. Paul Ricoeur argues that one of the key distinctions between

Genesis and other stories of the beginning is this gap: that creation was originally good and then something went wrong. Relationships of domination between men and women are part of what should be put right through atonement. Genesis 3:16 describes sin and its consequences, and it cannot be taken as a mandate for the way things should be.

The sin of Adam and Eve also results in the breakdown of the harmony of creation as a whole. The ground is cursed, and the human relationship with it will be one of hardship. This pattern of multiple breakdowns is carried forward in the story of Cain and Abel (Gen 4), in which Cain's jealousy and fratricide alienate him from God, from his people and from the ground.

These features of sin are generally carried through in the Old Testament and the New. However, whereas the law—the expression of God's will—was the Old Testament means of evaluating humanity, Jesus is God with us and becomes the standard for judging human attitudes and behavior. The most fundamental sin is rejection of Jesus, which is rejection of God.

One largely new emphasis in the New Testament is an emphasis on the power of sin as a force enslaving all humanity. The responsibility of human beings as individuals is assumed as in the Old Testament, but sin is also seen as something that controls us and as something that is universal and cosmic. This is vital for Christianity and relates to the way in which sin, although a central concept, is secondary. It is a derivative doctrine for Christianity. Salvation in Christ is always the primary doctrine and content. So sin is seen in a way retrospectively as that which has been overcome. In line with this, the universality of sin is necessary to demonstrate that all have need of Christ, the starting point being that Christ came to save the world.

This emphasis on the universality of sin is seen in Paul's use of Genesis in Romans 5. It is important to note that Paul is concerned with Adam only as a counterpart and contrast to Christ. He is not concerned primarily with speculation about the origins of sin but with emphasizing how salvation in Christ begins a new order. The order of sin, condemnation and death begun with Adam is exchanged for the order of acquittal and life through Jesus Christ (1 Cor 15:22).

Sin in Christian Teaching

Influences of Dualism

Christian thought about sin has been shaped, as in other areas, by a range of concerns and presuppositions, including the Bible interpreted in particular ways and in the light of particular influences. Most important in the case of sin is the influence on early Christian thought of Greek ideas, especially Greek dualism, which separated reality into two different types: the spiritual realm of the divine, of truth, light, good, rationality, and the material realm of the physical, of change, darkness, death and irrationality. Most crucially for Christianity this dualism associated the physical with evil, and it also associated maleness with the spiritual and rational but femaleness with the physical and irrational.

The New Testament uses the language of "flesh" and "spirit" (e.g., in Rom 8), which might sound like a similar dualism. However *flesh* in the New Testament means "human": "in human terms," "human nature," "human existence apart from God" and sins of the flesh are not solely physical (e.g., Gal 5:19-21). This is seen clearly in Colossians, which talks of the mind of the flesh (2:18) and above all in the Christian insistence that in Jesus, the Word became flesh.

Although Christian teaching has carried through many of the basic emphases of the Bible, it has also taken on the task of theorizing about the origins of sin, and here in particular we see the influence of these dualistic ideas (see Avis; Furlong; Webster).

Women as Eve

Early Christian thinkers directly blamed Eve rather than Adam for the beginnings of human sin. In doing so they drew on a wide range of Greek and Jewish presuppositions about women being inferior to men, the dualism that associated women with the negative and Greek mythologies about evil (e.g., the story of Pandora). This interpretation of Genesis began only with early Christianity. Eve was also taken to typify female nature, so that in Tertullian's notorious condemnation of women as the "devil's gateway" he states that "each of you is Eve. The sentence of God on this sex of yours lives in this age" (*De cultu feminarum* 1.1). Hence, in this view, women are also responsible for the death of Christ.

New Testament teaching in 1 Timothy 2:12-15 has been taken as based on this kind of thinking and as proof of the misogynism of Christianity, although there are alternative interpretations of this text. It is more usual for the New Testament to talk about Adam, not Eve, as the representative of sinful humanity (Rom 5; 1 Cor 15).

As if this was not bad enough for women, early Christian speculation also worked on the idea that the temptation offered by Eve to Adam was sexual. This tied in with dualism associating women with the physical and reinforced negative biblical models of women as temptresses. Jezebel and Delilah are much more familiar images in secular culture than are positive images such as Sarah or Judith. The influence of this pattern is seen in the notion of women as forbidden fruit, an image that regularly crops up in contemporary advertising.

Augustine: Original Sin, Sin and Sex

The association of sin with sexuality was taken further by Augustine's teaching, which has massively influenced Western Christianity and Western culture. There are elements in the Old Testament that talk of being born in sin, but these strands are essentially confessions of the extent of human sinfulness. In Romans there is a concern with universality of sin. Augustine was the first to develop a clear notion of the inherent and inherited sinfulness of human beings. He was working, in part, from a mistranslation of Romans 5:12 that "all sinned in Adam"; he was also concerned to show that babies need baptism. This, combined with his great sense of the power, universality and inevitability of sin, led to Augustine's doctrine of original sin. This sees all human beings as born sinful and guilty: "no sinner as yet in act and still new from his birth, but old in guilt." All are included and implicated in the sin of Adam and in its punishment.

The sin and punishment are passed down—here we come back to dualism again—through sexuality. Although Augustine does not see sexuality as necessarily sinful, he says that it always is sinful in practice because it is the primary example of the way our senses, our physical nature, are in revolt against our rationality and will overcome it. In Western culture the notion lingers that there is something inherently sinful about sex; hence the idea more than lingers in much Christian thinking that sexual sins are worse than any other kind of sin. Augustine was not blaming women more than men for sin, but with powerful presuppositions around that women are more physical, less rational and spiritual than men, and with powerful images like Eve we have the ingredients for a poisonous cocktail of ideas. The poisonous nature of the cocktail is seen in the witch hunts of the fifteenth century onwards, justified by Christian thinkers on the basis that women are more inclined to witchcraft than men, and it is seen in current attitudes to sexual infidelity and rape where women are likely to be blamed.

These ideas linger in often subconscious but still significant ways. Few Christians are likely to explicitly argue that women are more sinful than men, although they might want to argue that sex is particularly likely to lead us to sin. However, not only do Christian ideas of salvation argue against these kinds of dualism, but so do Christian ideas of sin. It is clear from the Bible that sin springs from and affects human rationality and spirituality as much as it does our physical nature, and these are inseparable. Also, sin must be seen as a going wrong of the originally good creation, and this is as true of our embodiedness as it is for our rationality. We must hold out against any continuing vestiges of the early Christian asceticism that suggested that our physical nature should be punished and denied. Our bodies and sexuality may be affected by sin as much as the rest of us, but they were equally created good and are included in salvation. There is nothing wrong with bodies, either female or male, and there is nothing inherently wrong with physical pleasure.

Sin as Pride

Feminist criticism has also focused on a strand of recent Christian thinking that emphasizes pride and self-assertion as the fundamental form or core of sin. Some scholars have suggested that these are male understandings and that it may be more appropriate for women to think of sin as lack of self-assertion or as wrongful dependency; being a doormat might be a form of sin (Alsford). This is in line with the scope of sin described above—that it includes a range of meanings, including active and passive, and that sin may take many different forms.

Sin and Oppression

This range of meanings for sin makes it particularly appropriate to identify oppression and domination as sinful. Feminist analysis highlights the range of levels on which oppression operates: it has to do with attitudes and expectations, social practices, legislation, economic realities, stereotypes. The network of forces that constitute and perpetuate oppression is an example and illustration of the network of elements constituting sin: individual and corporate, subjective and objective, active and passive, sin as a controlling power of which we are all victims in different ways and in which we also participate as individuals and communities. The life of a woman affected by the presupposition, inherited and reinforced from birth, that as a woman she is inferior is a powerful example and illustration of sin. It is hard to identify who is responsible for such a presupposition, and the chances are it is passed on and reinforced by the woman's mother, who is also a victim of it, as well as by society. It is a presupposition that will negatively affect others in her life, men and women and their relationships. And it is something she is likely to pass on to her daughters and sons. A man brought up in such a context would be personally responsible for lack of respect or acts of violence toward women, and yet at some levels he would also be a victim, codetermined from birth by his situation. Patriarchy not only gives us instances of sin but also illustrates the ways in which sin is more than the sum of individual sins and becomes a power that enslaves.

Sin and Salvation

Despite the negative history of sin it is a vital concept for women in its identification of wrongness and the ways in which that wrongness works. It is also vital because talk of sin, within Christian theology, always implies its opposite or solution—salvation.

Salvation in Christ is the inauguration of a new creation. Just as salvation replaces the old order of Adam, sin and death, many evangelical feminists would argue, so must it replace the subordination of women to male dominance. Just as sin affects and works on every level of existence, so too must salvation if it is to be as all-encompassing as sin. And the reason Augustine and others after him stressed sin so much was partly a desire to stress salvation even more. Jesus is the new standard for judging humanity, and he is the man for women, not only for men. In his behavior we see the treatment of women and men as equally in need of salvation. In his teaching and his practice Jesus disregards notions of purity that would have barred him from touching a menstruating woman or from talking to a Samaritan woman. There is nothing unclean or sinful about these women as women; they are to be judged according to the same standards as men.

Many of the attitudes and ideas described in this article work in an invisible way, on subconscious levels, and have been perpetuated within Christianity alongside a clear insistence on the universality of sin and guilt, on human equality in sin as in salvation. This latter must be maintained. Inclusiveness in our understandings of sin must match inclusiveness in our understandings of salvation. Both of these must be worked out on individual and personal levels and on the corporate levels of life within community, specifically within the church. Our understanding and identification of sin must always be only a step on the way to understanding salvation and putting it into practice.

Bibliography

S. Alsford, "Sin and Atonement in Feminist Perspective," in *Atonement Today*, ed. J. Goldingay (London: SPCK, 1995); P. Avis, *Eros and the Sacred* (London: SPCK, 1989); M. Furlong, *A Dangerous Delight* (London: SPCK, 1991); P. Ricoeur, *The Symbolism of Evil* (Boston: Beacon Press, 1967); A. Webster, *Found Wanting: Women, Christianity and Sexuality* (London: Cassell, 1995). SALLY ALSFORD

Paul has contrasted freedom (positive) with slavery (negative). In preparation for his exhortations about community life in Galatians 5:16—6:10, he now redefines the freedom to which the Galatian believers have been called as a positive kind of servitude based on and empowered by love. Paul reminds those who are so concerned about the law that the classic summary of all that Torah teaches about human relationships is "Love your neighbor as yourself" (Lev 19:18; Mt 22:39-40; Mk 12:31; Lk 10:27-28; Rom 13:8-10; Jas 2:8). The opposite of serving one another through love and loving the neighbor as oneself is allowing freedom to become a military outpost or staging area *(aphormē)* for the flesh (Gal 5:13).

The flesh-Spirit contrast throughout the parenesis section has to be understood in terms of the definition of Galatians 5:13. To "gratify the desires of the flesh" is to engage in behavior patterns that destroy the community, that is, to refuse to serve and love the neighbor (Gal 3:16). To "live by" or be "led" by the Spirit is to live in ways that build up the Christian community. The former is typified by the vices listed as "works of the flesh" (Gal 5:19-21). People who choose these paths demonstrate that they care nothing for the communal life of God's realm. By contrast, the life of the Spirit flowing through each individual Christian produces the "fruit" or virtues listed in Galatians 5:22-23, all of which enhance the communal life of those who are "all one . . . in Christ Jesus" (Gal 3:28).

The lists are framed by Paul's repetitive insistence that Torah cannot produce but does endorse the Spirit-led life and by the exhortation to the Galatian believers to conduct their lives in this way. Paul pointedly labels the vices "works" (Gal 5:19) and the virtues "fruit" (Gal 5:22); the former are the result of human ambition while the latter are the natural result of the life of the vine flowing through its attached branches (cf. Jn 15:1-17).

By the appeal to the metaphor of the vine, Paul makes the same point here that he makes in the parenesis section of Philippians: "I am able to do all things by the agency of the One who continually infuses me with power" (Phil 4:13). Because the old self ("flesh") has been crucified (Gal 2:19; 5:24) with Christ, the life of Christ living in the believer is able to produce an ethical lifestyle. The vices denounced and the virtues praised here are the same behaviors that were regarded as vicious and virtuous by general agreement among pagan and Jewish moralists of Paul's time. The lifestyle prescribed by Torah and achieved by the Stoic sage by dint of considerable effort and self-control Paul claimed for the Christian as a gift from the indwelling Spirit of Christ. After a few final admonitions pointedly directed against "those who . . . think they are something" (Gal 6:1-10), Paul moves to the closing section of his letter.

The Closing of the Letter (Gal 6:11-18)

In this short final section, Paul calls attention to his personal signature, which appears in larger letters than those of the secretary who has written the letter. He takes a few parting shots at the teachers, re-

Women & Philanthropy

Now in Joppa there was a disciple whose name was Tabitha, which in Greek is Dorcas. She was devoted to good works and acts of charity" (Acts 9:36). Dorcas exemplifies a spirit of philanthropy, which is often defined as "voluntary action for the public good" (Robert L. Payton, founding director of the Indiana University Center on Philanthropy). If this definition is carefully examined, it becomes evident that Dorcas was one of the finest examples of a philanthropist that can be found in the Bible or in secular history and literature. First, she acted voluntarily. She was under no obligation to perform good deeds—her actions weren't dependent on a salary. Second, she took action. She went beyond the rhetoric of philanthropy. Third, she acted on behalf of the public within her reach, especially those often ignored by the church and government of her day, such as widows and their children. Finally, she concentrated on actions that produced good results for her constituents. Her philanthropic example was so powerful that God chose to intervene and allow her more years than at first expected. He moved through Peter to restore her to life so that her devotion to "good works and acts of charity" could continue and that her skills, energy and caring spirit might be a blessing to many.

The Bible contains many examples of women who engaged in voluntary action for the public good, women who believed what Jesus would state in Matthew 25:40, "Truly I tell you, just as you did it to one of the least of these who are members of my family, you did it to me." A few biblical examples selected from the ages will serve to further illustrate philanthropic action by women.

A dramatic example of mass philanthropy occurred during the wilderness wanderings of the children of Israel. God commanded that they build a tabernacle so that they would have visible, tangible evidence of God's continual presence. This story, told in Exodus 35—36, states that men and women came, all who were of a willing heart, and voluntarily gave offerings. Women parted with precious possessions, especially jewelry. The Israelites were so generous when moved by a worthwhile cause and when invited by God to participate in the project that they had to be restrained from giving. As the text states, "What they had already brought was more than enough to do all the work" (Ex 36:7).

The Exodus story of philanthropic activity, an early example of women taking action for public good, is congruent with some of the basic premises of philanthropy and fund raising. According to charitable statistics compiled yearly (*Giving USA*, published annually by the American Association of Fund Raising Counsel Trust for Philanthropy), more than 85 percent of every charitable dollar comes from individuals, not corporations or foundations. Individual giving was typical of the Israelites, and women in the Bible are noted for their charity. People give because they are asked, and God invited participation in a project that was beneficial to all. Considerable research in the past decade has focused on women as donors. It comes as no surprise that women have always been generous with their time and money, but only in recent philanthropic history have women been studied as to their preferences and ways of giving—and the extent of their generosity as well as potential for giving to charitable causes has been noted. In this sense the Bible serves as a fine document charting women's philanthropic history.

A few highlights, therefore, of philanthropic action by women can be noted. For example, the author of Proverbs discussed a worthy woman and states that "she opens her hand to the poor, and reaches out her hands to the needy" (Prov 31:20) and that "the teaching of kindness is on her tongue" (Prov 31:26). The author concludes that "many women have done excellently, but you surpass them all," a fine accolade to a woman who performed all parts of her life exceedingly well.

The widow of Zarephath is another role model who gave of all she had. As the story is told in 1 Kings 17, Elijah asked her for a loaf of bread for him before she prepared the last meal with the meager provisions she had. She complied, even though it seemed that she would use up her food supplies by making the loaf of bread, and her reward was that she and her son continued to have the basic food supply they needed, for as long as it was needed.

An exceptional example of a philanthropic woman is the widow who gave her two mites as a temple offering. She gave literally all she had! Jesus noted her generosity and sacrifice and lauded her philanthropic act (Lk 21:1-4).

Paul wrote in Galatians, "So then, whenever we have an opportunity, let us work for the good of all, and especially for those of the family of faith" (Gal 6:10). Women can be justifiably proud of the excellent examples of philanthropic action performed by their spiritual ancestors and emulate those actions for the glory of God and the benefit of humankind.

LILYA WAGNER

---

emphasizing the nonimportance of circumcision, and then he ends as he began, with a blessing of "grace" and "peace" for the believers in Galatia (Gal 6:16-18, cf. Gal 1:3).

Bibliography. B. R. Gaventa, "The Maternity of Paul: An Exegetical Study of Galatians 4:19," in *The Conversation Continues: Studies in Paul and John in Honor of J. Louis Martyn,* ed. R. T. Fortna and B. R. Gaventa (Nashville: Abingdon, 1990) 189-201; J. L. Martyn, *Galatians,* Anchor Bible 33A (Garden City, N.Y.: Doubleday, 1997); F. J. Matera, *Galatians,* Sacra Pagina 9 (Collegeville, MN: Liturgical Press, 1992); S. K. Williams, *Galatians,* Abingdon New Testament Commentaries (Nashville: Abingdon, 1997); N. H. Young, "Who's Cursed—and Why? (Galatians 3:1)," *Journal of Biblical Literature* 117 (spring 1998) 72-92.

KRISTEN PLINKE BENTLEY AND SHARYN DOWD

EPHESIANS

Introduction

Ephesians is written as a letter. Many features of Paul's letters reflect the Greco-Roman and Jewish forms of letter writing of his day. Ephesians begins (Eph 1:1) by mentioning the writer, Paul, and the recipients. The three main elements of most of Paul's letters are also included: looking back to thank God for the readers' Christian profession and walk, teaching and exhortation. Yet Ephesians also differs from Paul's other letters in that he does not deal here with detailed local church issues, as in 1 Corinthians. There are no names of individuals, as in Romans, and there does not seem to have been an immediately obvious situation he was writing to (e.g., Philemon being a letter of recommendation or Philippians being a thank-you letter). The writing is therefore of broader interest and application, as are Romans, the Pastoral Epistles, 1 and

2 Peter, James, 1, 2 and 3 John, and Jude. Paul adapts the letter form for his own use, to communicate this Christian content to its recipients.

Acts 19:1-20 and Acts 20:31 tell of Paul's visits to Ephesus and his three-year ministry among the Christians there. His close links with the Ephesian church make it remarkable that he makes no personal references to individuals in this epistle. Along with the fact that the words "in Ephesus" (Eph 1:1) are not found in the earliest and best manuscripts, it is not possible to say with certainty that the letter is directed to the Ephesian church in particular. Some think that the "letter from Laodicea" (Col 4:16) could be the letter of the Ephesians. It may be that the words "in Ephesus" were inserted later in a manuscript in Ephesus to show that the letter had been originally circulated among the churches of Asia Minor, of which Ephesus was a major one.

The letter shows that Paul is keenly aware of the cultural and religious backgrounds of the readers. It seems likely that most of them had been converted from Gentile beginnings (Eph 2:11; 3:1), and even if they had encountered Judaism they would have been widely influenced by prevailing Hellenistic philosophies and pagan religions. Even to Gentiles Paul freely quotes and expounds the Hebrew Scriptures as part of their new heritage that is fulfilled in Jesus, the Messiah, who unites Jew and Gentile in himself (Eph 2:17-19). Paul writes to encourage (Eph 6:22) the recently planted Gentile church and to build it up. This he does by reminding its members who they once were outside of Christ and who they now are in Christ.

Paul writes this letter not to a church pastor or leaders but to "the whole community" (Eph 6:23) and "the saints" (Eph 1:1). In the New Testament, saints are never people canonized for special goodness after death; it is a term synonymous with living believers in Christ or brother or sister (which Paul prefers to use in other letters, e.g., 1 Thess) and is used nine times in Ephesians. The expectation is that all who belong to Christ—men, women and children—are being equally addressed. This is true of Scripture as a whole. While human history shows that theology has often traditionally been more the domain of male scholars, pastors or teachers, the Bible makes no such distinction between men and women. Both have equal access before God to his Word, and therefore men and women have the responsibility to read, understand and pass on to others its riches.

The writer calls himself Paul. Some scholars have maintained that this is a later follower of Paul, writing with his authority and expanding on the letter of Colossians. This view seeks to make sense of the apparent lack of some features in Paul's undisputed letters (such as writing to specific people with specific needs) and a lack of some of the topics (such as justification by faith) that are found in the Pauline letters. And for many commentators it does not detract from the authority of the letter within the New Testament canon.

However, it is a normal human experience that people write on different topics, with different words, to different people. It is also difficult to see why Paul's name should have been associated with the letter from such an early time if he was not the actual writer. While it is not without its difficulties, there is evidence that the Paul named at the beginning of the epistle is the author, the apostle Paul. During the letter there are hints that Paul was writing from prison (Acts records that Paul was detained in Jerusalem, Caesarea and Rome), as a direct result of his preaching to the Gentiles (Eph 3:1; 4:1; 6:20).

There is a remarkable similarity between Ephesians and Colossians. Much of the words and structure are the same, yet obviously not as a simple matter of copying. It is likely that Paul was writing the two letters around the same time, to differing groups, which may account for the similarities and the differences.

Outline

1:1-2	Paul's Introduction
1:3-32	Praise of God and Prayer for the Believers
2:1—3:21	What God Has Done for Gentile Christians
4:1-16	Gifts and Graces in the Church
4:17—5:14	Exhortation to Practical Godly Living
5:15—6:9	Mutual Respect and Submission in Various Relationships
6:10-24	Final Encouragement and Blessing

Commentary

Paul's Introduction (Eph 1:1-2)

Paul was the apostle to the Gentiles. In the New Testament *apostle* is used in three distinct ways: to describe the Twelve, who were symbolically patterned on the twelve tribes of Israel to denote continuity and fulfillment in the Christian church and Paul; to describe some of the early Christian workers such as Barnabas; and to describe more broadly the function of someone sent to proclaim Christ. The last category may be likened to our word *missionary.* Most apostles recorded in the New Testament are men. However, there is no indication that this confers greater propensity to leadership for men or that all apostles must always be men. It may be descriptive of what was culturally more acceptable for those days. Even against such prevailing patriarchal culture, Junia (Rom 16:7) is most likely a woman apostle of the missionary kind, commended for her prominence, probably in the hard work she and Andronicus were doing.

Paul's use of the word *grace (charis)* is a play on the usual word *greetings (chairein)* used in Greek letters, filling the greeting with specifically Christian content. "Peace" is a most Jewish of greetings, based on the Hebrew and Aramaic word *shalom.* He also differs from the usual closing words in letters of the day by using a blessing of grace to end (Eph 6:24).

One of the most intimate metaphors for God in Scripture is that of father. It is found eight times in Ephesians. The problem with human language is that it often conjures up images in our minds. *Father* is one of those words that has many human images associated with it. For some people, the father figure is someone good and kind and close—the type of image that is properly to be associated with God's fatherhood. For others, the model of earthly fatherhood experienced has been negative. This can often be transferred to their view of God, who becomes a person to be wrongly feared, not trusted or even hated. The problem of this lies in the fact that the word *father* is initially an analogy, born of what we know of human fatherhood.

Not everything associated with a human father is transferable to the biblical usage of *father* for God. The major obstacle of the image is that all human fathers, by definition, are male. Yet this is not true of God as Father. Maleness is a human characteristic, created by God to image him along with femaleness. But it cannot be said that God is male or, for that matter, female. Such an importation from the use of *father* is not warranted according to the whole of Scripture's teaching about God. In fact, Deuteronomy 4:16 expressly forbids the people of Israel from making idols in the form of male or female, animals or any other created thing, knowing that to do such a thing would be to reduce God to human form.

God is the Creator, and human beings image God; God does not image us.

"Parent" might be an appropriate way of thinking of God as Father, since his parental love and commitment are the ideas paralleled, not simply maleness. The Hebrew word *ab* ("father") is also capable of such a meaning and is a more inclusive term than the more narrowly restricted word for mother. *Children* (Eph 1:5, lit. "sons"; Eph 5:1, "children") as a description of believers also furthers the parental metaphor.

Praise of God and Prayer for the Believers (Eph 1:3-32)

God is not only intimately known as Father to Christians but also is described as the "Father of our Lord Jesus Christ" (Eph 1:3). This is not implying a literal male fathering but denoting the closeness of relationship that has always been true within the Godhead (*see* The Trinity).

Since Paul is writing to all the believers, it is an encouragement and reminder that "every spiritual blessing" is accessible to men and women (Eph 1:3). Christianity is not a religion in which the highest mysteries or blessings are reserved for a few. All believers, young and old, male and female, Jew and Gentile, are blessed with every spiritual blessing that heaven affords, and this has been in the mind of God from all eternity.

So also is God's great plan for Christians, that they should be holy. In many countries and cultures it is more acceptable for men to be less holy in their morals than are women. Sometimes standards in sexual ethics are harsher for women than for men. Women are often required to be virgins at marriage, for example, whereas men are not. Scripture requires the same high ethical standards and purity for men and women. Holiness means being set apart for God, being acceptable to God and also living a life worthy of God.

Paul describes the purpose of God for each believer as *hyiothesia* (lit. "adoption as a son"). Since Jesus is, from eternity, the only one in essence and being coequal with God the Father, by virtue of his holiness and relation with God able to be called Son, it stands to reason that Christians must enter into relationship with God another way. The Bible has many different ways of describing this, such as new birth, justification by faith, salvation, and "adoption" (Eph 1:5), which is found only in Paul's writings.

The purpose of adoption under Roman law was to perpetuate the family line, whereas the Jewish idea, which is the background here, was for the benefit of the child: to confer the full rights and privileges of the family.

The NRSV rightly changes "adoption as a son" to "adoption as his children." In the patriarchal culture of the day, to be adopted as a son denoted the highest grace in belonging to a new family, with all the rights and privileges a son but not necessarily a daughter would have enjoyed. Nowadays it may be somewhat confusing for women to read this. It may not seem to be much of a privilege to be treated like a son, as if being a daughter is not quite good enough. The point Paul is making is not that women are inferior and that God is lifting them up to be like men. The rights and privileges normally accorded to adopted sons in those days are likened to the closeness of relationship God is willing to bestow on all who follow him. Therefore it is much clearer to use *children* in modern culture. The privileged relationship of the beloved child to a committed parent is in mind.

Paul excites his readers with the greatness of all that Christ has done on their behalf. There is a strong message that Christians have always been known by God and that belonging to Christ has always been their destiny. This is always something that Christians see in retrospect, whereas before people become Christians it is always true that "whosoever will, may come." The New Testament consistently teaches the parallel truths of our free choice of God and his predestination of us.

Ephesians 1:11, 18 speak of the "inheritance" of the believer. In many countries inheritance is something that passes through the male line. This is not true of the biblical inheritance. It is given to all those, women and men, who are children of the living God, and it is something that Paul prays that the believers will increasingly come to appreciate and understand the greatness of.

The power of Christ is of cosmic dimensions. To sit at God's right hand is the place of ultimate power and authority. This is further described as being above every rule, authority, power and dominion, past and future. Many of the words used here would ring bells within the religious milieu of Asia Minor; Christ is greater than any local magic, religious rite, prevailing philosophy or spiritual power. It was well known that there were many religious sects that were powerful in Asia Minor. In Ephesus, Acts 19 informs us, Artemis or Diana was worshiped, as in the whole of the then province of Asia. Goddess worship was important in personal religion and in the social fabric. Acts 19:24 shows the silversmith Demetrius being fearful of the gospel because it would affect his business if people no longer bought silver idols of Artemis.

In Acts 19 there is no attempt by Paul to replace goddess worship with a male God. The maleness of Christ is never referred to in Scripture as important in terms of salvation or leadership. His humanity, that which is common to men and women, is the key to his identification with and salvation of human beings.

What God Has Done for Gentile Christians (Eph 2:1–3:21)

In Ephesians 2:10 Paul reminds the believers of their former life in unbelief, which he describes in the strongest terms: they were once dead in sin but are now alive in Christ. All that we are is through grace; God's favor is freely given, and "we are what he has made us." This is true of our redemption as Christians who are new creations in Christ. It is also important to remember that it is God who creates each individual. Genesis 1 records God's verdict on the initial creation of men and women as equally "very good." Throughout subsequent history men and women's dealings together have tended to engender the idea that women are somehow not quite as good as men. This is not a scriptural understanding. We are what God has made us, equally capable of good works that are to characterize our Christian walk.

In Ephesians 2:11 the NIV has "done in the body by the hands of men." The Greek has no ambiguous "men" but a compound word meaning "done by hand," even though circumcision was usually done by men. Obviously Paul's point is that this is something done by a human hand rather than by God.

Circumcision was the sign of the covenant of God with the Jewish people, from the time of Abraham onward. It denoted being part of the chosen people and therefore belonging to and being accepted by God. It was a sign in the flesh of what was to be a spiritual reality. Circumcision was only ever done to males, never to females. Boys were to be circumcised at eight days old, but no cutting was ever advocated for girls. In some countries female circumcision is practiced widely, for many traditional reasons, though this is not a biblical idea. The health hazards involved in female circumcision are too great a risk to life, and women and girls should be protected from this as a Christian principle of justice (*see* The Purpose and Value of Human Life).

Women were no less part of God's covenant people because of uncircumcision. Paul makes the point in Ephesians 4:3-6 that the physical expression of unity in Christ is not to do with circumcision but baptism, which is inclusive of men and women, Jew and Gentile. It is that which was done to the flesh of Jesus (Eph 2:14) in his sacrificial death that is the mark of belonging and the uniting factor of Christians, rather than circumcision of the flesh.

Paul addresses the Gentile believers and explains how Jews and Gentiles are now one in Christ. By doing this there is now "one new humanity." The NIV has "one new man out of the two," translating the Greek word *anthrōpos* as "man." The NRSV is correct to translate it as an unambiguous "humanity." The Greek word is probably reminiscent of the Hebrew *adam,* which is used at the creation in Genesis 1:27 to denote the specific name for Adam, the first human, and also a generic name for human beings or person. Because of the tendency for modern understanding of the English *man* to be exclusive of women, it is better to use a word that clearly encompasses men and women, which is the intention here. When Paul speaks of the "two" at this point (Eph 2:14-15), he is not thinking of men and women but of Jew and Gentile, who are to become one, in language reminiscent of the closest intimacy of the marriage relationship in Genesis.

"Members of the household of God" (Eph 2:19) are those who are in the house, which is another way of expressing being part of the family rather than a stranger. Although Paul couches his teaching in theoretical terms, this would have had practical implications in how believers would treat and welcome one another within the church. The local church should always show in word and in action the family belonging and inclusive welcome that the gospel proclaims. No one should ever feel an outsider.

"This mystery was not made known to humankind" (Eph 3:5) is rendered in the NIV as "not made known to men," which ambiguously throws up a false image of men as opposed to women being the normal vehicles through whom God communicates. The Greek is *hyiois tōn anthrōpōn,* or "sons [children] of people," a Semitic idiom meaning "having the characteristics of a human being," which is rendered much more clearly by the NRSV inclusive version.

In Ephesians 3:7, Paul describes himself as a "servant," using the Greek word *diakonos.* This word can be descriptive of an official function in the church (Rom 16:1, Phoebe; Phil 1:1) or mean a servant attitude. It is not always easy to distinguish between these meanings. Here it would seem to be less of an official designation and more of an explanation of the allegiance Paul has to the gospel of Christ and serving God through his ministry.

Ephesians 3:14-15 employs a word play, "the Father, from whom every family in heaven and on earth takes its name," where *patria* ("family") refers to *patēr* ("Father"). *Patria* refers to a family group linked to a single ancestor, or it can mean a family grouping, a clan or lineage, but it does not mean "fatherhood." This verse is not saying that all fatherhood is derived from the heavenly Father. It is much more likely that this is referring to families of angelic groupings or spirit powers in heaven (which explains the idea of "every family in heaven") that owe their original existence to God and over whom God has ultimate power (probably the meaning of "takes its name"). It may be God as Creator and all-powerful that is the point (Lincoln). If this is the case, Paul is prefacing his prayer for the believers with an understanding of the greatness of the one to whom he is praying.

Gifts and Graces in the Church (Eph 4:1-16)

Ephesians 4:1 seems to introduce the second section of the letter, which focuses on the practical and ethical outworking of life and lifestyle of the believer. However, there is no bifurcation between a doctrinal first section and an ethical second section. In Paul's writings there is no doctrine that cannot be put into practice, and there is no ethical command that does not rest clearly on theological and christological argument. The two are gloriously interwoven in Ephesians. Yet Paul introduces an "amen" at the end of Ephesians 3 to draw his doxology to a close, and he begins Ephesians 4 with an injunction to holy living because of ("therefore") all he has said in the first three chapters.

Humility, gentleness and patience are often virtues more associated with women than with men, and in many societies they are expected of women but not of men. Paul includes them in Galatians 5:22 as fruit of the Spirit. Such fruit is presented as a whole, each one of which should characterize every believer. There is no picking and choosing some fruit and not others, and certainly no fruit is gender specific. It may be more of a comment on our cultures that some aspects of godliness are not usually considered masculine, and a reminder of the biblical view that men, just as much as women, are required to be humble, gentle and patient, just as also to be kind, tenderhearted and forgiving (Eph 4:32).

Within the unity of the church Christ gives gifts to his people, for the building up of the church, which is described as "the body of Christ" (Eph 4:12). The gifts, which are not intended to be an exhaustive list, are apostles, prophets, evangelists, pastors and teachers. Because many of these functions are seen to be done by men in Scripture and in the church, the image they conjure up when reading them is that these are gifts for men, not women, and many people have therefore a mental image of men as the personification of these gifts. However, there is no such delineation of the gifts in Ephesians, and in a context speaking so much in terms of unity of the body and grace given to "each of us," the thought that such gifts would be for men only would be distinctly out of place. The allusion in Ephesians 4:8 to the Hebrew Scriptures (Ps 68:18, a psalm that probably had associations with the Jewish festival of Pentecost and hence the link with gifts for the church) is rendered "gave gifts to men" in the NIV, which perpetuates the stereotype of such gifting for men in the church. But the Greek word there, *anthrōpos,* is better rendered by "people" in the NRSV. God's gifts are for all members of the church, and the church can grow properly only when "each part is working properly" (Eph 4:16), and each member is encouraged to use and develop her or his God-given gifts.

Exhortation to Practical Godly Living (Eph 4:17—5:14)

Christians are described as those who have a new life, continually clothing themselves with a new self (lit. *anthrōpos,* "person," in older versions rendered as putting on the new man). This is not referring to conversion but to the ethical dimension of holiness that should characterize believers' lives and set them apart from others. Christians will be marked out by their loving kindness, truthfulness, control of anger, honest hard work and wholesome talk.

Paul uses his situation of imprisonment for the Lord as a spur to the believers' evidence of service (Eph 4:1), and beginning in Ephesians 5:1 he reminds them that they

Manipulation

Masters and mistresses of the art of manipulation abound in the biblical story. In some instances manipulation is condemned within the narrative—David's attempt to manipulate Uriah after impregnating his wife or Jezebel's orchestration of Naboth's murder—but some manipulative measures enable the fulfillment of the promises to Abraham. This is true particularly of manipulative actions by women.

Rebekah orchestrates the deception of Isaac by assisting Jacob to steal Esau's blessing, Tamar deceives and seduces Judah in order to continue her husband's line, Shiphrah and Puah save Israelite boys in Egypt, Jochebed and Miriam hatch a plan to save Moses. Rahab the prostitute shields the Israelite spies and engineers their escape, Jael convinces Sisera to come to her for protection and then murders him, Naomi and Ruth arrange a suggestive encounter with Boaz that prompts him to act as Ruth's redeemer. Michal saves the life of David, soon to be king; Esther flatters the king and saves her people; in later tradition, Judith seduces and murders the Assyrian commander, Holofernes (Jdt 8—13).

In almost all of these stories the character and role of the women as women enables their manipulations to succeed and God's purposes to be fulfilled. Jael and Judith, because they are women, are able to lure generals into vulnerable positions that prove to be fatal; Shiphrah and Puah are by virtue of their midwifery able to save Israelite baby boys; Esther uses her role as queen and her favor with the king; and Tamar and Ruth use their femininity to ensure the continuation of the lineage of the people, as well as of the Messiah (Mt 1:3, 5; Rahab also is named).

Such manipulations are sometimes the actions of those on the margins of power (Tamar, Ruth and Lot's daughters). In other cases only subterfuge is effective in the face of brutality (Shiphrah and Puah, Jochebed and Miriam, Rahab, Jael, Michal, Esther and Judith).

The question remains as to why such stories are less present in the New Testament than in the Old. Is it because women are given more central roles in the Gospels and Epistles, from Elizabeth and Mary to the women commanded to proclaim Jesus' resurrection and the women prominent in the early church? Is it because such stories of women's power through trickery are told in women's memory, and the New Testament is the product of male authors? Or is it that violence, patriarchy and oppression are dealt a blow so decisive and fatal that the manipulations of those who came earlier in the story are only a shadow of the good news that has arrived? Perhaps all of these reasons give a hint of the truth. Ultimately all such manipulation is not in keeping with the New Testament admonition of speaking the truth in love (Eph 4:15).

Bibliography

A. O. Bellis, *Helpmates, Harlots, Heroes* (Louisville, KY: Westminster John Knox, 1994); J. C. Exum and J. W. H. Bos, eds., *Reasoning with the Foxes, Semeia* 42 (Atlanta: Scholars Press, 1988); S. Niditch, *Underdogs and Tricksters* (San Francisco: Harper & Row, 1987); P. Trible, *God and the Rhetoric of Sexuality* (Philadelphia: Fortress, 1978).

SYLVIA C. KEESMAAT

---

are to be imitators of God in the same way that children imitate (we get the English word *mimic* from the Greek here) their parents. The familiar parental image in Scripture for God is that of Father. Here, however, that is not specified, and the natural image is of children imitating father and mother. Also, Christ and his model of self-giving sacrifice are to be the catalyst to holy living that is acceptable to God.

Fornication and impurity are to be outside the believers' experience and even their talking and thinking. This is speaking about sexual immorality outside of marriage, particularly of adultery (*see* Adultery). In those days it probably also included the specific idea of prostitution. Such things are still prevalent and are forbidden to Christians. While many people may think that sexual sins are practiced more by men than women or that men may have more propensity to temptation in the area of sexual ethics, Paul makes no such distinction and is probably more realistic. Such injunctions are applicable to men and women alike.

Mutual Respect and Submission in Various Relationships (Eph 5:15—6:9)

Ephesians 5:18 begins one of Paul's characteristically long and flowing sentences. Although there is a full stop after Ephesians 5:20, the main verb ("be filled") governs to the end of Ephesians 5:22 and thus forms a continuous flow of thought and argument. Foolishness is seen in its consequent behavior of debauchery, particularly in overindulgence in alcohol, which in many families is the cause of much suffering. Paul describes it as *asōtia* ("wastefulness"), which is the same word used for the son in the parable of Luke 15:13, although the English description of him is usually taken from the equivalent Latin word, *prodigal.*

Drunkenness (although not drinking of alcohol per se) is a foolish waste and is contrasted with the wisdom of the continual infilling of the Spirit.

The verb "be filled" (the present tense implying continuous action) is followed by five dependent participles: speaking in psalms, singing, making melody (Eph 5:19), giving thanks (Eph 5:20) and submitting to one another (Eph 5:21).

Referring to the submission of wives to their husbands, Ephesians 5:22 does not begin a new section, contra many of the Bible versions. In fact, Ephesians 5:22 does not have a main verb or even participle of its own, relying instead on the participle "submitting" (Eph 5:21). So it reads more like, "be filled with the Spirit . . . submitting to one another out of reverence for Christ; wives, to your husbands, as to the Lord." The importance of this is that it shows that the injunction to wives is not separate from the injunction to mutual submission of all believers within the body of Christ but flows from it. It shows that Paul is not requiring submission from wives only and therefore relegating wives to a subordinate place within marriage. It is clear that Paul prefaces the injunctions to husbands and wives with the command to submit to one another. He continues by outlining what this will mean for wives and what it will mean for husbands.

The command to submit to one another stands at the beginning not only of the section on wives and husbands but also up to Ephesians 6:9, where a series of relationships is specified: wives and husbands, children and fathers, slaves and masters. The form of this list of ethical injunctions was termed *Haustafel,* or household code, by Martin Luther. It may have been a recognized form in pre-Christian literature. In any case, it is a form that is used elsewhere in the New Testament (Col 3:18—4:1; 1 Pet 2:17—3:9; 1 Tim 2:8-15; 6:1-10; Tit 2:1-10; some being incomplete sets, others dealing with the whole range of relationships). It may be that the most vulnerable or easily exploited of the relationships are mentioned first, and in comparison with pre-Christian sources, it is remarkable that these often lesser-valued people are addressed with greater dignity within the body of Christ.

The command to submit is clear within marriage, but a different word, *hypakouō* ("obey"), is used for children to parents and slaves to masters. This word for obedience is used only once in reference to marriage, when in 1 Peter 3:6 Sarah is said to have "obeyed" Abraham. Scripture does not mandate that a wife give unquestioning obedience to a husband any more than a husband give unquestioning obedience to a

Hierarchicalism & Equality in the Home

The Bible presents two contrasting pictures of the male-female relationship in marriage. The first appears in Genesis 1 and 2 as a relationship of mutuality in equality; the second emerges in Genesis 3 when, as a consequence of the Fall, the creational model of equality is overturned by sin and is replaced by a hierarchical order. Readers can trace the degeneration of the marital relationship through the mutual blaming in Genesis 3, the advent of polygymy in Genesis 4, and the shift to a view of the wife as one more possession to be owned, used and replaced if the owner wishes. Women were first seen as the property of their fathers and then bartered to become the property of the husbands to whom they were given in marriage.

At the same time, the picture in the Old Testament is not one of unrelenting hierarchy. Individual women exercised political, religious and familial authority in ways that challenged the prevailing patterns of hierarchy:

Deborah served primarily as a judge and prophet within Israel and secondarily as the wife of Lappidoth (Judg 4:4—5:31).

Huldah, a prophet in Jerusalem and the wife of a temple officer, spoke out forcefully when the high priest consulted her about the nation's fate. Because of her forthright denunciation of religious corruption in Judah, King Josiah instituted major changes in the nation (2 Kings 22:11—23:25).

Abigail, wife of the wealthy Nabal, received God's approval and David's praise when she authoritatively overruled her husband's decisions and independently acted to reverse them in order to save him and their entire household from destruction (1 Sam 25).

In addition, the Song of Solomon describes the sexual equality of husband and wife throughout the poem: both the husband and wife display deference and care for the other's desires; neither one manipulates or dominates the other. The Song elaborates the "one flesh" relationship of Genesis 2:24-25.

Whereas the Old Testament patterns emerge indirectly through the narratives, the

New Testament addresses the issue of marital relationships directly. The two clearest teaching passages are found in 1 Corinthians 7 and Ephesians 5:21-32.

A hierarchical marital structure places the husband in the superordinate position and the wife as his subordinate. Yet in 1 Corinthians 7:3-5, the apostle Paul clearly states that both wife and husband have expectations that the other should meet. This is the only passage in the New Testament that discusses the *authority* one spouse has over the other, and Paul is careful to state symmetrically that the exercise of authority is always reciprocal in the marital relationship. Both husband and wife have the same rights over each other.

Paul also teaches mutual decision-making in 1 Corinthians 7:5: neither one is to impose his or her decision as spiritual leader over the other. Decision-making is based on consensual partnership.

It may be argued that this equality extends only to the sexual union in marriage, but the context (1 Cor 6:13-20) establishes that the "body" is God's temple, to be used for his honor, and thus encompasses much more than sexuality.

This becomes clearer in Ephesians 5:21-32 in which husbands, when they love their wives as their own bodies, image the love of Christ for his church. The sexual union of mutual concern for the fulfillment of one's spouse pictures the union of Christ and the church, and this is precisely the teaching of Ephesians 5.

Ephesians 5:22 is widely used to support a doctrine of hierarchy in Christian marriage, and the paragraphing in many Bibles enhances that interpretation by splitting verse 22 from its immediate context. Textually, this in indefensible because verse 22 does not contain a verb but infers it from Ephesians 5:21, in which submission is enjoined on all believers. Verse 21, in turn, contains the fourth *(submitting)* of four present participles that describe the visible evidences of being filled with the Spirit of God. This hinge verse sets down the principle of submission, which Paul then explores in 5:22—6:9, describing what it looks like for wives, for husbands, for children, for fathers, for slaves and for masters. In particular, a wife's submission to her husband is to be "as to the Lord": she has only one Lord (Christ), but her devotion to her husband is to be of the same quality as her devotion to God. A husband shows his love for his wife by following Christ's example of humility and self-sacrifice (clearly forms of submission). There is no hint in this passage that a husband exercises power or authority over his wife.

A pivotal interpretive question arises about the meaning of *head*. For a full examination of this issue, see the discussion in this volume on 1 Corinthians 11:3 and Ephesians 5:23. Any resolution of the hierarchy-versus-equality debate will turn, at least in part, on the meaning of *head* in both passages.

Some Christians base their support of hierarchical marital relationships on Genesis 3:16, 1 Corinthians 11:3 and Ephesians 5:23, arguing that hierarchy is now necessary because of the Fall and the ongoing presence of sin in the world. But a fundamental question must be asked: if God's *creational* intent for male-female relationships is mutuality in equality (now marred by sin), has God done anything to overturn the effects of the Fall? Those who espouse equality in marriage believe that part of the purpose of redemption in Jesus Christ is to establish a new community, the church, which will model God's intent for marital relationships in the midst of a sinful world. Does the gospel of Jesus Christ, in fact, have the power to transform the marital relationships between redeemed people, imparting to them the spiritual graces needed so that they can live together in mutually submissive love? The apostle Paul assumed not only that they could, but that they *must* as they live out their redemption before a watching world. ALICE P. MATHEWS

---

wife. "Be subject" in the NRSV is probably better understood as "be submissive," since the submission Paul is requiring is not something enforced but embraced voluntarily, out of love for Christ and for one another. Another way of thinking of it may be giving in. Giving in to others or compromising our needs or wishes is something that is necessary to make a relationship work and is eventually a mark of strength, not of weakness. The relationship advocated is not one of doormat to exploiter but of equals giving in at appropriate times to each other in love.

Wives are to be submissive to their husbands. The Greek word *andrasin* (from *anēr*) can mean men or husbands. Here it means husbands, since the words "their own" are used in the Greek. This is not an excuse for imagining subjection of all women to all men. Neither does this mean that the husband is to be lord over the wife. The NRSV has the correct nuance in saying, "as you are to the Lord."

The husband is not commanded to be head but is described in metaphorical terms as head of the wife. The word *head* has been explained in a number of different ways, variously as ruler, supreme, governor, boss, derivation or source. The word is capable of these meanings and is used as such in other contexts. However, the way a word is used in its particular context gives it its meaning. It does not make sense that Paul should be using all possible meanings of the word here. Since the context is the parallel not of the glorious ruling of Christ but of his self-giving sacrifice, it is likely that this is the most sensible reading. What the husband stands for when described as head is the caring, giving, sacrificial love that is like Christ.

Given that the word *head* means "boss" in many cultures, it is difficult not to see this as a text of terror. It can be terrifying to women to think that the Christian gospel might be advocating a secondary place for women, under men's dominance. It can also be terrifying to men to try and think up some way in which they are properly fulfilling a role as head. Some imagine this must be in leading spiritually, although the husband is not the priest of the family, since the Bible speaks of the priesthood of all believers, or in showing authority or in being the major decision maker or arbiter. However, the Bible never denies women the opportunity also to make decisions for themselves or on behalf of the family. When two people enter into marriage, they bring with them a variety of gifts and areas in which they are competent. In a good relationship each partner will seek to develop the gifts of the other, rather than fitting into mythically predetermined roles. There is no biblical mandate for husbands going out to earn their daily bread and women staying at home to bake it. Paul never specifies any cultural action or practical application from this passage, except that, when the husband loves his wife (Eph 5:25), he is fulfilling that role. Christians will find appropriate ways of expressing mutual submission within their marriages, cultures, giftings and personalities.

While Paul urges husbands to love their wives, he is not rigidly dictating that wives submit and husbands love. Obviously both do both, and this is further descriptive of what it means to submit to one another (Eph 5:21). Perhaps he uses the specific words to each grouping because that was an aspect they were not so good at doing. This same reasoning can be applied to the injunction to fathers.

The sacrificial nature of love is the parallel between the husband and Christ. It is true that Christ's sacrifice brings salvation, but the husband is not seen as the savior of the wife. Christ alone is Savior, for each individual within a family unit.

In quoting Genesis 2:24, Paul appears to be advocating the creation of a new family unit at marriage, with the forsaking of the old family ties (*see* Marriage). This does not mean an abandoning of wider family responsibilities, but in some cultures where the wife is forced to leave her family and become a virtual slave in the husband's family, this may have some force.

Nowhere is the husband called upon to be Christ to the wife. It is the loving intimacy of marriage that is a suitable parallel to the love of Christ and the church.

These verses cut across the human tendency to selfishness and ambition within marriage and extol the workable virtues of self-sacrifice, mutual submission, care and love that are the foundations for any successful marriage. Human love within marriage is something possible even for non-Christians, since marriage is part of God's will for creation as a whole. But the sort of sacrificial love seen in Christ is not possible on our own. It is no mistake that these injunctions are under the general command of needing to be filled with the Spirit. The world around us will take notice of marriages that are sacrificial, mutually submissive, forgiving and loving. They will want to know the Christ who can make such things possible.

Children are addressed with the command to obey their parents in the Lord. Paul quotes from the Mosaic Decalogue the commandment with the promise attached of the blessing that comes from obedience and that is passed through the generations to come. The fact that fathers are addressed probably means either there

---

Childbearing & Rearing

In many places of the world, it is tradition immediately after birth to lay the newborn baby on the mother's breast: flesh on flesh, enveloped in love, warmth and hope. A mother gazing tenderly upon her child, the fruit of sexual pleasure with her beloved, is a portrait of God looking lovingly upon creation (Gen 1:31). The intimacy of the ideal mother-child relationship resembles the love God has for us, children born of human desire but fashioned in the likeness of our Creator God. Jesus uses the analogy of a mother hen, who gathers the chicks and protects them under her wings, to refer to his love for the children of Jerusalem (Mt 23:37; Lk 13:34).

These word pictures speak a thousand words, rekindling within us shared emotional experiences of love, intimacy, protection and survival. They raise the central themes of parenthood, of dependency and bonding, of resemblance and likeness, of closeness and nurture and of the human need to be loved.

Scripture instructs mothers and fathers to love their children and to provide for their temporal and spiritual needs (1 Tim 5:8). The Judeo-Christian heritage has always taught that children are a gift from God. From the presentation of Samuel at the temple by Hannah (1 Sam 1:28) to Christ's words, "Let the little children come to me" (Mk 10:14), Christian teaching holds a high view of children. New life and new birth in Christ—even these New Testament words—reinforce the notion that children and parenting are special motifs in the experience of Christians.

But parenting is far from easy. There is more to rearing children than feeding and housing them. Children need to be instructed and disciplined (Eph 6:4). In Deuteronomy 11:18-20 we read: "You shall put these words of mine in your heart and soul, and you shall bind them as a sign on your hand. . . . Teach them to your children . . . when you are at home and when you are away . . . when you lie down and when you rise." As Christian parents, we are to never tire of telling our children the story of God's love and forgiveness, of miracles and commandments, of the Great Commission and our collective call to compassion. We are to continually remind one another of an eternal perspective. We need to help one another in the family to get on with the task of loving God and loving our neighbor as much as we love ourselves.

In a spiritual sense, the church is to be involved in the processes of bearing and rearing in the family of God, as new believers come to faith, join others for worship and then seek to be discipled in the faith and sent into various forms of ministry. As mothers nourish their children, hug them, protect them from danger and help them to fight evil with good, so in the church family we need to strengthen each other with spiritual food and with loving acts of kindness. How will the world know that we are people of faith? By the love that we show one to another (Jn 13:35; 1 Jn 3:23).

NANCY NASON-CLARK

were specific instances Paul was thinking of or in those days provoking children to anger was more of a problem for fathers than for mothers and something Paul felt a need to address. Although the injunction is specifically to fathers, it applies to mothers also.

Paul seems to expect fathers to take an active role in bringing up children. It is probably a Western preoccupation with the value of monetary rewards in the workplace over against the devalued role of parenthood that has often relegated looking after the children as purely the woman's task. This is not specified in Scripture, and there would be warrant for the responsibility of both parents in that the normal pattern God shows for family units is of wife, husband and children, not absent fathering (*see* Parental Influence). However, this verse is not advocating that it is the father's sole job to discipline and instruct children, rather than mothers. (In single-parent families this may be impossible.) Paul is dealing with a problem the fathers may specifically have had. He is encouraging them to take a more active part.

In his closing, Paul describes Tychicus as a "faithful minister in the Lord." The word used for "minister" is *diakonos,* the same word used by Paul of himself (Eph 3:7) and rendered by the NRSV as "servant" in that passage. Considering the official capacity of pastor that the word *minister* evokes, "servant" would be a better rendering here. Paul is not describing Tychicus as a church leader but referring to his faithfulness of service in all that he does.

Bibliography. A. T. Lincoln, *Ephesians,* Word Biblical Commentary 42 (Waco, TX: Word, 1990). CLAIRE M. POWELL

PHILIPPIANS

Introduction

In one of his homilies on Paul's letter to the Philippians, the early Greek bishop and theologian John Chrysostom remarked in reference to Euodia and Syntyche, the two coworkers of Paul mentioned in Philippians 4:2-3, "It appears to me that these women were the heads of the church at Philippi" (Homily 13). What is interesting is that the allusion is made so matter-of-factly. Chrysostom displays no indication that anyone would think of disputing his remark. The book of Acts, which does not always agree in perspective with information presented in the undisputed letters of Paul, is in accord here in regard to the importance of women in the church at Philippi. Though the narrative of Paul's encounter with Lydia and the women gathered at the place of prayer outside the gates of Philippi (Acts 16:11-15, 40) does not mention Euodia and Syntyche by name, it does indicate that the first converts in Philippi consisted of the household of Lydia, a community that Luise Schotroff suggests was most likely made up of women engaged in the same trade. It is likewise tempting to suggest, though difficult to demonstrate, that Lydia's influence in her home city of Thyatira resulted in a community there that also continued to have respect for women leaders within the church, since the criticism directed at "Jezebel" in Revelation 2:19-29 would hardly be necessary if she were not influential within that community.

That women predominated in the community at Philippi seems to have been more or less taken for granted by most scholars, at least implicitly. This approach may have contributed to the relative lack of interest in Philippians in comparison with Romans, Galatians and 1 and 2 Corinthians, as well as to the tendency to view the disputes hinted at in Philippians 2:1-5 as minor faults, the kind of disagreements one might find in any Ladies' Altar Society. However, the publication of Ernst Lohmeyer's commentary on Philippians (1928) emphasized the theme of the possibility of impending martyrdom for Paul and for the Philippian Christians. Since then, it has become easier to recognize that Paul's use of the example of the Christ who was obedient unto death (Phil 2) indicates that his purpose in writing to the Philippians had more to do with encouraging them to stand fast in the face of threatened persecution than with exhorting them to practice humility in minor everyday matters.

What kind of church was there at Philippi, and what was the danger that threatened it? While for a number of years the fragmentation theory, that the extant letter to the Philippians is composed of remnants of two or three letters, has held sway and has tended to obscure a clear answer to these questions, recent scholarship seems somewhat more inclined to recognize the integrity of the letter.

Outline

- 1:1-2 Salutation
- 1:3-26 Prologue
  - 1:3-11 *Koinōnia* in the Gospel from the Beginning
  - 1:12-26 Contrast Between Paul and Unworthy Leaders
- 1:27—4:4 Body
  - 1:27—2:5 Encouragement to Unity
  - 2:6-11 Example of Christ
  - 2:12-16 Encouragement to Obey
  - 2:17-18 Encouragement to Rejoice Despite Difficulties
  - 2:19-24 Praise of Timothy
  - 2:25-30 Praise of Epaphroditus
  - 3:1-2 Caution Against Judaizers
  - 3:3-14 Example of Paul
  - 3:15-17 Call to Imitate Paul and Positive Leaders
  - 3:18-19 Examples of Those Who "Walk" Differently from Paul
  - 4:1-4 Encouragement to Agreement Between Two Women Leaders
- 4:5-20 Epilogue
  - 4:5-13 Exhortation with Paul as Model
  - 4:14-20 *Koinōnia* in the Gospel from the Beginning
- 4:21-23 Salutation and Benediction

Commentary

Partnership and Support

If we regard Philippians as all of a piece and also take into account the remarks in 2 Corinthians 8:1-9 and 2 Corinthians 11:9, which refer to the Philippians and perhaps, though not as explicitly, to the Thessalonians, it is clear that Paul is writing to a community for which he has a high regard. If, additionally, we take the reference to Euodia and Syntyche (Phil 4:2-3) together with the narrative of the encounter with Lydia and the other women at prayer (Acts 16), this was a community in which women most likely were a sizable portion, if not a majority, of the community. It was one in which they exercised considerable influence as well. Indeed, the importance of Euodia and Syntyche is recognized by a growing number of modern scholars who display no awareness of the opinion of John Chrysostom. Some modern commentators hold that Euodia and Syntyche were prominent in the church at Philippi, probably among the *episkopoi* ("overseers") and *diakonoi* ("ministers") of Philippians 1:1. These commentators suggest that therefore their dispute might have posed a threat to the unity of the church, despite the fact that Paul appeals to them so courteously and refers to them so positively in Philippians 4:2-3.

The high regard in which Paul holds the Philippians is demonstrated throughout the letter in connection with the terminology of *koinōnia,* a Greek word that is difficult to translate into other languages. It is often rendered as "fellowship" or "partnership." Because its usage in the letters of Paul sometimes has reference to financial contributions, J. Paul Sampley has argued that, in particular in the letter to the Philippians, it is an illustration of a contractual financial agreement defined by the Roman notion of *societas,* though somewhat modified by including spiritual concerns. However, Sampley's interpretation neglects the references in Philippians 2:1; 3:10, which have no financial connection. In general, while Paul sometimes emphasizes the aspect of financial sharing when he uses the term *koinōnia,* its full meaning can by no means be restricted to financial considerations.

In surveying the use of *koinōnia* terminology in all the undisputed letters of Paul, it is evident from 1 Corinthians 1:9, Philemon 7, Romans 11:17 and possibly 2 Corinthians 6:14 that *koinōnia* is something one is called to or shares in by virtue of being Christian. It is used in connection with the Christians' relation with Jesus Christ (1 Cor 1:9), with the gospel (1 Cor 9:23; Phil 1:5; 4:15), with faith (Philem 7), with suffering and consolation (2 Cor 1:7; Phil 3:10), with grace (Phil 1:7), with the Eucharist (1 Cor 10:14-22) and with the Holy Spirit (2 Cor 13:13; Phil 2:1). Romans 15:25-27, Galatians 6:6 and possibly 2 Corinthians 9:13-14 indicate that in employing the term *koinōnia* in regard to monetary contributions Paul had in mind a reciprocity that went beyond financial considerations. The apostles, the Jewish Christians or someone who already has the faith shares it with the Gentiles, and they in turn share at least their material wealth (cf. Phil 1:19) with those who had given them spiritual riches. Romans 11:17, in which only the aspect of the Gentiles sharing in the spiritual riches of the Jews is mentioned, should be read in conjunction with Romans 12:13, where there is an exhortation to the financial contribution to "the needs of the saints" without the prior spiritual benefits being mentioned; in Romans 15:25-27, both aspects are present. In 1 Corinthians 9, supporting his argumentation with Jewish practice, Paul insists at great length on the right of an apostle to be financially supported by those to whom he ministers. Thus whenever Paul employs the term *koinōnia* or one of its cognates with emphasis on the financial aspect, the prior spiritual benefit that grounds the obligation to render such financial assistance must always be kept in mind. In many of the occurrences of *koinōnia* terminology, monetary factors appear to be at best implicit.

What is so unusual in the letter to the Philippians in regard to the financial aspect of *koinōnia* is that Paul indicates that he has accepted financial assistance (Phil 4:15-18; the cognate verb) from this community and from none other for his use from the beginning of their relationship. Likewise, Paul remarks in Philippians 1:5 on the Philippian Christians' *koinōnia* in the gospel with him "from the first day until now." He asserts in Philippians 4:3 that Euodia and Syntyche have "struggled beside me in the work of the gospel, together with Clement and the rest of my co-workers, whose names are in the book of life." All of this suggests that from the beginning and consistently throughout their relationship the Philippian Christians have shared with Paul the missionary labor of the gospel in addition to assisting him monetarily from their limited financial resources.

Given his staunch refusal to accept financial aid from his converts (1 Thess 2:7-9; 1 Cor 9:3-18; 2 Cor 11:9-10), it says much for Paul's regard of the maturity of the Philippian Christians that he would not hesitate to accept such assistance even from those whom he described in 2 Corinthians 8:2 as being in "the extreme depth of poverty" (lit.; other suggested translations are "dirt poor" or "rock-bottom poor"). There is some disagreement among scholars as to why the Philippian Christians were so poor. Some propose that this situation was due to Philippi being within a Romanized province and the provinces being generally poor, while others maintain that Macedonia seems to have been prosperous on the whole, so there must be some other reason for the poverty of the Christians. C. K. Barrett has suggested that the poverty was due to the fact that the Christians were persecuted; an additional factor may have been that many of the converts were women whose husbands did not become Christian and therefore who had little wealth under their control, or single women like Lydia who had to engage in a trade. Schotroff contends, against the common view of Lydia as a wealthy businesswoman who might have lived in somewhat easy circumstances, that Lydia and the group of women associated with her probably were closer to what we would refer to as the working poor.

Paul commends the churches of Macedonia who have contributed "even beyond their means" (2 Cor 8:3) for the relief of the church in Jerusalem, "pleading earnestly for the grace of the *koinōnia* of the *diakonia* [ministry] to the saints" (author's translation). The reason for Paul's willingness to accept the generosity of the Macedonian churches for himself (2 Cor 11:9) and for the Jerusalem community is indicated in 2 Corinthians 8:5: "they gave themselves first to the Lord and, by the will of God, to us." They did this, according to 2 Corinthians 8:2, "during a severe ordeal of affliction," which nonetheless overflowed in "abundant joy" and "a wealth of generosity." That "churches of Macedonia" in 2 Corinthians refers to the churches of Philippi and not those of Thessalonica seems indicated because of the reference to the severe ordeal of affliction that correlates closely with the situation described in Philippians 1:28-30; additionally, 2 Corinthians 8:9 echoes Philippians 2:5-11. While the Thessalonian churches also endured persecution for the faith (1 Thess 1:6), Paul clearly indicates in 1 Thessalonians 2:7-9 that at that time, and up to the time of writing the letter, he had refused to accept financial assistance from that community, and it is unlikely that the subject of the collection for Jerusalem had come up so early.

A Need for Discernment

Paul's high regard for the Philippian Christians is further apparent in the positive description of them evidenced in the opening thanksgiving of the letter as well as in the consistently courteous terms of address employed throughout. Nowhere in the epistle does Paul claim the title of apostle, father or mother to the community; the authority by virtue of which he exhorts them is based on mutual affection in Christ. Yet he clearly believes that this community that he regards so highly and loves so well is in danger and in need of his loving support, and Philippians 1:9-10 suggests that that danger is related to a need for increased discernment. He praises their overflowing love but prays that their love will "overflow more and more with knowledge and full insight to help you to determine what is best."

It seems probable that the particular situation in which discernment is called for has to do with the danger of, at the least, harassment from non-Christians. Philippians 1:27-30 makes clear that Paul perceives the community at Philippi to be under threat of persecution and even death, as he has depicted himself in Philippians 1:12-24. Pheme Perkins has suggested that since emperor worship was prevalent in Romanized cities like Philippi, the Christians there may have been conspicuous by their refusal to participate in such homage and thus subjected themselves to the danger of persecution. If this is the case, then the lack of harmony within the community (Phil 2:1-5) requires further investigation.

The full implications of the exhortation in Philippians 2:1-5, which introduces the narrative of the Christ who emptied himself, depend to some extent on how Philippians 2:5 is translated. A literal rendering might be "This think in you which also in Christ Jesus." The verb *phroneō* ("to think"), which is used in the first part of the construction in Philippians 2:5, is also employed twice in Philippians 2:2; it refers more to an inward disposition encompassing the will and emotions than simply to an intellectual attitude. The second part of the sentence lacks a verb; thus any translation requires some interpretation. The entreaty at the beginning of Philippians 2, as well as the specific counsels in Philippians 2:2-4, implies that some sort of disagreement was disturbing the harmony of the Christian community at Philippi; the reference to the disagreement between Euodia and Syntyche (Phil 4:2) reinforces this conclusion. The question raised by Philippians 2:5 is whether Paul is encouraging the Philippian Christians to the kind of courteous humility that makes for harmony within a group or is pleading that they should be willing to risk everything in a situation of threatened persecution. How much is he asking of this community that is so dear to him?

In the RSV translation of Philippians 2:5, "Have this mind among yourselves, which is yours in Christ Jesus," "this mind" can refer to the *phroneō* described in Philippians 2:2-4, an attitude of humility that strives for harmony, avoids selfishness and conceit, and looks to the interest of others. Philippians 2:6-11, then, might be an emphasis on Christ who gave the supreme example of humility. It does not necessarily imply that the humility asked of the Christians at Philippi has to go to the extreme that Jesus went to, but neither does it rule out that interpretation. In this respect it is almost as ambiguous as the literal rendering. In another sense, however, it clarifies the literal translation because it states that the reason they should be humble in their attitudes toward each other is that they are "in Christ Jesus." It is unseemly for them to allow discord among themselves because they have been made one in Christ.

The NRSV translation offers two alternatives: "Let the same mind be in you that was in Christ Jesus" or "Let the same mind be in you that you have in Christ Jesus." The second possibility is similar in meaning to the RSV rendering. But the first seems to somewhat more definitely indicate that Christ is an example to be followed, as does the Jerusalem Bible: "In your minds you must be the same as Christ Jesus." In this vein one might also propose, somewhat more literally, since the Greek employs the verb *phroneō,* "Let this thinking be in you which was also [the thinking] in Christ Jesus." This suggests that those who are one in Christ are being called to put on his attitude no matter what it costs, and not only when it concerns relations with each other.

In Philippians 2:6-11, Paul depicts the kind of attitude, or thinking, that Christ had, which led him to be obedient even to death on a cross. In Philippians 2:12, despite the NRSV translation "you have always obeyed me," the Greek more literally reads, "you have always obeyed." It seems more likely that the immediately ensuing charge, "work out your own salvation with fear and trembling; for it is God who is at work in you" (Phil 2:12-13), is rather a further appeal, as in Philippians 1:27-28, to stand fast in their obedience to God in this situation of threatened persecution, even if this requires obedience unto death. The use of the sublime example of Christ makes more sense if the exhortation is to remain steadfast under threat of persecution and death rather than to improve community relations.

The harsh threefold warning in Philippians 3:2 to beware of outside agitators who advocate circumcision may also be related to this threat of persecution and death. Since the Jews enjoyed a protected status within the Roman Empire, some in the Philippian community (perhaps Euodia or Syntyche) may have felt that identifying themselves as Jewish in the eyes of the Roman authorities by adopting Jewish identity markers such as circumcision would serve to deflect the threatened persecution. Or Paul might have been concerned that some might be considering such a solution, which he adamantly opposed. Thus the lack of harmony in the community that seems to lie below the surface of the remarks in Philippians 2:1-5 may be due to disagreement about how to deal with the threat of persecution. And the humility to which Paul exhorts all the Philippian Christians, including their leaders, is radical, nothing less than self-emptying in imitation of Christ, who "did not regard equality with God as something to be exploited, but emptied himself . . . and became obedient to the point of death."

Examples to Imitate: Paul and Christ

In Philippians 3:17, Paul asks the community to join in imitating his example, but the example he has just offered (Phil 3:7-11) is that of suffering the loss of all things other than the knowledge of Christ Jesus suffering and risen, a self-emptying that imitates the example of the one he confesses as "my Lord" (Phil 3:8; cf. 2:11). In Philippians 2:1 Paul has presumed the community's *koinōnia* in the Spirit; in Philippians 3:8-11 he defines his knowledge of Christ in terms of knowing the power of Christ's resurrection and the *koinōnia* of his sufferings. This twofold knowledge of Christ is all that Paul desires, and for it he gladly gives up everything else.

The language that Paul uses of Christ Jesus in Philippians 3:7-11 echoes that of the author of the book of Wisdom 7:8-10 in characterizing Woman Wisdom, except that Paul takes the comparison further. While Wisdom's writer discovers that in giving up precious goods to gain Wisdom, he gains every good thing together with her, Paul is so centered on the overwhelming "gain" of knowing Christ Jesus his Lord that he is not interested in any other gain. All other gains are cheerfully acknowledged as loss from his new perspective, which views everything through the lens of divine Wisdom. Writing to a community under threat of persecution and death and being in the same situation (Phil 1:30), he reminds his beloved Philippians of the hope they look forward to: "But our citizenship is in heaven, and it is from there that we are expecting a Savior, the Lord Jesus Christ. He will transform the body of our humiliation that it may be conformed to the body of his glory, by the power that also enables him to make all things subject to himself" (Phil 3:20-21).

Roman mosaic depicting women athletes in different events. (Philippians 3:13-14)

The exhortation to imitate Paul is repeated in Philippians 4:9, but what they have learned and heard and seen in Paul is not simply a model of the virtues in Philippians 4:8, which could be found in any upright pagan. Paul was a person who would stand up to Peter in arguing for freedom from Jewish ritual law, yet he would be solicitous to remind the Gentile Christians to care for the material needs of the poor Christians in Jerusalem. He was a person who would speak out for Christ even when perceiving himself as a less than imposing speaker, who would accept the consequences of his speaking out without bitterness, who was willing to be a fool for Christ's sake and who refused to glory except in the cross of Christ. Could he ask less of those who were so dear to him, especially when he had already begun to experience the joy that was the result? Could he wish for them anything less?

Can one then seriously contend that to this church in Philippi Paul was merely saying in Philippians 2:1-5, "Be nice to each other because you are Christians"? After all, this is not the Philippi Chamber of Commerce he is addressing, or the Greater Macedonia Ladies Sewing Circle. Euodia and Syntyche have labored with him in the gospel. If all he desired were for them to get along, would he have to plead by virtue of all they hold most sacred as well as by virtue of their affection for him? This is a Paul who is contemplating his death and who is yet filled with joy, but his joy will be complete if they will listen to him. He is not just asking them to do something difficult. He has discovered that the way of the cross leads to joy. The joy to which the Philippian Christians are exhorted throughout the letter is the joy that comes from following Christ, even in the way of the cross that leads to death, but beyond that, to the glorious transformation in which Christ will transform their lowly bodies to be conformed to the body of his glory (Phil 3:20-21).

One feminist scholar has maintained that texts similar to that of Philippians reflect a powerfully seductive mystique in which an army of Christian martyrs stands on the side of divine violence. However,

Elizabeth A. Johnson maintains that the death of Jesus reflects not his required passive victimization divinely decreed but rather a dialectic of disaster and powerful human love by which the God of Jesus enters into solidarity with those who suffer. Paul's exhortation to the Christians in Philippi can thus be viewed as an invitation to enter into that solidarity.

A caution has been expressed by some feminist exegetes, such as Elisabeth Schüssler Fiorenza, about uncritically encouraging women to espouse a willingness to accept a servile status. She points out that the gospel admonitions to become as servants are unequivocally addressed to males in positions of leadership. Sheila Briggs contends that in Philippians the tension created by the statement that a divine being becomes a slave is relieved because the christological enslavement is removed from any analogy with human enslavement by virtue of the fact that the human slave did not choose servile status, nor do humans choose to be born. Thus she maintains that the text does not give possibilities of liberation but rather such possibilities are claimed by it from the oppressed. If so, such claiming appears to be an exercise in eisegesis—reading into the text.

I would maintain that the text of Philippians does offer possibilities of liberation, particularly when read in conjunction with

Paul's Greetings to Female Colleagues

Paul's greetings to female colleagues usually occur toward the end of his letters. His typical closings include hortatory remarks, greetings, a wish of peace and a benediction. In Hellenistic letters the purpose of greetings was emotional expression. Greeting forms include the writer greeting someone, asking the addressee to greet someone or relaying a third party's greetings. In these letters a greeting verb is followed by an indication of the one greeting; the person greeted is named, and elaborating phrases emphasize some aspect of the greeting. Paul's letters follow this format.

Paul greets or mentions the following women coworkers in his letters: Apphia (Philem 2), Euodia and Syntyche (Phil 4:2), Junia (Rom 16:7), Mary (Rom 16:6), Nympha (Col 4:15), Phoebe (Rom 16:1), Prisca (Rom 16:3; 1 Cor 16:19), and Tryphaena and Tryphosa (Rom 16:12). Euodia and Syntyche and Prisca are called "fellow workers" *(synergous);* Junia is called an apostle and "countryman" (*synaichmalōtous,* pl.); Mary, Tryphaena and Tryphosa, "hard workers" *(kopiōsas, ekopiasen);* and Phoebe, a deacon *(diakonon).* These are the same terms Paul uses for his male associates. Other women greeted in passing include Persis (Rom 16:12), Rufus's mother (Rom 16:13), Julia, Nereus's sister and Olympas (Rom 16:15). Whenever greetings are to the "brethren" *(adelphoi)* or to a church community, women are included as indicated by the NRSV's translation of *adelphoi* as "brothers and sisters."

Three women Paul greets are of special interest as leaders in their churches: Phoebe, Junia and Nympha. Romans 16:1-2 uses two technical phrases in connection with Phoebe, "deacon of the church" *(diakonon tēs ekklēsias)* and "helper of many" *(prostatis pollōn).* Although the meaning of *deacon* is not self-evident, it was a church office (see Phil 1:1; 1 Tim 3:8-13). "Helper of many" is the equivalent of the Latin *patrona,* a word used only here in the New Testament but found in the Septuagint and in contemporary inscriptions for patronesses. Evidence strongly supports the idea that the person in Romans 16:7 is Junia, a female, not Junias, a male (see Brooten). No commentator until Aegidius of Rome (1245-1316) took this person to be male. While the term *apostle* is not defined, a missionary couple (like Prisca and Aquila) are "outstanding among the apostles," and thus a woman is clearly called an apostle. Nympha (Col 4:15) seems to have been a householder who provided a church with a place to meet and thus, like Chloe in Corinth (1 Cor 1:11), was probably the leader of a house church.

Paul's greetings to his female associates indicate that he worked with and valued the contributions of women to Christian mission, that he used the same technical terminology in relation to them that he did with his male associates and that he numbered women among his friends, supporters and fellow workers.

Bibliography

E. E. Ellis, "Paul and His Co-workers," *New Testament Studies* 17 (1971) 437-52; B. Brooten, "Junia . . . Outstanding Among the Apostles," in *Women Priests*, ed. L. Swidler and A. Swidler (New York: Paulist, 1977); T. Mullins, "Greeting as a New Testament Form," *Journal of Biblical Literature* 87 (1968) 418-26.

BONNIE BOWMAN THURSTON

Galatians 3:28, 1 Corinthians 12:13 and Colossians 3:11, which many modern scholars view as reflective of early Christian baptismal liturgy. While mindful of Schüssler Fiorenza's caution, I would suggest that the reason Paul can exhort the Philippian Christians, and more particularly the women among them, to follow Christ's example of self-emptying is because in becoming members of the Christian community the women of Philippi have become leaders in that community as well. The letter indicates that Paul had a high regard for this community, never addressing them in terms other than those of equal to equal. It is a community that has taken seriously its baptismal dignity and struggled with Paul in the gospel from the beginning. So the danger that Schüssler Fiorenza rightly cautions against applies less to the women of Philippi than to Christian women in our day. It is only to the degree that we have some sense of self-worth that we can voluntarily pour ourselves out.

Johnson recognizes the related danger of simplistically equating God's power with weakness in modern attempts to speak of a suffering God, because this can inculcate a feeling of helplessness in those who are oppressed. Nonetheless she maintains that the alternative to an impassible, omnipotent God is neither a victimized, helpless God nor silence on the subject. "On the contrary, speech about Holy Wisdom's suffering with and for the world points to an act of freedom, the freedom of love deliberately and generously shared" (270). It is precisely the crucified Christ whom Paul portrays as the power and the wisdom of God (1 Cor 1:24). It is this Christ, now risen, whom the Philippians, and all who suffer in our day, are encouraged to await as the Savior who will transform their bodies of humiliation to be conformed to the body of his glory.

Bibliography. E. A. Johnson, *She Who Is: The Mystery of God in a Feminist Theological Discourse* (New York: Crossroad, 1993); V. Koperski, "Feminist Concerns and the Authorial Readers in Philippians," *Louvain Studies* 17 (1992) 269-92; idem, *The Knowledge of Christ Jesus My Lord: The High Christology of Philippians 3:7-11*, Contributions to Biblical Exegesis and Theology 16 (Kampen, The Netherlands: Kok Pharos, 1996); L. Portefaix, *Sisters Rejoice: Paul's Letter to the Philippians and Luke-Acts as Received by First-Century Philippian Women*, Coniectanea Biblica, New Testament 20 (Stockholm: Almqvist & Wiksell International, 1988); L. Schotroff, *Lydia's Impatient Sisters: A Feminist Social History of Early Christianity*, trans. B. and M. Rumscheidt (Louisville, KY: Westminster John Knox, 1995).

VERONICA KOPERSKI

COLOSSIANS

Introduction

The biblical text cites Paul as the author of Colossians (Col 1:1), although dissimilarities between the style, theology and use of words in Colossians and that in the undisputed Pauline epistles has led to the suggestion that Colossians was written by a follower of Paul. Alternate explanations for these dissimilarities could be that Paul writes with Timothy (Col 1:1; 4:18), that the text of Colossians is too short to provide an accurate sample of the author's writing style, that Colossians contains many blocks of imported traditional texts or that some combination of these factors is at work. The many similarities between Colossians and Philemon, which is generally agreed to be Pauline, provide additional evidence in favor of Pauline authorship. It seems likely that Paul, in prison, wrote Colossians, Philemon and Ephesians at about the same time and asked Tychicus, accompanied by Onesimus, to take them to Ephesus and then to Colossae. He hoped that the runaway slave Onesimus would reconcile with his master in Colossae (Col 4:7-9; Philem 10-21). Paul was probably in Rome but may have been in Caesarea or Ephesus. If he was in Rome, then the date is in the mid-fifties to early sixties. Many of his supporters are with him as he writes.

Paul has never been to Colossae (Col 1:4, 7-9; 2:1). Although of waning importance, this small city was nonetheless cosmopolitan, home to varied cultural and religious expressions. The largely Gentile church at Colossae (Col 1:21, 27; 2:13) had received the gospel from Epaphras (Col 1:7-8; 4:12-13), who shares Paul's imprisonment (Philem 23). Paul thanks God for these brothers and sisters in Christ: they have faith and love for the saints, they heard and comprehended the grace of God, and the gospel is bearing fruit among them.

However, the Colossians have been taken in by false teachings and have adopted a number of unnecessary religious practices. The Colossians were treating peripheral issues, ceremonies, the worship of angels, visions and self-denial as the focus of their belief instead of Christ. Paul describes the false teachings (Col 2:9, 18, 21, 23; cf. Col 2:11, 16, 20, 21) and warns the Colossians against "the elemental spirits of the universe," "the rulers and authorities" and "worship of angels" (Col 2:8, 15, 18). Commentators have proposed a wide variety of identities for these false teachers and their teachings; it seems likely that a syncretism of various beliefs and practices was taking place. We can see Judaism reflected in references to circumcision and the sabbath (Col 2:11-13, 16), and Greco-Roman concerns reflected in the mentions of "knowledge," "philosophy" and "severe treatment of the body" (Col 2:3, 8, 23). Possible allusions to dualism, astrology, Gnosticism, asceticism and pagan mystery religions can also be seen (Col 2:16, 18, 20-21, 23).

Paul writes with Timothy to these Christians, whom he does not know personally but esteems nonetheless, to warn them against the false religions and the syncretism by which they are tempted. His primary way of attacking this heresy is by insisting on the centrality and all-sufficiency of Christ in Christian belief. The Colossians do not need these false traditions, ceremonies or practices to help them become complete in Christ because they are already complete. People whose minds and deeds were once estranged from and hostile to God are now holy and blameless. This message would have been all the more liberating and perhaps difficult to wholly accept for the women of Colossae. Women were perceived as the embodiment of shame in their culture. Yet now they are not only entitled but also required to claim a new, honorable and holy status in Christ.

A crucial thing to keep in mind when studying Colossians, as with any book of the Bible, is that unless otherwise indicated, all of it is addressed to children, women and men. For people of faith who view the Bible as the source of inspiration and instruction, the Bible's message is meant to be understood, absorbed and integrated into our lives. Thus the vast majority of commands and teachings contained in the Bible are addressed to men and women. Far too often discussions of women's roles start with a focus on those relatively few passages that have separate discussions of how men and women are to serve God. A far better approach to this issue is first to focus on the majority of texts that address how all brothers and sisters in the Lord are to serve their Lord, and then to examine those particular texts.

Outline

1:1-2	Opening: Authors and Audience
1:3-14	Thanksgiving and Prayer
1:15-23	The Person and Work of Christ
1:24—2:5	Paul's Struggles for the Church
2:6-23	Warnings to Live in Christ
3:1—4:6	Implications of Being in Christ
4:7-18	Closing: Greetings and Instructions

Commentary

Opening: Authors and Audience (Col 1:1-2)

This opening follows the standard ancient letter style by identifying the author and audience. It also contains a typical Pauline greeting of grace and peace. The many translations that have Paul addressing "holy and faithful brothers" (Col 1:2) do a grave disservice to the women of Colossae and of the church ever since the first century. The term *adelphoi* in Greek was used to include male and female persons; one can imagine that young people and children were meant to be included in Paul's vision of the church. Thus the NRSV'S translation of "brothers and sisters" is much to be preferred.

Thanksgiving and Prayer (Col 1:3-14)

A thanksgiving to God or the gods was a standard element in ancient letters. Paul incorporates this element in his letter and expresses his thankfulness for the faith of the saints in Colossae, which is based on a hope that centers on Christ (Col 1:3-8). The gospel "is bearing fruit and growing in the whole world" and among the Colossian Christians. This expansive description easily includes children, women and men as those for whom Paul is thankful. Epaphras first taught them the word of the truth. He is a *diakonos,* a minister (the same term that is used of Phoebe, Rom 16:1). One wonders whether the image of "bearing fruit and growing" (Col 1:6) would summon the image of pregnancy and birth to the minds of the Colossian women (cf. 2 Kings 19:30; Hos 9:16 for this image used of a people reproducing). If so, this would be for women a particularly relevant image of one's participation in God's work of creating life in the world. Childbearing was central and unique to a woman's experience and role in this culture (*see* Childbearing and Rearing). Women could closely identify with God's creation of life in the womb and the joy and labor (Col 1:10-11 talks of the strength needed to bear fruit) required in the process of giving birth to a child and of giving birth to a new child of God.

Paul's prayer is that the Colossians "be filled with the knowledge of God's will" (Col 1:9). In the Prison Epistles, knowledge is related to the mystery of Paul's gospel and its inclusion of Gentiles. The embracing of the Gentiles, who were considered unclean and were excluded from the innermost places of the temple, would have had significant parallels for Jewish and Gentile women, who had also been considered unclean and who were also excluded from those most holy places of the temple.

Thus women are included in Paul's prayer that the Colossians will "bear fruit in every good work," "grow in the knowledge of God," be "made strong," "prepared to endure," patient, able "to share in the inheritance of the saints" (Col 1:1-12; women's inclusion could not be taken for granted in the first-century world; *see* Women's Rights in Biblical Times). Men and women alike are given God's power so that they can live lives that please God and can be free "from the power of darkness." Children, slaves, women and even most men were always under the power of some other person, whether their *pater familias* (family head), master or husband. The advantages of being under a kind and loving power instead of under a cruel and hateful power would have been felt by these subordinate people in a multitude of ways every day of their lives. Women living in Roman cities, which were known to be dangerous after dark, would likely have been particularly fearful of the dangers presented by literal darkness. This image of being rescued from the power of darkness and brought into a kingdom would have struck a deep chord with women.

The Person and Work of Christ (Col 1:15-23)

This hymn of Christ, whether written by Paul or adopted by him from an earlier source, sets before the Colossians the person of Christ (Col 1:15-20). Only after Paul does this can he address the Colossians' lack of appreciation for Christ. In this hymn Christ is presented as the image *(eikōn)* of God. In Colossians 3:10, the Colossian women, children and men are told that their new selves are being renewed according to the image *(eikōn)* of God. Despite the fact that the Old Testament describes God in predominately adult male terms, women and children are now able to be God's image, to represent or be like God, to be revealers of God's glory and goodness.

Paul uses a rhetorical form common in New Testament letters, "you were once . . . but now you are," to show the transformation and reconciliation that Christ has brought about (Col 1:21-23). Colossian children, women and men are presented as holy, blameless and irreproachable (*anenklētos*, a judicial word). The culture was invested in keeping and presenting women blameless before and after marriage. Women were in many ways the keepers of the family's honor, and those women who were not able to maintain irreproachable conduct and reputation would bring shame on themselves and their families. Girls and women would have especially understood the importance and relief at being found blameless and irreproachable, free from shame. Christ presents men and women who were once estranged and hostile in mind as now "holy and blameless and irreproachable" (Col 1:22).

Paul's Struggles for the Church (Col 1:24—2:5)

In this section Paul describes his suffering and sacrifices on behalf of the Colossians. Paul is accepting submission and self-sacrifice for himself and holding it up as an honorable concern. Submission was more strongly urged upon the women, children and slaves of the New Testament culture than on free males (see the household code in Col 3:18—4:1). Yet here Paul voluntarily humbles himself and holds that humility as an honorable position. Women's roles required them to be humble, and this idea of honor through humility in their dealings with male family members (or shame in a positive sense) would have been a familiar one. For men, the images of soldiers and athletes suffering for the honor of their city would have been evoked by Paul's words.

Warnings to Live in Christ (Col 2:6-23)

As Paul writes these warnings against false teachings, he must have been aware that in other Christian communities some women had seemed to be particularly susceptible to false teaching (1 Cor 14:34; 1 Tim 5:11-13). This vulnerability could be because women in general received less teaching, were less familiar with the Old Testament and were less educated in rhetoric and discriminating, logical thinking. People of the time thought that women were rash and weak by nature (*Letter of Aristeas* 250; cf. Virgil *Aeneid* 4.568; *Testament of Reuben* 5; *2 Enoch* 31:6s), and yet Paul assumes that men and women can resist these empty deceits. Paul gives to women and men alike "a charter of Christian freedom" (O'Brien, 155). Women are told not to let anyone condemn or disqualify them. No one in the Colossian congregation is allowed to accept passively what others determine to be proper spirituality; women have the freedom from these false teachings and the responsibility to live their lives in Christ Jesus.

One wonders how the use of circumcision as an identifying mark (Col 2:11-13; see also Col 3:11; 4:11) would have struck

Ritual flagellation initiation rite for women, typical of ordeals in so-called mystery religions. (Colossians 2:20-23)

the women of Colossae. Although Jewish women would have often heard this term used in a broad way and would have understood themselves as included among the chosen people of the circumcision (Gen 17:10-14), only males carried this mark (Gen 17:23-27). Circumcised individuals were not allowed into the gymnasium. Some Jews even had the equivalent of plastic surgery to remove the evidence of circumcision. Most Gentile women would have been unfamiliar with circumcision among their family members. It is hard to imagine that this image would have been an inspiring one for the women and girls of the Christian community at Colossae—or for the uncircumcised men and boys. Nonetheless the explanation that all Christians were now granted a "spiritual circumcision," that is, they put off "the body of the flesh" (Col 2:11) and needed no external representation of this status, must have fallen on grateful ears. For Christians the external representation of this death to the flesh and rebirth through faith is baptism, in which all believers can fully participate, regardless of gender.

The Colossian Christians no longer need to submit to the rules of this world (Col 2:20-23): "Do not handle, Do not taste, Do not touch." Women can now handle, taste and touch, but more noteworthy is that women—often the object that was unclean and not to be touched (Lev 12; 15:1-33)—are now freed from this status.

Implications of Being in Christ (Col 3:1—4:6)

Paul's instruction for how to live one's life is tied to his emphasis that the Colossians are now full in Christ. Their life is to be lived in a certain way, not because it will fulfill some religious obligation but because people who belong to Christ are people of a high morality. The Colossians are to have a realized eschatology, that is, they are to live lives that claim and act out in the present the future truth of their glory in Christ. Because they are "God's chosen ones, holy and beloved" (Col 3:12), they can and must act with a morality and compassion and conscientiousness that reflects their chosen status.

To be in a public (or "revealed") position of honor or glory (Col 3:4) would be an unusual and perhaps uncomfortable experience for women. Any grasping of this sort of position for themselves would be dishonorable in their culture. Now, however, Christ has won honor for women, and they (and men as well) must passively receive it. Women's honorable status in the community would have been earned through following the roles prescribed by their culture; stepping out of their domestic roles or into any sort of public arena would have brought shame upon themselves and their families. They also would have been accustomed to having their honor protected by others; the men in their families would have been careful to do this. For women of this culture, passively accepting Christ's work on their behalf may have been easier than it was for the men of the first-century world and easier than it is for Christian women, children and men today.

With minds set on things above, the Colossians are to put to death immoral practices of the old self and are to clothe themselves with a new self that is "being renewed in knowledge according to the image of its creator" (Col 3:10). The description of this renewed self in Colossians 3:11 may disappoint those women who love the assertions of Galatians 3:28; though parallel in many ways, the description in Colossians 3:11 leaves out the statement "there is no longer male and female; for all of you are one in Christ Jesus" (see 1 Cor 12:13, which also leaves this out). This omission is due far more to Paul's concerns to customize his message to the need of his immediate audience than it is to any lack of commitment to women's full inclusion in the body of Christ. In Galatians, Paul is likely responding to the Jewish prayer, "Oh God, thank you that I am not a Greek or a slave or a woman" (Bruce, 275). Here in Colossians, however, Paul is more concerned with the unity in Christ of people from a variety of cultural backgrounds, Jewish and non-Jewish.

The instructions in Colossians 3:12-17 would have been freeing for the Colossian women. Now, as God's "holy and beloved" (Col 3:12; these terms are used of Christ and Israel, e.g., Is 43:20; Ps 105:5; 1 Pet 2:4, 6), they are to clothe themselves with love. As a public sign of a woman's status and priorities, clothes needed to be chosen carefully (see 1 Tim 2:8-10 for an example of women who were clothing themselves with the wrong priorities; see also 1 Cor 11:5-6, 13; Jas 2:2-3; 1 Pet 3:3); now their first priority is being clothed in Christian love. Their freedom in Christ does not, however, mean a freedom from responsibility. They are told to "teach and admonish one another," that is, to do the same sort of integral work that Paul and his coworkers did (Col 1:28; cf. 1 Thess 5:12; Tit 3:10). For women, who lived largely in the private, unseen world of small children, cooking utensils and dirty laundry, the all-inclusive assertion that everything they did "in word or deed" could be done in Jesus' name (Col 3:17) would have given an added value to their lives and their ability to honor and please God.

Colossians 3:18—4:1 is often described as a household code: a listing of moral obligations necessary to maintain order within the household. Similar codes can be found in Hellenistic and Jewish writings, as well as elsewhere in the New Testament (Eph 5:22—6:9; cf. 1 Tim 2:8-15; 6:1; Tit 2:1-10; 1 Pet 2:8—3:7). It is noteworthy that in his appropriation and modification of the form

Use & Abuse of Language

Because language is ubiquitous and central to human existence, the use and abuse of language are strongly tied. When we may be trying to communicate at one level, miscommunication may occur at another. Feminists have described how patriarchy is inscribed in language and culture. Thus a part of the feminist task has been unmasking patriarchy in the use of language, in biblical hermeneutics and in approaches to narrative, liturgy and everyday language.

This enterprise has been aided by changes in philosophy of language and science that have occurred in the last hundred years. Women in the past have done detailed exegeses of Scripture—Sarah Grimké and Margaret Fell, for example—but the flourishing of feminist approaches to Scripture and theology have depended on paradigm shifts in our perceptions of language.

The most important development has been the unmasking of constructions. Philosophers and sociologists have argued that much of our language has its origins in our imaginings and projections from ourselves. Thus when we use the word *God* we may be referring to the Creator of the universe or we may be imagining ourselves, stronger, bigger and more male. We could use the word *God* without any God existing; with the constant use and telling of stories of this God we come to believe this divine being has an objective existence. Many critiques of Western society—Marx, Weber and Freud, for example—were based on linguistic and philosophical arguments like these. In the late twentieth century the deconstructing of language has become widely associated with postmodernism.

Feminism and Language

While the unmasking of our constructive human activity has led to a deep skepticism, it has also freed us to ask questions we had never asked before. Is God the male God always depicted? Have we imagined and projected this God into our language, Scripture and culture? Is it true that women are not equal to men under God? We have begun to see how it may be patriarchy, language and culture that have legitimated the dominion of men over women. These questions have inspired most of the new uses of language in feminist biblical hermeneutics.

In the early years of the feminist-ordination debate, attention was given to understanding a few of Paul's statements in a way that they were consistent with the seemingly obvious meaning of Galatians 3:28 and Paul's practice of saluting his fellow women workers as equals (Rom 16). The issue is how we should balance the particular and the overall theme of Scripture. A constructive evangelical feminism has to pay special attention to the overall redemptive trajectory, while taking more seriously than others the need to find some way of reconciling the troubling passages to the whole.

The use of Scripture most associated with contemporary feminism is Paul Ricoeur's "hermeneutic of suspicion," used powerfully by Elisabeth Schüssler Fiorenza. She invites us to notice the absence of women in the biblical narrative and to imagine what was going on. This exercise can be liberating as women come to see that their presence has left traces. Taken too far, however, this method can lead us to discard Scripture as it is written.

Closely related is Rosemary Radford Ruether's notion of the "canon within the canon," choosing as inspired only those passages that speak and affirm the liberation of women. This too is a double-edged sword. Scripture is no longer authoritative when we become its ultimate judge. However, Scripture exhibits a degree of selectivity and refinement of meaning. Jesus does not stone the woman caught in adultery, as the law demands; Paul urges us not to believe him if he tells us something other than the gospel of Christ (Gal 1:8). And even Ruether's harshest critics are selective in the Scriptures they emphasize.

Reimagining is also a feminist tool, which in its extremes is purely an exercise of imagining God to be in our image. But reimagining can help us to counter the image of God many women have internalized as a harsh father. A reimagining can be a rereading of Scripture, which rediscovers in Scripture a God who proclaims Godself in love and motherly and birthing images for God. This is a much-needed exercise of healing for many women.

Inclusive language in liturgy and Bible translation also threatens to divide us. The translation of Psalm 1 is an illustration. Women read the psalm and feel excluded by its reiteration of "man." But if the psalm has also a christological reference, it cannot easily be translated to bear this double meaning and include women. In this case it may be an abuse of language to insist always on one translation for all purposes. The multiple meanings of Scripture need to be emphasized.

Biblical feminists would critique a complete deconstruction of the biblical text and God language, insisting that God is not just a projection. Nevertheless, cultures do impose layers of interpretation on God, often distorting the image of God. All language is human and imperfect. God cannot be portrayed sharply but "through a glass darkly." Biblical feminism would want to claim also that we can speak of God with integrity and faithfulness. We abuse language when we claim that our projections are not there or that we can control them. We abuse language when we mask its power but also when we deny it any validity in speaking of transcendence. The Bible still speaks today.

Bibliography

M. Hayter, *The New Eve in Christ: The Use and Abuse of the Bible in the Debate about Women in the Church* (Grand Rapids, MI: Eerdmans, 1987); E. Schüssler Fiorenza, *In Memory of Her: A Feminist Theological Reconstruction of Christian Origins* (New York: Crossroad, 1983); E. A. Johnson, *She Who Is: They Mystery of God in a Feminist Theological Discourse* (New York: Crossroad, 1992); N. C. Murphy, *Beyond Liberalism and Fundamentalism: How Modern and Postmodern Philosophy Set the Theological Agenda* (Valley Forge, PA: Trinity Press International, 1996); R. R. Ruether, *Sexism and God-Talk: Toward a Feminist Theology* (Boston: Beacon, 1983); E. Storkey, *Origins of Difference: The Gender Debate Revisited* (Grand Rapids, MI: Baker, 2001); E. Storkey and M. Hebblethwaite, *Conversations on Christian Feminism: Speaking Heart to Heart* (London: Harper Collins, 1999).

NICOLA HOGGARD CREEGAN

---

of a household code Paul does not directly challenge the social code of his time. He tells masters to treat their slaves justly, keeping their Master in heaven in mind, but he does not overturn the institution of slavery (for Paul, protecting the cause of Christ was always more important than trying to change or improve the secular culture; *see* Ancient and Modern Slavery). The code contains three pairs of reciprocal obligations that are motivated by the need to do all things in the name of the Lord. In the first pair wives are to "be subject" (*hypotassesthe*, plural reflexive imperative) to their husbands. This verb communicates a mutual submission arrangement in Ephesians 5:21; Paul did not use "obey" *(hypakouō)*, which is found in the instructions to children and slaves (Col 3:20, 22), and this instruction to wives is balanced by the instruction that husbands love (*agapaō*, Christian love) their wives and not make themselves a bitter taste in their wives' mouths (the verb *pikrainō*, "to make a sharp or bitter taste," here is reflexive).

The second pair of obligations (Col 3:20-21) is that children obey both parents and that fathers refrain from provoking their children (cf. Eph 6:1). No differentiation is made between girls or young children of both sexes, who would have been primarily within the sphere of mothers, and older boys, who were more likely to come within the sphere of their fathers. Children are addressed directly, as members of the community with the ability to hear and the responsibility to respond to these words; parents are not intermediaries between Paul's words and the children. The warning to fathers is a limitation to the standard father's role, which allowed for the customary beating of their children, and it indicates a sense of a father's complicity in family conflicts.

In the third pair of obligations (Col 3:22-23), the slaves receive noticeably lengthier instructions than do the masters (Col 3:22—4:1), perhaps in light of the Colossians' familiarity with the situation of the runaway slave Onesimus.

In Paul's further instructions (Col 4:2-6), he wants the Corinthian Christians to pray and to live their lives "wisely," with an awareness that "outsiders" would be watching their actions and listening to their speech. Believers needed to be conscientious, since many outsiders viewed Christians with great skepticism; for example, rumors that they practiced cannibalism and incestuous drunken orgies were widespread (see Minucius Felix *Octavius* 9).

When women in the early church sometimes broke from the customary behavior for women of that time, they could attract people to Christianity, or they could lead outsiders to draw the wrong conclusions. They needed to appear moral and upstanding by the broader society's cultural standards, but they were also required to exercise their freedom in Christ, practice their call by Christ (through Paul), evangelize, pray, resist false teachers, become strong in God and perhaps even challenge some of those cultural norms. This tension between wanting to stand up and speak out for Christ and needing to avoid attracting the wrong kind of attention would have been acutely felt. The Roman Empire was quick to quash any movement perceived as a threat to its rule and interests.

Modern women have the same sort of tensions. Many of us live lives that are different from those lives modeled for us by our mothers and grandmothers. We are in the workplace or home schooling, we are pastors or church leaders, we are facing evolving issues as mothers, wives and women in the twenty-first century. In our desire to be godly women, we want to follow the Bible's instructions in faith and practice, but there are often widely varying contemporary understandings of what that means. Should we alphabetize our spice rack and bring hot meals to sick neighbors? Should we iron all the clothes in our house? Should we witness to everyone we encounter and shout "Jesus loves you!" to rude motorists? At church should we teach, preach or vacuum the rugs at church? Or should we find some new combination of the traditional and untraditional roles that works best for each of us? We want to be in this world enough to be able to relate to it and bring a Christian presence to it, and we also want to uphold Christian understandings of what it means to be a godly woman, without being unnecessarily constrained by outdated or misinformed social understandings of that concept. And we need to strike this balance in a way that does not give outsiders any reason to criticize our faith.

Closing: Greetings and Instructions (Col 4:7-18)

In this closing of his letter, Paul sends personal greetings and instructions to individuals at Colossae. Of most interest to us is Paul's greeting to "Nympha and the church in her house" (Col 4:15). While it is hard to be sure what Nympha's role in this church would have been, as the named host and owner of a house large enough for the church (most homes would have been very small) she would have been at the least a respected member and patron of the church. Given the prominence of her name in association with this house church, she is most likely its leader.

Bibliography. F. F. Bruce, *The Epistles to the Colossians, to Philemon and to the Ephesians,* New International Commentary on the New Testament (Grand Rapids, MI: Eerdmans, 1984); P. T. O'Brien, *Colossians, Philemon,* Word Biblical Commentary 44 (Waco, TX: Word, 1982); J. J. Pilch and B. J. Malina, eds., *Handbook of Biblical Social Values,* rev. ed. (Peabody, MA: Hendrickson, 1998) esp. 10-15. SHIRLEY A. DECKER-LUCKE

1 THESSALONIANS

Introduction

1 Thessalonians represents the earliest of the Pauline Epistles and contains many of Paul's characteristic teaching emphases. It also reveals how much he loved the Thessalonian believers, his children in the faith. As an early New Testament book, 1 Thessalonians also provides insight into the lives, faith and sufferings of some of the first Christians. The major subject and hence the theme of 1 and 2 Thessalonians focuses on the return of the Lord. For this reason, scholars classify these two books as the eschatological epistles. The eschatological teaching of 1 Thessalonians remains mainly on a personal level as Paul responded to questions about what happened to believers who died before Christ's return. The apostle wrote more about pastoral concerns than doctrinal ones in the letter.

The first epistle to the church at Thessalonica claims Pauline authorship. The internal evidence of vocabulary, style and theology supports this claim. As for external evidence, church fathers such as Irenaeus, Tertullian and Clement of Alexandria acknowledged it as Pauline. Paul wrote 1 Thessalonians from Corinth. The Delphi Inscription, which indicates the time of the service of the proconsul Gallio, dates the beginning of Paul's Corinthian ministry in A.D. 50 (Acts 18:12). The apostle penned 1 Thessalonians either in this year or 51.

1 Thessalonians encourages believers to stand firm in the midst of life's trials. We must remain faithful and live with the expectation that Christ will return at any moment. The Lord's return is more than a doctrine; it is a promise. It has more than future implications. The second coming has a vital influence on how we conduct ourselves. We must live moral and holy lives, ever watchful for the return of our Lord.

Thessalonica stood as the largest and most important city in the Roman province and geographical area of Macedonia, that is, northern Greece. It was a free (self-governing) city and the capital of the province. It served as a commercial, transportation and seaport city, due to its location on the important east-west road called the Ignatian Way and on the Thermaic Gulf at the head of the Aegean Sea. Cassandra, a general of Alexander the Great, founded the city in 315 B.C. He named the city for his wife, Thessalonica, the daughter of Philip of Macedon and the half-sister of Alexander. The modern Greek city of Salonika is built on the same location as Thessalonica and reflects the ancient name.

Acts 17:1-9 relates Paul's initial ministry in Thessalonica. As was his custom, the apostle started his work in the Jewish synagogue. A good number of Jews, devout Greeks (Gentiles) and leading women responded to this ministry (Acts 17:4). Women enjoyed a higher status in Macedonia and Asia Minor than elsewhere. They held extensive economic rights, including the right over their dowry. They could buy, own and sell goods and property. Women's degree of freedom and opportunity depended on their rank in society. Women of the poorer classes experienced fewer privileges. The prominent women who became charter members of the church at Thessalonica were possibly wealthy landowners, since the primary source of wealth was land. They probably enjoyed a high measure of political power and social prestige (Arlandson, 130). Paul did not give the names of any of these women in 1 Thessalonians. The rhetorically skilled orators and writers of that time tried to avoid mentioning the names of living, honorable, socially prominent women unless the circumstances warranted it. They would more likely mention by name women connected to their opponents, dead women or women of questionable reputation (Witherington 1998, 506).

Paul's success in Thessalonica provoked hostility among unbelieving Jews. Consequently, they started a riot, hauled some believers before the city authorities and charged them with disloyalty to Caesar. The apostle realized it was time to leave so as to avoid bringing additional hardship on the Thessalonian believers. These Christians suffered persecution from the beginning of their commitment to Jesus Christ.

At the time of writing Silvanus (Silas, in Acts) and Timothy had just returned to Paul in Corinth from a mission to Macedonia (Acts 18:5). Timothy's good report about the Thessalonian church prompted the apostle to write the epistle. Timothy also might have brought with him a letter requesting instruction from Paul on various subjects. The apostle wrote 1 Thessalonians to accomplish several purposes. He wanted to encourage the Thessalonian believers as they faced intense persecution. He responded to criticism against his motives in Christian service by explaining how he had conducted his ministry in Thessalonica. The presence of low moral standards in Greece led the apostle to explain Christian standards for sexual morality. The death of some members in the congregation led to questions about how they would participate in the coming return of Christ. Paul answered these questions and gave the church instructions about relating to fellow believers, God's will and the healthy use of spiritual gifts.

Outline

1:1	Greeting
1:2-10	Thanksgiving for the Thessalonians
2:1-12	Paul's Defense of His Thessalonian Ministry
2:13—3:13	Paul's Relationship to the Thessalonians
2:13-16	Thanksgiving for the Thessalonians' Endurance of Persecution
2:17-20	Paul's Desire to Visit
3:1-5	Paul's Willingness to Send Timothy
3:6-10	Paul's Joy and Thanksgiving for the Thessalonians' Progress
3:11-13	Paul's Prayer for the Thessalonians' Spiritual Growth
4:1—5:22	Doctrinal and Ethical Exhortations
4:1-12	Instructions About the Christian Life
4:13—5:11	Instructions About the Return of the Lord
5:12-22	Instructions About Life in the Church
5:23-28	Conclusion: Prayer, Requests and Benediction

Commentary

Thanksgiving for the Thessalonians (1 Thess 1:2-10)

Paul and his missionary associates thanked God for the Thessalonians' response to the gospel. They expressed gratitude for what these readers were doing for Christ and for the Christian virtues that produced such effort, for God's choice of them, for the work of the Holy Spirit in their lives, for their imitation of Jesus and the missionaries, for their joyous endurance of persecution, for their example to other Christians in Greece, for their evangelistic work, for their deliverance from idolatry and for their expectation of the return of Jesus. The apostle addressed the Thessalonians as "brothers and sisters" more than twenty times in 1 and 2 Thessalonians.

Despite severe suffering, the response of the Thessalonians provided a model for all believers in Greece and in every place. This should encourage women living in the twenty-first century who suffer in any way as a result of their commitment to Jesus Christ. Women can influence others for God despite the obstacles placed in their path. The Thessalonians "sounded forth" the word of the Lord as an echo continues ringing out from a brass instrument (1 Thess 1:8). The fact that Paul described the Thessalonian believers as turning to God from idols indicates that most of these converts came from Gentile rather than Jewish backgrounds.

Paul's Defense of His Thessalonian Ministry (1 Thess 2:1-12)

Paul had encountered great difficulties while serving in Thessalonica, yet he refused to quit or even be discouraged. As a result, his Thessalonian ministry achieved great success. Now the apostle appeared to be defending himself against various charges brought by the Jews concerning his motives, actions and general behavior. They had forced him to leave Thessalonica prematurely. Since his departure the Jews had apparently carried on a slander campaign against him. Paul insisted that he had pure motives. His preaching was free from error, motivated by unmixed reasons, untainted by trickery or deceit. He contrasted his motives and methods with those of pagan priests, exorcists, magicians, prophets and philosophers. These pagans employed all kinds of tricks to take advantage of the gullible. Paul did not work in this way. He refused to accept money from a church to which he was ministering at the time, a practice that further distinguished him from pagan teachers, who charged all the trade would bear. He supported himself by manual labor and offerings from other churches.

Paul's defense of his Thessalonian ministry provides a good manual for Christian ministers—women and men—especially those who endure hardship for the Lord. Women, as well as men, should conduct their ministries with integrity. Their motivation should always be to please and serve God, not themselves or their personal agendas.

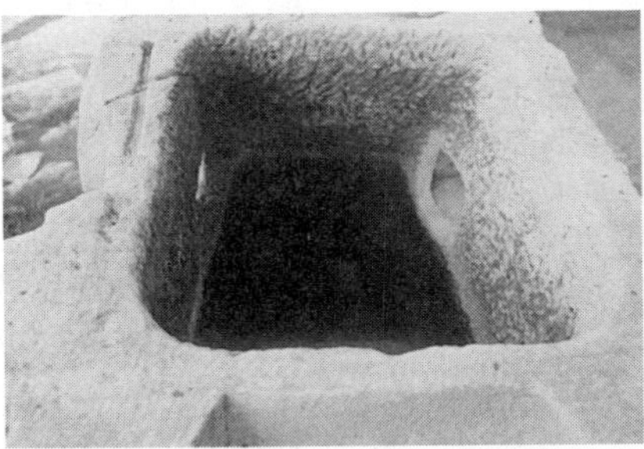

Trick statue with hollowed-out interior to conceal priest who could voice instructions that appeared to come from the god. (1 Thessalonians 2:3)

Where churches do not provide financial support for women in ministry, Paul's example offers guidance. Some women ministers may have to serve in a volunteer capacity, supporting themselves in bivocational service. Women can serve God in every occupation.

Paul noted that he had been "gentle" among the Thessalonians (1 Thess 2:7). A well-attested variant reading for "gentle" is "infants." Yet the apostle never referred to himself as a baby, and "infants" requires a radical change of metaphor that transforms the apostle quickly from a baby to a nursing mother. Paul compared himself to a gentle nursing mother and to a caring father. Christians need fatherly teaching and encouragement as well as motherly care. By using the female imagery to speak of his relationship to converts Paul recalled the Old Testament metaphor of the divine maternal care of God's people (*see* Images of God as Female). The Scriptures refer to God as a nursing mother to express the comfort and tender care that God gives (Is 66:13). A nursing mother provides a natural source of nourishment for her child, one designed by the Creator God. A mother's milk provides important antibodies to protect the newborn child against infectious diseases. Breastfeeding creates a special bond between a mother and her baby.

Nursing requires a mother's special commitment to her child by making physical and time demands on her. Through this unique relationship a child receives not only physical nourishment but also spiritual nurture. In showing her infant love, gentleness and caring through breastfeeding, a mother models God's love, compassion and

Paul's Use of Female Imagery

It is a little-known fact that Paul "uses maternal imagery more often than he does paternal imagery" (Gaventa 1996, 35). Female images surface in descriptions of Christ, calling, eschatological deliverance and especially ministry. Paul weaves Old Testament female personifications of divine wisdom into his christology (*see* Images of God as Female). The apostle uses birth imagery to describe his call (Gal 1:15; 1 Cor 15:8; *see* Birth Pain Imagery). And in his descriptions of eschatological deliverance, all creation groans, waiting to give birth—an image of eschatological hope (Rom 8:22; cf. Is 13:8). Believers likewise groan, awaiting not their birth but their adoption (Rom 8:23).

Birthing. Paul compares himself with a woman in labor, a conventional metaphor signifying anguish and anticipation (Gal 4:19). It is a second labor for Paul; he awaits not their birth but for Christ to be formed in his "little children" (Gaventa 1998, 32).

Nursing. In describing his apostolic leadership, Paul refers to himself as a wet nurse (1 Thess 2:7-8; cf. Num 11:12; *see* Occupations, Skills and Crafts of Women). He did not stop at giving the Thessalonians the gospel but shared with them his very substance (1 Thess 2:8), as a nurse does when she gives milk from her breast.

Nurse with child. (1 Thessalonians 2:7)

If, following Beverly Roberts Gaventa (1998, 24-26), the variant "infants" *(nēpioi)* is selected over the variant "gentle" (*ēpioi,* 1 Thess 2:7), then this nursing image is one of three familial figures that Paul employs in succession in order to clarify his motivations and style of ministry. Apostles are unassuming and guileless like infants (1 Thess 2:7), tender and self-giving like women who nurse (1 Thess 2:7-8) and directive like fathers who instruct and encourage (1 Thess 2:11). Together these familial figures reinforce ministry as connectedness.

The nursing image, axiomatic in antiquity for nurture and affection, radicalizes ministry by locating authority outside customary expectations (Gaventa 1996, 44; 1998, 33-34). Ecclesiastical authority is redefined as intimate relationality: in contrast to professional codes of conduct, Paul expresses his feelings of deep attachment and tenderness toward the Thessalonians. Imagery of nursing an infant further reconceptualizes ecclesiastical authority as self-giving vulnerability rather than demands for the rights of office. In the eyes of the world, this Christ-like style of ministry (Phil 2:5-8) is devalued and ridiculed (1 Cor 4:9-13).

Weaning. Chastising the Corinthians for being too spiritually immature to be weaned, Paul likens his task to a mother's, who diligently works to wean her child from milk to solid food (1 Cor 3:2).

The early church was aware of female images for ministry. Augustine noted that, like Christ, apostolic ministry resembled both fatherhood and motherhood (*Enarratio in Psalmum [Enarrations on the Psalms]* 101, PL 37, col. 1299). In the second-century *Acts of Paul,* milk rather than blood flowed from Paul's body (Gaventa 1996, 44). In the Priscilla catacombs in Rome, an ancient fresco depicts a woman suckling an infant; nearby a bishop appoints a woman with similar features to ministry. The third-century artist may have been drawing upon Paul's infant/nurse imagery to memorialize the nurturing, relational, self-giving style of the decedent's ministry (Houts), a style that Paul daringly advocates for all who minister.

Fresco from Priscilla catacomb depicting a woman's life as woman of prayer (Orans, center), mother suckling an infant (right), ordinand (left)

Bibliography

B. R. Gaventa, "Apostles as Babes and Nurses in 1 Thessalonians 2:7," in *Faith and History: Essays in Honor of Paul W. Meyer,* ed. J. Carroll, C. H. Cosgrove and E. E. Johnson (Atlanta: Scholars Press, 1990) 193-207; idem, "The Maternity of Paul: An Exegetical Study of Galatians 4:19," in *The Conversation Continues: Studies in Paul and John in Honor of J. Louis Martyn,* ed. R. T. Fortna and B. R. Gaventa (Nashville: Abingdon, 1990) 189-201; idem, "Our Mother St. Paul: Toward the Recovery of a Neglected Theme," *Princeton Seminary Bulletin* 17/1 (1996) 29-44; idem, *First and Second Thessalonians* (Louisville, KY: Westminster John Knox, 1998); M. G. Houts, "The Visual Evidence of Women in Early Christian Leadership," *Perspectives* 14/3 (1999) 14-18.

MARGO G. HOUTS

---

concern for those created in the divine image. This beautiful maternal metaphor shows how believers should serve others, seeing them, as it were, through a mother's eyes and feeling for them as from a mother's heart.

Paul's Relationship to the Thessalonians (1 Thess 2:13—3:13)

Thanksgiving for the Thessalonians' Endurance of Persecution (1 Thess 2:13-16)

Willingness to suffer for one's faith indicates its genuineness. In their suffering the Gentile majority in the Thessalonian church was following the example of Jewish Christians in Judea, who were being persecuted by their fellow Jews. As Paul thought about how the Jews killed Jesus and then persecuted his followers in Palestine and abroad, he launched into the harshest attack on them in any of his letters. Though some interpreters view Paul's strong judgment as anti-Semitic, he echoed the approach of Old Testament prophets who denounced their people for departing from God's ways.

God's wrath represents his abiding, universal opposition to evil. This becomes the final experience of those who continue in hostility toward God. Paul spoke of this wrath with certainty, yet uncertainty exists over whether he was referring to a specific instance of God's wrath, such as rejection of the nation of Israel after the Lord's crucifixion, the expulsion of the Jews from Rome in 49 or the coming destruction of Jerusalem in 70.

Paul's Desire to Visit (1 Thess 2:17-20)

Paul compared his enforced separation

from his Thessalonian friends with children's premature loss of their parents. In a climactic way the apostle expressed his affection for the Thessalonians. These believers were his hope, joy and crown of boasting before the Lord. Paul was describing his spiritual children. Women—as mothers, grandmothers, aunts or other family relationships—know the intense pride children bring in who they are as well as in their accomplishments. Children can be a mother's hope, joy and crown of boasting. Do we feel the same way toward our children in the faith? All women can participate in the spiritual birth and development of others. God calls all of us to make disciples.

Paul's Willingness to Send Timothy (1 Thess 3:1-5)

Greatly distressed by the intensity of the persecution that the Thessalonians faced, Paul sent Timothy to find out what was happening and to instruct the church further. Timothy could quietly return to the city because he was not as well known to the authorities as Paul. "To be left alone" (1 Thess 3:1) implies a sense of abandonment. Paul felt that the Thessalonians had a need greater than his own. He was willing to do without his beloved coworker, Timothy. God calls believers to put the needs of others above their own. Christian women can shine their light of influence in this dark world by practicing self-denial and putting others first, ordering their priorities according to God's Word.

The apostle had told the Thessalonian Christians that they would suffer persecution. He was indicating that suffering represents a normal part of Christian experience. Most believers will experience some form of suffering, whether mild or severe, because of their commitment to Jesus Christ. Women possess no exemption in this matter.

Paul's Joy and Thanksgiving for the Thessalonians' Progress (1 Thess 3:6-10)

Timothy's return with a report of the Thessalonians' steadfastness despite persecution produced Paul's renewed gratitude to God and intense prayer for an opportunity to see them. Their faithfulness in the face of difficulties encouraged the apostle in the midst of all his problems in Corinth. Timothy's encouraging report rejuvenated Paul. He could say he now really lived since he had the certainty his readers would continue to stand firm in the Lord. Paul's attitude toward these converts reflects that of a mother for her children. He felt such a sense of oneness with the Thessalonians that he felt renewed when he heard of their unwavering faith and love, as mothers really live when they know with certainty that their children are doing what they should be doing. Their achievements bring encouragement and renewal.

Paul's Prayer for the Thessalonians' Spiritual Growth (1 Thess 3:11-13)

Paul prayed that God would allow him to return to Thessalonica. He also prayed for the spiritual growth of his readers. Prayer has increasingly become an important area of ministry for women. These intercessory prayer efforts require time, commitment, perseverance and strength because the struggle is not against enemies of flesh and blood (Eph 6:12). Women have made a difference in the lives of their family members, in their country and in the spread of the gospel by approaching God's throne of grace boldly on behalf of others. Prayer unleashes God's power. It changes people according to the divine will. Women prayer warriors have greatly affected the kingdom of God.

Doctrinal and Ethical Exhortations (1 Thess 4:1—5:22)

Instructions About the Christian life (1 Thess 4:1-12)

Paul began to address the Thessalonians on particular ethical issues. He wanted them to lead lives that pleased God. God's will for his people is their sanctification, the process of being made holy or set apart, dedicated to God and God's purposes. Sanctification results in a changed lifestyle for believers. God sets Christians apart at their conversion. They live out that dedication in holiness as the Holy Sprit works to conform them to the image of Jesus Christ.

Sanctification involves not only believers' spiritual life but also their physical and sexual life. Sexual laxity characterized life in the first-century Roman Empire, especially in Greece. Many of the pagan cults featured inappropriate sexual expression in their practices, including sacred prostitution and lewd gestures as a part of worship. Some pagan religions taught that ritual coitus promoted fertility and blessing. In contrast, the New Testament condemns all promiscuity, whether in religious or secular settings (1 Cor 6:9-10; Eph 5:5). It affirms marriage as the appropriate vehicle for sexual expression (1 Cor 7:2; Heb 13:4; *see* Marriage). Jesus gave believers a higher standard, calling them to shun lustful thoughts (Mt 5:27-28).

The prevailing sexual laxity that Paul witnessed throughout the Roman Empire caused him to remind his readers that sexual purity represents the will of God. He exhorted the Thessalonians to "abstain from fornication" (*porneia,* 1 Thess 4:3). *Porneia* refers to all sexual immorality, including premarital sex, extramarital sex, homosexuality, lesbianism, rape and incest. Believers' holiness requires abstaining from such practices. As most pagans treated immorality with indifference, Gentile converts had great difficulty in making a clean break with their past. They needed the apostle's encouragement. His exhortation to sexual sanctification has much-needed relevance to the present age of sexual permissiveness. Sexual holiness gives value to God's gift of sex. It prevents the treatment of women and men as sex objects.

"Control your own body" (1 Thess 4:4) literally means "possess his own vessel." This expression has been interpreted as referring either to taking a wife or to controlling the body, particularly the male sexual organ. The first view claims the support of early church fathers, including Augustine. It also has the normal use of *ktasthai* ("acquire"). The principal argument against this view rests in the unnatural interpretation of *skeuos* ("vessel"). Also, some interpreters feel that this view promotes a low view of marriage and depreciates women by suggesting that the wife's primary function is that of satisfying her husband's sexual desires. Yet Paul desired that this vessel be honored, not dishonored and degraded. One could interpret this as the apostle's warning against relating to one's wife in a lustful manner. Living a sanctified life involves abstaining from any sort of sexual immorality, whether this involves the abuse of a wife in the passion of lust or the defrauding of a Christian brother through an adulterous relationship with his wife. Paul was warning the men among his readers that misconduct in marriage is just as much a sin as the offense of adultery (Witherington 1990, 141-43; *see* Adultery).

Other church fathers, such as Tertullian and Chrysostom, interpreted *skeuos* as "body." This translation has a partial parallel in other New Testament passages (2 Cor 4:7; Rom 9:22). Also, one Old Testament passage uses "vessel" in the same kind of context with special reference to the genitalia (1 Sam 21:5). Paul was dealing with the whole Christian community in the preceding verses. Taking *skeuos* as "body" avoids an abrupt transition to husbands. This view, however, strains the meaning of *ktasthai* and awkwardly applies *heautou* to *skeuos,* "his own body." This view offers the translation "that each of you learn to gain control over his own body." Whatever view one supports, Paul made it clear that God had not called believers to trifle with sexual impurity but to live a holy life.

In addition to maintaining moral purity, the Thessalonians needed to deepen their love for one another. They were already loving their fellow believers, yet all Christians in regard to Christian virtues can do even more.

Paul insisted on the necessity of work. In doing so he dignified manual labor, something upper-class Greeks and Romans despised. Evidently some people in the church had quit their jobs, possibly in anticipation of an imminent return of the Lord. The result was excessive excitement, meddling in the affairs of others and dependence on others for support. Meddling in the affairs of others as busybodies brings to mind the stereotype of gossiping women. Gossip has a destructive force; it destroys unity and trust and endangers relationships. Women as well as men must learn to control their tongues.

Instructions About the Return of the Lord (1 Thess 4:13—5:11)

The most potentially damaging problem that Paul addressed involved a serious misunderstanding of the impact of the Lord's return. As did many of the early Christians, the Thessalonians naively assumed that Christ would return during their lifetime. When some of their fellow believers died, they became concerned that these would miss some of the benefits of Christ's return. Paul reassured his readers that, far from being at a disadvantage, the Christian dead would take precedence over living Christians. At the return of Christ, the dead would rise first and go to meet the Lord. The dead would then be joined in the Lord's presence by living believers.

The event when the Christian living will be caught up with the dead in Christ to meet the descending Lord in the air is sometimes called the rapture because the Latin verb *rapere* means "caught up." Those who hold to a dispensational view of eschatology use the term *rapture* to describe a secret return of Christ to remove living believers prior to the persecution and suffering of the tribulation period. To them the events of 1 Thessalonians 4:13-18 are a pretribulation return of Christ. Others of different eschatological views see this as the glorious second advent of Christ occurring after the events of the tribulation (Mt 24:3-14). Still others identify the tribulation as a time of persecution in this age and do not regard it as a special time of difficulty at the end of the age (postmillennial eschatology). Secular Greek writings sometimes used the word translated "meet" (1 Thess 4:17, *parousia*) to describe how the people of a city would go out to meet a visiting king or general and accompany him back to their city in festal procession. This word has come to refer to Christ's return. Whatever the particular events connected with the Lord's return, the parousia will result in unending fellowship between Christ and his people.

Believers in Thessalonica were asking, When will the Lord return? Paul indicated that they did not need additional instruction about the timing of the return. For most human beings that event would occur suddenly, unexpectedly, like the coming of a thief. To make vivid the sudden, unexpected disaster that will come upon non-Christians engaged in their daily, ordinary pursuits Paul used the analogy "as labor pains come upon a pregnant woman" (1 Thess 5:3). The onset of labor points to the inevitable birth to follow. This image indicates that unbelievers will have no possible escape from God's judgment when the Lord returns. It conveys the urgency of being ready or prepared. Mothers know the sudden pain and helplessness when labor takes them by surprise. They have no opportunity to change their minds. Neither will non-Christians. Believers should prepare for the Lord's return by disciplined, godly living supported by attitudes of faith, love and hope. Paul wanted to discourage rationalistic speculation about the time of the parousia. He insisted that watching for Jesus' return involved consistent living in obedience to the Lord's commands.

Instructions About Life in the Church (1 Thess 5:12-22)

Paul urged believers to show respect for their leaders and the leaders to demonstrate understanding and acceptance of all members, especially those who persisted in trying behavior. The apostle did not give any clues to indicate the extent to which women participated in activities in the church in Thessalonica. He named neither male nor female leaders. Paul directed all of his readers to acknowledge God's sovereignty and providence by expressing thanks in all circumstances. He urged the Thessalonians to accept the gifts of the Spirit with an openness characterized by a discerning evaluation of the gift.

Conclusion: Prayer, Requests and Benediction (1 Thess 5:23-28)

Paul concluded his letter with a prayer for the consecration of his readers and a reminder of God's faithfulness in directing their sanctification. He requested prayer for himself and urged his friends to greet one another with the holy kiss of warmth and love. According to the *Apostolic Constitutions* (early fourth century), men were to kiss men and women were to kiss women. This prevented any hint of scandal. The kiss symbolized the bond that unites believers. Paul's benediction focused on his favorite concept—grace.

Bibliography. J. M. Arlandson, *Women, Class and Society in Early Christianity: Models from Luke-Acts* (Peabody, MA: Hendrickson, 1997); B. Witherington III, *The Acts of the Apostles: A Socio-Rhetorical Commentary* (Grand Rapids, MI: Eerdmans, 1998); idem, *Women and the Genesis of Christianity* (Cambridge: Cambridge University Press, 1990).

SHARON H. GRITZ

2 THESSALONIANS

Introduction

2 Thessalonians is unusual in that it contains apocalyptic material along with positive recommendations for social amelioration. Ordinarily apocalyptic literature focuses on the dire straits in which a society finds itself and predicts a worsening of the situation until God's final intervention. Apocalyptic literature is viewed with particular discomfort by women because it describes hostility that will be directed against them (Dan 11:37; Rev 12:13-17) and foretells dangers to which they, as nurturers and care givers, are particularly vulnerable. War, famine and natural disasters exact a horrible toll on women and on all that they hold dear. Jesus expressed the deepest fears of women as he walked the way of sorrows (Lk 23:27-31).

Upper-class, well-educated women had responded enthusiastically to Paul and Silas's original mission to Thessalonica (Acts 17:4) and were a significant part of the body of believers, so it is appropriate that anxieties common to women should be addressed. The city, located on the main road that stretched from east to west in the Roman Empire, had become the locus of persecution for Christians. As the afflictions worsened, it was natural to assume that the end of the world was at hand. The sufferers considered themselves powerless to do anything except to await deliverance from God.

In this epistle, the message is one of encouragement and common sense for those who are obsessed by the imminence of Christ's second coming. The believers apparently received a letter that falsely claims to have been sent by Paul, and they have been further confused by local prophets with doomsday predictions. The result is fear, frustration and dysfunction. Paul calls them to calmness of spirit, to orderly and constructive conduct and to faithful discharge of duty.

The ascription speaks of Silas and Timothy, with Paul sharing in the composition. Dual authorship is ascribed in several epistles, but triple authorship appears unique to the Thessalonian correspondence (cf. 1 Thess 1:1). Timothy, perhaps in company with Silas, delivered the first letter to the church at Thessalonica (1 Thess 3:2, 6). They appear to have joined Paul in composing a second treatise shortly after their return to Corinth in A.D. 51 or 52. Pauline authorship of the letter is sometimes questioned, as certain elements are unique to this epistle, but they may be explained by the input of other members of the composition team. Whether in writing, traveling, tent making or proclaiming the gospel, Paul is usually found as part of a team in which there is lively interaction.

Outline

1:1-4	Comfort for the Thessalonians
1:5-12	God Will Set All Things Right
2:1-12	Implications of the Second Coming
2:13—3:15	Positive Faith for Here and Now
3:16-18	Closing Greetings

Commentary

Comfort for the Thessalonians (2 Thess 1:1-4)

God is called "our Father," emphasizing more that God is the Father of all Christians than the Father, the first person of the Trinity. Through the grace of Christ we know the peace of God. The power of new life that restores broken harmonies is the gift of God as we know him in Jesus Christ.

Paul praises the Thessalonians, for their Christian witness has advanced even beyond their excellent showing from when last he wrote. He stresses their faith and love and the strong relationship between their faith and their lives. The ensuing fusion results in a correspondingly greater consideration for each other. This shows the apostle's prayer had been answered.

The apostle is proud of their "steadfastness and faith during all your persecutions and the afflictions that you are enduring." Steadfastness or patience suggests endurance of opposition but also hope of a speedy end to it in the second coming. "Father" here implies trust and reliance on God in Christ through all adversity. Their faith gives them power to endure.

God Will Set All Things Right (2 Thess 1:5-12)

Paul comforts the Thessalonians by pointing out how the righteous judgment of God shows itself. There will be everlasting reward for their faith and patience in their suffering for the gospel, along with punishment for their persecutors.

The Thessalonians' faith has been strengthened rather than weakened by adversity; they have been given power to endure all the ills that befall them. This is the surest indicator that there is a just God who cares for his people. He is nearer to them in affliction than in prosperity, thus giving proof of where his final judgment will fall between them and their persecutors.

God has given them a pledge that, however much evil seems to triumph, the victory would be theirs. Further, by these hardships they are being fitted for full citizenship as redeemed saints in Christ's kingdom. When the day of the Lord comes, the humble and faithful who have borne the assaults of the world will find that worldly judgments are overturned. God's justice, of which even now they have proof, will vindicate those who have kept faith. The wicked will suffer, and the righteous will reap their reward.

God's justice, like his wrath (Rom 1:18), is inherent in the nature of a moral universe. Because God is the ruler of that universe, retribution for sin is a part of life, either here or in the hereafter (Lk 16:25). In the deepest sense, punishment is separation from God, and reward is fellowship with him. Here the emphasis is on the final vindication of goodness and the punishment of evil. This is consolation for women, who so often suffer injustice without being able to defend themselves.

The mention of "flaming fire" recalls the appearance of Jehovah at Sinai (Deut 33:2; Ex 3:2; Is 66:15). The fact that Jesus is to be "revealed" suggests that what is unknown will become plain (see also Rom 2:5; 8:19; 1 Cor 1:7; 1 Pet 1:7, 13; 4:13). His glory, which is at present hidden from the mass of humankind, though glimpsed by faithful Christians, will become manifest. His presence, which is a reality for Christians on earth, will at his coming be made known to all. Jesus is to be revealed "from heaven." This is a material symbol of the final climax of history, when the baffling reflections in the mirror become clear (1 Cor 13:12).

"Those who do not know God" are presumably pagans. They will be punished because they have willfully disregarded the knowledge of God that they did possess. Humankind is judged on its response to the light that is given (Jn 3:18-19). Paul sees the last judgment as the consummation of what has already begun. The punishment will be "eternal destruction," separation "from the presence of the Lord and from the glory of his might." Paul emphasizes spiritual separation from God, not the material. He is interested in the essential contrast between the person who is in Christ now and forever, as over against the person who by rejecting Christ is forever a lost soul.

The apostle gives a word of comfort for any despondent Thessalonian (2 Thess 1:10), and women are particularly susceptible to despondency (*see* Depression). They are assured that their faith is real. Through all their stumbling and falling, their sense of unworthiness was the surest proof that they were still Christ's people and that they would take their place among his folk on his day. As proof of their faith, Paul and his cohorts add, "because our testimony to you was believed." Their preaching mission had borne ample fruit since then.

There is a prayer that the Thessalonians' virtues may by God's grace be so perfected that they will add luster to the Lord's coming. God is asked to make them "worthy of his call." Their example of Christian behavior will be a testimony to the Lord on his day. He will be glorified in them, and they will be glorified in him. To be known as Christ's people at his coming will be to share in the honor paid to him.

The text moves on to "the grace of our God and the Lord Jesus Christ." Grace is generally thought of as coming through Christ—the channel by which it flows from God, the source of all. Father and Son are regarded as the fountainhead of the love and favor that make possible the mutual glorification.

Implications of the Second Coming (2 Thess 2:1-12)

Excitement and unrest seem to have grown in Thessalonica since Paul's first letter. Talk about the second advent and judgment appear to have unsettled Christians' minds and habits. Some Thessalonians saw no need of working, for they felt the time was short, and others felt unready to meet their Lord. Therefore Paul deals with the signs that must precede the end. Before the last day, the lawless one, who is at present held in restraint, must appear in the world as the antithesis of all goodness yet likely to be mistaken for Christ. Until then, it is futile to talk as if the end of the world were already upon them.

Paul holds before the readers the certainty of the Lord's coming and what it will entail. At the Lord's advent, he had already told them, believers who are still alive will be gathered to meet him and the resurrected saints in the air (1 Thess 4:15-17).

Apparently the Thessalonians have received some sort of communication that has demoralized them. They have been misled by what has been said by others and from a fraudulent letter that purported to be from the apostolic team. The problem of false prophets and false missives was a real one in the early church, and women and men who were leaders of house churches had to use discrimination as to what documents and what teachers they would receive as genuine (Acts 12:12-17; 2 Jn 7-11; *see* 2 John; 3 John).

Order must be restored in a community that should be living and working soberly and prayerfully so that when the Lord comes, he should not find them off course. Instead, they were behaving like a ship that had been insecurely anchored, had broken from its moorings and was blown here and there by every rumor or chance remark that the end of the world has come. There is no reason to think that the end of the world is upon them (cf. Mt 24:26-27; Lk 17:23-24). The concern must be for the spiritual readiness of the people.

The apocalypse will not be realized "unless the rebellion comes first." God has a fixed order for the final events. The word *rebellion* (lit., "apostasy") refers to one of the unnatural portents and manifestations that precede the end of the world. It will take the form of a widespread and violent defiance to the authority of God. The rebellion is to be a definite event, an apocalyptic happening; it may conceivably be an earthly parallel to the revolt in heaven (Rev 12:7-12). Associated with the rebellion will come the revealing of "the lawless one," a man of sin whose character is the essence of evil. In the description, traits of persons ancient and modern may be discerned (e.g., Antiochus Epiphanes, Caligula, Nero, Napoleon, Stalin, Hitler), and with each appearance, there is agitated speculation that the end times are at hand.

The writers' efforts to instill calm indicate that there must have been near panic. Paul reminds his readers that he has gone over this ground with them and that the force of evil is still being restrained, a concept that might well speak to the heightened fright of women.

The lawless one will be the incarnation of evil, as Jesus was the incarnation of good. His father will be Satan, as Jesus' father is God. He will be able to do mighty works, and people will flock to him as he claims the rights of God for himself. However, Christ will destroy the lawless one and those who have followed him (cf. Dan 7:11; 8:25).

The result of rejecting God's truth will be moral and spiritual death as humankind falls under the evil spell and forfeits its chance of salvation. The two traditional aspects of antichrist—the demonic and the human—remind us that evil, like God's mercy that is new every morning, is the same in principle throughout the ages. It is a force of darkness calling mortals to its service and binding them fast in its chains. Evil as an abstraction must always be incarnated in human personalities. Evil is in all of us. Only when the evil in humankind is overcome, when antichrist is vanquished by Christ, will God's kingly rule be complete. Whether it comes quickly, as the early church believed, or whether slowly by the spread of the gospel, it is an act of God alone.

Positive Faith for Here and Now (2 Thess 2:13—3:15)

Christ loved the Thessalonians, and God chose them for salvation (2 Thess 2:13-17). He has honored them by choosing them to be first in his new order of creation and therefore an offering to himself. He chose them from the beginning, for their knowledge and experience of his loving grace had its roots in the mind and intention of God from before the world was made.

Salvation of humanity and deliverance from sin are grounded in the timeless will of God. They are the work of the Holy Spirit of God, recreating sinful people into the likeness of Christ. Hence the operation is mutual; the marks of Christian life are God's indwelling power in human beings, with a concomitant giving of themselves to God. The Lord's encouragement will speak to the depressing effect of persecution and to the uncertainty about the end.

The "word of the Lord" (2 Thess 3:1) is spoken of as if it were almost an independent spiritual force not relying on the eloquence and physical powers of the missionaries. In an expression used only of the honor due to God or Christ, Paul speaks of the gospel's triumph or glory. When the gospel is allowed to spread freely and is properly received, the results speak for themselves, as had happened at Thessalonica. There indeed the gospel was glorified.

The point of the intercession for which Paul asks is that his mission should be as successful in Corinth as it had been in Macedonia, but this is not being permitted (2 Thess 3:2-5). They should pray that the apostles may be delivered from perverse or wicked and evil men. It was just such local thugs who had been stirred up by Jewish opponents to Paul while he was in Thessalonica (Acts 17:5). The term *atopos* literally means "having no place or position" (i.e., in society). These ruffians stand in direct contrast to the upper-class women who were incited to hostility against Paul in Antioch of Pisidia (Acts 13:50). But here Paul's methods and message were warmly received by women.

Paul had had occasion in his first letter to caution the converts gently about the danger of allowing advent expectations to unsettle them. Some were reluctant to carry on their ordinary work. While their endeavors might have seemed profitless in view of the Lord's immediate return, it also provided a theological pretext for idleness. Since Christians were willing to share with others of the faith, the situation lent itself to serious exploitation by those who were indisposed to honest labor (2 Thess 3:6-15). Hence the stern injunction treated in threefold manner. First Paul cites his example of independence and self-support. He further appeals to the loafers to go back to their jobs. If these admonitions fail, he instructs the congregation to "have nothing to do" with the offending members, "so that they may be ashamed." The rule of the Thessalonians was that people were "to do their work quietly and to earn their own living."

The word *hēsychia,* sometimes applied to women's silence (1 Tim 2:11-12), means to refrain from meddling in other people's business and to tend to one's own affairs. In 1 Thessalonians 4:11, the same sense is found in the verbal form *hēsychazein.* The adjectival *hēsychios* speaks of a "quiet and peaceable life" (1 Tim 2:2). Cannot the use in 2 Thessalonians 3:12 inform our understanding of women's *hēsychia* in 1 Timothy 2:11-12? Does it indicate that women may not speak, or rather that they should avoid idleness, mind their own business and behave in a discreet fashion?

Women who so often must persevere in monotonous tasks may find special encouragement not to grow weary in their well-doing. There is much work to be done for the kingdom of God.

Closing Greeting (2 Thess 3:16-18)
Paul notes that there is little outward peace for the Thessalonians; they are subject to persecution, plagued by excited speculation about the imminence of the end of the world and have in their midst idle vagabonds. Paul invokes on their behalf the inward peace of God that alone can give confidence and courage. He adds "the Lord be with you all"—with mourners, with the distraught, with the victims of persecution, with those who need him most.

Bibliography. A. J. Malherbe, *Paul and the Thessalonians* (Philadelphia: Fortress, 1987); I. H. Marshall, *1 and 2 Thessalonians*, New Century Bible Commentary (Grand Rapids, MI: Eerdmans, 1983); L. Morris, *The First and Second Epistles to the Thessalonians*, New International Commentary on the New Testament (Grand Rapids, MI: Eerdmans, 1959); N. Williams, *The Epistles of St. Paul to the Thessalonians*, Moffat New Testament Commentary (London: Hodder & Stoughton, 1950).

JANET NASAMBU KASSILLY

1 TIMOTHY

Introduction

1 Timothy is one of three letters commonly referred to as the Pastoral Epistles. In them (1-2 Timothy and Titus), Paul addresses two former trainees in need of pastoral advice. Timothy is pastoring a church about ten years old in the provincial capital of Ephesus. Titus is pastoring a recent church plant on the island of Crete, off the coast of Asia Minor.

The issues addressed in 1 Timothy include false teaching, the choosing and training of church leaders, the handling of money and possessions, gender relationships, church discipline, church and family support of marginalized seniors, guidelines for pastor-parishioner relationships and the kind of prayer and demeanor suitable for worship. What is unusual about 1 Timothy, however, is the amount of space devoted specifically to women. This includes appropriate dress for women who lead in worship (1 Tim 2:9-10), behavior befitting women who teach (1 Tim 2:12-15), qualifications for women deacons (1 Tim 3:11), suitable pastoral relations with women (1 Tim 5:2), qualifications for women elders (1 Tim 5:9-10), correction of young widows (1 Tim 5:11-15) and familial responsibilities toward destitute widows (1 Tim 5:3-8, 16). In no other New Testament letter do women figure so prominently.

Church tradition places the writing of 1 Timothy somewhere between A.D. 62 and 63, shortly after Paul's first Roman imprisonment. Paul has left Timothy in charge of the Ephesian church while he goes on to Macedonia (1 Tim 1:3). Timothy's task at Ephesus is to command certain persons not to teach false doctrines any longer.

Paul hopes to join Timothy soon, but in the event that he is delayed he also wants Timothy to know "how one ought to behave in the household of God" (1 Tim 3:14-15). References to persistent sin, the need for a public rebuke and the concern that other leaders take warning point to a leadership crisis at Ephesus (1 Tim 5:19-20). The prominence given to women in the letter suggests that they are linked to this crisis.

A native of the Galatian town of Lystra, Timothy accompanied Paul on his missionary endeavors to Greece and Asia, traveled with him to Jerusalem with relief funds (Acts 20:4) and was with Paul during his first lengthy imprisonment (Phil 2:19-23). At the time of writing, he was pastoring the Ephesian church in Paul's stead—albeit with some timidity (1 Tim 4:11; 5:23; cf. 2 Tim 1:6-7; 2:22).

The city of Ephesus was the urban hub and provincial capital of Asia, the western part of modern Turkey. It housed the temple of Artemis, the Anatolian goddess of fertility, acclaimed as one of the seven wonders of the ancient world. In fact, the city was named the temple warden of Artemis (Acts 19:35). The religious and economic importance of the cult to Ephesus is evident from the two-hour-long chant "Great is Artemis of the Ephesians" (Acts 19:28-36). Added to this was the belief that the city possessed Artemis's image, supposedly fallen from Jupiter (Acts 19:35).

The cult of Artemis had great appeal, especially among the female population. Artemis, it was believed, was the child of Zeus and Leto, and the sister of Apollo. Because of the severity of her mother's labor, Artemis never married. Instead she turned to a male consort for company. This made Artemis and all her female adherents superior to men. Artemis was also seen as the mother goddess, the mother of life, the nourisher of all creatures and the power of fertility in nature. Maidens turned to her as the protector of their virginity, barren women sought her aid, and women in labor turned to her for help.

One of the challenges Timothy faced was that of false teaching of a syncretistic sort. There were at least five components to the false teaching. Esoteric knowledge was one component (1 Tim 6:20-21), involving "endless genealogies" (1 Tim 1:4), "profane myths" (1 Tim 4:7), controversies (1 Tim 1:4) and "meaningless talk" (1 Tim 1:6).

Asceticism was also a component. The order of the day was to abstain from certain foods (1 Tim 4:3-4) and to refrain from marriage (1 Tim 4:3). A belief that the resurrection had already happened (i.e., that we are wholly spiritual beings) motivated such restrictions (2 Tim 2:17-18; cf. Lk 20:34-35).

There was a dualistic component. The material world was something to be kept at an arm's distance and the spiritual realm something to be striven for. Withdrawal from the world was therefore in order, and fasting and sexual abstinence served to keep in check physical impulses (1 Tim 4:3-4).

The false teaching had a distinctly Jewish character. Those who sought to advance it were primarily from the circumcision group (Tit 1:10). Their aim was to be teachers of the Mosaic law (1 Tim 1:7; Tit 3:9). They devoted themselves to Jewish legends (Tit 1:14) and genealogies (1 Tim 1:4; Tit 3:9) and forbade certain foods (perhaps in line with Mosaic law; 1 Tim 4:3-4).

A further component was the positing of mediators through which contact between a material creation and a spiritual God was accomplished. Christ was held up as one such mediator—but only one of many efforts on God's part to bridge the gap (1 Tim 2:5).

That syncretistic teaching of this sort should make inroads at the Ephesian church is not surprising. The church was syncretistic in its religious practices from the start. Luke records that many believers early on confessed to practicing sorcery and publicly burned their books (Acts 10:13-20).

The influence of this heretical teaching can be judged from its impact on the leadership of the Ephesian church. Two leaders, Alexander and Hymenaeus, were expelled for promoting it (1 Tim 1:20). Other church leaders needed to be rebuked publicly for it (1 Tim 5:20). Its impact on the congregation was devastating. In its wake it left ruined households (Tit 1:11), "envy, dissension, slander, base suspicions" (1 Tim 6:4) and "wrangling" (1 Tim 6:5).

Women seem to have been a ready target of this aberrant teaching. The false teachers, Paul states, "make their way into households and captivate" them (2 Tim 3:6). Young widows seem to have been eager evangelists, going about "from house to house, . . . saying what they should not say" (1 Tim 5:13). That something more than nosiness or gossiping is involved is clear from Paul's evaluation that they "have turned away to follow Satan" (1 Tim 5:15).

Were any of the false teachers women? There is much to suggest a yes answer. "Going about from house to house, . . . saying what they should not say" indicates an active role (1 Tim 5:13). "Always being instructed and . . . never arriv[ing] at a knowledge of the truth" suggests a discipleship relationship (2 Tim 3:7). Women may not have been the primary offenders, but they seem to have been eager advocates. It may even be that these women got caught up in genealogizing and mythologizing (1 Tim 1:4; Tit 3:9) and used this kind of esoteric knowledge to gain the upper hand over the men in the congregation. This would clarify why women are the particular focus of Paul's teaching prohibition in 1 Timothy 2:12-15. It would also account for the fact that only here in Paul's letters do we find him telling younger widows to marry and rear a family (1 Tim 5:14).

Pauline authorship of the Pastoral Epistles has been hotly debated. One objection that bears on women's issues is the presence in the Pastorals of statements that seem at odds with Paul's affirmations of women elsewhere. Women at Ephesus are permitted neither to teach nor dominate a man (1 Tim 2:12). Women are said to be saved (or NIV [1973 ed.] "kept safe") through childbearing—if they continue in faith, love and holiness with propriety (1 Tim 2:15). Younger widows are to marry, to have children and to manage their homes (1 Tim 5:14). Younger women are to be trained to love their husbands and children, be hard workers at home and subject to their husbands (Tit 2:4-5).

Can such dicta come from the apostle who praised a woman for being "prominent among the apostles" (Rom 16:7), acknowledged two women as coworkers who contended at his side for the gospel (Phil 4:2-3), encouraged women to remain unmarried so that they could devote themselves to the Lord's work (1 Cor 7:34-35) and gave his judgment that a widow is happier if she does not remarry (1 Cor 7:40)? Nevertheless, there is much to support Pauline authorship internally and externally. The early fathers (e.g., Polycarp and Irenaeus) and canons cite them. In fact, only Romans and 1 Corinthians have more external support.

Outline

1:1-2	Paul's Opening Greeting
1:3-11	False Teaching, Round 1
2:1-7	Public Prayers
2:8-10	Appropriate Public Demeanor
2:11-15	Women Learners and Teachers
3:1-13	Qualifications for Church Leaders
4:1-5	False Teaching, Round 2
4:6-16	Pastoral Responsibilities
5:1-2	Correcting Older and Younger Parishioners
5:3-16	Widows in Ministry
5:17-25	The Elders in the Church
6:1-2	Slaves and Masters
6:2-10	False Teaching, Round 3
6:11-16	Paul's Closing Charge
6:17-21	Correcting the Attitude of Wealthy Parishioners

Commentary

Paul's Opening Greeting (1 Tim 1:1-2)

Paul begins by titling himself "an apostle of Christ Jesus." Although the claim is not an unusual one, its presence in a letter addressed to a close friend and colleague is surprising. Yet a look at the plural "grace be with you" that closes this letter shows that Paul has the Ephesian church as a whole in view. The opening reference to Paul's apostleship then makes sense. The situation at Ephesus warrants a strong-arm approach. "By the command of God" reinforces this impression.

The one who issues this order is "God our Savior." Outside of the Pastorals the epithet appears only twice (Lk 1:47; Jude 25). Its presence nonetheless is understandable in a letter to a pastor and church located in a city with the status of imperial temple warden, for the emperors were deemed saviors of the world. The number of women attached to the imperial cult is of interest. In Ephesus alone, fifteen women served as imperial high priest in the first three centuries of the Christian era.

Paul's apostleship also comes by the command of "Christ Jesus our hope," a phrase that is unique to 1 Timothy. Christ is our hope because he is the "one mediator between God and humankind" (1 Tim 2:5). The cult of Artemis, the goddess of hope for women, and the Greco-Roman plurality of religious mediators provide a fitting background for Paul's claim.

False Teaching, Round 1 (1 Tim 1:3-11)

Paul bypasses the standard thanksgiving and goes straight to the matter at hand. Timothy apparently was having second thoughts about his mission at Ephesus. So Paul has to tell him to "remain" and "instruct certain people not to teach any different doctrine" (1 Tim 1:3). "Different" doctrines included "myths" and "endless genealogies," which promote fruitless speculations. The teachers of these doctrines are graphically depicted as runners who have taken their eyes off the target, gone off the track and wandered into a wasteland of idle chatter. This happened because they set their sights on being "teachers of the [Mosaic] law," but without the knowledge to do so (1 Tim 1:6-7).

The false teachers' ignorance of the law prompts Paul to speak knowledgeably about it. He begins with affirmation: "We know that the law is good." But this is true only if the law is used properly (lit., "lawfully," 1 Tim 1:8). Although one might think of law as something that guides the steps of the law abiding, Mosaic law was intended for those who desired to live their lives without law. Transgressors against God head the list of the lawless. Into this group fall those who spurn divinely instituted authority, the nonreverent and those for whom nothing is sacred (cf. Ex 20:3-11).

Transgressions against neighbor come second. They include patricide and matricide, murder, sexual immorality, slave trading and lying and perjury (cf. Ex 20:12-16). It is worth noting that striking down one's mother is as serious an offense as killing one's father. This reflects a movement in first-century Roman law toward the parity of husband and wife. The wife's position in the household was equal to her husband's. She was addressed as *domina* ("mistress") not only by her children but also by her husband. "Adulterers and perverts" (NIV) can be more narrowly defined as immoral heterosexuals *(pornoi)* and homosexuals *(arsenokoitai)*. Same-sex relationships were commonplace in the first century among upper-class Greek males, particularly between a teacher and his prepubescent student (*see* Homosexuality). Sexual activity between women is rarely mentioned, although the love poems of Sappho (sixth century B.C.) and the colony of women on the island of Lesbos show that it existed.

Paul's vice list atypically lacks the tenth commandment, "You shall not covet." Instead Paul generalizes with "and whatever else is contrary to the sound teaching that conforms to the glorious gospel" (1 Tim 1:10-11). Not only is Mosaic law good, but also it is health-producing and gospel-conforming.

Public Prayers (1 Tim 2:1-7)

The opening "then" and the repeated "I urge" tie what follows to the preceding concerns about false teaching. The key terms are "all" (six times) and "humankind" (four times). There looks to be a narrow-minded spirit at work at Ephesus. God, however, desires that *all* be saved and Christ died for *all*. Public intercession for *all* people must therefore be the church's first priority and prayers for high-ranking public officials of foremost importance. High-ranking officials in Paul's day included women. City records name women in such roles as magistrates, priestesses and chief municipal officers. God desires also that *all* come to a knowledge of "the truth" about the "one God" (not the Greco-Roman many gods) and the "one mediator" and "human" Christ Jesus (1 Tim 2:3-6). The fact that God intervened to save a persecutor like Paul shows conclusively that God desires to save all.

Appropriate Public Demeanor (1 Tim 2:8-10)

Paul's instructions are now gender specific. He begins with a virtual command: "I will it" (lit.). There was a need for immediate correction. The corrective for the men is to stop lifting up their hands with anger and disputing. Although the posture was the acceptable form of the day, the prayer was not. The attitude must be devout (i.e., focused on God). Instead it was "with anger" (i.e., focused on one another).

The corrective for women also has to do with attitude. In the Greek text, 1 Timothy 2:9-10 lacks a subject and a main verb. The text is literally, "Likewise, the women . . ." The missing grammatical pieces must be supplied from what precedes: "Likewise *I want* the women *in every place to pray*." Paul affirms women who pray in public worship. This is because worship in the New Testament period was a cooperative enterprise of the whole (cf. 1 Cor 11:4-5). The only qualification is that they use sound judgment. Unsound judgment is "hair braided" with "gold ribbon," "pearls" and "expensive clothes." The corrective is not merely for wealthy women. Women aped the latest fashions in hairstyles and dress regardless of their social standing.

Women Learners and Teachers (1 Tim 2:11-15)

At 1 Timothy 1:11 the correction shifts from women praying to women learning. Paul's first correction is that women learn quietly. Although some translations have "in silence," this is not compatible with the Greek Socratic method of learning. The standard of propriety was calmness and self-control. This is how Paul uses the Greek adjective nine verses earlier. Intercession for public officials is urged so that believers may live "a quiet and peaceable life" (1 Tim 2:2).

Paul's second correction is that women learn "with full submission." While some interpreters leap to the conclusion that the submission is to one's husband, "let a woman learn" suggests nothing of the sort. Either submission to a teacher or "with self-control" better suits a learning context (cf. 1 Cor 14:32). What is often missed is that Paul affirms a woman's right to learn. Greco-Roman higher education for girls past the age of fourteen, though on the rise, was still not commonplace (*see* Expectations of Women).

Paul's third correction is found in 1 Timothy 2:12-15. 1 Timothy 2:12 is a point of contrast to the preceding verse: "Let a woman learn quietly . . . *but* for a woman to either-teach-or-*authentein* a man, I am not permitting." Despite claims to the contrary, Paul cannot be categorically prohibiting women from teaching, for in a letter written about the same time, Paul commands the older women in the church to teach the younger (Titus 2:3-5). Also, the ongoing sense of the present tense Greek verb points to a restriction specific to the current situation at Ephesus ("I *am not* permitting [*an Ephesian woman*]"). Nor can Paul be forbidding men to receive instruction from women, since the New Testament record shows that women did this very thing (e.g., Acts 18:26). The restriction is not women teaching men in public, for Paul affirms women prophets (1 Cor 11:5), whose task it was to speak words that "instruct" the entire congregation (1 Cor 14:19, 31). On the basis of 1 Corinthians 14:26, a woman can bring a teaching to the congregation just as readily as a man. Nor is Paul forbidding authoritative teaching, for women are praised elsewhere as apostles (e.g., Junia) and evan-

Women in Worship

Women assume a variety of cultic roles in the history of religions. In primitive religions in which divination and soothsaying play a prominent role, women often take the lead. The biblical reference to the "medium of Endor" (1 Sam 28:7) is one example. In the fertility cults, women were among the sacred prostitutes. Examples of cruelty to women can be found in the Hindu practice known as *sati* (widow sacrificing). In Islamic lands veiling and seclusion of women are the norm, and the circumcision of girls is still practiced, including clitoridectomy. Women of the Old Testament are usually viewed as finding a place between these extremes.

The Old Testament originated in a world in which the male took the public role and the female, almost exclusively, the private role. Patriarchy is the norm; matriarchy cannot be found.

The Old Testament record has been variously interpreted. Some interpreters perceive the data as presenting a patriarchal religion. Others see the Old Testament story as a patriarchal society out of which emerges the beginning of a more egalitarian status for women. Proponents of the first view point to such considerations as the fact that revelation came almost exclusively to men, as well as circumcision being administered only to the males. Moreover, the priesthood in Israel was exclusively male. Proponents of the second view emphasize that one must not take the phenomena of the Israelite society as normative but rather consider the peculiar and unique aspects of the material to correctly assess the guidance the Old Testament presents. Among these unique aspects would be the presence of women who were fully recognized to be prophets (Miriam, Deborah and Huldah); the openness of the office of Nazirite (an office comparable to the high priesthood in consecration) to women; women bringing sacrifices without a male representing them.

If it is considered important that there were no women priests in Israel, it should be remembered that the priestesses in the neighboring cults often were sacred prostitutes; and since the Old Testament was so inimical to the fertility cult, this alone might be considered a decisive factor in excluding women from the priesthood. Moreover, other reasons such as the fact that priesthood was considered a full-time vocation requiring such duties as the slaughtering of large animals, plus such considerations as periodic ritual uncleanness of women and the high value placed on the role of motherhood, would militate against women participating in the Israel's priesthood.

Some interpreters have even posited that women were not members of the covenant community. The strong consensus, however, is that this is not so. Simply because women were not required to appear three times a year at the sanctuary, as men were (Deut 16:16), does not exclude them from the membership in the community. We must acknowledge that in that society it was natural that men sometimes represent women, but there are too many evidences of women participating fully and independently in the worship of Israel to suppose they were excluded from membership.

It is difficult to discern any important change of the status of women in the apocryphal literature, except to note that like the protocanonical book of Esther, the deuterocanonical books of Judith and Susanna are devoted to the heroism and wisdom of women in the history of Judaism. One looks in vain for comparable contemporary literature.

The data on the church at worship is scant in the New Testament. It must be noted, however, that Apollos seems to have been instructed by Prisca and Aquila. Phoebe was a "deacon" *(diakonos),* a term used for Paul, Timothy, and many others. Paul takes for granted that women prophesy.

As in the Old Testament setting, the social context must be considered. While the data we possess are incomplete, we must consider the evidence we have. Apparently a type of feminism existed in the worship of Artemis (Acts 19:27). She apparently is a goddess who goes back to the Egyptians as Isis, to the Hurrians as Hepat, and is identified as Eve, "the mother of gods and men." This may explain why we find in some schools of ancient Judaism what seems a sharp antifeminist spirit, which is heard in such expressions as "the best way to destroy the law is to teach it to a woman" or the rabbinical prayer, "I thank you, Lord, that you have not made me . . . a woman." The more we learn of the social status of women in that culture the more astonishing is Jesus' relationship to women. His admonition to Martha that Mary had chosen the better part would hardly have merited the acclaim of the teachers of the law.

One school of interpreters has emphasized the way in which Jesus lifted the status of women, as well as Paul's words in Ephesians 5:21 that believers are to practice mutual submission, as clear evidence that the New Testament gives to each gender an equal opportunity for leadership in the church. Another school of interpreters emphasizes the words in 1 Timothy 2:11-15 as paramount and indicating that women are not to be regarded as equals in leadership but are to be in submission to males in worship as well as in the home.

There is archaeological evidence from the third and fourth century frescoes that women may have functioned as clergy in the early church. The evidence is difficult to assess, but some see evidence that the hair of the person officiating at the altar has been removed, and there appear to be markings which show that someone scratched below the chin looking for a beard. Whether this is proof that there were female celebrants in the early church and that in a later period efforts were made to obscure or destroy such evidence is hard to determine. If the art of the early frescoes does indicate that women functioned as clergy, it would suggest that the early church did not see 1 Timothy 2:11-15 as universally applicable.

In the medieval period the governance of the church was strictly limited to a celibate male hierarchy. Women, however, did take a significant role in the monastic orders. Each convent was under the jurisdiction of the hierarchy; and no examples have been found of women as celebrants of the mass. During this period the rail at the altar became common; its purpose was to limit the proximity of women to the altar. Nevertheless, it must be said that a form of worship took place in devotional reading, study, writing and singing. The apex of this activity may be seen in St. Teresa of Ávila (1515-1582), whose actions and writings so influenced the church that she was beatified in 1614 by Pope Paul V and declared a doctor in the church in 1970 by Pope Paul VI.

The Reformation did not significantly bring women into positions of leadership in governance or worship. While Martin Luther could speak eloquently of "the priesthood of all believers," his relegation of women to *Kinder und Küchen* is well known. John Calvin, despite his well-earned title as prince of exegetes and his aid to the harried and oppressed, still often betrays a male chauvinistic perspective in his writings (e.g., *Commentary on Ezekiel* 13:17).

It may be said that the more established the organized aspect of the church, the more difficult it has been to yield a leadership role to women. While women were welcomed in the ancillary role of music and financial support, there was little room for them in the governance and administration of the church. In the latter part of the twentieth century the effects of the women's suffrage movement and the entry of women into positions of leadership in society have forced a renewed examination of Scripture and ecclesiastical policies. It is the hope of many that permitting women's perspectives to enter the arena of theological reflection and combining them with male perspectives will result in something richer than the sum of its parts. We may hope that this will allow the church to present appropriate social models and more acceptable praise and worship.

CLARENCE J. VOS

gelists (e.g., Syntyche and Euodia) in roles comparable to that of Paul (Rom 16:7; Phil 4:2). And it is not women teaching men doctrine, for the concern in 1 Timothy is for sound *teaching* over against false teaching (lit., "different"; 1 Tim 6:3; cf. 1:3, 10; 4:6, 11).

The key phrase is curiously translated in the NIV and other versions as "have authority over a man." Although the Greek word *authentein* is commonly rendered this way, it is a meaning not attested in the Greek of Paul's day or earlier. Nor is it particularly logical. Although some translations have two prohibitions, the structure of 1 Timothy 2:12 demands a single, coherent idea (correlative "neither [slumber] nor [sleep]"), and logic demands that the general idea (exercise authority) precede the particular expression (teach). "Not teach authoritatively" is a possible construal of the correlative, but it does not fit the culture; the Greek Socratic method of teaching was dialogical, not dictatorial.

Tombstone of richly ornamented woman. (1 Timothy 2:9)

Paul had at his disposal a number of words that commonly bear the meaning "exercise authority." Yet he picked a word not found elsewhere in the New Testament and very rare outside of it. So there must be something about *authentein* that particularly suited the Ephesian situation. In sources roughly contemporary with Paul, it means "to have the upper hand" (*BGU* 1208), "powerful" (Philodemus) and "dominating" (Ptolemy *Tetrabiblos* 3.13 [#157]). Paul would then be saying that the Ephesian women are to stop teaching with a view to gaining the upper hand over the men (cf. Mt 6:20 for a similar construction).

1 Timothy 2:13-14 provides two reasons for Paul's restriction. "Adam was formed first, then Eve" is commonly thought to teach male leadership. But this is our culture speaking, where to be first is to have the advantage. "First . . . then" in Paul is nothing more than a temporal marker. A good example is found ten verses later, where Paul states that deacons must be tested "first" and only "then" be permitted to serve (1 Tim 3:10; cf. 1 Cor 15:46; 1 Thess 4:16-17). Another example is John the Baptist, who hardly had the advantage because he ministered before Jesus. Two, "Adam was not deceived, but the woman was deceived" (1 Tim 2:14). Some interpreters would say that Paul is asserting that women by nature are easily deceived. But this conflicts with scriptural teaching elsewhere and overlooks the fact that two men (not women) were expelled for false teaching and that due to personal deception (1 Tim 1:20).

Paul's use of Adam and Eve as the prototypical relationship suggests a battle of the sexes. The women of the church (undoubtedly egged on by the false teachers) were trying to gain the advantage over the men. The men in response were becoming angry and disputing what they were doing. The prestigious Ephesian cult of Artemis may have been partly to blame (Acts 19:34 and the two-hour Ephesian chant "Great is Artemis"). The belief that Artemis's priority in time placed all women in a position of superiority would go a long way toward explaining Paul's correctives. Artemis as woman's protector "through childbearing" would also explain Paul's correction that women will be saved through bearing *the* Child (1 Tim 2:15).

Qualifications for Church Leaders (1 Tim 3:1-13)

Concerns about worship leaders lead naturally to other leadership roles such as overseer and deacon (cf. Phil 1:1). It is common to interpret these roles as offices, but nothing in Paul's treatment justifies it. Paul explicitly talks of overseer as a "noble task" and not a worthy office (1 Tim 3:1). Although some scholars translate *episkopos* as "bishop" and understand the role in terms of a presiding officer, the basic sense of the word grouping is to "watch over" or "care for" and the role is pastoral in nature (cf. Acts 20:28; 1 Pet 5:2).

The specific duties of an overseer are not spelled out. The qualifications are, but they are not the ones of which we might readily think. The focus is on character, family, lifestyle and orthodoxy. Overseers are to be above reproach, have a good reputation with non-Christians, be forbearing and not be recent converts. They must also be the husband of one wife, lead their household well and have submissive and respectful children. An additional eight qualifications pertain to Christian lifestyle. Overseers must be clear-headed, of sound judgment and respectable. They must not be given to excesses such as drunkenness, punching, brawling or greed—and they must be a friend to strangers. The only qualification that is job-related is "an apt teacher" (1 Tim 3:2). Yet this too is situational. Inroads made by false teachers would make the ability to refute wrong teaching and present right teaching an urgent need.

Some interpreters argue that "married once only" (literally, "the husband of one wife") excludes women (1 Tim 3:2). But then it would also rule out the unmarried leader. "Submissive and respectful" children would exclude the married but childless leader. In reality, though, the unmarried and the childless are more accessible. Paul elsewhere counsels against (re)marriage for this reason (cf. 1 Cor 7:32-35). Certain qualifications apply more readily to women than to men. Respectability is required of female worship leaders (1 Tim 2:9), hospitality is expected of widowed leaders (1 Tim 5:10), and good household management was women's work. Virtually all the rest apply equally to both genders. The possible exceptions are punching and brawling.

The real oddity is the absence of "the wife of one husband" (both here and for women deacons in the next section), especially as it is required of widowed leaders two chapters later (1 Tim 5:9). Paul obviously did not think that this qualification applied to married women. One explanation is that women leaders were largely drawn from the ranks of the unmarried. Another is that men were culpable at this point and women were not. Marital faithfulness and submissive children were a greater challenge for males in that society. Men were largely the initiators in divorce and philandering. Men were also more prone to corporal punishment and physical violence. This would explain Paul's acknowledgment that the wife might feel compelled to leave her husband (1 Cor 7:10-11) and his command that fathers not embitter (Col 3:21) or exasperate their children (Eph 6:4).

In any event, Paul's mention of *univera* ("married once") should give us pause. There is enough cultural bias in the list of qualifications that due caution is needed. At 1 Timothy 3:8 Paul turns to deacons. Once again character, family, lifestyle and orthodoxy are at the fore. Qualifications for deacons closely parallel those for overseers, but the list is decidedly shorter. Character qualifications are only two in number. Deacons are to be worthy of respect and not prone to gossip (lit., "not double-tongued"; 1 Tim 3:8, 11). Family qualifications are virtual duplicates. Lifestyle qualifications match those for overseers in number but exceed them in degree. Deacons are not to be *addicted* to much wine or money. And deacons, like overseers, must be orthodox.

Two qualifications are unique to deacons: they must not be prone to gossip and must be blameless while receiving on-the-job training. This makes sense, if the primary responsibility of deacons was to care for the material needs of the local body of believers. Beyond this, caution needs to be exercised. It is hard to say what exactly distinguished an overseer and a deacon during the apostolic period. There is some merit in the suggestion that the distinction lay in the sphere of ministry. Hospitable and apt to teach fit well the person who opens his or her home as a meeting place and so *oversees* the church. Not prone to gossiping or drinking and a blameless ministry record fit well the house-to-house visitation role of the deacon.

Women deacons are singled out in 1 Timothy 3:11: "Women [deacons] likewise must be . . ." The qualifications closely parallel in word order and content those listed for male deacons. In fact, it is a woman deacon whom Paul applauds elsewhere (Rom 16:1). Some scholars translate, "[Their] wives, likewise . . ." But if Paul were turning to the wives of deacons, he would have written "*their* women likewise" or some other spousal linkage. It is true that the word *deaconess* is lacking. But the feminine form did not exist in the first century. The only available option was to use a gender-specific word like *gynē* and let the context clarify.

False Teaching, Round 2 (1 Tim 4:1-5)

On the note of Christ's universal lordship, Paul enters the ring for round two with the false teachers. The opening verses are prophetic in tone. Paul cites the Spirit's warning about a time when "some will renounce the faith" (cf. Acts 20:29-30). "The faith" is the common confession of the early church regarding Christ's incarnation, life, death, resurrection and ascension (see 1 Tim 3:16; cf. Acts 2:22-36). The reason they turn away from the faith is in order to pay "attention to deceitful spirits and teachings of demons" (1 Tim 4:1). What permits the deceit is a "seared" conscience that no longer has the ability to distinguish right from wrong.

That Paul understood recent happenings at Ephesus to be within the scope of "later times" (1 Tim 4:1) is clear from the concrete character of the two heretical prohibitions: "They forbid marriage and demand abstinence from foods" (1 Tim 4:3). Such thinking betrays a dualistic understanding of the world, where what is material is evil and what is spiritual is good (cf. 1 Cor 7:1). From the standpoint of the dualist, sex and certain foods would be a material pollution of the spiritual good.

Paul leaves the marital prohibition for 1 Timothy 5 and tackles dietary restrictions. His approach is to appeal to creation order as overriding particular religious scruples. The argument is presented in the form of a syllogism: Food is a part of creation. Everything God created is good. Therefore food is inherently good (cf. Mk 7:19; Acts 10:9-15). There is one qualification, however. The food must be "received with thanksgiving" and "by God's word" and so become "sanctified" (1 Tim 4:4-5). Whatever idolatrous (e.g., Deut 14:21) or hedonistic (e.g., 1 Cor 15:32) associations a particular food had, thanksgiving put it squarely in the realm of a God who created all things "very good" (Gen 1:31).

Pastoral Responsibilities (1 Tim 4:6-16)

Paul proceeds to give Timothy a pep talk about his pastoral responsibilities. The pastors' first responsibility is to the congregation. In particular, they are to give attention to three worship activities. The public reading of Scripture played a central role in Jewish and Christian liturgies. The exhortation (or sermon) followed the Scripture reading in the synagogue liturgy (e.g., Acts 13:15). It was much the same for early Christian worship. "Sound teaching" is probably shorthand for "the teaching of the apostles" (Acts 2:42). The primary apostolic task was to preserve and transmit Jesus' life and teachings (see 1 Cor 11:2; 2 Thess 2:15; 2 Pet 2:21). It was a task for which God held women (e.g., Junia [Rom 16:7]) and men (e.g., Andronicus [Rom 16:7]) accountable.

The pastors' second responsibility is to take care of themselves. To be effective in pastoral ministry, pastors must continue to be "nourished on the words of the faith and of the sound teaching" (1 Tim 4:6). Unsound teaching is identified as "profane myths" and "old wives' tales" (1 Tim 4:7). "Old women's fables" (not "tales") is an idiom of the day for an uninformed and unlearned opinion. The education of Greek women typically stopped at the marriageable age of fourteen, while the education of Greek men continued well into their thirties (and beyond for certain career choices). The idiom reflects a presumption that to be formally uneducated is to be ignorant.

Self-discipline is critical to effective ministry: "Train yourself in godliness" (1 Tim 4:7). Ministry is pictured as training for an athletic contest. As such, it involves hard work and much struggle. When it came to athletics, Greek men and women were on equal footing. There are numerous records of women who competed in the same kind of sporting events as men (e.g., chariot racing, cross-country, track and field, sword play, discus throw). Spiritual training is similarly gender inclusive. Women and men are described as colaborers

(Rom 16:3; Phil 4:3) and hard workers (Rom 16:6, 12) who "risked their necks" for Paul (Rom 16:3), "struggled beside [him] in the work of the gospel" (Phil 4:2-3) and ended up in prison with him (Rom 16:7; Col 4:10). Accordingly, the prize is of eternal consequence for both: promise for the present and future life and salvation for oneself and one's parishioners.

The Ephesian congregation looks to have been a bit more than Timothy bargained for. Paul points to Timothy's youth and timidity, which the congregation appeared to exploit. To offset these handicaps, Paul charges Timothy to teach in a commanding fashion. In addition to his demeanor, Paul calls on Timothy to "set . . . an example" for his parishioners. Paul sets forth five spheres where youth is often deficient: "in speech [i.e., daily conversation] and conduct, in love [i.e., unselfish giving], in faith, in purity" (1 Tim 4:12). If Timothy is diligent in these matters and gives himself wholly to them, then his parishioners will begin to take note of his spiritual growth and forget about his physical youth (or one's gender today).

Correcting Older and Younger Parishioners (1 Tim 5:1-2)

Paul turns next to the need for Timothy to treat his parishioners like family members. This is not unique to Christianity. Burial inscriptions and moralists laud those who treated the elderly as parents and peers as brothers and sisters. Paul's focus, however, is on correction. "An older man" is to be corrected "as . . . a father," an older woman as one's mother, and younger men and women as "brothers" and "sisters."

The Greek term for "older" ("elder") elsewhere in the New Testament generally denotes a position of leadership (e.g., Acts 14:23; 1 Tim 5:17; Titus 1:5; Jas 5:14). This was also the case in the culture at large, where the elderly were looked to for wisdom and leadership. There is good contextual support for seeing elder men and women here in much the same light. Two verses earlier, Paul refers to commissioning by "the council of elders," and in the verses that follow he treats two paid leadership positions staffed by the elderly (1 Tim 5:3-16, 17-25).

Widows in Ministry (1 Tim 5:3-16)

"Honor widows who are really widows" (1 Tim 5:3). There are good reasons for thinking that Paul is talking about a leadership position (*see* Widows). The terms are technical ones for enlistment and financial compensation. The qualifications parallel those for other leadership positions (1 Tim 5:9-10). And there is mention of an ongoing ministry; these widows committed themselves to praying for the church "night and day" (1 Tim 5:5).

The qualifications provide a rough idea of what was involved (1 Tim 5:9-10). Ministerial activities include showing hospitality, washing feet (a courtesy extended by the host or hostess to one's guests), and helping "the afflicted." The last one included caring for those in prison for their faith and providing shelter, food and clothing for the persecuted. Caring for orphans may have also been part of the job description. It was one of the major challenges that the church faced early on and would explain the good-parenting requirement. Home visitation is suggested by Paul's criticism that younger widows were "going about from house to house" (1 Tim 5:13 NIV). "Saying what they should not" points to some sort of teaching role (1 Tim 5:13; cf. Titus 2:3-4).

Only widows sixty years and older were to be put on the church's payroll. According to first-century mindset, this was the age when pressure to marry eased. "Younger widows" were not to be put on, for they lacked the self-control necessary to resist sexual temptation. Instead they should remarry, rear a family and manage their household. Paul's language may sound a bit sexist to the modern ear. But it makes sense in the Ephesian context. Paul's opinion elsewhere is that widows not remarry (1 Cor 7:8-9, 39-40). At Ephesus, however, they were ready targets for the false teachers, who made "their way into households" (2 Tim 3:6) and turned them into eager evangelists, going from house to house, saying things they ought not say.

Paul concludes with a command aimed at women who were heads of households: "If any believing woman has relatives [in her household] who are really widows, let her assist them; let the church not be burdened" (1 Tim 5:16). The Greek is a statement of fact: "*Since* there are Christian women . . ." This indicates that the Ephesian congregation included female CEOs.

Widows

Widows are silent ones, expressing their legal status as not spoken for (Heb. *almahan,* from the root *alem,* "unable to speak"). The New Testament *chēra* (Gk. from Indo-European *ghe,* "forsaken," "left empty") is a woman without a husband or a single, celibate woman. In first century A.D. *monandros* denoted a woman married only once, and *univera* was a term of approbation for widows who did not remarry.

The legal status of widows varied widely in biblical cultures. In Hebrew tradition widowhood was a misfortune and even disgraceful (Ruth 1:20-21). A widow could return to her family only if her bride price were repaid. She was expected to await levirate marriage or public refusal (Deut 25:5-10). Little provision was made for widows; as a consequence, God is viewed as their protector (Ps 68:5) who will "heed their cry" (Ex 22:23; Deut 10:18; Ps 146:9) and bring them justice. The covenant code links relationship to God with response to such poor and oppressed (see Ex 22:21-22; Deut 10:18; 14:28-29).

Prohibitions against oppressing widows and provisions for them include that every three years a widow should receive a portion of the produce tithe (Deut 14:28-29); that her garment is not taken in pledge (Deut 24:17-18); that she be invited to public festal meals (Deut 16:11, 14) and be allowed to glean vineyards and fields (Deut 24:19-24; cf. Ruth). Since according to Genesis 38:14, 19 widows wore special clothing, ignorance was no excuse for noncompliance with regulations. Women's status was lower than men's, and widows were the lowest women.

The widow's legal status improved in the Roman Empire. Roman widows functioned as independent, legal parties if their finances allowed. They could inherit from husbands and manage their own property. Augustan marriage laws encouraged younger widows to remarry; those under fifty who did not do so within a specified period were debarred from inheritance. Later, perhaps due to Christian influence, second marriages were discouraged and once-marrieds were honored.

In the New Testament, Paul mentions widows (1 Cor 7:8, 39-40; Rom 7:1, 3) and generally prefers they not remarry. In Mark, widows demonstrate Jesus' advocacy for the oppressed. The tradition in Luke contains extensive material on widows in the Gospel (Lk 2:36-38; 4:25-26; 7:11-17; 18:1-8) and Acts (Acts 6:1-7; 9:36-43). The longest New Testament passage on widows is 1 Timothy 5:3-16, which defines membership in and duties of the order of widows in the church. In James, true religion is evidenced by care of widows (Jas 1:27), echoing Jesus' teaching (Mk 12:38-44; Lk 20:46-47) and traditional teaching that caring for widows serves God (Hos 6:6; Mt 9:13; 25:40). In Revelation 18:7 the widow is used figuratively in contrast to the harlot of Babylon, who mistakenly thinks she will escape the humbling of widowhood.

While the widow generally was relegated to low social, economic and legal positions in the Roman world, the New Testament offers the possibility of status for the widow that includes specific, constructive duties and privileges within the Christian community and claim to benevolence from it.

Bibliography

J. M. Bassler, "The Widows' Tale: A Fresh Look at 1 Tim 5:3-16," *Journal of Biblical Literature* 103/1 (1984) 23-41; R.M. Price, *The Widow Traditions in Luke-Acts,* Society for Biblical Literature Dissertation Series 155 (Atlanta: Scholars Press, 1997); B. B. Thurston, *The Widows* (Minneapolis: Fortress, 1989).

BONNIE BOWMAN THURSTON

It fits the culture at large. Donors' records show that female CEOs were on the increase in the early centuries.

The Elders of the Church (1 Tim 5:17-25)

Paul proceeds next to instruct Timothy regarding elderly leaders as a whole. The first concern is that elders be duly compensated. Those who lead well are to receive "double honor [pay]." This is to be the case especially for elders who work long and hard at preaching and teaching. The emphasis is on how one leads. There were elders who did not lead well and were asked to step down because of it (e.g., Hymanaeus and Alexander, 1 Tim 1:20). This meant a double workload for some of the remaining elders.

The impact of false teaching on the leadership can be clearly seen. Accusations have been brought against some, and public rebuke of others is needed. Elders have stepped down, and there is an urgent need for replacements. The impact on Timothy is seen in Paul's two commands to stop receiving accusations that lack at least two witnesses and to stop laying hands on new recruits too quickly. Paul's mention of laying on of hands has led some scholars to think in terms of ordination. But the language and process of ordination are foreign to the first century.

Were there women in the ranks of elders? Nothing in the description of what elders did would exclude them. We see them praying and caring for the critically ill (Jas 5:14), helping the weak (Acts 20:35), refuting error (Tit 1:9), commissioning for service (1 Tim 4:14), preaching and teaching (1 Tim 5:17), shepherding (1 Pet 5:1-2) and guiding the flock (1 Tim 5:17) and perhaps handling monies (1 Pet 5:2). At heart, this was a group whose responsibility was to care for the spiritual life of the local congregation (Acts 20:28; 1 Tim 5:17; 1 Pet 5:2). When elders are singled out, it is because of how they do their job. It is not due to a position they hold or an authority they wield (1 Tim 5:17).

Slaves and Masters (1 Tim 6:1-2)

Paul concludes his letter with some pointed correctives for the rich and the poor. The economic poor in Greco-Roman society were primarily slaves (*see* Ancient and Modern Slavery). In most urban areas they constituted the majority. Slavery was a challenge for the church. To have full rights in God's kingdom and no rights in Caesar's kingdom must have been difficult for Christian slaves to handle. This was particularly so for female slaves. While women of standing benefited legally and socially from the Greco-Roman feminist movement, female slaves did not. The disparity between life inside and outside the church was especially problematic for those serving unbelieving masters. Female slaves were seen as possessions to be used however the master saw fit. This included satisfying their master's sexual whims.

Although Paul acknowledges that slavery is a "yoke," he calls Christian slaves to look on their masters, believers and nonbelievers, as "worthy of all honor" (1 Tim 6:1). The rationale is distinctly evangelistic: "that the name of God and the teaching may not be blasphemed." The bar is higher for slaves serving believing masters. The fact that believing masters at Ephesus maintained the economic status quo seems to have led Christian slaves to look on them as spiritual inferiors. So slaves are commanded to stop disdaining them (stronger than "not be disrespectful"). Even more, they are to show them affection. Though the economic reality was one of slave-master, the spiritual reality is that of brothers/sisters and so "beloved." Hence slaves are to serve their believing masters not merely well but better.

False Teaching: Round 3 (1 Tim 6:2-10)

The source of the slaves' disdain is identified as someone who "teaches otherwise." Paul does not provide specifics beyond a "depraved mind" that craves "controversy" and financial "gain." The false teachers were the ancient equivalent of today's con artists, who seek fame and fortune through putting on a *godly* show. Paul responds with warnings about the great peril that a desire for riches brings. First, there is enticement. Then they become ensnared like an animal in the trap of "many senseless and harmful desires." The desires are senseless in that they do not lead down the path of righteousness, and the thinking is harmful, for it plunges its victim into the waters of overwhelming ruin and destruction. Paul supports his warning with a popular maxim: "The love of money is *the* root of every kind of evil" ("a root," NRSV and others, 1 Tim 6:10). The sentiment is not his alone. Jewish and Greco-Roman moralists warned about the impact of greed on a person's life. Nor is Paul speaking theoretically. The Ephesian church is living proof: "In their eagerness to be rich some have wandered from the faith and pierced themselves with many pains" (1 Tim 6:10; cf. Mt 18:23-24).

Riches may be perceived by many to be gain. But "great gain" can be found only in self-sufficiency ("contentment," 1 Tim 6:6, 8). To be sufficient is to possess "food" and "clothing" (i.e., what nature provides). Food and covering constituted the basic necessities of first-century life for the Jew (Deut 10:18; Mt 6:25) and the non-Jew. Anything more than the basics was superfluous, "for we brought nothing into the world, so that we can take nothing out of it" (1 Tim 6:7).

Paul's Closing Charge (1 Tim 6:11-16)

Paul concludes with a final charge to "shun all this," "pursue righteousness," "fight the good fight of faith" and "take hold of the eternal life" (1 Tim 6:11-12). "All this" refers to the failings of the false teachers outlined in the previous verses. The first image is that of an animal stalking its prey ("pursue"). The prey for the believer is "righteousness" (right conduct), "godliness" (spiritual disciplines), "faith" (without the article), "love" (willful sacrifice), "endurance" (without wavering) and "gentleness" (gentle passions; 1 Tim 6:11). The second image is that of an athlete competing against a strong opponent ("fight the good fight of faith"). But the prize is beyond worth, namely, "eternal life."

Correcting the Attitudes of Wealthy Parishioners (1 Tim 6:17-21)

Paul finally turns to those who already possess wealth. Rather than denouncing the possession of wealth, Paul affirms that "God . . . richly provides us with everything for our enjoyment" (1 Tim 6:17). The early church depended on wealthy patrons, most of whom were women. Wealthy women supported Jesus (e.g., Lk 8:1-3) and Paul (Phoebe [Rom 16:1-2]). They also owned homes large enough to accommodate whole church gatherings (e.g., Mary [Acts 12:12], Nympha [Col 4:15], Lydia [Acts 16:4-5]).

Although Paul does not denounce riches per se, he does take issue with the arrogance and misplaced trust that wealth commonly spawns. The reality is that wealth will ultimately disappoint. It can be here one day and gone the next. God holds accountable those whom he has entrusted with the world's wealth to "do good," "be rich in good deeds" and be "generous and ready to share" (1 Tim 6:18).

LINDA L. BELLEVILLE

---

2 TIMOTHY

Introduction

Although most introductory matters have been covered in the preliminary to 1 Timothy, it is worth noting that features in 2 Timothy such as the frequent digressions about people as well as the more typical closing greetings and personal requests like that for a cloak make the letter's authenticity all the more probable.

Timothy and his situation, his youth and shyness (*see* the introduction to 1 Timothy), have often been remarked upon. Without making these characteristics central in interpreting the letters, it adds to the poignancy of the book if we remember that like many of us, Timothy seems to have sometimes felt himself in over his head. And the fact that Timothy's leadership was questioned helps to make these books particularly relevant to those who feel their calling doubted. In our era it is not always because of youth but because of gender. 2 Timothy may discuss women's issues far less specifically or directly than does 1 Timothy, but the overall situation speaks to women. To those whose situations thus resonate with the intended reader, Paul's encouragements and exhortations will also resound.

Outline

1:1-5	Greetings, Gratitude and Grounding
1:6-18	Attitude Toward Paul and the Gospel
2:1-13	Endurance and Good Teaching
2:14-26	The Dangers of Wrangling over Words
3:1-9	The Last Days: Unteachable Listeners and Deceitful Teachers
3:10—4:8	Paul's Example and Timothy's Charge
4:9-22	Final Greetings, Personal Details and Logistics

Commentary

Greetings, Gratitude and Grounding (2 Tim 1:1-5)

Paul's opening stresses personal elements, calling Timothy "my beloved child" and focusing on their respective backgrounds. Their closeness is made clear by Paul's constant prayers for him, recollection of Timothy's previous display of emotion and the knowledge that Paul has of Timothy's family, background and faith.

Because the New Testament was written at the beginning of the Christian movement, the believers portrayed almost always joined the community through individual conversions requiring a break with their previous lives. In this late letter of Paul, it is refreshing to see an acknowledgment that true faith can be in continuity with one's upbringing. Although he regards Timothy as his spiritual son, Timothy's relationship to and debt of gratitude to his mother and grandmother are not negated. There is affirmation of the role of the family in spiritual matters.

There is also a contrast between Paul's ancestral background and Timothy's. Paul says that he worships "with a clear conscience, as my ancestors did" (2 Tim 1:3), whereas Timothy has a sincere faith that lived also in his grandmother and mother. Paul uses a vague term instead of referring directly to his parents; this may be deliberate: Paul's pedigree is not bad, but Timothy's family is much more spiritually connected—it is not a set of traditions handed down for generations but a living faith shared by particular close family members.

Attitude Toward Paul and the Gospel (2 Tim 1:6-18)

This section weaves back and forth between Paul and Timothy, illustrating their close relationship. This can be traced eloquently by observing the pronouns used. Note, for instance, "the gift of God that is within you through the laying on of my hands; for God did not give us a spirit of cowardice" (2 Tim 1:6-7). Paul wants Timothy to realize that he is not on his own and by implication that Paul, in his sufferings, can draw comfort from Timothy's companionship.

Paul's references to the "shame" of being a prisoner points to a real burden borne by the apostle and his friends (see also 2 Tim 2:8, 14). Our culture is much less driven by concerns of honor and shame than was Paul's, yet it's easy to imagine the embarrassment of a spiritual advisor with a criminal record.

It appears that Timothy was not as assertive as Paul might have liked him to be. Where the NRSV renders "God did not give us a spirit of cowardice" (2 Tim 1:7), other translations employ the phrase "spirit of timidity" (NIV, NASB, RSV). It is likely that English does not have a word that fits *deilia* exactly (a word found only here in the New Testament). The best way to think of it is somewhere between cowardice and timidity: a lack of positive action due to a lack of confidence. Timothy is being challenged into positive action, but he is not being accused of cowardice. The remedy is not self-

Parental Influence

God blessed them, and God said to them, 'Be fruitful and multiply, and fill the earth and subdue it'" (Gen 1:28). With this mandate God called the first couple to marital partnership in parenting as well as in subduing and ruling over the rest of creation. Current research confirms the healthy results when fathers are actively involved in parenting their daughters and sons rather than leaving parenting to mothers. But the climb back to this original partnership has been slow and painful. The pain began when sin disrupted God's created order and resulted in the man's concentration on subduing the earth while the woman focused on child rearing, thus dividing what God had joined together. Biblical history records destructive examples of this division, such as Saul's castigation of Jonathan as a "son of a perverse and rebellious woman" (1 Sam 20:30) and David's noninvolvement in the training of his rebellious son Adonijah (1 Kings 1:6), possibly due to his polygamous family (children from polygamous families still report overwhelming noninvolvement of fathers). But Scripture also presents God's continuing call back to healthy partnership in parenting.

God models effective parenting with Israel and then with all who become his children through Christ. He affirms mothers by identifying himself with their special, universal role of breast feeding (Is 49:15) and comforting their children (Is 66:13), thus demonstrating the divine model for maternal care. By presenting himself as our Father while modeling nurturing characteristics normally labeled as maternal, however, God redefines the role of father in ways that challenge the cultural models undergirding paternal noninvolvement in parenting. God demonstrates his deep, unconditional love for his children by sacrificing Jesus to free us from sin's bondage, by holding us in his arms and blessing us, by protecting, feeding and providing for us, and by teaching us his ways. Thus he earns our trust before calling us to love and obey him. Christian parents are called to follow his example, with most Scriptures on parenting being addressed to parents together or to fathers rather than just to mothers.

God's modeling also blends varying parenting styles. Traditional cultures that value hierarchy and respect use frequent physical contact and holding of infants to comfort and quiet them. Cultures valuing individual achievement, however, rely more heavily on eye contact and talk to infants to comfort them but also to stimulate their learning of speech. Scripture portrays God using both styles in parenting his children. We receive comfort from his hands and are carried in his arms (Ps 37:24; Is 63:9) while he guides us with his eyes and his words (Ps 33:18; Is 30:21) and listens to us (1 Pet 3:12).

Scripture emphasizes the importance of communication between God and his children as he teaches us his ways. Biblically, respectful behavior includes talking, listening and asking questions rather than using silence to denote respect as in the traditional model. God's instructions in Deuteronomy 5—6 call for open communication in family relationships, with the parents being called to love and obey God and then to teach their children. Children's questions about God are to be answered rather than resisted (Deut 6:20-21). These instructions were given to people in the extremely difficult circumstances of moving as refugees from slavery to an unknown future. Rapid social change challenges parents now as it did then. The biblical model of family communication requires more time together than is acceptable in many traditional families. But for both types of families the rewards of following God's pattern meet our deepest longings that our children will become godly people blessed by our Lord. God's type of family communication helps to bridge the generation gap and also reduces the hypocrisy that so easily neutralizes parental training of children.

God also disciplines us to train us for godliness and to protect us from evil. He recognizes that our sinful natures cause us to resist his ways, so he warns us often and in great detail to control our disobedient impulses, to consider the consequences of our choices for ourselves and for our neighbors and to choose the future reward of heaven over the instant gratification of sin. He then calls us to train and discipline our children. This is hard work that is often emotionally uncomfortable, and our cultures can make it more difficult. Traditional cultures tend to view young children as incapable of being taught, or they share with some current child rearing theories the implicit assumption that children are innately good. Scripture, however, confirms that sin is innate in the hearts of children and leads them to resist parental training and discipline (Gen 8:21; Prov 22:15). Loving parents are therefore called to follow God's example in disciplining their children for training in godliness (Heb 12:7-11).

As we work toward God's ideal of family partnership in parental influence, Scripture encourages us to be faithful in our circumstances. Paul commends Timothy's faith, noting the godly influence of his mother and grandmother, who had taught him the Scriptures from his infancy (2 Tim 1:5; 3:15). Although Timothy's father is not mentioned, these women's parental influence on the young Timothy was effective and should encourage all women who lack a father's involvement in parenting. Paul calls Timothy his "dear son" (2 Tim 1:2) and exhibits a fatherly concern for the young man, giving us a worthy example. Within the Christian family, brothers and sisters can provide needed aspects of parental influence as we serve one another. God's model of parental partnership thus guides all Christians as we nurture our children, training them in godliness so that all of us will live as loving and obedient children of our heavenly Father.

KATHLEEN W. STUEBING

---

confidence—learning to feel better about yourself—but rather God-given power, love and self-discipline.

Furthermore, the second paragraph in this section (2 Tim 1:15-18) details examples of the two alternative behaviors. These verses are only the first of several sections mentioning people who deserted Paul as well as some few who stood by him. Phygelus and Hermogenes (2 Tim 1:15; neither mentioned elsewhere in the New Testament) are blameworthy in their turning away. But finding and identifying himself with the imprisoned Paul showed some bravery on Onesiphorus's part, bravery that Paul would like Timothy to emulate. Nor is the theme of battle and military far away. Timothy is to "share in suffering like a good soldier" (2 Tim 2:3).

There is the paradoxical contrast between our being called to act and our awareness that all our actions count for nothing—salvation is "not according to our works but according to . . . his grace" (2 Tim 1:9). Thus within the space of a few short sentences, Paul exhorts Timothy to "guard the good treasure" (2 Tim 1:14) having affirmed that "[God] is able to guard" (2 Tim 1:12). From that grace and in the knowledge of God's actions on our behalf, we, like Timothy, are to take our security, courage and boldness.

Our duty, like Timothy's, is to rekindle the gift we have inside us and guard the treasure we've been entrusted with, aware that God gives the gifts and does the preserving.

Endurance and Good Teaching (2 Tim 2:1-13)

What is called for is the strength to see the matter through, certain of the end. And that matter is the spread of the good news. From "guard the good treasure entrusted to you" (2 Tim 1:14), we may have been tempted to think in terms of preserving it safe and untouched by human hands. However, the teaching is not to be archived but passed on, entrusted "to faithful people who will be able to teach others" (2 Tim 2:2; the word translated "people" is the generic *anthrōpos* rather than a word that demands maleness).

The task involves sharing, and that may entail disappointing and hurtful relationships as well as those which bear fruit. The way is illustrated by three short metaphors (2 Tim 2:4-6). It is to be done single-mindedly, as a soldier must concentrate on one task; it is to be done according to the rules, as with the athlete; but it is to be done with the certainty of outcome, as with the farmer.

Paul has mentioned his imprisonment elsewhere in the book as well as in 2 Timothy 2:9. Being imprisoned, and especially being in chains, is extremely damaging to one's status: there is much shame. Here Paul begins to shift the focus, however. He knows he is not unique in this matter and, without making too much out of it, tries to set an example for Timothy.

The series of pairs (2 Tim 2:11-13) may be quotations from a hymn rather than Paul's composition. The initial two pairs take the form If we do X, Y will happen to us. The first concerns becoming a Christian: if we die with him, "we will also live with him" (2 Tim 2:11). The second is about living as a Christian, picking up on Paul's attitude of enduring: "if we endure, we will also reign with him" (2 Tim 2:12).

The next two take the form If we do X, he will do Y. These are about things going wrong: "if we deny him" and "if we lack faith" (2 Tim 2:12-13, author's translation). The second part of each pair is about God's response to these failures. "If we deny him, he will also deny us" (2 Tim 2:12) is the expected reciprocity and would be true not only of the Jewish-Christian God but also of gods and goddesses throughout the ancient world.

The final pairing requires more thought: "If we lack faith" is not coupled with the reciprocal "God will lack faith in us." Quite the opposite: "If we lack faith, he remains faithful—for he cannot deny himself" (2 Tim 2:13, author's translation). Lacking faith is not the same as refusing it. If we deny him, he will deny us, but if we lack faith in him, will he lack faith in us? No. Once within the relationship the dealings are not strictly reciprocal: we will be human and therefore fail, but he will be divine and constant. As is the case throughout this book, there is warning and comfort to be obtained here.

The Dangers of Wrangling over Words (2 Tim 2:14-26)

Continuing the theme of sharing, Paul tells Timothy he is not just to "remember" these things (2 Tim 2:8), he is to cause others to remember them as well. But genuine teaching and reminding are not a matter of quarreling.

If we are right to see Timothy's position as being analogous to today's female church leaders, then such passages as 2 Timothy 2:15 and 2 Timothy 2:24-25 may well apply across eras. Both passages contrast Timothy's role with the quarrels and squabbles around him. "Do your best to present yourself to God as one approved by him, a worker who has no need to be ashamed, rightly explaining the word of truth" (2 Tim 2:15) In the face of divisions and quarrels, it is important to have one's self-image linked to God's approval, not to anyone else's. Squabbles are not always to be answered with sharp and resounding argument; "the Lord's servant must not be quarrelsome but kindly to everyone, an apt teacher, patient, correcting opponents with gentleness" (2 Tim 2:24-25).

It is not merely quarrels over "stupid and senseless" things (2 Tim 2:23) that Timothy is to avoid. Others concern such fundamental matters as the doctrine of the resurrection. From Jesus' resurrection and the phenomena of Pentecost, it is easy to see how people could think that the resurrection had already taken place. Parts of Paul's writings could be so construed (see 2 Cor 5:17). As well as Hymenaeus and Philetus, some of the Corinthians and Thessalonians succumbed to this error (1 Cor 15; 2 Thess 2:2).

Even in such cases, it is up to God to grant repentance and a return to the truth. It is not Timothy's primary duty to debate, but rather to avoid profane chatter and controversies and instead to concentrate on righteousness, faith and love, and to be firm, patient and gentle.

2 Timothy 2:20 is a metaphor about different types of utensils, some of precious metals and others of wood or clay. The large house here stands for the church, and the different articles the different people or perhaps teachers. Paul explains what he means: one should strive to be numbered with the useful, special utensils (2 Tim 2:21). The metaphor should probably not be pushed further than that.

The Last Days: Unteachable Listeners and Deceitful Teachers (2 Tim 3:1-9)

Although Paul uses the phrase "in the last days" (2 Tim 3:1), for him that means the present, not twenty-something centuries in the future. The day of the Lord had not already come, but he did not think it was far away. Timothy is living in the last days and is told to avoid these people who err in the last days. Paul's description still applies: we and our culture are people of the last days—the messianic age.

A few specific sinful deeds are mentioned, but the list of vices is mostly about wrong attitudes. These people are repeatedly described as those who love, but they love themselves, money and pleasure rather than God. It is worth remembering that not all love is healthy. These people were "holding to the outward form of godliness but denying its power" (2 Tim 3:5). Timothy is told to have nothing to do with these people rather than to stand up to them.

The false teachers insinuate themselves into private homes (2 Tim 2:6; cf. 1 Tim 5:13; Tit 1:11) and ensnare women unsophisticated in theological discourse and gullible in their eagerness to learn (cf. 1 Tim 2:11as a countering measure). While some women are being victimized, others are assuming leadership roles in the heresy (1 Tim 4:7; 5:13-15; 2:12).

The victims are also portrayed in a negative light. These "silly women" are not only sinful and swayed by desires but also apparently incapable of learning, despite being instructed. If it is read out of context, the passage sounds offensive. How easy it is for some readers to think that a reference to "silly women" implies that women are prone to silliness, whereas a reference to "deceitful teachers" never seems to imply the analogous generalization. We need only to note that later in the letter Paul sends his greetings to Priscilla, who was not only instructed and arrived at the truth but also was able to instruct (Acts 18:26).

But the female victims are not the main focus of the passage. Timothy is to avoid people like these exploitative teachers because such teachers "will not make much progress" (2 Tim 3:9), but they may appear to make some progress. The caricature (2 Tim 3:6-7) is of one type of gullible person in Ephesus who might be susceptible to such evil teachers. The opening in 2 Timothy 2:6 makes clear that these women are not brought up as a topic in their own right but as the beginning of the explanation for the surprising advice to ignore them.

The naming of Jannes and Jambres, the Egyptian magicians (2 Tim 2:8, using the traditional names for Pharaoh's magicians, Ex 7:11; 9:11), coupled with the reputation of Ephesus for interest in magic (Acts 19:19), has led some scholars to speculate that the description "are always being instructed and can never arrive at . . . the truth" refers to these people's cravings for religious and occult novelties. Such people might fall victim to these false teachers, but not many others and not for long.

Paul's Example and Timothy's Charge (2 Tim 3:10—4:8)

This extended section starts and ends with Paul's example, but the middle contains imperatives for Timothy. As well as the formal-sounding charge "In the presence of God and of Christ Jesus . . . I solemnly urge you" (2 Tim 4:1), there is a short repeated phrase, "as for you" (2 Tim 3:14, 4:5). A better translation might be "You, on the other hand," indicating the contrast with the preceding material. The contrast is between those whose folly will be found out by their intended students and Paul's teaching of and example to Timothy.

It is likely that Paul mentions "Antioch, Iconium and Lystra" (2 Tim 3:11; cf. Acts 13-14) because Timothy is from Lystra. It is a reference to the beginnings of their history. This shows that Paul is not complaining but has Timothy's experiences and instruction in focus.

Good teaching is one obvious remedy for bad teaching. The famous verse about the inspiration and usefulness of Scripture (2 Tim 3:16) represents another strong antidote. Paul has in mind what we think of as the Old Testament (see 1 Tim 5:18; 2 Pet 3:15-16 for hints, however, of a possible authority for Christian teaching). In an era making the transition from oral-based culture to a literary one, hearing the living witness of the apostles was reckoned as even more special than having their exploits or thoughts on paper. If he could have had his way, he'd have visited, not written, and we'd have had a shorter New Testament.

Aware that he has finished his race, Paul reminds Timothy of the lasting influence of Scripture. If only he knew that his efforts (although not merely his) on behalf of Timothy would become Scripture and a comfort and challenge to generations of people!

In 2 Timothy 4:1, Paul has invoked an official-sounding formula. This is not one friend asking a favor of another but a matter of the utmost gravity. The duty commanded is all-encompassing: proclamation, persistence, patience and not only in bearing witness but also the convincing and rebuking we saw omitted from 2 Timothy 2:3.

A reminder about the distressing last days is followed by another exhortation. This is meant not only to reiterate the formal urging of 2 Timothy 4:2 but also to parallel Paul's career. It looks very much as though Paul is metaphorically passing on the torch to Timothy. This impression is confirmed by final verses of this section. Paul knows that he is being "poured out" (a metaphor he also used in his first imprisonment, Phil 2:17) and that his "time has come" (2 Tim 4:6). This section is not the grumbling of an old man but is constructed with Timothy in mind. For the end of Paul's race includes the rewards "which the Lord, the righteous judge, will give me on that day." It is Timothy's perseverance that Paul is trying to influence, as is clear from the ending of the sentence: "and not only to me" (2 Tim 4:8). This is a good model for our communication: talking, even talking about ourselves, can be other-directed as well.

Final Greetings, Personal Details and Logistics (2 Tim 4:9-22)

The letter turns to personal greetings, as do the ends of many of Paul's letters. Titus is the same man to whom the epistle of Titus was written. Mark and Luke are the Gospel authors. Crescens is otherwise unknown to us, but Demas is mentioned in two other passages (Col 4:14; Philem 24), always alongside Luke. His desertion is disappointing to Paul, but it may be a temporary setback; Paul also once regarded Mark as a deserter (Acts 15:37-38).

Tychicus's name is found in a few of the letters, notably Ephesians, where Paul called him "a dear brother and a faithful minister in the Lord" (Eph 6:21, cf. Col 4:7). Carpus is unknown otherwise, but Alexander the coppersmith is most likely the Alexander of 1 Timothy 1:20 (but not Acts 19:33-34).

The books and parchments that Paul requests are likely to have been copies of the Old Testament Scriptures or Paul's notes and perhaps even his copies of some letters.

Before the next round of personal names, Paul talks about his "first defense." This may be about a preliminary hearing during the present imprisonment or more likely the first of his Roman imprisonments (cf. Acts 28). This is because of the "lion's mouth" from which he was delivered (2 Tim 4:17). The phrase need not refer to anything specific; this was a common metaphor for danger but does not fit a preliminary trial verdict that leaves him in prison. Paul is most likely reminding Timothy (and himself) that he's been in this kind of situation before: last time everyone deserted him; this time there will be a handful around him, including, it is to be hoped, Timothy.

The final list of names again includes a

mixture of the familiar and unknown. The name Prisca is the name of which Priscilla is the diminutive form. She and her husband are mentioned several times in the New Testament, notably Romans 16:3-4. Neither Onesiphorus nor his household appear outside of 2 Timothy, although they have been mentioned in 2 Timothy 1:15-18. Erastus is also mentioned in Romans 16:23 and Acts 19:22, whereas Trophimus features in only Acts (Acts 20:4; 21:29). Of Eubulus, Pudens, Linus and Claudia little else is known; they are likely to have been local Christians.

The letter concludes with a final benediction. CONRAD GEMPF

TITUS

Introduction

The letter to Titus has been described as a preliminary draft of 1 Timothy. It addresses the same concerns and situations, uses the same vocabulary and adopts a similar tone. Like 1-2 Timothy, its dominant theme is combating the behavior and doctrines of false teachers. While 1 Timothy specifies the proper conduct for a church already established, Titus differs in giving instructions for installing officers in one or more congregations.

Authorship and date have been vigorously debated, as have been the identity and location of the person addressed. The letter bears the name of the apostle Paul and is addressed to Titus in Crete. Lively speculation notwithstanding, we are better served to study the letter on its own terms (*see* introduction to 1 Timothy).

In the distant past Crete had afforded women a high social position. Wall paintings show richly adorned women participating equally with men in diverse areas of life, including athletic, social and cultic activities. Many of the earliest religious representations are those of female deities. Important shrines of archaic goddesses still attracted the devotion of many in the New Testament period.

The Cretans had a proprietary attitude toward many forms of religious expression practiced throughout the Mediterranean world. On Crete, tradition said, the gods of the Greeks had their origin and from there their cults had spread. Even the Ephesian goddess Artemis was called "the Cretan lady of Ephesus."

On a Cretan mountain Zeus, king of the gods, and Hera his wife were said to have been born. There were still celebrations in the cave identified as their birthplace, and tourists visited the burial site of Zeus. Mystery rites were performed openly that were elsewhere conducted in secret.

The island was rich in myths, often based in earlier ritual. Cretan tales abounded of Zeus's abduction of Europa, of Minos and the minotaur, of Daedalus, Ariadne and the earth mother's sacred marriage with Iason to conceive Plutus, god of wealth.

The Cretans' forebears had long before dominated the Mediterranean world, and remnants of their civilization were still visible in the landscape. Athenians extolled as their greatest king, Theseus, who freed them from vassaldom to Crete. Despite the passage of many centuries, mainlanders still harbored feelings of hostility toward the denizens of the island.

The presence of Jewish communities in Crete is well attested from the first century B.C. until the fifth century A.D. Josephus, who was married to a Cretan Jewess, implies that they were easily misled (*Antiquities* 17.327; *Jewish Wars* 2.103).

Religious currents, pagan and Jewish, rendered Crete a particular challenge to the early church. The deviant doctrines addressed in the letter have marked similarities to those described in 1-2 Timothy. Based especially on the reference of 1 Timothy 6:20 to "what is falsely called knowledge," the heresy is often thought to lean toward an early strand of Gnosticism. Like the Cretans, Gnostics claimed a deeper knowledge of religious realities than was afforded to others. Both groups shared a predilection for powerful female figures and for stories of divine beginnings.

Outline

1:1-16	Organizing to Meet the Opposition
2:1-15	Applying Sound Doctrine to the Household of God
3:1-15	Advice for Christian Living

Commentary

Organizing to Meet the Opposition (Tit 1)

Elsewhere in the New Testament Titus is identified as a close Greek associate of Paul (Gal 2:1-3) who made a missionary trip to Dalmatia (2 Tim 4:10) and demonstrated administrative skills in the service of the Corinthian congregation (2 Cor 2:13; 7:6-16; 8:6, 16-23; 12:18). Church difficulties required Titus to remain in Crete, just as Timothy had been asked to remain at Ephesus (1 Tim 1:3-4). He was to resolve problems by appointing elders capable of overseeing churches and repudiating error.

The stipulation that an elder must be the husband of only one wife (Tit 1:6) may address Jewish polygamy. Even middle-class Jews could legitimately marry more than one nondivorced woman, a practice that continued until it was prohibited under the code of Justinian. The intention of the specification appears not to be the exclusion of women or of unmarried men but rather the restriction of a marital pattern that was unacceptable in a church including Jews and Gentiles.

Elders must be careful to create peace and harmony in their homes. A prerequisite is that the elders' children should not be "rebellious," the adjectival opposite of the verb *submit.* The negative implies disorderly conduct and a failure to fulfill one's responsibilities.

In Titus 1:7 the designation changes from "elder" *(presbyteros)* to "bishop" *(episkopos),* the terms at this stage apparently being synonymous. An elder must not be arrogant, disposed to anger or alcohol, and must not be a batterer. The term translated "violent" means literally "one who beats or rains blows on another." The instruction is repeated in 1 Timothy 3:3; elders and bishops must abstain from all violence, whether in the home or in the broader society.

Christian leaders must first understand Christian truth in order both to instruct the faithful and to rebuke opponents. A major duty is countering heresy as it appears in the Cretan congregations.

The troublemakers are described as "rebellious," just as earlier Titus was urged not to choose elders with rebellious children. They are full of empty chatter and an erring mindset—two characteristics of incipient Gnosticism. Here, however, those subscribing to a false doctrine are "especially those of the circumcision," a clear indication that they were Jews or had at least imbibed Jewish teaching.

Titus is to silence those who brought disruptive and deviant doctrine (cf. 1 Tim 1:3-4, 20; 2:12). Entire households are being led astray, a strong indicator of the involvement of women. In 2 Timothy 3:6-7 women are major targets in the heretics' invasion of private homes. This was a known strategy of several cults, most notably among the priests of Cybele, who gained female adherents by insinuating themselves into the domestic sphere (Menander, frag. 202). As the younger widows of Ephesus went from house to house "saying what they should not" (1 Tim 5:13), here the opponents are "teaching for sordid gain what it is not right to teach" (Tit 1:11). The Cretans were reputed to be the only people who did not consider dishonest gain a disgrace (Polybius *Histories* 6.46). Juvenal makes note of women who paid handsome-

Menopause

Mention of menopause in the Bible is usually in connection with the inability to bear children. Sarah's laughter at the announcement that she will bear a son in her old age is provoked by the fact that she "had stopped having a woman's periods" (Gen 18:11, Anchor Bible). The miracle of Sarah's conception is echoed in Elizabeth's pregnancy, which is offered to Mary as a sign of God's ability to initiate Mary's miraculous pregnancy: "Your relative Elizabeth in her old age has also conceived a son" (Lk 1:36).

In the stories of Sarah and Elizabeth, their postmenopausal state is seen as a category of barrenness, or inability to bear a child. When Sarah asks, "Withered as I am, am I still to know enjoyment?" (Gen 18:15, Anchor Bible) there is also the intimation that there has been the cessation of pleasurable sexual activity.

In the story of Ruth, Naomi is more questionably menopausal. Her address to her daughters-in-law suggests an improbable scenario: "Even if I thought there was hope for me, even if I should have a husband tonight and bear sons, would you then wait until they were grown?" (Ruth 1:12-13). Her deferral of her kinswoman's claim to marriage to Boaz suggests that she is at least perimenopausal; she is rewarded for her generosity of spirit when she vicariously bears a child through Ruth.

Given the restrictions the levitical law placed on women (menstruation was originally a time of ritual uncleanness), menopause would have signaled an era of enlarged personal freedoms for older women within the worshiping community. Anna "never left the temple but worshiped there with fasting and prayer night and day" (Lk 2:37).

In the New Testament, "older women," probably post- or perimenopausal, are given a specific role in teaching younger women in the church (Tit 2:3). There is also an ethic of care for senior widows, the church perpetuating the dying Christ's concern for the care of his mother in caring for widowed, postmenopausal women.

In the New Testament, interest in women's reproductive capacity is replaced with an interest in their spiritual fruitfulness. Priscilla teaches in her home without any hint given of her age; since no children are mentioned, it might be possible that Priscilla is either postmenopausal or, in Old Testament terminology, barren. Yet she is fruitful in her ministry. Under the new covenant, women are to be valued not for their reproductive capacity but for their ability to "bear fruit in every good work" (Col 1:10).

Contemporary secular authors have written about menopause and postmenopause as a time when women are no longer defined societally by their sexual attractiveness and can be valued for other attributes. Christian women find their worth throughout their lives in the knowledge that they have been created lovingly and are embraced by God's love from conception to death. They can see menopause as marking the commencement of a new season of maturity and serenity and be secure in the promise, "The righteous flourish like the palm tree. . . . In old age they still produce fruit; they are always green and full of sap, showing that the LORD is upright; he is my rock" (Ps 92:12, 14-15).

Bibliography

E. A. Speiser, *Genesis*, Anchor Bible 1 (Garden City, NY: Doubleday, 1964); G. Greer, *The Change* (New York: Fawcett Columbine, 1991) esp. 378-87; S. M. McKinlay and J. B. McKinlay, "The Impact of Menopause and Social Factors on Health," in *Menopause*, ed. C. B. Hammond et al. (New York: Alan R. Liss, 1989) 137-62.

MAXINE HANCOCK

---

ly for the visits of religious charlatans (*Satire* 6).

The couplet describing Cretans derives from an oracle of the seventh-century B.C. sage Epimenides (Tit 1:12). Though a native of Crete, he denounced certain aspects of his society. The original hexameter was quoted extensively in antiquity, principally to repudiate the Cretan insistence that Zeus was not only dead but also lay buried on their island—his tomb served as a tourist attraction. The theological implications of the god's demise struck at the heart of Greek religion and aroused widespread outrage. The continued propensity to distort established dogma posed a threat to the Christian community.

The theme of error springing from Judaism is reintroduced, not this time as bondage to the law but rather as "paying attention to Jewish myths" (Tit 1:14). These myths can scarcely be the stories from the biblical canon, a tradition for which the writer has the profoundest respect, but later Gnosticism was particularly adept at subverting the early stories of Genesis as a basis of its theology. Here Gnostic elements, including myth, are present but have not coalesced into the theological formulations that would follow.

"Myths" are part of the false doctrine in 1 Timothy, where they are called "old wives' tales" (1 Tim 4:7; cf. 1 Tim 1:4). The tale of Cupid and Psyche, with its profound psychological insight, is said to be an *anilis fibula*, "the tale of an old woman." Women were often the storytellers of antiquity, and ancient authors regarded some of their renditions as scurrilous because of the unfavorable light in which they cast the gods. Retelling brought revision and often a very different perspective from that of the original author. 1 Timothy 2:12-14 may represent an effort to control such a deviation and to reclaim the storytelling women to the sound teaching of the canonical Scriptures.

Applying Sound Doctrine to the Household of God (Tit 2)

The instructions that follow apply to individual households and to various constituencies within the household of the church. The concepts would be very close for those who met in house churches.

Titus is to teach elders to be "temperate, serious, prudent, and sound in faith, in love, and in endurance" (Tit 2:2). An elder is sometimes understood to be an "older" or "mature man" in the congregation (cf. NRSV), but the letter emphasizes throughout the preparation of officers to strengthen the church during a time of storm.

If *presbytēs* is best understood as a church officer, then the term *presbytis* is best understood not simply as an "old woman" but as a "female presbyter" (cf. Lampe, *A Patristic Greek Lexicon*, s.v., B.2). These women must be "reverent" (lit. "worthy of the priesthood"), again an indication that they must be fit for special function within the church. The ensuing qualification list is comparable to that for elders and bishops. Just as all elders should counter opposition with sound teaching, female elders must disseminate good doctrine.

Then follows a touching description of the mentoring of young women by those who have learned much from life. Elizabeth gave such mentoring to Mary as she anticipated a birth that would not be understood. Naomi mentored Ruth as she entered an alien society and found her way through social and economic distress to the blessings of a loving marriage and children.

Young wives reared in a pagan background may well have lacked family support as they struggled to adjust to marriage, care for children and cope with household management. Mature women in positions of Christian leadership could help them and inculcate moral qualities as well. They could teach the temperate use of alcohol, for its abuse was rampant among frustrated pagan women. Chastity was an important virtue in a world in which women were thought not to have a developed conscience and to be incurably lustful. The submissiveness here indicates orderly and responsible conduct toward their husbands. If these young women were leaders in the church, the obligation to fulfill all domestic duties would be the more necessary "so that the Word of God may not be discredited" (Tit 2:5).

"Young man" and "young/er men" are sometimes designations for a deacon or junior official (Elliott; Verner, 172-73; cf. Acts 5:6, 10). If the old and young men are official church leaders, it is likely that the old and young women are as well, whose conduct should be worthy of the priesthood and who teach what is good. Titus appears to be a young officer like Timothy, called to be a model to the congregation (1 Tim 4:12; 5:1; cf. Tit 2:15).

Detractors alleged that Christianity appealed principally to slaves, women and children. This being so, church leaders arose from within their ranks, and at least one pope was a former slave. Slaves composed part of the Roman *familia* and sometimes were entrusted with positions of financial, political and administrative importance. As Christians they should continue to show respect, rather than opposition, even if vested with greater churchly responsibility than their earthly masters. The honesty of Christian slaves and their eagerness to please should be powerful ornaments for the gospel.

Three times in this pericope appropriate behavior is enjoined to demonstrate the legitimacy of the gospel. Titus 2:5 and 2:8 seek to silence opposition, but only in reference to slaves is there a positive emphasis on evangelism.

Advice for Christian Living (Tit 3)

Exemplary conduct, responsible citizenship and peaceableness are expected of all believers. The strongest apologetic for the Christian faith is the constructive and Christlike attitude of its adherents.

The description of the false teachers is suggestive of later Gnosticizing traditions. Gnostics often constructed elaborate genealogies of celestial beings (cf. 1 Tim 1:4), engaged in specious arguments, debated precepts of Jewish law and tore at the fabric of revealed scriptural truth.

After appropriate and conscientious efforts at their reconstruction, it is best to let "anyone who causes divisions" (Tit 3:10; *hairetikos,* the Greek word from which we get the word *heretic*) go his or her way.

The letter closes with instructions for the deployment of Paul's companions. All of them are to seek to excel in good works so that their labors may not be fruitless. The church may be beset by error, but there are still those who remain faithful and seek to bring truth and righteousness to troubled congregations in Crete.

Bibliography. J. H. Elliott, "Ministry and Church Order in the New Testament: A Traditio-Historical Analysis," *Catholic Biblical Quarterly* 32 (1970) 367-91; D. C. Verner, *The Household of God: The Social World of the Pastoral Epistles* (Society for Biblical Literature Dissertation Series 71; Chico, CA: Scholars Press, 1983).

CATHERINE CLARK KROEGER

PHILEMON

Introduction

The letter to Philemon is the shortest and most personal of the thirteen epistles attributed to Paul, and its authorship is undisputed. Differing opinions exist, however, regarding the location of sender and recipient.

The traditional view is that Paul, imprisoned in Rome, has found solace in the ministrations of Onesimus, whom he has led to faith in Christ. The apostle faces an ethical dilemma: although he finds Onesimus helpful, he recognizes that Philemon, as master of the slave, has a prior claim on him. The honorable course is to reveal the circumstances and to throw himself and Onesimus on the kindness of the letter's recipients.

Paul wrote his letter in a society dependent on slavery. It was one part of a larger patriarchal system in which the basic unit was the household. Within the Hellenistic household there were three primary sets of relationships: master-slave, husband-wife and father-child. Their proper management had, since the time of Aristotle (*Politics* 1.2.1-14a; 1.5.1-2), been considered essential to the order of society. In contemporary thought, the quality of life in a household depended on the master. In Christian tradition, however, the wife was responsible for managing the household (1 Tim 5:14; cf. Prov 31:15-21).

Outline

1-3	Salutation and Greetings
4-7	Prayer
8-22	Body of Letter
23-25	Conclusion

Commentary

Salutation and Greeting (Philem 1-3)

The letter's opening uses the customary formula for ancient letters: sender to recipient, followed by greetings. Paul is the author, and his associate Timothy is included. The letter is addressed to Philemon, Apphia, Archippus and the church that meets in Philemon's house. The greetings are extended to the house church, for the content is a personal matter but also one intended for the congregation.

If Apphia is the wife of Philemon and Archippus the son, then the letter is a rather graceful effort to intrude into the life of a family whose home is the meeting place for a local church and a hospitality center for traveling missionaries. The letter demonstrates considerable effort in its address to a delicate situation. The matter is further complicated because Onesimus bears the missive.

Prayer (Philem 4-7)

This section of ancient letters frequently

contained praise intended to focus attention on the recipient and to secure a favorable response. Paul thanks God for Philemon's love and faith, which will be challenged if he is to show the grace of Christ to a sinner who has now become a saint.

The apostle has known refreshment in Philemon's home. The word *splanchna* ("hearts," NRSV) could refer to any of the affections or internal organs, including the womb. The term reappears when Onesimus is described as Paul's *splanchna* and Philemon is asked to "refresh my heart *(splanchna)* in Christ" (Philem 20). The recurrence is intentional, drawing Onesimus into the family circle of hospitality and acceptance.

Body of the Letter (Philem 8-22)

Paul bases his appeal on love rather than insisting on what is appropriate. Using feminine imagery, he introduces Onesimus as the son whom he has "birthed in bonds" (lit. Philem 10).

Paul uses slave terminology to assert that Onesimus is different now than in the past. Onesimus's name, which means "useful," becomes part of a word play employing standard terms for bad slaves ("useless," *achrēston*) and for good slaves ("useful," *euchrēston*). He states that he is not merely returning a useful slave to his master but one whose services Paul covets.

Whether Onesimus had been Philemon's slave or a disaffected brother, as Allen Callahan suggests, he is now a brother "in the flesh and in the Lord" (Philem 16). The family is asked to receive a former recalcitrant as one of its own.

The reintroduction of Onesimus will disrupt the balance of established relationships, probably with particular implications for Apphia. Hers would have been the

Ancient & Modern Slavery

The Hebrews, whose enslavement and deliverance is chronicled in the book of Exodus, endured a lengthy bondage in Egypt. The biblical narrative emphasizes Yahweh's concern for their plight and his salvific work in delivering them. Thereafter the Israelites were repeatedly enjoined to remember their own servitude and to deal with slaves compassionately (Deut 15:12-18).

Most slaves were taken as prisoners of war (cf. Deut 21:10). Individuals in debt or facing starvation might also sell themselves or their children into slavery to overcome their plight. Though Hebrews could own and bequeath foreign slaves, they were prohibited from owning fellow Hebrews as slaves (Lev 25:39-46). Fellow Hebrews were to be treated as hired servants and released after six years (Deut 15:12).

Slavery under the Romans sometimes offered prospects for education, a trade, career advancement and promotion to a responsible position. For example, Felix, the Roman procurator before whom Paul was tried (Acts 24:1-27), was a freed slave. Upon manumission (usually after a period of seven to twenty-one years), the freed person received Roman citizenship, the protection and advocacy of the former owner, and a means of earning a living.

By the time of the New Testament, there were restrictions governing when and how an owner might free his slaves. Rome was glutted with freed persons who had to compete against cheap slave labor, and it was they who had to be mollified with bread and games. A slave in uncertain situations might be better off not to seek emancipation. The early church was cautioned not to buy freedom for slaves but to encourage them to buy their own, on the theory that slaves who could earn enough to purchase their freedom could also provide for their own support thereafter.

Both male and female slaves were full recipients of the Holy Spirit (Acts 2:18), and the New Testament documents the presence and ministry of slaves (Mt 26:69-72; Mk 14:66-69; Lk 22:56-57; Jn 18:16-17; Acts 12:13-17). They are also mentioned in non-biblical writings as influential leaders in the church. At least one pope was a former slave, as was the author of the *Shepherd of Hermas*.

While Aristotle in previous centuries had denied the full humanity of slaves, the New Testament Scriptures insisted on their full equality. Other early Christian writings also called for righteous treatment of slaves and proper respect for their spiritual lives.

Slavery for the most part disappeared in Europe itself, but African slavery played a major role in the early development of the Americas and in the growth of commercial capitalism. It evolved into more than an economic institution: it represented the ultimate form of dehumanization. Had the virulent, more cruel nature which characterized modern slavery been prevalent in ancient times, the New Testament writers might well have taken a stronger stance against it.

Bibliography

S. S. Bartchy, *Mallon Chrēsai: First-Century Slavery and the Interpretation of 1 Corinthians 7:21*, SBL Dissertation Series (Missoula, MT: Scholars Press, 1973); D. B. Martin, *Slavery as Salvation: The Metaphor of Slavery in Pauline Christianity* (New Haven: Yale University Press, 1990).

BEVERLY E. MITCHELL AND CATHERINE CLARK KROEGER

---

responsibility to manage a household stretched by the inclusion of a worshiping community. Now she is asked to receive back a disruptive member of the family, for slaves were considered part of the Roman *familia*.

The relationship between mistress and household slaves was frequently a close one; literary evidence reveals that much of a slave's treatment lay in the hands of the mistress. In the case of Onesimus, a breach of trust must be overcome, though Paul's words may imply that there has been ill treatment on both sides. Onesimus's malfeasance has betrayed the administration of an orderly household, and wounds remain. These wrongs and injuries Paul asks to have charged to him.

Philemon owes his life to Paul, and Paul asks to have Onesimus received as himself. The guest room that is to be prepared reminds the family of the hospitality gladly afforded the apostle and now requested for Onesimus. He expresses a wish—that he might find profit from Philemon in the Lord. The term comes from the same stem as does the name Onesimus, again a subtle form of encouragement to do the right thing in a difficult circumstance. Slave and master must be useful in Christ's service. Even if Onesimus is returned to minister to Paul, he will remain "forever" (Philem 15) part of Philemon's family. Freed slaves continued to have a familial relationship and might derive from the former owner use of the family name, Roman citizenship, support in legal matters and bonds of affection.

Portrait of husband and wife inside Pompeian house. (Philemon)

Conclusion (Philem 23-25)

The letter closes with greetings from Paul's associates, including his companion Luke and two individuals with whom relationships were not always harmonious: Demas

(2 Tim 4:10) and Mark (Acts 15:37-39). Onesimus appears to have continued in ministry, for he was sent with Tychicus to the Colossians as an emissary and fellow citizen (Col 4:9).

If Onesimus was a slave, then we see at work a policy of openness and mutuality in reestablishing a relationship. The transformation of his character and life demands that he be received on equal footing, empowered to serve in the bonds of the gospel. His new identity has made him a full person, worthy of respect and of acceptance in the body of Christ.

Bibliography. A. D. Callahan, *Embassy of Onesimus: The Letter of Paul to Philemon* (Valley Forge, PA: Trinity Press International, 1997); L. A. Lewis, "An African American Appraisal of the Philemon-Paul-Onesimus Triangle," in *Stony the Road We Trod: African American Biblical Interpretation,* ed. C. H. Felder (Minneapolis: Fortress, 1991) 232-46; E. Lohse, *Colossians and Philemon: A Commentary on the Epistles to the Colossians and to Philemon,* trans. W. R. Poehlmann and R. J. Karris, Hermeneia, ed. H. Koester (Philadelphia: Fortress, 1971).

KRISTEN PLINKE BENTLEY

Priscilla, the Author of Hebrews

Discussion of the authorship of Hebrews can no longer be quelled by Origen's remark that God alone knows who wrote Hebrews. Clues are plentiful supporting a feminine author in general and Priscilla in particular (but *see* introduction to Hebrews).

Priscilla, like the author, was of Paul's intimate circle. Comparable patterns of thought and use of Scripture connect Pauline writings with Hebrews despite their divergent theology.

Sharing Paul's evangelistic work in a capacity of trust and responsibility (Acts 18:19), Priscilla could credibly have been traveling with Timothy (Heb 13:23). She was a colleague of both. The author of Hebrews, hoping to travel with Timothy but unwilling to delay the trip on his account, was at least on the same level as Timothy.

Internal evidence connecting the epistle with Rome includes the references to church leaders (Heb 13:7, 17, 24), the salutation "those from Italy" (Heb 13:24) and affinity with the Roman liturgy. In Rome Hebrews was known, circulated and esteemed. We have several manuscripts naming Rome or Italy as the place of origin. Priscilla was leader of a house church in Rome. Archaeological discoveries, reinforcing ancient church tradition, identify her with a noble Roman family (Spence-Jones). As a daughter of the nobility, she was trained in rhetoric, philosophy and oratory.

Priscilla had a ministry at Ephesus, destination of the epistle, judging from information such as the spiritual condition of that church, its history and theological concerns. Ephesus was the logical destination of Timothy's homecoming and the author's.

A match for his learning and eloquence, Priscilla took the lead in teaching Apollos (Chrysostom named her the sole tutor). Following her detailed instruction, Apollos was able to present, from Scripture, the messiahship of Jesus—a theme predominant in Hebrews.

Yet another clue links Priscilla with Hebrews. When Apollos came to Priscilla, his lack of knowledge was stated in terms of knowing only the baptism of John (Acts 18:25). Priscilla was certain to have taught him the difference between John's baptism and Christian baptism. The author of Hebrews gave instruction in "baptisms" (see Attridge, 164).

Priscilla is often dismissed by citing a "masculine" participle, *diegoumenon* ("telling"), in Hebrews 11:32. Note, however, that here, in the accusative case, masculine and neuter are identical in form. Since the participle is an adjective, modifying a person in general despite gender, the neuter would have been intended, in compliance with classical usage (Blass and Debrunner, 72-73, 76-77; cf. Hoppin, 49-52). A feminine voice is heard throughout the epistle. We find the parent-child relationship portrayed with tenderness and poignancy, interest in education, delineation of the compassion of Christ and keen compassion *for* Christ. A feminine voice is heard in the naming of women as models of faith, with direct and indirect allusions to many others. The inexplicable loss of the author's name so early in the letter's history bears mute testimony to female authorship.

Bibliography

H. W. Attridge, *The Epistle to the Hebrews* (Philadelphia: Fortress, 1989); F. Blass and A. Debrunner, *A Greek Grammar of the New Testament and Other Early Christian Literature* (Chicago and London: Univ. of Chicago Press, 1961); R. Hoppin, *Priscilla's Letter: Finding the Author of the Epistle to the Hebrews* (Fort Bragg, CA: Lost Coast Press, 2000); F. M. Schiele, "Harnack's 'Probabilia' Concerning the Address and Author of the Epistle to the Hebrews," *American Journal of Theology* (1905) 290-308; H. D. M. Spence-Jones, *The Early Christians in Rome* (London: Methuen, 1910); M. A. R. Tuker, "The Gospel According to Prisca," *Nineteenth Century* 73 (1913) 81-98.

RUTH HOPPIN

HEBREWS

Introduction

Hebrews represents a carefully composed, formal writing whose oratorical style suggests a tract or written sermon. Its ending suggests a letter even though it lacks the usual opening salutation. The author described the work as a "word of exhortation" (Heb 13:22), rooting this urgent sermon-letter in life and addressing believers who discovered that adverse circumstances over which they exercised no control could affect them. Hebrews reflects the writer's sensitive pastoral response to people in danger of relinquishing their Christian commitment. Wanting to strengthen the hearers so that they could stand firm in their faith, the author issued five warnings dealing with the danger of neglecting the salvation in Christ as a result of unbelief, apostasy or compromise.

Hebrews is anonymous, and any attribution of authorship must remain speculative. Its Greek language and style have high literary qualities, indicating some degree of education, especially in the art of rhetoric. This and other internal evidence suggest that the writer was a highly educated, Hellenistic, Jewish Christian who possessed a pastor's heart. Scholars have suggested Paul, Barnabas, Luke, Apollos, Priscilla and others as the author (*see* Priscilla, the Author of Hebrews). Why do some scholars believe Priscilla wrote this book, when no other New Testament book is attributed to a woman? Priscilla, like the writer of Hebrews, belonged to Paul's immediate circle and enjoyed Timothy as a colleague. She did not know Jesus from direct experience but received his teachings from others. Hebrews also expresses a marked sympathy for women (Heb 11:11, 31, 35). Its account of Sarah emphasizes her faith as she faced the challenges of a child in her old age (Heb 11:11). In contrast, the account in Genesis refers to her laughter of unbelief at the promise of a son (Gen 18:11-15). Some scholars have suggested a team effort by Priscilla and her husband, Aquila, since the author(s) moved easily from a first person singular to a first person plural. Also, the writing team or person knew about the persecution of believers in Rome. They served as leaders in the community addressed by the letter, knowing well its members' lack of spiritual maturity. Knowledgeable in Jewish Scriptures, they wrote of the tabernacle ritual but gave no hint of familiarity with temple procedure. The New Testament does not record Priscilla and Aquila as traveling to Jerusalem. If Priscilla wrote Hebrews or served as its primary writer, scribes may have tended to suppress this fact due to their prejudice against women.

The Greek title, "To the Hebrews," appeared in some early manuscripts but not necessarily in the original text. The frequent appeals to the Old Testament, the assumption that the readers knew Jewish ritual and the warnings against returning to Judaism suggest the author wrote to Jewish Christians. These believers had endured public abuse, imprisonment and the looting of their property, but they had not yet been called on to die for their faith. They hesitated to separate themselves decisively from Judaism, which enjoyed the protection of Roman law, because total commitment to the Christian way would bring risks. Instead of pressing ahead, they were inclined to come to a full stop in their spiritual progress, if not to slip back to a stage they had left. The epistle also implies the recipients were Hellenistic. All of the extensive Old Testament quotations follow the Septuagint, the Greek translation of the Hebrew Scriptures. Their knowledge of Israel's sacrificial ritual seems derived from their reading of the Old Testament and not from firsthand contact with the temple services. The words "you ought to be teachers" (Heb 5:12) may indicate the author addressed a group within a church rather than the whole fellowship. The author of Hebrews probably addressed comparatively well-educated Jewish Christians somewhere in the Mediterranean dispersion.

Clement of Rome quoted Hebrews authoritatively in A.D. 95. Consequently any date between 60 and 95 for its composition is possible. Most evidence points to a time of writing prior to 70. The description of the persecution endured (Heb 10:32-34) points to that under the emperor Claudius. The persecution predicted (Heb 12:4) implies the intensity of persecution during the reign of Nero in 64. Nor does the epistle mention the destruction of the temple in 70, an event of great importance to Jewish Christians. The writer's imminent expectation of the parousia (Heb 10:25, 36-39) and the reference to Timothy's release from prison (Heb 13:23) also point to a relatively early date.

During this period Christians in Rome and probably in other cities appear to have met as groups in house churches. Even though significant numbers of Gentiles had embraced Christianity, some groups continued to reflect their Jewish background. The remains of buildings of several stories dating to the second and third centuries indicate what characterized early house churches in Rome. Shops apparently occupied the ground floors, while prosperous families lived in the upper levels. For example, the house of Priscilla and Aquila must have served as a workshop, residence and meeting place (Rom 16:3-5). The multiplicity of house churches throughout large cities suggests why the early church had problems with diversity, disunity and a tendency toward independence. Hebrews gives evidence of tension between the readers and those currently recognized as leaders. The writer wanted to bring the two groups together and did not want the members of the house church to regard themselves as an autonomous fellowship or to isolate themselves from other household groups. These Jewish Christians were also experiencing social and physical persecution from Jews and Gentiles, tempting them to return to the Jewish community. The writer reminded them of the basis of their faith, Jesus Christ.

Hebrews represents a practical response to an urgent situation. The readers stood on the verge of taking action that would deny the Christian faith. Indeed, some had already defected from their number. Among those who remained, some had lost confidence in the effectiveness of their convictions. They might have questioned whether the past event of Jesus' sacrificial death had continuing efficacy. They had regressed from the bold commitment they had shown shortly after becoming believers when they had endured public abuse, imprisonment and loss of property. Attraction to traditions conflicting with the word of God caused unresolved tension between the community and its leaders. The writer proposed to stop this apostasy to Judaism, or perhaps a kind of heretical, gnosticizing Judaism influenced by Hellenistic ideas, by presenting the sufficiency and superiority of Christ. Christianity alone offered superior benefits and promises. All other religions lacked hope, failed to lead to a deeper knowledge of God and could not provide the power for holy living. Whether the delay of the parousia, social ostracism and impending persecution, neglect of fellowship, listening to heretical teachers, a general fading of enthusiasm or erosion of confidence caused the problems, the author wrote to warn readers against apostasy and to bring them back into the community of the faithful.

Outline

1:1—4:13	The Superiority of Christ's Person
1:1-3	The Superiority of Christ in the Revelation of God
1:4—2:18	The Superiority of Christ to Angels
3:1—4:13	The Superiority of Christ to Moses and Joshua
4:14—10:18	The Superiority of Christ's Work
4:14—7:28	The Superior Priesthood Demonstrated in Christ
8:1-13	The Superior Covenant Introduced by Christ
9:1—10:18	The Superior Sacrifice Offered by Christ
10:19—13:25	The Superiority of Christ's Power
10:19-39	An Appeal for Endurance
11:1-40	The Encouragement of Faith
12:1-13	The Experience of Discipline
12:14-29	A Warning Against Rejecting God
13:1-17	Final Exhortations
13:18-25	Benediction and Conclusion

Commentary

The Superiority of Christ's Person (Heb 1:1—4:13)

The Superiority of Christ in the Revelation of God (Heb 1:1-3)

The prologue establishes the theme of Hebrews' doctrinal division (Heb 1:4—10:18): the superiority of Christ. God has revealed himself to human beings in a variety of ways in the past, most clearly through the prophets, yet his revelation given through

Christ has superiority and finality. "In these last days" means that in Jesus the new age, the messianic age, has appeared. The writer's majestic descriptions of Jesus imply that in quality and quantity God had no more revelation to give other than what he had given in Jesus. Jesus Christ reveals what God is like. What an encouragement for women! The Gospels show Jesus as the friend of women who dared to talk with them in public. He risked his reputation and theirs by allowing them to travel as part of his group of disciples. He met their needs. He revealed great spiritual truths to them. He respected their work and their thinking. God cares for women as Jesus did. Women should want to know this God.

The Superiority of Christ to Angels (Heb 1:4-2:18)

Scriptural Proof of Christ's Superiority (Heb 1:5-14). The author uses seven quotations from the Old Testament, showing the authority of those Scriptures to prove to Jewish Christian readers the superiority of Christ to the angels. He interprets these Old Testament quotations christologically, taking passages originally referring to God or Israel's king and applying them to Christ. The Jews regarded angels highly as God's intermediaries in conveying the law to Moses. The writer identifies Jesus as the Son and the Creator who received worship from the angels. Angels are God's servants, created beings, and spirits who minister to believers. Like the Jews of ancient times, some women today place too much value on God's messengers at the expense of God. Jesus, superior over angels, should receive the focus.

A Warning Against Rejecting Christ's Superiority (Heb 2:1-4). The writer interrupts the flow of the argument by turning from proclamation to application. In the epistle's first warning passage are cautions against drifting away from the superior gospel of Christ. If the message the angels declared (the Mosaic law) led to the punishment of its violators, how much greater will be the punishment for those who neglect the great salvation declared through the Lord? The Old Testament does not speak of angels in connection with the giving of the law, but the New Testament mentions their presence (Acts 7:38, 53; Gal 3:19). Intertestamental and rabbinical Judaism did also (*see* Intertestamental History and Literature). Women have greater opportunities now than in any preceding age in terms of education, employment and achievement. The demands of their lives could cause them to neglect their spiritual needs. Women should heed the warning not to neglect the great salvation found in Jesus Christ.

The Reason for Christ's Incarnation (Heb 2:5-18). The nature of the work Jesus came to accomplish demanded the incarnation. The transcendent Son of God became a human being liable to death in order to achieve for women and men their glorious destiny designed by God. The writer quotes from Psalm 8, which usually is not seen as referring to the Messiah. In the original context it referred to humanity rather than to an individual (NRSV, "human beings"). The Greek text, however, reveals that the writer uses the singular to refer to the sovereign Christ. Christ's condescension—to be made for a brief while lower than the angels—set in motion a sequence of events in which his ultimate exaltation first required the abasement and humiliation associated with his death. His coronation and investiture with priestly glory and splendor provide assurance that the power of sin and death has been nullified and that humanity will one day fully realize its intended glory. The concept of the Messiah suffering would have been abhorrent to some Jews, yet God made his great and glorious Son perfect through sufferings. Christ's sufferings and death opened the way for others to participate in the glory of God as a result of deliverance from enslavement to the devil and the removal of their fear of death. The portrayal of Jesus as champion offers a word of comfort and encouragement to these Christians in crisis, helping them to look beyond their immediate trouble to the triumph that already had been secured for them. Because Jesus was in every respect perfectly and completely human, he can act on people's behalf as their high priest, fully able to understand their needs, suffering and temptations. Jesus understands and helps women and men in times of testing and temptation. He is their Champion. As high priest, Jesus has made a "sacrifice of atonement" (Heb 2:17) for the sins of people. This means a sacrifice that satisfies God's justice and turns away his wrath against sin. The Christian use of "atoning sacrifice" does not include the pagan idea of bribing a deity to appease his wrath. Although God's holiness and opposition to all evil demand a sacrifice, his love leads him to provide the means of atonement.

The Superiority of Christ to Moses and Joshua (Heb 3:1—4:13)

A Comparison of Christ and Moses (Heb 3:1-6). Moses and Jesus were faithful to God in fulfilling their respective offices. Moses was a servant of God in God's house. "House" means household, the people of God. In contrast, Jesus was God's exalted Son serving over that house. Jesus is worthy of greater honor than Moses because he was builder of the house rather than part of it, as was Moses. The writer demonstrates that faithful sonship is superior to faithful servanthood as an apologetic and pastoral response to the confusion of a dispirited congregation. He wants to persuade his readers to remain loyal to Christ in the presence of pressures that would encourage them to abandon their confession.

A Warning Against Unbelief (Heb 3:7-19). The author issues a second warning about the danger of refusing to believe God's Word, quoting Psalm 95 to extend a serious call to persevering discipleship. "Today" indicates a fresh moment of biography and history, conditioned always by the response of obedience or disobedience, of faith or unbelief. In comparing Christians with the ancient Israelites, the writer pictures both groups as people whose pilgrimage was almost over and who were on the verge of attaining what God had promised. Despite God's miraculous deliverance from Egypt, the Israelites grumbled against him and continued in disobedience and unbelief. Refusing to acknowledge God's presence and voice, they forfeited the possibility of entrance into his rest and failed to attain the goal of their redemption. The writer cautions readers that if they also harden their hearts, refuse to believe, turn away from the living God, sin, fail to persevere to the end, rebel and disobey, a worse thing will happen to them. They will not enter God's ultimate rest. To harden the heart means to disobey God and act in accordance with one's own desires. "Drift away" (Heb 2:1) and "turns away" (Heb 3:12) indicate that the readers faced the temptation of apostasy, willful rejection of the Christian faith. Jews might have contended that they served the same God as the Christians so that they would not be departing from God if they returned to Judaism. But to reject God's highest revelation, Jesus Christ, is to depart from him. The writer does not deal with the question of whether those who apostatized were genuine Christians but focuses only on the result, on practical, not theoretical matters. The author encourages readers to exhort one another so that none of them might be hardened by the deceitfulness of sin. Such exhortation often belongs to the role of mothers. Mothers have to teach their children about the deceitfulness of sin and train them not to allow the world's attractive pull to deceive them lest they develop hearts hardened to God's call.

A Comparison of Christ's Rest and Joshua's Rest (Heb 4:1-10). If the ancient Israelites, with all their advantages, failed to enter the rest, believers must beware lest they too fail to enter the blessing. The writer tempers the warning by the encouragement that God has not revoked the promise of entering his rest. The failure of the exodus generation to enter the promised rest did not nullify the reality and accessibility of that rest for future generations. There is a far better rest than that eventually found in Canaan by the believing Israelites. Christians inherit this rest, a state of completion and harmony when God's people will "cease from their labors" (Heb 4:10). What a wonderful promise for believing women who find their household labors repetitive and unending.

An Exhortation to Enter Christ's Rest (Heb 4:11-13). The rest is still available for believers, but they must "make every effort" to enter it. Believers enter God's rest through faith in his word of promise and obedient response to the voice of God in Scripture. The "word of God" (Heb 4:12) indicates every way in which God speaks to people and especially the word that came through Jesus Christ. The immediate context suggests the writer refers to God's message particularly in the text of Scriptures cited in Hebrews 3:7—4:11. The author does not mean the incarnate Word, Jesus. "Living and active" reveal the dynamic quality of God's revelation. Like a "two-edged sword," God's word penetrates the innermost recesses of one's being. One can hide no secrets from God. "Judge" represents a legal term. The word of God passes judgment on one's thoughts and motives. Nothing escapes the scope of this word. The writer expresses an overwhelming sense of the power involved in God's word. Only as people know this word can they obey it. Saturating themselves in the Scriptures will enable them to respond to the God who loves them.

The Superiority of Christ's Work (4:14—10:18)

The Superior Priesthood Demonstrated in Christ (Heb 4:14—7:28)

The Value of Christ's High Priesthood (Heb 4:14-16). Jesus is fully qualified to act as high priest. Because he is "great" and "has passed through the heavens," and because he remains sinless, Jesus can stand before God. Because he has known human temptations, he can stand alongside men and women. The writer emphasizes Jesus' full humanity and his solidarity with those exposed to weakness and temptation. Jesus knows the human condition. He understands us as no one else can. Knowing that Jesus serves as our high priest should motivate believers to hold fast to our confession as Christians and approach God boldly for help in time of need. The writer wants these believers to recognize the importance of prayer, especially since past loyalties pulled at them and renewed hostility confronted them. Those who pray effect a great difference in their lives and in the lives of those for whom they intercede.

A Comparison of Christ and Aaron (Heb 5:1-10). Aaron and Jesus displayed humility in refusing to exalt themselves to the office of high priest. God chose or appointed them from among others. Jesus, however, did not have to offer sacrifices for his sins as Aaron and the Aaronic high priests had to do. Also, the appeal to the order of Melchizedek, who as the first priest mentioned in Scripture is the archetype of all priesthood, validates Jesus' priesthood as different from and superior to the levitical priesthood. Christ enjoys a preeminence that removes him from the sphere of comparison with Aaron. He was without sin, and God summoned him to be a priest forever. This rendered the Aaronic institution obsolete. Christ's high-priestly offering culminated in his suffering death in perfect obedience to God's revealed will. Christian salvation is eternal because it is based on the sacrifice of Christ, which was once for all, never to be repeated and forever valid. "For all who obey him" (Heb 5:9) does not mean that believers earn their salvation by obedience. Instead believers respond in obedience to the call to trust Christ for salvation. They express their Christian faith through obedience in daily life.

The Warning Against Falling Away (Heb 5:11—6:20). Spiritual immaturity is addressed in Hebrews 5:11-14. The author writes to believers who appear unwilling to accept the deeper implications of faith and obedience. They should have been mature enough to serve as teachers, yet they have made little progress in the faith. They need to learn again the "basic elements of the oracles of God." "Basic elements" refers to elementary religious teaching as symbolized by the word *milk,* an image well understood by mothers of infants. The "oracles of God" probably refers to divine revelation in general. These Christians have forgotten the ABCs of the faith. They had sharply departed from the boldness and mature commitment they had shown earlier. The hope the writer expresses later regarding these readers (Heb 6:9) indicates he believes they possess maturity and wants to shame this community into assuming the responsibilities belonging to a spiritually mature group of Christians in a hostile society. Their lack of skill indicates a lack of "practice."

In Hebrews 6:1-3 the writer exhorts readers to progress. A strong foundation has been laid among the readers that could carry them to "perfection" or spiritual maturity. The six beliefs or practices can be interpreted as either Jewish or Christian. If all the references are to Jewish rituals, the writer pleads with the recipients to leave the teachings and practices of Judaism, which were preparatory for Christianity, and move on to Christian maturity. If these items refer to Christian teachings, the author's plea remains the same: press forward in the faith. "Repentance from dead works" may allude to the Jewish idea of attaining justification through works. "Instruction about baptisms" (note the plural) refers to purification ceremonies found in most religions of that day, including Judaism. Christian converts had to be taught the true meaning of Christian baptism, a single act, as well as the right approach to the various ablutions they encountered. "Laying on of hands" signifies the giving of blessing for Jews and the conferring of specific gifts for Christians. The "resurrection of the dead" and "eternal judgment" relate to the future.

In Hebrews 6:4-8 the writer warns against apostasy in the strongest possible terms. Can genuine Christians lose their salvation? The four verbal actions ("enlightened," "tasted the heavenly gift," "shared in the Holy Spirit," "tasted the goodness of the word of God") do seem to describe those who have professed Christ. "Fallen away" refers to committing apostasy. Individuals who fall away cannot be brought back to Christ because they openly disgrace him by their actions and try to recrucify the Son of God, an impossible act.

Interpretations of this passage include the following: (1) A true Christian can revert to a lost condition. (2) The author poses a hypothetical possibility: If a Christian could lose her salvation, then it would be impossible for her to be resaved. (3) The threatened judgment refers to loss of reward, not loss of salvation (see 1 Cor 3:12-15). (4) The writer addresses near-Christians rather than genuine Christians. These people have rejected God's grace even after experiencing something of it. (5) Professing Christians must show the genuineness of their faith by withstanding the pressure to apostatize. Christians must outwardly demonstrate their commitment by persevering against opposition and temptation. The moment professing believers abandon Christianity, they reveal that their faith was not real. It is not possible to be saved and lost from God's perspective, but it is apparently possible, based on appearances from a human perspective. The distinctive evidence of true Christianity is endurance. True believers will endure in their commitment to Christ because God will preserve them by his power.

The author of Hebrews wants readers to know that the consequences of abandoning Christianity are serious. If they turn from Christ, they will not find salvation anywhere else. He does not believe, however, that they will prove to be apostates. In fact, he reminds readers what they possess and what they had experienced as the result of God's redemptive activity through Christ. God's presence and salvation represent the undoubted reality of their lives. The writer pictures these believers as a well-watered and cultivated field capable of producing the useful harvest that God expects.

In Hebrews 6:9-12 we find an expression of confidence in perseverance. Recognizing the severity of the warnings, the writer assures readers that he has confidence they will persevere in their faith. Their previous compassion and love for others demonstrate their faith. The author does not want them to become lazy or listless but to endure in their commitment. They have not earned their salvation by their good works, but their service to others gives evidence of God's work in them. Many women have servant hearts; they delight in serving family members and others. They must not confuse these good works with the necessity of faith.

A reminder of God's unchangeable purpose is the focus of Hebrews 6:13-20. After exposing the danger of spiritual immaturity, the writer affirms the reliability of God's word of promise to the Christian community. The promise for Abraham (Gen 22:15-18) has its ultimate fulfillment in Christ and the church. God's promise and solemn oath—"two unchangeable things"—confirm his purpose. He gave his oath so that the people of God might know he would fulfill his promise. The word of promise confirmed with an oath reveals the irrevocable character of God's will. The promised salvation secured through the high-priestly ministry of Jesus is certain because God guaranteed it. Believers have a steadfast hope because through his sacrificial death Jesus has entered the presence of God on behalf of his people and has made it possible for them to approach God in priestly service. The "inner shrine behind the curtain" pictures the curtain that divided the holiest place, where the ark of God was kept, from the rest of the tabernacle. This curtain symbolized the barrier keeping sinful human beings away from the presence of God. Only the chief priest, a man, could ever pass that curtain and then only on the Day of Atonement. But Jesus' death split the curtain into two and made the way open for his followers, including women, to enter into God's presence.

The Melchizedek Order of Christ's Priesthood (Heb 7). The greatness of Melchizedek is taken up in Hebrews 7:1-10. Melchizedek was the mysterious figure described as the king of Salem and priest of the most high God (Gen 14:18-20). The name Melchizedek means "king of righteousness." The writer implies that true righteousness comes through his kind of priesthood. He was also king of Salem, probably an ancient name for Jerusalem, which signifies "king of peace." This implies that peace with God comes through this kind of priesthood. The author shows Melchizedek's superiority to Abraham by indicating that Melchizedek blessed Abraham and received tribute from him. Melchizedek's superiority to Abraham, the founder of the Israelites, also made him superior to the latter's descendants, including Levi, the father of the priestly tribe. "Without father, without mother" does not necessarily mean that Melchizedek had no parents but that the absence of the record is significant. The people of antiquity put much emphasis on a priest's genealogy. After the exile, certain priests whose genealogy could not be established were excluded from the priesthood as unclean (Neh 7:64). What was true of Melchizedek as a matter of record was true of Christ in a fuller and more literal sense. Melchizedek prefigured the messianic priest, Christ. He served as a precedent for a superior priesthood, the one to which Christ belongs. His position stood apart from the line of descent, and his ordination was apart from law. He presented an exception to the common interpretation of priesthood in the Old Testament, anticipating the ultimate displacement of the levitical priesthood. This royal priestly figure with no parentage, successor, beginning or end of life evoked the notion of a priest who continues in this office forever.

The superiority of Christ's priesthood is shown in Hebrews 7:11-28. The writer argues for the need for a new priesthood because the Levitical system did not provide perfection. A new priesthood also means a new law and a new covenant. These Jewish Christians were tempted to go back into Judaism, perhaps thinking that the law and the covenant were best for them. The writer of Hebrews rejects and tries to correct this belief, appealing to Melchizedek to prove that Jesus' priesthood was different from and superior to the Levitical priesthood. The old priesthood, sacrifices and covenant had been replaced by the new priest and the new covenant he secured with his sacrifice. The author develops the Melchizedek Christology primarily to prove the effectiveness of the Son's eternal priesthood. Christ's singular offering of himself put an end to the Levitical system of sacrifice. His continual access to the presence of God makes his priesthood effective and perpetual. Evidently the members of the house church doubt the ability of God to act decisively in the present on their behalf. The writer wants them to comprehend the reality of God's final action in Jesus and of Christ's present ability to help them face the difficulties of their circumstances. Women who face discouragement need this reminder. God acts on behalf of his daughters as well as his sons.

The Superior Covenant Introduced by Christ (Heb 8:1-13)

The writer contends the earthly Aaronic priesthood served as a model, a sketch and a shadow pointing to Christ. Christ achieved what the sacrificial action of the high priest on the great Day of Atonement foreshadowed. Jesus entered the heavenly sanctuary, the "true tent," where he has unrestricted access to God's eternal presence. This shows the eternal superiority of his priestly service to the ministry of the levitical high priest. The author describes Jesus as the "mediator of a better covenant." "Mediator" represents a legal term for one who arbitrates between two parties. Christ mediates between God and people. He establishes the new covenant. According to Jeremiah 31:31-34 the new covenant provides forgiveness of sins. It involves an inward and personal relationship with God open to all people. Everyone can know God through the new covenant in Jesus Christ. Consequently there is no longer any place for the old covenant.

The Superior Sacrifice Offered by Christ (Heb 9:1—10:18)

A Sacrifice That Cleanses Conscience (Heb 9:1-14). The author develops the superiority of the new covenant by pointing to the significance of the way of worship in the old one. He focuses not on the temple but on the long-vanished tabernacle. Only Jews in or near Jerusalem had access to the temple, but the Scriptures told all Jews everywhere about the tabernacle. The setup and use of the tabernacle reflected the ineffectiveness of the old covenant, which centered on external matters, such as foods, drinks and ceremonial washings. The division of the tabernacle into a front and rear compartment indicated that approach to God was not an easy matter. The old sanctuary consisted of a system of barriers between the worshiper and God. The cultic provisions allowed the people to approach God only through their representatives, the priests and the high priest. Only the high priest could enter the rear compartment, and then only once a year under strictly prescribed conditions. He must never enter without the sacrificial blood. Under the old covenant it was necessary to repeat sacrifices that were never adequate to remove sin, cleanse the conscience and achieve an unbroken relationship with God. But when Christ came and acted as the high priest and the perfect sacrifice, he purified and made perfect the conscience of believers. He entered the most holy place and offered his blood, thereby securing eternal redemption.

A Sacrifice That Removes Sin (Heb 9:15-28). Christ's death put the new covenant into effect, just as the death of the testator puts a will into effect. His death on the cross is the sacrifice of the new covenant corresponding to the animal sacrifices prescribed under the old covenant. All sacrificial blood is powerful, but Christ's blood is the most powerful medium because it achieved decisive purification and the removal of every barrier to the enjoyment of God. To deal with sin, there had to be a sacrifice—"without the shedding of blood there is no forgiveness of sins." But unlike all previous sacrifices, which needed to be repeated, Christ's sacrifice was once for all. Christ's single offering secured salvation and provided access to the inaccessible presence of God for women and men. The author identifies the Christian era as the "end of the age" (Heb 9:26). Yet he combines this thought with futuristic eschatology by a clear reference to the second coming of Christ. He "will appear a second time" for salvation, its consummation and perfection. Christ dealt with sin at his first coming.

A Voluntary, Unrepeatable Sacrifice (Heb 10:1-18). The author summarizes and emphasizes what was said previously concerning the failure of the law, Christ's final sacrifice and the forgiveness of sins. The law, as a shadow, anticipated the good things to come in Christ. Its sacrifices were unable to provide forgiveness. Even after making such sacrifices, the worshiper still had a painful consciousness of sin. In interpreting Psalm 40:6-8 christologically the author sees the words of the psalm as being spoken by Christ to God at the time of the incarnation. The writer emphasizes Christ's bodily existence to indicate his identification with the rest of humanity. Consequently his sacrificial death served also as an act of identification and made possible the participation of others in his consecration to the service of God. Jesus' active obedience in offering his body as a once-for-all sacrifice abolished the levitical priesthood and sacrificial system. His sufficient sacrifice in conformity to the will of God effectively removed obstacles to fellowship with him for the worshiping community. Jesus' saving action was performed in history, but it possesses a validity that transcends history.

The Superiority of Christ's Power (Heb 10:19—13:25)

An Appeal for Endurance (Heb 10:19-39)

By Approaching God Through Christ (Heb 10:19-25). This marks the beginning of the ethical or practical division of Hebrews. The contemplation of what Christ has done should stir his people to action. The writer reviews the benefits the believing community gained from the sacrifice of Christ. All believers, male and female, can now enter the Most Holy Place. The writer appeals for them to act responsibly because they exhibit a tendency to waver in their commitment to Christ and to each other and challenges them to approach God "with a true heart," presupposing a lack of sincerity on the readers' part. The sprinkling of the hearts signifies the cleansing effect of the blood of Christ on the inmost being. The washing of their bodies with "pure water" refers to baptism. Believer's baptism is more than an outward rite cleansing the body from ritual defilement. Baptism represents the outward sign of an inward cleansing from sin. The author exhorts them to "hold fast" to the confession of their "hope without wavering," implying a vacillation that undermined the integrity of Christian profession. The writer urges readers to "provoke one another to love and good deeds." Many women serve as effective role models in this area. The readers should not neglect meeting together for worship and should exhort one another to remain faithful. Persecution has caused some readers to be negligent about church attendance. Some have even returned to the Jewish synagogue.

By Fearing the Living God (Heb 10:26-31). Having spoken of their hope and the way in which Christ has opened up the path into God's presence, the author warns the readers of the alternative. If an individual rejects the sacrifice of Christ, there is no other one who can provide forgiveness for sins. The result can only be judgment, punishment and death. "Willfully persist in sin" refers not to someone who backslides, slips away or does not understand. It points to one who deliberately rejects the message of the gospel. For this person there is no hope. The sin of apostasy involves spurning the Son of God. This strong expression for disdain implies not only rejecting Christ but also despising him. The apostate regards Jesus' blood as a common thing, treating the death of Jesus like the death of any other person. Apostasy also means outraging the Spirit, who applies the grace of God. This insolent self-assertion disregards the respect due to others, in this case the respect due to the Holy Spirit.

By Considering Past Experiences and Future Reward (Heb 10:32-39). The writer has confidence that readers will recognize their peril and will demonstrate a quality of faithfulness and steadfast endurance consistent with their relationship with God through Christ and the goal set before them. He reminds them they had endured the persecution and implies they will face more such adversity. The writer and readers belong not to those who reject the gospel but to those who stand firm, the company of faith.

The Encouragement of Faith (Heb 11:1-40)

The Nature of Faith (Heb 11:1-3). The writer defines faith or faithfulness by two words, "assurance" and "conviction." Faith means trust or confidence in what God has promised for the future and a life of faithfulness and perseverance as a result. Faith represents the foundation of the Christian life. It gives meaning to things that have not yet happened and gives certainty that they will happen. Faith proves the reality of things not seen.

The Examples of the Faithful (Heb 11:4-40). The author illustrates faith and encourages readers in their walk of faith by listing Old Testament heroes and heroines who lived in faithfulness to God. In these examples we see faith as active obedience. Each champion of faith worked out his or her faith in different ways. Although the majority of these faithful were men, the author includes references to Sarah, Moses' parents, Rahab and women in general. Although Sarah laughed when first hearing that she was to have a child, her disbelief evidently turned to faith long before the birth of her son, Isaac (Gen 18:12). Like her husband, Abraham, Sarah had to believe that the God who made promises would honor his word, despite how impossible it must have seemed to her as a woman long past childbearing years. Sarah shared not only her husband's challenges and disappointments but also his dreams and blessings. She stood by his side through good and bad decisions, adversities and blessings, in youth and old age. The New Testament describes Sarah as one of the holy women of old because she willingly cooperated with her husband and with God (1 Pet 3:5). Moses' mother, Jochebed, emerged as a fearless and focused woman of faith. She circumvented the Egyptian edict to destroy her baby and cleverly protected her son. She acted as a caring and resourceful mother despite the evil around her. God saw her heart, heard her prayers and intervened in her behalf. Rahab, the Gentile prostitute, demonstrates that God does not restrict faith to those of acceptable race, background or gender. A prostitute initially seems an unlikely example of faith, yet Jews and Christians highly regard Rahab. James mentions her as an example to follow because her faith was not without works (Jas 2:25). Matthew lists her in the genealogy of the Lord as the wife of Salmon (Mt 1:5). Although Rahab came from a pagan people, she acted decisively out of her deep convictions about Yahweh, about whom she must have heard from the Hebrew spies. She risked her life for God's people. Rahab exercised her faith. Women who received their dead by resurrection included the widow of Zarephath and the Shunammite woman (1

Kings 17; 2 Kings 4).

All these figures of faith, male and female, possessed a strong future hope. They never saw the full working out of God's promises. The author employs the motifs of pilgrimage, sighting the target but not attaining it and the disavowal of a worldly goal. Throughout the chapter the writer shows how faith enables believers to endure suffering, even martyrdom. The capacity to endure suffering and death presupposes a relationship to the unseen world. The summary verses speak of people whose circumstances of poverty and persecution singled them out as undesirable from the viewpoint of the world. The writer of Hebrews, however, exclaims that the world was not worthy of them. They were the people of God and recipients of his blessings.

The Experience of Discipline (Heb 12:1-13)

The Example of Christ (Heb 12:1-3). The writer appeals to readers by using an athletic metaphor to compare the Christian life with a race. Contemporary women may be able to relate to this image better than their first-century counterparts since many of them participate in sports or fitness activity. The runners, believers, find themselves surrounded by a great "cloud of witnesses," the champions of faith. These witnesses are not heavenly spectators who observe the conduct of Christians, though some Bible scholars hold that view, but those who have given testimony by their examples. Christians can compete in the race of life well only by laying aside every impediment that hinders them from putting forth their best effort and running with perseverance. The author thinks of a distance race that requires endurance and sustained effort—not a sprint. The author directs the believers from the models of faithfulness in Israel's past under the old covenant to Jesus, the "pioneer and perfecter" of their faith. Like the readers, Jesus faced conflict in a hostile environment. Jesus endured the abject humiliation of crucifixion. God therefore vindicated him, enthroning Jesus in his presence. Believers must fix their gaze on Jesus and draw from his example the courage to display responsible commitment in their difficult situations. Jesus offers a model for Christians whenever they are tempted to become disheartened with the intensity of the opposition they encounter from society.

The Purpose of God (Heb 12:4-13). The author appeals to readers not to become discouraged by the discipline of suffering in light of its divine purpose. For believers, the cross transforms all affliction. The Savior, who suffered, will not lead his followers into meaningless trials. To help readers perceive the significance of the hardships they experience, the writer uses Proverbs 3:11-12 to demonstrate the essential and integral relationship between sufferings and a filial relationship with God. Sufferings are corrective in character. Such sufferings become disciplinary when God makes them a means for maturing his children spiritually and ultimately enabling them to participate in his holiness. Whenever the community of faith experiences unpleasantness, pain and adversity because they are Christians, they should recognize in these sufferings the pledge of the Father's love. Difficulties come to everybody, but they are easier to bear when one accepts them as meaningful.

A Warning Against Rejecting God (Heb 12:14-29)

Careless disregard for the blessings of the new covenant exposes these Jewish Christians to the threat of apostasy. Therefore the writer calls them to pursue peace and holiness as an expression of Christian maturity, urging them to be vigilant lest anyone fail to "obtain the grace of God." He uses Esau to exemplify an immoral, godless person who had contempt for his spiritual privileges and applies this example to apostates. The writer compares the old and new covenants under the imagery of two mountains in order to illustrate their basic differences. Mount Sinai symbolized the law, the sacrificial system and the Aaronic priesthood. The author focuses on the threatening aspects, judgment and fear connected with the giving of the law at Mount Sinai (see Ex 19—20; Deut 5). These things created an atmosphere of dread and confusion. The writer also stresses the immense distance that separated the worshipers from God under the old covenant. By contrast, believers have come to Mount Zion and to the city of the living God, the heavenly Jerusalem. The images of Mount Zion describe the realization of the eschatological hopes of God's people under the old and new covenants. God can be approached in the new covenant as opposed to the restriction on approaching him under the old covenant. Christians come to God, meeting him in joyful assembly, together with angels, the faithful men and women of God under covenants and Jesus. Believers respond gratefully to covenant blessings already experienced and to the certainty of the reception of the unshakable kingdom with authentic worship. The frank awareness of the awesome character of God's holiness deepens the worship experience.

Final Exhortations (Heb 13:1-17)

Exhortations for Social Life (Heb 13:1-3). The author encourages readers in their general Christian living. Believers cannot restrict worship to formal or informal expressions of praise and prayer. Instead, worship infuses every aspect of public and private life with the character of consecrated service to God. Worship of God should issue in "mutual love." Love reflects itself in showing hospitality and concern for other believers and in particular for strangers and any who are imprisoned or ill-treated. There were many itinerant missionaries in the first century. Filth and immorality characterized the public inns. Without hospitality in Christian homes the spread of the faith would have been much more difficult. Though conditions differ now, people respond to the warmth and intimacy of a home setting. Many women today embrace the ministry of hospitality, opening their homes and offering their creative talents to the Lord's service.

Exhortations for Home Life (Heb 13:4-6). The author stresses that believers should honor marriage because God takes seriously the marriage covenant (*see* Marriage). This affirms the significance and responsibility of the wife and the husband. He refers primarily to avoiding sexual immorality and unfaithfulness, but he might also be speaking out against sexual asceticism that viewed marriage as a lesser state than celibacy. He also warns about the dangers of materialism. Dependency on material things can become idolatry, taking away dependency on God. Unlike the uncertainty and temporal nature of riches, God never fails or forsakes his children.

Exhortations for Religious Life (Heb 13:7-17). Believers should treat their spiritual leaders with respect and follow their examples of faith. Those who exercise authority must also accept responsibility for their actions. The followers of Jesus Christ can rely on him and base their conduct on the certainty of his unchanging nature. Jesus' suffering had a specific purpose—to sanctify his people. Jesus' death "outside the city gate" of Jerusalem symbolized the rejection of the Jewish authorities. The writer appeals to the readers to leave the security and respectability of Judaism and go outside to Jesus regardless of the difficulties this decision might involve.

Benediction and Conclusion (Heb 13:18-25)

The author asks readers for their personal prayers. He also prays that God might enable them to do his will in all things. He gives information about Timothy and sends greetings to the rest of the church, confirming the view that this letter was not sent to a whole church but to a particular group within it.

Bibliography. W. L. Lane, *Hebrews 1—8* and *Hebrews 9—13,* Word Biblical Commentary 48 (Dallas: Word, 1991); B. Lindars, *The Theology of the Letter to the Hebrews,* New Testament Theology (Cambridge: Cambridge University Press, 1991); L. Morris, "Hebrews," in *The Expositor's Bible Commentary,* ed. F. E. Gaebelein (Grand Rapids, MI: Zondervan, 1981).

SHARON H. GRITZ

JAMES

Introduction

James is a difficult book to classify. It is almost, but not quite, a letter; there is an opening greeting but no closing benediction. It is almost, but not quite, a sermon; there is much advice but no structured argument. It is almost, but not quite, a wisdom treatise, like the book of Proverbs; but there is too much personal involvement for that. It consists of a series of thoughts and recommendations that are related but not systematically organized, explaining what is involved in living a Christian life. James's conviction that Christian faith is meaningless without a practical outworking comes across strongly. The focus moves from subject to subject apparently as different ideas came to mind. The writer does not follow the rules of classical logic, but allows one thought to lead on to another in a way that in the past might have been described as feminine, or in more recent years as postmodern, but in fact has many parallels in Hebrew wisdom thinking. At every stage, however, the concern is with how those who are servants (or slaves) "of God and of the Lord Jesus Christ" (Jas 1:1) should think and behave and live. James is not unconcerned with doctrine—the practical life of which he speaks stems from clear belief—but his primary concern is with what that belief means in the nitty-gritty of everyday life. There are parallels to this in the teaching of Jesus, and it is interesting to note the many echoes of the Sermon on the Mount that can be discerned within the book of James (Mt 5:12 in Jas 1:2, Mt 5:48 in Jas 1:4, Mt 7:7 in Jas 1:5, Mt 7:11 in Jas 1:17, and Mt 5:22 in Jas 1:19 are just a few of the examples from Jas1). James seems to have taken that sermon to heart.

We cannot be sure of the identity of the writer, although traditionally the book has been ascribed to Jesus' brother James. There is also little clue to the recipients. "The twelve tribes in the Dispersion" may indicate an intended Jewish readership but is just as likely to be a symbolic way of referring to Christians throughout the world. James may have had specific situations of persecution (Jas 1:2) or favoritism (Jas 2:1) in mind as he wrote, but his thoughts would apply across the board. What we can be sure of is that James's focus on the importance of down-to-earth, everyday behavior would have been especially relevant to those who saw themselves as of little account. As James pours out encouragement and challenge to his Christian family—the all-embracing "brothers" involves men, women and children—those, perhaps particularly women, who were engulfed by domestic responsibilities would have been reassured that any service they might give to God was far from irrelevant or worthless.

Because James jumps from one idea to another it is hard to produce a sequential outline, but the following structure gives some idea of his particular interests. He addresses Christians' attitude to problems (Jas 1:2-4, 12-15; 5:7-11), attitude to possessions (Jas 1:9-11, 16-18; 4:1-10, 13-16; 5:1-6) and attitude to people (Jas 2:1-16; 5:19-20). He also emphasizes listening and doing (Jas 1:19-27; 2:17-27; 4:17), wisdom (Jas 1:5-8; 3:1-2, 13-18) and speech (Jas 3:2-12; 4:11-12; 5:12-18).

Outline

1:1-27 Introduction to the Christian Life

2:1-26	Status in Christ
3:1—4:10	Use and Misuse of Speech
4:11—5:19	Reprise and Redevelopment

Commentary

Introduction to the Christian Life (Jas 1)

James 1 contains seven separate paragraphs, each dealing with what appears to be a separate topic. However, there is enough link between them to justify the conclusion that the chapter is not a collection of isolated thoughts but was composed at the same time.

James begins by speaking of the trials that he assumes all Christians will face (Jas 1:1-4). Trials, in this instance probably referring to persecution although the application is general, are not to be seen as a failure of faith or even as an unexpected intrusion. Rather, they are to be welcomed as a God-given means of strengthening faith and bringing maturity. Patient endurance or steadfastness is a positive Christian quality, and the cultivation of this characteristic will enable any trial to have a positive effect on Christians' spiritual lives. In this context, James 1:5-8 probably refers to the kind of wisdom needed to understand the reason for whatever trials Christians face. God does want them to understand, but spiritual discernment based on trust in God's sovereignty is needed. This kind of wisdom comes from God alone. There is no assurance here that if only they have the right kind of faith, then their every request will be granted, or even a promise that they will never remain in the dark over any issue.

The reference to wisdom reminds James that his readers need to have the right attitude to status as well as to problems. The danger of assuming that Christians should expect riches and that riches must mean God's blessing was as real as the danger of assuming that Christians should not face trials. James shows readers that the right attitude for believers is different. The poor Christians, including the believing women who had little public recognition or personal wealth, should be glad that they have abundant wealth and status in Christ regardless of any material possessions (Jas 1:9-11). And any rich Christians, including the wealthy businessmen who might have expected their status to carry over into the church, should be glad that their salvation is not dependent on passing possessions.

Again, as James's thoughts flow on, the temptation he has first in mind in James 1:12-15 is probably the temptation to underestimate one's status in Christ or to overestimate one's status in the world. Women throughout the world have been prone to the temptation to denigrate themselves and should perhaps take special note of James's words. It is easy to see that boasting about human status comes from one's pride, but it is often assumed that excessive humility is a sign of spirituality and comes from God. This is quite wrong. To underestimate the significance of life and status in Christ, to assume that although we have that life and status we are still insignificant nobodies, is as likely to lead to spiritual death as the assumption that human status does have spiritual significance. James's message about temptation has application to a whole range of other enticements, but given the context we should at least take this one seriously. James can in no way be seen as encouraging women or men to a self-deprecation that fails to acknowledge the power of the work of Christ's Spirit within them.

Far from tempting people into evil of

any kind, God gives only good gifts (Jas 1:16-18). Therefore every "generous act of giving," whether it comes from the wealthy or the poor, is inspired by and reflects God, who is the parent of all believers. The reference to God as "the Father of lights" in James 1:17 is paralleled by the reference to mothering, giving birth, in James 1:18, and it is hard to see this parallel as anything other than deliberate (*see* Birth Pain Imagery; Images of God as Female). The family likeness, illustrated by such characteristics as generosity (Jas 1:17), the ability to listen and the lack of anger (Jas 1:19-20), is brought about through "the word of truth" that has been "implanted" (Jas 1:21) into the believer.

Hearing that word is important. The "law of liberty" cannot be understood without hearing about it. But to have an intellectual appreciation of gospel truth and to think that that makes you into a Christian is self-deception. That kind of knowledge is no more lasting than your reflection in a mirror after you have moved on. Real blessing comes from knowing the gospel and living it out—which means ongoing moral purity, concern for the poor and control of speech and temper.

Status in Christ (Jas 2)

In James 2, the issue of right and wrong attitudes that was introduced in James 1 is further developed and theological backing is provided to justify James's conclusion that living out the Christian faith is a life-and-death matter.

A wrong attitude to possessions and to status can be reflected in a wrong attitude toward those who have possessions and status. Within the congregation of believers, to show favoritism to people just because they have status in the world is to negate the significance of faith in Jesus Christ. To organize the seating in a way that gives special importance to people because of their wealth or their education or maybe their gender is to imply that these factors take priority over the work of Christ. The contrast that James introduces, between the tawdry shoddiness of worldly wealth and Christ as the "glorious Lord," shows just how bad this kind of behavior was. To show favoritism to rich or to poor, to women or to men can never be justified by reference to the royal commandment to love one's neighbor. It seems likely that James is reflecting on a particular situation, and it may be that some had tried to excuse their partiality on the grounds that they were only trying to love the high-status people involved. James has no doubt that to show partiality because of wealth—as opposed to caring for rich and poor alike—is sin. It breaks God's law and is just as serious as committing adultery or murder. If they make judgments on the basis of worldly criteria, then they will be placed under such merciless judgment. There is a strong warning here to any who pay too much attention to external factors like fashion, jewelry or hairstyle when they make judgments about people.

Two additional arguments are given in support of James's position. First, the poor have been chosen by God to receive faith, and therefore to dishonor the poor is to dishonor God. Second, those who come from the higher social strata have caused many problems for the young churches, and therefore to honor them does not make sense.

James 2:14-16 provides a link to James's next topic. Christians must not only have a loving attitude to rich and poor alike but also must show loving actions, making sure that the material needs of all are met. Sympathizing with the poor is not much better than despising them if it doesn't lead to helpful action. Belief that does not affect behavior is a waste of time. It does not bring life.

James's development of this thought has sometimes been seen as controversial. His statements "Was not our ancestor Abraham justified by works" and "You see that a person is justified by works and not by faith alone" are seen as being in direct contradiction to Paul's statement "We hold that a person is justified by faith apart from works prescribed by the law" (Rom 3:28), or his argument in Romans 4 that Abraham was justified by faith and not by works. However, a closer examination reveals that Paul and James are using the words for faith and for works in different senses. For James, faith is intellectual assent to certain truths, whereas for Paul it is personal belief and commitment. For Paul works are acts of obedience to specific laws, whereas for James they are acts of love and kindness. James and Paul come to the same position via different routes. Paul wanted to stress that adherence to a legal code is not enough and that salvation cannot come through our own works, as we can never keep the whole law. But he is clear that faith is not faith unless it results in Christian living—that is, in works as James understands it. James wanted to stress that belief on its own is useless, not that works are enough but that faith must be indicated and shown to be true by works. Both target the necessity of faith in action. This kind of worked-out faith was demonstrated by Abraham, the high-reputation, righteous father of the nation, and by Rahab, the foreign prostitute. Maybe James is subtly pressing home his previous point that it is not whether one is on the top of the pile or the bottom that counts for men or for women but a worked-out faith in Jesus Christ.

The Use and Misuse of Speech (Jas 3:1—4:10)

It seems unlikely that James wrote with Christian women particularly in mind, and it is true that everything he says also relates well to men. However, it is interesting to note how closely the topics that concerned him relate to the lives of women. Conversation, which tends to be especially important to women, is picked out as the key area in which the believer can stand or fall. If Christian women and men can avoid letting their speech get out of control, then they can be confident of success in their attempt to live Christian lives.

A link with the previous concern about status is provided by the initial warning for would-be teachers. James is not suggesting that teaching is unnecessary or bad. On the contrary, he presents himself as a teacher. However, he warns teachers and taught alike against placing too much dependence on the reliability of any human teacher and points out that whatever status the role of teacher might bring may be outweighed by the spiritual accountability involved.

The abundance of dynamic images—horses, ships, fire, animal taming—brings out the importance that James places on this question of how speech is used. It is vital that the family likeness to God "the Lord and Father" (Jas 3:9) is shown in this area. It is not appropriate for Christians to participate in cursing, lying, thoughtlessness, unkind gossip, bragging or aggressive disputation. All of these have their origin in self-seeking covetousness. Godly talk, by contrast, is "first pure, then peaceable, gentle, willing to yield, full of mercy and good fruits" (Jas 3:17). Never being able to admit to a mistake or willing to lose an argument is by no means a sign of strength, and the threatening, do-not-dare-to-contradict-me approach is not a sign of wisdom. Destroying other people by aggressive and wounding words or using prayer as a means of trying to blackmail God into acceding to selfish demands is spiritual adultery, a betrayal of all that life in Christ implies.

All of this is somewhat daunting, and it is as if James, as his thoughts move on, suddenly realizes that it might sound as if what God requires is impossible. So in James 4:6-9 he refocuses: God's empowering and God's willingness to help come into the forefront of the picture. Because God "gives all the more grace," the devil can be defeated. Will power is involved, the believer must actively resist, but God's grace makes successful resistance possible. James wants them to be certain that that grace is freely available to all who recognize their need of it.

Reprise and Redevelopment (Jas 4:11—5:19)

As James's symphony of encouragement and challenge comes to an end, the themes introduced in James 1 and James 2 are repeated and taken one step further.

To speak "evil against one another," like having the wrong approach to status, is to put oneself in the place of a judge, not only of the individual involved but also of the law. Usurping the divine role in this way is presented as a serious matter (Jas 4:11-12).

To spend one's time seeking after worldly rewards is to ignore the fact that what counts are the values of heaven. James is not suggesting that business activities are wrong. But to see money making as an end in itself and to forget the transience of human values and even human life is foolish (Jas 4:13-17).

It is not impossible to be both godly and rich, but the suspicion creeps in here that those who have reached the top of the ladder in human terms are likely to have done so by treading on those who remain below, whether this was the intention or not. In the complex capitalistic context of our modern world, James's words should come home with particular force to those of us who live surrounded by the luxuries of Western society (Jas 5:1-6).

At this point, the rich oppressors of the establishment are separated from the family of God who must be patient until the time when true values will be seen for what they are and real rewards will be received. It may appear that worldly status and worldly possessions are what count in life, but believers should not doubt that "the coming of the Lord is near." Expectant steadfastness, involving endurance through the trials of life with hope and patience in suffering, is the attitude that they should cultivate, following Job's example (Jas 5:7-11).

Sarcophagus detail depicting an Orans (a woman praying with upraised arms). (James 5:16)

Speech and actions must be related. There should be no need for Christian believers to back up what they say with rash oaths of any kind. One's word should be surety enough. James is not making a specific point about the necessity of refusing to swear an oath in a court of justice but about the vital importance of keeping one's word. The condemnation of which he speaks is not so much for the speaking out of an oath but of the kind of unreliability that might make an oath necessary (Jas 5:12).

The tongue can be misused, but there are also right uses of speech, such as prayer, praise and confession. Wrong prayer will be ineffective, but there should be no misunderstanding about this; right prayer, stemming from right motives and in line with the will of God, is powerful. It is possible that James is speaking in James 5:15-16 of physical and spiritual healing, but his reference to the need for confession of sins and his earlier calls to endurance act as a warning against the assumption that Christians can expect all physical ailments to be automatically removed (Jas 5:13-18).

The loving attitude that leads people to take action and to provide for the material needs of those who lack should also lead to action in providing for the needs of the spiritually poor. Helping another person to return to a full, applied knowledge of the truth is about the greatest thing that a woman or a man can do. James is content to bring his recommendations to a close on that point (Jas 5:19-20).

Bibliography. J. B. Adamson, *James: The Man and His Message* (Grand Rapids, MI: Eerd-mans, 1989); P. H. Davids, *The Epistle of James: A Commentary on the Greek Text* (Grand Rapids, MI: Eerdmans, 1982); idem, *James*, New International Bible Commentary (Peabody, MA: Hendrickson, 1989); L. T. Johnson, *The Letter of James* (Garden City, NY: Doubleday, 1995); R. P. Martin, *James*, Word Biblical Commentary 48 (Waco, TX: Word, 1988); D. J. Moo, *James* (Grand Rapids, MI: Eerdmans, 1985); C. Freeman Sleeper, *James* (Nashville: Abingdon, 1998).

MARY J. EVANS

1 PETER

Introduction

This epistle deals with the faith, comportment and courage of believers enduring persecution or the threat of it. The occasion for the letter may have been the persecution under the emperor Nero (c. A.D. 64-68). How widely this may have spread throughout other parts of the Roman Empire is not known, but local persecutions occurred sporadically in Asia Minor.

The letter claims to be from "Peter, an apostle of Jesus Christ" (1 Pet 1:1), "an elder myself and a witness of the sufferings of Christ" (1 Pet 5:1). The early church unhesitatingly identified 1 Peter as written by the apostle. Eusebius described the church's recognition of 1 Peter as being equal to the "recognized letters" of Paul (*Ecclesiastical History* 3.25). Papias (A.D. 60-135) mentions 1 Peter and its composition in Rome (Eusebius *Ecclesiastical History* 2.15). Clement of Rome (30-101), the *Didache* and Polycarp (69-156) quote from every chapter. Second Peter 3:1 refers to 1 Peter. Irenaeus (130-200) quotes from 1 Peter by name (*Against Heresies* 4.9.2).

Some modern critics, however, have questioned Peter's authorship of the letter. In arguing for a pseudonymous letter, they point out that the historical situation appears to be later than the persecution of Nero during which Peter was presumably martyred. The Greek is that of a more literate author, the recipients are apparently Gentiles living in areas associated with the apostle Paul, and the concerns expressed are close to those identified with Paul.

Although Peter was described as "uneducated" (Acts 4:13), he was not necessarily illiterate. By law Jews were taught to read Scripture, write and work out mathematical sums (Mishnah, *Aboth* 5:2; Josephus *Against Apion* 2.25). Galilee, Peter's home province, was known to be bilingual (Mt 26:73; Greek and Aramaic). Fishermen such as Peter were middle-class business people who would need to use koine Greek as a trade language.

Peter's encounter with Jews from Pontus, Cappadocia and Asia (Acts 2:9) may have involved continuing communication, as the same locations are also mentioned in 1 Peter 1:1. Paul is not known to have visited the provinces of Bithynia (Acts 16:6-7), Pontus or Cappadocia.

The epistle shows knowledge of Mark, John, James, Paul, Luke, Matthew and Jesus. It touches on motifs known to be concerns of Peter, such as rejected stones (1 Pet 2:4, 7-8; Mk 12:10; Acts 4:11), silver as not being important (1 Pet 1:18; 3:3; Acts 3:6), prophecy (1 Pet 1:10-12; Acts 2:16, 30; 10:43), God as impartial judge (1 Pet 1:17; Acts 10:34, 42), Peter as witness (1 Pet 5:1; Acts 2:32), baptism (1 Pet 3:21; Acts 2:38), service (1 Pet 4:10-11; Acts 6:2-4), sin (1 Pet 1:18; Acts 2:40) and salvation for the household (1 Pet 3:20; Acts 2:39). The attitudes expressed are often those exhibited by Peter in the Gospels and the book of Acts.

In these 105 verses are more than 130 New Testament and 60 Old Testament quotations and allusions. In spite of this, 63 words occur that are unique in the New Testament. The document abounds in metaphors and similes. Because of the multiplicity of topics discussed and the inclusion of a doxology, some readers have failed to see clear arrangement and progression in the letter. Nevertheless, the progression of the letter can be outlined. Recipients of the letter are encouraged to "live in reverent fear during the time of [their] exile" (1 Pet 1:17) as they remember the good news (1 Pet 1:3-25) and grow in their salvation (1 Pet 2:1—5:11). A primary motif is that of the people of God as a family. In the initial spread of Christianity, the home became the platform for propagating the new faith in communities. Here family, friends and neighbors gathered to hear the message of the traveling evangelist, to worship and to discuss what they had heard. Interested persons who became part of the faith community not only observed the family from the outside but also were incorporated into its interior life. One might view the treatise as a discussion of the birth, development, character, relationships and conduct of the household of faith.

Outline

1:1-2 Greeting
1:3-25 Remember the Good News Announced to You
  1:3-12 Giving Birth to the Heirs of Promise
  1:13-25 Becoming Proactive Family Members
2:1—5:11 Growing in Salvation
  2:1-3 Alimentation of the New Child
  2:4-10 Integration into a Kinship Structure
  2:11-17 Submission Silences Critics Outside the Household
  2:18—3:12 Submission Silences Critics Within the Household
  3:13—4:19 The Household Making Sense of Suffering
  5:1-11 Humility Within the Household
5:12-14 Greetings Among Christ's Family

Commentary

Greeting (1 Pet 1:1-2)

The writer is identified as an apostle and a witness. As one of the Twelve (Lk 6:13-14) Peter had insisted on a replacement for Judas and specified that such an individual must have accompanied the original twelve from the time that John baptized Jesus until he ascended (Acts 1:21-22). These eyewitnesses were mandated to testify to their firsthand knowledge of the risen Christ (1 Cor 9:2).

The readers are Christians who had not seen Jesus. Although Jewish believers lived in these provinces (Acts 2:5-9), Gentiles appear to be Peter's focus. If so, then "exiles of the Dispersion" (1 Pet 1:1) is a metaphor referring to the Christian life in the world. J. H. Elliott maintains that the term *parepidēmos* refers to resident aliens deprived of full status as citizens. Thus there is a chasm between them and those enjoying full privileges. There were thousands of displaced persons in Asia Minor, and family identity becomes critically important to the disenfranchised (*see* Yahweh's Concern for the Disenfranchised).

Giving Birth to the Heirs of Promise (1 Pet 1:3-12)

Birthing imagery recurs throughout the document. This is an appropriate metaphor, for entrance into a family is possible only through birth or adoption. In the New Testament the verb *gennaō* is mainly used of a mother "bearing a child" but is also used for the father's act of begetting. We are told that the birthright is a living hope and an unfading inheritance. God has given new birth, usually considered a maternal gift, with an imperishable inheritance, ordinarily bequeathed by a father. Both aspects are intimately connected with familial continuity.

"Living hope" stood in contrast to the high infant mortality rate in the ancient world. Parents who could afford to do so often remained emotionally detached from a newborn until there was a reasonable prospect that the child could survive infancy. Unlike human inheritance, that from God never decays or fades and is always untainted. It cannot be lost, for it is "kept in heaven."

If the inheritance must be safely retained for use in the next generation, even more must the children be protected and guided until they can responsibly use what has been preserved for them. The child reaches maturity through a process of training that is often far from pleasant.

Enduring persecution because of their faith, these Christians are situated in the world so that their faith may become durable. Unlike gold, which can be destroyed, a durable faith will persist until Jesus' return.

Birth pangs had been necessary for the creation of a new people. Although Peter had initially not been able to accept Jesus' suffering, he now understood the necessity of the Messiah's agony and death. He had gained a comprehension denied to the prophets and angels. Though both were God's messengers, the ultimate revelation had come to those who heard and heeded the gospel.

Becoming Proactive Family Members (1 Pet 1:13-25)

Readers are invited metaphorically to belt up their flowing garments in order to have freedom of motion. Parent-child vocabulary reminds believers that they must be holy as God is holy, for the child is identified by her resemblance to the parent.

The metaphor of Father is reintroduced with the adjectival phrase "the one who judges all people impartially according to their deeds." This had been a hard lesson for Peter to learn. As a devout Jewish fisherman, Peter had been required to separate unclean from clean fish. By stages he learned that Samaritans and Gentiles could participate in the blessing of faith in Christ and that no one should be called unclean. Under pressure, Peter stopped eating with Gentiles but eventually defended Paul's and Barnabas's ministry to Gentiles. Though the addressees live as strangers away from their home, in danger of being treated unjustly, the Father is impartial; and freedom depends on an imperishable ransom.

The believers have been born anew by the "living and enduring word of God" (1 Pet 1:23). As God created the world by a word, now again there is creation for every believer by God's message. Unlike the Roman Empire, in which a victim of persecution could be denied status and legal rights, one can never be deprived of the rebirth. It is dependent upon the word of an eternal God. Mutual love arises from this new birth and develops a luxuriant growth leading to spiritual maturity.

Alimentation of the New Child (1 Pet 2:1-3)

In view of Christ's instruction that Peter should feed his lambs (Jn 21:15), the emphasis on nurture is well taken. Babies who lack the sucking instinct are in jeopardy. While some newborns begin to nurse naturally, others have no idea how or where to satisfy their hunger. They turn away from the breast and may resist vigorously, all the while crying because their most basic need is unsatisfied. Usually resistance stops once they have tasted milk.

Peter, who apparently had observed the nursing process, insisted that those who had tasted of Christ's grace should thirst after it. They may not have known where or how to find satisfaction, but the initial taste should lure the believer to growth in the Lord (Ps 34:8).

A newborn wants nothing so much as nourishment. It would be impossible to find a more apt metaphor for the ravenous desire of a new believer for the Word of God or for the diligent work that is required in assimilating that Word into one's life. Nursing requires intense effort and concentration. Yet with astonishing frequency the infant demands more feedings to fill its limited capacity. This too is part of the desire and reminds us that ingesting the will and Word of God is an ongoing process that must become a frequent practice.

By implication, God is portrayed as a nursing mother, an image used in the Old Testament (Is 49:15; Ps 131:2; *see* Images of God as Female). The milk is pure and provided without ambivalence. For the mother who could not or would not nurse her baby, mother's milk could be bought in the marketplace or a wet nurse hired. Though there was a risk of diluted or adulterated milk, this was often the choice of upper-class women in order to prevent attachment to an infant who might not survive.

Integration into a Kinship Structure (1 Pet 2:4-10)

A newborn was not automatically accepted as part of the family. Instead there was a formal ceremony in which the baby was laid on the floor in full view of assembled kinfolk. The father, in official recognition of the new arrival as his child, would take up the baby. Then followed reception into the larger family, clan and tribe. The newborn believer was similarly integrated into a larger group, a "spiritual house" (1 Pet 2:5; *oikos* may indicate house and temple).

"Coming" to Jesus (1 Pet 2:4) is a process, but it involves approach to a divinely constructed edifice. The "stone" is not simply a loose stone but the large, costly, polished marble stones that made up the temple in Jerusalem.

The cornerstone of this marvelous edifice was a stone that had previously been left in the quarry (Ps 118:22; Lk 20:17) but now was placed in the position of greatest honor. Thus the "living stone" gave stability and cohesion to the impressive building. Peter (whose name ["rock"] is *petros* rather than *lithos,* as in 1 Peter 2:4-8), contemplated the eternal Stone *(lithos)* that could not be moved or vacillate as he had done. Believers constitute building blocks of a spiritual temple. While the picture of a nursing infant is individual, the collective body of stones is communal.

The metaphor changes to that of priests within the temple. Each is given a specific assignment, but all work together to bring fitting worship to God. The new identity of this priesthood is spelled out in a dramatic list drawn from Exodus 19:4-6 and Isaiah 43:20. "Race" highlights direct descendants; "people" emphasizes common people as opposed to leaders. However, the descendants are "chosen"; the common people are for a possession. Though of obscure status, they hold a royal post. Unlike the descendants of Aaron and Phinehas, who claimed hereditary priesthood, entrance now comes with the new birth. Though once outside the fold of Israel, these believers are of holy stock and have a share with the people of God in the worship and mission of Yahweh. Theirs is the command "to proclaim the mighty acts of him who called you" (1 Pet 2:9).

The priestly functions are no longer divided by gender, birth, race or physical characteristic (e.g., Ex 28:1; Lev 21:17-21; 22:4-13). Every member of the congregation has the privilege and responsibility to represent God within and outside the congregation. The quotation in 1 Peter 2:10, a refrain from Hosea 2:23, declares all who believe to be part of the new Israel.

Submission Silences Critics Outside the Household (1 Pet 2:11-17)

These "aliens and exiles" should not seek to establish rights of citizenship in a "country" that indulges passions of the flesh—desires warring against their soul (2 Pet 2:11). Instead they should strive after good conduct so that nonbelievers might glorify God from having observed believers' good actions. The verb for "see" is *epopteuō* , a word also used in Greek mystery religion to denote a vision that brought knowledge. Those who saw the Christians' behavior would gain a practical knowledge of this new religion.

By their attitude and conduct, believers are to live honorably among the Gentiles. Two centuries earlier, two thousand Jewish families had been deported from Babylonia to Asia Minor, where they would serve as a stabilizing influence on restive local populations (Josephus *Antiquities* 12.150). Jews were known for their law-abiding lifestyle, one that the new people of God also needed to demonstrate.

The finite verb *hypotassō* is rendered "accept" (NRSV) or "submit yourselves" (NIV, KJV) but has a wide semantic range. Implied synonyms in 1 Peter 2:17 include "honor," "love," "fear." The literal meaning, "to place oneself under," or in military parlance, "to draw up behind," developed other meanings. Among these were to serve as an ally, identify or associate with, adhere to, or to relate in such a way as to make meaning (for the last, Polybius *Histories* 3.36.6-7; 18.15.40; "to bring under the influence of," see *Analytical Greek Lexicon,* 1970 l.c.). The term had also the sense of loyalty and of orderly and accountable behavior. In view of Peter's insistence that obedience must be yielded to God rather than to human beings (Acts 4:19; 5:29), one can hardly construe the term in this context as requiring a believer's absolute obedience. Rather, submission is a call for compliance with the structures necessary for the peaceful functioning of society and a discharge of all rightful obligations of citizenship.

In 1 Peter 2:17 an expanded commentary is given for the desired conduct. "Honor everyone" is a command with ramifications: persevere in fearing God and honoring rulers. As in 1 Peter 5:9, there is a call to family solidarity, for believers are brothers and sisters who share their faith and consequent afflictions with one another and with Christ.

Submission Silences Critics Within the Household (1 Pet 2:18—3:12)

In approaching the following directives, we must bear in mind that they were addressed to persons enduring persecution for their faith. Ancient philosophers maintained that the welfare of the political state depended on proper order within the household, a state in microcosm. The conduct of slaves, wives and children was therefore of paramount concern, especially in situations where the faith and lifestyle of Christians were considered to be damaging to the state and to society. Their conduct will provide an apologetic for Christianity. "By doing right you should silence the ignorance of the foolish." (The word for silence is "to muzzle," as one muzzles a dog to stop its barking.) If the Christians were doing good, their critics could find little basis for accusations, especially in those provinces to which the letter is addressed.

Household slaves were in part responsible for the harmony and cooperation necessary within the household. A careful differentiation is made between the constructive behavior that should be expected from Christian slaves and the abuse that they might suffer in consequence of professing their faith (1 Pet 2:18-25). A sound drubbing was considered effective in bringing the religious views of a slave into accord with those of the master. This view was held even by Christians (Augustine *Epistle* 185.21; 93.3, Council of Toledo 16.5.52.4). If a slave were recalcitrant, progressively more severe beatings should be employed to secure the desired result (MacMullen 65).

In theory, a slave might report excessive brutality on the part of a master to a Roman magistrate and thereby gain his or her freedom. But especially in a time of persecution, the reality was that a slave might deny Christ, run away or endure savage mistreatment. To be beaten for unruly conduct brought no reward from God, but suffering for the sake of the gospel was another matter. To remain with an abusive master could result in blessing as observers glorified God.

Unlike other New Testament instructions to slaves, there is no accompanying caution offered to Christian masters. This may bespeak a social situation that included slaves within the church but not the wealthier slave owners.

"In the same way" wives are bidden to cooperate with and honor their husbands as long as their conduct advances God's cause (1 Pet 3:1-6.) The purpose is clarified: that the husbands "may be won over" (*kerdainō,* 1 Pet 3:1). This term is a financial metaphor, literally signifying "they may gain a profit." The husbands, unconvinced of Christ's claims, are debits on a financial sheet. The purpose of the wives' loyalty and responsible conduct is redemptive. Nonbelieving husbands may be won, even when the wives are forbidden to speak of Christ, by "the purity and reverence" of their lives. In an age of promiscuity, sexual purity was a quality to be noted and prized. A husband had a right to his wife's fidelity, respect and propriety ("submission"). These are tools to bring him to Christ.

Not outward adornment but the ornament of a gentle and quiet spirit would win a nonbelieving spouse. In this lay a power more alluring than fashion. James Neil suggests that 1 Peter 3:3 should be rendered as a hendiadys, "gold-braided hair." Women would braid their hair, interweaving into it golden spangles and threads that glittered and twinkled with every movement of the head. (For braided hair as being seductive in the cult of Isis, see Apuleius *Golden Ass* 3.8-9; Xenophon *Anthia and Habrocomes* 1.11.5-6.) Plutarch remarked that flame-colored garments enraged husbands. The expense of elaborate embroidery with gold threads might better be dispensed to meet the needs of the poor. A gentle and quiet spirit is still the brightest ornament. "Quiet" *(hēsychios)* bespeaks a state of calm, restraint at the proper time, respect and affirmation (Spencer). According to Plutarch, this was a quality in short supply within the women's quarters (Plutarch *Peri Hēsychia)*.

The theme of adornment continues as the discussion turns to Sarah, "who obeyed Abraham and called him lord." "Lord" *(kyrios)* was a common deferential mode of address (e.g., "sir," Jn 12:21). The use of the present participle "calling" (1 Pet 3:6) may suggest not a single incident but a practice over time. *Kyrios* is well attested as the legal or technical name for a woman's male guardian and protector. Usually her father filled this role, but other male relatives could also fill it. Since Abraham was also her half-brother, Sarah may have named *(kaleō)* him as her *kyrios*. As they traveled further into the unknown, after the death of her father, Terah, Abraham appears to have become husband and legal protector.

Sarah's outstanding obedience appears to have been in following her husband as he left the ties and comforts of a brilliant civilization to follow God's call into an unknown land among an alien people. Her life was fraught with incredible difficulties, but she persisted as a devoted wife who shared her husband's call. Women may find it particularly difficult to be uprooted and to sever familiar ties. To find oneself among people who do not share one's faith is even worse. The thought of Sarah's journey of faith might give great encouragement to women living as strangers in an alien land.

There are, however, divergent opinions as to the writer's view of Sarah's obedience. Does it refer to the episode in which Abraham denied that he was married to her and allowed the king of Egypt to take her into his household? There are other possible options. One of the functions of the *kyrios* was to bestow the woman in marriage. Did Abraham in this capacity give her to another? If that is the point, then in the same way

Feminine Adornment

Feminine adornment refers to methods used to highlight a woman's appearance, and any study must consider cosmetics and jewelry.

Eye paint enhanced and enlarged the eyes and eyebrows but may also have reduced glare from the sun, deterred disease-carrying flies and alleviated dryness of the skin. Three Old Testament passages seem to disapprove of eye painting (2 Kings 9:30; Jer 4:30; Ezek 23:40), but Job 42:14 refers to Job's third daughter as Keren-happuch, the "horn of paint" or "antimony" (horn being a small container used for eye paint powder), and Job 42:15 refers to the same daughter with high regard. This passage could indicate that only the overuse of cosmetics was viewed with disapproval.

The use of perfume was hygienic and social. Since water was sometimes scarce, the more expeditious method of caring for the body was with oils and perfumes. Oils and ointments were essential for maintaining the skin in such a dry climate. Manufacture of these items required skilled workers and was an accepted vocation (1 Sam 8:13).

Jewelry was sometimes worn for superstitious reasons (e.g., as a good-luck charm). Many biblical passages mention jewelry, specific gemstones, metals, or bones, wood or plants from which jewelry was fashioned. Some ancient jewelry forms are necklaces, bracelets, armlets, anklets, hairpins and hair ornaments, pins for securing tunics, earrings, nose rings, finger rings, belts and pendants. Reportedly no gemstone deposits have been found in Palestine, but many are located in Egypt and Mesopotamia. This helps in understanding why much Israelite acquisition of gemstone jewelry came through trade, purchase or conquest (cf. Is 1).

In the Greco-Roman world, sumptuary laws (that is, laws regulating personal behavior) were passed from time to time, but they did little to restrain women's love of elegance and fashion. Classical statuary reveals the care with which fine fabric was draped about the female form and with which hair was arranged, often requiring the specialized labor of at least two slaves (cf. 1 Pet 3:4). Pearls were greatly prized, even though they were acquired at the risk of a pearl diver's life, and ostentation in jewelry and fine clothing required funds that might better be employed to feed the poor (cf. 1 Tim 2:9). The noble Roman widow Cornelia was once visited by women anxious to show off their jewels. When asked in turn to show her own, Cornelia summoned her two young sons, the Gracchi, and declared, "These are my jewels."

Bibliography

R. J. Forbes, *Studies in Ancient Technology,* 2d ed. (Leiden: E. J. Brill, 1965) 3:1-50, 8:194 n. 175, 195 n. 190; A. Lucas, *Ancient Egyptian Materials and Industries,* 3d ed. (London: Edward Arnold & Co.) 52-60, 99-119, 442-61.

MARSHA ELLIS SMITH

---

that Christ was a model to slaves, Christ is a model to wives. Sarah, like Christ, committed no sin, offered herself on behalf of another and placed her hopes in God (1 Pet 2:21-23; 3:18). Sarah was Christlike (1 Pet 3:4, 16) in giving her life as a potential sacrifice for Abraham, despite his unrighteous request that she misrepresent herself to Pharaoh as Abraham's sister (Gen 12:13; cf. 20:13).

As in 1 Peter 3:3, the focus was on Sarah's physical beauty, a factor that made her husband fearful for his life as he entered Egypt. Abraham demonstrated a lack of faith and obedience to God's promise in requiring Sarah to risk life and virtue for his self-preservation (Gen 12:12). Confronted with a life-threatening situation in a hostile, alien environment, she had little recourse but to comply. Sarah could hope only in God to deliver her, a deliverance that came through the affliction of Pharaoh and his house with plagues (Gen 12:17). Abraham appears as culpable in this story and in the similar episode with Abimilech (Gen 20). Abimilech's household is visited with sterility, and the truth of Sarah's and Abraham's relationship is revealed (Gen 20:3-7, 18). While Sarah is held guiltless, her husband is rebuked (Gen 20:9, 16). Far from being a blessing to all nations, his infidelity has made him a curse.

The introduction of Sarah as a figure to be emulated raises other considerations that must also be reviewed. The relationship of Sarah and Abraham was more of a mutual arrangement than a cursory reading of the preceding text might envisage. God commanded Abraham to obey Sarah's bidding when she perceived that Ishmael might be a threat to the safety of the newly weaned Isaac (Gen 21:10-12). The Hebrew text (Gen 21:9) tells us that Sarah had seen Ishmael "mocking" or "playing" with Isaac. The same verb is used in 2 Samuel 2:14 to describe a pretext for murderous action (see also Prov 26:19). Whatever the activity, Sarah perceived it as a threat to the newly weaned child.

Although some adolescent Bedouin lads are sent to make their way in the desert at this age, Abraham could not bear the thought. Sarah was adamant that Ishmael, along with Hagar, be removed from the home. Abraham obeyed not only in the case of Ishmael but also in the case of the sons of his concubines (Gen 25:6). The action seems cruelly unjust to Hagar and her son, but it gave the slave woman her freedom and Ishmael ascendancy among a tribal people. There does not appear to have been alienation, for Ishmael took part in the burial of Abraham (Gen 25:9).

When Paul turns to this story, he uses the

verb *diōkō* ("to persecute," "to mistreat") to intimate that Ishmael's treatment of Isaac was in some way abusive (Gal 4:29). In this his thought was similar to that of several rabbinic scholars. Sarah's dictum is described by Paul as a decree of Scripture (Gal 4:30) that Abraham was required to honor. Sibling rivalry and abuse are recurring themes in Genesis, and the deadly effects were averted by Rebekah in just such a separation of brothers (Gen 27:41-45; *see* Sibling Rivalry; Violence, Abuse and Oppression).

Even the best of biblical ancestors had their flaws, and Sarah should be claimed by

Elaborate hairdo requiring the work of several slaves as hairdressers. (1 Peter 3:3)

Christian women although she may not always have been admirable. The injunction is remarkable, however, in naming a spiritual ancestor who is female rather than male. Although there are many references to the faith and deeds of the fathers, those of mothers are far less prominent. Here spiritual heredity is traced from foremother to daughter, perhaps on the principle that endures to this day: a true Jew is one whose mother is a Jew (cf. Ps 86:16; 116:16; Prov 1:8; 6:20; 2 Tim 1:5). Godly women are called to place themselves in this tradition. The final clause of 1 Peter 3:6 describes the genuine daughter of Sarah: "as long as you do what is good and never let fears alarm you."

The fears of a woman might be based on intimidation and threats from an unbelieving husband. They might be similar to those that Sarah experienced in Pharaoh's court. Like Sarah, a Christian woman might find herself in an alien household with few defenses. In the context of 1 Peter 3, wives whose aim was to "win over" their husbands to Christianity might be fearful. Given away as child brides by families who would be unsympathetic to their Christian profession, these women had no recourse apart from God. Despite their predicament, they are enjoined to be fearless in their witness for Christ and to use good actions as a means of evangelism. But nowhere in this passage are women enjoined to endure abuse from their husbands. Rather, they are encouraged to maintain their witness for Christ and to demonstrate their faith by irreproachable conduct.

As a deterrent to possible abusive behavior on the part of believing husbands, a new set of instructions outlines the norm for Christian family living. The section begins with "in the same way" (1 Pet 3:7), connecting the submission of the husband to that of the wife, the household slaves and to the more general earlier commands. Lacking a finite verb, the exhortation of 1 Peter 3:7 is participial: "the men, in the same way, living with their wives as the weaker vessel." The use of the comparative indicates that husbands as well are considered vessels. A "vessel" denoted an implement of any kind, such as a utensil, furniture or equipment. Elsewhere in the New Testament, Paul is called a "chosen vessel" (Acts 9:15 KJV), and those who have matured in Christian virtues are vessels "to honor" (2 Tim 2:20-21 KJV). The simplest understanding of the image is that husbands should take into consideration that women generally possess less physical strength than do men.

The text, however, calls for husbands to honor their spouses as joint heirs with them. An heir is one who receives an inheritance and manages it. The concept of a woman as joint heir with her husband was a radical one in Jewish and Roman society. According to rabbinic tradition, sons inherited and daughters received maintenance (Mishnah, *Ketuboth* 4:6). A Roman woman upon marriage sank to the legal status of her husband's daughter and could claim only a daughter's inheritance—half that of a son. Here women are presented as coheirs of "the gracious gift of life," equal in the sight of God and of the believing community.

The husband who affirmed his wife in honor and equality would find power in his prayers. Abuse or degradation of his wife would bring an obstruction, an echo of Isaiah's injunction that God would not hear the prayers of the violent (Is 58:4). Significantly, New Testament calls for wifely submission are always accompanied with specific directives to prevent abuse on the part of the husband (Eph 5:28-29; Col 3:19).

A summary of the exhortation to husbands as well as the section about honorable conduct is found in 1 Peter 3:8-12. It is imperative that the call for endurance under persecution is not misapplied to other situations. This passage has been woefully misinterpreted in a way that has been destructive to many Christian homes.

The Household Making Sense of Suffering (1 Pet 3:13—4:19)

The mandates of 1 Peter 2:18—3:8 are not a call for slaves or women in all situations to endure abuse. Suffering that allows a perpetrator to continue the abusive conduct can never be redemptive. Rather, it enables sin that damages the soul of perpetrator and victim. In societies where there is legal redress for abuse, patient endurance

Holiness & Wholeness

To a suffering community, stigmatized, humiliated and persecuted, comes the call in the wilderness: "Be holy!" With this summons, 1 Peter inspires its audience with a new identity and new reference point for understanding their suffering. Their experience of persecution is a sign that eschatological judgment is begun and they will soon share in the glory of Christ. They are chosen and destined by the Father, made holy by the Spirit and purified by the work of Jesus Christ.

In the marvelous ascription of praise to God that follows, believers are invited into the realm of eschatological joy with lofty reminders of the marvelous gifts of grace. The carefully enumerated blessings of those who "rejoice" (1 Pet 1:8) become the inspiration for the instruction to live as a holy people unto God. The indicative gifts are followed by the imperatives of faith and hope. With the connective "therefore" comes the divine summons: "You shall be holy, for I am holy" (1 Pet 1:16). This quotation of Leviticus 19:2 refers the reader to the Old Testament code of holiness (Lev 17—26). The key word *holy* and its derivatives in the Old Testament indicate dedication to God and separation from the ungodly. Alignment to the holy God brings wholeness or shalom. Leviticus 19 defines holiness by God's nature; what is required is godly character in relation to God, others and even nature (*see* Men and Women as Stewards of the Environment): reverence, devotion, faithfulness, goodness, honesty, compassion, generosity, justice, love and purity. Those who call upon God (1 Pet 1:2; cf. Mt 6:9; Lk 11:2) are to live in holy relation to God, to a new family—the people of God—and to the world. As "obedient children" they demonstrate the nature of their "parent" in all of their conduct.

In the holiness code of 1 Peter 1:13—2:8, all of the main verbs are imperatives. The positive commands presume the gift of new birth. The metaphors express the focus of intent, exertion of the will and corresponding action. Gratitude for the good news of God's salvation, brought by the Holy Spirit, is to be expressed in mental readiness, sober attention and committed hope. Such wholehearted and single-minded devotion to the holy One results in holy conduct.

The negative command "do not be conformed" (1 Pet 1:14) recalls a pagan past of moral rebellion. The old desires of the unregenerate heart—selfish seeking of privilege, power and pleasure—are manifested in malice, guile, insincerity, envy and slander. Such desires are deadly, and believers are urged to rid themselves of and refrain from that which destroys relationship and wages war against the soul. By contrast, purification of the soul by obedience to the truth (the gospel) results in a social outcome—genuine and deep love within the community. Only in 1 Peter is the church referred to as siblings. Beyond the identity of family comes the more specific identifiers of "chosen race, royal priesthood, holy nation, God's own people." This family then is related to the Israel of old and to its mission to "proclaim the mighty acts of him who called you" (1 Pet 2:9). Those who have limited power and insecure livelihood in their culture are granted a new corporate identity. Intergroup strength and divine call are the foundation for security and mission.

The appeal to the human will in 1 Peter is always based on the source of new identity—spiritual birth. That new life, already a reality, is to yearn for the living word about the Lord, which sustains life. The nursing infant craving mother's milk becomes the symbol for the longing of growing believers. Growth into salvation comes by continuous appropriation of God's gift and may be recognized in experience. Holiness is gift and command, fact and process, individual and corporate, general and specific—and that is the nature of wholeness. The "holy life" is the whole life. It is manifested in all conduct: reverential fear of God as Judge as well as Father and genuine love for brother and sister in the Lord, which extends even to persecutors (1 Pet 3:9; cf. Mt 5:45). The courage "to submit" in unjust and terrifying circumstances "for the sake of the Lord" is a practical holiness in face-to-face encounters with real threats and fears and pains. Christ is lifted up as the perfect example in the face of such suffering. Just as he entrusted himself to God, so should his followers.

Yet, much misunderstanding has come from the instruction to "submit" because of a lack of knowledge about the situation behind 1 Peter. In a society in which emperor, master and husband had power and privilege, subject people, slaves and wives were at risk. There is nothing new here in the requirement of subordinate partners. "Submit" had been the rule of the culture for generations, and in this letter it is applied to those most tempted to rebel. What is revolutionary and new in 1 Peter is the acknowledgment of the injustice of the suffering and humiliation and the motivation given for submission. Rather than the appeal to a created order of superior-inferior, as the culture taught, believers are to submit "for the Lord's sake" (1 Pet 2:13). In the face of absolute power and with little opportunity for recourse, the strategy commanded is "do good" and "submit." Take what cannot be changed from the outside and change it from the inside. Do not simply endure as victims. Take action. Serve God. "Silence the ignorance of the foolish" (1 Pet 2:15).

This strategy is extended to women: "win over" your husbands (1 Pet 3:1). In a culture that required women to follow the religion of their husbands, conversion to Christ was a threat at the center of society, the home. Christian women with pagan husbands are already rebels. They are in danger. And yet, women are counseled to "not fear any terror." They are assigned a mission. Good conduct is presented as the means to godly ends. Living honorably within the institutions of society is elevated to the level of obedience to God and evangelism or witness. What is being urged is not conformity to society—that has already been denounced. The truth of their status as "free" is pronounced and then redirected to honor and love (1 Pet 2:16; cf. 1 Cor 9). In 1 Peter all are called to live as "servants of God." As a spiritual priesthood they "proclaim the mighty acts of [God]" (1 Pet 2:9). They offer spiritual sacrifices. Holiness in all conduct is the means of worship and witness.

As a result of their conversion and participation in a new community the believers addressed in 1 Peter experienced alienation and persecution. Their suffering threatened to overwhelm them. To this specific sociopolitical situation, the suffering of the faith community, 1 Peter employs a theological response found first in the old tradition of Exodus and then in its reapplication to the exiles in Isaiah. The chosen people of God are a holy people "sanctified for obedience." They are holy in the whole of life. Holiness in all conduct is promise and command. It is the way to wholeness. In the face of unjust suffering, when they are tempted to be afraid and despair, they are to hope and to trust. In the face of not belonging and no safety, they are to do good. God is faithful. God can be trusted and answers the cry of his people. God will vindicate the right and judge the wrong. Believers will not be put to shame but will be exalted when Christ is revealed. The word of God will accomplish the promise of exodus to a new life for the suffering church, just as it did in the past for Israel in exile. When they are helpless and have no control, God is still accomplishing good. Stand fast. Be encouraged. Be holy in all your conduct!

Bibliography

L. Goppelt, *A Commentary on 1 Peter* (Grand Rapids, MI: Eerdmans, 1993); J. R. Michaels, *1 Peter,* Word Biblical Commentary 49 (Waco, TX: Word, 1988); W. L. Schutter, *Hermeneutic and Composition in 1 Peter,* Wissenschaftliche Untersuchungen zum Neuen Testament, 2d series 30 (Tübingen: J. C. B. Mohr, 1989).

SHARON CLARK PEARSON

---

is more likely to be seen as codependence than as exemplary conduct.

The New Testament contains definite instructions to stop wrongful conduct of fellow believers and to hold the perpetrator responsible (Mt 18:15-17; 1 Cor 5:1-7; 1 Thess 5:14; 2 Thess 3:14-15; 1 Tim 5:20; Tit 3:10-11; Jas 5:19-20). The believing community must also recognize its duty to deliver the oppressed from the hand of the violent (Jer 21:12; 22:3). In contemporary societies where professing Christians are persecuted for their faith, they may still endure abuse as a consequence of their refusal to deny Christ.

How may these passages, written to people caught in persecution for the faith, be applied to situations that involve no oppression for one's faith? First, we can have an understanding that believers must demonstrate a lifestyle that can withstand criticism. Second, meeting mistreatment with kindness and exemplary conduct is a powerful response. Workers are to give conscientious service, even to disagreeable employers. Third, God calls husband and wife as coheirs to live joyfully with respect and love for one another. A distortion of this balance brings obstruction not only of effective prayer but also of true communion in marriage. All believers are called to unity of spirit, sympathy, love for one another, a tender heart and a humble mind.

Verbal abuse, a sin vehemently condemned in Scripture (Mt 5:21-22; 12:34-37; 15:18-20; Eph 4:29; Jas 3:2-10) although often condoned in contemporary Christian circles, is addressed in 1 Peter 3:9-10. Other misuse of language, such as untruth and word twisting, are also to be shunned (Ps 56:5-6).

Believers are called to faith rather than fear while sanctifying "Christ as Lord" (1 Pet 3:15). When the opportunity arises for persecuted believers to give a defense of their faith, they must be ready.

In the phrase "the hope that is in you" (1 Pet 3:15) the second person plural is used. This hope is among the community. Being in Christian community is another key for arresting fear. Hope is alive because its object is a living God and must be continuous. Outwardly Christians are gentle and respectful, while inwardly they maintain a good conscience in the knowledge that they have not sinned.

In the foregoing chapters the example and sufferings of Christ have been mentioned. Here we see voluntary suffering to promote a righteous cause. In similar cases believers may be called on to suffer if they are to remain faithful to Christ. On August 28, 1963, Martin Luther King Jr. said to those who had labored for racial justice, "You have been veterans of creative suffering. Continue to work with the faith that unearned suffering is redemptive." Suffering was a necessary corollary to advancing a righteous cause. By contrast, the horrible suffering inflicted on prisoners in concentration camps during World War II was not of their choosing and therefore was not redemptive.

The conduct of the sufferers must be irreproachable, or the power of witness is diminished. Here the example of Christ is paramount. Though wronged and vilified in his arrest and trial, he did not reciprocate but remained silent and respectful. Christ provides the example for the correct reason to suffer, not because of sin but "for sins" (1 Pet 3:18). He remained righteous while bringing sinners to God.

Christians are not to rejoice in all sufferings but only "insofar" as they are "sharing Christ's sufferings" (1 Pet 4:13). They may be vilified for bearing the name of Christ. The mere name of Christian would later become sufficient grounds for a death sentence. Believers would suffer "as Christians" and thereby glorify God because of that name. The suffering that remains steadfast under persecution is that which glorifies God.

The example of Christ has been given so that readers might "arm yourselves also with the same intention" (1 Pet 4:1). They were not to defend themselves with the weapons of earthly warfare but with those supplied by Christ. All forms of licentiousness, debauchery and idolatry must be abandoned. Promiscuity, drunkenness (*komoi* is a technical word for rites involving excessive use of wine) and idolatry were basic components of paganism.

What should believers do, since the time of judgment is near? They should be "serious," having a sound mind and showing self-control. They should also be temperate. The term *nēphō* refers to refraining from wine but metaphorically to being disciplined. The repeated call to sobriety stands in contrast to Plato's description of the blessed afterlife as being one of perpetual intoxication.

God's help is indispensable in the end times, especially during this time of persecution. Relationship with God should be coupled with relationships to human beings, involving love and hospitality, qualities that enabled the ministry of others. Hospitality was imperative to shelter traveling missionaries exposed to imminent danger and to afford them the opportunity of proclaiming the gospel in a community. The distribution of gifts within the family is according to God's choice, but the exercise of them is the responsibility of the faithful steward of the household regardless of gender (1 Pet 4:10-11; cf. Rom 12:6-8; 1 Cor 12; Eph 4:11-12).

Humility Within the Household (1 Pet 5:1-11)

We are given a touching mandate for feeding the flock of God. As Peter had been urged to feed the sheep, the command is now passed on to others. They are to serve without compulsion or in the hope of financial gain. Neither are they to "lord it over" those in their care (1 Pet 5:3; cf. 2 Cor 1:24). The term *katakyrieuō* occurs also in Matthew 20:25 and Mark 10:42 as Jesus announces that such control of power is unacceptable among his followers. Submission (*hypotassō*, 1 Pet 5:5) is here a matter of accepting instruction and guidance.

Greetings Among Christ's Family (1 Pet 5:12-14)

"She who is fellow elect in Babylon" (1 Pet 5:13, lit.) appears to be a specific individual, as is Mark (pace NRSV's "sister church"). The affection that Peter expresses for Mark may also be understood to extend to the unnamed woman.

Tradition maintains that Peter shared much with his wife, whose mother Jesus had healed (Mk 1:30-31). Paul speaks of the pair traveling together in a gospel ministry (1 Cor 9:5). Clement of Alexandria described their union as "blessed" and their feelings toward each other as "consummate" (Eusebius *Ecclesiastical History* 3.30). As she was led away to martyrdom, Peter shouted out to her, "My dear, remember the Lord."

If "she who is fellow elect" is a woman rather than a church, she may be the author's spouse. Her location is said to be Babylon, a code name for Rome in early Christian writings. Her name may have been withheld to protect her identity in a dangerous environment. Yet she may have wished to send a message to those among whom she had ministered and to encourage them in their time of tribulation to remember the Lord.

Such is the whole of Peter's message. Regardless of the affliction, comfort comes by remembering all that Christ has done for the redeemed.

Bibliography. D. Balch, *"Let Wives Be Submissive": The Domestic Code in 1 Peter* (Chico, CA: Scholars Press, 1981); J. H. Elliot, *Home for the Homeless* (Philadelphia: Fortress, 1981); R. MacMullen, *Christianizing the Roman Empire A.D. 100-400* (New Haven, CT: Yale University Press, 1984); J. M. A. Neil, *Everyday Life in the Holy Land* (London: Church Missions to Jews, 1953); A. B. Spencer, *Beyond the Curse* (Peabody, MA: Hendrickson, 1985).

CATHERINE CLARK KROEGER AND
AÍDA BESANÇON SPENCER

2 PETER

Introduction

2 Peter shares with other New Testament writings a conviction that eschatology and ethics are of a piece, that behavior in the present is conditioned by expectation of what is to come. This writing, like other early Christian writings, makes a connection between sexual continence and eschatological expectation (e.g., 1 Cor 7; Lk 20:34-36). The early church considered that sexuality would be excluded from the new age (e.g., Mk 12:25). Consequently, those who looked forward to the new heaven and the new earth regarded sexual restraint in this age as critical. Early Christianity thought that exercising self-control in the present was directly related to the future judgment (Acts 24:25). 2 Peter does not present a positive description of sexuality. Rather, we find a denigrating of the false teachers' enslavement to debauched sexuality and a polemical use of Scriptures that refer to sexual immorality. The letter's denunciation of licentiousness and extolling of sexual purity is typical of Christian writings with an eschatological focus (cf. 1 Thess 4:4-7; Rev 14:4).

Outline

1:1-2	Salutation
1:3-11	Homily on Godliness
1:12-21	Authority of Peter
2:1-22	Denunciation of the False Teachers
3:1-13	The Message of the Letter
3:14-18	Conclusion

Commentary

The message of the letter is bluntly simple, devoid of many of early Christianity's convictions and concerns. The writing is not concerned, for instance, with the cross of Christ and his resurrection, the process of becoming a Christian, such as we might find in the Gospels, and the new identity given believers, as we find in Paul. Neither does 2 Peter address the shape of communal worship, the division and nature of community responsibilities, how the church is to relate to the *polis,* or matters relating to Christian households, including the matter of sex within marriage.

The letter focuses solely on calling its hearers back to a particular aspect of the faith. The author considers his message so important that he intends his letter to be a constant reminder (2 Pet 1:12). It appears that the dissenting view—that there will be no judgment and that Christ will not come again—has gained significant ground among the readers. Those teaching this view are part of the community to which the letter is addressed, sharing common meals with the readers of the letter (2 Pet 2:13). Being at a distance, the author has only his words with which to challenge his readers, who may be young in the faith (2 Pet 2:18), with a message that is at odds with the false teachers, at odds with common sense and at odds with his readers' desires.

The message is at odds with the false teachers because while they say that Jesus will not return, the author claims he will, and while they say that enjoying the pleasures of the body is a good, the author claims that such is self-indulgence (2 Pet 2:13) and will lead only to destruction. The message of 2 Peter is also at odds with common sense, for the expectation that Jesus would appear again has begun to appear nonsensical. Some in the community scoff at the idea that Christ will come, saying that, since the first generation of believers has died, it is folly to hope for Christ's return (2 Pet 3:4). The false teachers say that things will go on as they are indefinitely. The author retorts that God has already demonstrated that God creates and destroys (2 Pet 3:5-6). Moreover, what appears to humans like a delay is not so in the divine agenda (2 Pet 3:8). God's slowness about bringing the end is connected to God's compassion, for God hopes that all would turn to God before the time of judgment (2 Pet 3:9; cf. 2 Pet 3:15). Furthermore, the message of 2 Peter is contrary to the natural desires of his readers. Whereas the false teachers deny that there is a coming judgment and so encourage believers in Jesus to yield to their natural passions, the author warns that God will come to judge the behavior of all, including believers. God will destroy those who have behaved unrighteously (2 Pet 3:7).

The Letter's Strategy: Emphasizing Peter's Authority

The daunting challenge of turning his addressees away from the persuasive arguments of the false teachers requires the author to be strategic. The most obvious strategy he uses in service of convincing his readers that Jesus will return at the judgment and that upright behavior matters is to appeal to Peter's authority. Scholars debate whether or not Peter the apostle wrote the letter. For various reasons, including the letter's highblown language and the late date implied by referring to Paul's letters as Scripture (2 Pet 3:16), many consider 2 Peter to be pseudonymous. A significant number of scholars regard the letter as written in Peter's name so as to convey to a particular community that its message accords with Peter's views. On the whole the issue of authorship is not overly important. 2 Peter's authority rests on its being in the Christian canon. It should be recognized, furthermore, that whether or not Peter wrote the letter, the letter's message is grounded on the apostle's authoritative knowledge. This fact is seen even more clearly if we accept what many take to be the best explanation for the similarities between the epistle of Jude and 2 Peter (e.g., Jude 4 and 2 Pet 2:1-3; Jude 5 and 2 Pet 2:5; Jude 6-7 and 2 Pet 2:4, 6; Jude 8-9 and 2 Pet 2:10-11). Most scholars hold that 2 Peter is dependent on Jude. When the author of 2 Peter used Jude in composing his letter, he reshaped the material so as to focus on Peter's credibility and unimpeachable apostolic credentials. The message that Jesus will come at the judgment is reliable because it comes from the apostle Peter.

The author claims that he, Simon Peter, is the one capable of reminding his readers of the truth. He focuses on the danger of forgetting (2 Pet 1:9) and the importance of remembering. What the author declares the readers must never forget is that they have been privileged to receive a faith equal to that of the apostle Peter (2 Pet 1:1). The faith equal to Simon Peter's is one that knows that the Lord Jesus Christ will return at the day of judgment and that in this time believers in Christ must live righteously. The letter focuses on the authority of Peter's knowledge by what it says and how it says it. (For a defense of Petrine authorship, see D. A. Carson, Douglas J. Moo and Leon Morris, *An Introduction to the New Testament* [Grand Rapids, MI: Zondervan, 1992], 433-38.)

The Foundation of Peter's Authority

The letter claims that the basis of Peter's authority is that he was a spectator of Christ's majesty (2 Pet 1:16-18), particularly at the transfiguration. Consequently the prophetic word that he gives in the letter is firm (2 Pet 1:19); in fact, it is the only reliable guide. The author strongly implies that scriptural prophecy supports his view and that he therefore is a spiritually gifted interpreter of prophecy (2 Pet 2:20-21).

Of the several interpretations of 2 Peter 1:20-21, the least reasonable is that which takes these verses out of their context and reads them as a statement about the divine inspiration of Scripture. These verses must be understood within the framework of, and as making a contribution to, the author's argument. 2 Peter 1:20-21 is not an abstract statement about the nature of the Bible. A more sensible, and widely held, interpretation sees these verses as referring to the Scriptures that have come to be called the Old Testament. In this view, the author is claiming that God's appointment of a Son was prophesied in the Old Testament (e.g., Ps 2) and this has surely come to pass (2 Pet 1:19). Likewise, the author's conviction about the coming of Jesus is prophesied and the author is the one who can correctly interpret the Old Testament Scriptures in this regard. His letter is a reminder of the predictions of the holy prophets and the commandment of their apostles (2 Pet 3:2). He is the authoritative interpreter. This view implies that there was dissension over whether Peter or the false teachers were the correct interpreters of the Old Testament. The letter, however, gives no evidence for such a disagreement.

Paul's letters, however, were a bone of contention (2 Pet 3:16). Furthermore, the writings of Paul, which the author and his audience regard as Scripture (2 Pet 3:15-16), refer to Jesus as God's Son and connect his Sonship to his coming in power at the end (1 Thess 1:10; 1 Cor 15:23-28). The author describes Paul's letters as confirming his viewpoint (2 Pet 3:15). While few scholars take this position, 2 Peter 1:16-21 can be understood as the author's declaration that his message is correct not only because he saw the majesty of God's Son and heard God's declaration of Jesus as Son. His message is true also because he knows how this event is connected to the future hope, for he is the one moved by the Holy Spirit to correctly interpret writings, such as Paul's, that speak of this.

This Message Is Peter's Last Words

2 Peter accentuates the authority of Peter not only by what it says about his unique role and abilities but also through how it says this. 2 Peter is ostensibly a letter, beginning with a salutation in which the sender identifies himself, followed by the name of the recipients and a wish for grace and peace. This is standard letter form. The writing closes with a doxology (2 Pet 3:18; cf. Rom 16:27). What 2 Peter does not contain is a normal letter body, including a thanksgiving section (e.g., 1 Cor 1: 4-9). The book moves directly from the epistolary salutation to a sermon on godliness (2 Pet 1:3-11), which precedes the author's admission that he knows himself to be dying (2 Pet 1:13-15).

2 Peter is often characterized as being a letter and a last will and testament. One strategy the author uses to increase the value placed on Peter's authority is to present Peter's exhortation as a deathbed speech. Within Hellenistic Judaism there was a tradition of patriarchs on the verge of death

giving ethical advice to their descendants (e.g., *Testaments of the Twelve Patriarchs*). Often the patriarchs' advice is based on having had a unique vision of heavenly things (e.g., *Testament of Naphtali* 5; *Testament of Joseph* 19). Likewise, Peter's advice in his last days is based on his special vision (2 Pet 1:16-18). Extracanonical early Christian literature, for example the *Acts of Thomas* (159-60), evidences a phenomenon similar to what is suggested for 2 Peter. The speaker's authority on the last things is accentuated by describing his words as his last.

The Message of the Letter

The readers are called to remember, now and in the future (2 Pet 1:12), that they are the ones who have true knowledge and the capacity for "everything needed for life and godliness" (2 Pet 1:3). The author affirms that the readers know nothing less than God who has called them to share in God's "own glory and goodness" (2 Pet 1:3). The message about which the author seeks to persuade his hearers concerns the "power and coming of our Lord Jesus Christ" (2 Pet 1:16).

The Power of Christ

The power inherent in Jesus is that believers may approach God's character and may share in the divine nature (2 Pet 1:4). Such capacity excludes debauchery (2 Pet 2:2) and is antithetical to being focused on and enslaved to bodily desires (2 Pet 2:10). Presumably the image of God shared by the author and his readers, unlike the image presented in the Greco-Roman pantheon, is that God is asexual. Becoming like God entails sexual continence. The power inherent in Jesus is that of escaping the corruption that is in the world because of passion (2 Pet 1:4; 2:20). It should be noted that in the Hellenistic Mediterranean world passion did not refer exclusively to sexual passion. Greco-Roman philosophical and religious thinkers considered that desire or passion was part of human nature and a trap from which it is necessary to be freed. The problem with passion is that one makes one's happiness or peace dependent on achieving or receiving what one desires, whether it be money, position or another person. Passion was understood to be a cruel master of humankind.

The solution to this human dilemma was to find the means by which to eradicate the passions. The Jewish thinker Philo advocated circumcision for "the excision of pleasure and all passions" (*On the Migration of Abraham* 92 [trans. Colson and Whitaker, LCL]). The Stoic philosopher Epictetus offered a way of life based on the understanding that "freedom is not acquired by satisfying yourself with what you desire, but by destroying your desire" (*Arrian's Discourses* 4.1.175 [trans. Oldfather, LCL]). 2 Peter claims that the way to escape slavery to the passions is to believe that God has granted believers the capacity to be Godlike (2 Pet 1:3), a state that by definition is free of entrapment to passion. Believers are privileged to share in God's nature and so to live cleansed of sin (2 Pet 1:9) and capable of virtue, wisdom, self-control, steadfastness, godliness, care for others and love (2 Pet 1:5-7). Rather than being captive to the passions, believers can partake of the nature of God.

The Coming of Christ

The truth according to 2 Peter concerns also the "coming of our Lord Jesus Christ" (2 Pet 1:16). The author is convinced that the faithful have received a promise (2 Pet 1:4; 3:13) that Jesus will return in concert

Drunken woman at banquet. (2 Peter 2:13)

with the judgment of God on unrighteousness (2 Pet 3:10). The Greek word for coming *(parousia)* in the phrase the "coming of our Lord Jesus Christ" is found also in the phrase the "coming of the day of God" (2

Pet 3:12). Here and elsewhere the author makes clear his conviction that the coming of Jesus is synonymous with the coming day of God and so with the inescapable judgment.

The Consequences of the Message

This conviction is, in the author's view, fundamental and critical. It is fundamental because without belief in the return of Jesus at the time of God's judgment on unrighteousness, theology is misguided. A proper understanding of God includes regarding God as Creator and Judge (2 Pet 3:5-7). God's righteous sovereignty is at the heart of all that is. The faithful Christian also believes that Jesus is Son of God and Savior. It is therefore certain that Jesus will return at the day of God and that unrighteousness will be judged and destroyed and a new heaven and earth full of righteousness established. This conviction is critical because it is integrally related to right conduct. On the basis of belief that Jesus Christ will come at the day of judgment, the faithful are capable of escaping the corruption of the world and are motivated to behave in a holy and godly manner (2 Pet 3:11; 3:14). According to the author, those who deny the coming of Jesus and the judgment of God act corruptly. For the author of 2 Peter, ethical behavior is directly connected to proper belief. It is essential to believe that Jesus will come at the time of God's judgment on unrighteousness. In order to drive his point home, the author vividly describes God's judgmental activities in the past (2 Pet 2:4-10).

There is no talk of the Spirit helping believers with their passions; the focus is on correct convictions. Proper knowledge will result in proper action (2 Pet 1:9). And proper action will result in a more secure calling and election and certainty of entrance into Christ's eternal kingdom (2 Pet 1:10-11).

Summary

The authority of the apostle Peter is invoked to underscore the importance of believing that Jesus will come at the judgment. The letter is concerned with persuading the faithful to hold onto this conviction, for the author's view is that lack of certainty about this matter leads to immoral living and ultimately to damnation. The letter does not indicate that currently the readers are living immorally. It is rather a letter of warning to people the author thinks are relatively stable (2 Pet 3:17) but who are being adversely influenced by false teachers. Unlike Paul's first letter to Corinth, this is not a letter addressed to people who are currently behaving badly. It is more like Paul's Galatian letter, in which the focus is on helping Christians maintain right belief in the face of an alternate gospel. The author's strategy is to denounce the false teachers as deviants from the true faith.

The author believes that a conviction about God's judgment will result in lives lived in expectation of the dramatic intervention of God at the "day of God" (2 Pet 3:12), when God comes in judgment and the present heavens and earth are burned up (2 Pet 3:7; 3:10). Those who believe in the manner advocated by the author will, however, escape. The author seeks to persuade his readers that attachment to the world as it is is equivalent to writing one's death warrant. The gift of God to those who believe, however, is the possibility of escaping the world's fate. The world is corruptible, and people who focus on the things of the world will be destroyed. The passions draw people to the world and away from God, and the passions can be overcome through conviction about the promise of God's judgment and the coming of the Lord Jesus Christ.

Bibliography. R. J. Bauckham, *Jude, 2 Peter,* Word Biblical Commentary 50 (Waco, TX: Word, 1983); A. B. Kolenkow, "The Genre Testament and Forecasts of the Future in the Hellenistic Jewish Milieu," *Journal for the Study of Judaism* 6 (1975) 57-71; J. H. Neyrey, "The Apologetic Use of the Transfiguration in 2 Peter 1:16-21," *Catholic Biblical Quarterly* 42 (1980) 504-19; D. F. Watson, *Invention, Arrangement and Style: Rhetorical Criticism of Jude and 2 Peter,* Society for Biblical Literature Dissertation Series 104 (Atlanta: Scholars Press, 1988).

L. ANN JERVIS

1 JOHN

Introduction

Living in the light and love of the Lord Jesus Christ is the challenge of 1 John. In explaining what this entails, the author touches on great central themes of Christian theology and ethics, such as sin, faith, forgiveness and love, which remain as relevant for our times as for that of the author. Who was this writer and what do we know of the circumstances for which the author wrote? While we will examine some possible answers to these questions, the historical setting, the recipients and the structure of 1 John provide an intriguing challenge for scholars and remain a mystery.

The Fourth Gospel—the Gospel of John—1 John, 2 John, 3 John and the Revelation to John all mention the name John in their title. Did the same author write them all? Which order were they written in? For whom were they written and why? Debate continues regarding whether the same author wrote the Fourth Gospel and the three letters. Opposing views exist, based on the same arguments concerning similarities and differences in style, language and concepts. But there is some general agreement that the Gospel of John and the letters of John have some relationship with similar themes and styles of writing.

Early church fathers and theologians Polycarp (himself a disciple of John), Irenaeus, Justin Martyr, Tertullian and Clement of Alexandria all supported the view that the apostle John was the author of the Fourth Gospel. There is still support today for this view. Some scholars think that there may have been a first draft of the Fourth Gospel (with John the apostle as the author) and that later after his death, his followers published a final version in Ephesus around A.D. 85. These scholars consider 1 John to have been written after the first draft but before the final version of the Gospel.

1 John does not reveal anything about its author, except that 1 John 1:1-4 strongly suggests the author was an eyewitness to the events. 2 John and 3 John, by contrast, state that they are from the elder (2 Jn 1; 3 Jn 1). Debate continues as to whether the same author wrote all three letters or whether there were two authors. It seems reasonable to hold that the apostle John was responsible for the Fourth Gospel regardless of whether he completed an initial draft and his followers the final version, and that a John known as the elder wrote 2 John and 3 John and also may have written 1 John.

Early traditions indicate that John planted churches in Ephesus. These may have been house churches, communities or fellowships, but they were people who accepted John the disciple in some sense as their leader. Irenaeus (A.D. 130-200) wrote that John was a leading ecclesiastical figure in Asia Minor and that many clergy traveled to Ephesus to learn from John.

John the elder addresses the second letter to the elect lady and her children (2 Jn 1). Some commentators treat this as a metaphor for the congregation, but nowhere else do we find the congregation or community referred to in this way. It is more likely that John has a specific lady in mind, and clues in the letter suggests that this lady may have been a woman church leader with a congregation under her care. The term *lady (kyria)* is the feminine form of "lord" *(kyrios),* and as *kyrios* is a guardian, master of a house or head of a family, then it may be argued that *kyria* is a female church leader and the children are the community in her care. Leaders in a house church or community had a responsibility in maintaining the purity of the gospel by the careful selection of appropriate teachers to receive into their homes. It is possible that these households became collecting stations for oral and written traditions, and hence the role of women house church leaders had great significance.

There were several groups in this community. First, there were Jewish Christians, some of whom were totally committed to the teachings of John. Others among them, while believing in Jesus, might have found it hard to accept him as Messiah and still had a strong loyalty to the Jewish law. They accepted the humanity of Jesus and show similarities to a group known as the Ebionites, who emphasized keeping the Jewish law, and some of their members also denied the deity of Christ.

Second, there were Hellenistic Christians in this community and also some Jewish Christians who lived in a Hellenistic environment. The Hellenistic dualism and some of the pre-Gnostic ideas of this background may have influenced them. Their difficulty would have been accepting the deity of Jesus Christ. Thus in the community there were groups having too low a view of Jesus Christ, emphasizing his humanity, and others who had too high a view of Jesus Christ and saw mainly his deity.

The third group, the opponents or secessionists, were those who had once embraced the teaching of John and had been followers in the Johannine community but clashed with John and perhaps with others in the community over matters of belief and behavior. It became impossible for them to remain within the Johannine community, and they had left (1 Jn 2:19).

The letters of John make it possible to trace the development of this community. 2 John reveals that the divisions in the community had deepened and that more people had left the community. Many deceivers have gone out into the world, those who did not confess that Jesus Christ has come in the flesh (2 Jn 7). 3 John indicates that there were now threats organizationally with a Diotrephes who refused to acknowledge the authority of the leadership and expelled believers from the community. The Johannine community disappeared leaving no records or heritage.

The letter recognizes and addresses the problems that have arisen within the Johannine community. John lays down the true doctrine in his teaching and defends it against the claims made by his opponents, the secessionists, who have gone out from the community. He emphasizes the reality and importance of the incarnation of Jesus Christ to the community. Along with this John emphasizes the humanity of Jesus, the reality of sin and the need to confess it, forgiveness found through Jesus Christ and his death, and the commandment to love. He is concerned that the believers have right doctrine and ethical behavior. His letter is a call to the community of believers to discern truth from falsehood and to walk worthy of the gospel in their behavior and to remember the incarnation of Jesus Christ.

1 John is referred to as a letter or epistle, but it lacks some of the elements of the genre letters. Some scholars consider the lack of an address, greetings and conclusion indicate that 1 John is more of a pamphlet, brochure or tract for wide distribution. Yet, within the writing, there is a tone of endearment and closeness characteristic of letters. I will adopt the traditional convention of referring to 1 John as a letter or epistle.

1 John contains parallels to the Fourth Gospel; in particular, the prologue in the Gospel and the introduction to 1 John have much in common with themes of light, life and the incarnation of Jesus Christ. The ending of the Gospel parallels the ending of the letter (Jn 21; cf. 1 Jn 5:14-21). Probably John had a draft of the Fourth Gospel, and some of what he wrote presupposes knowledge of the Fourth Gospel.

1 John does not fall into neat divisions or easy structure. There is one natural division, however, occurring at 1 John 3:11, which separates the letter into two halves. These are closely linked with light and love, key concerns in both. The first half concentrates on the difference between those who live in the light and those who live in darkness. The second half focuses on the quality of Christian life in the community.

Outline

Commentary

Prologue: The Word of Life Revealed (1 Jn 1:1-4)

The words "what we have heard, what we have seen with our eyes, what we have looked at and touched with our hands" are John's attempts to convey the reality of Jesus' entry into this world and human history. He experienced the word of life through his senses and showed that ordinary people may experience this word of life. Two important statements follow, resembling the prologue in the Fourth Gospel. The first is that life (eternal life) was with God, and second is that this life from God came into the world. John is eager for others to experience and embrace this word of life and find fellowship with John and the other disciples.

John uses the word *koinōnia* ("fellowship"), which has the basic root meaning "common" and expresses the most intimate kinds of human relationship with other related meanings of generosity, participation, partner and sharer. Two dimensions to this fellowship exist. In one there is the human fellowship among the Christian believers of the community; in a second dimension, there is fellowship with the Father and his Son Jesus Christ.

God Is Light: Walk in the Light (1 Jn 1:5—3:10)

Walking in Light or Walking in Darkness (1 Jn 1:5—2:2)

These verses begin a section concerning right thinking about God and the implications and consequences for Christian behavior and ethics. It intertwines theology and ethics.

1 John 1:5-7 is in the form of Hebrew parallelism, in which the second line may reinforce the idea of the first line, be part of a development or express the contrast to the first line. Here "God is light" is reinforced by "in [God] there is no darkness at all." God's character is emphasized in these phrases. Other examples of Hebrew parallelism are also found in these verses (e.g., "walking in darkness" and "walk in the light").

God as light is a concept rooted in the Old Testament. Moses experienced God in the burning bush, and God's presence was as fire for guidance during travel in the desert (Ex 3:2-4; cf. Ex 13). God's light eliminates the darkness physically and spiritually (Ps 18:28). Light is God's character (Ps 27:1). Jewish believers in the community would be familiar with this concept. If the Johannine community did have a first draft of the Fourth Gospel, then they would also be familiar with passages referring to Jesus as the light shining in the darkness (Jn 1:5) and the claim by Jesus, "I am the light of the world."

In 1 John 1:5 the statement is "God is light." There was a type of heretical belief of a pre-Gnostic nature appearing in the community. For these people, light was a metaphor for God. John is giving a positive message to the Christians still in the community, but at the same time he is setting up a defense of his teaching and a framework in which to refute the false teaching. 1 John 1:6-10 has six clauses, three of which are negative and probably refer to statements of the position held and hints of the nature of the heretical thinking by those outside the community. The other three positive counterparts are obvious challenges for the Johannine community to abide by.

The first pair of "if" clauses begin in 1 John 1:6, "If we say that we have fellowship with him while we are walking in darkness, we lie and do not do what is true." "Walking in darkness" refers to habitually living this way, choosing sin (darkness) rather than truth or light. If these passages refer to people outside of the community who may be bringing pressure to bear on those inside the Johannine community, then John is condemning them for their lying and deceptive behavior. The contrast comes in 1 John 1:7, "if we walk in the light as he himself is in the light," in other words, habitually living in God's way, then two results follow: fellowship with one another and cleansing from sin through the blood of Jesus. (Note here an implicit reference also to the humanity of Jesus, an aspect that will be in focus later.) There is a relationship between spiritual life and life in the community, and spiritual integrity seeks to ensure quality of community life.

"Cleansing" (1 Jn 1:7) shows the cleansing power of the blood of Christ, for implied in this word is the removal of that which is corrupting us, so that there are no ongoing effects and God may produce a permanent change. The second pair of clauses are "if we say that we have no sin" (1 Jn 1:8) and "if we confess our sins" (1 Jn 1:9). Walking in darkness is intensified to claiming sinlessness. The viewpoint of John's opponents was that everyday living was related to this world and separated from God; therefore sin, being of the world, did not affect their relationship with God. In response John intensified his statements. In 1 John 1:6 he said they do not do what is true. In 1 John 1:8 he says the truth is not in them. But the other side is the positive statement that confession of sin displays God's character of faithfulness and justice, which allows for forgiveness of sins ("letting go," e.g., letting go of a debt) and cleansing. 1 John 1:9 addresses the past, with sin forgiven, and the future, with cleansing from all unrighteousness.

1 John 1:10 introduces the start of the third pair of "if" clauses. It seems the opponents are claiming they have never sinned. John responds that the word is not in these people. What is meant by "the word"? One possible interpretation is that "word" refers to the Scriptures. Another possibility is that "word" refers to Jesus. This interpretation makes sense, since in the prologue John referred to the "word of life," which is a reference to Jesus. He also referred to the "truth" (1 Jn 1:8) and may be using terminology from the Fourth Gospel, where Jesus says, "I am the way, and the truth, and the life" (Jn 14:6), which lends support to the view of the word being Jesus. Perhaps John allowed both interpretations to be possibilities.

1 John 2:1-2 shows a shift in John's thinking as he turns to the members of the community who have remained. He uses a term of endearment, *teknia,* meaning "little children," to refer to all in the community, male and female. John acknowledged the possibility for members of the community to sin, in contrast to the claims of sinlessness by his opponents, and he assures his community that there is an advocate (*paraklētos,* one who is called alongside as a counselor), Jesus, for the times when they sin. The atoning sacrifice (*hilasmos,* a sacrifice made to placate an angry person) is the basis for Jesus' advocacy (1 Jn 2:2). Sin is covered, and God's righteous anger is appeased. This sacrifice is available for the

sins of the whole world, not just for an elite group.

Three Tests of Authentic Living in the Light of God (1 Jn 2:3-11)

In this section John gives three statements that test the authenticity of a person's Christian life. As was true in the previous "if" sections, each statement builds on what has gone before. John states that the reality of the claims "I have come to know him" (1 Jn 2:4), "I abide in him" (1 Jn 2:6) and "I am in the light" (1 Jn 2:9) are demonstrated by the way a person lives.

1 John 2:3-4 contains the key to this section. Knowing God must result in obedience to him. The perfect tense of the verb for the phrase "have come to know" (1 Jn 2:4) implies that while there was a time when the believer came into an experience of knowing God, there is an ongoing component to this knowing. It is expressed in daily life by obedience to God's commandments. Disobedience reveals that the person is a liar and that the truth (i.e., Christ) does not exist in that person's life. Notice the similarity to 1 John 1:8. Obedience involves willingly persevering and a desire for being obedient to the will of God.

1 John 2:6-8 gives "abiding in him" and "walking just as he walked" as the second test of an authentic Christian life. The Greek word translated "abide" refers to a two-way indwelling, the Christian indwelling in God and God indwelling the Christian. The present continuous tense of the verb has a sense of ongoing participation in God, resulting in living and walking as Jesus Christ did. The third test, 1 John 2:7-11, concerns obedience to the commandment to love. John describes it as an old and a new commandment (1 Jn 2:8), old in the sense that the Old Testament expresses this commandment but new also because Jesus Christ demonstrated its truth by laying down his life, the supreme example of love. His example and his living within the Christian enable this commandment to be fulfilled. His truth and light illuminate what is right conduct toward a brother or sister. The person unable to love and who hates is described by John as being in darkness and walking in darkness, being blind to the truthful nature of her or his actions (1 Jn 2:11).

Staying Strong Through Knowing the Father (1 Jn 2:12-17)

With the point made, John is able to give some praise and reassurance to the community. He uses terms of endearment and family—"little children," "fathers" and "young people." "Children" refers to the whole community, male and female. If women were excluded, it would have been more natural to commence with fathers. John writes that the sins of the children are forgiven and that they know the Father, something that is true of men and women (1 Jn 2:12, 14). The second letter of John, addressed to the elect lady and her children (2 Jn 1:1), suggests that the letter was written to a particular lady, probably the leader of a house church, and the children were the members of that community. If 1 John is written to the same community (and there is no reason to doubt that), then the use of "children" in 1 John 2:12 and 1 John 2:14 would refer to the whole community of believers that remain in fellowship in the Johannine community. In a similar manner the term *father* refers to mature adults, male and female, who have known him who is from the beginning. Therefore they provide a foundation for the young people in the community.

1 John 2:15-17 picks up on the theme of overcoming the world and recognizes the temptations that young people in particular face. The warning "do not love the world or the things in the world" (1 Jn 2:15) is followed by a list of three things that may lead the believer astray from doing the will of God and falling into the trap of loving the world of sin which stands in opposition to God. 1 John 2:16 defines these as the desire of the flesh, the desire of the eyes and the pride of riches (wealth and position in society).

Warning Against Antichrists (1 Jn 2:18-27)

The thought of being led astray by loving the world reminds John of those who have left the community. This time he refers to them as antichrists, and in this section we learn what were their main doctrinal errors.

"The last hour" (1 Jn 2:18) is eschatological language. The appearance of antichrists fits Jesus' description of what would take place in the last days. The opponents have left the community, and John considers them as never truly having been part of it. Note the progression to this point: walking in darkness, claiming sinlessness, claiming to have never sinned, not having the truth and now never having the truth and never belonging to the community of believers.

The first error of the antichrists or opponents is the denial that Jesus is the Christ. 1 John 4:1-6 elaborates this; the antichrists also do not confess that Jesus has come in the flesh and is from God. The incarnation of Jesus is the stumbling block for the opponents. God become flesh was unthinkable. In denying the Son, the opponents also denied the Father. Quite possibly they were claiming spiritual authority as they propounded their beliefs, and hence John reminds the community of believers that the holy One has anointed them, that they have knowledge and that they therefore must discern what is true (1 Jn 2:20, 26-27). They must remain grounded in what they heard from the beginning.

Children of God or Children of the Devil (1 Jn 2:28—3:10)

This is another section of reassurance and encouragement to the believers. The passage highlights the contrast between those who do right (1 Jn 2:28—3:3) with those who commit sin (1 Jn 3:4-6). Much of this passage spirals back on the previous ideas.

1 John 2:28 continues the eschatological theme with two phrases referring to the hope of Christ's return. The first, "when he is revealed," signifies the time is coming when Christ will be unveiled before the world. The second phrase, "at his coming," hints at the judgment of believers and nonbelievers when Christ returns. John reassures the believers that they will have no sense of shame if they abide in Christ. Knowing God's righteousness will lead them to imitate his righteousness in their daily living, and they may have confidence at his coming.

1 John 3:2 furthers this idea with the phrase "when he is revealed, we will be like him, for we shall see him as he is." The believers will see the reflection of his righteousness in their behavior and will see how through abiding in him their lives have been shaped into conformity with his. This is an encouragement to the community to continue to purify their lives.

1 John 3:4-10 changes the tack a little from the preceding verses to reflect the tensions between sin and doing what is right, between being a child of the devil and being a child of God. John uses the technique of accenting the positive by giving negative examples. Those who commit sin are guilty of lawlessness; they do not abide in Christ but are children of the devil because they imitate his works. John makes the contrast (1 Jn 3:9) when he states Christians do not sin because God's seed abides in them and they cannot sin because they have been born of God. Does this mean perfection is demanded? The answer is no, as John has explained earlier the advocacy of Jesus Christ and what should be done when Christians sin. The meaning cannot be that John expects that Christians will never sin. The key to understanding is the tenses of the verbs and participles. 1 John 3:6 (no one who abides in him sins") uses the present continuous tense. The sense is that of continuing to sin or an ongoing habit of sin. The second part of the verse contains the participle the "one who sins," again in the present tense with the same implication of continuing in sin. Habitual sin has no place in the life of the believer. The presence of Christ in the believer enables this to become reality.

The concluding verse of this section (1 Jn 3:10) reiterates John's constant refrain, what you are is revealed by the way you live. The challenge to live ethically in love is forwarded through the negative statements that those who do not do what is right are not from God; nor are those who do not love their brothers and sisters.

God Is Love: Consequences for the Children of God (1 Jn 3:11—5:13)

Children of God Love One Another (1 Jn 3:11-24)

Most commentators see a natural division at this stage with the letter being in almost equal halves, but the two halves are closely linked and both divisions have love and light as major themes. Gary Burge, in his commentary of the letters of John says, "The secession has torn the life of the Johannine community and the author is taking pains to rebuild that life. He does this by giving full stress to the gospel of loving one another."

Cain becomes a negative example of loving one another (1 Jn 3:12). Cain's actions were consistent with those of the evil one, and therefore Cain was working in conjunction with the evil one (cf. 1 Jn 3:8). Cain's envy and jealousy toward his brother and his righteous deeds is compared with that of the world (here the secessionists or opponents) toward the righteousness of the believers as they love one another. Christ's love in laying down his life for us is held up as the supreme example and model (1 Jn 3:16). This example of love is quickly translated into practical terms reflecting God's heart for the poor and needy. To see a brother or sister in need and to refuse help is not showing the love of God (1 Jn 3:17). The thought is that something is set aside that is personally valued and is precious. Christ did this in laying down or setting aside his life. John challenges the community that laying down their lives is the setting aside of that which is precious and valued to help their needy brother or sister. To fail to do so is to refuse life to the person. This practical love demonstrates the change: that the believer has passed from death to life (1 Jn 3:14).

1 John 3:19 reassures believers that they will know that they belong to the truth by the evidence of their obedience to this command to love. The action is reassurance for times of self-doubt by the members of the community (1 Jn 3:20). John links this obedience with faith or belief in the name of God's Son, Jesus Christ. Again, the Spirit is to enable the believer to abide in Christ and to live ethically in love.

Children of God Discern the Spirits (1 Jn 4:1-6)

At first glance this section appears to be completely separate. However, when one considers what was happening to this community, the relevance of this section is seen. The opponents of John had left the community but were obviously still troubling it and claiming spiritual authority for their beliefs and teaching. Advice to the community on how to discern the spirits would be natural. John sees the opponents as false prophets who have gone out into the world and refers to them as the antichrists or children of the devil in 1 John 2 and 1 John 3.

John warns of the need to test or discern the spirits, and 1 John 4:2-3 gives the necessary test: Every spirit that confesses that Jesus Christ has come in the flesh is from God, and every spirit that does not confess Jesus is not from God. The test is a theological confession. It acknowledges the incarnation, the deity of Jesus Christ and his messiahship. The careful reader will note that the negative statement in the second part of the test does not include the words "has come in the flesh." Perhaps John thought that this is understood and does not need repeating. This struggle of coming to terms with the humanity and deity of Christ occupied the early church for many years and was not finally settled until the Council of Chalcedon, which affirmed and built on the work of the Council of Nicea.

John writes that his children have conquered the opponents because of the abiding of Christ within them. Those outside the community are described as being "from the world," and it is obvious that they are being accepted and attracting followers (1 Jn 4:5). But John condemns their teaching as being of the world and associated with the darkness of the world in contrast to the light of the truth. The test of whether their doctrine is right doctrine or right confession for John has become the test of validating or invalidating claims to speak with the inspiration or authority of the Spirit as outlined in 1 John 4:2-3.

Children of God Love Because God First Loved (1 Jn 4:7-21)

John returns to his theme of love, and in these verses he explains the origin and motivation for love. His basic premise is that love is of God. The true believer demonstrates this in life. Hence the one who loves is born of God and knows God, for the character of God is revealed through that love. Failure to love invalidates the claim to know God (1 Jn 4:8). John defines love as the love revealed by God through his sending his only Son into the world to be the atoning sacrifice for our sins (1 Jn 4:10). God took the initiative. Because Jesus deals with sin, we are able to live through him. 1 John 4:11 comes to the heart of the issue: "Beloved, since God loved us so much, we also ought also to love one another." Theology, morality and ethics are involved. God's love is the basis for our human motivation and obligation to love one another: "We love because he first loved us" (1 Jn 4:19).

1 John 4:13-16 reveals the first appropriate human response to God's love is the confession that the Father has sent his Son as the Savior of the world. The second appropriate response follows in 1 John 4:16-21, being obedient to the command to love one another. The result is assurance that God abides in the believer and removes fear of punishment (eternal punishment) on the day of judgment. Love leaves no room for fear because self-interest and self-concern become secondary. Those who do not love their brothers and sisters who are visible cannot love God whom they have not seen (1 Jn 4:20-21).

Children of God Conquer the World (1 Jn 5:1-5)

John interprets loving God in human terms, using the analogy of the family. Friendship with parents involves accepting and loving their children. Women in present-day society demonstrate this very well as they show practical love and concern for the children of others. John reveals that our love for God (the parent) is shown in our love to one another (the children of God; 1 Jn 5:1-2).

1 John 5:4 links back to 1 John 5:1, where the person born of God is defined as the one who believes that Jesus is the Christ. The believer is being shaped in this world by God and overcomes it by not accepting its standards or lure and not being controlled by it.

The Testimony of God to His Son (1 Jn 5:6-13)

The preceding section finished with belief that Jesus is the Son of God. These next verses concern the witness to the Son to establish his validity.

1 John 5:6 refers to his coming by water and blood. Most scholars understand water as a reference to the baptism of Jesus and blood as his death. John Calvin applied both terms to the death of Christ, when blood and water flowed as his side was pierced. Both explanations, however, show the real humanity of Jesus in his death, a counter to the doctrine and rejection of the humanity of Christ held by the opponents of the Johannine community.

According to Judaism, three witnesses made for creditable witness. John writes of three witnesses to Jesus, namely, the Spirit, water and blood (1 Jn 5:8). Each is a witness to Jesus and is related to the other two by his death. 1 John 5:9-10 adds a further witness, the testimony of God, an inner testimony of eternal life, established by the Spirit in the hearts of believers (1 Jn 5:12-13).

Final Words (1 Jn 5:14-21)

Debate occurs as to whether these verses were part of 1 John or were appended later. Since they reflect themes that John has already mentioned, probably they were some extra points that John wished to make, and he added them as afterthoughts. Therefore they are a unity with 1 John.

1 John 5:14-15 is frequently misinterpreted. John says, "We know we have obtained the requests made of him," rather than promising we shall obtain, as the verses are often interpreted. They look forward to what a brother of sister ought to pray for. 1 John 5:16 indicates that prayer is for a brother or sister who is committing "what is not a mortal sin." The answer to the request is given: God will give life to the person. However, the injunction to pray does not cover praying for sin that is mortal. Many scholars have speculated on what is the mortal sin, with answers including blasphemy against the Holy Spirit or apostasy; later the church defined a list of mortal sins. I tend to agree with those who propose that mortal sin refers to unconfessed sin outside of the community. John has already shown how sin inside the community may be confessed and forgiven. Those outside the community, denying the fact of sin in their lives, do not have the means for confession and forgiveness. Those within the community have the light of Christ to show them the truth and to bring about conviction of sin so that it may be dealt with.

Bibliography. G. M. Burge, *The Letters of John: The NIV Application Commentary* (Grand Rapids, MI: Zondervan, 1996); D. M. Smith, *First, Second and Third John: Interpretation* (Louisville, KY: John Knox, 1991).

MARGARET A. MOTION

Atonement

Atonement ("at-one-ment") is an interesting word because it is so central to Christian thinking and yet so alien to contemporary secular culture. The word was first used by William Tyndale relatively late within Christian history. However, the basic idea to which it refers—reconciliation—has been at the foundations of Christianity from its birth.

This broad concept of restoring unity ("onement" in early English) is a familiar concept in contemporary culture and is a vital point of common ground between church and society. Talk of reconciliation presupposes that relationship has broken down, there is a need for restoration, something must be done.

The word *atonement* translates or refers to a range of words and concepts in the Bible. It is found fairly frequently in the Old Testament in the context of offerings, usually connected with priesthood and cultic practices. It refers to a process and practices intended to achieve reconciliation between God and human beings. The most widely known reference in this context would be the Day of Atonement. However, although in the Old Testament atonement may be achieved through the offering of life—the death of a sacrificial animal—it may also be achieved through the offering of incense, money or other goods, anointing with oil, piety (Prov 16:6).

In the New Testament the word *atonement* appears rarely or not at all in modern translations. However, it is still used to refer to a central concept or cluster of words and concepts within the New Testament and in Christian theology so that *atonement* is often used as another term for salvation. Broadly speaking the atonement means the work of Jesus Christ: reconciliation with God achieved in and through Jesus' life, death and resurrection.

However, atonement suggests more than the fact of reunification. It includes reference to making amends or reparation, and it thus also has a more specific focus on the means of salvation, or how reconciliation is achieved.

Christian theology does not have any one clear theory explaining precisely how salvation works. Atonement in the New Testament is often but not always linked with the death of Christ, and we might assume that reconciliation is achieved through suffering and death as sacrifice. However, language of sacrifice is rarer in the New Testament than we might expect, and although it is undoubtedly an important part of early Christian views, it is one of a range of different terms and images used to confess faith in atonement through Christ. For example, Christ is seen as a servant and as a victor as well as a sacrifice. Talk of atonement includes talk of redemption, ransom, liberation, healing or forgiveness. There is also a range of theories that developed within Christian theology. Some of these theories have been dramatically shaped by their cultural context as Christian thinkers have sought to explore the significance of Christ in terms that made sense to them and their contemporaries. For example, Tertullian talked of atonement as satisfaction, a payment to make up for a breach of law as in the Roman legal system; Anselm talked of the work of Christ as payment of a debt of honor owed by humanity to God, as a serf might owe a debt to a feudal lord.

It is important to note not only this range of images but also their cultural heritage and to see the need for ways of expressing the work of Christ that will be relevant and meaningful for our society and particularly, in the context of this work, for women.

Any discussion of atonement will have three particular reference points: why we need reconciliation (*see* Sin); how reconciliation is achieved, or the process of atonement; what reconciliation leads to, or the results of the atonement.

The Process of Atonement

The Action of God

For Christianity the process of atonement is always centered on the person of Jesus Christ. This is in line with the Old Testament emphasis on atonement coming about through God's provision and initiative. Sacrifices may be offered by human beings, but Yahweh is seen as the one making atonement on behalf of his people. Atonement in Christ is equally seen as God's action; God is the acting subject of the process. Atonement is a free gift due solely and totally to God's grace and love. Whatever patterns of leadership may be developed in Christian churches, including priesthood or not, and whatever significance is given to the Eucharist, there can be no suggestion that human effort or individuals accomplish atonement. Human beings are not saved by other human beings, and women are not saved by or through men any more than they are saved through gender roles such as motherhood (see 1 Tim 2:15 and commentary on Lk 11:27-28). Atonement is an act of God on behalf of human beings who are all equally in need of reconciliation.

Atonement Through Jesus' Life

Because Jesus is central as the sole means of atonement, we need a holistic view of his life, death and resurrection as part of the process. Western Christianity has tended to focus narrowly on Jesus' death in a way that has had negative implications for women. It is maybe this tendency that gives atonement particular connotations of suffering and punishment whereas its reference is much broader than this. For example, F. W. Dillistone uses friendship as one category for understanding the atonement. We can focus instead on the more inclusive category of incarnation as the means of reconciliation. This will allow us to explore familiar ideas, such as sacrifice, self-giving and atonement achieved by death, as well as less familiar ideas.

One such idea is that of Jesus' life as means of atonement. This is an important theme within Christian theology but is one that many Christian believers might find surprising and constructive. The giving of Jesus' life for us does not refer exclusively to the giving up of life in death but also to the living of Jesus' life. Atonement is achieved in part through Jesus' presence within human reality and through his being as the perfect and perfectly reconciled human. Not only *is* Jesus the presence of God with us by definition, Emmanuel, but his life shows us what humanity can and should be when lived in harmony with God and within the community of creation. An early theory of atonement known as recapitulation theory explains atonement as a process whereby Jesus repeats (recapitulates) and summarizes human existence by going through every stage of human life. By doing so without sin, he establishes a new way of being human. It is as if Jesus rewrites the DNA of human existence; he reprograms by going through the code and taking out the virus so that we can now live fully human lives as we were originally created to do. So Jesus' teaching, behavior and practice are not merely examples of how we should try to live. They are the establishment of the possibility. Jesus' radical treatment of women as friends and disciples, equal to men, his disregard for social and religious taboos, his overthrowing of patriarchal patterns of domination are not merely models of an ideal society. They are part of the means of making change possible.

Atonement Through Suffering and Death

The reason that this is true of Jesus in a way that is not true of other great human beings is that not only was he without sin, but he was also God incarnate. This life was not only the best possible human life, but it was also the action of the Divine. Claims that atonement is achieved through Jesus have always depended on the insistence that as well as being fully human, Jesus is fully divine. Estimates of Jesus' death rely equally on this presupposition.

One important implication of this is that the link between suffering and salvation in Jesus does not establish a similar link for human suffering. This is seen in the New Testament, which talks of salvation as exchange—righteousness for sin, life for death, peace and reconciliation for enmity and separation. Although there may be many who suffer for Christ in different ways, and although suffering may sometimes lead to good, still human suffering cannot be justified on this basis. Jesus' death is seen in sacrificial imagery as the redemptive death of the sinless offering, a death that atones for sin in our place and is therefore different from any other suffering and death. A strand in Christian thinking has seen the particular suffering of women as the appropriate penalty for women's weaker natures, greater sinfulness and peculiar responsibility for the Fall. While these assumptions about women's nature and role must be confronted and disputed, we must also remember that the penalty for sin has in any case been paid on our behalf (1 Pet 3:18)

These models of atonement rely on the notion that Jesus is a substitute for us. Something was achieved that we could not and now need not achieve. Jesus' life and death are vicarious, or on our behalf, and this is seen throughout the New Testament in assertions that Jesus came, lived, died for us. There is, however, another side to this coin; there are also ways in which Jesus is representative without being substitutionary. He is a model, but not in our place—symbolizing and typifying what is or should and can be true for each of us as well. This is true for the model of perfectly reconciled humanity that we see in Jesus. It is also true, in a rather different way, of Jesus' suffering.

Although Jesus' suffering and death are on one crucial level vicarious, suffering and death are also fundamental to human experience. Not only are Jesus' suffering and death done for us; they are also done with us, and this is part of the meaning of atonement. This is an important and sensitive area because the suffering of many has been justified or sanctified by identification with Christ, which can excuse the suffering and deny the need for action. Women have been seen by many as more Christlike, particularly as more likely to live vicariously. Even if this were true in practice, it is important that the reality of women's experience is neither denied nor turned into a necessary or a God-ordained fate.

Jesus typifies and represents perfect humanity as it should be, but he also enters into solidarity with the worst of human experience—being weak, oppressed, betrayed and abandoned, suffering and dying in rejection. In Paul's terms, he is "made . . . to be sin" (2 Cor 5:21); in the terms of Jürgen Moltmann, he enters into Godforsakenness.

Atonement thus happens through and within human history. Human experience and suffering are taken seriously. Their reality is affirmed. This is important as some Christian talk of salvation seems to offer a vision of a different plane of existence that has no connection with our present reality. This may lead us either to an otherworldly detachment and denial or to despair. However, the context of this affirmation of human suffering is that God enters into the human situation in order to transform it from within. The suffering of Jesus is not the end point but the basis for hope because it is part of the process of atonement—making amends, bringing about reconciliation. Jesus' cry from the cross has been interpreted as a cry of protest, the kind of protest that should be made by or on behalf of those who suffer and are abandoned.

This particular view of the atonement should make us take with the utmost seriousness all human experiences of suffering, oppression or abandonment as basic to the human situation but also as the place where the atonement should make a difference. We must be sure that our talk of salvation does not lead women who are abandoned, oppressed, used and abused, who feel inadequate, guilty or estranged to feel that their suffering is their fate or the role which Christianity assigns to them. Nor should they feel intimidated because their experience seems so far removed from the vision of reconciliation offered by Christianity. That vision must be rooted in the reality within which it was achieved and that it can transform.

Outcomes of Atonement

The New Testament talks of atonement as bringing about a new creation. It is a new beginning, and Christ is the one who makes it possible; he is the first reconciled human being (Col 1:15). "Adam" in Romans 5 refers to the first human beings who became estranged; Christ, the first of the new covenant, is the second Adam. Whereas the sin of Adam and Eve led to estrangement and, it can be argued, specifically to the subordination of women to male dominance, the order of reconciliation in the second Adam is an inclusive order of equality where "there is no longer Jew or Greek, . . . slave or free, . . . male and female" (Gal 3:28). Paul talks in Galatians about atonement as redemption from the curse of the law. It is also redemption from the curse of Genesis 3:16-19. Rather than trying to get back to being like Adam and Eve in the image of God before the Fall, Christians are to be conformed to the image of Christ, and this must include the radical vision of community we see in Jesus' life and relationships.

Although Western Christianity has often seen salvation as primarily or solely spiritual, between the individual and God on an inner and personal level this is not the only level on which reconciliation works. The biblical understanding of humanity does not separate human rationality and spirituality from our physical and social being, as early Christianity was to do. As sin affects every aspect of our being, so does atonement. This means that atonement affects not only our inward and subjective reconciliation with God but also deals with the forces of sin and evil as systems that enslave us, as outer, as objective, external, social and cosmic. And indeed the two are interconnected. Feminists have argued that the personal is political—we cannot separate the inner and private from the public and corporate. This is in line with biblical thinking about the nature of human existence, about sin and about reconciliation. Atonement is seen as liberation from bondage, from powers and principalities, and one contemporary application of this cluster of images is that atonement means freedom from systems of oppression.

Having said that atonement is the action of God and is not achieved by human beings, this does not mean that atonement is achieved for us without our involvement or irrespective of how we do or do not respond. This is another level on which Christ is representative but not substitutionary. The New Testament is full of calls to a new way of being and behaving because now we are in Christ and must become Christlike in our thinking, our relationships, our way of life (e.g., Rom 6; 1 Jn 2; Jas).

Of course atonement has to do with individual repentance and response to God. It is inward and subjective, and this is one level on which we must participate. But it also has to do with relationships with others, and reconciliation with God cannot be separated from reconciliation with others. Jesus talks of the need for reconciliation with one's brother before making an offering to God (Mt 5:24), and this emphasis is continued through the New Testament (e.g., Col 3:12-14). The change and exchange that are part of atonement must be made a reality in our lives and our church life on social and practical levels as well as inner and individual ways. They must be made a reality through our effort and involvement working with and through God's grace.

It has been argued that the radical patterns of life and behavior we see in Jesus and the first disciples cannot be put into practice in contemporary society: that processes of institutionalization, and with this patterns of power, hierarchy and domination are inevitable, given the nature of human society. And sometimes it seems impossible to change entrenched human structures and attitudes. But surely we cannot conclude that the gospel is impractical or impossible, that it cannot be implemented. Paul insists that we are a new creation. We are in the process of being changed (2 Cor 3:18; 5:16-21).

A more common line of argument within Christianity has been to say that women and men are equal spiritually, before God, but that this is consistent with patterns of leadership and subordination within the world. It is true that reconciliation is not yet fully achieved and will not be until the end. However, the vision of perfectly fulfilled future reconciliation is presented in the New Testament as a vision of hope that leads to change in the present. One great insight of contemporary theologies of liberation is the rediscovery of the imperative for action on practical, social, political and economic levels, for praxis as part of human being, part of Christianity and as inseparable from the inward and spiritual. This must be part of the ministry of reconciliation that Paul talks of in 2 Corinthians 5:11-21, and it is also part of conformity to the image of Christ as we see him in the Gospels.

Hope for reality of reconciliation on every level and in every aspect of being human must be related to the atonement achieved in Jesus Christ—where God's presence and forgiveness is seen in the midst of the human reality of estrangement. It must also be related to faith in the power of the Spirit to guide and shape the church as the redeemed community, the body of Christ. The Christian life is inevitably concerned with this tension of implementing a vision that contradicts sinful reality as we know it but that has the power to lead to real transformation.

Bibliography

P. S. Fiddes, *Past Event and Present Salvation: The Christian Idea of Atonement* (London: Darton, Longman & Todd, 1989); R. Wallace, *The Atoning Death of Christ* (London: Marshall, Morgan & Scott, 1981).

SALLY ALSFORD

2 JOHN

Introduction

2 John has often been regarded an outline for 1 John, although 2 John could as easily be its résumé. Commentators often determine the sequence of Johannine writings according to what seems to make sense. Thus 1 John is an extension of 2 John if the circumstances that in 2 John had been a threat have become reality in all churches of the "elder." This is what I think is the case.

The debate about the author of Johannine literature, as well as the date and the recipients, has produced manifold theories. Some scholars argue for a date in the late second century because they perceive apparent refutations of Gnosticism in it. This view precludes John the apostle from being the author and gives no other clues for author or audience. With other scholars, however, I believe that these works (including Revelation), traditionally attributed to John, have a common apostolic author and could have been written between 80 and 95 of the first century. In all of them development of pastoral and leadership problems is sensed as churches became older, that is, as they move toward the end of the century.

Comparing 2 John and 3 John, which are similar in language, style and approach and deal with the issue of itinerant teachers, will illuminate both letters and their meaning for readers today.

Almost nothing definitive can be claimed about the setting into which 2 John was written. However, the presuppositions stated above lead one to suspect that a leader in Asia Minor, around Ephesus, is the recipient (cf. the circle of churches [Rev 2—4], in which a man named John was the elder). John the apostle could still be a living witness of the old commandment, but his churches now have new leaders, several of whom may have been women. Churches usually met in homes, and there is evidence that the egalitarian outlook on human beings in Christianity attracted influential women. They opened their homes to the church when they became Christians, and naturally they served in them. The New Testament testifies to several such women: for example, Apphia (Philem 2), Prisca (1 Cor 16:19; Rom 16:3) and Nympha (Col 4:15; cf. Schüssler Fiorenza, 225), who by faithful service may have become overseers.

Itinerant preaching and teaching was a popular profession even in the secular realm. Christians used it, sometimes in the context of their secular work of trading, to spread the gospel. Hospitality to people who traveled and evangelized was important and a natural duty of a house-church leader. It does not surprise us to see how difficult this duty of hospitality became as the church grew bigger and older. Knowing who was a true teacher required spiritual discernment, and 2 John is an introduction to the subject from one of the last authentic authorities. The elder, if he was John, was too old now to visit his churches regularly, but it seemed he was to make one more visit because difficulties with false teachers had increased.

Gnostic tendencies in some leaders created strife in the church. "Those who do not confess that Jesus Christ has come in the flesh" (2 Jn 7) are, as in all Johannine literature, the false teachers and false teaching attacked in 2 John. This teaching developed out of the dualism of body and spirit that was posited in the ever-present, syncretistic Hellenistic religion and philosophy. Historical findings show that women were often attracted to ecstatic spirituality in their homes and promoted it there. Against such hyperspirituality our author demands obedience to the double commandment that "we have had from the beginning": Christ's commandment of love and truth (2 Jn 5). A person who has the spirit and the truth knows the Father; a person who doesn't is a deceiver.

Outline

1-3	Greetings
4-11	The Concern: Love and Truth
12-13	Announcement and Final Greetings

Commentary

Greetings (2 Jn 1-3)

The introductory term "elect lady" *(eklektē kyria)* is intriguing, but the elect lady's identity is disputed. Many interpreters think this is a poetic description of the church. However, as Lamar Wadsworth has shown

(2-3), there is no parallel or logical explanation for such an understanding. And there have been commentators who claimed that *eklektē* (Gk. "chosen") as well as *kyria* (Gk. "lady") could be proper names for women. *Kyria* could also be a title of respect for the lady of the house (where there was no male head, or *kyrios*) or possibly the house where the church met, whereas *eklektē* is an honorary title meaning everything up to "ordained." For these reasons as well as for the parallelism with 3 John, which is undoubtedly a personal letter, it is safe to assume that 2 John is written to a female church leader.

"Love and truth" seem to be two words directly or indirectly present in every verse of 2 John. There are among the lady's children some who are "walking in the truth," but the emphasis on "all who know the truth" and on "us" in the first verse show that some people have difficulty with the elder's truth. Among them possibly is the "elect lady" (or she before all others; note the second person singular in 2 Jn 5 and compare with Rev 2:20-23). The balance of love and truth is an important imperative, especially in women's ministries today, as it was for the elect lady. There is a tendency in women to accept what feels good and to not ask about the truth.

The Concern: Love and Truth (2 Jn 4-11)

Although in all Johannine literature it is important to refute the heresy of negating Jesus' deity, accepting the phrase "that Jesus Christ has come in the flesh" is not meant to be the only sign of orthodoxy. For Johannine churches it was a starting point. The emphasis on Jesus' body is important for God's saving work, and it also rescues believers from a Platonic spirituality in which spirit and body are strictly divorced and the body is declared evil.

Possibly the elder has one false teacher in mind and calls him "the deceiver and the antichrist" (note the singular in 2 Jn 7, 10-11). The pointedly impersonal address may mean that the author tries not to offend the church leader who favors such teaching or the teacher. However, he also clearly identifies the risks and expresses hope that the leader will understand what is at stake.

In 2 John 10-11 the elder asks for a revolutionary act of dissociation from the deceiver, showing that even greeting him means having a part in his "evil deeds." These deeds are not identified here, although Jude and 2 Peter 2 give insight.

Glimpse of life within women's quarters inside a Greek home. (2 John)

Announcement and Final Greetings (2 Jn 12-13)

The announcement of the elder's visit is a connecting point for 2 John and 3 John, suggesting the same time and similar place. The reference to "the children of your elect sister" has traditionally been interpreted as John's home church. However, these people could be believers in John's neighborhood who are led by the lady's relative or the children of the lady's sister, who also is a Christian.

Bibliography. M. Hengel and A. M. Schwemer, "Exkrus II: 'Sympatisanten' and judische Propaganda," in *Paulus zwischen Damaskus and Antiochien,* Wissenschaftliche Untersuchungen zum Neuen Testament 108 (Tübingen: Siebeck, 1998); E. Schüssler Filorenza, *Zu ihrem Gedächtnis . . . ; eine feministisch theologische Rekonstruktion der christlichen Ursprünge* (Munich, Mainz: Kaiser, Grünewald, 1988); L. Wadsworth, "Who Was the 'Chosen Lady' of 2d John?" *Priscilla Papers* 10/3 (1996): 1-5.

KSENIJA MAGDA

3 JOHN

Introduction

Nobody has ever doubted that 3 John is a personal letter to a prominent Christian, Gaius. The parallel with 2 John in structure and language, as well as the announcement of a (the same) visit by the elder, gives ground enough to think of 2 John as personal too. Accordingly, the final greetings in both letters show parallel familiarity. As Gaius is greeted by present friends in 3 John, so the "children of [the] elect sister" may be the lady's relatives who are close to the elder and thus a unifying factor between her and the elder.

As is the case in 2 John, nothing in 3 John is said about the place or date of origin. For reasons shown in the introduction to 2 John, I argue that John the apostle is the author and Ephesus a possible place of origin. However, the occasion for 3 John is evident: one of the leaders in the surrounding churches, Diotrephes, is fighting for authority and challenging the elder, the old overseer of several churches in the area. On several occasions Diotrephes has refused hospitality to itinerant teachers sent by the elder and is stirring up the church against his emissaries. Gaius, a prominent member in the church in this town but not necessarily in the same house church has, however, proven faithful to the elder (3 Jn 12) and is trustworthy to accept this recommendation about Demetrius, the traveling teacher.

Close to the end of first century, orthodoxy was not yet well defined, the churches lacked the Bible in a written form, and the first-generation apostles were not living. Even guidelines such as the second-century church practice manual, the *Didache,* with all its practical advice, did not exist yet. "Whoever does good is from God; whoever does evil has not seen God" (3 Jn 11) suggests that the church leaders should be helping members discern between right and wrong leaders. Diotrephes' love to be first and his malicious gossiping and unfriendliness toward brothers and sisters are therefore as easily identified as is Gaius's loving faithfulness.

In both 2 John and 3 John, leaders are being corrected for their inability to discern the teachers who can contribute to the well-being of their church. In 2 John the lady accepts false teachers too willingly; here Diotrephes doesn't accept the true ones. We may see them acting wrongly along typical gender lines, ontological or sociological in origin. She is accepting, caring and challenged by creativity and spirituality; he is strict, orthodox and stern. While the lady may sometimes lack the needed strictness, orthodoxy and sternness (perhaps through lack of learning opportunity and experience), Diotrephes lacks openness, acceptance and caring (perhaps because he "knows too much").

The need for both female and male leadership strengths becomes evident in the elder's guidelines for true teachers. They include orthodoxy and moral values as well as affection and acceptance of others, especially coworkers in Christ. In 3 John Diotrephes' character is lacking. His strict orthodoxy seems to produce moral inadequacies common to heretic teachers: they question apostolic authority, gossip, create enmities among churches and lack love (cf. Jude; 2 Pet 2).

Outline

1	Address
2-8	Praise for Gaius's Faithfulness

9-11	Against Diotrephes
12	Recommendation for Demetrius
13-15	Announcement and Greetings

Commentary

Address (3 Jn 1)

The introductory greeting is short but does not lack affection. In a setting where his authority is challenged, the elder appreciates having obedient people like Gaius. *Agapēte* ("beloved "; "dear friend" in NIV; 3 Jn 1-2, 5, 11) will therefore be the favorite term in this letter. It occurs four times in only fifteen verses.

Praise for Gaius's Faithfulness (3 Jn 2-8)

There is no hidden agenda—the elder praises Gaius. Gaius's soul is so well that one can only wish him bodily health accordingly. He walks "in the truth," and others testify to that fact. Both truth (3 Jn 3-4) and love (3 Jn 6) are evident in his life, especially in the way he treats real teachers of the gospel, accepting and equipping them for their ministry even under opposition. Thus Gaius takes part in their ministry, just as the one who welcomes the deceiver in 2 John participates in his evil deeds.

Against Diotrephes (3 Jn 9-11)

Gaius is a well-balanced Christian, in contrast to the lady in 2 John and Diotrephes here. Although the elder does not rebuke Diotrephes' Christology directly, the typically Johannine comment that "whoever does what is evil has not seen God" (3 Jn 11) shows what the elder thinks of this self-centered liar. Diotrephes is close to being labeled false.

Recommendation for Demetrius (3 Jn 12)

John indicates the occasion for writing this letter. Demetrius is coming to Gaius's church or town, and the elder wants to prevent unpleasant circumstances that occurred earlier, when the elder sent his letter of recommendation to the church directly. Demetrius should be accepted on the basis of a threefold testimony: from everybody; from the truth, meaning the Christ; and the elder and his coworkers. Gaius knows that the elder and his testimony are truthful at all times.

Announcement and Greetings (3 Jn 13-15)

The announcement of the visit (3 Jn 14) is not a main issue of the letter, as I think it is in 2 John. One can assume that the elder has to travel to his churches to reestablish doctrine in the lady's church and his authority in Diotrephes' church (3 Jn 10), so he will also visit Gaius. The letter ends with "peace" and greetings from friends to friends, leaving us with the feeling that regardless of the nasty situation, the elder's authority still means something to a bigger circle of people.

Bibliography. *See* bibliography for 2 John.

KSENIJA MAGDA

JUDE

Introduction

The epistle is ascribed to "Jude, a servant of Jesus Christ and brother of James" (Jude 1). References in the church fathers as well as internal evidence supports that most likely this was Jude, the brother of James, head of the Jerusalem church, and the brother of Jesus (Mt 13:55). The author was familiar with Palestinian, apocalyptic and Old Testament literature. The vocabulary, although fairly extensive, would not have been beyond the rhetorical skills expected of a traveling Jewish preacher.

Even less can be said about the destination of the letter. Syria, Asia Minor or Egypt are possibilities. The readers were largely Jewish Christians struggling with the problems of a Gentile environment. Although some scholars suggest Gnosticism as the nature of the heresy reflected in the epistle, more likely Richard Bauckham is correct in characterizing it as antinomianism—the idea that Christians were free in Christ not to abide by laws or rules, an idea also reflected in the Corinthian letters and Revelation.

Equally little is known about the date of the epistle, which may be as early as the 50s or as late as the 90s.

The character of the epistle is that of Palestinian apocalyptic Jewish Christianity. The author's accomplished use of exegesis is more like that found in the Qumran literature than in diaspora Judaism. He uses apocalyptic material like 1 Enoch and the account of Moses' death, and he shows a strong dependence on the Hebrew Bible rather than on the Greek Septuagint, the version widely used in the diaspora.

The epistle includes a large number of rare words that suggest a literary education as the author's background. Jude also uses a triplet style showing a concern for coherence and textual discourse (cf. Neyrey 27-29 for a detailed description of Jude's use of triplets).

Outline

1-2	Introduction
3-4	Purpose
5-16	Body of Letter
17-23	Relation to the Community
24-25	Conclusion

Commentary

Introduction (Jude 1-2)

The epistle begins in the usual style of Hellenistic letters: the sender is named, followed by his title or label of authority. The author cites as his authority that he is servant of Jesus Christ and brother of James. If he was the brother of Jesus, it is particularly interesting that he uses "servant" rather than "brother." Perhaps we can see his alignment of himself with his call to service rather than a reliance on his personal status.

Jude describes the receivers of his letter as "those who are called," "beloved in God" and "kept . . . for Jesus" (Jude 1). All three terms are perfect participles that indicate a state of being in God. God's love is bestowed in the call but also remains, keeping one safe. The concept of being kept recurs throughout the epistle. Further, this state of being in God conveys the meaning that to be called into God's love is to be enfolded and embraced. This stands in marked contrast to the treachery, hypocrisy and deceit of Jude's opponents.

The content of Jude's blessing, a usual component of Jewish and Christian letters, is unique because he excludes the concept of grace, common to most Christian forms, but includes "love." The use of love in this context is not found in any Jewish examples, and only one Christian example of blessing includes it. Love, mercy and peace make up the major themes of the epistle.

Purpose (Jude 3-4)

Jude establishes the epistle's dual purpose: "to write to you about the salvation we share" and to "appeal to you to contend for the faith that was once for all entrusted to the saints." When Jude refers to salvation, he probably refers to the corporate nature of Christianity, perhaps in contrast to the opponents who are causing strife within the community. The second phrase can be translated to indicate the emphasis on an aggressive posture; "to contend for the faith" is a figure taken from the athletic games.

Jude proceeds to describe the opponents in vivid terms (Jude 4): they have "stolen in among you," they are "designated for this condemnation," and they are ungodly persons "who pervert the grace of our God into licentiousness and deny our only Master and Lord, Jesus Christ." Although he continues to describe and denounce these opponents, their main characteristics are that they are deceptive and will be condemned by God because of their denial of the authority of Jesus and even God.

The deception of the opponents is graphically captured in the figure of having "stolen in." The connotation is of secret or even illegal entering into the community with wrong intentions. Jude further describes the opponents' condemnation by using examples from apocalyptic and Old Testament literature. The term *ungodly* implies immorality and suggests that their rejection of God's authority was in reference to moral behavior. Evidently they were rejecting God's spiritual grace and challenging his rules for their behavior within the community.

The Body of the Letter (Jude 5-16)

Jude introduces the body of the letter with the phrase "I desire to remind you." He proceeds in his usual style of triplets; three Old Testament examples illustrate his point that those who challenge God's authority will be punished: the exodus, the fallen angels, and Sodom and Gomorrah. All of these vivid illustrations would have been familiar to his readers. In the exodus, the unbelievers were destroyed; the angels were exiled from heaven and are "kept in eternal chains" for judgment; Sodom and Gomorrah underwent "eternal fire" (Jude 7).

Jude applies these examples to his opponents. This clarifies to some extent the problem in his community: they "defile the flesh," "reject authority" and "slander the glorious ones" (Jude 8). Defiling the flesh can be interpreted several ways but most likely has to do with sexual immorality. Rejecting authority is reflected in all three examples and probably here, as in Jude 4, implies not necessarily a christological heresy but behavior that rejects the laws of God. The third category is vague. The glorious ones could refer to angels, as in the Dead Sea Scrolls. If so, this would most likely relate to a rejection of their role in Judaism as guardians of the law of Moses.

Evidently these people were not only practicing their antinomianism but also teaching it, basing their authority on their dreams or prophetic visions (Jude 8), a common practice in apocalyptic Judaism and early Christianity as well as paganism. The word for dreams can also refer to authentic revelation but is most often used to refer to the "dreams" of false prophets (cf. Bauckham, 55).

Jude cites an example to illustrate a different point. Michael, a leading figure in apocalyptic literature, demonstrates that judgment belongs to God. Even Michael does not revile Satan in the dispute; this authority belongs to God. In contrast, the false teachers in the community "slander whatever they do not understand" (Jude 10). Out of this ignorance, they behave like "irrational animals." The irony is remarkable—the teachers claim spiritual insight from revelations but merely follow basic instincts like animals.

Jude follows this with a woe oracle (Jude 11), a common stylistic device in apocalyptic as well as prophetic literature to denote the role of a prophet delivering the judgment of God. He cites three more Old Testament examples to describe the false teachers and their coming condemnation. Like Cain, the teachers are godless, self-seeking, hostile to authority, a challenge to God's authority; they finally bring about the death of others. Like Balaam, they are greedy and lead people astray to benefit themselves. And like Korah, they rebel against God's authority. These examples underscore the problems of greed, a rejection of God's authority and an attempt to lead the people astray.

The heretics have plunged into the error of Balaam, the mercenary prophet who wanted to accept the wages offered by Balak, king of Moab, to curse the Israelites in their wilderness journey. God forbids Balaam to accompany Balak's messengers back to Moab, but when the messengers return with offers of still higher economic gain, Balaam begs to be allowed to go to Balak. Balaam is warned that he must proclaim only the oracles of God.

Once in Moab, Balaam blesses Israel; God will not allow him to curse them. Still eager to earn a reward, Balaam turns to another path to wreak havoc on the Israelites. The women of Moab are instructed to inveigle the men into union with cultic prostitutes (Num 31:16; 25:1-2; see also Rev 2:14). Israel became involved in the worship of Baal of Peor, in eating meat offered to the god and in ritual promiscuity. The error of Balaam involved the manipulation of women for the sake of his financial advantage.

Six metaphors are used to describe the heresy; they are images from each of the four regions of the physical world: air, earth, sea and heavens or space. All of them emphasize emptiness and futility, probably referring to the false teachers' vain words and arrogance. All of them illustrate nature gone awry—clouds without rain, trees without fruit, wandering stars. 1 Enoch is reflected here where even nature becomes chaotic when it does not follow God's laws. Jude points out that like nature when it goes astray from God's laws, the opponents reject the laws of God. It is implied that as disaster results from lawless nature, so disaster will result from the behavior of the false teachers.

Jude now quotes directly from 1 Enoch 1:9. This does not necessarily mean that he considered 1 Enoch part of the canon; Qumran also used apocalyptic literature in this way. He uses it to set the situation into an eschatological context. The opponents may be currently rejecting God's authority, but the Lord is eventually coming "to execute judgment on all" (Jude 15). "All" explicitly refers to the ungodly; the word is used four times in this verse as well as two additional times in the epistle. Jude 15-16 echoes the sins mentioned earlier, but here Jude directly relates them to speech. They speak harsh things; they are grumblers, finding fault, speaking arrogantly and flattering people for their own advantage (cf. Neyrey for a discussion of speech issues in Jude).

In this passage, Jude adds details about the opponents. Not only are they greedy, immoral, deceitful, out of control and arrogant about God's laws and authority. They also reject authority and insult the angels; they argue and dispute; they revile what they do not understand; they speak in arrogance against God. Jude notes the result of this behavior: severe punishment and destruction.

Relation to the Community (Jude 17-23)

The tone of the letter changes here. Jude urges the "beloved" to remember the Old Testament prophecy and the words of the apostles. The word for "you" is emphatic. His readers stand in marked contrast to the lawless behavior of the opponents. Jude admonishes his readers to build themselves up in the faith, pray in the Holy Spirit (perhaps in contrast to the false revelations of the opponents), keep themselves in the love of God, wait for the mercy of the Lord and have mercy on others.

Whereas the opponents claim the authority of false revelations, the community prays in the Holy Spirit. The opponents cause strife and division, whereas the community is building up; the opponents revile everyone, including God, whereas the community is admonished to "have mercy" and to keep themselves in God's love.

Conclusion (Jude 24-25)

The letter concludes with a traditional doxology adapted by Jude. The reference to "keep" completes Jude's emphasis on this concept throughout the epistle. Just as God is able to keep the wicked for destruction, he is able to keep his faithful ones from the dangers of the false teachers. The result of being kept is to be able to stand in God's glory with rejoicing. These terms suggest an eschatological connotation and emphasize the final result of salvation.

The doxology concludes with the components common to this form. References to the nature of God include his "majesty," which describes his awesome transcendence. *Power* is common to doxologies, but *authority* is rare. Jude underscores the sovereignty of God in his community in marked contrast to the views of the false teachers.

Bibliography. R. J. Bauckham, *Jude, 2 Peter,* Word Biblical Commentary 50 (Waco, TX: 1983); J. H. Neyrey, *2 Peter, Jude* Anchor Bible Commentary (New York: Doubleday, 1993).

REBECCA SKAGGS

REVELATION

Introduction

The book of Revelation has long been viewed as a book of mystery and intrigue, full of mythical beasts, bloodthirsty battles and seemingly unexplainable events. Many Christian readers through the ages have reacted to it in one of two ways. Some readers hate it, cannot understand what it is saying and so dismiss it as irrelevant to their life and faith, viewing it as a mistaken entry in Scripture, as Martin Luther believed. Other readers love its rich imagery and powerful reassurances. However Revelation strikes an individual, it is impossible to be neutral toward it, which is part of its purpose. The book seeks to encourage people of all eras, genders and nationalities to respond to the message of Jesus Christ. There can be no neutrality in the battles portrayed between good and evil; everyone is either a faithful witness of Christ or against him.

The authorship of Revelation is traditionally ascribed to John the apostle, the son of Zebedee, but there continues to be much debate over whether this is so. Another suggested author is John the elder, known to the churches of Asia Minor, or even that the text is the product of a school of John that ascribed it to its founder to add weight to its authority. There are arguments for and against each of these. But the work is the revelation of Jesus Christ, and it carries such an overwhelming message that the human intermediary is secondary.

However, what can be discerned about this skillful writer is important. His name was John, and he describes himself as a prophet, never as an apostle. He was well acquainted with and had a degree of authority over the churches in Asia Minor to whom he writes. He had been exiled to Patmos by the Roman authorities for his witness to the Christian faith. During this time he received a series of visions that he recorded for building up the churches, for Domitian's (A.D. 90-95) emphasis on emperor worship caused conflict between the ruling authorities and the Christian community and led to persecution. The churches also suffered from the infiltration of heretical teachings that threatened to undermine their consistency of witness in an already precarious situation. Although the message addresses the immediate needs of the seven churches, its wider message of hope and reassurance of the victory of Christ over all is relevant for Christians of all eras.

Two of the puzzling questions asked of Revelation are how it is to be interpreted and to what genre it belongs. Four traditional methods or approaches are generally proposed. The preterist approach interprets the book as relating only to the circumstances of the first-century readers. The futurist method finds its meaning in relating the whole text to the end times of history when all the prophecies will be fulfilled. The poetic or symbolic approach emphasizes the images and attempts to interpret their meaning in terms of values relevant to all eras; the historical method proposes an interpretation based on viewing the prophecies of Revelation as relating to historical events through the ages from the early church to the second coming. Each view has drawbacks and weaknesses, so a more effective approach is to use the most helpful aspect of each.

The answer to the question of genre is found within the book. The first word claims that it is an apocalypse (a "revealing" or "unveiling"), and one does not have to read far before it becomes clear that this apocalyptic piece of writing refers to the end times. At the same time it claims to be a prophecy and its writer a prophet, and its qualifications as a letter are also found within the opening paragraphs. On a most basic level Revelation is a letter to all churches that is simultaneously prophetic and apocalyptic.

Does Revelation have particular relevance to women, their faith and life? At first glance some women may reject it as a bloodthirsty, military, male-dominated book, but closer examination demonstrates that the book has at its heart the image of a faithful, pure woman who personifies the church in all its glory. The basic message of Revelation applies equally to women and men. It is a call for Christians to be faithful to Christ, to continue their witness even though they may suffer for it, some to the point of death. Reassurance is given that God is in control, however persistent evil may appear, and that ultimately God will bring about judgment and vindicate his people. Unbelievers and waverers are constantly encouraged to repent so that they too will share in the good things of God. Revelation begins by addressing the failings of the church but ends gloriously with the marriage of the purified church to the Lamb.

Outline

1:1-20	Prologue
2:1—3:22	Letters to the Seven Churches
4:1—5:14	Setting the Heavenly Scene

6:1—7:17	Seven Seals
8:1—19:21	Seven Trumpets
10:1—11:19	The Little Scroll and the Two Witnesses
12:1—13:18	The Woman, the Dragon and the Beasts
14:1-20	The Lamb and the 144,000
15:1—16:21	Seven Bowls of Wrath
17:1-18	The Great Harlot
18:1-24	The Fall of Babylon
19:1—22:21	Rejoicing in Heaven

Commentary

Prologue (Rev 1)

The prologue is made up of a title, motto, blessing and greeting. The title, which states that the book is a revelation of Jesus Christ to his followers, is reminiscent of the prophetic books (cf. Is 1:1). The motto briefly describes the contents of the revelations that "must soon take place" (Rev 1:1). A blessing is bestowed on all who read, hear and heed the prophecies. A similar blessing rounds off the book (Rev 22:7). The greeting (Rev 1:4-5) follows the format used in many New Testament letters (e.g., Eph 1:2).

The opening verses introduce hearers to themes that in varying modifications are carried through the rest of the vision. First we learn about the unveiling of things previously hidden that will take place in the future. We are reminded of the veil that was torn in two at Christ's death, opening up the way into the holy of holies in the temple. Here the veil is drawn back so that Christ can reveal what will take place. We see a distinct order in the line of communication: the revelation given by God to Jesus, to his servants via the angel and John.

John describes vividly and eloquently all that he experiences. In order to express heavenly sights and sounds and to convey these wonders to his readers, he uses images that are familiar to them from Jewish traditions and the Old Testament. He frequently uses the word *like* in his descriptions to help him and us to make sense of what he sees. If we had seen the same visions, we would use images familiar to our culture and experience to convey the same truths. John describes what he experienced in a way that he and his first-century readers could understand.

The Revelation of Jesus Christ was given by God to pass on to his servants, who include not only the congregations of the seven churches, to whom this circular letter is addressed, but also all his servants, male and female, in all times and places.

Throughout the book, what is heard is as important, if not more so, than what is seen. Revelation is primarily a message to be heard, with themes and motifs throughout that gradually build momentum. The best way to experience the nuances and capture the vivid description in all its richness and diversity is to hear the text read aloud. Throughout, all that John hears is interpreted by what he sees.

Often too much emphasis is placed on deciphering the images down to every detail, but this approach loses the effect and impact of the drama; the full meaning can be lost with the reader. If a single note in a piece of music is studied on its own, what does it convey about the piece as a whole? It can be played in various ways, but without the notes around it, that single note doesn't make much sense or give a good and balanced picture of the whole. But when it is played at the right time, it adds to the richness and meaning of the whole. So it is with Revelation. Deciphering every detail has the danger of detracting rather than enhancing. Revelation is a work to be heard, and it often urges those who have ears to hear to listen carefully to what is being said. Revelation is not chaotic but is ordered and structured, constantly moving forward to its triumphant conclusion.

The Pauline-like greeting (Rev 1:4-5) introduces the first-century recipients of this letter. In these few verses are themes that are later picked up throughout the text: the themes of seven, the throne, faithful witness and priests redeemed.

Although it is addressed to the seven churches, Revelation is intended for the whole of Christianity. It is a message for all who love Christ, freed from sin by his blood, to remain faithful to him. The inclusive nature is evident. All who are faithful witnesses are redeemed priests serving God. Gender is irrelevant, and trying to make it an issue only causes grief to those who then feel excluded from part of God's plan for his people. All are priests because of Christ's blood and not because of social favoritism, gender, race, position or wealth (cf. 1 Pet 2:9). The text carries a matter-of-fact warning that there will be a time of distress and judgment when Christ returns and all will see Christ in his glory.

In Revelation 1:8 God sets out some of his credentials. He is eternal, in all times and places. This verse introduces one of the themes that weaves through the text to enrich and give continuity the whole. Revelation then moves into John's vision of Christ (Rev 1:12-20). The descriptions are taken up and used to describe the sender of the messages to the seven churches, thus forging a link between the introductory paragraphs and the seven letters.

John falls into an ecstatic state in which the earthly fades away and the spiritual comes into clear focus. He hears and sees incredible sights and sounds that he is instructed to record and send to the seven churches. There is insufficient space here to discuss the transmission and receiving of visions, but we must accept that John, with his senses heightened by his worship on the Lord's day, had a vision in which he not only saw and heard amazing things but also took part and interacted with the characters.

John sees Christ among seven golden lampstands and describes his vision of Christ using imagery from the Old Testament. Each aspect of the figure has significance and points to an aspect of Christ's character. Seven golden lampstands represent the seven churches and mean that Christ is present with his church. (Within Revelation, numbers should not always be taken literally; many have a symbolic meaning. The number seven, for example, symbolizes perfection and completion.)

The figure of Christ is dressed in priestly and royal clothing, which demonstrates his function as mediator between God and his people. His wisdom and piercing spiritual insight, from which no one can escape, are indicated by the color of his hair and his eyes like fire. His feet cannot be shaken, and his thunderous voice, like the sound of a waterfall, blots out all other sounds. The force and power are so great that the ground would shake. In his hand he holds seven stars representing angels and his authority over supernatural beings. From his mouth protrudes a two-edged sword that denotes Christ's ability to bring judgment and peace with a word discerning the thoughts of the heart (cf. Heb 4:12).

The vision is so terrifying that John's senses are overloaded, and he is rendered unconscious. Jesus reassures him with a touch and tells him not to fear. Here we have the familiar, compassionate Jesus of the Gospels—his heavenly, holy appearance may inspire awe, but he is still the same. After calming John's fears, Jesus assures him of Christ's supremacy over all things, including death, because he has conquered death and is alive. Jesus instructs John to record all he sees. The remainder of Revelation is this record.

Letters to the Seven Churches (Rev 2—3)

In Revelation 2—3 are seven letters from Christ to seven of the churches in Asia Minor with whom John had a close relationship. The book of Revelation is addressed to these churches, and they are given individual messages of encouragement and reproof relevant to their situation. These letters introduce the main theme of Revelation: a call to a life of faithful witness to

Christ resulting in eternal reward or failure to comply, with unfaithfulness and lack of repentance resulting in punishment. Although they are aimed at specific situations in the first century, these letters can also be used as an encouragement for all Christians in all eras to remain faithful to Christ. The failings represented by the seven churches are reflected in many church situations through the ages, and the command to listen to what the spirit of God says and the call to repentance are as relevant today as they have ever been.

The messages to the churches follow the same format. They begin by stating who the letter is from; each letter uses a different description of Christ found in the vision of Revelation 1 and is addressed to the angel of the church who in some way represents the church in heaven. Each church is first commended for the positive areas of its life and worship and then reprimanded for its failings. The exceptions are the churches of Smyrna and Philadelphia, for which there is nothing but praise. There follows a call to repentance with promises of rewards for those who respond to what the spirit of God is saying and punishment for those who ignore it.

The church at Ephesus (Rev 2:1-7) was in the city known as the center for the worship of Diana, the fertility goddess, and the emperor cult. It had a strong Jewish community from which Paul launched his mission into Asia.

This Christian community is commended for its vigilance against heretics, those Christians who have weakened in the face of pressure to conform to the emperor cult and the Nicolaitan teaching. They have held on to the truth, but their enthusiasm for truth has led them to follow it so rigidly that they have forgotten love, the first principle of Christian faith. Their passion for rooting out those in error has overtaken their passion for Christ. Their efforts to act without love, in their own strength, will fail, and their refusal to repent and return to a way where love is their motivating factor will result in the loss of Christ's presence among them. Not loving brings destruction in this life and in the lives of individuals. Lack of true love deprives not only the unloved but also the one who refuses to love.

The NRSV translates Revelation 2:7 as "let anyone who has an ear listen" rather than "he who has ears to hear, let him hear," which many older translations use. Many women may be put off by the use of the male pronoun, but that could be said of much of the Bible, written as it was in patriarchal societies. The content of the message demonstrates that it is applicable for the whole church and not for men only. The NRSV conveys the sense and meaning of the text in a fuller and more helpful way; all are included, just as all are included in God's kingdom.

The Christian community at Smyrna (Rev 2:8-11) also found itself in the midst of a large Jewish community and a center dedicated to the emperor cult. These Christians are highly commended for their faithfulness in the face of adversity, and nothing negative is found against them. Their faithfulness has, however, had repercussions on their financial status. In a city renowned for its wealth, these Christians are materially poor. In order to prosper, trade workers had to belong to the city guilds, membership which included participating in the worship of the guilds' patron gods. Without such membership one could not work or earn a living.

The church had the second problem of no longer coming under the protection previously afforded to Christians as a Jewish sect. Christians were expected to take part in the emperor cult, and failure to do so meant persecution. The Romans insisted that conquered peoples take on Roman religion, which included paying homage and making sacrifices to the emperor as god. Judaism was exempt from this, and Jews were allowed to continue practicing their religion. It would appear that the Jewish community stirred up trouble for the Christians and maybe drew the Romans' attention to their noncompliance to the religious laws. The church at Smyrna was about to undergo persecution and was called to remain faithful, even if that meant martyrdom. In doing so it would receive great rewards from Christ.

Pergamum (Rev 2:12-17) was yet another center for emperor worship and also had temples dedicated to Zeus and Asclepius, both of whom bore the title savior and took the serpent as their symbol. Praised for its faithful witness, even after the execution of one of the congregation, the church at Pergamum still is rebuked. It has allowed the teaching of Balaam and the Nicolaitans to continue unchecked. Balaam, who at the instigation of Balak the king of Moab (Num 22; 25:1-3; 31:7-18) led the Israelites into error, had become synonymous with a teacher who leads the people of God into infidelity. Adherence to the Nicolaitans' teaching meant compromising with society, not remaining exclusively faithful to Christ. Failure to repent will bring severe punishment. Those who repent and remain faithful will be given spiritual nourishment, proclaimed innocent and given a new name to reflect their character and relationship with Christ.

The letter to the Thyatiran Christians (Rev 2:18-29) is the longest of the seven letters but follows the same format as the other letters. This congregation's promising record has been spoiled by its toleration of the teachings of a false prophet. The name Jezebel had become symbolic of someone who encouraged false beliefs and worship. (This was not the woman's real name; no one would name a daughter after such an infamous woman [2 Kings 9:22].) Not everyone in the church had been drawn into her web of deceit and sin, but they had sinned by tolerating these errors and allowing them to flourish. They are guilty for allowing the church to be compromised and for not protecting those weaker in the faith. The teachings of Jezebel, like the harlot of Babylon (Rev 17), caused Christians to become involved in spiritual idolatry and fornication. Jezebel is given the opportunity to repent, but if she does not choose to do so, she and her followers will be destroyed.

Accusations have been leveled against John claiming that his use of the name Jezebel to symbolize a woman with ideas different from his demonstrates a negative attitude toward women. This view says that he pictured women only in the traditional ways of his society—as pure and good, as brides (Rev 19:7-8; 21:2) or mothers (Rev 12), or as Jezebels and harlots. What this view fails to take into account is John's use of Old Testament imagery, in which a woman symbolizes the changing relationship of God with his people.

Sardis (Rev 3:1-6) was a commercial city on the major trade route through Asia Minor. During its history it had twice fallen due to its population's complacency. Instead of keeping watch at night, the city had slept while its enemies invaded. The fact that a number of public buildings had been started but never completed led to its reputation for apathy. John spiritualizes these themes to demonstrate the faults of the church, which seems to have been infected with the problems traditionally associated with the city. The church in Sardis had the appearance of a thriving community but had become spiritually lifeless. It is called to rouse from its slumber and apathy before it is overtaken by the sleep of death from which it will never awake. The church's deeds for Christ have been incomplete and substandard. It has not finished what it started, and it has failed to prepare for Christ's return. If the church wakes, shakes itself out of apathy and repents, then it too will be among those commended and rewarded. If not, then Christ will appear when they least expect it and attack them with his full fury. Their names, it is implied, will be removed from the book of life.

Like the church at Smyrna, the congregation at Philadelphia (Rev 3:7-13) is praised by Christ, who holds the keys to unlock the future. This community has remained faithful to Christ even though it is powerless in the face of opposition. But the church is reassured by the fact that Christ alone is in control of all that happens to them. Christ has put an open doorway in front of them through which he alone gives access, and they are given entry because of their faithful witness. On the other side of the door they will find themselves in the presence of God, a place of reward and security.

The encouragements to hold fast and patiently endure form the backbone of the message to the churches, not just in the seven letters but also throughout Revelation. The main theme that undergirds the visions and revelations is a plea to remain faithful and not to be led astray by fear of persecution, apathy, lack of love or the seductions of false teaching.

The final letter is addressed to the church at Laodicea (Rev 3:14-22), a prosperous commercial city known for its clothing industry, ophthalmic medical center and banking activities. Here the hot medicinal waters of Hierapolis (for healing) and the cold (refreshing) water of Colossae met, but the mixture of the two waters produced lukewarm, nauseating water that was not fit to drink. The spiritual condition of the church is reflected in this unhealthy water supply. The lukewarm state of the church meant it could offer neither healing nor refreshment. As such it was fit only to be spat out. The self-reliant, rich, complacent atmosphere of the city had permeated the Christian community, causing it to lose its distinctiveness and witness. Christ, however, offers a remedy if the church will repent and accept it. They think of themselves as rich but are in spiritual poverty; to this Christ offers what they cannot buy. They are spiritually blind in a city with ophthalmic experts; Christ offers salve to soothe the eyes and help them see. They have no clothing in a city famous for its garment industry; Christ provides white robes to wear. Christ is the answer to their failings. They are urged to "listen" and not to rely on their wealth. Christ waits for them to respond and accept his remedy, but he does not force it on them. The Laodiceans are given a choice—to welcome his help or not. To those who open the door to Christ, the gateway into the Father's presence will be opened.

By the end of Revelation 3, the seven letters are complete. The picture emerges of the church divided into two camps: those who remain faithful to the end and will receive their reward and those who are found to be unfaithful and will be punished. Revelation pays considerable attention to these themes. Some will be consistent in their witness to Christ; others will waver; still more, including those not in the church, will repent and acknowledge God; many refuse. Within the seven letters we see a microcosm of the church and the world, both in need of repentance. Much of the rest of Revelation gives the prophetic account of the battle between those who belong to Christ and those who do not. The seven churches set the scene for the remainder of the vision.

The whole of Revelation can, in one sense, be seen as the account of the cleansing and beautifying of the church. It begins with the failings being pointed out, and then the book gives opportunities for repentance and encouragements to continue in faithfulness until the process of refinement and purification has been made complete. The church is presented as the bride of Christ—pure, beautiful, without blemish.

Setting the Heavenly Scene (Rev 4—5)

Having set the scene on earth by commenting on seven specific churches, the vision moves on to set the stage where the scenes in the heavenly realm will be played out. This realm is unlike anything experienced by John on earth, but the two realms are linked by worship of the One on the throne. The realms, running parallel, from time to time overlap so that the scenes played out in one affect the other. The way for John into this world is through an open door in heaven through which the familiar voice invites him.

The essence of Revelation 4 is the description of ceaseless worship taking place in the throne room of heaven. At first the impression of the throne room is that of a cold, stark and frightening place. A throne, flashes of lightning and thunder emanating from it, stands in the center surrounded by twenty-four elders constantly worshiping the figure on the throne. They are accompanied by four creatures that also worship and sing. In the foreground is a sea of glass, smooth and cold to the touch. One on the throne is a figure described in terms of precious stones—cold, rigid, hard stone. The images seem frightening and unwelcoming. But for first-century readers such semiprecious stones convey not coldness or stonelike qualities but the reflection of light. Brilliant light everywhere reflects off every surface, and radiant light emanates from the One on the throne.

Here we are introduced to some of the heavenly characters who repeatedly contribute to the worship in heaven. Twenty-four elders, to represent the twelve tribes of Israel and the twelve apostles, act as royal priests in leading the worship. The four living creatures, supreme representatives of their kind, are covered with eyes; nothing goes unnoticed by these eyes, which are forever awake and vigilant. Both groups sing constantly in praise and worship of God.

In the midst of this worship, the One on the throne holds a sealed scroll. A search is made throughout all times and places to find someone eligible to open it. But to

John's bitter disappointment, no one is found. He doesn't know the contents, but intuition tells him that it is vital for the seals to be broken; the whole of the future depends on it. Out of his distress he hears one of the elders speak comforting words to him: John is not merely a spectator but a participant. There is after all one—only one—worthy to open the scroll, and that is the Lamb. John's sorrow and hopelessness turn around; all is not lost. All John's readers, familiar with the Old Testament, would understand the allusion to the Passover lamb (Ex 12), Isaiah's lamb led to the slaughter (Is 53:7) and the traditional names for the Jewish Messiah (Rev 5:5). They know beyond a doubt that this is Jesus.

Christ's conquering through the cross is made central and foremost in all that follows (Rev 5:6-10), the event on which all else hangs, without which there could be no Revelation, no future. His death and resurrection are of significance not only for believers. This act has repercussions for all, including the enemies of God, whereby their fate is sealed. Revelation has at its focal point the decision of all as to which category they fall into.

As the Lamb takes the scroll (Rev 5:7), he is worshiped by the creatures and elders in the same manner as the One on the throne. The Lamb is equal; it is his due. It is worth noting here that John's later attempts to worship an angel were rejected. If worship of the Lamb were erroneous, then rebuke would have followed. A countless number of angels and every creature in heaven and earth acknowledge the supremacy of the Lamb and in full voice worship him (cf. Phil 2:9-11). The one slain out of self-sacrifice regains his rightful position.

Seven Seals (Rev 6—7)

With the great crescendo of worship still ringing in John's ears, the time arrives for the unfolding of the future, the setting in motion of the last things that end in God's judgment. The opening of the seven seals inaugurates the first of three septets of disasters that rain down against the earth, its inhabitants and the enemies of God. The opening of the seals and the angelic trumpet calls (Rev 8—12) inflict partial disaster, whereas the emptying of the bowls of God's wrath brings final, complete destruction. Each septet is divided into an initial quartet of related plagues, followed by three more.

The first septet introduces the four horsemen of the apocalypse who with permission—all that happens is permitted and under the control of God—destroy a quarter of the earth. With the opening of the first four seals, four riders on horseback, each with a specific task, are called forward (Rev 6:1-8). They remind readers of the horses found in Zechariah (Zech 1:8; 6:2-8) sent by God to punish the nations who oppress his people.

The first, white horse is ridden by a divine and royal personage. His mission is to conquer. He represents Christian witness, picking up the theme from the seven letters with their call to conquer through witness. The rider of the second horse, the color of blood and the dragon (see Rev 12:3), is assigned to remove all peace from the earth. The third horse is the color of darkness, and its rider carries the symbol of famine. This famine is partial; it does not affect the vine crops, whose roots are deeper than those of the cereal crops.

The fourth horse, the color of decomposing flesh, is ridden by Death, and Hades follows close behind. Death and Hades are personified, and even in our society death is frequently pictured as a dark, shadowy, faceless person carrying a sickle. His role is to kill a quarter of earth's inhabitants using the plagues of the sword (rider 2) and famine (rider 3) and also by other means. Although they mark the onset of destruction, the seals also emphasize the continued desire of God to be merciful, to persuade by whatever means repentance in those remaining through the witness of the church.

The opening of the fifth seal indicates a shift in emphasis (Rev 6:9-11). The cry of the innocent for vengeance is characteristic of apocalyptic writing, but this will only take place after the allocated number of martyrs has been reached. Theirs is a plea for public justice rather than personal revenge, that those who have been publicly shamed will be publicly vindicated. Their faithfulness to Christ will be recognized while those responsible will suffer public humiliation (see the fate of the harlot, Rev 17:15—19:2). In the meantime the martyrs are instructed to wait and rest.

In response (Rev 6:12-17), the sixth seal unleashes the wrath of the Lamb on the earth in an act that plunges the world back into precreation chaos to clear the way for a new order. But before this can be possible, people must recognize God. Everyone runs to hide from the devastation, but there is no escape. The people see who has initiated the destruction; they are terrified but do not repent.

Before the final scroll is opened the scene changes while the question "Who is able to stand?" (Rev 6:17) is considered. The answer given: the servants of God sealed with his identification mark, the sign of ownership and protection. Until these 144,000 are sealed, the disasters are delayed and four angels assigned to hold back the winds that would do dreadful damage to the earth. Once they have been sealed, they receive protection, just as in the Old Testament the blood of the Passover lamb on the doorframes protected the Israelites from the angel of death (Ex 12:12-13). Later, those who worship the beast are sealed with a counterfeit mark (Rev 13:16-18).

Notice the different use of seals within this section. The seals on the scroll are the type made of wax bearing the name, mark or crest of the sender. Such a seal is to be broken only by the person authorized. The second, a seal in terms of a mark, denotes ownership.

John hears the number of those to be sealed and records that the number includes twelve thousand from each of the tribes of Israel (Rev 7:4-8). But the list does not correspond to traditional lists; instead, it represents the faithful remnant of Israel or believers in Christ and is symbolic of all those under God's protection.

The scene shifts again, this time looking forward to a time after the tribulation. Again there is no chronological order. Time as we know it does not exist. It can move backwards or forwards. When it stops, John catches a glimpse of a scene; then after a fleeting glance he sees another time and scene.

Again a great multitude representing the faithful who have come through the terrible tribulation, for which John is preparing the seven churches, worship the Lamb. In Revelation 5:13 the multitude celebrates the payment of their ransom; here they celebrate their place around the throne.

The Lamb becomes the shepherd to lead his flock into eternal life where, looking forward to Revelation 21:4, their tears will be wiped away. They will drink the water of life, in contrast to worshipers of the beast, who are given blood to drink (Rev 16:4-9). This section takes up the theme of endurance and assurance from the second and sixth letters to reassure the faithful that even though dreadful times are inevitable, they have a place waiting for them in eternity.

Seven Trumpets (Rev 8—9)

After the reassuring interlude, the vision returns to the opening of the seals—the seventh and final—but following its opening something unexpected happens. There is silence, which is as important as the noise and action of the previous scenes. The silence anticipates what is to take place next. It is an integral part of the action. One might expect the contents of the scroll to be revealed, but it isn't, and readers are kept in suspense. After all the noise, silence comes as a relief and an opportunity for the prayers of the saints to be heard as they raise to God a fragrant offering. In response (cf. Rev 6:9-10) the censor filled with fire is flung at the earth as a prelude to divine judgment. Each septet of disasters concludes with demonstrations of God's holiness modeled on Mount Sinai (Ex 19:16-17; see also Rev 11:19; 16:18; 4:5). During this silence seven trumpets are handed to the archangels to announce and warn of the impending plagues (cf. Ex 8—12) and as a call to repentance.

The first four trumpet calls form a distinct group resulting in plagues that destroy a third of the earth through ecological disasters. The first destroys vegetation essential for the production of oxygen and the sustaining of animal life. With the second a third of the sea creatures and ships are destroyed by the tidal waves produced by an enormous fireball and, possibly, by the melting of the ice cap and pollution. The third trumpet announces the fall of a great star from heaven. This fall poisons a third of the water supply, making it unsuitable for drinking. Thus another vital resource essential for survival is devastated. The final trumpet darkens the skies, reducing the amount of light and warmth necessary for a healthy life to penetrate the atmosphere. By the end of these plagues, the whole ecosystem is seriously damaged, and a situation reminiscent of precreation chaos is emerging.

An eagle announces that three woes, worse than anything experienced so far, are to inflict the earth.

Whereas the first four trumpets announce judgments that attack the world's resources, the fifth through seventh trumpets involve demonic activity.

At the sound of the fifth trumpet call the star, fallen from heaven, unlocks the bottomless pit, the place of evil spirits (Rev 9:1-11; cf. Lk 8:31, in which the spirits in the swine are sent to the abyss). From the pit emerges thick, black smoke that blocks out the remainder of the light and heat of the sun and makes the air unbreathable. Monstrous, locustlike creatures (cf. Ex 10:21-23) emerge to torture those not sealed by God. They were not to harm the vegetation, an unusual behavior for locusts, which normally ravage the countryside and crops. These creatures' target is to be people. The torture, although restricted in time, will be so great that victims will long for the relief of death, but their tormentors must not kill them. This is reminiscent of Joel 2, where an army of locusts, representing demonic forces, cause penitence. In Revelation, there is no repentance. This torture is the first woe announced by the eagle; two more are to follow.

The angel with the sixth trumpet releases the four angels, who wreak havoc by bringing about the destruction of a third of humankind (Rev 9:13-19). They release a great army with a terrifying appearance that kills with fiery, dragonlike breath. The incredible aspect of this episode is not the monstrous creatures or the deaths of so many but the fact that the survivors still refuse to repent (Rev 9:20-21). They are so hardened against God that no amount of torture, discomfort or terrifying experiences can move them to repentance. The objective is to bring them to repentance so that they do not suffer the eternal second death (Rev 20:14-15), but still they continue to worship idols, or more precisely the demonic forces behind the idols, rather than recognize the living God.

The Little Scroll and the Two Witnesses (Rev 10—11)

Two new scenes break into the septet of trumpet calls. The plagues resulted in the hardening of the hearts of the survivors, so another tactic to encourage repentance is formulated—the use of the word of God and two faithful witnesses to persuade by speech rather than force. This has the desired effect, and the episode concludes with penitence.

The prophetic word of God is presented to John in the form of a scroll (Rev 10). In order to receive the word, he is to imitate Ezekiel's action (Ezek 2:8—3:11) and eat the scroll. This action causes the words to be taken in, digested and understood. The initial sensation is one of pleasure. But as the contents of the scroll are digested and the reality of the words set in, it becomes bitter, for John can see the consequences of the words he must prophesy. These words, as does the gospel, will bring salvation for some and harsh judgment to others. In contrast to the scroll in Revelation 5, this scroll is open. The contents are not secret but are available for all to hear and respond to.

Following the giving of the prophetic words to John comes the episode of two witnesses of Christ whose words and actions cause repentance (Rev 11). But first John is given a measuring rod to calculate how many worship God. Those who do not worship are not measured but left to rampage through the city.

Measuring tools were used to symbolize the boundaries between good and evil; here the lines between the two groups are being drawn up, and the divide between them grows (Rev 11:1). The outer courts are left to the unbelievers, just as in Herod's temple the outer courts were the domain of the Gentiles. This circumstance protects the sacred from contamination. "Outside" can be seen not only in physical terms but also in terms of an attitude by which the possessors exclude themselves. Those who identify themselves primarily with unbelievers cannot be counted among the worshipers.

The two witnesses, two being the minimum number necessary for valid witness, represent the witness of the church in the world (Rev 11:3-14). Their role is to prophesy and bring the peoples to repentance. To this end they spend 1,260 days, the same amount of time the unbelievers trample the holy city (i.e., forty-two months of thirty days) prophesying and are given miraculous powers in order to help and protect them and give weight to their arguments.

After the allotted period of witness, the beast, the enemy of God, emerges from the bottomless pit to kill the two witnesses (Rev 11:7-10). As the witnesses represent the witness of the church, their killing could refer to a time of persecution resulting in martyrdoms. The bodies are left in the street to rot; representatives from across the world gloat over the witnesses' fate. Some go further and rejoice, celebrating by giving each other gifts. The source of their irritation and discomfort, those who had pricked their consciences, has been destroyed. Their savior, the beast, has rescued them from their torment.

But the rejoicing proves to be temporary. Three days later, echoing the resurrection of Jesus, the two witnesses are restored to life, to the horror and amazement of the onlookers. Those who had been publicly slain for their witness are publicly vindicated and rewarded by ascending to heaven. This would also be true for all those who remain faithful even through the times of persecution that were imminent. At their resurrection a tenth of the watching city is destroyed in a mighty earthquake reminiscent of those that shook the earth at Jesus' death and resurrection (Mt 27:51-54; 28:2), again adding to the similarities between Jesus and his witnesses. Those who suffer for him will be raised to life like him. Death has no hold over them, as Christ holds the keys of death and Hades (Rev 1:18). At this point, shaken to the core, the people finally repent. The faithful witnesses rather than the dreadful plagues bring repentance. The power of words spoken by faithful believers, even in the face of opposition, was and is essential to bring the gospel of Christ to unbelievers.

The second woe is complete (Rev 11:14-19), and the stage is set for the final woe (Rev 12:13—13:18). But first the final trumpet call instigates a liturgical interlude in which the words and songs look ahead to the future but speak as though it is already accomplished. This gives great reassurance to the believers in the seven churches and to all about to undergo persecution. They can look forward to a time when the kingdom of God is established and they will receive their hard-earned reward. Access to the holiest part of the temple of God is available to all (compare this with the opening of the earthly holy of holies at Christ's death, Mt 27:51-52). Again the formula demonstrating the holiness of God is used to round off the septet (see Rev 8:5; 16:17-21).

The Woman, the Dragon and the Beasts (Rev 12—13)

The main character of this episode is not the child or the supernatural figure of the dragon but the woman (Rev 12:1-6). The venue has moved to the earth, where a woman, portrayed as a queen of heaven, is about to give birth. Her appearance is one of brilliance, clothed in light, in marked contrast to the harlot dressed in garish apparel of purple and scarlet (Rev 17:4; 18:10).

Who is this woman, and what does she represent? As with much of Revelation, there are layers of meaning so that one symbol can at once represent a number of ideas that merge into each other. This is true of the woman. The most obvious interpretation is that she represents Mary the mother of Jesus, here pictured as a woman glorified, with her role as mother bearing eternal significance (*see* Mary the Mother of Jesus). Mary in a sense embodies all the faithful in Israel who have looked forward to the birth of the Messiah. This brings us into the next layer of meaning: she represents the ideal Israel as personified in the Old Testament image of a faithful wife or bride of Yahweh who gives birth to the Messiah (the Messiah comes from the faithful line of Israel). On a third level the woman represents the church, which, as a continuation of the Old Testament picture, becomes the faithful bride of Christ. The three images are fluid and hold each other together. In a sense the whole of the book of Revelation can be viewed as the story of this woman's children, the church, in its struggle to remain faithful to God in spite of many temptations.

The woman is about to give birth, the most vulnerable time for any woman. In the moments prior to the birth a red dragon—the age-old enemy of people, the one who tempted them to sin—appears to destroy the one who would seek to destroy him. The woman cannot get up and save herself and her child. She is in the hands of God, just as Israel and the church depend on God for survival and protection.

Without midwife or protector, the woman gives birth. What chance of survival do she and her child have against such an evil force—a picture of weakness and vulnerability versus strength and evil? What chance does the infant church—weak, few in number and vulnerable—have in the face of evil persecution? But just as with the woman, God gives a place of safety and nourishment to the church if it remains faithful to the end. On one level the dragon wishes to kill the child, Jesus, so that God's plans will be thwarted; on another, the dragon wants to destroy the church and its witness by temptations, persecution and whatever other means he has at his disposal.

The child is snatched away to safety, but the mother is left at the dragon's mercy. Exhausted and sore after childbirth, she nevertheless flees to the wilderness, where God has prepared a safe place for her to recover and rest. The pursuit of the woman is delayed while the dragon and his angels go into battle with the archangel Michael and his forces. Michael is victorious, and the dragon is exiled to earth, where he continues in his destruction and deception. The dragon takes this opportunity to resume his pursuit of the woman. Again she is protected. Failing once more to harm the woman, the dragon turns on the rest of her children, the church, in a twofold attack of persecution and deception, using the harlot of Babylon as one of his main weapons.

In Revelation 13 readers are introduced to two horrific beasts that join with the dragon to form an unholy trinity in direct opposition to God and the Lamb. The first beast, a conglomeration of the four beasts of Daniel's vision (Dan 7), emerges from the sea, the birthplace of chaos. In Daniel the beasts represent earthly empires; John's beast is often identified with the Roman Empire, which persecuted the church of God. The dragon, Satan, gives his authority, power and a throne to the beast, which is clearly meant to parody Jesus. It had been inflicted with wounds that should have killed it but instead had been restored to health. Just as the Lamb (Rev 5) equally shares the worship of the One on the throne, so the beast shares the worship ascribed to the dragon in wording that accurately parodies worship due to God alone. All those not belonging to God are taken in by the counterfeit, originating from the master of deception. The answer to the question "Who can fight against it?" (the beast) must wait until later in the book.

The beast is allowed by God to blaspheme for the same amount of time that the two witnesses prophesied. The beast's prophecies are the opposite of the message of the two witnesses. The beast, which personifies all that is in opposition to God, is also allowed to make war on the church, but all that it does is by divine permission. Even in the most horrendous of circumstances Christians are reminded that God is in control.

The dragon, having been banished from heaven, has set himself up in opposition to God by establishing his own kingdom, which closely parodies the true and original. This counterfeit kingdom is so good a copy that many people are taken in by it. Only those who have remained faithful to Christ can recognize its true character and see it for what it is. But even within the church some may be taken in. Stating the main theme of Revelation, a direct call (Rev 13:10) is made for the church to endure and persist in faith even unto death.

A second beast emerges from the earth to join the dragon and the first beast (Rev 13:11-18). The appearance of this beast is far more appealing than the last; the second beast looks like a lamb in a direct parody of the Lamb of God. But appearances can be deceptive. As soon as it speaks, it shows its true character. Speaking like the dragon, it is like a wolf in sheep's clothing (see Mt 7:15). This beast has the same authority as the first and works on its behalf to persuade the world to worship it. Just as at the beginning the dragon seduced humankind into sin, so this confederate with its silver tongue and deceptive lies leads the inhabitants of earth away from the worship of the true God. Among its tactics is the ability to perform all kinds of miracles that people cannot resist. Persuaded by this beast, the people make and worship an image of the first, which is then given life so that it can talk. Refusal to worship this idol is made a capital offense, just as those who refused to take part in emperor worship were persecuted. This demonstrates that idols are more than stone or metal. They have an evil force at work behind them. To give in to pressure from Rome and take part in the emperor cult meant to worship the evil behind the image.

In this parody of the divine Trinity the second beast could equally be the counterfeit of Christ, with the appearance of the Lamb, or of the Holy Spirit, who leads people to follow Christ and performs signs and wonders through God's people. Is the second beast sufficiently lamblike to deceive Christians? Some may be taken in, as in the church at Pergamum, but those who know Christ and his word will be able to discern true words from dragonish talk. All those who worship the beast will be marked with its sign, a counterfeit of the seal with which the saints of God are marked. Without the beast's mark, no one could work to earn a living.

At the end of Revelation 13 the two opposing forces are clearly identified. There are two parallel armies: on one side, God, Jesus and the saints; on the other side, the unholy trinity and all those with the beast's mark. The battle lines are drawn. Let battle commence.

The Lamb and the 144,000 (Revelation 14)

The action moves to the camp of the Lamb, where preparations for battle have been made (Rev 14:1-5). The Lamb and his followers (see Rev 7:1-3) are waiting for the battle to commence. While they wait they sing a song known only to themselves. Keeping it secret gives the song power. It is a song of redemption only for the redeemed.

Revelation 14:4, more than any other verse, has caused problems for many women because it suggests that sexual intercourse with a woman defiles a man. This idea was taken up by certain sections of the church, which then viewed women as the source of all temptation because of their sexuality and led to hostility and a low opinion of women. This is a clear misunderstanding of John's words. Throughout Revelation, fornication and idolatry are viewed in spiritual terms to refer to unfaithfulness toward God, and this verse must be interpreted in the light of that fact. Looking at Scripture as a whole, we see that sexual relations within marriage are good, right and proper. What is being spoken of here is purity. The saints have kept themselves pure and faithful to Christ alone. Abstinence from sexual activity was traditionally the way a soldier prepared for battle or a priest prepared to perform sacrifices. This verse is not intended to denigrate women. The 144,000 represent the faithful of the whole church, men and women, who become the spotless bride of the Lamb.

In contrast to the three woes, three angels appear with messages using similar phraseology (Rev 14:6-11). The first angel proclaims the gospel to all the nations. A further opportunity to repent is given, but time is running out. The second angel announces the fall of Babylon, the symbol of opposition, and the third carries a warning that those with the beastly mark will experience the full wrath of God and eternal torment. This fate is reserved for those who deliberately refuse to repent, even after repeated opportunities to do so, and align themselves with the beast and the harlot.

These angelic messages are followed by another message of encouragement for the church (Rev 14:12-13). Those who heed this message will be rewarded with eternal rest. Those who follow the beast will suffer eternal torment.

The reaping of the world's harvest gathers together everything for the final judgment, when the good and the evil are separated (Rev 14:14-20). The chaff and weeds, those belonging to the evil one, are collected and burned, while the good crops, the saints, are safely stored. This idea is repeated in the imagery of harvesting a crop of grapes (Rev 14:17-20). All are picked and thrown into the wine press, where instead of producing juice they produce blood. The blood represents judgment and punishment of God on unbelievers.

In John's Gospel (Jn 15) Jesus describes himself as the true vine and his followers as the branches who bear good fruit. In Revelation 14:18, the vine is of the earth, and even though the grapes are ripe, they are not part of the true vine but an earthly reproduction destined for destruction.

Seven Bowls of Wrath (Rev 15—16)

The time for the final septet of disasters has arrived. Whereas the previous two have caused partial destruction, this one releases the full wrath of God and climaxes in total destruction. As the angels prepare to commence, a glimpse of heaven is seen, looking toward the time when the beast has been defeated. This glimpse shows us the victorious army singing and worshiping God.

From the temple of heaven, now open to all, the seven angels emerge and are handed golden bowls full of God's wrath. This imagery is reminiscent of the golden censor full of incense or prayer of the saints (Rev 8:5). The martyrs are to be avenged and those responsible judged and punished. The temple is filled with the glory and wrath of God, and no one dare enter until the seven plagues are ended. In the Old Testament, when the presence of the Lord was in the temple no one could enter because of his holiness (Is 6:4).

The pattern of these seven plagues follows those of the seven trumpets with the theme of the retribution and punishment of the beast's followers. The first four plagues are based on the plagues of Egypt (Rev 16:1-9). These plagues represent elements of nature and are an attack on the followers of the beast, but the effect this time is destruction. Those who shed the blood of the martyrs now only have blood to drink—a fitting punishment. Even after these four plagues, survivors still curse God and refuse to repent. They have no intention of doing so.

The last three bowls of wrath target the forces of deception rather than individuals (Rev 16:10-21). The fifth strikes the heart of the beast's authority as its center of its worship is destroyed. The sores inflicted on its followers by the first bowl of wrath cause great pain. But still there is no repentance. With the sixth bowl the river Euphrates (the starting point for the invasion of Palestine in the Old Testament) dries up in readiness for the invasion of the kings from the east. At this point evil spirits from the dragon assemble the unbelieving kings for battle.

No one knows the time, the hour or the day when Christ will return (Rev 16:15; cf. Mt 24:44), so the church must remain faithful, awake, alert and on guard against the dragon that seeks to devour it.

With the pouring out of the contents of the seventh bowl God, in an announcement reminiscent of Jesus' cry from the cross—"It is finished"—states "It is done!" The final plague is unleashed on the earth, its inhabitants and the demonic forces. They receive the full vent of God's fury. A violent earthquake splits the great city, Babylon, into three, and other cities also fall. Islands and mountains disappear; huge hailstones drop on people, but there is nowhere left to hide. And still, incredibly, people curse God up to the end. They truly are hardened people.

The Great Harlot (Rev 17)

John is taken by one of the seven angels to witness God's judgment of the great harlot. Reproduced in Revelation 17 is the strong image of the harlot dressed in her finery and jewels. In one hand she holds a golden cup, and she is ready for her next client. She has used her charms to seduce; she sold her body to the rulers of the earth, who have been taken in by her seductive ways. The harlot is not based on a particular woman and is not intended to portray women in a negative light. Instead, she is an expansion of the Old Testament image of unfaithfulness to God being personified as an unfaithful wife who prostitutes herself. She is the opposite of the virtuous mother and bride who represents the faithful church.

The image of a whore demonstrates the seductive power of those things that lead people away from Christ and into partnership with the dragon and his colleagues. It is an image easy to understand because everyone recognizes the role of a prostitute and the destructiveness she inflicts on stable relationships. But it is not only individuals that the harlot destroys; her activities undermine the core of society, for her behavior damages marriage and family. Those who collude with the harlot are equally to blame for their unfaithfulness. Admittedly she used her seductive ways, but no one forced them into intimacy with her. They too are guilty of sin.

The harlot and the dragon are in league with each other. Their aim is to corrupt and seduce the faithful while blinding the whole of humanity to the truth with deception and lies about wealth and power. The harlot and her clients are responsible for the deaths of the saints. The original readers of the letter would see this image clearly, because for them the harlot was Rome and its rulers, with its worship of idols and emperor. Refusal to comply with Rome's demands for worship meant the death of faithful Christians.

There have been many interpretations about the "seven kings" (Rev 17:7-14). Some commentators have taken them to be various Roman emperors, while others have thought of them in terms of modern tyrannical leaders (e.g., Adolf Hitler). The relationship to any historical figures can only be guessed at. The important fact is not in deciphering the detail in an attempt to work out a date for the events mentioned but to note that these rulers hand over their authority to the beast. They become his subjects and join together to do battle against the Lamb. What an encouragement for the believers in the first century to be told that even though times are bleak, they and not society are on the winning side because their leader is the King of kings and Lord of lords.

The final destruction of the harlot is brought about by those who used her (Rev 17:15-18). Those she had seduced now turn on her. There was never love or respect but only lust for power, wealth and pleasure. They take all she has and leave her naked and humiliated. Then they kill and burn her. God uses the harlot's clients as the instrument of her destruction. She is destroyed by the ones she sought to corrupt and destroy (cf. Jer 41:30-31; Ezek 23:1-27).

The Fall of Babylon (Rev 18)

Now that the harlot of Babylon is destroyed, a song of triumph echoes from the heavens. The great city that affected everyone's life and livelihood is left in ruins. This ruination affects the city but also all who slept with her. With the city destroyed so too is the trade, the means of earning a living. A voice from heaven instructs the faithful to leave the city so that they are not caught up in the destruction (Rev 18:4-8).

The voice of triumph from heaven (Rev 18:2) contrasts with the voices of lament and wailing from those who used the harlot to become wealthy and powerful or to gain power and prestige (Rev 18:9). All this destruction has come about because of the death of the saints who faithfully stood firm against wickedness. The saints, like the two witnesses, were killed because their words of truth were like torture to the unfaithful. Now God has avenged the saints' cry for vengeance (Rev 6:10).

Rejoicing in Heaven (Rev 19—22)

The vision reaches the part that all the saints have eagerly anticipated. Heaven resounds with the sound of worship. The familiar characters of previous liturgical scenes are present.

The worship turns into rejoicing over the forthcoming marriage of the Lamb (Rev 19:7-10). The bride, the church, has made herself ready for her marriage to the Lamb by remaining faithful to him and not allowing herself to be corrupted or tainted by harlot-inspired ideas or ways. She has not been seduced by those things that the harlot found so enticing: fine clothes, wealth, power and prestige. She did not covet any of those things but in simplicity kept herself pure. Her love for the Lamb was so great that she would forego all the attractions of the world to remain loyal to him. Her bridal gown is made from the most costly of materials—the righteous deeds of the saints—and as such is pure, uncorrupted and beautiful.

John uses the imagery of a bride to symbolize God's intimate relationship with his church and the image of the harlot to symbolize those who oppose him. The opposition have sold themselves to the beast, the harlot's pimp, while the bride has been redeemed by Christ.

Revelation 19:9 demonstrates one of the peculiarities of the book. The church is the bride, but at the same time the saints are invited guests at the wedding feast. Those who are invited to the wedding are blessed. To be invited to a wedding feast is a great joy and privilege, an opportunity to join in and celebrate with the couple, to share their happiness. This is no exception, although the emotions will be overwhelming, on a scale never thought possible.

Overcome, John falls at the angels' feet in worship. He is immediately rebuked, for the angel is a fellow servant of God (Rev 19:10). Only God is worthy to be worshiped, however divine other heavenly beings may appear. To worship anyone other than God is idolatry, the error of those who worship the beast.

A rider, who clearly represents Jesus, stands in readiness with his armies assembled to wreak judgment on the armies of the beast (Rev 19:11-16). Heaven is open wide so that everyone on earth will see his arrival (see Mt 24:23-27). In readiness for the ensuing battle, an angel gathers all the carrion birds together. No one will be left to bury the dead, so their bodies will be left to the scavengers. Contrast this with the wedding supper of the Lamb to which the saints are invited.

The beast and the ruler of earth go into battle against the white rider and his army (Rev 19:19-21). The beast is captured and, along with the false prophet, is thrown alive into the lake of fire. The remainder of the beast's army are killed and eaten by the birds. Reading or listening to this would induce some waverers in the faith to stop and take notice.

With the beast and the false prophet languishing in the lake of fire, the third part of the unholy alliance, the dragon—Satan—is seized and bound for a thousand years (Rev 20:1-3). During this time he is unable to deceive, accuse or do any more harm. His power has been curtailed.

During this thousand years Christ reigns with his faithful followers, those who had been martyred and those who refused to worship the beast (Rev 20:4-6). They have all been raised to life, and death no longer has any power over them. Only the dead in Christ are resurrected at this point.

Covenant & Community

Covenant is not a uniquely biblical idea. In entering into covenantal agreements to secure the ordered arrangement of their lives, the ancient Israelites were engaging in a practice widespread in the ancient Near East. Our best evidence, from the Hittite Empire, reveals a variety of treaty forms to accommodate parity and vassal agreements. Of greatest interest to us are the suzerain/vassal treaties.

These treaties normally opened with a preamble, in which the principal party is introduced by name and his position and authority established. This was followed by a historical prologue, recounting the past relations between the two treaty parties. By reiterating the benefactions of the suzerain, the merit of maintaining the relationship was commended to the vassal. Next the stipulations of the covenant were outlined, with particular emphasis on the requirement for gratitude and loyalty on the part of the vassal. A clause followed that specified the place where the document was to be preserved and the requirements for regular reading of the treaty. A list of witnesses to the treaty (usually the gods of the parties to the treaty) was then included. Blessings and curses were invoked for keeping or violating the treaty. The ancient Near Eastern pattern is not exactly replicated in the biblical context of covenant, but it provides a context in which that concept can be understood. The vassal treaty pattern is seen most clearly in the book of Deuteronomy, with echoes in other covenant narratives (e.g., Ex 19—24).

In the Old Testament, covenants are frequently used as a means of articulating the relationship that exists between two parties. When God is portrayed as entering into covenant relationship with human beings, the emphasis is on God's sovereignty and the grateful response called forth from humanity by what God has done for them. The establishment of a covenant is generally designated by the phrase "to cut a covenant" *(karat berith)*. Divinely initiated covenants are followed by an act of commitment and are frequently sealed with a fellowship meal. Throughout the Old Testament, God is shown as entering into covenant commitment to God's people, always with a view to improving their situation.

Covenant and Community in the Old Testament

The Beginnings of Covenant Relationship

There is some debate about where the beginning of covenant relationship in the Old

Testament ought to be located. The word *covenant* first appears in Genesis 6:18. However, the relationship between God and humanity in which the covenant-making action of God is grounded is established in the creation narratives. In these archetypal stories of divine-human community, we have a depiction of the ideal state of humanity. The open and trusting relationship is epitomized in the picture of God walking in the garden in the cool of the evening, seeking to converse with God's image bearers.

The violence done to this relationship by the human quest for autonomy (Gen 3) radically alters the situation. Trust is turned to suspicion, openness to a desire for concealment, harmony to alienation. Yet God does not abandon humanity to the consequences of their rebellion. In the midst of pronouncing the inevitable judgment on their willful disobedience, God provides for their needs, clothing their nakedness (Gen 3:21). This is the first testimony to God's will to create and re-create conditions in which human beings can live in relationship to God and continue to be what God made them to be.

The story of the Fall is not the end of human disobedience. The succeeding chapters recount an escalation of evil, until God despairs of all humanity except Noah and his family. The preservation of Noah is described as covenantal (Gen 6:18), as is God's subsequent undertaking never again to so punish humanity (Gen 9:8). This latter commitment is accompanied by a sign, the rainbow.

The covenant with Abraham begins to reveal the trajectory of God's purposes for humanity. The covenant is preceded by a call and a promise (Gen 12:1-3). Abram is called to leave behind his old life and to go forward in trusting obedience to God. In response to this trust, God promises to make of him a great nation, so that he might be a blessing to the nations. This call is given covenant formality in Genesis 15:1-21, with the promise of land being added to the reiterated promise of offspring. The sign of the covenant is given in Genesis 17:11-14. Thus Abram and Sarai are elected by God to be the means of God's blessing the nations. The call, signified by a change of name to Abraham and Sarah, is on the basis of God's grace and is depicted as the means whereby God's grace shall be revealed to the world. Blessing for the nations comes through relationship to Israel, because God is with them (Gen 26:28-30; 30:27). Genesis 17 makes it clear that this covenant is not just with Abraham but for Abraham and Sarah. She is to be the mother of the chosen people, and a son of Abraham by another woman will not count. Hagar, the concubine of Abraham, also receives a covenant similar to that of her master. She too will have offspring so numerous that they cannot be counted (Gen 16:10). In response to God's covenant, Hagar gives God a name, the only person recorded in Scripture to have done so.

The God Who Makes Covenants

Throughout the Bible, covenant is essentially relational. To understand the meaning and purpose of God's covenant activity it is necessary to understand something of the God who stands behind the covenant.

In the ancestral narratives, God is known by various names. In the context of God's covenant dealings with Moses, God's name is revealed. This name, Yahweh, has been the subject of much debate. It is based on the verb "to be," but the Hebrew grammar is ambiguous. The name can be read as a simple verb *(qal)* or as a causative (*Hiphil)* in present or future tense in the third person; thus either "he is," "he will be" or "he brings into being." In Exodus 3:14 God provides a gloss on his name—"I AM WHO I AM"; "I will be who I will be"; "I create [cause to be] what I create" or "I will bring into being what I will bring into being." Fundamentally the divine name is active and dynamic. It attests that Yahweh's nature will be revealed through divine action, manifest in human history.

As the Old Testament narrative unfolds, the vicissitudes of the human heart stand in marked contrast to the constancy of God. This constancy is described in terms of two characteristics. God's *hesed,* or steadfast love, testifies to God's faithfulness and utter dependability. This aspect of the divine nature is manifest in covenant making and in God's persistent intention to redeem and restore continually rebellious humanity. The second divine characteristic is *sadiq,* or righteousness. God's image bearers are called to exhibit this quality in their lives; it is a quality found in Noah and Abraham and sought in Israel.

The Mosaic Covenant

The Mosaic covenant builds on the covenant with Abraham. The promise of offspring has been abundantly realized, and God declares an intention to fulfill the promise of land (Ex 6:4). Having brought the people out of Egypt, God declares that Israel is to be God's "treasured possession" (Ex 19:5). That this is an act of gracious election is underlined by the affirmation that "indeed, the whole earth is mine," yet Israel is to be "priestly kingdom" and "a holy nation" (Ex 19:5-6). These two terms refer to two dimensions of the one calling. As a royal priesthood Israel is called to mediate God's righteousness to the nations. They do so as a holy nation, a people set apart as the possession of a holy God and at the same time a nation being transformed into the likeness of the holiness of God (Lev 19:2). These terms make it plain that the covenant mediated through Moses is not, as Israel later came to think, a matter of exclusive privilege. Rather, it is congruent with God's intention in Abraham to bless the nations through God's chosen people.

The essential element of the Mosaic covenant is the divine promise. God, on the basis of prior self-disclosure, calls for a response of grateful obedience from the people. In affirming the relationship, God makes further promises concerning Israel and the world. Only after the people have responded, affirming God's covenant (Ex 19:8), is the covenant "sealed" by the sacrificial rite and celebrated in the fellowship meal. It mattered that the whole people took part in this ceremony, after having affirmed the covenant. The specific inclusion of women shows that this was not just for leaders or even just for men.

What it means for Israel to be God's special possession is spelled out. The short answer to the question is given in the Decalogue, or ten words (commandments) given to Moses. After the dreadful apostasy of the people jeopardizes the covenant relationship, the implications of being a holy people are set out in much greater detail. Because all of life was included in the concept of being a covenant people, it was vital that women, men and children saw the covenant as belonging to them. It would be the responsibility of women to ensure that many of the covenant requirements were carried out. Under Nehemiah and Ezra, care was taken to reacquaint women and men with the law and to ensure that they understood it (Neh 8:1-8). A special covenant demanded that Israelites would marry only within the covenant community (Ezra 10:3).

The stipulations for maintaining the proper conditions for living in covenant relationship are further articulated in the book of Leviticus. These stipulations are referred to generally as the law. While some of the provisions of the law are difficult for us to comprehend, certain underlying principles are clear. The purpose of the law was to ensure that God was always, and in all things, acknowledged as the one who ruled over Israel. The life of God's people was to be ordered in a way that reflected the divine rule over all creation, and the conduct of relationships was to reflect the righteousness of God. All people were to be treated with justice and integrity, and the vulnerable and the dispossessed were to be treated preferentially.

The Davidic Covenant

Despite acknowledging the sovereignty of God, Israel, having entered the land that God had promised, longed for a king like the other nations. This plea is ultimately but reluctantly granted by God. The establishment of the monarchy inaugurates a new era in Israel's life (2 Sam 7). Yet God continues to be faithful, and God's covenant promises are refocused in the light of the new administration.

In the covenant with David the promises to Abraham and Moses are broadened and particularized. The covenant promises are located particularly in the king and his offspring. The house of David is described as exercising everlasting rule, a promise that in the light of Israel's later history is generally interpreted in terms of the image of "the root of Jesse" (Is 11:10). This messianic hope becomes an increasingly significant theme in the later stages of Israel's history.

Under the Davidic monarchy Israel experienced what might be considered the high point of national achievement. However, the people of God show every sign of forgetting who they are. The Davidic covenant was sometimes seen as a means of automatically fulfilling the obligations of the Mosaic covenant and relieving the people of responsibility rather than a way of strengthening and encouraging them in that responsibility. Confidence in the provision of the sovereign God is replaced by trust in the political institutions. The burgeoning temple ritual emphasizes the form rather than the substance of the sacrificial action. Concern for the vulnerable is subjugated to the desire to accumulate wealth (Amos 8:4-6). The people grow complacent, believing themselves secure, since the temple is seen as a talisman of God's presence with them (Jer 7:4). A growing dissonance between the lives of God's people and their espoused belief in God as their protector and Lord leads to repeated warnings by the prophets that such carelessness of the divine call will not go unpunished. Ultimately the judgment comes, and the people of God are exiled, with neither king nor temple.

A New Covenant

The bleak experience of exile forced God's people to reassess their understanding of the covenant relationship. Out of this soul searching comes a conviction that God is faithful. The prophets of the exile (Jeremiah, Ezekiel, Isaiah 40—55) affirm that God's promises stand and that Israel has a part to play in their fulfillment. At the same time they understand that this will not come about through the nation of Israel. The covenant community is redefined in terms of the faithful remnant, those who have remained faithful to God. Through this remnant God will continue the redemptive program begun in Abraham.

In Jeremiah 30—31 there is an assurance of return to the Promised Land, of restoration under messianic leadership, of renewal not only of the covenant but also of the whole creation. It is a picture of radical renewal, in which the most deeply rooted human tendencies will be reversed (Jer 31:22), yet set in the context of the Mosaic promise (Jer 30:22). It is easy to think of this as a new covenant—the law is now inscribed on the hearts of God's people (Jer 31:31-34). Yet the law was always a matter of the heart (Deut 10:16; 30:6). The Septuagint translates *hadash* ("new") by the Greek *kainos,* which could suggest a qualitatively new dimension being added to the existing covenant rather than a new covenant. This new dimension is revealed in Jeremiah 31:34, in the radical forgiveness of sins.

God's Purposes Fulfilled: Jesus Christ

In Jesus Christ we find the means by which this radical alteration to the covenant can be achieved. In Christ's once-for-all sacrifice the way is opened for the forgiveness of sins that Jeremiah envisages. Jesus is the fulfillment of the law (Mt 5:17). He is the one in whom the covenant promise of rest, so long deferred (Ps 95:11), is made available (Mt 11:28; Rev 14:13).

With the coming of the Messiah, the shape of the covenant community is radically redefined. No longer is membership based on keeping of the law. Rather, the focus is on the things of the heart, most notably a willingness to give up all and follow Jesus

(Mt 4:19; 8:19-22; 16:24). Established familial relationships are secondary to divine allegiance (Mk 3:35). Those who thought themselves the privileged holders of divine truth, the priests, Pharisees and Sadducees, find themselves marginalized in the divine plan, while those who experienced life on the margins found at last their place in the kingdom of God.

Jesus identifies as his own those who recognize him as the one in and through whom God's covenant purposes for humanity are being realized. This new community centered on Christ is made up of those who share something of Martha's understanding that the Nazarene carpenter is the Messiah, God made present in human form (Jn 11:27). Its life comes from the willingness of many, like the Samaritan woman (Jn 4:7-29), to allow the incarnate One to transform their lives.

The People of the New Covenant

For those who had followed Jesus throughout his ministry, the death, resurrection and ascension of the Messiah was a time of profound crisis. The ongoing life of the community was made possible by holding tenaciously to Jesus' promise that his people would not be left alone but would be guided and comforted by the Spirit of God (Jn 16:7-15). The communal life of the triune God becomes the life of the community of the risen Christ (*see* The Trinity). The power of God present among the disciples in the person of the Holy Spirit enables them to proclaim the good news of their risen Lord, adding many to their number (Acts 2:14-42). When the infant church faces daunting opposition, the Spirit of God encourages and emboldens the faithful (Acts 4:31). This same Spirit indwells the believers and shapes their life together to be the community of the divine covenant.

The challenge for the early church was to articulate what it meant to live as God's people in this renewed covenant—to be the body of Christ. In Christ God's people discover anew what it means to be a royal priesthood, called to proclaim God's saving grace (1 Pet 2:9). The church is the "Israel of God" (Gal 6:16), whose offering to God is the sacrifice of holy lives (Rom 12:1). These themes of covenant renewal and reappropriation are developed extensively in Peter's epistles. Incorporation into the body of Christ through baptism is seen in terms of God's redemptive purposes in the covenant with Noah (1 Pet 3:18-22). The purpose of divine election is for Peter as it was in God's call of Israel: that as God's precious possession, a holy nation, the people of God might declare God's grace to the world (1 Pet 2:9)

Paul radically reinterprets the promises of the covenant. He declares that since the covenant promises are affirmed in Jesus, all those who give their lives to him are heirs to those promises (Rom 4:13-22). The land that Abraham was promised is cast not as Canaan but the world (Rom 4:13). Paul thus affirms that God's promised grace transcends the limitations of ethnic territory and national ideology and extends to all the peoples of the earth, a concern reflected in his mission (e.g., Rom 15:22-25). The concern to enlarge the covenant community should not obscure the relationship of God's promises to the stewardship of the land. As people of God's promises, Christians must remember that, as in the book of Deuteronomy, the covenant binds people to the good land. The responsibility for stewardship of the environment, which was humanity's from the outset (Gen 1:28), persists (*see* Men and Women as Stewards of the Environment; Monotheism).

Eschatological Realization

While the indefinite "the days are coming" of Jeremiah is largely fulfilled in the coming of Jesus, there is a sense in which we still await the full realization of the glorious prophecies of that time. God's covenant promises have been fulfilled in Christ, and God's covenant purposes are being worked out in the present. But the culmination of that process is yet ahead. All Scripture looks forward to the time when God will make all things new, in fulfillment of God's original purposes. God's plan in salvation history has been the restoration of all relationships in the wake of the Fall. Yet there is no going back to Eden. Rather, salvation history carries us forward to a new heaven and a new earth (Rev 21:1). God's redemptive purposes take us from the communion of the garden to the community of the holy city (Rev 21:4), where God will again dwell among God's people. JILL MCCOY

Later, all those who have died come alive to be judged.

After the thousand years Satan is released and allowed to deceive the nations, gathering them again for battle (Rev 20:7-10). Some still align themselves with Satan and join his army. Maybe they did not know about the previous battles and were taken in by the master of deception. Or perhaps they believed they were fighting on the side of right, liberation and justice. Or maybe they wanted to do battle with Christ. They surround the camp of the saints but are defeated when fire falls from heaven. Satan is thrown into the lake of fire, from where there is no escape, to join his compatriots to be tormented for eternity.

All the dead have now been raised to life and stand before the throne of God (Rev 20:11-15). Heaven and earth no longer exist, so there is nowhere to hide from God's presence. All the faithful have already been raised to life (Rev 20:4-5) and having been redeemed by Christ are not included among those being judged. Judgment is reserved for those whose names are not written in the Lamb's book of life. Books containing a record of the deeds of each person are opened, and according to the contents they are judged.

It appears that the dead are judged by their works rather than upon their acceptance of Christ, contrary to the belief that salvation is by faith alone through grace. This begs some questions. No one on his or her merits is good enough to satisfy God's demands—that is why Jesus sacrificed himself—but people are judged on the basis of their deeds. This could mean that all the deeds are judged to be evil, so all are thrown into the fire; this answer would solve the problem. But maybe from the foundation of the world some, known only to God, did have their names written in the book of life and did meritorious deeds but then had been seduced by the harlot and therefore did not do the deeds in the name of Christ. Perhaps if they had not been seduced they may have accepted Christ but were deviously deceived. Perhaps once the devil and his deceptive influences have been made powerless, those that followed them could see him for what he is and come out from under the spell. Have they been given another chance? Will God in his infinite mercy, knowing their innermost being, judge in their favor? There are so many buts and maybes. It is a sticky question that no one can answer. Just like the sealed scroll (Rev 5) that no one could open, this is a question that only the Lamb can answer.

Bride led to new home by husband. (Revelation 21:2)

However, judgment is made. Those whose names are not found in the Lamb's book of life are thrown into the lake of fire, where they will be alienated from God's presence.

Death and Hades are the last enemies to be destroyed. Now there is no death. Just as at the beginning of creation there was no death, so now with the new creation death does not exist. Death was the punishment for sin. With no sin there is no death.

A new heaven and earth are created.

The new Jerusalem descends from heaven like a beautiful bride dressed for her husband. Everything is new, pure and beautiful. God will now live with his people as he had planned from the beginning of creation. Then his plan had been spoiled through rebellion and sin. God had given people freedom of choice, but they used it to reject him. All those in this new creation have already chosen him freely. Paradise has been restored. There are no tears, death, mourning, crying or pain. All those things that came into being as a result of sin no longer exist. Heaven and earth are beginning all over again.

Revelation 21:9-27 contains a vision of the new Jerusalem, its measurements and the materials of its construction. Contrast this with the city of Babylon, which sought power and authority by aligning itself with the beast, and failed. No special place of worship is necessary, for God is with his people, and his presence means that sources of light are no longer needed. The gates of the city are always open to those whose names are in the Lamb's book of life but closed to any unclean thing or person. This suggests that the punishment of unbelievers is a separation from God. They are eternally tormented by seeing what they could have had but have rejected.

John is shown the river of life flowing from the throne of God (Rev 22:1-7). All life comes from God. The river is surrounded by fruit trees with different fruit for each month. This new community has all its needs—food, water, light—met by God.

John is returned to his own time and instructed to proclaim the revelation to as many people as possible (Rev 22:6-21). Time is running out. The events John saw in the visions are soon to take place, and Christ is soon to return.

The book of Revelation begins and ends with a blessing on those who remain faithful to God and heed the message contained in it. A final warning is given to anyone who might be tempted to alter the messages contained within the book. Anyone who adds to or takes from the prophecy will be suitably punished either by intensifying the plagues on them or by removing their rewards. Again and finally an emphasis is on the fact that Jesus is the originator of all the visions and his words are trustworthy and true. Revelation 21:21 ends with a benediction reminiscent of those in New Testament letters.

The Bible brings us full circle. It begins with creation and ends with the new creation. The end is really the beginning.

Bibliography. J. P. M. Sweet, *Revelation* (London: SCM, 1990); E. Schüssler Fiorenza, *Revelation: Vision of a Just World* (Minneapolis: Fortress, 1991). KEREN E. MORRELL

Identification & Credits for Illustrations

1. (p. 11) Figure of a woman grinding grain, Egypt, Old Kingdom, Dynasty 5, 2500-2350 B.C.
Limestone; height 19.5 cm., width 8.2 cm.
Harvard University—Museum of Fine Arts Expedition, 12.1486.
Courtesy of the Museum of Fine Arts, Boston.

2. (p. 21) Four Astarte figurines.
Clay, around 1000 B.C.
Courtesy of Erich Lessing/Art Resource, NY.

3. (p. 26) "Reserve Head" of a woman, Egypt, Giza, tomb G 4440, Old Kingdom, Dynasty 4, reign of Khufu (Cheops), 2585—2560 B.C.
Limestone; height x width x depth: 30 x 21 x 26 cm (11 13/16 x 8 1/4 x 10 1/4 in.).
Harvard University—Museum of Fine Arts Expedition, 14.719.
Courtesy of the Museum of Fine Arts, Boston.

4. (p. 30) Pharaoh's daughter finds the infant Moses in the Nile River.
Fresco, synagogue, Dura Europos, Syria.
Courtesy of The Jewish Museum, NY/Art Resource, NY.

5. (p. 84) Rampant lion. Hittite, 9th century B.C.
Orthostat from the palace of King Kapara, Tell Halaf, Syria.
Courtesy of Erich Lessing/Art Resource, NY.

6. (p. 126) Hathor headed crystal pendant, Sudan (el Kurru), Dynasty 25, reign of King Piye, 747-716 B.C.
Rock crystal and gold; height: 5.4 cm (2 1/8 in.).
Harvard University—Museum of Fine Arts Expedition, 21.321.
Courtesy of the Museum of Fine Arts, Boston.

7. (p. 150) Peasant couple harvesting.
Wallpainting in the vaulted tomb chamber of Sennutem (No. 1), a necropolis officer of the early Ramessid Period (Dynasty 18), in the cemetery of Deir el-Medina, Luxor-Thebes, Egypt.
Courtesy of Erich Lessing/Art Resource, NY.

8. (p. 198) Elijah on Mount Carmel.
Fresco, synagogue, Dura Europos, Syria.
Courtesy of The Jewish Museum, NY/Art Resource, NY.

9. (p. 199) The royal seal of the Hittite King Tudhalija IV from a message to the King of Ugarit, Ras Shamra.
Seal imprint on a clay tablet; 1250-1220 B.C.
Courtesy of Erich Lessing/Art Resource, NY.

10. (p. 206) Woman at a window.
Detail of a furniture; ivory, formerly gilded; from Arslan Tash (Hadatu), Syria, 8th century B.C.
Courtesy Réunion des Musées Nationaux/Art Resource, NY.

11. (p. 210) Elamite prisoners led into exile by an Assyrian soldier.
Detail of a bas-relief from the palace of Ashurbanipal (668-627 B.C.); gypseous alabaster.
Courtesy of Erich Lessing/Art Resource, NY.

12. (p. 250) Darius I the Great (550-486 B.C.) giving audience.
Detail of a relief in the Treasury of the Palace at Persepolis, 491-486 B.C., Persia.
Courtesy of SEF/Art Resource, NY.

13. (p. 306) Funeral ceremony. Women dancing and playing the tambourine.
From Saqqara; Dynasty 19.
Courtesy of Scala/Art Resource, NY.

14. (p. 314) Slave girl dressing a lady for a feast.
Detail of a wallpainting in the tomb of Nakht, scribe and priest under Pharaoh Thutmosis IV (Dynasty 18, 16th-14th century B.C.) in the cemetery of Sheikh Abd al-Qurnan.
Courtesy of Erich Lessing/Art Resource, NY.

15. (p. 325) Sarcophagus and lid with representations (portraits) of husband and wife, Italic, Etruscan; Findspot: Vulci, Etruria, Italy Early Hellenistic Period, Late 4th or early 3rd century B.C.
Peperino tufa (volcanic stone); height x width x depth: 88 x 73 x 210 cm (34 5/8 x 28 3/4 x 82 11/16 in.).
Gift of Mr. and Mrs. Cornelius C. Vermeule III, 1975.799.
Courtesy of the Museum of Fine Arts, Boston.

16. (p. 339) Lekythos, Greek; Object place: Athens, Attica, Greece, Early Classical Period, about 480-470 B.C.; The Brygos Painter.
Ceramic, Red Figure; height: 33.2 cm (13 1/8 in.).
Francis Bartlett Fund, 13.189.
Courtesy of the Museum of Fine Arts, Boston.

17. (p. 345) Centauromachy painter. Young woman holding a mirror [spindle].
Red figure pyxis; classical period, 430 B.C.
Courtesy Réunion des Musées Nationaux/Art Resource, NY.

18. (p. 351) Skyphos (cup) of Corinthian type, Greek, South Italian, Late Classical Period, about 330-320 B.C.; Alabastra Group.
Ceramic, Red Figure; height x width with handles: 9.7 x 16 cm (3 13/16 x 6 5/16 in.). Mary L. Smith Fund, 69.28.
Courtesy of the Museum of Fine Arts, Boston.

19. (p. 359) A wooden statue of a non-Egyptian woman from the tomb of Useri at Beni Hasan carrying a child on the mother's back in the fold of her garments.
©The Trustees of the National Museums of Scotland.

20. (p. 378) The "Sarcophagus of Mourning Women," a column-type sarcophagus, found in the Phoenician royal necropolis at Sidon.
Pentilic marble; 4th century B.C.
Courtesy of Erich Lessing/Art Resource, NY.

21. (p. 412) Kylix, Greek; Object place: Athens, Attica, Greee, Classical Period, about 470 B.C. Douris Ceramic, Red Figure; height: 75 cm (29 1/2 in.); diameter: 21.5 cm (8 7/16 in.).
Catharine Page Perkins Fund, 97.369.
Courtesy of the Museum of Fine Arts, Boston.

22. (p. 451) Two Hittite dignitaries sitting at a table drinking.
Basalt funeral stele from Troas, Turkey; late Hittite, 9th century B.C.
Courtesy of Erich Lessing/Art Resource, NY.

23. (p. 466) Fertility figure.
Terracotta from Jerusalem, Iron Age II, 9th-7th century B.C.
Courtesy of Erich Lessing/Art Resource, NY.

24. (p. 481) Babylonian tablet with inscription.
Terracotta (605-562 B.C.); late Iron Age.
Courtesy of Erich Lessing/Art Resource, NY.

25. (p. 487) Procession of offering bearers, Egypt (Deir el-Bersha, tomb of Djehuty-nakht, no. 10A), Middle Kingdon, Late Dynasty 11 or Early Dynasty 12, 2008-1836 B.C.
Wood, painted; length: 66.36 cm (26 1/8 in.).
Harvard University—Museum of Fine Arts Expedition, 21.326.
Courtesy of the Museum of Fine Arts, Boston.

26. (p. 496) The Temple of Aaron.
West wall mural, synagogue of Dura Europos, Syria; c. A.D. 239.
Courtesy of The Jewish Museum, NY/Art Resource, NY.

27. (p. 497) Fragments of a krater (mixing bowl) with girls playing, Greek; Object place: Athens, Attica, Greece, Classical Period, about 470-460 B.C.; Manner of the Leningrad Painter.
Ceramic, Red Figure; length (max.) of a: 26.7 cm (10 1/2 in.), length (max.) of b: 16.3 cm (6 7/16 in.).
James Fund and by Special Contribution, 10.191a-b.
Courtesy of the Museum of Fine Arts, Boston.

28. (p. 540) Early Christian sarcophagus.
Detail depicting woman at a tomb. Museo Pio Cristiano, Vatican Museums.
Courtesy of Scala/Art Resource, NY.

29. (p. 557) The victorious army of Titus with the spoils from Jerusalem.
Marble; Arch of Titus, Rome; c. A.D. 90.
Courtesy of Alinari/Art Resource, NY.

30. (p. 572) Sarcophagus of Plotinus.
3rd-4th century A.D.; Museo Gregoriano Profano, Vatican Museums.
Courtesy of Scala/Art Resource, NY.

31. (p. 574) Healing of the woman with the issue of blood.
Fresco; Catacombe dei SS. Marcellino e Pietro, Rome.
Courtesy of Scala/Art Resource, NY.

32. (p. 598) Christ and the Samaritan woman.
Fresco; Catacombe di S. Callisto, Rome.
Courtesy of Scala/Art Resource, NY.

33. (p. 624) Artemis of Ephesus.
Statue; Museo Nazionale, Naples.
Courtesy of Scala/Art Resource, NY.

34. (p. 625) Martyrion of Philip at Hierapolis, Turkey.
Courtesy of Tom Cottingim.

35. (p. 641) Disc with Dionysiac relief, Greek; Object place: said to have come from Athens, Greece, Hellenistic Period, 2nd-1st century B.C.
Pentelic marble (?); diameter: 26.2 cm (10 5/16 in.).
Helen and Alice Colburn Fund, 37.1152.
Courtesy of the Museum of Fine Arts, Boston.

36. (p. 644) Teaching Center of Thecla, Silifke, Turkey.
Courtesy of Tom Cottingim.

37. (p. 650) Bell krater (mixing bowl), Greek, South Italian; Place of manufacture: Apulia, Italy, Late Classical Period, about 380-370 B.C.

Ceramic, Red Figure; height: 28.6 cm (11 1/4 in.); diameter: 33 cm (13 in.).
Otis Norcross Fund, 69.951.
Courtesy of the Museum of Fine Arts, Boston.

38. (p. 661) Breaking of the Bread.
Early Christian fresco.
Courtesy of Scala/Art Resource, NY.

39. (p. 711) Young women in bikinis.
Roman mosaic; Villa del Casale, Piazza Armerina, Sicily.
Courtesy of Scala/Art Resource, NY.

40. (p. 717) Ritual flagellation and winged demon.
Fresco at Villa dei Misteri, Pompeii.
Courtesy of Scala/Art Resource, NY.

41. (p. 724) Hollow statue, Pergamum, Turkey.
Courtesy of Tom Cottingim.

42. (p. 725) Old nurse with a baby, Greek; Place of origin: Tanagra, Boiotia, Greece, Early Hellenistic Period, about 325-300 B.C.
Terracotta; height: 12.9 cm (5 1/8 in.).
Contribution, 01.7842.
Courtesy of the Museum of Fine Arts, Boston.

43. (p. 726) Orante. Scenes from the life of a deceased woman in the chamber of the Velatio.
Early Christian fresco, 2nd half of the 3rd century A.D., Priscilla Catacombs, Rome.
Courtesy of Scala/Art Resource, NY.

44. (p. 741) Funerary monument of Aththaia, daughter of Malchos, Roman Provincial; Object Place; Gnathia, Apulia, Italy, Imperial Period, Palmyrene Group II, 2nd half of the 2nd century A.D.
Limestone; height x width: 55 x 42 cm (21 11/16 x 16 1/2 in.).
Gift of Edward Perry Warren in memory of his sister, 22.659.
Courtesy of the Museum of Fine Arts, Boston.

45. (p. 761) Portrait of Paquio Proculo and his wife.
Roman fresco from Pompeii.
Courtesy of Scala/Art Resource, NY.

46. (p. 779) Orante (praying woman).
Center panel of the "Sarcophagus of the Trees"; marble, c. A.D. 375.
Courtesy of Erich Lessing/Art Resource, NY.

47. (p. 787) Head of a woman.
Flavian period, Musei Capitolini, Rome.
Courtesy of Alinari/Art Resource, NY.

48. (p. 795) Bell krater, Greek, Sicilian; Object place: Sicily, Italy, Late Classical Period, about 400-380 B.C.; The Chequer Group.
Ceramic, Red Figure; height: 36.2 (14 1/4 in.); diameter: 37.7 cm (14 13/16 in).
Partial gift of Peter and Mary Lee Aldrich, 1995.840.
Courtesy of the Museum of Fine Arts, Boston.

49. (p. 811) Calyx krater (mixing bowl) with scenes of abduction and pursuit, Greek; Object place: Athens, Attica, Greece, Classical Period, about 460-450 B.C.; Niobid Painter.
Ceramic, Red Figure; height: 48 cm (18 7/8 in.); diameter: 50 cm (19 11/16 in.).
Mary S. and Edward J. Holmes Fund, 1972.850.
Courtesy of the Museum of Fine Arts, Boston.

50. (p. 837) Loutrophoros, Greek; Object place: Athens, Attica, Greece, Classical Period, about 450-425 B.C.
Ceramic, Red Figure; height x diameter of lip: 75.3 x 25.3 cm (29 5/8 x 10 in.).
Francis Bartlett Donation, 03.802.
Courtesy of the Museum of Fine Arts, Boston.

Index of Articles

Scripture Index

Genesis

2 Chronicles

Ezra